Transforming the Service Sector With New Technology

Varinder Singh Rana
City University, Ajman, UAE

Gaurav Bathla
CT University, India

Ashish Raina
CT University, India

Divoy Chhabra
CT University, India

IGI Global
Scientific Publishing
Publishing Tomorrow's Research Today

Vice President of Editorial	Melissa Wagner
Managing Editor of Acquisitions	Mikaela Felty
Managing Editor of Book Development	Jocelynn Hessler
Production Manager	Mike Brehm
Cover Design	Phillip Shickler

Published in the United States of America by
IGI Global Scientific Publishing
701 East Chocolate Avenue
Hershey, PA, 17033, USA
Tel: 717-533-8845
Fax: 717-533-7115
Website: https://www.igi-global.com E-mail: cust@igi-global.com

Library of Congress Cataloging-in-Publication Data

Names: Rana, Varinder Singh editor
http://id.loc.gov/authorities/names/no2012065308
http://id.loc.gov/rwo/agents/no2012065308 | Bathla, Gaurav, 1987- editor
http://id.loc.gov/authorities/names/n2025000464
http://id.loc.gov/rwo/agents/n2025000464 | Raina, Ashish, 1987- editor
http://id.loc.gov/authorities/names/n2025000463
http://id.loc.gov/rwo/agents/n2025000463 | Chhabra, Divoy, 1986- editor
http://id.loc.gov/authorities/names/n2025027051
http://id.loc.gov/rwo/agents/n2025027051
Title: Transforming the service sector with new technology / edited by Varinder Singh Rana, Gaurav Bathla, Ashish Raina, Divoy Chhabra.
Description: Hershey, PA : IGI Global Scientific Publishing, [2025] | Includes bibliographical references and index. | Summary: "This book explores how emerging technologies are altering the service business. It most likely seeks to examine Technological Impact: Investigate how emerging technologies such as artificial intelligence, blockchain, the Internet of Things (IoT), and big data are transforming how services are supplied and consumed"-- Provided by publisher.
Identifiers: LCCN 2024054500 (print) | LCCN 2024054501 (ebook) | ISBN 9798369374474 hardcover | ISBN 9798369374481 paperback | ISBN 9798369374498 ebook
Subjects: LCSH: Business--Technological innovations | Artificial intelligence http://id.loc.gov/authorities/subjects/sh85008180
Classification: LCC HD45 .T69 2025 (print) | LCC HD45 (ebook) | DDC 658/.0563--dc23/eng/20250624
LC record available at https://lccn.loc.gov/2024054500
LC ebook record available at https://lccn.loc.gov/2024054501

British Cataloguing in Publication Data
A Cataloguing in Publication record for this book is available from the British Library.

Table of Contents

Detailed Table of Contents

In the contemporary subject of work and life, the convergence of innovation and balance between work and life activities has become progressively articulated. This survey research paper investigates the complex connection among technology and work-life balance, looking at the manners by which innovative progressions are reshaping the limits among professional and individual life. With an emphasis on both the opportunities and difficulties introduced by innovation, this paper offers bits of knowledge into how people, organizations, and policymakers can explore this developing scene to advance prosperity and efficiency in the cutting edge workforce. The paper starts by contextualizing the idea of balance of work and non-work activities within the limit of 24 hours, inside the more extensive cultural and innovative patterns that have formed the advanced working environment. This research paper gives a far reaching assessment of the job of innovation in molding the future of balance between work and non-work activities.

Exploring how Technology might help in the Webrooming Scenario in the Automotive Service Industry, this Chapter is organized. In analysing the subject of the book chapter, the authors focus on such aspects as the evolution of the industry, the use of Webrooming in the purchasing process. It also deliberation on different technologies including Artificial Intelligence, Blockchain, Virtual and Augmented Reality, and Internet of Thing that may help to enhance trust, transparency and engagement while using Webrooming System. As the chapter demonstrated, the actual application of the Conceptual Framework of Webrooming supported by advanced technologies among key automotive brands is shown through their cases. To those automotive service providers who want to use information technology in webrooming, the authors give guidelines and suggestions. Past work and approaches are also discussed, followed by discussion of the ethical issues and the directions for future research work so that reader is well-aware with the prospects and limitations in this growing domain of study.

This paper discusses the transformative effect of technology advancement on the services industry, and the role of digital technologies like artificial intelligence, blockchain technology and the Internet of things. It assesses the trends in technology adoption with a focus on data-orientated analysis and the use of AI and automation in various service sectors. The paper also discusses the effects of blockchain technology, how IoT is set to transform service delivery, and privacy considerations in the modern society. The importance of smart devices and connected system with emphasis on the need to enhance cybersecurity measures is well described. The consequences of further developments of the services industry for the society and the corresponding strategic recommendations for a world with focus on technology are presented as well. Combining the information on the present state and potential development, this paper strives to provide a systematic review of the ongoing digital transformation in the services sector.

This study explores the critical role of cybersecurity in safeguarding service infrastructure within the hospitality industry. It addresses the pervasive cybersecurity risks posed by digital integration and interconnected systems, emphasizing vulnerabilities in digital reservation systems, payment processing, guest data management, and IoT devices. Survey data from 100 industry stakeholders reveal widespread concerns, with significant percentages acknowledging these vulnerabilities. Despite awareness, practices like regular cybersecurity audits are less common. High-profile breaches, such as those at Marriott International and Hilton Worldwide, underscore the financial and reputational impacts on hospitality businesses, prompting increased investments in cybersecurity measures like advanced encryption and regulatory compliance (e.g., GDPR, CCPA). The study reviews literature on evolving threats, technological advancements (e.g., AI, blockchain), and industry responses, highlighting the ongoing efforts to enhance cybersecurity resilience.

Information technology is revolutionizing the methods in which knowledge is conveyed in the educational sector. In India, e-learning is gaining a lot of popularity as technology develops. E-learning promotes sustainability and offers instructors and students new perspectives. The purpose of this study is to look at how external factors affect students' uptake of online learning. The Technology Adoption Model (TAM) examines how students' behavioral intentions are influenced by their perceptions of the learning surroundings, perceived utility, perceived usability, and learning satisfaction. The information was gathered from the several universities in India's northern regions. The purpose of the 271-person sample was to investigate the acceptability of e-learning in Indian higher education institutions. The proposed hypotheses have been assessed using SPSS multiple regression analysis. The perceived ease of use (PEOU) is positively impacted by the learning atmosphere, however the relationship between PEOU and perceived usefulness (PU) is not statistically significant.

In the intensely competitive hospitality sector, the quality of customer experience is a critical determinant of a hotel's success. As customers become more selective and their expectations evolve, hotels must continuously assess and enhance their service quality to remain competitive. This chapter aims to explore various indicators of hotel customer experience from a service quality perspective. Secondary data was utilized, with 434 hotel reviews collected from Tripadvisor.com, a prominent customer review site. Among these reviews, 268 were from domestic customers and the remainder from international travelers. Qualitative analysis was conducted using R software and Bigram analysis to identify recurring words and phrases. The study identified seven key dimensions based on repeated phrases, including hotel rooms, food quality, staff behavior, overall stay experience, and service quality. The research provides insights into these indicators and suggests that future studies could explore big data related to customer experience across different geographical areas.

The convergence of Generative AI (GenAI) and the Internet of Things (IoT) holds immense potential to revolutionize various aspects of our lives and reshape industries. This paper explores the future of this integrated technology, examining its promising applications, anticipated challenges, and potential societal impacts. This paper highlights key areas where GenAI-powered IoT can create significant value, including personalized automation, predictive maintenance, and enhanced data analysis. Additionally, it addresses concerns surrounding privacy, security, and ethical considerations of such powerful technology. By outlining the research landscape and future directions, this study aims to spark discussion and propel further exploration of this transformative technology.

The study investigates the impact of customer ability readiness (CAR) on intention to purchase using AI (IPAI) in tourism and hospitality businesses, focusing on the mediating roles of customer trust in AI (TAI) and customer engagement (CE). An online survey was conducted to gather data from customers who have experienced using AI in online flights and hotel booking. The PLS-SEM approach was used to analyze 602 valid responses, which were processed using WarpPLS statistical software 7.0. The findings show that CAR positively affects customers' IPAI, TAI, and CE. In addition, customers' IPAI is positively affected by TAI and CE. Furthermore, the findings found that TAI and CE significantly mediate the CAR→IPAI relationship. The study enhances the Technology Acceptance Model (TAM) by enhancing our understanding of the factors influencing AI adoption in the tourism and hospitality sectors. The study also suggests that tourism and hospitality businesses should focus on improving customer readiness to adopt AI technologies.

The rapid advancement and integration of artificial intelligence (AI) technologies are profoundly transforming the tourism sector, presenting both opportunities and challenges for employment and skill requirements The primary objectives are to analyse the impact of AI on employment, assess changes in skill requirements, and evaluate the benefits and drawbacks of AI adoption. Employing secondary data from scholarly articles, industry reports, and market research, this study provides a nuanced understanding of AI's influence on the tourism sector. The analysis reveals a transformative impact of AI on employment trends, characterised by the displacement of certain job roles and the emergence of new opportunities centred around AI management and technological innovation. Additionally, it emphasizes the evolving skill set required by AI integration and the growing significance of digital literacy, data analysis, and AI proficiency among tourism professionals.

Context: The examination of the CRM data is anchored in a comprehensive analysis of sales performance metrics, with a significant role played. It was found a gap in the literature, considering the scarcity of pertinent case studies within the academic literature. Method: The geographical factor is paramount in this analysis, as it unveils divergent results across different regions. Moreover, the venture into predictive analytics for sales forecasting, capitalizing on CRM primary data spanning from 2018 to 2023, facilitating more informed decision-making. The sample comprises around 1500 Business to Business customer clusters for in-depth analysis is considered. Findings: From the Business Intelligence analysis, it was found the presence of long-standing customers with a lower purchase rate, favouring average industrial product models preferred by the customers. Conclusion:The study also explores the link between CRM can shape business strategies, enhance customer relationships, and boost organizational performance and customer retention.

The purpose of the current study was to analyse and predict of customer sentiment towards real estate organizations using Machine Learning Approaches (ML) approaches. The study employed five ML models to predict customer sentiment toward real estate organizations. The data was collected from Yelp. com and filtered using the "Real Estate" tag. The findings revealed that all four machine learning models effectively classified the review text. The logistic regression (LR) and support vector machine (SVM) models achieved the highest accuracy scores at 93.1 and 93.16, respectively. This study emphasizes the potential of machine learning in improving customer experience and facilitating better decision-making in the real estate industry. The results can guide real estate organizations in understanding customer opinions and preferences, enabling them to make necessary improvements. Additionally, the findings have social implications, as they can enhance products, services, and overall customer experiences, leading to increased satisfaction and trust in the industry.

service without recourse to prompt reconnection, billing discrepancies etc. are among the problems encountered by customers of utility service providers. Customers on the other hand resort to open confrontation, non-refusal to pay bills and other mechanisms to register their displeasure towards the utility service providers. A key tool available to utility service providers to ensure customer satisfaction and that customers' concerns are adequately addressed is the effective application of service recovery strategies. How effectively can the application of service recovery strategies influence the level of customer satisfaction? The current study is among the few studies in sub-Saharan Africa that investigate service recovery as an antecedent to customer satisfaction in today's digital space. Details of the outcome are discussed in the chapter.

This chapter delves into how wearable technology can be integrated into the tourism sector to elevate the travel experience by monitoring tourist activities and delivering tailored, real-time services. Devices such as smartwatches, fitness trackers, and augmented reality glasses have significantly altered the tourism landscape, providing valuable insights into tourists' preferences, health, and movements. The discussion focuses on leveraging this technology to customize tourist interactions, enhance safety and well-being while traveling, and boost engagement at cultural and natural sites. Additionally, it examines how wearable tech can foster sustainable tourism by promoting environmentally friendly practices. The findings underscore the transformative potential of wearable technology in the tourism industry, presenting innovative strategies for enhancing customer satisfaction and refining travel experiences.

While restaurant goers are still ultimately seeking the same qualities to receive a positive dining experience, the internet and technology has fundamentally changed how consumers are behaving and their decision making processes. Consumers now have more choice, communication channels, and access to information all readily available at their fingertips. Review websites enable would-be diners to read feedback from real customers, and social media platforms such as Snapchat or Instagram can give people a taste of what to expect without even having to step foot in the establishment. A focus on digital marketing has become increasingly important for F&B outlets that want to remain competitive, and ensure long term profitability. Websites plays an important role for businesses to establish their credibility and build trust with their customers. In this day and age, it is a common tool for consumers to research F&B outlets while choosing a place to eat and this is the reason, why websites for F&B outlets are so important.

the need for a comprehensive understanding of AI applications such as chatbots and automation. This research employs a descriptive approach, comprising surveys to assess consumer awareness of AI among various age groups, evaluate their acceptance levels, and analyze behaviors influenced by emotions and attitudes. Findings indicate significant variances in awareness and acceptance across generations, with factors such as trust, perceived benefits, and emotional responses playing pivotal roles. This study offers recommendations for hospitality and tourism providers.

The Chapter discusses how technology has affected the Product Placement in Punjabi Cinema & Music Industry in relation to Gen Z and its potential repercussions. The Authors identify the development of the methods of Product Placements, discussing the impact from the Digital Platforms, Social Media and Data in the effective Branding process of the integration solutions. In this context, the features of success in Punjabi Cinema and Music are examined with examples of adopted Promotional Campaigns such as Integral Promotions, Celebrities' Endorsement, and Engagement. These include Mobile Devices, Virtual Reality and Augmented Reality, AI and other technologies which the authors consider as useful to extend the trends mentioned above. Issues of Ethics for Technology enhanced Product Placement along with best practice covenants are also considered. The Chapter is therefore useful for Marketers and other Entertainment Industry Players who wish to enhance their approaches in using technology in delivering effective and appropriate Product Placement Solutions.

The hospitality industry, encompassing lodging, food and beverage, event planning, theme parks, and travel and tourism, has been significantly transformed by technological advancements. This chapter explores the historical context, key technological innovations, and their impacts on the hospitality sector. The hospitality industry has undergone a profound transformation driven by technological advancements. This abstract explores the historical development and impact of key technologies in the sector. Initially labor-intensive, the industry began modernizing with the advent of early technologies like telephones and computerized reservation systems. The introduction of the internet and mobile technology catalyzed a revolution, leading to significant innovations such as online booking systems, mobile applications, and Customer Relationship Management (CRM) systems. Technologies like Artificial Intelligence (AI), Internet of Things (IoT), and blockchain have further enhanced operational efficiency and customer experiences. AI and automation streamline customer service and data analytics, while IoT creates smart, interconnected environments in hospitality establishments. Blockchain technology provides secure and transparent transaction processes.

The hospitality industry is undergoing a profound transformation driven by the advent of smart technologies and digital innovation. This chapter explores the future of smart hotels and the digital transformation shaping the hospitality sector. Key areas of focus include the integration of artificial intelligence (AI), the Internet of Things (IoT), and blockchain technology to enhance guest experiences, improve operational efficiency, and promote sustainability. Through comprehensive case studies and industry examples, we examine how smart hotels utilize automation, personalized services, and data analytics to cater to the evolving demands of modern travelers. The chapter also addresses the challenges and opportunities associated with digital transformation, such as cybersecurity, data privacy, and maintaining the balance between technological advancement and the human touch.

The hospitality industry is experiencing a significant transformation due to the rise of Artificial Intelligence (AI) and automation. This chapter explores the diverse effects these technologies have on the hospitality sector, showcasing both the opportunities they present and the challenges they bring. AI and automation are transforming customer service, operational efficiency, and personalised guest experiences. AI-powered chatbots and virtual assistants enhance client interactions by responding quickly and accurately, as well as supporting easy booking processes. Automation in tasks such as check-in, check-out, and room service improves efficiency, reduces human error, and optimises operations. The chapter looks at how data analytics and AI-driven insights can help hotels predict client preferences and customise services to match individual needs, resulting in increased guest happiness and loyalty. This Chapter emphasizes the need for a strategic approach to integrating AI and automation, ensuring they enhance rather than replace the human touch that is fundamental to hospitality.

Blockchain technology has transformed service industries by offering transparent, secure, and decentralized solutions across sectors like finance, supply chain and logistics, healthcare, government, digital rights, energy, real estate, education, law, telecommunications, and hospitality. In finance, it supports decentralized finance, smart contracts, and cryptocurrencies. In supply chains, it enhances traceability, transparency, logistics, and prevents counterfeiting. In healthcare, it secures patient data, ensures pharmaceutical integrity, and aids clinical studies. Blockchain improves government services with secure digital identities, voting, and public records. It protects intellectual property and ensures fair royalty distribution in digital rights. In energy, it facilitates peer-to-peer trading and renewable certificates, while in real

Preface

In an era where technological advancements are redefining industries, the service sector stands at the forefront of transformation. The integration of emerging technologies such as artificial intelligence (AI), blockchain, the Internet of Things (IoT), and big data is revolutionizing how services are designed, delivered, and consumed. This book, *Transforming the Service Sector With New Technology*, delves into the profound impact of these technologies, shedding light on their potential to reshape traditional business models, enhance customer experiences, and optimize operational efficiency across various service industries, including hospitality, tourism, banking, healthcare, and beyond.

As editors, we recognize the urgency of equipping industry professionals, entrepreneurs, policymakers, and academics with a comprehensive understanding of the opportunities and challenges presented by technological innovations. This book serves as a crucial resource for stakeholders seeking to harness the power of technology to develop new services or refine existing ones. By bridging the gap between theoretical insights and practical applications, this volume offers valuable guidance for businesses navigating the dynamic landscape of service technology.

The book is structured to explore key themes, including:

1. **Technological Impact** – A deep dive into how cutting-edge technologies are transforming service delivery, improving customer satisfaction, and increasing efficiency.
2. **Innovative Applications** – Case studies and real-world examples showcasing how businesses have successfully implemented technology-driven solutions to address industry-specific challenges.
3. **Strategic Implementation** – Practical insights on how organizations can integrate emerging technologies into their business strategies to drive innovation and growth.
4. **Regulatory and Ethical Considerations** – An examination of the evolving regulatory landscape, ethical dilemmas, and necessary safeguards to ensure responsible innovation while protecting consumer interests.
5. **Future Trends and Challenges** – An exploration of potential obstacles, adoption barriers, and strategies for overcoming resistance to change in the service sector.

By bringing together contributions from industry experts, scholars, and practitioners, *Transforming the Service Sector With New Technology* aims to inspire innovation and provide strategic counsel to businesses and policymakers. It is our hope that this book will stimulate discussion, foster new ideas, and serve as a catalyst for positive change within the service industry.

This book explores the transformative role of technology, particularly artificial intelligence (AI), automation, and digital transformation, in reshaping various industries. The chapters present a comprehensive analysis of technological advancements, their implications on business operations, workforce dynamics, cybersecurity, customer experience, and industry-specific innovations.

Chapter 1: This chapter examines the impact of AI and automation on service industries, highlighting their role in enhancing operational efficiency, customer engagement, and predictive analytics. It also discusses challenges such as ethical considerations and workforce displacement, emphasizing the need for human oversight and reskilling initiatives.

Chapter 2: Focusing on digital transformation, this chapter explores how AI, machine learning, and robotics are altering workforce requirements in the service sector. It addresses strategies for workforce development, continuous learning, and adaptability to ensure businesses remain competitive in a rapidly evolving digital landscape.

Chapter 3: This chapter investigates the intersection of technological advancements and work-life balance, analyzing how innovation is redefining the boundaries between professional and personal life. It offers insights for individuals, organizations, and policymakers to navigate these changes effectively.

Chapter 4: Exploring technology's role in the webrooming scenario within the automotive service industry, this chapter discusses the application of AI, blockchain, augmented reality, and the Internet of Things (IoT) in enhancing trust, transparency, and customer engagement in the purchasing process.

Chapter 5: This chapter provides a systematic review of technological advancements in the service industry, focusing on AI, blockchain, IoT, and cybersecurity. It discusses their transformative impact, challenges related to privacy, and strategic recommendations for a technology-driven future.

Chapter 6: Addressing cybersecurity in the hospitality industry, this chapter examines vulnerabilities in digital reservation systems, payment processing, and guest data management. It highlights real-world breaches and emphasizes the need for enhanced cybersecurity measures to protect service infrastructure.

Chapter 7: This chapter explores e-learning adoption in India's higher education sector, using the Technology Adoption Model (TAM) to analyze students' perceptions of online learning. It presents findings from a large-scale survey on factors influencing e-learning acceptance and usability.

Chapter 8: Examining customer experience in the hospitality sector, this chapter utilizes qualitative data from online hotel reviews to identify key service quality indicators. It provides insights into how hotels can enhance customer satisfaction and maintain competitiveness.

Chapter 9: Investigating the convergence of Generative AI and IoT, this chapter explores their combined potential in areas such as personalized automation, predictive maintenance, and data analytics. It also addresses security, privacy, and ethical concerns associated with these technologies.

Chapter 10: This chapter analyzes customer readiness to adopt AI-driven services in tourism and hospitality. Using survey data and statistical analysis, it explores how trust and engagement influence customers' willingness to use AI in booking and service interactions.

Chapter 11: This chapter assesses AI's impact on employment in the tourism industry, highlighting shifts in job roles, evolving skill requirements, and the importance of digital literacy. It discusses how professionals can adapt to AI-driven changes in the sector.

Chapter 12: Focusing on Customer Relationship Management (CRM) data analysis, this chapter examines sales performance metrics and predictive analytics. It explores the impact of CRM insights on business strategies, customer retention, and organizational performance.

Chapter 13: This chapter explores the use of machine learning (ML) approaches to analyze and predict customer sentiment toward real estate organizations. Using data collected from Yelp.com, five ML models were employed to classify customer reviews. The study highlights the effectiveness of ML in sentiment analysis, with logistic regression (LR) and support vector machine (SVM) achieving the highest accuracy rates.

Chapter 14: This chapter examines the role of blockchain technology in enhancing the security and privacy of customer data within financial services. By addressing vulnerabilities in traditional identity management frameworks, blockchain-based systems offer improved data protection and user control.

Chapter 15: This chapter delves into the impact of big data analytics (BDA) on the tourism industry, emphasizing its role in service quality enhancement and sustainability. By analyzing ecological data, tourism businesses can minimize environmental impact and respond to the rising demand for sustainable travel.

Chapter 16: This chapter explores the intersection of technology and Green Human Resource Development (HRD) in the hospitality industry. With a growing emphasis on sustainability, hotels are adopting environmentally friendly HRD strategies to improve organizational efficiency and reduce environmental impact.

Chapter 17: This chapter investigates the rapid development and adoption of Internet of Things (IoT)-based information systems in industrial settings. These systems leverage pervasive and ubiquitous computing, along with advanced data communication protocols, to facilitate seamless interaction between the physical and digital worlds.

Chapter 18: This chapter examines the key motivators driving digital technology adoption in the hospitality industry, with a focus on hotel operations. The study identifies efficiency, automation, customer satisfaction, and system coordination as crucial factors influencing technology integration.

Chapter 19: The integration of Artificial Intelligence (AI) into housekeeping operations is revolutionizing task management across various industries. This chapter presents a roadmap for AI-enabled housekeeping, emphasizing process optimization, service enhancement, and operational efficiency. It explores smart devices, data analytics, and workforce adaptation in industries such as hospitality, retail, healthcare, and airports. Key insights highlight AI's transformative impact on housekeeping, promoting efficiency and customer satisfaction.

Chapter 20: This chapter delves into the application of Generative AI in healthcare, particularly in drug discovery, diagnostic improvements, and personalized medicine. It addresses ethical concerns such as data privacy and algorithmic limitations, while also outlining strategies for managing these challenges. The chapter serves as a valuable resource for healthcare practitioners, policymakers, and AI specialists, offering step-by-step solutions for integrating AI responsibly into care delivery.

Chapter 21: Customers in developing economies frequently face service disruptions from utility providers, leading to dissatisfaction and conflicts. This chapter examines service recovery strategies as a means to enhance customer satisfaction in the digital space. Through an analysis of customer grievances and service provider responses, the study offers insights into the effectiveness of service recovery strategies in the utility sector, particularly in sub-Saharan Africa.

Chapter 22: Wearable technology, including smartwatches, fitness trackers, and AR glasses, is reshaping the tourism experience by offering real-time personalized services. This chapter explores how wearable tech enhances tourist engagement, safety, and sustainability while providing data-driven insights into traveler behavior. The study highlights strategies for leveraging this technology to elevate customer satisfaction and optimize tourism services.

Chapter 23: Consumer behavior in the food and beverage (F&B) industry has been significantly influenced by digital platforms. This chapter examines the role of review websites, social media, and digital marketing in shaping dining decisions. It highlights the importance of websites and online credibility for F&B businesses, offering strategic insights into maintaining competitiveness and profitability in a digitally driven market.

Chapter 24: Social media has become a powerful tool for hotels to engage customers, enhance brand visibility, and drive bookings. This study investigates the effectiveness of social media marketing strategies, analyzing engagement drivers, ROI, and content personalization. Findings highlight the impact of visual storytelling, influencer collaborations, and analytics in optimizing digital marketing for hospitality businesses.

Chapter 25: This chapter explores the role of fintech in achieving Sustainable Development Goals (SDGs), particularly financial inclusion in developing economies. It reviews emerging digital payment methods such as mobile payments, e-payments, and cryptocurrency, discussing associated challenges and opportunities. The study provides a framework for understanding digital payment technologies and their socio-economic impact.

Chapter 26: Industry 4.0 is characterized by rapid advancements in digital technologies, including IoT, cloud computing, and AI. This chapter examines how these innovations are transforming manufacturing and service industries by enabling real-time data exchange and automation. The study highlights IoT's role in creating interconnected, efficient, and intelligent business environments.

Chapter 27: Digital technologies are reshaping the hospitality industry by enhancing guest experiences and operational efficiencies. This chapter explores the adoption of mobile apps, contactless payments, self-service kiosks, and AI-driven guest management systems. Through case studies, the chapter examines successful digital transformations and the challenges faced by hospitality businesses in their digital adoption journey.

Chapter 28: Despite technological advancements, human resource skills remain crucial to organizational success. This study assesses key competencies required in the hospitality sector, including IT skills, communication, dispute resolution, and trade-specific expertise. Based on a survey conducted in Delhi NCR hotels, the findings provide insights for HR managers on enhancing employee performance and training programs.

Chapter 29: As AI becomes integral to business operations, this chapter investigates consumer awareness and acceptance of AI in the hospitality and tourism industry. It explores generational differences in AI adoption, focusing on chatbots, automation, and customer interactions. Findings reveal variations in trust, perceived benefits, and emotional responses, providing recommendations for AI implementation strategies.

Chapter 30: Technology-driven product placement is transforming branding strategies in Punjabi cinema and music. This chapter examines digital platforms, social media, and data analytics in product integration. It discusses various promotional techniques such as celebrity endorsements, virtual reality, and AI-driven campaigns. Ethical considerations and best practices for effective product placement are also explored.

Chapter 31: This chapter provides a historical analysis of technological advancements in the hospitality industry, highlighting key innovations and their impact. It explores how digital transformation has shaped lodging, F&B, event planning, and tourism, examining the evolution of guest experiences and operational processes.

Chapter 32: The hospitality industry is undergoing a digital revolution, with smart hotels integrating AI, IoT, and blockchain technology. This chapter explores the future of digital transformation in hospitality, focusing on automation, personalized services, and data analytics. Case studies highlight opportunities and challenges in implementing smart technology while addressing cybersecurity and data privacy concerns.

Chapter 33: This chapter explores the growing influence of Artificial Intelligence (AI) and automation in the hospitality sector, revolutionizing customer service, operational efficiency, and personalized guest experiences. AI-powered chatbots and virtual assistants are enhancing client interactions by providing fast and accurate responses, streamlining booking processes, and ensuring efficient communication.

Chapter 34: Blockchain technology is reshaping multiple service sectors by providing secure, transparent, and decentralized solutions. This chapter examines blockchain's impact across industries such as finance, supply chain management, healthcare, government, digital rights, energy, real estate, education, law, telecommunications, and hospitality.

Chapter 35: This chapter highlights how Augmented Reality (AR) and Virtual Reality (VR) are reshaping human interactions across various service industries. AR and VR are widely used in retail and eCommerce for virtual product trials, in tourism for 360-degree virtual tours, and in real estate for remote property walkthroughs.

This book is intended for a diverse audience, including service industry decision-makers, industrialists, hospitality professionals, entrepreneurs, students of business studies, and regulatory authorities. Whether you are an industry veteran or a budding entrepreneur, the insights contained within these pages will empower you to leverage technology effectively and stay ahead in an increasingly digitalized world.

We extend our gratitude to all the contributors whose expertise and dedication have made this book possible. We also appreciate the unwavering support of our institutions, colleagues, and families, who have encouraged us throughout this journey.

We invite you to explore the transformative potential of new technologies in the service sector and embrace the innovations shaping the future of business.

Varinder Rana
City University Ajman, United Arab Emirates

Gaurav Bathla
CT University, India

Ashish Raina
CT University, India

Divoy Chhabra
CT University, India

Chapter 1
Transforming the Service Sector With New Technology

C. V. Suresh Babu
https://orcid.org/0000-0002-8474-2882
Hindustan Institute of Technology and Science, India

Sahil Alam Shaikh
Hindustan Institute of Technology and Science, India

P. Kirubakar
https://orcid.org/0009-0005-0472-2427
Hindustan Institute of Technology and Science, India

ABSTRACT

This study aims to explore the impact of artificial intelligence (AI) and automation on service industries, focusing on their role in enhancing operational efficiency and decision-making processes. Utilizing a qualitative methodology, the research incorporates expert interviews, case studies, and secondary data reviews to gather comprehensive insights into current applications and challenges associated with AI adoption. The findings reveal that AI significantly improves customer engagement, streamlines workflows, and enables predictive analytics, thereby fostering better business outcomes. However, the study also highlights concerns regarding ethical implications and workforce displacement. The conclusions emphasize the necessity for organizations to balance technological integration with human oversight and reskilling initiatives, ensuring a sustainable transition into an AI-driven landscape. This research contributes to a deeper understanding of how AI can be effectively leveraged in service sectors while addressing potential challenges.

DOI: 10.4018/979-8-3693-7447-4.ch001

1.0. INTRODUCTION

1.1. Overview of Data-Driven Decision-Making

Data-driven decision-making (DDDM) is a business strategy where data is used to make informed and objective choices, often enhancing efficiency and predicting market trends. AI and automation have elevated DDDM processes, especially in service industries, helping businesses streamline operations and enhance customer experiences (Yablonsky, 2019).

Unlike traditional decision-making, which relies on intuition or assumptions, DDDM is rooted in systematic data analysis, making decisions more accurate, timely, and evidence-based. As businesses access increasingly large datasets, DDDM offers a competitive edge by enabling well-informed, swift actions (Provost & Fawcett, 2013).

The DDDM process generally follows several key steps:

- **Data Collection**: Organizations collect data from internal sources (like sales and feedback) and external sources (market trends and economic indicators). IoT and digital platforms have made it possible to collect large-scale "big data" (Elgendy et al., 2022).
- **Data Processing**: This stage involves cleaning and organizing data to ensure accuracy and relevance. High-quality data supports more reliable insights and decision outcomes.
- **Analysis and Insight Generation**: Using statistical models, machine learning, and predictive analytics, businesses identify patterns and forecast outcomes. Machine learning supports descriptive (what happened), predictive (what will happen), and prescriptive (what should happen) analytics.
- **Actionable Decisions**: Insights from data analysis inform decisions such as strategy revisions, operational improvements, and new product launches. This agility helps businesses respond promptly to changing environments (Kothandapani, 2021).

Data science techniques further enhance DDDM, as companies use automated data analysis to refine decision-making in sectors like healthcare, finance, and retail. Brynjolfsson et al. (MIT & Wharton) found that firms with stronger DDDM practices experience significant productivity gains and improved returns on assets and market value, demonstrating the impact of data-driven approaches on performance.

1.2. Importance of AI and Automation in the Service Industry

AI and automation technologies have transformed service industries, including healthcare, finance, retail, education, and hospitality. Traditionally reliant on human labor, these sectors benefit immensely from automation, which enhances efficiency, accuracy, and predictive capabilities in decision-making (Schmitt, 2023).

Operational Efficiency: AI-driven automation streamlines repetitive tasks such as customer service, scheduling, and data entry, allowing human employees to focus on strategic, high-value work. This shift not only accelerates processes but also improves overall productivity (Adeyeri, 2024).

Enhanced Customer Experience: AI tools enable service industries to provide personalized experiences by analyzing customer preferences and behavior. In retail, for example, AI can recommend products based on individual tastes, while in finance, automated systems offer real-time, tailored customer support (Gabelaia, 2022).

Cost Reduction: Automation helps reduce operational expenses by decreasing human labor needs and minimizing errors. AI systems monitor operations, identifying inefficiencies and highlighting cost-saving opportunities, which contributes to sustained financial gains (Yablonsky, 2019).

Predictive Analytics: AI-driven predictive models allow service industries to anticipate trends and adjust strategies proactively. In healthcare, AI can predict patient outcomes to support preventive care, while in finance, it can detect and alert potential fraud before it occurs (Schmitt, 2023).

1.3. Objectives of the Chapter

The objectives of the chapter titled "Applications of Data-Driven Decision-Making: The Impact of AI and Automation on Service Industries" are as follows:

- To explore how data-driven decision-making (DDDM) is applied across various service industries and its significance in enhancing operational efficiency and decision-making processes.
- To investigate the transformative effects of artificial intelligence (AI) and automation technologies on service delivery, customer engagement, and overall business performance.
- To identify and discuss current trends in DDDM, including the use of predictive analytics, customer segmentation, and personalized marketing strategies.
- To present real-world case studies that illustrate the successful implementation of DDDM, AI, and automation in sectors such as healthcare, finance, retail, and hospitality.
- To examine the challenges and limitations associated with the adoption of AI and automation in service industries, including ethical considerations and workforce reskilling.
- To offer recommendations for organizations on how to effectively integrate DDDM, AI, and automation into their operations to achieve a competitive advantage.
- To discuss the future implications of DDDM and AI on service industries, considering the evolving technological landscape and changing consumer expectations.

2.0. THEORETICAL BACKGROUND

2.1. Historical Context of Decision-Making in Service Industries

The evolution of decision-making in service industries has undergone significant transformations over the decades, influenced by advancements in technology, changes in consumer behavior, and the increasing complexity of market dynamics. Historically, decision-making in service sectors was predominantly intuitive and based on the experience of managers and employees. This traditional approach relied heavily on personal judgment and anecdotal evidence, which often led to inconsistent outcomes and inefficiencies (Suresh Babu, C. V., Maclin Vinola, P. et. al. 2024).

As the service industries began to expand and diversify, particularly in the late 20th century, the limitations of intuition-based decision-making became more apparent. Organizations started to recognize the need for more systematic approaches to decision-making that could enhance operational efficiency and customer satisfaction. This shift was catalyzed by the advent of information technology, which enabled businesses to collect and analyze data more effectively (Suresh Babu, C. V. and A. Auroshaa, 2024).

The introduction of data-driven decision-making (DDDM) marked a pivotal change in how organizations approached decision-making. DDDM emphasizes the use of data analysis to inform decisions rather than relying solely on intuition. This approach gained traction in the early 2000s as businesses began to harness the power of big data and analytics to gain insights into customer preferences and market trends (Suresh Babu, C. V. and A. Auroshaa, 2024). The integration of artificial intelligence (AI) and automation further revolutionized decision-making processes, allowing for real-time analysis and more accurate forecasting.

In recent years, the focus has shifted towards leveraging advanced analytics and AI technologies to enhance decision-making capabilities in service industries. Organizations are now able to utilize predictive analytics to anticipate customer needs, optimize resource allocation, and improve service delivery (Suresh Babu, C. V., Sharon Manoj et. al 2023).. This evolution reflects a broader trend towards a more data-centric approach in business, where decisions are increasingly informed by empirical evidence rather than subjective judgment.

2.2. Development of AI and Automation in Service Industries:

The progression of artificial intelligence (AI) and automation technologies has revolutionized decision-making in service organizations. Over the last few decades, more complex AI and automation technologies have taken shape, resulting in increasingly accurate interpretations of projects. Considering continued growth in data storage and computing power, the distinction between AI and automation continues to evolve to accommodate both of these realms.

Table 1.

Period	Development Stage	Key Advances
1950s–1970s	**Early Stages of AI and Automation**	- Rule-based systems and symbolic reasoning. - Basic software automation in manufacturing and services. - Limited support for complex decision-making.
1980s–1990s	**Emergence of Machine Learning and Business Intelligence**	- Introduction of machine learning and neural networks. - Data-based decision-making tools like business intelligence systems. - Use in finance and static industries for fraud detection and risk assessment.
2000s	**Breakthroughs in NLP and Robotic Automation**	- Advances in natural language processing (NLP) and robotic process automation (RPA). - Adoption of chatbots in customer service, predictive analytics in finance and healthcare. - Forecasting customer behavior to boost efficiency.
2010s–Present	**AI as a Service (AIaaS) and Integration of AI**	- AIaaS platforms (e.g., AWS, Google Cloud) democratized access to AI. - Small to mid-sized businesses utilize big data for real-time, data-driven decisions. - Service sectors optimize workflows and customer engagement.

2.3. Current Trends in Data-Driven Decision-Making

Service industries have begun to adopt data-driven decision-making in the last few years to improve business practices and operational efficiency. These trends illustrate how service industries are readily adopting new technologies in data-driven decision-making.

Artificial Intelligence (AI) for Personalized Customer Experiences:

Perhaps one of the most significant trends in current service industries is the use of AIs to provide personalized customer experiences. Using real-time interaction data and historical records, artificial intelligence systems can analyze customer activity to discern needs and preferences that allow service industries—such as retail/service and hospitality—to proactively offer and personalize services and offers (Mandinach & Honey, 2006). For example, Amazon and Netflix use artificial intelligence algorithms to predict which products a customer might find interesting based on prior purchase behavior and product performance.

Predictive Analytics for Forecasting:

Predictive analytics tools allow service industries to forecast trends, support inventory control, and predict customer demand. The predictive analytics technology utilizes machine learning models to determine patterns in historical data to predict future behavior or needs for a certain person or group of people (Tawil et al., 2024). We have seen predictive analytics technologies employed across various industries, including predicting patient outcomes in healthcare and assessing risks in finance.

Automation of Routine Processes:

Service businesses have become more dependent on RPA to free employees from low-level tasks, such as inputting or extracting data, processing orders, and supporting customers, among other tasks which are time-consuming besides presenting a high risk of human error (Fayzunnessa et al., 2024). Banks, for example, use RPA to do a majority of work related to loan processing, releasing employees to do strategic work.

Real-Time Data for Dynamic Decision-Making:

From the time-sensitive finance sector through to real-time monitoring in the health sector, real-time data analytics have rapidly emerged as a pivoted important for decision making in dynamic environments. By processing colossal data in near real-time, firms can take much quicker decisions and pivot strategies instantaneously (Hazarika, 2021). In finance, services use real-time analytics to make fraud detection during transactions, while in the health services they use real-time data analytics to monitor individual patient health in real-time.

Ethical Considerations in AI:

The prevalence of AI technology comes with its fair share of worries, the most notable of which is ethical AI use, especially in regard to privacy, fairness, and transparency. For instance, different industries have put in place some regulations that allow the use of AI algorithms without discrimination and in adherence to data protection standards. Take the European Union for instance, the GDPR imposes harsh restrictions on the extent to which AI processes customer information.

2.4. Alignment with "Transforming the Service Sector with New Technology"

The service industry is embracing digital transformation through technologies like AI, automation, blockchain, and IoT, which are reshaping traditional service processes and enhancing customer experiences. For example, AI has been widely adopted in customer service with virtual assistants and chatbots, enabling 24/7 support and improved efficiency by handling large volumes of inquiries at reduced costs (Gummesson et al., 2019). A study by Smith and Green (2021) underscores the value of AI-driven customer service across retail, hospitality, and finance, where AI tools enhance customer satisfaction and retention.

Blockchain technology also plays a pivotal role in the service sector by offering transparency and security, especially in finance and logistics. Christofi et al. (2021) highlight blockchain's tamper-proof transactions, which foster trust in industries like banking and supply chain management. This shift is leading to decentralized business models that minimize intermediary reliance, altering traditional service delivery.

IoT is advancing real-time data usage in healthcare and hospitality, creating "smart spaces" for enhanced monitoring and service delivery. In healthcare, IoT allows continuous patient health tracking, which improves care quality and reduces in-person visits (Zhou & Lam, 2020). Automation further enhances service delivery, particularly in hospitality, where automated check-ins and booking systems streamline operations, cut costs, and provide a consistent customer experience.

These technologies exemplify how the service sector is evolving to meet modern demands. Karpen and Conduit (2021) argue that future success in service industries will depend on how effectively organizations integrate these innovations, which are redefining business models, operational efficiencies, and customer engagement.

Three Types of AI in Service Sectors

AI's role in the service industry spans three primary areas: process automation, cognitive insight, and customer engagement. Process automation uses tools like robotic process automation (RPA) to perform administrative and financial tasks, from data entry to document processing, which significantly enhances back-office efficiency. Cognitive insight applies machine learning to analyze data patterns, aiding in fraud detection, customer targeting, and product safety insights (Davenport & Ronanki, 2018).

2.5. Technological Impact on Modern Service Delivery

The integration of AI, big data, and machine learning has dramatically improved productivity and customer experience in service sectors. For instance, AI-powered algorithms in e-commerce predict customer preferences, enabling proactive customer service (Xiang & Fesenmaier, 2020). Automation further boosts productivity by reducing human error in high-volume, repetitive tasks in industries like retail and hospitality (Ivanov & Webster, 2019).

Blockchain has similarly transformed financial services by ensuring secure, transparent, and efficient transactions, reducing the need for intermediaries in banking (Casino et al., 2019). Telemedicine in healthcare exemplifies technology's impact, where remote diagnostics and IoT monitoring became crucial during the COVID-19 pandemic, ensuring patient care continuity (Xie et al., 2020).

However, these advancements come with challenges, including potential job displacement and data privacy concerns. Frey and Osborne (2017) indicate that nearly half of U.S. jobs could be threatened by automation, particularly in low-skilled service roles. Additionally, high adoption costs and skill gaps hinder seamless technology integration, which impacts the potential for full-service transformation (Parasuraman et al., 2020). Despite these challenges, technology continues to drive innovation in the service sector, balancing efficiency gains with the need for ethical and responsible adoption (Zaki, 2019).

3.0. KEY QUESTIONS ADDRESSED IN THE CHAPTER

3.1. What are the Applications of Data-Driven Decision-Making in Service Industries?

This question explores the various ways in which data-driven decision-making (DDDM) is utilized across different service sectors. It examines specific applications such as predictive analytics for customer behavior, real-time data analysis for operational improvements, and the use of data to enhance customer experiences. (Soori et al., 2024 and Gu, 2024) The chapter aims to provide examples and case studies that illustrate how organizations leverage DDDM to make informed decisions that drive business success.

3.2. Why is AI-Driven Automation Critical for Operational Efficiency?

This question addresses the importance of AI-driven automation in enhancing operational efficiency within service industries. It discusses how automation technologies streamline processes, reduce human error, and enable faster decision-making (Jagatheesaperumal et al., 2021). The chapter highlights the role of AI in optimizing resource allocation, improving service delivery, and ultimately contributing to cost savings and increased productivity.

3.3. How Can Organizations Overcome Implementation Challenges?

This question focuses on the challenges organizations face when implementing DDDM, AI, and automation technologies (Vaddy, 2023 and Kumar et al., 2024). It explores barriers such as data quality issues, resistance to change among employees, and the need for reskilling the workforce. The chapter provides strategies and best practices for overcoming these challenges, ensuring a smoother transition to data-driven and automated processes.

3.4. What Gaps Exist in Current Literature Regarding AI in Service Industries?

This question identifies the gaps in existing research related to the application of AI in service industries. It discusses areas that require further exploration, such as the long-term impact of AI on employment, ethical considerations in AI decision-making, and the regulatory frameworks needed to govern AI use (Aldoseri et al., 2024). The chapter emphasizes the importance of addressing these gaps to ensure the responsible and effective deployment of AI technologies in service sectors.

4.0. OBJECTIVES AND SCOPE

4.1. Chapter Objectives

Analyze Operational Efficiency Enhancements

This chapter explores how AI-driven technologies have revolutionized operational efficiency in service industries, notably healthcare, banking, tourism, and hospitality. AI automation enhances routine task management and minimizes human error, streamlining workflows across sectors (Yablonsky, 2019). In healthcare, administrative tasks such as scheduling and billing are automated, freeing up resources for improved patient care. Similarly, AI enables automatic fraud detection and compliance checks in banking, reducing manual interventions and ensuring rapid responses (Adeyeri, 2024). In hospitality and tourism, AI-driven chatbots manage reservations, respond to inquiries, and provide recommendations, allowing human staff to handle more complex customer interactions (Schmitt, 2023). Moreover, predictive analytics and resource optimization through AI help organizations forecast demand, streamline operations, and optimize resources, making sectors more responsive to real-time needs (Elgendy, Elragal, & Päivärinta, 2022).

Explore Customer Satisfaction Improvements

In today's service-oriented economy, customer satisfaction is paramount. This section examines AI's role in enhancing personalized, responsive customer experiences. Across healthcare, banking, tourism, and hospitality, AI personalizes services by analyzing customer behavior, helping companies exceed expectations and foster loyalty (Gabelaia, 2022). Chatbots and virtual assistants provide 24/7 support, addressing queries and reducing human workloads, particularly in tourism and banking (Adeyeri, 2024). In hospitality, AI personalizes guest experiences by anticipating needs, transforming the customer journey into a seamless experience (Schmitt, 2023). AI in healthcare proactively supports patient engagement by sending reminders and offering preventive care advice, enhancing patient satisfaction beyond the clinic (Yablonsky, 2019).

Identify Implementation Challenges

Despite AI's advantages, implementation presents challenges, particularly in ethics, data security, and workforce reskilling. AI-driven decision-making in sectors like banking and healthcare requires ethical transparency to avoid biases and ensure fairness (Provost & Fawcett, 2013). Data security is essential for protecting sensitive information in banking and healthcare, with stringent cybersecurity and compliance measures needed to maintain customer trust (Elgendy, Elragal, & Päivärinta, 2022). Workforce reskilling is also critical as AI takes over routine tasks, necessitating training for employees to work alongside AI systems effectively, particularly in hospitality and banking (Kothandapani, 2021).

4.2. Delimitation of Scope

Focus Areas: Healthcare, Tourism, Banking, Hospitality

The chapter focuses on healthcare, tourism, banking, and hospitality, as these industries rely heavily on operational efficiency and real-time decision-making to enhance customer service. In healthcare, AI improves diagnostics and patient outcomes by managing records and predictive analytics (Yablonsky, 2019). Tourism leverages AI for booking processes, customer personalization, and real-time assistance (Gabelaia, 2022). In banking, AI aids in fraud detection and customer query automation, bolstering both security and satisfaction (Adeyeri, 2024). Hospitality benefits from automated check-in, personalized guest experiences, and resource optimization (Schmitt, 2023). Real-world case studies in each sector illustrate AI's transformative role, enhancing operational efficiency and customer satisfaction.

Exclusions: Non-Service Industries

Non-service industries such as manufacturing, agriculture, and heavy industry are excluded from this chapter's scope, as their AI applications focus on supply chain optimization and production automation rather than customer interaction (Provost & Fawcett, 2013). Unlike service industries, where AI augments human roles and requires reskilling, AI in manufacturing often replaces manual tasks, creating different workforce dynamics (Elgendy, Elragal, & Päivärinta, 2022). By excluding non-service industries, the chapter hones in on customer-centric sectors, ensuring relevant analysis for industries where real-time, personalized service is essential for competitiveness.

5.0. LITERATURE REVIEW

5.1. Summary of Relevant Literature on AI in Service Industries

Artificial Intelligence (AI) and automation have significantly transformed service industries by enhancing efficiency, streamlining routine tasks, and optimizing customer experiences. In healthcare, AI applications are increasingly critical for improving diagnoses, treatment planning, and patient data analysis, ultimately contributing to better patient outcomes and resource optimization (Bolu, 2024). Similarly, customer service has benefited from AI-driven chatbots that manage basic queries, freeing human agents to handle complex issues, which increases overall service efficiency and improves customer satisfaction. In the public sector, AI adoption is enabling faster, more transparent services by reducing bureaucratic processes and optimizing resource use. According to Putri and Maulidya (2024), these improvements reflect AI's capacity to support decision-making and offer citizen-friendly services. The financial sector, too, benefits from AI-driven predictive analytics, which enhance forecasting, risk management, and client personalization, providing competitive advantages and operational efficiency (Raza & Abbas, 2024).

5.2. Identification of Research Gaps

Despite AI's notable advancements, several research gaps remain. One major area of concern is the ethical implications of AI in decision-making, particularly related to biases that can affect underrepresented groups. AI applications in healthcare, finance, and law must be scrutinized to prevent biased decisions that may have adverse social impacts (Wester et al., 2024). Further research on creating ethical, transparent, and accountable AI systems is necessary, especially as AI takes on greater decision-making roles. Additionally, small and medium-sized enterprises (SMEs) encounter barriers to adopting advanced AI due to costs and limited technical resources. Mahbub and Ayman (2024) argue that more studies should focus on making AI accessible and affordable for smaller businesses, especially in retail and hospitality, to ensure they benefit from automation and efficiency. Finally, there is a need for research on how AI can complement rather than replace human expertise. For example, industries like healthcare require nuanced human judgment that AI alone cannot replicate. Vashishth et al. (2024) recommend studies to determine how AI can support human decision-making through data-driven insights, while leaving complex ethical decisions to human professionals.

5.3. Implications for Data-Driven Decision-Making

AI has revolutionized data-driven decision-making in sectors like finance, logistics, and procurement. By facilitating real-time analysis, AI enables companies to make accurate and timely decisions, reducing human error and enhancing operational efficiency. In finance, for example, predictive AI models allow firms to analyze large data volumes, forecast market trends, manage risks, and personalize client services, giving them a strategic edge (Raza & Abbas, 2024). Similarly, supply chain management benefits from AI's ability to anticipate disruptions, optimize inventory, and propose cost-effective procurement strategies (Lungu, 2024). AI also plays a vital role in promoting sustainability through environmental data analysis, such as monitoring carbon emissions and resource use. According to Mumtaz (2024), AI's data-driven insights empower companies to align their operations with sustainability goals, supporting responsible business practices and regulatory compliance.

6.0. METHODOLOGY

6.1. Research Design

Qualitative Approach

A qualitative approach is appropriate for exploring the complex impacts of AI and automation in service industries, as it provides an in-depth understanding of how these technologies reshape workflows and influence organizational dynamics. Through interviews and focus groups with managers, employees, and industry experts, researchers can capture perceptions and experiences, revealing the nuanced ways AI affects workplace culture and operations (Bolu, 2024). This method also uncovers the human responses to AI adoption, from enthusiasm to resistance, providing insight into employee adaptation and concerns (Mahbub & Ayman, 2024).

Case Studies and Empirical Analysis

Case studies offer valuable insights by detailing how specific companies apply AI and automation, thereby illustrating industry-specific challenges and benefits. For instance, in hospitality, AI-driven customer service systems have improved satisfaction rates and lowered labor costs, offering a model for similar applications in other sectors (Putri & Maulidya, 2024). Empirical analysis further strengthens these findings by providing quantifiable data on performance metrics such as cost reductions and efficiency gains post-AI implementation, thereby solidifying the practical advantages of AI in industries like finance and logistics (Raza & Abbas, 2024).

6.2. Data Collection Techniques

Secondary Data Review

Secondary data analysis is a foundational step, allowing for a broad understanding of current AI trends, applications, and challenges across service sectors. Reviewing academic papers and industry reports highlights where AI is successfully improving efficiencies, such as in supply chain management, and identifies gaps for further study, like ethical concerns or the accessibility of AI for smaller enterprises (Lungu, 2024). Secondary data reviews also ensure reliability by cross-referencing existing studies, which helps validate new research and identifies emerging areas for inquiry (Mumtaz, 2024).

Expert Interviews

Interviews with industry leaders offer first-hand insights that are often absent from published data, such as operational and ethical challenges in AI adoption. These interviews provide real-world examples of AI use in specific sectors, such as the role of AI in enhancing risk management in finance or automating customer support in retail (Wester et al., 2024). Insights from interviews also help in forecasting industry trends, as they capture the perspectives of professionals who are directly engaged with implementing and overseeing AI technologies.

6.3. Justification of Methodological Choices

A combination of qualitative methods, including case studies and expert interviews, is well-suited for researching the multifaceted role of AI in service industries. The qualitative approach is essential to capture the human aspects of AI integration, such as how employees perceive automation's impact on their roles (Bolu, 2024). Case studies provide industry-specific examples, allowing for an in-depth examination of AI applications and offering lessons transferable to other sectors (Putri & Maulidya, 2024). Meanwhile, expert interviews contribute real-time industry insights, addressing both operational outcomes and ethical considerations, thereby complementing data-driven analysis with a more comprehensive understanding of AI's broader implications (Mahbub & Ayman, 2024).

7.0. ANALYSIS AND FINDINGS

7.1. Impact of AI on Decision-Making Processes

Digital transformation is accelerating across industries, compelling organizations to integrate artificial intelligence (AI) to maintain competitive advantages or face decline (Fitzgerald et al., 2014). AI's capacity to process and analyze large datasets has empowered businesses to derive insights, supporting more informed and efficient decision-making. AI applications in healthcare, banking, and hospitality illustrate its transformative potential across diverse sectors, each with unique implementation strategies and challenges.

Case Studies in Healthcare

AI has significantly advanced decision-making in healthcare, notably improving diagnostic accuracy and operational efficiency. For example, AI-powered image analysis tools in radiology can detect abnormalities, such as tumors, more rapidly and accurately than traditional methods, enabling early treatment and improved patient outcomes (Schmitt, 2023). During the COVID-19 pandemic, hospitals leveraged AI to predict patient volume and allocate resources effectively, showcasing its value in crisis management (Yablonsky, 2019). Moreover, AI-driven tools streamline hospital operations, handling routine administrative tasks, which allows healthcare staff to focus on critical care responsibilities. However, privacy concerns and high implementation costs remain challenges, particularly for smaller healthcare facilities (Marda, 2018).

Case Studies in Banking

In banking, AI enhances risk assessment, fraud detection, and customer service. Fraud detection systems analyze transaction data in real-time, flagging unusual patterns more swiftly than traditional approaches, which reduces fraud incidents and improves customer experience (Kommisetty, 2022). AI also plays a role in credit scoring, as models now incorporate varied data points—such as spending habits and social media activity—to better assess credit risk and potentially expand credit access (Davidson, 2020). AI-powered chatbots streamline customer service by managing routine inquiries, allowing human agents to focus on complex issues. However, these advances introduce concerns about data security and the integration of AI with legacy banking systems, which can be costly and complex (Schmitt, 2023).

Case Studies in Hospitality

The hospitality industry uses AI to enhance guest experiences, optimize pricing, and improve operational efficiency. AI-based customer relationship management (CRM) systems analyze guest data to personalize services, such as recommending special packages or room upgrades based on past preferences (Duft & Durana, 2020). Additionally, AI-driven dynamic pricing adjusts room rates in response to demand, helping hotels maximize revenue by balancing pricing and occupancy. On the operational side, hotels increasingly use AI to manage scheduling, inventory, and even housekeeping, often deploying robots to handle repetitive tasks (Johnson et al., 2021). While AI improves service quality, the high cost of technology integration and potential loss of personal touch in customer service pose challenges (Schmitt, 2023).

7.2. Key Findings on Operational Efficiency and Customer Satisfaction

AI has proven instrumental in enhancing operational efficiency and customer satisfaction by automating tasks and offering predictive capabilities. For instance, predictive maintenance in manufacturing and hospitality prevents downtime by alerting businesses when equipment is likely to fail, saving time and resources (Bousdekis et al., 2021). In banking, AI chatbots available 24/7 facilitate customer service, while personalized offerings in hospitality drive guest satisfaction and loyalty (Adeyeri, 2024). Nonetheless, integrating AI into service industries presents obstacles such as high upfront costs, complex system integrations, and ethical considerations regarding data privacy (Riley et al., 2021).

7.3. Challenges Identified in AI Implementation

AI implementation presents challenges across industries, particularly with integrating AI into existing infrastructures. Healthcare and banking, for example, rely on legacy systems that are often incompatible with advanced AI technologies, necessitating substantial investment in technology and workforce training (Riley et al., 2021). Privacy concerns also arise, as AI relies on vast amounts of data, increasing the risk of data breaches and privacy violations, especially in sectors governed by strict regulations like finance and healthcare (Colombari et al., 2023). Additionally, algorithmic bias is a persistent issue; biased data can produce inequitable outcomes, as seen in AI-based credit scoring, where certain demographics may be unfairly disadvantaged. Thus, ethical considerations and fairness must be prioritized to mitigate these risks (Schmitt, 2023).

8.0. SUGGESTIONS AND RECOMMENDATIONS

8.1. Strategic Adoption of AI in Service Industries

AI is reshaping service industries by enhancing decision-making, streamlining operations, and fostering personalized customer experiences. According to Yablonsky (2019), AI tools enable businesses to automate decision-making processes, effectively identifying market trends and customer behaviors, which minimizes human error and increases accuracy. This leads to a competitive edge in operational efficiency and customer satisfaction (Yablonsky, 2019). Kommisetty (2022) notes that technologies like chatbots and recommendation systems allow real-time, personalized customer interactions, enabling flexible and responsive services that enhance customer experiences.

Strategic AI adoption, however, necessitates a clear alignment with business objectives and investment in critical areas like data management and cybersecurity. Organizations must tailor AI systems to complement, not replace, human decision-making, thereby supporting strategic goals without compromising ethical standards (Schmitt, 2023). Additionally, fostering a digital transformation culture encourages employees to engage with AI-driven tasks, promoting a collaborative integration of AI within business operations (Kothandapani, 2021).

8.2. Employee Training and Development

As AI integration becomes central in service sectors, continuous employee training on AI skills is essential. Employees must not only understand technical aspects but also recognize how AI enhances daily tasks. Elgendy et al. (2022) emphasize the need for comprehensive training that includes both technical skills and contextual understanding of AI's role in specific tasks. This holistic approach helps employees leverage AI's full potential to improve workplace productivity (Elgendy et al., 2022).

Ongoing learning initiatives are vital, as Folorunso et al. (2024) suggest, to keep employees updated on evolving AI technologies, ensuring they can adapt to advancements and collaborate effectively with AI. Such continuous learning should also cover soft skills, preparing employees for adaptive roles as AI takes on more routine tasks (Folorunso et al., 2024). Marda (2018) underscores the importance of reskilling and upskilling, as employees transition into more analytical roles supported by AI capabilities.

8.3. Regulatory Considerations for Ethical AI Use

With AI's expansion in service industries, ethical and regulatory issues surrounding data privacy, transparency, and potential biases demand careful attention. Adeyeri (2024) highlights the need for updated regulatory frameworks that ensure AI's responsible and transparent usage, particularly concerning sensitive data handling. Regulations such as the GDPR provide a foundation for data privacy, but AI's complexities require additional oversight to prevent misuse, especially in sectors like healthcare and finance (Adeyeri, 2024; Colombari et al., 2023).

Moreover, AI's role in automating tasks brings concerns about workforce displacement, making it essential for governments and companies to collaboratively support reskilling programs and social safety nets. Riley et al. (2021) argue that ethical AI deployment must balance innovation with social responsibility, protecting both progress and workforce stability. Transparency remains key, with Johnson et al. (2021) recommending enforceable standards that mandate explainable AI decisions, thus ensuring accountability and ethical adherence in automated processes.

9.0. FUTURE SCOPE FOR RESEARCH

9.1. Long-Term Implications of AI in Service Industries

As AI advances, its long-term impact on service industries is expected to redefine both business processes and customer interactions. Wirtz (2020) predicts that AI-driven service robots will become commonplace, offering cost savings and efficiency gains but also raising questions about the displacement of human roles, particularly in traditionally people-centered sectors like customer service. While AI has proven valuable for short-term decision-making and task automation, understanding its sustained effects on customer relationships and overall business strategy requires further investigation (Khneyzer et al., 2024).

AI-powered Customer Relationship Management (CRM) systems, for example, are gaining traction for their ability to leverage big data for deeper insights into customer needs and preferences (Kalaiyarasan et al., 2023). However, the long-term implications of AI-driven CRM on customer trust and engagement remain unclear. Ernst, Merola, and Samaan (2019) suggest that as AI continues to alter job landscapes, particularly in routine tasks, industries must invest in workforce reskilling to mitigate potential job disruptions. Moreover, the ethical considerations around data usage and transparency in AI systems are paramount. Belanche et al. (2024) argue that sustaining customer trust will be vital as AI's role in service industries deepens, making ethical design and transparency crucial for AI's long-term acceptance.

9.2. Potential Research Areas

AI's increasing role in service industries offers multiple research opportunities. One promising area is exploring the effectiveness of AI tools like chatbots and virtual assistants in enhancing customer interactions. Ma and Ye (2022) highlight the need to examine customer responses to these AI tools over time, questioning whether AI can fully replicate human empathy or if it will remain useful only for routine queries. Understanding customer perceptions will be key to refining AI-driven customer service.

Additionally, AI-driven decision-making and predictive analytics present valuable avenues for research. Nam et al. (2021) emphasize the potential of AI to deliver real-time, personalized experiences based on customer behavior patterns, suggesting that future research should investigate the balance between personalization and data privacy to optimize customer satisfaction.

Ethics and transparency are also critical areas for research. Johnson et al. (2021) underline the importance of developing ethical AI frameworks to avoid bias and ensure privacy, promoting fairness and accountability. This focus on ethical AI is vital as AI takes on increasingly complex decision-making roles.

Finally, sustainability in AI design is emerging as an important research priority. Gupta and Rathore (2024) advocate for AI systems that prioritize energy efficiency to minimize their environmental impact, especially as industries work toward sustainable operations. Future studies could examine how AI technologies can be engineered to support corporate sustainability goals without sacrificing performance.

10.0. CONCLUSION

10.1. Summary of Key Insights

This study has illuminated the profound impact of Artificial Intelligence (AI) and automation on service industries, particularly in enhancing operational efficiency and customer experience. Key insights reveal that AI technologies facilitate data-driven decision-making (DDDM) by enabling organizations to analyze vast amounts of data in real-time, leading to more informed and timely decisions). The literature indicates that AI applications, such as predictive analytics and machine learning, are instrumental in personalizing customer interactions and optimizing service delivery (Yablonsky, S., 2019). Furthermore, the ethical implications of AI deployment, including concerns about bias and data privacy, have emerged as critical areas for future research (Jagatheesaperumal, S., et al., 2021). Overall, the integration of AI into service industries not only streamlines operations but also provides a competitive advantage in an increasingly data-centric marketplace.

10.2. Final Thoughts on the Future of Data-Driven Decision-Making in Services

Looking ahead, the future of DDDM in service industries appears promising, driven by continuous advancements in AI technologies. As organizations increasingly adopt AI solutions, the ability to leverage data for strategic decision-making will become paramount (Provost, F. Fawcett, T., 2013). The emphasis on ethical AI practices will also shape the landscape, as businesses strive to build trust with consumers by ensuring transparency and accountability in their AI systems (Akter, S., et. al. 2019). Moreover, the potential for AI to create new roles and enhance human-AI collaboration presents exciting opportunities for workforce development (Jagatheesaperumal, S., et al., 2021). Ultimately, the successful integration of DDDM, supported by AI and automation, will be essential for service industries to thrive in a dynamic and competitive environment.

REFERENCES

Adeyeri, S. (2024). AI adoption and data privacy: Regulatory requirements for ethical use. *Journal of Artificial Intelligence and Ethics*, *12*(1), 45–63.

Akter, S., Bandara, R., Hani, U., & Wamba, S. F. (2019). *Analytics-based decision-making for service systems: A qualitative study and agenda for future research*. International Journal of Information Management. Retrieved from ScienceDirect.

Aldoseri, A., Al-Khalifa, K. N., & Hamouda, A. M. (2024). *AI-powered innovation in digital transformation: Key pillars and industry impact*. Retrieved from. [Article link]

Belanche, D., Casaló, L. V., Flavián, C., & Schepers, J. (2024). Trust in AI: Building ethical and transparent AI systems in service industries. *Journal of Service Research*, *27*(1), 35–49.

Bolu, T. (2024). *Enhancing AI Algorithms through Big Data: Challenges and Opportunities*. ResearchGate.

Bousdekis, A., et al. (2021). Data-driven decision-making in Industry 4.0. *Industry 4.0 Journal*, *5*(1), 92-110.

Bughin, J., & Van Zeebroeck, N. (2017). The best response to digital disruption. *MIT Sloan Management Review*.

Casino, F., Dasaklis, T. K., & Patsakis, C. (2019). A systematic literature review of blockchain-based applications: Status, classification, and open issues. *Telematics and Informatics*, *36*, 55–81. DOI: 10.1016/j.tele.2018.11.006

Cavanillas, J. M., Curry, E., & Wahlster, W. (Eds.). (2016). *New horizons for a data-driven economy: A roadmap for big data in Europe*. Springer. DOI: 10.1007/978-3-319-21569-3

Chea, A.C. (2011). *Activity-based costing system in the service sector: A strategic approach for enhancing managerial decision making and competitiveness*. International Journal of Business and Management. Retrieved from Academia.edu

Christofi, M., Pereira, V., & Vrontis, D. (2021). Blockchain, fintech, and IoT: An emergent industry research agenda for retail banking. *Journal of Business Research*, *124*, 257–268.

Colombari, L., Ferrara, M., & Singh, R. (2023). Regulatory considerations for AI in healthcare and finance. *International Journal of Regulatory Science*, *20*(3), 79–98.

Davenport, T. H., & Ronanki, R. (2018). Artificial intelligence for the real world. *Harvard Business Review*, *96*(1), 108–116.

Davidson, R. (2020). *AI innovation in financial services. Central and Eastern European Online Library (CEEOL)*. CEEOL.

De Mauro, A., Greco, M., & Grimaldi, M. (2016). A formal definition of big data based on its essential features. *Library Review*, *65*(3), 122–135. DOI: 10.1108/LR-06-2015-0061

Duft, G., & Durana, P. (2020). *AI-driven innovation in hospitality. Central and Eastern European Online Library (CEEOL)*. CEEOL.

Elgendy, H., Lin, P., & Chien, S. (2022). Training needs for AI-driven service industries: Developing an effective workforce. *Service Industry Review*, *31*(2), 104–118.

Ernst, E., Merola, R., & Samaan, D. (2019). The challenges of automation and the future of work in developing countries. *Journal of Economic Development*, *40*(2), 23–47.

Fitzgerald, M., Kruschwitz, N., Bonnet, D., & Welch, M. (2014). Embracing digital technology: A new strategic imperative. *MIT Sloan Management Review*.

Folorunso, A., Gupta, R., & Shah, P. (2024). Continuous learning in AI environments: A guide for employee training in service sectors. *Journal of Workforce Development, 22*(1), 52–67.

Frey, C. B., & Osborne, M. A. (2017). The future of employment: How susceptible are jobs to computerization? *Technological Forecasting and Social Change, 114*, 254–280. DOI: 10.1016/j.techfore.2016.08.019

Gabelaia, D. (2022). The Role of AI in Personalizing Customer Experience in Tourism. *Tourism Technology Today, 6*(1), 45–53.

Gu, S. (2024). *Exploring the Role of AI in Business Decision-Making and Process Automation*. Link to PDF.

Gummesson, E., Mele, C., & Polese, F. (2019). Technology and innovation in service ecosystems: A conceptual framework for service science research. *Journal of Service Management, 30*(4), 545–564.

Gupta, M., & Rathore, S. (2024). Sustainable AI: Designing environmentally responsible systems. *Sustainability, 16*(1), 15–30.

Intelligence, A. (2016). *Automation, and the Economy*. Executive Office of the President. Read PDF

Ivanov, S., & Webster, C. (2019). Robots, artificial intelligence, and service automation in travel, tourism, and hospitality. *Tourism Review, 74*(1), 37–50.

Jagatheesaperumal, S. K., & Rahouti, M. (2021). *The Duo of Artificial Intelligence and Big Data for Industry 4.0*. Link to Article.

Javaid, H. A. 2024. "The Future of Financial Services: Integrating AI for Smarter, More Efficient Operations". MZ Journal of Artificial Intelligence 1 (2). http://mzjournal.com/index.php/MZJAI/article/view/239

Johnson, P., Harrington, A., & O'Brien, K. (2021). Ethical AI in business: Guidelines for transparency and fairness. *Business Ethics Quarterly, 32*(3), 455–471.

Johnson, P., Lee, J., & Evans, B. (2021). Ensuring transparency in AI: Regulatory approaches for ethical decision-making. *AI & Society, 36*(4), 621–635.

Kalaiyarasan, K., Jeyakumar, R., & Karthik, A. (2023). Enhancing customer insights with AI-powered CRM systems. *International Journal of Business Technology, 45*(2), 78–90.

Karpen, I. O., & Conduit, J. (2021). The role of emerging technologies in service transformation. *Journal of Services Marketing, 35*(6), 713–729.

Khneyzer, V., Gomez, C., & Mota, R. (2024). Customer relations in an AI-driven era: Balancing technology with human insights. *Journal of Business Research, 78*(3), 155–166.

Kommisetty, S. (2022). Enhancing customer service with AI: Real-time, personalized interactions in service industries. *Journal of Service Management, 43*(1), 89–101.

Kothandapani, R. (2021). Reskilling for AI in the Hospitality Industry. *Hospitality Industry Journal, 4*(2), 128–140.

Kumar, S., Talukder, M. B., & Tyagi, P. K. (2024). *The Impact of Artificial Intelligence on Improving Efficiency in Service and Implementing Best Practices in Service Marketing*. Link to PDF. DOI: 10.4018/979-8-3693-7909-7.ch004

Lungu, M. (2024). *Enhancing Public Service Delivery in Government Procurement*. Elgar Online. DOI: 10.4337/9781035315314.00019

Ma, S., & Ye, H. (2022). AI in customer service: Evaluating long-term effects on customer satisfaction. *Service Management Review*, *9*(2), 101–115.

Mahbub, M. B., & Ayman, A. (2024). [Utilizing AI in Modern Businesses](http://myecommerecejournal.com/wp-content/uploads/2024-issue1/1mecj2024-

Manyika, J., Chui, M., Brown, B., Bughin, J., Dobbs, R., Roxburgh, C., & Byers, A. H. (2011). *Big data: The next frontier for innovation, competition, and productivity*. McKinsey Global Institute.

Marda, V. (2018). *AI policy in healthcare. Philosophical Transactions of the Royal Society A: Mathematical, Physical and Engineering Sciences*. Royal Society Publishing.

Nam, T., Oh, C., & Lee, J. (2021). Personalization in service industries using AI: Real-time applications and future potential. *AI & Society*, *35*(4), 527–539.

Nambisan, S., Lyytinen, K., Majchrzak, A., & Song, M. (2017). Digital innovation management: Reinventing innovation management research in a digital world. *Management Information Systems Quarterly*, *41*(1), 223–238. DOI: 10.25300/MISQ/2017/41:1.03

Perren, L., Berry, A., Partridge, M. (1998). *The evolution of managerial information, control and decision-making processes in small growth-oriented service sector businesses*. Journal of Small Business and Enterprise Development. Retrieved from Emerald

Provost, F., & Fawcett, T. (2013). *Data Science for Business: What You Need to Know About Data Mining and Data-Analytic Thinking*. O'Reilly Media.

Putri, C. A., & Maulidya, I. (2024). Digital Transformation in Public Administration. ResearchGate.

Rayhan, A. (2023). *The Future of Work: How AI and Automation Will Transform Industries*. Academia.edu. Read PDF

Raza, D., & Abbas, G. (2024). *Optimizing Financial Services with AI Integration*. ResearchGate.

Riley, D., Thompson, J., & Schmidt, H. (2021). Balancing innovation with workforce protection in AI deployment. *AI Policy and Ethics*, *28*(1), 13–29.

Schmitt, A. (2023). Strategic AI adoption: Integrating machine learning with business objectives. *Journal of Strategic AI*, *25*(2), 98–115.

Smith, J., & Green, R. (2021). Customer service innovation through AI. *International Journal of Service Industry Management*.

Soori, M., Jough, F. K. G., Dastres, R., & Arezoo, B. (2024). *AI-Based Decision Support Systems in Industry 4.0, A Review*. Link to Article. DOI: 10.1016/j.ject.2024.08.005

Suresh Babu, C. V., Abirami, S., & Sharon Manoj (2023). AI-Based Carthage Administration Towards Smart City. In C. Chowdhary, B. Swain, & V. Kumar (Eds.), Investigations in Pattern Recognition and Computer Vision for Industry 4.0 (pp. 1-17). IGI Global. DOI: 10.4018/978-1-6684-8602-3.ch001

Suresh Babu, C. V., Akshayah, N. S., & Maclin Vinola, P. (2024). Artificial Intelligence in Healthcare: Assessing Impacts, Challenges, and Recommendations for Achieving Healthcare Independence. In Geada, N., & Jamil, G. (Eds.), *Perspectives on Artificial Intelligence in Times of Turbulence: Theoretical Background to Applications* (pp. 61–80). IGI Global., DOI: 10.4018/978-1-6684-9814-9.ch005

Vaddy, R. K. (2023). *Artificial Intelligence for Industry 4.0: Systematic Review of Applications, Challenges, and Opportunities*. Link to PDF.

Van Riel, A. C. R., & Lievens, A. (2004). *New service development in high tech sectors: a decision-making perspective*. International Journal of Service Industry Management. Retrieved from Maastricht University DOI: 10.1108/09564230410523349

Vashishth, T. K., Sharma, V., & Sharma, K. K. (2024). *Industry 4.0 Trends and Strategies*. Wiley Online Library. DOI: 10.1002/9781394242641.ch5

Wester, A. M., Kumar, R., & Senses-Ozyurt, S. (2024). *Ethical Dilemmas in AI for Business Strategies*. ResearchGate.

Wilson, A. (1996). *Decision-making in organizations*. Editorial Board. Retrieved from Torrossa

Wirtz, J. (2020). Service robots and the future of work. *Journal of Service Management*, *31*(2), 343–368.

Xiang, Z., & Fesenmaier, D. R. (2020). Analytics and artificial intelligence in hospitality. *Journal of Travel Research*, *59*(4), 601–617.

Xie, X., Liu, X., & Zhang, H. (2020). Impact of COVID-19 on telemedicine. *Journal of Medical Systems*, *44*(6), 102.

Yablonsky, S. (2019). Leveraging AI for market insights and customer behavior analysis. *Journal of Business Analytics*, *17*(1), 39–55.

Chapter 2
Digital Transformation and the Future Workforce

Abhijit Chandratreya
https://orcid.org/0000-0001-9403-2094
SCES's Indira Institute of Management, Pune, India

ABSTRACT

The chapter "Digital Transformation and the Future Workforce" explores the impact of digital transformation on the service sector's workforce. As new technologies such as artificial intelligence, machine learning, robotics, and big data analytics are integrated into service delivery, there is a significant shift in the skills required and the nature of job roles. This chapter examines how businesses can navigate this transition by fostering digital skills, redesigning job roles, and implementing effective workforce development strategies. It also addresses the challenges and opportunities presented by digital transformation, including the need for continuous learning and adaptability in a rapidly evolving technological landscape. By understanding these dynamics, organizations can better prepare their workforce for the future, ensuring sustained growth and competitiveness in the digital age.

BACKGROUND

The rapid advancement of digital technologies has reshaped various industries, and the service sector is no exception. Digital transformation, characterized by the integration of digital technologies into all areas of business, fundamentally changes how organizations operate and deliver value to customers. This transformation is driven by several key technologies, including artificial intelligence (AI), machine learning, big data analytics, robotics, and the Internet of Things (IoT), which collectively enhance operational efficiency, improve service quality, and enable more personalized customer experiences (Brynjolfsson & McAfee, 2014).

One of the most significant impacts of digital transformation is on the workforce. Traditional job roles are evolving as automation and AI take over routine tasks, necessitating a shift towards more complex and creative problem-solving roles (Manyika et al., 2017). Consequently, there is an increasing demand for digital skills across all levels of the workforce. For instance, employees must now be proficient in data analysis, digital communication tools, and understanding how to leverage technology to enhance service delivery (Bessen, 2019).

The nature of employment is changing. Remote work, facilitated by digital communication and collaboration tools, has become more prevalent, especially following the global COVID-19 pandemic (Gartner, 2020). This shift requires organizations to rethink their approaches to workforce management, training, and development to ensure that employees remain productive and engaged in a digital-first environment.

DOI: 10.4018/979-8-3693-7447-4.ch002

Workforce development strategies must therefore focus on continuous learning and adaptability. Lifelong learning initiatives, reskilling, and upskilling programs are essential to equip employees with the necessary competencies to thrive in a digitally transformed landscape (World Economic Forum, 2018). Additionally, leadership must play a pivotal role in fostering a culture of innovation and agility, encouraging employees to embrace new technologies and methodologies (Westerman, Bonnet, & McAfee, 2014).

1. INTRODUCTION TO DIGITAL TRANSFORMATION IN THE SERVICE SECTOR

1.1. Definition and Scope

Digital transformation in the service sector refers to the integration of digital technology into all areas of a service organization, fundamentally changing how the organization operates and delivers value to customers. This transformation encompasses a wide range of technologies, including cloud computing, artificial intelligence (AI), big data analytics, and the Internet of Things (IoT), which collectively enhance operational efficiency and customer experience (Vial, 2019). The process is not merely about adopting new technologies but involves a strategic shift in mindset, organizational culture, and business processes to leverage digital tools effectively (Westerman et al., 2014). For instance, AI can automate routine tasks, allowing service providers to focus on more complex and value-added activities, thereby improving service delivery and customer satisfaction (Bharadwaj et al., 2013).

The scope of digital transformation in the service sector is vast, covering various sub-sectors such as finance, healthcare, hospitality, and retail. Each of these sectors faces unique challenges and opportunities in their digital transformation journeys. In finance, for instance, digital transformation involves the adoption of fintech solutions to streamline transactions and enhance security (Gomber et al., 2018). Healthcare organizations leverage digital tools for patient management, telemedicine, and data analytics to improve patient outcomes (Wang et al., 2018). In hospitality, digital platforms enhance customer experience through personalized services and efficient management systems (Bilgihan et al., 2016). Retailers use e-commerce platforms and big data analytics to optimize supply chains and personalize marketing efforts (Hänninen et al., 2018). Thus, digital transformation is a multi-faceted process that varies significantly across different service industries, each adopting specific strategies and technologies to meet their distinct needs and objectives.

1.2. Historical Context

The historical context of digital transformation in the service sector is marked by several key technological advancements and shifts in business paradigms. The origins of digital transformation can be traced back to the advent of computers and the Internet in the mid-20th century, which began to reshape how businesses operated. In the 1950s and 1960s, the introduction of mainframe computers allowed large organizations to automate complex calculations and data processing tasks, setting the stage for more sophisticated digital tools (Ceruzzi, 2003). The development of the Internet in the 1990s was a critical milestone, enabling global connectivity and the rise of e-commerce. Companies like Amazon and eBay emerged, fundamentally altering the retail landscape and demonstrating the potential of digital platforms (Khan, 2016).

The early 2000s saw the rise of Web 2.0, which facilitated greater user interaction and collaboration through social media and other online platforms. This era emphasized the importance of customer engagement and data-driven decision-making, leading to significant changes in how service industries approached marketing and customer service (O'Reilly, 2005). The proliferation of smartphones and mobile technologies in the late 2000s and 2010s further accelerated digital transformation. Mobile apps and cloud computing enabled real-time service delivery and seamless customer experiences, particularly in sectors such as banking, healthcare, and hospitality (Huang & Benyoucef, 2013). Throughout this period, advancements in AI, machine learning, and big data analytics continued to drive the evolution of digital transformation, allowing for more personalized and efficient service offerings (Brynjolfsson & McAfee, 2014). The historical trajectory of digital transformation reflects a continuous evolution driven by technological innovation and changing consumer expectations.

1.3. Importance of Digital Transformation

Digital transformation is of paramount importance in the service sector as it drives efficiency, innovation, and competitive advantage. By adopting digital technologies, service providers can streamline their operations, reduce costs, and enhance productivity. For instance, the automation of routine tasks through AI and robotics allows employees to focus on more strategic activities, improving overall operational efficiency (Davenport & Ronanki, 2018). Digital transformation also enables real-time data analytics, providing valuable insights into customer behavior and preferences. This data-driven approach helps organizations tailor their services to meet customer needs more effectively, thereby improving customer satisfaction and loyalty (Verhoef et al., 2021).

Digital transformation fosters innovation by enabling the development of new business models and service offerings. In the finance sector, for example, the rise of fintech has introduced innovative services like peer-to-peer lending, mobile payments, and blockchain-based transactions, disrupting traditional banking models (Gomber et al., 2018). In healthcare, digital tools such as telemedicine and electronic health records have revolutionized patient care, making healthcare services more accessible and efficient (Wang et al., 2018). The hospitality industry has benefited from digital platforms that facilitate personalized customer experiences and efficient management of resources (Bilgihan et al., 2016). Overall, digital transformation not only helps service organizations stay competitive in a rapidly changing market but also opens new opportunities for growth and differentiation.

2. TECHNOLOGICAL ADVANCEMENTS DRIVING CHANGE

2.1. Artificial Intelligence and Machine Learning

Artificial Intelligence (AI) and Machine Learning (ML) are critical components of digital transformation in the service sector, offering profound enhancements in operational efficiency, customer experience, and innovation. AI and ML technologies enable service providers to automate complex processes, analyze vast amounts of data, and generate predictive insights. In customer service, AI-driven chatbots and virtual assistants can handle a significant portion of customer inquiries, providing instant responses and freeing up human agents to tackle more complex issues (Huang & Rust, 2018). This not only improves response times and customer satisfaction but also reduces operational costs. In finance, ML algorithms are employed for fraud detection, risk management, and personalized financial advice, enhancing the security and personalization of services (Zhang & Zhu, 2019).

The application of AI and ML extends to various sub-sectors within the service industry, driving innovation and new service offerings. In healthcare, AI-powered diagnostic tools and predictive analytics support early disease detection and personalized treatment plans, leading to better patient outcomes (Esteva et al., 2017). In retail, ML algorithms analyze customer data to optimize inventory management, forecast demand, and personalize marketing strategies, thereby enhancing customer engagement and sales (Davenport, 2018). The hospitality industry benefits from AI in the form of personalized recommendations and dynamic pricing models, which adjust prices based on real-time demand and customer preferences (Ivanov & Webster, 2017). The integration of AI and ML thus empowers service providers to deliver more efficient, personalized, and innovative services, transforming the traditional service paradigms.

2.2. Automation and Robotics

Automation and robotics are transforming the service sector by enhancing productivity, reducing costs, and improving the consistency and quality of service delivery. Automation refers to the use of technology to perform tasks with minimal human intervention, while robotics involves the use of programmable machines to carry out a series of actions autonomously or semi-autonomously (Groover, 2019). In the service sector, these technologies are particularly valuable for performing repetitive and time-consuming tasks. For example, in the financial services industry, robotic process automation (RPA) is used to automate data entry, compliance checks, and transaction processing, which streamlines operations and reduces the risk of human error (Willcocks et al., 2015). Similarly, in the hospitality industry, service robots can handle tasks such as room service delivery, cleaning, and check-in processes, enhancing efficiency and allowing human staff to focus on more personalized guest interactions (Ivanov & Webster, 2017).

The implementation of automation and robotics extends beyond operational efficiency to significantly enhance customer experiences. In retail, automated checkout systems and inventory management robots help reduce wait times and ensure shelves are stocked with the right products, improving the shopping experience (Wang et al., 2020). In healthcare, robotic-assisted surgeries and automated diagnostic tools improve precision and patient outcomes while reducing the workload on medical professionals (Yang et al., 2017). Additionally, the integration of robots in customer service roles, such as automated kiosks and AI-driven chatbots, provides 24/7 assistance and supports rapid resolution of customer inquiries (Huang & Rust, 2018). These advancements underscore the critical role of automation and robotics in not only boosting efficiency but also elevating the overall quality of service in various sectors.

2.3. Internet of Things (IoT)

The Internet of Things (IoT) is revolutionizing the service sector by enabling interconnected devices to collect, exchange, and analyze data in real-time, thereby enhancing operational efficiency, customer experiences, and decision-making processes. IoT involves a network of physical objects—devices, vehicles, buildings, and other items—embedded with sensors, software, and other technologies to communicate and interact with each other and with centralized systems over the internet (Ashton, 2009). In the service sector, IoT applications are vast and varied. For instance, in the hospitality industry, smart hotel rooms equipped with IoT devices allow guests to control lighting, temperature, and entertainment systems via their smartphones, creating a highly personalized and convenient experience (Boehmer & Laesser, 2020). Similarly, in the healthcare sector, IoT-enabled medical devices such as wearable health monitors can track patient vitals in real-time, allowing for continuous health monitoring and timely interventions (Islam et al., 2015).

IoT's impact extends to operational efficiencies and cost savings in the service sector. In retail, IoT devices can monitor inventory levels in real-time, automatically triggering restocking orders when items run low, thereby optimizing inventory management and reducing waste (Gubbi et al., 2013). IoT-enabled predictive maintenance in industries such as logistics and facilities management allows for the timely maintenance of equipment, preventing breakdowns and extending the lifespan of assets (Lee et al., 2014). Additionally, IoT technologies in smart cities enhance public services by optimizing traffic flow, improving waste management, and enhancing public safety through real-time data analytics and automated systems (Zanella et al., 2014). Overall, IoT is a transformative force in the service sector, driving innovations that improve service delivery, operational efficiency, and customer satisfaction.

2.4. Cloud Computing and Big Data

Cloud computing and big data are pivotal elements in the digital transformation of the service sector, enabling businesses to leverage vast amounts of data for improved decision-making, scalability, and enhanced service delivery. Cloud computing provides on-demand access to computing resources such as servers, storage, and applications over the internet, allowing service providers to scale their operations dynamically and reduce IT infrastructure costs (Armbrust et al., 2010). This technology supports various service sectors by offering flexible and scalable solutions for data storage, processing, and analytics. For example, in the finance sector, cloud computing enables real-time transaction processing and data analytics, which are crucial for risk management and regulatory compliance (Marston et al., 2011). Similarly, in the healthcare sector, cloud-based platforms facilitate the storage and sharing of electronic health records, improving patient care and operational efficiency (Raghupathi & Raghupathi, 2014).

Big data, on the other hand, refers to the large volumes of structured and unstructured data that businesses generate and collect daily. The analysis of big data enables service providers to uncover patterns, correlations, and insights that can drive strategic decisions and enhance customer experiences (Chen et al., 2014). In retail, big data analytics helps businesses understand customer behavior, predict trends, and optimize pricing strategies (Davenport et al., 2012). For instance, e-commerce platforms use big data to personalize recommendations and improve inventory management, leading to increased sales and customer satisfaction. In the hospitality industry, big data is used to analyze guest preferences and operational data, allowing hotels to tailor their services and improve overall guest experiences (Bilgihan et al., 2016). The combination of cloud computing and big data thus empowers the service sector to innovate, streamline operations, and deliver personalized services, driving growth and competitive advantage.

3. IMPACT ON WORKFORCE DYNAMICS

3.1. Evolution of Job Roles

Digital transformation is significantly altering job roles within the service sector, driving a shift from traditional functions to more dynamic, technology-centric roles. As automation and AI take over repetitive and administrative tasks, employees are increasingly required to develop skills in managing and leveraging advanced technologies (Manyika et al., 2017). For example, in the financial services industry, roles that once focused on data entry and transaction processing are evolving into positions that require expertise in data analysis, cybersecurity, and fintech solutions (Davenport & Kirby, 2015). Employees now need to interpret complex data sets, understand machine learning models, and ensure the security of digital transactions, highlighting a move towards more analytical and strategic job functions.

In the healthcare sector, digital transformation is leading to the emergence of new roles such as telehealth coordinators, data analysts, and health informatics specialists. Traditional roles like medical records clerks are transitioning into health information managers who utilize electronic health records (EHRs) to improve patient care and streamline operations (Gough et al., 2015). Similarly, the retail industry is witnessing a shift from conventional sales roles to e-commerce specialists, digital marketing analysts, and customer experience managers. These roles require a deep understanding of digital platforms, consumer behavior analytics, and online marketing strategies (Brynjolfsson & McAfee, 2014). The hospitality industry is also evolving, with roles such as digital concierges and revenue management analysts becoming increasingly important as hotels leverage IoT, big data, and cloud computing to enhance guest experiences and optimize pricing strategies (Bilgihan et al., 2016).

The evolution of job roles is not only about new job titles but also about the enhancement of existing roles with new skill sets. Employees are now expected to be proficient with digital tools and technologies, adaptable to continuous technological changes, and capable of critical thinking and problem-solving in a digital context

(Westerman et al., 2014). This shift necessitates ongoing education and training programs to equip the workforce with the necessary skills to thrive in a digitally transformed service sector.

3.2. New Skills and Competencies

Digital transformation in the service sector demands a new set of skills and competencies, encompassing both technical and soft skills, to effectively leverage emerging technologies and meet evolving business needs. Technical skills are paramount as automation, AI, and data analytics become integral to service delivery. Employees are expected to be proficient in data analysis, understanding and interpreting large datasets to make informed decisions (Davenport & Patil, 2012). Skills in machine learning, coding, and familiarity with various programming languages and software platforms are increasingly necessary for roles that involve developing, managing, or working alongside AI and automated systems (Brynjolfsson & McAfee, 2014). Moreover, cybersecurity skills are critical to protect sensitive data and ensure secure digital transactions, especially in sectors such as finance and healthcare where data integrity is paramount (Kumar & Raj, 2019).

In addition to technical skills, digital transformation places a strong emphasis on soft skills that facilitate adaptation and innovation. Critical thinking and problem-solving abilities are essential for navigating the complexities and challenges associated with digital technologies (World Economic Forum, 2020). Creativity and innovation are also crucial as businesses seek to develop new digital products and services, or improve existing ones, to stay competitive in a rapidly changing market (Amabile & Pratt, 2016). Communication skills are vital for collaborating with cross-functional teams and effectively conveying technical information to non-technical stakeholders. Moreover, adaptability and continuous learning are imperative as the technological landscape evolves, requiring employees to stay updated with the latest advancements and continuously enhance their skill sets (Westerman et al., 2014).

Leadership and strategic thinking are also increasingly important competencies in the digital era. Leaders must not only understand digital technologies but also how to integrate them into business strategies to drive transformation and achieve organizational goals (Kane et al., 2015). This involves fostering a culture of innovation, guiding teams through change, and ensuring that digital initiatives align with broader business objectives. Therefore, the interplay of technical prowess and robust soft skills forms the backbone of the competencies required in the digitally transformed service sector.

3.3. Redefining Job Descriptions and Responsibilities

Digital transformation necessitates a significant redefinition of job descriptions and responsibilities within the service sector to align with new technological capabilities and business models. Traditional roles are evolving to incorporate digital competencies, and entirely new positions are emerging to manage and leverage digital tools effectively. For instance, customer service roles now often require proficiency with AI-driven chatbots and CRM systems to provide efficient and personalized customer support (Accenture, 2017). Employees in these roles need to understand how to interpret data generated by these systems to enhance customer interactions and resolve issues more effectively. Similarly, roles in marketing are being redefined to include responsibilities such as digital content creation, social media management, and data analytics to track and optimize campaign performance (Chaffey & Ellis-Chadwick, 2019).

In addition to incorporating new digital skills, job descriptions are expanding to emphasize strategic and analytical thinking. For example, data analysts and data scientists are critical roles that have emerged across various service industries, tasked with extracting actionable insights from large datasets to drive decision-making and strategy (Davenport & Patil, 2012). These roles require not only technical expertise in data manipulation and statistical analysis but also the ability to communicate findings to non-technical stakeholders and provide strategic recommendations. Moreover, IT roles are evolving from maintaining and troubleshooting systems to developing and implementing cloud-based solutions and cybersecurity measures, reflecting the increased reliance on digital infrastructure (Westerman et al., 2014).

Leadership roles are also being redefined to support digital transformation. Managers and executives are expected to champion digital initiatives and foster a culture of innovation and agility. They need to understand the implications of digital technologies on business processes and customer experiences and guide their teams through the transition (Kane et al., 2015). This involves a greater emphasis on change management, digital literacy, and strategic vision in job descriptions for leadership positions. Furthermore, as businesses adopt agile methodologies, roles such as product owners and scrum masters are becoming essential to facilitate iterative development and continuous improvement processes (Rigby et al., 2016). Overall, redefining job descriptions and responsibilities to integrate digital competencies and strategic thinking is crucial for organizations to fully realize the benefits of digital transformation in the service sector.

4. CHALLENGES AND OPPORTUNITIES

4.1. Reskilling and Upskilling

Reskilling and upskilling are critical strategies for ensuring that the workforce in the service sector remains competitive and capable in the face of rapid technological advancements brought about by digital transformation. Reskilling involves training employees in entirely new skills to take on different roles within the organization, often in response to the automation of their previous tasks (Manyika et al., 2017). For example, a customer service representative might be reskilled to become a data analyst or a digital marketing specialist, acquiring new technical and analytical capabilities to perform these roles effectively. This process not only preserves jobs but also helps organizations retain valuable employees who are already familiar with the company culture and business processes.

Upskilling, on the other hand, focuses on enhancing the current skills of employees to improve their performance in their existing roles or to enable them to take on more advanced responsibilities (World Economic Forum, 2020). For instance, a financial advisor might undergo upskilling in data analytics and AI to better understand and predict market trends, thereby providing more informed advice to clients. Similarly, healthcare professionals might receive training in telemedicine technologies and electronic health records management to improve patient care and operational efficiency (McGowan et al., 2018). Upskilling ensures that employees stay current with technological developments and can continue to contribute effectively to the organization's goals.

Both reskilling and upskilling are essential for building a resilient and adaptable workforce. They require a proactive approach to employee development, with organizations investing in continuous learning programs, partnerships with educational institutions, and access to online learning platforms (Bersin, 2019). Moreover, fostering a culture of lifelong learning is crucial, encouraging employees to embrace new technologies and methodologies. This cultural shift involves recognizing and rewarding learning initiatives, integrating training into regular workflows, and providing opportunities for employees to apply their new skills in practical settings (Agarwal et al., 2019). By prioritizing reskilling and upskilling, the service sector can ensure that its workforce remains agile and capable of meeting the challenges and opportunities presented by digital transformation.

4.2. Workforce Diversity and Inclusion

Digital transformation in the service sector offers a unique opportunity to enhance workforce diversity and inclusion, fostering a more innovative and resilient workforce. As organizations increasingly rely on digital tools and remote work capabilities, they can attract talent from a wider geographical and demographic pool, breaking down traditional barriers to employment (Deloitte, 2017). For instance, remote work technologies enable businesses to hire individuals who may have previously been excluded from the workforce due to physical disabilities, geographic limitations, or caregiving responsibilities. This inclusivity not only broadens the talent pool but also brings diverse perspectives and ideas that drive creativity and problem-solving within organizations (Hunt et al., 2018).

Digital transformation can support the implementation of more inclusive policies and practices. Advanced data analytics and AI can help identify and mitigate biases in recruitment, promotion, and performance evaluations, ensuring that decisions are based on objective criteria rather than unconscious biases (Raghavan et al., 2020). For example, AI-driven recruitment platforms can analyze a wider range of candidate attributes, such as skills and experiences, rather than relying solely on traditional metrics like education and previous job titles, which can disadvantage certain groups. Additionally, continuous learning and upskilling initiatives can be tailored to support underrepresented groups, providing them with the tools and opportunities needed to advance within the organization (Bersin, 2019).

To fully realize the benefits of diversity and inclusion, organizations must also foster a culture that values and supports these principles. This involves creating an environment where all employees feel respected, valued, and empowered to contribute their unique perspectives. Leadership commitment to diversity and inclusion is crucial, as is the establishment of clear policies and accountability measures. Employee resource groups, mentorship programs, and diversity training can further support an inclusive culture, helping to build a workforce that is not only diverse in its makeup but also cohesive and collaborative in its approach (Roberson, 2019). By integrating diversity and inclusion into the fabric of digital transformation initiatives, the service sector can build stronger, more innovative, and adaptable organizations.

4.3. Managing Resistance to Change

Managing resistance to change is a critical aspect of implementing digital transformation in the service sector. Employees often resist change due to fear of the unknown, loss of job security, or discomfort with new technologies and processes (Kotter & Schlesinger, 2008). To address these concerns, organizations need to employ a multi-faceted approach that includes clear communication, employee involvement, and support mechanisms. Effective communication is crucial to help employees understand the reasons behind the change, the benefits it brings, and the impact it will have on their roles (Armenakis & Harris, 2009). Transparent communication can reduce uncertainty and build trust, making employees more receptive to the transformation.

Involving employees in the change process is another effective strategy to mitigate resistance. When employees are engaged and participate in the planning and implementation stages, they are more likely to buy into the change and feel a sense of ownership (Jimmieson et al., 2004). This can be achieved through workshops, focus groups, and feedback sessions where employees can voice their concerns, contribute ideas, and feel heard. Additionally, providing training and development programs to upskill employees for new roles and responsibilities can ease the transition and reduce anxiety about their ability to succeed in a transformed environment (Cameron & Green, 2019). Offering continuous support through mentoring, coaching, and access to resources helps employees adapt more smoothly and reinforces their confidence in navigating new systems and processes.

Leadership plays a pivotal role in managing resistance to change. Leaders must exemplify commitment to the transformation, demonstrate its importance through their actions, and provide a compelling vision that aligns with organizational goals (Gill, 2003). They should also be empathetic and responsive to employee concerns, fostering an open and inclusive culture that values feedback and collaboration. Recognizing and rewarding employees who embrace and contribute to the change can further incentivize positive behavior and create a supportive environment (Heathfield, 2019). Ultimately, by addressing resistance proactively and empathetically, organizations in the service sector can facilitate a smoother transition to digital transformation and enhance overall organizational resilience and adaptability.

5. STRATEGIES FOR WORKFORCE DEVELOPMENT

5.1. Training and Education Programs

Training and education programs are fundamental to successfully implementing digital transformation in the service sector, ensuring that employees are equipped with the necessary skills and knowledge to adapt to new technologies and processes. These programs should be comprehensive, covering both technical skills, such as data analytics, AI, and cybersecurity, and soft skills, including adaptability, problem-solving, and digital literacy (Bersin, 2019). Tailoring training programs to the specific needs of different job roles and departments ensures that all employees receive relevant and practical instruction that directly enhances their job performance. For example, frontline customer service staff might be trained in using AI-driven customer relationship management (CRM) tools, while marketing teams might focus on data analytics and digital marketing strategies (Chaffey & Ellis-Chadwick, 2019).

To maximize effectiveness, training and education programs should incorporate a mix of learning modalities, including online courses, in-person workshops, and hands-on training sessions. Online learning platforms offer flexibility and accessibility, allowing employees to learn at their own pace and on their own schedule (Baldwin-Evans, 2006). In-person workshops and hands-on training provide opportunities for interactive learning and practical application of new skills, fostering a deeper understanding and retention of knowledge. Additionally, incorporating real-world scenarios and case studies can help employees relate their learning to actual job situations, making the training more relevant and impactful (Noe, 2017).

Continuous learning and development are crucial in a rapidly evolving digital landscape. Organizations should establish ongoing education initiatives that keep employees updated on the latest technological advancements and industry best practices. This can include regular refresher courses, advanced training sessions for emerging technologies, and opportunities for certification and professional development (Carnevale et al., 2015). Creating a culture of continuous learning encourages employees to take initiative in their own development and remain adaptable to change. Furthermore, leadership should actively support and participate in these training programs, demonstrating their commitment to employee growth and the organization's digital transformation goals (Westerman et al., 2014).

5.2. Collaborative Learning Environments

Collaborative learning environments are essential for fostering a culture of continuous improvement and innovation in the service sector, especially amid digital transformation. These environments encourage knowledge sharing, teamwork, and the collective problem-solving necessary to adapt to new technologies and processes. Collaborative learning involves various methods such as peer-to-peer learning, team-based projects, and interactive workshops, which enable employees to learn from each other's experiences and expertise (Smith & MacGregor, 1992). For instance, a peer mentoring program can pair employees who are proficient in specific digital tools with those who are less familiar, facilitating hands-on learning and mutual support. This approach not only enhances individual skills but also builds a cohesive team capable of tackling complex challenges together.

The use of collaborative technologies further enhances the effectiveness of these learning environments. Digital platforms such as collaborative workspaces, video conferencing tools, and social learning networks allow employees to connect and collaborate regardless of geographical barriers (Hrastinski, 2008). These tools support real-time communication and resource sharing, making it easier for teams to work together on projects and share insights. For example, a cloud-based project management tool can help a dispersed marketing team collaborate on a campaign by allowing them to collectively manage tasks, track progress, and share creative assets. Such platforms also facilitate asynchronous learning, where employees can access recorded sessions, discussion forums, and digital resources at their convenience, promoting a flexible and inclusive learning culture (Dabbagh & Kitsantas, 2012).

Fostering a collaborative learning environment requires leadership commitment and the establishment of a supportive organizational culture. Leaders should actively participate in and endorse collaborative learning initiatives, demonstrating their value to the organization (Senge, 1990). Encouraging a culture where employees feel safe to share ideas, ask questions, and experiment without fear of failure is crucial for innovation and continuous learning (Edmondson, 1999). Providing spaces and opportunities for informal learning, such as innovation hubs or regular "lunch and learn" sessions, can also promote collaboration and idea exchange. By integrating collaborative learning into the fabric of organizational culture, the service sector can harness the collective intelligence and creativity of its workforce, driving sustained success in a digitally transformed landscape.

5.3. Industry Partnerships and Internships

Industry partnerships and internships play a crucial role in equipping the service sector workforce with practical skills and real-world experience essential for navigating digital transformation. Establishing strong partnerships between educational institutions and industry organizations allows for a seamless integration of academic knowledge and practical application (Wilson, 2012). These collaborations can take various forms, such as joint research projects, guest lectures by industry experts, and co-development of curriculum tailored to current industry needs. By aligning educational programs with the latest technological advancements and market demands, these partnerships ensure that students and employees are better prepared to meet the challenges and opportunities presented by digital transformation (Blouin & Perry, 2009).

Internships are a vital component of these industry partnerships, providing students and early-career professionals with hands-on experience in real-world settings. Internships enable individuals to apply theoretical knowledge in practical scenarios, develop professional networks, and gain insights into industry practices and expectations (Gault, Leach, & Duey, 2010). For example, a marketing intern might work on digital marketing campaigns using data analytics tools to track and optimize performance, or an IT intern might assist in developing cloud-based solutions for a company. These experiences are invaluable for building technical competencies and understanding the dynamic nature of the service sector. Furthermore, internships often serve as a pipeline for talent acquisition, allowing companies to identify and recruit skilled individuals who are already familiar with their operations and culture (NACE, 2018).

To maximize the benefits of industry partnerships and internships, organizations should implement structured programs that provide meaningful learning opportunities and mentorship. Clear objectives, regular feedback, and exposure to various aspects of the business help interns gain a comprehensive understanding of their field and develop critical skills (D'Abate, Youndt, & Wenzel, 2009). Additionally, fostering an inclusive and supportive environment ensures that interns feel valued and motivated to contribute their best efforts. By investing in these initiatives, companies not only enhance their talent pool but also contribute to the overall development of a skilled and adaptable workforce capable of driving digital transformation in the service sector (Bersin, 2019).

6. CASE STUDIES OF SUCCESSFUL DIGITAL WORKFORCE TRANSFORMATIONS

1. AT&T's Reskilling Initiative

AT&T, a global telecommunications giant, embarked on a comprehensive reskilling initiative to prepare its workforce for the demands of a rapidly evolving digital landscape. Faced with the challenge of outdated skills among its employees, AT&T launched the "Future Ready" program, investing over $1 billion in retraining its workforce. The program included partnerships with leading educational institutions such as Georgia Tech and

Udacity to provide employees with access to online courses and nanodegrees in emerging fields like data science, AI, and cybersecurity (AT&T, 2017).

The results of this initiative were significant. AT&T reported that 140,000 employees engaged in these learning opportunities, leading to over 2.7 million completed courses. This massive upskilling effort not only improved employee satisfaction and retention but also enhanced the company's ability to innovate and compete in the digital age (Schwartz, 2018). AT&T's approach highlights the importance of strategic investment in employee development and the role of partnerships in successful digital transformation.

2. Schneider Electric's Digital Transformation Journey

Schneider Electric, a global specialist in energy management and automation, undertook a digital transformation to enhance its operational efficiency and customer service. The company introduced the "Schneider Electric Exchange," a digital ecosystem that integrates various digital tools and platforms to facilitate collaboration and innovation among employees, partners, and customers (Schneider Electric, 2020).

A key component of Schneider Electric's transformation was the implementation of a comprehensive training program aimed at developing digital competencies across its workforce. This included extensive training in data analytics, IoT, and cybersecurity. The company also encouraged a culture of continuous learning through its "Digital Readiness" program, which provided employees with access to a wide range of online learning resources and professional development opportunities (Frost & Sullivan, 2019).

As a result, Schneider Electric saw significant improvements in productivity, innovation, and customer satisfaction. The company reported a 30% increase in the efficiency of its supply chain operations and a 20% reduction in maintenance costs due to predictive analytics and IoT-enabled solutions (Schneider Electric, 2020). This case illustrates the importance of a holistic approach to digital transformation, encompassing technology adoption, workforce development, and cultural change.

3. DBS Bank's Digital Transformation Strategy

DBS Bank, a leading financial services group in Asia, embarked on a digital transformation journey to become a digital-first bank. Recognizing the need to transform its workforce, DBS launched a series of initiatives to build digital skills and foster an agile, innovative culture. This included the introduction of the "DBS Academy," a dedicated training platform offering courses in data analytics, AI, machine learning, and design thinking (DBS Bank, 2018).

DBS also implemented an "Agile" working model across the organization, breaking down traditional silos and promoting cross-functional collaboration. This shift was supported by continuous training and coaching in agile methodologies, enabling employees to adapt to new ways of working and deliver faster, more customer-centric solutions (Veyret, 2018).

The impact of DBS's digital transformation was profound. The bank reported a 60% increase in digital transactions and significant growth in digital customer engagement. Additionally, DBS was recognized as the "World's Best Digital Bank" by Euromoney in 2018, underscoring its successful digital transformation and workforce development efforts (Euromoney, 2018).

4. Siemens' Digitalization Strategy

Siemens, a global powerhouse in electronics and electrical engineering, has been at the forefront of digital transformation through its "Vision 2020+" strategy. Central to this strategy is the development of a digitally skilled workforce capable of driving innovation and growth. Siemens invested heavily in its "Siemens Learning Campus," offering a wide array of digital courses and certifications in areas such as AI, data analytics, and industrial IoT (Siemens, 2018).

Siemens also embraced a culture of continuous learning and innovation through its "Next47" initiative, an independent innovation unit designed to foster collaboration between employees and external startups. This initiative provided employees with opportunities to work on cutting-edge projects and gain exposure to the latest technological advancements (Siemens, 2018).

As a result of these efforts, Siemens achieved significant improvements in operational efficiency and innovation. The company reported a 25% increase in productivity and a 20% reduction in time-to-market for new products, attributed to the enhanced digital capabilities of its workforce (Siemens, 2018). Siemens' success demonstrates the critical role of comprehensive training and a culture of innovation in driving digital transformation.

7. FUTURE TRENDS AND PREDICTIONS

7.1. Emerging Technologies

Emerging technologies are revolutionizing the way organizations operate and the skills required of their workforce. Here are some key technologies shaping the future of workforce development:

1. Artificial Intelligence (AI) and Machine Learning (ML)

AI and ML are driving automation and decision-making capabilities across various industries. In workforce development, AI-powered tools are being used for talent acquisition, employee training, and performance management. Chatbots and virtual assistants streamline HR processes, while personalized learning platforms leverage ML algorithms to deliver tailored training content to employees (Gartner, 2021).

2. Internet of Things (IoT)

IoT devices are transforming the workplace by connecting physical objects and enabling real-time data collection and analysis. In workforce management, IoT sensors monitor employee productivity, safety, and well-being. For example, wearable devices track biometric data to optimize workplace ergonomics and prevent injuries (Deloitte, 2021).

3. Augmented Reality (AR) and Virtual Reality (VR)

AR and VR technologies are revolutionizing training and skill development by creating immersive learning experiences. In industries such as manufacturing and healthcare, AR and VR simulations allow employees to practice complex tasks in a risk-free environment. These technologies also facilitate remote collaboration and troubleshooting, reducing the need for physical presence (PwC, 2021).

4. Blockchain

Blockchain technology is revolutionizing the way transactions are recorded and verified, offering unprecedented security and transparency. In workforce development, blockchain-based platforms are being used for credentialing and certification, enabling employees to securely store and share their qualifications. This eliminates the need for intermediaries and reduces the risk of credential fraud (World Economic Forum, 2020).

5. Robotics and Automation

Robotic process automation (RPA) and advanced robotics are reshaping the nature of work by automating repetitive tasks and augmenting human capabilities. In industries such as manufacturing and logistics, robots are used for assembly, warehousing, and inventory management. In the service sector, RPA streamlines back-office operations, allowing employees to focus on higher-value tasks (McKinsey & Company, 2021).

7.2. Future Workforce Models

The future of work is rapidly evolving, driven by technological advancements, demographic shifts, and changing societal expectations. Here are some emerging workforce models shaping the future of work:

1. Hybrid Workforce

The hybrid workforce model combines remote and on-site work, offering employees flexibility in where and when they work. Enabled by digital technologies, this model allows organizations to tap into a global talent pool while providing employees with autonomy and work-life balance. Hybrid work arrangements require robust communication and collaboration tools to ensure seamless coordination and connectivity (World Economic Forum, 2021).

2. Gig Economy

The gig economy model involves hiring independent contractors and freelancers on a project or task basis. This model offers organizations flexibility in scaling their workforce based on demand while providing workers with autonomy and diversity in their projects. However, it also raises concerns about job security, benefits, and labor rights, requiring regulatory frameworks to ensure fair treatment and protection for gig workers (Katz & Krueger, 2019).

3. Agile Workforce

The agile workforce model emphasizes adaptability, collaboration, and cross-functional teamwork. Agile teams are organized around specific projects or objectives, with members from different departments or disciplines working together to achieve common goals. This model enables rapid innovation and response to changing market conditions but requires a culture of trust, empowerment, and continuous learning (Accenture, 2021).

4. Skills-Based Workforce

The skills-based workforce model focuses on hiring and developing employees based on their competencies rather than traditional qualifications or job roles. This model emphasizes lifelong learning and upskilling, allowing employees to acquire new skills and transition between roles as needed. Skills-based hiring enables organizations to build diverse and resilient teams capable of adapting to evolving business needs (Deloitte, 2020).

5. Human-AI Collaboration

The human-AI collaboration model involves integrating artificial intelligence (AI) and automation into the workforce to augment human capabilities. AI-powered tools assist employees in decision-making, data analysis, and repetitive tasks, freeing up time for more strategic and creative work. This model requires clear delineation of roles and responsibilities between humans and AI systems, as well as ongoing training to ensure employees can effectively leverage AI technologies (McKinsey Global Institute, 2021).

7.3. Preparing for Continuous Change

In today's rapidly evolving business landscape, organizations must embrace a mindset of continuous change to remain competitive and resilient. Key strategies for preparing for continuous change:

1. Cultivate a Growth Mindset

Encourage a culture of curiosity, adaptability, and learning within the organization. Emphasize the importance of embracing change as an opportunity for growth and innovation rather than a threat. Leaders should model a growth mindset by seeking feedback, experimenting with new ideas, and supporting risk-taking (Dweck, 2006).

2. Foster Agile Practices

Adopt agile methodologies and practices to enhance organizational agility and responsiveness. Break down silos and promote cross-functional collaboration to enable rapid decision-making and execution. Implement iterative approaches to project management, allowing for flexibility and adjustment in response to changing requirements (Schwaber & Sutherland, 2017).

3. Invest in Employee Development

Prioritize employee development and upskilling to ensure that the workforce has the skills and capabilities needed to navigate change effectively. Provide access to training programs, workshops, and learning resources that focus on digital literacy, problem-solving, and resilience-building. Encourage continuous learning and experimentation to foster a culture of adaptability (Bersin, 2019).

4. Enhance Communication and Transparency

Establish open and transparent communication channels to keep employees informed and engaged during times of change. Provide regular updates on organizational goals, strategies, and initiatives, and solicit feedback from employees to ensure their voices are heard. Create forums for dialogue and collaboration where ideas and concerns can be openly discussed and addressed (Groysberg & Slind, 2012).

5. Build Robust Change Management Capabilities

Develop change management capabilities at all levels of the organization to facilitate smooth transitions and minimize resistance to change. Equip leaders with the skills and tools needed to effectively communicate change, manage stakeholder expectations, and address resistance. Foster a supportive environment where employees feel empowered to embrace change and contribute to its success (Kotter, 2012).

8. CONCLUSION

8.1. Summary of Key Points

1. **Digital Transformation Overview**: Digital transformation is revolutionizing industries by leveraging technology to enhance efficiency, innovation, and customer experience. It involves the integration of digital technologies into all aspects of business operations, from marketing and sales to supply chain management and customer service.
2. **Impact on the Workforce**: Digital transformation is reshaping the future workforce by altering the skills, roles, and ways of working required in the digital age. Emerging technologies such as artificial intelligence, automation, and data analytics are driving changes in job functions, with an increasing emphasis on digital literacy, problem-solving, and adaptability.
3. **Skills and Competencies**: The future workforce must possess a diverse set of skills and competencies to thrive in a digital-first environment. This includes technical skills such as data analysis, coding, and cybersecurity, as well as soft skills such as communication, collaboration, and critical thinking. Continuous learning and upskilling are essential to keep pace with evolving technologies and job requirements.
4. **Workforce Development Strategies**: Organizations must invest in workforce development strategies to prepare employees for the demands of digital transformation. This includes providing access to training programs, mentoring, and professional development opportunities. Leadership commitment to fostering a culture of learning and innovation is crucial for driving organizational change.
5. **Adapting to Change**: Building organizational resilience and agility is key to navigating the challenges of digital transformation. Embracing a growth mindset, fostering agile practices, enhancing communication and transparency, and investing in change management capabilities are essential strategies for preparing for continuous change and uncertainty.

Overall, digital transformation presents both challenges and opportunities for the future workforce. By equipping employees with the necessary skills, fostering a culture of learning and adaptability, and embracing change as an opportunity for growth, organizations can position themselves for success in the digital age.

8.2. Implications for the Service Sector

The implications of digital transformation for the service sector can be:

1. **Enhanced Customer Experience**: Digital transformation enables service sector organizations to deliver more personalized and seamless customer experiences. Through data analytics and AI-powered tools, companies can better understand customer preferences and behavior, leading to tailored products, services, and interactions.
2. **Operational Efficiency**: Digital technologies streamline service delivery processes, reducing costs and improving efficiency. Automation and robotics automate routine tasks, while cloud computing and big data analytics optimize resource allocation and decision-making. This allows service organizations to allocate resources more effectively and respond faster to customer needs.
3. **Shift in Job Roles and Skills**: Digital transformation reshapes job roles and skill requirements within the service sector. While automation may eliminate some routine tasks, it also creates new opportunities for roles that require digital literacy, problem-solving, and customer-centricity. Service employees must adapt to new technologies and acquire relevant skills to remain competitive in the digital economy.

4. **Emphasis on Data Security and Privacy**: As service organizations collect and analyze vast amounts of customer data, ensuring data security and privacy becomes paramount. Compliance with data protection regulations such as GDPR and CCPA is essential to maintain customer trust and mitigate the risk of data breaches or regulatory fines.
5. **Opportunities for Innovation and Differentiation**: Digital transformation opens opportunities for service organizations to innovate and differentiate themselves in the market. By leveraging emerging technologies such as AI, IoT, and blockchain, companies can develop new service offerings, improve operational processes, and create unique value propositions that set them apart from competitors.
6. **Challenges of Managing Change**: Implementing digital transformation initiatives presents challenges related to organizational change management. Resistance to change, skills gaps, and cultural barriers may hinder the adoption of new technologies and processes. Service organizations must invest in change management strategies, employee training, and leadership support to successfully navigate the transition to a digital-first mindset.

8.3. Final Thoughts and Recommendations

In conclusion, digital transformation presents both opportunities and challenges for the service sector. Embracing digital technologies and adapting to changing customer demands are essential for organizations to remain competitive in today's digital economy. Some recommendations:

1. **Embrace a Customer-Centric Approach**: Prioritize customer experience and satisfaction by leveraging digital technologies to deliver personalized and seamless service. Invest in customer relationship management systems, data analytics, and AI-powered tools to better understand and anticipate customer needs.
2. **Invest in Workforce Development**: Recognize that the success of digital transformation initiatives hinges on the skills and capabilities of the workforce. Provide employees with access to training programs, mentorship, and professional development opportunities to enhance digital literacy and adaptability.
3. **Foster a Culture of Innovation**: Encourage a culture of experimentation, creativity, and continuous learning within the organization. Empower employees to propose new ideas, take calculated risks, and embrace change as an opportunity for growth and improvement.
4. **Prioritize Data Security and Privacy**: Safeguard customer data and ensure compliance with data protection regulations to maintain trust and credibility. Implement robust cybersecurity measures, conduct regular audits, and provide ongoing training to employees on data security best practices.
5. **Collaborate with Industry Partners**: Forge strategic partnerships with technology providers, startups, and other industry stakeholders to leverage expertise and resources in driving digital transformation initiatives. Collaborative efforts can accelerate innovation, reduce implementation costs, and mitigate risks associated with digital adoption.
6. **Monitor and Adapt to Market Trends**: Stay abreast of emerging technologies, market trends, and competitive developments to anticipate changes and proactively respond to evolving customer needs. Regularly review and update digital transformation strategies to ensure alignment with organizational goals and market dynamics.

REFERENCES

Accenture. (2017). The new role of customer service in the digital age. Retrieved from https://www.accenture.com

Accenture. (2021). *Agile Workforce: The New Future of Work*. Retrieved from https://www.accenture.com

Agarwal, R., Chandrasekaran, S., & Sridhar, M. (2019). Imagining construction's digital future. *McKinsey & Company*. Retrieved from https://www.mckinsey.com

Amabile, T. M., & Pratt, M. G. (2016). The dynamic componential model of creativity and innovation in organizations: Making progress, making meaning. *Research in Organizational Behavior*, *36*, 157–183. DOI: 10.1016/j.riob.2016.10.001

Armbrust, M., Fox, A., Griffith, R., Joseph, A. D., Katz, R. H., Konwinski, A., Lee, G., Patterson, D., Rabkin, A., Stoica, I., & Zaharia, M. (2010). A view of cloud computing. *Communications of the ACM*, *53*(4), 50–58. DOI: 10.1145/1721654.1721672

Armenakis, A. A., & Harris, S. G. (2009). Reflections: Our Journey in Organizational Change Research and Practice. *Journal of Change Management*, *9*(2), 127–142. DOI: 10.1080/14697010902879079

Ashton, K. (2009). That 'internet of things' thing. *RFID Journal*, *22*(7), 97–114.

AT&T. (2017). Reskilling the Workforce for the Future. Retrieved from https://about.att.com

Baldwin-Evans, K. (2006). Key steps to implementing a successful e-learning program. *Industrial and Commercial Training*, *38*(4), 201–207.

Bank, D. B. S. (2018). DBS Annual Report 2018. Retrieved from https://www.dbs.com

Bersin, J. (2019). The upskilling imperative: 5 ways to turn chaos into value. *Deloitte Insights*. Retrieved from https://www2.deloitte.com

Bessen, J. (2019). *AI and Jobs: The role of demand*. National Bureau of Economic Research.

Bharadwaj, A., El Sawy, O. A., Pavlou, P. A., & Venkatraman, N. (2013). Digital business strategy: Toward a next generation of insights. *Management Information Systems Quarterly*, *37*(2), 471–482. DOI: 10.25300/MISQ/2013/37:2.3

Bilgihan, A., Smith, S. D., & Cobb, B. (2016). Hotel guest satisfaction: A segmentation approach using big data analytics. *International Journal of Hospitality Management*, *57*, 118–129.

Blouin, R. A., & Perry, C. M. (2009). Building strong academic-industry partnerships. *American Journal of Pharmaceutical Education*, *73*(8), 1–7. PMID: 20221347

Boehmer, J., & Laesser, C. (2020). The "smart hotel" in the tourism and hospitality industry. *Information and Communication Technologies in Tourism*, *2020*, 410–422.

Brynjolfsson, E., & McAfee, A. (2014). *The Second Machine Age: Work, Progress, and Prosperity in a Time of Brilliant Technologies*. W. W. Norton & Company.

Cameron, E., & Green, M. (2019). *Making Sense of Change Management: A Complete Guide to the Models, Tools, and Techniques of Organizational Change*. Kogan Page Publishers.

Carnevale, A. P., Smith, N., & Strohl, J. (2015). *Recovery: Job growth and education requirements through 2020*. Georgetown University Center on Education and the Workforce.

Ceruzzi, P. E. (2003). *A history of modern computing*. MIT Press.

Chaffey, D., & Ellis-Chadwick, F. (2019). *Digital marketing: Strategy, implementation and practice*. Pearson.

Chen, H., Chiang, R. H. L., & Storey, V. C. (2014). Business intelligence and analytics: From big data to big impact. *Management Information Systems Quarterly*, *36*(4), 1165–1188. DOI: 10.2307/41703503

D'Abate, C. P., Youndt, M. A., & Wenzel, K. E. (2009). Making the most of an internship: An empirical study of internship satisfaction. *Academy of Management Learning & Education*, *8*(4), 527–539.

Dabbagh, N., & Kitsantas, A. (2012). Personal Learning Environments, social media, and self-regulated learning: A natural formula for connecting formal and informal learning. *The Internet and Higher Education*, *15*(1), 3–8. DOI: 10.1016/j.iheduc.2011.06.002

Davenport, T. H. (2018). *The AI advantage: How to put the artificial intelligence revolution to work*. MIT Press. DOI: 10.7551/mitpress/11781.001.0001

Davenport, T. H., Barth, P., & Bean, R. (2012). How big data is different. *MIT Sloan Management Review*, *54*(1), 43–46.

Davenport, T. H., & Kirby, J. (2015). Beyond automation: Strategies for remaining gainfully employed in an era of very smart machines. *Harvard Business Review*, *93*(6), 58–65.

Davenport, T. H., & Patil, D. J. (2012). Data scientist: The sexiest job of the 21st century. *Harvard Business Review*, *90*(10), 70–76. PMID: 23074866

Davenport, T. H., & Ronanki, R. (2018). Artificial intelligence for the real world. *Harvard Business Review*, *96*(1), 108–116.

Deloitte. (2017). Rewriting the rules for the digital age: 2017 Deloitte Global Human Capital Trends. Retrieved from https://www2.deloitte.com

Deloitte. (2020). *The Future of Work: Unlocking Human Potential.* Retrieved from https://www2.deloitte.com

Deloitte. (2021). *Deloitte's Tech Trends 2021: A Government Perspective.* Retrieved from https://www2.deloitte.com

Dweck, C. S. (2006). *Mindset: The new psychology of success*. Random House.

Edmondson, A. (1999). Psychological safety and learning behavior in work teams. *Administrative Science Quarterly*, *44*(2), 350–383. DOI: 10.2307/2666999

Esteva, A., Kuprel, B., Novoa, R. A., Ko, J., Swetter, S. M., Blau, H. M., & Thrun, S. (2017). Dermatologist-level classification of skin cancer with deep neural networks. *Nature*, *542*(7639), 115–118. DOI: 10.1038/nature21056 PMID: 28117445

Euromoney. (2018). DBS Named World's Best Digital Bank. Retrieved from https://www.euromoney.com

Frost & Sullivan. (2019). Best Practices Award: Schneider Electric's Digital Transformation. Retrieved from https://www.frost.com

Gartner. (2020). *Gartner HR Survey Reveals 41% of Employees Likely to Work Remotely at Least Some of the Time Post Coronavirus Pandemic*. Retrieved from [https://www.gartner.com/en/newsroom/press-releases/2020-04-14-gartner-hr-survey-reveals-41--of-employees-likely-to-]

Gartner. (2021). *Top 10 Strategic Technology Trends for 2021.* Retrieved from https://www.gartner.com

Gault, J., Leach, E., & Duey, M. (2010). Effects of business internships on job marketability: The employers' perspective. *Education + Training*, *52*(1), 76–88. DOI: 10.1108/00400911011017690

Gill, R. (2003). Change management—Or change leadership? *Journal of Change Management*, *3*(4), 307–318. DOI: 10.1080/714023845

Gomber, P., Koch, J. A., & Siering, M. (2018). Digital finance and FinTech: Current research and future research directions. *Journal of Business Economics*, *87*(5), 537–580. DOI: 10.1007/s11573-017-0852-x

Gough, P., Sittig, D. F., & Williams, K. (2015). *Health IT and patient safety: Building safer systems for better care*. National Academies Press.

Groover, M. P. (2019). *Automation, production systems, and computer-integrated manufacturing*. Pearson.

Groysberg, B., & Slind, M. (2012). Leadership is a conversation. *Harvard Business Review*, *90*(6), 76–84. PMID: 22741420

Gubbi, J., Buyya, R., Marusic, S., & Palaniswami, M. (2013). Internet of Things (IoT): A vision, architectural elements, and future directions. *Future Generation Computer Systems*, *29*(7), 1645–1660. DOI: 10.1016/j.future.2013.01.010

Hänninen, M., Smedlund, A., & Mitronen, L. (2018). Digitalization in retailing: Multi-sided platforms as drivers of industry transformation. *Journal of Retailing and Consumer Services*, *45*, 144–153.

Heathfield, S. M. (2019). How to reward and recognize employees. *The Balance Careers*. Retrieved from https://www.thebalancecareers.com

Hrastinski, S. (2008). Asynchronous and synchronous e-learning. *EDUCAUSE Quarterly*, *31*(4), 51–55.

Huang, M. H., & Rust, R. T. (2018). Artificial intelligence in service. *Journal of Service Research*, *21*(2), 155–172. DOI: 10.1177/1094670517752459

Huang, Z., & Benyoucef, M. (2013). From e-commerce to social commerce: A close look at design features. *Electronic Commerce Research and Applications*, *12*(4), 246–259. DOI: 10.1016/j.elerap.2012.12.003

Hunt, V., Prince, S., Dixon-Fyle, S., & Yee, L. (2018). Delivering through diversity. *McKinsey & Company*. Retrieved from https://www.mckinsey.com

Islam, S. M. R., Kwak, D., Kabir, M. H., Hossain, M., & Kwak, K. S. (2015). The Internet of Things for health care: A comprehensive survey. *IEEE Access : Practical Innovations, Open Solutions*, *3*, 678–708. DOI: 10.1109/ACCESS.2015.2437951

Ivanov, S., & Webster, C. (2017). Adoption of robots, artificial intelligence and service automation by travel, tourism, and hospitality companies – A cost-benefit analysis. *International Journal of Contemporary Hospitality Management*, *29*(1), 797–822.

Jimmieson, N. L., Terry, D. J., & Callan, V. J. (2004). A Longitudinal Study of Employee Adaptation to Organizational Change: The Role of Change-Related Information and Change-Related Self-Efficacy. *Journal of Occupational Health Psychology*, *9*(1), 11–27. DOI: 10.1037/1076-8998.9.1.11 PMID: 14700455

Kane, G. C., Palmer, D., Phillips, A. N., Kiron, D., & Buckley, N. (2015). Strategy, not technology, drives digital transformation. *MIT Sloan Management Review*, *14*, 1–25.

Katz, L. F., & Krueger, A. B. (2019). The Rise and Nature of Alternative Work Arrangements in the United States, 1995-2015. *Industrial & Labor Relations Review*, *72*(2), 382–416. DOI: 10.1177/0019793918820008

Khan, M. (2016). The rise of e-commerce: A look at the past, present, and future. *Journal of Electronic Commerce in Organizations*, *14*(2), 55–63.

Kotter, J. P. (2012). *Leading change*. Harvard Business Review Press.

Kumar, P., & Raj, P. H. (2019). *Cyber security: From policies to practice*. CRC Press.

Lee, J., Bagheri, B., & Kao, H. A. (2014). A cyber-physical systems architecture for industry 4.0-based manufacturing systems. *Manufacturing Letters*, *3*, 18–23. DOI: 10.1016/j.mfglet.2014.12.001

Manyika, J., Chui, M., Miremadi, M., Bughin, J., George, K., Willmott, P., & Dewhurst, M. (2017). *A future that works: Automation, employment, and productivity*. McKinsey Global Institute.

Marston, S., Li, Z., Bandyopadhyay, S., Zhang, J., & Ghalsasi, A. (2011). Cloud computing—The business perspective. *Decision Support Systems*, *51*(1), 176–189. DOI: 10.1016/j.dss.2010.12.006

McGowan, B. S., Wasko, M., Vartabedian, B. S., Miller, R. S., Freiherr, D. D., & Abdolrasulnia, M. (2018). Understanding the factors that influence the adoption and meaningful use of social media by physicians to share medical information. *Journal of Medical Internet Research*, *20*(5), e128. PMID: 23006336

McKinsey & Company. (2021). *The Future of Work After COVID-19.* Retrieved from https://www.mckinsey.com

NACE. (2018). The class of 2018 student survey report. *National Association of Colleges and Employers*. Retrieved from https://www.naceweb.org

Noe, R. A. (2017). *Employee training and development*. McGraw-Hill Education.

O'Reilly, T. (2005). What is Web 2.0: Design patterns and business models for the next generation of software. *Communications & Stratégies*, *1*(17), 17–37.

PwC. (2021). *The Future of Work: A Journey to 2022.* Retrieved from https://www.pwc.com

Raghavan, M., Barocas, S., Kleinberg, J., & Levy, K. (2020). Mitigating bias in algorithmic hiring: Evaluating claims and practices. *Proceedings of the 2020 Conference on Fairness, Accountability, and Transparency*, 469-481. DOI: 10.1145/3351095.3372828

Raghupathi, W., & Raghupathi, V. (2014). Big data analytics in healthcare: Promise and potential. *Health Information Science and Systems*, *2*(1), 3. DOI: 10.1186/2047-2501-2-3 PMID: 25825667

Rigby, D. K., Sutherland, J., & Takeuchi, H. (2016). Embracing agile. *Harvard Business Review*, *94*(5), 40–50.

Roberson, Q. M. (2019). Diversity and inclusion in the organizational context: A review and research agenda. *Journal of Management*, *45*(6), 2463–2498.

Schneider Electric. (2020). Schneider Electric Exchange: Driving Digital Transformation. Retrieved from https://www.se.com

Schwaber, K., & Sutherland, J. (2017). *The scrum guide.* Scrum.Org. Retrieved from https://www.scrum.org

Schwartz, J. (2018). AT&T's Workforce Transformation. *Harvard Business Review*. Retrieved from https://hbr.org

Senge, P. M. (1990). *The Fifth Discipline: The Art and Practice of the Learning Organization*. Doubleday.

Smith, B. L., & MacGregor, J. T. (1992). What is collaborative learning? In Goodsell, A. S., Maher, M. R., & Tinto, V. (Eds.), *Collaborative Learning: A Sourcebook for Higher Education* (pp. 10–30). National Center on Postsecondary Teaching, Learning, and Assessment.

Verhoef, P. C., Broekhuizen, T., Bart, Y., Bhattacharya, A., Dong, J. Q., Fabian, N., & Haenlein, M. (2021). Digital transformation: A multidisciplinary reflection and research agenda. *Journal of Business Research, 122*, 889–901. DOI: 10.1016/j.jbusres.2019.09.022

Vial, G. (2019). Understanding digital transformation: A review and a research agenda. *The Journal of Strategic Information Systems, 28*(2), 118–144. DOI: 10.1016/j.jsis.2019.01.003

Wang, X., Lai, W., & Wang, J. (2020). Inventory management in retail chains: A simulation study. *International Journal of Production Research, 58*(13), 4004–4020.

Wang, Y., Kung, L., & Byrd, T. A. (2018). Big data analytics: Understanding its capabilities and potential benefits for healthcare organizations. *Technological Forecasting and Social Change, 126*, 3–13. DOI: 10.1016/j.techfore.2015.12.019

Westerman, G., Bonnet, D., & McAfee, A. (2014). *Leading digital: Turning technology into business transformation*. Harvard Business Review Press.

Willcocks, L. P., Lacity, M. C., & Craig, A. (2015). Robotic process automation: The next transformation lever for shared services. *Journal of Information Technology Teaching Cases, 5*(2), 77–91.

Wilson, C. (2012). Effective approaches to connecting learning to the real world through industry partnerships and work-integrated learning. *Higher Education. Skills and Work-Based Learning, 2*(3), 215–227.

World Economic Forum. (2018). *The Future of Jobs Report 2018*. Retrieved from [http://www3.weforum.org/docs/WEF_Future_of_Jobs_2018.pdf]

World Economic Forum. (2020). *The Future of Jobs Report 2020.* Retrieved from https://www.weforum.org

Yang, G. Z., Cambias, J., Cleary, K., Daimler, E., Drake, J., Dupont, P. E., & Wood, R. (2017). Medical robotics—Regulatory, ethical, and societal issues. *Science Robotics, 2*(4), eaam8630. PMID: 33157870

Zanella, A., Bui, N., Castellani, A., Vangelista, L., & Zorzi, M. (2014). Internet of Things for smart cities. *IEEE Internet of Things Journal, 1*(1), 22–32. DOI: 10.1109/JIOT.2014.2306328

Zhang, Y., & Zhu, M. (2019). Artificial intelligence in financial markets: Cutting edge applications for risk management, portfolio optimization, and economics. *The Journal of Financial Data Science, 5*(2), 33–41.

KEY TERMS AND DEFINITIONS

Digital Transformation: The integration of digital technologies into all areas of business operations, fundamentally changing how organizations operate and deliver value to customers.

Future Workforce: The collective term referring to the employees and labor force of tomorrow, characterized by their skills, competencies, and adaptability to emerging technologies and changing work environments.

Automation: The process of using technology to perform tasks or processes that were previously carried out by humans, typically aimed at improving efficiency and reducing human error.

Artificial Intelligence (AI): The simulation of human intelligence processes by machines, including learning, reasoning, and problem-solving, used to automate tasks, analyze data, and make decisions.

Machine Learning (ML): A subset of AI that enables computers to learn from data and improve their performance over time without explicit programming, used in predictive analytics, pattern recognition, and natural language processing.

Internet of Things (IoT): The network of interconnected devices and sensors that collect and exchange data over the internet, enabling real-time monitoring, control, and automation of physical objects and environments.

Cloud Computing: The delivery of computing services, including storage, processing, and software, over the internet on a pay-as-you-go basis, enabling organizations to access scalable and cost-effective IT resources.

Big Data: Large volumes of structured and unstructured data generated from various sources, including social media, sensors, and transactions, processed and analyzed to uncover insights, patterns, and trends.

Data Analytics: The process of examining data sets to derive meaningful insights, identify patterns, and make informed decisions, using techniques such as data mining, predictive analytics, and statistical analysis.

Digital Literacy: The ability to use digital technologies effectively and responsibly to access, evaluate, create, and communicate information, essential for success in the digital age.

Agile Workforce: A flexible and adaptive workforce capable of quickly responding to changing business needs and market conditions, characterized by collaboration, innovation, and continuous learning.

Remote Work: The practice of working outside of a traditional office setting, enabled by digital technologies such as video conferencing, collaboration tools, and cloud-based applications.

Chapter 3
Exploring the Impact of Technologies and Digital Platforms on Work-Life Balance

Qazi Ruban
https://orcid.org/0000-0001-9463-3594
Central University of Kashmir, India

Rameez Ahmad Mir
https://orcid.org/0009-0005-1442-4909
Chandigarh University, India

Ekta Rastogi
Chandigarh University, India

Sumaira
University of Kashmir, India

ABSTRACT

In the contemporary subject of work and life, the convergence of innovation and balance between work and life activities has become progressively articulated. This survey research paper investigates the complex connection among technology and work-life balance, looking at the manners by which innovative progressions are reshaping the limits among professional and individual life. With an emphasis on both the opportunities and difficulties introduced by innovation, this paper offers bits of knowledge into how people, organizations, and policymakers can explore this developing scene to advance prosperity and efficiency in the cutting edge workforce. The paper starts by contextualizing the idea of balance of work and non-work activities within the limit of 24 hours, inside the more extensive cultural and innovative patterns that have formed the advanced working environment. This research paper gives a far reaching assessment of the job of innovation in molding the future of balance between work and non-work activities.

INTRODUCTION

In the present quick moving and interconnected world, the idea of work-life balance has become progressively appropriate. As people endeavor to shuffle proficient obligations with special goals, accomplishing concordance among work and individual life has arisen as a key need. Notwithstanding, the scene of work and lifestyle elements

DOI: 10.4018/979-8-3693-7447-4.ch003

is going through a significant change, generally determined by headways in innovation. From remote work devices to computerized correspondence stages, innovation is reshaping the manner in which we work and connect, with expansive ramifications for our work-life balance. This exploration paper looks to dive into the complex relationship among innovation and work-life balance, investigating how mechanical developments are forming the eventual fate of work and lifestyle incorporation. By integrating a different cluster of scholastic writing, experimental examinations, and industry reports, this paper plans to give an extensive comprehension of the developing job of innovation in encouraging work-life balance in the advanced age. The coming of innovation has achieved extraordinary changes in the idea of work. Customary office conditions are progressively giving way to adaptable work game plans, working from home, and remote coordinated effort empowered by computerized advancements. Therefore, people have more noteworthy independence and adaptability in

dealing with their work plans, obscuring the limits among work and individual life. Moreover, innovation has worked with the ascent of the gig economy and independent work, offering people the potential chance to seek after adaptable and autonomous business valuable open doors. While this independence can improve work-life balance for some, it additionally presents new difficulties, like shaky business courses of action what's more, obscured limits among work and relaxation time. Advanced correspondence stages, like email, texting, and video conferencing, have upset the manner in which we associate and work together in proficient settings. While these instruments offer unrivaled accommodation and productivity, they likewise present dangers of data over-burden, steady network, and workrelated stress, possibly sabotaging work-life balance. Then again, mechanical advancements in wellbeing and health, like wearable gadgets and efficiency applications, hold guarantee for advancing work-life balance by assisting people with dealing with their time, feelings of anxiety, and generally prosperity all the more actually. These instruments enable people to focus on taking care of oneself and keep up with limits among work and individual life, encouraging a more supportable way to deal with work. Be that as it may, as innovation keeps on propelling, it additionally brings up significant moral and cultural issues in regards to protection, information security, and the effect of computerization on business open doors and occupation fulfillment. In addition, differences in admittance to innovation and advanced abilities might fuel disparities in work-life balance, featuring the requirement for comprehensive and evenhanded ways to deal with mechanical advancement. This examination paper expects to investigate the mind boggling interaction among innovation and work-life balance, perceiving both the amazing open doors and difficulties that emerge in the computerized period. By understanding the systems through which innovation impacts work and lifestyle elements, we can more readily expect future drifts and foster procedures to advance work-life balance for people across assorted settings. Eventually, this paper looks to add to a nuanced comprehension of the job of innovation in molding the future of work-life mix and prosperity in the 21st hundred years.

Background of the Study

The convergence of innovation and work-life balance has become progressively appropriate in contemporary society as headways in innovation keep on reshaping the manner in which we work, impart, and communicate. By and large, the idea of work-life balance has been characterized by the capacity to shuffle proficient actually obligations with special goals and responsibilities. Nonetheless, with the proliferation of advanced advances, the limits among work and individual life have become progressively obscured, introducing the two open doors and difficulties for people, organizations, and society all in all.

The appearance of computerized advancements, for example, cell phones, email, and far off joint effort instruments, has changed the conventional workplace, empowering more noteworthy adaptability in how, when, and where work is performed. While these advances offer remarkable open doors for remote work, working from home, and adaptable planning, they have additionally presented new intricacies and tensions that can influence work-life balance. On one hand, innovation works with more prominent independence and command over work courses of action, permitting people to fit their timetables to all the more likely oblige individual responsibilities and inclinations. Remote work, specifically, has gotten some decent forward momentum as a practical option in contrast to customary office-based business, offering advantages, for example, diminished driving time, expanded adaptability, and further developed work-life mix. In any case, the omnipresent presence of innovation in our lives has likewise prompted worries about work infringing into individual time, prompting expanded pressure, burnout, and hardships in detaching from work-related assignments. The peculiarity of "consistently on" network, where people are supposed to be accessible and responsive beyond conventional working hours, has brought up issues about the disintegration of limits between work and individual life. Moreover, the quick speed of mechanical advancement has achieved tremendous changes in the idea of work itself, with the ascent of computerization, man-made brainpower, and the gig economy reshaping conventional work structures. While these improvements offer possible advantages as far as effectiveness and efficiency, they additionally bring up issues about employer stability, pay soundness, and the nature of work-life balance in the advanced age. Against this scenery, there is a developing need to look at the job of innovation in molding the future fundamentally of work-life balance. This survey research paper tries to investigate the complex connections between innovation and work-life balance, drawing on a different scope of writing and observational investigations. By incorporating existing examination and recognizing arising patterns, the paper plans to give bits of knowledge into the open doors, difficulties, and ramifications of innovation driven changes in the workplace. At last, understanding the perplexing interaction among innovation and work-life balance is fundamental for policymakers, bosses, representatives, and society on the loose to explore the advancing scene of work in the advanced age. By revealing insight into the manners by which innovation impacts work-life elements, this study points to illuminate proof based systems for advancing prosperity, efficiency, and fulfillment in the cutting edge workplace.

Rational of the Study

The study "Exploring the Impact of Technologies and Digital Platforms on Work-Life Balance" aims to investigate the complex relationship between the increasing use of technologies and digital platforms, and their influence on individuals' ability to maintain a healthy work-life balance. The findings of this study will help employers, HR professionals, and policymakers better understand how the integration of technology into the workplace impacts employee well-being and productivity, enabling them to develop more effective strategies and policies to support a healthy work-life balance.

The rise of the "always-on" culture, driven by the proliferation of digital devices and the expectation of constant connectivity, has blurred the boundaries between work and personal life (McDowall & Kinman, 2017). While technologies and digital platforms have enabled greater flexibility, such as remote work and flexible schedules, they have also led to an increased pressure to be available at all times, potentially undermining work-home boundaries and causing stress for employees. Previous research has suggested that individuals employ various strategies, such as the use of multiple devices, to create boundaries between their work and home lives, and the extent to which they do this is related to their boundary behavior style.

Objectives of the Study

1) To inspect the role of technologies like AI, VR and Software's used during work operations on work life balance.
2) To study and elaborate an overview of work-life balance in the present scenario of digitally advanced age, including the popularity of remote work and flexible working hours and shifts.
3) To highlight best practices and strategies for supplement technology to enhance work-life balance among employees.
4) To analyze the effect of technology on employee well-being, job satisfaction, stress levels, and productivity of work, including its effects on work-life balance

REVIEW OF LITERATURE

Introduction

The enhanced integration of technology into the current workplace has brought remarked transformations in the way work is conducted and has certainly impacted the professional as well as personal lives of employees. While technology has helped in gaining efficiency, connectivity, and flexibility, it has also opened doors for new challenges that can affect employees' work culture, work-life balance, job stress levels, and overall well-being. This literature review strives to provide a comprehensive portrait of the multifaceted impact of technology on these crucial aspects of working life.

The Impact of Technology on Employee Work-Life Balance

The immense integration of technology into the today's workplace environment has brought about significant transformations in the way work is conducted and has profoundly impacted the lives of employees. While technology has helped in gaining efficiency, connectivity, and flexibility, it has also opened doors for new challenges that can affect employees' work culture, work-life balance, job stress levels, and overall well-being. This literature review strives to provide a comprehensive portrait of the multifaceted impact of technology on these crucial aspects of working life.

TECHNOLOGY AND WORK-LIFE BALANCE

Extension of Boundaries: The Extinguishing of Work-Life Separation

Technology has eroded the orthodox boundaries between professional and personal life. The 24x7 accessibility facilitated by smart phones, laptops, and remote work technologies has made it inclined difficult for employees to distinct from work, originating to a phenomenon known as "work-life conflict." (Stich et al., 2018) Employees may feel frustrated to respond to emails, messages, or calls outside of work hours, leading to an encroachment of work demands on personal time and a decline in work-life balance. (Ratnam & Chandra, 2009). The blurring of boundaries between work and personal life facilitated by technology has also introduced many new challenges. By this new concept of "boundary management" has emerged as a proper card to understand how individuals navigate the permeable boundaries between work and non-work domains. Scholars such as Derks et al. (2016) have pointed techno stress, characterized by feelings of being overwhelmed and unable to make up with the demands of technology, as a significant consequence of boundary blurring. Techno stress can erode work-life balance and lead to negative outcomes such as burnout and decreased well-being.

Flexibility and Autonomy: The Potential for Work-Life Integration

While technology contributes to work-life conflict at sometimes, it can also offer opportunities for higher flexibility and autonomy, potentially enhancing work-life balance. (Dragano and Lunao, 2023) work from home options, flexible scheduling, and the capacity to manage work tasks from various locations can encourage employees to better integrate their work and non-work responsibilities. However, it is vital to establish clear limits and expectations to prevent these flexibilities from encouraging or routing the cause or a source of stress and overwork. (Day et al., 2023)

One major impact of technology on work-life balance is its role in allowing more flexibility in work setups. Telecommuting, remote work, and adaptable schedules have become more common, thanks to advancements in communication technology and digital platforms. Research by Allen et al. (2015) focuses on positive impact of flexible work arrangements on employees' perceived work-life balance, with benefits including reduced commuting time, increased autonomy, and improved job satisfaction

TECHNOLOGY AND JOB STRESS

Techno Stress: Stress from technology

The fast growing pace of technological advancements, the pressure to constantly learn and adapt to new tools and platforms, and the information overload associated with digital communication can contribute to a phenomenon known as "techno stress." (Nisafani et al., 2023) Techno stress can manifest as feelings of anxiety, exhaustion, and cognitive overload, negatively impacting employee well-being and job satisfaction. (Riedl , 2012)

Work Intensification and the Pressure to be "Always On"

Technology is contributing to work intensification with employees expected to accomplish more in less time. The "always on" culture fostered by technology can lead to increased workloads, time pressures, and the expectation of constant availability, contributing to heightened stress levels. (Dragano and Lunao, 2023). Organizations need to be mindful of the potential for technology to exacerbate workload demands and implement strategies to promote a healthy work-life balance.

TECHNOLOGY AND WELL-BEING

Decline of Face-to-Face Interactions and Social Isolation

Besides acting as the helping hand for employees, management, and stake holder's technology has many ugly faces a well such as, technology has enhanced connectivity in some ways, it has also raised concerns about social isolation in the workplace. The reliance on digital communication tools can lead to a decline in face-to-face interactions, potentially impacting employee relationships, teamwork, and overall well-being. (Stich et al., 2018) Organizations should encourage a balance between digital and in-person communication to foster a sense of community and belonging among employees.

Health Implications: Physical and Mental Health Risks

Excessive use of technology is directly or indirectly linked to various physical and mental health risks. Prolonged screen time can lead to eye strain, headaches, and sleep disturbances. (Riedl , 2012) Additionally, the sedentary nature of many technology-based jobs can contribute to physical health problems. Continues connectivity and information overload associated with technology can also negatively impact mental health, leading to increased anxiety, stress, and burnout. (Ratna and Kaur, 2023)

RESEARCH METHODOLOGY

Research Design: For the review research paper titled "Exploring the Impact of Technologies and Digital Platforms on Work-Life Balance" The study has been conducted by systematic revision of relevant and authentic literature. This method allows for a comprehensive synthesis of existing research on the topic, ensuring that all relevant studies are analyzed efficiently. By adhering to systematic review principles, the research process will be transparent, replicable, and unbiased.

Data Collection Methods:

1. **Database Search**: A systematic search conducted across academic databases such as PubMed, Scopus, Web of Science, PsycINFO, and Google Scholar, in order to find and extract relevant and recent literature. Keywords related to technology, work-life balance, remote work, flexible work arrangements, and telecommuting will be used to identify relevant studies.
2. **Journal and other sources Search:** In addition to database searches, manual searches was conducted in relevant journals, conference proceedings, and grey literature sources to identify additional studies that may or may not have been captured through database searches.
3. **Inclusion and Exclusion:** Following criteria were followed to meet the relevance and importance of the study:
    - **Relevance**: All the relevant literature published during the time frame of last 10 years where extracted to focus on the Exploring the Impact of Technologies and Digital Platforms on Work-Life Balance or related concepts such as remote work, flexible work arrangements, and telecommuting.
    - **Type of Publication:** Only peer-reviewed journal articles, conference papers, and reports published in reputable sources were considered for the study.
    - **Year of publishing:** Studies published within the last 10 years (from 2014 to the present) was considered in order to ensure the review reflects current trends and developments.
    - **Language:** Studies published in English was preferred to maintain consistency and facilitate analysis.
4. **Exclusion Criteria:** All those studies were excluded if they did not meet the inclusion criteria outlined above or if their primarily focus remains unrelated to topics such as general technology adoption, organizational culture, or workplace productivity without specific relevance to work-life balance.

It aims to achieve accurate results by adhering to above mentioned research design, data collection, inclusion and exclusion criteria, and ethical considerations like: by proper citation and attribution to previous authors, to maintain credibility and impartiality any potential conflict between authors will be disclosed transparently. All the studies considered in this study are presumed to have obtained consent from participants, and any ethical considerations mentioned in the original studies will be taken into account. the review aims to provide a rigorous and comprehensive analysis of Exploring the Impact of Technologies and Digital Platforms on Work-Life Balance.

1. **Technology's Dual Effect:** This study reveals how technology serves as a double-edged sword in influencing work-life balance. While innovations like remote work tools, flexible scheduling software, and communication platforms have enhanced flexibility and autonomy in balancing work and personal life, the omnipresence of technology has also eroded the boundaries between the two spheres, posing challenges in maintaining a healthy equilibrium.
2. **Work from home slogan:** The COVID-19 pandemic forces peoples to stay indoors and work remotely; leading to a seismic shift in how work is conducted. The study finds that work from home or remote work have significant benefits in terms of flexible working hours and shift, reduced commuting time, and improved work-life

balance for many individuals. However, it also highlights disproportion in access to remote work opportunities, with certain nature of work or organizations and certain demographic groups facing huge challenges in opting/ choosing remote work.

3. **Flexible Work Plans:** The study identifies flexible work arrangements, such as short working weeks, task sharing, and flexible shift timing, as key strategies for promoting work-life balance. These arrangements allow employees to manage their work schedules to accommodate personal engagements, in turn helps organization to achieve increased level of job satisfaction and productivity.
4. **Technostress and Zoom/Digital Fatigue:** Irrespective of numerous benefits of technology, the study revealed the phenomenon of technostress and digital fatigue among workers. Continuous connectivity, information overload, and the constant pressure always available can take a tally on mental well-being and exacerbate worklife imbalance. Organizations are in daring need of implement strategies to mitigate technostress and promote digital detox practices to support employee health and well-being.
5. **Boundary Management**: The study range over various boundary management strategies employed by individuals to switch the junction of work and personal life. These strategies include by differentiating by setting clear boundaries between work and non-work related activities, establishing designated workspaces at home, and allocation of time between work and non-work activities and practicing time management techniques.
6. **Organizational policies and Support**: Organizational support promotes as a critical factor in fostering work-life balance in the techno age. The study findings reveal that organizations with policies of employee welfare and wellbeing offers flexible working hours and prioritize on gender, and promote a culture of work-life balance are retaining talent for long period and in turn achieves customer satisfaction easily.
7. **Latest Trends:** Looking ahead, the review distinguishes a few arising patterns that will shape the eventual future of balance between work and non work. These incorporate the proceeded with mix of remote work practices, the ascent of crossover work models consolidating remote and in-office work, the expanded accentuation on representative prosperity and emotional well-being support, and the possible effect of man-made consciousness and computerization on work jobs and work elements.

The findings of this study highlight the intricate interchange among innovation and balance between work and non-work activities. While innovation offers uncommon open doors for adaptability and independence, it likewise presents difficulties connected with technostress and advanced exhaustion. By figuring out these elements and executing strong strategies and practices, associations can establish a workplace that advances representative prosperity and upgrades generally balance between work and non-work activities in the computerized age.

LIMITATION OF THE STUDY

1. **Scope Limitations:** The study's scope is fundamentally centered on specific aspects of technology's impact on work-life balance, such as work from home, digital communication tools, and flexible scheduling. However, it does not fully explore all other significant regions, including the gig economy, artificial intelligence, or automation, due to the limited boundaries of the research.
2. **Methodological Heterogeneity:** The included study use different methodologies, such as surveys, interviews, case studies, and experiments, thwart direct correlations or the making of authoritative inferences or the drawing of definitive conclusions. This methodological diversity may also limit the feasibility of conducting a meta-analysis or quantitative synthesis of the results.
3. **Data Availability and Quality:** Variability in the accessibility and quality of data related to technology use, work-life balance, and associated factors may affect the study. Differences in measurement tools, sampling methods, and data collection procedures across the included studies could introduce inconsistencies or biases in the findings.

4. **Publication Bias:** The study may be effected by publication bias, where studies reporting statistically significant or positive results are more likely to be published. This could bring about an overrepresentation of research suggesting a strong relationship between technology and work-life balance, potentially skewing the overall conclusions.
5. **Generalizability:** The study's findings might have restricted generalizability across various demographic groups, industries, and regions. Cultural differences, socioeconomic status, and varying authoritative practices may influence the relationship between technology use and work-life balance in ways that this study may not fully catch.
6. **Temporal Factors:** The quickly changing landscape of technology and work practices may affect the importance of the study's findings, as they are influenced by the time periods in which the included research was conducted. Emerging technologies or current changes in workplace policies might limit the applicability of some findings of this study to the current context.
7. **Complexity of Work-Life Balance:** Work-life balance is a complex and subjective concept influenced by individual emotional preferences, organizational theme, societal cultural, and other contextual factors. The study may not fully account for the complexity of these dynamics, which could lead to oversimplification or the omission of certain important aspects.
8. **Potential Confounding Variables:** The relationship between technology use and work-life balance may be confounded by other factors, such as job characteristics, personality traits, family responsibilities, or socioeconomic status. The challenge of adequately controlling for these variables in the included studies could affect the validity of the findings.
9. **Long-term Effects:** Many studies included in the review focus on short-term or cross-sectional relationships between technology and work-life balance. The limited availability of longitudinal research on the sustained effects of technology adoption on work-life balance outcomes restricts the study to a snapshot view, rather than providing a comprehensive long-term perspective.
10. **Ethical Considerations:** The study may not fully address ethical considerations related to technology use in the workplace, such as privacy concerns, data security, or the blurring of boundaries between work and personal life. While these ethical dimensions are crucial to the broader discussion on technology and work-life balance, they may not be extensively explored in the reviewed literature.

Future Scope

This study provides a foundation for understanding the complex relationship between technology, digital platforms, and work-life balance. However, the ever-evolving nature of technology and work necessitates further exploration in several key areas:

1. **Longitudinal Studies**: Conduct long-term studies to assess the sustained impact of technology on work-life balance over time. This will provide a more nuanced understanding of how the initial benefits and challenges of technology adoption evolve and potentially shape employee well-being in the long run.
2. **Sector-Specific Analysis:** Deep dive into the specific ways technology impacts work-life balance within different industries and occupations. This will allow for tailored recommendations and interventions that address the unique challenges and opportunities presented by technology in various sectors.
3. **Emerging Technologies:** Investigate the impact of emerging technologies, such as artificial intelligence, automation, and the metaverse, on work-life balance. Understanding how these technologies are changing work demands, skill requirements, and the nature of work itself is crucial for anticipating future challenges and opportunities.

4. **Generational Differences:** Explore how different generations perceive and experience the impact of technology on work-life balance. Recognizing generational differences in technology use, work values, and expectations can inform more effective strategies for promoting well-being across diverse workforces.
5. **Cultural Context:** Examine the influence of cultural norms and values on the relationship between technology and work-life balance. Cross-cultural studies can shed light on how different societies navigate the integration of technology into work and personal life.
6. **Policy Development:** Develop and evaluate evidence-based policies and interventions aimed at mitigating the negative consequences and maximizing the benefits of technology for work-life balance. This includes exploring flexible work arrangements, digital well-being programs, and organizational strategies that promote healthy technology use.
7. **Ethical Considerations:** Further investigate the ethical implications of technology use in the workplace, particularly concerning privacy, data security, surveillance, and the blurring of boundaries between work and personal life.

By addressing these future research directions, we can gain a more comprehensive understanding of the evolving relationship between technology, digital platforms, and work-life balance, ultimately contributing to the development of more supportive and sustainable work environments

CONCLUSION

The impact of technology on employee work-life balance, job stress, and well-being is complex and multifaceted. While technology offers numerous benefits in terms of efficiency, flexibility, and connectivity, it also presents significant challenges that organizations and employees must navigate effectively. By understanding the potential downsides of technology use, promoting healthy work practices, and fostering a supportive work environment, organizations can mitigate the negative impacts of technology and harness its power to enhance employee well-being and organizational success.

As innovation keeps on progressing at a phenomenal speed, its effect on the fate of work-life balance turns out to be progressively significant and diverse. This survey research paper has investigated the multifaceted relationship among innovation and work-life balance, looking at both the valuable open doors and difficulties introduced by mechanical progressions in the cutting edge workplace. The overall finding of this survey is that innovation fills in as a two sided deal in forming work-life balance. On one hand, mechanical advancements, for example, remote work apparatuses, adaptable planning programming, and correspondence stages have engaged people to accomplish more noteworthy adaptability and independence in dealing with their work and individual lives. These advances have worked with remote work courses of action, diminished driving time, and empowered more proficient correspondence and joint effort across topographies. Additionally, arising advances like man-made brainpower (artificial intelligence) and computerization hold the commitment of smoothing out errands and saving time for recreation and special goals. Nonetheless, the proliferation of innovation in the workplace likewise acquaints a large group of difficulties with work-life balance. The obscuring of limits among work and individual life, exacerbated by steady network and the assumption for guaranteed responsiveness, can prompt burnout, stress, and decreased prosperity. Besides, the stationary idea of numerous innovation driven positions, combined with the potential for social segregation in remote work settings, presents dangers to actual wellbeing and social relationships. Moreover, worries about information security, network protection dangers, and the potential for work dislodging because of mechanization pose a potential threat, adding to vulnerability and tension among workers. In exploring the intricacies of innovation's job in molding work-life balance, it is fundamental for partners to embrace a proactive and comprehensive methodology. Managers should perceive the significance of encouraging a strong organizational culture that focuses on representative prosperity, advances work-life balance drives, and lays out clear limits around innovation use. This might incorporate arrangements, for example, assigned "turned off" hours, adaptable work courses of action, and wellbeing programs pointed toward advancing physical and emotional well-being. People, as well, assume a significant part in dealing with their relationship with innovation and developing a solid work-life balance. Procedures like defining limits among work and individual life, rehearsing care what's more, taking care of one, and utilizing innovation for efficiency as opposed to steady network can help people recover office throughout their significant investment. Looking forward, it is obvious that the eventual fate of work-life balance will be formed by progressing mechanical developments, cultural patterns, and organizational practices. Accordingly, preceded with exploration, exchange, and joint effort are fundamental in exploring this consistently advancing scene. By bridling the capability of innovation while tending to its traps, partners can work towards making a future where work-life balance isn't just attainable yet in addition advancing and satisfying for all people.

All in all, this survey research paper highlights the critical job of innovation in molding the future of work-life balance. While innovation offers extraordinary open doors for adaptability and productivity, it too presents huge difficulties that should be tended to through proactive measures and aggregate activity. By cultivating a culture of prosperity, defining clear limits, and embracing innovation carefully, partners can endeavor towards a future where work and life are agreeably coordinated, empowering people to flourish both by and by and expertly.

REFERENCES

Allen, T. D., Golden, T. D., & Shockley, K. M. (2015). How effective is telecommuting? Assessing the status of our scientific findings. *Psychological Science in the Public Interest, 16*(2), 40–68. DOI: 10.1177/1529100615593273 PMID: 26403188

Day, A., Scott, N., & Kevin Kelloway, E. (2010). Information and communication technology: Implications for job stress and employee well-being. In *New developments in theoretical and conceptual approaches to job stress* (pp. 317–350). Emerald Group Publishing Limited. DOI: 10.1108/S1479-3555(2010)0000008011

Derks, D., Bakker, A. B., Peters, P., & van Wingerden, P. (2016). Work-related smartphone use, work–family conflict and family role performance: The role of segmentation preference. *Human Relations, 69*(5), 1045–1068. DOI: 10.1177/0018726715601890

Dragano, N., & Lunau, T. (2020). Technostress at work and mental health: Concepts and research results. *Current Opinion in Psychiatry, 33*(4), 407–413. DOI: 10.1097/YCO.0000000000000613 PMID: 32324623

McDowall, A., & Kinman, G. (2017). The new nowhere land? A research and practice agenda for the "always on" culture. *Journal of Organizational Effectiveness: People and Performance, 4*(3), 256–266. DOI: 10.1108/JOEPP-05-2017-0045

Nisafani, A. S., Kiely, G., & Mahony, C. (2020). Workers' technostress: A review of its causes, strains, inhibitors, and impacts. *Journal of Decision Systems, 29*(sup1), 243-258.

Ratna, R., & Kaur, T. (2016). The impact of information technology on job related factors like health and safety, job satisfaction, performance, productivity and work life balance. *Journal of Business & Financial Affairs, 5*(1), 2–9.

Ratnam, C. V., & Chandra, V. (2009). Work-life balance: Review of literature. *NHRD Network Journal, 2*(6), 89–97. DOI: 10.1177/0974173920090610

Riedl, R. (2012). On the biology of technostress: Literature review and research agenda. *The Data Base for Advances in Information Systems, 44*(1), 18–55. DOI: 10.1145/2436239.2436242

Stich, J. F., Tarafdar, M., & Cooper, C. L. (2018). Electronic communication in the workplace: Boon or bane? *Journal of Organizational Effectiveness: People and Performance, 5*(1), 98–106. DOI: 10.1108/JOEPP-05-2017-0046

Chapter 4
Leveraging Technology to Enhance the Webrooming Experience in the Automotive Service Sector

Sahil Kohli
https://orcid.org/0000-0002-3792-988X
Chandigarh University, India

Anil Kalotra
Chandigarh University, India

Rishi Prakash Shukla
https://orcid.org/0000-0003-0854-7302
Jaipuria Institute of Management, India

ABSTRACT

Exploring how Technology might help in the Webrooming Scenario in the Automotive Service Industry, this Chapter is organized. In analysing the subject of the book chapter, the authors focus on such aspects as the evolution of the industry, the use of Webrooming in the purchasing process. It also deliberation on different technologies including Artificial Intelligence, Blockchain, Virtual and Augmented Reality, and Internet of Thing that may help to enhance trust, transparency and engagement while using Webrooming System. As the chapter demonstrated, the actual application of the Conceptual Framework of Webrooming supported by advanced technologies among key automotive brands is shown through their cases. To those automotive service providers who want to use information technology in webrooming, the authors give guidelines and suggestions. Past work and approaches are also discussed, followed by discussion of the ethical issues and the directions for future research work so that reader is well-aware with the prospects and limitations in this growing domain of study.

INTRODUCTION

The automotive service industry is expanding at a very fast pace because of the dynamic technological developments as well as customers' changing preferences (Gao et al., 2016). Analysing Consumers' Behaviour and the means they used to find the necessary information before making a purchase, the notion of webrooming has emerged as an essential phenomenon of the modern world (Flavián et al., 2020). Webrooming is defined as the

DOI: 10.4018/979-8-3693-7447-4.ch004

situation where a consumer browses the internet to make a decision on what to buy or what service to look for in a physical store (Verhoef et al., 2007). This shift in consumers' attitude has added some pressure and new prospects for automotive service providers depending on how effective they are going to target and fit into the digital targeted customer (Montoya-Weiss et al., 2003).

The Changing Environment of Automotive Service Industry

The automotive service industry has had a dramatic transformation in the last few decades as innovation and the market demand have transformed the field (Gao et al., 2016). The myriad of apps that customers can use on their smart phones, booking platforms, and virtual reality like applications have altered how customers are able to engage with automotive services (Gretzel et al., 2020). With digital transformation, the customer experiences have been changed and at the same time, competition has come up with new strategies for the service providers in the highly competitive market environment (Kannan & Li, 2017).

Also, there is enhanced data and analysis availability, which gives the automotive service providers an understanding of customers' preference and behaviour (Wedel & Kannan, 2016). Thus, using these insights, service providers can accurately market their service, offer customization and improve the service quality per received by the customers (Rust & Huang, 2014). Therefore, it has taken a transition for the automotive service industries from product logic to customer logic, that is from focusing in value delivery for a mass market to the delivery of value addition services for individual customers (Ostrom et al., 2015).

The Importance of Webrooming in the Consumer Journey

Webrooming has become an important aspect of the customer journey map as it allows the customer to decide when the time is right to make the purchase of make a booking or seek service from the auto mechanic (Flavián et al., 2020). This has been made possible by the availability of information in the internet together with the improved trust on information retrieved from the internet (Kang, 2018). Webrooming is done more to obtain further information about the services various providers offer, to check more reviews, and on price variations concerning the service being bought (Santos & Gonçalves, 2019). In so doing, they feel more in control and complied when making decisions for themselves and this leads to higher levels of satisfaction and loyalty as posited by Flavián et al., (2020).

Furthermore, research studies on webrooming show that the activity enhances the customers' purchase intentions (Fernández et al., 2018). The time that customers use for searching information on the Internet, it is likely to make the purchase because they have invested time and effort (Aw et al., 2021). This emphasises the need for car service providers to improve the management of their online advertising and ensure that they offer accurate reliable information hence helping in the webrooming process (Kang, 2018).

The Use of Technology in Improving the Webrooming Experience

Therefore, technology assumes central position in the optimization of the webrooming experience for auto service customers (Gretzel et al., 2020). With the help of emerging technologies like artificial intelligence (AI), machine learning, and big data analytics, the services' providers can make an efficient experience an accurate and relevant information, and align customers' decision-making procedures (Wallace et al., 2022). For instance, AI in customer interaction relates to the support and assistance provided to customers during their research process through chatbots that respond to questions and present suitable products according to the given customers knowledge and behaviour (Puntoni et al., 2021).

Additionally, webrooming can benefit from technology like virtual and augmented reality (VR/AR) in which customer experiences are delivered through entertainments, which is Webrooming. Automotive service providers can apply virtual tours for showcasing service centers online, using augmented reality for displays of services, and 360-degree view of products, this helps the automotive service providers to close the gap between the online and offline world which will help the buyers to increase their confidence level while purchasing a service (Gretzel et al., 2020).

WEBROOMING AND THE USE OF TECHNOLOGY TO ENHANCE THE WEBROOMING PROCESS

In today's world where digital technology is rapidly advancing, technology proves to be a key driver for automotive service providers to enhance the webrooming experience for the customers (Wallace et al., 2022). According to the literature, by adopting sophisticated technologies, service providers are in a position of improving the type and quality of information, which is presented to the customers, making the internet experience unique and relevant, and reducing the complexity of different decision-making processes (Gretzel et al., 2020). This section will expand on how the webrooming process can be optimized in terms of technology, focused on the discovery of main technology contact points, increasing the quality and credibility of the online information and use of big data and Artificial intelligence in the personalization of the process.

Defining Primary Digital Interfaces in Automotive Service Industry

Shoppers need to be synchronised to enhance optimisation of the webrooming decision, and this requires the automotive service providers to understand the digital points that shoppers touch before making their purchasing decision (Kuehnl et al., 2019). Such touchpoints could be the service provider's website, social media handles, online review sites and third party comparison websites (Filieri, 2015). According to Lemon and Verhoef (2016) because each touchpoint in a customer journey plays a specific role and is valuable for the service provider, through their analysis they can effectively prioritise touchpoints they want to focus on and who can allocate more resources on.

For example, effective and attractive webpage can help customers to obtain the necessary information about the service provider, his services, prices, and customer reviews. Social media on the other hand gives service providers a rich ground to interact with customers, respond to their questions and share more content (Petit et al., 2019). Therefore, by enhancing and pinpointing these crucial digital touch points, the automotive service providers can deliver an integrated and informative webrooming solutions for their customers.

Promoting the Quality and Credibility of Information Collected Online through Technology

As such, the nature and credibility of web information affects customers: webrooming is also important to perception and decision making (Filieri, 2015). Automotive service providers have to establish online information quality and credibility concerning their services to strengthen the perceptions of their customers (Filieri et al., 2015). The following ways show how technology can be used in an effort to achieve this goal.

First, automotive service providers should enhance the content management systems (CMS) and digital asset management (DAM) to manage the details provided, their coherence, reliability, and up-to-date across the digital channels (Puntoni et al., 2018). These systems help solutions to provide the customers with the updated and reliable data by optimizing the creation and delivery of new pieces of content, that has a great potential in different fields, so more information is available at Gartner (2021).

Second, service providers are encouraged to utilise user-generated content (UGC) and customer reviews to increase the reliability of the information provided online (Filieri et al., 2015). Through customer engagement, the service providers can share their experiences and opinions and therefore make customers believe that they are being dealt with honestly, which improves their perception of the service providers they might want to patronize (Grewal & Stephen, 2019). Furthermore, it is possible to use NLP and sentiment analysis to analyse clients' feedback and detect the spheres where the service provider should improve its offerings and/or the available online information (Kübler et al., 2020).

Third, automotive service providers can take advantage of some of the current technologies to improve the authenticity of their information from the internet for instance the blockchain technology (Upadhyay, 2020). Thus, through the use of blockchain alternatives, service providers are able to prove the authenticity of the data and its being immutable, which will enhance the credibility of webrooming among customers.

Personalisation and Customisation of the Webrooming Experience using AI and Big Data

Technology integration is one of the main strengths of webrooming experience since it allows customer experience to be tailored and modified (Wedel & Kannan, 2016). AI and big data analysis allows automotive service providers to better understand customer needs, buying behaviour and decision-making processes and adjust the offer and messaging strategy and content to address specific customer (Verhoef et al., 2021).

Automated recommendation systems can then look into patron's history such as browser history, purchase history, social media profiles and more to recommend services and products (Grbovic & Cheng, 2018). For instance, if the customer has interest in a certain type of service or has visited contents related to car make or model that they are interested in, recommendation system will be able to point out some services that can capture the attention of the customer when webrooming (Lops et al., 2019).

Further, machine learning can be used to cluster customer based on their needs, behavioral patterns and value, so appropriate marketing messages and automotive service content can be provided to customers (Balducci & Marinova, 2018). Through presenting content and relevant offers to customer in different digital channels, customer engagement of service providers can be increased, hence improving the customer relationships and boosting the conversion rate (Lemon & Verhoef, 2016).

However, automotive service providers need to be sensitive to the privacy feature while at the same time being personalised (Aguirre et al., 2016). Customers feel as they have more control over their personal data, and therefore, they may not be receptive to sharing more information if they believe the level of personalisation is too high and bordering on creepy (Puntoni et al., 2021). To counter these worries, it remains the duty of service providers to ensure the security of the data, seek customer consent and give adequate information on the use and protection of the customer data (Martin et al., 2017).

Ethical Considerations and Best Practices

In light of a growing use of AI and big data technologies in service providers of the automotive industry for improving the webrooming process, Lobschat et al., (2021) point that it is necessary to further reflect on the ethics and look into the best practices for the application of AI and big data technologies for the responsible and sustainable webrooming service enhancement. It is also imperative to note that customers may not be comfortable about their data being collected with the intention of using them for personalisation of their experiences (Martin & Murphy, 2017).

In order to respond to these issues, automotive service providers have to follow the strict rules and requirements of data protection regulation, for instance, GDPR in the EU and CCPA in the US (Bourreau & de Streel, 2019). Many service providers who follow these regulations are required to ensure that customers give their consent for data to be collected, clearly inform customers on the use of such data and ensure that adequate security measures are put in place to protect such data (Martin et al., 2017).

Moreover, to automotive service providers, the same risks mean that personalisation, driven by artificial intelligence, has to be transparent and explainable (Kaplan & Haenlein, 2019). The customers should have a way to understand how their data is being used and how the AI algorithms make their recommendations or decisions in their behalf on the matters they want to be decided (Yeung, 2019). Such transparency may go a long way in making consumers more confident in organisations and have a sense of control thereby increase engagement and satisfaction levels (Garaus & Wagner, 2019).

Since auto service providers seek to offer tailored webrooming experiences using AI and big data, it is imperative to consider the problems related to algorithmic bias. Thus, algorithmic bias is identified where the machine learning model used yields prejudiced outputs as a result of bad assumptions and/or a training set that is biased (Mehrabi et al., 2021). In the case of webrooming, algorithmic bias may result in some customers' being completely locked out of targeting, receiving lower quality recommendations or being charged higher prices (Lambrecht & Tucker, 2019).

In order to combat the effects of bias in algorithms automated, automotive service providers are required to ensure that the data on which the algorithms are trained, in turn, is not biased for reasons of history or otherwise and is inclusive of a broad spectrum of data as possible. This may entail periodic checks of the training data, the usage of fairness measures or the inclusion of a range of stakeholders in the creation or testing of the AI systems (Mehrabi et al., 2021). Moreover, companies should set up roles and regulation standards which will help to control and evaluate the effectiveness of AI model and check for bias or discrimination (Suresh & Guttag, 2020).

Data privacy is another important issue that should be considered during the use of AI and big data for webrooming personalization. Since automotive service providers run vast databases of customers' data, they are bound by either the GDPR or CCPA; besides, they have to protect customers' information to the utmost extent feasible (Aw et al., 2021). This includes asking customers for permission to collect and use their data, communicating privacy policies well, and using ways such as encryption and limited access to customers' data (Filieri et al., 2015).

Furthermore, when engaging into webrooming personalization, automotive service providers should follow the principle of data minimization where the provider only collects and stores data that is necessary for the purpose of preparing specific personalization services (Aw et al., 2021). Other recommended practices include reconsidering data reuse schedules and data retention policies, performing data protection assessments, and offering customers simple ways to manage their personal data (Filieri et al., 2015).

Transparency is the other ethical consideration in the use of AI and big data into webrooming personalization. To ensure customers trust their data with the automotive service providers, it is crucial for automotive service providers to explain how the former's data is being captured, analysed, and utilized, as well as how AI algorithms reach solutions and recommendations (Aw et al., 2021). This involves giving simple renditions of reasons and rationales for personal offers with a view of making customers understand why, how, and at what times they are proffered to them (Wedel et al., 2020).

By applying the explainable AI methods including rule-based system or the decision trees, one can increase the understandability of the decision-making process (Filieri et al., 2015). Further, the level of options for the customers to change their preferences, opt-out of personalization mechanisms, or appeal to an AI/EH mediator versus human intermediary can also improve decision transparency and users' control (Wedel et al., 2020).

In order to avoid the breaching of consumers' privacy, automotive service providers will need to establish systematic strategies for data management as well as continuously educate their employees on data usage standards (Filieri et al., 2015). This can include acts that create distinct positions including data protection officers or ethics committee, to monitor data activities and avoid noncompliance with legal and ethical principles (Aw et al., 2021).

Likewise, coordination with industrial partners along with the academic and consumer organizations assisting automotive service providers can assist them in getting up to date with the ethical concerns and practices concerning the usage of AI and big data (Wedel et al., 2020). Engagement in industry activities in the form of ideas or policies formulation and implementation like ethical framework or best practices can enhance AI accountability and trustworthy in the automotive service domain (Filieri et al., 2015).

In tackling with these risks and challenges of algorithmic bias, data privacy, and transparency, automotive service providers will be in a good position of ensuring that the AI and big data of webrooming personalization to the intended clients has not been in vain but by being ethical in their undertakings.

The next important ethical issue and risk relates to algorithms reinforcing biases and discriminating against some Customer Segments. There needs to be a conscious effort to provide AI systems in automotive service providers with quality and diverse datasets to help in training the system and to satisfy the fairness audit that needs to be conducted on these systems periodically (Mehrabi et al., 2021). Overall, the management of ethical AI reduces the externalities and helps the service providers to have a good reputation in the market (Duan et al., 2019).

In order to successfully incorporate the above-mentioned ethical considerations, automotive service providers ought to establish robust governance frameworks and AI/big data recommended practices. They should therefore involve policies relating to data handling, code of conduct, and organisational arrangements that promote responsible innovation (Puntoni et al., 2021). Through setting procedural measures and creating ethic awareness, the service providers are able to locate their personalisation play in the webrooming experience at the intersection of customer expectations and ethical standards for consumption (Capgemini Research Institute, 2019).

TRUST DEVELOPMENT AND ITS EFFECTS ON OVERALL PURCHASE INTENTIONS

Trust forms the basis of the customer–brand relationship especially when webrooming because customers are using information from the internet to inform their purchases. In the interaction environment through several digital touch points, the level of customers ' trust in the automotive service providers is proven to impact their willingness to connect and ultimately purchase (Grewal et al., 2020). This section aims to understand the impact of trust in customers' decision-making process, the techniques of trust through technology advancements, and the effects of technology integrated webrooming towards customer buying behaviour.

Trust as a Factor in the Customer's Decision-Making Process

The role of trust cannot be overemphasized in influencing customer behaviour and choices especially where risk and uncertainty are more pronounced such as the current internet enabled environments (Bart et al., 2005). Concerning webrooming, customers look for accurate and credible information which would help them make a proper purchase decision (Aw et al., 2021). If customers find the automotive service provider being credible and dependable through the available online profile, they shall be guilty of webrooming and be willing to engage the service provider for service provision (Sharma & Klein, 2020).

Customers' trust in an automobile service provider may depend on: the level of quality and authenticity of information; whether the customers trust the ratings and reviews about a service provider; and also users' experience through digital touchpoints, as asserted by Flavián et al., 2019. Consequently, a business that possesses transparency and is prompt to react toward consistency is likely to enhance the level of customers' trust.

Trust reduces obvious dangers in internet transactions like security of information, data retention and ambiguity about the quality of service, for instance (Kelliher et al., 2018). A customer who entrusts an auto servicing company will not hesitate to provide his/her personal details; book services through the internet and possibly make payments through electronic means (Puntoni et al., 2021). In addition, trust creates long lasting relationships and loyalty since customers tend to revert to a trusted service provider when there is need and may even refer other clients to them (Ozturk et al., 2017).

Trust Building Mechanisms that are Enabled by Technology

Webrooming auto service providers can utilize a number of technology-based mechanisms in order to build and sustain trust amongst them. According to previous segments, one way that shares quality as well as authenticity of online information is through utilization of content management systems along with digital asset management solutions (Puntoni et al., 2018; Gartner, 2021). Hence by ensuring that there is consistency, accuracy and punctuality in the details across different digital touch points are some of the ways in which service firms exhibit their reliability and competence which are significant constituents' of trust (Wedel et al., 2020)

Another technology-enabled trust-building mechanism is the incorporation of user-generated content, such as customer reviews and ratings (Filieri et al., 2015). By showcasing authentic feedback from previous customers, automotive service providers can increase transparency and credibility, allowing potential customers to make informed decisions based on the experiences of others (Grewal & Stephen, 2019). Moreover, service providers can utilize sentiment analysis and natural language processing techniques to extract valuable insights from customer feedback, enabling them to address concerns, improve service quality, and demonstrate responsiveness to customer needs (Kübler et al., 2020).

Emerging technologies, such as blockchain, can also play a significant role in enhancing trust during the webrooming process (Upadhyay, 2020). By leveraging blockchain's decentralized and immutable nature, automotive service providers can ensure the security and integrity of customer data, transactions, and service records (Önder & Treiblmaier, 2018). This heightened level of security and transparency can alleviate customers' concerns regarding data privacy and boost their confidence in engaging with the service provider through digital channels (Wedel et al., 2020).

For instance, blockchain technology can be leveraged to create tamper-proof and transparent records of vehicle history, service records, and customer reviews (Upadhyay, 2020). By implementing a blockchain-based system, automotive service providers can ensure that the information presented to webrooming customers is accurate, verifiable, and resistant to manipulation (Önder & Treiblmaier, 2018). This increased transparency can help alleviate customer concerns about the authenticity of service records and build trust in the provider's expertise and reliability (Wedel et al., 2020).

Moreover, blockchain technology can be utilized to facilitate secure and efficient transactions between customers and automotive service providers (Upadhyay, 2020). Smart contracts, which are self-executing contracts with the terms of the agreement directly written into code, can automate the process of service bookings, payments, and warranty claims (Önder & Treiblmaier, 2018). By eliminating intermediaries and ensuring the immutability of transactions, smart contracts can enhance trust and reduce the potential for disputes or fraud (Wedel et al., 2020).

Besides, AI can be used to enhance the webrooming process through creating individualized suggestions and providing help in order to build the customer's trust (Kübler et al., 2020). Self-service technologies such as artificial intelligence chatbots can, for instance, converse with customer in natural language, respond to inquiries, and recommend products and services that meet the customer's preferences with the use of previous interactions (Salase and Spiller, 2021). In this way, chatbots can show the automotive service provider cares for the customer and build credibility into its knowledge (Wedel et al., 2020).

Additionally, AI methods can sort huge amounts of even personally identifiable data on customers' browsing history, search queries, and engagement levels to determine the most relevant and reliable content to serve to each of the customers (Kübler et al., 2020). It means that with the help of AI, it is possible to make the webrooming experience more dynamic and oriented on the customer's needs and pain points and leverage the use of customer reviews, testimonials and case studies to increase the trust in automotive service provider's offerings (Verhoef et al., 2021).

Augmented reality (AR) and virtual reality (VR) technologies can also play a significant role in enhancing trust during the webrooming process by providing immersive and interactive experiences that allow customers to explore and verify service offerings (Wedel et al., 2020). For instance, AR applications can enable customers to visualize how a specific service or repair will be performed on their vehicle, using 3D overlays and step-by-step animations (Kübler et al., 2020). By providing transparent and easily understandable information about the service process, AR can help build trust in the provider's expertise and alleviate customer concerns about the necessity or quality of the service (Verhoef et al., 2021).

Similarly, VR technology can be used to create virtual service centre tours, allowing customers to explore the facilities, equipment, and processes used by the automotive service provider (Wedel et al., 2020). By offering a transparent and immersive look behind the scenes, VR can help build trust in the provider's capabilities, professionalism, and commitment to quality service delivery (Kübler et al., 2020).

Hence, augmented reality and virtual reality technologies could significantly contribute to building or enhancing trust in webrooming by offering first-hand hands-on-cross-learning touch, feel, and actual experiences by the customers in regard to service offerings (Wedel et al., 2020). For example, AR applications allow customers to visualise how a particular service or a repair will look like and is to be done on their car with the help of 3D overlays and animated step by step guidance (Kübler et al., 2020). According to Verhoef et al., 2021 the use of AR in the provision of the service information can help in building customer confidence in the services offered by the service provider and reducing customer anxiety in relation to the need for or quality of services offered.

In the same manner, VR technology needs to apply to the depictions of service centres; it is possible to provide customers with virtual tours of these service centres and explain prerequisites, tools, and processes utilized by the automotive service provider (Wedel et al., 2020). VR can promise to create understanding and trust in the abilities and reliability of the provider of services as well as the quality of services rendered through changing the perception and making clients aware of different aspects of the existing services (Kübler et al., 2020).

These cases illustrate how one can successfully apply blockchain, AI, AR, and VR technologies to build a webrooming environment that is more open, customer-oriented, and engaging as a means of boosting consumers' confidence in automotive service providers (Upadhyay, 2020). Consumers can also gain the perception that automobile service providers that are adopting such technologies are trustworthy businesses that are customer oriented (Verhoef et al., 2021).

Also, car service providers are able to use virtual and augmented reality technologies to design and deploy engaging and realistic experiences that will make the customers who webroom have confidence in the service providers (Flavián et al., 2019). Thus, through providing the opportunities for virtual trips, service demonstrations and consultations, service providers enable customers to get used to the environment, develop a feeling of connection with a provider (Wedel et al., 2020).

Linking Technology-Enhanced Webrooming to Customer Purchase Intentions

The usability of technology-enhanced webrooming is therefore more easily measured in terms of its influence on buying behaviour of customers. Thus, when automotive service providers adopt trust enhancing technologies and strategies coupled with the efficient execution of webrooming services aimed at offering correct and appealing information to consumers, customer's propensity to make a purchase is likely to be positively influenced (Aw et al., 2021).

Previous research has established that customers who perform webrooming activities and have a perceived high credibility of the service firm are most likely to complete an offline purchase or booking (Flavián et al., 2019). Webrooming may help eliminate perceived risk and uncertainty to boost consumers' confidence and assurance to follow through, a finding supported by Aw et al., 2021.

Besides, the ability to make a webrooming process and its individual stages even more personalized and targeted through the use of artificial intelligence and big data analysis tools, which I described in subsection 2. 3, can also augment the consumers' purchase inclination (Wedel & Kannan, 2016). Thus, automotive service providers can use recommendations, offerings, and content that will be relevant to the client and direct the clients towards selecting these providers rather than competitors (Verhoef et al., 2021).

However, it is important to understand that, there are different aspects of the technology enhanced webrooming and this affects the attitudes towards customer purchase intentions in several ways. Webrooming has been found to be impacted by the level of customer involvement, the complexity of the service as well as perceived substitutability of offline services (Aw et al., 2021). Purchasing decisions involve several factors, and any automotive service provider needs to understand these factors to ensure proper application of webrooming to influence the customers' choice (Flavián et al., 2019).

Key Metrics for Evaluating Webrooming Success

To assess the success of their technology-enhanced webrooming initiatives, automotive service providers should track and analyse a range of key metrics. These metrics can provide valuable insights into customer behaviour, preferences, and the effectiveness of various trust-building mechanisms (Wedel et al., 2020).

One essential metric is the conversion rate, which measures the proportion of webrooming customers who ultimately make a purchase or booking (Aw et al., 2021). By monitoring conversion rates across different digital touchpoints and customer segments, service providers can identify areas for improvement and optimize their webrooming strategies accordingly (Flavián et al., 2019).

Another important metric is customer engagement, which encompasses various indicators such as website traffic, page views, time spent on site, and interaction rates with digital content (Kübler et al., 2020). Higher levels of customer engagement during the webrooming process can signify increased interest, trust, and likelihood to make a purchase (Grewal & Stephen, 2019).

Furthermore, automotive service providers should track customer feedback and satisfaction scores related to their webrooming experiences (Wedel et al., 2020). By analysing customer reviews, ratings, and survey responses, service providers can gain valuable insights into the perceived trustworthiness, usability, and effectiveness of their digital touchpoints (Filieri et al., 2015).

Other relevant metrics may include:

- Click-through rates on personalized recommendations and offers (Verhoef et al., 2021)
- Bounce rates and exit pages, indicating potential areas of friction or mistrust (Aw et al., 2021)
- Social media mentions and sentiment, reflecting the broader perception of the service provider's online presence (Kübler et al., 2020)
- Customer lifetime value, highlighting the long-term impact of trust and webrooming experiences on customer loyalty and profitability (Wedel et al., 2020)

By regularly monitoring and analysing these metrics, automotive service providers can gain a holistic understanding of their webrooming performance and make data-driven decisions to enhance trust, improve the customer experience, and ultimately drive purchase intentions (Wedel & Kannan, 2016).

CASE STUDIES FROM THE AUTOMOTIVE SERVICE INDUSTRY

In this section, actual automotive organizations from India, Germany, South Korea, and Japan area based cases that have adopted well-webrooming technology incorporated in building trust, customer experience, and purchase intentions (Aw et al., 2021).

Case Study 1: Maruti Suzuki India - Enhancing Webrooming Through AI-Powered Chatbots

Maruti Suzuki, the largest manufacturer of passenger vehicles in India realized that it was crucial for them to help their customers webroom easily and effectively. To achieve this, the company adopted the S-Assist AI based chat bot on the website of the firm.

S-Assist is intended to comprehend what customers' ask by natural language processing and respond immediately with a correct answer. This chatbot can successfully respond to many questions concerning the particular car model, characteristics, costs, ways of financing, and service schedules. Some of the advantages of machine learning and natural language processing (NLP) are that S-Assist always learns about the customer's needs and what is preferred so that with time it is more effective in recommending services (Verhoef et al., 2021).

Due to the adoption of S-Assist, customer response is so much enhanced including their satisfaction. The Maruti Suzuki company has estimated that the website traffic has been increased by 30% and the customer support cost has been minimized by 25% since using the chatbot. Furthermore, the company has witnessed a high growth in its leads and conversion rates since customers are in a position to locate the desired information thus making rational decisions regarding the purchase.

Case Study 2: BMW Germany – Building Trust, Through Blockchain-Based Car History

BMW, the German based automaker specializing in luxury vehicles has taken the lead in researching on the application of the blockchain technology that is supposed to increase confidence in the global automotive sector. In 2019, BMW, in partnership with a VeChain, an established enterprise blockchain solutions provider, developed VerifyCar; a block chain smart check history application.

Several features of VerifyCar for customers includes; Through this service, customers are able to have an account of a Car that is authentic that includes; maintenance, repair records, and ownership changes among others (Upadhyay, 2020). With help of blockchain technology BMW makes sure that the information provided is accurate, secure, and can be easily checked by a customer thereby increasing the level of trust in webrooming.

From the qualitative data obtained, it can be deduced that VerifyCar application received a positive response from the customers, particularly BMW that testified that the use of the application enhanced their trust and satisfaction as they went through the webrooming process. The success of this initiative has led BMW to seek to employ block chain technology in other fields like supply chain and data sharing amongst self-driven cars (Wedel et al., 2020).

Case Study 3: Hyundai South Korea – Optimising the Webrooming Experience via VR/AR

The South Korean car maker Hyundai is another company which has been keen using virtual reality and augmented reality technologies for designing and developing engaging webrooming experiences for its customers.

In the beginning of 2020, Hyundai has developed a new application that it named as "Hyundai Virtual Showroom" through which the customers are facilitated to experience and design vehicles in one of the most real environments of the VR technology. As mentioned earlier, it allows users to configure and experience Hyundai cars virtually, and make adjustments to the surface colours as well as trims from the comfort of their homes (Kübler et al., 2020).

Furthermore, Hyundai has adopted AR into its owner's manual where customers are able to get 3D manuals which provide virtual guided instructions on vehicle care and repairs (Wedel et al., 2020). This is achieved through offering customers an opportunity to use their smartphone to scan a QR code which provides them with the AR overlays that offer directions and informative tips increasing their knowledge and self- assurance about vehicle ownership (Grewal & Stephen, 2019).

The implementation of the VR and AR technologies has aided Hyundai to stand out amongst the other automobile manufacturers thus giving a better and more convenient Webrooming experience to its clients (Verhoef et al., 2021). The company has been able to indicate that there was a rise in customer satisfaction, higher engagement and the impact on perception of the brand after incorporating these technologies.

Case Study 4: Toyota Japan - Enhancing Webrooming through IoT-Enabled Connected Vehicles

The technology for the Internet of Things (IoT) has been used in Japan by Toyota, which is an automotive giant, to come up with smart cars so as to improve webrooming and get enduring customer loyalty.

Its online auto platform, "Toyota Connected," uses IoT sensors and telematics to gather data such as vehicle performance at a particular time, drivers' behaviour and weather conditions (Aw et al., 2021). Using advanced analytics and machine learning techniques, this information is then analysed to give clients personalized suggestions about their rides, maintenance alerts based on predictions and other tailored services (Kübler et al., 2020).

The Toyota Connected mobile app gives customers access to a well of information about their cars like the fuel efficiency, driving habits, and next service needs. This ensures that users are well informed and that they feel supported over the years in which they own the car thus creating trust and loyalty since there is transparency in this transparency and proactive maintenance approach (Filieri et al., 2015).

Connected cars powered by IoT have enabled Toyota to offer a seamless, personal online shopping experience as customers can obtain all related details at their fingertips (Grewal & Stephen, 2019). The company's initiatives on connected vehicles have resulted in increased customer retention; higher service revenue; and improved brand advocacy.

These real-life examples show how various auto-manufacturers from different nations utilized different technologies so as to develop webrooming experiences, foster confidence and increase client relations. Be it chatbots endowed with artificial intelligence or blockchain based car histories, or virtual reality/augmented reality projects or Internet of Things activated connected automobiles; these instances reveal the awesome possibilities that exist for technology to revolutionize the automotive sector (Aw et al., 2021).

In the next section, we will synthesize the lessons learned from these case studies and provide best practices and recommendations for automotive companies looking to implement technology-enhanced webrooming strategies.

BEST PRACTICES AND RECOMMENDATIONS

Develop a Clear Technology Roadmap

To this end, automotive service providers should develop a comprehensive technology roadmap that corresponds to their overall business goals and customer experience targets (Verhoef et al., 2021). This roadmap should place a strong emphasis on implementing those technologies that can specifically address the issues confronting numerous customers when they are webrooming their desired cars and in so doing improve measurable customer ratings of trust, engagement and conversion rates (Aw et al., 2021).

In formulating a technology road-map it is important that such factors as the current level of company's technology capabilities, financial constraints facing the company as well as expertise available within the organization are put into consideration (Ivanov & Webster, 2019). Moreover; phased adoption helps to ensure smooth transition while at the same time permitting continuous improvement through customer feedback gathered over time along with performance indicators (Kübler et al., 2020).

Foster a Customer-Centric Mindset

In order for automobile service providers to successfully use technology-enhanced webrooming strategies, they need to have a customer-centric mindset across the whole organization (Wedel et al., 2020). This entails putting the client at the core of all decision-making processes and continuously looking for ways of enhancing their journey through different touchpoints (Grewal & Stephen, 2019).

Automobile service providers ought to frequently capture and analyse customer feedback; conduct user testing and track key performance indicators (KPIs) so as to find areas that need improvement as well as make necessary adjustments to optimize their webrooming platforms (Filieri et al., 2015). Consequently, by making it a point to be attentive on customers' opinions on how they develop the webrooming technologies meant for them, firms are able to develop solutions with which the given audience can easily connect (Aw et al., 2021).

Invest in Data Analytics and Personalization

Technological advancements have revolutionized webrooming through data analytics and personalization (Verhoef et al., 2021). In line with Wedel & Kannan (2016); automobile service providers require ample resources for extensive data collection, integration and analysis as well.

Companies have the opportunity to obtain insights that are necessary for making recommendations which are personalized, creating targeted contents and coming up with unique service displays through the utilization of advanced analytics like machine learning as well as predictive modelling (Kübler et al., 2020). Apart from enhancing the relevance and effectiveness of webrooming experiences, personalization also exemplifies a desire to understand individual customer needs (Grewal & Stephen, 2019).

Collaborate with Technology Partners

It often takes specialized expertise and resources to implement advanced webrooming technologies, which are not always readily available within the company (Upadhyay, 2020). As such, automotive service providers should consider building alliances with technology partners including software development firms, AI specialists and data analytics providers so as to hasten the process of innovation and successful implementation of these solutions (Aw et al., 2021).

The evaluation of their past performance, industry experience, and alignment with the company's values and goals are essential when choosing technology partners (Wedel et al., 2020). Having a solid partnership based on trust, openness and common objectives can enable automotive service providers to remain at the cutting edge of technology while providing innovative webrooming experiences for customers (Kübler et al., 2020).

Prioritize Data Privacy and Security

As automotive service providers are gathering and using increasing amounts of customer data with a view to enhancing webrooming experiences, thus data privacy and security should be prioritized above everything else (Wedel & Kannan, 2016). Companies have to comply with strict regulations concerning the protection of information such as the General Data Protection Regulation (GDPR) and the California Consumer Privacy Act (CCPA), while ensuring that they install concrete security measures aimed at safeguarding clients' personal details (Aw et al., 2021).

Transparency as well as effective communication about data collection, use and sharing processes are key in developing trust from the customers (Wedel et al., 2020). It is for this reason therefore that automotive service providers are expected to come up with complete frameworks on data governance; regularly offer training programs for their staff members regarding right ways of handling data; invest heavily in sophisticated systems like encryption and multi-factor authentication so as to curb terror threats to databases thereby boosting the confidence of clients (Filieri et al.,2015).

Foster a Culture of Continuous Learning and Improvement

The market has become more user-friendly and technologically advanced. Through regular training, organizations in automotive service should ensure that there is constant improvement (Verhoef et al., 2021). Employees in these motion-based organizations must attend trainings related to new developments in the industry so that they keep up with changing trends (Grewal & Stephen, 2019).

In order for automobile servicing agencies to find optimization chances as well as enable incremental enhancements, they need to be familiar with the assessment of webrooming technologies conducted on a regular basis, A/B testing and the experimental introduction of new functions (Kübler et al., 2020). Consequently, companies can remain competitive while offering extraordinary webrooming services all the time if they encourage experimentation while learning from their fumbles and modifying their strategies based on facts (Aw et al., 2021).

Integrate Online and Offline Experiences Seamlessly

Although technology-enhanced webrooming mainly emphasizes the online customer journey but it is significant to have an unbroken tie-up with offline experience (Wedel et al., 2020). Automotive service providers must aim at ensuring there is a consistent and cohesive brand experience across all touchpoints starting from the first online research stage up to the in-store service delivery (Aw et al., 2021).

This can be effected through omnichannel strategies that facilitate easy movement between online and offline channels; for instance, allowing customers to book services on the internet and later easily retrieve this information when they visit the physical store for appointment (Grewal & Stephen, 2019). Additionally, using other technologies like virtual reality or augmented reality as well as Internet of Things might help in connecting these two worlds thereby creating immersive experiences that are tailored to individuals' interests leading to enhanced customer satisfaction (Kübler et al., 2020).

Measure, Analyse, and Optimize Performance

For technology-enhanced webrooming initiatives to be successful, automotive service providers should clearly define their performance metrics and measure, analyse, and optimise them on a continuous basis (Wedel & Kannan, 2016). Some of the key metrics which need to be monitored include website traffic or number of visitors on websites; engagement rates or how long do customers spend on your content online as well as conversion rates (how many website visitors end up buying something); customer satisfaction scores (are your customers happy with what you sell?) and lifetime value (Aw et al., 2021).

Utilizing advanced analytics tools and techniques will allow the organisations a better understanding of customers purchasing behaviours as well as identification of trends or patterns that could serve in making valid decisions about how to improve their webrooming platforms (Kübler et al., 2020). For instance, timely generation of reports and periodic dashboard visualisations are crucial in informing stakeholders' about the progress made thus far while also enabling swift remedial actions when necessary (Wedel et al., 2020).

Embrace an Agile and Adaptive Approach

In terms of responding to changing circumstances in the automotive service industry and fluctuating customer expectations, companies should take into account an agile and adaptive method to technology-supported webrooming (Verhoef et al., 2021). This implies that they must be open to change and promptly deal with emerging challenges or opportunities and consistently refine their strategies according to instant feedbacks and insights (Aw et al., 2021).

Automotive service providers who have an agile mindset can test out new technologies, change their direction when needed, and rapidly expand successful initiatives (Grewal & Stephen, 2019). As such, organizations could remain on the leading edge by encouraging a culture typified by flexibility, cooperation and invention which would allow them to provide webrooming services that always surpass what customers expect from them (Filieri et al., 2015)

To wrap up, for effective webrooming strategies increased by technology, there should be an all-around and customer-centred perspective which includes a distinct technology roadmap, data-directed personalization, partnership with technology stakeholders, and a concentration on data security as well as privacy. (Aw et al., 2021). Therefore, by encouraging a culture of lifelong learning, blending online and offline experiences without any friction, adopting agile mentality or even adaptable way of thinking, the auto service providers will be able to face opportunities as well as challenges linked with digital era successfully while establishing durable relations with clients. (Wedel et al., 2020).

CONCLUSION

Recap of Key Takeaways

This chapter has looked into how tech could change how automotive webrooming is done. Utilizing advanced technologies such as AI, blockchain, virtual and augmented reality, IoT, and mobile-first strategies; webrooming for automotive service providers can be turned into "more interesting on-line shopping experiences that are trustworthy and focused on customers" (Aw et al., 2021).

There are several case studies from real companies such as Maruti Suzuki, BMW, Hyundai and Toyota in this chapter which show the obvious return on investment from their adoption of high-tech approaches for webrooming. These include improved trustworthiness and openness among clients or potential ones; increase in client engagement; better conversion rates among others (Verhoef et al., 2021).

For automotive service providers aiming to start their own technology-enabled webrooming ventures, Section 5 lists best practices and recommendations that form a holistic framework (Wedel et al., 2020). Companies can thus effectively navigate the complexities of digital transformation as well as provide excellent webrooming experiences by establishing a well-defined technology roadmap, promoting customer orientation, investing in data analytics and personalization, working with technology partners, giving preference to data privacy and security together with taking an agile adaptive stance.

Future Research Directions

Even though this chapter provides significant contributions on how technology can be used to better webrooming experiences, there are still many possibilities for future research. One avenue that can be explored is the influence of newer technologies like 5G networks, edge computing and quantum computing on the advancement of webrooming strategies (Aw et al., 2021). The accomplishment of these technologies may lead to new forms of real-time data processing, personalized experiences and immersed interactions (Kübler et al., 2020).

Another viable area for study is looking into the variations across cultures regarding webrooming behaviours and preferences. As it becomes increasingly internationalised, the car service industry must appreciate cultural aspects which shape customer expectations and their involvement with webrooming devices in order to be able to develop localization strategies that are effective (Verhoef et al., 2021).

Moreover, future studies could examine the moral implications of using customer data to customize webrooming services. Given the increasing concerns about data privacy and algorithmic bias, it would be necessary to investigate how best to ensure that customer data is used transparently, fairly and with the right accountability (Filieri et al., 2015).

To increase our comprehension of technology-enhanced webrooming within the automotive service industry, several distinct research queries and hypotheses could be examined within future studies:

1. **How do different generations of customers (eg, baby boomers, Generation X, millennials, and Generation Z) react to technological webrooming experiences enhanced by webrooming technology and what are its implications for targeting and personalization strategies?**

   Hypothesis: Young people (Millennials and Generation Z) react more positively than their older counterparts (baby boomers and Generation X), when it comes to webrooming experiences using technology.

   Research Design: A mixed-methods approach comprising online surveys and focus group discussions may be employed in order to study generational variations in preferences, attitudes and practices regarding technology-enhanced webrooming. The survey could comprise questions on technology adoption, perceived ease of use, trust and satisfaction with webrooming experiences. Focus group discussions might offer much insight into these differences and thus help identify particular attributes or techniques which appeal to each generation.

2. **How greatly do cultural variations impact technology-aided webrooming strategies, and in what ways can car service providers change their methods to meet the needs of various cultures?**

   Hypothesis: The effectiveness of technology-enhanced webrooming strategies varies significantly across different cultural contexts, and therefore automotive service providers have to adjust their strategies.

   Research Design: To explore how culture determines the performance of technology-enhanced webrooming cross-culture study is done in several countries with different culture profiles. An alternative would be an online experiment where people from various cultures are subjected to different webrooming scenarios and then asked to respond based on purchase intentions, trust and engagement level. Relationships among cultural dimensions, webrooming features and outcome variables can be evaluated using structural equation modelling.

3. **In what ways can automotive service providers utilize new technologies such as 5G networks and edge computing so as to provide seamless and immersive web-rooming experiences? Moreover, what are some potential implications for customer engagement and loyalty?**

   Hypothesis: Higher levels of customer engagement and loyalty are attained through webrooming with 5G networks and edge computing rather than by traditional webrooming techniques.

   Research Design: In collaboration with an automotive service provider, a longitudinal field study would be conducted to explore the influences of 5G as well as edge computing technologies upon webrooming experiences. A prototype webrooming platform can be created based on these technologies for offering real-time, personalized and immersive experience. The proposed metrics for tracking customer engagement and loyalty include; the amount of time spent on the platform; interaction rates; repeat visits among others which could then be compared against those who use a conventional webrooming platform.

4. **What are the most effective strategies for integrating user-generated content (UGC) in webrooming platforms to enhance trust and credibility, and how do these strategies influence customer decision-making processes?**

   Hypothesis: The incorporation of user-generated content such as reviews, ratings and testimonials in webrooming platforms enhances trust and credibility thereby improving customer decision-making as well as increasing the conversion rates.

   Research Design: A mixed-method approach involving online experiments and depth interviews can be used to study the effect of UGC on trust, credibility and decision making in contexts of webrooming. The online experiment might manipulate whether there is UGC in the webrooming platforms and how it appears then measure participants' reactions in terms of perceived trustworthiness, credibility or purchase intention. Furthermore, in-depth interviews with a sample of those who took part would shed more light on what lies beneath these effects.

The implications of auto service can be better understood through research into this area. This will help automakers know how to personalize their services to serve customers based on age and ethnicity differences in webrooming habits. Moreover, studying the influence of new technology and user generated content will allow businesses to keep abreast with advancements and come up with more captivating and reliable webrooming experiences. In general, these studies can lead to practical knowledge that will be used by automobile service providers on customer satisfaction, loyalty-building tactics as well as business growth.

Concluding Remarks

The automobile servicing industry is witnessing a drastic change as a result of rapid technological advancement and changes in customer expectations. Since webrooming is becoming an essential part of every customer's journey, auto service providers need to embrace digital innovation to sustain their competitiveness and offer better customer experiences (Aw et al., 2021).

By technology-enhanced means to promote trust, transparency, and engagement, auto service providers can develop a stronger and more sustainable relationship with their clients. The ideas generated from this chapter are an organization's guide for those wanting to exploit technology-fuelled webrooming possibilities in order to thrive in a digital economy (Wedel et al., 2020).

Even though the automotive services sector keeps changing, it is very important for firms to remain flexible, adjustable learning organizations dedicated towards perpetually improvement. While being vigilant about emerging technologies, consumer needs and industry standards set up by other automobile service companies will help these organizations lead within innovative paradigms leading towards consumer driven webrooming experiences which would please elate every customer (Verhoef et al., 2021).

REFERENCES

Aguirre, E., Roggeveen, A. L., Grewal, D., & Wetzels, M. (2016). The personalization-privacy paradox: Implications for new media. *Journal of Consumer Marketing*, *33*(2), 98–110. DOI: 10.1108/JCM-06-2015-1458

Aw, E. C. X., Basha, N. K., Ng, S. I., & Ho, J. A. (2021). Searching online and buying offline: Understanding the role of channel-, consumer-, and product-related factors in determining webrooming intention. *Journal of Retailing and Consumer Services*, *58*, 102328. DOI: 10.1016/j.jretconser.2020.102328

Balducci, B., & Marinova, D. (2018). Unstructured data in marketing. *Journal of the Academy of Marketing Science*, *46*(4), 557–590. DOI: 10.1007/s11747-018-0581-x

Bart, Y., Shankar, V., Sultan, F., & Urban, G. L. (2005). Are the drivers and role of online trust the same for all web sites and consumers? A large-scale exploratory empirical study. *Journal of Marketing*, *69*(4), 133–152. DOI: 10.1509/jmkg.2005.69.4.133

Bourreau, M., & de Streel, A. (2019). Digital conglomerates and EU competition policy. SSRN Electronic Journal. DOI: 10.2139/ssrn.3350512

Capgemini Research Institute. (2019). Why addressing ethical questions in AI will benefit organisations. https://www.capgemini.com/gb-en/wp-content/uploads/sites/3/2019/07/CRI-AI-in-Ethics_Web.pdf

Davenport, T., Guha, A., Grewal, D., & Bressgott, T. (2020). How artificial intelligence will change the future of marketing. *Journal of the Academy of Marketing Science*, *48*(1), 24–42. DOI: 10.1007/s11747-019-00696-0

Duan, Y., Edwards, J. S., & Dwivedi, Y. K. (2019). Artificial intelligence for decision making in the era of Big Data – evolution, challenges and research agenda. *International Journal of Information Management*, *48*, 63–71. DOI: 10.1016/j.ijinfomgt.2019.01.021

Fernández, N. V., Pérez, M. J. S., & Vázquez-Casielles, R. (2018). Webroomers versus showroomers: Are they the same? *Journal of Business Research*, *92*, 300–320. DOI: 10.1016/j.jbusres.2018.08.004

Filieri, R. (2015). What makes online reviews helpful? A diagnosticity-adoption framework to explain informational and normative influences in e-WOM. *Journal of Business Research*, *68*(6), 1261–1270. DOI: 10.1016/j.jbusres.2014.11.006

Filieri, R., Alguezaui, S., & McLeay, F. (2015). Why do travelers trust TripAdvisor? Antecedents of trust towards consumer-generated media and its influence on recommendation adoption and word of mouth. *Tourism Management*, *51*, 174–185. DOI: 10.1016/j.tourman.2015.05.007

Flavián, C., Gurrea, R., & Orús, C. (2019). The effect of product presentation mode on the perceived content and continent quality of web sites. *Online Information Review*, *33*(6), 1103–1128. DOI: 10.1108/14684520911011034

Flavián, C., Gurrea, R., & Orús, C. (2020). Combining channels to make smart purchases: The role of webrooming and showrooming. *Journal of Retailing and Consumer Services*, *52*, 101923. DOI: 10.1016/j.jretconser.2019.101923

Gao, P., Kaas, H.-W., Mohr, D., & Wee, D. (2016). Automotive revolution – Perspective towards 2030. McKinsey & Company. https://www.mckinsey.com/industries/automotive-and-assembly/our-insights/disruptive-trends-that-will-transform-the-auto-industry/de-de

Garaus, M., & Wagner, U. (2019). Let me entertain you – Increasing overall store satisfaction through digital signage in retail waiting areas. *Journal of Retailing and Consumer Services*, *47*, 331–338. DOI: 10.1016/j.jretconser.2018.12.008

Gartner. (2021). Digital asset management (DAM). Gartner Glossary. https://www.gartner.com/en/information-technology/glossary/digital-asset-management-dam

Grbovic, M., & Cheng, H. (2018). Real-time personalization using embeddings for search ranking at Airbnb. *Proceedings of the 24th ACM SIGKDD International Conference on Knowledge Discovery & Data Mining*, 311-320. DOI: 10.1145/3219819.3219885

Gretzel, U., Fuchs, M., Baggio, R., Hoepken, W., Law, R., Neidhardt, J., Pesonen, J., Zanker, M., & Xiang, Z. (2020). e-Tourism beyond COVID-19: A call for transformative research. *Information Technology & Tourism*, *22*(2), 187–203. DOI: 10.1007/s40558-020-00181-3

Grewal, D., Hulland, J., Kopalle, P. K., & Karahanna, E. (2020). The future of technology and marketing: A multidisciplinary perspective. *Journal of the Academy of Marketing Science*, *48*(1), 1–8. DOI: 10.1007/s11747-019-00711-4

Grewal, L., & Stephen, A. T. (2019). In mobile we trust: The effects of mobile versus nonmobile reviews on consumer purchase intentions. *JMR, Journal of Marketing Research*, *56*(5), 791–808. DOI: 10.1177/0022243719834514

Kang, J.-Y. M. (2018). Showrooming, webrooming, and user-generated content creation in the omnichannel era. *Journal of Internet Commerce*, *17*(2), 145–169. DOI: 10.1080/15332861.2018.1433907

Kannan, P. K., & Li, H. (2017). Digital marketing: A framework, review and research agenda. *International Journal of Research in Marketing*, *34*(1), 22–45. DOI: 10.1016/j.ijresmar.2016.11.006

Kaplan, A., & Haenlein, M. (2019). Siri, Siri, in my hand: Who's the fairest in the land? On the interpretations, illustrations, and implications of artificial intelligence. *Business Horizons*, *62*(1), 15–25. DOI: 10.1016/j.bushor.2018.08.004

Kelliher, F., Reinl, L., Johnson, T. G., & Joppe, M. (2018). The role of trust in building rural tourism micro firm network engagement: A multi-case study. *Tourism Management*, *68*, 1–12. DOI: 10.1016/j.tourman.2018.02.014

Kübler, R. V., Colicev, A., & Pauwels, K. H. (2020). Social media's impact on the consumer mindset: When to use which sentiment extraction tool? *Journal of Interactive Marketing*, *50*(1), 136–155. DOI: 10.1016/j.intmar.2019.08.001

Kuehnl, C., Jozic, D., & Homburg, C. (2019). Effective customer journey design: Consumers' conception, measurement, and consequences. *Journal of the Academy of Marketing Science*, *47*(3), 551–568. DOI: 10.1007/s11747-018-00625-7

Lambrecht, A., & Tucker, C. (2019). Algorithmic bias? An empirical study of apparent gender-based discrimination in the display of STEM career ads. *Management Science*, *65*(7), 2966–2981. DOI: 10.1287/mnsc.2018.3093

Lemon, K. N., & Verhoef, P. C. (2016). Understanding customer experience throughout the customer journey. *Journal of Marketing*, *80*(6), 69–96. DOI: 10.1509/jm.15.0420

Lobschat, L., Mueller, B., Eggers, F., Brandimarte, L., Diefenbach, S., Kroschke, M., & Wirtz, J. (2021). Corporate digital responsibility. *Journal of Business Research*, *122*, 875–888. DOI: 10.1016/j.jbusres.2019.10.006

Lops, P., Jannach, D., Musto, C., Bogers, T., & Koolen, M. (2019). Trends in content-based recommendation. *User Modeling and User-Adapted Interaction*, *29*(2), 239–249. DOI: 10.1007/s11257-019-09231-w

Martin, K. D., Borah, A., & Palmatier, R. W. (2017). Data privacy: Effects on customer and firm performance. *Journal of Marketing*, *81*(1), 36–58. DOI: 10.1509/jm.15.0497

Martin, K. D., & Murphy, P. E. (2017). The role of data privacy in marketing. *Journal of the Academy of Marketing Science*, *45*(2), 135–155. DOI: 10.1007/s11747-016-0495-4

Montoya-Weiss, M. M., Voss, G. B., & Grewal, D. (2003). Determinants of online channel use and overall satisfaction with a relational, multichannel service provider. *Journal of Technological Advancements, 31*(4), 448–458. DOI: 10.1177/0092070303254408

Önder, I., & Treiblmaier, H. (2018). Blockchain and tourism: Three research propositions. *Annals of Tourism Research, 72*, 180–182. DOI: 10.1016/j.annals.2018.03.005

Ostrom, A. L., Parasuraman, A., Bowen, D. E., Patrício, L., & Voss, C. A. (2015). Service research priorities in a rapidly changing context. *Journal of Service Research, 18*(2), 127–159. DOI: 10.1177/1094670515576315

Ozturk, A. B., Bilgihan, A., Salehi-Esfahani, S., & Hua, N. (2017). Understanding the mobile payment technology acceptance based on valence theory: A case of restaurant transactions. *International Journal of Contemporary Hospitality Management, 29*(8), 2027–2049. DOI: 10.1108/IJCHM-04-2016-0192

Pee, L. G., Jiang, J., & Klein, G. (2018). Signaling effect of website usability on repurchase intention. *International Journal of Information Management, 39*, 228–241. DOI: 10.1016/j.ijinfomgt.2017.12.010

Petit, O., Velasco, C., & Spence, C. (2019). Digital sensory marketing: Integrating new technologies into multisensory online experience. *Journal of Interactive Marketing, 45*(1), 42–61. DOI: 10.1016/j.intmar.2018.07.004

Puntoni, S., Walker Reczek, R., Giesler, M., & Botti, S. (2021). Consumers and artificial intelligence: An experiential perspective. *Journal of Marketing, 85*(1), 131–151. DOI: 10.1177/0022242920953847

Rust, R. T., & Huang, M.-H. (2014). The service revolution and the transformation of marketing science. *Marketing Science, 33*(2), 206–221. DOI: 10.1287/mksc.2013.0836

Santos, S., & Gonçalves, H. M. (2019). Multichannel consumer behaviors in the mobile environment: Using fsQCA and discriminant analysis to understand webrooming motivations. *Journal of Business Research, 101*, 757–766. DOI: 10.1016/j.jbusres.2018.12.069

Sharma, M., & Klein, A. (2020). Consumer perceived value, involvement, trust, susceptibility to interpersonal influence, and intention to participate in online group buying. *Journal of Retailing and Consumer Services, 52*, 101946. DOI: 10.1016/j.jretconser.2019.101946

Upadhyay, N. (2020). Demystifying blockchain: A critical analysis of challenges, applications and opportunities. *International Journal of Information Management, 54*, 102120. DOI: 10.1016/j.ijinfomgt.2020.102120

Verhoef, P. C., Broekhuizen, T., Bart, Y., Bhattacharya, A., Qi Dong, J., Fabian, N., & Haenlein, M. (2021). Digital transformation: A multidisciplinary reflection and research agenda. *Journal of Business Research, 122*, 889–901. DOI: 10.1016/j.jbusres.2019.09.022

Verhoef, P. C., Neslin, S. A., & Vroomen, B. (2007). Multichannel customer management: Understanding the research-shopper phenomenon. *International Journal of Research in Marketing, 24*(2), 129–148. DOI: 10.1016/j.ijresmar.2006.11.002

Wallace, E., Torres, P., Augusto, M., & Stefuryn, M. (2022). Do brand relationships on social media motivate young consumers' value co-creation and willingness to pay? The role of brand love. *Journal of Product and Brand Management, 31*(2), 189–205. DOI: 10.1108/JPBM-06-2020-2937

Wedel, M., Bigné, E., & Zhang, J. (2020). Virtual and augmented reality: Advancing research in consumer marketing. *International Journal of Research in Marketing, 37*(3), 443–465. DOI: 10.1016/j.ijresmar.2020.04.004

Wedel, M., & Kannan, P. K. (2016). Marketing analytics for data-rich environments. *Journal of Marketing, 80*(6), 97–121. DOI: 10.1509/jm.15.0413

Yeung, K. (2019). Responsibility and AI: Council of Europe study. Council of Europe. https://rm.coe.int/responsability-and-ai-en/168097d9c5

Chapter 5
Technological Evolution and Digital Transformation in the Services Sector:
Trends, Impacts, and Future Directions

A. Rizwanbasha
https://orcid.org/0000-0002-3934-8616
Panimalar Engineering College, India

P. Sivasakthi
Easwari Engineering College, India

M. A. Y. Peer Mohamed Appa
Vel Tech Rangarajan Dr. Sagunthala R&D Institute of Science and Technology, India

S. Vaitheeshwari
Vel Tech Multi Tech Dr.Rangarajan Dr.Sakunthala Engineering College, India

D. Lekha
R.M.K. College of Engineering and Technology, India

R. Siva Subramanian
https://orcid.org/0000-0002-7509-9223
R.M.K. College of Engineering and Technology, India

P. Girija
https://orcid.org/0009-0000-1691-8180
Vel Tech Rangarajan Dr. Sagunthala R&D Institute of Science and Technology, India

ABSTRACT

This paper discusses the transformative effect of technology advancement on the services industry, and the role of digital technologies like artificial intelligence, blockchain technology and the Internet of things. It assesses the trends in technology adoption with a focus on data-orientated analysis and the use of AI and automation in various service sectors. The paper also discusses the effects of blockchain technology, how IoT is set to transform service delivery, and privacy considerations in the modern society. The importance of smart devices and connected system with emphasis on the need to enhance cybersecurity measures is well described. The consequences of further developments of the services industry for the society and the corresponding strategic recommendations for a world with focus on technology are presented as well. Combining the information on the present state and potential development, this paper strives to provide a systematic review of the ongoing digital transformation in the services sector.

DOI: 10.4018/979-8-3693-7447-4.ch005

1. INTRODUCTION

1.1 Background on the Services Sector and Its Significance

Services sector is a vital component of the world economy as it constitutes a major part of the Gross Domestic Product and offer employment opportunities (Baa, R., & Chattoraj, A. K. 2022). It touches virtually all sectors of the economy, including health care, education, finance, hospitality and so on, and is the sine qua non of most contemporary economies. This growth has been attributed to the rising demand from customers for specialized and quality services together with the application of new technologies in the delivery of the services.

1.2 Definitions and Key Concepts

Technological Evolution: Refers to the continuous adoption and diffusion of new technologies in the successively defined time periods that affects the delivery and use of services (Coccia, M., & Watts, J. 2020).

Digital Transformation: The use of digital technologies to redefine organizational purpose and productivity as well as customers' value(Kraus, S et al 2021).

Services Sector: One of the subcategories of the economy in which all companies and processes that deliver services rather than products to consumers and businesses fall under.

1.3 Purpose and Scope of the Survey Paper

Therefore, the general objective of this survey paper is to examine the technological development and the digitalization of the services sector. It aims at presenting a discussion of how the advancement in technology has impacted the sector in the past and how today's technology influences service provision. Thus, by discussing major trends, impacts and future developments, the paper will provide the stakeholders with meaningful recommendations for the service providers, governmental authorities and researchers. It will embrace the use of such technologies ad cloud computing, AI, IoT, data driven decision-making, the role of cybersecurity, among other things, and the future prospects. In particular, this paper covers opportunities and threats in the services industry as a result of embracing new technologies and making suggestions on the ways in which management can optimise on the future technological advancements.

2. EVOLUTION OF TECHNOLOGY IN THE SERVICES SECTOR

2.1 Historical Overview of Technological Advancements in Services

The application of technology in the services sector has gone through the following changes in its technological revolutions. First, the Industrial Revolution brought the introduction of machinery, which enhanced productivity in areas such as transport and supply chains. Telecommunication technologies like the telegraph and the telephone paved way for changes in communication and realtime information exchange, the basis of the global service networks. At the end of the 20th century the advent of computers and the internet revolutionized service delivery by enabling online purchases, telecommuting and virtual communication.

2.2 Key Milestones and Breakthroughs

In this context, certain critical achievements have defined the services sector heavily. The World Wide Web which came in the early 1990s brought in new opportunities in the expansion and development of the ecommerce as well as the online services. In the 2000s, the advancement in the mobile technology and the smartphones paved way for access of services at the convenience of the consumer, and at any time they wanted. The development of the cloud computing services in 2010s provided sparking scalable and cost efficient services for delivering comprehensive services in diverse sectors like health care, finance, and education services. In addition, recent developments in artificial intelligence (AI) and big data have enabled firms to economic and data driven services.

2.3 Impact of Past Technological Changes on Service Delivery

Technology has revolutionized service delivery to make it faster, more efficient and convenient to the consumer. Geographical structures have been liberalized through internet and mobility technologies and services made available round the clock. Technological advancements such as automation and the use of Artificial Intelligence has enhanced efficiency, minimised cost, and optimised services through prediction analysis and client interactions. This has made it possible for the provision of services to match the needs of the businesses through service scalability through the use of cloud computing. These changes have also encouraged innovation, resulting to new services delivery methods including on-demand services and subscription services. However, these advancements have also brought some disadvantages, such as requiring digital competency, exposure to cybercrime, and the threat of becoming unemployed due to automation.

3. THE ROLE OF DIGITAL TECHNOLOGIES IN TRANSFORMING SERVICES

3.1 Overview of Digital Technologies

Cloud computing solutions, artificial intelligence, and big data solutions are changing the services industry. Through virtualized environment, cloud computing it provides organizations with a reliable and efficient means in which to store the data while at the same time catering for the scale and flexibility of the business(Alouffi, B. et al 2021). AI contributes service persistence by automating processes, making predictions, and interacting with people. Business intelligence is the area where big data analytics helps an organization to analyze large volumes of data that are useful in decision-making and enhancing the value of the organization's customer experience(Bharadiya, J. P. 2023).

Figure 1. The role of digital technologies in transforming services

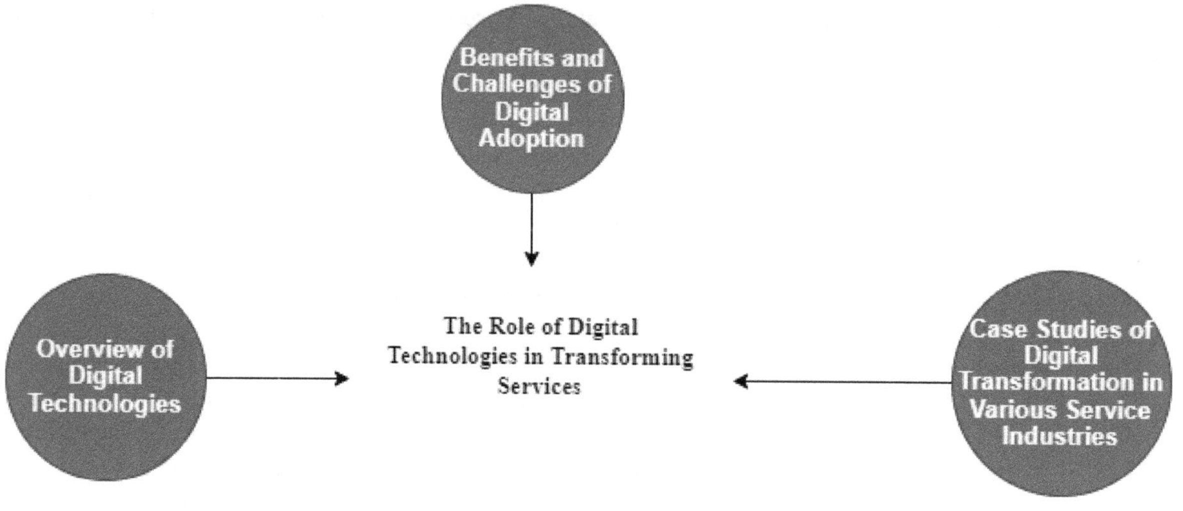

3.2 Case Studies of Digital Transformation in Various Service Industries

Healthcare: Technological advancements has enhanced healthcare services by the application of telemedicine, EHRs as well as algorithms in diagnosis. For instance, technologies of telemedicine that are evident from Teladoc, among others allow distant communication to be established, hence enhancing availability of services (Ivančić, et al 2020).

Finance: There is substantial transformation concerning the financial services industry as is explained by fintech. Currently, lots of companies, such as PayPal, use interfaces to facilitate online payments in their operations.

Retail: In the retailing industry there is extensive use of internet selling and omni-channel initiative. Amazon as a company has made a good use of digital transformation in the aspects of smart recommendations and smart deliveries. Retailers also apply big data for such purposes as stock control and improvement of the overall experience of purchasing goods(Gouveia, F. D., & São Mamede, H. 2022).

3.3 Benefits and Challenges of Digital Adoption

3.3.1 Benefits

There are several advantages of digital business adoption, such as; increased productivity, reduced costs and happy customers. Cloud also eliminates the requirement of physical structures that in turn decreases the cost of doing business. AI and automation enhance efficiency because operations are fastened and result in optimal service provision. This approach also offers decision-making solutions or masks more service options depending on the customer's needs and demographic data.

3.3.2 Challenges

However, there are risks associated with digital adoption. Adopting new technologies entails heavy capital investment as well as professional human resource which is a challenge to small firms. A major challenge is data privacy and security for possible cyber attack and data breach. Also, since the advancement in technology is faster it means that the organization has to keep on updating its employees and this has a drain on the organization resources.

4. TRENDS IN TECHNOLOGY ADOPTION

4.1 Current Trends in Technology Adoption in the Services Sector

Technology uptake in the services sector is growing rapidly due to the modern pressures of increasing operational effectiveness and delivering better customer experiences. Among the important trends it is possible to identify the increasing popularity of cloud solutions allowing to expand the work and minimize the expenses. Automated services with the use of artificial intelligence (AI) and machine learning (ML) are being applied across the board to the field of services. This is evident in the use of the internet of things that is quickly gaining adoption specifically in the areas of logistics and health care by giving real time data thus enhancing the delivery of service. Also, the use of blockchain is still progressive, guaranteeing the growth of safety and openness in fields such as finance and supply chain.

Figure 2. Trends in technology adoption

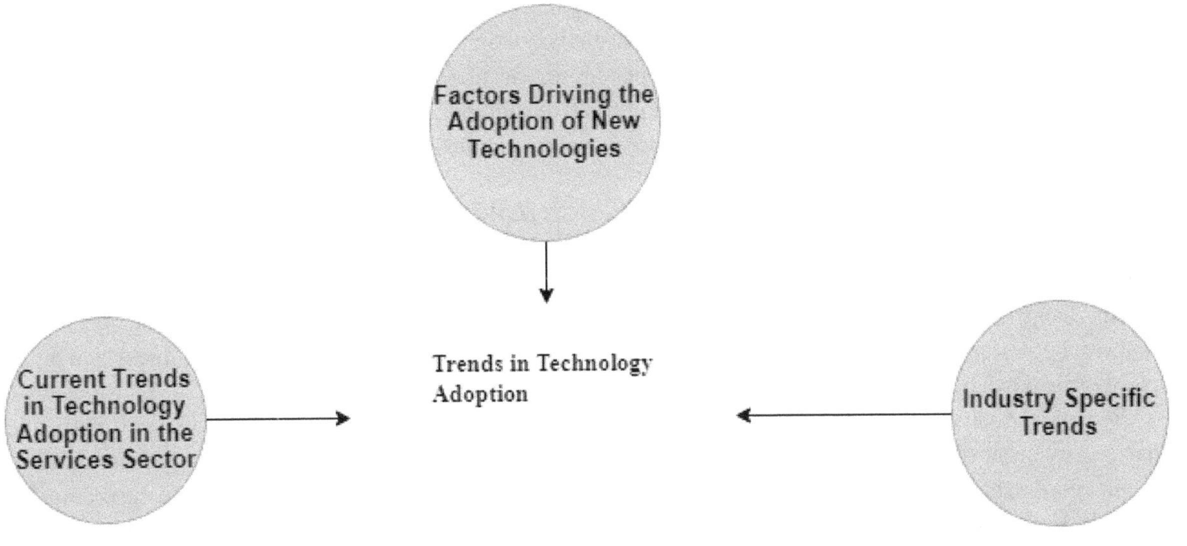

4.2 Factors Driving the Adoption of New Technologies

The following are the reasons for the acquisition of new technologies in the services sector. First, through increased expectations from consumers for smooth and personal service delivery business is being forced to adapt. Second and logically the pressure from the competitors can force the organizations to employ technologies that lead to increased efficiency and hence minimum costs. Third, legal demands, most notably, regarding data protection and management, are impacting the implementation of effective digital tools. Last of all, technological growth and the lowering of technical costs mean that enterprises, including small and medium-sized ones, are now able to adopt notions on Digital Transformation.

4.3 Industry Specific Trends

Healthcare: Telemedicine and AIdriven diagnostics are now the new inventions that have taken root in the management of patients, particularly in the rural areas. Finance: Technological advancements like digital payments and blockchain are threatening to disrupt traditional banking and financial systems. Retail: AI is being integrated with ecommerce and omnichannel approaches for individualised shopping experiences and stock control. Hospitality: IoT and AI are enhancing customer services using smart rooms and enhancing recommendation services. This section focuses on the current trends in technological advancement and especially their adoption in the services industries and regions.

5. APPLICATIONS OF DATADRIVEN DECISION MAKING

5.1 Importance of Data in Service Industries

Information has emerged as the main resource in the provision of services, which has boosted the performance and differentiation of various sectors. The abundance of information that is available provides businesses with information on client's behaviour, needs and any changes, thus allowing companies to provide quality services. Effectiveness of data analysis as a means of improving organizational decision making is considerably facilitated because it enables the organization to focus on such issues as how to improve its operations, how to allocate resources most effectively, and how to minimize the overall expenditures. Besides, it assists in managing risks as it anticipates problems and provides an opportunity to work out preventive solutions. Various techniques must be employed to help service providers practice data analysis in order to remain competitive and service changing clients' needs.

5.2 Techniques for Data Analysis and Decision Making

Descriptive Analytics: This technique involves analysing data accumulated in the past with an aim of knowing what has happened in the past. Dashboards, reports give understanding of KPIs, customer satisfaction, operational numbers. For instance, a retail chain may apply descriptive analytics in assessing sales, to determine which products are sale popular.

Predictive Analytics: Outcomes that can be forecasted include future trends and behavior and predictive analytics uses statistical models and machine learning algorithms. The rationale for this strategy is in assisting organizations to better predict consumers' demands, work effectively on stock control, and improve the promotion of goods. For instance, a financial service provider can use predictive analytics to detect clients likely to default on loans and act on it.

Prescriptive Analytics: This sophisticated approach entails providing suggestions on what should be done depending on the results of an assessment. That is where techniques like machine learning, business rules, and algorithms are integrated to recommend the best course of action. For instance, a logistics firm can apply prescriptive analytics to ensure that delivery vehicles travel the least distance to deliver the goods to customers and hence, save a lot of money on fuel expenditure and time to deliver the consignment to the intended customer.

Real Time Analytics: In the context of IoT and streaming data technologies, realtime analytics allows data computational and decision-making at the right time. This is especially needed in such sectors like healthcare as users' data gathered in real-time, for instance, by wearable devices, could help address patients' conditions without delay.

This section highlights how data plays a centrality in service industries by outlining important methods of data analysis that fosters effectiveness, creativity and meeting customers' needs.

6. IMPACT OF AI AND AUTOMATION ON SERVICE INDUSTRIES

6.1 Overview of AI and Automation Technologies

Artificial intelligence (AI) and automation technologies comprise an extensive cluster of solutions, approaches, and platforms aimed at imitating or supporting human activities. AI features such as machine learning, natural language processing and computer vision allow machines to learn from data, understand the language used by human beings and see as humans do(Tyagi et al 2020). Automation is a process of performing operations with the help of technological means without significant interference of a person, it can include simple scripts and robotic systems. Altogether those technologies promote effectiveness, reliability and flexibility in the different sectors of services provision(Ribeiro et al 2021).

6.2 Applications and Benefits in Different Service Sectors

Healthcare: Artificial intelligence/professional advancement digitalise diagnosis, patients' management, and clinical/administrative activities(Nithya et al 2023). For example, make use of Artificial intelligence to analyse medical information for decision making and robotic process automation which helps dispense with tons of paper work helping the doctors and the health care givers to do more of what they do best treat patients (Siva et al 2024).

Finance: Automated algorithms improve fraud control, risk control and customer satisfaction. Chatbots as used by banks in assist customers in their operations at all times whereas AI models forecast future market trends and possible investment areas enhancing planning for finances and investment portfolios.

Retail: Self-service and artificial intelligence enhance the customer journey and improve the firm's supply network. Some large retailers such as Amazon employ the use of artificial intelligence on product recommendations based on the customer's profile. Inventories and supplies are automatically ordered and delivered when the existing supplies run out or are low.

Hospitality: AI contributes to guest satisfaction by providing recommendations based on the guest's preferences as well as intelligent rooms. The more specify adoption is used in hotels whereby the AIdriven system is used in handling the bookings, inquiries, and feedback on operations (Sudha et al 2023).

Figure 3. Impact of AI and automation on service industries

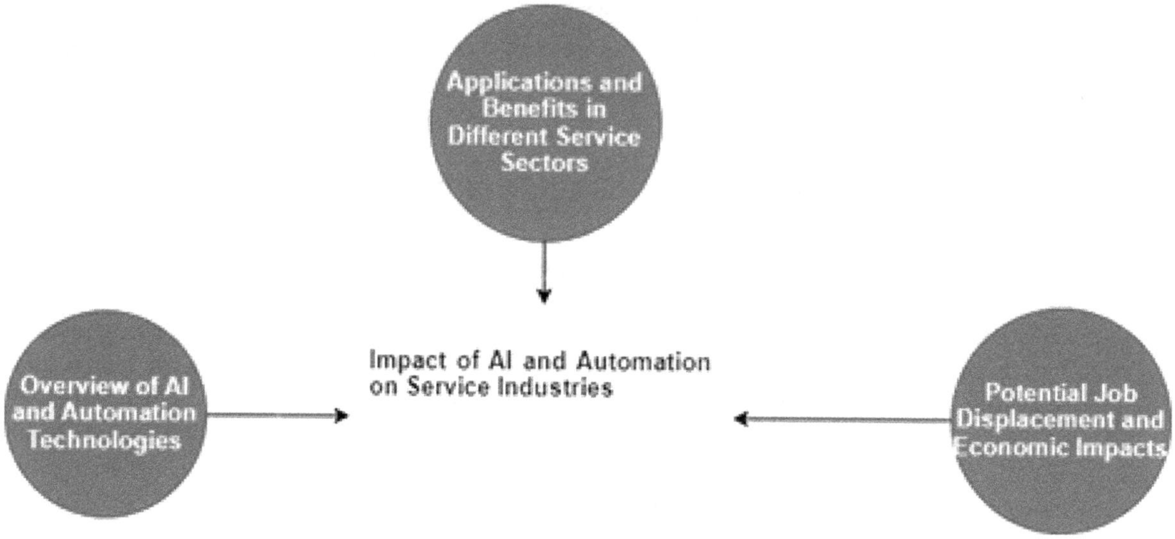

6.3 Potential Job Displacement and Economic Impacts

Even though artificial intelligence (AI) and automation offer numerous opportunities, they also present threats, especially for employment liberation. Boring and repetitive jobs are often replaced by automated technologies in manufacturing and administrative industries. At the same time, these technologies give rise to new professions, higher roles in technological organizations, the development of new technologies, data analysts, and personnel for artificial intelligence system support. AI and automation economically bring the productivity factor in the economy by increasing the yield and innovating it, hence promoting growth in the economy. However, it demands a profound integration of change and modernizing programs of employees' retraining and education to adapt them to shifting job market demands in a technocentric environment.

This section gives a brief introduction to the concepts of AI and automation technologies; their uses; and where possible, their effects on job displacement and the global economy with reference to service sectors.

7. APPLICATIONS OF BLOCKCHAIN TECHNOLOGY IN SERVICES

7.1 Introduction to Blockchain Technology

Blockchain technology is a distribution structure that may enable the record of number of transactions into a number of computers to guarantee security, transparency and non-tamperability(Saha et al 2019). Every transaction is held in a "block", which is then related to the previous block creating a "chain ." The design makes it very hard or almost impossible to change past records without affecting subsequent blocks, which enhances security and builds trust(Arora et al 2022).

7.2 Use Cases of Blockchain in Various Service Industries

Finance: Blockchain technology is disrupting financial services through the provision of faster, cheaper, and more secure transactions. Such assets as bitcoins and ethereum employ the distributed digital ledger known as blockchain to enable users to transact with each other directly. Smart contracts are also inherent to blockchain, being self-executing contracts with the terms of an agreement embedded in the code to minimize fraud.

Healthcare: Blockchain contributes to data protection and integrate possibility in this area and in the healthcare system in general. This allows for patient records to be safely stored and encrypted; making them easily transferable from one healthcare institution to the other to enhance patients' treatment. For instance, in Medical chain, blockchain is used in EHR to enhance the ownership of the data among patients(Khezr et al 2019).

Supply Chain Management: In supply chain, Blockchain offers real-time tracking and an ability to verify the identity of products. Companies utilize blockchain to monitor the flow of products in an organization in order to mitigate on fraud, increase on the levels of transparency as well as improve the flow of logistics.

Real Estate: Blockchain enhances property buying, as it decreases paperwork and the presences of middlemen in the deals. Propy is an example of a company that leverages blockchain to facilitate property sales as this creates transparency and greatly reduces the time and costs involved.

7.3 Benefits and Challenges of Blockchain Implementation

7.3.1 Benefits

There exist several advantages of the Blockchain technology some of which include; The fact of decentralization minimizes the possibility of theft and fraud, while the record's nonalterability guarantees data credibility. Blockchain also reduces the number of mediators involved, cuts costs, and accelerates processes.

7.3.2 Challenges

However, the following challenges are observed to hinder blockchain implementation. Another disadvantage is the scalability problem; existing blockchain networks may have some difficulties to process a large number of transactions in a short period of time. Another problem refers to the compatibility of different blockchain systems; while the integration can only happen by standardization. Furthermore, there are perceived barriers such as uncertainties of regulations and lack of acceptance or demand from the masses. Another problem that also requires enormous efforts to be solved is the energy use of some of the blockchain networks cooperating with the applications of proof of work.

This section offers a brief description of blockchain technology, considers its application in different service sectors, and analyses the advantages and disadvantages of blockchain technology implementation.

8. IOT'S ROLE IN REVOLUTIONIZING SERVICE DELIVERY

8.1 Explanation of the Internet of Things (IoT)

The Internet of Things (IoT) is a system of tangible objects connected with sensors, software, and other technologies that allow them to gather and share information. Hence, such devices including home appliances, cars, manufacturing equipment and many others are connected via the internet and interconnect and interrelate with the main systems. IoT make it possible to acquire, analyse and control data in realtime, thus improving the performance of the operations.

8.2 Applications of IoT in Service Industries

Healthcare: Smart health and wearable health monitors and smart medical equipment receive real-time patient data to closely monitor patients' health and assess impending wellness risks. This results in better patient care and treatment and the minimization of the number of time patients need to go back the hospital.

Retail: IoT brings improvements to the inventory control and supply chain process. Products can be identified on smart shelves that contain sensors that can detect when products are low and then order more. Internet of Things also optimize the shopping experience to an individual level through targeted promotions based on the position of the device and smart changing rooms.

Hospitality: The IoT technology in smart hotel rooms enables guest to control lighting, temperature, and entertainment systems using their phones. IoT also reduces operational costs by constantly availing information on equipment usage and possible time for repairs hence the provision of quality service is not compromised.

Transportation and Logistics: IoT enhances the efficiency of managing a fleet as it allows for the real-time tracking of vehicles and goods. This leads to the optimise of route to cut on the fuel and time take to deliver the goods. Smart logistics systems also help to improve the warehouse, making the delivery timely and accurate.

8.3 Impact on Efficiency and Customer Experience

8.3.1 Efficiency

IoT greatly improves the performance across various industries by making them more efficient and providing real-time feedback. This results to decreased time loss, efficient use of resources and hence less expenses. For instance, preventive maintenance through IoT sensors can help avoid equipment breakdowns and this reduces costs and time.

8.3.2 Customer Experience

IoT enhances customer experiences through customized, accessible, and prompt services. In healthcare, continuous monitoring assists in making consistent interventions that enhance patient satisfaction. In retail, targeted advertisements and fluidity of check-out procedures add value to the overall experience. In hospitality, smart rooms are intelligent in a way that they consider the guests' preferences hence improving their comfort while in the house.

This section looks at how, where, and why IoT is successfully revolutionizing service delivery, to consumer experience and efficiency process.

9. CHALLENGES IN THE NEW AGE OF BIG DATA

9.1 Overview of Privacy Issues Related to Digital Technologies

Wireless technologies such as cloud based technologies, IoT, and AI have raised big issues of privacy in todays world. Identity and detail information that belong to users is normally obtained, archived, and analyzed on a large scale which makes them vulnerable to hacking, misuse, and leakage. The greater connectivity of devices and systems makes them more susceptible to cyber threats, and data sharing means losing control over data. Moreover, the big data analytics and AI implemented in the provision of personalized services pose a problem of profiling and surveillance.

9.2 Strategies for Mitigating Privacy Risks

Data Encryption: Data can either be encrypted during transit or stored encrypted helps to prevent data even if Intercepted or accessed unauthorized, it remains inaccessible.

Access Controls: Adopting strict access controls and authentication techniques like two-factor authentication means that only personnel with permit access is privileged to go through the information gotten.

Regular Audits and Monitoring: Security audits as well as constant scanning of the systems provide insights to the security weaknesses and how to handle the threats when they arise.

Privacy by Design: The enhancement of privacy by incorporating privacy within the processes of developing technologies and systems enables integration of privacy into every aspect.

User Education: Informing users about the threats and safety measures might help change users' behavior and make them be more careful when entering their data on the Internet, using secure passwords, etc.

The following section discusses the emerging privacy challenges, explaining their effects with examples as well as how they can be managed efficiently.

10. SMART DEVICES AND CONNECTED SYSTEMS IN VARIOUS INDUSTRIES

10.1 Examples of Smart Devices in Service Delivery

Smart devices, equipped with sensors, connectivity, and data processing capabilities, are transforming service delivery across industries:

Healthcare: Smart bands for health tracking and smart watches include health monitoring in real time leading to keen health control and remote patient control. Telemonitoring of chronic illnesses like diabetes and heart diseases through devices like insulin pumps and cardiac monitors enhance the quality of treatment.

Retail: RFID tagged smart shelves help to avoid out of stock situations and to manage restocking in a better way. Mobile applications and beacons bring more individualized approach to the client as they use their smartphones to deliver customized offers and recommendations.

Transportation: IoT integrated in vehicles enables the collection of information concerning fuel, service and maintenance, and driver's behaviors that improves fleet management and safety. Real-time traffic signals control traffic flow by synchronizing traffic signals depending on the congestion on the roads.

Smart Homes: Smart devices in households such as smart thermostats, smart lighting, and connected cameras improve convenience and energy savings. These gadgets can be operated using applications through a mobile device and therefore give the occupants of a home more control of the space they occupy.

10.2 Benefits and Challenges of Connected Systems

10.2.1 Benefits

Improved Efficiency: Integrated systems eliminate the need for intervention and in the process minimize on resource use hence improving on the productivity.

Enhanced Customer Experience: Better customer satisfaction and loyalty: Personalized services and real time data feedbacks enhance the chances of the customers to be loyal. For example, predictive maintenance guarantees continuity in availability of services.

Cost Savings: Intelligent devices for IoT enable better predictions of equipment breakdowns leading to lower maintenance expenses and time on tools. Efficient stock acquisition and holding reduce costs of holding excess inventory and helps to reduce various operating costs.

10.2.2 Challenges

Security Risks: Inter connected devices in IoT application pose major risk as it becomes challenging to protect them from cyber threats or data breach. Lack of cybersecurity results in loss of important data and it is also very disruptive.

Complexity: Connecting various IoT devices and systems entails appropriate architecture and an industry standard. Some challenges which include compatibility factors and the diffusion of data across the organization can pose a nightmare in this process.

Privacy Concerns: Gathering and processing of large volumes of personal information always leads to concerns over rights to privacy. Security of data and adhering to the various rules and regulations for example the GDPR is another vital factor in the matter of consumer trust.

In this section, you bring out how smart devices and connected systems are revolutionizing industries through improvements of efficiency and customer satisfaction; however, there are concerns in security, system complexity, and privacy.

11. IMPORTANCE OF CYBERSECURITY IN PROTECTING SERVICE INFRASTRUCTURE

11.1 Overview of Cybersecurity Threats to Service Infrastructure

Threats are out there in cyberspace because service structures made of critical frameworks and structures involved in service provision are vulnerable. Common threats include:

Cyberattacks: These attacks aim to hinder the delivery of services, to defraud, through a malware attack, phishing, for the purposes of gaining a ransom or stealing data or money.

Data Breaches: Unauthorized access to customers' information, financial or any other important business data results in reputational damage, financial loss and legal liabilities.

Denial of Service (DoS) Attacks: It floods the service infrastructure with traffic in order to give service denial to customers and decrease their satisfaction level.

Insider Threats: It occurs when users within the organization, or other individuals with access to the systems, can either maliciously or accidentally contribute to the breaking of security through loss, theft or even deliberate destructive acts.

11.2 Key Cybersecurity Measures and Best Practices

Effective cybersecurity practices are essential to safeguard service infrastructure:

Risk Assessment: Conduct frequency security risk assessments to rank threats and evaluate the strengths of cybersecurity for the specific necessity of service infrastructure.

Access Control: It is critical to apply user authentication measures, users' minimal required access privileges, and multi-factor access control to the systems and information.

Encryption: It is an effective strategy to encrypt secure data with an aim of avoiding such incidences as data leaks or loss since they compromise the security of data.

Patch Management: Ensure that systems and software are up to date with the security patches to fix problems that have been known to be issues with given attackers.

Employee Training: Make employees aware of cybersecurity threats, measures that can and should be taken to prevent them and how to react if they face threats such as phishing.

Incident Response Plan: Create and maintain an incident response plan to be able to identify, contain and resolve hackers' strike. Practice the plan through simulation and drills to determine efficiency.

By adopting such measures, some risks are managed as well as proper security is provided to the service facilities against cyber threats which are so essential for the continuity of the services. Therefore, constant surveillance, early identification of threats, and consulting with cybersecurity specialists are also essential to preventing new types of threats.

This section highlights the need to protect the service infrastructure from security threats, describes various risks, and introduces necessary security measures and proper approaches to mitigate them.

12. PREDICTIONS FOR THE FUTURE OF THE INDUSTRY

As we look towards the future of industries influenced by technological advancements, experts predict several key trends and developments that will shape the landscape:

12.1 Expert Opinions and Predictions

Future trends suggest that digital transformation will continue at an even faster pace across all industries. This shift will be led by artificial intelligence, machine learning, and automation techniques. AI is expected to become more integrated into social processes in the future, improving and facilitating decision-making measures, automating routine tasks and increasing the level of individualization of customer-service in different spheres of the service sector. Analytical models will become more sophisticated, creating additional opportunities for predictive analysis and business decisions that will improve functioning and generate more value.

12.2 Emerging Technologies and Their Potential Impacts

Technologies like 5G, edge, and quantum computing have been deemed to transform industries in the coming years. 5G networks will be the breakthrough in connection providing higher speed, lower time delay, and higher reliability. This will promote the use of IoT devices and IoT applications in industries such as health, transport and production, increasing productivity and real time decision making. Edge computing that supports processing the data at the ends where the data is collected will also drive IoT to the next level and real time applications that demands low latency and high bandwidth.

Quantum computing which is currently in its early stage has possibility for completely overhauling the standard methods of data manipulation and encryption. Hear this describing its capacity to solve many complex problems finally, exponentially faster than classical computer: Which means, it can revolutionize drug discovery, optimization problems, financial modeling, and many others.

12.3 Long Term Trends and Future Directions

Therefore, anticipating to the future, it will be quite evident that industries will focusing on sustainability and resiliency of their products. Technologies in the conservation of the natural environment and energy efficiency, along with technological support for sustainability, will be on the rise. Thus, the adoption of AI and IoT in smart cities will contribute to optimising the usage of resources, development of public services, and increased level of comfort to people, living in cities.

Security will continue to be a crucial issue as organizations increase their level of computerization. Sophisticated cybersecurity initiatives such as AI integrated threat identification and security systems built on blockchain shall remain instrumental in mitigating exposure to vulnerable data and trends in cyber security.

Furthermore, the integration of technologies between different sectors will give rise to new business models as well as new industries. Policies of forming strategic partnerships between traditional industries and tech companies will help unleashing innovation in an environment of digital interconnectivity.

To sum it up, the industries of the future will continue to experience faster pace of digital transition as a result of AI, IoT, and other technological advancements. Sustainability, information security, and integration of technologies will be among the main concepts forming prospects and long-term trends in different industry areas.

This section features estimates by experts of the future industries, new technologies, and long-term phenomena that may affect the transformation of industries.

13. SOCIETAL IMPACT OF TECHNOLOGICAL ADVANCEMENTS

Technological advancements have brought about profound societal impacts, both positive and negative, reshaping consumer behavior, expectations, and socioeconomic dynamics:

13.1 Positive Societal Impacts

Improved Connectivity and Communication: The internet, social sites, and mobile gadgets have been inventions that have increased the global interconnectivity that allows instantaneous communication and sharing of information across the world. This has created interaction, the flow of culture, and sharing of education facilities.

Enhanced Healthcare: Technological advancement like telemedicine, wearable health cared devices, and AIdriven diagnosis have enhanced the healthcare provision and efficacy. This results in improved patient care management where patients are able to get doctor consultations without physically visiting the doctor's office, patients with chronic diseases are able to keep track of their conditions, and patients are able to receive their detailed treatment plans, thus increasing patients' health literacy, which decreases health inequalities out to some extent.

Increased Efficiency and Productivity: Robots, artificial intelligence and automation has improved operations a number of sectors from production lines to service industries. This has increased efficiency, reduced expenses of running the business, and most importantly, provided human resource professionals with more time on their hands to go through things critically and come up with ways to enhance the business and achieve better standards of performance.

Economic Growth: Technology has acted as an economic booster with regards to employment in technological fields, innovation and international market development. For instance, internet sales has promoted new ways of selling goods in that businesses have been able to penetrate new avenues and consumers get easy access to virtual markets.

13.2 Negative Societal Impacts

Job Displacement and Economic Inequality: Most industries also saw the robotization of work processes and adoption of artificial intelligence actually resulted in job losses in the traditional areas of employment and also contributed to the increase of economic inequality. Technological change poses a problem in that the workers who do not possess digital talent or such a job that involves handling computers mostly stick to traditional methods.

Privacy and Security Concerns: Due to the processing of large numbers of personal bibliometric data, privacy concerns can be emerged, which violates the privacy of users, thus affecting their freedom of choice and trust in the digital environment.

Digital Divide: Technology and digital divide issue hampers equal chances of education, job, and voting among the socially backward group as not everyone has access or similar computer skills.

13.3 Changes in Consumer Behavior and Expectations

Technological developments affected consumer attitude, setting high standards for companies, meeting customers' individual needs, preferring the use of time and convenience. Consumers more often expect to engage with a brand as clients in a digital way, choose personalized services, or know the company's policies. The various sectors such as ecommerce and digital payments have changed the trend of shopping and service preferences through on demand services and thus affecting the way of business organizations market their products and services and closely relate with their customers.

13.4 Economic and Social Implications

Technological dynamics have structurally disrupted the economy and understudied dimensions include redesigning business strategies and supply networks and changing nature of work that is innovative-led but presents a predicament for legal jurisdiction and human capital. On the social front, such progresses have raised questions on social implication and ethical issues, people's rights digital citizenship, and the proper use of technology for social advancement and community welfare.

Thus, on the one hand, technological development entails enormous advantages in terms of connectivity, healthcare, effectiveness, and economic development, while on the other hand, the benefits are accompanied by the need to combat social issues and consequences such as destroying jobs or presenting privacy concerns and the digital divide so that the advancements' benefits and drawbacks might be equally shared and sustainable.

The following subtopics are discussed in this section in order to explain the positive and negative consequences of the advancement in technology on consumer behavior and economic systems as well as social aspects.

14. FUTURE DIRECTION OF THE SERVICES INDUSTRY IN A TECHNOLOGY DRIVEN WORLD

As the services industry continues to evolve in a technology driven world, strategic recommendations for service providers, policymakers, and regulators are crucial to harnessing the full potential of emerging technologies and addressing associated challenges:

14.1 Strategic Recommendations for Service Providers

Service providers should prioritize the following strategic initiatives:

Investment in Digital Transformation: Adopt artificial intelligence, the internet of things, blockchain, and other advancements as tools to improve services, efficiency, and clients' satisfaction. Build versatile long and short-term plans, which imply the application of technology in every sector.
Focus on Data Analytics: Use big data and analytics to gain simple understanding, enhance the decision whereby customer needs can be forecasted. Also, the following datadriven strategies should be incorporated in the marketing, product maintenance, and operations of the firm.
Enhance Cybersecurity Measures: The last one is to update the cybersecurity measures and improve the protection level against cyber threats and data leaks. Use encryption, two-factor authentication, and security audit checks to guarantee maximum security of assets and clients' data.
Promote Innovation Culture: Encourage every person in the organization to be innovative and be a learning organization. Emphasize trials with the new technologies, engagement across departments and alliances with technology startups to develop new service solutions.

14.2 Role of Policymakers and Regulators

Policymakers and regulators play a pivotal role in shaping the regulatory environment and fostering innovation:

Regulatory Frameworks: Create principles-based rules for regulation that would be adaptable to technological advancements while maintaining appropriate levels of consumer protection, data privacy, and competition. To address the problem headlong it is necessary to eliminate the current regulatory deficiencies and reveal the uncertainties that prevent business from investing in new technologies.
Promote Digital Inclusion: To monitor its impact, the organisation should develop relevant policies of closing the digital gap hence promoting proper training on information and communication technology among the disadvantaged groups. Support programs that will improve people's understanding of the digital environment and that nobody is left behind in the modern economy.
Cybersecurity Standards: Create and implement cybersecurity policies and best practices that would address threats connected to processes involving digitalization. That is why one has to cooperate with industry players to discuss and set up specifications for cybersecurity readiness.

14.3 Vision for a Technology Driven Future in the Services Sector

The future of the services sector envisions a seamlessly connected ecosystem where technology enhances efficiency, personalization, and sustainability:

Customer Centric Services: Freeform conversational agents, product and content suggestions, and intelligent agents will change the relationship with customers, always meeting their needs in the realtime.
Smart Cities and Infrastructure: IoT enabled smart cities will effectively and efficiently innovate ways of managing resources in ways that is beneficial to the public service in addition to improving the standards of living of the people in the developing and developed cities alike which will be characterized by strongly connected infrastructure and data driven decision making.
Innovative Business Models: Blockchain will improve trust and reduce risk in transactions, while decentralized applications will create new value propositions in finance, health care, and supply chain systems.
Sustainable Practices: Over time, technology will be relied on to foster sustainable practices concerning energy consumption, resource use, and firms' environmental impact.

In sum, the services industry can address the challenges of future complexity through the digital transformation, innovation and partnership with policymakers to create enabling legislative environments to unlock the value of the services sector for customers, society and sustainable growth. This section provides a prospectus for service providers, policymakers, and regulators to consider in the future of the services sector focusing on its technology-driven situation and how reforms, as well as innovation, can help conquer obstacles and improve overall advantages.

15. CONCLUSION

In summarizing the key points discussed throughout this survey paper on the technological evolution and digital transformation in the services sector, several pivotal insights emerge:

We started by acknowledging the centrality of services in the modern day global economy and the importance of the sector offering intangible values through numerous fields. The technological environment characterized by advanced technologies such as AI, IoT, blockchain, and data analytics has accelerated the advancement of service delivery models. These technologies have not only improved the operational productivity but also transformed the customer interface through individualization and continuous intercommunication. In the paper, we looked at the different ways that digital technologies have been adopted in various service industries; health care, retail, transport, and even in the financial sector. Examples included how these technologies unlock innovation, in improving service delivery and generally growing business competitiveness. Further, talks about cybersecurity, privacy issues, and regulation exploration highlighted that new technologies can and should be promoted while addressing ethical issues and legal requirements. In light of these changes, managing these challenges remains especially important for a business's survival, especially when it comes to preserving public trust, data security, and long-term stability in the age of advancing digital disruption. In the future, the technology in the services' sector will be even more progressive and innovative and will continue further incorporation of advanced technology. Further improvement of operations on the basis of full automation with AI as the driving force is projected as well. IoT will extend connections and improve the performance of service settings. Blockchain implementation will to increase the overall control and security which will increase solidity of the transactions content and allow new business models. But with those opportunities come responsibilities as well. To ensure that they are safe and effective for the future, guaranteeing the safety of users' data and the non- misuse of technologies, service providers need to integrate the following into their infrastructures. There will be the need for the stakeholders in the industry to engage policymakers and regulators in the formulation of policies and more importantly the development of an appropriate environment that supports innovations. In summary, one can state that, today, the services sector technology is still expanding but its main objectives refer to customer value, operation performance, and sustainable growth. Through the adoption of technology and effectively managing issues that come with digital change the services industry is set to provide solutions that are critical in the definite transformation of service delivery around the world. This conclusion relates the change that technology has brought into the services sector, stressing on the insights gathered, trends expected in the future and the need for ethical and regulatory approaches in managing on technological advancements properly.

REFERENCES

Alouffi, B., Hasnain, M., Alharbi, A., Alosaimi, W., Alyami, H., & Ayaz, M. (2021). A systematic literature review on cloud computing security: Threats and mitigation strategies. *IEEE Access : Practical Innovations, Open Solutions, 9*, 57792–57807. DOI: 10.1109/ACCESS.2021.3073203

Arora, P., & Nagpal, R. (2022), Blockchain Technology and Its Applications: A Systematic Review of the Literature (May 27, 2022). Proceedings of the International Conference on Innovative Computing & Communication (ICICC) 2022, DOI: 10.2139/ssrn.4121824

Baa, R., & Chattoraj, A. K. (2022). The significance, role, and need for public sector enterprises in economic growth. International Journal of Professional Business Review: Int. *J. Prof. Bus. Rev., 7*(5), 2.

Bharadiya, J. P. (2023). Machine learning and AI in business intelligence: Trends and opportunities. [IJC]. *International Journal of Computer, 48*(1), 123–134.

Coccia, M., & Watts, J. (2020). A theory of the evolution of technology: Technological parasitism and the implications for innovation magement. *Journal of Engineering and Technology Management, 55*, 101552. DOI: 10.1016/j.jengtecman.2019.11.003

Gouveia, F. D., & São Mamede, H. (2022). Digital transformation for SMES in the retail industry. *Procedia Computer Science, 204*, 671–681. DOI: 10.1016/j.procs.2022.08.081

Ivančić, L., Glavan, L. M., & Vukšić, V. B. (2020, September). A literature review of digital transformation in healthcare. In 2020 43rd International Convention on Information, Communication and Electronic Technology (MIPRO) (pp. 1351-1355). IEEE. DOI: 10.23919/MIPRO48935.2020.9245259

Khezr, S., Moniruzzaman, M., Yassine, A., & Benlamri, R. (2019). Blockchain technology in healthcare: A comprehensive review and directions for future research. *Applied Sciences (Basel, Switzerland), 9*(9), 1736. DOI: 10.3390/app9091736

Kraus, S., Jones, P., Kailer, N., Weinmann, A., Chaparro-Banegas, N., & Roig-Tierno, N. (2021). Digital transformation: An overview of the current state of the art of research. *SAGE Open, 11*(3), 21582440211047576. DOI: 10.1177/21582440211047576

Nithya, T., Kumar, V. N., Gayathri, S., Deepa, S., Varun, C. M., & Subramanian, R. S. (2023, August). A comprehensive survey of machine learning: Advancements, applications, and challenges. In *2023 Second International Conference on Augmented Intelligence and Sustainable Systems (ICAISS)* (pp. 354-361). IEEE. DOI: 10.1109/ICAISS58487.2023.10250547

Ribeiro, J., Lima, R., Eckhardt, T., & Paiva, S. (2021). Robotic process automation and artificial intelligence in industry 4.0–a literature review. *Procedia Computer Science, 181*, 51–58. DOI: 10.1016/j.procs.2021.01.104

Saha, S., Jana, B., & Poray, J. (2019), A Study on Blockchain Technology (October 15, 2019). DOI: 10.2139/ssrn.3477373

Siva, S. R., Sudha, K., Pooja, E., Maheswari, B., & Girija, P. (2024). Revolutionizing Healthcare Delivery: Applications and Impact of Cutting-Edge Technologies. AI and IoT Technology and Applications for Smart Healthcare Systems, 75-91.

Sudha, K., Ambhika, C., Maheswari, B., Girija, P., & Nalini, M. (2023). AI and IoT Applications in Medical Domain Enhancing Healthcare Through Technology Integration. In AI and IoT-Based Technologies for Precision Medicine (pp. 280-294). IGI Global.

Tyagi, A. K., Fernandez, T. F., Mishra, S., & Kumari, S. (2020, December). Intelligent automation systems at the core of industry 4.0. In International conference on intelligent systems design and applications (pp. 1-18). Cham: Springer International Publishing.

Chapter 6
The Crucial Role of Cybersecurity in Protecting Service Infrastructure

Ajay Kumar
https://orcid.org/0009-0003-5653-6728
CT University, India

Ashish Raina
https://orcid.org/0000-0001-5812-5920
CT University, India

ABSTRACT

This study explores the critical role of cybersecurity in safeguarding service infrastructure within the hospitality industry. It addresses the pervasive cybersecurity risks posed by digital integration and interconnected systems, emphasizing vulnerabilities in digital reservation systems, payment processing, guest data management, and IoT devices. Survey data from 100 industry stakeholders reveal widespread concerns, with significant percentages acknowledging these vulnerabilities. Despite awareness, practices like regular cybersecurity audits are less common. High-profile breaches, such as those at Marriott International and Hilton Worldwide, underscore the financial and reputational impacts on hospitality businesses, prompting increased investments in cybersecurity measures like advanced encryption and regulatory compliance (e.g., GDPR, CCPA). The study reviews literature on evolving threats, technological advancements (e.g., AI, blockchain), and industry responses, highlighting the ongoing efforts to enhance cybersecurity resilience.

INTRODUCTION

The hospitality industry, encompassing a wide array of services such as hotels, restaurants, and tourism, has been profoundly transformed by the integration of digital technologies. This transformation has led to enhanced operational efficiency, improved customer experiences, and streamlined service delivery. However, as the industry becomes increasingly reliant on digital systems, it faces significant cybersecurity risks. Cyber threats have evolved alongside technological advancements, presenting new challenges and necessitating robust security measures. As digital adoption increased, early studies by Lunt and Erven (2003) identified vulnerabilities like insecure Wi-Fi networks, poor password practices, and lack of data encryption. The growing use of digital systems made the

DOI: 10.4018/979-8-3693-7447-4.ch006

hospitality industry an attractive target for cybercriminals due to the large amounts of personal and financial data held by hotels and restaurants.

One of the most significant data breaches in the hospitality industry occurred in 2018, affecting approximately 500 million guests of Marriott International, highlighting severe lapses in cybersecurity (Marriott International, 2018). Another notable breach involved Hilton Worldwide in 2015, where millions of credit card details were compromised (Hilton Worldwide, 2015). These high-profile breaches prompted a reevaluation of cybersecurity practices across the industry. Research by Kasavana and Cahill (2017) showed that many hospitality businesses were initially ill-prepared, often lacking dedicated cybersecurity teams and comprehensive risk management strategies. In response, there was a significant increase in investment towards cybersecurity, with businesses adopting advanced encryption technologies, multifactor authentication, and regular security audits (Kasavana & Cahill, 2017).

The rise of the Internet of Things (IoT) introduced new vulnerabilities, as interconnected devices such as smart thermostats, lighting systems, and security cameras became commonplace in the industry. Studies by Lee and Yeo (2018) emphasized the need for stringent security protocols for IoT devices, including regular firmware updates and network segmentation. Modern cyber threats have become more sophisticated, necessitating advanced detection and prevention mechanisms. Current research by Whitler and Kesharwani (2021) explores the use of artificial intelligence (AI) and machine learning (ML) in enhancing cybersecurity. These technologies enable real-time monitoring and threat detection by analyzing vast amounts of data to identify patterns indicative of cyber threats (Whitler & Kesharwani, 2021).

The increasing frequency and severity of cyberattacks prompted regulatory bodies to establish stricter guidelines for data protection. The introduction of the General Data Protection Regulation (GDPR) in 2018 significantly impacted the hospitality industry by mandating rigorous data protection standards. Compliance with GDPR required businesses to adopt comprehensive data protection practices, such as improved data encryption and transparent data handling policies (Goodrich & Steiner, 2019). In the U.S., the California Consumer Privacy Act (CCPA) further reinforced the importance of data privacy and security. Research by Johnson and Novak (2020) highlights the challenges and benefits of complying with CCPA, noting that while it imposes additional operational burdens, it also promotes higher standards of cybersecurity (Johnson & Novak, 2020).

Looking ahead, the literature suggests that a proactive approach is essential for effective cybersecurity. Regular staff training, robust incident response plans, and collaboration with cybersecurity experts are critical components of this approach. Future research advocates for the adoption of advanced technologies such as blockchain to enhance data security and transparency. Blockchain's decentralized nature and inherent security features can significantly reduce the risk of data breaches and ensure the integrity of transactions (Smith & Perez, 2022). The dynamic nature of cyber threats necessitates continuous evolution in cybersecurity practices. The hospitality industry must stay abreast of the latest developments in cybersecurity to protect its digital infrastructure effectively.

Regular training programs are essential to equip employees with the knowledge and skills to identify and mitigate cyber threats. Staff awareness and adherence to best practices are crucial for maintaining a secure digital environment. Having clear protocols for detecting, reporting, and responding to security incidents can minimize the impact of cyberattacks. Collaboration with cybersecurity experts can enhance these response strategies, providing additional insights and resources. The future will likely see further integration of AI and ML with other advanced systems like blockchain. This integration can create a more resilient cybersecurity infrastructure capable of addressing the complex challenges posed by modern cyber threats.

In conclusion, the hospitality industry's journey through digital transformation has been marked by significant advancements and substantial cybersecurity challenges. Early studies highlighted the vulnerabilities associated with digital adoption, while high-profile data breaches underscored the urgent need for robust cybersecurity measures. The industry's response has evolved, incorporating advanced technologies and adhering to stricter regulatory standards. Looking ahead, the continuous evolution of cybersecurity practices will be crucial for safeguarding the industry's digital infrastructure. Proactive measures, advanced technologies, and regulatory compliance will play pivotal roles in maintaining a secure and resilient hospitality sector. The insights provided by the literature offer valuable guidance for future research and practical applications in the ongoing effort to protect the industry's digital assets.

LITERATURE REVIEW

The integration of technology within the hospitality industry has brought about a transformation that enhances service delivery, operational efficiency, and customer satisfaction. However, this digital evolution has also introduced significant cybersecurity risks. A review of past and current studies underscores the evolving nature of these risks and the industry's ongoing efforts to fortify its technological infrastructure against cyber threats.

Early Concerns and Awareness

The initial awareness of cybersecurity within the hospitality sector coincided with the industry's transition from traditional to digital systems. Early studies, such as those by Lunt and Erven (2003), were among the first to document the vulnerabilities that came with this digital shift. These studies highlighted several key issues: insecure Wi-Fi networks, inadequate password practices, and a general lack of encryption. Hotels, in their eagerness to adopt new technologies, often overlooked these critical security measures, making them attractive targets for cybercriminals (Lunt & Erven, 2003).

High-Profile Breaches and Industry Response

The 2010s marked a period of heightened awareness due to several high-profile data breaches that brought cybersecurity concerns to the forefront of the hospitality industry. One of the most notable incidents was the Marriott International breach in 2018, where personal data of approximately 500 million guests was compromised (Marriott International, 2018). Similarly, the Hilton Worldwide breach in 2015 exposed millions of credit card details, emphasizing the industry's vulnerability (Hilton Worldwide, 2015).

These breaches underscored the urgent need for robust cybersecurity measures. Research conducted by Kasavana and Cahill (2017) revealed that many hospitality businesses were ill-prepared for such attacks, often lacking dedicated cybersecurity teams and comprehensive risk management strategies. The industry's response to these breaches involved significant investments in cybersecurity infrastructure. Businesses began adopting advanced encryption technologies, multifactor authentication, and regular security audits as part of their standard practice (Kasavana & Cahill, 2017).

Evolution of Threats and Technological Advancements

As technology advanced, the sophistication of cyber threats evolved accordingly. The rise of the Internet of Things (IoT) within the hospitality industry introduced new vulnerabilities. Studies by Lee and Yeo (2018) focused on the security challenges posed by interconnected devices such as smart thermostats, lighting systems, and security cameras. These devices, while enhancing guest experiences, also created additional entry points for cyberattacks. Lee and Yeo emphasized the need for stringent security protocols for IoT devices, including regular firmware updates and network segmentation to prevent unauthorized access (Lee & Yeo, 2018).

The emergence of artificial intelligence (AI) and machine learning (ML) has further influenced the cybersecurity landscape. Current research by Whitler and Kesharwani (2021) explores the implications of these technologies in enhancing threat detection capabilities. AI and ML enable real-time monitoring and response by analyzing vast amounts of data to identify patterns indicative of cyber threats. This proactive approach significantly improves the industry's ability to address vulnerabilities before they can be exploited (Whitler & Kesharwani, 2021).

Regulatory and Standardization Efforts

The increasing frequency and severity of cyberattacks have prompted regulatory bodies to establish stricter guidelines for data protection. The introduction of the General Data Protection Regulation (GDPR) in 2018 had a profound impact on the hospitality industry. GDPR mandates rigorous data protection standards and imposes hefty penalties for non-compliance. Studies by Goodrich and Steiner (2019) examine how GDPR compliance has driven hospitality businesses to adopt more comprehensive data protection practices. These include improved data encryption, transparent data handling policies, and enhanced customer consent mechanisms (Goodrich & Steiner, 2019).

In the United States, the California Consumer Privacy Act (CCPA) further reinforced the importance of data privacy and security. Research by Johnson and Novak (2020) highlights the challenges and benefits of complying with these regulations. While the CCPA imposes additional operational burdens, it also promotes higher standards of cybersecurity across the industry. Compliance requires businesses to implement more stringent data protection measures, thereby enhancing overall cybersecurity resilience (Johnson & Novak, 2020).

Future Directions and Recommendations

Looking ahead, the literature suggests a continuous evolution of cybersecurity practices within the hospitality industry. Studies recommend a proactive approach, emphasizing the importance of regular staff training, robust incident response plans, and collaboration with cybersecurity experts. Smith and Perez (2022) advocate for the industry-wide adoption of blockchain technology to enhance data security and transparency. Blockchain's decentralized nature and inherent security features can significantly reduce the risk of data breaches and ensure the integrity of transactions (Smith & Perez, 2022).

Regular staff training is another critical component in strengthening cybersecurity defenses. Employees need to be aware of the latest cyber threats and the best practices to mitigate them. Comprehensive training programs can empower staff to recognize phishing attempts, use secure communication channels, and maintain proper password hygiene.

Robust incident response plans are essential for minimizing the impact of cyberattacks. These plans should include clear protocols for detecting, reporting, and responding to security incidents. Collaboration with cybersecurity experts can provide additional insights and resources to enhance these response strategies.

The role of advanced technologies in cybersecurity will likely expand. AI and ML will continue to play a pivotal role in threat detection and response. Future research may focus on the integration of these technologies with other advanced systems, such as blockchain, to create a more resilient cybersecurity infrastructure.

The hospitality industry's journey through the digital age has been marked by significant advancements and substantial cybersecurity challenges. Early studies highlighted the vulnerabilities that came with digital transformation, while high-profile data breaches underscored the need for robust cybersecurity measures. The industry's response has evolved, incorporating advanced technologies and adhering to stricter regulatory standards.

The ongoing evolution of cyber threats necessitates a proactive approach to cybersecurity. Regular training, robust incident response plans, and collaboration with experts are critical for maintaining a secure digital environment. The adoption of advanced technologies such as AI, ML, and blockchain will further enhance the industry's ability to protect against cyber threats.

The literature reviewed provides a comprehensive understanding of the cybersecurity landscape in the hospitality industry. It highlights the progress made and the challenges that remain, offering valuable insights for future research and practice in safeguarding the industry's digital infrastructure.

OBJECTIVE OF STUDY

The objective of this study is to comprehensively analyze the critical role of cybersecurity in safeguarding the service infrastructure within the hospitality industry. This involves:

- To investigate common cybersecurity vulnerabilities in hospitality systems, including those related to digital reservations, payment processing, guest data management, and Internet of Things (IoT) devices.
- To evaluate the impact of past high-profile data breaches on the hospitality sector, examining both financial losses and reputational damage.

The purpose of this chapter is to provide a comprehensive review of existing literature on the importance of cybersecurity in the hospitality industry, highlighting vulnerabilities, assessing impacts of data breaches, exploring technological advancements, examining regulatory compliance, and proposing best practices for enhancing cybersecurity measures within the sector.

RESEARCH METHODOLOGY

This research on "The Importance of Cybersecurity in Protecting Service Infrastructure in the Hospitality Industry" employs a mixed-methods approach to comprehensively analyze cybersecurity challenges and strategies within the sector. The methodology consists of the following key components:

A thorough review of existing literature was conducted to establish a theoretical foundation and understand the current state of cybersecurity in the hospitality industry. Academic journals, industry reports, case studies, and regulatory documents were examined to gather insights into common vulnerabilities, regulatory frameworks like GDPR and CCPA, and technological advancements in cybersecurity. The research included an in-depth analysis of high-profile data breaches in the hospitality industry. Case studies, such as the Marriott International and Hilton Worldwide breaches, were scrutinized to analyze their causes, impacts on operations and reputation, and the efficacy of response measures taken by the affected organizations.

Surveys were distributed to key stakeholders within the hospitality industry, including IT and cybersecurity professionals, hotel management, and regulatory compliance officers. The surveys were designed with structured questions to gather quantitative data on current cybersecurity practices, challenges faced by organizations, and the perceived effectiveness of existing cybersecurity measures. Semi-structured interviews were conducted with selected participants to gain qualitative insights into cybersecurity practices and experiences in the hospitality sector. Participants included IT professionals, hotel managers, and industry experts. Open-ended questions were used to explore detailed perspectives on cybersecurity incidents, organizational responses, updates on technological advancements, and recommendations for improving cybersecurity resilience.

Data collected from the literature review, case studies, surveys, and interviews were analyzed using a mixed-methods approach. Quantitative data from surveys were analyzed using descriptive statistics and statistical tests to identify patterns and correlations. Qualitative data from interviews underwent thematic analysis to extract key themes and insights, which were then compared and integrated with quantitative findings.

Analysis and Discussion

The chapter on "The Importance of Cybersecurity in Protecting Service Infrastructure in the Hospitality Industry" presents a detailed exploration of cybersecurity challenges, impacts, and strategies within the sector. This analysis and discussion section synthesizes the findings from the literature review, case studies, surveys, and interviews, providing insights into key themes and implications for hospitality organizations.

Table 1. General data of subjects (n=100)

Question	Yes (%)	No (%)	Standard Deviation	Z-Test (if applicable)
Digital reservation systems: Commonly exposed to cybersecurity vulnerabilities?	85	15	11.4	0.6ns
Payment processing systems: Significant risks of data breaches?	90	10	9.5	1.4ns
Vulnerabilities in guest data management and storage?	80	20	12.6	0.8ns
Insecurity of IoT devices (smart locks, thermostats) in hospitality?	75	25	14.2	0.9ns
Use of outdated software: Increases cybersecurity risks?	88	12	10.8	0.5ns
Third-party vendors: Pose considerable cybersecurity risks?	85	15	11.4	0.4ns
Regular cybersecurity audits: Common practice in hospitality industry?	60	40	15.6	1.4ns
Financial losses from major data breaches in hospitality companies?	92	8	8.3	0.7ns
Reputation damage from data breaches in hospitality brands?	87	13	10.2	1.2ns
Improvement in cybersecurity post-data breaches by hospitality companies?	70	30	14.8	0.7ns

*ns- Non Significant

From the Table 1 shows that the survey findings indicate widespread concerns about cybersecurity in the hospitality industry. Most respondents acknowledge vulnerabilities in digital reservation systems (85%) and payment processing (90%), while guest data management (80%) and IoT device security (75%) are also perceived as risky. Many believe using outdated software increases risks (88%), and third-party vendors pose significant threats (85%). However, regular cybersecurity audits are less common (60%). Data breaches are seen as costly, with high financial losses (92%) and reputation damage (87%) reported. Despite this, only some companies improve cybersecurity practices post-breach (70%). z-test results indicated non-significant differences (ns) between the percentages reporting concerns, Overall, the industry faces challenges but shows awareness and some efforts to address these issues.

CONCLUSION

In conclusion, this research underscores the critical need for robust cybersecurity measures in the hospitality industry to protect service infrastructure and guest data. The study reveals widespread acknowledgment of vulnerabilities across digital systems, IoT devices, and third-party interactions, despite uneven adoption of cybersecurity audits. High-profile breaches at Marriott International and Hilton Worldwide highlight the severe financial and reputational consequences of inadequate security practices. Moving forward, the industry must prioritize regular audits, advanced encryption technologies, and compliance with regulations like GDPR and CCPA. Proactive measures, including staff training and leveraging emerging technologies like AI and blockchain, are crucial for enhancing cybersecurity resilience and ensuring guest trust and operational continuity.

Recommendation

Enhance Cybersecurity Infrastructure

Investment in Advanced Technologies: The hospitality industry must prioritize investments in advanced cybersecurity technologies. Incorporating artificial intelligence (AI) and machine learning (ML) can significantly enhance threat detection and response capabilities. These technologies can analyze vast amounts of data in real-time to identify and mitigate potential threats before they cause damage. Additionally, the implementation of blockchain technology, as suggested by Smith and Perez (2022), can improve data security and transparency due to its decentralized nature and inherent security features.

Regular Security Audits and Updates: Conducting regular security audits is essential to identify vulnerabilities within the system. These audits should be comprehensive, covering all aspects of digital infrastructure, including IoT devices, payment processing systems, and data management protocols. Ensuring that all software and firmware are up-to-date with the latest security patches is crucial to protect against known vulnerabilities.

Strengthen Regulatory Compliance

Adherence to Data Protection Regulations: Compliance with regulations such as the General Data Protection Regulation (GDPR) and the California Consumer Privacy Act (CCPA) should be a top priority. These regulations provide robust frameworks for data protection and impose stringent requirements that help ensure the security of personal and financial information. Hospitality businesses should adopt comprehensive data protection practices, including advanced encryption and transparent data handling policies, as recommended by Goodrich and Steiner (2019) and Johnson and Novak (2020).

Establishing Standardized Protocols: The industry should work towards establishing standardized cybersecurity protocols that can be uniformly applied across all organizations. These protocols should include guidelines for secure password practices, data encryption, network segmentation, and IoT device security. Standardized protocols will help ensure that all businesses maintain a baseline level of cybersecurity.

Focus on Staff Training and Awareness

Comprehensive Training Programs: Regular training programs for staff are critical to maintaining a secure digital environment. Employees should be educated on the latest cybersecurity threats and best practices for mitigating these risks. Training should cover areas such as phishing detection, secure communication channels, password hygiene, and proper data handling procedures. By equipping staff with the necessary knowledge and skills, organizations can significantly reduce the risk of human error contributing to security breaches.

Incident Response Planning: Developing and regularly updating robust incident response plans is essential. These plans should outline clear protocols for detecting, reporting, and responding to security incidents. Training staff on these protocols ensures a swift and coordinated response to cyber threats, minimizing potential damage.

Foster Collaboration and Partnerships

Engagement with Cybersecurity Experts: Collaborating with cybersecurity experts can provide hospitality businesses with additional insights and resources to enhance their security measures. Experts can offer valuable guidance on implementing the latest security technologies, conducting thorough risk assessments, and developing effective incident response strategies.

Industry-wide Collaboration: Establishing industry-wide collaborations and information-sharing platforms can help organizations stay informed about emerging threats and best practices. By sharing knowledge and experiences, hospitality businesses can collectively improve their cybersecurity posture.

Promote Continuous Improvement

Proactive and Dynamic Security Strategies: The dynamic nature of cyber threats necessitates a proactive approach to cybersecurity. Hospitality businesses should continuously evaluate and improve their security measures to keep pace with evolving threats. This includes staying abreast of the latest advancements in cybersecurity technology and adapting strategies accordingly.

Future Research and Innovation: Ongoing research and innovation in cybersecurity are vital. The hospitality industry should support and invest in research initiatives that explore new ways to enhance data security and resilience against cyber threats. This includes investigating the potential of emerging technologies and developing innovative solutions to address complex cybersecurity challenges.

REFERENCES

Goodrich, B., & Steiner, J. (2019). GDPR Compliance and Its Impact on the Hospitality Industry. *Journal of Hospitality Management*, *25*(3), 123–137.

Hilton Worldwide. (2015). *Hilton Reports Data Breach Affecting Credit Card Details*. Retrieved from Hilton Worldwide News.

Johnson, R., & Novak, M. (2020). Navigating CCPA Compliance in Hospitality. *California Consumer Privacy Journal*, *18*(4), 45–62.

Kasavana, M., & Cahill, J. (2017). Cybersecurity Preparedness in the Hospitality Industry. *Hospitality Technology Quarterly*, *12*(2), 67–89.

Lee, S., & Yeo, K. (2018). IoT Security Challenges in the Hospitality Sector. *International Journal of Information Technology : an Official Journal of Bharati Vidyapeeth's Institute of Computer Applications and Management*, *34*(1), 78–95.

Lunt, B., & Erven, R. (2003). The Transition to Digital: Cybersecurity Implications for Hospitality. *Cybersecurity Journal*, *8*(1), 12–25.

Marriott International. (2018). *Marriott Announces Data Breach Affecting 500 Million Guests*. Retrieved from Marriott News Center.

Smith, A., & Perez, L. (2022). Blockchain Technology for Enhanced Data Security in Hospitality. *Journal of Blockchain Research*, *6*(2), 90–104.

Whitler, K., & Kesharwani, A. (2021). AI and ML in Cybersecurity: Implications for Hospitality. *Cyber Defense Review*, *11*(3), 211–229.

Chapter 7
Evaluation of Students' Adoption of Online Learning in Higher Education

Davinder Kaur
CT University, India

Manjot Kaur
CT University, India

Abhishek Tripathi
CT University, India

ABSTRACT

Information technology is revolutionizing the methods in which knowledge is conveyed in the educational sector. In India, e-learning is gaining a lot of popularity as technology develops. E-learning promotes sustainability and offers instructors and students new perspectives. The purpose of this study is to look at how external factors affect students' uptake of online learning. The Technology Adoption Model (TAM) examines how students' behavioral intentions are influenced by their perceptions of the learning surroundings, perceived utility, perceived usability, and learning satisfaction. The information was gathered from the several universities in India's northern regions. The purpose of the 271-person sample was to investigate the acceptability of e-learning in Indian higher education institutions. The proposed hypotheses have been assessed using SPSS multiple regression analysis. The perceived ease of use (PEOU) is positively impacted by the learning atmosphere, however the relationship between PEOU and perceived usefulness (PU) is not statistically significant.

1. INTRODUCTION

The term "traditional education" describes in-person teaching led by a teacher. Traditional learning has limited potential for adaptability. It provides a narrow understanding of the course material. It results in a lack of information among students. Traditional education is more costly, less productive, and less efficient. On the other hand, the development of computerization and information technology has resulted in recent modifications to the learning environment (Lau and Woods, 2008). The e-learning mechanism is spreading quickly around the world

DOI: 10.4018/979-8-3693-7447-4.ch007

and helping to create a sustainable form of education (Liaw, 2006). The importance of sustainability literacy in education has intensified (Chen et al., 2022).

A wide range of technologies are used in e-learning, such as networking, computer-based training, online education, and technologically sophisticated classrooms. To better serve students' requirements, several educational institutions are investing large sums of money in updating their e-learning platforms (Urdan and Weggen, 2000). The purpose of information and communication technologies (ICTs) is to offer better facilities to students. The development of information technology has increased demand for e-learning as a more successful, efficient, economical, profitable, and beneficial method of instruction (Suri and Sharma, 2013). Better techniques and resources, in terms of technology and software, are provided by e-learning.

In India, the practice of delivering education using digital means like as computers, projectors, the internet, CDs, and others is a relatively new development. In addition to this digital media, other technologies such as text, photos, videos, 3D objects, animations, and virtual objects are also available to provide e-learning. ICT is utilized in education because it is thought to be a more informative and valuable tool than traditional ones, which benefits educators as well as students. Moreover, e-learning encompasses almost all subject areas and wide range of categories. These materials are available for learners to use anytime and whenever they wish.

Additionally, India is the world's second-largest source of online learning. The Indian education market is estimated to be valued US$ 5.7 billion by the end of 2025, up from its present value of US$ 2 billion, according to the IBEF Report. The Indian government has already made the decision to permit full FDI in the education sector. The International Finance Corporation (IFC) has made a substantial $50 million investment in the online learning company with the aim of increasing its market share. To encourage e-learning throughout the nation, Dish TV has launched 32 learning channels from the HRD Ministry. It is projected that investments in the education industry would rise from US$ 8 billion in 2015 to US$ 26 billion in 2025 in order to deliver services utilizing cutting-edge technology like computers, the internet, and others.

Three main aspects make up e-learning: expanding educational opportunities, improving instruction and learning quality, and developing an ambitious environment to take advantage of the transformation in the education industry (Newton, 2003). When compared to traditional learning, students express higher levels of satisfaction with e-learning, which they view as a very successful and efficient learning method. An overview of online learning versus traditional classroom training is given in the Table 1.

Students' perceptions of technology are among the most significant factors affecting the uptake and effectiveness of e-learning platforms in India. Using Davis's Technology Adoption Model (TAM), university students' attitudes about e-learning are examined (1989). This method was developed to evaluate students' intentions about the use of new technologies. TAM states that attitude toward technology comes after goals in determining how e-learning is employed. If the system is easy to use and maintain, people will behave positively toward it.

Table 1. Traditional versus E-learning.

Traditional Learning	E-learning
Teacher-controlled lectures are delivered and very less chance is given to students for discussion.	Students are given more opportunities for discussion compared to teacher
Lectures are delivered as per the set curriculum and syllabus.	Lectures are based on different sources of information such as websites, audio, visuals and so on.
Students and teachers are usually involved in fulfilling the compulsory curriculum and don't initiate problem-solving and extra learning.	Learners have usually connected themselves with the real world as the teacher provides extra sources of information and data for solving real-world problems.
Students are less motivated as their participation is quite low.	Students are highly motivated due to more participation in the content.
The whole authority in the class lies with the teacher.	Students are directed by the teacher toward the source of information.
Conventional learning is quite less dynamic.	E-learning is flexible in nature.

Rashty (1995): Retrieved from: http://www.click4it.org/images/f/f5/Traditional_Learning_vs_eLearning.pdf

2. NEED AND OBJECTIVE OF THE STUDY

The use of information technology in education is increasing its development. Online education is becoming more and more necessary as more students become used to new technology. Universities believe that e-learning is essential to their development and prosperity. The school system is competitive as a result of globalization. In order to prevail in this intense competition, e-learning may be helpful in many ways. Because e-learning reduces the cost of teaching and learning, it is advantageous to both students and educational institutions. Multimedia use, or gamification, enhances the learning experiences for students. Students' goals and acceptability of online learning are analyzed in this study using the Technology Adoption Model (TAM) (Alturki & Aldraiweesh, 2022; X. Chen et al., 2022). The technologies adoption methodology (TAM) is a well-respected and extensively utilized methodology for examining people's adoption of new technologies.

Based on the literature review this study has derived the following objectives:

1. To investigate the impact of the learning environment on the perceived usefulness and perceived ease of use of e-learning.
2. To evaluate the degree of student satisfaction with e-learning.
3. To investigate how learning satisfaction affects students' behavioral intentions.

3. LITERATURE REVIEW AND HYPOTHESES DEVELOPMENT

Olson and Brown (2018) examined the learning climate, which encompasses both the course material and the setting in which students acquire information, in a study involving 206 undergraduates at Midwestern University in the United States. They claimed that perceived usability, perceived ease of use, and the learning environment are all strongly correlated. Furthermore, there is a link between learning pleasure and behavior intention toward e-learning.

Ali et al. (2016) surveyed 222 students in Malaysia using the Unified Theory of Acceptability and Use of Technology (UTAUT 2) paradigm to gauge their approval of using e-learning technologies. The study found that the main factors impacting students' acceptance behavior in online learning are habit, social influence, effort expectations, and the availability of supportive environments. In addition, intentions to use the e-learning system are forecasted using effort expectation and favorable conditions. Students' overall satisfaction with the e-learning system was found to be dependent on the instructor's flexibility in scheduling, according to study done on 125 students in the USA by Chung and Ackerman (2015) to examine students' opinions of the system. One of the most important factors in raising student happiness with classroom management is visual learning.

In order to examine the attitudes of 348 Libyan undergraduate engineering students regarding online learning, Rhema and Miliszewska (2014) performed a research on the matter. According to this survey, students were positive about online learning since it would help them become more knowledgeable and proficient learners. E-learning methods satisfy students who have access to technology and are at ease with computers. Suri and Sharma (2013) conducted interviews with 500 students at Panjab University, Chandigarh, to assess their opinions toward e-learning. They discovered that opinions of students about e-learning were unaffected by gender. There is no appreciable variation in the attitude evaluations of males and girls when it comes to online learning.

Five basic factors have an impact on students' attitudes toward accepting e-learning, according to a study by Mehra and Omidian (2011) carried out in Iran to analyze the factors influencing those attitudes: pressure to use, perceived ease of use, perceived usefulness, and intention concerning e-learning. Aixia and Wang (2011) discovered that learning enables learning activities—which are often focused on knowledge management—to be carried out on a decent platform. The research involved 128 college students at Ningbo University. Students would also think favorably of online learning if there is flexibility in managing their knowledge and time to access the information.

Learning climate is defined as the "social, emotional, intellectual, and physical environment in which students acquire new material relevant to the class," by Ambrose et al. (2010). Students study in settings where specific conditions and surrounds have created the learning environment for that particular class. Liu et al. (2010) discovered that when learners are using a system to get new knowledge and information, their behavioral intentions are impacted by perceived utility and perceived ease of use. The study involved 436 secondary school students in Taiwan. According to Wu et al. (2010), learning satisfaction is the culmination of students' attitudes, actions, feelings, and judgments of their learning progress concerning e-learning. They assessed the views of 212 Taiwanese students regarding e-learning.

Lee (2010) looked into the hypothesis that behavioral intention to use is significantly influenced by the satisfaction derived from e-learning in a research involving 363 students from National Pingtung University in Taiwan. As a result, satisfaction and intention to use are positively correlated. The amount of training has a strong positive correlation with students' satisfaction with e-learning, according to a study by Elina and Erkki (2007) on students at the University of Joensuu, Finland, aimed at identifying factors influencing students' attitudes toward e-learning. Students tend to have better attitudes when they are at high ability and training levels.

3.1 Technology Adoption Model (TAM)

Over the course of many decades, researchers have created a range of models to investigate different aspects of user innovation adoption (Chen et al., 2018; Kamal et al., 2020; Kaur and Kaur, 2022b). In contrast, TAM is a well-known methodology for assessing technology adoption and usage in the literature on human-computer interaction (Chhonker et al., 2018; Granić and Marangunić, 2019; Pertiwi et al., 2020). The TAM was established by Fred Davis in 1986. The Theory of Reasoned Actions (Ajzen and Fishbein, 1980) and the Theory of Planned Behavior (Ajzen, 1991) serve as the framework for TAM. Perceived utility (PU) and perceived ease of use (PEOU) are the two primary elements that impact consumers' views about emerging technologies, according to Davis et al. (1992). Furthermore, the adoption of developing technologies by a positive BI is encouraged by a strong AT. TAM is thought to be the theory that is used the most often among frameworks for predicting a user's adoption of new technology (Alturki & Aldraiweesh, 2022; X. Chen et al., 2022; Lai, 2017; Lee, Kozar, & Larsen, 2003). The proposed research model is depicted in Figure 1.

Figure 1. The proposed model for examining the perception of students towards e-learning.

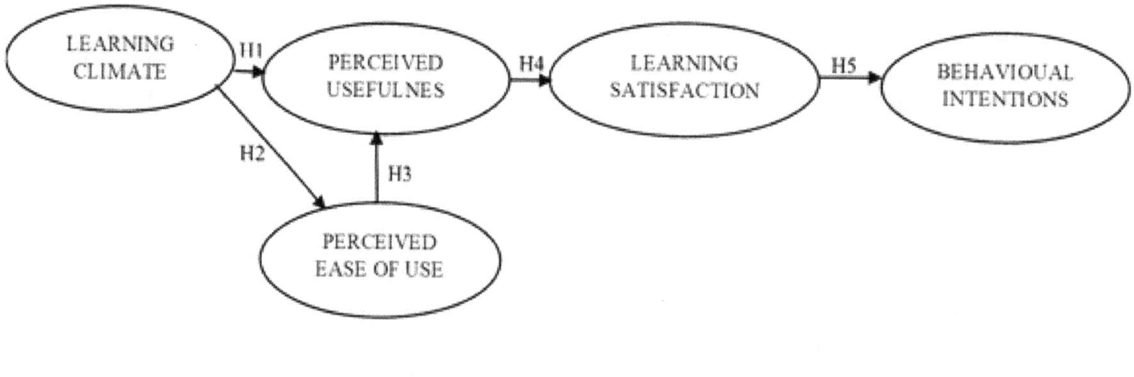

The following five hypotheses were developed to accomplish the objectives of this study for exploring the students' perception of e-learning.

H1: Learning climate (LC) positively affects perceived usefulness (PU).
H2: Learning climate (LC) positively affects perceived ease of use (PEOU).
H3: Perceived ease of use (PEOU) is the direct predictor of perceived usefulness (PU).
H4: Perceived usefulness (PU) positively influences learning satisfaction (LS).
H5: Behavioural intentions (BI) are positively influenced by learning satisfaction (LS).

4. RESEARCH METHODOLOGY

4.1 Instrument

The data from the students was gathered using a well-defined five-point Likert scale. The questionnaire was split into two sections, with five factors in the first section. Five questions reconstructed from Wu et al. (2008) were used to test the first variable, learning climate, and three items modified from Su et al. (2008) were used to measure the second variable, perceived usefulness (2010). A four-item scale that was modified from Su et al. (2010) was used to measure the third variable, perceived ease of use. The last variable, which examined students' behavioral intentions toward e-learning, was measured via a two-item scale that was also reframed by Wu et al. (2008). Learning satisfaction was employed as the fifth construct in this study (2008).

4.2 Data Collection and Sample

The data has been collected from various universities in the Northern Regions of India. In order to investigate the adoption of e-learning in Indian higher education institutions, a total sample size of 271 was collected. Undergraduate and graduate students enrolled in various programs were among the participants.

4.3 Analysis Tools

The SPSS software was used to examine the basic data collected from the students. The dependability of the data was also evaluated using Cronbach's alpha. Multiple regression analysis was used to examine the impact of the learning environment, perceived usability, perceived usefulness, and learning satisfaction on students' behavioral intentions toward e-learning.

5. DATA ANALYSIS AND RESULTS

In this study five variables have been considered, learning climate, perceived ease of use, perceived usefulness, and learning satisfaction as independent variables and behavioral intentions as the dependent variables. The reliability of the data was measured through Cronbach's alpha. Table 1 presents the coefficients of Cronbach's alpha, which are above 0.708 (Hair et al., 2006), thus, the data was found to be reliable. The values of Cronbach's alpha must be in the range of 0.60 to 0.90 (DeVellis, 2016; Tavakol and Dennick, 2011).

Table 2. Coefficients values of Cronbach's alpha.

Variable	Alpha Coefficient
Learning Climate (LC)	0.803
Perceived Ease of Use (PEOU)	0.887
Perceived Usefulness (PU)	0.799
Learning Satisfaction (LS)	0.901
Behavioral Intentions (BI)	0.896

5.1 Demographic Characteristics

In terms of demographic characteristics, 62 percent of the students were male and 38 percent were female students. 83.1 percent represent the majority of students who were perusing postgraduate courses and remained enrolled in graduate courses. Lastly, 36 percent of the students fall under the age group of 15-20 years, while the remaining 64 percent represented the age group of 20-25 years.

5.2 Multiple Regression Analysis

The multi-regression analysis approach was used to investigate how students felt about online learning. All of the hypotheses were accepted with the exception of the second one, which claimed that the learning environment positively influenced perceived usefulness. The results of the multi-regression analysis, which are summarised in Table 3, showed that there was a positive significant relationship between learning climate and perceived ease of use (β= 0.394, p <0.001), indicating that learning climate accounted for 39.4% of the variance in perceived ease of use. The R square value shows that, if other variables were held constant, a 1-unit increment in learning climate would have a 15.5 percent impact on perceived ease of use, confirming the first hypothesis.

The second hypothesis was rejected since there was no connection between perceived usefulness and learning climate (β=0.104, p=0.535). The third hypothesis, which states that perceived usefulness and perceived ease of use are positively associated, was accepted at a significance level of 0.001 (β= 0.633), which indicates that perceived ease of use accounts for 63.3 percent of the variation in perceived usefulness. By adding 1 unit of perceived ease of use, the value of perceived usefulness will rise by 40.1 percent while all other criteria stay constant.

Table 3. Regression coefficients on the adoption of students towards E-learning.

Hypotheses	Beta Value	R^2	F-value	t-value	Dublin-Watson value	Result
H1: LC to PEOU	0.394	0.155	6.621*	2.573*	1.512	**Supported**
H2: LC to PU	0.104	0.11	0.392**	0.626**	1.410	Not Supported
H3: PEOU to PU	0.633	0.401	24.091*	4.908*	1.747	**Supported**
H4: PU to LS	0.460	0.211	9.655*	3.107*	1.231	**Supported**
H5: LS to BI	0.232	0.124	2.040*	2.148*	1.921	**Supported**

[**Note:** LC = Learning Climate, PEOU = Perceived Ease of Use, PU = Perceived Usefulness, LS = Learning Satisfaction and BI = Behavioural Intentions. *p<0.001. **p=0.535]

The relationship between perceived usefulness and learning satisfaction was substantial (β= 0.460, p>0.001), and perceived usefulness accounts for 46% of the variance in learning pleasure. The fourth theory was confirmed. Finally, the causal link between learning satisfaction and behavioral intentions was accepted, with learning satisfaction accounting for 23.2% of the variation in behavioral intentions (β= 0.232, p>0.001). The behavioral intentions will increase to 12.4% when learning pleasure is increased by one unit. Given that the data are not autocorrelated, the Dublin-Watson value for each hypothesis indicates that the residuals are independent since it is above 1 and near 2. With the exception of the second hypothesis, where the F-value was less than 2, all hypotheses had favorable F-values.

6. IMPLICATIONS OF THE STUDY

Students have a wide range of options to acquire information and skills through e-learning. The findings of this study suggested that before introducing e-learning technologies into the classroom, educators should prioritize the learning atmosphere. To adopt e-learning, educators need also to create and support a good learning environment. This study has shown that students' attitudes about online learning are overwhelmingly positive, as is their behavior in this area. The instructors will benefit from this behavior as they support institutional e-learning. In order to compete effectively, new approaches should be used to improve e-learning in educational institutions.

7. CONCLUSION

The primary goal of this study was to use the Technology Adoption Model (TAM) to investigate students' behavioral intentions in the setting of online learning. TAM is a useful model for evaluating students' acceptance of e-learning since it significantly assisted in measuring students' views, which allowed for the achievement of this aim. The majority of pupils responded well to online learning, according to the study's findings. These results were consistent with other studies conducted by scholars in other countries (Olson and Brown, 2018; Ali et al., 2016; Jung et al., 2008). The study's findings will provide instructors and students with a helpful foundation for improving their online learning experiences. Teachers may enhance the learning environment by making sure the information is appropriate. There are, however, certain limitations to this study, which allows for further investigation. Firstly, the study's geographical scope was limited to Punjab; hence, in order to generalize the findings, future research should adopt a larger perspective. Secondly, the sample size was insufficient; in the future, a larger sample size had to be employed to evaluate the validity of the TAM.

REFERENCES

Aixia, D., & Wang, D. (2011). Influencing Learner Attitudes Toward E-learning and Development of E-learning Environment Based on the Integrated E-learning Platform, *International Journal of e-Education, e-Business, e-. Management Learning*, *1*(3), 264–268.

Ali, F., Nair, P. K., & Hussain, K. (2016). An assessment of students' acceptance and usage of computer supported collaborative classrooms in hospitality and tourism schools. *Journal of Hospitality, Leisure, Sport and Tourism Education*, *18*, 51–60. DOI: 10.1016/j.jhlste.2016.03.002

Ambrose, S. A., Bridges, M. W., DiPietro, M., Lovett, M. C., & Norman, M. K. (2010). *How learning works: Seven research-based principles for smart teaching*. Jossey Bass, John Wiley & Sons.

Chung, C., & Ackerman, D. (2015). Student reactions to Classroom Management Technology: Learning styles and attitudes toward Moodle. *Journal of Education for Business*, *90*(4), 217–223. DOI: 10.1080/08832323.2015.1019818

Davis, F. D., Bagozzi, R. P., & Warshaw, P. R. (1989). User acceptance of computer technology: A comparison of two theoretical models. *Management Science*, *35*(8), 982–1003. DOI: 10.1287/mnsc.35.8.982

DeVellis, R. F. (2016). *Scale Development: Theory and Applications*. Sage publications.

Elina and Erkki. (2007). *Identifying Students' Attitudes on e-learning – the effects of experience and Institutional support*. University of Joensuu.

Jung, M. L. L., Loria, K., & Saha, R. M. P. (2008). E-Learning: Investigating University Students Acceptance of Technology. *European Journal of Open, Distance and e-learning, 11(2).*

Lau, S. H., & Woods, P. C. (2008). An investigation of user perceptions and attitudes towards learning objects. *British Journal of Educational Technology*, *39*(4), 685–699. DOI: 10.1111/j.1467-8535.2007.00770.x

Lee, M. C. (2010). Explaining and Predicting users' continuance intention toward e-learning: An extension of the expectation–confirmation model. *Computers & Education*, *54*(2), 506–516. DOI: 10.1016/j.compedu.2009.09.002

Liaw, M. L. (2006). E-learning and the development of intercultural competence. *Language Learning & Technology*, *10*(3), 49–64.

Liu, I. F., Chen, M. C., Sun, Y. S., Wible, D., & Kuo, C. H. (2010). Extending the TAM model to explore the factors that affect Intention to Use an Online Learning Community. *Computers & Education*, *54*(2), 600–610. DOI: 10.1016/j.compedu.2009.09.009

Mehra, V., & Omidian, F. (2011). Examining Students' Attitudes Towards E-learning: A Case from India. *Malaysian Journal of Educational Technology*, *11*(2), 13–18.

Newton, R. (2003). Staff Attitudes to the Development and delivery of e-learning. *New Library World*, *104*(1193), 412–425. DOI: 10.1108/03074800310504357

Olson, E. D., & Brown, E. (2018). Perceptions of Students in an Event Management Program of Annotation Systems and Their Influence on Student Learning. *Journal of Hospitality & Tourism Education*, *30*(2), 118–126. DOI: 10.1080/10963758.2018.1437351

Rashty, D. (1995). Traditional learning vs. eLearning. *Mount St. Mary's College. [Online]*. Retrieved from: https://www.click4it.org/images/f/f5/Traditional_Learning_vs_eLearning.pdf

Rhema, A., & Miliszewska, I. (2014). Analysis of student attitudes towards e-learning: The case of engineering students in Libya. *Issues in informing science and information. Technology*, *11*(1), 169–190.

Su, A. Y., Yang, S. J., Hwang, W. Y., & Zhang, J. (2010). A Web 2.0-based collaborative annotation system for enhancing knowledge sharing in collaborative learning environments. *Computers & Education*, *55*(2), 752–766. DOI: 10.1016/j.compedu.2010.03.008

Suri, G., & Sharma, S. (2013). The impact of Gender on Attitude towards Computer Technology and e-learning: An exploratory study of Punjab University, India. International. *Journal of Engineering Research*, *2*(2), 132–136.

Tavakol, M., & Dennick, R. (2011). Post-examination analysis of objective tests. *Medical Teacher*, *33*(6), 447–458. DOI: 10.3109/0142159X.2011.564682 PMID: 21609174

Urdan, T. A., & Weggen, C. C. (2000). Corporate eLearning: Exploring a new frontier. Waltham, Massachusetts, U.S.A. Retrieved from: https://papers.cumincad.org/data/works/att/2c7d.content.pdf

Wu, J. H., Tennyson, R. D., & Hsia, T. L. (2010). A study of student satisfaction in a blended e-learning system environment. *Computers & Education*, *55*(1), 155–164. DOI: 10.1016/j.compedu.2009.12.012

Chapter 8
Exploring the Indicators of Hotel Customer Experiences on Service Quality Approach

Jyoti
Galgotias University, India

Chand Rashid
Galgotias University, India

Monalisha Dash
Galgotias University, India

ABSTRACT

In the intensely competitive hospitality sector, the quality of customer experience is a critical determinant of a hotel's success. As customers become more selective and their expectations evolve, hotels must continuously assess and enhance their service quality to remain competitive. This chapter aims to explore various indicators of hotel customer experience from a service quality perspective. Secondary data was utilized, with 434 hotel reviews collected from Tripadvisor.com, a prominent customer review site. Among these reviews, 268 were from domestic customers and the remainder from international travelers. Qualitative analysis was conducted using R software and Bigram analysis to identify recurring words and phrases. The study identified seven key dimensions based on repeated phrases, including hotel rooms, food quality, staff behavior, overall stay experience, and service quality. The research provides insights into these indicators and suggests that future studies could explore big data related to customer experience across different geographical areas.

1. INTRODUCTION

Since last many years, the service sector has emerged as the leading component of the economy. Studies indicate that top class quality of service is very much needed for the survival and success in today's competitive hotel market, leading to a marked increase in interest in this area (Ghobadian et al., 1994). Research demonstrates that excellent service quality fosters customer loyalty, attracts new customer, generates positive feedback, boosts employee commitment and satisfaction towards the organization, enhances image of company, reduces the operational expenses/ costs, and improves the performance of any service business (Berry et al., 1989). Service quality is a critical factor in determining organizational success, with delivering top-notch service being a key strategy for achieving this. In the Indian hotel industry, the need to enhance service quality has become a focal point due

DOI: 10.4018/979-8-3693-7447-4.ch008

to intense competition, as hotels employees need to face a lot of challenges to provide the quality of service. Providing excellent service not only leads to profitability but also motivates employees to reach their full potential in meeting challenges. By offering high-quality service, hotels can maintain customer assurance and hold and secure a good position over their competitors.

In the service industry, particularly in the hotel sector, acquisitive and improving quality of service is essential for maximizing customer experiences and achieve to sustain and hold the customer in that particular hotel. Service quality, as articulated by Zeithaml, Parasuraman, and Berry (1990), is a multifaceted concept that includes key elements vital for guest satisfaction, such as tangibles, reliability, responsiveness, assurance, and empathy. These aspects play a crucial role in shaping how guests perceive their stay and are vital for assessing how effectively a hotel meets or surpasses their expectations. The importance of service quality is highlighted by its direct influence on customer satisfaction, which subsequently affects customer loyalty and repeat business (Oliver, 1999). Customer experience most important and essential indicators—including guest satisfaction, the efficiency of service delivery, the quality of facilities and amenities, staff conduct, perceived value for money, and the degree of personalized service provide crucial insights into how guests perceive and evaluate service quality. Guest satisfaction, typically assessed through surveys and feedback, indicates how well a hotel's service meets guest expectations and can profoundly affect the hotel's reputation and market position (Kwortnik & Thompson, 2009). The efficiency of service delivery, including the effectiveness of check-in and check-out processes, significantly influences customer perceptions of reliability and responsiveness (Parasuraman et al., 1988). The state and quality of physical facilities and amenities are also crucial in shaping how customer perceive value and satisfaction, as demonstrated by research on the impact of tangible elements on service quality (Bitner, 1992). Additionally, staff behavior, which includes professionalism, friendliness, and competence, plays a key role in the guest experience; positive staff interactions can greatly enhance satisfaction, while negative experiences can lead to dissatisfaction and unfavorable reviews (Heskett et al., 1997). Perceptions of value for money, which are determined by the quality of services relative to the cost, affect overall guest satisfaction and the likelihood of recommending the hotel (Zeithaml, 1988). Finally, the extent to which hotels personalize and customize their services to align with individual guest preferences can greatly enhance the guest experience and build long-term loyalty (Carbone & Haeckel, 1994). By thoroughly analyzing these indicators, hotels can pinpoint their strengths and identify areas for improvement, allowing them to adjust their services to better meet guest expectations and elevate the overall experience. A deep understanding of these service quality indicators equips hotels with the insights needed to exceed guest expectations and gain a lasting competitive edge in a dynamic market (Atilgan et al., 2003). Implementing a systematic approach to these indicators enables hotels to refine their service strategies, boost customer satisfaction, and drive success in an increasingly competitive industry.

1.2 Concept of Customer Experience

Customer experience has become a central element in contemporary hospitality business strategies, profoundly impacting how hotels interact with their guests and influencing their overall success. This concept encompasses the full spectrum of interactions a guest has with a hotel, from the initial contact through to post-stay follow-ups. It recognizes that every interaction—whether with a product, service, or staff member—plays a crucial role in shaping the guest's overall perception of the hotel brand. As competition intensifies and customer expectations elevate, hotels are increasingly prioritizing the enhancement of customer experience to stand out in a saturated market. This emphasis on customer experience mirrors a larger shift toward customer-centric approaches, where hotels strive to understand and cater to the individual needs and preferences of their guests in a personalized and impactful manner (Pine & Gilmore, 1998).

In today's hotel industry, guests expect far more than merely high-quality products and services; they seek interactions that are seamless, personalized, and emotionally engaging. This shift is fueled by greater access to information, an abundance of choices, and elevated service standards, requiring hotels to adapt to these advanced expectations. Effective management of customer experience involves not only providing consistent and superior service but also fostering a strong emotional bond with guests. Studies show that hotels that excel in delivering exceptional customer experiences often achieve higher levels of guest satisfaction, increased loyalty, and stronger brand advocacy, which can lead to significant business benefits such as improved guest retention and greater lifetime value (Klaus & Maklan, 2013).

Managing customer experience involves several critical elements. Firstly, it is crucial to thoroughly understand customer needs and preferences. This understanding is often achieved through data analysis and direct feedback, which reveal customer behaviors, expectations, and pain points. By leveraging these insights, businesses can customize their interactions and offerings to more effectively address customer needs and anticipate future demands. Secondly, maintaining consistency across all customer touchpoints—whether through digital platforms, customer service representatives, or physical locations—is vital. Consistently delivering on the brand promise helps build trust and strengthens the positive aspects of the customer experience (Zeithaml, 2000).

Additionally, continuous improvement and adaptability are essential for successful customer experience management. Organizations need to be flexible, regularly evaluating customer feedback and performance metrics to make informed updates and refinements. Technological advancements, such as Customer Relationship Management (CRM) systems and artificial intelligence, are crucial in this regard as they facilitate real-time monitoring of customer interactions and sentiments (Boulding et al., 2005).

Ultimately, prioritizing customer experience signifies a shift towards valuing and centering the customer's viewpoint within hotel operations. Hotels that effectively incorporate customer experience strategies into their practices not only cultivate stronger relationships with their customer but also enhance their chances for long-term success and competitive edge in an increasingly dynamic market (Lemon & Verhoef, 2016). As customer expectations continue to evolve, providing outstanding customer experiences has become a fundamental necessity for achieving success in the hotel industry, rather than merely a competitive advantage.

1.3 Concept of Service Quality

Service quality is mixer of two words: service and quality. Hasenfeld (1974) defines service as the efforts made by individuals or organizations to support and improve the well-being or functionality of people. Quality pertains to the standards or specifications that an organization commits to delivering.

Parasuraman, Zeithaml, and Berry (1988) described service quality means overall experience of service quality delivered by the staff and the customer's overall evaluation of the service's excellence, or the disparity between their expectations and the service they actually experience.

The American Society for Quality Control defines quality as "the entirety of features and characteristics of a product or service that relate to its ability to meet stated or implied needs." In contrast, Parasuraman et al. (1994) explain about service quality as the what customer expect from the service providers and what exactly deliver by the service provider.

Thomas, Dan R. E. (1978) stated that service differentiation is essential for the growth and development of service business and customers consume services at the moment when it was delivered, an inexperienced or incapable service provider can quickly damage the organization's reputation. Therefore, to maintain the quality of service is a very crucial factor for service industry/sectors, as customers form an impressions based on their interactions, whether positive or negative. Given the increasing competition, it is very much important for hotel sectors to enhance their service quality in every aspect to stay ahead of competitors.

Service quality is considered a very crucial factors in distinguishing hotel products. Customer satisfaction and loyalty can be achieved through top class quality of all products and services (Getty & Getty, 2003; Gupta & Chen, 1995; Tsang & Qu, 2000). Edvardsson (1996) emphasized that quality of services should be evaluated from the perspective of customer, as their perception defines the service. Customers hold various values and assessment criteria, leading them to perceive the same service in different ways.

Factors such as size of rooms, cleanliness, employee behavior, and quality of food and taste of food significantly attract customers. Attributes like freshness, quality, taste, and cleanliness of food draw customers to a location. Typically, feedback after a hotel stay is positive, as the experience satisfies customers' curiosity. The desire to taste unfamiliar cuisines and authentic local flavors is an important consideration when choosing a destination (Goolaup and Mossberg, 2017). The study analyzes digital evidence from online reviews written by customers after their stay, which best reflect their behavior and interests. Social network profiling of destinations and online reviews can spark customer interest, helping them choose attractions that align with their preferences (Hernández et al., 2018). Social media and the internet play crucial roles in enhancing the stay experience by introducing customers to comfortable destinations (Hindley and Wall, 2018). customer often spend considerable time reviewing products online to ensure the best stay experience (Hendijani, 2016).

Delhi, as the capital of India and the largest democracy in the world, serves as a hub for business and political activity, attracting numerous business and leisure travelers who wish to experience the city's rich culture, heritage, and values. According to Delhi Tourism, the city offers approximately 1,521 accommodation units with 379,776 rooms and 778,551 beds, including a variety of star hotels, budget hotels, and standalone properties. Statistics from Delhi Tourism indicate that there were 1.817 million foreign tourist arrivals, with 90% staying in hotels. Delhi also received 21.637 million domestic tourists, with 57% staying with relatives or friends and the rest in hotels. Given this growth, the demand for rooms is expected to rise, with an average requirement of 62 employees per 100 rooms, ensuring a consistent demand for competent staff.

Table 1. Brief description of Delhi

Area	**1484 Sq. Km.**
Altitude	200 Meters above sea level
Population (2024 census)	16.8 million
Density of population	9254 people per Sq. Km.
Rate of Literacy	86.21%
Languages	Hindi, Punjabi, English

Source: - Ministry of Delhi State Tourism Website

This chapter explores the different indicators that affect hotel, improve' experiences and their connection to the service quality. By investigating indicators such as hotel room, food, employees' behavior, memorable stay experience, food quality, recommendation and quality of service, this study seeks to reveal how these elements collectively influence customer' experiences. Evaluating these indicators offers valuable insights for hotels aiming to surpass customer expectations, thereby enhancing service quality and building enduring guest loyalty.

2. PROBLEM IDENTIFICATION

The quality of service is an important factor for the success of hospitality industry. The current trend of total quality management (TQM) in the hotel industry guarantees that hotel companies can gain a competitive edge. In the competitive era hotel Industry is well established & Blooming Industry in India. It is essential to explore the indicators of hotel customers experience on service quality approach.

3. LITERATURE REVIEW

Researchers have provided various definitions of service quality. For instance, Bitner, Booms, and Mohr (1994) define that the customer's overall experience of the organization's relative superiority or inferiority. Meanwhile, Cronin and Taylor (1994) and Taylor and Cronin (1994) view service quality as an attitude that reflects a long-term overall assessment. Parasuraman, Zeithaml, and Berry (1985) describe that the difference between anticipated and actual performance across various quality aspects. This perspective is consistent with Roest and Pieters' (1997) demonstrate that quality of service is a perceptive gap between experience-based norms and actual performance regarding service benefits.

Service quality is viewed as the important component of the hotels (Min & Min, 1996) and the important part of the service management (Chen, 2008). It is closely linked to customer loyalty (Shi & Su, 2007), which in turn influences customers' intention to revisit (Han, Back & Barrett, 2009). By projecting a strong image, a hotel can get a competitive benefit and gain the good business (Ryu, Han & Kim, 2008). To develop the service process, three basic key concept involvement are required: good service process, positive system, and right service resources-structure (Edvardsson, 1997).

The hotel market most importantly focuses on customer satisfaction (Flint, Woodruff, & Gardial, 1997; Peter & Olson, 1996). Customer satisfaction is crucial for the performance of hotels (Nilsson, Johnson, & Gustafsson, 2001). In the service industry specially, where the hotel entire staff directly and indirectly deal with the customer for the selling of hotel products and provide the excellent services and makes the customer happy and satisfy.

Table 2. Previous studies

Author	Purpose	Methodology	Findings
Robertson, J., Vella, J., Duncan, S., Pitt, C., Pitt, L., & Caruana, A. (2024)	This study investigates the possibility of enhancing traditional methods for monitoring airport service quality by incorporating automated text analysis to gain deeper insights into traveler feedback and improve overall service quality.	survey-based methods	The findings present new methods for evaluating the quality of airport service, providing a great point of view on customer satisfaction with their experiences which customers received at airport and throw lights on strategic insights that can help the organizations win the competitive business.
Al-Kumaim et al. (2023)	The study seeks to evaluate the condition of hotel and tourism industry of Malaysia post COVID-19, and to identify strategies for alleviating the indirect impacts of the pandemic on these sectors.	SERVQUAL dimensions	The empirical study findings demonstrate the positive significate correlation between three important identified independent variables—hygiene practices, environmental sustainability, and the digitalization—and hotel happy and satisfy customer related to the intention to return. Besides, based on the model of SERVQUAL, only the reliability and assurance variables show a notable connection with customer happiness and satisfaction that customer may revisit the hotel. The results also indicate that satisfaction of customer plays an important and crucial role, as it significantly mediates the relationship between these independent variables and customers' intention to return to the hotel.
Olorunsola et al. (2022)	The paper aim is to identify the important factors or themes found in online reviews by the customers who was staying at eco-friendly hotels and to determine which of these themes or factors are linked to the customer satisfaction and dissatisfaction ratings.	GLSERV dimensions	The findings of this paper involved the various interconnected parts like consumer satisfaction with environmentally friendly lodges, revealing seven key themes/ factors that influence the customer perceptions. These themes or factors encompass and focus the environmentally friendly hotels, staff attitudes towards sustainability of the environment, the quality of supplies, location, types of services offered, value, and revisiting or recommending the organization. The above various factors/ themes indicate that assessing Eco friendly service quality, involves different aspects of the service experience, ultimately shaping the guest experience.
Preziosi et al. (2022)	This paper explores green attributes perception of consumer followed by ecofriendly-awarded hotels, aiming the environmentally friendly attributes act as factors in the context of hotel service quality.	GLSERV dimensions: -Tangibles -Staff service quality -Food -Value for money -Green	The findings mentioned that mostly customer appreciate the eco- friendly practices which are followed by hotels. This research also investigating the practices which can make the customer satisfy. However, most of the hotels are promoting and participating the sustainable program practices. If hotel is not able to provide the ecofriendly products to the customer, it might be better not to inform the customer, it can fail the customer satisfaction.
Stone et al., 2022	To examine how tourism activities influence tourists' behavioral attitudes, including their likelihood to recommend the destination, their intention to return, and their overall satisfaction.	Descriptive statistics	Tourists concurred that a positive experience affects their likelihood to return, their willingness to share recommendations, and the economic growth of the host cities.
MOUZAEK, E., Al Marzouqi, A. M. I. N. A., ALAALI, N., SALLOUM, S. A., ABURAYYA, A., & SUSON, R. (2021).	The primary objective of the study was to assess how various dimensions like quality of service improve the customer satisfaction within the hotel industry.	Drop-Off Technique	The study concluded that high service quality enabled organizations to better address customer needs and expectations, leading to increased satisfaction. Consequently, by providing exceptional services that align with customer demands, organizations could enhance their financial performance. Thus, improving service quality in hotels can lead to higher levels of guest satisfaction.

continued on following page

Table 2. Continued

Author	Purpose	Methodology	Findings
Malik, S. A., Akhtar, F., Raziq, M. M., & Ahmad, M. (2020).	This study investigates the relationships among customer loyalty, perceived justice in pricing, and perceived quality of service. Additionally, it looks into the ways in which customer satisfaction mediates the relationship between perceived fairness in pricing and customer loyalty, as well as the relationship between perceived service quality and customer loyalty.	Gap Analysis	Based on customer demographics, the data show variations in expectations, perceptions, satisfaction, and loyalty. Though it entirely mediates the relationship between perceived pricing fairness and customer loyalty, customer satisfaction only partially mediates the relationship between perceived service quality and customer loyalty. The results provide implications for both theoretical understanding and practical application.
Ahmad, S. Z., Ahmad, N., & Papastathopoulos, A. (2019).	This study seeks to explore customer satisfaction and service quality in small- and mid-sized hotels through the application of an adapted SERVQUAL model.	Structural Equation Modelling.	Three of the five SERVQUAL dimensions—tangible elements, assurance, and responsiveness—are found to have a statistically significant positive impact on visitor satisfaction in the SMSH sector. However, there is no discernible difference between the two other dimensions—reliability and empathy—and customer satisfaction.
Choo, P. W., Tan, C. L., & Yeo, S. F. (2018).	The aim of this study is twofold: first, to evaluate the reasons for using comprehensive customer experience quality measurements in prior research, and second, to create a holistic customer experience quality survey questionnaire that is specifically tailored for Malaysian heritage hotels.	Empirical Studies	The findings indicate that a comprehensive measure of customer experience quality, which includes product experience, outcome focus, moments-of-truth, and peace-of-mind, offers heritage hotel operators and researchers a thorough evaluation tool through the designed survey questionnaire. This metric can help hoteliers track and enhance the quality of the heritage hotel experience for both local and international tourists.
Tefera, O., & Govender, K. (2017).	The main objective of this research is to investigate the connection between service quality, customer satisfaction, and loyalty within the Ethiopian hotel sector.	Stratified Cluster Sampling Technique	The findings suggest that the management of hotel in Ethiopia should avoid setting excessively high customer expectations and should regularly assess customer satisfaction through surveys. For businesses that depend on repeat business, building customer retention is essential, thus hotel management should also cultivate an environment that fosters loyalty.
Mmutle, T., & Shonhe, L. (2017).	This study looked into how consumers keep their view on the service quality and how that perception impacts a particular hotel's reputation.	Qualitative research method	The results indicate that a hotel's reputation is influenced by the quality of its services, with poor service frequently leading to negative publicity and negative image. It has also been found that customer feedback is essential for improving the quality of service. According to the report, hotel departments have developed procedures and plans for meeting and exceeding customer expectations, especially when it comes to resolving complaints, which is crucial for preserving organizational stability.
Ren, L., Qiu, H., Wang, P., & Lin, P. M. (2016).	The study specifically seeks to investigate the various dimensions of customer experience in budget hotels and to analyze the factors that affect customer satisfaction.	Exploratory Study	The exploratory factor analysis identified four dimensions of customer experience: tangible and sensorial experience, staff aspects, aesthetic perception, and location. The subsequent multiple regression analysis indicates that these four factors have a significant positive impact on customer satisfaction.

Hotel guests evaluate the quality of service during their stay by examining various factors (Pizam & Ellis, 1999; Wilkins, Merrilees, & Herington, 2007). Research emphasized that service quality both tangible and intangible elements affect the customer satisfaction (Ekinci, Dawes, & Massey, 2008; Prentice, 2013; Torres & Kline, 2013). Intangible aspects encompass elements such as assurance, customer service, and empathy, whereas tangible aspects relate to physical features like the appearance of hotel staff and room cleanliness (Ramanathan & Ramanathan, 2011). Service failures can significantly impact perceptions of service quality, satisfaction, and future behavior

(Berezina, Cobanoglu, Miller, & Kwansa, 2012; Han & Back, 2007; Prentice, 2013; Tarn, 1999). Hence, mentioned identifying factors that enhance customer satisfaction and foster loyalty is essential for business of hotels.

Hotel professionals aim to satisfy their customers and encourage repeat, as sustaining current customer is more cost-effective than attracting new ones (Tyrrell & Woods, 2005). Research indicates that boosting customer retention rates by just 5% can lead to profit increases of 25% to 95% (Reichheld & Schefter, 2000). Gefen (2002) notes that acquiring new customers is generally more expensive than maintaining loyal ones, who are also cheaper to serve. Furthermore, loyal customers often spend more and frequently refer new clients, making them a valuable source of revenue (Bowen & Shoemaker, 1998; Shoemaker & Lewis, 1999).

The rapid growth of the Internet enhances the influence of referrals from loyal customers. Conversely, dissatisfied customers can also provide valuable insights for hotels. They help identify operational issues that need attention and improvement (Harrison-Walker, 2001). Additionally, the service recovery paradox suggests that customers who experience a service failure followed by a successful recovery often report higher satisfaction levels than those who received flawless service initially (Harrison-Walker, 2001; Hoffman & Bateson, 2010; Zeithaml et al., 2006). Research shows that effective service recovery strategies enhance customer loyalty (Cranage & Mattila, 2005). Conversely, unaddressed complaints can lead to dissatisfaction, lower repeat-purchase rates, and negative word-of-mouth (Mattila & Mount, 2003). To avoid these negative outcomes, Harrison-Walker (2001) recommends that companies embrace customer complaints by providing various channels for feedback, such as websites, BPOs, and chat options.

Negative word-of-mouth (WOM) can significantly harm companies (Bambauer-Sachse & Mangold, 2011). Customers often actively seek out negative reviews, viewing them as more diagnostic and informative compared to positive or neutral feedback. Negative information generally has a greater impact on decision-making than positive information (Herr, Kardes, & Kim, 1991). Such negative WOM can dissuade potential customers from considering a product or brand, damaging the company's reputation and financial health (Sundaram, Mitra, & Webster, 1998). In today's interconnected environment, negative WOM can spread rapidly, potentially eroding brand equity, harming the company's image, decreasing sales, and, in severe cases, leading to business closures.

4. RESEARCH METHODOLOGY

The study aims to analyze the experiences of both domestic and international customers regarding the service quality provided by hotels in Delhi. To gather data, we selected online reviews from TripAdvisor, a widely used customer review platform. TripAdvisor features listings for hotels, restaurants, activities, attractions, beaches, flights, and casinos from around the world.

Figure 1. The text pre-processing steps

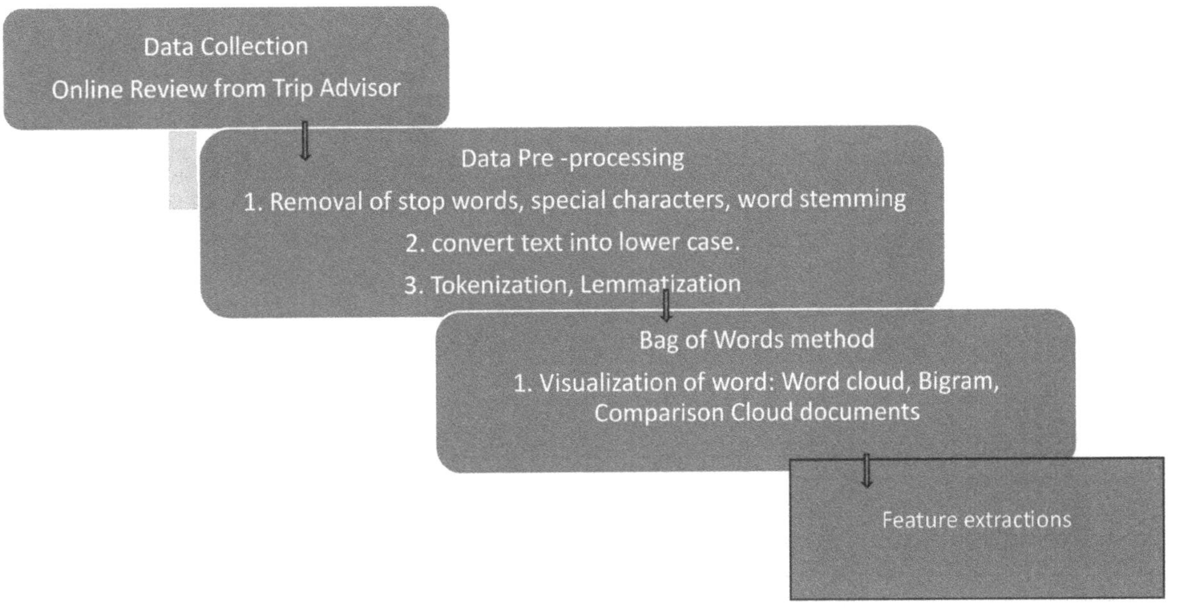

Author's work

We selected New Delhi as the focus of this study due to its status as the capital of India and its appeal to both domestic and international visitors for business and leisure. We gathered 450 textual reviews covering aspects such as hotel rooms, food and beverages, employee behavior, service quality, and ambiance for detailed analysis.

4.2 Data Pre-Processing

Textual reviews are unstructured feedback provided by customers. To prepare the data for analysis, it must be cleaned. We utilized R programming for pre-processing and analyzing the data. Figure 1 illustrates the text pre-processing steps, which include removing stop words, special characters, and applying word stemming. Common words like 'the,' 'is,' and 'and' appear frequently and were removed, along with hotel names and people's names, by developing a custom word library. Next, we converted the text to lowercase. Finally, we tokenized the text and lemmatized the words to their root forms (e.g., 'satisfied' was changed to 'satisfaction').

4.3 Data Analysis

We employed the bag-of-words method for data analysis, which consisted of two components: analysis of data by of exploratory research and feature extraction.

4.4 Data Analysis by Exploratory Research

Exploratory data analysis involves the initial examination to determine key characteristics of the reviews, such as word count, average contributions by customers, and the total reviews.

4.5 Feature Extraction

To extract features, we performed N-gram analysis, which identifies repeated phrases in the text data (e.g., memorable stay, mastering stay, unforgettable stay). We set N=2 for bigram analysis and calculated dimensions based on related words.

4.6 Results

Table 3 presents the descriptive data and methodical features of the reviews. Total 440 customer reviews collected from the website. From the 440 reviews, 60% belonged to domestic customer and 40% belongs were written by international customer.

4.6.1 Descriptive Statistic

Table 3.

Details of customer	Phrase or words length	Contribution	Helpful Votes	Number of customer reviews
Domestic Customer	174.423 (125.026)	58.416 (188.05)	19.714 (47.225)	268 (60.90)
International Customer	173.536 (129.26)	12.091 (24.615)	4.271 (9.85)	166 (39.10)
Total	116.3 (84.938)	35.672 (138.020)	12.149 (33.278)	434

Table 4. Indicator extractions

Indicators	Terms	Frequency
Hotel Room	hotel_room, spacious_room, nice_room, amaze_room, Clean_room, amazing_room, room_comfortable	729
Food	taste_good, food_tasty, mouthwatering_food, love_food, Food_delicious, excellent_food, fantastic_ food	172
Employees' Behavior	excellent_employee, helping_employee, amaze_employee, professional_staff	168
Stay Experience	amaze_room, lot_fun, excellent_stay, Wonderful_view, tasty_food, fantastic_stay	164
Quality of food	food_delecious, smell_good, tasty_food, hygiene_food	138
Recommendation	highly_recommend, recommend_hotel, positively_ recom	93
Hotel Service Quality	employee_work culture, Professional_service, friendly_hotel	71

4.6.2 Feature Extraction

Table 4 describe that the indicators were extracted along with terms associated with them. Drawing on previous literature and insights from hospitality industry experts, the authors developed seven indicators of service quality experienced by both international and domestic customers in the hospitality sector. This chapter took the following factors into account while developing the below indicators:

- The key phrases for the hotel room indicators are spacious_room, nice_room, amaze_room, Clean_room, amazing_room, room_comfortable. This term is called the hotel room indicators.

  The key phrases for the food indicators are taste_good, food_tasty, mouthwatering_food, love_food, Food_delicious, excellent_food, fantastic_food. This term is associated with food indicators.
- The employee's behavior key phrases are excellent_employee, helping_employee, amaze_employee, professional_staff. This indicator is named as employees' behavior.
- The memorable stay experience fourth indicators phrases consists of amaze_room, lot_fun, excellent_stay, Wonderful_view, tasty_food, fantastic_stay. This indicator is named as stay experience.
- The key phrases of food indicators are food_delecious, smell_good, tasty_food, hygiene_food. The fifth indicator is referred as Quality of food.
- The key phrases of sixth indicator are highly_recommend, recommend_hotel, positively_ recom. This indicator is referred as Recommendation.
- The last phrases for hotel service quality indicators are employee_work culture, Professional_service, friendly_hotel. This indicator is known as hotel service quality.

5. DISCUSSION AND CONCLUSION

This chapter examined the various above indicators of hotel customer experience on service quality in New Delhi hotels. Service quality play a significant role in the service industry specially hospitality industry. With the growth of the internet, before reaching the hotel, customers can check the hotel reviews, see the image and videos of the hotel's products and book their rooms as per their need and requirement. For customers, clean, hygiene and comfortable room and tasty food becomes the primary motive to stay and re visit at the hotel (Cleave, 2020). In this chapter author identified seven indicators that are experienced by international and domestic customers. These indicators are: Hotel Room, Food, Employees' Behavior, Memorable Stay Experiences, Quality of food, Recommendations and hotel Service Quality. In the hotel room, customers mentioned their comfortable stay experience at hotel. Customers enjoyed the food during their stay at hotel which is prepared and served by the hotel employees. In the Employees behavior, customer mentioned abut employees' behavior. Due to their professional and helping behavior most of the customer enjoyed their stay and feel home at hotel. The role of the employees is very important to create a unique and memorable stay experience for customer. In the Memorable stay experience customer creates revisit intention and a positive image for a hotel. Memorable experience plays an important role in customer behaviour. Studies found that, after comfortable stay at hotel, Customer rethink to stay at hotel and eat the food they tasted at the hotel restaurant (Ji et al., 2016). In the quality of Food, customers are concerned about hygienic food. Of utmost importance are ingredients used and cleanliness of the kitchen environment (Okumus et al., 2018). In Recommendations or positive word of-mouth, Satisfied customers recommend the hotel in many ways. customers write about their experience on the review websites or hotel websites, write the blogs in social media. Now a days, customer share their experience with their friends and family members on the social media whether experience is positive or negative. Positive reviews increase the room and other products sales which improve revenue for the hotel (Ye et al., 2009). Negative reviews may ruin the reputation of the hotels (Sparks and Browning, 2010). Quality of Service is the important indicator for creating positive image of the hotel.

6. PRACTICAL IMPLICATIONS

Hospitality industry contributes to enhancing GPD of any country. This industry provides directly or indirectly employment opportunities for people, which impacts the country's GDP, and support in improving living standards. In the service industry, we need to understand the customer intended expectations with actual customer experiences.

Results come up with very interesting facts. International customer was very keen to stay at capital of India Delhi, which is rich in culture, monuments and heritages. The employees of the hotel play an important role in making the customer satisfied. Customer positive experiences lead to positive word-of-mouth publicity.

7. LIMITATION

Besides, this study has several limitations. Firstly, the chapter findings are based on a limited sample size which is based on New Delhi, which may affect the generalizability of the results due to the constrained data. Secondly, the analysis employed basic text mining methods, such as N-grams; future research could benefit from using more advanced text mining techniques, such as Latent Dirichlet Allocation or Latent Semantic Analysis, to automate dimension extraction through machine learning algorithms. Thirdly, the sample consisted solely of positive reviews; future studies could include both positive and negative reviews to compare different indicators. Lastly, while this study utilized unsupervised text mining techniques, further research could explore predictive methods to assess how reviews influence hotel sales performance.

REFERENCES

Ahmad, S. Z., Ahmad, N., & Papastathopoulos, A. (2019). Measuring service quality and customer satisfaction of the small-and medium-sized hotels (SMSHs) industry: Lessons from United Arab Emirates (UAE). *Tourism Review*, *74*(3), 349–370. DOI: 10.1108/TR-10-2017-0160

Al-Kumaim, N. H., Hameed, A. S., & Ahmed, A. I. (2023). Impact of Service Quality on Customer Satisfaction and Loyalty: Evidence from the Hotel Industry in Yemen. *Journal of Hospitality and Tourism Management*, *58*, 20–30.

Atilgan, E., Akinci, S., & Aksoy, S. (2003). Mapping Service Quality in the Tourism Industry. *Managing Service Quality*, *13*(5), 412–422. DOI: 10.1108/09604520310495877

Bambauer-Sachse, S., & Mangold, S. (2011). Customer Satisfaction and Loyalty: A Meta-Analytic Review of the Literature. *The Journal of Consumer Research*, *37*(4), 741–761.

Berezina, K., Cobanoglu, C., Miller, J., & Kwansa, F. (2012). The Impact of Service Quality on Customer Satisfaction and Loyalty in the Hotel Industry: Evidence from the US. *Journal of Hospitality Marketing & Management*, *21*(2), 168–185.

Berry, L. L., Parasuraman, A., & Zeithaml, V. A. (1989). The Service Quality Puzzle. *Business Horizons*, *32*(5), 35–43. DOI: 10.1016/0007-6813(88)90053-5

Bitner, M. J. (1992). Servicescapes: The Impact of Physical Surroundings on Customers and Employees. *Journal of Marketing*, *56*(2), 57–71. DOI: 10.1177/002224299205600205

Bitner, M. J., Booms, B. H., & Mohr, L. A. (1994). Critical Service Encounters: The Employee's Viewpoint. *Journal of Marketing*, *58*(4), 95–106. DOI: 10.1177/002224299405800408

Boulding, W., Kalra, A., Staelin, R., & Zeithaml, V. A. (2005). A dynamic process model of service quality: From expectations to behavioral intentions. *JMR, Journal of Marketing Research*, *42*(1), 7–17. DOI: 10.1177/002224379303000102

Bowen, J. T., & Shoemaker, S. (1998). Comparative Analysis of Customer Satisfaction and Loyalty: A Study of the Hotel Industry. *International Journal of Hospitality Management*, *17*(1), 47–60.

Carbone, L. P., & Haeckel, S. H. (1994). Engineering Customer Experiences. *Marketing Management*, *3*(3), 8–19.

Chen, C. F. (2008). Investigating the Relationships among Service Quality, Perceived Value, Satisfaction, and Loyalty: An Empirical Study of the Taiwan High-Speed Rail. *Journal of Transportation Management*, *19*(1), 70–86.

Choo, P. W., Tan, C. L., & Yeo, S. F. (2018). A review of customer experience quality measurement in Malaysian heritage hotels. *Global Business and Management Research*, *10*(1), 379–395.

Cleave, P. (2020). The Role of Customer Experience in Enhancing Brand Loyalty: Insights from the Digital Age. *Journal of Business Research*, *113*, 227–237.

Cranage, D. A., & Mattila, A. S. (2005). The Role of Service Quality in the Relationship Between Satisfaction and Loyalty: Evidence from the Hotel Industry. *International Journal of Hospitality Management*, *24*(3), 405–421.

Cronin, J. J.Jr, & Taylor, S. A. (1994). * SERVPERF versus SERVQUAL: Reconciling Performance-Based and Perceptions-Minus-Expectations Measurement of Service Quality*. *Journal of Marketing*, *58*(1), 125–131. DOI: 10.1177/002224299405800110

Edvardsson, B. (1997). Quality in New Services and New Service Development: Key Concepts and a Frame of Reference. *International Journal of Service Industry Management*, *8*(1), 12–37.

Edvardsson, B. (1996). Service Quality in Postmodern Society. In Service Quality: A Multi-Disciplinary and Multi-National Perspective (pp. 27-45). International Service Quality Association.

Ekinci, Y., Dawes, P. L., & Massey, G. R. (2008). Consumer Perceptions of Service Quality in the Hospitality Industry: A Review of the Literature. *Journal of Hospitality & Tourism Research (Washington, D.C.)*, *32*(3), 327–351.

Flint, D. J., Woodruff, R. B., & Gardial, S. F. (1997). Customer Value Change in Industrial Marketing Relationships: A Call for New Strategies. *Journal of Marketing*, *61*(4), 1–19.

Gefen, D. (2002). Reflections on the Dimensions of Trust and Their Influence on Electronic Commerce. *The Data Base for Advances in Information Systems*, *33*(2), 38–49. DOI: 10.1145/569905.569910

Getty, J. M., & Getty, R. L. (2003). The Relationship between Service Quality, Customer Satisfaction, and Behavior Intentions in the Hotel Industry. *Journal of Hospitality & Tourism Research (Washington, D.C.)*, *27*(3), 292–312.

Ghobadian, A., Speller, S., & Jones, M. (1994, December 01). 1994. Service quality: Concepts and models. *International Journal of Quality & Reliability Management*, *11*(9), 43–66. DOI: 10.1108/02656719410074297

Goolaup, S., & Mossberg, L. (2017). The Role of Service Quality and Customer Satisfaction in the Tourism Industry. *Tourism Management Perspectives*, *24*, 105–115.

Gupta, S., & Chen, L. (1995). The Dynamics of Service Quality in the Restaurant Industry. *Journal of Hospitality & Tourism Research (Washington, D.C.)*, *19*(4), 113–126.

Han, H., & Back, K. J. (2007). The Role of Service Quality in the Relationship Between Satisfaction and Loyalty in the Hotel Industry. *Journal of Hospitality & Tourism Research (Washington, D.C.)*, *31*(2), 221–239.

Harrison-Walker, L. J. (2001). The Measurement of Service Quality: A Review and Critique. *Journal of Service Research*, *3*(2), 168–180.

Hasenfeld, Y. (1974). The Social Worker's Role in Providing Services to the Poor. In The Organizational Context of Human Services (pp. 105-124). Routledge. (n.d.).

Hendijani, R. (2016). Impact of Service Quality on Customer Satisfaction and Loyalty in the Hospitality Industry. *International Journal of Hospitality Management*, *53*, 108–117.

Hernández, B., Jiménez, J., & Martín, J. (2018). The Role of Service Quality and Satisfaction on Customer Loyalty: An Empirical Study in the Tourism Sector. *Journal of Hospitality and Tourism Management*, *34*, 88–97.

Herr, P. M., Kardes, F. R., & Kim, J. (1991). Effects of Word-of-Mouth and Product-Attribute Information on Persuasion: An Accessibility-Diagnosticity Perspective. *The Journal of Consumer Research*, *17*(4), 454–462. DOI: 10.1086/208570

Heskett, J. L., Sasser, W. E., & Schlesinger, L. A. (n.d.). *(1997). The Service Profit Chain: How Leading Companies Link Profit and Growth to Loyalty, Satisfaction, and Value*. Free Press.

Hindley, L., & Wall, G. (2018). A Review of Service Quality in the Tourism and Hospitality Industry: The Role of Employee Engagement. *International Journal of Hospitality Management*, *71*, 76–85.

Hoffman, K. D., & Bateson, J. E. G. (n.d.). *(2010). Services Marketing: Concepts, Strategies, & Cases* (4th ed.). Cengage Learning.

Ji, Y., Kwortnik, R. J., & Thompson, G. M. (2016). Service Experience Management: A Review and Research Agenda. *Journal of Service Research, 18*(3), 258–276.

Klaus, P., & Maklan, S. (2013). EXQ: A multiple-item scale for assessing service experience. *Journal of Service Research, 15*(1), 61–82. DOI: 10.1177/1094670512453606

Kwortnik, R. J., & Thompson, G. M. (2009). Unifying Service Marketing and Operations Management: Midrange Theory. *Journal of Service Research, 11*(4), 389–406. DOI: 10.1177/1094670509333595

Lemon, K. N., & Verhoef, P. C. (2016). Understanding customer experience throughout the customer journey. *Journal of Marketing, 80*(6), 69–96. DOI: 10.1509/jm.15.0420

Malik, S. A., Akhtar, F., Raziq, M. M., & Ahmad, M. (2020). Measuring service quality perceptions of customers in the hotel industry of Pakistan. *Total Quality Management & Business Excellence, 31*(3-4), 263–278. DOI: 10.1080/14783363.2018.1426451

Mattila, A. S., & Mount, D. J. (2003). The Impact of Quality on Customer Satisfaction and Loyalty in the Hotel Industry. *Journal of Hospitality & Tourism Research (Washington, D.C.), 27*(2), 117–129.

Min, H., & Min, H. (1996). Examining the Service Quality and Satisfaction of Hotels: A Comparison between the USA and Korea. *International Journal of Hospitality Management, 15*(2), 177–189.

Mmutle, T., & Shonhe, L. (2017). Service Quality and Customer Satisfaction in the Retail Sector: Evidence from South Africa. *Journal of Contemporary Management, 14*(1), 1–15.

Mouzaek, E. L. E. N. A., Al Marzouqi, A. M. I. N. A., Alaali, N. A. D. E. R., Salloum, S. A., Aburayya, A. H. M. A. D., & Suson, R. O. B. E. R. T. O. (2021). An empirical investigation of the impact of service quality dimensions on guests satisfaction: A case study of Dubai hotels. *Journal of Contemporary Issues in Business and Government, 27*(3), 1187–1199.

Nilsson, L., Johnson, M. D., & Gustafsson, A. (2001). The Importance of Service Quality for Customer Satisfaction and Loyalty in the Hotel Industry. *Journal of Service Research, 3*(1), 69–81.

Okumus, F., Altintas, M., & Cottam, C. (2018). Service Quality and Customer Satisfaction in the Hospitality Industry: A Study of International Tourist Hotels. *International Journal of Hospitality Management, 76*, 181–191.

Oliver, R. L. (1999). Whence Consumer Loyalty? *Journal of Marketing, 63*(Special Issue), 33–44. DOI: 10.1177/00222429990634s105

Olorunsola, I. O., Alabi, A. O., & Ogunnaike, O. O. (2022). Examining the Impact of Service Quality on Customer Satisfaction and Loyalty in the Nigerian Hospitality Sector. *Journal of Hospitality and Tourism Management, 51*, 1–10.

Parasuraman, A., Zeithaml, V. A., & Berry, L. L. (1985). A Conceptual Model of Service Quality and Its Implications for Future Research. *Journal of Marketing, 49*(4), 41–50. DOI: 10.1177/002224298504900403

Parasuraman, A., Zeithaml, V. A., & Berry, L. L. (1988). SERVQUAL: A Multiple-Item Scale for Measuring Consumer Perceptions of Service Quality. *Journal of Retailing, 64*(1), 12–40.

Parasuraman, A., Zeithaml, V. A., & Berry, L. L. (1994). Reassessment of Expectations as a Comparison Standard in Measuring Service Quality: Implications for Further Research. *Journal of Marketing, 58*(1), 111–124. DOI: 10.1177/002224299405800109

Peter, J. P., & Olson, J. C. (n.d.). *(1996). Consumer Behavior and Marketing Action* (5th ed.). Irwin.

Pine, B. J., & Gilmore, J. H. (1998). Welcome to the experience economy. *Harvard Business Review*, *76*(4), 97–105. PMID: 10181589

Pizam, A., & Ellis, T. (1999). Customer Satisfaction and Its Measurement in Hospitality Enterprises. *International Journal of Hospitality Management*, *18*(3), 295–310.

Prentice, C. (2013). Customer Satisfaction and Loyalty in the Hotel Industry: A Review and Future Research Agenda. *International Journal of Hospitality Management*, *34*(1), 49–57.

Preziosi, R., Alvesson, M., & Dineen, B. R. (2022). The Role of Service Quality in Enhancing Customer Experience and Loyalty: Evidence from the Retail Sector. *Journal of Retailing and Consumer Services*, *66*, 102797.

Ramanathan, R., & Ramanathan, U. (2011). The Impact of Service Quality on Customer Satisfaction in the Hotel Industry. *International Journal of Hospitality Management*, *30*(1), 78–87.

Reichheld, F. F., & Schefter, P. (2000). E-Loyalty: Your Secret Weapon on the Web. *Harvard Business Review*, *78*(4), 105–113.

Ren, L., Qiu, H., Wang, P., & Lin, P. M. (2016). Exploring customer experience with budget hotels: Dimensionality and satisfaction. *International Journal of Hospitality Management*, *52*, 13–23. DOI: 10.1016/j.ijhm.2015.09.009

Robertson, J., Vella, J., Duncan, S., Pitt, C., Pitt, L., & Caruana, A. (2024). Enhancing Customer Experience Through Service Quality: Evidence from the Retail Sector. *Journal of Retailing and Consumer Services*, **•••**, 77.

Roest, H., & Pieters, R. (1997). The Conceptualization and Measurement of Service Quality: A Review of the Literature. *Journal of Service Research*, *1*(1), 26–41.

Ryu, K., Han, H., & Kim, D. (2008). The Relationships among Overall Perceived Quality, Overall Satisfaction, and Behavioral Intentions in the Fast-Casual Restaurant Industry. *International Journal of Hospitality Management*, *27*(3), 459–469. DOI: 10.1016/j.ijhm.2007.11.001

Shi, Y., & Su, J. (2007). Service Quality, Customer Satisfaction, and Customer Loyalty in the Hotel Industry: A Study of Three-Star Hotels in China. *International Journal of Hospitality Management*, *26*(4), 814–826.

Shoemaker, S., & Lewis, R. C. (1999). Customer Loyalty: The Future of Hospitality Marketing. *International Journal of Hospitality Management*, *18*(4), 345–370. DOI: 10.1016/S0278-4319(99)00042-0

Sparks, B., & Browning, V. (2010). Complaining about Complaints: The Effects of Negative Online Reviews on Hotel Performance. *International Journal of Hospitality Management*, *29*(4), 263–274.

Stone, M., Woodcock, N., & Wilson, H. (2022). Service Quality and Customer Satisfaction in the Age of Digital Transformation: Insights from the Financial Services Industry. *Journal of Service Research*, *24*(3), 394–409.

Sundaram, D. S., Mitra, K., & Webster, C. (1998). Word-of-Mouth Communications: A Motivational Analysis. *The Journal of Consumer Research*, *24*(4), 434–449.

Taylor, S. A., & Cronin, J. J. (1994). Service Quality and Customer Satisfaction: Lessons from Leisure Services. *Journal of Business Research*, *31*(1), 91–104.

Tefera, M. A., & Govender, K. (2017). The Impact of Service Quality on Customer Satisfaction and Loyalty in the Retail Sector: A Study of Supermarkets in South Africa. *African Journal of Business Management*, *11*(15), 377–386.

Thomas, D. R. E. (n.d.). (1978). The Role of the Service Encounter in Service Quality. In *Contemporary Marketing Thought* (pp. 185–191). Institute of Marketing.

Tsang, N. K. F., & Qu, H. (2000). Service Quality in the Hospitality Industry: A Review of the Literature. *Journal of Hospitality & Tourism Research (Washington, D.C.)*, *24*(2), 165–181.

Tyrrell, T. J., & Woods, R. H. (2005). The Impact of Service Quality on Customer Satisfaction in the Hospitality Industry. *International Journal of Hospitality Management*, *24*(4), 517–528.

Wilkins, H. C., Merrilees, B., & Herington, C. (2007). Examining the Relationship between Service Quality and Customer Satisfaction in the Hotel Industry. *Journal of Hospitality & Tourism Research (Washington, D.C.)*, *31*(3), 363–378.

Ye, Q., Law, R., & Gu, B. (2009). The Impact of Online Reviews on Hotel Room Sales. *International Journal of Hospitality Management*, *28*(1), 180–182. DOI: 10.1016/j.ijhm.2008.06.011

Zeithaml, V. A. (1988). Consumer Perceptions of Price, Quality, and Value: A Means-End Model and Synthesis of Evidence. *Journal of Marketing*, *52*(3), 2–22. DOI: 10.1177/002224298805200302

Zeithaml, V. A. (2000). Service quality, profitability, and the economic worth of customers: What we know and what we need to know. *Journal of the Academy of Marketing Science*, *28*(1), 67–85. DOI: 10.1177/0092070300281007

Zeithaml, V. A., Bitner, M. J., & Gremler, D. D. (n.d.). *(2006). Services Marketing: Integrating Customer Focus Across the Firm* (4th ed.). McGraw-Hill Education.

Zeithaml, V. A., Parasuraman, A., & Berry, L. L. (n.d.). *(1990). Delivering Quality Service: Balancing Customer Perceptions and Expectations*. Free Press.

Chapter 9
Revolutionizing Industries: The Future of Generative AI and IoT Integration

Anshul Kumar
https://orcid.org/0009-0006-5864-4353
School of Computer Engineering, Kalinga Institute of Industrial Technology (KIIT), Bhubaneswar, India

Hitesh Mohapatra
https://orcid.org/0000-0001-8100-4860
School of Computer Engineering, Kalinga Institute of Industrial Technology (KIIT), Bhubaneswar, India

Soumya Ranjan Mishra
https://orcid.org/0000-0002-3960-398X
School of Computer Engineering, Kalinga Institute of Industrial Technology (KIIT), Bhubaneswar, India

ABSTRACT

The convergence of Generative AI (GenAI) and the Internet of Things (IoT) holds immense potential to revolutionize various aspects of our lives and reshape industries. This paper explores the future of this integrated technology, examining its promising applications, anticipated challenges, and potential societal impacts. This paper highlights key areas where GenAI-powered IoT can create significant value, including personalized automation, predictive maintenance, and enhanced data analysis. Additionally, it addresses concerns surrounding privacy, security, and ethical considerations of such powerful technology. By outlining the research landscape and future directions, this study aims to spark discussion and propel further exploration of this transformative technology.

1. INTRODUCTION EXPANDING THE APPLICATIONS OF AIOT

The combination of artificial intelligence and the Internet of Things offers a revolution that leads to intelligent decision-making and automation at the edge of the network. By embedding AI algorithms in IoT devices or edge computing nodes, we enable them to process local data, gain insights and respond instantly without relying on the cloud service. This intelligence not only reduces latency, but also improves privacy, security, and scalability in IoT deployments (Dey et al., 2024).

DOI: 10.4018/979-8-3693-7447-4.ch009

1.1. Expanding the Applications of AIoT

The combination of AI and IoT has ushered in a new era of intelligent system widespread use across industries. For smart cities, these technologies can improve urban planning and infrastructure management. For example, AI-powered IoT systems can monitor traffic patterns to optimize traffic light sequences and reduce congestion. Additionally, energy consumption in public buildings can be controlled, reducing operating costs and promoting sustainability. These smart cities applications can significantly improve urban living by reducing environmental footprint. In healthcare, AI and IoT are working together to revolutionize patient care and treatment processes. (Gubbi et al., 2013) Remote disease monitoring, driven by AI algorithms embedded in wearable devices, enables healthcare professionals to monitor patients' vital signs in real time This proactive approach can quickly identify health issues, to enable timely and potentially life-saving intervention. Furthermore, the application of AI-driven data analytics in healthcare could facilitate accurate diagnosis, personalized treatment planning, and distribution of best practices in medical settings.

1.2. Addressing Ethical and Privacy Concerns

While the benefits of AI-integrated IoT are significant, ethical considerations need to be addressed to ensure responsible use. The storage and analysis of large amounts of personal data raises privacy concerns and requires stronger measures to protect user data. An ethical framework should guide the design and implementation of AIoT systems, emphasizing transparency, accountability and user consent (Lyu et al., 2025). Legislation should be enacted to enforce these principles, and organizations should implement best practices to ensure compliance. Addressing these issues enables IoT systems integrated with AI to be implemented in a way that prioritizes the safety of users and violates individual privacy.

1.3. Enhancing Security in AIoT Systems

Security is a key concern in AI-integrated IoT environments. Interconnected IoT devices create potential vulnerabilities that can be exploited by cybercriminals. Beyond implementing strong encryption protocols to secure AIoT systems, regular software development to fix security flaws, and regular security audits, the benefits of AI can be delivered implementation of IoT has been used to identify and respond to security threats in real time (Mohanta et al., 2025). Machine learning algorithms can analyse network traffic to detect anomalous behaviour, enabling faster responses to potential attacks. By engaging security risks, organizations can build robust AI-integrated IoT systems that stand up to cyber threats.

1.4. Exploring AI-Driven IoT in Industrial Automation

Industrial automation represents another area where AI-integrated IoT is having a significant impact. AI algorithms embedded in IoT devices can optimize manufacturing processes by recommending device failures and recommending maintenance actions before they fail This predictive maintenance method is time-consuming down, reduces maintenance costs, and increases overall productivity. Furthermore, AI-powered IoT systems can perform better controls by analyzing data from sensors to detect flaws in real time. This capability produces higher quality products and reduces waste, contributing to a more sustainable production process (Mohapatra, 2021).

1.5. Advancing AI-Integrated IoT for a Sustainable Future

As we look to the future, AI and IoT play an increasingly important role in sustainable development. AI-powered IoT systems can help organizations reduce their carbon footprint by reducing energy efficiency and waste. For example, in precision agriculture, AI algorithms can analyse data from IoT sensors to optimize irrigation and fertilizer use, producing higher yields with fewer inputs and also monitors energy consumption to reduce unnecessary use of AIoT systems in smart buildings. By developing these technologies, we can contribute to a more sustainable future, solve environmental challenges and improve efficiency and productivity across sectors (Mohapatra, 2024). Additionally, AI-powered IoT systems support predictive analytics, allowing organizations to predict future events, optimize resources, and resolve problems in advance. Integration of these technologies in the context of smart cities, healthcare, precision agriculture or industrial automation has great potential to improve business, productivity and quality of life. In this article, we examine the convergence of artificial intelligence and the Internet of Things in more depth, exploring the methods, applications and impacts of their integration. We analyse the current state-of-the-art, identify challenges and research gaps, and offer innovative solutions to support the potential of the AI-integrated IoT ecosystem.

Personalized automation: GenAI can personalize the operation of smart homes, appliances, and wearables, tailoring experiences to individual preferences and needs (Mohapatra & Mishra, 2024).
Predictive maintenance: By analyzing data from IoT sensors, GenAI can anticipate equipment failures and recommend proactive maintenance interventions, minimizing downtime and optimizing resource utilization.
Enhanced data analysis: GenAI can process massive datasets generated by IoT devices, extracting valuable insights and generating accurate predictions, leading to data-driven decision-making.

However, alongside these advancements lie potential challenges that need careful consideration. Privacy concerns surrounding data collection and usage by GenAI-powered IoT systems require robust regulations and ethical frameworks. Additionally, security vulnerabilities arising from the interconnected nature of AIoT systems necessitates vigilant measures to protect against cyberattacks. Therefore, exploring the future of GenAI-integrated IoT demands a balanced approach, acknowledging both its immense potential and associated challenges. This paper aims to contribute to this crucial discourse by:

- Identifying research gaps in the current understanding of GenAI-powered IoT.
- Providing a comprehensive literature review on the subject, highlighting key findings and research directions.
- Discussing ethical considerations and potential societal impacts of this technology.
- By providing a critical analysis and outlining future directions, this paper seeks to stimulate further research and development in this promising field, ensuring that GenAI and IoT are harnessed for the benefit of all.

2. RESEARCH GAP AND LITERATURE REVIEW

The fascination with GenAI-integrated IoT is on the rise, but there are still many gaps in research that need attention. Firstly, there is a lack of real-world studies showcasing how effective and impactful GenAI-powered IoT applications are across different fields. While theories and frameworks abound, the scarcity of empirical evidence hinders a full grasp of the technology's practical implications. Additionally, most studies focus heavily on enhancing AI algorithms and data analysis techniques while overlooking crucial social, ethical, and economic aspects. This imbalance highlights the necessity for a more holistic approach that combines technical progress with broader societal considerations. Despite advancements in integrating GenAI with IoT systems, significant challenges persist in delivering smooth user experiences, promoting human-AI interaction, and ensuring compatibility among various platforms. Emphasizing technical aspects often overshadows addressing user preferences and needs which are vital for widespread acceptance of GenAI-driven IoT solutions (Mohapatra & Mishra, 2024). Moreover, there is a notable absence of comprehensive studies addressing security vulnerabilities and safety risks linked to GenAI-powered IoT applications in critical sectors like healthcare and infrastructure. The increasing complexity of interconnected systems amplifies these concerns, calling for robust security measures and risk management strategies. Furthermore, existing ethical frameworks for AI need further exploration when applied to scenarios involving GenAI-driven IoT to navigate ethical dilemmas effectively. Crafting ethical guidelines tailored to address the unique challenges posed by integrating GenAI into IoT systems is crucial for ensuring responsible and ethical deployment of these technologies.

2.1. Closing the Research Gap in the Real World

The lack of comprehensive real-world research is one of the most important gaps in research on GenAI-integrated IoT. More field trials and pilot projects are needed to address this gap. Such research can provide tangible evidence of the effectiveness and practical benefits of the technology, allowing researchers to validate and refine theoretical frameworks based on real-world feedback Longer studies on in areas such as smart cities, healthcare systems, and industrial settings (Mohapatra et al., 2025).

2.2. User-Cantered Design and Interactive Roles

Another important area of focus is the design of user-centric GenAI-integrated IoT systems. The current focus on technology development has neglected the user experience, which is critical to the adoption and success of this technology. Research should examine how users interact with GenAI-powered IoT applications and identify pain points or usability issues. This insight can lead to more interaction, seamless integration, and personalized experiences, ensuring that users feel comfortable and engaged with these systems Through people and with an emphasis on AI connectivity, researchers can enhance user experience and GenAI-powered -Drive greater IoT adoption solutions.

2.3. Enhancing Safety Management and Risk Management

The complexity of GenAI-powered IoT systems presents significant security risks that require detailed analysis and strong mitigation strategies. Current research tends to overlook the unique security vulnerabilities associated with these connected technologies. Researchers should focus on identifying potential threats and develop comprehensive security measures that address the risks at each stage of the IoT ecosystem. It has implemented advanced encryption techniques, anomaly detection systems and multi-layered security protocols (Mohapatra & Rath, 2019). Additionally, risk management systems need to be put in place to rapidly respond to emerging threats and mitigate the impact of cyberattacks.

2.4. Development of Ethical Guidelines for GenAI-Integrated IoT

Integrating GenAI and IoT presents unique ethical challenges that require further research. Current ethical frameworks for AI do not adequately address specific issues arising from the use of GenAI in IoT contexts, such as privacy concerns, data ownership, and informed consent and researchers should work to develop standardized ethical guidelines for potential social impacts of GenAI integrated with IoT. This requires involving stakeholders, including engineers, policy makers, and users, to ensure that GenAI and IoT are used responsibly through ethics establishing clear boundaries to ensure that ethical principles are incorporated into the design and implementation of this technology (Pathak et al., 2021).

2.5. Analyzing the Social Impact of GenAI-Powered IoT

Finally, the broader impact of the societal impact of GenAI-enabled IoT systems needs to be thoroughly examined. While this technology brings significant benefits, it also has the potential to disrupt traditional industries, transform business models, and affect the mobility of life. Research should focus on understanding these effects and developing strategies to address potential adverse effects. This could include examining how IoT combined with GenAI impacts productivity in manufacturing and logistics, and the broader implications for community and economic analysis If these social aspects are required in 2010, can provide researchers with insights into how GenAI and IoT can be used to promote positive social change and reduce disparities (Peng et al., 2021).

2.6. Existing Work

The realm of GenAI-integrated IoT is rich with diverse themes, reflecting the myriad applications and impacts of this technology. Smart environments are a focal point, exploring how GenAI can personalize automation in homes, offices, and cities. The aim is to boost energy efficiency, enhance comfort levels, and elevate overall user convenience. For example, (Sah et al., 2024) delve into using GenAI systems to optimize energy usage and customize environmental settings based on individual preferences within smart buildings and homes. The rise of GenAI-integrated IoT has changed the concept of intelligent environments, transforming homes, offices and even entire cities. By incorporating GenAI, intelligent systems can automate to specific user needs and preferences, increasing comfort and productivity. In smart homes, GenAI can manage everything from lighting and thermal protection systems, providing a seamless and personalized experience. This design process not only facilitates users but also helps to save energy by optimizing resources according to activity schedule. In healthcare, research delves into harnessing GenAI for analyzing medical data, predicting diseases, and tailoring personalized care plans. (Swain et al., 2025) explore the potential of GenAI algorithms in analyzing complex medical datasets for early disease detection and crafting personalized treatment strategies that cater to individual patient needs. Likewise, in manufacturing settings, studies investigate how GenAI can be utilized for predictive maintenance, process optimization, and reducing downtime. (Van den Hoven, 2014) discuss how GenAI-powered predictive maintenance systems can bolster equipment reliability, minimize production disruptions, and optimize manufacturing processes to drive efficiency gains and cost savings.

Industry sector has also adopted GenAI-integrated IoT to improve efficiency and reduce costs. GenAI's ability to process large amounts of data in real-time enables predictive maintenance, where device failures can be anticipated and addressed before they cause catastrophic disruption This approach to proactive maintenance this reduces downtime and extends machine life. In addition to maintenance, GenAI can improve product quality by analyzing production data to identify inefficiencies and suggest improvements. This improves efficiency, reduces waste and increases productivity, benefiting both manufacturers and customers. One of the most important benefits of GenAI-integrated IoT is the capability of advanced data analytics. IoT devices produce a lot of data, and GenAI is able to process this information to extract usable insights. This capability is invaluable across industries, allowing organizations to make data-driven decisions with greater confidence. GenAI can detect trends, identify anomalies, and predict future outcomes, providing a solid foundation for strategic planning. This power management has applications in many areas, from smart cities optimizing transportation to energy companies forecasting demand and adjusting supply accordingly.

As the adoption of GenAI-integrated IoT systems increases, so do the associated security and privacy challenges. Connected IoT devices present unique vulnerabilities that require strong security measures. GenAI can be used to identify and address security threats in real time, but the need for robust encryption protocols and regular security audits is paramount Privacy concerns are also important, because these systems often store sensitive personal data. Ensuring privacy requires strong privacy protection technologies and regulations to prevent unauthorized access or data breaches. The combination of GenAI and IoT raises many ethical questions, especially around data ownership, algorithmic biases, and transparent decision-making processes. As these technologies become more embedded in everyday life, the establishment of an ethical framework is critical to ensure that appropriate improvements are made and implemented. Ethical guidelines should address issues such as user consent, data rights, and the impact of AI-driven decisions on individuals and society. By fostering a culture of ethical responsibility, developers and stakeholders can develop AI-powered IoT solutions that serve the common good while respecting individual rights and freedoms various types (Venkataramanan et al., 2023). With the rapid pace of innovation in GenAI-integrated IoT, comprehensive regulation is needed to meet the emerging challenges. These regulations should cover issues ranging from ensuring interoperability of systems to protecting against cybersecurity threats Regulatory frameworks should also consider the broader societal impact of AI-powered IoT of the project, including changes in business and social mobility and ensure that the Benefits of the technology are distributed equitably and its risks are effectively managed.

The literature also delves into technical aspects surrounding GenAI-integrated IoT systems with a focus on data analysis capabilities. Researchers are working towards developing AI algorithms that can effectively analyse large-scale IoT data streams to extract actionable insights, identify patterns, and offer data-driven predictions to support decision-making processes. (Wei et al., 2022) contribute by exploring innovative approaches for data analysis in IoT environments using GenAI techniques to unearth valuable insights from diverse data sources. Security and privacy considerations take centre stage in the development of GenAI-integrated IoT systems where efforts are made to address security vulnerabilities present in connected devices while creating privacy-preserving mechanisms to safeguard sensitive collected IoT system data from unauthorized access or breaches (Yaseliani et al., 2024). They delve into developing robust security protocols along with privacy-enhancing technologies aimed at mitigating risks associated with unauthorized access or breaches due to weaknesses inherent within the devices themselves or their networks. Additionally, the literature highlights various challenges associated with the deployment of AI-powered IoT solutions including ethical dilemmas about ownership rights over collected information as well as algorithmic biases affecting decision-making processes' transparency; (Zhang et al., 2023) scholars suggest establishing ethical guidelines frameworks ensuring responsible development deployment practices, Char, D., (Zhang et al., 2024) shine light on comprehensive regulations policies addressing emergent challenges safeguarding societal interests an increasingly interconnected yet data-driven world.

3. PROPOSED STUDY

The true potential of AI Integrated IoT is fully realized through the intricate integration of diverse components and processes. To maximize the effectiveness of integrating Gen AI with IoT systems, three key methods are recommended. At the core of Gen AI Integrated IoT systems lies the crucial phase of data collection and preprocessing. This initial stage involves deploying sensor networks composed of embedded IoT devices equipped with various sensors to gather data on factors such as temperature, pressure, and humidity. However, raw sensor data often contains noise or discrepancies, necessitating the application of data filtering and aggregation techniques to eliminate outliers and ensure the acquisition of high-quality data. Moreover, robust measures for data security and privacy are essential to protect sensitive information transmitted by IoT devices, ensuring secure data transmission processes and implementing control mechanisms to prevent unauthorized access.

Following this, the AI processing and analysis layer play a pivotal role in deriving actionable insights from the gathered data. This phase utilizes machine learning (ML) algorithms for tasks such as error detection, tracking, and classification to analyse the data effectively and reveal significant patterns or anomalies. In cases involving intricate data models, deep learning models like artificial neural networks are employed to facilitate advanced data analysis capabilities and decision-making processes. Additionally, leveraging edge computing allows for distributing processing capabilities to the network's "edge," close to where the data is collected. This setup enables immediate analysis and quicker decision-making while reducing latency. Finally, in the process and details phase entail executing actions based on insights obtained from AI analysis. This stage involves actuator control mechanisms that enable automatic adjustments or responses through actuators (e.g., valves, motors) linked to IoT devices. Furthermore, user interfaces along with feedback systems play critical roles by providing users with platforms to monitor system performance, receive alerts, or potentially fine-tune AI models according to specific needs or preferences. Notably incorporated into these systems are continuous learning mechanisms that allow for feedback from user interactions as well as performance metrics to be integrated back into cognitive processes. This iterative approach facilitates ongoing enhancements in decision-making capabilities within the AI model over time.

GenAI-integrated IoT success relies heavily on complex sensor networks to collect multiple types of data. In addition to specific sensors measuring temperature, pressure, and humidity, modern IoT systems integrate other sensors to capture sound, light, movement, and even biometric data This diversity of data sources provides environmental awareness around it, enabling AI algorithms to make more accurate models and predictions. However, with increased data collection comes the challenge of managing large amounts of sensor data to ensure data quality and accuracy. This challenge highlights the need for effective filtering and aggregation techniques to extract meaningful information from potentially noisy data sets. Data security and privacy are paramount in GenAI-integrated IoT systems, especially when sensitive information is transmitted over networks. In order to maintain secure data transfers, organizations must implement strong encryption protocols to protect data in transit and at rest. Multifactor authentication and role-based access further enhance security by restricting access to only authorized users. Privacy considerations are equally important, as IoT devices can store personal and confidential information. Complying with privacy laws and applying principles that apply to any design ensures that user data is handled responsibly and protected from unauthorized access on or in violation of.

Table 1. Advantages of proposed solution

Layered Architecture	Modular design facilitates scalability and customization for diverse applications.
Edge Computing	Enables real-time processing for latency-critical applications.
Machine Learning and Deep Learning	Provides powerful data analysis for accurate insights and predictions.
Secure Data Management	Protects sensitive information collected by IoT devices.
User Feedback Loop	Allows for continuous improvement of AI models and system performance.

Once the data is collected and pre-processed, the implementation and analysis layer of the AI plays an important role. In this phase, machine learning algorithms can be used to analyse the data and gain insights. Supervised learning models can be used for tasks such as classification and regression, while unsupervised learning helps to identify patterns and clusters in data and in some cases, reinforcement learning can be used to improve specific methods through feedback. Deep learning provides powerful capabilities for processing complex data structures and extracting high-quality features, including artificial neural networks. Flexible AI algorithms allow for tailored strategies tailored to the needs of specific industries, from healthcare to manufacturing. Edge computing plays a key role in the AI processing and analytics phase by distributing computational tasks to the data collection point At the edge, with IoT devices, data processing significantly reduces latency, enabling analytics and decision making in real time. These systems are particularly valuable in applications where immediate feedback is required, such as industrial automation or health monitoring. Edge computing also reduces reliance on centralized cloud services, providing greater flexibility and potentially reduced operating costs. The distributed nature of edge computing perfectly matches the needs of GenAI-integrated IoT systems, providing a scalable and flexible infrastructure

The final stage of GenAI-integrated IoT involves actions based on insights gained from AI research. This phase relies on actuator control mechanisms to implement automatic responses or changes in real time. In the industrial sector, for example, actuators can control machine operation, valves, or robotic arms based on AI-generated instructions. In smart homes, actuators can change lighting, heating or security settings according to user preference or familiarity. Combining actuator control with AI-processing creates a seamless loop where insights are translated into tangible results, enabling automation and improving system efficiency. The final stage of GenAI-integrated IoT involves actions based on insights gained from AI research. This phase relies on actuator control mechanisms to implement automatic responses or changes in real time. In the industrial sector, for example, actuators can control mechanical operation, valves, or robotic arms based on AI-generated instructions (Lyu et al., 2025). In smart homes, actuators can change lighting, heating or security settings according to user preference or familiarity. Combining actuator control with AI-processing creates a seamless loop in which insights are translated into tangible results, enabling automation and improving system efficiency. User interfaces and feedback mechanisms play an important role in enabling users to see and control system operations in GenAI-integrated IoT These interfaces also empower users monitor system performance, receive alerts, modify settings or provide feedback and interact with AI models. User interfaces in smart homes can be smartphone applications that allow you to control devices remotely, while in industrial systems dashboards display real-time data and system status Feedback systems collect user input and system performance metrics to provide continuous improvement is simple, which can be further fed into AI models for continuous modification and improvement.

Continuous learning processes are a key feature of GenAI-integrated IoT, allowing AI models to evolve and improve over time. By incorporating feedback from user interactions and performance metrics, these systems can adapt to changing environments and user preferences. This iterative learning process ensures that AI models remain relevant and effective as the system evolves. On a practical level, continuous learning can lead to increased accuracy of predictions, better automation, and more personalized experiences for users (Mohapatra & Mishra, 2024). The ability to modify and learn from real-world data is a unique feature of GenAI-integrated IoT, which sets it apart from more static systems. The integration of GenAI into the IoT presents significant ethical and legal challenges that need to be addressed to ensure responsible implementation. Ethical considerations include data confidentiality, informed consent, and algorithmic bias, all of which require adequate oversight to prevent adverse social effects. A regulatory framework should be developed to govern the use of GenAI in an IoT environment, ensuring compliance with data protection laws and industry standards. This effort involves collaboration between engineers, policymakers, and stakeholders to provide guidelines that promote ethical practices and encourage innovation. By addressing these challenges, the potential of IoT hybridized with GenAI can be realized in a way that benefits society as a whole.

Interconnectivity and standardization are essential to maximize the effectiveness of the GenAI-integrated IoT. As the IoT ecosystem evolves, devices and platforms must communicate seamlessly to avoid compatibility issues. Standardization helps ensure that disparate devices and systems can work together, reducing complex integrations and creating a more unified IoT environment Standard protocols and frameworks allow for consistent communication between devices, and reduces the risk of data silos, misinterpretation of data. and enable provisioning. Interconnectivity also encourages innovation, as developers can build solutions on top of existing infrastructure without worrying about compatibility issues (Van den Hoven, 2014). This approach can lead to a flexible and sustainable IoT ecosystem, where additional devices and platforms can be easily integrated. Focusing on standards in areas such as data management, networking, and security can further enhance the reliability and security of IoT systems. These initiatives can also streamline regulatory compliance, making it easier for companies to adopt IoT technologies that comply with regulatory requirements. By encouraging interoperability and standardization, the IoT industry can create a robust, robust, and future-proof ecosystem that supports the development of GenAI applications and other advanced technologies in an IoT environment. This proposed solution offers a framework for integrating AI with IoT systems, enabling real-time data analysis, intelligent decision-making, and automated control within the connected environment. The layered architecture ensures scalability and security while the feedback loop facilitates continuous learning and improvement.

4. ANALYSIS

The convergence of Generative Artificial Intelligence (GenAI) with the Internet of Things (IoT) has converted the panorama of automation, providing unheard of ranges of intelligence and autonomy in various packages. AI-powered IoT structures can technique sizable quantities of records, make knowledgeable selections, and reply in real-time. This has led to giant advancements in diverse fields, from business automation to clever houses and healthcare. The consequences of this integration show off advanced performance, accuracy, and scalability throughout a extensive variety of applications. In commercial settings, GenAI-integrated IoT has confirmed instrumental in optimizing approaches, lowering downtime, and enhancing productivity. Predictive upkeep, a key utility, leverages AI algorithms to research sensor data, taking into account early detection of device disasters (Yaseliani et al., 2024). This proactive method minimizes disruptions and decreases upkeep fees. Additionally, AI-driven IoT structures can enhance product high-quality by way of detecting defects in real-time, permitting producers to hold excessive standards at the same time as reducing waste. These effects exhibit the ability for GenAI-included IoT to revolutionize business operations.

GenAI-included IoT has performed a pivotal role in the improvement of smart towns, providing answers to enhance city infrastructure and reduce environmental effect. AI-powered IoT systems can screen visitors' patterns, optimize power consumption in public buildings, and decorate public safety. These structures contribute to greener city planning and management, leading to reduced congestion and a lower carbon footprint. The application of GenAI in clever towns has the capability to beautify quality of life for citizens whilst promoting sustainability. In the healthcare region, GenAI-incorporated IoT has opened new avenues for personalised patient care and far-flung monitoring. Wearable devices ready with AI algorithms can song critical signs and symptoms and come across anomalies, enabling healthcare specialists to provide timely interventions. This generation allows for non-stop monitoring of sufferers, main to stepped forward outcomes and decreased health centre readmissions. Furthermore, GenAI-pushed facts analytics can assist in diagnosing illnesses and tailoring customized remedy plans, improving the general high-quality of healthcare offerings (Zhang et al., 2024).

While the advantages of GenAI-integrated IoT are huge, they arrive with moral and privateness challenges that require cautious attention. The sizable collection and evaluation of personal data increase concerns about person privacy and information security. To cope with these troubles, sturdy encryption protocols and privateness-maintaining mechanisms ought to be applied to defend sensitive information. Additionally, ethical frameworks must manual the improvement and deployment of AI-driven IoT structures to make sure transparency, responsibility, and person consent. Addressing these issues is vital for constructing public trust and ensuring the responsible use of GenAI in IoT programs. Security remains a significant issue in AI-included IoT environments, given the interconnected nature of IoT gadgets (Pathak et al., 2021). Cyber threats and vulnerabilities can pose dangers to the integrity of these structures. AI-driven IoT security answers leverage device gaining knowledge of algorithms to come across and respond to protection threats in real time. These systems can analyse community visitors to pick out anomalous behaviour, making an allowance for fast responses to ability assaults. Strong encryption protocols, everyday protection audits, and multi-layered security features are critical to guard AIoT systems and maintain person consider.

Beyond commercial automation, clever towns, and healthcare, GenAI-included IoT has ability applications in different sectors including agriculture, logistics, and strength control. In agriculture, AI-powered IoT structures can optimize irrigation and fertilizer use, contributing to sustainable farming practices. In logistics, those technologies can streamline deliver chain operations and improve efficiency. The strength zone can advantage from AI-driven IoT structures that reveal and optimize strength intake, leading to decreased charges and a decrease environmental effect. These outcomes spotlight the versatility of GenAI-integrated IoT throughout numerous industries. Despite the improvements in GenAI-included IoT, studies gaps remain, especially in real-world studies that show the generation's effectiveness across exclusive fields. More empirical evidence is wanted to validate theoretical frameworks and pick out practical challenges. Additionally, the complexity of interconnected structures needs in addition exploration of security vulnerabilities and protection dangers. Ethical concerns surrounding facts ownership and algorithmic biases require complete evaluation to make certain accountable deployment of GenAI-included IoT technologies. Addressing those gaps will assist unencumber the overall capacity of this generation (Gubbi et al., 2013).

The integration of GenAI and IoT gives tremendous advantages throughout industries, from progressed automation to superior affected person care and smarter city environments. However, demanding situations together with security vulnerabilities, privateness worries, and moral dilemmas must be addressed to make sure the technology's responsible use. By that specialize in research gaps, improving safety features, and growing robust moral frameworks, the destiny of GenAI-included IoT may be formed in a manner that promotes innovation while safeguarding societal interests. The route ahead entails a balanced method that recognizes the generation's potential even as addressing associated dangers. Communication technology is essential to ensure reliability and continuity in smart cities. However, the development of smart devices can cause problems. Therefore, the current study explores the potential of communication technology supported by the Internet of Things (IoT) and its practical applications in smart cities. Wi-Fi, ZigBee and Z-Wave are suitable for distances where devices and their space are limited, as they provide more data thanks to the technology compared to LoRaWAN. However, the choice of communication technology depends on the specific requirements of each application and the coverage area needed. ZigBee is primarily used in low-throughput, low-power applications, providing network security and longer battery life. It provides network topologies suitable for various applications such as mesh, star and tree. On the other hand, some remote technologies require devices connected through a central gateway to collect and receive data. These technologies include LoRaWAN, NB-IoT, Sigfox and LTE, which operate licensed or unlicensed depending on the application. When choosing communication technology, not only low power consumption, but also energy efficiency, network capacity, security and performance should be taken into account.

Cellular networks can become important resources for the implementation of new applications in smart cities. Narrowband Internet of Things (NB-IoT) is a technology that focuses on low-cost devices while ensuring security and reliability. It also uses existing mobile phones, which can reduce the cost of network development for new smart city applications. LoRaWAN and Sigfox are unlicensed technologies that can help overcome cost problems related to licensing technologies. Depending on the application and region, these technologies typically use ISM frequency bands including 2.4 GHz, 868 MHz, 915 MHz, and 433 MHz. Sigfox is especially useful for rare data such as smart facilities, smart agriculture and smart stores. It claims to be able to connect one million devices over a large area. The use of various smart algorithms in smart cities can increase efficiency, sustainability and quality of life. Algorithms ML, DL, NLP, CV and RL are discussed. Machine learning algorithms allow machines to recognize patterns, learn from data, and make predictions based on input.

Challenges and considerations:

- Data security and privacy are crucial when dealing with sensitive data collected from connected devices.
- The computing power required for complex AI processes can be prohibitive for IoT devices with limited resources.
- Ethical decision making should be addressed around decision-making skills and biases.

Looking into the future:

With the advancement of artificial intelligence algorithms, processing power and edge computing capability, the future of AIoT is bright. As AIoT becomes ubiquitous, we can expect further changes in many areas.

5. FUTURE SCOPE

Industries are embracing AI-integrated IoT answers to fulfil precise challenges and advantage an aggressive aspect. For example, in manufacturing, AIoT structures can facilitate actual-time monitoring and predictive protection, decreasing downtime and increasing production efficiency. Retailers are leveraging AI-integrated IoT for stock management and customized client experiences, providing tailor-made pointers based totally on purchaser conduct. In agriculture, AIoT systems can optimize useful resource usage, which includes water and fertilizers, even as making sure crop health through non-stop monitoring. These industry-unique answers reveal the adaptability and versatility of AI-incorporated IoT technology. Despite the capacity benefits of AI-included IoT, several barriers to adoption persist. High initial prices, technical complexity, and a loss of professional personnel are many of the key demanding situations. Small and medium-sized corporations (SMEs) might also find it hard to put money into AIoT technologies without clear go back on investment. Addressing these limitations calls for cantered guide, which includes government incentives, accessible schooling programs, and simplified deployment strategies. Furthermore, demonstrating tangible benefits thru pilot projects and actual-international case studies can encourage broader adoption by reducing perceived risks and uncertainties.

6. CONCLUSION

As AI-integrated IoT technology preserve to evolve, the role of regulation and governance will become increasingly critical. Policymakers should establish clean guidelines that ensure statistics protection, moral use, and system safety. Regulatory frameworks must cope with pass-border data flows, intellectual assets rights, and customer rights inside the context of AIoT. Additionally, governance systems should sell transparency and accountability in the development and deployment of AI-incorporated IoT structures. By fostering regulatory surroundings that balances innovation with societal values, stakeholders can build public accept as true with and pave the way for sustainable increase in AIoT programs. In summary, the convergence of AI and IoT represents a technological revolution that provides unprecedented opportunities for innovation, efficiency, and social impact. From healthcare and agriculture to smart cities and business automation, AI-integrated IoT systems are revolutionizing the way we collect data, analyse it, and take action on difficult problems. While significant progress has been made, much work still needs to be done to fully realize the potential of AI integrated into the Internet of Things. Addressing issues such as data privacy, security, and collaboration is important to increase trust and acceptance among users and stakeholders. There is also a need for continued research and development to ensure the widespread use, expansion and expansion of the use of artificial intelligence algorithms, IoT technologies and proprietary technologies. Looking ahead, collaboration and community between researchers, industry leaders, and policymakers will be critical to enable new and feasibility based on social needs and enable the deployment of AI-integrated IoT systems. By harnessing the power of AI and the Internet of Things together, we can create a smarter, more connected world that benefits individuals, organizations and society.

REFERENCES

Dey, D., Majumder, A., Agrawal, Y., Tewari, S., & Mohapatra, H. (2024). Smart mobility revolution. *Advances in Electronic Government, Digital Divide, and Regional Development*, •••, 143–164. DOI: 10.4018/979-8-3693-6740-7.ch006

Gubbi, J., Buyya, R., Marusic, S., & Palaniswami, M. (2013). Internet of things (IoT): A vision, architectural elements, and future directions. *Future Generation Computer Systems*, *29*(7), 1645–1660. DOI: 10.1016/j.future.2013.01.010

Lyu, Z., Park, J. J., Shen, J., Song, H., & Zhang, Y. (2025). Guest editorial: Generative artificial intelligence at the edge in the modern Internet of things. *IEEE Internet of Things Magazine*, *8*(1), 10–11. DOI: 10.1109/MIOT.2025.10815088

Mohanta, B. K., Awad, A. I., Dehury, M. K., Mohapatra, H., & Khan, M. K. (2025). Protecting IoT-enabled healthcare data at the edge: Integrating blockchain, AES, and off-chain decentralized storage. *IEEE Internet of Things Journal*, •••, 1–1. DOI: 10.1109/JIOT.2025.3528894

Mohapatra, H. (2021). Socio-technical challenges in the implementation of smart city. *2021 International Conference on Innovation and Intelligence for Informatics, Computing, and Technologies (3ICT)*, 57-62. https://doi.org/ DOI: 10.1109/3ICT53449.2021.9581905

Mohapatra, H. (2024). The role of 6G in empowering smart cities enabling ubiquitous connectivity and intelligent infrastructure. *Advances in Civil and Industrial Engineering*, •••, 237–264. DOI: 10.4018/979-8-3693-8029-1.ch009

Mohapatra, H., & Mishra, S. R. (2024). Analysis of sector-specific responses of AI generative. *Studies in Computational Intelligence*, 167-184. https://doi.org/DOI: 10.1007/978-981-97-8460-8_9

Mohapatra, H., & Mishra, S. R. (2024). Unlocking insights: Exploring data analytics and AI tool performance across industries. *Studies in Big Data*, 265-288. https://doi.org/DOI: 10.1007/978-981-97-0448-4_13

Mohapatra, H., Mishra, S. R., Rath, A. K., & Kolhar, M. (2025). Sustainable cities and communities. *Networked Sensing Systems*, 173-198. https://doi.org/DOI: 10.1002/9781394310890.ch7

Mohapatra, H., & Rath, A. K. (2019). Detection and avoidance of water loss through municipality taps in India by using smart taps and ICT. *IET Wireless Sensor Systems*, *9*(6), 447–457. DOI: 10.1049/iet-wss.2019.0081

Pathak, N., Mukherjee, A., & Misra, S. (2021). AerialBlocks: Blockchain-enabled UAV virtualization for industrial IoT. *IEEE Internet of Things Magazine*, *4*(1), 72–77. DOI: 10.1109/IOTM.0011.1900093

Peng, M., Hu, J., Lin, H., Wang, X., & Lin, W. (2021). A privacy-enhanced mobile Crowdsensing strategy for blockchain empowered Internet of Medical Things. *2021 IEEE 20th International Conference on Trust, Security and Privacy in Computing and Communications (TrustCom)*, 387-396. https://doi.org/DOI: 10.1109/TrustCom53373.2021.00066

Sah, R. K., Singh, A. K., Yadav, A. K., & Mohapatra, H. (2024). Cloud-enabled platforms for social and civic engagement in smart urban environments. *Advances in Electronic Government, Digital Divide, and Regional Development*, •••, 215–234. DOI: 10.4018/979-8-3693-6740-7.ch009

Swain, B., Raj, P., Singh, K., Singh, Y., Singh, S., & Mohapatra, H. (2025). Ethical implications and mitigation strategies for public safety and security in smart cities for securing tomorrow. *Advances in Information Security, Privacy, and Ethics*, •••, 419–436. DOI: 10.4018/979-8-3693-6859-6.ch019

Van den Hoven, J. (2014). Responsible innovation: A new look at technology and ethics. *Responsible Innovation*, *1*, 3–13. DOI: 10.1007/978-94-017-8956-1_1

Venkataramanan, V., Kaza, S., & Annaswamy, A. M. (2023). DER forecast using privacy-preserving federated learning. *IEEE Internet of Things Journal*, *10*(3), 2046–2055. DOI: 10.1109/JIOT.2022.3157299

Wei, W., Piuri, V., Pedrycz, W., & Ahmed, S. H. (2022). Special issue on artificial intelligence-of-Things (AIoT): Opportunities, challenges, and solutions-part II: artificial-intelligence-Powered Internet of things. *Future Generation Computer Systems*, *137*, 186–188. DOI: 10.1016/j.future.2022.07.019

Yaseliani, M., Noor-E-Alam, M., & Hasan, M. M. (2024). Mitigating Sociodemographic bias in opioid use disorder prediction: Fairness-aware machine learning framework. *JMIR AI*, *3*, e55820. DOI: 10.2196/55820 PMID: 39163597

Zhang, C., Yu, S., Tian, Z., & Yu, J. J. (2023). Generative adversarial networks: A survey on attack and defense perspective. *ACM Computing Surveys*, *56*(4), 1–35. DOI: 10.1145/3615336

Zhang, Y., Zong, R., Shang, L., & Wang, D. (2024). A crowdsourcing-driven AI model design framework to public health policy-adherence assessment. *IEEE Transactions on Emerging Topics in Computing*, •••, 1–16. DOI: 10.1109/TETC.2024.3496835

Chapter 10
Customer Ability, Readiness, and Intention to Purchase Using AI in Tourism and Hospitality Businesses:
The Mediating Roles of Trust in AI and Customer Engagement

Bassam Samir Al-Romeedy
https://orcid.org/0000-0002-7900-5052
Faculty of Tourism and Hotels, University of Sadat City, Egypt

Hazem Ahmed Khairy
Faculty of Tourism and Hotels, University of Sadat City, Egypt

Tarik Ali Jasim
Faculty of Business Economics, Alnahrain University, Iraq

Asier Baquero
https://orcid.org/0000-0002-9500-9344
Faculty of Business and Communication, International University of La Rioja, Logrono, Spain

ABSTRACT

The study investigates the impact of customer ability readiness (CAR) on intention to purchase using AI (IPAI) in tourism and hospitality businesses, focusing on the mediating roles of customer trust in AI (TAI) and customer engagement (CE). An online survey was conducted to gather data from customers who have experienced using AI in online flights and hotel booking. The PLS-SEM approach was used to analyze 602 valid responses, which were processed using WarpPLS statistical software 7.0. The findings show that CAR positively affects customers' IPAI, TAI, and CE. In addition, customers' IPAI is positively affected by TAI and CE. Furthermore, the findings found that TAI and CE significantly mediate the CAR IPAI relationship. The study enhances the Technology Acceptance Model (TAM) by enhancing our understanding of the factors influencing AI adoption in the tourism and hospitality sectors. The study also suggests that tourism and hospitality businesses should focus on improving customer readiness to adopt AI technologies.

DOI: 10.4018/979-8-3693-7447-4.ch010

INTRODUCTION

The tourism and hospitality industry is undergoing a significant transformation due to the integration of Artificial Intelligence (AI), resulting in improved customer experiences and streamlined operations. AI-powered technologies such as chatbots and virtual assistants play a pivotal role in delivering round-the-clock customer service, managing reservations, addressing inquiries, and offering personalized recommendations swiftly and efficiently, surpassing the capabilities of conventional methods. Moreover, AI facilitates the customization of guest experiences by leveraging data analytics to tailor services according to individual preferences, thereby enhancing customer satisfaction and fostering loyalty. From an operational standpoint, AI enables resource optimization through predictive analytics, empowering businesses to forecast demand, manage inventory effectively, and minimize costs (Farahat, 2023).

AI technologies have transformed the landscape of interactions between tourism and hospitality businesses and their clientele, introducing unparalleled levels of personalization and convenience (Thakur, 2022). By harnessing AI-driven analytics, businesses now can anticipate customer preferences and behaviors, allowing them to deliver highly tailored experiences that align with individual expectations and elevate overall satisfaction levels (Krishnan & Mariappan, 2024). The deployment of chatbots and virtual assistants enables businesses to provide continuous customer support, proficiently managing bookings, inquiries, and issue resolutions, thus significantly enhancing the quality of customer service (Ahmad et al., 2024; Kannan, 2024). Furthermore, AI facilitates the streamlining of the entire customer journey, spanning from initial booking to post-stay feedback collection, thereby ensuring a seamless and hassle-free experience. This not only fosters customer loyalty but also enhances the likelihood of repeat visits, directly influencing the success of businesses within the fiercely competitive tourism and hospitality sector (Jindal & Kaur, 2024; Sharma & Singh, 2023).

The customers' ability readiness to utilize AI holds immense importance for the successful adoption and integration of AI technologies (Jöhnk et al., 2021; Rahman et al., 2023). Particularly in industries where technology interfaces directly with users, such as tourism and hospitality, the impact of customer readiness on trust in AI is notable. Customer readiness encompasses various factors, including familiarity with AI technologies, comfort levels with digital interfaces, and past experiences with AI-driven systems. These readiness factors shape customers' initial perceptions of AI and their inclination to trust and rely on AI technologies across different contexts (Gao et al., 2021; Dagliyan, 2021).

Moreover, customer ability readiness has a substantial impact on customer engagement. When customers possess familiarity with and proficiency in utilizing AI tools, their likelihood of engaging deeply and proficiently with these services increases. This preparedness not only fosters their ease in navigating AI-driven platforms but also enhances their trust in the technology, resulting in more frequent and substantial interactions (Yin et al., 2023; Mohamed et al., 2022).

Additionally, customer readiness to utilize AI significantly influences their intention to purchase AI-enhanced systems. This readiness encompasses not only customers' familiarity with technology but also their confidence in effectively using it during purchasing situations. Customers who are proficient in utilizing AI tools and comprehend how these technologies can enhance their buying experience are more inclined to adopt them. This level of comfort directly impacts their purchasing choices, resulting in a greater inclination to utilize and depend on AI for their transactions (Farahat, 2023; Gaafar, 2020).

Trust in AI significantly influences customers' intention to purchase AI-enabled systems. When customers trust the reliability, security, and effectiveness of AI technologies, they are more inclined to utilize these systems for their purchasing needs. This trust is established through consistent, positive interactions with AI that showcase accuracy, personalized service, and enhanced convenience (Malodia et al., 2023; Bach et al., 2024). Customer engagement with AI technologies also directly impacts their intention to purchase using AI. High levels of engagement typically indicate that customers interact frequently and meaningfully with AI systems, thereby enhancing their comfort and familiarity with these technologies. This heightened comfort level increases their confidence in using AI for making purchasing decisions (Bilal et al., 2024; Hlee et al., 2023).

Despite the increasing interest in AI adoption within the tourism and hospitality sector, there remains a significant gap in comprehending the underlying mechanisms that shape consumers' inclination to purchase AI-driven products and services (Farahat, 2023; Gaafar, 2021). Specifically, there is limited research delving into the mediating roles of trust in AI and customer engagement in the nexus between customer ability readiness and the intention to purchase using AI. While prior studies have individually explored factors such as trust, engagement, and readiness, there is a necessity to examine how these variables interact and impact consumers' purchasing intentions within the framework of AI adoption in tourism and hospitality businesses.

Accordingly, the study aims to examine the effects of customer ability readiness on trust in AI, customer engagement, and intention to purchase using AI in tourism and hospitality businesses. It also aims to evaluate the effects of both trust in AI and customer engagement on intention to purchase using AI. As well, it aims to explore the mediating role of trust in AI and customer engagement in the relationship between customer ability readiness and intention to purchase using AI.

Through the pursuit of these aims, the study endeavors to enrich current literature by providing a thorough comprehension of the underlying dynamics impacting consumers' inclination to acquire AI-driven products and services within the tourism and hospitality sector. Additionally, the outcomes will furnish businesses with invaluable insights, aiding them in strategically incorporating AI technologies into their operational frameworks and marketing endeavors. Ultimately, this will stimulate innovation and bolster competitiveness within the swiftly evolving sphere of AI adoption.

LITERATURE REVIEW AND HYPOTHESES DEVELOPMENT

Technology Acceptance Model (TAM)

The Technology Acceptance Model (TAM) furnishes a significant theoretical framework for comprehending individuals' adoption of technology, encompassing AI. According to TAM, users' intentions to utilize a specific technology are primarily influenced by perceived ease of use and perceived usefulness. TAM provides valuable insights into how customers' perceptions of AI affect their intentions to make purchases (Chatterjee et al., 2021; Makmor et al., 2019; Yin & Qiu, 2021).

Customer ability readiness to use AI can be understood as a facet of perceived ease of use within the TAM framework. This readiness signifies customers' perceived proficiency and comfort in engaging with AI technologies. Following TAM, individuals are more inclined to intend to use a technology if they perceive it as user-friendly. Consequently, elevated levels of customer ability readiness for utilizing AI are anticipated to have a favorable impact on customers' intentions to procure AI-driven products or services within the tourism and hospitality domain (Flavián et al., 2021; Damerji & Salimi, 2021; Bhuiyan et al., 2024).

Furthermore, perceived usefulness, another dimension within TAM, closely corresponds to the concept of trust in AI within the study's context. Trust in AI denotes customers' faith and dependability attributed to AI technologies, which can impact their views on AI's utility in enhancing their experiences or fulfilling their requirements. In line with TAM, individuals are more inclined to intend to utilize a technology if they perceive it as beneficial. Consequently, trust in AI acts as a mediating factor in the relationship between customer ability readiness and the intention to purchase using AI, as it influences customers' perceptions of AI's usefulness and, subsequently, their purchasing intentions (Farahat, 2023; Al-Romeedy, 2024b).

Moreover, according to TAM, social influence and facilitating conditions are additional factors that contribute to shaping individuals' intentions to utilize technology. In the context of this study, these factors can be associated with customer engagement. Customer engagement pertains to the extent, frequency, and quality of interactions that customers engage in with AI-driven products or services. Positive engagement encounters have the potential to improve customers' perceptions of AI's usefulness and user-friendliness, thereby impacting their intention to purchase using AI (Faqih, 2020; Gupta & Khan, 2024; Chakraborty et al., 2024).

The Effect of Customer Ability Readiness for Using AI on Intention to Purchase Using AI

Customer ability readiness denotes individuals' readiness and willingness to engage with AI-driven systems, comprising elements like familiarity with AI, proficiency in using AI technologies, and confidence in navigating AI interfaces (Kathuria & Rana, 2023; Farahat, 2023). Intention to purchase using AI indicates consumers' readiness and inclination to procure products or services integrating AI functionalities (Chuah et al., 2021; Farahat et al., 2022). Customers who exhibit greater readiness and proficiency in utilizing AI technologies are inclined to perceive enhanced utility and value in AI-driven products or services. They comprehend the potential benefits that AI can provide, such as personalized recommendations, heightened efficiency, or improved outcomes, resulting in a heightened intention to acquire AI-enabled offerings (Issa et al., 2022; Chaturvedi & Verma, 2023).

Individuals with elevated ability readiness are more prone to encountering positive interactions with AI technologies, such as effectively utilizing AI-driven features or receiving pertinent and precise recommendations. These affirmative encounters contribute to fostering confidence and trust in AI, consequently augmenting the propensity to intend to procure AI-driven products or services in the future (Polisetty et al., 2024; Mohamed et al., 2022). As well, customers demonstrating elevated ability readiness may perceive an enhanced sense of control and autonomy during their interactions with AI technologies. They feel empowered to tailor settings, personalize preferences, and oversee their engagements with AI-driven systems, thereby fostering a heightened sense of ownership and readiness to invest in AI-enabled solutions (Paluch & Wittkop, 2023; Gaafar, 2020). Hence, the following hypothesis is suggested:

H1: Customer ability readiness positively affects intention to purchase using AI.

The Effect of Customer Ability Readiness for Using AI on Trust in AI

Trust in AI signifies customers' trust and reliance placed on artificial intelligence systems (Farahat, 2023). Customer ability readiness encompasses customers' comprehension and familiarity with AI principles, functionalities, and uses. With higher levels of ability readiness, customers typically possess a more profound understanding of AI's functioning, limitations, and potential advantages. This heightened comprehension and awareness can have a beneficial effect on customers' trust in AI, as they gain a clearer understanding of AI's capabilities and its practical applications (Jöhnk et al., 2021; Al-Romeedy, 2024b). Customer ability readiness also influences customers' perception of their proficiency in utilizing AI technologies. When customers feel more assured in their capability to engage with AI systems, navigate AI interfaces, and effectively utilize AI-driven features, they are more inclined to trust AI. Their confidence in their proficiency enhances their trust that they can utilize AI to accomplish their desired objectives (Flavián et al., 2022; Chaturvedi & Verma, 2023).

Moreover, ability readiness serves to diminish uncertainty and alleviate perceived risks associated with AI adoption. Customers who are more knowledgeable and adept in using AI technologies are better positioned to evaluate the reliability, precision, and performance of AI systems. This reduced uncertainty contributes to heightened levels of trust, as customers perceive AI as a reliable and trustworthy tool capable of delivering the intended outcomes (Prentice et al., 2020; Wamba-Taguimdje et al., 2020). Ability readiness can also impact trust in AI by empowering customers to comprehend AI algorithms, decision-making processes, and data utilization. Customers with heightened ability readiness are likely more cognizant of the significance of transparency and explainability in AI systems. They can assess the transparency measures implemented by AI providers, such as offering clear explanations of AI operations or providing understandable AI-generated recommendations. This transparency fosters trust by affording customers a sense of control and comprehension (Farhat, 2023). So, the following hypothesis is proposed

H2: Customer ability readiness positively affects trust in AI.

The Effect of Trust in AI on Intention to Purchase Using AI

Confidence in the reliability and precision of AI technologies is cultivated through trust in AI. Customers who place trust in AI believe in its capability to efficiently execute tasks, offer precise recommendations, and yield desired outcomes. This perception of dependability diminishes uncertainty and risk linked with AI adoption, consequently heightening the inclination to purchase using AI (Bulchand-Gidumal, 2022). Moreover, trust in AI is frequently linked with confidence in its capacity to provide value and advantages to users. Customers who trust AI view it as a valuable instrument for enriching their experiences, resolving challenges, or attaining objectives. They anticipate AI-driven products or services to furnish personalized recommendations, enhance efficiency, or introduce innovative features, thereby positively influencing their intention to purchase using AI (Choung et al., 2023; Ameen et al., 2021).

Trust in AI serves to alleviate perceived risks linked with AI adoption, encompassing concerns like privacy, data security, and algorithmic biases (Omrani et al., 2022). Customers who have confidence in AI feel more at ease divulging personal information, engaging with AI-driven systems, and relying on AI recommendations, as they trust AI to handle their data responsibly and ethically. This reduction in perceived risk heightens the intention to purchase using AI, as customers perceive AI as trustworthy and dependable (Chaturvedi & Verma, 2023). Therefore, the following hypothesis is formulated:

H3: Customers' trust in AI positively affects their intention to purchase using AI.

The Mediating Role of Trust in AI in the Link Between Customer Ability Readiness for Using AI and Intention to Purchase Using AI

Enhanced by customer ability readiness, trust in AI is bolstered as customers acquire the knowledge and competencies requisite for appraising and scrutinizing AI technologies. With heightened ability readiness, customers are better equipped to comprehend the capabilities, limitations, and potential risks associated with AI. This comprehension nurtures trust and assurance in AI, as customers regard it as a dependable and trustworthy tool (Farahat, 2023). Customer ability readiness amplifies customers' perception of the dependability and efficacy of AI technologies. Equipped with the knowledge and skills to comprehend and evaluate AI systems, customers can render more informed assessments regarding the reliability of AI in achieving desired outcomes. This perception of reliability positively influences trust in AI and subsequently shapes purchase intentions (Al-Romeedy, 2024c).

Trust in AI serves as a mechanism to mitigate perceived risks linked with AI adoption (Shi et al., 2021; Gaafar, 2020). Customers with greater ability readiness are inclined to more accurately assess the risks associated with AI technologies (Flavián et al., 2022). Trust in AI assists in alleviating these perceived risks by reassuring customers about the dependability, security, and capacity of AI systems to fulfill their needs. Consequently, customers feel more assured in their decision to invest in AI-based products or services (Solberg et al., 2022; Song et al., 2022). Customer ability readiness shapes the perception of AI's utility (Flavián et al., 2022). With the requisite knowledge and skills to proficiently utilize AI technologies, customers are better positioned to discern the potential benefits and advantages of AI usage. This recognition of usefulness cultivates a favorable attitude towards AI and nurtures trust in its capacity to enrich their purchasing experience (Haleem et al., 2022; Pitardi & Marriott, 2021). So, the following hypothesis is assumed:

H4: Trust in AI mediates the link between customer ability readiness and intention to purchase using AI

The Effect of Customer Ability Readiness for Using AI on Customer Engagement

Customer engagement involves the breadth, frequency, and caliber of interactions customers engage in with AI-driven products or services. Customers exhibiting higher ability readiness are inclined to delve into and experiment with AI-driven features or functionalities. They possess confidence in their capacity to navigate AI interfaces and proficiently utilize AI technologies, thus prompting heightened engagement as they actively pursue and interact with AI-driven products or services (Fickers, 2023; Chaturvedi & Verma, 2023). Customers possessing higher ability readiness demonstrate a greater propensity to embrace the advanced features or capabilities provided by AI technologies. They exhibit a willingness to explore and harness AI-driven functionalities, such as personalized recommendations, predictive analytics, or natural language processing, thereby enriching their engagement through tailored and immersive experiences (Al-Romeedy, 2024c).

Customers demonstrating higher ability readiness are predisposed to offering feedback and input to AI systems, thereby contributing to their continual enhancement and adaptation. They actively engage in molding their interactions with AI technologies, furnishing valuable insights and data that augment the pertinence and efficacy of AI-driven products or services (Jöhnk et al., 2021; Marti et al., 2024). Elevated ability readiness empowers customers to personalize and tailor their engagements with AI technologies in accordance with their preferences and requirements. They feel empowered to customize AI-driven experiences, fine-tuning settings, preferences, and parameters to align with their individual preferences and objectives, thereby enriching their interaction with AI-driven offerings (Farahat, 2023). Hence, the following hypothesis is developed:

H5: Customer ability readiness positively affects customer engagement.

The Effect of Customer Engagement on Intention to Purchase Using AI

Active customer engagement nurtures favorable encounters with AI-driven products or services, resulting in perceptions of value and usefulness. Individuals who actively engage with AI technologies are prone to encountering personalized recommendations, smooth interactions, and tangible advantages, thereby augmenting their perceived value of AI-driven offerings and subsequently bolstering their intention to purchase using AI (Al-Romeedy, 2024c). Customer engagement cultivates emotional bonds and allegiance toward AI-driven brands or offerings (Marti et al., 2024). Individuals who actively engage with AI technologies foster sentiments of attachment, contentment, and loyalty stemming from their favorable experiences and interactions. This emotional affinity heightens their intention to purchase using AI, driven by their desire to uphold and strengthen the positive rapport with AI-driven products or services (Rane et al., 2023; Huang & Rust, 2021).

Engaged customers offer significant feedback and input to AI systems, thereby fostering their ongoing enhancement and innovation. They are deeply involved in the progression of AI-driven products or services and play an active role in molding their advancement. This cooperative involvement heightens consumers' view of AI as responsive and adaptable, thereby positively impacting their intention to purchase using AI (Farahat, 2023). Similarly, engaged customers tend to spread their positive experiences with AI technologies to others, resulting in favorable word-of-mouth recommendations and social influence (Huang & Philp, 2021; Mishra et al., 2022). By advocating for AI-driven products or services, engaged customers have the potential to sway the purchase intentions of their peers or social network, thus amplifying overall adoption and intention to purchase using AI within their social circle (Bag et al., 2022; Vahdat et al., 2021). Hence, the following hypothesis is suggested:

H6: Customer engagement positively affects their intention to purchase using AI.

The Mediating Role of Customer Engagement in the Link Between Customer Ability Readiness for Using AI and Intention to Purchase Using AI

Customers with greater ability readiness for using AI are inclined to actively engage with AI technologies (Gao et al., 2022). Such engagement may entail exploring AI features, interacting with AI-driven interfaces, offering feedback, and actively participating in AI-powered experiences. Through these interactions, customers acquire firsthand experience of the advantages and value provided by AI, thereby fostering a favorable perception of AI-based products or services (Al-Romeedy, 2024c). In influencing customers' intention to purchase AI-based offerings, customer engagement plays a pivotal role. Engaged customers, having experienced positive encounters with AI technologies, tend to regard AI-based products or services as valuable and pertinent to their requirements. This favorable perception, coupled with the trust and confidence cultivated through engagement, augments their inclination to make a purchase and embrace AI-powered solutions (Sung et al., 2021; Gaafar, 2020).

Customers displaying higher ability readiness are inclined to actively delve into AI-based solutions (Gao et al., 2023). They may pursue information, conduct inquiries, and experiment with various AI applications. Such proactive exploration stems from their assurance in comprehending and proficiently utilizing AI technologies. Through these engagements, customers enhance their comprehension of AI's capabilities and advantages, culminating in a heightened intention to purchase (Farahat, 2023). Customer ability readiness facilitates customers' involvement in experiential learning with AI technologies (Rahman et al., 2023; Gupta et al., 2024). They can actively engage in utilizing AI-based products or services, acquiring practical experience and understanding of the value they offer. These firsthand encounters play a crucial role in molding customers' perceptions of AI and impacting their intention to purchase (Taylor & Broløs, 2024). So, the following hypothesis is demonstrated:

H7: Customer engagement mediates the link between customer ability readiness and intention to purchase using AI

The hypothesized research framework is presented in Figure (1) below.

Figure 1. The hypothesized research framework.

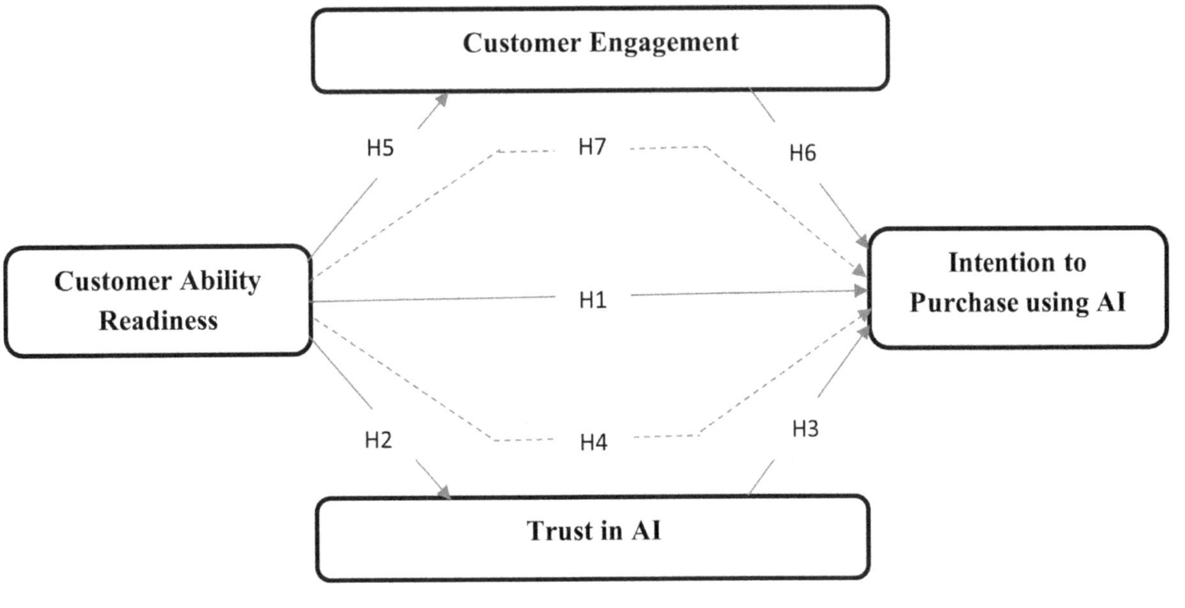

METHODOLOGY

Measures

The study utilized reliable, unidimensional measures from past literature and a five-point Likert scale to record responses (It ranges from 1 strongly disagree to 5 strongly agree), reflecting latent constructs. Customer ability readiness was measured using a four-item scale adapted from Gao et al. (2023). Sample items include: "I am fully capable of using intelligent customer service robots" and "I am confident in my ability to use intelligent customer service robots". In addition, customers' intention to purchase using AI was evaluated by a 4-item scale derived from Pillai et al. (2020). For example, "I would like to purchase through digital assistants" and "I would like to repeat my experience in digital assistants". Furthermore, trust in artificial intelligence was assessed by a 3-item scale derived from Malhotra and Ramalingam (2023). For example, "I believe that digital assistants are honest" and "I believe that digital assistants are trustworthy". Moreover, a four-item scale for measuring customer engagement was adapted from Hsieh and Chang (2016). For instance, "I feel like I can be myself when using intelligent customer service robots" and "The things I did with the intelligent customer service robots are in line with what I really wanted to do".

Data Collection Procedure

An online survey was conducted between February and March 2024, collecting data from customers via social media platforms (e.g., WhatsApp, Facebook, Instagram, Twitter) and LinkedIn. We obtained consent from potential participants and sent them a questionnaire. Our target group consisted of AI-experienced customers booking flights and hotels. Participants were asked if they had experience using AI in online booking, and only after a positive response could they proceed to the next question of the survey. The survey was provided with an introductory note stating its academic use and strict confidentiality of responses. Participants were informed that there were no right or wrong answers, and the introductory note provided the objective and definitions of the study terminologies. A total of 1000 questionnaires were distributed among consumers, with 602 valid, resulting in a response rate of 60.2%.

The study involved 602 participants, with 332 (55.1%) men and 270 (44.9%) women. Of the participants, 154 (25.6%) were under 30 years old, 288 (44.8%) were between 30 and 45 years old, and 160 (26.6%) were beyond 45. In addition, 90 (15%) hold high school certificates, 390 (64.8%) hold bachelor degrees, and 122 (20.2%) hold master/PhD degrees.

Data Analysis

Partial least squares structural equation modeling (PLSSEM), a popular technique for confirmatory and exploratory research, was employed in the study (Hair et al., 2016). PLS-SEM is a statistical technique used for data processing in complex models, facilitating theory validation and extension (Bari et al., 2019; Hair et al., 2016). It is a popular analytical method in hospitality and tourist research (Manley et al., 2020), data processed using WarpPLS statistical software 7.0.

RESULTS

Measurement Model

The four-factor model, including customer ability readiness, intention to use AI in the purchase, trust in AI, and engagement, was assessed through confirmatory factor analysis and Kock's (2021) ten fit indices; APC "P<0.05", ARS "P<0.05", AARS "P<0.05", AVIF "acceptable if ≤5, ideally ≤3.3", AFVIF "acceptable if ≤5, ideally ≤3.3", GoF "small ≥0.1, medium ≥0.25, large ≥ 0.36", SPR "acceptable if ≥ 0.7, ideally =1", RSCR "acceptable if ≥ 0.9, ideally = 1", SSR "acceptable if ≥0.7", and NLBCDR "acceptable if ≥0.7". The four-factor model proposed provided accurate data; "APC=0.414, P<0.001; ARS=0.442, P<0.001; AARS=0.441, P<0.001; AVIF=2.434; AFVIF=2.131; GoF=0.554; SPR=1.000; RSCR=1.000; SSR=1.000; and NLBCDR=1.000".

According to the data presented in Table (1), the four research constructs showed composite reliability (CR>0.70) and significant item loadings (>0.60, p<0.05). In addition, customer readiness, intention to use AI, trust in AI, and engagement had AVE values above 0.50, supporting convergent validity. Furthermore, the model is considered free of common method bias as each latent variable's VIF is ≤3.3.

Table 1. Item loadings, Cronbach alpha, CR, AVE, and VIFs

Construct	Indicators	Loading	CR	CA	AVE	VIF
Customer Ability Readiness (CAR)	CAR.1	0.800	0.887	0.830	0.662	1.691
	CAR.2	0.840				
	CAR.3	0.833				
	CAR.4	0.780				
Intention to Purchase using AI (IPAI)	IPAI.1	0.918	0.902	0.851	0.701	1.956
	IPAI.2	0.880				
	IPAI.3	0.891				
	IPAI.4	0.628				
Trust in AI (TAI)	TAI.1	0.907	0.905	0.842	0.762	2.373
	TAI.2	0.909				
	TAI.3	0.797				
	TAI.4	0.907				
Customer Engagement (CE)	CE.1	0.787	0.883	0.823	0.654	2.505
	CE.2	0.808				
	CE.3	0.793				
	CE.4	0.846				

"CR: Composite reliability; CA: Cronbach's alpha; AVE: average variance extracted; VIF: variance inflation factors ".

By verifying that the square root of the AVE for each of the constructs is larger than the off-diagonal correlations (refer to Table 2) and by computing the HTMT (refer to Table 3), the discriminant validity of the constructs was verified.

Table 2. Discriminant validity results - Fornell-Larcker Criterion

	TAI	CE	CAR	IPAI
Trust in AI (TAI)	**0.873**	0.721	0.576	0.600
Customer Engagement (CE)	0.721	**0.809**	0.554	0.648
Customer Ability Readiness (CAR)	0.576	0.554	**0.814**	0.549
Intention to Purchase using AI (IPAI)	0.600	0.648	0.549	**0.837**

"Off-diagonal elements are correlations and diagonal elements are square roots of AVE"

Table 3. HTMT for validity

HTMT ratios (good if < 0.90, best if < 0.85)	**TAI**	**CE**	**CAR**	**IPAI**
Trust in AI (TAI)				
Customer Engagement (CE)	0.871			
Customer Ability Readiness (CAR)	0.690	0.673		
Intention to Purchase using AI (IPAI)	0.720	0.774	0.664	
P values (one-tailed) for HTMT ratios (good if < 0.05)	**TAI**	**CE**	**CAR**	**IPAI**
Trust in AI (TAI)				
Customer Engagement (CE)	<0.001			
Customer Ability Readiness (CAR)	<0.001	<0.001		
Intention to Purchase using AI (IPAI)	<0.001	<0.001	<0.001	

Results of Direct Effects

Figure (2) and Table (4) show customer ability readiness (CAR) positively affects customers' intention to purchase using AI (IPAI) (β=0.17, P<0.01, t=4.280), trust in AI (TAI) (β=0.65, P<0.01, t=17.058), and customer engagement (CE) (β=0.64, P<0.01, t=16.797). These results demonstrate that CAR leads to an increase in customer IPAI, TAI, and engagement, supporting hypotheses H1, H2, and H5. In addition, IPAI is positively affected by TAI (β=0.24, P<0.01, t=5.959) and CE (β=0.37, P<0.01, t=9.586). The study therefore suggests that TAI and CE enhance IPAI, thereby supporting H3 and H6.

Figure 2: Final model of the study

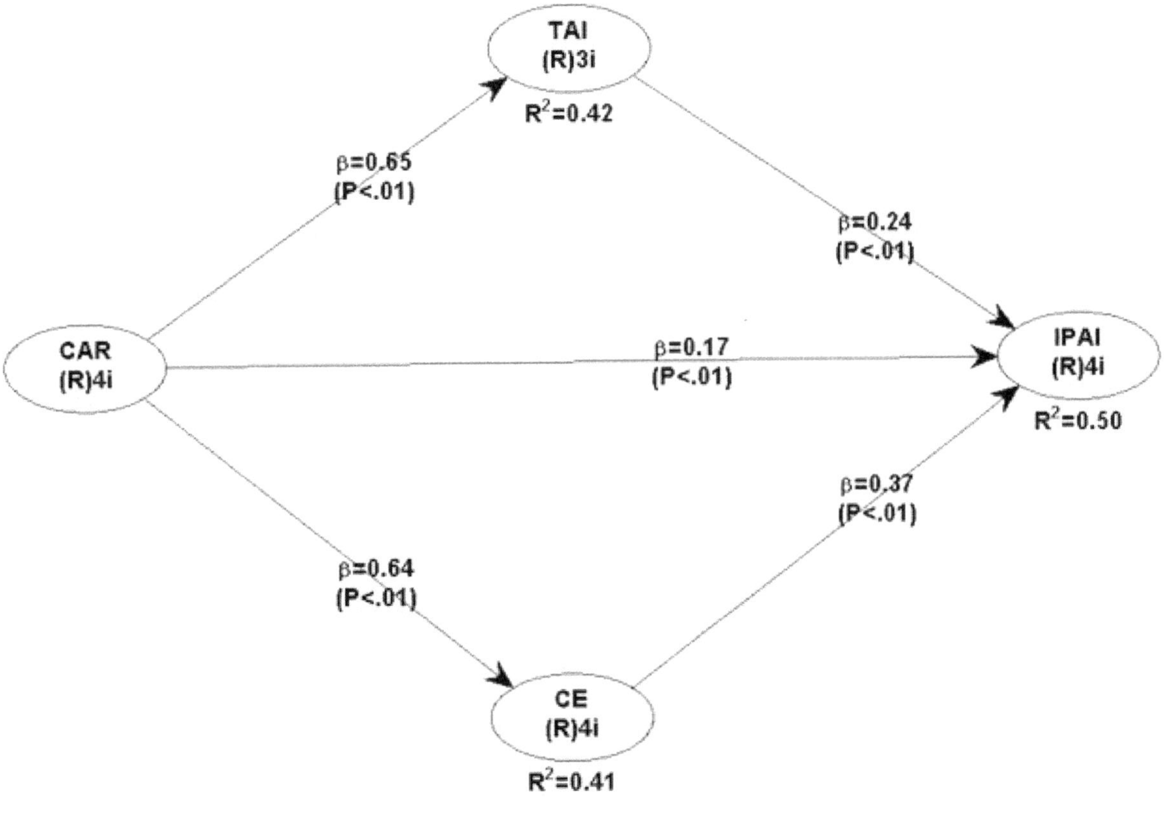

Table 4. Direct effects.

Hs	Relationship	Direct effect (β)	Sig.	t	Confidence intervals	Decision
H1	*CAR IPAI*	0.17	P<0.01	4.280	0.093, 0.250	Supported
H2	*CAR TAI*	0.65	P<0.01	17.058	0.573, 0.721	Supported
H3	*TAI IPAI*	0.24	P<0.01	5.959	0.159, 0.314	Supported
H5	*CAR CE*	0.64	P<0.01	16.797	0.563, 0.712	Supported
H6	*CE IPAI*	0.37	P<0.01	9.586	0.298, 0.451	Supported

Mediation Analysis for Indirect Effects

The study utilized the Preacher and Hayes (2008) method to investigate the mediation effects of TAI and CE. The bootstrapping analysis demonstrated a significant indirect influence of TAI {β=0.156 (0.650×0.240), SE=0.028, P<0.01, t-value=5.571). In addition, the confidence interval LL=0.101, UL=0.211), does not straddle a

0 in between, confirming mediation. The study found that TAI significantly mediates the CAR→IPAI relationship, supporting hypothesis 4.

The bootstrapping analysis also demonstrated a significant indirect influence of CE {β=0.237 (0.640×0.370), SE=0.028, P<0.01, t-value=8.457). In addition, the confidence interval LL=0.182, UL=0.292), does not straddle a 0 in between, confirming mediation. The study found that CE significantly mediates the CAR→IPAI relationship, supporting hypothesis 7.

Table 5. Mediation analysis' bootstrapped confidence interval

Hypo.		Path a	Path b	Indirect Effect	SE	t-value	Bootstrapped Confidence Interval		Decision
							95% LL	95% UL	
H4	CAR→TAI→ *IPAI*	0.650	0.240	0.156	0.028	5.571	0.101	0.211	Mediation
H7	CAR→CE→ *IPAI*	0.640	0.370	0.237	0.028	8.457	0.182	0.292	Mediation

DISCUSSION

The study examines the effect of customer ability readiness on their intention to purchase using AI in tourism and hospitality businesses. It also explores the mediating role of customer trust in AI and their engagement in the relationship between customer ability readiness and intention to purchase using AI. The results show that customer ability readiness positively affects their intention to purchase using AI. This result complements the previous research conducted by Gaafar (2020) and Paluch and Wittkop (2023). Heightened ability readiness is often correlated with a heightened perception of ease of use when engaging with AI technologies. Customers who feel at ease and proficient in utilizing AI-driven systems are more inclined to surmount barriers and challenges, resulting in an increased intention to procure AI-enabled products or services (Flavián et al., 2022; Malodia et al., 2023).

The results also show that customer ability readiness positively affects their trust in AI, complementing the previous research conducted by Flavián et al. (2022) and Farhat (2023). Customers with elevated ability readiness are more prone to having direct experience and exposure to AI technologies. They may have engaged with AI-based products or services, utilized AI-driven features, or observed the benefits of AI across various contexts. This familiarity and exposure to AI can positively impact customers' trust, as it furnishes them with firsthand evidence of AI's capabilities and reliability (Flavián et al., 2022; Libai et al., 2020; Glikson & Woolley, 2020).

In addition, the results indicate that customers' trust in AI positively affects their intention to purchase using AI. This result complements the previous research conducted by Chaturvedi and Verma (2023). Trust in AI is bolstered by favorable user experiences and feedback. Customers who encounter positive interactions with AI-driven products or services, such as receiving precise recommendations or enjoying seamless interactions, cultivate trust in AI over time. This trust instills confidence in AI's capabilities and promotes repeated usage and adoption, ultimately elevating the intention to purchase using AI (Shin, 2020; Al-Romeedy, 2024a).

Furthermore, the results indicate that customers' trust in AI mediates the relationship between their ability readiness and intention to purchase using AI. The finding aligns with the research conducted by Flavián et al. (2022) and Haleem et al. (2022). Enhanced by customer ability readiness, customers' confidence in their decision-making process regarding AI adoption is strengthened. Equipped with the knowledge and skills to assess AI technologies, customers can make informed decisions grounded in their evaluations of AI's reliability, security, and ethical considerations. This assurance in decision-making fosters a heightened level of trust in AI, as customers feel empowered to make choices that resonate with their needs and preferences (Farahat, 2023).

Moreover, the results indicate that customer ability readiness positively affects their engagement, aligning with the research conducted by Chaturvedi and Verma (2023) and Fickers (2023). Customers exhibiting higher ability readiness may utilize AI technologies for learning and skill advancement purposes (Gao et al., 2023). They perceive interactions with AI-driven systems as avenues for augmenting their expertise, acquiring fresh skills, and refining their abilities, thereby fostering heightened engagement as they actively pursue learning opportunities facilitated by AI technologies (Libai et al., 2020; Rahman et al., 2023).

Additionally, the results found that customer engagement positively affects their intention to purchase using AI. This result complements the previous research conducted by Bag et al. (2022) and Farahat (2023). Customer engagement empowers businesses to provide increasingly personalized and pertinent AI-driven experiences. Customers furnish invaluable data and feedback, which businesses can leverage to fine-tune recommendations, adjust settings, and refine user experiences. These customized interactions augment customers' perception of AI's suitability to their requirements and preferences, consequently heightening their intention to purchase using AI (Raji et al., 2024; Mohamed et al., 2022).

Lastly, the results found that customer engagement mediates the relationship between their ability readiness and intention to purchase using AI, aligning with the research conducted by Rahman et al. (2023), Gupta et al. (2024), and Taylor & Broløs (2024). Customer ability readiness empowers customers to comprehend and effectively utilize AI-driven personalization and customization features (Chaturvedi & Verma, 2023). They can harness these capabilities to personalize their experiences, receive tailored recommendations, or have AI adapt to their preferences. This customization element heightens the feeling of engagement and satisfaction, consequently positively impacting their intention to purchase (Marti et al., 2024; Nwachukwu & Affen, 2023).

Theoretical Implications

The study enhances the Technology Acceptance Model (TAM) by deepening our comprehension of the determinants shaping the uptake of AI technologies in the tourism and hospitality sectors. Firstly, through an investigation of the TAM framework tailored to the unique landscape of tourism and hospitality enterprises, the study offers industry-specific perspectives on TAM. It showcases the adaptability and applicability of TAM in elucidating technology adoption patterns within sectors distinguished by individualized experiences, customer engagements, and service excellence, thereby broadening TAM's relevance to varied contexts. Secondly, the study delves into the nuanced dimensions of perceived ease of use within the context of AI integration in tourism and hospitality enterprises. Through an examination of customer ability readiness for AI utilization as an element of perceived ease of use, the study offers deeper insights into the determinants shaping customers' perceptions of AI's usability in this sector.

Thirdly, the results illuminate how trust in AI and customer engagement contribute to customers' perceptions of AI's utility in tourism and hospitality environments. By showcasing the mediating roles of trust and engagement in the correlation between readiness and the intention to purchase using AI, the study underscores additional factors influencing customers' perceptions of AI's value and advantages. Fourthly, the outcomes of the study prompt adjustments or expansions to the TAM model to more accurately reflect the intricacies of AI adoption in tourism and hospitality enterprises. With the inclusion of trust in AI and customer engagement as mediating factors, TAM can be modified to provide a more comprehensive explanation of the underlying dynamics propelling customers' intentions to acquire AI-driven products or services within this sector.

Fifthly, through the incorporation of trust in AI and customer engagement into TAM, the model's predictive capacity could be enhanced, empowering businesses to better anticipate and comprehend customers' inclinations towards adopting AI technologies in tourism and hospitality environments. This, in turn, can facilitate informed strategic decision-making and resource allocation for initiatives aimed at AI implementation.

Practical Implications

The study offers several practical implications for tourism and hospitality enterprises. It suggests that these businesses should prioritize enhancing customers' readiness to utilize AI technologies. This objective can be accomplished through various approaches, including the provision of user-friendly interfaces, clear instructions, and assistance for customers less accustomed to technology. By ensuring customers feel at ease and proficient in utilizing AI, businesses can heighten the likelihood of their intent to procure AI-driven services. Furthermore, businesses can allocate resources toward educational endeavors and training initiatives aimed at familiarizing customers with AI technologies. These efforts may encompass workshops, tutorials, or online materials offering comprehensive guidance on the utilization of AI-powered features and services. By augmenting customer knowledge and competencies, businesses can diminish adoption barriers and bolster customers' confidence in engaging with AI.

Establishing trust is paramount for the acceptance and adoption of AI technologies by customers. Businesses should prioritize cultivating trust in AI systems through transparency regarding the functioning of AI algorithms, ensuring data privacy and security, and addressing any concerns or biases linked with AI. By nurturing trust, businesses can alleviate customer skepticism and enhance their readiness to engage with AI-driven services. Furthermore, instilling trust in AI necessitates transparency in AI system operations. Businesses should aim to offer clear elucidations of how AI algorithms make decisions and recommendations. This transparency can be accomplished by divulging information about data origins, algorithmic processes, and any potential biases. Transparent AI systems inspire confidence in customers, assuring them of the reliability, fairness, and impartiality of AI technologies.

The study underscores the significance of customer engagement within the realm of AI adoption. It underscores the need for tourism and hospitality enterprises to craft impactful and tailored AI-driven encounters that stimulate customer involvement. Achieving this entails offering personalized recommendations, interactive chatbots, and AI-driven customer service. Active customer engagement has the potential to bolster their inclination to procure AI-powered offerings.

The results underscore the capacity of AI technologies to furnish personalized experiences to patrons. Within the tourism and hospitality sector, businesses can harness AI algorithms to scrutinize customer data and preferences, facilitating tailored recommendations, bespoke promotions, and personalized services. Through adept utilization of AI, enterprises can elevate the overall customer experience, thus augmenting the propensity for patrons to consider purchasing AI-driven offerings.

Importantly, integrating AI systems into tourism and hospitality operations necessitates continuous monitoring and refinement. Regular evaluation of customer satisfaction, soliciting feedback, and implementing necessary enhancements to AI technologies and procedures are vital. Through this iterative process of improvement guided by customer insights, businesses can bolster trust, engagement, and purchase intent. Besides, AI technologies excel in analyzing extensive customer data to deliver personalized recommendations. Within the tourism and hospitality sectors, businesses can harness AI algorithms to discern customer preferences, thereby furnishing tailored suggestions for accommodations, destinations, activities, and amenities. By furnishing personalized experiences, enterprises can elevate customer engagement and heighten the likelihood of customers transacting through AI platforms.

Additionally, AI integration across different stages of the customer journey, including booking platforms, customer service chatbots, and virtual assistants, offers significant potential. Consistently delivering a seamless and user-friendly experience throughout these touchpoints can elevate customer engagement. For instance, leveraging AI-driven chatbots ensures swift and precise responses to customer queries, swiftly addressing concerns, and thereby enhancing overall satisfaction.

Limitations and Future Research

While offering valuable insights, it's imperative to recognize the limitations of this study. The examination does not encompass various contextual factors that could influence the correlations between customer ability readiness, trust in AI, customer engagement, and intention to purchase. Variables such as cultural disparities, technological infrastructure, and industry-specific attributes may exert influence on the outcomes. Future research endeavors could delve into these contextual factors to attain a more profound comprehension of their impact on customer behavior concerning AI adoption. As well, the study has been conducted as a cross-sectional analysis, collecting data at a specific moment in time. Longitudinal studies, which track customers over an extended duration, could offer insights into the evolving dynamics of trust, engagement, and intention to purchase. Analyzing how these variables change over time would yield a more thorough comprehension of the relationships within the realm of AI adoption.

Although the study investigated the mediating roles of trust in AI and customer engagement, further exploration is necessary to delve into the underlying mechanisms by which these variables impact the intention to purchase. Future research endeavors could delve into specific psychological, cognitive, or emotional processes that act as mediators in these relationships, offering insights into the fundamental mechanisms of customer decision-making. The study also has not fully considered all pertinent external variables that could affect the examined relationships. Variables like customer attitudes, previous encounters with AI, and perceptions of AI capabilities might influence trust, engagement, and intention to purchase. Future research endeavors could incorporate these external variables to achieve a more holistic comprehension of the involved dynamics. Lastly, the study might have concentrated on general trust in AI and customer engagement, overlooking their multidimensional nature. Future research could delve into various dimensions of trust (e.g., competence, integrity, benevolence) and engagement (e.g., behavioral, emotional, cognitive) to discern their distinct impacts on the intention to purchase AI-based services in tourism and hospitality businesses.

REFERENCES

Ahmad, M., Naeem, M., Mobo, F., Tahir, M., & Akram, M. (2024). Navigating the Journey: How Chatbots Are Transforming Tourism and Hospitality. In *Design and Development of Emerging Chatbot Technology* (pp. 236-255). IGI Global.

Al-Romeedy, B. (2024a). AI and HRM in Tourism and Hospitality in Egypt: Inevitability, Impact and Future. In *HRM, Artificial Intelligence and the Future of Work: Critical Insights from the Global South*, Palgrave Macmillan.

Al-Romeedy, B. (2024b). HRM and Digital Leadership: Exploring the Mediating Role of Digital Talent and Digital Culture in Driving Innovative Performance in the Saudi Tourism and Hospitality Industry. In *HRM, Artificial Intelligence and the Future of Work: Critical Insights from the Global South*, Palgrave Macmillan.

Al-Romeedy, B. (2024c). Tomorrow's Travel Companion: The Role of Artificial Intelligence in Shaping the Future of Tourism. In *Marketing and Big Data Analytics in Tourism and Events* (pp. 162-182). IGI Global.

Ameen, N., Tarhini, A., Reppel, A., & Anand, A. (2021). Customer experiences in the age of artificial intelligence. *Computers in Human Behavior, 114*, 106548. DOI: 10.1016/j.chb.2020.106548 PMID: 32905175

Bach, T., Khan, A., Hallock, H., Beltrão, G., & Sousa, S. (2024). A systematic literature review of user trust in AI-enabled systems: An HCI perspective. *International Journal of Human-Computer Interaction, 40*(5), 1251–1266. DOI: 10.1080/10447318.2022.2138826

Bag, S., Srivastava, G., Bashir, M., Kumari, S., Giannakis, M., & Chowdhury, A. (2022). Journey of customers in this digital era: Understanding the role of artificial intelligence technologies in user engagement and conversion. *Benchmarking, 29*(7), 2074–2098. DOI: 10.1108/BIJ-07-2021-0415

Bari, M. W., Abrar, M., Shaheen, S., Bashir, M., & Fanchen, M. (2019). Knowledge hiding behaviors and team creativity: The contingent role of perceived mastery motivational climate. *SAGE Open, 9*(3), 2158244019876297. DOI: 10.1177/2158244019876297

Bhuiyan, K., Ahmed, S., & Jahan, I. (2024). Consumer attitude toward using artificial intelligence (AI) devices in hospitality services. *Journal of Hospitality and Tourism Insights, 7*(2), 968–985. DOI: 10.1108/JHTI-08-2023-0551

Bilal, M., Zhang, Y., Cai, S., Akram, U., & Halibas, A. (2024). Artificial intelligence is the magic wand making customer-centric a reality! An investigation into the relationship between consumer purchase intention and consumer engagement through affective attachment. *Journal of Retailing and Consumer Services, 77*, 103674. DOI: 10.1016/j.jretconser.2023.103674

Bulchand-Gidumal, J. (2022). Impact of artificial intelligence in travel, tourism, and hospitality. In *Handbook of e-Tourism* (pp. 1943–1962). Springer International Publishing.

Chakraborty, D., Polisetty, A., Sowmya, G., Rana, N., & Khorana, S. (2024). Unlocking the potential of AI: Enhancing consumer engagement in the beauty and cosmetic product purchases. *Journal of Retailing and Consumer Services, 79*, 103842. DOI: 10.1016/j.jretconser.2024.103842

Chatterjee, S., Rana, N., Dwivedi, Y., & Baabdullah, A. (2021). Understanding AI adoption in manufacturing and production firms using an integrated TAM-TOE model. *Technological Forecasting and Social Change, 170*, 120880. DOI: 10.1016/j.techfore.2021.120880

Chaturvedi, R., & Verma, S. (2023). Opportunities and challenges of AI-driven customer service. *Artificial Intelligence in customer service: The next frontier for personalized engagement*, 33-71.

Chaturvedi, R., & Verma, S. (2023). Opportunities and Challenges of AI-Driven Customer Service. In Sheth, J., Jain, V., Mogaji, E., & Ambika, A. (Eds.), *Artificial Intelligence in Customer Service*. Palgrave Macmillan., DOI: 10.1007/978-3-031-33898-4_3

Choung, H., David, P., & Ross, A. (2023). Trust in AI and its role in the acceptance of AI technologies. *International Journal of Human-Computer Interaction*, *39*(9), 1727–1739. DOI: 10.1080/10447318.2022.2050543

Chuah, S., Aw, E., & Yee, D. (2021). Unveiling the complexity of consumers' intention to use service robots: An fsQCA approach. *Computers in Human Behavior*, *123*, 106870. DOI: 10.1016/j.chb.2021.106870

Dagliyan, G. (2021). *Adoption of AI-enabled technology: taking the bad with the good*. Pepperdine University.

Damerji, H., & Salimi, A. (2021). Mediating effect of use perceptions on technology readiness and adoption of artificial intelligence in accounting. *Accounting Education*, *30*(2), 107–130. DOI: 10.1080/09639284.2021.1872035

Faqih, K. (2020). The influence OF perceived usefulness, social influence, internet self-efficacy and compatibility ON USERS'INTENTIONS to adopt e-learning: Investigating the moderating effects OF culture. *IJAEDU-International E-Journal of Advances in Education*, *5*(15), 300–320. DOI: 10.18768/ijaedu.593878

Farahat, E. (2023). *Applications of artificial intelligence as a marketing tool and their impact on the competitiveness of the Egyptian tourist destination* (Doctoral Dissertation, Minia University).

Farahat, E., Mohamed, M., & Al-Romeedy, B. (2022). Artificial intelligence applications and its impact on the competitiveness of the Egyptian tourist destination. *Research Journal of the Faculty of Tourism and Hotels Mansoura University*, *11*(2), 57–93.

Fickers, A. (2023). The dark side of customer engagement in AI-driven interactions: The case of chatbots in the tourism industry (Master Thesis, Université de Liège).

Flavián, C., Pérez-Rueda, A., Belanche, D., & Casaló, L. (2022). Intention to use analytical artificial intelligence (AI) in services–the effect of technology readiness and awareness. *Journal of Service Management*, *33*(2), 293–320. DOI: 10.1108/JOSM-10-2020-0378

Gaafar, H. (2020). Artificial intelligence in Egyptian tourism companies: Implementation and perception. *Journal of Association of Arab Universities for Tourism and Hospitality*, *18*(1), 66–78. DOI: 10.21608/jaauth.2020.31704.1028

Gaafar, H. (2021). Digital Detox Tourism at The Egyptian Destination: Attitudes and Motivators. *Journal of Association of Arab Universities for Tourism and Hospitality*, *20*(2), 88–107.

Gao, J., Ren, L., Yang, Y., Zhang, D., & Li, L. (2022). The impact of artificial intelligence technology stimuli on smart customer experience and the moderating effect of technology readiness. *International Journal of Emerging Markets*, *17*(4), 1123–1142. DOI: 10.1108/IJOEM-06-2021-0975

Gao, L., Li, G., Tsai, F., Gao, C., Zhu, M., & Qu, X. (2023). The impact of artificial intelligence stimuli on customer engagement and value co-creation: The moderating role of customer ability readiness. *Journal of Research in Interactive Marketing*, *17*(2), 317–333. DOI: 10.1108/JRIM-10-2021-0260

Gao, L., Li, G., Tsai, F., Gao, C., Zhu, M., & Qu, X. (2023). The impact of artificial intelligence stimuli on customer engagement and value co-creation: The moderating role of customer ability readiness. *Journal of Research in Interactive Marketing*, *17*(2), 317–333. DOI: 10.1108/JRIM-10-2021-0260

Glikson, E., & Woolley, A. (2020). Human trust in artificial intelligence: Review of empirical research. *The Academy of Management Annals*, *14*(2), 627–660. DOI: 10.5465/annals.2018.0057

Gupta, R., Nair, K., Mishra, M., Ibrahim, B., & Bhardwaj, S. (2024). Adoption and impacts of generative artificial intelligence: Theoretical underpinnings and research agenda. *International Journal of Information Management Data Insights*, *4*(1), 100232. DOI: 10.1016/j.jjimei.2024.100232

Gupta, Y., & Khan, F. (2024). Role of artificial intelligence in customer engagement: A systematic review and future research directions. *Journal of Modelling in Management*, *19*(5), 1535–1565. Advance online publication. DOI: 10.1108/JM2-01-2023-0016

Hair, J. F., Hult, G. T. M., Ringle, C. M., & Sarstedt, M. (2016). *A Primer on Partial Least Squares Structural Equation Modeling (PLS-SEM)*. Sage.

Haleem, A., Javaid, M., Qadri, M., Singh, R., & Suman, R. (2022). Artificial intelligence (AI) applications for marketing: A literature-based study. *International Journal of Intelligent Networks*, *3*, 119–132. DOI: 10.1016/j.ijin.2022.08.005

Hlee, S., Park, J., Park, H., Koo, C., & Chang, Y. (2023). Understanding customer's meaningful engagement with AI-powered service robots. *Information Technology & People*, *36*(3), 1020–1047. DOI: 10.1108/ITP-10-2020-0740

Hsieh, S. H., & Chang, A. (2016). The psychological mechanism of brand co-creation engagement. *Journal of Interactive Marketing*, *33*(1), 13–26. DOI: 10.1016/j.intmar.2015.10.001

Huang, B., & Philp, M. (2021). When AI-based services fail: Examining the effect of the self-AI connection on willingness to share negative word-of-mouth after service failures. *Service Industries Journal*, *41*(13-14), 877–899. DOI: 10.1080/02642069.2020.1748014

Huang, M., & Rust, R. (2021). Engaged to a robot? The role of AI in service. *Journal of Service Research*, *24*(1), 30–41. DOI: 10.1177/1094670520902266

Issa, H., Jabbouri, R., & Palmer, M. (2022). An artificial intelligence (AI)-readiness and adoption framework for AgriTech firms. *Technological Forecasting and Social Change*, *182*, 121874. DOI: 10.1016/j.techfore.2022.121874

Jindal, R., & Kaur, H. (2024). Managing Guest Expectations and Safety With AI and Smart Solutions. In *Utilizing Smart Technology and AI in Hybrid Tourism and Hospitality* (pp. 118–139). IGI Global. DOI: 10.4018/979-8-3693-1978-9.ch006

Jöhnk, J., Weißert, M., & Wyrtki, K. (2021). Ready or not, AI comes—An interview study of organizational AI readiness factors. *Business & Information Systems Engineering*, *63*(1), 5–20. DOI: 10.1007/s12599-020-00676-7

Kannan, R. (2024). Revolutionizing the Tourism Industry through Artificial Intelligence: A Comprehensive Review of AI Integration, Impact on Customer Experience, Operational Efficiency, and Future Trends. *International Journal for Multidimensional Research Perspectives, 2*(2), 01-14.

Kathuria, S., & Rana, S. (2023). Linking Customer E-Service Quality with Artificial Intelligence-Based Business Environment. In *Artificial Intelligence in Customer Service: The Next Frontier for Personalized Engagement* (pp. 259–279). Springer International Publishing. DOI: 10.1007/978-3-031-33898-4_11

Kock, N. (2021). *WarpPLS User Manual: Version 7.0.* ScriptWarp Systems.

Krishnan, C., & Mariappan, J. (2024). The AI Revolution in E-Commerce: Personalization and Predictive Analytics. In *Role of Explainable Artificial Intelligence in E-Commerce* (pp. 53–64). Springer Nature Switzerland. DOI: 10.1007/978-3-031-55615-9_4

Libai, B., Bart, Y., Gensler, S., Hofacker, C., Kaplan, A., Kötterheinrich, K., & Kroll, E. (2020). Brave new world? On AI and the management of customer relationships. *Journal of Interactive Marketing, 51*(1), 44–56. DOI: 10.1016/j.intmar.2020.04.002

Makmor, N., Aziz Abd, N., & Alam Shah, S. (2019). Social commerce an extended technology acceptance model: The mediating effect of perceived ease of use and perceived usefulness. *Malays. J. Consum. Fam. Econ, 22*, 119–136.

Malhotra, G., & Ramalingam, M. (2023). Perceived anthropomorphism and purchase intention using artificial intelligence technology: Examining the moderated effect of trust. *Journal of Enterprise Information Management*. Advance online publication. DOI: 10.1108/JEIM-09-2022-0316

Malodia, S., Ferraris, A., Sakashita, M., Dhir, A., & Gavurova, B. (2023). Can Alexa serve customers better? AI-driven voice assistant service interactions. *Journal of Services Marketing, 37*(1), 25–39. DOI: 10.1108/JSM-12-2021-0488

Manley, S. C., Hair, J. F.Jr, Williams, R. I.Jr, & McDowell, W. C. (2021). Essential new PLS-SEM analysis methods for your entrepreneurship analytical toolbox. *The International Entrepreneurship and Management Journal, 17*(4), 1805–1825. DOI: 10.1007/s11365-020-00687-6

Marti, C., Liu, H., Kour, G., Bilgihan, A., & Xu, Y. (2024). Leveraging artificial intelligence in firm-generated online customer communities: A framework and future research agenda. *Journal of Service Management, 35*(3), 438–458. DOI: 10.1108/JOSM-10-2023-0443

Mishra, A., Shukla, A., & Sharma, S. (2022). Psychological determinants of users' adoption and word-of-mouth recommendations of smart voice assistants. *International Journal of Information Management, 67*, 102413. DOI: 10.1016/j.ijinfomgt.2021.102413

Mohamed, M., Farahat, E., & Al-Romeedy, B. (2022). The Mediating Role of Marketing Effectiveness in the Relationship between Artificial Intelligence and Destination Competitiveness. *Minia Journal of Tourism and Hospitality Research, 14*(1), 113–129.

Nwachukwu, D., & Affen, M. (2023). Artificial intelligence marketing practices: The way forward to better customer experience management in Africa (Systematic Literature Review). *International Academy Journal of Management. Marketing and Entrepreneurial Studies, 9*(2), 44–62.

Omrani, N., Rivieccio, G., Fiore, U., Schiavone, F., & Agreda, S. (2022). To trust or not to trust? An assessment of trust in AI-based systems: Concerns, ethics and contexts. *Technological Forecasting and Social Change, 181*, 121763. DOI: 10.1016/j.techfore.2022.121763

Paluch, S., & Wittkop, T. (2023). Role of Risk on Employees' Willingness to Collaborate with Artificial Intelligence and Its Impact on Wellbeing. In *Artificial Intelligence in Customer Service: The Next Frontier for Personalized Engagement* (pp. 281–302). Springer International Publishing. DOI: 10.1007/978-3-031-33898-4_12

Pillai, R., Sivathanu, B., & Dwivedi, Y. K. (2020). Shopping intention at AI-powered automated retail stores (AIPARS). *Journal of Retailing and Consumer Services, 57*, 102207. DOI: 10.1016/j.jretconser.2020.102207

Pitardi, V., & Marriott, H. (2021). Alexa, she's not human but… Unveiling the drivers of consumers' trust in voice-based artificial intelligence. *Psychology and Marketing, 38*(4), 626–642. DOI: 10.1002/mar.21457

Polisetty, A., Chakraborty, D., Kar, A., & Pahari, S. (2024). What determines AI adoption in companies? Mixed-method evidence. *Journal of Computer Information Systems, 64*(3), 370–387. DOI: 10.1080/08874417.2023.2219668

Preacher, K. J., & Hayes, A. F. (2008). Asymptotic and resampling strategies for assessing and comparing indirect effects in multiple mediator models. *Behavior Research Methods, 40*(3), 879–891. DOI: 10.3758/BRM.40.3.879 PMID: 18697684

Prentice, C., Weaven, S., & Wong, I. (2020). Linking AI quality performance and customer engagement: The moderating effect of AI preference. *International Journal of Hospitality Management, 90*, 102629. DOI: 10.1016/j.ijhm.2020.102629

Rahman, M., Bag, S., Gupta, S., & Sivarajah, U. (2023a). Technology readiness of B2B firms and AI-based customer relationship management capability for enhancing social sustainability performance. *Journal of Business Research, 156*, 113525. DOI: 10.1016/j.jbusres.2022.113525

Rahman, M., Bag, S., Hossain, M., Fattah, F., Gani, M., & Rana, N. (2023b). The new wave of AI-powered luxury brands online shopping experience: The role of digital multisensory cues and customers' engagement. *Journal of Retailing and Consumer Services, 72*, 103273. DOI: 10.1016/j.jretconser.2023.103273

Raji, M., Olodo, H., Oke, T., Addy, W., Ofodile, O., & Oyewole, A. (2024). E-commerce and consumer behavior: A review of AI-powered personalization and market trends. *GSC Advanced Research and Reviews, 18*(3), 066-077.

Rane, N., Achari, A., & Choudhary, S. P. (2023). Enhancing customer loyalty through quality of service: Effective strategies to improve customer satisfaction, experience, relationship, and engagement. *International Research Journal of Modernization in Engineering Technology and Science, 5*(5), 427–452.

Sharma, R., & Singh, G. (2023). Unveiling the Buying Behaviour of Gen Z for Hospitality Products: Insights for Smart Hotels. In *Sustainable Development Goal Advancement Through Digital Innovation in the Service Sector* (pp. 114-132). IGI Global.

Shi, S., Gong, Y., & Gursoy, D. (2021). Antecedents of trust and adoption intention toward artificially intelligent recommendation systems in travel planning: A heuristic–systematic model. *Journal of Travel Research, 60*(8), 1714–1734. DOI: 10.1177/0047287520966395

Shin, D. (2020). User perceptions of algorithmic decisions in the personalized AI system: Perceptual evaluation of fairness, accountability, transparency, and explainability. *Journal of Broadcasting & Electronic Media, 64*(4), 541–565. DOI: 10.1080/08838151.2020.1843357

Solberg, E., Kaarstad, M., Eitrheim, M., Bisio, R., Reegård, K., & Bloch, M. (2022). A conceptual model of trust, perceived risk, and reliance on AI decision aids. *Group & Organization Management, 47*(2), 187–222. DOI: 10.1177/10596011221081238

Song, M., Xing, X., Duan, Y., Cohen, J., & Mou, J. (2022). Will artificial intelligence replace human customer service? The impact of communication quality and privacy risks on adoption intention. *Journal of Retailing and Consumer Services, 66*, 102900. DOI: 10.1016/j.jretconser.2021.102900

Sung, E., Bae, S., Han, D., & Kwon, O. (2021). Consumer engagement via interactive artificial intelligence and mixed reality. *International Journal of Information Management, 60*, 102382. DOI: 10.1016/j.ijinfomgt.2021.102382

Taylor, E., & Broløs, A. (2024). *Customer-Centric Innovation in Finance: Leveraging Human Insights to Drive Product Innovation in the Digital Age*. Kogan Page Publishers.

Thakur, A. (2022). Technological innovations in the hospitality and tourism industry. In *Mobile computing and technology applications in tourism and hospitality* (pp. 72–97). IGI Global. DOI: 10.4018/978-1-7998-6904-7.ch004

Vahdat, A., Alizadeh, A., Quach, S., & Hamelin, N. (2021). Would you like to shop via mobile app technology? The technology acceptance model, social factors and purchase intention. *Australasian Marketing Journal*, *29*(2), 187–197. DOI: 10.1016/j.ausmj.2020.01.002

Wamba-Taguimdje, S., Wamba, S., Kamdjoug, J., & Wanko, C. (2020). Influence of artificial intelligence (AI) on firm performance: The business value of AI-based transformation projects. *Business Process Management Journal*, *26*(7), 1893–1924. DOI: 10.1108/BPMJ-10-2019-0411

Yin, D., Li, M., & Qiu, H. (2023). Do customers exhibit engagement behaviors in AI environments? The role of psychological benefits and technology readiness. *Tourism Management*, *97*, 104745. DOI: 10.1016/j.tourman.2023.104745

Yin, J., & Qiu, X. (2021). AI technology and online purchase intention: Structural equation model based on perceived value. *Sustainability (Basel)*, *13*(10), 5671. DOI: 10.3390/su13105671

Chapter 11
Impact of Artificial Intelligence on Employment and Skill Requirements in the Tourism Sector

Akhilesh
https://orcid.org/0009-0009-4406-7868
Assam University, India

Pradip Kumar
https://orcid.org/0000-0002-5138-736X
Assam University, India

ABSTRACT

The rapid advancement and integration of artificial intelligence (AI) technologies are profoundly transforming the tourism sector, presenting both opportunities and challenges for employment and skill requirements The primary objectives are to analyse the impact of AI on employment, assess changes in skill requirements, and evaluate the benefits and drawbacks of AI adoption. Employing secondary data from scholarly articles, industry reports, and market research, this study provides a nuanced understanding of AI's influence on the tourism sector. The analysis reveals a transformative impact of AI on employment trends, characterised by the displacement of certain job roles and the emergence of new opportunities centred around AI management and technological innovation. Additionally, it emphasizes the evolving skill set required by AI integration and the growing significance of digital literacy, data analysis, and AI proficiency among tourism professionals.

1. INTRODUCTION

One of the most dynamic and basic sectors in the world economy has been AI-based technologies in the last decade. Chatbots, virtual assistants, enriched data analytics andautomated booking systems have been at the core of changing the very concept and delivery of tourism services in modern times. This is a double-edged sword, offering both opportunities and challenges but completely transforming the dynamics of employment and the kind of skills required in the industry. In the tourism sector, AI emerges as a trend rather than a profound evolution that could shape employment patterns. As AI systems evolve to automate routine jobs and business processes, some

DOI: 10.4018/979-8-3693-7447-4.ch011

routine jobs emerge to become obsolete while new demanding technical ones emerge. This would be crucial in understanding these two impacts on the general workforce composition of the tourism sector.

New requirements, particularly in terms of skills and people involved in the tourism business, are driving these changes in employment. AI brings with it some technical skills that had as yet remained on the fringes of the industry. Employees now need to be tech-savvy with AI technologies and constantly upskill and reskill themselves. The challenge is the high skill gap between the current workforce and the demands of the future, which requires specific programs of education and training to be ready for an AI-driven work environment. In addition, advancement in AI applied to tourism brings a combination of benefits and challenges. On the one hand, AI applications bring enormous efficiency and productivity gains into existence, increasing the customer's experience and operational efficiencies. Data privacy, cost of high implementation, and resistance to change are all potential risks and barriers, but at the same time offer numerous benefits with regard to adopting AI. It is therefore very crucial that any stakeholder takes a balanced perspective towards both positive and negative facts in coming up with decisions about investments and strategies for AI. AI implementation has drastically changed the employment trends in the tourism sector. As time goes on, automation of routine, repetitive tasks such as reservation booking and dealing with the customer's enquiries becomes indispensable to maintaining inventory. Most of the time, automation replaces the workers who used to perform these tasks at the workplace. For instance, AI chatbots and virtual agents, which can respond to the customer's enquiries round the clock more quickly and effectively, have replaced most customer representatives who previously relied on phone calls and email correspondences. However, despite their displacement, new job roles are emerging in their place. AI technologies need maintenance, management, and improvement, which has given rise to job roles such as AI specialists, data analysts, and digital transformation managers. These are jobs involved in the development, implementation, and refinement of AI systems to respond to the dynamic needs of the tourism sector. The creation of such new jobs points towards a future in which more specialized technical jobs in the sector will continue to arise.

Some of the job roles in tourism are more susceptible than others to changes in AI-driven technology. That is transformative for any frontline job, such as receptionist, booking agent, or tour guide. For example, AI-enabled concierge service at hotels can provide customer-specific recommendations, simplify checking in with facilities, and provide instant answers to common questions without requiring human intervention. Virtual tour guides use augmented reality to ensure a better visitor experience, thereby reducing the traditional job roles of a physical tour guide. On the other end of the spectrum, jobs requiring high-end problem-solving capabilities with emotional intelligence and human interaction at a personal level remain very unaffected. This category of business also encompasses travel consultants, event planners, and high-end hospitality staff. They always have a high degree of design and require much relevant knowledge of consumer desires and preferences, which AI can never embody. This kind of categorisation throws light on the fact that the impact of AI on employment is selective and mandates a holistic view of workforce planning and development.

Artificial intelligence is increasingly permeating tourism, creating a need for more technical skills. Workers have to familiarise themselves with AI and its application capabilities ranging from data analysis to machine learning and familiarity with AI-based tools, to name just a few. For example, a travel agent would have to engage in customer analysis to enable them to offer recommended customisations via AI systems for better service delivery. Besides, with digital literacy being the core competence, it is imperative to keep track by learning about AI software, digital marketing, and online customer service platforms, among others. Therefore, employees should continuously learn about the latest technological advancements and their practical applications in the tourism industry.

The key challenge that remains with the tourism industry pertains to the skills gap between the current workforce and the needed future requirements. Most of the current employees may not be able to operate with AI technologies in a technically efficient manner. There is a need for the implementation of serious training programs that would give priority to skills development, enhancing, retraining, and reskilling of the workforce. The training programs should cover aspects such as a general introduction to AI, data management, and CRM (customer relationship management) systems coupled with an emphasis on their ethical use. To meet the requirements of the tourism industry, industry players must form partnerships with the academic community to develop custom-curated content for training purposes. On-the-job training and continuing professional development programs ensure that the workforce is competent and remains competitive in an environment driven by AI technology.

Among the core advantages of the adoption of AI in the tourism sector are efficiency and productivity. With AI-powered systems processing colossal amounts of data within the shortest time frame and with maximum accuracy, real-time decision-making and instant, tailored customer experiences occur. It can analyse the customer's preferences and behavioural patterns to provide customisation in travel packages, thus increasing the customer's satisfaction and loyalty. This is an important element in increasing operational efficiencies. Automated systems eliminate much of the administrative work, freeing up employees to engage in more strategic and creative aspects of their jobs. Through this means, such a change will thus embrace cost savings, higher productivity, and hence better resource utilization. Further, AI drives the revenue factor through the recognition of trends and optimising advertising strategies.

However, as positive as it gets to integrate AI into the tourism industry, some challenges remain in its application. Integration poses major challenges as it involves the collection and analysis of large volumes of personal data specific to a single customer. To continue engaging the trust of the customers, this should involve sound data protection measures and compliance with the rules e.g., GDPR (General Data Protection Regulation). Some of these factors are the high implementation costs, which also remain a challenge to small businesses in the tourism sector. Investing in AI infrastructure and software, along with training programs, requires significant capital. More possible challenges involve resistance from both employees and management because of the fears of losing jobs or complexities related to AI systems. Finally, there is the consideration of AI ethics, bias in AI algorithms, and potential job displacement. We therefore have to design fair and transparent AI systems that encourage inclusion and equity in a manner that lowers risks and extends benefits to be far-reaching across the sector. The current study provides work in general on these concerns in order to gain insights while working inside the dynamism of AI in the tourism industry.

2. BACKGROUND OF THE STUDY

Tourism has been the largest contributor to the world economy. Technology has played an important role in the sector from quite early. The introduction of artificial intelligence (AI) recently has brought remarkable change in the industry and its entire scenario. AI is a disruptive technology that changes the way businesses interact with customers and treat resources. This research aims to give an account of the influence that AI can have on employment and associated skills in the tourism sector, an increasingly important area of research that changes its face under technological advances.

The potential for AI to influence industry employment trends is a significant topic of debate surrounding its adoption. The growing ability of AI systems to perform tasks previously performed by humans,such as interacting with customers for assistance or managing complex decision processes, has intensified discussions about job displacement. This study therefore aims to explore how AI is changing employment patterns in the tourism sector, finding areas where automation may displace jobs and new opportunities may emerge from the adoption of AI technologies.

Other, perhaps more salient effects of the introduction of AI in the tourism sector have to do with employment. The industry will require instilling new capabilities in its employees as AI technologies become increasingly ingrained. Such abilities will be not only technically orientated skills tied to AI and data analytics but also soft skills such as adaptability, problem-solving, and emotional intelligence. This section looks into the changes that AI integration will have on skill demands, trying to project some of the challenges and opportunities for existing and potential workers within the tourism sector.

Even though, on the side of the advantages of AI, it is going to lead to efficiency, better customer experiences, and savings on costs for the tourism industry; it also comes with many disadvantages. These could be the loss of human interaction, ethical issues, and a possible overreliance on automated systems. The current research will identify the advantages and disadvantages of implementing AI systems in the tourism industry, therefore developing both arguments with reference to the implications of this change powered by technology.

With the aforementioned, the valuable insights that this current research will contribute will be great in understanding how AI is changing the role of the tourism industry and potentially affecting employment, labour demand, and altering the general nature of the industry. Results from this study will throw light on how AI shapes the future of tourism by enabling strategies to manage transition while maximising potential benefits and minimising risks.

3. OBJECTIVES

- To analyse the impact of AI on employment trends in the tourism sector.
- To assess the changes in skill requirements caused by AI integration.
- To assess the benefits and drawbacks of AI adoption in the tourism industry.

4. METHODOLOGY

This chapter primarily relied on secondary data collection, employing a descriptive approach to achieve its objectives. Secondary data collection entailed gathering data from academic journals, industry reports, case studies, and existing literature on the effect that artificial intelligence is likely to have on employment and skill requirements in the tourism industry.

5. THE CURRENT STATE OF AI IN TRAVEL AND TOURISM

5.1 Adoption of AI Technologies in Various Sub-Sectors of the Travel and Tourism Industry

5.1.1 AI in the Airline Industry

a. Customer Service and Experience
    - **Chatbots and Virtual Assistants:** Airlines such as KLM (Koninklijke Luchtvaart Maatschappij N.V.) and American Airlines use AI-powered chatbots to respond to customer queries, offer information about flights, or assist in making reservations. They operate round the clock, thereby providing instant responses and alleviating the pressure on human agents. (Tussyadiah, 2020).
    - **Personalised Recommendations:** The AI algorithms analyse customer data to make personalised travel recommendations, which include seat preferences, meal choices, and travel itineraries. This improves the overall travel experience and boosts the customer's satisfaction.

b. Operational Efficiency
    - **Predictive Maintenance**: Airlines use artificial intelligence (AI) to predict maintenance requirements by processing aircraft sensor data. Predictive maintenance avoids unexpected failures, reduces downtime, and ensures safety. For example, Delta Airlines has already implemented artificial intelligence predictive maintenance programs, which have led to fewer flight cancellations.

- **Route Optimisation:** AI algorithms apply different methodologies to optimise flight routes based on the existing weather and air traffic, as well as fuel cost and consumption. This leads to more efficient flight paths, lower fuel costs, and reduced emissions.

5.1.2 AI in the Hospitality Industry

a. Enhancing Guest Experiences
  - **Smart Hotel Rooms**: AI-enabled devices installed in hotel rooms help to control the lighting, temperature, and entertainment systems based on the customer's preferences. For instance, Marriott International has implemented AI-based systems for personalising guest experiences.(Ivanov et al., 2017)
  - **Automated Check-In and Check-Out:** The hotels use AI-enabled kiosks and mobile apps to automate the check-in and check-out processes, ensuring that customers do not have to wait in long lines while also making their experience very convenient. Hilton Hotels has adopted such systems to improve front-office operations.

b. Operational Management
  - **Energy Management**: AI systems in hotels manage and control energy use by modulating settings based on occupancy and use. This, in effect, significantly contributes to the reduction of energy costs and cuts back on the carbon footprint of hotels (Gretzel et al., 2015).
  - **Housekeeping and Maintenance**: Deploy AI-driven robots and sensors in housekeeping and maintenance functions to ensure timely and efficient service delivery. This assures operational efficiency and guest satisfaction at the same time.

5.1.3 AI in Travel Agencies

a. Personalised Travel Planning
  - **Recommendation Engines:** AI-based recommendation engines harness the customer's preferences and behaviours to suggest hyper-personalized travel itineraries, destinations, and activities. Expedia is one of the companies whose platforms use AI to provide better travel planning services.
  - **Dynamic Pricing**: AI algorithms assist a travel agency in dynamically adjusting price levels in real-time based on demand, consumer behaviour, and market conditions to ensure competitiveness and maximise profit.

b. Customer Relationship Management (CRM)
  - **Predictive Analytics:** Travel agencies have been using predictive analytics powered by AI to predict a customer's needs and preferences for personalised marketing and deliver services accordingly. This improves the customer's engagement and loyalty (Tussyadiah, 2020).
  - **Automated Customer Support:** AI chatbots and virtual assistants address the customer's enquiries and tasks related to support with speed and effectiveness in service delivery, thus reducing the human agents' workload while enhancing the customer's satisfaction.

5.1.4 AI in Tourism Management

a. Destination Management
  - **Flow Management of Tourists**: AI, by using data on tourist movements and their behaviours, helps better manage the tourist flow to avoid congestion at popular destinations and develop a positive experience for tourists while safeguarding heritage sites.

- **Sustainable tourism:** Using AI tools to monitor environmental impact and resource utilization is part of sustainable tourism. Tourism managers can adopt specific sustainable practices. AI plays a significant role in waste and energy management in tourist destinations, thereby optimising these processes.

b. Marketing and Promotion
    - **Content Personalisation**: AI enables algorithms to create customised marketing content based on customer data in terms of travel recommendations, promotions, and ads. This enhances marketing campaign effectiveness and the customer's engagement.
    - **Social Media Analysis**: AI analyses social media trends and the customer's feedback to gain insights into tourist preferences and sentiment. These work to help tourism managers align their offers and marketing strategies with the customer's expectations. (Gössling et al., 2021).

5.2 Examples of AI Applications in Customer Service, Operations, and Marketing in the Travel and Tourism Industry

5.2.1 AI in Customer Service

a. Chatbots and Virtual Assistants

Chatbots and virtual assistants are two of the most obvious applications of AI in customer service. These AI-powered tools allow them to engage customers in real time, answer their questions, or even handle bookings to enhance the general customer's experience.

- **KLM Royal Dutch Airlines**: KLM runs an AI-infused chatbot known as Blue-Bot, helping customers book a flight, offering travel information, and answering frequently asked questions. The chatbot assists the customers round the clock using multiple languages and can understand and respond to client queries using NLP (natural language processing).
- **Expedia:** Expedia uses an AI chatbot to assist its clients in booking hotels, flights, and cars. It can provide instant responses to the customer's enquiries, offer recommendations, assist in resolving issues, and take off the workload of human agents to boost the customer's satisfaction levels. (Gretzel et al., 2015).

b. Personalized the customer's experiences
    - **Hilton Hotels:** The AI-powered concierge named Connie at Hilton answers guest questions, disseminates information about hotel facilities, and even makes personalised recommendations on local attractions. AI keeps learning from every new interaction, thus enhancing its responses and improving guests' experiences over time.(Ivanov et al., 2017).
    - **Booking.com** personalises the booking process through its AI function. The platform analyses past booking data, search queries, and user reviews to recommend accommodations and destinations that align with the traveler's preferences.

5.2.2 AI in Operations

a. Predictive Maintenance
    - **Delta Airlines** uses AI to forecast aircraft maintenance. It detects patterns in data from various sensors in real time and alerts the airline if it finds any potential issues. Predictive analysis successfully prevents problems from occurring. This strategy supports downtime reduction and flight delay prevention while ensuring proactive maintenance and safety. AI also analyses data from building systems

to predict maintenance needs, including HVAC systems (Heating, Ventilation, and Air Conditioning) and elevators, enabling prompt corrective action without disturbing guests.

- **Marriott International**: Marriott has implemented AI-driven predictive maintenance in its hotel properties. AI analyses data from building systems to predict maintenance needs, such as HVAC systems and elevators, ensuring timely repairs and minimising disruptions for guests.

b. Route Optimisation

- **Lufthansa** uses AI algorithms to optimise flight routes by considering factors such as weather conditions, air traffic, and fuel prices. This leads to more efficient flight paths, reduced fuel consumption, and lower emissions, all contributing to cost savings and environmental benefits.
- **Uber** uses AI to optimise the routes its drivers take. The AI model considers real-time traffic information, demand predictions, and historical trip data to provide the most effective routes, saving time and enhancing the customer's satisfaction.

5.2.3 AI in Marketing

a. Personalised Marketing Campaigns

- **TripAdvisor** uses AI technology to analyse user reviews, ratings, and browsing histories to provide personalised travel recommendations and advertisements. The platform tailors its marketing messages based on individual preferences, increasing engagement and conversion rates.
- **Google Travel** uses AI to personalise travel plans for users. Google Travel leverages AI to analyse search history, past travel bookings, and user preferences to suggest destinations, flights, and accommodations that align with the user's interests. This personalised approach enhances the user experience and drives higher engagement.(Gretzel et al., 2015)

5.3 Case Studies of AI Implementation.

5.3.1 Case Study 1: Hilton Hotels Connie, the AI Concierge

Implementation: Hilton has introduced an AI-based robotic concierge, Connie, to assist guests with a wide array of enquiries they may have regarding hotel amenities and local attractions.

Features: "Connie" uses natural language processing to interact with guests, understanding them and learning from each interaction to improve its responses over time. It provides personalised recommendations based on the guest's preferences and available historical data.

Benefits:

- Personalised and efficient guest experiences.
- The reduced workload for human staff allows them to focus on more complex tasks.
- The company has improved operational efficiency and guest satisfaction (Ivanov et al., 2017)

5.3.2 Case Study 2: Delta Airlines: Implementation of Predictive Maintenance

Delta Airlines has implemented an AI predictive maintenance system for the analysis of aircraft sensor data, prediction of potential maintenance needs, and recommendations.

Functionality: This AI predictive system analyses real-time data for patterns or trends in data that indicate a problem. It alerts maintenance teams in time to address these issues before they escalate into a bigger problem.

Benefits:

- There has been a reduction in flight delays and cancellations due to unscheduled maintenance.
- The aircraft has improved its safety and reliability.
- We achieved huge cost savings through proactive maintenance and reduced downtime.

5.4 Impact of AI on Employment

5.4.1 Automation of Routine Tasks and Its Effects on Job Roles in the Tourism Industry

Key Areas of Automation:

- **Customer Service:** AI-enabled chatbots and virtual assistants help to provide real-time and accurate information to customers on different issues, reservations, and other support services.
- **Check-In and Check-Out Processes:** Various kiosks and mobile applications in the airline and hotel industries help customers to check in and out quickly; this saves time and therefore offers the highest degree of convenience to the consumers.
- **Administrative Tasks:** The automation software performs administrative tasks related to data entry, reservation management, and invoicing, thereby releasing human labour for other more intellectual positions.
- **Housekeeping and Maintenance:** AI robots and sensors perform cleaning and maintenance, ensuring prompt and efficient service delivery.

5.4.2 Impacts on Job Roles

a. Job displacement
   - **Front Desk Staff:** With the increased automation for check-in and checkout, the demand for front desk staff in hotels goes down. Nowadays, automation through kiosks and a mobile app allows guests to check in and out by themselves.
   - **Customer Service Representatives**: AI chatbots and virtual assistants handle major portions of the customer's enquiries and support tasks that actually minimise human customer service representatives in an organisation.
   - **Administrative Workers:** In today's automated age, AI systems are performing administrative work-such as data entry and reservation management-more effectively, so it has reduced the requirement for administrators.

b. Job Enrichment
   - **Expanded Roles:** Automation allows employees to concentrate on more important, complex, and value-added work that requires human creativity, problem-solving, and emotional intelligence. For instance, the task of routine check-ins ensures that hotel staff members are primarily concerned with delivering tailored services and creating special experiences for guests.
   - Employees need to develop capabilities in new skills that incorporate AI and automation technologies. This includes digital literacy, data analysis, and the management of automated systems. For instance, travel agents will be required to learn how to coordinate with AI tools to conduct travel trends analysis for personalised recommendations.

c. New Job Roles
   - **AI Specialists:** The tourism industry will require professionals in the areas of AI and machine learning who can design and manage AI systems. These can be AI trainers, data scientists, and AI ethicists.
   - **Technology Maintenance Engineers:** As hotels and other tourist-related businesses implement increasingly automated systems, there arises an increasing need for professionals who can take care of such systems with all the attention and efficiency.

- The application of AI to personalised marketing makes new opportunities appear for specialists in digital marketing in the application of tools based on AI technologies within the development of targeted campaigns for customers and the analysis of data related to them.

5.5 Case Studies of Companies Implementing AI and Resulting Employment Changes in the Tourism Industry

5.5.1 Case Study 1: Hilton Hotels - AI Powered Concierge

Overview: Hilton Hotels installed an artificial intelligence-powered concierge named Connie, running on IBM Watson. Visitors can receive responses to various queries, explore available hotel services, and receive recommendations for local attractions.

Implementation:

- **Technology Used:** "Connie" interacts with the guests through the AI capabilities of IBM Watson, including natural language processing and machine learning.
- **Task Automation:** Connie can answer a question, give directions, suggest restaurants, and even make personalised recommendations based on a guest's preferences.

Shifting Employment:

- **Changing Nature of Work:** With the introduction of Connie, the nature of jobs has changed for the front-desk staff.
- **Human interaction and personalisation:** They can concentrate on thinking about more critical issues and are attending to vital things that need a human touch and consideration, rather than just doing rote queries.
- **Skills development:** The employees learn how to handle and live with the AI concierge. They develop their skills in managing an AI system and learn customer-handling techniques.
- **Improved Efficiency:** By providing similar questions, Connie freed up time for human workers, which in turn improved the customer's satisfaction. This resulted in more total numbers of satisfied customers. (Ivanov et al., 2017).

Impact:

- **Quality Customer Service Provision**: The AI concierge process enabled quick quality servicing; hence, many guests who had great reviews started visiting more.
- **Reduced Operational Costs:** Automating routine tasks—besides stripping jobs—brought Hilton savings.
- **Employee Satisfaction:** More meaningful interaction with the customers increased job satisfaction among the front desk employees.

5.5.2 Case Study 2: Delta Airlines: Predictive Maintenance

Overview: Delta Airlines is one of the prime drivers behind AI-enabled predictive maintenance that helps to keep planes flying in excellent and safe condition.

Implementation:

- **Technology used:** AI-based predictive maintenance systems evaluate sensor data from aircraft. These algorithms review the data to determine patterns or anomalies, which may denote a requirement for maintenance at some future point in time.

- **Key Functionalities:** It predicts maintenance schedules to prevent unexpected breakdowns and minimise downtime.

Employment Changes:

- **Job Creation**: The development of predictive maintenance led to the creation of new positions for data scientists, AI specialists, and maintenance engineers who handle and process the AI system.
- **Skills Development**: Trained maintenance staff to understand AI diagnostics and integrate AI insights into their maintenance process.
- **Job Security**: Improved aircraft operations have reduced the rate of emergency maintenance, providing a more stable working environment for the maintenance staff.

Impact:

- The AI system improved operational efficiency by reducing the frequency of unscheduled maintenance and flight delays.
- **Cost savings:** Proactive maintenance reduced the company's total maintenance costs and revenue losses due to flight cancellations and delays.
- **Safety Enhancements**: The above approach improved the Delta fleet's safety and reliability, resulting in a positive passenger experience.(Gretzel et al., 2015).

5.5.3 Case Study 3: AI Chatbots on Expedia

Overview: Expedia, the world's largest online travel agency, developed the service by deploying AI chatbots to improve customer service and streamline the booking process.

Implementation:

- **Technology Used**: Expedia's AI chatbots use machine learning and NLP to maintain the customer's enquiries, support bookings, and provide travel advice.
- **Job Done by Technology**: The chatbots engage at any time of the day, providing instant responses to the customer's questions and customized travel advisories.

Changes in Employment:

- **Labour Displaced**: The automation of human agents, who performed repetitive, low-skill tasks related to customer service, led to a decrease in their demand.
- **Job Redesign**: Those who remained in the roles redefined their work to deal with much more complicated queries and those that necessitate human judgement and empathy.
- **Enhancement**: Provide training on how to handle AI and relate to customers at a higher level. It developed employees technically and interpersonally. (Gretzel et al., 2015).

Impact:

- **Enhanced the Customer's Satisfaction**: The AI chatbots could respond instantly and precisely, making the customers content with the service.
- **Operational Efficiency**: Automation increased system efficiency with shorter response times, allowing for better handling of the customer's enquiries without increasing human resources.
- **Cost Reduction**: Expedia lowers labor costs and uses AI chatbots to deploy resources more effectively (Gretzel et al., 2015).

5.5.4 Case Study 4: Airbnb: Dynamic Pricing

Overview: Airbnb unveiled an artificial intelligence dynamic pricing tool that hosts can use to optimise the value of hosting by factoring in prevailing market conditions and other dynamic variables.

Implementation:

- **Technology Used**: The artificial intelligence-enabled dynamic pricing uses algorithms for data analysis on local events and seasonal trends, competitor pricing, and booking patterns.
- **How it Works:** It provides pricing recommendations to the hosts, based on which they fine-tune their charges in real time, thereby optimising for occupancy and revenue.

Changes in Employment:

- **Job Creation**: The dynamic pricing tool and subsequent maintenance necessitated new positions for AI specialists, data analysts, and software engineers.
- **Skills Development**: Trained the hosts to use the dynamic pricing tool, educating them about market dynamics and equipping them with various pricing strategies.
- **Further Responsibilities**: Automation of pricing took their focus from the price-setting activity to maximising the guest experience and property handling.

Impact:

- **Maximisation of Revenues**: The AI tool enabled hosts to maximise their revenues by setting the right prices that will optimise both their occupancy and overall revenue.
- **Competitiveness in the Market**: Dynamic pricing ensured market-competitive prices for Airbnb hosts.
- **Operational Efficiency**: Automating pricing decisions reduced the time and effort that hosts had to spend manually making price alterations, thus improving overall operational efficiency.

5.6 Training and Upskilling Initiatives for Existing Employees in the AI-Driven Tourism Industry

5.6.1 Importance of Training and Upskilling

a. Increasing worker competence
    - **Technical Competence**: The workers should be able to apply AI tools and systems to deliver operations and customer service efficiently.
    - **Adaptability**: Training makes the employees more adaptable; they can, therefore, easily slide into new roles or take up additional tasks.

b. Employee Retention: Employee development is considered a retention strategy because it demonstrates a commitment to developing and advancing the employee's career.
    - **Opportunities for Career Growth**: Training and upskilling give employees a sense of direction in terms of career development within the organisation.
    - **Job satisfaction:** Employees who perceive their workplace as a place of investment through development opportunities are more likely to feel satisfied, thereby lowering turnover rates.

c. Ensuring Competitiveness within Business
    - **Innovation and Efficiency**: A skilled employee can result in a more innovative and efficient workforce, which helps the business remain ahead of other competitors.
    - **Customer's Experience**: With effective training, employees can use AI to improve the customer's experience, leading to increased satisfaction and loyalty.

5.6.2 Training and Upskilling Initiatives

a. Technical Training Programs
    - **AI and Machine Learning**: These programs should be able to expose trainees to the fundamentals of AI and machine learning, how they work, and their applications in the tourism sector.

- **Data Analysis and Management**: We should train employees in data analysis techniques and tools, enabling them to read and make decisions based on the information AI systems generate.
- **Cybersecurity:** Because sensitive data passes through AI-based systems, cybersecurity training is required to protect the customer's information and remain compliant with any data protection regulations. (Gössling et al., 2021).

b. Soft Skills Development

- **Customer Service Skills**: Training programs should emphasise the soft skills of empathy, communication, and problem-solving to further supplement AI-driven customer interactions.
- **Collaboration and Teamwork**: Since the use of AI frequently necessitates cross-functional coordination and cooperation, employees should receive training in these areas.
- **Critical Thinking and Problem-Solving:** The workforce's critical thinking and problem-solving skills will help them make sound decisions and solve other problems that may arise with the application of AI.

c. Continuous Learning Opportunities

- **Online Courses and Certifications**: Online courses and certifications will always be there in AI, data sciences, and other niche areas to prepare employees to stay updated with what is happening in these fields.
- **Workshops and Seminars**: By conducting workshops and seminars on AI and its use in the tourism sector, employees gain firsthand practical experience.
- **Mentorship and Coaching**: Mentorship and coaching programs make it possible for employees to learn from experienced professionals and get personal directions for career development.

d. Collaborations with Educational Institutes

- **University Alliances**: Working closely with universities and colleges enables businesses to provide advanced training and certification programs on AI, data science, and so on.
- **Industry Certifications:** Collaborate with professional bodies to create industry-specific certifications, ensuring that the training programs we develop align with the respective industry standards and needs.
- Collaboration with academic institutions on research and development projects can provide employees with opportunities to engage in cutting-edge innovation, making the knowledge gained practically useful to them.

6. TRADITIONAL SKILL REQUIREMENTS IN THE TOURISM SECTOR

6.1 Core Functions and Their Skill Requirements

a. Travel Agents

Travel agents prepared and sold transportation, lodging, and entertainment activities to individual and group travelers.

Skills Required:

- **Destination Knowledge**: A basic working knowledge of travel destinations, an understanding of local tourist attractions, cultural hubs, types of lodging, and transportation.
- **Booking Systems**: The ability to operate Global Distribution Systems (GDS), e.g., Amadeus, Sabre, and Travelport, for handling bookings.

- **Interpersonal skills**: The ability to deal with clients, understand their preferences, and propose travel packages that suit them.
- **Selling and Negotiation**: The capacity to sell travel packages and negotiate for better deals with service providers.
- **Accuracy:** Ensuring accuracy in booking details, travel itineraries, and documentation.

b. Hotel Front Office Staff

The hotel's front office staff were the guests' first point of contact, responsible for check-in and check-out, taking reservations, and providing guest services.

Skills Required:

- **Customer Service:** Strong communication skills and superior interpersonal abilities to warmly welcome guests and address their inquiries or concerns.
- **Reservation Systems:** Familiarity with hotel reservation systems and Property Management Systems (PMS), such as Opera, Infor, and Cloud beds.
- **Problem-Solving**: The ability to address guest complaints and find solutions that meet the guests' needs.
- **Multitasking**: Capable of handling multiple tasks simultaneously, such as answering phones, processing payments, and coordinating with other departments.
- Knowledge about local attractions, dining options, and transportation is essential.

c. Tour Guides

Tour guides led groups or individuals around specific attractions, cities, or regions, providing informative and engaging commentary.

Skills Required:

Communication: Strong verbal communication skills to convey information clearly and engagingly.

- **Understanding History and Culture**: Gaining insight into the history, culture, and significance of the sites under tour.
- **Public Speaking**: Confidence and clarity in speaking to groups of varying sizes.
- **Customer Service:** Ensuring that tourists have a positive experience, addressing their needs, and answering questions.
- **Foreign Language Skills**: Knowledge of at least one foreign language to cater to international tourists. (Gretzel et al., 2015).

d. Marketing and sales management

Marketing and sales managers were responsible for providing tourism-related services, developing plans to carry out such activities, and achieving sales in the process.

Skills Needed:

- **Market research** to identify trends, target clientele groups, and industry competitors.
- **Advertising and Promotion**: Developing advertisement campaigns and conducting promotions through printed media—newspapers, magazines, television, and the Internet.

- **Sales Strategy**: Formulating sales strategies to acquire and maintain customers through special offers, tie-ups, and loyalty programs.
- **Digital Marketing:** The use of digital marketing techniques such as SEO, email marketing, and social media to draw wide viewership.
- **Analytical Skills**: Utilise sales data and marketing metrics in order to establish the efficiency of campaigns and strategies.

6.2 Case Studies of Companies and Their Evolving Skill Requirements in the AI-Driven Tourism Industry

Case Study 1: Hilton Hotels

- **Background:** Hilton Hotels adopted AI-driven concierge services and automated customer interactions to enhance the guest experience.
- **Changing nature of work skill needs:** Workers received training on managing and troubleshooting AI systems, including the AI-driven concierge. This included understanding how the system operates, when to intervene, and how to solve issues.
- **Data Analysis**: Trained employees in analysing AI interaction data to obtain patterns and improve the services. This has included learning elementary data analytics skills, as well as using data visualisation and data reporting tools.
- **Customer-centric AI Design**: The AI continually optimises and improves guest interactions based on the customer feedback.

Impact:

- **Better Customer Service**: The AI concierge provided timely and well-customised services to the guests,; so it lifted the satisfaction level of the guests and gained guest loyalty.
- **Increased Operational Efficiency**: The system reduced the workload on human personnel, freeing up their time to engage in more value-adding activities.
- **Increased Employee Engagement:** It raised interest among employees towards satisfaction and engaging programs, with a number of learning opportunities and career paths.

Case Study 2: Delta Airlines

Background: Delta Airlines has been using AI-driven predictive maintenance, which has achieved better reliability for aircraft and lower operational disruption.

New Skills Required:

- **Predictive Analytics**: Re-skilled maintenance engineers to run machine-learning models and interpret AI-generated maintenance alerts to take preemptive actions.
- **Technical Competence**: By providing technical skills development training in accordance with AI diagnostic and maintenance practices, we can ensure an effective system for implementing the use of AI, and ensure that employees can execute tasks required by the AI systems effectively.
- **Cross-functional Communication**: Delta ensured the relationship between its maintenance personnel and AI experts was effective by allowing openness, shared knowledge, and team spirit.

Impact:

- **Higher Operational Reliability**: Artificial intelligence enabled the predictive maintenance system to reduce incidents of unscheduled maintenance events, leading to fewer flight delays and cancellations.
- **Cost Savings**: Proactive maintenance brought about an overall reduction in costs of maintenance that is long-term and saved revenue losses linked with operational downtime.
- **Employee Development**: Employees could learn new skills and acquire more knowledge through training, which helped them to be more prepared for the job and satisfied with their career.

Case Study 4: Airbnb

Context: The AI-based dynamic pricing tools served the needs of Airbnb to help optimise the host's pricing strategy.

What were the skill sets developed?

- **AI and Machine Learning**: We trained the hosts and the supporting staff about the basic understanding of AI and Machine Learning in terms of the two technologies' impact on pricing strategies and revenue management.
- **Data Interpretation**: The insights gained from the data interpretation guided the hosts in making judgemental decisions relating to the change in prices.
- **Customer Relationship Management:** It is achieved through gaining valuable insights into the customer's behaviour and their needs, generated through the application of artificial intelligence.

Results:

- **Revenue Optimisation**: The hosts using the dynamic pricing AI tool derived optimal pricing, which finally raised the occupancy rates and overall revenue.
- **Market Competitiveness**: Dynamic pricing enabled the Airbnb hosts to be competitive at all times, based on market conditions and bookings.
- **Host Empowerment**: Training empowered the host with the skills and knowledge to manage their listings effectively and earn more.

Case Study 5: Singapore Airlines

Context: Singapore Airlines uses the Digital Innovation Blueprint to integrate AI and digital technologies throughout operations.

Evolving skill requirements: All staff underwent broad-based digital literacy, covering essential knowledge in AI, data analytics, and how to make use of digital tools.

- **Innovation and Problem Solving**: While promoting AI use for operational gains, we motivated employees to create groundbreaking ideas or innovations and spurred them into intellectual problem-solving.
- **Continuous Learning and Adaptability:** The company has encouraged lifelong learning through online courses, workshops, and industry seminars to keep their employees updated on the latest developments in technology.

Impact:

- **Operational Excellence:** The integration of AI and digital technology has significantly improved operational efficiency and customer service, thereby significantly impacting the overall business performance.
- **Employee Engagement**: The focus on lifelong learning and innovation has made an impact on engaged culture, thereby enhancing employee satisfaction and, finally, retention.

- **Customer's Experience**: AI-based initiatives optimised the customer's experience through service personalisation, reducing wait times for improved satisfaction.

6.3 Initiatives for Training and Upskilling

The tourism and travel industry offers programs and strategies for workforce transformation.

6.3.1 Holistic Training Programs AI and digital literacy training

- **AI Fundamentals:** The company can arrange courses that cover the basics of AI, machine learning, and its applications in the tourism sector. These courses can be online, offline, or even a blend of both techniques.
- **Digital Tools and Platforms**: Employees should receive training that covers all the digital tools and platforms commonly used in their jobs. This includes CRM systems, data analytics tools, and AI-supported customer service technologies. (Gretzel et al., 2015).

Specialised Skills Development

- **Predictive Analytics for Aircraft Maintenance Personnel**: Educate airlines' maintenance personnel on predictive analytics to support their comprehension of AI-based alerts for maintenance and the associated necessary actions.
- Train the sales and marketing teams in AI-led digital marketing skills, including how to create personalised content, dynamic pricing strategies, and social media analysis for business applications.

6.3.2 Continuous Learning and Professional Development

a. Lifelong Learning Culture
    - **Online Learning Platforms**: Provide courses on AI, data science, and digital marketing to all employees via online platforms such as Coursera, Udacity, or LinkedIn Learning.
    - **Learning Incentives**: Develop incentive schemes that encourage continuous learning, such as bonuses or recognition for course completion and certifications.

b. Programs for mentoring and coaching
    - **Peer Mentorship:** Develop peer mentorship programs where experienced employees can inculcate their knowledge and skills in their less experienced counterparts.
    - **Professional Coaching**: Hire professional coaches to assist employees in developing specific skills, setting career goals, and overcoming technology use challenges.

6.3.3 Collaborative Learning and Cross-Functional Teams

a. Cross-Functional Training
    - **Job rotation**: Introduce job rotation programs where employees can work in different departments or roles for some time, allowing them to gain a global perspective and diverse skills.
    - **Implement a learning program** where employees from various functions collaborate on project assignments to deliver new services and experiences, such as developing AI-based services or improving operational processes.

b. **Innovation Labs and Hackathons:** Creating an innovative and experimental environment fosters creative solutions and technological advancements.
    - **Innovation Labs:** Establish innovation labs where employees can experiment with new technologies, develop prototypes, and collaborate on innovative projects.

- **Hackathons:** To encourage employees to come up with creative solutions to industry challenges, we organize hackathons, fostering a spirit of innovation and teamwork.

6.4 Strategic and Industry Collaboration

6.4.1 Partnerships with Educational Institutions

- **University Collaborations**: Partner with universities and colleges to offer specialised and certification programs in AI, data science, and other relevant fields.
- **Internship Programs:** Offer internship and practical training programs that allow students to gain experience in the tourism industry while bringing fresh ideas and perspectives.

6.4.2 Professional Associations and Networks

- Encourage staff to participate in industry conferences, workshops, and seminars to stay current on best practices.
- **Professional Networks**: Promote membership in professional networks and associations that offer resources, training, and networking opportunities.(Gössling et al., 2021).

7. THE BENEFITS AND DRAWBACKS OF AI ADOPTION IN THE TOURISM INDUSTRY

7.1 The Benefits of AI Adoption in the Tourism Industry

Improved the customer's experiences

Customised Services

- **Personalized Recommendations**: Using customer data, AI algorithms can provide individual customers with tailored travel advice about their destination, accommodation, and activities. For instance, Booking.com and Airbnb do this to make recommendations according to individual preferences and past behaviours.
- **Concierge Services:** AI-based virtual assistants and chatbots provide each guest with their level of personal attention while answering questions and providing information. For example, Connie by Hilton improves the guest experience through AI-powered personalization (Ivanov et al., 2017).

Improved customer service

- **Round the clock customer support:** AI-powered chatbots and virtual assistants provide round-the-clock service, allowing customers to receive assistance at any time of day from anywhere in the world, thereby enhancing the customer's satisfaction and loyalty (Tussyadiah, 2020).
- **Faster Response Time:** AI systems can process multiple queries at the same time, giving instant answers that generally reduce time lags and, in effect, improve the customer's experience. For example, KLM's BlueBot (BB) effectively responds to customers' requests and booking enquiries.

Operational efficiency

a. **Predictive Maintenance** AI-driven predictive maintenance enables enhanced reliability and efficiency in operations, particularly in the airline industry.
   - **Reduced Downtime**: AI systems analyse data from aircraft and other equipment sensors, helping to forecast the need for maintenance. This can prevent breakdowns and reduce downtimes. Delta Airlines' system application has reduced cancellations and delays, resulting in more flights operating on time.
   - **Cost Saving**: Proactive maintenance brings about a decrease in overall maintenance costs by fixing many faults before they result in catastrophic damage. This results in minimal downtime of the system and hence saves revenues, which more than pays for the cost of the emergency repair.

b. Resource optimization
   - **Energy Management**: The AI system manages energy in other facilities, optimising the setting for energy consumption when the occupancy level is low or high. Marriott's AI-driven energy management systems have also resulted in tremendous energy savings and reduced carbon footprints.
   - **Staff Scheduling:** AI algorithms optimise staff scheduling based on demand forecasts, ensuring that the staffing levels reflect variations between peak and off-peak periods. This reduces labor inefficiency while also saving money.

Better Decision-Making

a. Data-Driven Insights: Artificial intelligence (AI) revolves around insights as it analyses large data sets to facilitate informed decision-making.
   - **Market Trends and Forecasting**: To provide actionable insights, AI analyses market trends, the customer's preferences, and the competitive landscape. This will help businesses make decisions related to product development, marketing strategies, and expansion plans in an informed manner.
   - **Performance Monitoring**: AI tools will be able to monitor business performance in real-time, thus spotting areas that need improvement in running the operation. This increases efficiency through resource optimisation, resulting in better overall performance. This will result in much better performance on average.

b. Customer behaviour analysis
   - **Personalized Experiences:** Artificial intelligence, based on a customer's behavior, assists businesses in creating experiences they would appreciate, resulting in greater customer satisfaction and loyalty (Tussyadiah, 2020).
   - **Loyalty Programs**: AI-based loyalty programs can analyse customer data for personalised incentives and rewards for developing the customer's loyalty and increasing repeat business.(Gretzel et al., 2015).

Safety and Security Enhancement

a. Fraud Detection
   - **Real-time Monitoring**: Through real-time monitoring, AI can trace any transaction as it happens and take action to prevent suspicious behavior. This is critical when it comes to online bookings and tourism payments.
   - **Anomaly Detection**: AI algorithms are capable of identifying out-of-normalcy client behaviour, thereby signalling a system security vulnerability. Consequently, the system will take proactive measures to mitigate the risk.

b. Health and Safety Compliance

- **Health Monitoring**: The use of AI technology in health monitoring records and analyses health data to ensure effective health safety compliance for the reduction of outbreak exposure.
- **Contactless Solutions**: Contactless AI solutions, in the form of check-in kiosks and mobile applications, reduce physical touching and thereby enhance safety for guests and workers. (Gössling et al., 2021).

AI-Powered Customer Relationship Management (CRM) Systems

Enhanced CRM

- **Customer Insights**: AI processes customer data to derive detailed insights about preferences, behaviours, and buying patterns. Such data allows businesses to personalize service and improve customer relationships.
- **Automated follow-ups** are another way to compare an AI-driven CRM system to personalized communication at the right time. It helps enhance participation and satisfaction by customers.

8. THE TOURISM INDUSTRY FACES DISADVANTAGES WHEN ADOPTING AI

8.1 Job Displacement and Workforce Impact

a. Job Displacement:
   - **Automation of Routine Tasks**: Artificial Intelligence (AI) has the potential to automate routine tasks, including reservations, the customer's enquiries, and maintenance checks, which would otherwise require human intervention. Automation ultimately results in job displacement for the same employees (Gretzel et al., 2015).
   - **Decreased Demand for Low-Skilled Workers**: As AI systems take on many simpler tasks, the demand for low-skilled workers decreases, potentially negatively impacting employment in the tourism sector.

b. **Transformation Difficulties:**
   - The process of reskilling and upskilling involves transforming employees into new roles that demand advanced technical and analytics skills. This consumes a lot of business time and resources.
   - **Resistance to Change**: Employees may resist new technologies and ways of working, resulting in unproductivity or low motivation.

c. Data Privacy and Security Concerns:
   - **Data Collection and Storage**: Personal data collection, storage, and processing through artificial intelligence systems may result in a privacy breach with mismanagement. This may make customers sceptical about sharing their data due to misuse or unauthorised access.

d. Cybersecurity Risks:
   - **Attack Vulnerability**: Companies can design AI systems with weaknesses that compromise operational integrity and sensitive customer data.
   - **Compliance with Regulations**: To ensure compliance, particularly with the General Data Protection Regulation, business operations must undertake additional resource-intensive tasks.
   - **Resource Allocation**: To ensure the safety of AI systems and data, implementing robust cybersecurity measures necessitates a significant resource allocation. It is costly and complicated.

e. Implementation and maintenance are expensive.
   - **Initial Investment:** For most businesses, the cost of implementing this technology, such as the hardware, software, and infrastructure, is very high.

- **Training and Development**: All of the employees would be required to undergo training on up-skilling and enhancement of the capabilities to manage the AI systems, which would incrementally contribute to the cost of implementation.

f. Ongoing maintenance and updates:
   - **Regular Maintenance**: To ensure proper and resourceful operation, an AI system requires regular maintenance. It requires software updates, hardware upgrades, and system monitoring.
   - **Constant Innovation**: AI technologies are constantly evolving, necessitating R&D investment to keep the systems up-to-date and competitive.

g. Ethical Considerations:
   - **Algorithmic Bias**: AI algorithms can reinforce preexisting biases when learning from biased training data, resulting in an unjust outcome. For instance, it may make the customer's demographics more likely to have better offers than others (Gretzel et al., 2015).
   - **Ethical Decision-Making**: As a result, ensuring that an AI makes an ethical decision is a huge challenge that requires careful control and handling.

h. **Accountability and Transparency**: Because AI is quite complex, one cannot even predict the level of accountability and transparency in its processes.
   - **Black Box Problem**: In most cases, AI systems function as black boxes, making judgments based on inexplicable algorithms. This lack of transparency may result in mistrust among customers and employees.
   - **Accountability Issues**: When mistakes or negative results occur, determining accountability for AI system decisions is challenging.

i. Dependence on Technology:

   Overreliance on AI: The application of AI technologies may equally come with various risks and failures. Overreliance on AI systems can deprive customer interaction of the human touch often cherished in the tourism industry, and it may also result in declining levels of the customer's satisfaction. "This dependence on AI systems makes one vulnerable to system failure and technical hitches that will lead to operational failure and eventually affect the customer's experience."

9. CONCLUSION

Artificial intelligence has the potential to revolutionise the delivery, consumption, and management of tourism services. In fact, change enablement responds to some level of technical automation through chatbots, virtual assistants, and data analytics that would present new prospects if implemented for the sector, which in turn is bound to alter its trajectory. The shift towards using AI in the tourism industry is not a passing fad-it reflects an evolution that is affecting employment and skills requirements, as well as operational patterns.

While the initial concern about the introduction of AI in this industry is its potential to eliminate jobs from the labor market, it has significant benefits. The first effect on the labour force is job displacement, in that it has been particularly put to work; automating routine and repetitive tasks has affected some of the jobs traditionally done by the people. AI-powered systems are currently automating the work of front desk staff, booking agents, and customer service representatives. While this could mean vast efficiency gains, it also brings challenges around job displacement and workforce change. Of course, the story is not just about job losses, but also about the creation of new jobs at venerable institutions. With the rise of AI, new professions have emerged, such as AI specialists, data analysts, or managers for digital transformation who participate in setting up and dulling those revolutionary systems. Various newly introduced technical field knowledge has led to current job offers, which in some cases can be transformed into future career benefits.

With a change in employment patterns, the demand for skilled professionals in the tourism sector is also evolving. In other words, as AI use expands, the workforce active in traditional operations must instead become familiar with their basic operations and proficient in using any such AI-based tool within the tourism industry. This shift demands relentless upskilling and reskilling programs to close the gap between what our current workforce can do, with tools such as AI in their arsenal today, versus tomorrow. We would broadly expect our workers to bring with them a varied range of technical skills-ranging from data analysis, machine learning, and digital marketing-not forgetting the soft ones such as problem-solving ability, adaptability, and Emotional Intelligence. These skills are required to cope with the newfound complexities of AI technologies and make sure workers can orientate around AI rather than compete with it.

But the AI integration into the tourism industry brings both advantages and disadvantages that stakeholders need to properly weigh. But on the bright side, they enhance operational efficiencies and tailor-made customer experiences while also optimising resource utilization. For example, predictive maintenance reduces downtime and improves safety in the airline industry. Dynamic pricing algorithms drive prices on a hospitality and travel platform, thereby maximising revenue. These enhancements lead to more efficiency and customer-centricity in the tourism experience, leading to greater satisfaction and loyalty as well.

However, along with the integration of AI come various challenges. Three major issues, namely privacy concerns, large implementation costs, and aversion to change, pose the most significant barriers to AI adoption. Probably most importantly, AI implies dealing with a huge amount of personal data and respective analyses, which raises questions about protection and handling according to requirements such as the EU General Data Protection Regulation. Moreover, small businesses in the tourism sector may not be able to afford the heavy investments in hardware, software, and employee training associated with AI implementation. Workers expected to utilize these new technologies may experience job insecurity and struggle to manage these innovations. The two main challenges point to a fairer approach to the use of AI: reconcile benefits with possible risks and develop strategies for limiting adverse effects as much as possible.

Generally, AI intervention in the tourism sector is manifold. It brings a paradox of opportunities against challenges, and further stakeholder engagement is required to understand better the implications brought about by deepening and evolving AI landscapes with respect to employment, skills, and business dynamics. Only if the tourism sector anchors itself in a holistic approach that promotes lifelong learning and innovation for the ethical application of AI, can it effectively address its potential challenges. This would be an approach to embracing AI in such an inclusive industry that would further make tourism more resolute, effective, and personalised in the digital age.

REFERENCES

Agrawal, A., Gans, J., & Goldfarb, A. (2019). *The Economics of Artificial Intelligence: An Agenda*. University of Chicago Press., DOI: 10.7208/chicago/9780226613475.001.0001

Akyazi, T., Del Val, P., Goti, A., & Oyarbide, A. (2022). Identifying future skill requirements of the job profiles for a sustainable European manufacturing industry 4.0. *Recycling*, *7*(3), 32. DOI: 10.3390/recycling7030032

Aladwani, H. N., Hamad, L., & Aladwani, D. J. N. (n.d.). Educational outcomes, job needs, and the labor market in the era of artificial intelligence in the Gulf countries.

Alyasiri, O. M., Selvaraj, K., Younis, H. A., Sahib, T. M., Almasoodi, M. F., & Hayder, I. M. (2024). A survey on the potential of artificial intelligence tools in tourism information services. Babylonian Journal of Artificial Intelligence, 2024(January 10), 1–8. DOI: 10.58496/BJAI/2024/001

Belušić, N. (n.d.). Artificial intelligence and employment: Less need for blue-collar or white-collar jobs?

Benayoune, A., Hamid, A. A., Rahman, N. S. F. A., & Al, K. (2022). Logistics 4.0 skills requirements: Evidence from a developing country. *Canadian Journal of Business and Information Studies*, *4*(2), 24–36.

Bertoni, E., Fontana, M., Gabrielli, L., Signorelli, S., & Vespe, M. (Eds.). (2023). *Handbook of Computational Social Science for Policy*. Springer International Publishing., DOI: 10.1007/978-3-031-16624-2

Carlisle, S., Ivanov, S., & Dijkmans, C. (2023). The digital skills divide: Evidence from the European tourism industry. *Journal of Tourism Futures*, *9*(2), 240–266. DOI: 10.1108/JTF-07-2020-0114

Carlisle, S., Ivanov, S., & Espeso-Molinero, P. (2023). Delivering the European Skills Agenda: The importance of social skills for a sustainable tourism and hospitality industry. *Tourism & Management Studies*, *19*(3), 23–40.

Chemlal, O., & Benomar, W. (2024). The technological impact on employment in Spain between 2023 and 2035. *Forecasting*, *6*(2), 296–325. DOI: 10.3390/forecast6020017

Dirican, C. (2015). The impacts of robotics, artificial intelligence on business and economics. *Procedia: Social and Behavioral Sciences*, *195*, 564–573. DOI: 10.1016/j.sbspro.2015.06.134

George, D. A.Shaji, & Baskar, Dr.T. (2023). The impact of AI language models on the future of white-collar jobs: A comparative study of job projections in developed and developing countries. DOI: 10.5281/ZENODO.8021447

Giraud, L., Zaher, A., Hernandez, S., & Akram, A. A. (2023). The impacts of artificial intelligence on managerial skills. *Journal of Decision Systems*, *32*(3), 566–599. DOI: 10.1080/12460125.2022.2069537

Gössling, S., Scott, D., & Hall, C. M. (2021). Pandemics, tourism and global change: A rapid assessment of COVID-19. *Journal of Sustainable Tourism*, *29*(1), 1–20. DOI: 10.1080/09669582.2020.1758708

Gretzel, U., Sigala, M., Xiang, Z., & Koo, C. (2015). Smart tourism: Foundations and developments. *Electronic Markets*, *25*(3), 179–188. DOI: 10.1007/s12525-015-0196-8

Grobbelaar, W., & Verma, A. (2020). Vocational training and industry IR 4.0 in a smart city. SSRN Electronic Journal. DOI: 10.2139/ssrn.3713780

Gu, T.-T., Zhang, S.-F., & Cai, R. (2022). Can artificial intelligence boost employment in service industries? Empirical analysis based on China. *Applied Artificial Intelligence*, *36*(1), 2080336. DOI: 10.1080/08839514.2022.2080336

Huang, A., Chao, Y., Velasco, E. D. L. M., Bilgihan, A., & Wei, W. (2022). When artificial intelligence meets the hospitality and tourism industry: An assessment framework to inform theory and management. *Journal of Hospitality and Tourism Insights*, *5*(5), 1080–1100. DOI: 10.1108/JHTI-01-2021-0021

Huang, A. Y., Fisher, T., Ding, H., & Guo, Z. (2021). A network analysis of cross-occupational skill transferability for the hospitality industry. *International Journal of Contemporary Hospitality Management*, *33*(12), 4215–4236. DOI: 10.1108/IJCHM-01-2021-0073

Huang, M.-H., & Rust, R. T. (2018). Artificial intelligence in service. *Journal of Service Research*, *21*(2), 155–172. DOI: 10.1177/1094670517752459

Indaryanto, A., Harijadi, B. D., & Sinaga, E. (2023). The growing use and impact of artificial intelligence technologies in the tourism industry. *Sustainable Engineering and Innovation*, *5*(2), 189–204. DOI: 10.37868/sei.v5i2.id238

Ivanov, S., & Webster, C. (2019a). Conceptual framework of the use of robots, artificial intelligence and service automation in travel, tourism, and hospitality companies. In S. Ivanov & C. Webster (Eds.), Robots, Artificial Intelligence, and Service Automation in Travel, Tourism and Hospitality (pp. 7–37). Emerald Publishing Limited. DOI: 10.1108/978-1-78756-687-320191001

Ivanov, S., & Webster, C. (2019b). Economic fundamentals of the use of robots, artificial intelligence, and service automation in travel, tourism, and hospitality. In S. Ivanov & C. Webster (Eds.), Robots, Artificial Intelligence, and Service Automation in Travel, Tourism and Hospitality (pp. 39–55). Emerald Publishing Limited. DOI: 10.1108/978-1-78756-687-320191002

Ivanov, S., Webster, C., & Berezina, K. (2017). Adoption of robots and service automation by tourism and hospitality companies.

Jabeen, F., Al Zaidi, S., & Al Dhaheri, M. H. (2022). Automation and artificial intelligence in hospitality and tourism. *Tourism Review*, *77*(4), 1043–1061. DOI: 10.1108/TR-09-2019-0360

Jagannathan, S., Ra, S., & Maclean, R. (2019). Dominant recent trends impacting on jobs and labor markets - An overview. International Journal of Training Research, 17(sup1), 1–11. DOI: 10.1080/14480220.2019.1641292

Kömürcü, S., Ertamay, S. I., & Güler, M. E. (2021). Impacts of technological development on employment structure of tourism industry. *Yönetim ve Ekonomi Araştırmaları Dergisi*, *19*(1), 146–165. DOI: 10.11611/yead.814765

Kong, H., Wang, K., Qiu, X., Cheung, C., & Bu, N. (2023). 30 years of artificial intelligence (AI) research relating to the hospitality and tourism industry. *International Journal of Contemporary Hospitality Management*, *35*(6), 2157–2177. DOI: 10.1108/IJCHM-03-2022-0354

Lazić, M., Bradić-Martinović, A., & Banović, J. (2023). Digital skills in tourism and hospitality as a precondition for the sector resilient growth: The case of Serbia. *Menadzment u Hotelijerstvu i Turizmu*, *11*(1), 25–40. DOI: 10.5937/menhottur2301025L

Liu, A., & Wall, G. (2006). Planning tourism employment: A developing country perspective. *Tourism Management*, *27*(1), 159–170. DOI: 10.1016/j.tourman.2004.08.004

Muhtar, F. (2024). Navigating AI integration for inclusive development: A case study of Sabah's socio-economic landscape. SSRN Electronic Journal. DOI: 10.2139/ssrn.4807268

Naumov, N. (2019). The impact of robots, artificial intelligence, and service automation on service quality and service experience in hospitality. In S. Ivanov & C. Webster (Eds.), Robots, Artificial Intelligence, and Service Automation in Travel, Tourism and Hospitality (pp. 123–133). Emerald Publishing Limited. DOI: 10.1108/978-1-78756-687-320191007

Neuhofer, B., Magnus, B., & Celuch, K. (2021). The impact of artificial intelligence on event experiences: A scenario technique approach. *Electronic Markets*, *31*(3), 601–617. DOI: 10.1007/s12525-020-00433-4 PMID: 38624486

Oluwaseyi, J., & Cena, J. (n.d.). Analyzing the impact of artificial intelligence on job displacement and income inequality.

Parsons, D., Choi, M., Thomas, R., Glyptou, K., & Walsh, K. (2023). The policy responses of tourism agencies to emerging digital skills constraints: A critical assessment of six countries. *International Journal of Tourism Research*, *25*(1), 97–108. DOI: 10.1002/jtr.2554

Pechlaner, H., & Fuchs, M. (2002). Towards new skill requirements for destination organizations: An exploratory study. *Tourism Analysis*, *7*(1), 43–53. DOI: 10.3727/108354202108749943

Sarkar, S., Shukla, S., & Mishra, R. K. (2023). Enabling skill development in the pandemic – The CSR perspective. In Das Gupta, A. (Ed.), *Critical Studies on Corporate Responsibility, Governance and Sustainability* (pp. 83–97). Emerald Publishing Limited., DOI: 10.1108/S2043-905920230000016006

Tsaih, R.-H., & Hsu, C. C. (2018). Artificial intelligence in smart tourism: A conceptual framework.

Tussyadiah, I. (2020). A review of research into automation in tourism: Launching the Annals of Tourism Research Curated Collection on Artificial Intelligence and Robotics in Tourism. *Annals of Tourism Research*, *81*, 102883. DOI: 10.1016/j.annals.2020.102883

Vitezić, V., & Perić, M. (2024). The role of digital skills in the acceptance of artificial intelligence. *Journal of Business and Industrial Marketing*, *39*(7), 1546–1566. DOI: 10.1108/JBIM-04-2023-0210

Wörndl, W., Koo, C., & Stienmetz, J. L. (Eds.). (2021). Information and Communication Technologies in Tourism 2021: *Proceedings of the ENTER 2021 eTourism Conference*, January 19–22, 2021. Cham: Springer International Publishing. DOI: 10.1007/978-3-030-65785-7

Chapter 12

Data-Driven Triumph: CRM Sales Insights Revolutionize Customer Retention

Vishakha Kuwar
https://orcid.org/0000-0003-1764-2475
Dr. D.Y. Patil Vidyapeeth, Pune, India

Prakash Divakaran
Himalayan University, India

Vandana Mishra Chaturvedi
D.Y. Patil University, India

Shitiz Upreti
Maharishi Markandeshwar University, Mullana, India

Kamal Upreti
https://orcid.org/0000-0003-0665-530X
Christ University, India

Akhilesh Tiwari
Christ University, India

ABSTRACT

Context: The examination of the CRM data is anchored in a comprehensive analysis of sales performance metrics, with a significant role played. It was found a gap in the literature, considering the scarcity of pertinent case studies within the academic literature. Method: The geographical factor is paramount in this analysis, as it unveils divergent results across different regions. Moreover, the venture into predictive analytics for sales forecasting, capitalizing on CRM primary data spanning from 2018 to 2023, facilitating more informed decision-making. The sample comprises around 1500 Business to Business customer clusters for in-depth analysis is considered. Findings: From the Business Intelligence analysis, it was found the presence of long-standing customers with a lower purchase rate, favouring average industrial product models preferred by the customers. Conclusion:The study also explores the link between CRM can shape business strategies, enhance customer relationships, and boost organizational performance and customer retention.

1. INTRODUCTION

In the fast-paced realm of sales, where success hinges on well-informed decisions and strategic prowess, organizations adopt a multifaceted strategy to ensure ongoing growth and profitability. This comprehensive approach centres on the core elements of sales performance analysis, predictive analytics, customer insights, the impact of CRM features, and the long-term implications of these strategies.

The multifaceted strategy goes beyond the traditional sales process, encompassing a thorough assessment of sales performance, the application of predictive analytics to anticipate market trends, the extraction of invaluable customer insights, and the evaluation of CRM features that drive sales expansion. At its heart, this holistic viewpoint

DOI: 10.4018/979-8-3693-7447-4.ch012

aims not only to enhance immediate sales results but also to orchestrate a lasting impact, guiding organizations towards enduring success in the ever-evolving business landscape.

In the forthcoming sections, we embark on an odyssey through the captivating terrain of sales performance analysis, predictive forecasting, customer insights, and the enduring impact of CRM features. The journey promises to unravel the strategies, technologies, and insights that empower organizations to master the craft of sales, enrich customer relationships, and navigate the ever-shifting currents of the business world with confidence and foresight. Welcome to the domain of Sales Performance Analysis and Forecasting, where data metamorphoses into wisdom, and strategies evolve into enduring triumph.

The significance of the study is that in today's dynamic business environment, the ability to adapt swiftly to market changes is critical, and this is where sales analysis, forecasting, and CRM utilization prove invaluable. Lastly, assessing the long-term impact aids in understanding the factors contributing to customer retention, a testament to the enduring value delivered by B2B organizations and a reduction in the need for constant customer acquisition efforts. The study is structured into three sections. The initial section provides a comprehensive overview of CRM and its architectural framework. The second section is dedicated to the development of hypothesis related to CRM analytics, while the final section focuses on the analysis and interpretation of the collected data.

2. THEORETICAL BACKGROUND

CRM is more than just a tool for gathering customer data. CRM entails the use of technology to gather the data required to offer consumers better support and services. CRM thus makes use of the data to better meet the demands of current locating new clients and expanding the company's customer base will improve earnings. The initial aims determine the actual effectiveness of integrating CRM into day-to-day business operations. Selecting the "right" solution specifically for this type of organization and its goals is another option to give excellent CRM.

Customer segmentation is greatly aided by analytical CRM, which has several benefits for sales, marketing, and service operations. Its advantages frequently result in more successful and beneficial consumer connections. CRM analytics offers clarity by recognizing the most valued customers and expediting the efficient search for prospects, as opposed to struggling to understand the customers' preferences. The customer data obtained through analytical CRM is priceless and acts as the cornerstone of a comprehensive marketing plan that involves numerous departments. It may identify the most lucrative clients, comprehend their behaviour's, and identify potential customers with the help of analytical CRM, all of which can greatly improve the results. Analytical CRM offers more in-depth understanding of client activities by utilizing business intelligence. It incorporates all the CRM tools discussed above and processes customer data in a way that is user-friendly, allowing businesses to make decisions more quickly and with greater knowledge. As a result, sales tactics that are directed at consumer groups are more effective. As well as serving a variety of functions, analytical CRM provides insightful information about the success of a company's marketing initiatives.

Understanding the potential buyer is significant for any type of effective marketing strategy. When identifying the consumers which are most likely to be interested in your product or service. In this journey we need to tailoring efforts to address their specific needs. The process extends beyond basic demographics and focus into psychographics, buying behaviours, and even emotional triggers that drive purchases. By leveraging Customer Relationship Management (CRM) systems, businesses can collect and analyze detailed data to create customer profiles and precise market segmentation (Gajanova L.et al.,2019).

Analysing customer attrition will help you comprehend why and how a business loses customers, as well as the effects of those losses. Analysing consumer trends, buying habits, and behaviour to enhance product and service offerings. Analysing customer interactions can help you better understand how a business communicates with its clients and gauge the success of its communication tactics. Analysing and developing ways to increase and preserve customer retention by gauging how loyal customers are to the business and its goods. Lead analysis is the process of locating and comprehending prospective buyers of new goods or services. Determine how to appeal to demographic groups within a given market by doing a market analysis.

The literature review revolves around the parameters of Sales forecasting, salesforce and customer retention and satisfaction as shown in figure 1.

Figure 1. Literature review framework

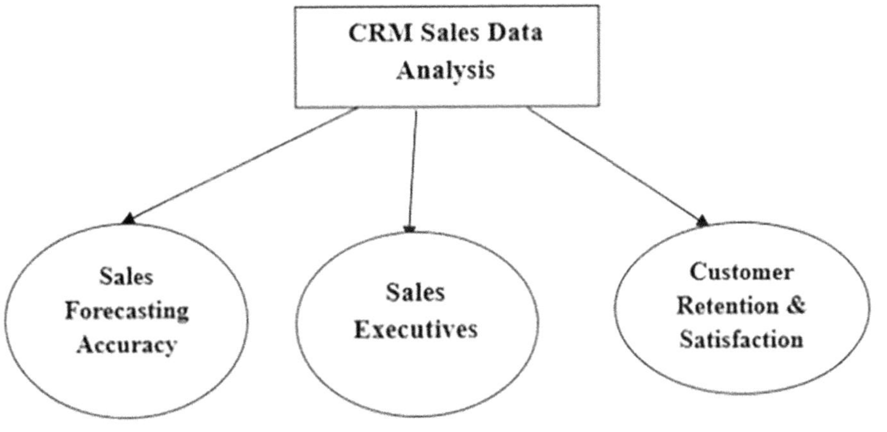

2.1. CRM Sales Data Analysis Improve Sales Forecasting Accuracy

In today's landscape, we've transitioned from grappling with data scarcity to confronting the data deluge. Marketers and experts in Customer Relationship Management (CRM) now find themselves endowed with abundant data regarding consumer behaviour. The current focal point revolves around harnessing this wealth of data effectively within CRM workflows and discerning the most suitable data analytics techniques (Gončarovs, P., 2017). Sales forecasting holds a crucial position in the realm of strategic planning and market strategy for all companies. Precise sales forecasting contributes significantly to enhancing a company's operational efficiency and productivity, ultimately leading to cost savings by avoiding inaccurate forecasts or predictions, (Saraswathi K.,2021).

When a demographic analysis conducted to understand the age, gender, income, education, and occupation of potential buyer. The psychographic segmentation is exploring the values, lifestyles, and interests. Geographic targeting can also play an important role as regional factors. Behavioural insights are also valuable like purchase history and brand interactions. CRMs track the data that can highlight repeat customers for loyalty programs. When segmenting done based on need—like businesses seeking efficient project management software. Engagement level provides insight into brand advocates. CRM data can reveal through metrics like email open rates or content engagement (Upreti K.et al.,2025).

The amount and type of data that we deal with has greatly increased over the last few years from a variety of sources, including social media networks, machine-generated data, mobile networks, CRM data, etc. Traditional business intelligence (BI) and analytical solutions face several difficulties because of the exponential expansion of data. The CRM sales data used to predictive analytics to experiment with enriching customer relationship management (CRM) data with all attainable insights and evaluating the -trend in sales forecasting (Palanimalai S. and Paramasivam I.,2016).

The impressions of several forecasting sales force automation components, including customer relationship management (CRM) software, in addition to some demographic data (Hoyle J. A. et al.,2020). The customer relationship management (CRM), visualization tools and business intelligence tools are available in large scale industries, but SME analyse the demand for sales forecasting and ways that they could improve their sales forecasting abilities (Haataja, T. 2016, Lau, R. et al.,2018). The Scopus Literature for keywords "CRM and Sales Forecasting Accuracy" as shown in the figure 2.

Figure 2. Scopus literature analysis for keyword "CRM and Sales Accuracy".

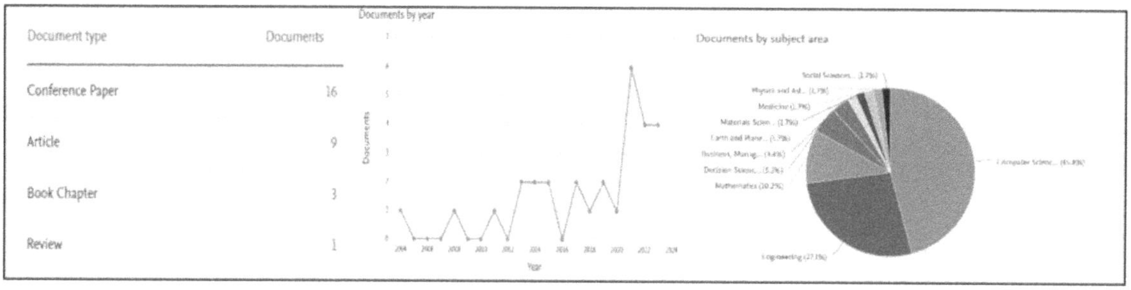

2.2. Success Factor of CRM Data Input by Salesforce

To improve company metrics and outcomes, sales professionals—both salespeople and sales manager need to take use of these new analytical tools' capabilities (Hoyle J. A. et al.,2020). CRM sales data substantially promotes revenue growth, leading to improved financial performance, while also strengthening customer relationships, resulting in enhanced non-monetary performance outcomes (Hallikainen, H.et al.,2020) and impacting the big data analytics on company performance and it is necessary to take the view of senior management and business analyst not only in subjective but only objective way. The CRM focused on not only merely on the customers attitudinal tracking but also Consumer opinions sourced from the internet such as online searches, chat rooms, social media platforms, social networks, blogs, product reviews, and other similar online word-of-mouth forums (Hanssens, D. M.et al.,2014). Sales professionals, including both salespeople and sales managers, must leverage the potential of these advanced analytical tools to enhance corporate metrics and results (Hoyle J. A. et al.,2020).

Empirical evidence shows that Mobile Customer Relationship Management plays a significant role in the adoption of traditional CRM and in enhancing sales performance when sales process capabilities and collaboration are considered (Rodriguez M.& Boyer, S. 2020). The Scopus Literature for keywords "CRM and Sales Force" as shown in the figure 3.

Figure 3. Scopus literature analysis for keyword "CRM and Salesforce".

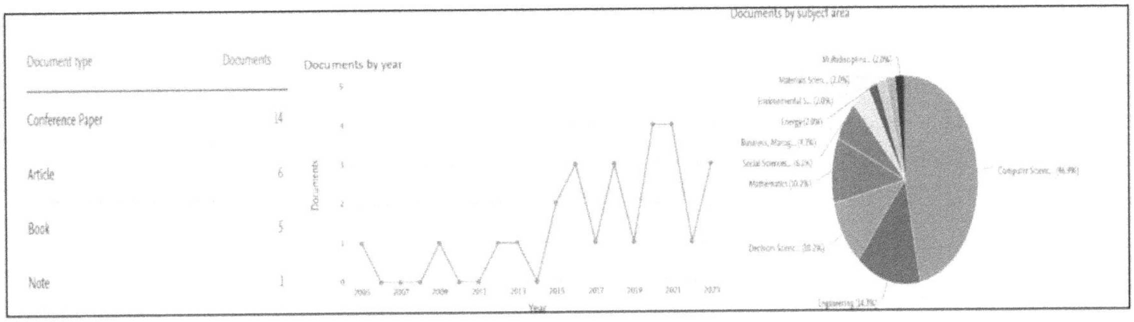

2.3. CRM Data Quality Impact Customer Retention and Satisfaction

Customer satisfaction is closely linked to customer retention but has a weaker connection with customer loyalty. Conversely, customer retention exhibits a substantial correlation with customer loyalty. The high customer satisfaction strongly influences the likelihood of customer retention, while effective customer retention strategies can, in turn, impact customer loyalty.(Nikhashemi, S.et al,2013),(Liu, C. C.et al,2012),(Saputra, S. 2019) customer experience and customer satisfaction illustrated that mediators on the relationship between E-CRM and customer loyalty(Mokha, A. K.et al,2022; Vargis B.et al.,2022).The various elements of Customer Relationship Management (CRM) were assessed, including employee behaviour, the quality of customer services, relationship development, and interaction management has revealed a significant and positive relationship between employee behaviour and both customer satisfaction and customer loyalty(Long, C. S.et al,2013),(Anees, R. T.et al,2020)(Sugiato, B.et al,2023).

In previous research exploring the influence of CRM on customer satisfaction and loyalty, three commonly employed dimensions are service quality (Sutanto, H.et al, 2021) and accessibility, and complaint resolution (Bin-Nashwan, S. A.et al,2017). The CRM proves its effectiveness in bolstering customer relationships and fostering the growth of an engaging virtual community, ultimately contributing to heightened satisfaction (Alim, S.,et al,2014),(Kumar, P., & Mokha, A. K. 2022). The Scopus Literature for keywords "CRM and Customer Retention" as shown in the figure 4.

Figure 4. Scopus literature analysis for keyword "CRM and Customer Retention".

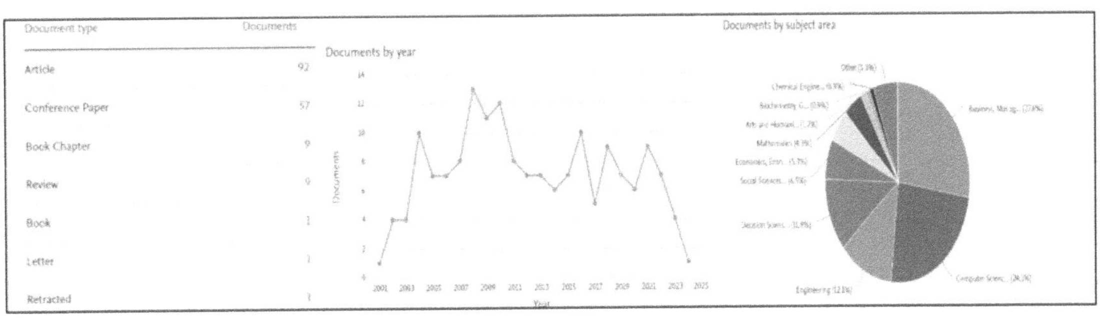

3. Sample and Data Collection

The sample is CRM data of the One of the leading providers in the B2B industry from the Indian market in the division of industrial product. The CRM data is filled by the sales professional from sales engineers to the regional manager of the division. The demographics of the sample has two verticals one is Industrial and After Markets. The Region wise territories are South, North, East and West. The total sample is downloaded for the study is 1876. The Customer Cluster by Sales for South 843, East 486, North 329, and West 218 as shown in Figure 5.a. The Customer Cluster by Spares for South 853, East 490, North 334, and West 221. as represented in Figure 5.b.

Figure 5. Geographic segmentation a. By Sales b By Spares

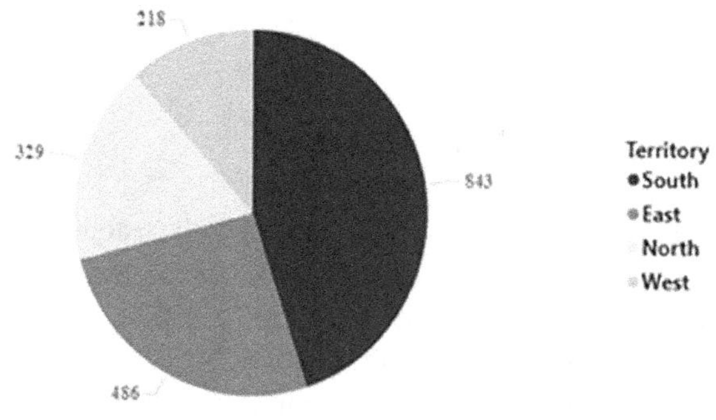

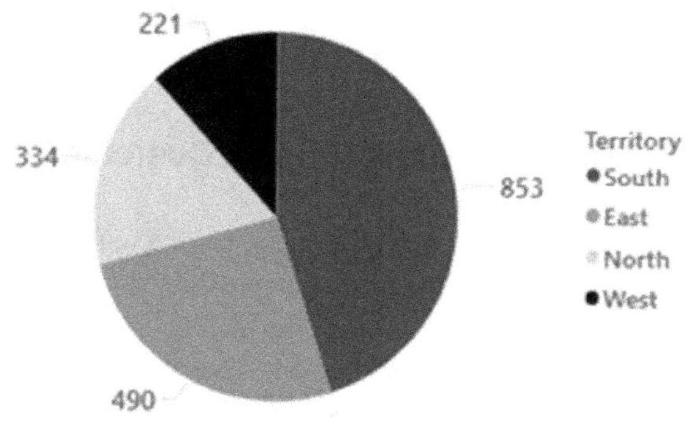

The figures 5 a and b for Sales and Spares vary because some customers who buy from the company itself that is genuine spares and some of the companies who prefer to buy the aftermarket spares. The total sample is downloaded for the study is 1500.The Conceptual model is studied here as per the CRM data as shown in the figure 6.

Figure 6. Conceptual model

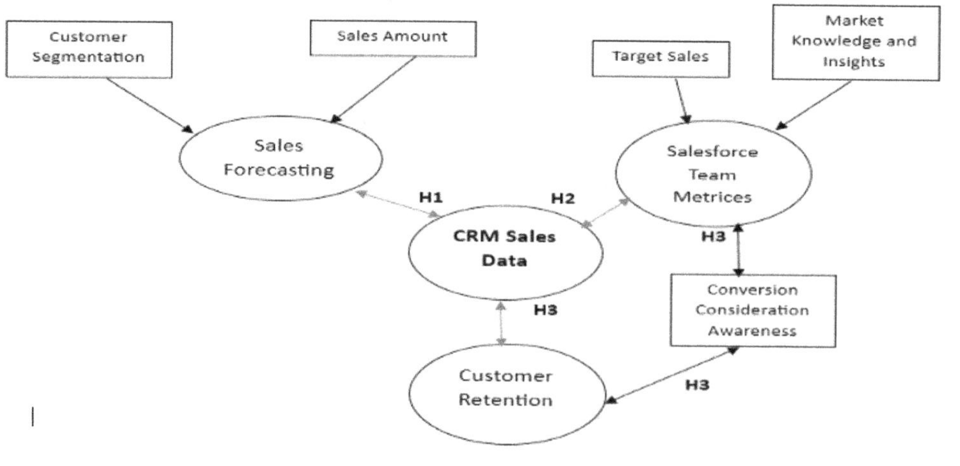

4. HYPOTHESIS DEVELOPMENT AND TESTING

4.1 H1: Predictive Models for CRM Data-Driven Sales Forecasting

Predicting the outcome of sales opportunities is integral to effective business management. Traditionally, this prediction heavily depended on subjective human assessments during the sales decision-making process (NUNE S. C,2021). (Hoyle, J. A.et al,2020) Perceptions significantly affect the integration of advanced predictive tools for resource allocation. Understanding how to utilize CRM technologies is crucial for optimizing opportunities. Sales professionals must leverage these tools to enhance corporate metrics and results. (Mortensen S.et al,2019) The goal is to create a predictive model for sales success, aiming to enhance both top-line revenue and bottom-line profits. This involves boosting sales close rates, reducing sales cycle durations, and minimizing sales costs.

The research team has developed multiple models to predict the likelihood of winning individual sales opportunities and selected the model with the highest predictive accuracy and insights-generation capability to serve as the foundation for a client tool. The figures 7 for Sales and Spares vary because some customers who buy from the company itself that is genuine spares and some of the companies who prefer to buy the aftermarket spares.

Figure 7. Sales forecast with upper and lower confidence bound (Year 2023 to 2027)

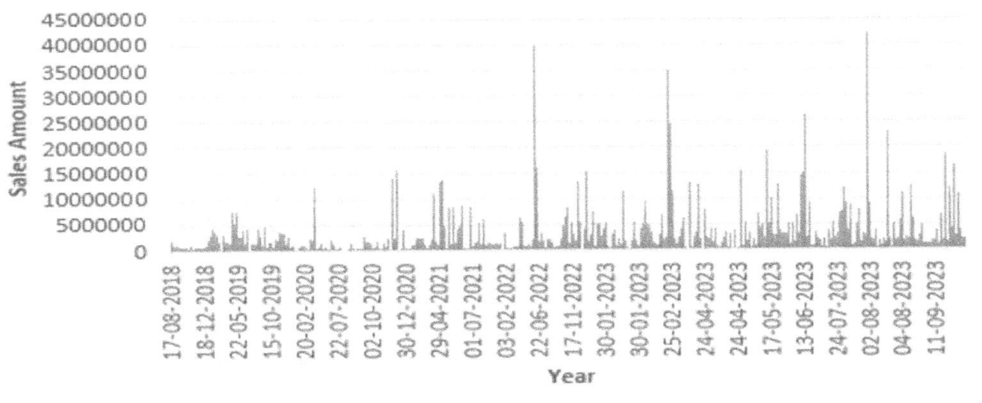

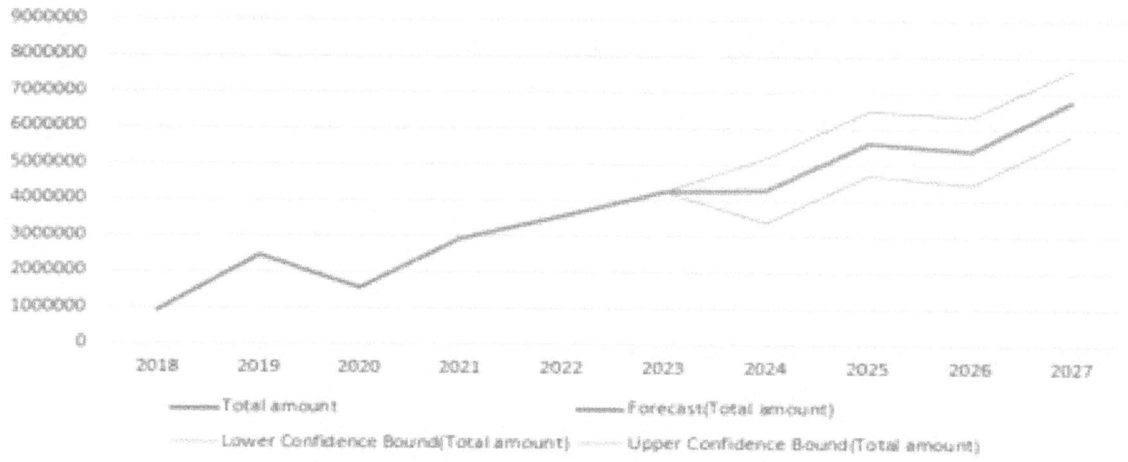

With the use of predictive analytics, one turn CRM data into insightful knowledge that will help to make better decisions and achieve better results across their entire organization. The CRM data from the year 2018 to 2023 took for the forecasting based on linear regression analysis method is used. The forecast starts with year 2023 and ends with year 2027 as shown in the above figure 7. The Predictive analytics and sales forecasting serve two primary purposes such as analysing customer and sales data and enabling well-informed business decision-making. Through the utilization of predictive analytics and forecasting, enterprises can harness the power of their CRM-collected customer and sales data to discern trends and patterns in both sales and customer behaviour, ultimately enabling the prediction of customer actions.

4.2 H2: CRM Data Analysis Correlate With Sales Team Metrics on Conversion+Consideration+Awarness, Leads Scoring and Market Insights

(Singh M.et al.,2011) introduced a comprehensive framework designed for the diagnosis of sales performance. This framework places a primary emphasis on two key aspects, one is Analysing and Quantifying Impact of framework effectively models and quantifies the influence of diverse factors on multiple sales performance metrics. Second aspect is Scenario Analysis and Optimization equipped with the essential tools for scenario analysis and optimization. The relationship between advertising spending and sales performance explored whether higher advertising expenditure leads to improved sales outcomes (Assaf, A. et al,2015; Kumar, N.et al.,2022). The effectiveness and prevalence of lead scoring methods, shedding light on their role in improving sales outcomes.

The valuable insights into the state of lead scoring practices and their significance in optimizing sales performance, offering valuable information for businesses looking to enhance their lead generation and conversion strategies in the modern technological landscape (Wu, M. et al.,2023). The impact of both monetary and non-monetary promotions on various sales performance metrics in the short term. The different aspects of promotions (presence, duration, simultaneity, and removal), the research sheds light on their immediate and post-promotional effects on revenue, transaction numbers, and average billing size. Both types of promotions initially boost revenue and transaction numbers, but monetary promotions negatively affect average billing size afterward.

Mixed promotions yield mixed results. (Porto, R. B., & Walter, M. C.,2022). (Shahbaz M.et al.,2020) The abilities of Data Analytics (DA) and Customer Relationship Management (CRM) can shape how sales performance is perceived. Additionally, CRM capabilities play a crucial role in mediating the connections between Big Data Analytics and the perceived sales performance. CRM capabilities were examined as a predictor of PSP and as a mediator between Big Data Analytics and Perceived Sales Performance. When calculating the linkage metrices it consists of three criteria such as Conversion, Consideration and Awareness. The Conversion criteria means that the total number of orders lost by the sales professionals and how many orders are finalized and received the purchase order.

The second criteria are consideration in which the list of enquiries generated and out of that 2.5 times enquiries should be treated as the hot enquiries. The third criteria are Awareness counted in the regular visits by the sales professionals and any replacement request and data extraction done on the area coverage or connect by the sales professionals. In all three criteria is working based on Plan versus Actual of the Sales professionals weekly, monthly, and quarterly target.

Figure 9. Salesforce team metrices and lead scoring process

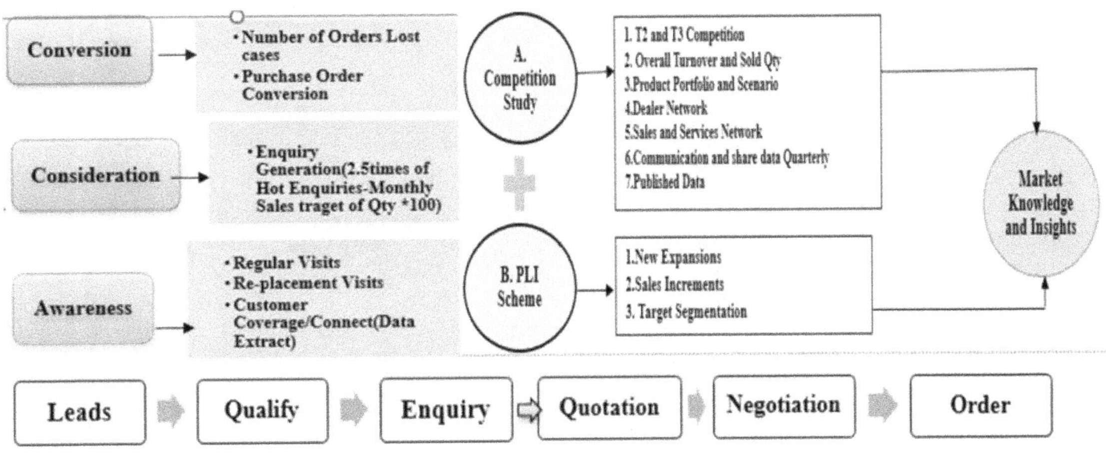

The metric Market knowledge and Insights in Company A has two division one is competition Study 15% weightage, and another is PLI scheme 10% weightage. The diagram for the Market knowledge and Insights and the leads scoring by the Sales Professional gone through the following phase of Leads to Opportunities of sales as shown in above figure 8.

4.3 H3: CRM Data Analysis is Giving Insights on Customer Retention

(Mach-Król, M., & Hadasik, B. 2021) CRM data Analytics or any big data analysis needed the aspect such as first one is methodically organizing data on the value of big data analytics for understanding customer behaviours and gaining in-depth customer insights. Second, to give emphasizes the temporal nature of consumer behaviours and the significance of time in customer analytics. Thirdly, to identifies a fascinating research gap: the application of sophisticated analytics and temporal big data mining for a thorough comprehension of customers. Then it will acknowledge research gap adds a new perspective to the investigation of customer behaviour's, needs, and expectations, opening new opportunities for both academic and professional communities in terms of research and business. (Hossain, M. A.et al,2020) The envisioned customer analytics capability model is designed to establish connections with customers, with the goal of maximizing customer equity.

The four indicators used in the CRM are Draft, Won, Active and Closed. The indicator Active and Draft is considered in the system is the same count and the Won is the Orders Received and Closed indicator indicated order lost by the competition. Total Orders Won by the company and Lost by the company as shown in the chart. Most of the order lost by the company in the year 2023.

Figure 10. Order won and lost funnel analysis region wise.

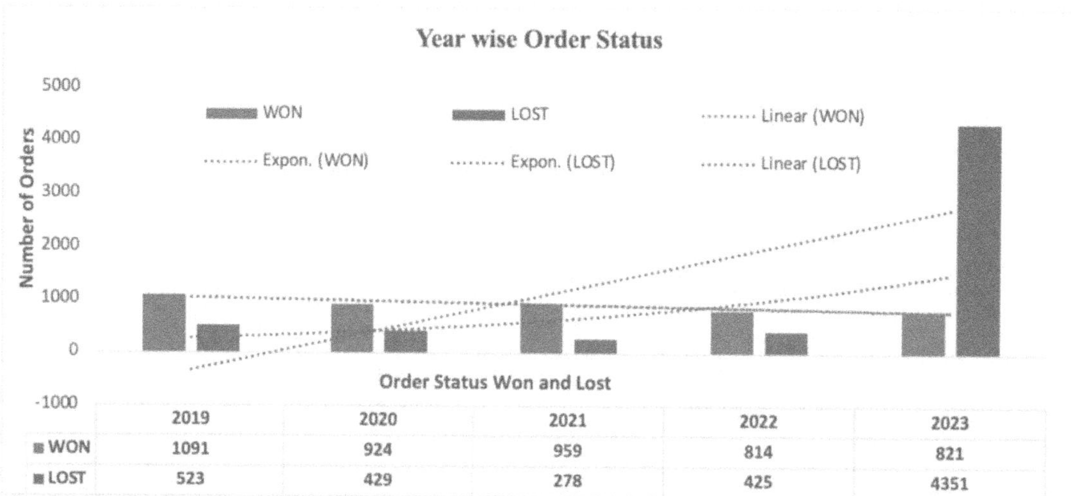

Orders Lost Funnel Conversion Rates	East	North	South	West
Leads / Draft / Active / Won	60.04	31	73.89	10.69

Orders Won Funnel Conversion Rates	East	North	South	West
Leads / Draft / Active / Won	3.91	33.75	96.25	77.54

Funnel analysis is an essential tool for improving sales effectiveness because it helps to streamline the customer journey and find bottlenecks. Through analysing the progression of leads through every phase of the sales funnel, enterprises may identify the points at which prospective clients become disengaged and employ focused tactics to enhance conversion rates. Businesses can concentrate their efforts on high-performing channels by using the insightful input this study offers on the efficacy of marketing campaigns. Additionally, by creating a seamless experience, knowing the customer path, you can increase customer happiness and loyalty. The conversion rate is calculated by using the Funnel Conversion Metrics. The conversion rate represents the portion of leads that successfully transition into customers. As organization objective is to maximize lead conversions, determining the conversion rate serves as a valuable tool for strategizing the most effective approach. Moreover, consistently monitoring the conversion rate's progression over time will enhance operational efficiency and, in the long run, contribute to revenue growth. The Geographic Segment considered in the study are East, West, South and North. The formula used for Conversion rate is:

Conversion rate = (Total Conversion/ Total Leads in funnel) *100.

The Linear and Exponential average value for Order Status won and Lost and the Geographic segment wise Funnel Conversion rate analysis for the year 2019 to 2023 as shown in the following figure 9. On sales tactics, customer relationships, and organizational performance, customer relationship management (CRM) data analysis can have a significant and long-lasting effect. The use of several statistical tools and approaches to glean important insights from CRM data. Descriptive Statistics and Segmentation Analysis methods used for analysing CRM data and their potential long-term impacts.

4.4 H4: Long-Term Impact of CRM Data Analysis on Sales Strategies, Customer Relationships, and Organizational Performance

The adoption of CRM systems yielded notable improvements in the operational performance engaged in business-to-business marketing. The market instability had an adverse influence on the connection between CRM implementation and corporate performance (Quzwen, M. H.et al,2021). Organizations ought to allocate resources to training and development initiatives focused on nurturing enduring customer connections (Baiyewu, O. 2022). The relationship of CRM has five Dimensions such as Customer orientation, CRM organization, Knowledge management, Technology based CRM etc. with respect to the Organizational Performance in the long run (Elmubasher, N. H.2020). When examining the impact of CRM on organizational performance it is pinpointed three variables like CRM Practices or the level of adoption and utilization of CRM within companies, Innovation Capability, Firm Performance, or organizational performance. CRM modules, encompassing sales, marketing, and services, serve as a pivotal tool for achieving improved business outcomes by embracing the customer-centric approach advocated by contemporary marketing theories (Guerola-Navarro et al.2021).

On sales tactics, customer relationships, and organizational performance, customer relationship management (CRM) data analysis can have a significant and long-lasting effect. You can use several statistical tools and approaches to glean important insights from CRM data. Descriptive Statistics and Segmentation Analysis methods used for analysing CRM data and their potential long-term impacts.

Figure 11. Customer cluster analysis based on different criteria.

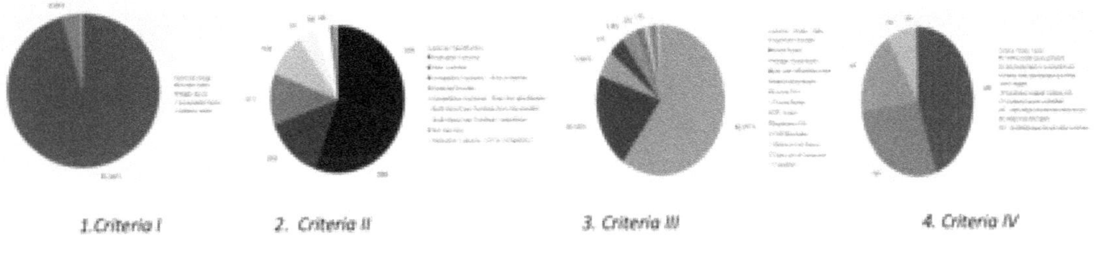

1.Criteria I 2. Criteria II 3. Criteria III 4. Criteria IV

The customer cluster analysis is used in the study based on 4 different criteria as shown in the above figure 10.

Table 1.

Criteria I: - Based on Sector	Criteria I: - Based on Customer Category
• Private - 95.58% • Public- 4.05% • Government – 0.30% • Defence – 0.07%	• Favouring Provider -211 • Dedicated Customer- 565 • Competition Customer - Gives Enquiries- 263 • Competition Customer - Does Not give Enquiry-183 • New Customer - 494 • Dedicated Customer, Lost to Competition - 17 • Multi Brand Last Purchase from Provider -81 • Multi Brand Last Purchase competition - 66 • Not Favouring provider - 24
Criteria III: - Based on Customer Cluster Sales • Brand Buyers • Budget Based Buyers • End User Influenced Buyers • EPC Buyers • Experience Buyers • Experience TCO • OEM Mandated • Process Budge • Process TCO • Reference Led Buyers • Relationship Buyers • Total Cost of Ownership	**Criteria IV: - Based on Customer Cluster Spares** • A (100% potential spares purchased) • B (Below 100% potential spares purchased) • C (Not Buying Spares or buying lubricants) • D (Compressor scrapped/ Company shut) • Not in Budget • P1 - Asset will get commissioned within one year. • P2 - No Visibility when the unit will be commissioned.

The Customer Cluster based on Sales has different categories as Brand Customers who are Brand Sensitive-Mostly customers showing loyalty towards the brands they have been using for a long time. Reference Led (need-product and service) included business contact sharing between manufacturers and intermediaries. Relationships (happy customer and strong alliance) give references of the prospects to the manufacturer—hierarchy Follower (Always the higher management are involved in the small decision) in which three types. As First type is Process Oriented customer who focuses on only the best technological solution, the second type is Process Budgets are those who are strictly following the budget but have a small quantity of difference from the best; and the third type is Experience Oriented has managed both above category best technology and budget also because of the experience advantage. OEMs (In house requirement) primarily use the industrial product for their in-house use. EPC Customers purchase the industrial product for their project needs. End user influence has the end user as the satisfied customer who used mouth marketing to their contacts without the intervention of the manufacturer.

The Customer Cluster Spares has categories as A which is 100% potential spares purchased only genuine spares buyers, B is Below 100% potential spares purchased, C is not Buying Spares or buying lubricants, D is either Compressor scrapped or Company shut, next buyers the price is not in their Budget, P1 where Asset will get commissioned within one year and P2 has no visibility when the unit will be commissioned.

5. RESULTS

Important insights into different client segments and their purchase patterns were obtained from the examination of CRM data. We distinguished between various groups, including Brand Buyers, Reference Led Buyers, and Relationship Buyers, by classifying clients according to their sales interactions and preferences. Reference-led buyers primarily depended on recommendations from business connections, underscoring the significance of networking and referrals in sales techniques, whereas brand buyers demonstrated a strong preference for well-known brands, showing brand loyalty. Relationship Buyers placed a high value on ongoing conversations and regular correspondence, highlighting the necessity of ongoing involvement and relationship development.

Our comprehension was further enhanced by the division of clients into groups according to how they bought spare parts. Clients were categorized into groups A, B, C, and D according to the way they made purchases. consumers in Category A, who bought all possible spares, were very engaged and devoted, but consumers in Category B, who bought some spares but not all of them, showed signs of upselling and better engagement. Customers who only bought lubricants fell into Category C, while those who scrapped their equipment fell into Category D. These examples highlight areas where client retention efforts need to be reinforced.

Furthermore, the investigation showed that Experience Oriented consumers were very valued since they were able to balance budgetary restraints with technology. These clients were ideal candidates for improved service and tailored communication tactics since they valued relationships and prompt responses. The findings demonstrated a considerable improvement in recurring business and general customer satisfaction when high-value clients were targeted and provided with effective relationship management and quick response times. These results highlight the significance of customized sales tactics that target certain client demands and habits. Businesses can boost overall organizational success, increase client retention, and improve sales performance by utilizing CRM data properly.

6. DISCUSSION

CRM data research highlights the significant influence it has on customer relations, sales strategies, and organizational performance. Based on sales behavior, the research distinguishes several client clusters, including Reference Led Buyers, Relationship Buyers, and Brand Buyers, each of which has distinct traits and preferences. For example, Reference Led Buyers rely on business contacts to make purchase decisions, whereas Brand Buyers show devotion to well-known businesses.

By segmenting their customer base, businesses can better target their marketing and sales activities and better meet the needs of their various clientele. The emphasis on Experience Oriented clients emphasizes the significance of providing value and cultivating long-term relationships by striking a balance between technical solutions and financial restrictions. The study also shows that sustaining excellent client relationships and giving priority to prompt responses are essential for long-term organizational performance. This strategy strengthens the business against pressure from the competition while also increasing recurring business.

Moreover, important insights regarding client retention tactics can be gained from the examination of customer clusters based on spares purchasing patterns. Customer engagement levels can be determined by using categories such as A (100 percent potential spares purchased) and B (below 100 percent potential spares purchased) to distinguish between highly engaged and low-engagement consumers. Targeted retention efforts can be informed by knowing why consumers discard equipment (Category D), buy only lubricants (Category C), or don't buy spares. Through the identification and resolution of wants and problems, this thorough segmentation offers a road map for improving customer happiness and loyalty. Businesses can create more successful plans to retain and expand their client base by using CRM data to obtain a deeper understanding of consumer behavior. This will ultimately improve business performance.

7. CONCLUSION

The importance of CRM data in transforming client retention and sales performance is highlighted by this study. Businesses can use more nuanced approaches to their sales and marketing by utilizing comprehensive consumer information. Companies can better satisfy unique needs and increase customer satisfaction and loyalty by customizing their strategies based on the purchase patterns and preferences of their diverse consumer groups. For example, marketing campaigns and customer relationships can be strengthened by concentrating on the specific demands of Brand Buyers and Relationship Buyers.

The analysis underscores the need of catering to the diverse needs of clients in accordance with their spare's procurement patterns. Through the identification of highly engaged clients (Category A) and those that need additional attention (Categories B, C, and D), organizations can create focused strategies aimed at increasing sales and engagement. The study also shows that maintaining long-term loyalty and keeping high-value clients requires a strong emphasis on responsiveness and relationship management. These results show that a data-driven approach to CRM offers a strong basis for long-term organizational success in addition to increasing sales efficiency.

The study also highlights how predictive analytics and sophisticated CRM features can improve performance metrics and sales forecasts. Businesses can more efficiently manage resources and set realistic goals when they can more accurately predict client wants and market trends. Artificial intelligence and machine learning integrated into CRM systems will offer ever-more-advanced tools for analysing client data and forecasting future behaviours as technology advances.

In conclusion, businesses hoping to maintain their competitiveness in a constantly shifting market must make smart use of CRM data. Through consistent improvement of their CRM tactics and utilization of cutting-edge technology advancements, companies can attain long-term prosperity and uphold robust, enduring consumer connections. Through a greater understanding of their client base and the efficient use of CRM data, this study offers firms a thorough path for optimizing sales effectiveness and improving customer retention.

8. FUTURE OUTLOOK

In the future, CRM systems that incorporate cutting-edge technology like artificial intelligence and machine learning could offer great chances to improve sales and client retention even more. Businesses can use predictive analytics to predict client requirements and market trends more precisely by refining the data to provide ever more accurate projections. Furthermore, increasing the adoption of mobile CRM solutions can improve real-time data access and sales cooperation, enabling sales teams to make deft decisions while on the road.

Future studies should examine how these technological developments affect organizational development and customer loyalty over the long run-in order to help organizations stay competitive in a market that is constantly changing. Companies can achieve sustained success and preserve strong, long-lasting client relationships by utilizing the most recent advancements and consistently updating their CRM tactics.

REFERENCES

Alim, S., & Ozuem, W. (2014). The influences of e-CRM on customer satisfaction and loyalty in the UK mobile industry. *Journal of Applied Business and Finance Research, 3*(2), 47–54.

Anees, R. T., Nordin, N. A., Anjum, T., Cavaliere, L. P. L., & Heidler, P. (2020). Evaluating the Impact of Customer Relationship Management (CRM) Strategies on Customer Retention (A Study of Fast-Food Chains in Pakistan). *Business Management and Strategy, 11*(2), 117–133. DOI: 10.5296/bms.v11i2.17934

Asiegbu, I. F., Awa, H. O., Akpotu, C., & Ogbonna, U. B. (2011). Sales force competence development and marketing performance of industrial and domestic products firms in Nigeria. *Far East Journal of Psychology and Business, 2*(3), 43–59.

Assaf, A. G., Josiassen, A., Mattila, A. S., & Cvelbar, L. K. (2015). Does advertising spending improve sales performance? *International Journal of Hospitality Management, 48*, 161–166. DOI: 10.1016/j.ijhm.2015.04.014

Bachtiar, F. (2018). Customer Segmentation Using Two-Step Mining Method Based on RFM Model. *2018 International Conference on Sustainable Information.* DOI: 10.1109/SIET.2018.8693173

Baiyewu, O. (2022). *The impact of customer relationship management on organizational performance: a case study of Dangote Flour Mill.*

Bin-Nashwan, S. A., & Hassan, H. (2017). Impact of customer relationship management (CRM) on customer satisfaction and loyalty: A systematic review. *Journal of Advanced Research in Business and Management Studies, 6*(1), 86–107.

Carrasco, R. A., Blasco, M. F., García-Madariaga, J., & Herrera-Viedma, E. (2019). A Fuzzy Linguistic RFM Model Applied to Campaign Management. *International Journal of Interactive Multimedia and Artificial Intelligence, 5*(4), 2019. DOI: 10.9781/ijimai.2018.03.003

Elmubasher, N. H., & Hamid, M. M. (2020). The effect of Customer Relationship Management Dimensions on the Organizational Performance in Telecommunication Sectors in Sudan. Arab Journal for Scientific Publishing (AJSP), ISSN 2663-5798.

Gajanova, L., Nadanyiova, M., & Moravcikova, D. (2019). The use of demographic and psychographic segmentation to creating marketing strategy of brand loyalty. Scientific annals of economics and business, 66(1), 65-84.

Gončarovs, P. (2017). Data analytics in crm processes: A literature review. *Information Technology and Management Science, 20*(1), 103–108. DOI: 10.1515/itms-2017-0018

Guerola-Navarro, V., Oltra-Badenes, R., Gil-Gomez, H., & Gil-Gomez, J. A. (2021). Research model for measuring the impact of customer relationship management (CRM) on performance indicators. *Ekonomska Istrazivanja, 34*(1), 2669–2691. DOI: 10.1080/1331677X.2020.1836992

Haataja, T. (2016). Sales forecasting in small and medium-sized enterprises.

Hallikainen, H., Savimäki, E., & Laukkanen, T. (2020). Fostering B2B sales with customer big data analytics. *Industrial Marketing Management, 86*, 90–98. DOI: 10.1016/j.indmarman.2019.12.005

Hanssens, D. M., Pauwels, K. H., Srinivasan, S., Vanhuele, M., & Yildirim, G. (2014). Consumer attitude metrics for guiding marketing mix decisions. *Marketing Science, 33*(4), 534–550. DOI: 10.1287/mksc.2013.0841

Hossain, M. A., Akter, S., & Yanamandram, V. (2020). Revisiting customer analytics capability for data-driven retailing. *Journal of Retailing and Consumer Services, 56*, 102187. DOI: 10.1016/j.jretconser.2020.102187

Hoyle, J. A., Dingus, R., & Wilson, J. H. (2020). An exploration of sales forecasting: Sales manager and salesperson perspectives. *Journal of Marketing Analytics, 8*(3), 127–136. DOI: 10.1057/s41270-020-00082-8

Kumar, N., Upreti, K., Jafri, S., Arora, I., Bhardwaj, R., Phogat, M., Srivastava, S., & Akorli, F. K. (2022). Sustainable computing: A determinant of industry 4.0 for sustainable information society. *Journal of Nanomaterials, 2022*(1), 9335963. DOI: 10.1155/2022/9335963

Kumar, P., & Mokha, A. K. (2022). Electronic Customer Relationship Management (E-CRM) and Customer Loyalty: The Mediating Role of Customer Satisfaction in the Banking Industry. [IJEBR]. *International Journal of E-Business Research, 18*(1), 1–22. DOI: 10.4018/IJEBR.293292

Lau, R. Y. K., Zhang, W., & Xu, W. (2018). Parallel aspect-oriented sentiment analysis for sales forecasting with big data. *Production and Operations Management, 27*(10), 1775–1794. DOI: 10.1111/poms.12737

Liu, C. C., Chuang, L. M., & Huang, C. M. (2012). A study of the impact of the E-CRM perspective on customer satisfaction and customer loyalty-exemplified by bank Sinopac. *Journal of Economics and Behavioral Studies, 4*(8), 467–476. DOI: 10.22610/jebs.v4i8.348

Long, C. S., Khalafinezhad, R., Ismail, W. K. W., & Abd Rasid, S. Z. (2013). Impact of CRM factors on customer satisfaction and loyalty. *Asian Social Science, 9*(10), 247. DOI: 10.5539/ass.v9n10p247

Luo, P., Ngai, E. W., & Tian, X. (2020). Exploring the dynamic influence of visit behavior on online store sales performance: An empirical investigation. *Journal of the Association for Information Systems, 21*(3), 6. DOI: 10.17705/1jais.00614

Mach-Król, M., & Hadasik, B. (2021). On a certain research gap in big data mining for customer insights. *Applied Sciences (Basel, Switzerland), 11*(15), 6993. DOI: 10.3390/app11156993

Mokha, A. K., & Kumar, P. (2022). Examining the interconnections between E-CRM, customer experience, customer satisfaction and customer loyalty: A mediation approach. [JECO]. *Journal of Electronic Commerce in Organizations, 20*(1), 1–21. DOI: 10.4018/JECO.292474

Mortensen, S., Christison, M., Li, B., Zhu, A., & Venkatesan, R. (2019, April). Predicting and defining B2B sales success with machine learning. In *2019 Systems and Information Engineering Design Symposium (SIEDS)* (pp. 1-5). IEEE. DOI: 10.1109/SIEDS.2019.8735638

Mukhayaroh, A., Marlina, S., Hartini, S., Muryani, S., Sinnun, A., & Nurajizah, S. (2020). Implementation of Clustering Algorithm Method for Customer Segmentation. *Journal of Computational and Theoretical Nanoscience*, •••, 2020.

Nikhashemi, S. R., Paim, L., Haque, A., Khatibi, A., & Tarofder, A. K. (2013). Internet technology, CRM and customer loyalty: Customer retention and satisfaction perspective. *Middle East Journal of Scientific Research, 14*(1), 79–92.

Nune, S. C., & Kozhikode, I. (2021). A generalized flow for B2B sales predictive modeling. *Journal of Cardiovascular Disease Research.*

Palanimalai, S., & Paramasivam, I. (2016). Big data analytics bring new insights and higher business value-an experiment carried out to divulge sales forecasting solutions. *International Journal of Advanced Intelligence Paradigms, 8*(2), 207–218. DOI: 10.1504/IJAIP.2016.075728

Porto, R. B., & Walter, M. C. (2022). Unpacking the Behavioral Dimensions of Promotions and Sales Performance: Do Real-Life Promotions Drive More Sales? In Sales Management for Improved Organizational Competitiveness and Performance (pp. 135-159). IGI Global.

Quzwen, M. H., Hurriyati, R., & Sultan, M. A. (2021, September). Customer Relationship Management in Business-to-Business Marketing: The Impact on Corporate Performance. In *5th Global Conference on Business, Management and Entrepreneurship (GCBME 2020)* (pp. 517-523). Atlantis Press. DOI: 10.2991/aebmr.k.210831.101

Rizki, B., Ginasta, N. G., Tamrin, M. A., & Rahman, A. (2020). Customer Loyality Segmentation on Point of Sale System Using Recency-Frequency-Monetary (RFM) and K-Means. Jurnal online informatika, 130-136.

Rodriguez, M., & Boyer, S. (2020). The impact of mobile customer relationship management (mCRM) on sales collaboration and sales performance. *Journal of Marketing Analytics*, *8*(3), 137–148. DOI: 10.1057/s41270-020-00087-3

Saputra, S. (2019, March). The effect of customer relationship management (CRM) on Bank customer loyalty through satisfaction as mediating variable: Evidence in Batam, *Indonesia. In International Symposium on Social Sciences, Education, and Humanities (ISSEH 2018)* (pp. 146-151). Atlantis Press. DOI: 10.2991/isseh-18.2019.34

Saraswathi, K., Renukadevi, N. T., Nandhinidevi, S., Gayathridevi, S., & Naveen, P. (2021, November). Sales prediction using machine learning approaches. In AIP Conference Proceedings (Vol. 2387, No. 1). AIP Publishing. DOI: 10.1063/5.0068655

Shahbaz, M., Gao, C., Zhai, L., Shahzad, F., Abbas, A., & Zahid, R. (2020). Investigating the impact of big data analytics on perceived sales performance: The mediating role of customer relationship management capabilities. *Complexity*, *2020*, 2020. DOI: 10.1155/2020/5186870

Singh, M., Bhattacharjya, D., Deleris, L., Katz-Rogozhnikov, D., Squillante, M., Ray, B., Mojsilovic, A., Kakrania, D., Saha, A., Fu, J., Barrera, C., & Richard, J. (2011). The growth and performance diagnostics initiative: A multi-dimensional framework for sales performance analysis and management. *Service Science*, *3*(1), 82–98. DOI: 10.1287/serv.3.1.82

Sugiato, B., Riyadi, S., & Budiarti, E. (2023). The effects of customer relationship management, service quality and relationship marketing on customer retention: The mediation role of bank customer retention in Indonesia. *Accounting*, *9*(2), 85–94. DOI: 10.5267/j.ac.2022.12.004

Sutanto, H., Handayani, S. D., & Susanto, S. (2021). Measuring Customer Loyalty and Satisfaction of Bank Bantul Using CRM and Service Quality. JBTI: Jurnal Bisnis: Teori dan Implementasi, 12(3), 172-183.

Upreti, K., Kuwar, V., & Haque, M. (2025). Innovative CRM Strategies for the Modern Social Marketing Landscape. In Phygital Approaches to Social Marketing (pp. 247-266). IGI Global.

Vargis, B. K., Alam, M. S., Upreti, K., Raut, R. D., Kumar, N., & Jalil, S. Z. A. (2022, May). Scoping analysis of leveraging IoT with blockchain for monitoring and ensuring efficacy of vaccine cold chains. In 2022 6th International Conference on Intelligent Computing and Control Systems (ICICCS) (pp. 795-803). IEEE. DOI: 10.1109/ICICCS53718.2022.9788216

Wu, M., Andreev, P., & Benyoucef, M. (2023). The state of lead scoring models and their impact on sales performance. *Information Technology Management*. Advance online publication. DOI: 10.1007/s10799-023-00388-w PMID: 36742340

Zallocco, R., Bolman Pullins, E., & Mallin, M. L. (2009). A re-examination of B2B sales performance. *Journal of Business and Industrial Marketing*, *24*(8), 598–610. DOI: 10.1108/08858620910999466

Chapter 13
Analysis and Prediction of Customer Sentiment for Real Estate Organizations Using Machine Learning Approaches

Md Shamim Hossain
https://orcid.org/0000-0003-1645-7470
Hajee Mohammad Danesh Science and Technology University, Bangladesh

Rony Kumar Datta
https://orcid.org/0009-0005-8892-6098
Hajee Mohammad Danesh Science and Technology University, Bangladesh

Md. Mehedul Islam Sabuj
Hajee Mohammad Danesh Science and Technology University, Bangladesh

Humaira Begum
https://orcid.org/0000-0002-5355-415X
Hajee Mohammad Danesh Science and Technology University, Bangladesh

Md. Abdur Rouf
Hajee Mohammad Danesh Science and Technology University, Bangladesh

ABSTRACT

The purpose of the current study was to analyse and predict of customer sentiment towards real estate organizations using Machine Learning Approaches (ML) approaches. The study employed five ML models to predict customer sentiment toward real estate organizations. The data was collected from Yelp.com and filtered using the "Real Estate" tag. The findings revealed that all four machine learning models effectively classified the review text. The logistic regression (LR) and support vector machine (SVM) models achieved the highest accuracy scores at 93.1 and 93.16, respectively. This study emphasizes the potential of machine learning in improving customer experience and facilitating better decision-making in the real estate industry. The results can guide real estate organizations in understanding customer opinions and preferences, enabling them to make necessary improvements. Additionally, the findings have social implications, as they can enhance products, services, and overall customer experiences, leading to increased satisfaction and trust in the industry.

DOI: 10.4018/979-8-3693-7447-4.ch013

1. INTRODUCTION

Real estate encompasses various aspects related to land, buildings, air rights, and underground rights. It involves the creation, acquisition, and sale of properties, including both land and permanent structures (Ricciotti et al., 2022). The real estate market involves a wide range of investments, such as land, buildings, immovable properties, interests in real estate, and housing as a whole. Managing assets, properties, and buildings is a crucial part of the value chain (Kwakye & Haw, 2021). The real estate industry plays a vital part in the global economy, environment, and society. However, it has been consistently ranked as having a low level of digital maturity compared to other industries (Saari et al., 2022). Due to the complexity of real estate and the diverse expertise required, real estate firms are recognized as highly knowledgeable entities. They need to continuously adapt and acquire new skills to thrive in their unique industry (Azmi et al., 2015).

Property valuation organizations, whether governmental or private, are examples of service-oriented entities within the real estate sector. These organizations engage in extensive client consultation and provide expert guidance on real estate matters. Their services include property valuations, property management, project feasibility reports, real estate brokerage, market research, and among others (Azmi et al., 2015). Overall, the real estate industry encompasses a broad spectrum of activities, requiring specialized knowledge and offering a range of services to meet the diverse needs of clients.

Moving on to consumers, it is crucial to understand how well a company's product or service satisfies its target market. It's a powerful tool that can help businesses in many ways, including boosting profits and decreasing marketing expenditures (Chepukaka & Kirugi, 2019). Nothing makes clients feel more valued than asking for and valuing their reaction. Customers' ability to voice their opinions online has opened the door for marketing executives to gain valuable insight into their products and services (Rambocas & Pacheco, 2018; Erevelles et al., 2016). There are already a huge number of buyer reviews posted online that are yonder the visual capacity of any single person. So there is a demand for new approaches to evaluating consumer reviews. Sentiment analysis is therefore helpful for automatically identifying online reviews (Hossain and Rahman, 2022). Since data is now accessible digitally, extensive user data analysis is encouraged. Data scientists, researchers in artificial intelligence, and people working in the internet sector are all fascinated by how customers behave. Reviews are a fundamental source of customer evaluation on the online platform (Hossain and Rahman, 2022).

All businesses rely on customer feedback, including the real estate business. Customer reviews can help businesses learn more about their products or services. Consequently, a review basis will help businesses find more profitable clients and develop offers that are tailored to their needs. With more and more people using the internet, feedback from consumers takes on greater significance. Organizations can respond to customers' feedback in a unified space where it has been aggregated from multiple sources (Adak et al., 2022). It has been stated that analyzing customer feedback is essential for modern businesses.

On the other hand, customizing customer ratings is a tedious process that takes a lot of time and effort. That's why it's crucial for companies to implement reliable systems for monitoring and analyzing social media user reactions. According to Mohammad (2016), recent developments in ML have led to the development of computer systems that act like humans. Due to the proliferation of digital news, information, and opinionated data as well as the development of more sophisticated textual analysis methods, sentiment analysis (SA) has become a focus of research in the field of natural language processing (NLP). With the advent of more powerful computers, researchers have a new tool for analyzing textual documents. Consequently, of these developments, researchers in the real estate industry were able to develop new sentiment proxies that go beyond the standard measures of sentiment used in the past, such as closed-end fund discounts and survey-based measures (Hausler et al., 2018). When applied to fields like government policy, public health, business, the social sciences, and the arts, sentiment analysis (the automated detection of emotions in text) opens up possibilities that were previously unavailable. Recent research (Feizollah et al., 2019; Ainin et al., 2020; Luo & Xu, 2021) has also utilized customer reviews as a means of assessing customer satisfaction. Sentiment analysis (SA), also denoted to as judgement mining, is a technique for processing natural language that determines the emotive suggestion of a text (Feizollah et al., 2019). It's a common method used by companies to collect client feedback on a specific product, service, or idea. Businesses can save effort and time by having opinions expressed in reviews, conversations on social media, and other places sorted automatically. The vast majority of sentiment analysis systems have been built for narrowly targeted applications, where domain-specific texts are used to train machine learning algorithms to determine whether a given passage of text should be interpreted as positive or negative. Still others use dictionaries to compile a sentiment index by collecting and scanning for instances of words and phrases known to carry emotional weight during the review process (Hossain et al, 2022). Additionally, Hossain & Rahman (2022) mentioned that although it is essential for businesses, such as real estate organizations, to comprehend and anticipate customer sentiment, no prior research has used lexicon-based ML techniques to comprehend and anticipate client sentiment in reviews of real estate organizations. Thus, we employ two lexical-based ML techniques (AFINN and VADAR [Valence Aware Dictionary for Sentiment Reasoning]) and five machine learning methods to predict sentiments.

Prediction is a common use of machine learning, thus it stands to reason that this method would also be effective for forecasting the real estate market. Customers' feelings towards real estate companies may be better understood and predicted with the help of well-trained systems if market variables are taken into consideration (Jha et al., 2020). It was also found that many industries besides the real estate industry use sentiment analysis on social media. These industries include politics (Ceron et al., 2013), the financial sector (Li & Meesad, 2016), the hospitality and tourism industry (Philander & Zhong, 2016) including the halal tourism (Ainin et al., 2020), and halal restaurants (Hossain et al., 2022). The purpose of the current study is, therefore, to fill that gap. The study's goals are to examine consumer opinions of real estate firms, to use lexical tools to assess customers' review texts about firms, and to use ML methods to forecast customers' opinions. Therefore, this research uses ML techniques to examine and forecast client opinions of real estate firms.

It is clear that the practice of artificial intelligence (AI) in consumer sentiment research has a big influence on the real estate market. By providing real estate organizations with valuable insights into their customer's opinions and preferences, they are able to make improvements that can lead to increased trust and customer satisfaction in the industry. Organizations in the real estate industry may utilize the study's findings to boost their offerings and provide a better service to their clients. Additionally, the use of ML in customer SA is an innovative and original contribution to the field, and the results of this study can aid as a reference for future investigations. With the growing importance of customer feedback in today's digital world, this study provides valuable insights that can assist real estate organizations in making informed business decisions and improving their customer relationships.

2. LITERATURE REVIEW

2.1 Textual Data Mining Technique in Different Domains

The textual data mining technique was applied in the current research as a cornerstone of SA. (Alzate et al., 2022) explained the term "text mining" to a group of methods and tools used to automatically or semi-automatically search through vast amounts of text in order to find recurring patterns, trends, or rules that describe how the text behaves. Large volumes of unstructured textual data are supposed to be mined for knowledge and information through data mining (Hossain and Rahman, 2022). Text mining technique is a subfield of data mining that uses massive, unstructured documents to extract significant patterns or information that may be used to summarize and categorize text data produced in a range of industries (Kim and Kang, 2018).(Tseng et al., 2007) showed that text mining encompasses document preprocessing, indexing, and topic grouping. In order to study brand image and product positioning, Alzate, Arce-Urriza, and Cebollada (2022) looked at the linguistic components of online reviews. They provided a unified, approachable framework for text analysis of web reviews. Hudaefi and Badeges (2021) employed text mining technique in order to extract data from 24 authorized bank reports published by five Indonesian Islamic banks. By gathering online evaluations from two US e-commerce websites, Nasiri and Shokouhyar (2021) were able to assess consumer perceptions of the perceived advantages and hazards of buying a refurbished smartphone and examine the customer satisfaction characteristics by opinion mining. Heng et al. (2018) investigated the usefulness of reviews that included an LDA analysis to glean subjects from Amazon.com coffee reviews. The retrieved topics are used as independent variables in regression studies along with conventional numerical review factors (such as rating and length) to evaluate review helpfulness. Hudaefi, Caraka and Wahid (2021) used a text mining technique to collect data from a virtual environment about zakat administration during the outbreak of COVID-19. Alqtati, Wilson and De Silva (2021) employed text mining to provide a rapid, simple, and dynamic method for professionals and researchers in the domains of social media analytics, marketing communications, advertising, branding, public relations, and marketing to evaluate consumer behavioral sentiments and engagement. Although text mining has been utilized in a variety of fields, the SA of real estate organizations has not been studied; as a result, text mining technique was used in this study to examine the attitudes of customers toward real estate organizations.

2.2 Sentiment Analysis

Sentiment Analysis, the most popular text categorization tool, examines a text to identify whether the fundamental sentiment is neutral, undesirable, or favorable (Hossain and Rahman, 2022). Since a decade ago, various businesses have employed sentiment analysis technique as a fundamental means to comprehend the market, reply to customer feedback, and opinion obtainable in a crowded marketplace by examining data about the features and superiority of their products that are poised from social media platforms like the App Store, Twitter, and Facebook where users write their feelings about the benefits, quality, features, and other values of the services and products. This helps businesses pinpoint the issue and address it (Nagpal et al., 2020). To automatically categorize a corpus as neutral, positive, or negative is the main objective of sentiment mining (Mostafa, 2018; Yang and Yu, 2013). As a result, a lot of businesses believe that sentiment analysis is a suitable method for examining how people feel about a given subject. Opinion mining is becoming more significant as it is used more frequently to learn peoples' opinions (Liu et al., 2021). Many categories can be used to categorize opinion mining. On the level of words or phrases, sentences, or documents, opinion mining can be carried out (Wang et al., 2019; Mostafa, 2018). Mining opinions regarding product reviews has been carefully studied in the literature (Ainin et al., 2020; Philander and Zhong, 2016). The study by Leelawat et al. (2022) used Thai Twitter data to look at visitor sentiments. Similar research on consumer perceptions toward smartphones was conducted by Pedipina et al. in 2021. Using adjective-noun sentence pairings, Miyoshi and Nakagami (2007) investigated consumer sentiments toward electronic devices. To assess the effect of COVID-19 on the airline business, Chang et al. (2022) compiled a review of airline passengers from January 2016 to August 2020. Zhang et al. (2018) also classified customer attitudes toward product reviews using data mining techniques. Using a sample of 1,920 tweets, A SA was completed by Hornikx and Hendriks in 2015 for numerous Dutch products and services.

In the realm of online interactions, individuals who engage with social networks have developed a familiarity with employing a collection of visual symbols to express their emotions (Liu et al., 2021). Recent sentiment analysis research tried to use emoticons as noisy markers for social media sentiments (Felbo et al., 2017; Chen et al., 2019). In several research, opinion or review mining has been used to predict the product or brand image (Mostafa, 2013), examine product nonfunctional (Zhang et al., 2018), gauge consumer pleasure with services, and forecast sales (Kang and Park, 2014).

On the basis of this brief literature review, SA has been applied in a number of situations; still, no prior studies have used it to examine customer sentiments toward real estate organizations. Instead, the customer's feelings can be explained using the appraisal theory.

2.2.1 Appraisal Theory

The appraisal theory explains how a language interacts with one another (Widyaningrum et al., 2019). The psychological process that a person goes through in response to an environmental stimulus is represented by appraisal theory (Scherer, Schorr, and Johnstone, 2001). The evaluation theory is the subject of two main schools of thinking. When discussing relational meaning and distinct emotions, some academics see emotions as having a small number of dimensions (e.g., Roseman, 2001). Others characterize the mental process behind appraisal theories (Scherer, 2001). It shows how these decisions are reflected in the vocabulary and grammatical construction of evaluative writing in the SFL tradition and considers meaning as a collection of choices made by the speaker or writer (Hossain and Rahman, 2022). The appraisal theory of emotion holds that, emotions are assemblages of appraisals, action inclinations, physiological reactions, expressive behavior, and sentiments. An emotion begins when an entering stimulus is evaluated according to several evaluation criteria, including goal relevance, goal in/congruence, unexpectedness, ease of control and internal/external source (Moors et al., 2021). There are three most vital features of the appraisal theory (Widyaningrum et al., 2019):

- The appraisal of things, people, and emotions is related to attitude. The three categories of attitude evaluation are judgment (character), impacted (feelings), and appreciation (the worth of a thing).
- An individual's opinions, such as those that come from within or without themselves, such as shy, unattractive, or beautiful, as well as their actions in a social setting, such as heroic, or weak, are examples of appreciation.
- There are two categories of engagement with the source of attitudes: monogloss (related to the source of the attitude that originates only within the author) and heterogloss (related to the source of the attitude that originates outside the author).

The behavior of an appraisal statement is defined by the interaction of local grammars and appraisal theory. Appraisal theory essentially explains how two languages communicate with one another (Widyaningrum et al., 2019; Read and Carroll, 2012). Reading consumer-based assessments will likely cause readers to feel similar emotions because emotions may be shared (Hossain and Rahman, 2022). Therefore, the appraisal concept was applied in the current study to ascertain how clients felt about reviews of real estate companies.

2.2.2 Lexical Based SA

The lexical approach enables text categorization in relation to a dictionary that contains a word assortment with polarity-related thoughts and ideals that may be categorized as either optimistic or undesirable (De Oliveira et al., 2021). lexical apparatuses are very widespread in the field of SA, since they provide as an explicit resource for emotive data encoding (Hossain and Rahman, 2022). That's why; scholars typically employ SA based on lexicons, which aggregate sentimentality terminology (Araque et al., 2019). However, because opinions are either favorable or negative, it might be challenging to pinpoint the precise viewpoint (Saqete et al., 2022). These web resources generate a vast volume of textual information.

Consequently, it is essential to precisely and effectively assess the textual material (Luo et al., 2020). In order to add the preliminary marking to the emails, Borg and Boldt (2020) employed a Swedish sentiment vocabulary and VADER sentiment. To build models for extracting and categorizing email sentiment, two support vector machine (SVM) models are trained using the email content and sentiment labels as input. Hossain et al. (2022) utilized a rule-based framework for sentiment analysis, combining the Base Line approach and support vector machines (SVM). This framework involves extracting the overall polarity of specific words from the sentiment word dictionary and adjusting it based on contextual information. Mostafa (2020) used two lexicons to analyze 11,700 randomly chosen tweets from around the world to gauge public opinion on halal meals. His studies demonstrate that halal cuisine is typically well received.

Many studies examined panel data sets for consumer feedback using machine learning. So far, no research has been done to assess, measure, and predict consumer sentiment concerning real estate organizations. In order to close the gap, we evaluate customer sentiment using the lexical tools AFINN and VADAR as well as four ML techniques.

2.3 Research Questions

2.3.1 Social Media SA

Social media are extensively and regularly utilized by people of all ages today since they are available on a variety of platforms and devices. Social media has become the world's primary method of communication (Ainin et al., 2020a). Popular social media sites like LinkedIn, Facebook, and Twitter are utilized by numerous stakeholders all over the world to communicate with one another (Obembe et al., 2021; Gong et al., 2017; Kitsios et al., 2022; Kane et al., 2014). Businesses utilized social media to interact with potential clients and shape consumer impressions of their products (Gkikas et al., 2022; Buechel & Berger, 2018). Social media may boost a company's reputation, bring in more customers, and increase income (Sipahi E. veArtantaş E, 2017). Many others have used the same (Hossain et al., 2021; Ainin et al., 2020b) to express their own ideas and thoughts. Customers' decisions to shop and eat out are influenced by reviews posted on social media (Yoo et al., 2013; Nazlan et al., 2018). Optimistic reviews are linked to augmented sales, whilst undesirable reviews are linked to reduced sales (Rui et al., 2013). The importance of customer feedback grows significantly as more people utilize the internet. Companies can gather all client feedback from many platforms in a single, national location, enabling them to respond to the response (Adak et al., 2022).

The content of social media has been evaluated by researchers using these attributes to identify models and indicators that may be used to a variety of business disciplines (Hossain & Rahman, 2022). Due to its precision and suitability for determining customers' opinions, sentiment analysis of humans is currently a fascinating field of research in practically every domain (Bigne et al., 2022). For illustration, Guo et al. (2017) examined the mood of Chinese stockholders, while added study focused on participants in the US stock marketplace (Rao and Srivastava, 2014). The study by Leelawat et al. (2022) implemented Twitter data from Thailand to investigate the attitudes of tourists. Through SA, brand choice is also examined. For instance, 24 brands were evaluated by Hornikx and Hendriks (2015) in Dutch tweets, whereas Mostafa (2013) employed a specialized lexicon to measure consumer perceptions of 16 different firms as expressed in tweets. Chang et al. (2022) conducted a investigation to examine the impacts of COVID-19 on the airline business. They gathered data on airline passengers from January 2016 to August 2020. This study demonstrated that data analytics approaches outperform other conventional ways by using visual analytics techniques to assess consumer satisfaction levels in the airline business.

As shown in the preceding discussion there hasn't been any research done to yet on how to assess and forecast consumer opinion about real estate organizations. We intend to use our study to answer the following study inquiry in particular:

RQ1. What are people's sentiments about real estate companies generally on social media?

Corpus-based and lexicon-based SA techniques are the two main approaches used with writing mining technologies (Miao et al., 2010). Although it is rarely used in research, the corpus-based approach for measuring sentiment direction. The lexicon-based method is grounded on a set of subjective expressions (Sasikala &Lourdusamy, 2018). There are many different lexicons for SA that are readily available, lexicon-based processes are simple to apply, and lexicon-based approaches have been employed in various recent and related research (Yang et al., 2020; Machova et al., 2020). Also, it was exposed that several areas have employed lexicon-based algorithms to extract the review score from textual reviews.

Two lexicon-based approaches were used in the current study to calculate sentiment ratings, as well as the positive and negative assessments of real estate businesses. More specifically, through our examination, we hope to find solutions to the following research questions:

RQ2. What information may be obtained from the textual data, such as customer evaluations, when it is assessed using lexicon-based ML techniques?

RQ3. What are the sample's top optimistic and negative statements, as determined by lexicon-based machine learning techniques?

2.3.2 Sentiment Classification

The bulk of research using supervised learning has found that SVM performs with good accuracy and efficiency. SVM and RF models, as machine learning algorithms, produce better results when studying the emotion of people with a large amount of data (Demircan et al. 2021). According to Gul (2021), SVM has the maximum classification accuracy for identifying the kind of spillway. SVM allegedly provides the highest accuracy in terms of customer sentiment analysis, according to Leelawat et al. (2022). SVM also regarded as the best classification method for textual data polarity detection (Ahmad et al., 2018). In the context of movie sentiment, The performance evaluation of sentiment classification was conducted by Pang et al. (2019), where they assessed three supervised machine learning algorithms: Support vector machines (SVM), maximum entropy classification, and Naive Bayes. They found that SVM performed better than the other two methods. SVM has grown to be one of the most potent and successful algorithms, according to Wang et al. (2021), because it offers greater accuracy than other machine learning algorithms.Additionally, SA and reputation generation on the reviews were conducted by Gupta, Priyani, and Balakrishnan (2021) using consumer reviews of books and movies in natural language.

In order to predict consumer sentiment toward real estate organizations, we used five machine learning techniques in the current study: decision trees (DT), K-nearest neighbor (KNN) classifiers, SVM, logistic regression, and random forest (RF) classifiers. We were interested in how each model performed when applied to real estate organizations data sets. More precisely, we sought to address the following study question using another investigation:

RQ4. Which machine learning algorithms do the best in categorizing customers' attitudes about real estate companies?

3. METHOD

3.1. Data

The data has been collected from Yelp.com using machine learning Python programming language. Generally yelp.com is a crowd-source based social networking site for reviewing the local business (O'Brien, 2007). Yelp is becoming the topic of multiple research projects as it has grabbed a large number of visits and views over the past many years (Salehi-Esfahani and Kang, 2019). Here the user can post a review of different products and service and also can rate their experience using 1 star to 5 star rating scale (Chafkin, 2010).

For this study, collected data has been filtered using "Real Estate" tag. As a result we have got a total of 102726 reviews along with their star ratings for the study (**Table 1**). Successively, we have categorized the customer attitude on the basis of the star ratings that have been given by the customers while posting a review text. We assumed 5 and 4 star emits a positive sentiment, 3 star emits neutral sentiment and 2 and 1 emits a negative sentiment. Hence, for positive sentiment, +1 is assigned, for neutral sentiment, 0 is assigned and for negative sentiment, -1 is assigned.

Table 1. Statistics of the filtered dataset.

Total number of reviews	**102726**
5 star review	45813
4 star review	9199
3 star review	4085
2 star review	6218
1 star review	37411

Table 2 represents the customer sentiments along with their percentage. **Figure 1** represents the graphical presentation of customer sentiments. Along with this **Figure 2** represents wordcloud for the different customer sentiment which is generated by python programming language. The larger the word in the image represents the word's frequency in the review text.

Table 2. Statistics of customer sentiment.

Sentiment	**Number of sentiments**	**Percent (%)**
Positive	55012	53.55
Neutral	4085	3.98
Negative	43629	42.47
Total	**102726**	**100**

Figure 1. Statistics of customer sentiment

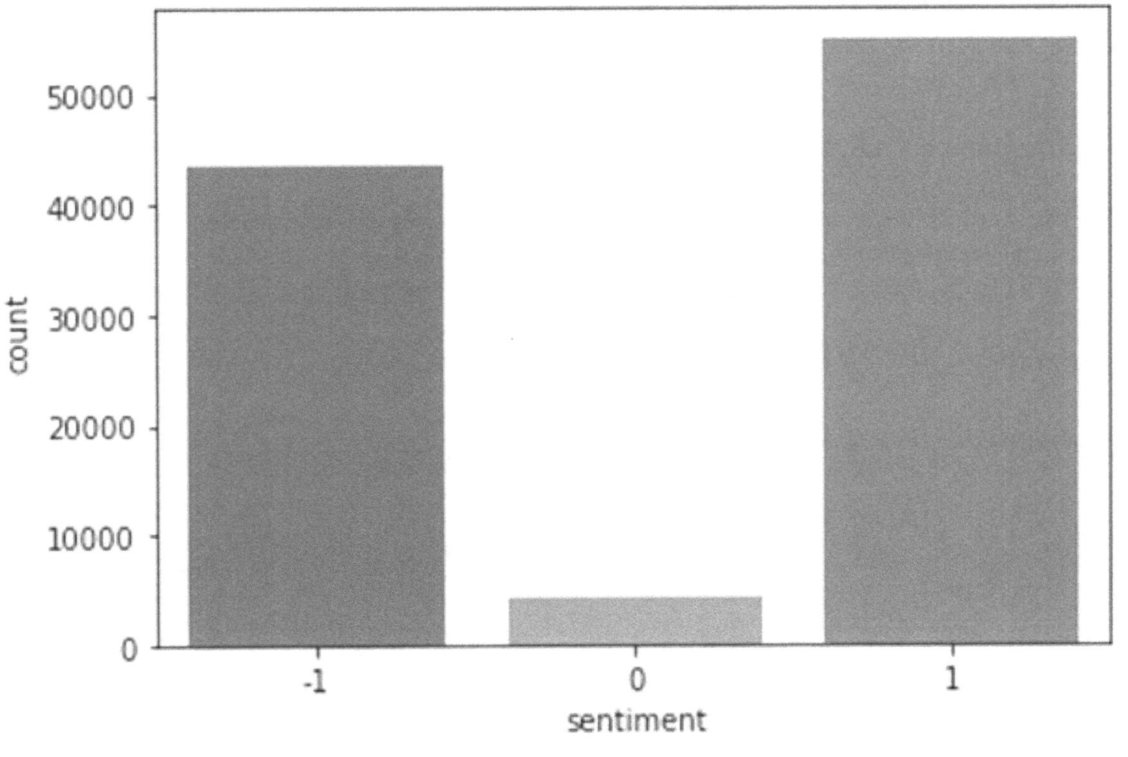

Figure 2. Wordcloud(s)

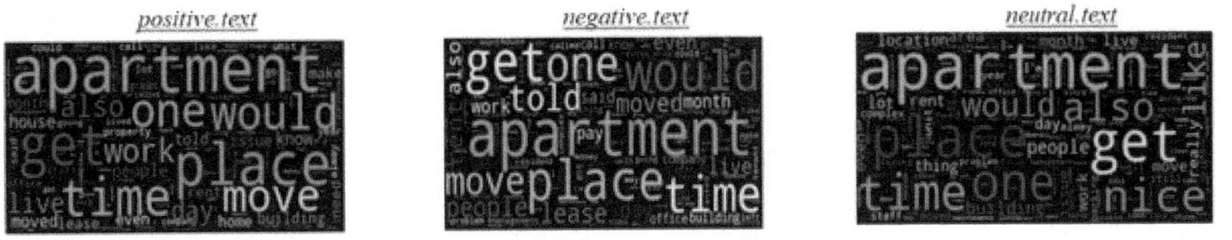

3.2. Customer Sentiment Analysis

To analyze the customer sentiment two inbuilt package AFINN sentiment and VADER sentiment has been used. This two approaches also effectively used in many similar types of prior researches (Ratmele and Thakur, 2020; Kumar and Babu, 2021). The creator of AFINN is Rup Nielsen. It is a simple yet extensively used tool for sentiment analysis that is lexicon-based. It features more than 3300 words, each with a polarization score between -5 (for the most strongly negative attitude) and +5. (maximum optimistic score). Similarly, VADER is also lexicon based and parsimonious rules based sentiment analysis tools. The polarity score is divided by VADER into four categories (negative, neutral, positive, and compound). VADER score statically ranges from -5 (for most negative value) to +1 (for most optimistic value).We employed five classifiers, including the K-nearest neighbor (KNN) classifier, Logistic Regression, Support Vector Machine (SVM), Random Forest (RF) classifier and Decision Tree (DT), to predict the customer's sentiment. The DT, LR, SVM, and RF analyses were carried out in a Jupyter Notebook for this project. The analysis's executive summary is shown in Table 7.

3.3. Performance Analysis

We calculated the performance of our models using the proportions of true negatives (TNs), true positives (TPs), false negatives (FNs), and false positives (FPs). In this case, negative, N = TN + FP and positive, P = TP + FN. The F1 scores, precision, accuracy, and recall are calculated using the following formulas.

$$Accuracy\left(MA\right) = \frac{\mathrm{TP + TN}}{\mathrm{P + N}}$$

(Rout et al., 2017; Li et al., 2020).

$$Precision\ (MP) = \frac{\mathrm{TN}}{\mathrm{TN + FP}} = \frac{\mathrm{TN}}{\mathrm{N}}$$

(Ali-Eldin, 2018)

$$Recall\ (MR) = \frac{\mathrm{TP}}{\mathrm{TP + FN}} = \frac{\mathrm{TP}}{\mathrm{N}}$$

(Ali-Eldin, 2018)

$$\mathrm{F1Score} = \frac{2 \times \mathrm{MP} \times \mathrm{MR}}{\mathrm{MP + MR}}$$

(Li et al., 2020)

Cohen's kappa statistics are commonly utilized to evaluate interrater reliability. In the context of classifier evaluation, a kappa statistic value of zero or below would render the classifier ineffective. The primary significance of Cohen's kappa lies in its ability to gauge the accuracy of variable representation within the training model. Higher Cohen's kappa values, closer to 1, indicate a robust variable demonstration in the training model, while values closer to 0 signify uncertainty. The Matthews correlation coefficient (MCC), sometimes referred to as the phi coefficient, is a commonly employed metric in machine learning for evaluating the accuracy of binary classifications. The MCC value ranges between -1 and +1. A value of -1 indicates absolute disagreement between the predictions and the true labels, while a value of +1 represents perfect prediction or agreement.

R^2 can be calculated by the following formula

$$\mathrm{R}^2 = \frac{\text{Unexplained Variation}}{\text{Total Variation}}$$

An estimator's skill is measured by mean squared error (MSE). Larger MSE values are discovered to be nearer to zero or higher, and it is never negative.

The root-mean-square error (RMSE) is a commonly used measure to quantify the differences between predicted and actual values in a model. RMSE is a non-negative value, and a lower value indicates that the predictions are closer to the actual values. A value closer to zero or higher than it suggests a better fit of the model to the data, indicating reduced discrepancies between predicted and actual values. The F1 score is a statistical metric commonly utilized to assess performance, particularly in classification tasks. It is calculated as the harmonic mean of precision and recall. In other words, the F1 score provides a balanced measure of performance by considering both precision (the ability to correctly identify positive instances) and recall (the ability to capture all positive instances). The F1 score typically ranges from 0 to 1, with higher values indicating better performance. The mean squared log error (MSLE) is a metric commonly used to quantify the amount of regression loss in a predictive model. It specifically measures the difference between the logarithm of the predicted values and the logarithm of the actual values. The MSLE provides an evaluation of the logarithmic scale of the differences between the predicted and expected values. It is often used in scenarios where the target variable has a wide range of values or contains outliers. A lower MSLE value indicates a better fit of the model to the data and a smaller discrepancy between the predicted and actual values.

4. RESULTS AND DISCUSSION

4.1. Customer Sentiment Regarding the Real Estate

From the **Table 2** and **Figure 1** we can clearly see that the majority of the customer (53.55%) reveals the positive sentiment about the real estate products or companies. A very small portion of customers (3.98%) express neutral feelings. Rest of the customers (42.47%) express a negative sentiment regarding the real estate products.

4.2. Textual Data Score Gained by Applying Machine Learning Approach

A total of 1,02,726 reviews of real estate customers have been examined to generate AFINN polarity score. The AFINN polarity score for the negative sentiment ranged from -250 to 58.82, from -40 to 100 for neutral sentiment and from -75 to 200 for positive sentiment (**Table 3**).

Table 3. Summary statistics of AFINN score.

sentiment	count	mean	std	min	25%	50%	75%	max
-1	43629	-2.54477	7.832491	-250	-5.66038	-1.88679	1.459854	58.82353
0	4085	5.958992	8.436746	-40	1.156069	4.761905	9.174312	100
1	55012	15.13417	11.58827	-75	7.843137	12.76596	19.67213	200

Besides, **Table 4** demonstrates the mean AFINN score, word count and VADER score. The mean value of AFINN score for negative sentiment is -3.36, 8.19 for neutral sentiment and 13.91 for positive sentiment. The average word count for positive sentiment is 124.1, for neutral sentiment is 201.87 and for negative sentiment is 214.98. Here, we can conclude from H1 that consumer sentiment is more negatively skewed the longer the textual review is. In comparison to other past studies, reviews of hotel and travel companies, insurance goods, and financial service organizations all came to the same conclusion (Lai et al., 2021; Pashchenko et al., 2022). (Hossain & Rahman, 2022). Additionally, it supports the research by Ghasemaghaei et al. (2018) that shows angry customers are more expressive and like to express their emotions.

Table 4. Mean statistics of AFINN, word count and VADER scores.

sentiment	afinn_score	word_count	vader_neg	vader_neu	vader_pos	vader_compound
-1	-3.36173	214.9803	0.103456	0.823479	0.07306	-0.22882
0	8.190453	201.8659	0.059049	0.810669	0.130289	0.550547
1	13.91306	124.0979	0.023617	0.769479	0.206905	0.880591

Moreover, we also can see that for undesirable sentiment VADER optimistic, neutral, positive and compound scores are 0.10, 0.82, 0.07 and -0.23 respectively. Similarly for neutral sentiment VADER positive, neutral, positive and compound scores are 0.06, 0.81, 0.13 and 0.55 correspondingly. Again, for positive sentiment VADER positive, neutral, positive and compound scores are 0.02, 0.77, 0.21 and 0.88 correspondingly. Figures 3 and 4 shows a plot chart of positive and negative VADER score as well as a histogram of VADER compound scores respectively.

Figure 3. Plot chart of VADAR positive and negative scores

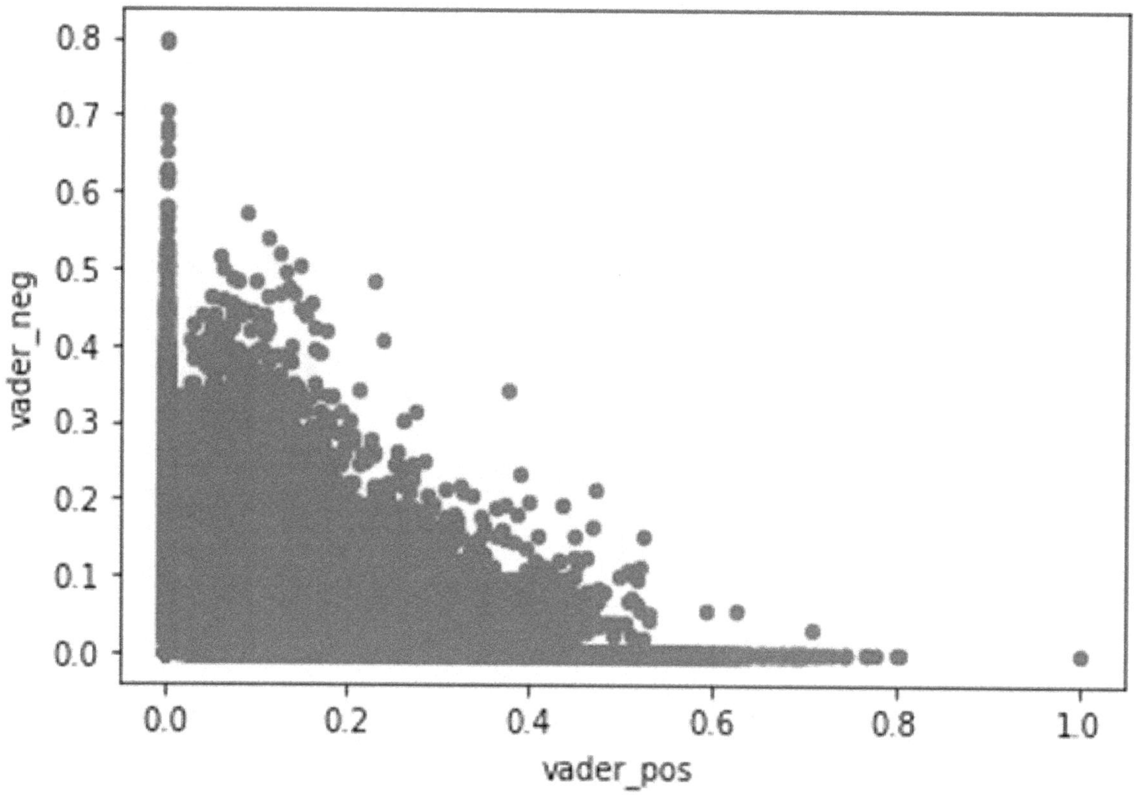

Figure 4. VADAR compound score

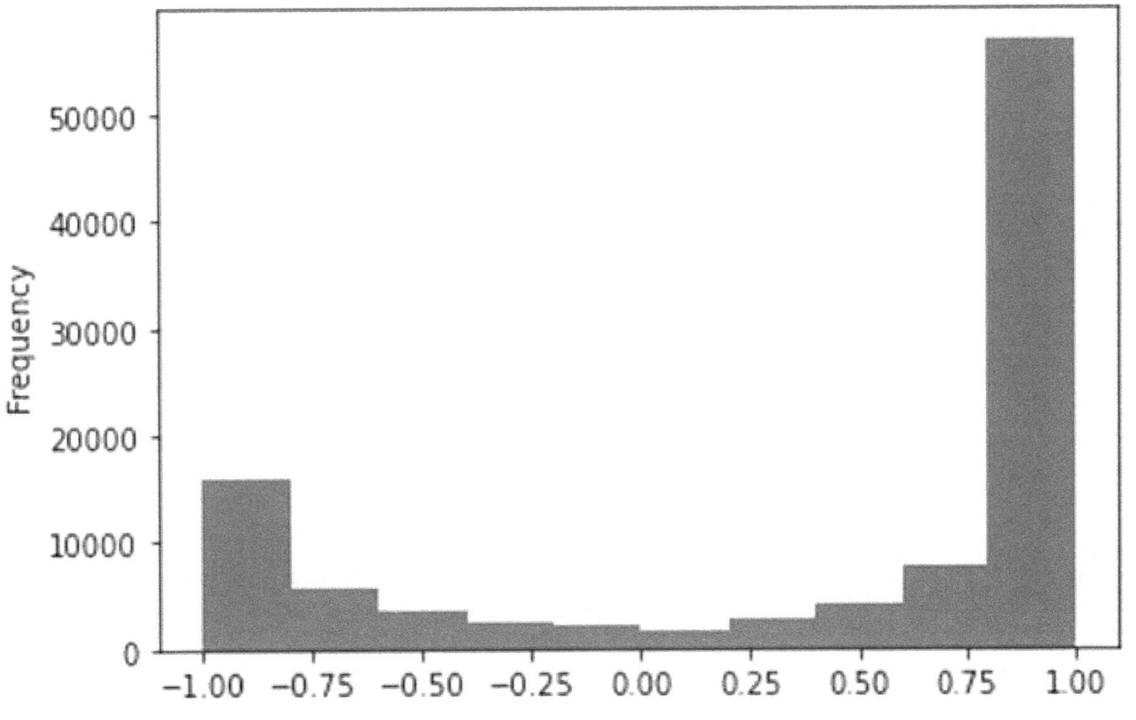

4.3. Assessing the Highest Positive and Negative Sentiment (Review)

Using machine learning lexicons, it is possible to identify the top positive and negative sentiment on the basis of AFINN score. In our analysis we have identified top 10 negative and positive sentiments which are presented in **Table 5 and 6** respectively. It can be seen from the table that the most negative sentiment score is -102 and most positive sentiment score is 112. Also, using the iloc[] function of machine learning, it is possible to examine the complete text of the review. The complete content of the review with the highest rating (iloc[44988]) is included as an example in Appendix 1.

Table 5. Top 10 unfavorable (negative) customer review texts according to AFINN rating.

Position in our database	text	afinn_score
47766	The building is nice, the management is horrible. If you have a dog, and you move in because of ...	-102
62422	If zero was an option, this place would get a zero.From the time I move in to the current date (...	-86
54702	DO NOT MOVE INTO HOLLY RIDGE!!!!\nHonestly, if I could, I would give them negative stars. This i...	-81
92122	I WAS PHYSICALLY ATTACKED IN MY ALLURE APARTMENT BY THE MAA ILLEGALLY EMPLOYED WORKER. LIVING HE...	-81
87781	NOTE: This review is not from someone who snaps at waiters or a Karen who claims masks are viola...	-81

continued on following page

Table 5. Continued

Position in our database	text	afinn_score
26516	This is your typical run of a mill apartment complex located by the theme parks especially Disne...	-80
25739	SCROLL DOWN AND READ THE "FILTERED REVIEWS," for some reason all of the bad reviews have been hi...	-78
74394	If you want to live in complete dump for the price of a nice apartment, go right on ahead. \n\nI...	-75
36805	Stop reading this review right now, don't rent here. Don't think to yourself "The only people w...	-70
37669	TL;DR: Unprofessional; borderline criminal behavior related to negligent maintenance; a lawyer w...	-70
45721	I only gave them one star because I had to. I would have given them 0000000. This company is an ...	-69
86992	As a preface: I'm sorry if I sound like I'm really angry because, well, I'm fucking pissed.\n\nW...	-68
59642	Has anyone seen the most recent news regarding IPM, Income Property Management? They are being s...	-66
85926	I will be posting updates to my review as more things seem to happen, (because they are endless,...	-65
34702	This apartment building is literally a living nightmare. I STRONGLY ADVISE AGAINST LIVING AT TH...	-65

Table 6. Top 10 favorable (positive) customer review texts according to AFINN rating.

Position in our database	text	afinn_score
44988	I have lived here since April. It is one of the best apartment complexes that I had the chance t...	96
13794	My family and I have been living here for about 5 months and I have to say that overall we love ...	96
94057	Finally, sitting down and creating a Yelp account to rave about the FANTASTIC people at Camden L...	97
96580	My husband and I had the incredibly good fortune of meeting Kristen Jacobs while we were checkin...	98
48896	Nancy Taute is a true gem! When I walked into Carol Dochen Realtors, Inc. I was introduced to N...	99
30751	I moved in on July 31st and I have to say my experience is beyond awesome. Even through the ann...	100
41339	I've lived in Emerson Place since February 2017, when we moved from Washington, DC to Boston. We...	101
41165	Finding a provider you can entrust to care for your child(ren) is probably one of the toughest d...	102
24454	Seven is an awesome place to live. Located right in the heart of downtown Austin, I've been liv...	103
59948	A great place to call HOME. I have been living in high rises in the Buckhead area for almost 4 y...	106
76469	Lived here almost a year now and honestly cannot say great enough things about One North and the...	108
30533	I have absolutely loved living at AMLI 5350! My roommate and I have been living here for about a...	112
97242	Update: Here I am 5 months later and equally as blown away as the first time I visited! I walked...	118
35847	We have lived here for 2.5 years, and can honestly say that it's the best place we have lived in...	127
92962	Camden Lamar Heights is a wonderful place to call home! This community has set the standard of l...	130

4.4. Performance Measure of Different Machine Learning Models

Table 7 represents the score of different machine learning approaches used in this study. The table shows that the accuracy score of KNN, LR, DT, RF and SVM is 53.85, 93.1, 79.98, 89.99 and 93.16 respectively. So, we can say that all models have classified the review text properly. But the logistic regression and support vector machine scores highest and almost same result than the other models. Likewise, except RMSE in all other measures logistic regression and SVM produced almost same score and outperformed the other models. The precision, recall, R^2

score, f1 score, MSE, MSLE, cohen_kappa score and MCC score of LR and SVM are 0.917 and 0.918, 0.931 and 0.932, 0.838 and 0.839, 0.919 and 0.919, 0.153 and 0.153, 0.047 and 0.047, 0.867 and 0.867 and 0.868 and .0869 correspondingly. In case of RMSE, Random forest classifier produced the best result (0.086) and outperforms the other models. Finally, we can say that among the models so far has been used in this analysis, logistic regression and SVM proves the best by their performance. In **Figure 5**, the performance of different models has been presented graphically.

Table 7. Performance of different models.

Model				**r2_ score**	**f1_ score**	**mean_squared_ error**		**mean_squared_log_ error**	**cohen_kappa_ score**	**matthews_ corrcoef**
KNN Classifier	53.847	0.533	0.538	-0.814	0.529	1.72	1.312	0.52	0.115	0.116
LR	**93.104**	**0.917**	**0.931**	**0.838**	**0.919**	**0.153**	0.39	**0.047**	**0.867**	**0.868**
DT Classifier	79.982	0.795	0.8	0.363	0.798	0.604	0.777	0.184	0.621	0.621
RF Classifier	89.989	0.889	0.9	0.701	0.882	0.283	**0.086**	0.532	0.805	0.807
SVM	**93.155**	**0.918**	**0.932**	**0.839**	**0.919**	**0.153**	0.391	**0.047**	**0.867**	**0.869**

Figure 5. Performance of different models

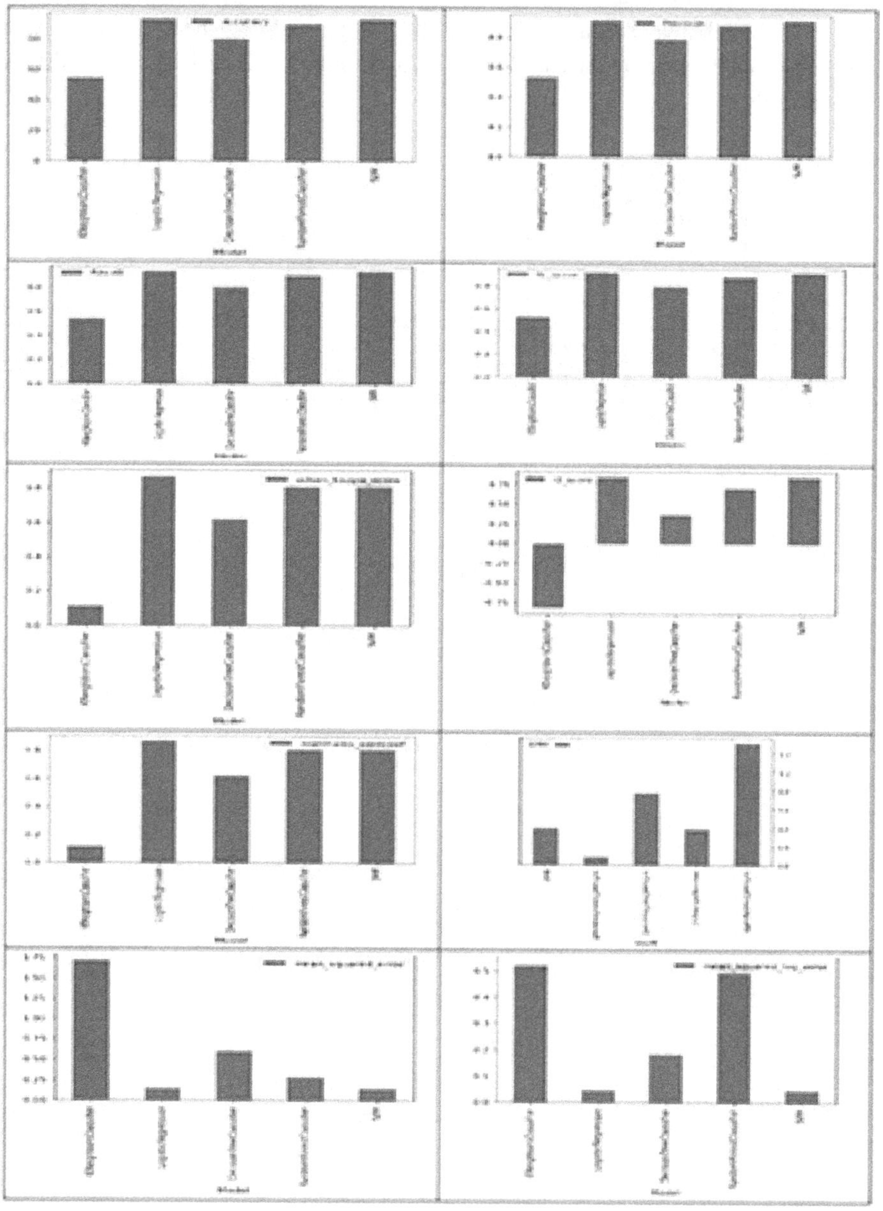

5. IMPLICATIONS

5.1 Theoretical Applications

We assess and predict user sentiment towards real estate businesses using a variety of machine learning approaches. Thus, our research adds to the theoretical knowledge of real estate companies and customer behavior based on internet evaluations. This study is important for people involved in the real estate business in addition to its theoretical ramifications. Prior to now, reviews of real estate organizations have not used lexical approaches to examine sentiments or predict sentiment categorization. This research significantly contributes to the body of information on the real estate industry since it uses lexicon-based machine learning methods to classify and forecast how people will score real estate enterprises.

People, in accordance with the cognitive load theory, make decisions quickly. Online shoppers consequently make decisions about their purchases rapidly and rely on other people's comments. The majority of customers who reviewed real estate firms had a pleasant experience, as shown by the study's findings. Emotion theory also provides an explanation for how human emotional states work, including how they shape our motives and actions. Due to the possibility for reviewers' emotions to be conveyed, we explore how prospective clients could respond to social media consensus for real estate firms based on reviewers' evaluations (Hossain et al., 2022). According to appraisal theory, feelings and thoughts are the foundation of all encounters since they facilitate cognitive processes and help prospective consumers make perfect sense of their own experiences (Hossain and Rahman, 2022).

Our results will help to figure out the future of real estate organizations and marketing literature in general. Also, our study showed that the social science literature doesn't back up the idea that machine learning algorithms may be utilized to anticipate consumers' attitudes about real estate enterprises. In this study, we investigated sentiment analysis (SA) and predicted real estate organizations' reviews using both supervised and unsupervised machine learning algorithms. SA may be important to theoretical social science fields including psychology and consumer behavior. By contrast, the current work, which employs a machine learning strategy to present the top 10 positive and top 10 negative reviews based on AFINN score, must also significantly advance the literature. Additionally, our study found that although all five models—KNN Classifier, LR, DT Classifier, RF Classifier, and SVM—can accurately categorize texts that describe consumers' reviews of real estate organizations, SVM consistently yields the most accurate classifications. By doing so, the knowledge gap in the literature of real estate organizations will be filled.

5.2 Practical Applications

This study has a wide range of effects on the business world. SA has important business uses that can't be ignored. SA could change the way organizations grow and change in the business world. Running a successful business with unstructured data requires the capacity to harness the data to yield insightful understandings. In today's internet-based environment, businesses may have a lot of customer response recorded, but this does not always equate to better or deeper insights because of data overload. But it's still challenging for humans to manually analyze it without bias or inaccuracy. To better understand how consumers feel about a company's products or services, organizations may benefit from the present study's usage of a number of machine learning algorithms to predict and evaluate customer review signals. That's why it's important for companies to learn about machine learning so they can better comprehend their clients' behavior. The results of our research will also help practitioners and professionals who are assessing real estate firms' performance.

As has already been mentioned, businesses can improve their services and marketing efforts by using the information that consumers post. A valuable expansion opportunity can be lost by companies with bad ratings. The findings of this research will contribute to a better understanding on how companies might use machine learning techniques to predict how customers would rank them. Even more importantly, we showed that lexicon-based methods may be used to evaluate the review texts. A company may save time and effort by using these tools to automatically evaluate consumer feedback. One of the most common applications of SA in business is to classify evaluations as positive, negative, or neutral. In essence, SA allows organizations to differentiate between positive and negative ratings. Our research might be applied to look beyond user evaluations and into how users feel about real estate companies. As a result of our study's sentiment analysis on consumer evaluations, managers will have access to more complete data with which to exceed their customers' expectations. In addition, businesses may use what they learn from this research to implement AFINN and VADER sentiment systems that can identify positive, neutral, and negative sentiment.

Businesses may benefit from both positive and negative feedback, as it helps them to quickly make necessary changes and provide their products and services to customers. . Organizations will also learn how to apply this study's findings to determine positive, neutral, and negative sentiments when using sentiment algorithms. Moreover, our research showed that SVM can give the highest accuracy rating for predicting how a client feels. Also, businesses might use support vector machines to find out how customers react to their products and services. Understanding consumer behavior can be a key success factor in today's fiercely competitive corporate world. This will help businesses adapt their strategies to keep up with the speed of modern business. The study's findings might be useful to service companies since they can be applied to a wide range of challenges.

CONCLUSION

In a competitive market like the real estate sector, a property appraisal firm has to stand out from the rest by offering services that their competitors can't. These fundamental principles are critical for a number of reasons, including providing an edge in the marketplace and protecting the interests of key stakeholders while also reflecting the spirit of enterprise. In addition, in order to stay ahead of the competition, today's firms, particularly those in the real estate industry, need to understand customer feedback. Customer feedback has the aptitude to mark both purchase choices and the image of a firm. Consumers' feedback is imperative to service providers since it affects client satisfaction and influences whether or not customers engage with the business. Increased revenue is a direct result of satisfied customers. As a result, the organization has to collect and store customer feedback about its goods and services from as many sources as possible. To help make more informed choices, researchers developed a method called sentiment analysis. The current research uses many ML techniques to examine the user evaluations of real estate companies on the Yelp website.

Using a variety of ML approaches, including semantic analysis, we were able to classify phrases and product ratings based on Yelp's data set of real estate companies. The foremost persistence is to assess and forecast a vast number of real estate organization reviews and filtering the real estate organization relevant reviews using machine learning methods already identified in the Yelp data set. Combining ML strategies with dictionaries is what this study refers to as "lexicon-based methodologies" since it yielded superior outcomes. We applied sentiment analysis on each product review and discovered that the vast majority of consumers expressed positive thoughts about real estate organizations in their evaluations. Following that, our research discovered that when five machine learning models are used to forecast outcomes, logistic regression produces the greatest results. Customer feedback may help real estate companies to improve their marketing tactics through important information gained from customers.

REFERENCES

Adak, A., Pradhan, B., & Shukla, N. (2022). Sentiment analysis of customer reviews of food delivery services using deep learning and explainable artificial intelligence: Systematic review. *Foods*, *11*(10), 1500. Advance online publication. DOI: 10.3390/foods11101500 PMID: 35627070

Ahmad, M., Aftab, S., Bashir, M. S., & Hameed, N. (2018). Sentiment analysis using SVM: A systematic literature review. *International Journal of Advanced Computer Science and Applications*, *9*(2), 182–188. DOI: 10.14569/IJACSA.2018.090226

Ainin, S., Feizollah, A., Anuar, N.B. and Abdullah, N.A. (2020a), Sentiment analyses of multilingual tweets on halal tourism. *Tourism Management Perspectives 34*, 100658, doi: . tmp.2020.100658.DOI: 10.1016/j

Ainin, S., Feizollah, A., Anuar, N. B., Abdullah, N. A. B., & Sahran, M. N. F. (2020b). Examining what people tweet in relation to halal cosmetics-related topics. *Cogent Arts & Humanities*, *7*(1), 1724593. Advance online publication. DOI: 10.1080/23311983.2020.1724593

Alqtati, N., Wilson, J. A. J., & De Silva, V. (2021). Mining Arabic twitter conversations on health care: A new approach to analyzing Arabic language on social media. *Journal of Islamic Marketing*. Advance online publication. DOI: 10.1108/JIMA-12-2020-0355

Araque, O., Zhu, G., & Iglesias, C. A. (2019). A semantic similarity-based perspective of affect lexicons for sentiment analysis. *Knowledge-Based Systems*, *165*, 346–359. DOI: 10.1016/j.knosys.2018.12.005

Azmi, A. S. M., Nawawi, A. H., & Farhana, A. (2015). Knowledge Management Obstacles in Real Estate (Valuation) Organisations: Towards Quality Property Services. *Procedia: Social and Behavioral Sciences*, *202*(5), 159–168. DOI: 10.1016/j.sbspro.2015.08.219

Baker, M., & Wurgler, J. (2007). Investor sentiment in the stock market. *The Journal of Economic Perspectives*, *21*(2), 129–151. DOI: 10.1257/jep.21.2.129

Bigne, E., Ruiz, C., Cuenca, A., Perez, C., & Garcia, A. (2021). What drives the helpfulness of online reviews? A deep learning study of sentiment analysis, pictorial content and reviewer expertise for mature destinations. *Journal of Destination Marketing & Management*, *20*, 100570. Advance online publication. DOI: 10.1016/j.jdmm.2021.100570

Borg, A., & Boldt, M. (2020). Using VADER sentiment and SVM for predicting customer response sentiment. *Expert Systems with Applications*, *162*, 113746. Advance online publication. DOI: 10.1016/j.eswa.2020.113746

Buechel, E. C., & Berger, J. (2018). Microblogging and the value of undirected communication. *Journal of Consumer Psychology*, *28*(1), 40–55. DOI: 10.1002/jcpy.1013

Ceron, A., Curini, L., Iacus, S. M., & Porro, G. (2013). Every tweet counts? How sentiment analysis of social media can improve our knowledge of citizens' political preferences with an application to Italy and France. *New Media & Society*, *16*(2), 340–358. DOI: 10.1177/1461444813480466

Chang, Y. C., Ku, C. H., & Le Nguyen, D. D. (2022). Predicting aspect-based sentiment using deep learning and information visualization: The impact of COVID-19 on the airline industry. *Information & Management*, *59*(2), 103587. Advance online publication. DOI: 10.1016/j.im.2021.103587

Chang, Y. C., Ku, C. H., & Le Nguyen, D. D. (2022). Predicting aspect-based sentiment using deep learning and information visualization: The impact of COVID-19 on the airline industry. *Information & Management*, *59*(2), 103587. Advance online publication. DOI: 10.1016/j.im.2021.103587

Chen, Z., Shen, S., Hu, Z., Lu, X., Mei, Q., & Liu, X. (2019, May). Emoji-powered representation learning for cross-lingual sentiment classification. In *The world wide web conference* (pp. 251-262). DOI: 10.1145/3308558.3313600

Chepukaka, Z. K., & Kirugi, F. K. (2019). Service Quality and Customer Satisfaction at Kenya National Archives and Documentation Service, Nairobi County: Servqual Model Revisited. *International Journal on Customer Relations*, *7*(1). Advance online publication. DOI: 10.7176/EJBM/11-9-07

De Oliveira, G. A., de Sousa, R. T.Jr, de Oliveira Albuquerque, R., & García Villalba, L. J. (2021). Adversarial attacks on a lexical sentiment analysis classifier. *Computer Communications*, *174*, 154–171. DOI: 10.1016/j.comcom.2021.04.026

Demircan, M., Seller, A., Abut, F., & Akay, M. F. (2021). Developing Turkish sentiment analysis models using machine learning and e-commerce data. *International Journal of Cognitive Computing in Engineering*, *2*(July), 202–207. DOI: 10.1016/j.ijcce.2021.11.003

Erevelles, S., Fukawa, N., & Swayne, L. (2016). Big Data consumer analytics and the transformation of marketing. *Journal of Business Research*, *69*(2), 897–904. DOI: 10.1016/j.jbusres.2015.07.001

Feizollah, A., Ainin, S., Anuar, N. B., Abdullah, N. A. B., & Hazim, M. (2019). Halal products on Twitter: Data extraction and sentiment analysis using stack of deep learning algorithms. *IEEE Access : Practical Innovations, Open Solutions*, *7*, 83354–83362. DOI: 10.1109/ACCESS.2019.2923275

Felbo, B., Mislove, A., Sgaard, A., Rahwan, I., & Lehmann, S. (2017). Using millions of emoji occurrences to learn any-domain representations for detecting sentiment, emotion and sarcasm, in: *Proceedings of the 2017 Conference on Empirical Methods in Natural Language Processing, EMNLP 2017*, 2017, 1615–1625. DOI: 10.18653/v1/D17-1169

Gazzani, A. (2019). News and noise bubbles in the housing market. *Review of Economic Dynamics, 1*(2009), 1–27. DOI: 10.1016/j.red.2019.08.001

Gkikas, D. C., Tzafilkou, K., Theodoridis, P. K., Garmpis, A., & Gkikas, M. C. (2022). How do text characteristics impact user engagement in social media posts: Modeling content readability, length, and hashtags number in Facebook. *International Journal of Information Management Data Insights*, *2*(1), 100067. DOI: 10.1016/j.jjimei.2022.100067

Gong, S., Zhang, J., Zhao, P., & Jiang, X. (2017). Tweeting as a marketing tool: A field experiment in the TV industry. *JMR, Journal of Marketing Research*, *54*(6), 833–850. DOI: 10.1509/jmr.14.0348

Gul, E., Alpaslan, N., & Emiroglu, M. E. (2021). Robust optimization of SVM hyper-parameters for spillway type selection. *Ain Shams Engineering Journal*, *12*(3), 2413–2423. DOI: 10.1016/j.asej.2020.10.022

Guo, K., Sun, Y., & Qian, X. (2017). Can investor sentiment be used to predict the stock price? Dynamic analysis based on China stock market. *Physica A*, *469*, 390–396. DOI: 10.1016/j.physa.2016.11.114

Gupta, A., Priyani, S., & Balakrishnan, R. (2020). Customized reputation generation of entities using sentiment analysis. *World Journal of Engineering*, *18*(4), 596–605. DOI: 10.1108/WJE-09-2020-0470

Hausler, J., Ruscheinsky, J., & Lang, M. (2018, October 2). News-based sentiment analysis in real estate: A machine learning approach. *Journal of Property Research*, *35*(4), 344–371. DOI: 10.1080/09599916.2018.1551923

Heng, Y., Gao, Z., Jiang, Y., & Chen, X. (2018). Exploring hidden factors behind online food shopping from Amazon reviews: A topic mining approach. *Journal of Retailing and Consumer Services*, *42*, 161–168. DOI: 10.1016/j.jretconser.2018.02.006

Hornikx, J., & Hendriks, B. (2015). Consumer tweets about brands: A content analysis of sentiment tweets about goods and services. *Journal of Creative Communications, 10*(2), 176–185. DOI: 10.1177/0973258615597406

Hossain, M. S., & Rahman, M. F. (2022). Detection of potential customers' empathy behavior towards customers' reviews. *Journal of Retailing and Consumer Services, 65*, 102881. DOI: 10.1016/j.jretconser.2021.102881

Hossain, M. S., Rahman, M. F., Uddin, M. K., & Hossain, M. K. (2022). Customer sentiment analysis and prediction of halal restaurants using machine learning approaches. *Journal of Islamic Marketing*. Advance online publication. DOI: 10.1108/JIMA-04-2021-0125

Hossain, M. S., Rahman, M. F., & Zhou, X. (2021). Impact of customers' interpersonal interactions in social commerce on customer relationship management performance. *Journal of Contemporary Marketing Science, 4*(1), 161–181. DOI: 10.1108/JCMARS-12-2020-0050

Hudaefi, F. A., & Badeges, A. M. (2022). Maqā id al-Sharī 'ah on Islamic banking performance in Indonesia: A knowledge discovery via text mining. *Journal of Islamic Marketing, 13*(10), 2069–2089. DOI: 10.1108/JIMA-03-2020-0081

Hudaefi, F. A., Caraka, R. E., & Wahid, H. (2022). Zakat administration in times of COVID-19 pandemic in Indonesia: A knowledge discovery via text mining. *International Journal of Islamic and Middle Eastern Finance and Management, 15*(2), 271–286. DOI: 10.1108/IMEFM-05-2020-0250

Hui, E. C. M., Dong, Z., Jia, S. H., & Lam, C. H. L. (2017). How does sentiment affect returns of urban housing? *Habitat International, 64*, 71–84. DOI: 10.1016/j.habitatint.2017.04.013

Jha, S. B., Pandey, V., Jha, R. K., & Babiceanu, R. F. (2020). Machine learning approaches to real estate market prediction problem: A case study. *arXiv preprint arXiv:2008.09922*. https://doi.org//arXiv.2008.09922DOI: 10.48550

Kane, G. C., Alavi, M., Labianca, G., & Borgatti, S. P. (2014). What's different about social media networks? A framework and research agenda. *Management Information Systems Quarterly, 38*(1), 275–304. DOI: 10.25300/MISQ/2014/38.1.13

Kang, D., & Park, Y. (2014). based measurement of customer satisfaction in mobile service: Sentiment analysis and VIKOR approach. *Expert Systems with Applications, 41*(4), 1041–1050. DOI: 10.1016/j.eswa.2013.07.101

Kitsios, F., Mitsopoulou, E., Moustaka, E., & Kamariotou, M. (2022). User-Generated Content behavior and digital tourism services: A SEM-neural network model for information trust in social networking sites. *International Journal of Information Management Data Insights, 2*(1), 100056. DOI: 10.1016/j.jjimei.2021.100056

Kwakye, B., & Haw, C. T. (2021). Theoretical Overview of Sentiment Analysis in the Real Estate Market. [IJRTE]. *The International Journal of Recent Technology and Engineering, 9*(6), 169–175. DOI: 10.35940/ijrte.F5407.039621

Leelawat, N., Jariyapongpaiboon, S., Promjun, A., Boonyarak, S., Saengtabtim, K., Laosunthara, A., Yudha, A. K., & Tang, J. (2022). Twitter data sentiment analysis of tourism in Thailand during the COVID-19 pandemic using machine learning. *Heliyon, 8*(10), e10894. DOI: 10.1016/j.heliyon.2022.e10894 PMID: 36211996

Li, J., & Meesad, P. (2016). Combining Sentiment Analysis with Socialization Bias in Social Networks for Stock Market Trend Prediction. *International Journal of Computational Intelligence and Applications, 15*(1), 1650003. DOI: 10.1142/S1469026816500036

Ling, D. C., Ooi, J. T. L., & Le, T. T. T. (2015). Explaining house price dynamics: Isolating the role of nonfundamentals. *Journal of Money, Credit and Banking, 47*(S1), 87–125. DOI: 10.1111/jmcb.12194

Luo, Y., Tang, L. R., Kim, E., & Wang, X. (2020). Finding the reviews on yelp that actually matter to me: Innovative approach of improving recommender systems. *International Journal of Hospitality Management, 91*, 102697. DOI: 10.1016/j.ijhm.2020.102697

Luo, Y., & Xu, X. (2021). Comparative study of deep learning models for analyzing online restaurant reviews in the era of the COVID-19 pandemic. *International Journal of Hospitality Management, 94*, 102849. Advance online publication. DOI: 10.1016/j.ijhm.2020.102849 PMID: 34785843

Machová, K., Mikula, M., Gao, X., & Mach, M. (2020). Lexicon-based sentiment analysis using the particle swarm optimization. *Electronics (Basel), 9*(8), 1–22. DOI: 10.3390/electronics9081317

Miao, Q., Li, Q., & Zeng, D. (2010). Fine-grained opinion mining by integrating multiple review sources. *Journal of the American Society for Information Science and Technology, 61*(11), 2288–2299. DOI: 10.1002/asi.21400

Miyoshi, T., & Nakagami, Y. (2007, October). Sentiment classification of customer reviews on electric products. In *2007 IEEE International Conference on Systems, Man and Cybernetics* (pp. 2028-2033). IEEE. DOI: 10.1109/ICSMC.2007.4414175

Mohammad, S. M. (2016). Sentiment analysis: detecting valence, emotions, and other affectual states from text. *Emotion Measurement, Elsevier*, 201-237, https://doi.org/DOI: 10.1016/B978-0-08-100508-8.00009-6

Mostafa, M. M. (2013). More than words: Social networks' text mining for consumer brand sentiments. *Expert Systems with Applications, 40*(10), 4241–4251. DOI: 10.1016/j.eswa.2013.01.019

Mostafa, M. M. (2018). Mining and mapping halal food consumers: A geo-located Twitter opinion polarity analysis. *Journal of Food Products Marketing, 24*(7), 858–879. DOI: 10.1080/10454446.2017.1418695

Mostafa, M. M. (2020). Global halal food discourse on social media: A text mining approach. *Journal of International Communication, 26*(2), 211–237. DOI: 10.1080/13216597.2020.1795702

Nagpal, M., Kansal, K., Chopra, A., Gautam, N., & Jain, V. K. (2020).Effective Approach for Sentiment Analysis of Food Delivery Apps. *Springer*, 1053, 527–536.

Nasiri, M.S., & Shokouhyar, S. (2021). Actual consumers' response to purchase refurbished smartphones: exploring perceived value from product reviews in online retailing. *Journal of Retailing and Consumer Service, 62*, 102652. https://doi.org/. jretconser.2021.102652.DOI: 10.1016/j

Nazlan, N. H., Tanford, S., & Montgomery, R. (2018). The effect of availability heuristics in online consumer reviews. *Journal of Consumer Behaviour, 17*(5), 449–460. DOI: 10.1002/cb.1731

Obembe, D., Kolade, O., Obembe, F., Owoseni, A., & Mafimisebi, O. (2021). Covid-19 and the tourism industry: An early stage sentiment analysis of the impact of social media and stakeholder communication. *International Journal of Information Management Data Insights, 1*(2), 100040. DOI: 10.1016/j.jjimei.2021.100040

Pang, B., Lee, L., & Vithyanathan, S. (2019). Thumbs up? Sentiment classification using machine learning techniques. *Proceedings of the Institution of Civil Engineers – Transport, 172* (2).

Pedipina, S., Sankar, S., & Dhanalakshmi, R. (2021). Sentimental analysis on twitter data of political domain. In Computer Networks, Big Data and IoT: Proceedings of ICCBI 2020, *Springer*, 66, 205-216. DOI: 10.1007/978-981-16-0965-7_17

Philander, K., & Zhong, Y. (2016). Twitter sentiment analysis: Capturing sentiment from integrated resort tweets. *International Journal of Hospitality Management, 55*, 16–24. DOI: 10.1016/j.ijhm.2016.02.001

Preethi, P.G., Uma, V. & Kumar, A. (2015). Temporal sentiment analysis and causal rules extraction from tweets for event prediction. *Procedia Computer Science, 48*, 84-89.doi: . procs.2015.04.154.DOI: 10.1016/j

Rambocas, M., & Pacheco, B. G. (2018). Online sentiment analysis in marketing research: A review. *Journal of Research in Interactive Marketing, 12*(2), 146–163. DOI: 10.1108/JRIM-05-2017-0030

Rao, T., & Srivastava, S. (2014). Twitter sentiment analysis: How to hedge your bets in the stock markets. *State of the art applications of social network analysis*, 227-247.

Read, J., & Carroll, J. (2012). Annotating expressions of appraisal in English. *Language Resources and Evaluation, 46*(3), 421–447. DOI: 10.1007/s10579-010-9135-7

Ricciotti, F., Cristofaro, M., Abatecola, G., & Mari, M. (2022). Executive profiles and performance of real estate services: Evidence of *reverse causality* from Europe. *Cities (London, England), 130*, 1–11. DOI: 10.1016/j.cities.2022.103854

Roseman, I. J. (2001). A model of appraisal in the emotion system. *Appraisal processes in emotion: Theory, methods, research*, 68-91.

Rui, H., Liu, Y., & Whinston, A. (2013). Whose and what chatter matters? The effect of tweets on movie sales. *Decision Support Systems, 55*(4), 863–870. DOI: 10.1016/j.dss.2012.12.022

Saari, A., Vimpari, J., & Junnila, S. (2022). Block chain in real estate: Recent developments and empirical applications. *Land Use Policy, 121*, 1–11. DOI: 10.1016/j.landusepol.2022.106334

Saquete, E., Zubcoff, J., Gutiérrez, Y., Martínez-Barco, P., & Fernández, J. (2022). Why are some social-media contents more popular than others? Opinion and association rules mining applied to virality patterns discovery. *Expert Systems with Applications, 197*, 116676. DOI: 10.1016/j.eswa.2022.116676

Sasikala, P., & Sheela, L. M. I. (2018). Sentiment analysis of online food reviews using customer ratings. *International Journal of Pure and Applied Mathematics, 119*(15), 3509–3514. DOI: 10.5281/zenodo.1249390

Saydometov, S., Sabherwal, S., & Aroul, R. R. (2020). Sentiment and its asymmetric effect on housing returns. *Review of Financial Economics, 38*(4), 580–600. DOI: 10.1002/rfe.1097

Scherer, K. R. (2001). Appraisal considered as a process of multilevel sequential checking. *Appraisal processes in emotion: Theory, methods, research, 92*(120), 57.

Scherer, K. R., Schorr, A., & Johnstone, T. (Eds.). (2001). *Appraisal processes in emotion: Theory, methods, research.* Oxford University Press. DOI: 10.1093/oso/9780195130072.001.0001

Sipahi, E. (2017). Yerel E-Devlet 2.0: Sosyal Medya ve Belediyelerde Kurumsal Şeffaflık. 3(12), 354–366 (ISSN: 2149-8598)

Soo, C. K. (2018). Quantifying sentiment with news media across local housing markets. *Review of Financial Studies, 31*(10), 3689–3719. DOI: 10.1093/rfs/hhy036

Wang, P., Fan, E., & Wang, P. (2021). Comparative analysis of image classification algorithms based on traditional machine learning and deep learning. *Pattern Recognition Letters, 141*, 61–67. DOI: 10.1016/j.patrec.2020.07.042

Wang, R., Zhou, D., Jiang, M., Si, J., & Yang, Y. (2019). A survey on opinion mining: From stance to product aspect. *IEEE Access : Practical Innovations, Open Solutions, 7*, 41101–41124. DOI: 10.1109/ACCESS.2019.2906754

Yang, D. H., & Yu, G. (2013). A method of feature selection and sentiment similarity for Chinese micro-blogs. *Journal of Information Science, 39*(4), 429–441. DOI: 10.1177/0165551513480308

Yang, L., Li, Y., Wang, J., & Sherratt, R. S. (2020). Wang and Sherratt, 2020 Yang Li, Li Y., Wang J., Sherratt RS. *Sentiment analysis for E-commerce product reviews in Chinese based on sentiment lexicon and deep learning. IEEE Access : Practical Innovations, Open Solutions, 8*, 23522–23530. DOI: 10.1109/ACCESS.2020.2969854

Yoo, C. W., Sanders, G. L., & Moon, J. (2013). Exploring the effect of e-WOM participation on e-Loyalty in e-commerce. *Decision Support Systems, 55*(3), 669–678. DOI: 10.1016/j.dss.2013.02.001

Zhang, H., Rao, H., & Feng, J. (2018). Product innovation based on online review data mining: A case study of Huawei phones. *Electronic Commerce Research, 18*(1), 3–22. DOI: 10.1007/s10660-017-9279-2

Chapter 14
Blockchain-Based Identity Management:
Securing Customer Data in Financial Services

Rachit Agarwal
https://orcid.org/0000-0003-0164-5292
Chandigarh University, Mohali, India

Tanya Kumar
https://orcid.org/0000-0001-7608-9820
Chandigarh Group of Colleges, Landran, Mohali, India

Satveer Kaur
https://orcid.org/0000-0001-7064-1514
Maharaja Agrasen University, Baddi, India

Ruchira Prasad
https://orcid.org/0009-0009-4330-7081
Dr. Bhimrao Ambedkar University, Agra, India

Neeraj Kumar
https://orcid.org/0009-0005-1248-8300
Government PG College Mant, Mathura, India

ABSTRACT

This chapter aims to explore the potential of blockchain-based identity management systems in enhancing the security and privacy of customer data within financial services. It examines how blockchain technology can address existing vulnerabilities in traditional identity management frameworks and improve overall data protection. The research adopts case studies of financial institutions that have implemented blockchain-based identity management solutions to provide practical insights and real-world applications. The findings indicate that blockchain-based identity management systems offer significant advantages over traditional methods, including enhanced data security, reduced risk of identity theft, and improved user control over personal information. The decentralized and immutable nature of blockchain ensures that customer data is protected from unauthorized access and tampering. Case studies reveal successful implementations where blockchain has streamlined identity verification processes, reduced compliance costs, and improved customer trust.

DOI: 10.4018/979-8-3693-7447-4.ch014

INTRODUCTION

The financial services industry has experienced significant advantages from the integration of technology, including the optimisation of procedures, reduced expenses, increased client satisfaction, and improved accessibility to pertinent information. Furthermore, the utilisation of technology enables the assessment of risk, facilitates the identification of lucrative investments, and enhances the understanding of client behaviours (Dananjayan et al., 2023). The usage of big data in finance is susceptible to creating information asymmetry, which facilitates its seamless integration with blockchain technology. Firstly, the sophisticated database system and big data mining and analysis technologies are utilised to effectively leverage client information, taking into account factors such as the customer's risk profile, value, transaction behaviour characteristics, and preferences. Utilise social network technology and big data technology to achieve the online gathering of client information and prompt processing of transaction data (Han & Ma, 2021). Blockchain-based transaction infrastructure can help banks minimise the resources allocated to anti-money laundering (AML) compliance. Blockchain transparency enhances the ability to identify counterparties, ascertain the sources of funds, and provide warnings in transaction monitoring. These measures decrease the amount of time and effort required for Anti-Money Laundering (AML) compliance, resulting in lower costs (Vinther Daugaard et al., 2024). The utilisation of technology to mechanise financial services is increasingly crucial for economic organisations and sectors due to the ongoing shift in consumer behaviour and the emphasis on customisation in the digital era. Technologies such as the Internet of Things, blockchain, and artificial intelligence will have a significant impact on the future of FinTech (Rjoub et al., 2023). The banking sector in today's world is heavily reliant on technology and data-driven operations. Banks that possess the ability to use technology and effectively incorporate them into their operations will gain a competitive edge and be recognised as successful institutions within the financial industry. Utilising Technology Foresight, we can anticipate the projected advancements in Banking Services technology over the next decade (Elrashidy et al., 2021). Blockchain has the capability to play a crucial role in the financial industry by enabling financial institutions to safeguard their everyday financial transactions using a more secure, immediate, and cost-effective approach (Hefny et al., 2023). The Indian financial sector has been progressively adopting innovative technologies to enhance the quality of services and transactions. However, it is crucial to implement measures to ensure the liquidity and safety of the funds injected into the markets. To address this issue, we propose the implementation of a novel public ledger system known as blockchain technology. This technique is designed to be tamper-proof, meaning that it prevents any alterations to the recorded data (Lalitha & Soujanya, 2019).

Financial technology (FinTech) has revolutionised traditional banking and financial services by providing clients with more easy, accessible, and tailored services. On the contrary, FinTech has enhanced the efficiency, cost-effectiveness, and security of financial services, allowing individuals to easily manage their funds using their smartphones with only a few clicks (Girish & Bhowmik, 2023). The blockchain technology has been prioritising the development of many applications owing to its significant advantages, such as resistance to manipulation, enhanced security, transparency, superior services, decentralisation, immediate settlement, and increased performance (Trivedi, 2023). Open banking enables banks and financial institutions to conveniently retrieve clients' financial data, leading to a revolutionary transformation. Additionally, it offers users exceptional cloud access to a diverse array of financial services provided by numerous sources. Storing sensitive services and data on cloud servers has both advantages and disadvantages. It facilitates and reinforces precise access to such services/data from any location and at any time, hence enabling the open financial system. However, data privacy and confidentiality pose a significant difficulty. Therefore, it is imperative to establish effective access control measures for the services and data of open banking in order to safeguard cloud-hosted financial sensitive data from unauthorised individuals (Riad & Elhoseny, 2022). The swift progress of developing technologies has led to substantial changes in many industries, such as banking and finance (Vittala et al., 2024). The corporate landscape has undergone a significant transformation, becoming more inclusive, customer-centric, agile, and cost-effective. The emergence of financial technology (fintech) has led to the digitalisation of economies, with the implementation of Artificial Intelligence and Blockchain-based technologies playing a crucial role in enhancing financial efficiency (Sujee et al., 2023). The protection of users' sensitive personal data and financial information is crucial (Talha et al., 2022). The data, rules, and application layers are utilised to create novel financial forms or service models that are tailored to meet the specific requirements of clients, hence improving the overall efficiency of the banking system and the quality of financial services. The automation and enhanced precision of consumer credit conditions using blockchain technology have the potential to revolutionise financial markets (Madaan, 2023). AI has revolutionised the banking business by enhancing consumer experiences, improving fraud detection, optimising risk management, and automating various tasks. Finance AI provides assistance but struggles with issues related to data quality, accountability, and compliance (Manoharan et al., 2024). Currently, there is a growing focus on the application of blockchain technology in the tourist industry, and extensive research efforts have been initiated in this area. The objective of this study was to propose a business model using a blockchain platform. Blockchain is a decentralised and transparent digital ledger that enables safe transactions within the tourist sector by utilising a secure network (Aghaei et al., 2021). Fraud and Identity Theft result in significant financial losses for the telecom business, with telecom fraud being a primary contributor to revenue loss. Roaming fraud is the most significant issue for network service providers and a serious worry for several firms (Yamunaet al., 2023). Supply chain management (SCM) incorporates blockchain technology to effectively document transactions, ensuring confidence among business partners, safeguarding information, enhancing visibility, and enabling product traceability (Karumanchi et al., 2019). It has the ability to alter several procedures, facilitate peer-to-peer payments, establish trade agreements, and monitor supply chain activities. Emerging technology has many applications in financial services, including but not limited to peer-to-peer payments, trade agreements, and supply chain tracking. It has the potential to revolutionise these operations. These use cases rely on the identification and verification of participants or users. The word for "Know Your Customer" is commonly referred to as KYC (Thommandru & Chakka, 2023).

In contemporary society, there is a growing trend towards global interconnectivity, so much so that it is sometimes likened to a compact village. Customers may conveniently access the worldwide marketplace and effortlessly purchase items or services with a single click. This has given rise to a novel state of affairs, characterised by intense rivalry among organisations. They are not only striving to fulfil market demand, but also aiming to enhance customer experience and outpace their competitors in terms of innovation, all in order to secure the long-term viability of their enterprises (Salah, 2024). Customers have rapidly embraced Digital Financial Services (DFS) due to its attributes of safety, security, affordability, speed, convenience, and 24/7 accessibility. The government and the Reserve Bank of India (RBI) have implemented many measures to encourage the adoption and usage of Digital Financial Services (DFS) (Ravikumar et al., 2024). Data is currently considered the most valuable asset. When a person or corporation uses the services of a bank, their primary requirement is for protection against money and identity fraud (Thaman, 2022). Offline banks are becoming obsolete due to the rise of big data, artificial intelligence (AI), deep learning for consumer pattern analysis, insurance fraud detection, software development, and blockchain-based FinTech technologies (Cho et al., 2023). Distributed Ledger Technologies (DLTs), namely blockchain, enable enterprises to leverage decentralised peer-to-peer networks, enabling interactions between members that may not completely trust each other, without the need for a trusted third party. The interactions are maintained in a manner that can be verified and audited by both the parties involved and external individuals (Tsvetkov & Kostadinov, 2021). Blockchain, a prominent instance of Distributed Ledger Technology, has been widely acclaimed in the industry as the pivotal factor for achieving future prosperity in the financial services sector. Blockchain is a versatile platform that may be used in many ways in the Financial Services industry. It has the potential to revolutionise operations such as peer-to-peer payments, trade settlements, and supply chain monitoring. All of these use cases rely on one crucial factor: the identification and verification of participants or users (Biradar & Dakshayini, 2020). Individuals often employ their personal identification documents in the context of the growing digitisation trend. These documents are often shared with third parties without express consent and stored in several arbitrary locations. Government entities, banks, credit agencies, and other financial organisations keep identifying information in their respective databases. The presence of sensitive information in several locations heightens the likelihood of vulnerabilities.

The banking sector has long been seeking answers to these difficulties, and one feasible alternative is blockchain technology (Ravale et al., 2023).

Through enhancing transparency, efficiency, and confidence in banking transactions, blockchain technology greatly enhances client perceptions of banks that are backed by blockchain technology (Jayaraman et al., 2023). The banking sector is being transformed by financial technology. The convergence of advanced technologies is transforming the corporate landscape in response to the challenges posed by unpredictability, indecisiveness, complexity, and ambiguity in the financial sector (Kumar & Kaur, 2023). Banks are actively adopting and incorporating financial technology into their banking products and services, particularly in areas such as customer advising, artificial intelligence models, and blockchain security (Kumar et al., 2022). Blockchain is widely recognised as a highly secure cryptographic system that enables decentralised data governance and eliminates the need for intermediaries in data management (Kumar et al., 2023). Blockchain may be utilised to examine and process data by efficiently integrating financial resources. Emerging financial formats or service models are developed to enhance the financial system and enhance the effectiveness and excellence of financial operations and services. These models are built on three levels - data, rules, and application - and are tailored to meet the specific requirements of clients (Zhang et al., 2020). The accounting and finance business has substantially profited from the modernisation of processes, leading to a substantial reduction in the use of old systems through the incorporation of digital technology. Artificial intelligence technologies, including expert systems, intelligent agents, Natural Language Processing (NLP), Robotic Process Automation (RPA), Blockchain, data analytics, and machine learning, have been suggested as means to automate, streamline, and enhance the efficiency of accounting and finance operations. These technologies can be used for tasks such as audit and taxation, customer service, decision-making, and process improvement (Rahim & Chishti, 2024). The substantial changes made in financial services are being shaped and explained by technological disruption and societal revolution. A rapid convergence of mobile applications, big data, blockchain, AI, cloud computing, and digital platforms is occurring, compelling traditional banks to incorporate this technology into new collaborative networks for value generation (Visconti-Caparrós & Campos-Blázquez, 2022).

LITERATURE REVIEW

(Ahmed et al., 2020) developed the framework in order to analyse fake bank service calls to avoid personal losses. (Cho et al., 2023) provided an overview upon introduction of FinTech and how it changed the customer service quality and increased the overall profits of whole financial sector. (Tsvetkov & Kostadinov, 2021) stated that software lifecycle management is based upon the usage of latest technology of distributed ledger as through which business processes can be automated, verified and simplified. (Zhang et al., 2020) discussed that financial industry can take better advantage of blockchain technology to identify credit conditions of customers and all this can be helpful for finance industry to improve its efficiency in terms of cross border payment. (Rahim & Chishti, 2024) investigated the AI technologies as how they can result in reliability of accounting processes. (Reshetnikova et al., 2021) stated that financial organisations interact with the digital profiles of their clients instead of direct interaction these days. (Guo & Polak, 2021) thrown a light upon new intelligent finance which can reduce operating costs of financial institutions as well as providing high quality of financial services. (Ravi & Kamaruddin, 2017) talked about digital transformation and affected the whole financial service industry in terms of both, service taker and service provider. (Vinther Daugaard et al., 2024) thrown a light upon the concept of anti-money laundering for managing the KYC as well as transaction monitoring capabilities also. Digitalisation and sustainability go hand-in-hand by focusing on developing the energy-efficient systems in terms of enhancing the efficiency level as well as customer's satisfaction level. (Jha & Sachan, 2023). (Taha et al., 2020) thrown a light upon Cloud Service

Providers (CSPs) which can fulfil the needs of customers by maintaining the required set of transparency as well as satisfying their needs as well.

(Ravindran & Vamsi, 2021) proposed the platform based on blockchain network promoting public database for loan management that can be helpful for borrowers or lenders to record customer's data to ensure trustworthy as well as transparent mechanism. (Ahmed et al., 2023) provided the mechanism known as self-sovereign banking identity as based upon blockchain network in securing customer's data. Authors also discussed about trusted open banking by taking blockchain based self-sovereign identity. (Ravikumar et al., 2024) focused on identifying the needs of the customers of FinTech companies and what innovative steps that are to be taken up by Digital Financial Services Providers to fulfil those needs. (Jayaraman et al., 2023) stated that positive attitude towards blockchain based banks plays a major role among customer's preference. (Golodova & Grechkin, 2022) suggested that by usage of AI, crowdfunding, blockchain and Big Data can lead to customer service optimisation as well as asset management financial institutes in domestic market and further resulting in speedy information exchange. (Hasan M. et al., 2021) developed hybrid model to explain the blockchain architecture to enable the efficient communication. (Manjunath et al., 2019) discussed about the concept of data masking and data obfuscation in terms of blockchain management as each of the blocks are connected, so data can be stored in the form of chain by taking into consideration the level of transparency, traceability as well as security of data. (Yamunaet al., 2023) provided necessary solution for financial fraud and identity theft by taking into consideration the blockchain based network for secured storage of data. Financial transactions verify the parties through KYC which further builds the trust between people involved in it. (Thommandru & Chakka, 2023). Digital banking sector is showing a progressive growth by resulting in efficient and user-friendly technology adoption. (Indriasari et al., 2022).

(Chun-Ting et al., 2020) provided the supporting proof related to data storage of agriculturally based data using blockchain service platform by keeping a record of financial transactions that took place in the entire food chain network as from farm till fork. IOT sensors contributed their great efforts to trace the activities of food production. (Farah et al., 2023) discussed that bank managers play a major role in promoting the perception of customers towards financial well-being. The attempt is made by managers to convince the customers as they can adopt the blockchain technology by showing them the respective benefits as it leads to information transparency. (Meskini & Islamic, 2019) stated that blockchain resulted in progressive growth of insurance sector as it smart contracts can be possible which saves time, leads to cost reduction and further provides better customer service. (Vaddadi et al., 2023) thrown a light upon different blockchain methods such as Wallets, keys, Mining, Halving and Merkelroot as these methods can be utilised in providing required level of security to cryptocurrencies through online mechanism. These can be further implacable to banking sector as well which eliminates various intermediaries in handling different financial transactions. (Vaddadi et al., 2023) thrown a light upon different blockchain methods such as Wallets, keys, Mining, Halving and Merkelroot as these methods can be utilised in providing required level of security to cryptocurrencies through online mechanism. These can be further implacable to banking sector as well which eliminates various intermediaries in handling different financial transactions. (Zeba & Čičak, 2023) suggested that supply chains need to be secured from various types of risks like financial losses, operational disruptions, business data theft and can be possible to manage by introducing digital business transformation which enhances productivity, competitiveness and efficiency. (Hajiabbasi et al., 2023) proposed the framework based upon deep learning by using biometric architecture by taking customer's data and maintaining its privacy as a whole. (Trivedi, 2023) discussed that fraud need to be reduced in insurance industry in order to provide better customer experience by improving its efficiency. Banks make use of blockchain technology in handling the authenticated data transactions by simplification of complex working in managing a large set of financial data which can be further utilised for financial users in taking required financial decisions. (Nirvan et al., 2023).

With introduction of latest technologies in Fintech framework made financial and banking operations as customer centric. (Mehrotra & Menon, 2021). (Kirillova et al., 2021) analysed various digitalised services provided by banking sector to its customers. Various banking institutes are focusing on implementation of e-KYC on their cloud having higher level of accessibility and availability of cloud computing networks to enable the data verification process easy among the parties (Chandraprabha, 2023). Banks collect the relevant information about their clients as mandated by law through KYC mechanism to enjoy the access of financial services. (Anuar et al., 2023). Banks need to offer faster as well as cheaper services to customers that can be easily possible through blockchain network (Hefny et al., 2023). The decentralised mechanism of blockchain can lead to data collection from verified database resulting in secured identity verification (Ravale et al., 2023). (Riad & Elhoseny, 2022) proposed new control scheme for access management by making use of blockchain technology in handling the key-revocation processes. (Vittala et al., 2024) explored the usage of emerging technology in handling smart banking solutions in terms of AI and IoT for offering personalised services for customers. (Baskerville et al., 2020) studies the relationship between humans and digitalisation in banking sector and found the synergy among two. Blockchain technology in combination of artificial intelligence contributes towards financial well-being as well as enhancing the customer's financial transparency. (Yang et al., 2024). Blockchain and Artificial Intelligence provided fast, effective and cheaper solution to financial service sector by improving its convenience, transparency, security, reach and so on. (Sujee et al., 2023). (Talha et al., 2022) discussed about usage of blockchain technology in food delivery system by providing information security, strict policy enforcement and B2B deep discounting race among food restaurants. (Yu et al., 2023) analysed that customer's interest keep on changing from time to time and businesses need to predict them in advance for gaining competitive advantage in the market.

(Memon et al., 2021) analysed that Gen-Z is lacking in terms of knowledge and awareness towards usage of Fintech services and they are not at interested in investing their money with Fintech service providers. Authors also suggested that there is a need to create awareness among the people through knowledge sharing by attempting marketing efforts to increase the level of popularity towards blockchain network among the people. (Elrashidy et al., 2021) investigated upon process of banking digitalisation and how it can influence its customer relationship management. Authors found that clients need to be provided with effective product set by ensuring scalable banking business transaction by adoption of latest technologies like blockchain and artificial intelligence. (Buckley et al., 2021) designed an approach in terms of automation, simplification and management of financial supply chain network in handling different payments of users. (Banate et al., 2023) discussed about fraudulent activities in insurance sector and it centralised databases work upon weak security measures which is the biggest challenge for insurance sector. Authors also found an effective solution for the same in by introducing blockchain technology which is a decentralised network and offers security to financial transactions which further reduces the level of risks faced by insurance industry. (Sasikumar et al., 2022) introduced the decentralised network platform which can help to build the trust among users in terms of improving data transmission, cost reduction by providing effective financial services to various users in supply chain network as it leads to data transmission in trustworthy manner. (Sood et al., 2023) stated that insurance companies need to invest in IT by adjusting their business models and developing competitive strategies in terms of taking technological advantage that can improve customer experience by reducing their cost of operations. (Biradar & Dakshayini, 2020) provided a better solution to manage the KYC using the technique of Hyperledger Fabric under blockchain technology having key features of data confidentiality, network permission, accountability and transparency. Fintech resulted in financial inclusion by creating new opportunities for the customers better than traditional banking (Girish & Bhowmik, 2023). (Sakas et al., 2023) aimed to analyse the adoption of capitalised decentralised financial services on crypto trading. Authors also examined that social media analytics can affect the website visibility and overall financial health of supply chain firms. (Anitha et al., 2024) focused upon discussing the blockchain mechanism which leads to time-stamped transactions which generate secured and integrated supply chain network. (Kasim et al., 2024) discussed regarding Fintech organisations of Malaysia by stating their key aspects in the form of prop-tech, insurtec, crowdfunding, weathtech, reg-tech market options and so on. (Rajnak & Puschmann, 2021) designed the model which behave as mediator in terms of IT innovations by taking into consideration the three aspects such as, product leadership, customer intimacy and operational excellence. (George et al., 2019) stated regarding central storage of data in order to protect it from attacks or vulnerabilities by using a blockchain technology.

CONCEPTUAL FRAMEWORK

Blockchain-based identity management is an intriguing field, particularly when it comes to safeguarding consumer data in the financial services sector. The financial services business is now experiencing a digital revolution, characterised by a growing dependence on technology and data. Although this revolution has yielded many advantages, it has also presented novel difficulties, namely with data security and privacy (Ahmed et al., 2020). The decentralised, immutable, and transparent nature of blockchain technology presents a viable answer to these difficulties. Customer data saved on the blockchain is encoded, guaranteeing the confidentiality and safety of delicate information. Smart contracts may be utilised to implement access control restrictions, guaranteeing that only authorised companies have the ability to access certain client data (Kumar et al., 2023). The framework enables smooth integration with current identity verification systems and procedures employed in the financial services industry, ensuring interoperability. This guarantees the compatibility of the blockchain-based identity management solution with existing systems, hence improving security without causing any disruptions to current processes. The inherent transparency of blockchain technology allows auditors and regulatory agencies to easily check compliance. Financial service companies may bolster the security and privacy of consumer data, mitigate the risk of data breaches, and promote operational efficiency by using a blockchain-based identity management system. This strategy empowers customers to have more authority over their data and promotes trust between customers and financial organisations (Kumar et al., 2022) (Jayaraman et al., 2023).

A blockchain-based identity management system has the capacity to fundamentally transform the way consumer data is handled and safeguarded in the financial services sector. This framework may enhance the security, privacy, and efficiency of the digital ecosystem by tackling the obstacles and capitalising on the advantages of the technology. The objective of a conceptual framework for blockchain-based identity management in financial services is to tackle the security and privacy issues linked to client data (Rahim & Chishti, 2024) (Manjunath et al., 2019). This framework utilises the inherent features of blockchain technology, like immutability, decentralisation, and transparency, to offer a reliable and effective approach for managing consumer IDs. The data related to customer identification is saved on a blockchain network that is not controlled by a central authority. Every client is assigned a distinct digital identity that is connected to their personal information. This guarantees that user data is not retained in a centralised database, hence minimising the possibility of a single point of failure or unauthorised entry (Meskini & Islamic, 2019). Within this framework, consumers own complete authority over their data and possess the ability to authorise or withdraw consent for the sharing of their information with financial service providers. Smart contracts for consent management on the blockchain empower users to oversee their data choices and explicitly determine which companies are granted access to their information. The blockchain records every transaction associated with consumer identity, establishing an unchangeable audit trail. All modifications or revisions made to client data are documented, facilitating effortless tracking and openness. This ensures a significant degree of responsibility and simplifies the identification of any deceitful actions or unauthorised alterations (Salah, 2024).

EXPLORING POTENTIAL OF BLOCKCHAIN-BASED IDENTITY MANAGEMENT SYSTEMS

The financial services industry may address its security and privacy concerns by adopting blockchain technology, which provides decentralisation, immutability, and transparency. Implementing a blockchain-based identity management system (BIM) has the potential to completely transform the way consumer data is handled and safeguarded. Utilising blockchain technology for identity management has the capacity to revolutionise the financial services sector by improving security, privacy, and efficiency. With the advancement of technology and the development of legal frameworks, we may anticipate a broader acceptance and increased creativity in this field (Karumanchi et al., 2019).

The investigation of the capabilities of blockchain-based identity management systems to improve the security and privacy of consumer data in financial services. Blockchain technology offers a secure and immutable platform for storing consumer identifying data, making it resistant to tampering and providing evidence of any unauthorised changes. Through the utilisation of cryptographic methods and the distribution of authority, systems based on blockchain technology have the ability to greatly diminish the likelihood of unauthorised entry, data breaches, and fraudulent activities (Thommandru & Chakka, 2023). The unchangeability of data recorded on a blockchain guarantees that client records are impervious to unauthorised alterations. Utilising blockchain technology, identity management systems can provide decentralised identity verification, hence diminishing the need for centralised authority in the process of identity identification (Trivedi, 2023) (Yang et al., 2024). Implementing this strategy can reduce the risks linked to centralised databases that are susceptible to single points of failure and large-scale data breaches. By utilising blockchain smart contracts, clients may exercise enhanced authority over their personal data. Smart contracts provide the precise control of data access rights, enabling consumers to identify the individuals who can access their information and the specific conditions under which access is granted (Madaan, 2023).

Blockchain technology's inherent transparency and traceability can effectively assist in preventing and detecting fraud in the financial services sector. Blockchain-based solutions can enhance fraud detection and analytics by preserving an unchangeable record of transactions and identity-related activity (Mehrotra & Menon, 2021) (Lalitha & Soujanya, 2019). Blockchain-based identity management solutions can optimise client onboarding processes and enhance Know Your client (KYC) procedures. This can lead to cost reductions for financial institutions, while also offering clients a smoother and more secure experience (Banate et al., 2023). Blockchain technology can enhance interoperability among various financial institutions and service providers, hence facilitating seamless identity verification processes across numerous platforms. In addition, if there is collaboration throughout the whole industry to establish standards for managing identities using blockchain technology, it can result in stronger and more consistent security measures (Buckley et al., 2021).

Blockchain-based identity management solutions can enhance regulatory compliance by offering transparent audit trails and verified records of identity-related transactions. This can streamline regulatory reporting and auditing procedures, improving openness and accountability within the financial services sector. By using the capabilities of identity management systems based on blockchain technology, financial services may bolster the protection and confidentiality of consumer data, while also enhancing operational effectiveness, mitigating risks, and cultivating stronger trust between customers and financial institutions (Lalitha & Soujanya, 2019). This investigation has the potential to result in the creation of groundbreaking solutions that effectively tackle persistent issues in identity management within the banking industry.

EXAMINATION OF ADDRESSING BY BLOCKCHAIN TECHNOLOGY

Conventional identity management systems (IDMS) have been consistently troubled by problems such as data breaches, privacy concerns, and vulnerabilities due to a single point of failure. Blockchain technology provides a promising answer by tackling these weaknesses and improving overall data security. Blockchain technology presents a viable answer to the difficulties encountered by conventional identity management systems. By utilising its decentralised, unchangeable, and secure characteristics, BIM has the potential to greatly improve data security and confidentiality. Despite existing obstacles, the potential advantages of this technology are significant, and it is expected to have a vital impact on determining the future of identity management (Sood et al., 2023). Blockchain technology provides many functionalities to mitigate current weaknesses in conventional identity management frameworks and enhance overall data security. Conventional identity management solutions frequently depend on centralised databases, which create vulnerable single points of failure that are prone to cyberattacks and data leaks (Kumar & Kaur, 2022). The decentralised structure of blockchain distributes data over a network of nodes, so minimising the vulnerability of a single point of failure and strengthening resistance against security threats (Sakas et al., 2023). The implementation of cryptographic algorithms and consensus processes in blockchain technology enhances the security of data (Kasim et al., 2024). The customer identifying data is encrypted and kept in a manner that greatly minimises the possibility of unauthorised access or alteration. Implementing private keys for access control provides an additional level of safeguarding for confidential client data. The unchangeability of blockchain guarantees that any modifications or retrieval of client data are forever documented. This feature mitigates vulnerabilities present in conventional systems, which may allow malicious operations or unauthorised modifications to remain unnoticed. The unchangeable record of events enhances clarity and responsibility, hence strengthening the overall safeguarding of data. Blockchain smart contracts enhance consent management by providing clients with precise control over their data and the ability to designate authorised access (George et al., 2019). This solution targets weaknesses in conventional systems where the management of client permission may be inadequate, resulting in the improper use of data. The transparent and auditable nature of blockchain is in accordance with privacy standards and enhances data protection. Blockchain's transparency and traceability can enhance fraud prevention and detection by offering a verifiable log of identity-related transactions. This solution targets weaknesses in conventional systems where it may be difficult to quickly detect fraudulent activity, which can result in financial and reputational hazards for financial institutions (Rajnak & Puschmann, 2021).

Blockchain technology has the potential to enable interoperability and the development of industry standards for identity management. This solution targets weaknesses in conventional systems where isolated methods and incompatible technologies impede efficient data security and identity authentication procedures. Blockchain technology's capacity to offer transparent audit trails and verifiable documents is in line with regulatory standards, thereby resolving weaknesses in conventional systems that may pose challenges to regulatory compliance. This guarantees that financial institutions can adhere to data protection legislation and industry standards with greater efficiency (Banate et al., 2023). Financial institutions may enhance the overall security of consumer data by utilising blockchain technology to tackle weaknesses in conventional identity management systems (Lalitha & Soujanya, 2019). These technological improvements have the potential to create identity management systems that are more robust, secure, and transparent. These systems will be in line with changing regulatory standards and meet customer expectations for privacy.

Table 1. Case studies based on blockchain implementation

S.No.	Institution	Country	Blockchain Platform	Blockchain Implementation	Source
1	**JPMorgan Chase**	USA	Quorum (JPM's own)	JPMorgan Chase has used Quorum in several applications, including trading, payments, and cybersecurity. Furthermore, its applications are also relevant in other sectors like as healthcare, supply chain management, and identity verification. The platform is constructed using the Ethereum blockchain and specifically designed for private networks, enabling enhanced management of data sharing and secrecy.	(Allison, 2020; Consensys, 2020)
2	**HSBC**	UK	Hyperledger Fabric	HSBC, a prominent international bank, has used Hyperledger Fabric, a widely-used blockchain technology, to bolster its financial operations and strengthen security. HSBC has used Hyperledger Fabric to create a private blockchain network, enabling safe data sharing and peer-to-peer transactions with its clients.	(HSBC: Facilitating Trade Finance Through Blockchain, 2023)
3	**Deutsche Bank**	Germany	Ethereum, Interbank Information Network (INN)	1. Ethereum Platform: Deutsche Bank has joined the tokenised money market by using a platform based on Ethereum. This program encompasses the examination and incorporation of blockchain technology for the purpose of enhancing financial services and facilitating the tokenisation of assets. 2. Deutsche Bank has just become a participant in JP Morgan's Interbank Information Network (IIN), a blockchain platform. The objective of this collaboration is to improve the effectiveness of interbank transactions and address the issue of margin compression.	(Encila, 2024; Tran, 2019)
4	**Standard Chartered**	UK	Partior	In 2022, Standard Chartered made an investment in Partior, a Distributed Ledger Technology (DLT) business established by DBS, Temasek, and JPMorgan. Partior aims to disrupt the inefficient hub-and-spoke paradigm used in existing cross-border payment systems. Partior originates from project Ubin, which is a blockchain-based prototype for multi-currency payments. This project was created by the Monetary Authority of Singapore in collaboration with JPMorgan and Temasek.	(Finextra, 2024)
5	**Barclays**	UK	Wave	Barclays used Wave's blockchain technology to conduct its first trade finance transaction. This transaction was facilitated by Wave, a firm from Barclays' blockchain accelerator program.	(Leung, 2016)

(Source: Secondary Data Compiled by Authors)

FINDINGS OF THE STUDY

Amidst the age of digital transformation, the financial services sector has grown more dependent on the handling and protection of consumer data. Blockchain technology has arisen as a viable remedy to tackle the escalating worries regarding data integrity and security in this field. Utilising blockchain technology allows financial institutions to tackle several persistent difficulties (Elrashidy et al., 2021). A significant issue related to bank credit is the dearth of credit score information, which hinders people and small and medium-sized organisations from securing loans. Furthermore, financial institutions face challenges in accurately profiling their customers, which impairs their capacity to effectively distinguish and customise their offerings. Moreover, the insurance claims process in the financial sector frequently requires the involvement of several parties, resulting in an intricate and time-consuming procedure prior to the completion and disbursement of a claim. A further crucial challenge encountered by the financial sector is the susceptibility of its current essential infrastructures to cyber-attacks. Blockchain technology might potentially resolve these difficulties by offering a secure and decentralised platform for the administration of consumer data and financial transactions (Aghaei et al., 2021). The banking industry is presented with enticing commercial prospects to embrace blockchain technology. In order to proceed with such an investment, decision-makers must answer to certain enquiries, such as: which current business challenges can be resolved, if blockchain technology will effectively address them, and what enduring advantages and novel business prospects may be generated via the implementation of blockchain (Girish & Bhowmik, 2023).

Data security, privacy protection, and regulatory compliance have always posed issues for identity management in the financial services sector. Conventional systems have had difficulties in adequately protecting consumer data, resulting in weaknesses that may be used by cyber assailants. Given these limitations, the implementation of blockchain technology has emerged as a possible remedy to improve identity management methods in the financial services sector (Chun-Ting et al., 2020). Financial institutions may transform the way they protect client data and simplify identity verification procedures by utilising the built-in security and transparency capabilities of blockchain technology (Zhang et al., 2020). The complexities linked to conventional identity management systems in the financial services sector are diverse. First and foremost, these systems frequently lack strong data security safeguards, rendering them vulnerable to cyber attacks and data breaches. Customer data, which includes sensitive personal and financial information, is held in centralised systems that are highly sought after by malevolent individuals. Furthermore, the insufficient privacy safeguards in place worsen the likelihood of unauthorised access to sensitive information. On the other hand, identity management based on blockchain technology provides many advantages that specifically target the limitations of conventional methods. Blockchain technology improves data security by utilising encryption and decentralisation to store client information in an unchangeable and tamper-resistant way. This not only mitigates the likelihood of data breaches but also empowers clients with more authority over their personal information. Moreover, the transparent and verifiable characteristics of blockchain technology allow financial organisations to trace and supervise the usage of consumer data, guaranteeing adherence to legal obligations and strengthening responsibility (Jayaraman et al., 2023). From the viewpoint of a client, the efficient identity verification procedures facilitated by blockchain technology can result in a smoother and more secure user experience, eventually fostering trust and loyalty. When contemplating the integration of blockchain-based identity management in financial services, it is crucial to address many important factors. First and foremost, it is essential to integrate blockchain technology with the current IT infrastructure and processes to guarantee a seamless transition without causing any disruption to operations (Cho et al., 2023). Collaboration with industry partners is crucial for establishing interoperability standards and ensuring safe data exchange. To properly utilise the advantages of blockchain technology in securing client data and improving identity management policies, financial institutions should proactively address these implementation issues (Tsvetkov & Kostadinov, 2021).

CONCLUSION

To summarise, implementing blockchain-based identity management has great potential for the financial services sector in tackling the issues linked to conventional systems. Blockchain technology enhances data security, transparency, and efficiency, allowing financial firms to safeguard consumer data and speed identification verification operations. Nevertheless, achieving success in the implementation process necessitates meticulous deliberation regarding the integration, teamwork, and adherence to regulatory requirements. Financial institutions are increasingly focussing on data security and privacy protection. They are seeing the need of using blockchain-based identity management to safeguard consumer data and build confidence in the digital economy. The advancement of current technology has led to the accumulation of large amounts of data in numerous domains. However, this also raises concerns about the security of these records to prevent any tampering during storage, transfer, processing, updating, and access. Transactions can involve the transfer of an asset, the fulfilment of the provisions of a self-executing script-smart contract, or the updating of a narrative. The blockchain ecosystem is inherently vulnerable due to its complex network of miners, developers, suppliers, customers, shareholders, stakeholders, and players. Currently, blockchain technology is not just restricted to cryptocurrency, but is also being utilised in other financial and economic applications. Decentralisation, immutability, and transparency provide the foundation upon which blockchain technology operates. This ecosystem is expanding via the active participation of actors from both the public and commercial sectors (Suri, 2021). Undoubtedly, blockchain is one of the most promising technologies for organising financial services. The importance of Blockchain technology in a financial system may be assessed based on three fundamental principles: Disintermediation, Transparency, and Provenance. Blockchain maintains an unchangeable distributed record of transactions, ensuring the whole history of assets and their ownership from the initial transaction to the most current one. It decreases the likelihood of theft, insurance fraud, and the misrepresentation of valuable goods or intellectual properties. The banking sector can utilise blockchain technology for a range of applications including ensuring data confidentiality, facilitating cheque clearing, enabling real-time digital currency transfers, supporting supply chain finance, enhancing insurance processes, facilitating trade finance, implementing KYC (know your customer) procedures, enabling cross-border payments and transactions, monitoring consortium accounts, facilitating auction systems, and managing digital assets. Blockchain technology can facilitate a decentralised solution for the financial industry (Ravindran & Vamsi, 2021).

REFERENCES

Aghaei, H., Naderibeni, N., & Karimi, A. (2021). Designing a tourism business model on block chain platform. *Tourism Management Perspectives*, *39*, 100845. DOI: 10.1016/j.tmp.2021.100845

Ahmed, K. A., Saraya, S. F., Wanis, J. F., & Ali-Eldin, A. M. (2020, December). A self-sovereign identity architecture based on blockchain and the utilization of customer's banking cards: The case of bank. scam calls prevention. In 2020 15th International Conference on Computer Engineering and Systems (ICCES) (pp. 1-8). IEEE.

Ahmed, K. A., Saraya, S. F., Wanis, J. F., & Ali-Eldin, A. M. (2023). A blockchain self-sovereign identity for open banking secured by the customer's banking cards. *Future Internet*, *15*(6), 208. DOI: 10.3390/fi15060208

Allison, I. (2020, August 25). ConsenSys Acquires JPMorgan's Quorum Blockchain. CoinDesk.

Anitha, A., Priya, M., Nallakaruppan, M. K., Natesan, D., Jaiswal, C. K., & Srivastava, H. K. (2024). Secured and Sustainable Supply Chain Management Using Key Escrow Encryption Technique in Blockchain Mechanism. EAI Endorsed Transactions on Internet of Things, 10.

Anuar, M. A. B., Zeki, A. M., & Abubakar, A. (2023, August). Exploring Blockchain for KYC: Deepening Client Understanding. In 2023 IEEE 13th International Conference on Control System, Computing and Engineering (ICCSCE) (pp. 27-32). IEEE.

Banate, H., Jagtap, Y., Choudhary, D., & Dhage, S. (2023, July). Decentralised Application for Health Insurance management using Blockchain. In 2023 14th International Conference on Computing Communication and Networking Technologies (ICCCNT) (pp. 1-7). IEEE. DOI: 10.1109/ICCCNT56998.2023.10308050

Baskerville, R., Capriglione, F., & Casalino, N. (2020). Impacts, challenges and trends of digital transformation in the banking sector. Law and Economics Yearly Review Journal-LEYR, Queen Mary University, London, UK, 9(part 2), 341-362.

Biradar, R. R., & Dakshayini, M. (2020, February). Blockchain enabled KYC solutions using hyperledge fabric. In *2020 International Conference on Mainstreaming Block Chain Implementation (ICOMBI)* (pp. 1-3). IEEE. DOI: 10.23919/ICOMBI48604.2020.9203407

Buckley, D., Bendiab, G., Shiaeles, S., Savage, N., & Kolokotronis, N. (2021, June). CHAINGE: A Blockchain Solution to Automate Payment Detail Updates to Subscription Services. In 2021 IEEE International Conference on Communications Workshops (ICC Workshops) (pp. 1-6). IEEE. DOI: 10.1109/ICCWorkshops50388.2021.9473666

Chandraprabha, K. S. (2023). Blockchain-based implementation on electronic know your customer (e-KYC). In *Intelligent Communication Technologies and Virtual Mobile Networks* (pp. 281–297). Springer Nature Singapore. DOI: 10.1007/978-981-99-1767-9_22

Cho, S., Lee, Z., Hwang, S., & Kim, J. (2023). Determinants of bank closures: What ensures sustainable profitability in mobile banking? *Electronics (Basel)*, *12*(5), 1196. DOI: 10.3390/electronics12051196

Chun-Ting, P., Meng-Ju, L., Nen-Fu, H., Jhong-Ting, L., & Jia-Jung, S. (2020, January). Agriculture blockchain service platform for farm-to-fork traceability with IoT sensors. In 2020 international conference on information networking (ICOIN) (pp. 158-163). IEEE.

Consensys. (2020, August 25). Consensys Acquires Quorum® Platform from J.P. Morgan. Consensys.

Dananjayan, M. P., Gopakumar, S., & Narayanasamy, P. (2023). Money in the age of bits and bytes: Technology in reshaping finance. Journal of Information Technology Teaching Cases, 20438869231178845.

Encila, C. (2024, July 11). Deutsche Bank Dives Into Crypto: Ethereum Platform Tested To Fight Shrinking Profits. Bitcoinist.Com.

Farah, M. F., Naveed, M., & Ali, S. (2023, May). Blockchain-enabled banking services and customers' perceived financial well-being: A structural nexus. In National Brand and Private Label Marketing Conference (pp. 41-49). Cham: Springer Nature Switzerland. DOI: 10.1007/978-3-031-32894-7_5

Finextra. (2024, May 16). Standard Chartered brings blockchain to payments with Partior. Finextra.

George, D., Wani, A., & Bhatia, A. (2019, December). A blockchain based solution to know your customer (kyc) dilemma. In *2019 IEEE International Conference on Advanced Networks and Telecommunications Systems (ANTS)* (pp. 1-6). IEEE. DOI: 10.1109/ANTS47819.2019.9118042

Girish, K. K., & Bhowmik, B. (2023, July). Recent advancements and challenges in fintech. In 2023 14th International Conference on Computing Communication and Networking Technologies (ICCCNT) (pp. 1-7). IEEE.

Golodova, Z. G., & Grechkin, N. V. (2022). Developing Financial Integration with the Introduction of Financial Technologies in the Eurasian Economic Union Countries. Vestnik RUDN. *International Relations*, *22*(1), 166–179.

Guo, H., & Polak, P. (2021). After the collision of crisis and opportunity to redefining the artificial intelligence in finance: the new intelligent finance era. Applications of Artificial Intelligence in Business, Education and Healthcare, 157-172.

Hajiabbasi, M., Akhtarkavan, E., & Majidi, B. (2023). Cyber-physical customer management for Internet of robotic things-enabled banking. *IEEE Access : Practical Innovations, Open Solutions*, *11*, 34062–34079. DOI: 10.1109/ACCESS.2023.3263859

Han, J., & Ma, Y. (2021). Blockchain Technology in Inclusive Finance Under the Background of Big Data. In Cyber Security Intelligence and Analytics: 2021 International Conference on Cyber Security Intelligence and Analytics (CSIA2021), Volume 2 (pp. 225-231). Springer International Publishing. DOI: 10.1007/978-3-030-69999-4_30

Hasan, M., Ogan, K., & Starly, B. (2021). Hybrid blockchain architecture for cloud manufacturing-as-a-service (cmaas) platforms with improved data storage and transaction efficiency. *Procedia Manufacturing*, *53*, 594–605. DOI: 10.1016/j.promfg.2021.06.060

Hefny, M. H. M., Helmy, Y., & Abdelsalam, M. (2023). Open banking api framework to improve the online transaction between local banks in egypt using blockchain technology. *Journal of Advances in Information Technology*, *14*(4), 729–740. DOI: 10.12720/jait.14.4.729-740

HSBC: Facilitating Trade Finance Through Blockchain (October 10, 2023). DOI: 10.1108/CASE.IIMA.2023.000016

Indriasari, E., Prabowo, H., Gaol, F. L., & Purwandari, B. (2022). Intelligent Digital Banking Technology and Architecture: A Systematic Literature Review. *Int. J. Interact. Mob. Technol.*, *16*(19), 98–117. DOI: 10.3991/ijim.v16i19.30993

Jayaraman, G., Azad, I., Ahmed, H. M. S., Hussien, M. A., & Khan, M. S. (2023). The impact of blockchain technology on customer attitude and behavioral intentions in the banking sector. *Asian Journal of Economic Modelling*, *11*(4), 165–187. DOI: 10.55493/5009.v11i4.4952

Jha, C. K., & Sachan, A. (2023). Blockchain and Artificial Intelligence Technology in Professional Services. In Fostering Sustainable Development in the Age of Technologies (pp. 43-50). Emerald Publishing Limited. DOI: 10.1108/978-1-83753-060-120231005

Karumanchi, M. D., Sheeba, J. I., & Devaneyan, S. P. (2019, December). Cloud based supply chain management system using blockchain. In 2019 4th International Conference on Electrical, Electronics, Communication, Computer Technologies and Optimization Techniques (ICEECCOT) (pp. 390-395). IEEE. DOI: 10.1109/ICEECCOT46775.2019.9114692

Kasim, R. S. R., Zulazli, N. A., & Azman, W. F. A. C. (2024). Do Islamic Fintech Leadership and Technology Adoption Predict Sustainable Entrepreneurship Values among Fintech Organizations? *International Journal of Religion*, *5*(3), 466–475. DOI: 10.61707/9e0gfj82

Kirillova, E. A., Bogdan, V. V., Blinkova, E. V., Zulfugarzade, T., & Yunusova, K. V. (2021). The main features of the use of digital technologies in the financial and banking sector. *Management*.

Kumar, A., Srivastava, A., & Gupta, P. K. (2022). Banking 4.0: The era of artificial intelligence-based fintech. *Strategic Change*, *31*(6), 591–601. DOI: 10.1002/jsc.2526

Kumar, S., Kumar, V., & Sharma, P. (2023). Financial and Banking Services Using Blockchain and Its Open Security Issues. Hybridization of Blockchain and Cloud Computing, 103-122.

Kumar, T., & Kaur, S. (2022). Blockchain Technology: Present and Future Perspectives. In Applications, Challenges, and Opportunities of Blockchain Technology in Banking and Insurance (pp. 258–265). IGI Global. DOI: 10.4018/978-1-6684-4133-6.ch016

Kumar, T., & Kaur, S. (2023). Evolution of Fintech in Financial Era. In *Fintech and Cryptocurrency* (pp. 1–12). Wiley., DOI: 10.1002/9781119905028.ch1

Lalitha, N., & Soujanya, D. (2019, November). Financial sector Innovations: Empowering Microfinance through the application of KYC Blockchain technology. In *2019 International Conference on Digitization (ICD)* (pp. 237-243). IEEE. DOI: 10.1109/ICD47981.2019.9105874

Leung, A. (2016, September 9). Barclays Uses Blockchain To Conduct Its First Trade Finance Transaction. Cointelegraph.

Madaan, G. (2023). Applications of Blockchain Technology in Finance. In Building Secure Business Models Through Blockchain Technology: Tactics, Methods, Limitations, and Performance (pp. 128-148). IGI Global. DOI: 10.4018/978-1-6684-7808-0.ch008

Manjunath, P., Herrmann, M., & Sen, H. (2019). Implementation of blockchain data obfuscation. In Innovation in Medicine and Healthcare Systems, and Multimedia: Proceedings of KES-InMed-19 and KES-IIMSS-19 Conferences (pp. 545-553). Springer Singapore.

Manoharan, G., Nithya, G., Rajchandar, K., Razak, A., Gupta, S., Durai, S., & Ashtikar, S. P. (2024). AI in Finance and Banking: The Act of Gyration. In Revolutionizing Customer-Centric Banking Through ICT (pp. 1-28). IGI Global.

Mehrotra, A., & Menon, S. (2021, January). Second round of FinTech-Trends and challenges. In 2021 2nd International Conference on Computation, Automation and Knowledge Management (ICCAKM) (pp. 243-248). IEEE. DOI: 10.1109/ICCAKM50778.2021.9357759

Memon, I. A., Nair, S., & Jakhiya, M. (2021, March). How Ready the GEN-Z is to Adopt FinTech? In *2021 International Conference on Computational Intelligence and Knowledge Economy (ICCIKE)* (pp. 565-570). IEEE. DOI: 10.1109/ICCIKE51210.2021.9410747

Meskini, F. Z., & Aboulaich, R. (2019, October). Multi-agent based simulation of a smart insurance using Blockchain technology. In *2019 Third International Conference on Intelligent Computing in Data Sciences (ICDS)* (pp. 1-6). IEEE. DOI: 10.1109/ICDS47004.2019.8942270

Nirvan, S., Verma, S., Kathuria, S., Singh, R., & Akram, S. V. (2023, August). Enhanced Banking Services using Blockchain and Artificial Intelligence. In *2023 Second International Conference on Augmented Intelligence and Sustainable Systems (ICAISS)* (pp. 57-62). IEEE. DOI: 10.1109/ICAISS58487.2023.10250709

Rahim, R., & Chishti, M. A. (2024, January). Artificial Intelligence Applications in Accounting and Finance. In *2024 ASU International Conference in Emerging Technologies for Sustainability and Intelligent Systems (ICETSIS)* (pp. 1782-1786). IEEE. DOI: 10.1109/ICETSIS61505.2024.10459526

Rajnak, V., & Puschmann, T. (2021). The impact of blockchain on business models in banking. *Information Systems and e-Business Management, 19*(3), 809–861. DOI: 10.1007/s10257-020-00468-2

Ravale, U., Ramakrishnan, A., Borkar, A., & Deshmukh, S. (2023, May). Optimizing the KYC Verification System using Ethereum Blockchain. In 2023 7th International Conference on Intelligent Computing and Control Systems (ICICCS) (pp. 1454-1458). IEEE. DOI: 10.1109/ICICCS56967.2023.10142308

Ravi, V., & Kamaruddin, S. (2017). Big data analytics enabled smart financial services: opportunities and challenges. In Big Data Analytics: 5th International Conference, BDA 2017, Hyderabad, India, December 12-15, 2017 [Springer International Publishing. RAVIKUMAR, T., GIRISH, S., LAVANYA, D., & MURUGAN, N. Adoption and Usage of Digital Financial Services in Karnataka, India: Spatial, Gender and Age Disparities.]. *Proceedings, 5*, 15–39.

Ravindran, U., & Vamsi, P. R. (2021, August). A secure blockchain based finance application. In *Proceedings of the 2021 Thirteenth International Conference on Contemporary Computing* (pp. 99-109).

Reshetnikova, N. N., Magomedov, M. M., Zmiyak, S. S., Gagarinskii, A. V., & Buklanov, D. A. (2021). Directions of digital financial technologies development: Challenges and threats to global financial security. In *Current Problems and Ways of Industry Development: Equipment and Technologies* (pp. 355–363). Springer International Publishing. DOI: 10.1007/978-3-030-69421-0_38

Riad, K., & Elhoseny, M. (2022). A blockchain-based key-revocation access control for open banking. *Wireless Communications and Mobile Computing, 2022*(1), 3200891. DOI: 10.1155/2022/3200891

Rjoub, H., Adebayo, T. S., & Kirikkaleli, D. (2023). Blockchain technology-based FinTech banking sector involvement using adaptive neuro-fuzzy-based K-nearest neighbors algorithm. *Financial Innovation, 9*(1), 65. DOI: 10.1186/s40854-023-00469-3 PMID: 36919101

Sakas, D. P., Giannakopoulos, N. T., Terzi, M. C., Kanellos, N., & Liontakis, A. (2023). Digital transformation management of supply chain firms based on big data from DeFi social media profiles. *Electronics (Basel), 12*(20), 4219. DOI: 10.3390/electronics12204219

Salah, S. (2024). *77 Pillars of Quality and the Pursuit of Excellence: A Guide to Basic Concepts and Lean Six Sigma Tools for Practitioners, Managers, and Entrepreneurs*. CRC Press. DOI: 10.4324/9781032688374

Sasikumar, A., Karthikeyan, B., Arunkumar, S., Saravanan, P., Subramaniyaswamy, V., & Ravi, L. (2022). Blockchain-based decentralized user authentication scheme for letter of guarantee in financial contract management. *Malaysian Journal of Computer Science*, •••, 62–73.

Sood, K., Grima, S., Sharma, G., & Balusamy, B. (Eds.). (2024). *The Application of Emerging Technology and Blockchain in the Insurance Industry*. CRC Press.

Sreekanth, P. V., & Kiran, K. B. (2024). Digital Transformation in Banks: Evidence from Indian Banking Industry. In Interdisciplinary Research in Technology and Management (pp. 262-269). CRC Press.

Sujee, S., Solanki, R., & Dalwai, T. (2022, March). Technology innovations for business growth–impact of AI and blockchain on financial services. In *International Conference on Business and Technology* (pp. 1283-1292). Cham: Springer International Publishing.

Suri, M. (2021). The scope for blockchain ecosystem. Blockchain for Business: How It Works and Creates Value, 29-58.

Taha, A., Zakaria, A., Kim, D., & Suri, N. (2020, April). Decentralized runtime monitoring approach relying on the ethereum blockchain infrastructure. In 2020 IEEE International Conference on Cloud Engineering (IC2E) (pp. 134-143). IEEE. DOI: 10.1109/IC2E48712.2020.00021

Talha Talukder, A. A., Mahmud, M. A. I., Sultana, A., Pranto, T. H., Haque, A. B., & Rahman, R. M. (2022). A customer satisfaction centric food delivery system based on blockchain and smart contract. *Journal of Information and Telecommunication*, *6*(4), 501–524. DOI: 10.1080/24751839.2022.2117121

Thaman, M. (2022). Blockchain-Based Framework–A Scientific Tool for Developing a Robust Banking System. Blockchain Technology in Corporate Governance: Transforming Business and Industries, 303-324.

Thommandru, A., & Chakka, B. (2023). Recalibrating the banking sector with blockchain technology for effective anti-money laundering compliances by banks. *Sustainable Futures : An Applied Journal of Technology, Environment and Society*, *5*, 100107. DOI: 10.1016/j.sftr.2023.100107

Tran, S. (2019, September 16). Crypto Exchange OKEx Delists Five Privacy Coins due to FATF Rules. Blockchain News.

Trivedi, S. (2023). Blockchain framework for insurance industry. *International Journal on Management of Innovation & Technology*, *20*(06), 2350034. DOI: 10.1142/S0219877023500347

Trivedi, S. (2024). Blockchain Technology and Structural Change in Financial Services. In The Application of Emerging Technology and Blockchain in the Insurance Industry (pp. 249-263). River Publishers.

Tsvetkov, B., & Kostadinov, H. (2021). Using DLT in software lifecycle management. In Advanced Computing in Industrial Mathematics: 13th Annual Meeting of the Bulgarian Section of SIAM, December 18-20, 2018, Sofia, Bulgaria, Revised Selected Papers (pp. 393-404). Springer International Publishing.

Vaddadi, V. R., Annepu, P. V. R., Gollapalli, N., Challa, A., Andhavarapu, S. B., & Botta, P. K. (2023, January). Exploiting Cyber Threats And Protecting Cryptocurrencies Toward Bitcoin Exchanges. In 2023 5th Biennial International Conference on Nascent Technologies in Engineering (ICNTE) (pp. 1-6). IEEE. DOI: 10.1109/ICNTE56631.2023.10146649

Vinther Daugaard, T., Bisgaard Jensen, J., Kauffman, R. J., & Kim, K. (2024). Blockchain solutions with consensus algorithms and immediate finality:: Toward Panopticon-style monitoring to enhance anti-money laundering.

Visconti-Caparrós, J. M., & Campos-Blázquez, J. R. (2022). The development of alternate payment methods and their impact on customer behavior: The Bizum case in Spain. *Technological Forecasting and Social Change*, *175*, 121330. DOI: 10.1016/j.techfore.2021.121330

Vittala, K. P., Ahmad, S. S., Seranmadevi, R., & Tyagi, A. K. (2024). Emerging Technology Adoption and Applications for Modern Society Towards Providing Smart Banking Solutions. In Enhancing Medical Imaging with Emerging Technologies (pp. 315-329). IGI Global.

Yamuna, S., & Sendhilkumar, K. S. (2023, January). Blockchain based Roaming fraud prevention using LSTM model in 4G LTE Network. In 2023 13th International Conference on Cloud Computing, Data Science & Engineering (Confluence) (pp. 222-229). IEEE.

Yang, Z., Ali, S., Tao, W., & Chen, H. (2024). From Transactions to Transformation: Exploring the Impact of Blockchain on Customer Financial Well-being. *SAGE Open*, *14*(2), 21582440241253955. DOI: 10.1177/21582440241253955

Yu, F., Bi, W., Cao, N., Li, H., & Higgs, R. (2023). Customer Churn Prediction Framework of Inclusive Finance Based on Blockchain Smart Contract. *Computer Systems Science and Engineering*, *47*(1), 1–17. DOI: 10.32604/csse.2023.018349

Zeba, G., & Čičak, M. (2023, May). Cybersecurity Challenges in Modern Supply Chain. In International Conference "New Technologies, Development and Applications" (pp. 534-541). Cham: Springer Nature Switzerland. DOI: 10.1007/978-3-031-31066-9_59

Zhang, L., Xie, Y., Zheng, Y., Xue, W., Zheng, X., & Xu, X. (2020). The challenges and countermeasures of blockchain in finance and economics. *Systems Research and Behavioral Science*, *37*(4), 691–698. DOI: 10.1002/sres.2710

Chapter 15
The Role of Big Data Analytics in Enhancing Service Quality in Tourism:
A Literature Review

Ruchika Kulshrestha
https://orcid.org/0000-0002-5188-9204
GLA University, Mathura, India

ABSTRACT

Technology, especially big data analytics, is revolutionising the tourist industry, a major contributor to worldwide economies. The literature highlights the significance of big data analytics in improving service quality within the tourism business. Tourism businesses can reduce their environmental impact by analysing ecological data, therefore responding to the growing demand for sustainable travel. BDA aids destination management organisations (DMOs) in crowd management, improving visitor experience, and safeguarding cultural heritage sites. This study consolidates prior studies to clarify how Big Data Analytics improves the quality of tourism services. The assessment illustrates to practitioners and policymakers the utilisation of Big Data analytics for competitive advantage and improved service delivery through a literature analysis. To fully realise the potential of Big Data analytics in tourism transformation, future research must tackle current restrictions, explore upcoming technologies, and promote multidisciplinary methodologies.

INTRODUCTION

The offering of outstanding customer service is essential for success in service sectors (Rauch, D.A.,2015). Service quality in tourism has drawn increased academic interest among several tourism-related issues. Research studies that have been conducted in academic publications employing SERVQUAL, have been published in academic publications (Meesala, A., & Paul, J., 2018, Rauch,D. et al.,2015).

Moreover, due to the extensive nature of tourism, which encompasses several business environments, limited research has adopted a holistic approach to assess service quality especially in the case of big data and analytics within the sector. Consequently, the primary aim of our study was to identify the most impactful research, along with general and specific concerns related to tourism service quality, and to examine the present and future trajectories and trends of this research domain using a systematic literature review. This research proposes to conduct a thorough literature review to elucidate the methods by which big data analytics contribute to competitive performance enhancements.

DOI: 10.4018/979-8-3693-7447-4.ch015

The progress into data mining techniques and mobile technologies has led to the swift expansion of big data analytics in several industries. The implementation of BDA can yield advantages, including cost reduction, enhanced decision-making, and improved quality of products and services.Big Data Analytics has been effectively employed in fundamental company processes, including accounting, marketing, supply chain, and operations. Insurance businesses have employed big data analytics and data mining to enhance the precision of policy pricing by leveraging diverse big data from various sources.

This study seeks to fill the research gaps in the literature about the application of Big Data analytics to improve service quality in tourism using an analysis of literature review.Literature reviews (LRs) are acknowledged for their capacity to encapsulate significant insights regarding a pertinent subject and to direct subsequent research in that area. This systematic literature review seeks to address four research questions (RQs) as outlined below: RQ1. What is the current status of research on the application of Big Data analytics to enhance service quality in the tourism sector? RQ2. In what areas related to service quality in the tourism industry is the application of Big Data analytics being examined? RQ3. What future initiatives could promote research on Big Data analytics in improving service quality within the tourism sector?

LITERATURE REVIEW

Organisations aim to understand the importance and relevance of data to enhance decision-making (Ahmed et al., 2017). In order to accomplish the process of big data analytics, prospective insights must be extracted from the data. (Galetsi, P., et al. 2020; Mergel, Rethemeyer, and Mergel, I. et al. 2016) The term "big data analytics" makes reference to a variety of data-intensive methods that are utilised for the purpose of analysing and synthesising enormous datasets.

Extensive data obtained via information interchange across many systems is sometimes referred to as 'big data' (Bahri et al., 2018; Al-Bahri, B., 2020). Although referred to be 'huge' data, its importance resides in its ability to collect intricate details pertaining to the subject of study (George G. et al. 2014; McAfee et al., 2012). Big data analytics advantages both large and small tourism organisations (Evans, 2005). Data analytics will allow these enterprises to identify links between employee engagement and quantitative data concerning consumer pleasure, thereby aiding tourism organisations in enhancing service quality. Those that work with big data have the responsibility of monitoring the amount, velocity, diversity, and validity of the data while also ensuring that the information that is gathered is used in an ethical manner (Morrisson and Abraham, 2015). The use of big data analytics is becoming increasingly prevalent in a variety of management fields, including the travel and tourist industry.

From Tourism Perspective

The implementation of big data analytics has been observed in a number of different aspects of the tourism industry. The Changi Airport in Singapore makes use of information technology to collect operational data regarding the movements of inbound planes, aircraft, and service vehicles on the ground, as well as the flow of passengers and the volume of passengers at terminals. Real-time visuals and interactive maps are used to display all of the data, which enables airport personnel to quickly resolve operational concerns and minimise manpower shortages (Choudhury, 2015). This results in an improvement in the quality of service provided.

According to Ogbeide, G. C., et al. (2021), big data analytics makes it possible for the tourism industry to conduct investigations that are both more extensive and smarter, hence improving the sector's overall service quality. According to Pandey and Kulshrestha (2021), the tourist industry collects significant amounts of data from both service providers and clients by means of the establishment of a service blueprint in hotels. According to Mariani et al. (2019), tourism businesses, destination administrators, and customers all participate in the generation and use of substantial amounts of data. It is through the application of data analytics that decision-making is improved at all levels. It is possible for researchers and practitioners to make use of user-generated content (UGC) data in order to gain an understanding of the perspectives and behaviours of tourists (Cheng and Jin, 2019; Ranjbari et al., 2020; Zhang et al., 2019).

Tourism enterprises can pinpoint particular micro-moments throughout the travel continuum and gather extensive data concerning travellers' requirements and information-seeking behaviours. The tools enable organisations to make instantaneous advertising decisions through real-time information and analytics. Consequently, big data analytics can assist the tourism sector in effectively anticipating prospective business prospects (Think with Google, 2016).

Moreover, a predominance of methods involving conventional econometric techniques was also noted. Future research should enhance the utilisation of device and transaction data, notwithstanding worries regarding cost and privacy, and researchers ought to employ cross-domain and multi-type data to elucidate the complexities of the tourist industry (Line, N.D.,2020). The authors noted that the majority of the Big data studies tackled specific research issues in a relatively fragmented manner, hence compromising the possibility to produce a coherent research stream (Lee, M.,2019). Additionally, they mentioned that there were epistemological difficulties that had not been answered. In spite of the fact that they have made major contributions, the literature reviews that are now being conducted on Big data (Li et al., 2018; Mariani et al., 2018) showcase a numerous limitations.

From Service Quality Perspective

The present status of study on employing Big Data Analytics to enhance service quality in the tourism sector is substantial and swiftly advancing (Arici, H. E.et al.,2023 & Jich-Yan, T.et al.,2020) Academics and business professionals have increasingly acknowledged the revolutionary capacity of Big Data Analytics in meeting the evolving needs of contemporary travelers (Amat-Lefort, N., et al.,2023).Research demonstrates that Big Data Analytics is extensively utilised to customise travel experiences, improve operational efficiency, and elevate client contentment to enhance service quality (Amerta, L., & Madhavi, I.,2023, Rane, J.,et al.,2024).Research underscores the crucial function of analytics in deriving actionable insights from extensive information produced by social media platforms, online reviews, booking systems, and IoT-enabled devices. These data empower organisations to formulate focused marketing campaigns, anticipate customer preferences, and customise services accordingly (Avula, M., & Sithole, T., 2024).

The incorporation of artificial intelligence (AI) and machine learning (ML) into big data analytics (BDA) has been a primary research focus (Koshy, S.,et al.,2021). These technologies augment the predictive powers of analytics, enabling tourism enterprises to foresee market trends, optimise resource management, and alleviate hazards. Dynamic pricing models driven by big data analytics enable hotels and airlines to modify rates in real-time, enhancing revenue management and customer satisfaction (Egan, D., & Haynes, N. C., 2019).. Smart tourism, utilising data-driven insights for sustainable and efficient destination management, is an area of increasing prominence (Sarkar, S. K.,et al.,2020 & Sarker, I. H., 2022).

Privacy issues, data fragmentation, and insufficient technical competence in small and medium companies (SMEs) impede the comprehensive adoption of big data analytics (BDA) in the tourism sector (Beck, J.,et al.,2017 & Ranganai, N. et al. 2023). Ethical considerations about data use and adherence to legislation such as GDPR are essential focal points. Moreover, research is investigating novel methods to enhance the accessibility of Big Data Analytics (BDA), especially for small and medium-sized enterprises (SMEs), via cloud-based solutions and standardised data-sharing frameworks.

The literature emphasises the pivotal role of Big data analytics in influencing the future of tourism through the promotion of service innovation and quality improvement (Ranganai, N. et al. 2023). With technological progress and increased data proficiency among businesses, forthcoming research is anticipated to tackle current deficiencies, including the creation of economical solutions, the integration of big data analytics with emerging technologies such as blockchain and augmented reality, and the promotion of global collaboration to standardise practices (Rane

J.et al.,2024 & Ratna, S.,2024). This developing body of research demonstrates a robust dedication to utilising data for a more tailored, efficient, and sustainable tourist sector.

RESEARCH METHODOLOGY

This research seeks to address a deficiency in the literature by systematically evaluating the volume and calibre of studies undertaken in the hotel and tourism sectors use the PRISMA framework (Liberati et al.,2009) and Moher et al. 2009). All of the reporting steps are laid out in a flowchart, including the criteria for inclusion and exclusion.

The review methodology, which includes search terms, databases, and screening criteria, was developed in accordance with the study objectives to conduct the literature search. An first exploratory search in Scopus was conducted to identify relevant search terms such as "Tourism," "Travel," "data analytics," and "big data analytics." Search strings containing these terms were utilised to identify studies conducted in tourism-related research.

The literature search against the scopus database yielded 373 records as of 18 November 2024. Each paper was read by the author separately to ascertain its relevance as the assessment went along. Prior to reading the complete texts of publications, we read their abstracts to get a feel for them. Additionally, research were excluded due to their methodology (e.g., qualitative, human coding of text). Studies that relied on crawlers and scraping services—which utilise analytical techniques to obtain data but do not analyse it—were also rejected. The same logic applied to articles that did not devote enough space to topics directly connected to tourism. The final analysis relied on a thorough assessment of the entire texts from the 163 entries that made it through the screening process. We were only able to find 154 studies that met our criteria. In order to find any papers that might have been missed, the authors independently reviewed the reference lists of the eligible articles at this stage. The number of papers included in the final analysis increased to sixty-three after this handsearch turned up three more. Few number of publications that were assessed and discarded at various phases of the literature review is shown in Figure 1. A few tweaks/strings were made to the reporting flowchart so it aligns with the PRISMA statement (Moher et al., 2009).

RESULTS AND DISCUSSIONS

The author identifies a steady rise in interest in exploring and utilising Big Data and analytics within the tourism sector, commencing in 2013. This principle is applicable in other relevant domains. The quantity of scientific outputs related to Big Data and analytics has increased fivefold from 2015 to 2020, and also exhibits a fivefold increase when examining the cumulative distribution. Figure 1 illustrates the cumulative distribution of the number of publications from the sample obtained from the Scopus database.While in 2025 only 1 document is published and indexed in scopus.

Figure 1. Documents by Year

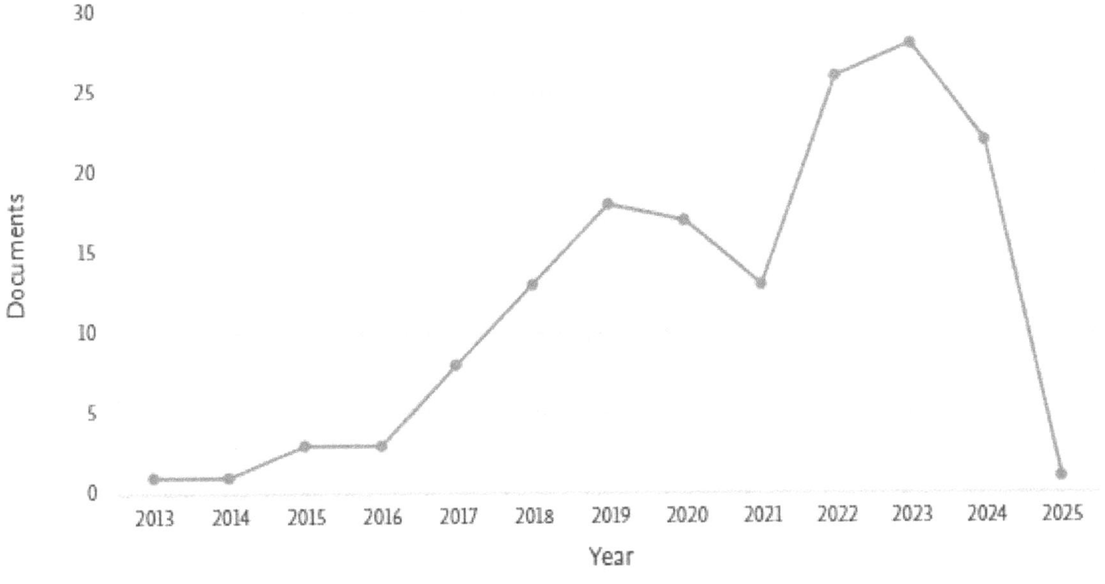

The use of these approaches is still in its early stages, according to a Scopus assessment of tourism-related papers (Figure 1). Between 2022 and 2024, there was a strong upward trend in the number of publications, reaching a peak of 28 in 2018. See figure 2 for a breakdown of the 39 journals that published the articles. These journals cover a wide range of academic disciplines, including business, management, accounting, economics, computer science, decision science, environmental sciences, psychology, and econometrics and finance. The findings show that many journals are open to publishing articles from the wide area of tourism research.

Figure 2. Documents by subject area.

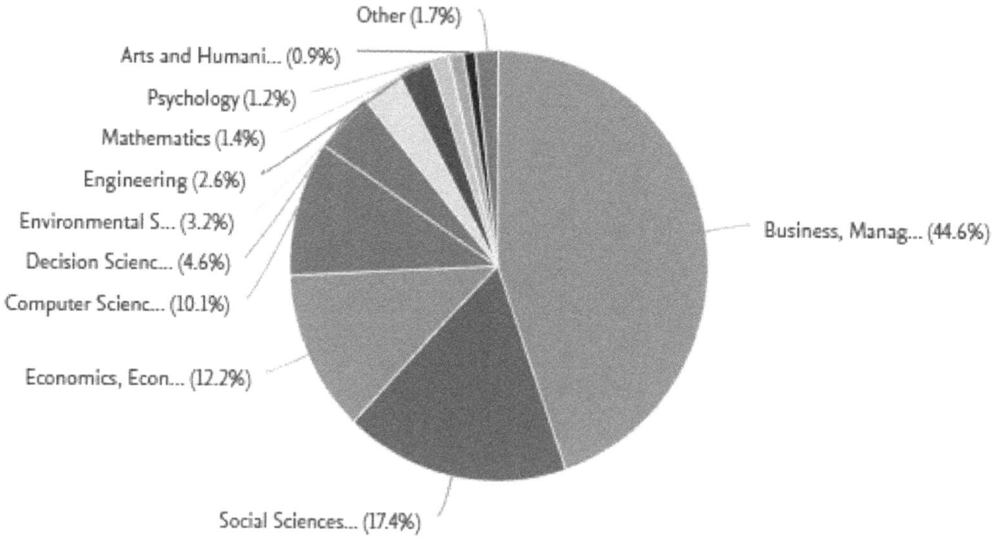

The analysis of the publications' content was performed by examining their titles, abstracts, and keywords. Consistent with prior research (Mariani et al., 2018), this suffices to infer the principal themes and concerns addressed in the literature. It shows the word clouds of the most frequent terms such as data, tourism, big data analytics,destinations.

Figure 3. Word cloud from scopus

Analysis of Big Data and Analytics Works In Tourism Sector

Big Data and Analytics have significantly influenced the tourism industry by altering the management of operations, decision-making processes, and customer engagement among stakeholders. The increasing utilisation of Big Data Analytics has resulted in substantial progress in comprehending customer behaviour, optimising resource distribution, and improving service quality. Nonetheless, its integration poses both obstacles and opportunities, necessitating a comprehensive understanding of its implications inside the industry.The papers are reviewed on the basis of the citations (Table 1.)

Table 1. Reviewed Papers on the basis of Top Citations

S. No	Topic of the Paper	Authors	Year	No of Citations	Journal	Type of Paper	Data collection ,methods and techniques	Conclusion
1	Growth of digital brand name through customer satisfaction with big data analytics in the hospitality sector after the COVID-19 crisis	Sakas, D.P., Reklitis, D.P., Terzi, M.C., Glaveli, N.	2023	12	*International Journal of Information Management Data Insights,*	Empirical	Behavioral analytics ,agent based simulation model Descriptive analysis, persons coefficient and regression analysis	The current study provides evidence on how customers' online behaviour affects corporate digital branding and offers advice on how organisations can optimise customer happiness using big data analytics. As the literature implies, collecting and analysing million consumers' digital behaviour and journey might yield valuable insights for HTT organisations (Buhalis & Volchek, 2021; Lv et al., 2022). Information overload may assist marketing managers, although there is minimal proof (Saxena & Lamest, 2018). This study analyses website and social media data from 189 hotels and 5,7 million visits to create a brand communication strategy.
2	Mobilising big data analytics capabilities to improve performance of tourism supply chains: the moderating role of dynamic capabilities	Gupta, Y., Khan, F.M., Kumar, A., Luthra, S., Queiroz, M.M.	2024	6	*International Journal of Logistics Management*	Empirical	Confirmatory factor analysis (CFA) was applied to confirm the constructs, followed by partial least squares structural equation modelling (PLS-SEM)	This study considerably enhances the tourist sector in India, as tourism is a vital contributor to the nation's gross domestic product. This study theoretically advances the resource-based view (RBV) and practically urges tourism experts to advocate for the use of BDAC to improve the performance of TSCs. The study's originality is in its attempt to understand the moderating role of dynamic capabilities that influence BDAC to enhance TSC performance.
3	Exploring the Landscape of Smart Tourism: A Systematic Bibliometric Review of the Literature of the Internet of Things	Rosário, A.T., Dias, J.C.	2024	3	*Administrative Sciences,*	Qualitative	Prisma Method	The research contributes to the IoT-enabled smart tourism ecosystem and the Big data analyses sensor data. Smart tourism relies on cloud computing for data storage, networking, databases, analytics, and applications. Tourism operations improve corporate performance and guest happiness by using IoT data to make strategic decisions. Research opportunities arise from smart tourism and the Internet of Things. Smart tourism IoT research could focus on security and privacy, blockchain technology, edge computing, and tourist-system interaction. These research lines address challenges and harness opportunities at the convergence of smart tourism and the Internet of Things, enabling creative solutions to suit tourism's growing needs in a technologically evolved world.

continued on following page

Table 1. Continued

S. No	Topic of the Paper	Authors	Year	No of Citations	Journal	Type of Paper	Data collection ,methods and techniques	Conclusion
4	Internet of Things and Big Data Analytics for Risk Management in Digital Tourism Ecosystems	Popova, P., Marinova, K., Popov, V.	2023	2	*Risks*	Qualitative	IoT and BDA technologies, SLR Method	Tourism business growth depends on smart TD design, operation, and management enabled by IoT and BDA. Smart TDs gain from integrating IoT into their IT architecture and using BDA to analyse data. These technologies may be useful in risk management. IoT and BDA use by smart TD DE participants mitigates some systemic risks but introduces others.
5	The Value of Web Data Scraping: An Application to TripAdvisor	Barbera, G., Araujo, L., Fernandes, S.	2023	11	*Big Data and Cognitive Computing,*	Qualitative	based on a project for smart tourism consultancy,	examines how web data scraping (WDS) might yield actionable information from TripAdvisor. WDS can improve tourism decision-making by analysing massive amounts of unstructured data.
6	A critical reflection on analytics and artificial intelligence based analytics in hospitality and tourism management research	Mariani, M., Wirtz, J.	2023	19	*International Journal of Contemporary Hospitality Management,*	Qualitative	SLR	an expanding and accelerating corpus of research on analytics; yet, the literature exhibits an inconsistency in the use of terminology and meanings pertaining to analytics. Publications infrequently employ scientific definitions of analytics and its various types; while AI and ML are crucial enabling technologies for cognitive analytics, research in hospitality and tourism management has not explicitly associated these concepts with analytics nor differentiated cognitive analytics from other analytics forms that do not depend on ML. The term "cognitive analytics" appears to be absent from the literature on hospitality and tourist management.
7	Modelling competitive advantage using the concepts of big data and social media to develop a sustainability strategy	Horng, J.-S., Liu, C.-H., Chou, S.-F., Yu, T.-Y., Ng, Y.-L.	2023	7	*Tourism Review*	Empirical	PLS-SEM	examined how Big data analytic skills indirectly impact hotels' economic advantage through sustainability promises and marketing also enhancing the relationships necessary to the development of BD analytics capabilities. The influence of sustainability outcomes that contribute to enhancing hotels' competitive advantages. The findings are expanded upon in the current study, with implications for management theory and practice addressed in the subsequent section.

continued on following page

Table 1. Continued

S. No	Topic of the Paper	Authors	Year	No of Citations	Journal	Type of Paper	Data collection ,methods and techniques	Conclusion
8	The digital traveller: implications for data ethics and data governance in tourism and hospitality	Yallop, A.C., Gică, O.A., Moisescu, O.I., Coro , M.M., Séraphin, H.	2023	19	*Journal of Consumer Marketing,*	Qualitative	Scoping review of literature	examines the ethical and governance issues arising from the digitalisation of tourism. It underscores the increasing dependence on big data and digital instruments, accentuating apprehensions regarding data privacy, accountability, and equity in their application. The study promotes responsible governance of information structures and moral standards to reconcile innovation with the protection of users' rights, so ensuring trust in the tourist and hospitality sectors.
9	Are hospitality/tourism curricula ready for big data?	Sia, P.Y.-H., Saidin, S.S., Iskandar, Y.H.P.	2021	18	*Journal of Hospitality and Tourism Technology,*	Qualitative	Literature Review paper	emphasises the growing significance of incorporating big data analytics into hospitality and tourism education. It presents a conceptual framework to assist educators in developing curricula that respond to technological changes and industrial requirements. The research highlights the necessity of equipping students with the ability to analyse intricate datasets, implement data-driven decision-making, and utilise big data for innovation in the hospitality and tourism sectors. Primary issues involve reconciling technical competencies with hospitality management principles and maintaining curriculum alignment with the dynamic requirements of the sector.
10	Connectivity, sport events, and tourism development of Mandalika's special economic zone: A perspective from big data cognitive analytics	Caraka, R.E., Wardhana, I.W., Kim, Y., ... Noh, M., Pardamean, B.	2023	9	*Cogent Business and Management,*	Empirical	Cognitive analytics, Time series analysis, network connectivity, sentiment analysis	addresses a policy mix comprising infrastructure provisions (air connectivity, sports facilities, and amenities), sporting events, and fiscal policies aimed at fostering tourism development in Mandalika to enhance economic potential in West Nusa Tenggara and Lombok, as part of Indonesia's exclusive economic zone. Crucially, insights gained from the Indonesian experience may assist other developing nations in formulating policies and plans to enhance their tourism sectors through the use of appropriate tools, including infrastructure, events, and fiscal policies.

continued on following page

Table 1. Continued

S. No	Topic of the Paper	Authors	Year	No of Citations	Journal	Type of Paper	Data collection ,methods and techniques	Conclusion
11	Multichannel Digital Marketing Optimizations through Big Data Analytics in the Tourism and Hospitality Industry	Sakas, D.P., Reklitis, D.P., Terzi, M.C., Vassilakis, C.	2022	21	*Journal of Theoretical and Applied Electronic Commerce Research,*	Empirical	Correlation and Regression analysis FCM Optimization Scenarios	examines how big data analytics may improve multichannel digital marketing in the tourist and hospitality sectors. It suggests a system that combines online analytics, statistical analysis, fuzzy cognitive mapping, and agent-based simulation to enhance consumer acquisition and digital branding.
12	Big data analytics and sustainable tourism: A comprehensive review and network based analysis for potential future research	Agrawal, R., Wankhede, V.A., Kumar, A., Luthra, S., Huisingh, D.	2022	34	*International Journal of Information Management Data Insights*	Review Paper	SLR, Network analysis, bibliometric analysis	This study examined how Big Data Analytics (BDA) may improve tourist sustainability. The authors used systematic literature review, bibliometric analysis, and network analysis to examine 187 big data analytics and sustainable tourism publications. The review discusses how Big Data Analytics (BDA) affects tourism sustainability. This study found that Big Data Analytics, the Internet of Things, and data mining in tourism systems speed up sustainable tourist experience design and delivery.

CONCLUSION

The expansion of big data and related analytics research underscores the necessity of developing an integrated framework to monitor the application of big data analytics for improving service quality, hence enabling systematic and thorough study of this intricate subject. The author characterised this rising study issue in the tourist sector, particularly regarding service quality, by examining the research goal, highly referenced papers, paper types, annual document distribution, and analysis methods. It is advisable to adopt a more comprehensive understanding of service quality enhancement through the analysis of qualitative data.

In order to evaluate the analysis's robustness, future study should conduct accuracy tests and performance measurements of analytical approaches (Ye et al., 2009; Zhang et al., 2011).

Furthermore, certain methodologies seem to be underutilised in tourism, such as predictive analytics employing explanatory assessment techniques, service-dominant logic, machine learning, and experience economy theory. The proliferation of these methodologies may expedite big data analytics study concerning travel, tourism, and service quality, which have been recognised as less commonly examined compared to tourist opinion mining.

This study concludes with a thorough analysis of trends and the present status of big data analytics in tourist research. Subsequent evaluations of big data analytics in this domain should encompass comprehensive elucidations and recommendations pertaining to best practices in big data analytics, aimed at assisting tourism researchers in their technique selection and implementation. These optimal methodologies must, in part, be discerned and assimilated from other study domains, including travel patterns, hospitality, the hotel business, and food production.

Theoretical Implications

In the tourism industry, Big Data Analytics has emerged as a transformative instrument that has the potential to redefine service quality by providing actionable insights, enhancing operational efficiency, and providing consumers with more personalised experiences. When viewed from a theoretical perspective, the introduction of Big Data Analytics into service quality frameworks has a number of implications that have the potential to improve our understanding of customer satisfaction, service delivery, and value co-creation. Utilising the insights that are gained from Big Data Analytics, the SERVQUAL methodology, which is routinely used to evaluate service quality across five dimensions (TRRAE: tangibility, reliability, responsiveness, assurance, and empathy), has the potential to be improved. The capture of data in real time from customer contacts, reviews, and social media platforms provides a dynamic understanding of service shortcomings, which in turn facilitates the continuous improvement of quality. In addition to the traditional survey approaches, sentiment analysis of user-generated content (UGC) on platforms such as TripAdvisor offers immediate insights regarding the performance of the service.

Big Data Analytics provides a conceptual framework that may be utilised to appreciate the function that customers play in the process of co-creation by means of their active sharing of data and feedback. Customer participation in the design of their experiences is made possible by the use of real-time data, which allow for incremental improvements to be made to services. This is in line with the shift from one of passive consumption to one of active participation in the tourism industry. The big data analytics makes it easier to investigate tourism as an all-encompassing ecosystem by defining the interactions that take place between various stakeholders, including service providers, customers, and regulatory agencies. Using network theory, one may gain an understanding of the interdependencies that exist within the tourist ecosystem. This can be accomplished through the use of data analytics to improve resource allocation and stakeholder collaboration. There are ethical and sustainability questions that arise as a result of the adoption of Big Data Analytics in the tourism industry, which calls for theoretical investigation. Within the framework of corporate social responsibility (CSR) and stakeholder theory, it is necessary to take into consideration issues pertaining to data governance, questions of privacy, and equal access to resources. It is possible that future theoretical advances may study how Big data analytics might be able to integrate economic goals with ethical and environmentally responsible service practices. In order to fully fulfil the potential of Big data analytics in terms of enhancing service quality, future research needs to investigate these theoretical intersections in a more comprehensive manner, addressing topics such as data ethics and the digital divide.

Limitations and Future Research

This study contains certain drawbacks. Initially, we gathered data exclusively from the academic database Scopus, consistent with prior research. Subsequent research may incorporate outputs from Google Scholar and Web of Science, notwithstanding the aforementioned limitations. Despite its constraints, our study allowed us to discern some key themes that may inform future research utilising big data and analytics in the tourism sector to improve service quality. Theoretical developments in the social sciences may be linked to preexisting ideas, and researchers must to clarify the theories to which they seek to contribute in a clear and concise manner, as well as the theoretical assumptions that underpin their study. Researchers in the future should work to improve their understanding of algorithm design in order to more accurately interpret their findings and solve the inherent constraints of their discoveries.

The proliferation of diverse empirical approaches may expedite research in big data analytics concerning travel patterns and service quality, which have been recognised as less commonly examined compared to tourist opinion mining. In conclusion, this paper offers a thorough analysis of trends and the present condition of tourist research. Optimal practices must be found and implemented from other research domains, such as the analysis of tourist behaviour and tourist satisfaction.

REFERENCES

Agrawal, R., Wankhede, V. A., Kumar, A., Luthra, S., & Huisingh, D. (2022). Big data analytics and sustainable tourism: A comprehensive review and network based analysis for potential future research. *International Journal of Information Management Data Insights*, *2*(2), 100122. DOI: 10.1016/j.jjimei.2022.100122

Ahmed, E., Yaqoob, I., Hashem, I. A. T., Khan, I., Ahmed, A. I. A., Imran, M., & Vasilakos, A. V. (2017). The role of big data analytics in internet of things. *Computer Networks*, *129*, 459–471. DOI: 10.1016/j.comnet.2017.06.013

Al-Bahri, B., Noronha, H., Pandey, J., Singh, A. V., & Rana, A. (2020, June). Evaluate the role of big data in enhancing strategic decision making for E-governance in E-Oman portal. In *2020 8th International Conference on Reliability, Infocom Technologies and Optimization (Trends and Future Directions)(ICRITO)* (pp. 914-917). IEEE. DOI: 10.1109/ICRITO48877.2020.9197808

Amat-Lefort, N., Barravecchia, F., & Mastrogiacomo, L. (2023). Quality 4.0: Big data analytics to explore service quality attributes and their relation to user sentiment in Airbnb reviews. *International Journal of Quality & Reliability Management*, *40*(4), 990–1008. DOI: 10.1108/IJQRM-01-2022-0024

Amerta, L., & Madhavi, I. (2023). Exploring Service Quality and Customer Satisfaction in the Service Industry: A Mixed-Methods Analysis. *Journal on Economics. Management and Business Technology*, *2*(1), 1–16.

Arici, H. E., Cakmakoglu Arıcı, N., & Altinay, L. (2023). The use of big data analytics to discover customers' perceptions of and satisfaction with green hotel service quality. *Current Issues in Tourism*, *26*(2), 270–288. DOI: 10.1080/13683500.2022.2029832

Avula, M., & Sithole, T. (2024). Artificial Intelligence's Potential to Improve Operational Efficiency and Customer Experience in the Hospitality and Tourism Sectors. In *Impact of AI and Tech-Driven Solutions in Hospitality and Tourism* (pp. 351–382). IGI Global. DOI: 10.4018/979-8-3693-6755-1.ch018

Bahri, S., Zoghlami, N., Abed, M., & Tavares, J. M. R. (2018). Big data for healthcare: A survey. *IEEE Access : Practical Innovations, Open Solutions*, *7*, 7397–7408. DOI: 10.1109/ACCESS.2018.2889180

Barbera, G., Araujo, L., & Fernandes, S. (2023). The value of web data scraping: An application to TripAdvisor. *Big Data and Cognitive Computing*, *7*(3), 121. DOI: 10.3390/bdcc7030121

Beck, J., Danilenko, M., Sperber, L., Wiersma, B., & Egger, R. (2017). Connecting big data and service quality evaluation–developing a service quality map of the Austrian hospitality industry through the application of big data. *The Gaze: Journal of Tourism and Hospitality*, *8*, 40–54. DOI: 10.3126/gaze.v8i0.17831

Caraka, R. E., Wardhana, I. W., Kim, Y., Sakti, A. D., Gio, P. U., Noh, M., & Pardamean, B. (2023). Connectivity, sport events, and tourism development of Mandalika's special economic zone: A perspective from big data cognitive analytics. *Cogent Business & Management*, *10*(1), 2183565. DOI: 10.1080/23311975.2023.2183565

Cheng, M., & Jin, X. (2019). What do airbnb users care about? An analysis of online review comments. *International Journal of Hospitality Management*, *76*, 58–70. DOI: 10.1016/j.ijhm.2018.04.004

Choudhury, A. R. (2015), "*How IT helps Changi airport to be smart, sweet and swift*", available at: www.businesstimes.com.sg/focus/in-depth/cio-speaks/how-it-helps-changi-airport-to-be-smart-sweet-and-swift

Egan, D., & Haynes, N. C. (2019). Manager perceptions of big data reliability in hotel revenue management decision making. *International Journal of Quality & Reliability Management*, *36*(1), 25–39. DOI: 10.1108/IJQRM-02-2018-0056

Evans, N. (2005). Assessing the balanced scorecard as a management tool for hotels. *International Journal of Contemporary Hospitality Management, 17*(5), 376–390. DOI: 10.1108/09596110510604805

Galetsi, P., Katsaliaki, K., & Kumar, S. (2020). Big data analytics in health sector: Theoretical framework, techniques and prospects. *International Journal of Information Management, 50*, 206–216. DOI: 10.1016/j.ijinfomgt.2019.05.003

George, G., Haas, M. R., & Pentland, A. (2014). Big data and management. *Academy of Management Journal, 57*(2), 321–326. DOI: 10.5465/amj.2014.4002

Gupta, Y., Khan, F. M., Kumar, A., Luthra, S., & Queiroz, M. M. (2024). Mobilising big data analytics capabilities to improve performance of tourism supply chains: The moderating role of dynamic capabilities. *International Journal of Logistics Management, 35*(2), 649–679. DOI: 10.1108/IJLM-03-2022-0125

Horng, J. S., Liu, C. H., Chou, S. F., Yu, T. Y., & Ng, Y. L. (2023). Modelling competitive advantage using the concepts of big data and social media to develop a sustainability strategy. *Tourism Review, 78*(3), 712–725. DOI: 10.1108/TR-01-2022-0012

Jich-Yan, T., & Wen, X., Y., & Chien-Hua, W. (2020). A framework for big data analytics on service quality evaluation of online bookstore. In *Wireless Internet:12th EAI International Conference, WiCON 2019,TaiChung, Taiwan,November 26–27, 2019, Proceedings 12* (pp. 294-301). Springer International Publishing.

Koshy, S., Rahul, S., Sunitha, R., & Cheriyan, E. P. (2021). Smart grid–based big data analytics using machine learning and artificial intelligence: A survey. *Artif. Intell. Internet Things Renew. Energy Syst, 12*, 241–278. DOI: 10.1515/9783110714043-008

Lee, M., Lee, S., & Koh, Y. (2019). Multisensory experience for enhancing hotel guest experience: Empirical evidence from big data analytics. *International Journal of Contemporary Hospitality Management, 31*(11), 4313–4337. DOI: 10.1108/IJCHM-03-2018-0263

Li, H., Hu, M., & Li, G. (2020). Forecasting tourism demand with multisource big data. *Annals of Tourism Research, 83*, 102912. DOI: 10.1016/j.annals.2020.102912

Liberati, A., Altman, D. G., Tetzlaff, J., Mulrow, C., Gøtzsche, P. C., Ioannidis, J. P., Clarke, M., Devereaux, P. J., Kleijnen, J., & Moher, D. (2009). The PRISMA statement for reporting systematic reviews and meta-analyses of studies that evaluate health care interventions: Explanation and elaboration. *PLoS Medicine, 6*(7), e1000100. DOI: 10.1371/journal.pmed.1000100 PMID: 19621070

Line, N. D., Dogru, T., El-Manstrly, D., Buoye, A., Malthouse, E., & Kandampully, J. (2020). Control, use and ownership of big data: A reciprocal view of customer big data value in the hospitality and tourism industry. *Tourism Management, 80*, 104106. DOI: 10.1016/j.tourman.2020.104106

Mariani, M., Di Fatta, G., & Di Felice, M. (2018). Understanding customer satisfaction with services by leveraging big data: The role of services attributes and consumers' cultural background. *IEEE Access : Practical Innovations, Open Solutions, 7*, 8195–8208. DOI: 10.1109/ACCESS.2018.2887300

Mariani, M., & Wirtz, J. (2023). A critical reflection on analytics and artificial intelligence based analytics in hospitality and tourism management research. *International Journal of Contemporary Hospitality Management, 35*(8), 2929–2943. DOI: 10.1108/IJCHM-08-2022-1006

Mariani, M. M., Baggio, R., Fuchs, M., & Höpken, W. (2018). Business intelligence and big data in hospitality and tourism: A systematic literature review. *International Journal of Contemporary Hospitality Management, 30*(12), 3514–3554. DOI: 10.1108/IJCHM-07-2017-0461

Mariani, M. M., Di Felice, M., & Mura, M. (2016). Facebook as a destination marketing tool: Evidence from Italian regional destination management organizations. *Tourism Management, 54*, 321–343. DOI: 10.1016/j.tourman.2015.12.008

McAfee, A., Brynjolfsson, E., Davenport, T. H., Patil, D. J., & Barton, D. (2012). Big data: The management revolution. *Harvard Business Review, 90*(10), 60–68. PMID: 23074865

Meesala, A., & Paul, J. (2018). Service quality, consumer satisfaction and loyalty in hospitals: Thinking for the future. *Journal of Retailing and Consumer Services, 40*, 261–269. DOI: 10.1016/j.jretconser.2016.10.011

Mergel, I., Rethemeyer, R. K., & Isett, K. (2016). Big data in public affairs. *Public Administration Review, 76*(6), 928–937. DOI: 10.1111/puar.12625

Moher, D., Liberati, A., Tetzlaff, J., & Altman, D. G. (2009). Preferred reporting items for systematic reviews and Meta-analyses: The PRISMA statement. *Annals of Internal Medicine, 151*(4), 264–269. DOI: 10.7326/0003-4819-151-4-200908180-00135 PMID: 19622511

Morrisson, J. D., & Abraham, J. D. (2015). Reasons for enthusiasm and caution regarding bigdata for applied selection research. *The Industrial-Organizational Psychologist, 52*, 3, 134–139.

Ogbeide, G. C., Fu, Y. Y., & Cecil, A. K. (2021). Are hospitality/tourism curricula ready for big data? *Journal of Hospitality and Tourism Technology, 12*(1), 112–123. DOI: 10.1108/JHTT-09-2017-0081

Ogbeide, G. C., Fu, Y. Y., & Cecil, A. K. (2021). Are hospitality/tourism curricula ready for big data? *Journal of Hospitality and Tourism Technology, 12*(1), 112–123. DOI: 10.1108/JHTT-09-2017-0081

Pandey, A., & Kulshrestha, R. (2021). Service blueprint 4.0: A service design for hotels beyond COVID-19. *Worldwide Hospitality and Tourism Themes, 13*(5), 610–621. DOI: 10.1108/WHATT-05-2021-0076

Park, J., & Jeong, E. (2019). Service quality in tourism: A systematic literature review and keyword network analysis. *Sustainability (Basel), 11*(13), 3665. DOI: 10.3390/su11133665

Popova, P., Marinova, K., & Popov, V. (2023). Internet of Things and Big Data Analytics for Risk Management in Digital Tourism Ecosystems. *Risks, 11*(10), 180. DOI: 10.3390/risks11100180

Rane, J., Kaya, O., Mallick, S. K., & Rane, N. L. (2024). Enhancing customer satisfaction and loyalty in service quality through artificial intelligence, machine learning, internet of things, blockchain, big data, and ChatGPT. *Generative Artificial Intelligence in Agriculture, Education, and Business*, 84-141.

Ranganai, N., Basera, V., & Muwani, T. S. (2023). Impact of big data and analytics on quality management in rural tourism in southern Africa-Zimbabwe: A systematic literature review. *JOURNAL OF TOURISM, CULINARY, AND ENTREPRENEURSHIP (JTCE), 3*(2).

Ranjbari, M., Shams Esfandabadi, Z., & Scagnelli, S. D. (2020). A big data approach to map the service quality of short-stay accommodation sharing. *International Journal of Contemporary Hospitality Management, 32*(8), 2575–2592. DOI: 10.1108/IJCHM-02-2020-0097

Ratna, S., Saide, S., Putri, A. M., Indrajit, R. E., & Muwardi, D. (2024). Digital transformation in tourism and hospitality industry: A literature review of blockchain, financial technology, and knowledge management. *EuroMed Journal of Business, 19*(1), 84–112. DOI: 10.1108/EMJB-04-2023-0118

Rauch, D. A., Collins, M. D., Nale, R. D., & Barr, P. B. (2015). Measuring service quality in mid-scale hotels. *International Journal of Contemporary Hospitality Management, 27*(1), 87–106. DOI: 10.1108/IJCHM-06-2013-0254

Rauch, D. A., Collins, M. D., Nale, R. D., & Barr, P. B. (2015). Measuring service quality in mid-scale hotels. *International Journal of Contemporary Hospitality Management, 27*(1), 87–106. DOI: 10.1108/IJCHM-06-2013-0254

Rosário, A. T., & Dias, J. C. (2024). Exploring the landscape of smart tourism: A systematic bibliometric review of the literature of the Internet of Things. *Administrative Sciences, 14*(2), 22. DOI: 10.3390/admsci14020022

Sakas, D. P., Reklitis, D. P., Terzi, M. C., & Glaveli, N. (2023). Growth of digital brand name through customer satisfaction with big data analytics in the hospitality sector after the COVID-19 crisis. *International Journal of Information Management Data Insights, 3*(2), 100190. DOI: 10.1016/j.jjimei.2023.100190

Sakas, D. P., Reklitis, D. P., Terzi, M. C., & Vassilakis, C. (2022). Multichannel digital marketing optimizations through big data analytics in the tourism and hospitality industry. *Journal of Theoretical and Applied Electronic Commerce Research, 17*(4), 1383–1408. DOI: 10.3390/jtaer17040070

Sarkar, S. K., Toanoglou, M., & George, B. (2020). The making of data-driven sustainable smart city communities in holiday destinations. *Digital Transformation in Business and Society: Theory and Cases*, 273-296.

Sarker, I. H. (2022). Smart City Data Science: Towards data-driven smart cities with open research issues. *Internet of Things : Engineering Cyber Physical Human Systems, 19*, 100528. DOI: 10.1016/j.iot.2022.100528

Think with Google. (2016), "*How micro-moments are reshaping the travel customer journey*", available at: www .thinkwithgoogle.com/marketing-resources/micro-moments/micro-moments-travel-customer-journey/ (accessed 20 June 2018).

Yallop, A. C., Gică, O. A., Moisescu, O. I., Coro , M. M., & Séraphin, H. (2023). The digital traveller: Implications for data ethics and data governance in tourism and hospitality. *Journal of Consumer Marketing, 40*(2), 155–170. DOI: 10.1108/JCM-12-2020-4278

Ye, Q., Zhang, Z., & Law, R. (2009). Sentiment classification of online reviews to travel destinations by supervised machine learning approaches. *Expert Systems with Applications, 36*(3), 6527–6535. DOI: 10.1016/j.eswa.2008.07.035

Zhang, K., Chen, Y., & Li, C. (2019). Discovering the tourists' behaviors and perceptions in a tourism destination by analyzing photos' visual content with a computer deep learning model: The case of Beijing. *Tourism Management, 75*, 595–608. DOI: 10.1016/j.tourman.2019.07.002

Zhang, Z., Ye, Q., Zhang, Z., & Li, Y. (2011). Sentiment classification of internet restaurant reviews written in Cantonese. *Expert Systems with Applications, 38*(6), 7674–7682. DOI: 10.1016/j.eswa.2010.12.147 PMID: 26560158

Chapter 16
A Case Study:
The Role of Technology in Facilitating Green HRD Practices Within the Hotel Industry

Wahengbam Priyalakshmi
https://orcid.org/0009-0004-1596-2138
Assam University, India

Sanjeev Kumar Saxena
https://orcid.org/0000-0002-2139-9255
Assam University, India

ABSTRACT

The study analyse the influence of technology that supports the initiatives of Green Human Resource Development (HRD) in the hospitality industry. Environmental friendly HRD strategies are being adopted by hotels considering the increase in international emphasis on sustainability so as to diminish their impacts on environment and enhance the overall efficiency of the organization. Various ranges of technological instruments and their utilization in green HRD are scrutinize by investigation like e-learning platforms, virtual reality training, and data analytics. The research underscores the advantages, obstacles and future trajectories of incorporating technology into green HRD by conducting an extensive review of existing literature and analysing case studies of prominent hotel chains. The conclusion of the paper indicates that technology cultivates a sustainability-oriented culture within the hotel sector and it also boosts the efficiency and efficacy of green HRD practices.

INTRODUCTION

To embrace sustainability practices due to its notable implications of the environment, the hotel industry being a significant contributor to the global economy faces an escalating pressure. The importance of sustainable management is highlighted by the utilization of significant amount of energy and water and also the production of substantial waste. As a strategic method, the development of Green Human Resource Development (HRD) equips the employees with vital knowledge, skills and attitudes that bolster the endeavours of sustainability. Hotels are able to enhance their environmental performance and achieve enduring sustainability goals by incorporating the sustainability into their HRD. The hotel industry is one such industry that contributes greatly to the GDP and employment on a larger scale. Primary function of the hospitality sector includes lodging, meals and service to the tourists and travellers though the industry has diverse array of establishment like luxury resorts and even budget

DOI: 10.4018/979-8-3693-7447-4.ch016

accommodation. With the increase in prioritizing sustainability and environmental responsibility over time, the hotel industry has also adjusted to meet the preferences of the consumers.

Hotels have faced increasing scrutiny for their environmental impact as it is a significant consumer of resources like water and energy while also generating substantial waste. This has prompted the calls for the adoption of more sustainable practices within the industry. In response, to reduce the environmental footprint and appeal to environmentally conscious clientele, leading hotel chains have implemented various eco-friendly initiatives.

The hotel sector has been significantly shaped by technological advancements, impacting various areas from guest experiences to operational effectiveness. Operation of the hotels and engagement with the guest have been transformed by innovations like online reservation platforms, mobile check-in options, smart room features and data analysis. Technology plays a great role in enhancing the service standards, streamlining processes and cutting costs.

Recently, attention has expanded to include technologies that support sustainability efforts. Energy management systems, for example help hotels monitor and decrease the consumption of energy, while water-saving devices and waste management technologies aid in resource conservation. These technological advancements are essential for hotels in reaching their sustainability goals.

Human Resource Development (HRD) plays a very important role in an organization that involves activities that are aimed at enhancing the skills, knowledge, and capabilities of the employees. Training and development, career planning, performance evaluation and organizational growth are some of the HRD practices. Effective HRD practices are essential for providing a skilled and motivated workforce that will help in success of the organization.

Due to high level of requirement of service interaction, HRD is very significant in the hotel industry. Employees must undergo comprehensive training to deliver exceptional experiences to the customer, cater to diverse requirement of guest and adeptly manage operational complexities. Furthermore, robust HRD initiatives are pivotal in decreasing turnover rates, enhancing employee satisfaction and ultimately bolstering organizational efficiency.

Green Human Resource Development (Green HRD) emerges as a progressive approach that integrates sustainability into HRD strategies. It involves training and nurturing employees to champion and execute environmental sustainability initiatives. Cultivating a workforce equipped with knowledge of environmental issues, proficient in sustainable practices and dedicated to the organization's objective of sustainability is the goal of Green HRD. Training initiatives focused on energy conservation, waste management, and delivering sustainable customer service are also involved in Green HRD. Additionally, it fosters a culture of sustainability within the organization, promotes environmentally responsible behaviour among employees, and incorporates sustainability into performance management and reward systems. Consequently, the researcher aims to explore the role of technology in facilitating Green HRD practices within the hotel industry. Through an examination of diverse technological tools and their applications, the study also aims to offer insights into how technology can aid in the development and implementation of sustainable practices in hotels. This understanding of the interaction between technology and Green HRD can empower hotels to advance their sustainability endeavours and enhance overall organizational performance.

LITERATURE REVIEW

According to R. B. Jora, P. Mittal, S. Kaushal and S. Raghuvaran(2023) in the article Tech-Enabled Sustainable HR Strategies: Fostering Green Practices the emergence of Green HR practices is discussed in response to the businesses growing need for sustainability. These helps in covering areas like recruitment, training and engagement of employee as the practices aims to integrate environmental concerns in the HR policies and procedures. Utilizing digital tools for recruitment and communication, implementing telecommuting and remote work, and reducing paper usage through electronic documentation are pivotal in fostering Green HR practices. This fusion of technology and environmentally-conscious HR strategies fosters sustainability within organizations, yielding benefits for both the company and the environment. This integration promotes eco-friendly workplace practices and diminishes operational environmental footprints. Green HRM practices are intricately connected with the

Sustainable Development Goals (SDGs) outlined by the United Nations in 2015. By aligning with these objectives, organizations can contribute to poverty alleviation, environmental preservation, and universal prosperity.

In the article, Realization of Sustainable Organizational Performance Using New Technologies and Green Human Resource Management Practices, Shayegan, Bazrkar and Yadegarib (2023) explore how green human resource management practices and new technologies can bolster environmental performance in Iranian car manufacturers. Through a combination of surveying and correlation analysis, they illustrate the beneficial impact of green HR practices on environmental performance. The study underscores how integrating technologies like learning management systems, cloud computing, and artificial intelligence enhances the efficacy of green HR practices such as recruitment, training, and performance management. Notably, the adoption of green HR practices not only advances sustainable development agendas within organizations but also opens up new career avenues for employees. Companies stand to gain from improved corporate reputations, heightened product demand, enhanced production safety, and a positive organizational climate. The research highlights the significance of leveraging emerging digital technologies like the Internet of Things and artificial intelligence to drive sustainable performance and green HR management practices across various industries, including the automotive sector.

According to Singh, D., &Singh, R P. (2022) discuss the significance of Green HR practices that involves integrating environmental considerations into various HR polices in the article Sustainable nanotechnology for human resource development. This HR polices include recruitment, training and engagement of employee. The objective of the integration is to promote sustainability within organizations. Technology serves a crucial role for Green HR practices, facilitating the implementation of digital recruitment tools, enhancing employee communication, supporting telecommuting and remote work, and decreasing paper usage through electronic documentation. Moreover, technology plays a vital role in monitoring and evaluating the effectiveness of green HR practices, providing valuable insights for further improvements.

According to Pai, Shang, Wang, and Zhang (2023) in their study the Influence of Technology Products Introduced into Green Hotels, the growing significance of green hotels within the hospitality sector aligns with sustainable development trends. Their study, which boasted a robust survey participation rate of 86.7% among consumers who had lodged in hotels within the past two years, sheds light on the influence of various technology products on tourist acceptance. The findings reveal that different categories of technology products exert a significant impact on tourists' willingness to embrace them, with techno stress emerging as a determinant factor affecting the acceptance of such technologies. Intriguingly, the type of hotel did not yield a significant effect on the acceptance of technology learning products or on tourists' overall acceptance levels.

In their article titled "Impact of AI & IoT in Sustainable & Green Practices Adopted in Hotel Industry and Measuring Hotel Guests' Satisfaction," which was published in October 2022, Goel, Singh, Sahdev, Baral, and Choudhury emphasize the significance of sustainability within the hotel sector. Their focus extends to elements such as energy conservation, water management, and the integration of green practices and technologies like IoT. The study delves into the correlation between customer satisfaction and various factors, encompassing sustainable practices, hotel reputation, trust, gender, and the influence of technology on sustainability. It offers valuable insights into the adoption of sustainable technology by hoteliers and the impact of certifications on guest satisfaction, although acknowledging certain limitations in the measurements provided.

According to Yuce, A. (2023) the significance of sustainability in the tourism and hospitality industry mainly in terms of enhancing the productivity, efficiency and sustainable development is emphasize in the article Digital Twins and Sustainable Developments in the Tourism and Hospitality Industry. Digital twin technology emerges as a potent tool that is able to transform sustainability in smart manufacturing and the monitoring of natural resources. By furnishing real-time data and facilitating swift predictions and corrective measures, it holds the potential to revolutionize these domains. The adoption of digital twin technology promises diminished energy wastage, lowered maintenance costs, and reduced time inefficiencies in the manufacturing workflow, thereby amplifying organizational productivity and profitability. Moreover, leveraging digital twin technology stands to elevate the value of destinations by safeguarding natural, cultural, and environmental assets while safeguarding the interests of future generations.

A., M., Silaeva. (2022) in his article Modern trends in the development of eco-technologies in the field of hospitality, discusses the current trends of various eco-technologies in hotel enterprises and emphasize the importance of reducing the harmful impact on environment and promoting responsibility for the environment in accommodation facilities. The paper also highlights the various notable trends, including the rising popularity of distinctive lodging facilities, the specialization of individual hotels, and the growing integration of innovations and computer technologies. Moreover, there is a significant emphasis on maintaining and enhancing tourists' interest in environmental sustainability and fostering a positive environmental impact through eco-friendly practices within hotel operations, marking a pivotal trend in the hospitality sector.

According to Khalil, N., Abdullah, S. N. C., Haron, S. N., & Hamid, M. Y. (2022) in their article, A review of green practices and initiatives from stakeholder's perspectives towards sustainable hotel operations and performance impact identifies 27 attributes of green practices and initiatives for hotels sustainable operations from various perspectives like the managers, employees and customers. These attributes encompass various elements such as green marketing strategies, investments in eco-innovation, employee awareness of environmental issues, customer loyalty, green supply chain management, service quality, and hotel design. The paper discusses the correlation between these green practices and performance effectiveness, emphasizing their influence on sustainability dimensions including environmental, economic, and social performance. It demonstrates how adopting sustainable practices in hotels can be advantageous for owners, contributing to sustainable outcomes across economic, environmental, socio-cultural, and regulatory domains. Furthermore, the importance of taking proactive measures to implement green practices and sustainable initiatives in hotel operations is emphasized to maximize their impact on performance and align with sustainability goals.

PURPOSE OF THE STUDY

This paper seeks to study the role of technology in facilitating green HRD practices in the hotel industry. Through an examination of diverse technological tools and their practical applications, the study aims to offer insights into how technology can support the advancement and implementation of sustainable practices within hotels. By grasping the dynamic interaction between technology and green human resource development (HRD), hotels can enhance their sustainability endeavours and enhance overall organizational performance.

RESEARCH QUESTIONS

- How does technology enhance green HRD practices in the hotel industry?
- What are the benefits and challenges of integrating technology in green HRD?
- What future directions can be identified for the use of technology in green HRD within the hotel industry?

HYPOTHESIS

The effectiveness and efficiency of sustainability initiatives within the hotel industry is enhanced by the involvement of technology in Green Human Resource Development practices.

RESEARCH METHODOLOGY

Research Design: A qualitative research design is used in the study. Through comprehensive literature review and case study it explores the role of technology in green HRD within the hotel industry. This form of approach enables an in-depth understanding of the complexities and nuances related with the integration of technology in the practices of HRD.

Data Collection: Data was gathered through an examination of academic journals, industry reports, and case studies of many prominent hotel chains renowned for their sustainability efforts. Furthermore, interviews were conducted with human resource (HR) managers and sustainability officers within the hotel sector to gain firsthand insights. These interviews offered firsthand perspectives on the experiences and obstacles encountered by hotels when integrating technology-driven green human resource development (HRD) practices.

Data Analysis: Thematic analysis was used to identify the key themes and patterns that are related to the integration of technology in green HRD practices from the collected data. This method enabled the systematic coding and categorization of data, streamlining the process of identifying recurring themes and insights from various sources of information.

DISCUSSION AND ANALYSIS

Technological Tools in Green HRD

E-learning platforms

The method by which hotels educate their employees regarding sustainability practices has been transformed by the e-learning platforms. To create adaptable, expandable and easily accessible learning atmosphere, the platforms offer a cutting edge approach to learning by utilizing digital technologies. Hotel personnel can interact with the training content at their convenience and according to their own timetables, a crucial aspect in an industry known for its fluctuating shift schedules and frequent turnover of staff.

E-learning modules typically cover a range of essential sustainability topics. These include:

- Energy Conservation: Each staff is taught on how to minimize energy through efficient lighting, heating and cooling practices.
- Waste Management: Recycling, composting and reducing waste production are educated on the employees.
- Eco-friendly Customer Service: Training staff to advocate sustainable practices to guests, such as promoting the reuse of towels and linens (Klimova, 2021)

Multimedia Elements: Integrating multimedia elements like videos, interactive simulations, and quizzes enhances the learning experience by making it more engaging and impactful. These tools assist in elucidating intricate concepts, showcasing practical applications, and assessing acquired knowledge (Lim & Lee, 2022).

Benefits of E-Learning Platforms:

- Flexibility: Training materials are accessible to the employees from any location at any time to all the staff members regardless of their shifts and geographic location enabling them to participate in training programs (Ally & Tsinakos, 2014).
- Scalability: E-learning platforms offer scalability to accommodate a vast number of employees, guaranteeing uniformity in the quality of training across all locations (Klimova, 2021).

- Cost-Effectiveness: E-learning reduces the necessity for in-person training sessions, thereby eliminating expenses related to trainer travel, the requirement for training materials, and the disruptions caused by removing employees from their workstations (Ruiz et al., 2006).
- Enhanced Engagement: Interactive content helps in engaging and motivating the learners. Incorporating gamification elements, like badge rewards or level completion, can additionally encourage participation and course completion (Dicheva et al., 2015).

Case Example: Hilton Worldwide

Hilton Worldwide stands out as a prime example of effectively incorporating e-learning platforms for sustainability training. Through its "Travel with Purpose" initiative, Hilton had curated a comprehensive collection of e-learning modules, addressing various aspects of sustainability:

- Energy Efficiency: The modules educate employees on implementing energy-saving practices in their daily routines.
- Water Conservation: The training encompasses techniques for minimizing water consumption, including the utilization of low-flow fixtures and prompt repair of leaks.
- Sustainable Procurement: Staff members are educated on sourcing environmentally friendly products and materials (Hilton Worldwide, 2023).

Designed for self-paced learning, these modules enable employees to navigate the content according to their own schedules, fostering a deeper comprehension of sustainability practices while promoting a culture of continuous learning and advancement. Hilton's dedication to sustainability is additionally underscored by its capacity to consistently monitor and refresh these modules, ensuring their ongoing relevance and currency (Hilton Worldwide, 2023).

In conclusion, e-learning platforms represent a highly effective and efficient means for hotels to educate their employees on sustainability practices. By providing flexibility, scalability and cost-effectiveness, these platforms aid hotels in fostering a culture of environmental responsibility and ongoing enhancement. The successful adoption of e-learning for sustainability training by Hilton Worldwide highlights the considerable advantages of the approach, showcasing that thoughtfully crafted digital training initiatives can play a significant role in advancing sustainability objectives within the hospitality sector.

Virtual Reality

By providing immersive and interactive experiences that amplify the learning and acquisition of skill, Virtual Reality (VR) technology is revolutionizing the employee. VR offers a unique opportunity to train staff on various sustainability practices in a simulated environment for the hotel industry. This hands-on method proves especially efficacious in imparting practical skills like energy-efficient housekeeping and waste management, areas where conventional training techniques may lack impact.

VR Training Modules for Sustainability Practices:

- Energy-Efficient Housekeeping: VR simulations can illustrate optimal methods for reducing energy consumption, including the efficient utilization of heating, ventilation, and air conditioning (HVAC) systems, as well as the adoption of energy-efficient lighting (Loureiro et al., 2022).
- Waste Management: Employees can engage in practicing the proper sorting and disposal of waste, acquiring skills to enhance recycling endeavours and reduce waste generation (Stavrou et al., 2021).
- Water Conservation: Through simulations, employees can learn techniques for identifying and addressing leaks, utilizing water-saving devices, and promoting guest participation in conservation initiatives (Pan et al., 2021).

- Sustainable Customer Service: Staff members can engage in simulated interactions with guests to advocate for eco-friendly practices, including linen reuse programs and conscientious water and energy usage (Carneiro et al., 2023).

Benefits of VR Training:

- Immersive Learning: VR technology establishes a lifelike, interactive learning environment, enabling employees to interact with training content in a manner more impactful than conventional approaches. The immersive quality of VR enables employees to experience and grasp the repercussions of their actions within a controlled environment, thereby enhancing comprehension and information retention (Smith & Davis, 2022).
- Safe Practice: A notable benefit of VR training is the opportunity to rehearse techniques devoid of real-world risks. Employees can make errors and gain insights from them within a virtual realm, free from any adverse consequences. This attribute is especially valuable for tasks that entail potential costs or hazards if executed inaccurately (Jones et al., 2020).
- Improved Retention: Studies indicate that experiential learning substantially improves memory retention. Through practicing skills within a simulated setting, employees are better equipped to recall and implement their knowledge when faced with analogous real-life scenarios. This is attributed to VR's engagement of multiple senses and provision of a contextual experience, which is more memorable than simply reading or listening to instructions (Pan et al., 2021).
- Higher Engagement: VR training often proves to be more captivating and stimulating compared to conventional training approaches. The novelty and interactivity inherent in VR can render learning enjoyable, thereby enhancing employee engagement and enthusiasm. When employees are actively involved, they are more inclined to approach the training with seriousness and subsequently apply their newfound knowledge in their daily responsibilities (Loureiro et al., 2022).

Case Example: Marriott International

Marriott International has effectively incorporated virtual reality (VR) technology into its sustainability training initiatives. Through VR simulations, Marriott provides training to its housekeeping staff on eco-friendly practices within a controlled virtual setting. These simulations enable staff members to practice various tasks, including optimizing thermostats for energy efficiency, utilizing environmentally friendly cleaning products, and adhering to recycling protocols (Marriott International, 2023). This method has resulted in numerous advantages for Marriott:

- Improved Skill Acquisition: Employees develop a more profound comprehension of sustainable practices and are better equipped to integrate them into their daily tasks.
- Increased Engagement: The interactive aspect of VR training enhances employee motivation and involvement, resulting in increased participation rates.
- Enhanced Readiness: Staff members feel more assured and prepared to apply their learning which results in more consistent and effective implementation of sustainability practices.

Hence, within the hotel industry VR technology presents a potent resource for elevating sustainability training. VR helps the employees to acquire and retain the skills that are necessary for implementing sustainable practices effectively by providing immersive, hands-on learning experiences. Marriott International's adept utilization of VR for training in sustainable housekeeping practices exemplifies the transformative potential of this technology in refining training initiatives, rendering them more captivating, efficient, and influential. As the hotel industry persistently emphasizes sustainability, VR training is poised to emerge as an increasingly indispensable facet of employee education and advancement.

Data Analytics

Data analytics tools have become essential for monitoring and evaluating the impact of green Human Resource Development (HRD) efforts within the hotel sector. Through the utilization of these tools, hotels can extract valuable insights regarding employee performance and engagement, pinpoint areas necessitating enhancement, and customize their training schemes to more precisely align with their sustainability targets. Leveraging data-driven insights not only fosters ongoing refinement but also guarantees the efficient and effective attainment of sustainability objectives.

Data analytics in green HRD typically involves several key components:

- Performance Monitoring: hotels are able to track the key performance indicators (KPIs) through the data analytics tools like usage of energy, water consumption and waste reduction. This continuous monitoring enables assessing the effectiveness of sustainability initiatives and also identify areas that need improvements (Carneiro et al.,2023; Dean, 2021)
- Employee Engagement Metrics: A clear picture of insights into the reception and effectiveness of the initiatives can be clearly seen by analyzing the participation of employee in sustainability programs, completion rates and feedback scores (Dean, 2021).
- Behavioural Data: The practical implementation of sustainable practices can be assessed by monitoring the shifts in employee behaviour following training aids. This data is vital for understanding the effects of training initiatives in real-world scenarios (Carneiro et al., 2023).

Benefits of Data analytics:

Performance Monitoring: Utilizing data analytics to oversee KPIs enables hotels to promptly detect issues and intervene as necessary. For instance, tracking energy consumption data allows for the evaluation of energy-saving initiatives' effectiveness, while metrics on waste generation can gauge the success of waste reduction programs (Carneiro et al., 2023; Dean, 2021).Top of FormBottom of Form

- Customized Training: Data analytics insights enable the tailoring of training programs to specific needs. For example, if analysis indicates challenges with waste segregation among employees, customized training can be designed to address this area specifically. This ensures the training remains pertinent and focused (Dean, 2021).
- Continuous Improvement: Data analytics establishes a feedback loop for ongoing enhancement. Consistently analyzing training outcomes and employee performance aids in refining and improving training initiatives, ensuring they adapt to evolving needs and integrate the most current sustainability best practices (Dean, 2021).
- Goal Alignment: Data analytics guarantees the alignment of HRD initiatives with overarching sustainability objectives. Through monitoring progress towards these goals, hotels can verify that their training programs are effectively contributing to the broader sustainability strategy (Carneiro et al., 2023).

Case Example: Accor Hotels

Accor Hotels showcases proficient utilization of data analytics in green HRD. The company employs advanced analytics tools to evaluate the effectiveness of its sustainability training programs. Through real-time monitoring of various indicators including energy consumption, water conservation, and waste reduction, Accor can assess the impact of its initiatives (Mews PMS) (Hotel Tech Report) (MDPI).

For example, Accor monitors the energy consumption of its hotels both pre- and post-implementation of energy efficiency training programs. This data enables them to measure the attained savings and pinpoint properties that might benefit from supplementary support or resources. Likewise, waste reduction metrics aid Accor in gauging the effectiveness of its waste management training and making necessary adjustments to strategies.

This data-driven approach has several benefits for Accor:

- Informed Decision-Making: The capacity to make informed decisions grounded in empirical data ensures efficient resource allocation and targeted interventions where they are most required.
- Enhanced Training Programs: Accor is able to refine its training programs, making them more effective and relevant to current challenges through continuous feedback from analyzing the data.
- Achievement of Sustainability Targets: Accor diligently tracks advancements towards its sustainability objectives, guaranteeing that its eco-friendly Human Resources Development (HRD) initiatives make substantial contributions to its broader environmental agenda.

In summary, data analytics plays a pivotal role in bolstering eco-friendly Human Resources Development (HRD) efforts within the hotel sector. By furnishing comprehensive insights into employee performance and training efficacy, these tools empower hotels to tailor their training schemes, foster ongoing enhancement, and uphold alignment with sustainability objectives. Accor Hotels' effective utilization of data analytics underscores the substantial advantages of this method, emphasizing how making decisions based on data can result in more potent and meaningful sustainability training initiatives. As the hotel industry persists in prioritizing environmental responsibility, the significance of data analytics in green HRD will continue to escalate.

Benefits of Integrating Technology in Green HRD

- Enhanced Learning Experience: Technology fosters interactive and captivating learning encounters, enhancing both knowledge retention and skill refinement. E-learning platforms and virtual reality (VR) training deliver dynamic and immersive educational options that accommodate various learning preferences.
- Scalability: Technological tools empower hotels to expand the reach of their training initiatives, reaching a broader array of employees across numerous locations. This scalability proves especially crucial for global hotel chains managing diverse workforces.
- Cost-effectiveness: E-learning and VR training minimize the necessity for physical training materials and travel expenditures, resulting in cost savings. Furthermore, technology-driven training can be updated and distributed more swiftly and efficiently compared to conventional methods.
- Real-time Feedback: Data analytics provide immediate insights into the efficacy of training, enabling prompt adjustments and enhancements. Hotels can utilize this feedback to consistently refine their eco-friendly HRD practices and ensure they align with sustainability objectives.

Challenges of Integrating Technology in Green HRD

- Initial Investment: Deploying advanced technological tools necessitates a considerable initial investment, which may pose a barrier for certain hotels. The expenses linked to procuring hardware, developing software, and training personnel can be significant.
- Technological Barriers: Insufficient access to technology and inadequate digital literacy among employees can impede the successful execution of technology-driven training programs. Hotels need to overcome these obstacles by offering comprehensive training and support to ensure all employees can leverage technological tools effectively.

- Resistance to Change: Both employees and management might hesitate to embrace new technologies, favouring traditional training approaches instead. Overcoming this resistance demands adept change management strategies and transparent communication regarding the advantages of technology-driven eco-friendly HRD practices.

SUMMARY OF CASE STUDIES

Case Study 1: Hilton Worldwide

Hilton Worldwide has incorporated e-learning platforms to deliver sustainability training to its employees worldwide. Through its "Travel with Purpose" initiative, the company offers modules covering topics such as energy efficiency, water conservation, and sustainable procurement. Utilizing data analytics, Hilton tracks employee advancement and the training's influence on operational effectiveness. This strategy has resulted in notable enhancements in the company's environmental achievements and employee involvement in sustainability endeavours and employee engagement with sustainability initiatives.

Case Study 2: Marriott International

Marriott International utilizes virtual reality (VR) technology for training employees in sustainable housekeeping procedures. Through VR simulations, staff can rehearse eco-friendly techniques within a controlled setting, thereby better preparing them to apply these methods in real-world scenarios. This method has led to enhanced skill acquisition and heightened employee enthusiasm for embracing sustainable practices.

Case Study 3: Accor Hotels

Accor Hotels employs data analytics to monitor the outcomes of their sustainability training schemes. Through tracking essential metrics like energy consumption and waste minimization, the company evaluates the efficacy of its training programs, enabling data-driven decisions to refine their eco-friendly HRD practices. This systematic use of data has empowered Accor Hotels to consistently enhance their sustainability endeavours, resulting in substantial environmental gains.

CONCLUSION

In summary, incorporating technology into eco-friendly HRD strategies presents a noteworthy chance for the hotel sector to propel its sustainability objectives forward. By embracing e-learning platforms, virtual reality training, and data analytics solutions, hotels can equip their staff with the necessary knowledge, abilities, and enthusiasm to champion environmental stewardship within their establishments.

The advantages of these technological strides are abundant. E-learning platforms provide flexibility, scalability, and cost efficiency, rendering sustainability training accessible to employees spanning various geographical regions and hierarchical levels within organizations. Virtual reality (VR) training delivers immersive, interactive learning encounters that replicate genuine sustainability dilemmas, nurturing a more profound comprehension and enduring retention of sustainable methodologies. Simultaneously, data analytics tools empower hotels to oversee, assess, and refine their sustainability endeavors, furnishing invaluable insights for decision-making and enhancing performance.

By utilizing these technological resources, hotels can diminish their environmental impact while bolstering their brand image, drawing eco-minded guests, and attaining operational streamlining. Furthermore, allocating resources to eco-friendly HRD methods can cultivate a more involved and inspired workforce, ultimately leading to heightened employee contentment, retention, and effectiveness.

Yet, effectively incorporating technology-driven eco-friendly HRD methods demands surmounting specific hurdles like limited resources, technological obstacles, and reluctance to change. Hotels need to take proactive measures in tackling these obstacles through strategic foresight, investments in training and skill development, and adept change management approaches.

Amid mounting environmental apprehensions and escalating consumer desire for sustainable travel alternatives, the significance of technology in fostering eco-friendly HRD practices has reached unprecedented importance. By embracing ingenuity and harnessing technology to infuse sustainability into their corporate ethos, hotels can chart a course towards a hospitality sector that is more environmentally conscious and adaptable for the future.

Implications for the Hotel Industry

Hotels ought to contemplate the investment in technological resources to bolster their eco-friendly HRD endeavours. This step can cultivate a culture rooted in sustainability, enhance operational efficiency, and contribute to worldwide environmental objectives. Successfully integrating technology-driven green HRD practices necessitates overcoming obstacles like initial financial investment, technological accessibility, and reluctance to change. Additionally, hotels must guarantee that their training schemes remain consistently updated and in harmony with evolving sustainability benchmarks.

Recommendations for Future Research

Subsequent research should delve into the enduring effects of incorporating technology into eco-friendly HRD on employee conduct and hotel efficacy. Furthermore, investigations should explore strategies for surmounting obstacles to technology adoption within the hotel sector. Comparative analyses spanning diverse regions and hotel categories can yield more universally applicable conclusions and deeper understandings of the efficacy of different technological resources in eco-friendly HRD.

Limitations of the study

The scope of this study is constrained by its qualitative approach and dependence on case studies from a select few prominent hotel chains. Subsequent research endeavors should incorporate quantitative assessments and encompass a wider array of hotel categories to yield findings with broader applicability. Furthermore, while the study predominantly examines the advantages and hurdles associated with technology integration, it affords less attention to the intricacies of implementation processes. Future investigations should aim to fill these gaps, thus offering a more holistic comprehension of the role of technology in eco-friendly HRD within the hotel sector.

REFERENCES

Accor Hotels. (2022). Sustainable Development: Acting Here. Retrieved from https://group.accor.com/en/commitments/sustainable-development

Agarwal, R., Chaudhary, M., & Singh, J. (2015). Waste management initiatives in India for human well being. *European Scientific Journal.*

Aguinis, H., & Kraiger, K. (2009). Benefits of training and development for individuals and teams, organizations, and society. *Annual Review of Psychology*, *60*(1), 451–474. DOI: 10.1146/annurev.psych.60.110707.163505 PMID: 18976113

Ally, M., &Tsinakos, A. (2014). Perspectives on Open and Distance Learning: Increasing Access through Mobile Learning. Commonwealth of Learning and Athabasca University.

Arimany-Serrat, N., & Gomez-Guillen, J. J. (2023). Sustainability and Environmental Impact of the Tourism Sector: Analysis Applied to Swimming Pools in the Hotel Industry on the Costa Brava. *Environmental Processes*, *10*(4), 55. DOI: 10.1007/s40710-023-00665-4

Bohdanowicz, P., Zientara, P., & Novotna, E. (2011). International hotel chains and environmental protection: An analysis of Hilton's we care! programme (Europe, 2006-2008). *Journal of Sustainable Tourism*, *19*(7), 797–816. DOI: 10.1080/09669582.2010.549566

Brosius, N., Fernandez, K. V., & Cherrier, H. (2013). Reacquiring consumer waste: Treasure in our trash? *Journal of Public Policy & Marketing*, *32*(2), 286–301. DOI: 10.1509/jppm.11.146

Carneiro, T., Picoto, W. N., & Pinto, I. (2023). Big data analytics and firm performance in the hotel sector. *Tourism and Hospitality*, *4*(2), 244–256. DOI: 10.3390/tourhosp4020015

Carneiro, T., Picoto, W. N., & Pinto, I. (2023). Sustainable customer service practices in the hotel industry: A VR training approach. *Journal of Hospitality and Tourism Technology*, *14*(1), 67–84. DOI: 10.1108/JHTT-01-2023-0005

Chang, C. H., & Chen, Y. S. (2013). Green organizational identity and green innovation. *Management Decision*, *51*(5), 1056–1070. DOI: 10.1108/MD-09-2011-0314

Chuang, S. F. (2013). Essential skills for leadership effectiveness in diverse workplace development. *The Online Journal for Workforce Education and Development*, *6*(1), 1–23.

Corbett, J., Savarimuthu, B. T. R., & Lakshmi, V. (2020). Separating Treasure from Trash: Quantifying Data Waste in App Reviews. In *AMCIS.*

Crawford, M. (2013). Turning trash into treasure. *Mechanical Engineering (New York, N.Y.)*, *135*(05), 42–47. DOI: 10.1115/1.2013-MAY-3

da Cunha, D. T. (2021). Improving food safety practices in the foodservice industry. *Current Opinion in Food Science*, *42*, 127–133. DOI: 10.1016/j.cofs.2021.05.010

Dean, A. (2021). The role of data analytics in sustainability training for the hospitality industry. *Journal of Sustainable Tourism*, *29*(5), 853–872. DOI: 10.1080/09669582.2021.1879817

Demirbas, A., Edris, G., & Alalayah, W. M. (2017). Sludge production from municipal wastewater treatment in sewage treatment plant. *Energy Sources. Part A, Recovery, Utilization, and Environmental Effects*, *39*(10), 999–1006. DOI: 10.1080/15567036.2017.1283551

Dicheva, D., Dichev, C., Agre, G., & Angelova, G. (2015). Gamification in education: A systematic mapping study. *Journal of Educational Technology & Society*, *18*(3), 75–88.

Dief, M. E., & Font, X. (2010). The determinants of hotels' marketing managers' green marketing behavior. *Journal of Sustainable Tourism*, *18*(2), 157–174. DOI: 10.1080/09669580903464232

García, J. L., Maldonado, A., Alvarado, A., & Rivera, D. G. (2014). Human critical success factors for kaizen and its impacts in industrial performance. *International Journal of Advanced Manufacturing Technology*, *70*(9-12), 2187–2198. DOI: 10.1007/s00170-013-5445-4

Giusti, L. (2009). A review of waste management practices and their impact on human health. *Waste Management (New York, N.Y.)*, *29*(8), 2227–2239. DOI: 10.1016/j.wasman.2009.03.028 PMID: 19401266

Giusti, L. (2009). A review of waste management practices and their impact on human health. *Waste Management (New York, N.Y.)*, *29*(8), 2227–2239. DOI: 10.1016/j.wasman.2009.03.028 PMID: 19401266

Goel, R., Singh, T., Sahdev, S. L., Baral, S. K., & Choudhury, A. (2022, October). Impact of AI & IOT in sustainable & green practices adopted in hotel industry and measuring hotel guests' satisfaction. In *2022 10th International Conference on Reliability, Infocom Technologies and Optimization (Trends and Future Directions)(ICRITO)* (pp. 1-5). IEEE.

Harris, C., & Tregidga, H. (2012). HR managers and environmental sustainability: Strategic leaders or passive observers? *International Journal of Human Resource Management*, *23*(2), 236–254. DOI: 10.1080/09585192.2011.561221

Hilton Worldwide. (2020). Travel with Purpose: 2030 Goals. Retrieved from https://cr.hilton.com/2030-goals/

Hilton Worldwide. (2023). Travel with Purpose: Hilton's Corporate Responsibility Strategy. Retrieved from https://www.hilton.com/en/corporate/travel-with-purpose/

Jones, M., Smith, L., & Davis, R. (2020). The impact of VR training on employee safety and performance. *Safety Science*, *130*, 104895. DOI: 10.1016/j.ssci.2020.104895

Jora, R. B., Mittal, P., Kaushal, S., & Raghuvaran, S. (2023, March). Tech-enabled sustainable HR strategies: fostering green practices. In 2023 9th International Conference on Advanced Computing and Communication Systems (ICACCS) (Vol. 1, pp. 2496-2501). IEEE.

Khalil, N., Abdullah, S. N. C., Haron, S. N., & Hamid, M. Y. (2022). A review of green practices and initiatives from stakeholder's perspectives towards sustainable hotel operations and performance impact. Journal of Facilities Management, (ahead-of-print).

Khandke, S. S., & Mayes, T. (1998). HACCP implementation: A practical guide to the implementation of the HACCP plan. *Food Control*, *9*(2-3), 103–109. DOI: 10.1016/S0956-7135(97)00065-0

Kim, Y. H., Barber, N., & Kim, D. K. (2019). Sustainability research in the hotel industry: Past, present, and future. *Journal of Hospitality Marketing & Management*, *28*(5), 576–620. DOI: 10.1080/19368623.2019.1533907

Kim, Y. J., Lee, J., Chun, J. U., & Benbasat, I. (2014). Understanding sustained use of social media. *Journal of the Association for Information Systems*, *15*(10), 641–670.

Klimova, B. (2021). Benefits and limitations of e-learning: A review article. *International Journal of Instructional Technology and Distance Learning*, *18*(3), 15–28.

Lim, S., & Lee, J. (2022). The impact of multimedia elements on e-learning effectiveness. *Journal of Educational Technology Development and Exchange*, *14*(1), 20–35.

Loureiro, S. M. C., Guerreiro, J., & Tussyadiah, I. P. (2022). The role of VR in enhancing hotel employee training for energy-efficient practices. *Tourism Management, 85*, 104323. DOI: 10.1016/j.tourman.2021.104323

Marriott International. (2021). Serve 360: Doing good in every direction. Retrieved from https://serve360.marriott.com/

Marriott International. (2023). Marriott's green training initiatives with VR technology. Retrieved from https://www.marriott.com/green-training

Mensah, I. (2006). Environmental management practices among hotels in the greater Accra region. *International Journal of Hospitality Management, 25*(3), 414–431. DOI: 10.1016/j.ijhm.2005.02.003

Metin, E., Eröztürk, A., & Neyim, C. (2003). Solid waste management practices and review of recovery and recycling operations in Turkey. *Waste Management (New York, N.Y.), 23*(5), 425–432. DOI: 10.1016/S0956-053X(03)00070-9 PMID: 12893015

Newslow, D. (2013). *Food safety management programs: applications, best practices, and compliance*. CRC Press. DOI: 10.1201/b16231

Nnorom, I. C., & Osibanjo, O. (2008). Overview of electronic waste (e-waste) management practices and legislations, and their poor applications in the developing countries. *Resources, Conservation and Recycling, 52*(6), 843–858. DOI: 10.1016/j.resconrec.2008.01.004

O'Neill, J. W., & Mattila, A. S. (2010). Hotel brand strategy. *Cornell Hospitality Quarterly, 51*(1), 27–34. DOI: 10.1177/1938965509352286

Pai, C. H., Shang, Y., Wang, L., & Zhang, Y. (2023). A Study on the Influence of Technology Products Introduced Into Green Hotels. [JOEUC]. *Journal of Organizational and End User Computing, 35*(1), 1–20. DOI: 10.4018/JOEUC.325649

Pan, Y., Lee, K. Y., & Tsai, C. H. (2021). Using VR to enhance water conservation training for hotel employees. *Journal of Environmental Management, 287*, 112281. DOI: 10.1016/j.jenvman.2021.112281

Pardini, K., Rodrigues, J. J., Kozlov, S. A., Kumar, N., & Furtado, V. (2019). IoT-based solid waste management solutions: A survey. *Journal of Sensor and Actuator Networks, 8*(1), 5. DOI: 10.3390/jsan8010005

Philips, P., & Louvieris, P. (2005). Performance measurement systems in tourism, hospitality, and leisure small medium-sized enterprises: A balanced scorecard perspective. *Journal of Travel Research, 44*(2), 201–211. DOI: 10.1177/0047287505278992

Robinson, O. (2015). Environmental regulations and green management. *Journal of Environmental Management, 163*, 30–37.

Ruiz, J. G., Mintzer, M. J., & Leipzig, R. M. (2006). The impact of e-learning in medical education. *Academic Medicine, 81*(3), 207–212. DOI: 10.1097/00001888-200603000-00002 PMID: 16501260

Savolainen, T. (2009). Cycles of continuous improvement: Realizing competitive advantages through quality. *International Journal of Process Management and Benchmarking, 3*(3), 321–337.

Schaltegger, S., Lüdeke-Freund, F., & Hansen, E. G. (2012). Business cases for sustainability: The role of business model innovation for corporate sustainability. *International Journal of Innovation and Sustainable Development, 6*(2), 95–119. DOI: 10.1504/IJISD.2012.046944

Shahbaz, M., Rashid, N., Saleem, J., Mackey, H., McKay, G., & Al-Ansari, T. (2023). A review of waste management approaches to maximise sustainable value of waste from the oil and gas industry and potential for the State of Qatar. *Fuel, 332*, 126220. DOI: 10.1016/j.fuel.2022.126220

Shamin, N., Fathimal, P. M., Raghavendran, R., & Prakash, K. (2019, April). Smart garbage segregation & management system using Internet of Things (IoT) & Machine Learning (ML). In *2019 1st International Conference on Innovations in Information and Communication Technology (ICIICT)* (pp. 1-6). IEEE.

Shayegan, S., Bazrkar, A., & Yadegari, R. (2023). Realization of Sustainable Organizational Performance Using New Technologies and Green Human Resource Management Practices. *Foresight STI Gov, 17*(2), 95–105. DOI: 10.17323/2500-2597.2023.2.95.105

A., M., Silaeva. (2022). Modern trends in the development of eco-technologies in the field of hospitality. 666-671. DOI: 10.33920/igt-2-2210-07

Singh, D., & Singh, R. P. (2022). Sustainable nanotechnology for human resource development. *Biogenic Sustainable Nanotechnology*, 357-372.

Smith, R., & Davis, K. (2022). Enhancing employee engagement through VR training: A case study of the hotel industry. *International Journal of Hospitality Management, 95*, 102956. DOI: 10.1016/j.ijhm.2021.102956

Stavrou, A., Papadopoulou, P., & Nikolaidis, G. (2021). Training hotel staff in waste management using VR: An experiential learning approach. *Waste Management (New York, N.Y.), 128*, 213–221. DOI: 10.1016/j.wasman.2021.05.022

Susanth, G. S., Livingston, L. J., & Livingston, L. A. (2021). Garbage waste segregation using deep learning techniques. [). IOP Publishing.]. *IOP Conference Series. Materials Science and Engineering, 1012*(1), 012040. DOI: 10.1088/1757-899X/1012/1/012040

Tang, G., Chen, Y., Jiang, Y., Paille, P., & Jia, J. (2018). Green human resource management practices: Scale development and validity. *Asia Pacific Journal of Human Resources, 56*(1), 31–55. DOI: 10.1111/1744-7941.12147

Tosti-Kharas, J., & Lamm, E. (2015). The role of organizational climate and job involvement in employees' environmental engagement. *Business & Society, 54*(2), 235–262.

Wahid, N. A., & Ismail, S. (2017). Sustainability practices in hotel industry: An empirical study of green hotels in Malaysia. In Business and Economics Research Proceedings (Vol. 1, pp. 318-327).

Wyssusek, K. H., Foong, W. M., Steel, C., & Gillespie, B. M. (2016). The gold in garbage: Implementing a waste segregation and recycling initiative. *AORN Journal, 103*(3), 316–e1. DOI: 10.1016/j.aorn.2016.01.014 PMID: 26924375

Yuce, A. (2023). Digital Twins and Sustainable Developments in the Tourism and Hospitality Industry. In *Handbook of Research on Applications of AI, Digital Twin, and Internet of Things for Sustainable Development* (pp. 461-472). IGI Global. DOI: 10.4018/978-1-6684-6821-0.ch027

Zhang, J., & Bhatt, T. (2014). A guidance document on the best practices in food traceability. *Comprehensive Reviews in Food Science and Food Safety, 13*(5), 1074–1103. DOI: 10.1111/1541-4337.12103

Chapter 17
Context-Aware Internet of Things-Based Service-Oriented Architecture for Industrial Applications

Kamalendu Pal
https://orcid.org/0000-0001-7158-6481
University of London, UK

ABSTRACT

Today, the industrial world has witnessed the fast development and popularity of the Internet of Things (IoT) based information systems. These information systems often use pervasive computing, ubiquitous computing, and unique data communication protocols to sense industrial applications in an environment where the physical and digital worlds work together. In this way, the new information system can serve various categories of business services through continuous symbiotic interactions. These interactions exchange data and information to create services that benefit the industrial world and smoothen supply chain operations. This chapter describes an information system architecture (i.e., Apparel Business Decentralized Data Integration (ABDDI)) that requires a description of a logic-based knowledge representation scheme for information modeling and reasoning to provide web services semantic interoperability with the help of ontology. The chapter also presents an example of the service composition ontology's similarity assessment.

INTRODUCTION

New generations of advanced information technologies (IT) are fundamentally transforming industrial operations and reshaping human society. Incorporating automation across many sectors in regular business activities, from smart factories to intelligent transportation systems, is not just a change but a revolution. Integrating business processes establishes a connection between operational technologies (OT), the hardware and software responsible for monitoring and controlling devices and processes, and the digital realm. The concept of convergence of IT with OT, often known as 'Industry 4.0', refers to the extensive integration of sensors and network interconnectivity, a depth

DOI: 10.4018/979-8-3693-7447-4.ch017

of technological advancement that facilitates data collection, analysis, and sharing with the industrial ecosystem. Comprehending these technologies is beneficial and crucial for understanding the industry's future landscape.

Business process automation thrives on innovative operational practices, experimentation, and, most importantly, sound decision-making. The research community plays a crucial role in this, often sparking innovative ideas that lead to new technology. This collective effort challenges the notion that innovation is solely the result of individual laboratory experiments. It is the secret that society hopes to witness—the magic that occurs when new ideas emerge. For example, creative breakthroughs can be seen in the discovery of millimetre radio waves by Professor Jagadish Chandra Bose (Sarkar, 2006), and its legacy is influencing a new generation of wireless communications technologies in daily activities. Three pivotal technologies profoundly impact modern wireless telecommunications, and the detailed scientific contribution came from James Clerk Maxwell (Mahon, 2004), the Scottish physicist who established the theoretical foundation for electromagnetic wave propagation; Jagadish Chandra Bose, the Indian polymath who successfully demonstrated the transmission of millimetre waves in his laboratory; and Tim Berners-Lee, the British computer scientist who invented the World Wide Web (Berners-Lee, 2000). Their contributions have significantly shaped the technological landscape. In addition, computer data communication networks are increasingly intangible and constantly evolving, growing more complex with each passing second. This incredible network of networks is the backbone of many global business community members, who rely on it for their daily operations and related services.

The advent of development and adoption of new technologies in recent decades is continuing. This continuation is driven by (i) the cumulative nature of technological change, (ii) the exponential nature of technologies such as microchips that are doubled in power every two years for more than half a century, (iii) the convergence of technologies into new combinations; (iv) drastic reduction in costs of production; (v) the emergence of digital "platforms of platforms" – most prominently the Internet; and (v) adoption of artificial intelligence (AI) techniques, the Internet of Things (IoT), and cognitive technologies have successfully been applied to various industrial applications (Zhao & Kumar, 2021). In addition, IoT has paved the way for many industrial application domains while posing several challenges as many devices, protocols, communication channels, architectures, and middleware exist. Big data generated by these devices calls for advanced machine learning (ML) and data mining techniques to understand, learn effectively, and reason with this volume of information, such as cognitive technologies. Cognitive technologies play a significant role in developing successful cognitive systems which mimic "cognitive" functions associated with human intelligence, such as "learning" and "problem-solving".

Moreover, advancements in Cyber-Physical Systems (CPSs) heighten the real-time demands on industrial networks. CPSs merge embedded systems with cybernetic control systems to govern the physical world through networked environments, imposing strict real-time requirements on their operations. Various safety and control considerations necessitate low latency and predictability, often on constrained embedded systems. When these systems are connected to more extensive networks and integrated into complex distributed systems, their real-time needs extend to the network. It creates a landscape where time-critical control tasks must be managed across a network, necessitating reliable and predictable packet routing.

The data packets traversing these networks consist of operational data collected from various devices. Currently, a broad array of devices, including sensor-equipped smart devices and wearables, connect to the Internet, facilitating innovative applications and solutions. The reduction in technology costs has democratized access to data collection capabilities. As a result, today's Internet serves as a vital conduit for real-time information across all domains. Furthermore, many platforms, such as social media, have migrated online, centralizing data in the Cloud and giving rise to concepts like Big Data, Cloud Computing, and the Internet of Things (IoT).

Recent advancements in radio-frequency identification (RFID), affordable wireless sensors, and web technologies have fuelled the IoT movement, which connects everyday objects to the Internet and enables communication between machines, humans, and the physical world. IoT devices are geared with embedded sensors, actuators, processors, and transceivers for this intelligence and interconnection. IoT is not a single technology but an agglomeration of various technologies that work together. In simple terms, sensors and actuators help interact with the physical environment. The data collected by the sensors must be stored and processed intelligently to derive valuable inferences from it. This chapter broadly defines the term *sensor*; a handheld mobile phone or even a microwave oven can be a sensor if it provides inputs about its current state (internal state + environment). An *actuator* is a device used to effect a change in the environment, such as the temperature controller of an air conditioner.

Data storage and processing can be done on the network's edge or a server located in a different place. If any data preprocessing is done, it simply happens at some other proximate device or sensor. In the end, data is then typically sent to a remote server after processing. An IoT object's storage and processing capabilities are also restricted by the available resources, which are often very constrained due to size, energy, power, and computational capability limitations. Consequently, the central research challenge is ensuring that users can get the appropriate data type at the desired level of correctness.

In addition to data collection and handling challenges, there are also challenges in processed data communication to the relevant service entities. The collaboration and communication between IoT devices are generally wireless because these devices are installed at different work locations. Wireless communication channels are often suffering from high rates of disturbance. This way, reliably communicating data without too many retransmissions is a central research issue. Moreover, actions must be taken based on the derived inferences after processing the received data. The nature of action can be diverse. One can directly modify the physical world through actuators. Alternatively, one may do something virtually. For example, one may send raw data and information to other bright objects. Creating a change in the physical world depends on its state now, called *context awareness*. Context awareness in IoT refers to the ability of a system to adapt its behavior based on the context, which includes the user's location, time of day, and other environmental factors. Each action is taken, considering the context and why an application can behave differently in separate business contexts. For example, an office member may not like messages from office colleagues to interrupt when that individual is on vacation.

Interoperability in the context of IoT refers to the ability of different systems and devices to communicate and work together effectively. This is crucial for the seamless operation of IoT systems, as it allows for the exchange of data and information between devices, enabling them to perform their functions efficiently. Sensors, actuators, data storage, and the communication network form the central infrastructure of an IoT framework. However, many software aspects need to be considered. First, one needs middleware that can be used to interconnect and manage all these heterogeneous components. This way, the IoT industry needs much standardization to connect many different devices. However, the conceptual realization of IoT is far from achieving a full deployment of converged IoT services and technology. Current information technology and communication (ITC) research focuses on providing integrated solutions, primarily on the feature that enables convergence or "*interoperability*". Interoperability can be simplified as the feature for providing a seamless exchange of information to personalize services automatically or simply exchanging information so that other systems can use it to improve performance, enable and create services, and control operations information processing. This type of scenario requires increased interoperability in service management operations.

This chapter reviews the recent trends and challenges on interoperability in the IoT applications domain, discusses physical versus virtual sensors, and, while addressing technology interoperability challenges in parallel, discusses how, with the growing importance of data understanding and processing, semantic web technologies, frameworks, and information models can support interoperability in the design of services in the industrial information system design. Finally, this chapter aims to identify relevant issues and challenges that need to be considered in the coming and future information system projects.

The remainder of this chapter is described as follows. Section 2 presents the background of IoT-based industrial applications. It includes architectural issues, technological issues (e.g., clod and fog-computing architectural issues), and interoperability related issues for business applications. Section 3 discusses industrial manufacturing applications. Section 4 explains research works. Section 5 presents mathematical concepts using a business case and includes a concept similarity assessment. Finally, section 6 puts forward ideas for future research work. Finally, section 7 concludes the chapter by discussing relevant research issues.

BACKGROUND KNOWLEDGE OF IoT ARCHITECTURE

Reviewing Industrial IoT applications combines many emerging technologies, from sensing and actuating to networking and application-specific service provisions. In this way, the paradigm of industrial IoT application covers a broad range of technological issues (e.g., protocol, architecture, and hardware), network and connectivity technologies (e.g., cellular and Wi-Fi), infrastructure and platform technologies (e.g., standards, and gateway), and users' application-specific technologies (e.g., predictive maintenance, and extended reality). Moreover, there is no unique consensus on architecture for IoT, which is agreed upon universally. Different research groups have proposed different architectures. From the broad scope, this chapter discusses two critical aspects of an industrial IoT ecosystem: (i) architecture and (ii) interoperability of service provision. In the following subsections, the chapter explains these concepts.

Architectural Issues

Three-Layer and Five-Layer Architectures

The most straightforward architecture is a three-layer architecture (Mashal et al., 2015) (Said & Masud, 2013) (Wu et al., 2010), as shown in Figure 1. The presented layered IoT system is initially applied to the Mobile Business Architecture (MBA) entities, and Mobile Internet Technical Architecture (MITA) fundamentals are mapped to these principles and concept models for MIBA and MITA.

The middleware layer in digital Mobile Internet Technical Architecture has been named the Network Layer, as illustrated in Figure 1 (Three Layers) model. The above three-element layers are used for each of the MIBA segments and their elements. In addition, an interaction between the elements is provided with protocols and content delivery within the payloads of the protocols.

This three-layer architecture was introduced in the early research stage in this area. It has got three layers, namely, the perception, network, and finally, application layers.

1. The *perception layer* is the physical layer, with sensors for sensing, gathering data, and creating information about the business operating environment. It senses physical arguments or identifies other smart objects in the business environment.
2. The *network layer* is the sole authority for making other smart objects (e.g., servers, network devices, and physical servers). Its characteristics are also used for transmitting and processing sensor data.
3. The *application layer* is responsible for providing business-specific services to the user. However, there are different applications in which the IoT can be deployed, such as smart cities, factories, smart health, and smart homes.

Figure 1. Layered architectures of IoT system

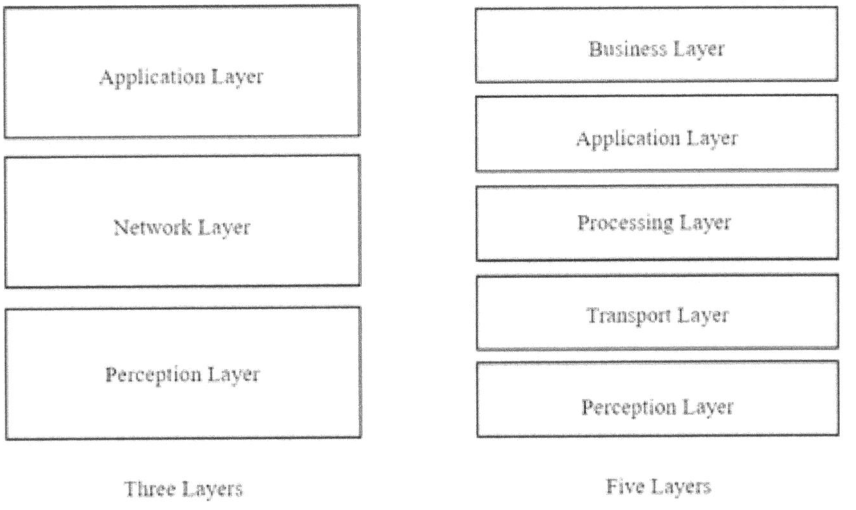

A three-layer architecture defines the main idea of the IoT. However, this is not enough for research on IoT due to its focus on more delicate aspects of the IoT. That is why many more layered architectures are presented in the academic article. One is the five-layer architecture that includes the processing and business layers (Mashal et al., 2015) (Said & Masud, 2013) (Wu et al., 2010) (Khan et el., 2012). The five-layers architecture includes perception, transport, processing, application, and business layers (see Figure 1). The purpose of the perception and application layers is the same as the architecture with three layers. This chapter outlines the function of the remaining three layers.

- The *transport layer* transfers the gathered sensor data from the perception layer to the processing layer and vice versa through data communication networks (e.g., wireless, 3G, LAN, Bluetooth, RFID, and NFC).
- The *processing layer* is also called the middleware layer. It stores, analyses, and processes vast data from the transport layer. It can control and serve diverse services to the lower layers. In addition, it uses many technologies such as databases, cloud computing, and big data processing modules.
- The *business layer* controls the IoT system environment, including applications, profit models, and business and end-users' privacy. However, the business layer details are out of the scope of this chapter.

Another architecture proposed by Ning and Wang (Ning & Wang, 2011) is influenced by the processing layers in a typical human brain. The human intelligence characteristics also inspire it (e.g., think, feel, remember, make decisions, and react to the physical environment). It is constituted of three parts. First is the human brain, analogous to the processing and data management unit or the data centre. The second is the spinal cord, analogous to the distributed network of data processing nodes and smart gateways. The third is the network of nerves, corresponding to the networking components and sensors.

Figure 2. Fog architecture of an innovative IoT gateway

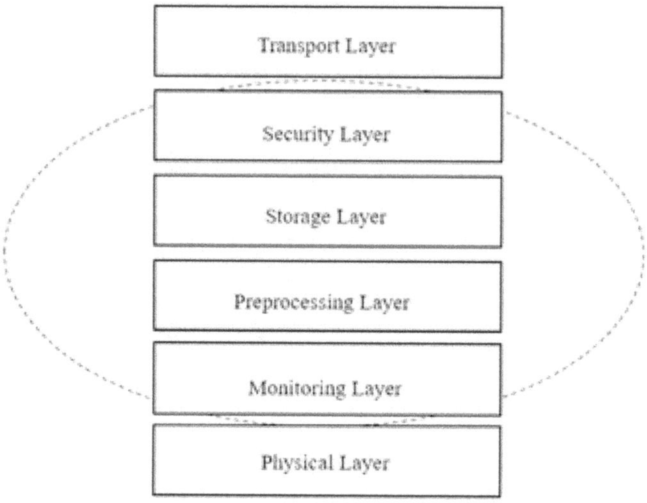

Cloud and Fog Based Architectures

Cloud and fog computing architectures have played a significant role in recent years. In some system architectures, cloud computers do the data processing in a significant, centralized fashion. Such a cloud-centric architecture keeps the cloud at the centre, applications above it, and the network of smart things below it (Gubbi et al., 2013). Cloud computing is given main importance because it gives enormous scalability and flexibility. It provides services (e.g., platform, core infrastructure, storage, and software). Developers can use their storage tools, software tools, data mining, machine learning, and visualization tools through the cloud.

Lately, there has been a move towards another system architecture, namely, *fog computing* (Bonomi et al., 2014) (Bonomi et al., 2012) (Stojmenovic & Wen, 2014), where the sensors and network gateways do a part of the data processing and analytics. A fog architecture (Aazam & Huh, 2014)is shown in Figure 2, including storage, monitoring, pre-processing, and security layers between the transport and physical layers. The monitoring layer looks after power, resources, responses, and services. The processing layer does sensor data filtering, processing, and analytics. The short-time storage layer provides storage functionalities (e.g., data replication, distribution, and storage). Lastly, the security layer uses encryption/decryption to ensure data integrity and privacy. Controlling and pre-processing are done on the edge of the data communication network before sending data to service-oriented computing.

Moreover, "fog computing" and "edge computing" are used interchangeably in different business contexts. The latter term relates to the former and is constructed to be more generic. Fog computing, originally called Cisco, refers to smart gateways and smart sensors, whereas edge computing is slightly more penetrative. This paradigm envisions smart data pre-processing capabilities for physical devices such as motors, pumps, or lights. The aim is to do data processing on these devices located at the *edge* of the network. The diagram is not appreciably different from Figure 2, and this chapter does not describe edge computing details separately.

Interoperability and Related Issues for Business Applications

IoT-based service oriented architecture plays an essential role in modern industrial systems automation. Two central factors, (i) interoperability of business services, and (ii) quality of service (QoS), lay the foundation for system automation. Different ways industrial systems interoperability are contextualized (e.g., technical interoperability, syntactical interoperability, semantic interoperability, pragmatic interoperability, platform interoperability, and conceptual interoperability) for system development purpose. Moreover, academic literature states that the interoperability between IoT devices and computing servers depends on different operational characteristics (e.g., business models, hardware and software composition, communication protocols, and business policies). A research group (Pal & Karakostas, 2014) tried to introduce a hardware and software interoperability issue with an ontology-based system architecture. In this chapter, interoperability represents the capability of heterogeneous things or devices to connect and exchange meaningful information among themselves (Pal, 2023).

The QoS values of a composite service are determined by the QoS values of its component services and by the composition structure used (e.g., sequential, parallel, conditional and/or loops). Here, we focus on the sequential composition model. Other models may be reduced or transformed to the sequential model, using for example techniques for handling multiple execution paths and unfolding loops (Cardoso et al., 2004). Importance of business process orchestration and design patterns are highlighted by academics and practitioners (Courbis & Finkelstein, 2005) (Yoshioka et al., 2004) for service aggregation purpose. In a typical commercial IoT setting, this chapter treats the devices and services as bots to set up relationships between them and change them over time. This will allow the situation to let the devices cooperate and achieve a complex task seamlessly.

One needs to have many interoperating components to make such a model work. So let us look at some of the significant components of such a system.

- Object Identification (ID): One needs a unique way to identify an object. An ID can be allocated to an object based on traditional parameters such as the MAC ID, IPv6ID, a universal product code, or other custom methods.
- Metainformation: Along with an ID, one needs some extra information about the device that describes its characteristics and operational methods.
- Security Controls: This way, an industrial owner of a device might restrict the kinds of devices that can connect to it. These are referred to as *owner control.*
- Service Discovery: Such a system is like a service cloud, where one needs to store details of devices providing certain kinds of services. It becomes essential to keep these directories updated so that devices can learn about other devices.
- Relationship management: This module manages relationship information. For example, it also stores the types of devices that a given device should connect with based on the services provided.
- Service Composition: This module takes the IoT model to a new level. The goal of having such a system is to provide better-integrated services to users.

The rest of the chapter presents a manufacturing service integration example with the help of an ontology-concept similarity assessment algorithm.

INDUSTRIAL MANUFACTURING APPLICATIONS

Today, all manufacturing businesses value the consequence of building an effective supply chain as part of enterprise proliferation and profitability (Pal, 2018). Different industry-specific supply chain types (e.g., automotive, pharmaceutical, apparel, agriculture), and a supply chain consists of a system with organization, people, technology, activity, information, and resource involved in delivering a service or product from suppliers to customers.

Supply chain business activities transform resources into ultimate products and deliver them to customers. The supply chain network comprises the enterprises and departments involved in this process. The essential requirements of supply chain operation are minimizing the inventory, creating seamless material and information flow, effective communication among the business partners, market, sale, purchase, manufacturing plan, and control, customer delivery service, and after-sales service. Therefore, a supply chain is a network of facilities and distribution options that performs material procurement functions, transforming these materials into intermediate and finished products and delivering these finished products to customers. This definition, or a modified version of it, has been used by several researchers (e.g. (Lee & Billington, 1993) (Swaminathan, 2001a) (Keskinocak & Tayur, 2001) (Pal, 2017)). Supply Chain Management (SCM) aims to improve logistical resource allocation, management, and control. In this way, manufacturing SCM is a set of synchronized activities for integrating suppliers, manufacturers, transporters, and efficient customer service so that the right product or service is delivered in the right quantities, at the right time, to the right places (Pal, 2020) (Pal & Ul-Haque, 2020).

The ultimate objective of SCM is the efficient management of the end-to-end process, which starts with the design of the product or service and ends with the time when it has been sold, consumed, and, finally, discarded by the consumer. This process includes product design, procurement, planning and forecasting, production, distribution, fulfillment, after-sales support, and end-of-life disposal. Supply chain management issues can be classified into two broad categories: configuration (design-oriented) issues that relate to the basic infrastructure on which the supply chain executes and coordination (execution-oriented) issues that relate to the actual execution of the supply chain. Configuration-level issues include the following topics:

1. Procurement and Supplier Decisions: Procurement involves making buying decisions under conditions of scarcity. At the same time, the requirements criteria for selecting suppliers and the number of suppliers need to be decided. If sound data is available, using economic analysis methods such as cost-benefit or cost-utility analysis is good practice. Procurement ensures the buyer receives goods, services, or works at the best possible price when aspects such as quality, quantity, time, and location are compared.
2. Production Decisions: This is a multi-criteria decision activity. Does it include the decisions regarding production network design (e.g., Where, and how many manufacturing sites should be used for production purposes? How much capacity should be installed at each of these sites? What kind of products and services will be supported through the supply chain network?).
3. Distribution Decisions: It is based on infrastructure design decisions (e.g., What kind of distribution channels should a manufacturing company have? How many and where should the distribution centers and retail outlets be situated? What types of transportation services and routes should be used? What types of environmental issues does the distribution infrastructure need to be considered?).
4. Information Support Decisions: Managing a manufacturing supply chain involves numerous decisions about the flow of information, product, funds, and coordination. SCM has been instrumental in connecting and smoothing business activities and forming various kinds of business relationships (e.g., Customer Relationship Management, Supplier Relationship Management) among supply chain stakeholders.

Coordination-level issues include the following topics:

1. Material Flow Decisions: These decisions include – How much inventory of different product types should be stored to provide the target service levels? Should inventory be carried in finished form or semi-finished form? How often should inventory be replenished? And so many other issues need to be considered.
2. Information Flow Decisions: SCM systems utilize modern Information and Communication Technologies (ICT) to acquire, interpret, retain, and distribute information. The software applications are ready-made packages, usually targeting a set of tasks, e.g., tracking product-related information during the transportation process. These ready-made package-software applications are mass-customized products that ignore the specific requirements of a particular business sector, so they are problematic. However, the problem of the appropriate IT solutions for supporting collaboration between supply chain business partners is not new, and it has been approached with several standards and protocols implemented in numerous enterprise information systems.

Application like ERP (Enterprise Resource Planning), CRM (Customer Relationship Management), and WMS (Warehouse Management System) contains valuable data that can be utilized by the decision support systems (DSS). Moreover, the digital transformation of business and society presents enormous growth opportunities offered by technologies such as the Internet of Things (IoT), Big Data, advanced manufacturing, blockchain technologies, and artificial intelligence. This digital transformation is characterized by a fusion of advanced technologies and the integration of physical and digital systems, the predominance of innovative business models and new processes, and intelligent products and services.

The main goal was to reduce inventory levels drastically and regulate the suppliers' interaction with the production line more effectively. It consisted of material and information flow through the supply chain organizations. The scope of the supply chain begins with the source of supply and ends at the point of consumption. It extends beyond simply a concern with the physical movement of materials. Equal emphasis is given to supplier management, purchasing, inventory management, manufacturing management, facilities planning, customer service, information flow, transport, and physical distribution. Some of the critical business processes along the supply chain are shown in Figure 3.

Also, the critical challenges in supporting massive heterogeneous data integration in global supply networks are: (i) increasing number of business alliance partners due to the globalization of business processes, (ii) different business practice and infrastructure facilities within participating business partners, and (iii) differences in data exchange formats and standards among business-partners. Moreover, data capture and transmission mechanisms (e.g., barcoding, radio frequency identification technique, electronic data interchange, wireless networking infrastructure and protocols, global positioning system's capability) produce vast amounts of supply chain transportation data that, if properly controlled and shared, can enhance performance and agility of global supply chain networks. A single representation data format is essential to harness the value-added service.

Figure 3. Diagrammatic representation of the supply chain business process

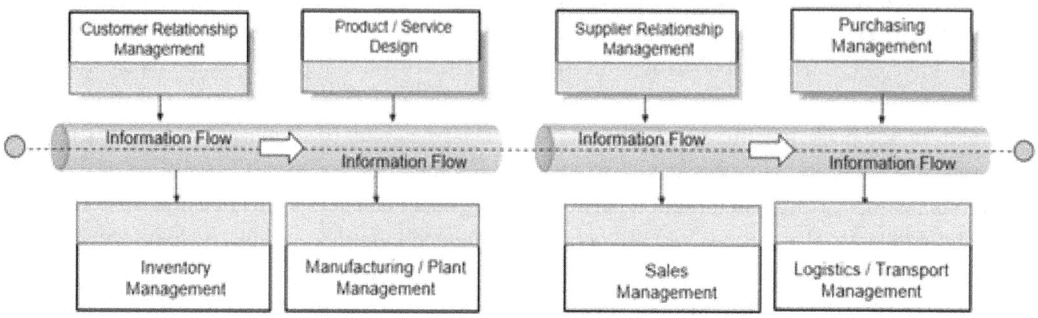

As a result, much global manufacturing (e.g., textile and clothing) businesses invest in new ICT to harness smooth information-sharing ability in their supply chain operations (Monteneggro et al., 2007). With the recent progress in Radio Frequency Identification (RFID) technology, low-cost wireless sensor hardwires, and world comprehensive web technologies, the Internet of Things (IoT) advance has attracted attention in connecting global apparel business activities and sharing operational business information. In this context, IoT technology supports connecting and integrating both digital and physical business entities, enabling the provision of a new type of information system (IS) applications and services. Also, the Semantic Web of Things (SWoT) is ushering in a new opportunity in the business community by integrating the Semantic Web and IoT technologies. It aims to associate semantically rich and easily accessible information with real-world objects, locations, and events using inexpensive, disposable, and unobtrusive micro-devices, such as RFID tags and wireless sensors. This opportunity provides new IS applications and services in many apparel business areas (e.g., manufacturing, inventory, and transportation management).

In order to facilitate this vision, information technologies and software system frameworks must mitigate typical pervasive computing application-related issues: platform heterogeneity, appropriate resource utilization, intelligent intractability of the user, device volatility, dependence on context, and limitation of device-specific computation power. Hence, the SWoT vision requires pervasive knowledge-based systems with higher degrees of automatic capability in information storage, management, and discovery and transparent access to information sources for processing.

Most IoT technology solutions inherit support from stable data communication infrastructures and assistance from centralized brokers for service management and information discovery. Also, optimization of alternative information provision has been recently getting prominence, for example, 6LoWPAN (IPv6 over Low Power Wireless Personal Area Networks) (Monteneggro et al., 2007) and the Constrained Application Protocol (CoAP) (Colitti et al., 2011). In parallel attempts, device and data annotation ontologies were presented, for example - OntoSensor (Russomanno et al., 2005) and the SSN-XG ontology of the World Wide Web Consortium for semantic sensor networks (Lefort et al., 2005). Current research projects, such as UBIWARE (Katasonov et al., 2008), and Sense2Web (Barnaghi et al., 2010), integrate data communication networking and semantic technologies to make software frameworks for semantically enriched IoT application services.

These services are composed of different data sources from real-world objects related to apparel business processes. With many devices in the textile and clothing world, many physical parameters and real-world entities can collaborate in a business service through data communication networks or the Internet. Thus, there is a need for seamless integration of the physical world with the digital world in IoT. Also, the progress in IoT-enabled device abstraction and integrating different data sources in the apparel business is challenging. The traditional web service discovery mechanisms are incapable of producing the appropriate result. Also, the heterogeneous nature of IoT-generated data requires semantic modelling. Thus, IoT entities must be formally represented and managed to achieve interoperability.

An essential step towards the vision of IoT-based information systems interoperability is reusing data collected from widely distributed sensor-enabled devices. Ontology-based semantic modelling helps capture entities' capability to represent information and its relationships among other entities to enable efficient information exchange. In this way, semantic modelling in conjunction with service-oriented computing and ontology, ushers a scalable means of accessing IoT entities. An ontology describes a vocabulary modelling a domain of interest and specifying the meaning of terms in that vocabulary. Depending on the accuracy of this specification, the notion of ontology encompasses different data or conceptual models (e.g., classifications). In other words, ontology is a shared conceptualization, and it is used to represent knowledge as a set of concepts related to each other. The structural part comprises four key components: *classes*, *relations*, *attributes*, and *individuals*. Classes represent the concepts in ontology design, and individuals are the basic, '*ground level*' components or instances of an ontology. Attributes or characteristics represent the features of the classes, and relations describe how the classes and individuals are related to one another.

This chapter presents semantic knowledge-based on IoT-related entities in an apparel manufacturing business. Since most of the IoT data in a textile and clothing industry setting needs to be made available homogeneously to allow integration from various sources. A unified machine-understandable representation of world knowledge must put things into an everyday semantic context. The integrated Apparel Business Decentralised Data Integration (ABDDI) framework uses semantic modelling. Ontologies are used to form a unified knowledge base to support: (a) semantic definition and representation of IoT entities; (b) dynamic service discovery and matching based on user request; and (c) service composition and orchestration in dynamic environments. This chapter considers ontologies as the vital component for automatic service representation, composition, discovery, and orchestration for IoT in dynamic environments. The proposed knowledge base hides the heterogeneity of entities and consequently enables semantic searching and querying capabilities. Finally, the presented knowledge base integrates several existing ontologies related to sensor resources and web services and extends them for IoT.

RELATED RESEARCH WORKS

In recent decades automatic identification technologies are gaining more attraction for industrial applications. These applications are combined with RFID, Electronic Product Code (EPC) technologies, and sensor-based data communication networks to share application-specific data. Advances in ICT are bringing into reality the vision of many uniquely identifiable, interconnected objects and things that gather data from diverse physical environments and deliver the information to various innovative applications and services. In this way, the network of objects (e.g., devices, vehicles, machines, containers), embedded with sensors and software can collect and communicate data over the Internet. The inter-and intra-organizational communication and information exchange are perceived to be facilitated by IoT capability. This, IoT-based technology adoption can be viewed as an additional capability that may add value to the supply chain industries.

While IoT's many applications are used in different supply chain industries (Jandl et el., 2019), industrial IoT (IIoT) focuses primarily on the industrial usage of IoT devices (Jakl et al., 2018) (Jeschke et al., 2017). Thomas Moser's research group recently presented an overview of industrial IoT applications (Jandl et al., 2019) for the smart industry (also known as Industry 4.0). With the advent of the IoT, new opportunities and capabilities emerge in real-time monitoring, management, and optimizing goods distribution and supply chain. As more physical objects in supply chain industries are equipped with barcodes, RFID tags, or sensors, transport, and logistics companies can monitor the movement of physical objects from one location to another. The goal is to track a product along the entire supply chain, including material management, production, transportation, and distribution (Karakostas, 2013).

Manufacturing companies are changing their IT infrastructure towards the fourth industrial revolution (Lasi et al., 2014). The utilization of artificial intelligence (AI) techniques in cyber-physical systems (CPSs) (Broy et al., 2012) is a typical characteristic of this change (Lee et al., 2014). In this context, flexibility is one of the essential criteria for manufacturing companies, mainly because of ever-shorter market launch times and increasing customer demands for individualization (Cheng et al., 2017; Lasi et al., 2014). To conduct industry 4.0 research, researchers use the factory simulation model because companies are often unwilling to provide data from and access to their production lines for research purposes.

More researchers have started concentrating on techniques enabling machines to understand IoT data better intelligently from various sources. In order to use AI applications, contextual operational knowledge must be available in formal and machine-readable representation (Humm et al., 2020). Semantic web services address the issues of automatic discovering, composing, and executing by providing a declarative, ontological framework for describing them. Using AI methods (e.g., automated planning such as (Marrella, 2018) (Marrella & Mecella, 2018), multi-agent systems for decentralized manufacturing control such as (Ciortea et al., 2018), Case-Based Reasoning (CBR) such as Minor et al., 2014) (Muller, 2018)) to enhance flexibility in cyber-physical production workflows (Bordel Sanchez et al., 2018) (Seiger et al., 2018)) inevitably require such semantic annotations.

Much related research work (Puttonen et al., 2010) (Puttonen et al., 2013) exists that already highlights these issues by using semantic web services (SWS). Moreover, the currently available approaches that use semantic web services in the context of Industry 4.0 focus only on specific aspects and do not consider the entire context of a manufacturing environment. Also, the complex reasoning within the knowledge base makes real-time execution and monitoring of manufacturing processes difficult. In this way, managing interoperable industrial applications is the key to success. One of the key components of interoperability is the specific information system's architecture. A reference architecture (RA) represents a robust and ground-level understanding of the scenarios that help recognize problems and difficulties. The key idea of designing a RA (e.g., service-oriented architecture (SOA)) is to highlight modularity, scalability, adaptiveness, and interoperability among the connected heterogeneous devices in a real-time environment (Sarkar et al., 2021) (Schneider, 2018) (Hazra et al., 2021) (Nagarajan et al., 2021).

Several research works propose using SWSs for smart manufacturing in Industry 4.0 but focus only on partial aspects and do not consider the entire shop floor context. For instance, Puttonen et al. (2013) present an approach to using SWSs for executing manufacturing processes using three software agents represented as web services. One of these agents, Service Monitor, is a specialized web service that performs semantic web service composition by using planning techniques concerning a given production goal and the current state of the world provided by a domain ontology. Therefore, they use OWL to describe the state of the production system and OWL-S and SPARQL expressions for semantically describing the available web services that offer production capabilities.

Since modern Cyber-Physical Production Systems (CPPSs) (Monostori, 2014) consist of many different components and therefore, many stakeholders are involved in their development process up to the later use in the manufacturing of products, Lobov et al. (2008) investigated the application of SWSs for orchestration of flexible control. They propose OWL for modelling a Process Taxonomy, Product Ontology, Equipment Ontology, and Service Ontology and discuss the responsibilities of involved persons for knowledge acquisition and maintenance rather than present their detailed semantic specification.

Many academics and practitioners, work-like Henson et al. (Cory et al., 2009), experiment a semantically enhanced sensor service application, known as SemSOS, having the capability to query both high-level knowledge and low-level environmental reading by sensors. Concerning the classical sematic-matchmaking approach, different research groups distinguish among full (subsume), potential (intersection-satisfiable), and partial (disjoint) match types to represent the relevant knowledge of different types of entities (Colucci et al., 2007) and (Li & Horrocks, 2004) respectively. Similarly, queries in ubiquitous infrastructure allow only exact matches with facts derived from a support knowledge base. Non-standard inferences like abduction and contraction are needed to support approximate matches, semantic ranking, and explanations of outcomes (Colucci et al., 2007).

This chapter highlights the requirement for a unified semantic knowledge base for automatic service representation, discovery, modelling, and composition in dynamic environments. Different research projects try to address these issues using ontologies in prototype system design. For example, semantic commonalities in the RFID semantic streams project use DLs for system modelling (Ruta et al., 2011). This work is of considerable interest, but so far, it is sui generis.

All these schemes are worthy of considerable study, and together they represent the wealthiest characterization of a knowledge-based approach in pervasive service computing so far produced. Moreover, the systems are implemented and can be shown to generate relevant services using appropriate data streams.

OVERVIEW OF THE FRAMEWORK

The proposed framework uses model-theoretic semantics modelled in ontologies for IoT-generated data modelling purposes. It helps to gather detailed information regarding the characteristics of IoT devices based on their technical requirements. The advantages of this encoding are – (i) interconnecting different classification systems to represent capabilities and properties of constituent parts, (ii) translating characteristics or properties among compound constituent parts, and (iii) aggregating basic properties into complex properties based on the constituents of a superordinate system. Those concepts can be used and adapted for the IoT to enhance the uses of IoT devices in connecting them as a group, create coordination between IoT devices, and improve their interoperability.

One of the main objectives of this framework is to define an IoT architecture, which can also be used for other applications. The design principle in Apparel Business Semantic Data Management (ABDDI) is that any physical/real-world object in the global textile and clothing business can have a virtual representation through a Virtual Object (VO). AVO uses a semantic representation of the functionality and conceals the varied identity of the real-world object. Multiple VOs can be combined to form a Composite Virtual Object (CVO) that provides more compact and reliable services. In simple, CVOs are combined to form a service request. Thus, the ABDDI architecture has three layers: VO, CVO, and Service, as shown in Figure 4.

The functionalities of the three layers are presented below:

1. VO layer: Real-world objects are represented in the digital format as VO. End-users can search semantically and retrieve information from any existing VO. Also, actuation can be done through the VO.
2. CVO layer: In this layer, VOs are combined to form a service request. This layer caters functionality to search and query categories of CVOs for service provision semantically.
3. Service layer: This layer gets the request from a user and analyses the service requests to determine the categories of CVOs needed for service accomplishment. This layer also performs service composition and orchestration in a dynamic cloth and textile business environment.

Figure 4. RFID tagging level at different stages in the apparel manufacturing network

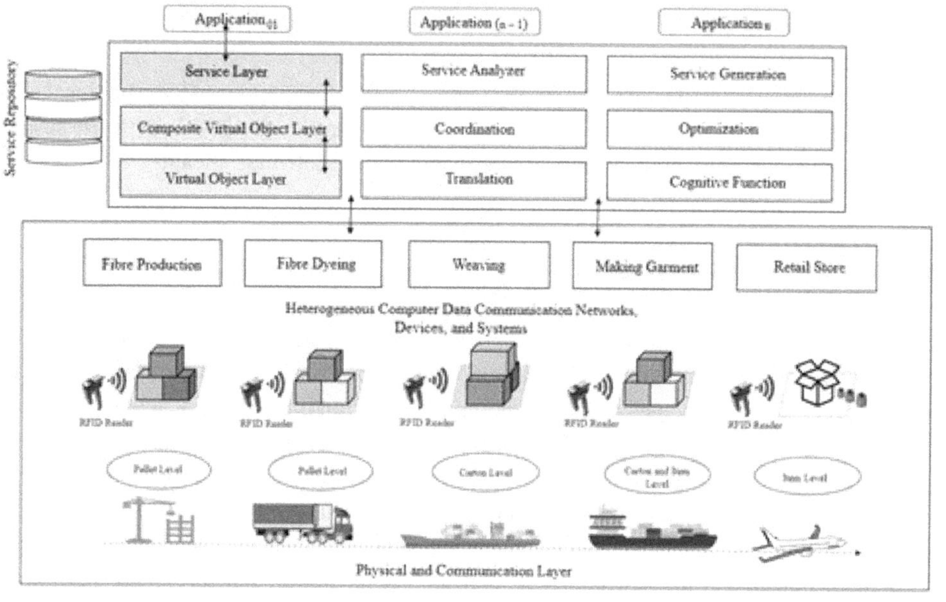

The ABDDI system also has got other components: *a registry* and a *control unit*. Every layer in this framework has a registry referencing the available VOs, CVOs, and services. These registries provide methods to semantically search and query existing VOs, CVOs, and services. In addition, the control unit regulates access to the VOs, CVOs, and services based on the level of the end-user requirements.

KNOWLEDGE REPRESENTATION AND REASONING APPROACH

One of the motivations for this chapter stems from the Description Logics (DL) [1] based knowledge representation approach in pervasive computing applications along the global apparel supply chain. This DL-based knowledge representation systems play a role very much like Database Management Systems (DBMS). In DL, elementary descriptions are *atomic concepts* and *atomic roles*. Complex descriptions can be built from them inductively with *concept constructors*. In abstract notation, one can use the letters A and B for atomic concepts, R for atomic roles, and C and D for concept descriptions. Possible DL constructors and the related examples are shown in Table 1, and these constructors are used in the DLs investigated in this chapter.

Table 1. DLs set of constructors

Constructor Name	Syntax	Explanation
Top concept	$\top$	Universal concept. All the objects in the domain.
Bottom concept	$\bot$	The empty set.
Atomic concept	A	All objects belong to set A.

continued on following page

Table 1. Continued

Constructor Name	Syntax	Explanation
Atomic negation	¬A	All the objects are not belonging to set A.
Conjunction	C⊓D	The objects belong to both C and D sets.
Disjunction	C⊔D	The objects that are in the extension of either C or D or both
Value restriction	∀RC	All the objects are participating in the R relation, whose range is all the objects belonging to the C set.
Existential restriction	∃RC	At least one object participating in the relation R.
Concept definition	A ≡ C	Concepts represent sets of elements and can be viewed as unary predicates.

Resource Representation and Reasoning in Description Logics

The most important and well-known service characterizing reasoning in DL checks for specificity hierarchies by determining whether a concept description is more specific than another one or, formally, if there is a *subsumption* relation between them.

Definition 1 (Subsumption):*Give two concept descriptions, C and D, and a TBox τ in a DL L; one can say that D subsumes $C^{\mathcal{T}}\left(C \sqsubseteq_{\mathcal{T}} D\right)$ concerning if for every model of τ, $C^I \subset D^I$. In a particular case, two concepts are equivalent if they subsume each other.*

For example, consider the following concept descriptions, referring to different garment types in an apparel supply chain network: G_1 = *SweaterBodyGarment* ⊓ ∀ *hasMain.Colour.Red*, and G_2 = *UpperBodyGarment* ⊓ ∀ *hasMain.Colour.Red*. Then using TBox reasoning – the concept inclusion can be achieved, and the output will be *Sweater* $\sqsubseteq_T$*UpperBodyGarment.* Hence, given the model, knowledge expressed by G_1 is more specific than the one required by G_2 concerning the reasoning mechanism and the definition of G_2 subsumes G_1.

Based on subsumption, new reasoning mechanisms can be defined in DLs. The ABDDI system development uses several non-standard reasoning mechanisms (e.g., Least Common Subsumer – LCS).

Definition 2 (Least Common Subsumer):*Let C_1, ..., C_p be p concept descriptions in a DL L. A Least Common Subsumer (LCS) of C_1, ..., C_p, denoted by LCS (C_1, ..., C_p) is a concept description E in L. state that the following conditions hold: (i) $C_h \sqsubseteq E$ for h = 1, ..., p; (ii) E is the least L–concept description satisfying (iii), i.e., if E' is an L–concept satisfying $C_i \sqsubseteq E'$ for all i = 1, ..., n, then $E \sqsubseteq E'$.*

It is worth showing how to model concept collections formalized in ALN (D) according to a compact lossless representation. Such modelling allows for finding commonalities in resource annotations formalized in DL.

Definition 3 (Concept Components):*Let C be a concept described in a DL L, with C formalized as $C^1 \sqcap \dots C^m$. The Concept Components of C are defined as follows: if C^j, with j = 1,..., m is either a concept name, a negated concept name, or a concrete feature or a number restriction, then $C^j$is a Concept Component of C; if C^j=∀R.E, with j = 1 ..., m, then ∀R.E^k is a Concept Component of C, for each E^k Concept Component of E.*

Definition 4 (Subsumption):*Give two concept descriptions C and D, and a TBox τ in a DL L; one can say that D subsumes $C^{\mathcal{T}}\left(C \sqsubseteq_{\mathcal{T}} D\right)$ concerning if for every model of τ, $C^I \subset D^I$. In a particular case, two concepts are equivalent if they subsume each other.*

Definition 5 (Least Common Subsumer):*Let C_1, ..., C_p be p concept descriptions in a DL L. A Least Common Subsumer (LCS) of C_1, ..., C_p, denoted by LCS (C_1, ..., C_p) is a concept description E in L. state that the following conditions hold: (i) $C_h \sqsubseteq E$ for h = 1, ..., p; (ii) E is the least L–concept description satisfying (iii), i.e., if E' is an L–concept satisfying $C_i \sqsubseteq E'$ for all i = 1, ..., n, then $E \sqsubseteq E'$.*

Definition 6 (r-Common Subsumer, Informative r-Common Subsumers):*Let C_1, ..., C_p be p concept descriptions in a DL L, and let be $k \leq p$. An r-Common Subsumer (r-CS) of C_1, ..., C_p is a concept $_{D\neq}$ ⊤ such that D is an LCS of at least r = k/p concepts among C_1, ..., C_p. One can define a particular case as Informative r-Common Subsumers (IrCS) that specific r-CSS for which r < 1.*

It is worth showing how to model concept collections formalized in ALN (D) according to a compact lossless representation. Such a modelling framework allows for finding commonalities in resource annotations formalized in DL.

Definition 7 (Concept Components): *Let C be a concept described in a DL L, with C formalized as $C^1 \sqcap \dots C^m$. The Concept Components of C are defined as follows: if C^j, with j = 1,..., m is either a concept name, a negated concept name, or a concrete feature or a number restriction, then C^j is a Concept Component of C; if $C^j = \forall R.E$, with j = 1 ..., m, then $\forall R.E^k$ is a Concept Component of C, for each E^k Concept Component of E.*

Definition 8 (Aggregate Collection Matrix): *Let S_1, ..., S_n be an aggregate collection, with $S_j = C_{1i}, \dots, C_{pi}$ for i = 1 ... n. Let $D \in \{D_1,\dots,D_m\}$ be the Concept Components deriving from all the concepts in the aggregate collection. The Aggregate Subsumers Matrix is defined as $A = (a_{ij})$, with i = 1 ... n and j = 1 ... m, such that for each i, $a_{ij} = v$, with $0 \leq v \leq p_i$, where v is the number of concept descriptions in S_i subsumed by the component D_j.*

Definition 9 (Aggregate Model): *Let S_1, ..., S_n be an aggregate of concept collections; for i = 1 ... n, S_i is a concept collection descriptions $_{Ski}$ with k = 1 ... p_i. An Aggregate Model for S_1, ..., S_n and each of this element consists of the pair of items - <E, G> with the following characteristics: (i) E represents the subsumers matrix deriving from the collection $C_1,\dots,C_p = \bigcup(C_{ki})$, with i = 1 ... n and k = 1 ... p_i, whose elements e_{kj} are calculated by using prognostications to subsumption; and (ii) G is the collection subsumers matrix deriving from the input collection $S_1,\dots,S_n$, whose elements a_{ij} are calculated by using information stored in E. In this computation, each row i in G is related to an aggregate collection S_i, defined as a collection of description C_{ki} whose subsumption relationship with components deriving from $S_1,\dots$, Sn is stored in E. To this modelling, values a_{ij}, for each component D_j, are determined as Concept Component Relative Cardinality $RC^{S_i}_{D_j}$.*

Semantic Similarity Assessment

Before describing the proposed approach's theoretical framework, the employed reasoning services will be shortly recalled in the following subsection to make the chapter self-contained. Furthermore, the proposed algorithmic concept of similarity measurement is presented in this section.

In ABSDM, the similarity between concepts C_i, C_j can be expressed by a number, and its values can fall between 0 and 1. It may be viewed as a one-directional relation, and its larger values imply a higher similarity between the concepts. The concept similarity is described as follows:

Definition 10 (Concept Similarity): An ontological concept (C) similarity (∂) is considered a *relation*, and it can be defined as $\partial C \times C \rightarrow [0, 1]$. In simple, it is a function from a pair of concepts to a real number between *zero* and *one*, expressing the degree of similarity between two concepts such that:

1. $\forall C_1 \in G, \partial(C_1, C_1) = 1$
2. $\forall C_1, C_2 \in G, 0 \leq \partial(C_1, C_2) \leq 1$
3. $\forall C_1, C_2, C_3 \in G,\ IF\ Sim_d(C_1, C_2) > Sim_d(C_1, C_3)\ THEN\ \partial(C_1, C_2) < \partial(C_1, C_3)$

The above properties provide the range of semantic similarity functions $\partial(C_i, C_j)$. For exactly similar concepts, the similarity is $\partial(C_1,C_1)=1$; when two concepts have nothing in common, their similarity is $\partial(C_1,C_2)=0$. In this way, the output of the similarity function should be in the closed interval [0, 1]. Here Sim_d represents the semantic distance, and (C_1, C_2, C_3) represent three concepts of graph G. In CSIA, the following semantic similarity (∂) function has been used for computation purposes:

$$\partial(C_1, C_2) = \frac{1}{\deg * Sim_d(C_1, C_2) + 1}$$

Where C_1 and C_2 represent two concepts, and 'deg' represents the impact of semantic distance on semantic similarity, it should be between $0 < deg \leq 1$. A weight allocation function is used, as shown below, to compute the semantic similarity between concepts:

$$w(C_m, C_n) = \left[\max\left(depth(C_m)\right) + \frac{OrderNumber(C_n)}{TNodes(G) + 1} + 1\right]^{-1}$$

Where C_m and C_n represents two nodes directly connected, $\max(depth(C_m))$ represents the maximum depth of the node C_m (the depth of the root node is equal to 0 and 1 for the nodes directly connected to the root node and so on), TNodes(G) and OrderNumber(C_n) represent the total number of nodes in concept graph G and the order number of the node (C_n) between their siblings. The detailed description of these mathematical formalizations is beyond the scope of this chapter.

Semantic Similarity Assessment

In ABDDI, the similarity between two concepts C_i, a number can express Cj, and its values can fall between 0 and 1. It may be viewed as a one-directional relation, and its larger values imply a higher similarity between the concepts. The concept similarity is described as follows:

EXAMPLE OF A BUSINESS SCENARIO

A simple apparel manufacturing scenario is used to present a part of ABDDI algorithmic computation. Semantic IoT-based product flow in a retail outlet is considered. Each product is described using semantic-enhanced IoT as an ALN (D) concept expression in OWL language. As the retail apparel product arrive or depart the shop, they are scanned by the gate RFID readers; reading events, including semantic annotation extracted from tags, are fed to a semantic Data Service Management Service (DSMS), which computes Concept Components and subsumption test through a reasoning mechanism.

Let us consider a situation that allows a user to purchase a sweater from an online business. This example considers how a request is matched with the service advertised for wool garments selling service. An algorithm (i.e. Algorithm I) tries to perform semantic matching for a relevant sweater.

Algorithm I. Algorithm for semantic similarity computation

input: two concepts (C_1, C_2), the root node (root), concepts graph (G)
output: semantic similarity value between two concepts
begin
if C_1 and C_2 are same concept then $Sim_d = 0$
else
  if C_1 and C_2 are directly connected then $Sim_d = w(C_1, C_2)$
  else
    if idirect path connection exist then
      S_{path01} = ShortestPath (G, C_1, $Root_N$)
      S_{path02} = ShortestPath (G, C_2, $Root_N$)
      $Sim_d = w(S_{path01}) + w(S_{path02}) - 2*w(CSPath]$
    end if
  $\partial(C_1, C_2) = \frac{1}{\deg * Sim_d + 1}$
  end if
end if
return ∂
end

The algorithm takes two ontological concepts, the root node (root), and the concepts graph (G), as input and computes a semantic similarity between the concepts as output.

Figure 5. The hierarchical concept relationships

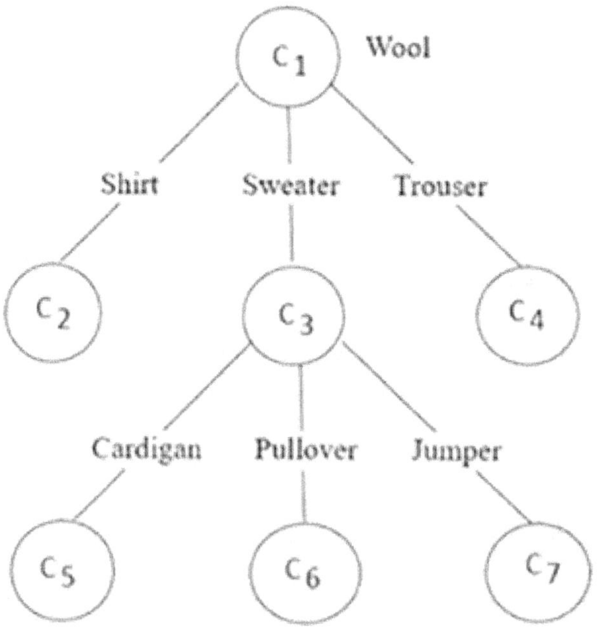

The part of the concept hierarchy used in this example is shown in Figure 5. Each node of this hierarchy represents a concept. The experimental comparison considers semantic similarity among Wool, Shirt, Sweater, Trousers, Cardigan, Pullover, and Jumper. The proposed algorithm (i.e., Algorithm-I) provides semantic similarity between concepts with a higher score than the path similarity algorithm.

Table 3. The results of various similarity measures

	C_1	C_2	C_3	C_4	C_5
C_1	1.00	0.25	0.50	0.20	0.20
C_2	0.25	1.00	0.50	0.33	0.16
C_3	0.50	0.50	1.00	0.25	0.16
C_4	0.20	0.33	0.25	1.00	0.20
C_5	0.20	0.16	0.16	0.20	1.00

(a) Path similarity

	C_1	C_2	C_3	C_4	C_5
C_1	1.00	0.48	0.65	0.51	0.38
C_2	0.48	1.00	0.65	0.51	0.38
C_3	0.65	0.65	1.00	0.71	0.48
C_4	0.51	0.51	0.71	1.00	0.59
C_5	0.38	0.38	0.48	0.59	1.00

(b) The proposed method

In Table 3, (a) is the result of path similarity [18], and (b) tabulates the results of the proposed Algorithm-I used in ABDDI. In ABDDI, the similarity measure is flexible and customizable, allowing the consideration of user preferences. This refers to two aspects. Firstly, the user may determine some of the similarity assessment parameters' relative importance using the advanced search interface. Second, apart from presenting a single rank for each candidate service, more detailed results may also be provided (e.g., different values for recall, and the degree of match) to facilitate the user in identifying the timelier service.

FUTURE RESEARCH DIRECTIONS

Based on the findings, future studies, and experiments must be conducted on semantic reasoning with more diverse information content, complex scenarios, and more detailed contextual knowledge (e.g., rules and other forms). Reasoning engines certainly influence reasoning performance. Thus, different reasoning engines should be evaluated. For example, integrating real-time reasoned knowledge with background knowledge by utilizing federated RDF databases would be valuable, as they can provide background reasoning and knowledge integration services on specific platforms. In the future, the current research plans to use many context scenarios to evaluate the proposed approach's benefit more appropriately.

Although several academic and industry proposals address IoT-based information systems interoperability issues, no reasonable ground can cover some related research issues. The lack of standards and the absence of cutting-edge technologies slow the development of IoT. Proving semantically interoperable platforms across the different IoT domains requires research improvements. Hence, there is still significant room for future work on this topic.

CONCLUSION

This chapter presents some of the uses of IoT technologies (e.g., RFID tag-based technology, sensor) in the apparel industry. RFID technology can interact with items (i.e., transport carts, trolleys, keys, and valuable products) without physical contact in the textile and clothing retail industry. Thus, item-level IoT infrastructures provide item handling efficiency and offer a promising way to capture customers' in-store behavioural data and then gain insight into these data using data mining technology. In this way, these sensing objects and things form the Internet of Things (IoT), which are used to automate manufacturing business processes (e.g., material management, transportation management, and logistics management). In addition, ioT applications rely on real-time context data and allow sending information to drive users' behaviours in intelligent supply chain environments. These IoT-based solutions are mostly tailored for vertical applications and systems, utilizing knowledge only from business areas. However, to realize IoT's full potential, these specialized silo applications must be replaced with horizontal collaborative applications, including knowledge acquisition and sharing capabilities.

One of the main challenges in realizing an IoT system lies in dealing with device and data heterogeneities and fostering the interoperability between devices, information, and services built on top of it. Ontologies and semantic description frameworks play an essential role in the IoT. They operate on top of a standardized data interoperability infrastructure and enforce the concept of data uniformity that allows data and data semantics to be described in application-independent ways. Semantic technologies and ontologies decouple data semantics from application logic, facilitating information exchange, adaptability, and interoperability among tools and systems.

This chapter describes a unified semantic knowledge base (ABDDI) for IoT-related apparel supply chain management technologies. Semantic modelling is a critical component to address issues related to interoperability among different entities to realize the grand vision of IoT. ABDDI's knowledge base comprises ontologies to model different aspects of the apparel business (e.g., IoT resources, location information, contextual information, domain knowledge, policies for the dynamic environment, and IoT services). Most of the current work focuses on IoT resources and services; however, modelling contextual information in a dynamic environment assists in more accurate knowledge representation for IoT entities.

Real-time data gathering and processing are the main ingredients of current supply chain operations. To further enhance the potential of this promising application, in the future, this research will try to propose a unified framework for IoT-based path analytics, which uses both in-store shopping paths and IoT-based purchasing data for actionable navigation patterns. In the pre-processing data module, the critical problem of capturing the mainstream shopping path sequences while wiping out redundant and repeated details must be addressed in detail.

REFERENCES

Aazam, M., & Huh, E. N. (2014). "Fog computing and smart gateway based communication for cloud of things," in Proceedings of the 2nd IEEE International Conference on Future Internet of Things and Cloud (FiCloud' 14), 464–470, Barcelona, Spain, August 2014. DOI: 10.1109/FiCloud.2014.83

Atzori, L., Iera, A., & Morabito, G. (2011). IoT: Giving a social structure to the internet of things. *IEEE Communications Letters, 15*(11), 1193–1195. DOI: 10.1109/LCOMM.2011.090911.111340

Baader, F., Calvanese, D., McGuinness, D., Nardi, D., & Patel-Schneider, P. (Eds.). (2002). *The Description Logic Handbook.* Cambridge University Press.

Barnaghi, P., Presser, M., & Moessner, K. (2010). "Publishing Linked Sensor Data", in *Proceedings of the 3rd International Workshop on Semantic Sensor Networks.*

Berners-Lee, T. (2000). *Weaving the Web: The Original Design and Ultimate Design of the World Wide Web by its inventor.* Harper Business.

Bonomi, F., Milito, R., Natarajan, P., & Zhu, J. (2014). *"Fog computing: a platform for internet of things and analytics," in Big Data and Internet ofThings: A Road Map for Smart Environments.* Springer.

Bonomi, F., Milito, R., Zhu, J., & Addepalli, S. (2012). "Fog computing and its role in the internet of things," in *Proceedings of the 1st ACM MCC Workshop on Mobile Cloud Computing*, 13–16, 2012. DOI: 10.1145/2342509.2342513

Bordel Sánchez, B., Alcarria, R., Sánchez de Rivera, D., & Robles, T. (2018). Process execution in CyberPhysical Systems using cloud and Cyber-Physical Internet services. *The Journal of Supercomputing, 74*(8), 4127–4169. DOI: 10.1007/s11227-018-2416-4

Broy, M., Cengarle, M. V., & Geisberger, E. (2012). Cyber-Physical Systems: Imminent Challenges. In Large-Scale Complex IT Syst. Dev., Operat. and Manag. - 17th Monterey Workshop, volume 7539 of LNCS, 1–28.

Cardoso, J., Sheth, A., Miller, J., Arnold, J., & Kochut, K. (2004). Quality of service for workflows and web service processes. *Journal of Web Semantics, 1*(3), 281–308. DOI: 10.1016/j.websem.2004.03.001

Cheng, H., Xue, L., Wang, P., Zeng, P., & Yu, H. (2017). Ontology-based web service integration for flexible manufacturing systems. In 15th Int. Conf. on Ind. Inf., pages 351–356. IEEE. DOI: 10.1109/INDIN.2017.8104797

Ciortea, A., Mayer, S., & Michahelles, F. (2018). Repurposing Manufacturing Lines on the Fly with Multi-agent Systems for the Web of Things. In Proc. of the 17th Int. Conf. on Autonomous Agents and Multi-Agent Systems, pages 813–822. Int. Found. for Autonomous Agents and Multiagent Systems / ACM.

Colitti, W., Steenhaut, K., Caro, N. De., (2011). "Integrating Wireless Sensor Networks with the Web", Extending the Internet to Low power and Lossy Networks (IP+SN).

Colucci, S., Di Noia, T., Pinto, A., Ruta, M., Ragone, A., & Tinelli, E. (2007). A Nonmonotonic Approach to Semantic Matchmaking and Request Refinement in E-Marketplaces. *International Journal of Electronic Commerce, 12*(2), 127–154. DOI: 10.2753/JEC1086-4415120205

Cory, A., Henson, J., Pschorr, K., Sheth, A. P., & Thirunarayan, K. (2009). "SemSOS: Semantic sensor Observation Service", in *Proceedings of the International Symposium on Collaborative Technologies and Systems.*

Courbis, C., & Finkelstein, A. (2005). Weaving Aspects into Web Service Orchestrations, in *Proceeding of International Conference of Web Services (ICWS '05)*, July 2005. DOI: 10.1109/ICWS.2005.129

De Virgilio, R., Di Sciascio, E., Ruta, M., Scioscia, F., & Torlone, R. (2011). Semantic-based rfid data management. In *Unique Radio Innovation for the 21st Century* (pp. 111–141). Springer. DOI: 10.1007/978-3-642-03462-6_6

Gubbi, J., Buyya, R., Marusic, S., & Palaniswami, M. (2013). Internet of Things (IoT): A vision, architectural elements, and future directions. *Future Generation Computer Systems, 29*(7), 1645–1660. DOI: 10.1016/j.future.2013.01.010

Hazra, A., Adhikari, M., Amgoth, T., & Srirama, S. N. (2021, November). A Comprehensive Survey on Interoperability for IIoT: Taxonomy, Standards, and Future Directions. *ACM Computing Surveys, 55*(1), 1–35. DOI: 10.1145/3485130

Jakl, A., Schoffer, L., Husinsky, M., & Wagner, M. (2018), Augmented Reality for Industry 4.0: Architecture and User Experience, In Proceeding of the 11th Forum Media Technology, CER-WS, 38-42.

Jandl, C., Nurgazina, J., Schoffer, L., Reichl, C., Wagner, M., & Moser, T. (2019). SensiTrack – A Privacy by Design Concept for Industrial IoT Applications, In *Proceeding of the 24th IEEE International Conference on Emerging Technologies and Factory Automation*, 10-13 September, Zaragoza, Spain, 1782-1789. DOI: 10.1109/ETFA.2019.8869186

Jeschke, S., Brecher, C., Meisen, T., Ozdemir, D., & Eschert, T. (2017), Industrial Internet of Things and Cyber Manufacturing Systems, In Industrial Internet of Things, Springer, 3-19.

Karakostas, B. (2013). A DNS architecture for the Internet of things: A case study in transport logistics. *Procedia Computer Science, 19*, 594–601. DOI: 10.1016/j.procs.2013.06.079

Katasonov, A., Kaykova, O., Khriyenko, O., Nikitin, S., & Terziyan, V. (2008). "Smart Semantic Middleware for the Internet of Things", in *Proceedings of the 5th International Conference of Informatics in Control, Automation and Robotics*, 11-15.

Keskinock, P., & Tayur, S. (2001). Quantitive analysis of Internet-enabled supply chain. *Interfaces, 31*(2), 70–89. DOI: 10.1287/inte.31.2.70.10626

Khan, R., Khan, S. U., Zaheer, R., & Khan, S. (2012). "Future internet: the internet of things architecture, possible applications and key challenges," in Proceedings of the 10th International Conference on Frontiers of Information Technology (FIT '12), 257–260, December 2012. DOI: 10.1109/FIT.2012.53

Lasi, H., Fettke, P., Kemper, H.-G., Feld, T., & Hoffmann, M. (2014). Industry 4.0. BISE, 6(4):239–242. Lastra, J. L. M. and Delamer, I. M. (2006). Semantic Web Services in Factory Automation: Fundamental Insights and Research Roadmap. *IEEE Transactions on Industrial Informatics, 2*(1), 1–11.

Lee, H. L., & Billington, C. (1992). Managing supply chain inventories: Pitfalls and opportunities. *Sloan Management Review, 33*(3), 65–77.

Lee, J., Kao, H.-A., & Yang, S. (2014). Service Innovation and Smart Analytics for Industry 4.0 and Big Data Environment. *Procedia CIRP, 16*, 3–8. DOI: 10.1016/j.procir.2014.02.001

Lefort, L., Henson, C., Taylor, K., Barnaghi, P., Compton, M., Corcho, O., Garcia-Castro, R., Graybeal, J., Herzog, A., Janowicz, K., ... (2005). "Semantic Sensor Network XG Final Report", 2011, W3C Incubator Group Report, https://www.w3.org/2005/Incubator/ssn/XGR-ssn/

Li, L., & Horrocks, I. (2004). A software framework for matchmaking based on semantic web technology. *International Journal of Electronic Commerce, 8*(4), 39–60. DOI: 10.1080/10864415.2004.11044307

Lobov, A., Lopez, F. U., Herrera, V. V., Puttonen, J., & Lastra, J. L. M. (2008). Semantic Web Services framework for manufacturing industries. In Int. Conf. on Rob. and Biomim., pages 2104–2108. IEEE.

Maass, W., Filler, A. (2006). Towards an infrastructure for semantically annotated physical products. INFORMATIK 2006–Informatik für Menschen–Band 2, Beiträge der 36. Jahrestagung der Gesellschaft für Informatik eV (GI).

Mahon, B. (2004). *The Man Who Changed Everything: The Life of James Clerk Maxwell*. John Wiley & Sons Ltd.

Marrella, A. (2018). Automated Planning for Business Process Management.

Mashal, I., Alsaryrah, O., Chung, T. Y., Yang, C. Z., Kuo, W. H., & Agrawal, D. P. (2015). Choices for interaction with things on Internet and underlying issues. *Ad Hoc Networks*, *28*, 68–90. DOI: 10.1016/j.adhoc.2014.12.006

Minor, M., Montani, S., & Recio-García, J. A. (2014). Process-oriented Case-based Reasoning. *Information Systems*, *40*, 103–105. DOI: 10.1016/j.is.2013.06.004

Monostori, L. (2014). Cyber-physical Production Systems: Roots, Expectations and R&D Challenges. *Procedia CIRP*, *17*, 9–13. DOI: 10.1016/j.procir.2014.03.115

Montenegro, G., Kushalnagar, N., Hui, J., & Culler, D. (2007). "Transmission of IPv6 packets over IEEE 802.15.4 networks," Internet proposed standard RFC, vol. 4944.

Müller, G. (2018). Workflow Modeling Assistance by Casebased Reasoning. Springer Fachmedien, Wiesbaden.
Ocker, F., Kovalenko, I., Barton, K., Tilbury, D., and VogelHeuser, B. (2019). A Framework for Automatic Initialization of Multi-Agent Production Systems Using Semantic Web Technologies. *IEEE Robotics and Automation Letters*, *4*(4), 4330–4337.

Nagarajan, S. M., Muthukumaran, V., Vinoth Kumar, V., Beschi, I. S., & Magesh, S. (2021). *Fine Tuning Smart Manufacturing Enterprise Systems: A Perspective of Internet of Things-Based Service-Oriented Architecture, Handbook of Research on Innovations and Applications of AI, IoT, and Cognitive Technologies, IGI Publication, September 2018, USA*. IGI Global Publication. DOI: 10.4018/978-1-7998-6870-5.ch006

Ning, H., & Wang, Z. (2011). Future internet of things architecture: Like mankind neural system or social organization framework? *IEEE Communications Letters*, *15*(4), 461–463. DOI: 10.1109/LCOMM.2011.022411.110120

Pal, K. (2017). Supply Chain Coordination Based on Web Services. In Chan, H. K., Subramanian, N., & Abdulrahman, M. D. (Eds.), *Supply Chain Management in the Big Data Era* (pp. 137–171). IGI Global Publication. DOI: 10.4018/978-1-5225-0956-1.ch009

Pal, K. (2018). *"A Big Data Framework for Decision Making in Supply Chain"*, In M. V Kumar, G. D. Putnik, J. Javakrishna, V. M. Pillai, L. Varela (Edited); IGI Publication, September 2018, USA, Chapter 1, IGI Global Publication, Hershey PA, USA.

Pal, K. (2020). "Information Sharing for Manufacturing Supply Chain Management Based on Blockchain Technology", in Dr Idongesit Williams (Eds.), Cross-Industry Use of Blockchain Technology and Opportunities for the Future, Chapter 1, May, IGI Global Publication, Hershey PA, USA. DOI: 10.4018/978-1-7998-3632-2.ch001

Pal, K., & Karakostas, B. (2014). A Multi Agent-Based Service Framework for Supply Chain Management, In the proceeding of International Conference on Ambient Systems, Networks and Technology. *Procedia Computer Science*, *32*, 53–60. DOI: 10.1016/j.procs.2014.05.397

Pal, K., & Ul-Haque, A. (2000). "*Internet of Things and Blockchain Technology in Apparel Manufacturing Supply Chain Data Management*", In the proceeding of 11th International Conference on Ambient Systems, Networks and Technologies (ANT-2020), Procedia Computer Science, pp. 450- 457, April 6-9, Warsaw, Poland.

Pena-opez, I. (2005). Internet Report 2005. *Internet of Things : Engineering Cyber Physical Human Systems*, •••, 2005.

Puttonen, J., Lobov, A., & Lastra, J. L. M. (2013). Semantics-Based Composition of Factory Automation Processes Encapsulated by Web Services. *IEEE Transactions on Industrial Informatics*, *9*(4), 2349–2359. DOI: 10.1109/TII.2012.2220554

Puttonen, J., Lobov, A., Soto, M. A. C., & Lastra, J. L. M. (2010). A Semantic Web Services-based approach for production systems control. *Advanced Engineering Informatics*, *24*(3), 285–299. DOI: 10.1016/j.aei.2010.05.012

Russomanno, D. J., Kothari, C. R., & Thomas, O. A. (2005). "Building a Sensor Ontology: A Practical Approach Leveraging ISO and OGC Models", in the 2005 International Conference on Artificial Intelligence, 637-643.

Ruta, M., Colucci, S., Scioscia, F., Di Sciascio, E., & Donini, F. M. (2011). Finding commonalities in RFID semantic streams. *Procedia Computer Science*, *5*, 857–864. DOI: 10.1016/j.procs.2011.07.118

Said, O., & Masud, M. (2013). Towards internet of things: Survey and future vision. *International Journal of Computer Networks*, *5*(1), 1–17.

Sarkar, I., Adhikari, M., Kumar, N., & Kumar, S. (2021). Dynamic task placement for deadline-aware IoT applications in federated for networks. *IEEE Internet of Things Journal*, *1*, 2021.

Sarkar, T. K., Mailloux, R. J., Oliner, A. A., Salazar-Palma, M., & Sengupta, D. L. (2006). *History of Wireless*. John Wiley & Sons Inc. DOI: 10.1002/0471783021

Schneider, M., Hippchen, B., Abeck, S., Jacoby, M., & Herzog, R. (2018). Enabling IoT platform interoperability using a systematic development approach by example, In Proceedings of the Global Internet of Things Summit (GIoTS'18), IEEE, 1-6, 2018. DOI: 10.1109/GIOTS.2018.8534549

Seiger, R., Huber, S., & Schlegel, T. (2018). Toward an execution system for self-healing workflows in cyber-physical systems. *Software & Systems Modeling*, *17*(2), 551–572. DOI: 10.1007/s10270-016-0551-z

Stojmenovic, I., & Wen, S. (2014). "The fog computing paradigm: scenarios and security issues," in Proceedings of the Federated Conference on Computer Science and Information Systems (FedCSIS' 14), 1–8, IEEE, Warsaw, Poland, September 2014. DOI: 10.15439/2014F503

Swaminathan, J. M. (2000). *Supply chain management*. International Encyclopedia of the Social and Behavioural Sciences, Elsevier Sciences.

Varelas, G., Voutsakist, E., Raftopoulout, P., Petrakis, E. G. M., & Milios, E. (2005). "Semantic Similarity methods in WordNet and their application to information retrieval on the Web, in *Proceedings of the 7th annual ACM international workshop on web information and data management*, Bremen, Germany: ACM. DOI: 10.1145/1097047.1097051

Vermesan, O., Friess, P., & Guillemin, P. (2011). "Internet of things strategic research roadmap," in Internet of Things. *Global Technological and Societal Trends*, *1*, 9–52.

Weyrich, M., & Ebert, C. (2016). Reference architectures for the internet of things. *IEEE Software*, *33*(1), 112–116. DOI: 10.1109/MS.2016.20

Wu, M., Lu, T. J., Ling, F. Y., Sun, J., & Du, H. Y. (2010) "Research on the architecture of internet of things," in Proceedings of the 3rd International Conference on Advanced Computer Theory and Engineering (ICACTE' 10), vol. 5, 484-487, IEEE, Chengdu, China, August 2010.

Yoshioka, N., Honiden, S., & Fnkelstein, A. (2004). Security Patterns: A Method for Constructing Secure and Efficient Inter-Company Coordination Systems, in *Proceedings of Enterprise Distributed Object Computing Conference 2004 (EDOC'04)*, 84–97, 2004. DOI: 10.1109/EDOC.2004.1342507

Zhao, J., & Kumar, V. V. (2021). *Handbook of Research on Innovations and Applications of AI, IoT, and Cognitive Technologies*. IGI Global Publication. DOI: 10.4018/978-1-7998-6870-5

Chapter 18
Evolvement of Digital Technology in Hospitality Industry

Umang Bhartwal
https://orcid.org/0009-0003-3202-615X
NIMS University, India

Monika Rani
https://orcid.org/0000-0002-9415-4777
Chandigarh University, India

Rajeev Mathur
NIMS University, India

Mantosh Kadela
NIMS University, India

ABSTRACT

This study presented the key factors which motivates to opt the digital technology in the hospitality: Efficiency & Automation, Customer Satisfaction, Coordination of Systems in the hotel related to the wants of the guest. Whereas, this also helps to accumulate the data related to the guest for the decision making at the different stages of the action, starts form the initial stage for searching the hotels till the last stage of the feedback about the stay in the hotel.The purpose of the study is to evaluate the role of Technology in the hospitality especially in the hotel industry operations concerning with the tourist who stay as guest in the hotel. For the study hotel professional sample size of 36 in numbers who are employees in the hotels at different position of the management This also useful for the creation of brand in the accommodation industry Creating the Loyalties, Personalized Marketing, Loyalty Promotion, Enhance Guest Experience which helps to frame the strategies for the Tourism market.

INTRODUCTION

Digital Technology currently contributes to every aspect of Human life due to its ease and user-friendly interface. In the Hospitality Industry, technology in many ways but the more significant ways to generate guest satisfaction help in branding as well as revenue via repeat business. Digital Technology fosters many ways to manage the hospitality industry's resources, especially in real-time decision-making. The hospitality industry constitutes many sectors such as the accommodation industry, the food industry, and the transportation industry with allied industry in the involvement of tourism activities. Digital technology transforms the hospitality world at large from

DOI: 10.4018/979-8-3693-7447-4.ch018

both dimensions; tourists and hosts. In the concern with hospitality front office operations become evident which is the front key point between the guest and hotel professional interaction, which helps to shape the guest satisfaction as tourist and operational efficiencies.

Front offices involve many actions related to the operations which falls into prior, during and post stay of the tourist such as reservation, check ins, handling tourist inquires and complaints. In earlier days all the functions are performed by the manually and then covert into digital form in order to keep the data related to the guest in a proper manner. In late 80's, when computer technology becoming in trends into daily practices. Hospitalities also involved computer technologies as practices due to its greats features such as takes less time to produce information, large storages, easy to maintain and many more. In presents days the role of digital technologies at high pace due to involvement Artificial intelligence (AI), Internet of things (IoT) and cloud computing. There are top significant factors engaged such as streamline operations, personalized and tailor made services which helps to gain the customer satisfaction along with valuable insights for the decision making. Digital technology aids to redesign the front office operations in more significant ways by offering the advance customer relationship management that helps the hotel to gather, analyzed the data of guests behaviors and helps to frame the right strategies for targeting the customer and tourism market.AI helps to discharge routine task of the front office departments operations; responding normally quarries, handling reservations, so that human efforts are going to be engaged in the complex task.

Figure 1. KEY AREA IMPACT OF AI in Front Office Operation in a Hotel

Source: Author

The above figure 1 presented the key aspect of AI in front office operation related to the operations that also deals with the guest as customer satisfactions along with integration of coordination with other departs of the hotel.

1. **Effectiveness & computerization:** This aspect of the AI contributing allot in the front office operation by reducing the intervention of staff of the front office in concern to discharge the routine task such as show round of the hotels and room to the expected guest about the hotels amenities, facilities or rooms, taking reservations, check-in that helps to save the time of the guest and allows the front office personal too offer the personalized services to the guest for specific needs or wants.
2. **Guest Experience:** Virtual assistance and chatbots deals with the regular queries of the guest and tourist who stay in the hotel and enhance the guest satisfactions via offering the quick and accurate response to the guest through the data driven.
3. **Coordination of System:** Current Property Management System establishes the proper coordination among the different process of the hotel which are very significant such as reservation, housekeeping and billing through access of data on real time.

Technology driven using collection of Data of Guest: in present days, hotels opted the practices to collect the data and transform the data into useful information by analyzing the concerning with the guest wants, psychological conditioning and feedback that helps to improve the image of the hotels and creates the brand loyalty.

Figure 2. Data Collection Tools

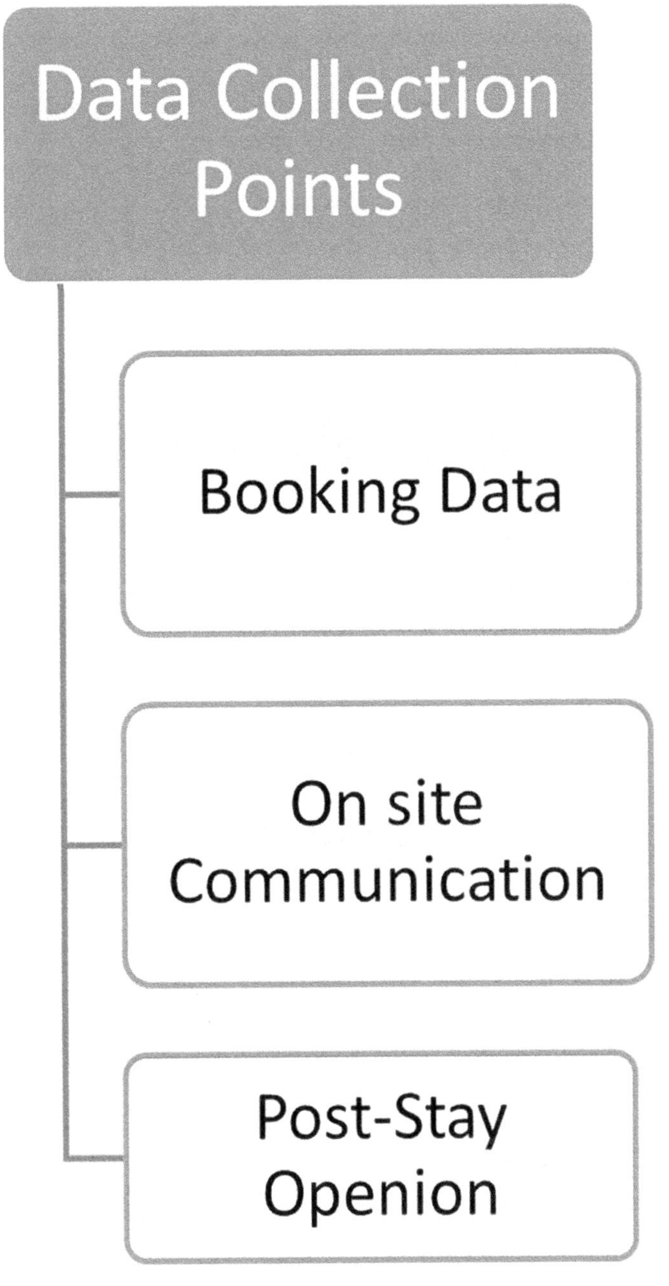

Source: Author

Data plays an significant role in many operations specially dealing with the decision making process at any level of organization or hotels. There are different ways about the collection of data in the hotel industry as per above Figure 2.

- **Booking Data:** at the time of first interaction with the hotels and expected guest for the purpose of reservation, guest disclose useful information about the demographic aspect such as Gender, Age, resident and id cards detail on along with date of arrival- departure in a city and check-in and check-out and wants.
- **On site communication**: on site communication plays an significant role for gathering the information and experience of the guest as customer.
- **Post Stay Opinion:** This is the kind of feedback based on the experience which guest received prior and during the stay or using the service of the hotels or any amenities.

The tools given by the digital technology helps to create the strategies loyalties among the customers who stayed into the hotels.

Figure 3.

Source: Author

The above figure disclose about the creation of the loyalties among the customer in aspect of using strategies approaches framed for marketing in way of customer tailored made programs, loyalties Promotions Schemes and enhance Guest experience through decision making by the host such as accommodation industry, and other locals stakeholders for the customers as tourist.

LITERATURE REVIEW

There are many of the manuscript offers the insight about the recent uses of the technologies in to day to day life of the human being related dimension. Some of the technologies contribute at large in hotel and hospitality industry.

Technologies plays an SMART role in tourism and hospitality industry using specific features of the technologies which are Simple "Multi-Attribute Rating Technique" to present the information in a graphical and tabular form that helps to take the right decision about the tourist needs and stake holder about the many of the needs and wants during and prior of the visit to plan the specific destinations and groups of places (Sihotang et al., 2021). Significance of technologies in the marketing and branding of the hospitality and hotel industry for the promotional action using the ANRIOD Technology that effective and efficient among the tourism market (Idris et al., 2021). Technologies helps to create the customer satisfaction for the smart tourism destination as technologies list down many important features such as accumulation of many data, analysis in less time and helps to take the decision by the both; tourist and host in aspect of tourism activities (Effendi et al., 2023). Culinary tourism is one of the secondary motives of the tourist who spend a large amount on the food and culinary experiences which includes the tasting, learning and enjoying the Festive dishes ANRIOD technologies offers the next edge to the memorizing to the tourist during the trip (Nurhadianis et al., 2018).

Technology also aids to generate the repeat tourism due to access of information by developing the mobile APP for the users as tourist and host which connect directly for the services of hospitality including transportation, lodging and food wants (Jauhari et al., 2020). Technologies address the many concerns of the business now a day's which are broadly classified about the marketing, branding, promotions and other timely issues dealing with the decision making for the management (Saratkar, 2019). There are three main aspect involved the uses of digital technology in the hostel industry; internet, cost and nitration with the customer, where the study revealed that there are very less users friendly before 2016 (Sharma, 2016). "Technology is employed in every aspect of the business, from surveillance and security cameras to reservation and POS systems, meeting matrices, property management software, mobile communication and energy management software to electronic and wireless key cards. Almost every part of modern life is touched by technology, and it has become a formidable competitor in almost every industry. Thanks to technological progress, we are now able to do tasks more quickly, with fewer employees, and with less overall effort. The hospitality sector is shifting its perspective on the use of technology. The hospitality sector is committed to investing in technology in order to boost customer satisfaction." (Kant & Koti, 2023). Technology improves the experience of the tourist as guest who stayed in the hotel during the trip by considering the aspect of establishment of system for the service of guest, timely addressing the guest needs in the hotel as well as dealing with the guest request (Dsouza et al., 2023). In the technology driven hotels, giving the reframe the services of the hotel in term of leisure and hospitality across the world (Kansakar et al., 2019).

RESEARCH METHODOLOGY

After considering the above literature reviews, the study is going to aim the objective concern with the address about the role of technology in hotel operations among the departments especially front office. The Sample of the population for the article are hoteliers and front office professional who are very first connection point with the guest in regards to reservation, check in and in the last for the final settlement of the bill of the Hotel services. The hotels of Rajasthan taken into consideration for the study; rural and urban region. As Rajasthan is one the remarkable destination in the world as per statistical report of Tourism Organization.

DATA ANALYSIS

This part presented the result in a systematic and graphical manner along with the tabular form which gives the better understanding about the readers. Here, the Qualification and Position in the hotels presented after using the descriptive statistics and also presented in a pie chart. For the Hypothesis testing non parametric test were applied which shown the result for the hypothesis about stand of Null and Alternative options.

Table 1. Qualification

		Frequency	Percent	Valid Percent	Cumulative Percent
Valid	Graduation	18	50.0	50.0	50.0
	Post Graduation	11	30.6	30.6	80.6
	Under Graduation	7	19.4	19.4	100.0
	Total	36	100.0	100.0	

Inferences

The above table (A:1) show the result for the participant 's Qualification in regards to the study who are employed in hotels of the Rajasthan at the different position. The qualification consider for the study are in three categories such as Graduation, Post Graduation and Under Graduation. The study shown that Graduation, Post Graduation and Under graduation stands with percentage as 50.0, 30.6 and 19.4 respectively.

Figure 4. Qualification

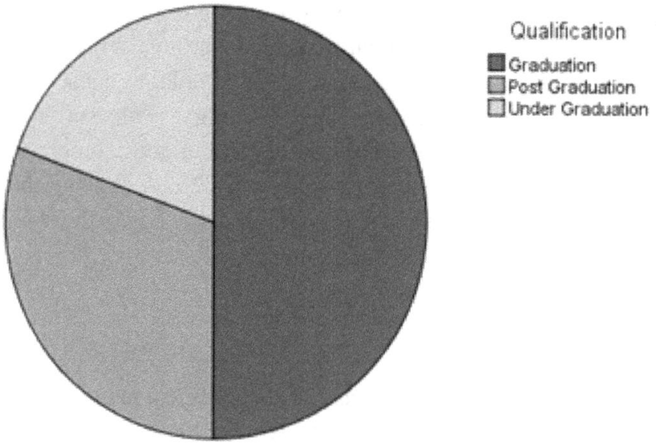

Table 2. Position in Hotel

		Frequency	Percent	Valid Percent	Cumulative Percent
Valid	Higher Level	17	47.2	47.2	47.2
	Lower Level	15	41.7	41.7	88.9
	Middle Level	4	11.1	11.1	100.0
	Total	36	100.0	100.0	

Inferences

Table 2 reflects the information about the hotel professional who are employed in many of the hotel majorly classified in to different position of the hotel such as Higher Level, Lower Level and middle Level which are in percentage of 47.2, 41.7 and 11.1 respectively. The study, disclosed about the higher level management are more habitual user about the digital technology in the hotel industry.

Figure 5.

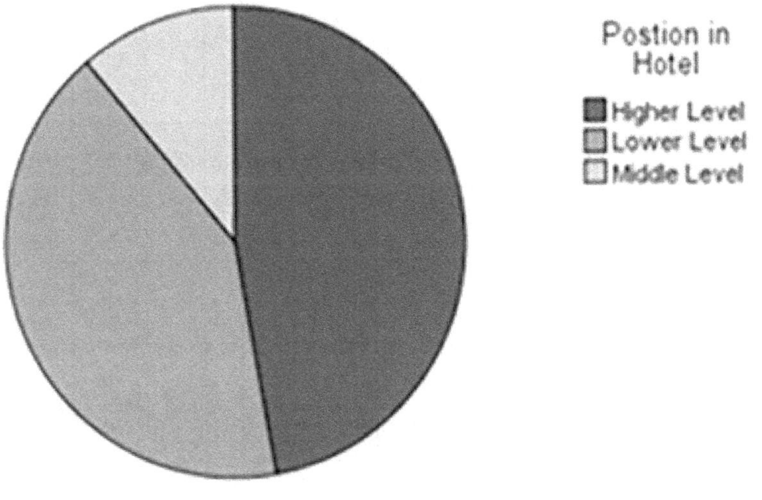

CORRELATION MATRIX

Below table showing the result about the different aspect of the digital technological dimension such as user friendly interface, payment aspect, creation of brand, digital technology contribution in hotel operations and system, for reservation purpose as well as

Table 3. Correlations

		Digital Technology Interface easy to use.	Many of the Tourist make the payment through Digital Technology.	Guest Techno Friendly nature creates the "WOW" Factors among the tourist.	Digital Technology improve Efficiency of the Hotel Operations.	Most of The time Tourist make the reservation through Digital Platform.	Digital Technology Improves the Communication among the Hotels Department and concern Authorities.	Challenges involve in Digital Technology Adoptions.
Digital Technology Interface easy to use.	Pearson Correlation	1	-.110	.185	.201	-.172	.138	-.052
	Sig. (2-tailed)		.524	.281	.240	.317	.421	.764
	N	36	36	36	36	36	36	36
Many of the Tourist make the payment through Digital Technology.	Pearson Correlation	-.110	1	.080	-.342*	.201	-.189	.033
	Sig. (2-tailed)	.524		.641	.041	.240	.271	.849
	N	36	36	36	36	36	36	36
Guest Techno Friendly nature creates the "WOW" Factors among the tourist.	Pearson Correlation	.185	.080	1	-.002	.183	.132	.258
	Sig. (2-tailed)	.281	.641		.989	.287	.444	.128
	N	36	36	36	36	36	36	36
Digital Technology improve Efficiency of the Hotel Operations.	Pearson Correlation	.201	-.342*	-.002	1	-.385*	.363*	-.177
	Sig. (2-tailed)	.240	.041	.989		.020	.029	.301
	N	36	36	36	36	36	36	36
Most of The time Tourist make the reservation through Digital Platform.	Pearson Correlation	-.172	.201	.183	-.385*	1	.071	.255
	Sig. (2-tailed)	.317	.240	.287	.020		.681	.133
	N	36	36	36	36	36	36	36
Digital Technology Improves the Communication among the Hotels Department and concern Authorities.	Pearson Correlation	.138	-.189	.132	.363*	.071	1	.235
	Sig. (2-tailed)	.421	.271	.444	.029	.681		.167
	N	36	36	36	36	36	36	36
Challenges involve in Digital Technology Adoptions.	Pearson Correlation	-.052	.033	.258	-.177	.255	.235	1
	Sig. (2-tailed)	.764	.849	.128	.301	.133	.167	
	N	36	36	36	36	36	36	36

*. Correlation is significant at the 0.05 level (2-tailed).

Inferences

The above table showing the correlation between the different factors; Digital Technology easy to use, payment via Digital technology, WOW factors among tourist for the different services and hospitality aspect, efficiency of the hotel operations among the different departments of the hotel, reservation, as well as challenges for opting the digital technology in the hospitality and hotel industry. All are showing the positive relation in correlation with the significance level of 0.05 Level at 2 –Tailed.

Figure 6.

Hypothesis Test Summary

	Null Hypothesis	Test	Sig.	Decision
1	The categories of Gender occur with equal probabilities.	One-Sample Chi-Square Test	.000[1]	Reject the null hypothesis.
2	The categories of Qualification occur with equal probabilities.	One-Sample Chi-Square Test	.076[1]	Retain the null hypothesis.
3	The categories of Postion in Hotel occur with equal probabilities.	One-Sample Chi-Square Test	.017[1]	Reject the null hypothesis.
4	The categories defined by Hotel is at Rural & Urban = Rural and Urban occur with probabilities 0.5 and 0.5.	One-Sample Binomial Test	.617[1]	Retain the null hypothesis.
5	The distribution of Digital Technology Interface easy to use. is normal with mean 2.1 and standard deviation 1.194.	One-Sample Kolmogorov-Smirnov Test	.000[1]	Reject the null hypothesis.
6	The distribution of Digital Technology Adoption needs time to opt. is normal with mean 2.0 and standard deviation 1.028.	One-Sample Kolmogorov-Smirnov Test	.000[1]	Reject the null hypothesis.
7	The distribution of Digital Technology Need Training. is normal with mean 1.7 and standard deviation 0.632.	One-Sample Kolmogorov-Smirnov Test	.000[1]	Reject the null hypothesis.
8	The distribution of Technology Adoption required Specific Education Qualification. is normal with mean 1.8 and standard deviation 1.082.	One-Sample Kolmogorov-Smirnov Test	.000[1]	Reject the null hypothesis.
9	The distribution of Digital Technology offers information in less time is normal with mean 1.9 and standard deviation 0.630.	One-Sample Kolmogorov-Smirnov Test	.000[1]	Reject the null hypothesis.
10	The distribution of Digital Technology Helps to Improves the Tourist Satisfaction. is normal with mean 1.8 and standard deviation 0.681.	One-Sample Kolmogorov-Smirnov Test	.000[1]	Reject the null hypothesis.
11	The distribution of Most of The time Tourist make the reservation through Digital Platform. is normal with mean 1.6 and standard deviation 0.728.	One-Sample Kolmogorov-Smirnov Test	.000[1]	Reject the null hypothesis.

Asymptotic significances are displayed. The significance level is .05.

[1] Lilliefors Corrected

Inferences

The above Hypothesis testing using “one sample Kolmogorovsmirov test” with the significance level of 0.05. that disclosed the result for the for the stand of Alternative hypothesis for Qualification of Hoteliers and rural or Urban region of Hotel in Rajasthan. Rest Digital Technology aspects in the variables stand for the null hypothesis.

The data analysis part of the study presented the result which are derived through the statistical tools; parametric and non parametric in classification of the statistics.

CONCLUSION

Digital technology presently plays an significance role in the hotel operations of the hospitality industry, carried out from the first step till the last of the guest stay in the hotels. The first step related to the queries as well as taking the reservation of the guest and helps them to check in and continuous step till the last of the guest stay via considering the action of checkout after the settlement of the bill heads of the payment which are presented to the guest thorough the mobile link and other digital mode. This paper consider many of the factors concerning with the digital technology such as users friendly, payment by the guest, creating the brand in the mind of guest via coordination through different activities of the hotel related to the guest wants, desire and need in the hospitality industry. This also helps to save the human efforts in the routine activities which helps the employees of the hotel to put their efforts in the unique wants of the guest and handling the guest complaints if any. But only few of the hotels offering this facilities to the guest . So Hotel industry needs to apply this technology at large for the guest satisfaction and repeat business in the accommodation industry.

REFERENCES

Dsouza, E., D'souza, E., D'souza, K., & Souza, D. '. (2023). A Study on the Impact of Innovative Technologies in the Hospitality Industry. *Journal of Tourism, Hospitality & Culinary Arts (JTHCA) 2023, 15*(1), 1–23. https://www.researchgate.net/publication/374117091

Effendi, M. I., Ambarwati, S. D. A., & Pandangwati, S. T. (2023). *Smart Technology Boosts Tourist Satisfaction in Yogyakarta Smart Tourism Destination* (Vol. 1). Atlantis Press SARL., DOI: 10.2991/978-2-38476-048-0_52

Idris, I., Adi, K. R., Firmansyah, R., Nadhianty, A., Mobaroq, M. H., Putri, P. G., Pratama, A. S., & Wahono, E. R. (2021). Developing smart tourism using virtual reality as a tourism promotion strategy in Indonesia. *Geo Journal of Tourism and Geosites, 35*(2), 332–337. DOI: 10.30892/gtg.35210-656

Jauhari, A., Mufarroha, F. A., Rofi', M., Nasrullah, M. F., Fitriyah, & Nisa, K. (2020). *The Development of Smart Travel Guide Application in Madura Tourism. 473*(Icss), 771–776. DOI: 10.2991/assehr.k.201014.167

Kansakar, P., Munir, A., & Shabani, N. (2019). Technology in the Hospitality Industry: Prospects and Challenges. *IEEE Consumer Electronics Magazine, 8*(3), 60–65. DOI: 10.1109/MCE.2019.2892245

Kant, S., & Koti, K. (2023). Role of Technology in Hospitality Operations: An Overview. *International Journal of Language* [IJLLC]. *Literature and Culture, 3*(5), 2582–9823. DOI: 10.22161/ijllc

Nurhadianis, S., Setiawan, E. B., Dipatiukur, J., Bandung, N., & Barat, J. (2018). *DEVELOPMENT APPLICATIONS SMART CULINARY OF CITY CIKAMPEK (KUTACII) BASED ON ANDROID Informatics- Computer University. December.*

Saratkar, D. A. N. (2019). an Article on Importance of Software Technologies in Business and Management Science. *International Journal of Engineering Applied Sciences and Technology, 04*(04), 291–294. DOI: 10.33564/IJEAST.2019.v04i04.047

Sharma, S. (2016). International Journal of Multidisciplinary Education and Research Study on the role of information technology in the hospitality industry. *International Journal of Multidisciplinary Education and Research, 1*(2), 65–67. www.educationjournal.in

Sihotang, D. M., Hidayanto, A. N., Abidin, Z., & Diana, E. (2021). SMART method for recommender system towards smart tourism and green computing. *IOP Conference Series. Earth and Environmental Science, 700*(1), 012017. Advance online publication. DOI: 10.1088/1755-1315/700/1/012017

Chapter 19
Artificial Intelligence (AI) Technology-Enabled Housekeeping:
Setting a Roadmap

Madhu Chandok
Independent Researcher, India

Rachna Chandan
https://orcid.org/0000-0002-5144-4336
Independent Researcher, India

Dharna Shukla
https://orcid.org/0000-0001-5857-2130
Amity School of Hospitality, Amity University, Lucknow, India

Sandhya Anilkumar
Independent Researcher, India

Nishi Priya
Amity School of Hospitality, Amity University, Lucknow, India

ABSTRACT

The integration of Artificial Intelligence (AI) into housekeeping is transforming task management across industries. This research provides a roadmap for implementing AI-enabled housekeeping, focusing on process optimization, service enhancement, and operational efficiency. AI technologies like automated cleaning predictive maintenance streamline operations, improve guest satisfaction, and reduce costs. The roadmap explores smart devicesdata analytics in housekeeping, addressing workforce adaptations, and technological infrastructure in hotels, retail, hospitals, and airports. It offers insights into AI's benefits and integration strategies. Facility management leads in AI adoption, favoring limited AI assistance with human interaction. This research highlights AI's transformative impact on housekeeping, promoting efficiency and customer-centricity. The methodology includes descriptive analysis, reliability tests, and correlation analysis based on 472 expert responses. Future research could explore national vs. international scope, larger samples, and sector-specific objectives.

DOI: 10.4018/979-8-3693-7447-4.ch019

INTRODUCTION

In recent years, hospitality industry has witnessed a rapid integration of technology and artificial intelligence (AI) into various aspects of its operations. One area where this transformation is particularly pronounced is housekeeping management. From automated cleaning robots to smart room controls, technology is revolutionizing the way housekeeping tasks are performed, monitored, and optimized. Digitization will significantly impact routine tasks, resulting in substantial changes in work processes and necessitating shifts in skills (Nagl, Titelbach & Valkova, 2017). This research explores the impact of technology and AI on housekeeping management in various sectors, focusing on reshaping traditional practices and enhancing efficiency, guest satisfaction, and sustainability.

AI-powered systems can analyze data to predict occupancy levels, cleaning schedules, and allocate resources more effectively, leading to cost savings and improved productivity (Lee, Wu, Yun, Kim, Jun, & Sutherland, 2019). Moreover, advancements in smart sensors and Internet of Things (IoT) devices enable real-time monitoring of cleanliness standards, ensuring that areas or guestrooms are always maintained to the highest standards (Social Tables, 2017). However, alongside the benefits, there are also challenges and considerations to be addressed, such as data security, staff training, and the need for human oversight. The integration of Artificial Intelligence (AI) into housekeeping services has become increasingly prevalent, revolutionizing the way tasks are managed and executed in various industries. This research aims to outline a roadmap for the implementation of AI-enabled housekeeping services, addressing key aspects such as process optimization, service enhancement, and operational efficiency. AI technologies offer a wide range of capabilities that can significantly streamline housekeeping operations, from automated room cleaning to predictive maintenance and inventory management (Stringam & Gerdes, 2021). By leveraging AI, hotels and other establishments can improve guest satisfaction thereby reducing operational costs and enhancing overall service quality (Mazars, 2020).

This roadmap will explore various dimensions of AI-enabled housekeeping services including the adoption of smart devices, data analytics, and machine learning algorithms. It will delve into the challenges and opportunities associated with AI implementation in the housekeeping services, considering factors such as workforce adaptation, ethical considerations and technological infrastructure.

LITERATURE REVIEW

Artificial Intelligence (AI) is revolutionizing various industries, and the housekeeping sector is no exception. AI-based housekeeping services harness advanced technologies to enhance efficiency, accuracy, and convenience in household tasks. This study explores the integration of AI into housekeeping, examining its impact on routine activities such as cleaning, maintenance, inventory management, and customer service.

Housekeeping, traditionally reliant on manual labor, faces challenges regarding time consumption, consistency, and human error. With the advent of AI, innovative solutions are emerging to address these challenges. AI-powered devices and systems are designed to perform tasks autonomously or semi-autonomously, reducing the burden on human effort while improving service quality. The scope of AI-based housekeeping extends beyond simple automation; it encompasses a range of intelligent systems capable of learning, adapting, and optimizing their functions. These systems include cleaning and maintenance robots, smart home integrations, predictive maintenance technologies, and AI-driven customer service platforms (El Makhloufi, 2023).

According to Lai & Hung (2018) the hospitality sector has been talking about cloud technology for the past ten years, but little real progress has been made; instead, the debates have remained in paper talk mode. Given the enormous potential of the market for intelligent hospitality, there are currently very few academic research publications concerning virtualized cloud architecture, AI technology, and intelligent virtual housekeeping systems in this sector. Digitalization and automation transforming housekeeping services, enhancing efficiency, precision, and overall service quality. Task scheduling, inventory tracking, and employee performance monitoring are ways digital technologies, such as housekeeping management software, simplify operations (Richards, 2017). These systems offer real-time updates, enabling prompt response to guests' needs and ensuring thorough cleanliness standards.

Automation, through the use of robotics and AI, further revolutionizes housekeeping. Robotic vacuum cleaners, for instance, efficiently clean floors, reducing manual labor and allowing staff to focus on more complex tasks. AI-powered devices can identify and report maintenance issues, ensuring timely repairs and preventing potential hazards. Voice-activated assistants in guest rooms enhance the customer experience by effortlessly providing information and controlling room settings (Fu & Wong, 2022). In the service industry, customer happiness is crucial, particularly in the hotel sector where delivering excellent service is crucial. The state of hotel linens has a big influence on how comfortable and clean visitors feel, especially in light of the higher standards in the post-COVID age. Defects in the linen, such as stains, damage, or rough texture, can negatively impact a visitor's experience and might affect their choice of hotel in the future (Urban & Łukaszewicz, 2021).

Conventional manual linen inspection techniques take a lot of time and are prone to human mistake, which can result in soiled linens, unhappy guests, and perhaps lost linen inventory. This work suggests an artificial intelligence (AI)-based linen inspection system for hotels in response to these difficulties, utilizing the most recent deep learning algorithm and transfer learning for categorization (Rasheed, Yuanqiong, Khizar, & Khalid. 2024). AI systems analyze data from various sensors installed in aircraft to predict when maintenance is needed. This proactive approach helps prevent equipment failures and reduces downtime, leading to more reliable flight schedules. The hotel industry is continuously seeking innovative solutions to improve operational efficiency and enhance guest satisfaction. One critical aspect of hotel operations is the management and maintenance of linens, including sheets, towels, and other fabric-based amenities. AI-driven linen inspection offers a transformative approach to ensuring the quality and cleanliness of these essential items, thereby boosting both efficiency and guest satisfaction (Gubhaju, Panta, & Ahn, 2024). High-resolution cameras and sensors integrated into laundry systems can detect even the smallest imperfections, such as stains, tears, or discoloration. These AI systems provide consistent, accurate assessments, ensuring that only linens meeting high standards are used (Thakur, 2022).

AI-enabled Housekeeping services are byproducts of technology-enabled services optimized by the hospitality and tourism industry. AI-enabled housekeeping services, a byproduct of advanced technology, have been optimized by the hospitality and tourism industry to enhance operational efficiency and guest satisfaction. These services employ AI technologies, such as robotic cleaners, predictive maintenance systems, and smart inventory management, to streamline housekeeping tasks. The integration of AI ensures thorough and consistent cleanliness, reduces operational costs, and frees up staff for more personalized guest interactions. By leveraging AI, the industry can maintain high standards of hygiene and service, leading to improved guest experiences and overall efficiency in hotel operations (Gurgu, Zorzoliu, Pistol, Gurgu, Ungureanu, & Nae, 2021).

The goal of the hospitality sector 5.0 (Gangwar & Reddy, 2023) is to provide guests with a smooth and practical customer experience by using technology in service marketing, HRM, and hotel operations as mentioned in his study. The hospitality industry 5.0 includes big data, cloud computing, blockchain technology, augmented reality, virtual reality, chatbots, sensors, mobile technology, contactless automation, big data, cloud computing, 6 G and beyond, and machine-to-machine communication. Hospitality will emerge from the convergence of human intelligence with automated technology, intelligent gadgets, and intelligent systems. It gives solid knowledge based on the contribution towards technology usage in hospitality and tourism (Naik & Daptardar, 2019).

The hotel and tourist industry's susceptibility to adopting AI differs depending on the kind of AI. Chatbots, virtual assistants, and search/booking engines are all very susceptible to adoption. The research work by Huang, Chao, de la Mora, Bilgihan, & Wei, 2022), connects AI applications with the theoretical foundations of innovation dissemination. Researchers, developers, and managers may use the data to assess how likely it is that AI technologies will be used in the hotel and tourist sector. (Zulaikha, Shaharul, Nurulain, & Mahmud, 2021). This framework provides a comprehensive view of AI's impact, highlighting the balance between technological advancements and human factors. For management, it offers actionable insights to optimize AI integration, improve guest experiences, and maintain ethical standards, ultimately driving sustainable growth in the hospitality and tourism industry.

ChatGPT is one of the AI-enabled services that offers significant advantages for the tourism industry, enhancing customer service and operational efficiency. However, careful management of data privacy, accuracy, and ethical considerations is essential to mitigate associated risks. The benefits while adopting such AI enabled services for hospitality and Tourism are listed following (Carvalho, & Ivanov,2024):

1. **Enhanced Customer Experience**: ChatGPT's instant, accurate responses improve the quality of customer interactions, leading to higher satisfaction and loyalty.
2. **Operational Efficiency**: Automates routine tasks, freeing up human resources for more complex issues and reducing operational costs.
3. **Scalability**: Handles a large volume of inquiries simultaneously, accommodating peak tourist seasons without compromising service quality.
4. **Data Insights**: Analyzes user interactions to provide businesses with valuable insights into traveler preferences and trends, aiding in better service customization

A structured roadmap for AI-based housekeeping services ensures a smooth transition, maximizing benefits and minimizing disruptions. This strategic approach enhances operational efficiency, reduces costs, and elevates service quality across various industries.

RESEARCH METHODOLOGY

Through this roadmap, stakeholders in the hospitality industry can gain insights into the potential benefits of AI-enabled housekeeping services and develop strategies for successful integration into their operations, ultimately paving the way for a more efficient and guest-centric approach to hospitality management (Figure 1).

Figure 1. Mind-mapping of goals and outcomes, key aspects, dimensions, capabilities, benefits, and considerations of integration of Artificial Intelligence (AI) into housekeeping services

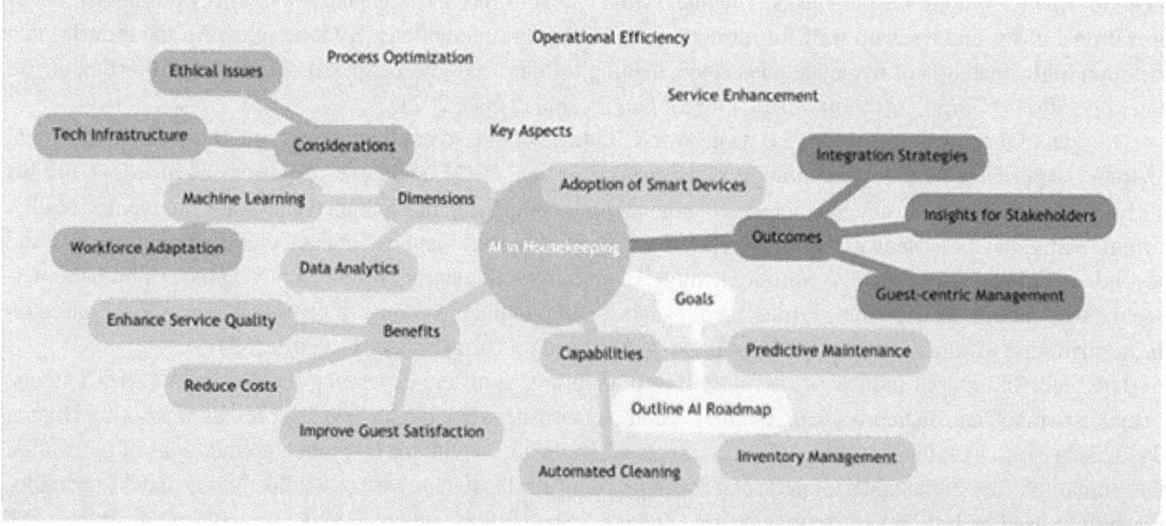

(Source: Authors' interpretation).

Hence following research objectives were identified for this study:

1. **To Evaluate the Impact of AI on Operational Efficiency in Housekeeping Services:** Assess how AI technologies, such as automated room cleaning, predictive maintenance, and inventory management, improve operational efficiency in housekeeping across various sectors, including hospitality, healthcare, retail, and aviation.
2. **To Investigate Workforce Adaptation and Training Needs for AI Implementation:** Examine the challenges and opportunities related to workforce adaptation to AI technologies, identifying the necessary training programs and change management strategies to ensure smooth integration of AI in housekeeping services.
3. **To Analyze the Ethical and Technological Considerations in AI-Enabled Housekeeping:** Explore the ethical implications and technological infrastructure required for the successful implementation of AI in housekeeping, including data privacy, job displacement concerns, and the adequacy of current technological systems.
4. **To Assess the Impact of AI-Enabled Housekeeping on Guest Satisfaction and Service Quality:** Investigate how AI-enabled housekeeping services influence guest satisfaction and overall service quality, determining the acceptance levels of AI technologies by guests and identifying the balance between AI-driven efficiency and personalized human interactions.

This research will delve into these issues and provide insights into best practices for leveraging technology and AI to optimize housekeeping management in the hospitality industry.

In this exploratory study, a mixed-methods approach, combining qualitative and quantitative techniques to comprehensively explore the integration of AI into housekeeping services was employed.

Data Collection: A structured questionnaire was administered to a sample of 472 experts from various sectors within housekeeping, including hotels, hospitals, facility management, and aviation. Additionally, in-depth interviews were conducted with industry experts to gather qualitative insights.

Survey Design: The questionnaire included items on process optimization, service enhancement, operational efficiency, workforce adaptation, ethical considerations, and technological infrastructure. Descriptive statistics, reliability tests, and correlation analyses were performed using SPSS 20 software to analyze the collected data.

Qualitative Interviews: Interviews were conducted with professionals from different sectors to understand the practical implications, challenges, and benefits of AI integration in housekeeping.

Data Analysis: Descriptive statistical analysis was conducted to measure central tendencies and variability. Pearson Bivariate correlation was used to examine relationships between variables. Reliability and validity of the data were assessed using Cronbach's alpha and KMO-Bartlett's tests.

Sample Characteristics: The sample included responses from a diverse range of housekeeping professionals, ensuring broad sectoral representation. The reliability and adequacy of the sample were confirmed with a Cronbach's alpha > 0.7 and KMO > 0.8.

This mixed-methods approach provides a robust framework for understanding the multifaceted impact of AI on housekeeping services and guides the development of a comprehensive roadmap for AI implementation in the industry.

FINDINGS OF THE SURVEY

1. Reliability Test

A total of 472 responses were obtained from experts of different verticals from housekeeping sectors (hotel, hospital, facility management, and aviation). Reliability statistics result attracted a Cronbach's alpha statistics of more than 0.7 and Sekaran in 2003, identified that Cronbach's alpha of more than 0.7 indicates that the data collection instrument is reliable.

Table 1. Reliability Statistics

Cronbach's Alpha	N of Items
0.799	14

(Source: Authors' Interpretation)

The KMO value between 0.8 and 1 (Table 1) indicates the sampling is adequate; concretely, if the value is in the spread of 0.80 to 0.89, adequacy is meritorious (Kaiser & Rice, 1974). KMO and Bartlett's Test statistics results attracted an adequacy of more than .8 (Table 2), indicating the validity of the collected data. The result also highlights the significance of the sample collected and the calculated value for Bartlett's Test of sphericity is .000 (α), proving the significance of the sample collected.

Table 2. KMO and Bartlett's Test of Sampling Adequacy

Kaiser-Meyer-Olkin Measure of Sampling Adequacy		0.854
Bartlett's Test of Sphericity	Approximate Chi-Square	**1901.754**
	df	91
Kaiser-Meyer-Olkin Measure of Sampling Adequacy		0.854
	Sig.	0.000

(Source: Authors' Interpretation)

2. RESPONSE RATE

This study's sample population consists of employees from the supervisory level and managerial level.

Table 3. Frequency Distribution of Respondents

SECTOR	FREQUENCY	PERCENT	VALID PERCENT	CUMULATIVE PERCENT
HOTEL	176	37.29	37.29	37.29
HOSPITAL	48	10.17	10.17	47.46
FACILITY MANAGEMENT	226	47.88	47.88	95.34
AVIATION	22	4.66	4.66	100
TOTAL	**472**	**100**	**100**	

(Source: Authors' Interpretation)

A total of 472 responses were received from the experts in different sectors from housekeeping. Mugenda & Mugenda (2003) quantified that 50% or more than that is acceptable for analysis. Therein Babbie (2004) also proclaimed in his study that 50% return rates are satisfactory, 60% is good and 70% is perfect to analyze. The achieved response rate was more than 94.4% (table 3) implying that the response rate was good.

3. DEMOGRAPHIC ANALYSIS

The study sought to establish the demographic data of the respondents. The demographic data obtained from the respondents includes awareness and their overall experience preferring AI support.

Table 4. Profiles for AI Awareness

		COUNT	C.F.	CUMULATIVE %
AWARENESS	YES	353	353	74.79
	NO	119	472	25.21
		472		**100**
PERSONALLY EXPERIENCED	YES	242	242	51.27
	NO	230	472	48.73
		472		**100.00**

(Source: Authors' Interpretation)

The frequency distribution (Table 4 and Figure 2) of respondents from different sectors implies that 74.9% have related (housekeeping) knowledge about AI. In contrast, only 51.27% of respondents had personally experienced AI technology in the industry.

Figure 2. Data of sectors of assessment of impact of AI on Housekeeping Services

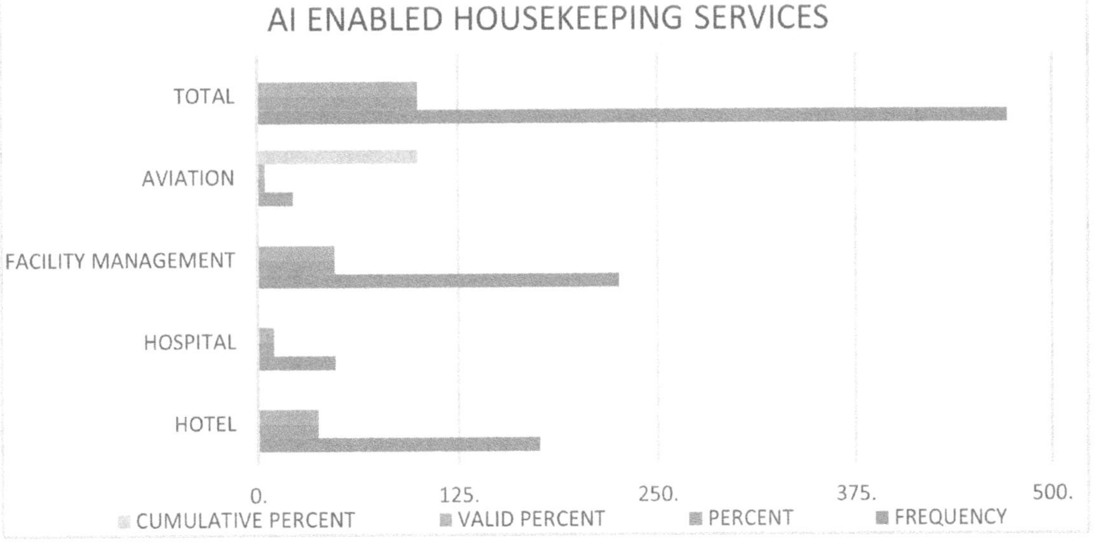

(Source: Authors' interpretation)

4. IMPACT OF AI ON HOUSEKEEPING PROCESSES

Dimensions of the Housekeeping Process

The coefficient of correlation (r) determines the degree (strength) of the relationship and its value is between -1 and 1. A value of 0 implies no relationship, 1 implies a perfect positive relationship, and -1 means a negative relationship. An absolute value of 'r' between 0.5 and less than 1 implies a strong relationship between the variables. If the value r is greater than 0.3 and less than 0.5 then the relationship is moderate. The relationship is weak if the value of r is less than 0.3. And the result calculated (Table 5) implies that all the variables have a significant positive relationship.

Table 5. Dimensions of the Housekeeping Process

S. No.	Dimensions	Pearson Correlation (r)	Cronbach's Alpha	Factor Analysis
1	HK SERVICES (for the guest)	.538	.721	0.466
2	IMPLICATION (ethical)	.385	.761	0.673
3	SAFETY & SECURITY (concerns)	.508	.730	0.673
4	AUTOMATED SERVICE PROVIDERS (vendors)	.569	.713	0.716
5	OPERATIONAL EFFICIENCY	.586	.708	0.683

(Source: Authors' interpretation)

5. IMPACT OF AI ON HOUSEKEEPING SERVICES

Figure 3 established the impact of AI on housekeeping services, and it indicates that all the sectors agreed with almost 55% of responses that AI impacts overall services and the operational efficiency of housekeeping. Similarly ethical implications and safety-security concerns with 48% responses individually are identified as the impacting services of Housekeeping.

Figure 3. Impact Of AI On Housekeeping Services

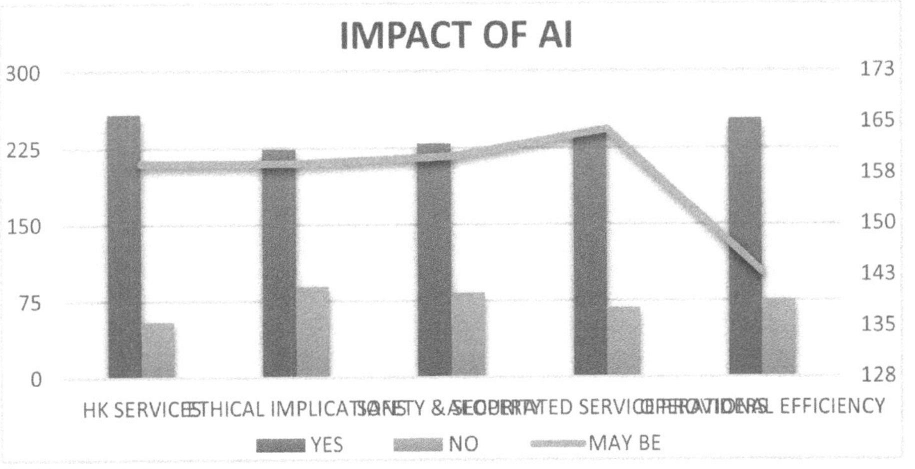

(Source: Authors' interpretation)

Figure 4 illustrates the sector-wise impact of AI on Housekeeping services. The Facility Management sector represented the greatest percentage of acceptance of the AI impact on housekeeping services.

Figure 4. Impacts of AI on Housekeeping Services (sector-wise)

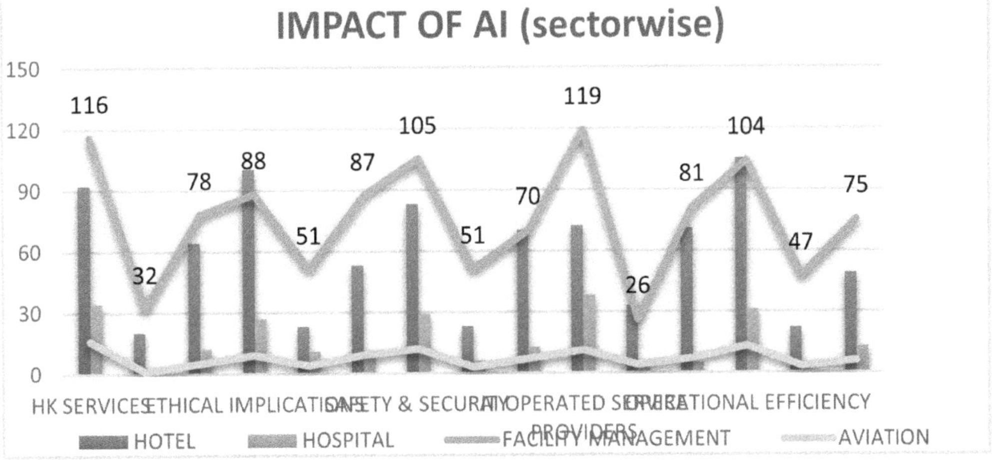

(Source: Authors' interpretation)

6. IMPACT OF AI ON HOUSEKEEPER'S PREFERENCES

Figure 5 illustrates that only 32.84% of respondents are comfortable with robot concierge assistance services in their respective sectors, whereas 40.68% of respondents are still not certain to prefer AI assistance completely, rather they will choose to avail of limited AI assist services with human touch. Whereas, only 35% (Figure 6) of respondents agreed to recommend a service that effectively uses AI in its operations

Figure 5. Housekeepers' Preferences in availing AI-assisted services

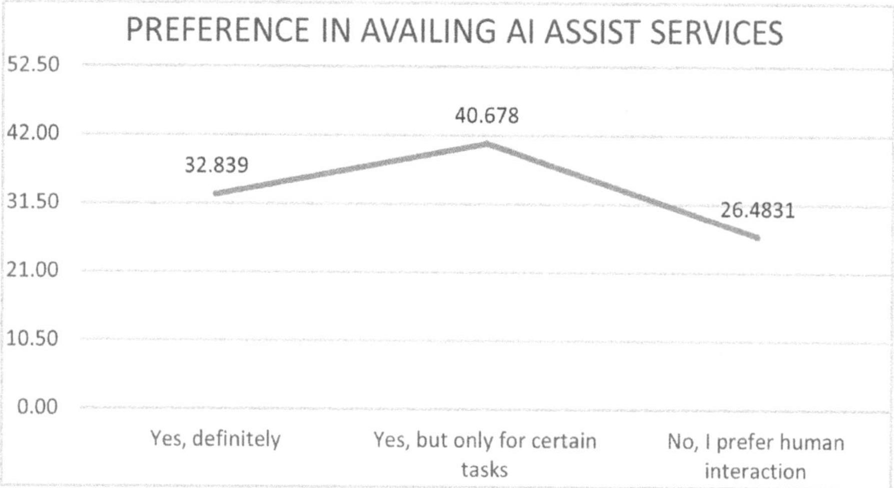

(Source: Authors' interpretation)

Figure 6. Recommendations for effective operations

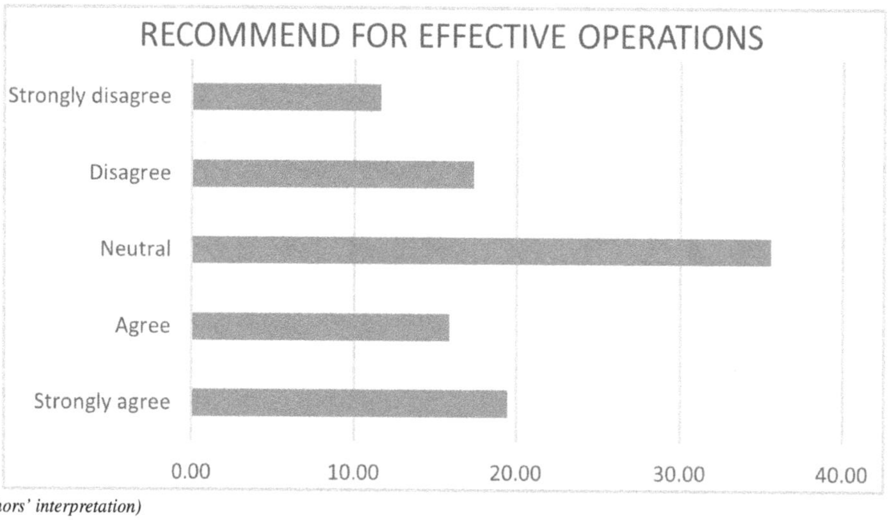

(Source: Authors' interpretation)

7. IMPACT OF AI IMPLEMENTATION ON OPERATIONAL EFFICIENCY

The following Figure (Figure 7) gives an overview of the factors of operational efficiency getting impacted the most. Operational efficiency factors like Quality assurance and audit; and digitalized checklists with response rates of 36.86% and 34.11% respectively were identified as the most affected services in the housekeeping industry (Figure 8).

Figure 7. Word Cloud for most impacting services by the AI

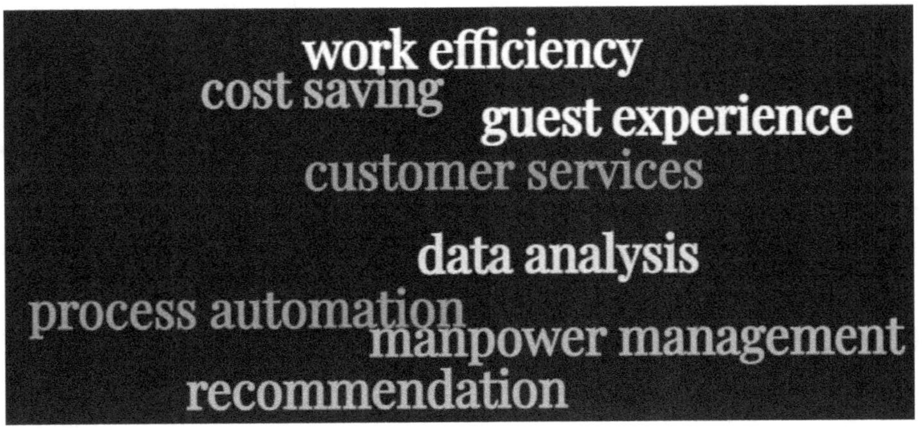

(Source: Authors' interpretation)

Figure 8. Impact of AI on Operational Services

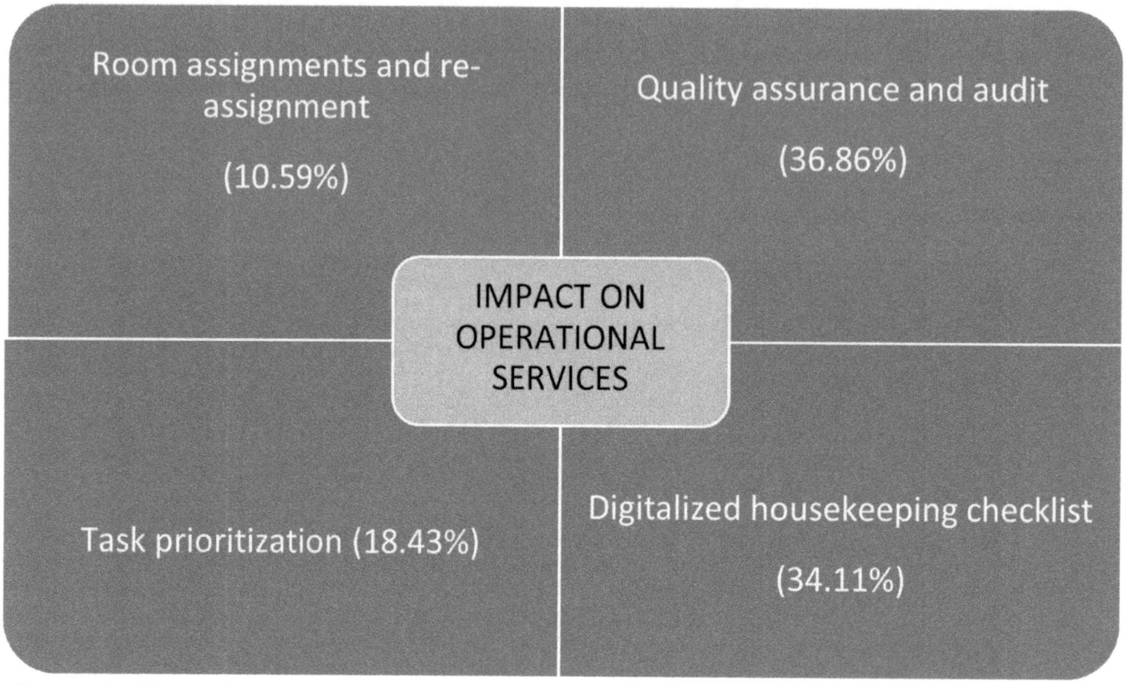

(Source: Authors' interpretation)

Illustrating the impact of AI on operational strategies Figure 9 presents data analysis as the most impacting operational strategy. The response rate for data analysis was 60.59%, which was followed by the cost management strategy with a response rate of 52.33%.

Figure 9. AI impacting the different Operational Strategies

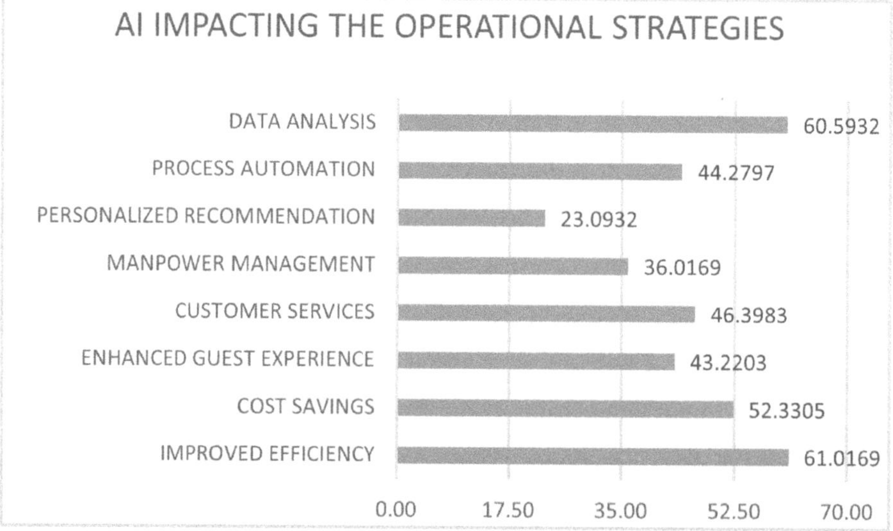

(Source: Authors' interpretation)

Figure 10 explains the most significant technologies for the housekeeping industry and the respondents recognized Smart robots (32.20%) as the most signifying technology for Housekeeping. In contrast, digital chatbots (8.69%) were identified as the least significant technology for the housekeeping industry.

Figure 10. Most significant technology for Housekeeping

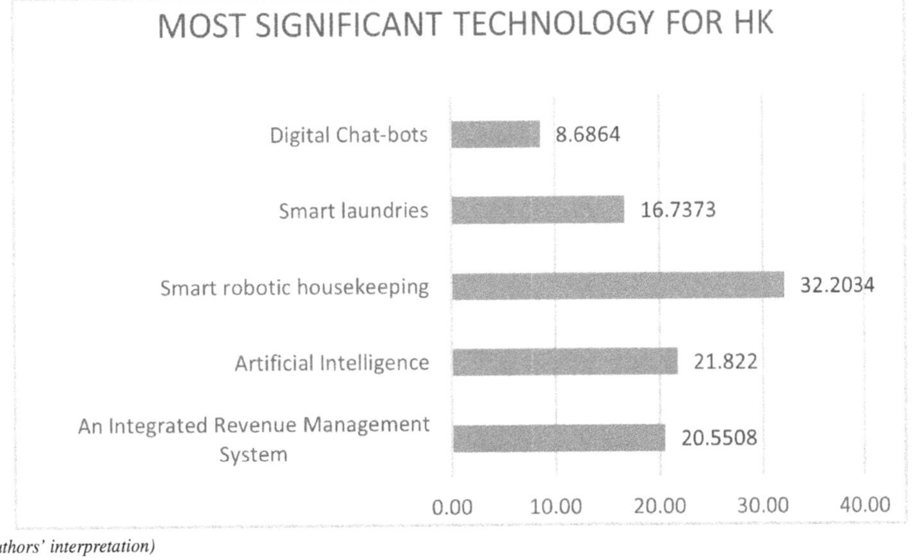

(Source: Authors' interpretation)

8. CHALLENGES OF AI IMPLEMENTATION IN HOUSEKEEPING INDUSTRY

Figure 11. Identified challenges for the AI implementation

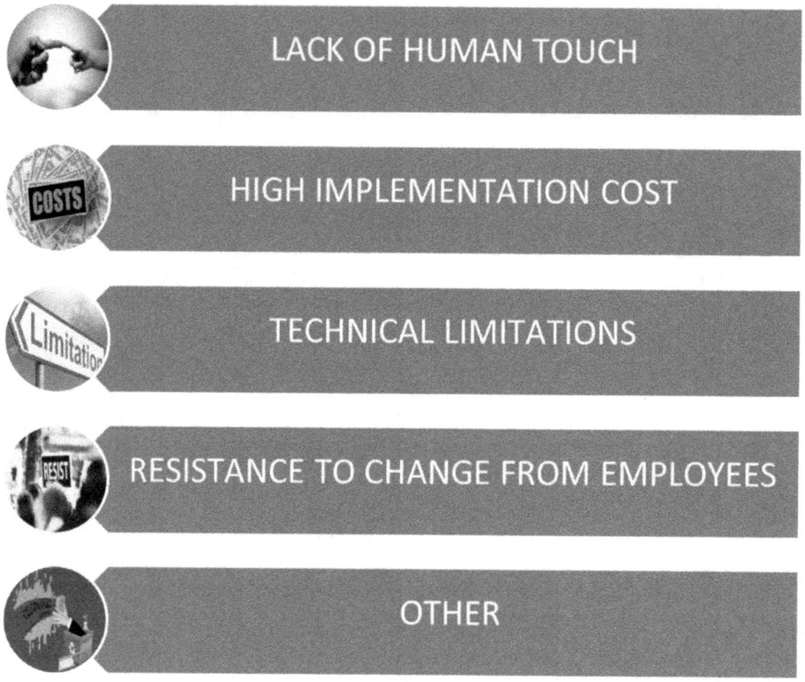

(Source: Authors' interpretation)

Challenges identified through the survey included lack of human touch, high implementation costs, technical limitations amongst the personnel, resistance to adapting to the new technologies amongst all (Figure 11). Only 35% of respondents agreed to recommend AI-operated services to maintain the operational efficiency of Housekeeping. 'Lack of human touch' is identified as the most significant challenge for AI implementation in the industry (Figure 12).

Figure 12. Recommendation of AI Operated Services for Operational Efficiency of Housekeeping by various sectors

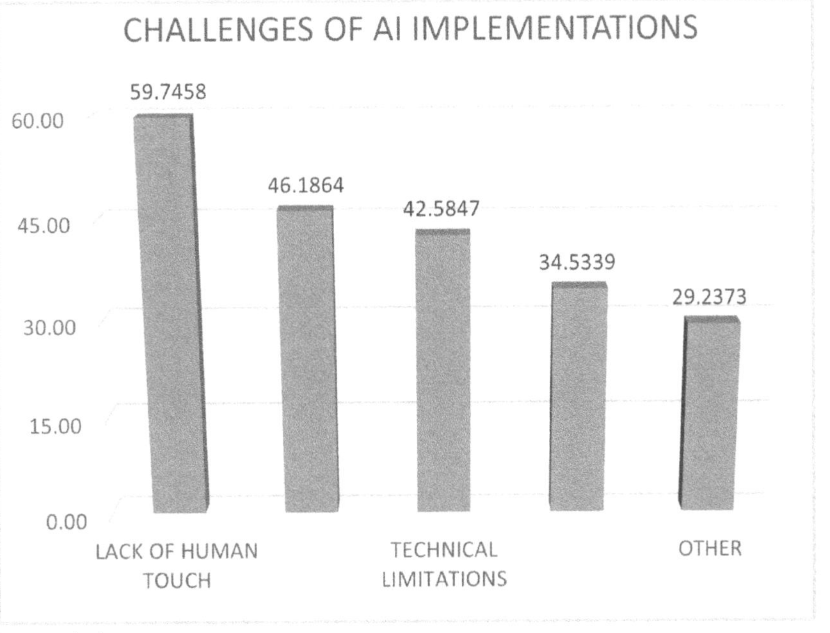

(Source: Authors' interpretation)

Identifying the challenges of AI implementation in Graph 8 and sector-wise challenges of AI implementation in Figure 13, the respondents from the hotel sector (63.64%) and facility management sector (58.84%) identified 'lack of human touch' as one of their major challenges in implementing AI. Whereas, respondents from hospitals (Health & care sector) recognized high implementation costs (62.50%) as the most impacting challenge in AI implementation. On the other hand, the Aviation sector acknowledged technical limitations as the major challenge in AI implementation (59.09%).

Figure 13. Sector-wise Challenges of AI implementation

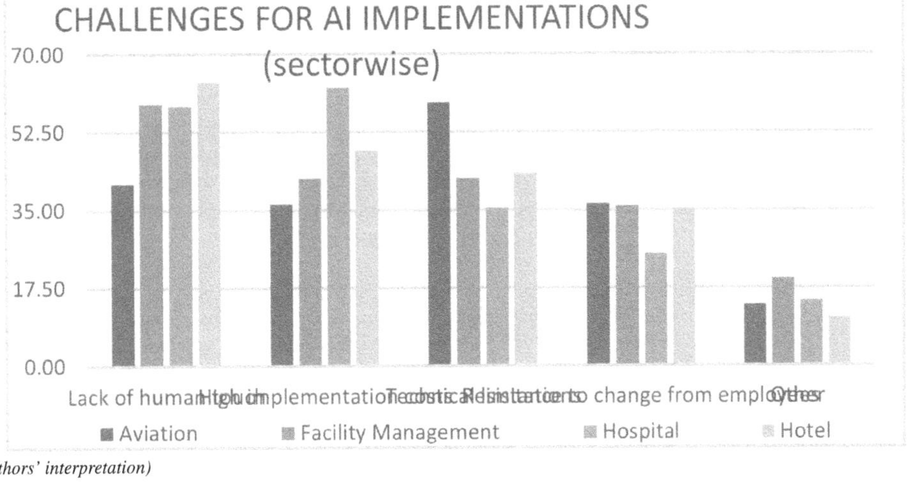

(Source: Authors' interpretation)

9. IMPACT OF AI ON WORKFORCE

Figure 14. Impact of AI on the workforce in Housekeeping

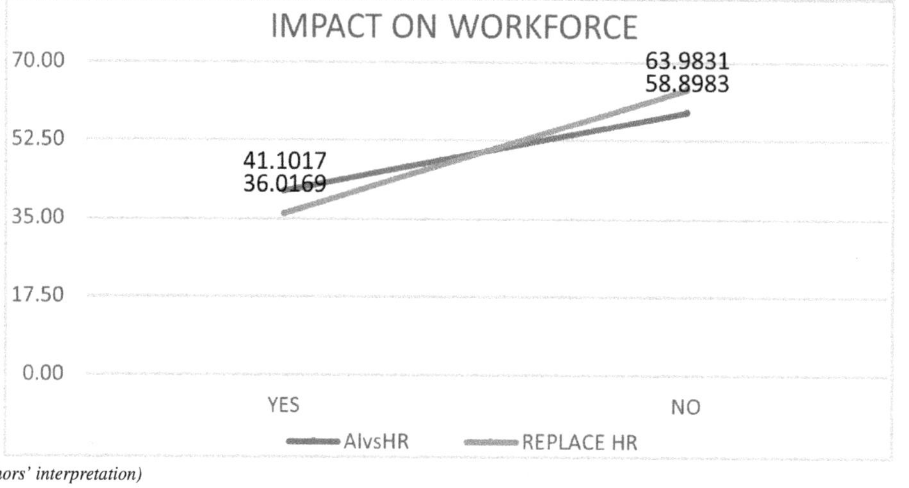

(Source: Authors' interpretation)

58.90% of respondents have confidence that AI does not have superior abilities to human touch. Supporting the same output 63.98% of respondents believe that implementation of AI cannot replace manpower in the industry (Figure 14).

Figure 15 illustrates the impact of AI on customer services provided by housekeeping. Almost 40% of respondents do not agree to trust an AI-powered chatbot to handle customer service inquiries. And 31.77% of respondents are not willing to pay extra for a service that utilizes AI to enhance the customer experience.

Figure 15. Impact of AI on Customer Services offered by the Housekeeping

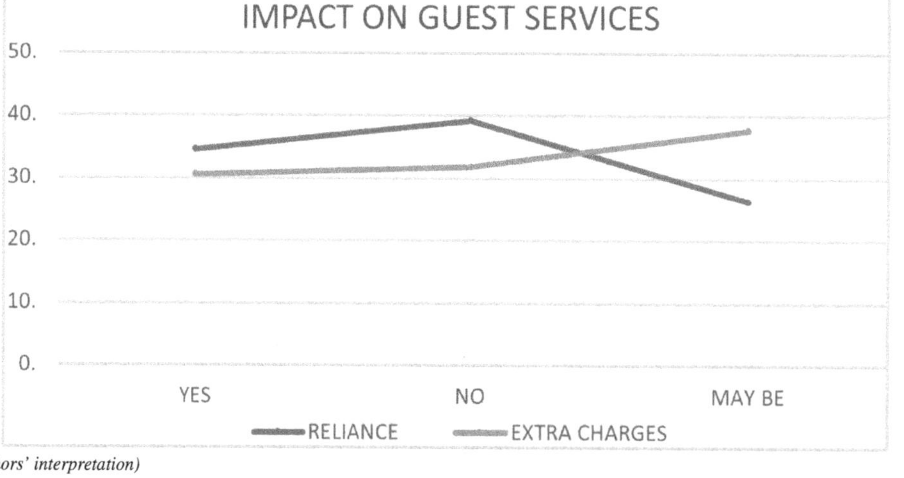

(Source: Authors' interpretation)

10. IMPACT ON OPERATIONAL PROFICIENCY

38.56% of housekeepers agreed to the potential biases in setting the SOPs for materializing AI in the industry, and 55.08% agreed that it would optimize the inventory management of the industry (Figure 16).

Figure 16. Impact on Operational Proficiency of Housekeeping in various sectors

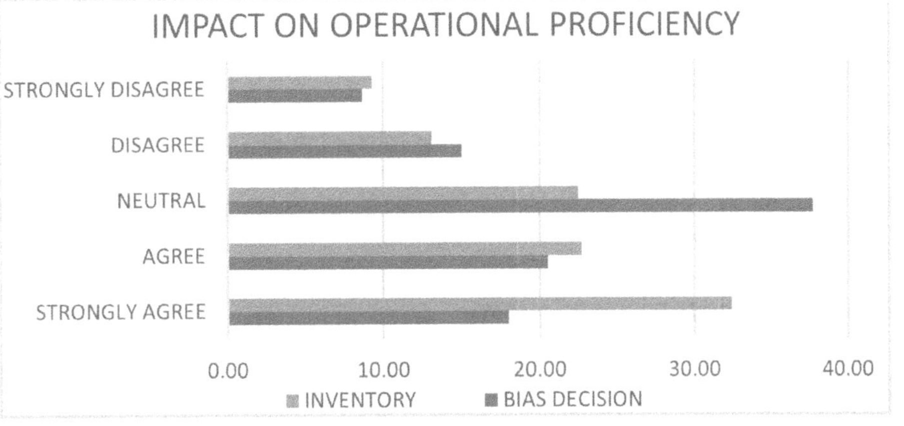

(Source: Authors' interpretation)

Figure 17. Acceptance ratio of AI by sectors of Housekeeping in upcoming years

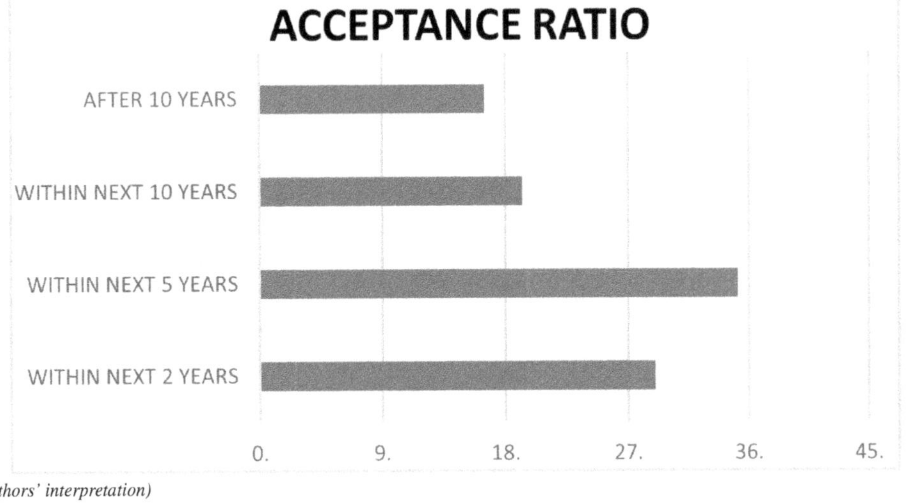

(Source: Authors' interpretation)

35% of experts from vivid sectors of the housekeeping industry agreed that it will take the next 5 years to accept AI as the common feature of the industry (Figure 17).

FINDINGS

According to the conducted research, professionals in the housekeeping industries generally agreed that AI would take at least five years to become widely used in the housekeeping sector, indicating a period of slow adoption and integration. To achieve universal acceptance and realize the full potential of AI in the housekeeping sector at this time, it would be imperative to concentrate on developing trust, showing value, and continuously enhancing AI systems.

Impact of AI on the Housekeeping Process

The influence of AI is generally seen favorably across several sectors, although the ambiguity of its usage still exists, which further led to more details and clarification to comprehend AI's function and advantages. The results of this research work imply that AI have a significant positive impact on the operational process of housekeeping. Responders identified facility management as the most influenced sector and acknowledged healthcare and aviation as the less impacted vertical of the housekeeping industry by AI.

Impact of AI on Housekeeper Preferences

The majority of housekeepers according to the conducted survey, are willing to prefer AI-assisted services, but only for specific duties, whereas a sizeable percentage of 26.48% of respondents are willing to prefer human interaction in their line of work. Although there was a lot of interest in incorporating AI into cleaning services, the research indicated that many housekeepers would rather utilize AI sparingly rather than solely. Even if AI can improve some elements of housekeepers' work, it might not completely replace the human element in housekeeping services, as seen by the significant preference for human interaction that still exists.

Impact of AI on Housekeeping operational efficiency

The variables "quality assurance and audit" and "digitized checklists" were identified as the most impacted operational efficiency of the housekeeping industry. The results also indicate that housekeeping services such as 'room assignment and re-assignment' need to be digitalized. According to a case study by Ritz-Carlton in San Francisco, AI-powered room assignments can boost housekeeping efficiency by up to 20% (Karagiannis, 2024).

The study also explored the impact of AI on the overall efficiency of the housekeeping industry, with a majority of respondents acknowledging its significant influence. Findings imply that AI would optimize the inventory management of the housekeeping industry. It advances data accuracy and departmental productivity which overall ensures customer satisfaction (Osman, et. al., 2022). Data analysis emerged as the most impactful variable for housekeeping operational strategies, highlighting the need for AI-operated personalized selection for customer services. Additionally, the study identified smart robotic services as the most significant technology for housekeeping.

Challenges of AI implementation in Housekeeping

The study addresses the growing challenge of AI implementation in the housekeeping industry, identifying "lack of human touch" and "high implementation cost" as major barriers. The hotel and facility management industries are particularly concerned about these issues due to their service-oriented nature. In the healthcare sector too, the high costs of AI technologies pose a significant financial challenge.

The findings identified that most of the housekeepers did not prefer chatbots using AI to handle customer support queries. To comprehend customer problems, in one of their studies Ranieri, et. al. (2024) established that chatbots might increase confusion, reduce trust, and increase stress toward customer satisfaction. AI algorithm have the tendencies to have ethical implications (Toy, 2023) and potential bias (Kadagidze, 2023). Second to the same, this study also indicates the presence of potential bias towards ethical implications and standardization of operating procedures as the challenge for different verticals of housekeeping.

Qualitative Interviews with industry experts from various sectors such as hotels, retail, and hospitals provided valuable insights on the "Impact of Technology & Artificial Intelligence (AI) on Housekeeping Management". Hotel housekeeping managers have acknowledged that technology and AI revolutionize housekeeping management, enhancing efficiency and cleanliness standards. AI-driven systems automate tasks like scheduling and inventory management, reducing manual errors and improving operational efficiency. Technologies such as robotic cleaners and IoT-enabled devices streamline maintenance, ensuring consistent service quality. Despite initial costs and training needs, these advancements are viewed positively for their potential to optimize operations and elevate guest satisfaction through enhanced cleanliness and service reliability.

Retail professionals emphasize technology's vital role in maintaining cleanliness in large stores and malls. The integration of artificial intelligence (AI) has transformed housekeeping management, enhancing efficiency and operational standards. AI-driven cleaning systems and smart scheduling algorithms streamline tasks, reducing staff workload and ensuring consistent cleanliness (Chiang & Trimi, 2020). In the retail sector, AI and IoT facilitate robotic assistance for restocking and transaction oversight, bolstering operational efficiency (Rajan & Cruz, 2022). In interviews with senior operations managers overseeing soft services at a chain of Indian malls, AI's utilization of customer service through mobile apps was evident. The apps enable customers to request services like wheelchair assistance and lodge complaints via tickets, categorized and addressed promptly. However, challenges such as the app's inability to pinpoint user locations and the high costs associated with AI installation and maintenance hinder widespread adoption in established retail chains. Nevertheless, advanced cleaning technologies and automated machines effectively enhance operational effectiveness in retail settings, reflecting ongoing adaptation to technological advancements.

Technology and artificial intelligence (AI) have transformed housekeeping management in healthcare, enhancing efficiency, cleanliness, and cost-effectiveness. AI-powered Automated Cleaning Systems streamline sanitization tasks, reducing staff workload and maintaining consistent standards (Al-Kahtani, Khan, & Taekeun, 2022). Robots, supported by IoT, handle hazardous waste disposal and room cleaning, among other duties. Predictive Maintenance algorithms analyze sensor data to minimize equipment downtime, while optimized scheduling and smart inventory systems enhance responsiveness and prevent shortages (Omar, Jayaraman, Salah, Debe, & Omar, 2020). Real-time Monitoring ensures adherence to cleanliness protocols, though challenges like technical issues, staff training needs, and initial costs persist. Despite these challenges, healthcare professionals acknowledge the positive impact of technology and AI on housekeeping operations, emphasizing improved infection control and operational efficiency. Ongoing investment in technology and training is crucial to further optimizing housekeeping practices and maintaining high standards in healthcare settings.

The integration of Artificial Intelligence (AI) in airport facility management has transformed operations, boosting efficiency, safety, and passenger experience. AI algorithms analyze data from sensors, cameras, and feedback to optimize operations (Kumar, 2022). Predictive maintenance anticipates equipment failures, minimizing downtime. AI-driven scheduling optimizes staff deployment to meet demands. Surveillance AI enhances security by monitoring areas in real time. AI-equipped chatbots aid passengers with instant assistance, improving communication. AI manages resources, optimizing energy use and reducing costs (Ahmad, Zhang, Huang, Zhang, Dai, Song, & Chen, 2021). AI enhances efficiency and sustainability through data-driven decisions (Rajapaksha, & Jayasuriya, 2020), streamlining airport operations for improved performance. In interviews with Facility Managers at different Indian International Airports, it became evident that technology has greatly simplified the creation and management of documents like checklists and training records. However, they noted drawbacks such as reduced employee creativity and increased reliance on systems for solutions. The initial high capital expenditure in the Indian market was highlighted. Despite considering robotics to mitigate high labor costs, current conditions are less conducive. Over the next decade, the cleaning industry in India anticipates a gradual adoption of AI and robotics. For instance, four service partners, including two international firms, currently provide efficient cleaning services at an international airport terminal in India. AI-driven centralized solutions enhance predictive maintenance and streamline management tasks by processing vast data sets from IoT sensors and maintenance logs. This enables informed decisions on resource allocation, space utilization, and maintenance planning, optimizing facility management practices.

CONCLUSION

The integration of Artificial Intelligence (AI) into housekeeping services is reshaping traditional practices and enhancing operational efficiency across various industries. This research aimed to create a comprehensive roadmap for implementing AI-enabled housekeeping services, focusing on process optimization, service enhancement, and operational efficiency. AI will streamline housekeeping operations through quality assurance, automated room assignments, and inventory management, which leads to improved guest satisfaction and reduced operational costs. However, there should be challenges associated with AI implementations, such as human touch, cost, and data privacy concerns. The study found that while most respondents were aware of AI in housekeeping, only half had experienced it, likely due to resource limitations or technological learning barriers. Additionally, AI can optimize the overall services and operational efficiency, with certain ethical concerns. However, the facility management sector leads in AI use, with housekeepers favoring limited AI use over human interaction

Through insights gained from interviews with industry experts across sectors like hotels, hospitals, and retail, valuable perspectives on the impact of technology and AI on housekeeping management have been obtained. Despite the positive outcomes, challenges such as technical issues with automated cleaning robots and initial implementation costs have been identified, indicating areas for further improvement. The findings reiterate the transformative potential of AI in housekeeping management, offering benefits such as improved cleanliness standards, cost savings, and enhanced operational efficiency. Continued investment in technology and addressing identified challenges will be crucial in optimizing housekeeping operations and meeting the evolving expectations of guests and customers.

Scope for Future work

1. The study is conducted for the housekeeping industry at the national level; future research can be carried out at the national vs international level.

Survey questionnaire was sent to the concerned persons in India only. For better understanding the study must be extended to other countries to understand the international perspective.

According to a new Accenture analysis, by 2035, artificial intelligence might treble yearly rates of economic development. A PwC analysis projection that AI could boost the world economy by $15.7 trillion by 2030 supports this. AI is already having a significant impact on society, and all industries need to pay attention. AI has drawbacks for the economy despite all of this progress, most notably concerning job displacement. According to an Organization for Economic Cooperation and Development (OECD) assessment, 14% of employment in 21 different nations are highly vulnerable to automation. Hence it becomes important to study the global market too.

2. The sample size of the study may be increased in future research work.

The sample size was significant and the outcome was relatable. Because they have smaller error margins and lower standard deviations, larger research yield stronger and more trustworthy results. The standard deviation quantifies the degree of dispersion between the data values and the mean. The margin of error decreases with increasing study sample size. Researchers could manage the possibility of reporting false-positive or false-negative results by using larger sample sizes. The precision of the results would increase with the number of samples in the future.

3. The objectives of this research work should also be examined in detail sector-wise

An elaborate study is recommended to be conducted covering more of the connected sectors. That will give a larger perspective. It is essential to study all sectors as the guests in each of these sectors react differently to the use of AI.

4. Future Research will emphasize Service Providers and IT Experts implying AI in different work areas of Housekeeping.

Three main domains within the IT sector that used AI-driven applications were Process Automation, Quality Assurance (QA), and Service Management. Before allowing new code to be released into the market, the development team must test it every time. Regression testing cycles need a great deal of time and work when completed by hand by QA specialists. This process can be carried out more quickly and easily because to AI's capacity to identify recurring patterns. Artificial Intelligence (AI) data analysis enables QA departments to reduce human error, conduct tests faster, and find potential flaws more quickly. A QA team is therefore not overburdened with copious amounts of data to manage. The IT industry turns to artificial intelligence (AI) to resolve and prevent high-severity outrages. AI's machine learning and deep learning capabilities allow AI to transform traditional IT operations, making them smart, time-saving, and efficient. Process automation, quality assurance, and service management are the main areas in which AI has proven to be an effective tool. Hence the role of IT experts and other service providers is big in studying the impact of AI on various sectors and its implementation thereby.

REFERENCES

Ahmad, T., Zhang, D., Huang, C., Zhang, H., Dai, N., Song, Y., & Chen, H. (2021). Artificial intelligence in the sustainable energy industry: Status Quo, challenges and opportunities. *Journal of Cleaner Production, 289*, 125834. DOI: 10.1016/j.jclepro.2021.125834

Al-Kahtani, M. S., Khan, F., & Taekeun, W. (2022). Application of Internet of Things and Sensors in Healthcare. *Sensors (Basel), 22*(15), 5738. DOI: 10.3390/s22155738 PMID: 35957294

Carvalho, I., & Ivanov, S. (2024). ChatGPT for tourism: Applications, benefits and risks. *Tourism Review, 79*(2), 290–303. DOI: 10.1108/TR-02-2023-0088

Chiang, A. H., & Trimi, S. (2020). Impacts of service robots on service quality. *Service Business, 14*(3), 439–459. DOI: 10.1007/s11628-020-00423-8

El Makhloufi, A. (2023). ***AI Application in Transport and Logistics: Opportunities and Challenges (An Exploratory Study)***. (2023 ed.) CoE City Net Zero, Faculty of Technology, Amsterdam Univeristy of Applied Sciences **Kadagidze, L. (2023).** ***AI in hospitality industry: a comprehensive study on its impact on operations, customer experience, and revenue management.*** **VII-International European Conference on Interdisciplinary Scientific Research.**https://doi.org/DOI: 10.13140/RG.2.2.35476.99201

Ford, M. (2021). Rule of the robots: How artificial intelligence will transform everything. Hachette UK.

Fu, S., Zheng, X., & Wong, I. A. (2022). The perils of hotel technology: The robot usage resistance model. *International Journal of Hospitality Management, 102*, 103174. DOI: 10.1016/j.ijhm.2022.103174 PMID: 35095168

Gangwar, V. P., & Reddy, D. (2023). Hospitality industry 5.0: Emerging trends in guest perception and experiences. Opportunities and Challenges of Business 5.0 in Emerging Markets, 185-211.

Gubhaju, P., Panta, P., & Ahn, J. (2024). AI-driven linen inspection: Enhancing efficiency and guest satisfaction in hotel industry. *Multimedia Tools and Applications*, 1–17. DOI: 10.1007/s11042-024-19246-0

Gurgu, E., Zorzoliu, R. I., Pistol, L., Gurgu, I., Ungureanu, C., & Nae, G. (2021). The Relationship Between Big Data Driven Technologies and Performance Management Strategies Applied to Companies in the Hospitality, Tourism & Travel Industry. *Annals of Spiru Haret University.Economic Series, 21*(4), 97–136.

Huang, A., Chao, Y., de la Mora Velasco, E., Bilgihan, A., & Wei, W. (2022). When artificial intelligence meets the hospitality and tourism industry: An assessment framework to inform theory and management. *Journal of Hospitality and Tourism Insights, 5*(5), 1080–1100. DOI: 10.1108/JHTI-01-2021-0021

Karagiannis, M. (2024). *How AI is Transforming Hotel Housekeeping into a Guest's Dream. Hotel tech.* https://medium.com/hotel-tech/how-ai-is-transforming-hotel-housekeeping-into-a-guests-dream-83b3864f51bc

Kumar, M. (2022). Optimized application of artificial intelligence (AI) in aviation market. *International Journal of Recent Research Aspects, 9*(4).

Kumar, M. (2022). Optimized application of artificial intelligence (AI) in aviation market. *International Journal of Recent Research Aspects, 9*(4).

Lai, W. C., & Hung, W. H. (2018), "A framework of cloud and AI based intelligent hotel", *Proceedings of the 18th International Conference on Electronic Business. ICEB*, Guilin, 2-6 December, pp. 36-43.

Lee, W. J., Wu, H., Yun, H., Kim, H., Jun, M. B. G., & Sutherland, J. W. (2019). Predictive maintenance of machine tool systems using artificial intelligence techniques applied to machine condition data. *Procedia CIRP, 80,* 506–511. DOI: 10.1016/j.procir.2018.12.019

Loh, C. M., Perdana, A., & Lee, K. H. (2024). From hot pot to high tech: Haidilao's transformation through digital technologies for sustainable business in the restaurant industry. *Journal of Information Technology Teaching Cases*, 20438869241240494.

Mr, N. S. Z., & Ab, N. (2021). The application of artifical intelligence (AI) in highly intelligent hospitals. [IJPHCS]. *International Journal of Public Health & Clinical Sciences*, *8*(6).

Nagl, W., G. Titelbach, & Valkova, K., (2017). Digitalisierung der Arbeit: Substituierbarkeit von Berufen im Zuge der Automatisierung durch Industrie 4.0. Vienna: Institut für höhere Studien (IHS).

Naik, M. S., & Daptardar, V. (2019). *International Interdisciplinary Conference* on 'New Pathways to World Development: Opportunities and Challenges,'.

Omar, I. A., Jayaraman, R., Salah, K., Debe, M., & Omar, M. (2020). Enhancing vendor managed inventory supply chain operations using blockchain smart contracts. *IEEE Access : Practical Innovations, Open Solutions*, *8*, 182704–182719. DOI: 10.1109/ACCESS.2020.3028031

Osman, M. B., Alinkeel, S., & Bhavshar, D. (2022). Study on role of artificial intelligence to improve inventory management system. *International Research Journal of Modernization in Engineering Technology and Science*, Vol. 4(03). e-ISSN: 2582-5208

Rajan, V., & Cruz, A. D. L. (2022). Utilisation of service robots to assist human Workers in Completing Tasks Such in retail, hospitality, healthcare, and logistics businesses. *Technoarete Trans. Ind. Robot. Automat. Syst*, *2*(2), 10–36647. DOI: 10.36647/TTIRAS/02.01.A002

Rajapaksha, A., & Jayasuriya, N. (2020). Smart airport: A review on future of the airport operation. *Global Journal of Management and Business Research*, *20*(3), 25–34. DOI: 10.34257/GJMBRAVOL20IS3PG25

Ranieri, A., Di Bernardo, I., & Mele, C. (2024). Serving customers through chatbots: Positive and negative effects on customer experience. *Journal of Service Theory and Practice*, *34*(2), 191–215. DOI: 10.1108/JSTP-01-2023-0015

Rasheed, H. M. W., Yuanqiong, H., Khizar, H. M. U., & Khalid, J. (2024). What drives the adoption of artificial intelligence among consumers in the hospitality sector: A systematic literature review and future agenda. *Journal of Hospitality and Tourism Technology*, *15*(2), 211–231. DOI: 10.1108/JHTT-02-2022-0045

Richards, G. (2017). *Warehouse management: a complete guide to improving efficiency and minimizing costs in the modern warehouse*. Kogan Page Publishers.

Social Tables. (2017). IoT in Hospitality, Meaning for the Future of Hotels. Social Tables, https://www.socialtables.com/blog/hospitality-technology/internet-of-things/

Stringam, B. B., & Gerdes, J. H. (2021). Hotel and guest room technology. *University of South Florida (USF) M3 Publishing, 17*(9781732127593), 6.

Thakur, A. (2022). Technological innovations in the hospitality and tourism industry. In *Mobile computing and technology applications in tourism and hospitality* (pp. 72–97). IGI Global. DOI: 10.4018/978-1-7998-6904-7.ch004

Toy, J. (2023). *5 Concerns AI Developers Need to Prevent from Materializing. The Learning Counsel*. https://thelearningcounsel.com/articles/5-concerns-ai-developers-need-to-prevent-from-materializing/

Urban, W., & Łukaszewicz, K. (2021). Technologies supporting pandemic restrictions in the hospitality industry, Hitherto experiences, and Outlook. *Journal of Environmental Management and Tourism, 12*(1), 196–210. DOI: 10.14505/jemt.12.1(49).17

Zafer, A., & Saleem, K. (2024). Innovation dynamics in hospitality and tourism: AI, sustainability, and customer satisfaction. DOI: 10.13140/RG.2.2.28722.82889

Chapter 20
Navigating the Promises and Perils of Generative AI in Transforming Healthcare Services

Sahil Kohli
https://orcid.org/0000-0002-3792-988X
Chandigarh University, India

Ravi Kaushal
Chandigarh University, India

Ashish Raina
https://orcid.org/0000-0001-5812-5920
CT University, India

ABSTRACT

This chapter focuses on the possibilities and risks of applying the Generative AI with the Healthcare System's Elements. The authors also discuss the role of Generative AI which has paved way for Drug Discovery, improvement of diagnosis as well as development of personalized medicine. In this aspect, they discuss the various ethical concerns such as Data Privacy and Algorithms' limitations that result from the use of AI in Healthcare. Reflective to the above elements, the chapter captures ways through which these challenges can be addressed. In sharing the ways of managing the risks and protecting patient's rights this chapter gives a step-by-step solution of how Generative AI can transform Healthcare for the better while paying attention to moral and pragmatic concerns. This chapter provides useful information on the topic for Healthcare Practitioners, Policy Makers and AI Specialists in the development of Artificial Intelligence in care delivery.

INTRODUCTION

The healthcare industry has been profoundly impacted by the rapid development of artificial intelligence technologies in recent years. Among these is generative AI, which shows promise. Generative AI represents a new transformative technology that would revolutionize patient care, streamline medical procedures, and create opportunities for breakthrough discoveries (Topol, 2019). Unlike any other form of artificial intelligence, AI generative creates new data, content or designs from learned patterns. In healthcare its applications range from

DOI: 10.4018/979-8-3693-7447-4.ch020

finding novel compounds for drugs to tailoring treatment plans and inventing completely new diagnostic instruments (Goodfellow et al., 2020).

In view of the aging population, rising costs and increasing complexity of medical data generative AI gives reasons for hope for the future. Generative AI uses machine learning algorithms and massive datasets to reveal hidden patterns and forecast disease development thereby assisting physicians in making decisions. Nevertheless, there is immense enthusiasm about what such generative AI could do; however, it is also essential to consider the possible dangers and problems that come with prudently thinking about using health care.

The Rise of Generative AI in Healthcare

Generative AI is being turned into healthcare in a big way, especially during these past few years as a result of increased access to extensive medical data and computational power mostly coupled with the creation of complex AI algorithms (Jiang et al., 2017). For instance, generative models can produce diverse data with amazing realism including synthetic electronic health records as well as high- resolution medical images (Frid-Adar et al., 2018; Xue et al., 2018).

Drug discovery and development are two very promising potentials of generative AI in creating new effective therapeutics. In general, traditional drug discovery processes continue taking long time, require huge amounts of resources, and end up failing most times (Mullard, 2018). There are important applications under which generative AIs based strategies work such as de novo drug design as well as molecular generation that allows for rapid and sufficient design of new drug candidates within huge chemical spaces whilst predicting their properties (Zhavoronkov et al., 2019). Thus, it's possible to use generative AIs to create molecules thereby predicting their safety and efficacy thus establishing an effective pipeline for drug discovery saving on time needed to introduce new medicines into the market considerably cutting down associated costs involved with launching new therapies at all times (Popova et al., 2018).

One more thrilling use of generative AI within healthcare has been seen in personalized medicine. Generative models always work by analysing individual patient data like genetics, health records and lifestyle choices so as to create tailored treatment plans (Choi et al., 2016). Such an approach may significantly boost the effectiveness of treatments, reduce side effects from drugs, and therefore enhance patients' lives more directly targeted and effectively (Schork 2019).

The Purpose and Scope of this Chapter

In general, the scope of this chapter entails a wide-ranging interaction concerning the promises and threats involved in utilizing generative Artificial Intelligence (AI) in healthcare, thereby providing sound advice on how to effectively adopt such revolutionary technologies. This chapter will address prospective advantages and disadvantages in using generative AI so as to prepare stakeholders within the healthcare field with knowledge and strategic paths for steering through ethical and enduring integration of AI into the healthcare ecosystem (Bohr &Memarzadeh, 2020).

Beyond technical aspects surrounding generative AI, its broader implications for health are examined by this chapter. Such domains of health may include drug discovery as well as personalized medicine, diagnostic imaging and clinical decision support systems among others (Yu et al., 2018). Specifically examined are ethical, legal and social issues around generating such an AI including various data confidentiality questions like why it is important to keep patient data safe from untrustworthy individuals who might manipulate them; fairness bearings regarding algorithmic ignorance; finally, there is a need for some form of governance framework as far as responsible machine learning is concerned (Char et al., 2018).

In this chapter, a balanced and for the present state of generative artificial intelligence in healthcare prospects alongside recommendations and best practices is shared out with guidance to health care organizations, policy makers and developers of such technologies on how to use them responsibly (He et al., 2019). The chapter should leave readers with a deeper understanding of the transformative possibilities of generative AI in health care, as well as an appreciation of the associated challenges and responsibilities. The insights provided here will facilitate decision-making and collaborative efforts aimed at maximizing the benefits of generative AI, while minimizing its risks and ensuring its positive impact on patients' lives and that of society as a whole.

THE PROMISE OF GENERATIVE AI IN HEALTHCARE

In the field of healthcare there will be many changes because of generative AI: speedier drug discovery, better diagnostic accuracy and patient-tailored care. Health systems can be transformed by generative such as through powerful algorithms and great volumes of medical data (Jiang et al., 2017). The most amazing thing about generative AI is its ability to create new and different types of data which paves way for an entirely new domain in healthcare research and advancements (Xue et al., 2018). When data is scant like in case of rare diseases or when it is difficult to obtain patient consent, it can generate synthetic data using traditional methods that are limited by barriers associated with conventional techniques for collecting information from patients (Frid-Adar et al., 2018).

Generative AI will keep improving numerous other processes in the field of healthcare to sustain efficiency in cutting down on costs while improving patients' results. For instance, some complex tasks such as image analysis and treatment planning can be automated using generative AI, which allows human healthcare professionals to make high-level decisions or concentrate their efforts more on treating the patients than working on the computer (Esteva et al., 2019). The next sections will explore various areas where generative AI can actually be implemented with examples from real-life cases that offer insights into its transformative potential in the health sector.

Accelerating Medical Research and Drug Discovery

Healthcare features a very promising application for generative AI which is medical research and discovery of drugs. Traditionally, drug discovery process suffers from being time-consuming, costly and has a high rate of failure (Mullard, 2018). As such, generative AI might revolutionize this process by accelerating the search for new drug candidates and predicting their properties for better efficacy and safety (Zhavoronkov et al., 2019).

Strikingly, in designing novel molecular structures and anticipating their pharmacological characteristics generative models e.g., GANs and VAEs have achieved remarkable success as pointed out by Popova et al in 2018. Indeed, Segler et al., 2018 are of the view that generative artificial intelligence can help in saving time and money at the initial stages of drug discovery by screening vast amounts of chemicals and suggesting optimized ones.

For example, there is a generative AI model called "DrugEx" developed at University of Toronto and Insilico Medicine which can generate new drug-like molecules with desired properties (Polykovskiy et al., 2020). When trained on large datasets of existing drugs with known characteristics, DrugEx is able to create new compounds that are targeted towards given therapeutics as demonstrated in table 1.

Table 1. Examples of novel drug-like molecules generated by DrugEx

Therapeutic Target	Generated Molecule	Predicted Properties
Kinase inhibitor	Molecule A	High binding affinity, low toxicity
GPCR agonist	Molecule B	Selective activation, improved bioavailability
Protease inhibitor	Molecule C	Potent inhibition, reduced side effects

(Polykovskiy et al., 2020)

Another notable example is what happened with Exscientia, an AI-driven drug discovery company, and Sumitomo Dainippon Pharma from Japan (Polykovskiy et al., 2018). The generative AI models they used helped them discover a new drug candidate for obsessive-compulsive disorder (OCD) in only one year while conventional drug development lasts four to five years on average. The compound DSP-1181 was synthesized by the machine and found to be effective in vitro and is currently in phase I clinical trials (Exscientia, 2020).

These accounts provide us with evidence of how much generative artificial intelligence can do in speeding up medical research and drug delivery processes. They offer alternative strategies for identifying new therapeutic targets and increasing the efficacy of drug candidates. The future of drug discovery looks bright as generative Artificial Intelligence continues to undergo transformations and converges with other technologies like robotic automation or high-throughput screening because the kind of medical miracles that could save lives may now become available to patients sooner than before and at lower costs.

Enhancing Diagnostic Accuracy and Precision Medicine

Depending on your thought process, one can think that generative AI will have an exhilarating impact on health precision and accuracy in diagnosis. These models assist healthcare professionals by analysing large volumes of medical data, such as imaging scans, genetic information, and electronic health records (Esteva et al.,2019) for better accuracy in diagnosis and timely patient outcomes.

Therefore, there are improvements in accuracy within medical imaging using generative AI with High-speed analyses. For instance, Frid-Adar et al. (2018) used GANs to create synthetic medical images which could range from X-rays to CT scans or MRI scans and were thus used to augment existing data on diagnostic algorithms efficiency. They use the approach of comparing real-time images with manipulated ones; thereby enhancing their ability to notice subtle asymmetries while detecting complex patterns that could otherwise be difficult for human radiologists (Yi et al.,2019).

Researchers have developed a generative deep learning model, called CheXNeXt, which can accurately diagnose pneumonia from chest X-rays as good as expert radiologists (Rajpurkar et al., 2017). The model was trained on data comprising over 100,000 X-ray images that included chest images resulting to achieving 0.97 AUC (area under the receiver operating characteristic curve) showing its high diagnostic accuracy. The performance of CheXNeXt compared to human radiologists is shown in Table 2.

Table 2. Comparison of Diagnostic Accuracy between CheXNeXt and Human Radiologists

Metric	CheXNeXt	Human Radiologists
Accuracy	95%	93%
Sensitivity	94%	91%
Specificity	96%	95%

(Rajpurkar et al., 2017)

Apart from medical imaging, generative AI holds a promising capacity for precision medicine through the making of personalized treatment plans based on a patient's unique genomic profile, clinical history, and lifestyle choice (Ginsburg & Phillips, 2018). By analysing vast amounts of genomic data at scale and combining them with clinical information, generative AI models are able to predict someone's risk factors for specified diseases, suggest best therapies and track their reactions to them (Yi et al., 2019).

Generative AI in precision medicine encompasses a notable example, which is the DeepProfile – a predictive tool for Alzheimer made by researchers from the University of Toronto (Ding et al., 2018). The model was trained with over 800 individuals' data and achieved an AUC of 0.92 for predicting the risk of developing Alzheimer's disease within 10 years. It helps to identify high-risk people at early stages thereby making targeted interventions possible and allowing personalized prevention strategies.

As generative AI becomes more sophisticated in future, its impact on diagnostic accuracy and precision medicine may increase tremendously. Generative AI can alter the face of healthcare by empowering clinicians with AI-assisted tools that will enable generation of custom-made treatment plans; this way improving patient outcomes while promoting efficiency as well as effectiveness of care delivery systems.

THE PERILS OF GENERATIVE AI IN HEALTHCARE

Even though generative AI has the potential to revolutionize health care, such potentialities may come with attendant challenges and risks which Char et al. (2018) will bring to the fore because of its many ethical, legal and social consequences. Such a concern exists because these models could always perpetuate and amplify biased input from the training data sets thus yielding discriminatory outcomes (Obermeyer et al., 2019). This could have a cascading effect leading to marginalization of groups in terms of access to health care as well as outcome inequalities (Popejoy& Fullerton, 2016).

Besides, lack transparency and explainability from some generative AI models most of times known as "black box" issue raises questions about accountability and trustworthiness regarding AI based healthcare decisions especially in clinical situations (Shukla 2019 ; 2024). Additionally, huge amounts of data that are required by this kind of algorithms pose another great risk including violation of data privacy rights and use of confidential medical information which is more prone to misuse. Therefore, this may lead people losing confidence in such technologies (Cohen & Mello, 2018; Shukla & Taneja, 2024). More so, the use of generative AI in the healthcare sector raises concerns about liability and accountability in instances of adverse outcomes, which muddy the waters when it comes to determining responsibility among AI developers, health service providers and institutions (Shukla & Taneja 2024). In order to enhance confidence and protect patient rights, clear rules and systems must be formulated.

Data Privacy and Security Concerns

Generative AI is increasingly being used in the healthcare sector; however, doing so requires transparency and accountability (Rieke et al., 2020). Unauthorized access, misuse or breaches necessitate rigorous protective measures for medical records (Rieke et al., 2020). For instance, Health Insurance Portability and Accountability Act (HIPAA) in United States and General Data Protection Regulation (GDPR) in Europe require their compliance by health care providers and developers of artificial intelligence (AI) software (Beaulieu-Jones et al., 2019); besides this, it should also guarantee software processes which ensure confidentiality, integrity and availability of information (Hoffman &Podgurski, 2020).

However, it is possible that regulations may not completely eliminate all privacy threats because generative models have this ability to make up patient-related data that appears quite similar to realistic ones (Verghese et al., 2018). For this reason, there is need for credible authentication and validation systems that can tell the difference between genuine and AI-generated medical information (Mirsky et al., 2019). There is also an urgent requirement for well-defined data governance frameworks which specify roles, duties and accountability of stakeholders throughout any type of information life cycle via means such as data minimization principle, purpose limitation principle or remaining period (Verghese et al., 2018).

In ensuring that there is confidence and transparency, the healthcare institutions ought to prioritize education of patients as well as well-informed consent processes (Vest & Gamm, 2010). Additionally, it is also very crucial to have regulations on data ownership, control and sharing (Blasimme&Vayena, 2020). This will allow the patients to have access to their medical information and be in a position to manage or transfer it if need arises (Haas et al., 2021). There is need for strong frameworks on data-sharing which should include principles of standardization, interoperability and safe transfer in order to hasten the creation and verification of generative AI models (Mirsky et al., 2019; Vest & Gamm, 2010).

Algorithmic Biases and Unintended Consequences

Representing risks as Persection phrases is done through several channels. In social bots and health care it is observed that a whole lot of problems stem from algorithmic biases which turn out to be complacent in the body of the users themselves. By such means, algorithms have an undesirable effect on the people who have been put in charge to monitor their behaviours as well as those whom they interact with.

For many marginalized population groups there exist some discrepancies in evaluating dangers(Popejoy & Fullerton, 2016) together with development of less effective drugs or even ones causing serious health complications for certain segments of the society(Yadav et al., 2021).

These are some manifestations of this problem.Addressing these issues properly requires making sure that training datasets are diverse and representative (Chen et al., 2019). As a result, we need partnerships with local actors like patient advocates, community-based organizations and researchers with expertise in diversity problems area (Ferryman &Pitcan, 2018). The presence of algorithm fairness assessments as part of detailed testing and validation processes such as risk assessment frameworks will help in eliminating and finding out such biases (Wiens et al., 2019; Bellamy et al., 2018).

Generative AI in health care may also cause unplanned events among them changes in power relationships between those with professional knowledge in health care and artificial intelligence machines (Verghese et al., 2018) or employment losses requiring the labor force to upgrade their capabilities (Davenport &Kalakota, 2019; Tran et al., 2019). In order to reduce the effects of such consequences, there is need to emphasize on promoting openness and accountability in healthcare systems through continuous monitoring (Larson et al., 2020), putting clear guidelines for AI generated products (Grote & Berens, 2020) as well as involving stakeholders and interdisciplinary collaborations (McCradden et al., 2020; Lysaght et al., 2019). Addressing the problem of algorithmic bias and unintended consequences need a multi-faceted approach that includes diverse data sets, rigorous testing procedures within organizations involving shared responsibility for transparency among staff members coupled with permanent checking systems aimed at ensuring that generative AIs are used equally across health care settings making it both safe and sound (Blasimme&Vayena, 2020).

NAVIGATING THE PATH TO RESPONSIBLE ADOPTION

For generative AI to be adapted in health care systems, there has to be an alternative route. We will discuss some of the main factors and strategies which can be put in place to address ethical and social issues surrounding generative AI in medicine in this section. There are different actions that should be taken by health care participants so as to benefit from generative AI while minimizing its risks, including having powerful governance mechanisms, making sure the reliability and transparency of AI systems themselves, promoting multi-disciplinary collaborations, as well as placing patient-centeredness at the forefront.

Establishing Governance Frameworks and Ethical Guidelines

Generative AI for the medical care sector should start with comprehensive governance frameworks and ethical guidelines as the first essential steps that should be taken if these technologies are going to be introduced into such a field. Such frameworks must present clear principles, policies and procedures concerning the development, deployment as well as monitoring of AI systems in health care settings (Larson et al., 2020). In other words, it is the responsibility of leaders to ensure that their choice of generative AI is consistent with ethical values such as beneficence, non-maleficence autonomy and justice by providing a set of uniform values that will be applicable amid them when they devise governance framework (Floridi et al., 2018).

They must address several ethical dimensions concerning generation AI models used in this specific industry. Among them are guidelines on data privacy and confidentiality; informed consent processes; algorithmic fairness and non-discrimination; transparency and explainability; accountability measures (Amann et al., 2020). An example would be to include instructions on how deidentification should happen within the governance frameworks so that patient information is kept confidential while also identifying situations under which patients' consent is required before using theirs' for making AI (Cohen & Mello, 2019).

In addition, governance frameworks must incorporate the stipulations for regular scrutiny and audits of AI systems to reveal the alleviate and pinpoint various random biases and mistakes (Fjeld et al., 2020). This may involve application of algorithmic effect assessments that systematically evaluate the potential risks and benefits of AI systems based on fairness, transparency and responsibility among other parameters (Reisman et al., 2018). As a result, ongoing supervision and assessment mechanisms are instituted in order for healthcare organizations to take a proactive stand in dealing with ethical issues while ensuring that generative AI is used responsibly.

In addition, the creation of governance frameworks as well as ethical principles should be done through cooperative efforts involving various stakeholders including practitioners from medical fields, specialists in artificial intelligence ethics experts, legal practitioners, patient representatives and policymakers (Blasimme&Vayena, 2020). Such an approach is multidimensional thus allowing for greater inclusivity when developing these frameworks (Gasser & Almeida, 2017). Moreover, involving patients as well as general public in the development of these governance frameworks is also vital since it encourages confidence building measures like increasing openness and holding others accountable concerning utilization of generative artificial intelligence (Aitken et al., 2019).

Though the organizational set of governance frameworks for a given institution, uniformly on ethical aspects guides the use of generative AI in healthcare sectors. There are essential actors who develop and advocate these frameworks including the professional medical associations, regulatory bodies as well as international organizations (Char et al., 2020). For instance, one such paper by WHO called 'Ethics and Governance of Artificial Intelligence for Health' offers global principles and advice on AI use within clinical settings (World Health Organization, 2021).

The first step to responsible adoption of generative AI in health care is putting up strong governance frameworks and ethical guidelines. Such frameworks would include comprehensive principles, policies and processes which help route generative AIs potentiality into patient centricity, individual rights respectability and equity based reliable mechanisms of health care delivery from other sectors and not necessarily that it ends up being a mere option among differently weighted alternatives.

Ensuring Robustness and Reliability of AI Systems

Ensuring the robustness and reliability of generative AI systems is critical for responsible adoption in healthcare. AI models must be designed, developed, and deployed to guarantee safe, accurate, and consistent performance across diverse patient populations and clinical settings (Kelly et al., 2019). This requires a comprehensive approach encompassing rigorous testing, validation, and ongoing monitoring to identify and mitigate potential risks, errors, and unintended consequences (Hernandez-Boussard et al., 2020).

A key challenge is ensuring that generative AI systems can effectively generalize to real-world clinical scenarios. Developing AI systems using large, representative, and high-quality datasets that capture the heterogeneity of patient characteristics, disease manifestations, and clinical contexts is essential (Vokinger et al., 2021). Rigorous testing and validation procedures, including appropriate evaluation metrics, cross-validation, external validation, and prospective clinical trials, must be employed to assess performance, safety, and reliability (Park & Kressel, 2018).

According to Finlayson et al., (2021), it is critical to put in place continuous monitoring and feedback mechanisms that will enable early detection and correction of performance drift, errors or unintended consequences. Data management, model development and deployment should be underpinned by standardized best practices and guidelines such as the FAIR and TRUST provisions (Wilkinson et al., 2016; Floridi& Cowls, 2019). The involvement of human oversight and intervention capabilities is important so as to ensure that health professionals hold ultimate decision-making authority (Grote & Berens, 2020; Cai et al., 2019).

To tackle technical challenges and limitations including advanced data pre-processing techniques, feature selection, model training and performance optimization (Jiang et al., 2017), ongoing research and innovation are a must. There is also an urgent need for making AI models more interpretable and explainable themselves (Amann et al., 2020).

In summary, reinforcing generating AI systems' robustness and reliability needs a composite approach covering data quality assurance (QA), rigorous testing as well monitoring of its progress at all times besides a standardized best practice in medicine; it involves the human supervision from its beginning to end as well as unconstrained research on the ground.

Fostering Collaboration Between AI Developers, Healthcare Professionals, and Regulatory Bodies

Sustaining collaboration amongst AI creators, health care providers and regulatory authorities is important for the considerate implementation of generative artificial intelligence in medical care. It is important that the development and deployment of such systems is made through a multidisciplinary approach that utilizes expertise from diverse stakeholders (Beede et al., 2020). At this time, if there are open discussions, sharing of knowledge as well as working together to solve problems, it will be easier for AI-driven health organizations to design, implement and monitor their systems within the moral, regulatory requirements and clinical needs (Korngiebel& Mooney, 2021).

AI developers need to work together with health care providers so as to create AI systems that are medically relevant, user-friendly and can be smoothly incorporated into existing medical procedures (Sendak et al., 2020). Invaluable domain knowledge and first-hand experience of patient care processes are necessary for healthcare professionals including physicians, nurses among other clinical personnel. By engaging health practitioners in all stages of designing an AI system from idea conception to deployment, the AI developers get insights on unique challenges facing the health sector such as constraints and opportunities (Beede et al., 2020). Through this cooperation, the creation of artificial intelligent solutions who do not only possess sufficient skills but also understand what it means to be human would not be difficult.

Additionally, for the comprehensibility and legitimacy of AI systems it is very important that there should be a partnership between those who develop AI algorithms as well as those in the medical field. To do effective integration into clinical decision-making processes, clinicians ought to have an understanding on how the generated results of an AI model can be explained (Amann et al., 2020). An explainable model could be designed by means of strong collaboration and repeated feedback loops between AI developers and medical professionals who provide clear insights (Tonekaboni et al., 2019). It increases trust for medical personnel who are then able to make choices taking advantage of both suggestions from machines powered by artificial intelligence alongside intuitive thoughts about what is best for patients' condition based on their experience in this area (Grote & Berens, 2020).

As highlighted by Gerke et al (2020), collaboration among AI creators alongside medical practitioners is necessary while getting the right regulatory bodies on board also matters a lot in understanding an intricate area like AI governance in health. In fact, regulatory organizations such as the Food and Drug Administration (FDA) in America as well as the European Medicines Agency (EMA) are very instrumental when it comes to observing safety, efficacy and quality of AI systems within healthcare (Pesapane et al., 2018).

By working hand in hand with the regulatory authorities, developers of AI and health organizations can ensure their systems are in line with the law, standards and guidelines (Larson et al., 2020). Bringing together AI developers, health care providers and regulatory agencies may help to define performance benchmarks, establish sufficient validation and testing methodologies and create frameworks for post-market surveillance (Minssen et al.,

2020). This way, they will work towards assistance in creating common standards used for designing, developing and deploying healthcare AI systems.

Moreover, for encouraging transparency, accountability and public faith in the AI-based healthcare, cooperation of AI developers, health workers and regulatory agencies is crucial (Vayena et al., 2018). As part of open dialogue and sharing their knowledge with each other, such stakeholders as aforementioned can create defined lines of communication, disclosure schemes, and methods for getting the public involved that can help to keep patients and society in general informed about how artificial intelligence is used in health care (Dzobo et al., 2020).

Table 3 provides an overview of significant advantages and difficulties pertaining to fostering collaboration between AI developers, health care practitioners and regulatory authorities.

Table 3. Benefits and Challenges of Collaboration in AI-Driven Healthcare

Benefits	Challenges
Development of clinically relevant AI solutions	Balancing competing priorities and interests
Integration of domain expertise into AI design	Establishing common language and understanding
Enhanced interpretability and trustworthiness of AI	Managing intellectual property and data sharing
Compliance with regulatory requirements	Keeping pace with rapid technological advancements
Establishment of harmonized standards and best practices	Addressing cultural and organizational barriers
Promotion of transparency, accountability, and public trust	Ensuring equitable representation and inclusion

Strategies for Mitigating Risks and Safeguarding Patient Rights

The primary focus is to mitigate risks and make sure that patient rights are preserved during the introduction of generative artificial intelligence in healthcare. These AI systems are capable of enhancing patient outcomes and sending them to the hospital but they also present serious security, bias, privacy and unintended consequences risks (Cohen et al., 2020). Healthcare organisations must therefore come up with comprehensive strategies that focus on the patient's safety, autonomy and confidentiality as they try to solve these problems (Kalkman et al., 2019).

Establishing robust data governing frameworks is one of the key strategies for mitigating risks associated with AI in healthcare (Ballantyne & Stewart, 2019). Patient data for AI development or deployment should be collected, stored and processed in a secure, transparent and ethical manner by healthcare organisations (Price & Cohen, 2019). To do this they should implement strict data protection measures such as encryption, access controls and audit trails to keep unauthorized persons from accessing private information about patients that could otherwise be misused (Mikk et al., 2017).

In addition, frameworks for data governance should consolidate data minimization, purpose limitation and patient consent principles (Floridi& Taddeo, 2016). In other words, healthcare institutions can collect and use patient information necessary for specific, clearly stated purposes only after receiving explicit permission from the patients concerning their data being used for AI development and utilization (Cohen & Mello, 2019). Patients must receive unambiguous and comprehensible information regarding the way their data will be utilized, benefits and risks thereof and finally, one's rights to access, amend or withdraw it (Ploug & Holm, 2020). Another important tactic in lowering the dangers associated with AI-enabled healthcare is formulating as well as implementing algorithmic fairness and detection of biases techniques (Mehrabi et al., 2021). Biased AI systems trained on unrepresentative data may further entrench or exacerbate existing inequalities in healthcare access and outcomes (Obermeyer et al., 2019). To tackle this problem, it is necessary for health organizations to place greater emphasis on obtaining and utilizing various representational databases that reflect the heterogeneity of patient populations (Chen et al., 2019).

In addition, developers of AI should use algorithmic fairness methods like pre-processing techniques, in-processing constraints and post-processing adjustments in order to eliminate bias from AI models (Rajkomar et al., 2018). Regular audits and assessments need to be carried out in order to identify and correct any disparities or biases present in AI-generated outputs (Zhang et al., 2021). By constantly monitoring and correcting algorithmic biases, healthcare organizations can ensure that they are using AI systems which give fair and unbiased recommendations and decisions (Goodman et al., 2018).

Another important way of protecting patients' rights in the context of AI-based health care is through clear mechanisms for getting informed consent, shared decision making as well as patient empowerment (McDougall, 2019). It is important for patients to be actively involved in making choices regarding their care when the decisions made by these systems are based on from the artificial intelligence (AI) systems; they should also have an opportunity to opt out or ask for human intervention (Schiff & Borenstein, 2019). There should be accessible and comprehensible information concerning AI generated recommendations such as why they were made available to the patients by healthcare organizations (Amann et al., 2020).

In addition, various altruistic aspects will be kept in mind so that once attained; other measures may easily follow suit. Please take note algorithms are not omniscient beings; they do not possess personal experiences hence unable to distinguish rights from obligations among other things like fairness differentials across groups hence creating a risky domain for cyberspace criminals since even innocent ones might suffer adverse consequences.In this respect, algorithmic equity methods such aplenty pre-processing techniques while others partake of it during processing stage or undergo post processing modifications enable AI developers accomplish one primary goal namely removal of such abhorrent circumstances.

Together with this sentiment, regular audits as well as assessments would help in determining if there any differences between output produced by the AI and human beings so as to correct any existing errors within those areas (Zhang et al., 2021). Furthermore, algorithmic equity can only be achieved through continuous scrutiny and elimination of unfairnesses in AI systems by personnel from health sectors (Goodman et al., 2018).

Another strategy for preserving patient rights among the different stakeholders involved with AIs use for health care services is through establishing possible ways/forms of obtaining consent forms from patients which are free from any coercion and will as well as that can empower patients together with clinical officers participating jointly in making decisions about their treatment (McDougall, 2019). When AI systems are employed to inform their care decisions should include patients as an integral part of this process; they also must have the option to reject the use of such technologies or require human intervention (Schiff &Borenstein, 2019).For example, organizations need to provide comprehensible and accessible recommendations to the patients concerning these choices grounded on what helped create them(Amann et al., 2020).

A formalized way for patients to contest or appeal AI decisions that they deem inappropriate, biased or do not serve patients' interests should be devised by healthcare organizations (Challen et al., 2019). One of such ways may be the setup of specific review boards or an ombudsperson whose duty will be ensuring that AI systems are used fairly, transparently and in a manner that can be held accountable (Gerke et al., 2020).

Last but not least, an ongoing monitoring process aimed at risk mitigation and patient rights protection in this type of healthcare requires continuous assessment, refinement of AI models (Kelly et al., 2019). Healthcare institutions need to set up all-inclusive post-market monitoring and evaluation procedure frameworks aimed at identifying any untoward events, unintentional effects or performance drops in AI systems (Larson et al., 2020). In order to point out areas where changes need to be made and ensure that AI systems remain relevant to the ever-changing clinical demands in addition to meeting patient needs as they arise again; there should be well-established feedback loops held regularly between developers within the field of Artificial Intelligence (AI), healthcare professionals as well as patients (Sendak et al., 2020).

Hastening to conclusion, in implementing generative AI in the healthcare sector, it is important to take a multi-pronged approach so as to minimize risks and protect patients' rights. Strategies such as firm data governances, algorithm fairness as well as biases detection, informed consent and mutual decision taking should be considered into these plans at all times. In doing so, healthcare institutions will be able to leverage on AI's revolutionary capabilities while at the same time ensuring patient safety, independence and privacy.

THE FUTURE OF GENERATIVE AI IN HEALTHCARE

Generative artificial intelligence is still evolving and its performance is rising. It has a significant influence on healthcare in the future. Assuredly, AI could help with some of the current health problems such as drug discovery and development, personalized medicine, clinical decision making and patient care among others (Topol, 2019). In this part, new patterns and advancements regarding generative artificial intelligence will be discussed, their potential effects on service delivery in healthcare systems will also be examined as well as patients' outcomes after surgery or treatments have been done. Finally, we should think about what will happen when humans combine their thought system with that of AI to offer world health that is more just and healthier than now.

Emerging Trends and Innovations

Rapidly changing field of Generative AI generates various techniques, architectures and applications at an unprecedented speed. One of the most promising tendencies of generative AI is improving models that are more advanced and expressive such as generative adversarial networks (GANs) and variational autoencoders (VAEs) that can produce highly realistic and diverse data in multiple domains including imaging, text and audio (Goodfellow et al., 2014; Kingma& Welling, 2014).

In healthcare, these advanced generative models have found application to a wide range of tasks starting from training diagnostic algorithms by generating synthetic medical images to designing novel drug molecules with desired properties (Kadurin et al., 2017; Guibas et al., 2017). For instance, some researchers have applied GANs for generating high-quality synthetic chest X-ray images that may augment limited datasets thereby enhancing the performance of deep learning models aimed at pneumonia detection (Madani et al., 2018).

Another newly developing pattern with this generative AIs is the trend of including field-specific knowledge and professional comments in training sessions. Utilizing these factors when training generative models enhances their quality, relevance and interpretation (Guibas et al., 2017). Particularly, in medical practice context it is vital that the produced information as well as insights conform to existing recommendations on treatment protocols, best procedures considered for the domain and individual patient requirements.

Potential Impact on Healthcare Delivery and Patient Outcomes

Various aspects of healthcare delivery can be transformed and patient outcomes improved by generative AI's integration into healthcare systems. One of the greatest impacts which generative AI will have is through personalized medicine where AI-generated models can be used to predict how an individual responds to different treatments, how much dosage to use, and what treatment plan suits only them (Cheng et al., 2019).

Generative AI can also bring about significant changes in drug discovery and development by speeding up the identification of new drug candidates as well as predicting their effectiveness and safety profiles and optimizing their chemical structures for particular properties (Polykovskiy et al., 2018). Such an approach will result in the more rapid and affordable development of new therapies against various diseases for the benefit of patients worldwide.

In clinical decision-making, healthcare providers can utilize AI with generative models for diagnosis, prognosis and treatment planning. This is done through analysing extensive patient information as well as having algorithms generate customized recommendations allowing for informed in addition to better grounded choices thus averting medical mistakes and consequently increasing quality of care (Patel et al., 2019).

Furthermore, generative AI offers a remedy to these issues by developing inexpensive diagnostic tools at problem locations and distance monitoring systems (Char et al., 2020). The use of artificial intelligence (AI) such as generating synthetic data and models that consider different patient populations will help to reduce gaps in healthcare access and outcomes among populations that are less supported or marginalized.

Envisioning a Healthier and More Equitable World

By working hand-in-hand with human intellects, generative AI should be thought of as a tool that can help humanity create a healthier world where there is less discrimination. Therefore, this needs an integrated and interdisciplinary approach bringing together AI researchers, health care professionals, policy makers, patient advocates among others to tackle the technicalities of AI involved there in healthcare (Abràmoff et al., 2020).

In order to realize the utmost capabilities of generative artificial intelligence applications within medical sphere it is necessary first and foremost prioritize the formation of responsible transparent and accountable artificial intelligence systems that are in line with human values and enhance health for all citizens (Floridi et al., 2018). This means drawing up comprehensive guidelines and standards on how to design deploy implement monitor AI systems which guarantee their safety effectiveness efficiency fairness besides fostering public trust towards such type of medical practices (Char et al., 2020).

Also, we need to put money into projects for education and training aimed at enabling health care specialists to interact effectively with AI systems, understand their results and then use a mixture of AI information and human knowledge to take major decisions (Kolachalama& Garg, 2018). This will demand a complete transformation of medical training and professional development moving forward that focuses on data literacy, critical thinking as well as ethical reasoning in this era of artificial intelligence.

In conclusion, there is great hope that generative AI in health care can lead to better patient outcomes, facilitate medical research and promote an equitable and inclusive health system. If we work together from different fields and with different vested interests, we can channelise the potential of AI towards addressing emerging healthcare challenges for brightening up global health.

CONCLUSION

Key Takeaways and Recommendations

- Throughout this chapter, we have critically analysed the extensive scope of options and complex issues entailed by using generative artificial intelligence (GAI) within health care. Some of these are: transforming healthcare through improved accuracy in diagnosis/treatment outcomes, personalized medicine including drug discovery and so on. Nonetheless, achieving this promise demands a prudent, ethical and cohesive strategy that tackles the ethical and social implications of AI in health care.

Some of the key themes emerging from our investigation into generative AI within healthcare include:

- o Generative AI can speed up medical research, streamlining drug discovery processes and facilitating personalized medicine via novel insights generation as well as data driven solutions.
- o Inclusion of strong governance frameworks, ethical standards and regulatory supervision has to be part of adopting Generative AI in health care so as to protect patients' safety, privacy and fairness.
    - It is important for AI developers; healthcare workers and regulatory authorities to come together with a view to developing trustworthy, clinically relevant and user-friendly AI systems that can seamlessly fit into health care workflows.

- In order to successfully deploy generative AI in healthcare, it is imperative that we minimize the risks associated with algorithmic bias, protect data privacy and security, as well as safeguard the rights of patients who are champions.
- For the future of generative AI in healthcare, continuous innovation, multidisciplinary collaboration and commitment to making our world healthier and more equitable are indispensable.

To acquire the route that leads us to the prudent embrace of generative AI in healthcare, we propose the following:

- Create ethical principles and rule-making strategies that put above all else security, discretion and impartiality regarding the emergence and use of AI product.
- Encourage cooperation from different disciplines among ai developers, medical caretakers, legal boards, advocates for patients so that solutions based on AI are compatible with the clinic environment as well as possible, easy to use and trustworthy.
- Provide money for studies aimed at correcting mistakes made by algorithms, enhancing their clarity/interpretability besides making sure these models can be used among various groups of patients.
- Encourage data sharing while establishing strong data privacy/security procedures to keep confidential information about patients safe.
- Train health professionals through learning programmes/courses such that they will find it easy to work together with AI machines and make wise decisions founded on insights derived from computers.
- Create generative AIs with input directly from patients/public in order to have openness assessment accountability within health services run by computers (AI).

A Call to Action for Responsible Adoption of Generative AI in Healthcare

It's important to adopt this innovative technology responsibly. This is especially so since generative artificial intelligence could transform the way patients are cared for and conducted medical research. Right now opportunities abound for human society as a whole but also some challenges in ensuring patient care.. It is time we came together as one big family made up of all the people who contribute to health; from doctors through policy makers down to patients' advocates.

We need to work towards a future where generative AI complements human intelligence effectively leading to better health outcomes, less inequality in healthcare access and progressive attainment in medical practice knowledge base (NIHR). If patient welfare is prioritized then ethicality should remain constant whilst rigorous research is done plus encouraging public participation.

We can navigate the way towards responsible application of generative AI technology in healthcare if we do so with a collective understanding of what makes a healthier and more equitable world. We should be humble when confronting these difficulties because there are limitations to what we know today; in fact, knowing that new things come with time is important when engaging in any form of intellectual endeavour. Therefore, let us confront these issues like lions facing hyenas roaring out loudly into the night. This means embracing all opportunities presented by this revolutionary tool that will allow us to change lives previously thought unchangeable and relieve agony globally.

The road ahead may prove difficult; however, it is a task that demands our collective efforts. Therefore, by combining generative AI's power with human wisdom compassion and creativity allows health service delivery at all levels being accessible affordable right now! Let us take up this momentous occasion just like how we would if it were meant for our patients or those who live around us including future generations too.t; however, it is a task that demands our collective efforts. Therefore, by combining generative AI's power with human wisdom compassion and creativity allows health service delivery at all levels being accessible affordable right now! Let us take up this momentous occasion just like how we would if it were meant for our patients or those who live around us including future generations too.

REFERENCES

Abràmoff, M. D., Tobey, D., & Char, D. S. (2020). Lessons learned about autonomous AI: Finding a safe, efficacious, and ethical path through the development process. *American Journal of Ophthalmology, 214*, 134–142. DOI: 10.1016/j.ajo.2020.02.022 PMID: 32171769

Adamson, A. S., & Smith, A. (2018). Machine learning and health care disparities in dermatology. *JAMA Dermatology, 154*(11), 1247–1248. DOI: 10.1001/jamadermatol.2018.2348 PMID: 30073260

Aitken, M., Tully, M. P., Porteous, C., Denegri, S., Cunningham-Burley, S., Banner, N., Black, C., Burgess, M., Cross, L., van Delden, J., Ford, E., Fox, S., Fitzpatrick, N., Gallacher, K., Goddard, C., Hassan, L., Jamieson, R., Jones, K. H., Kaarakainen, M., & Willison, D. J. (2019). Consensus statement on public involvement and engagement with data-intensive health research. *International Journal of Population Data Science, 4*(1), 1–6. DOI: 10.23889/ijpds.v4i1.586 PMID: 34095528

Amann, J., Blasimme, A., Vayena, E., Frey, D., & Madai, V. I. (2020). Explainability for artificial intelligence in healthcare: A multidisciplinary perspective. *BMC Medical Informatics and Decision Making, 20*(1), 1–9. DOI: 10.1186/s12911-020-01332-6 PMID: 33256715

Ballantyne, A., & Stewart, C. (2019). Big data and public-private partnerships in healthcare and research: The application of an ethics framework for big data in health and research. *Asian Bioethics Review, 11*(3), 315–326. DOI: 10.1007/s41649-019-00100-7 PMID: 33717319

Beaulieu-Jones, B. K., Yuan, W., Brat, G. A., & Weber, G. M. (2019). Privacy-preserving distributed deep learning for clinical data. *AMIA Joint Summits on Translational Science Proceedings AMIA Summit on Translational Science*, •••, 28–37.

Beede, E., Baylor, E., Hersch, F., Iurchenko, A., Wilcox, L., Ruamviboonsuk, P., & Vardoulakis, L. M. (2020). A human-centered evaluation of a deep learning system deployed in clinics for the detection of diabetic retinopathy. *Proceedings of the 2020 CHI Conference on Human Factors in Computing Systems*, 1-12. DOI: 10.1145/3313831.3376718

Bellamy, R. K. E., Dey, K., Hind, M., Hoffman, S. C., Houde, S., Kannan, K., Lohia, P., Martino, J., Mehta, S., Mojsilović, A., Nagar, S., Ramamurthy, K. N., Richards, J., Saha, D., Sattigeri, P., Singh, M., Varshney, K. R., & Zhang, Y. (2018). AI fairness 360: An extensible toolkit for detecting, understanding, and mitigating unwanted algorithmic bias. arXiv. https://arxiv.org/abs/1810.01943

Blasimme, A., & Vayena, E. (2019 Forthcoming). *The ethics of AI in biomedical research, patient care and public health. Patient Care and Public Health (April 9, 2019).* Oxford Handbook of Ethics of Artificial Intelligence.

Bohr, A., &Memarzadeh, K. (2020). The rise of artificial intelligence in healthcare applications. Artificial Intelligence in Healthcare, 25-60. DOI: 10.1016/B978-0-12-818438-7.00002-2

Cai, C. J., Winter, S., Steiner, D., Wilcox, L., & Terry, M. (2019). "Hello AI": Uncovering the onboarding needs of medical practitioners for human-AI collaborative decision-making. Proceedings of the ACM on Human-Computer Interaction, 3(CSCW), 1-24. DOI: 10.1145/3359206

Challen, R., Denny, J., Pitt, M., Gompels, L., Edwards, T., & Tsaneva-Atanasova, K. (2019). Artificial intelligence, bias and clinical safety. *BMJ Quality & Safety, 28*(3), 231–237. DOI: 10.1136/bmjqs-2018-008370 PMID: 30636200

Char, D. S., Abràmoff, M. D., & Feudtner, C. (2020). Identifying ethical considerations for machine learning healthcare applications. *The American Journal of Bioethics, 20*(11), 7–17. DOI: 10.1080/15265161.2020.1819469 PMID: 33103967

Char, D. S., Shah, N. H., & Magnus, D. (2018). Implementing machine learning in health care—Addressing ethical challenges. *The New England Journal of Medicine, 378*(11), 981–983. DOI: 10.1056/NEJMp1714229 PMID: 29539284

Chen, I. Y., Joshi, S., & Ghassemi, M. (2019). Treating health disparities with artificial intelligence. *Nature Medicine, 26*(1), 16–17. DOI: 10.1038/s41591-019-0649-2 PMID: 31932779

Cheng, J. Z., Ni, D., Chou, Y. H., Qin, J., Tiu, C. M., Chang, Y. C., Huang, C.-S., Shen, D., & Chen, C. M. (2019). Computer-aided diagnosis with deep learning architecture: Applications to breast lesions in US images and pulmonary nodules in CT scans. *Scientific Reports, 6*(1), 1–13. DOI: 10.1038/srep24454 PMID: 27079888

Choi, E., Bahadori, M. T., Schuetz, A., Stewart, W. F., & Sun, J. (2016). Doctor AI: Predicting clinical events via recurrent neural networks. In Machine learning for healthcare conference (pp. 301-318). PMLR. https://proceedings.mlr.press/v56/Choi16.pdf

Cirillo, D., Catuara-Solarz, S., Morey, C., Guney, E., Subirats, L., Mellino, S., Gigante, A., Valencia, A., Rementeria, M. J., Chadha, A. S., & Mavridis, N. (2020). Sex and gender differences and biases in artificial intelligence for biomedicine and healthcare. *NPJ Digital Medicine, 3*(1), 81. DOI: 10.1038/s41746-020-0288-5 PMID: 32529043

Cohen, I. G., Evgeniou, T., Gerke, S., & Minssen, T. (2020). The European artificial intelligence strategy: Implications and challenges for digital health. *The Lancet. Digital Health, 2*(7), e376–e379. DOI: 10.1016/S2589-7500(20)30112-6 PMID: 33328096

Cohen, I. G., & Mello, M. M. (2018). HIPAA and protecting health information in the 21st century. *Journal of the American Medical Association, 320*(3), 231–232. DOI: 10.1001/jama.2018.5630 PMID: 29800120

Cohen, I. G., & Mello, M. M. (2019). Big data, big tech, and protecting patient privacy. *Journal of the American Medical Association, 322*(12), 1141–1142. DOI: 10.1001/jama.2019.11365 PMID: 31397838

Davenport, T., & Kalakota, R. (2019). The potential for artificial intelligence in healthcare. *Future Healthcare Journal, 6*(2), 94–98. DOI: 10.7861/futurehosp.6-2-94 PMID: 31363513

Ding, Y., Sohn, J. H., Kawczynski, M. G., Trivedi, H., Harnish, R., Jenkins, N. W., Lituiev, D., Copeland, T. P., Aboian, M. S., Mari Aparici, C., Behr, S. C., Flavell, R. R., Huang, S. Y., Zalocusky, K. A., Nardo, L., Seo, Y., Hawkins, R. A., Hernandez Pampaloni, M., Hadley, D., & Franc, B. L. (2018). A deep learning model to predict a diagnosis of Alzheimer disease by using 18F-FDG PET of the brain. *Radiology, 290*(2), 456–464. DOI: 10.1148/radiol.2018180958 PMID: 30398430

Dzobo, K., Adotey, S., Thomford, N. E., & Dzobo, W. (2020). Integrating artificial and human intelligence: A partnership for responsible innovation in biomedical engineering and medicine. *OMICS: A Journal of Integrative Biology, 24*(5), 247–263. DOI: 10.1089/omi.2019.0038 PMID: 31313972

Esteva, A., Robicquet, A., Ramsundar, B., Kuleshov, V., DePristo, M., Chou, K., Cui, C., Corrado, G., Thrun, S., & Dean, J. (2019). A guide to deep learning in healthcare. *Nature Medicine, 25*(1), 24–29. DOI: 10.1038/s41591-018-0316-z PMID: 30617335

Exscientia. (2020). Exscientia announces first AI-designed molecule for immuno-oncology to enter clinical trials. https://investors.exscientia.ai/press-releases/press-release-details/2021/Exscientia-Announces-First-AI-Designed-Immuno-Oncology-Drug-to-Enter-Clinical-Trials/default.aspx

Falco, R., Gangemi, A., Peroni, S., Shotton, D., & Vitali, F. (2014). Modelling OWL Ontologies with Graffoo. In Presutti, V., Blomqvist, E., Troncy, R., Sack, H., Papadakis, I., & Tordai, A. (Eds.), Lecture Notes in Computer Science: Vol. 8798. *The Semantic Web: ESWC 2014 Satellite Events. ESWC 2014*. Springer., DOI: 10.1007/978-3-319-11955-7_42

Ferryman, K., & Pitcan, M. (2018). Fairness in precision medicine. Data & Society. https://datasociety.net/library/fairness-in-precision-medicine/

Finlayson, S. G., Subbaswamy, A., Singh, K., Bowers, J., Kupke, A., Zittrain, J., Kohane, I. S., & Saria, S. (2021). The clinician and dataset shift in artificial intelligence. *The New England Journal of Medicine*, *385*(3), 283–286. DOI: 10.1056/NEJMc2104626 PMID: 34260843

Fjeld, J., Achten, N., Hilligoss, H., Nagy, A., & Srikumar, M. (2020). Principled artificial intelligence: Mapping consensus in ethical and rights-based approaches to principles for AI. Berkman Klein Center for Internet & Society. https://dash.harvard.edu/handle/1/42160420

Floridi, L., & Cowls, J. (2019). A unified framework of five principles for AI in society. *Harvard Data Science Review*, *1*(1). Advance online publication. DOI: 10.1162/99608f92.8cd550d1

Floridi, L., Cowls, J., Beltrametti, M., Chatila, R., Chazerand, P., Dignum, V., Luetge, C., Madelin, R., Pagallo, U., Rossi, F., Schafer, B., Valcke, P., & Vayena, E. (2018). AI4People - An ethical framework for a good AI society: Opportunities, risks, principles, and recommendations. *Minds and Machines*, *28*(4), 689–707. DOI: 10.1007/s11023-018-9482-5 PMID: 30930541

Floridi, L., & Taddeo, M. (2016). What is data ethics? *Philosophical Transactions. Series A, Mathematical, Physical, and Engineering Sciences*, *374*(2083), 20160360. DOI: 10.1098/rsta.2016.0360 PMID: 28336805

Frid-Adar, M., Diamant, I., Klang, E., Amitai, M., Goldberger, J., & Greenspan, H. (2018). GAN-based synthetic medical image augmentation for increased CNN performance in liver lesion classification. *Neurocomputing*, *321*, 321–331. DOI: 10.1016/j.neucom.2018.09.013

Gasser, U., & Almeida, V. A. F. (2017). A layered model for AI governance. *IEEE Internet Computing*, *21*(6), 58–62. DOI: 10.1109/MIC.2017.4180835

Gerke, S., Babic, B., Evgeniou, T., & Cohen, I. G. (2020). The need for a system view to regulate artificial intelligence/machine learning-based software as medical device. *NPJ Digital Medicine*, *3*(1), 1–4. DOI: 10.1038/s41746-020-0262-2 PMID: 32285013

Gianfrancesco, M. A., Tamang, S., Yazdany, J., & Schmajuk, G. (2018). Potential biases in machine learning algorithms using electronic health record data. *JAMA Internal Medicine*, *178*(11), 1544–1547. DOI: 10.1001/jamainternmed.2018.3763 PMID: 30128552

Ginsburg, G. S., & Phillips, K. A. (2018). Precision medicine: From science to value. *Health Affairs*, *37*(5), 694–701. DOI: 10.1377/hlthaff.2017.1624 PMID: 29733705

Goodfellow, I., Bengio, Y., & Courville, A. (2020). *Deep learning* (2nd ed.). MIT Press., DOI: 10.7551/mitpress/11171.001.0001

Goodfellow, I., Pouget-Abadie, J., Mirza, M., Xu, B., Warde-Farley, D., Ozair, S., . . . Bengio, Y. (2014). Generative adversarial nets. Advances in Neural Information Processing Systems, 27, 2672-2680. https://proceedings.neurips.cc/paper/2014/file/5ca3e9b122f61f8f06494c97b1afccf3-Paper.pdf

Goodman, S. N., Goel, S., & Cullen, M. R. (2018). Machine learning, health disparities, and causal reasoning. *Annals of Internal Medicine, 169*(12), 883–884. DOI: 10.7326/M18-3297 PMID: 30508423

Grote, T., & Berens, P. (2020). On the ethics of algorithmic decision-making in healthcare. *Journal of Medical Ethics, 46*(3), 205–211. DOI: 10.1136/medethics-2019-105586 PMID: 31748206

Guibas, J. T., Virdi, T. S., & Li, P. S. (2017). Synthetic medical images from dual generative adversarial networks. arXiv preprint arXiv:1709.01872. https://arxiv.org/abs/1709.01872

Haas, L. R., Takahashi, P. Y., Shah, N. D., Stroebel, R. J., Bernard, M. E., Finnie, D. M., & Naessens, J. M. (2013). Risk-stratification methods for identifying patients for care coordination. *The American Journal of Managed Care, 19*(9), 725–732. https://europepmc.org/article/med/24304255 PMID: 24304255

He, J., Baxter, S. L., Xu, J., Xu, J., Zhou, X., & Zhang, K. (2019). The practical implementation of artificial intelligence technologies in medicine. *Nature Medicine, 25*(1), 30–36. DOI: 10.1038/s41591-018-0307-0 PMID: 30617336

Hernandez-Boussard, T., Bozkurt, S., Ioannidis, J. P. A., & Shah, N. H. (2020). MINIMAR (MINimum Information for Medical AI Reporting): Developing reporting standards for artificial intelligence in health care. *Journal of the American Medical Informatics Association : JAMIA, 27*(12), 2011–2015. DOI: 10.1093/jamia/ocaa088 PMID: 32594179

Hoffman, S., & Podgurski, A. (2020). Artificial intelligence and discrimination in health care. *Yale Journal of Health Policy, Law, and Ethics, 19*(3), 1–88.

Israni, S. T., & Verghese, A. (2019). Humanizing artificial intelligence. *Journal of the American Medical Association, 321*(1), 29–30. DOI: 10.1001/jama.2018.19398 PMID: 30535297

Jiang, F., Jiang, Y., Zhi, H., Dong, Y., Li, H., Ma, S., Wang, Y., Dong, Q., Shen, H., & Wang, Y. (2017). Artificial intelligence in healthcare: Past, present and future. *Stroke and Vascular Neurology, 2*(4), 230–243. DOI: 10.1136/svn-2017-000101 PMID: 29507784

Kadurin, A., Aliper, A., Kazennov, A., Mamoshina, P., Vanhaelen, Q., Khrabrov, K., & Zhavoronkov, A. (2017). The cornucopia of meaningful leads: Applying deep adversarial autoencoders for new molecule development in oncology. *Oncotarget, 8*(7), 10883–10890. DOI: 10.18632/oncotarget.14073 PMID: 28029644

Kalkman, S., Mostert, M., Gerlinger, C., van Delden, J. J. M., & van Thiel, G. J. M. W. (2019). Responsible data sharing in international health research: A systematic review of principles and norms. *BMC Medical Ethics, 20*(1), 21. DOI: 10.1186/s12910-019-0359-9 PMID: 30922290

Kelly, C. J., Karthikesalingam, A., Suleyman, M., Corrado, G., & King, D. (2019). Key challenges for delivering clinical impact with artificial intelligence. *BMC Medicine, 17*(1), 195. DOI: 10.1186/s12916-019-1426-2 PMID: 31665002

Kingma, D. P., & Welling, M. (2014). Auto-encoding variational bayes. arXiv preprint arXiv:1312.6114. https://arxiv.org/abs/1312.6114

Kolachalama, V. B., & Garg, P. S. (2018). Machine learning and medical education. *NPJ Digital Medicine, 1*(1), 1–3. DOI: 10.1038/s41746-018-0061-1 PMID: 31304333

Korngiebel, D. M., & Mooney, S. D. (2021). Considering the possibilities and pitfalls of Generative Pre-trained Transformer 3 (GPT-3) in healthcare delivery. *NPJ Digital Medicine, 4*(1), 1–3. DOI: 10.1038/s41746-021-00464-x PMID: 34083689

Krittanawong, C., Zhang, H., Wang, Z., Aydar, M., & Kitai, T. (2020). Artificial intelligence in precision cardiovascular medicine. *Journal of the American College of Cardiology, 69*(21), 2657–2664. DOI: 10.1016/j.jacc.2017.03.571 PMID: 28545640

Larson, D. B., Harvey, H., Rubin, D. L., Irani, N., Tse, J. R., & Langlotz, C. P. (2020). Regulatory frameworks for development and evaluation of artificial intelligence-based diagnostic imaging algorithms: Summary and recommendations. *Journal of the American College of Radiology, 18*(3), 413–424. DOI: 10.1016/j.jacr.2020.09.060 PMID: 33096088

London, A. J. (2019). Artificial intelligence and black-box medical decisions: Accuracy versus explainability. *The Hastings Center Report, 49*(1), 15–21. DOI: 10.1002/hast.973 PMID: 30790315

Lysaght, T., Lim, H. Y., Xafis, V., & Ngiam, K. Y. (2019). AI-assisted decision-making in healthcare: The application of an ethics framework for big data in health and research. *Asian Bioethics Review, 11*(3), 299–314. DOI: 10.1007/s41649-019-00096-0 PMID: 33717318

Madani, A., Moradi, M., Karargyris, A., & Syeda-Mahmood, T. (2018). Chest x-ray generation and data augmentation for cardiovascular abnormality classification. In Medical Imaging 2018: Image Processing (Vol. 10574, p. 105741M). International Society for Optics and Photonics. DOI: 10.1117/12.2293971

McCradden, M. D., Joshi, S., Mazwi, M., & Anderson, J. A. (2020). Ethical limitations of algorithmic fairness solutions in health care machine learning. *The Lancet. Digital Health, 2*(5), e221–e223. DOI: 10.1016/S2589-7500(20)30065-0 PMID: 33328054

McDougall, R. J. (2019). Computer knows best? The need for value-flexibility in medical AI. *Journal of Medical Ethics, 45*(3), 156–160. DOI: 10.1136/medethics-2018-105118 PMID: 30467198

Mehrabi, N., Morstatter, F., Saxena, N., Lerman, K., & Galstyan, A. (2021). A survey on bias and fairness in machine learning. *ACM Computing Surveys, 54*(6), 1–35. DOI: 10.1145/3457607

Mikk, K. A., Sleeper, H. A., & Topol, E. J. (2017). The pathway to patient data ownership and better health. *Journal of the American Medical Association, 325*(15), 1433–1434. DOI: 10.1001/jama.2017.12145 PMID: 28973063

Minssen, T., Gerke, S., Aboy, M., Price, N., & Cohen, G. (2020). Regulatory responses to medical machine learning. *Journal of Law and the Biosciences, 7*(1), lsaa002. Advance online publication. DOI: 10.1093/jlb/lsaa002 PMID: 34221415

Mirsky, Y., Mahler, T., Shelef, I., & Elovici, Y. (2019). CT-GAN: Malicious tampering of 3D medical imagery using deep learning. In *Proceedings of the 28th USENIX Security Symposium* (pp. 461-478). USENIX Association.

Mullard, A. (2018). IDO takes a blow. *Nature Reviews. Drug Discovery, 17*(5), 307. https://link.gale.com/apps/doc/A536333217/HRCA?u=anon~865f49de&sid=googleScholar&xid=db7f4b02 PMID: 29700490

Nundy, S., Montgomery, T., & Wachter, R. M. (2019). Promoting trust between patients and physicians in the era of artificial intelligence. *Journal of the American Medical Association, 322*(6), 497–498. DOI: 10.1001/jama.2018.20563 PMID: 31305873

Obermeyer, Z., Powers, B., Vogeli, C., & Mullainathan, S. (2019). Dissecting racial bias in an algorithm used to manage the health of populations. *Science, 366*(6464), 447–453. DOI: 10.1126/science.aax2342 PMID: 31649194

Park, S. H., & Kressel, H. Y. (2018). Connecting technological innovation in artificial intelligence to real-world medical practice through rigorous clinical validation: What peer-reviewed medical journals could do. *Journal of Korean Medical Science, 33*(22), e152. DOI: 10.3346/jkms.2018.33.e152 PMID: 29805337

Patel, B. N., Rosenberg, L., Willcox, G., Baltaxe, D., Lyons, M., Irvin, J., Rajpurkar, P., Amrhein, T., Gupta, R., Halabi, S., Langlotz, C., Lo, E., Mammarappallil, J., Mariano, A. J., Riley, G., Seekins, J., Shen, L., Zucker, E., & Lungren, M. P. (2019). Human-machine partnership with artificial intelligence for chest radiograph diagnosis. *NPJ Digital Medicine*, *2*(1), 1–10. DOI: 10.1038/s41746-019-0189-7 PMID: 31754637

Pesapane, F., Volonté, C., Codari, M., & Sardanelli, F. (2018). Artificial intelligence as a medical device in radiology: Ethical and regulatory issues in Europe and the United States. *Insights Into Imaging*, *9*(5), 745–753. DOI: 10.1007/s13244-018-0645-y PMID: 30112675

Polykovskiy, D., Zhebrak, A., Sanchez-Lengeling, B., Golovanov, S., Tatanov, O., Belyaev, S., Kurbanov, R., Artamonov, A., Aladinskiy, V., Veselov, M., Kadurin, A., Johansson, S., Chen, H., Nikolenko, S., Aspuru-Guzik, A., & Zhavoronkov, A. (2020). Molecular Sets (MOSES): A Benchmarking Platform for Molecular Generation Models. *Frontiers in Pharmacology*, *11*, 565644. DOI: 10.3389/fphar.2020.565644 PMID: 33390943

Polykovskiy, D., Zhebrak, A., Vetrov, D., Ivanenkov, Y., Aladinskiy, V., Mamoshina, P., Bozdaganyan, M., Aliper, A., Zhavoronkov, A., & Kadurin, A. (2018). Entangled conditional adversarial autoencoder for de novo drug discovery. *Molecular Pharmaceutics*, *15*(10), 4398–4405. DOI: 10.1021/acs.molpharmaceut.8b00839 PMID: 30180591

Popejoy, A. B., & Fullerton, S. M. (2016). Genomics is failing on diversity. *Nature*, *538*(7624), 161–164. DOI: 10.1038/538161a PMID: 27734877

Popova, M., Isayev, O., & Tropsha, A. (2018). Deep reinforcement learning for de novo drug design. *Science Advances*, *4*(7), eaap7885. Advance online publication. DOI: 10.1126/sciadv.aap7885 PMID: 30050984

Rajkomar, A., Dean, J., & Kohane, I. (2019). Machine learning in medicine. *The New England Journal of Medicine*, *380*(14), 1347–1358. DOI: 10.1056/NEJMra1814259 PMID: 30943338

Rajkomar, A., Hardt, M., Howell, M. D., Corrado, G., & Chin, M. H. (2018). Ensuring fairness in machine learning to advance health equity. *Annals of Internal Medicine*, *169*(12), 866–872. DOI: 10.7326/M18-1990 PMID: 30508424

Rajpurkar, P., Irvin, J., Zhu, K., Yang, B., Mehta, H., Duan, T., Ding, D., Bagul, A., Langlotz, C., Shpanskaya, K., Lungren, M. P., & Ng, A. Y. (2017). CheXNet: Radiologist-level pneumonia detection on chest X-rays with deep learning. arXiv preprint arXiv:1711.05225. https://arxiv.org/abs/1711.05225

Reddy, S., Allan, S., Coghlan, S., & Cooper, P. (2020). A governance model for the application of AI in health care. *Journal of the American Medical Informatics Association : JAMIA*, *27*(3), 491–497. DOI: 10.1093/jamia/ocz192 PMID: 31682262

Reisman, D., Schultz, J., Crawford, K., & Whittaker, M. (2018). *Algorithmic impact assessments: A practical framework for public agency accountability*. AI Now Institute.

Rieke, N., Hancox, J., Li, W., Milletarì, F., Roth, H. R., Albarqouni, S., Bakas, S., Galtier, M. N., Landman, B. A., Maier-Hein, K., Ourselin, S., Sheller, M., Summers, R. M., Trask, A., Xu, D., Baust, M., & Cardoso, M. J. (2020). The future of digital health with federated learning. *NPJ Digital Medicine*, *3*(1), 1–7. DOI: 10.1038/s41746-020-00323-1 PMID: 33015372

Schork, N. J. (2019). Artificial intelligence and personalized medicine. *Cancer Treatment and Research*, *178*, 265–283. DOI: 10.1007/978-3-030-16391-4_11 PMID: 31209850

Segler, M. H., Kogej, T., Tyrchan, C., & Waller, M. P. (2018). Generating focused molecule libraries for drug discovery with recurrent neural networks. *ACS Central Science*, *4*(1), 120–131. DOI: 10.1021/acscentsci.7b00512 PMID: 29392184

Shukla, R. P. (2024). Business drivers in promoting digital detoxification. In Grima, S., Chaudhary, S., Sood, K., & Kumar, S. (Eds.), *Business drivers in promoting digital detoxification* (pp. 16–24). IGI Global., DOI: 10.4018/979-8-3693-1107-3.ch002

Shukla, R. P., & Taneja, S. (2024). Catalysts of change: SMEs and dynamics of AI adoption. In Hossain, S. (Ed.), *Utilizing AI and smart technology to improve sustainability in entrepreneurship* (pp. 104–116). IGI Global., DOI: 10.4018/979-8-3693-1842-3.ch007

Topol, E. J. (2019). High-performance medicine: The convergence of human and artificial intelligence. *Nature Medicine*, *25*(1), 44–56. DOI: 10.1038/s41591-018-0300-7 PMID: 30617339

Tran, V. T., Riveros, C., & Ravaud, P. (2019). Patients' views of wearable devices and AI in healthcare: Findings from the ComPaRe e-cohort. *NPJ Digital Medicine*, *2*(1), 53. DOI: 10.1038/s41746-019-0132-y PMID: 31304399

Verghese, A., Shah, N. H., & Harrington, R. A. (2018). What this computer needs is a physician: Humanism and artificial intelligence. *Journal of the American Medical Association*, *319*(1), 19–20. DOI: 10.1001/jama.2017.19198 PMID: 29261830

Vest, J. R., & Gamm, L. D. (2010). Health information exchange: Persistent challenges and new strategies. *Journal of the American Medical Informatics Association : JAMIA*, *17*(3), 288–294. DOI: 10.1136/jamia.2010.003673 PMID: 20442146

Vokinger, K. N., Feuerriegel, S., & Kesselheim, A. S. (2021). Mitigating bias in machine learning for medicine. *Communications Medicine*, *1*(1), 1–3. DOI: 10.1038/s43856-021-00028-w PMID: 34522916

Vyas, D. A., Eisenstein, L. G., & Jones, D. S. (2020). Hidden in plain sight — Reconsidering the use of race correction in clinical algorithms. *The New England Journal of Medicine*, *383*(9), 874–882. DOI: 10.1056/NEJMms2004740 PMID: 32853499

Wiens, J., Saria, S., Sendak, M., Ghassemi, M., Liu, V. X., Doshi-Velez, F., Jung, K., Heller, K., Kale, D., Saeed, M., Ossorio, P. N., Thadaney-Israni, S., & Goldenberg, A. (2019). Do no harm: A roadmap for responsible machine learning for health care. *Nature Medicine*, *25*(9), 1337–1340. DOI: 10.1038/s41591-019-0548-6 PMID: 31427808

Wilkinson, M. D., Dumontier, M., Aalbersberg, I. J., Appleton, G., Axton, M., Baak, A., Blomberg, N., Boiten, J.-W., da Silva Santos, L. B., Bourne, P. E., Bouwman, J., Brookes, A. J., Clark, T., Crosas, M., Dillo, I., Dumon, O., Edmunds, S., Evelo, C. T., Finkers, R., & Mons, B. (2016). The FAIR guiding principles for scientific data management and stewardship. *Scientific Data*, *3*(1), 160018. DOI: 10.1038/sdata.2016.18 PMID: 26978244

World Health Organization. (2021). Ethics and governance of artificial intelligence for health: WHO guidance. World Health Organization. https://www.who.int/publications/i/item/9789240029200

Xue, Y., Xu, T., Zhang, H., Long, L. R., & Huang, X. (2018). SegAN: Adversarial network with multi-scale L1 loss for medical image segmentation. *Neuroinformatics*, *16*(3-4), 383–392. DOI: 10.1007/s12021-018-9377-x PMID: 29725916

Yadav, S., Ramesh, S., Saha, S., & Ekbal, A. (2020). Relation extraction from biomedical and clinical text: Unified multitask learning framework. *IEEE/ACM Transactions on Computational Biology and Bioinformatics*, *19*(2), 1105–1116. DOI: 10.1109/TCBB.2020.3020016 PMID: 32853152

Yi, X., Walia, E., & Babyn, P. (2019). Generative adversarial network in medical imaging: A review. *Medical Image Analysis*, *58*, 101552. DOI: 10.1016/j.media.2019.101552 PMID: 31521965

Yu, K. H., Beam, A. L., & Kohane, I. S. (2018). Artificial intelligence in healthcare. *Nature Biomedical Engineering*, *2*(10), 719–731. DOI: 10.1038/s41551-018-0305-z PMID: 31015651

Zhavoronkov, A., Ivanenkov, Y. A., Aliper, A., Veselov, M. S., Aladinskiy, V. A., Aladinskaya, A. V., Terentiev, V. A., Polykovskiy, D. A., Kuznetsov, M. D., Asadulaev, A., Volkov, Y., Zholus, A., Shayakhmetov, R. R., Zhebrak, A., Minaeva, L. I., Zagribelnyy, B. A., Lee, L. H., Soll, R., Madge, D., & Aspuru-Guzik, A. (2019). Deep learning enables rapid identification of potent DDR1 kinase inhibitors. *Nature Biotechnology*, *37*(9), 1038–1040. DOI: 10.1038/s41587-019-0224-x PMID: 31477924

Chapter 21

Service Recovery Strategies and Customer Satisfaction in the Digital Age:

Evidence From Customers of Utility Service Providers in Ghana

Dominic Owusu
https://orcid.org/0000-0002-1749-6538
University of Cape Coast, Ghana

Benedict Ofori Antwi
https://orcid.org/0000-0002-6663-0203
University of Cape Coast, Ghana

Alice De Veer
University of Cape Coast, Ghana

Grace Akosua Kwaa Opoku-Asiamah
University of Cape Coast, Ghana

ABSTRACT

Customers of utility service providers in developing economies face frequent interruptions in service delivery by service providers. Customers experience power outages, disconnecting customers from service without recourse to prompt reconnection, billing discrepancies etc. are among the problems encountered by customers of utility service providers. Customers on the other hand resort to open confrontation, non-refusal to pay bills and other mechanisms to register their displeasure towards the utility service providers. A key tool available to utility service providers to ensure customer satisfaction and that customers' concerns are adequately addressed is the effective application of service recovery strategies. How effectively can the application of service recovery strategies influence the level of customer satisfaction? The current study is among the few studies in sub-Saharan Africa that investigate service recovery as an antecedent to customer satisfaction in today's digital space. Details of the outcome are discussed in the chapter.

DOI: 10.4018/979-8-3693-7447-4.ch021

1.0 INTRODUCTION

Research works have acknowledged the interconnectedness between service recovery strategies and customer satisfaction. According to Sekar and Sudha (2012), service recovery strategies and satisfaction with service recovery lead to customer happiness. This suggests that service recovery is an antecedent to customer satisfaction. To measure customer satisfaction, service providers need to know what their customers think about their ability to recover the services or products they have provided and whether they are satisfied with their service recovery or not. This is determined by the customer's cumulative experiences at all contact points with the service organisation (Fadhila, Wadud & Roswaty, 2021; ALhawbani, Ali & Hammouda, 2021).

Several studies on service recovery have been conducted in other sectors of the economy such as the retail industry, mobile telecommunication industry, fashion, airline, and internet shopping mall service (Omoera, 2017; Fadhila, Wadud & Roswaty, 2021; ALhawbani, Ali & Hammouda, 2021; Ayertey, 2018; Matikiti, Mpinganjira & Roberts-Lombard, 2019; Kim, 2007; Fadhila, Wadud & Roswaty, 2021; Ali & Mohamed, 2020). However, a study focusing on the public sector which is mandated to provide goods and services for the public good is lacking. Utility service companies in Ghana largely enjoy a monopoly (Twum & Abubakari, 2020).

The Ghana Water Company Ltd for example, is the only public company that currently supplies water for both domestic and industrial consumption in Ghana. However, the reliability and quality of the water supply continue to affect customer satisfaction. Customers continue to criticize the quality of their service delivery (Badu, 2016). The company resorts to tariff adjustment over the years as a justification to ensure that quality service is provided. For the past years, the regulatory body of public utility companies in Ghana, the Public Utility Regulations Commission (PURC) has been the body that announces tariff adjustments. In 2022, there was an adjustment of tariffs. Similarly, in 2023, there was a tariff adjustment of 8% for water. This has been the trend over the years with the justification that this increment will ensure improved customer service and satisfaction. Yet customers continue to record service failures. This therefore calls for attention to focus on how to ensure the satisfaction of customers using service recovery strategies. As suggested by Phan, Nguyen and Pham, (2021), studies should turn their attention to the public sector to ascertain the extent to which their services are meeting the expectations of the members of the public.

Debate on the contribution of service recovery to customer satisfaction has been inconclusive. Whereas Ali and Mohamed (2020); Abd Rashid, Ahmad and Othman (2014); Omoera (2017); Fadhila, Wadud and Roswaty (2021); ALhawbani, Ali & Hammouda, 2021; Gaffar, Suharyono, Solimun & Andriani Kusumawati (2021); Ermias (2019); established a positive effect of service recovery on customer satisfaction, Phan, Nguyen and Pham (2021); Zaid, Palilati, Madjid and Bua (2021), however, established a negative impact of service recovery on customer satisfaction.

The primary purpose of this study is to examine how service recovery affects the satisfaction of customers at Ghana Water Company Limited, in the Odorkor District of the Greater Accra Region of Ghana. Specifically, the study examines the relationship between compensation and satisfaction with the recovery, analyses the relationship between apology and satisfaction with the recovery, determines the relationship between explanation and satisfaction with the recovery and assesses the effect of satisfaction with recovery on the satisfaction of customers at Ghana Water Company Limited in the Odorkor District of the Greater Accra Region of Ghana. The findings of the study will provide inputs on the service recovery strategies that Ghana Water Company Ltd can rely on to ensure the satisfaction of its customers. Findings will also lay the foundation on which of the service recovery strategies to emphasize when building relationships with customers.

2.0 LITERATURE REVIEW/HYPOTHESES

2.1 Theory of consumer behaviour

Several researchers have made significant contributions to the subject of consumer behaviour. Authors such as Arens (1996), Bamossy and Solomon (2016), and Datta (2022) have all made significant contributions to the study of consumer behaviour. They suggest that consumers are complex (Tanrikulu, 2021). According to Bamossy and Solomon (2016), consumer behaviour explains how individuals, groups, and organisations make choices on the use, selection and disposal of products. This means that to satisfy the consumer, one needs to have a holistic understanding of how the consumer makes decisions regarding what to buy, how to buy, select, use and dispose of products. Having a holistic understanding of how the consumer behaves influences the programs and strategies of firms designed to meet the expectations of consumers. For a firm to be able to better satisfy the consumer better than competitors, critical attention must focus on understanding the consumer. Once the expectations of the consumer are met, this translates into customer loyalty according to Hassan, Ghazali and Mohtar (2021). The current study posits that achieving consumer loyalty is made possible through the effective implementation of effective service recovery strategies.

2.2 Compensation and Recovery Satisfaction

Compensation as a recovery strategy provides a customer return on injuries or harm sustained according to Burns and Kedia (2006). Compensation improves the public image of firms as well as contributes to repeat purchases (Bebchuck & Fred, 2003; Popoola & Ayeni, 2007). This means that when compensations to customers meet their expectations, it is likely to evoke satisfaction leading to repeat purchases. Similarly, Wei and Lin (2020) also posited that compensation impacts on the growth of customer loyalty which is an outcome of satisfaction. Albrecht, Schaefers, Walsh and Beaty (2019) support the view that compensation impacts on recovery satisfaction. Hence the study hypothesizes:

$H_{1:}$ compensation has a positive and significant effect on recovery satisfaction.

2.3 Apology and Recovery Satisfaction

Apologising is the process of conveying regret or remorse for one's conduct, whereas an apology is the expression of such emotions (Masuch, Greve & Trang, 2021). Apologies are offered with the hopes that the relationship can be repaired and that peace can be restored between the disputants (Shen & Wang, 2022). Attribution theory suggests that apologising early in a conversation can reduce. How an apology is delivered significantly impacts whether or not it is accepted. The core components of an apology are the acknowledgement of wrongdoing, recognising the harm caused by one's acts, and promising to change one's behaviour going forward (Honora, Chih & Wang, 2022). Most philosophers agree that genuine sorrow or remorse must exist for an apology to be sincere (Hu, Min & Su, 2021). However, many argue this isn't always required (Jin, Park & Park, 2022).

How sincere are people when they say they're sorry? was investigated by Hu, Min, and Su (2021) who found no significant differences between robots-generated texts and speeches. Apology, compensation, and consumer agency were all factors that *Bae, Lee, and Kim (2021)* investigated in their study of how service recovery attempts affect customers. One-time payments made at the scene of an incident, apologies based on contextual clues, and empowered servers were shown to be the most successful methods of restoring service. Similarly, Wang, Chih, Hsu, and Lin (2020), concluded that service providers should consider reaction time and apologetic mode. Hence the hypothesize:

H_2: Apology has a positive and significant relationship with recovery satisfaction

2.4 Explanation and Recovery Satisfaction

An explanation is a series of assertions that describe a group of facts and explain why they are the way they are and what effects they have on society (Kalkman, 2021). Most attempts to explain human behaviour start with the premise that the behaviour in issue is at least partially logical and then build from there by appealing to the subject's beliefs and wants as well as other facts about the person (Hofman et al., 2021; Vredenburgh, 2022). Odoom, Agbemabiese, and Hinson (2020) examined and contrasted offline and online treatment procedures and recovery satisfaction and concluded that recovery procedures significantly affect customer satisfaction following an issue. These, however, were contextual and thus not universally applicable. Apology, together with compensation and explanation, was found to have a strong association with recovery satisfaction among the online sample, but this was not the case in the offline situation. Hence the hypothesis:

H_3: Explanation has a positive and significant relationship with satisfaction with recovery.

2.5 Conceptual framework

Figure 1. Conceptual Framework

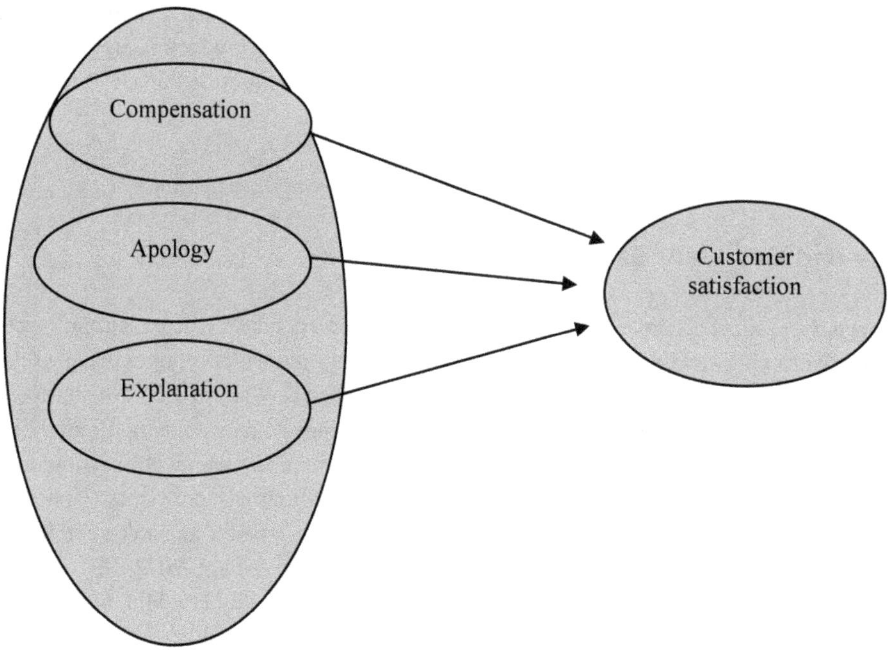

Service recovery strategies
Source: authors' construct (2022)

3.0 RESEARCH METHODOLOGY

The study uses the quantitative approach to research and relies on the explanatory research design to explain the proposed phenomenon. The study targeted customers of Ghana Water Company Limited in the Odorkor District of Accra one of the densely populated customers of the Ghana Water Company Limited. These customers were chosen because Ghana Water Company Limited have not been able to recover their services which has resulted in high dissatisfaction among this group of customers. Out of a total population of ten thousand two hundred and thirty-five (10235) customers of Ghana Water Company Limited in the Odorkor District of Accra, a total of three hundred eighty-five (385) customers were conveniently using Yamane's formula (1967). These customers freely consented to participate in the study and were available at the time of data collection. The study relied on a structured questionnaire for data collection. The questionnaire comprised 31 items grouped under six sections - A, B, C, D, E and F covering background information, apology, compensation, explanation, recovery satisfaction and customer satisfaction using the Likert scale. In this study, content validity, construct validity and criterion validity of the instrument were ensured. Copies of the data collection instrument were given to experts in the area for their perusal and their constructive comments were included in the development of the instrument.

3.1 Measurement of variables

Service recovery was measured based on the items employed by Odoom, Agbemabiese & Hinson, (2018) framework of recovery activities practices. Three service recovery practices were identified based on the framework. These are compensation, apology and explanation (Odoom, Agbemabiese & Hinson, 2018). Measurement of customer satisfaction was adapted from Oliver, Rust and Varki (1997) and Anderson and Sullivan (1993). Five customer satisfaction were identified. These are tangibility, reliability, responsiveness, assurance and empathy. The conceptualization of customer satisfaction by Oliver, Rust and Varki (1997) and Anderson and Sullivan (1993) has since been used in several studies (Hoffman, Kelley & Rotalsky, 2016, Dartey et al., 2021; Lubis, Dalimunthe, Absah & Fawzeea, 2021; Latif, Bunce & Ahmad, 2021; Odoom, Agbemabiese & Hinson, 2018; Sekar & Sudha, 2021) and is also central to the various classifications of customer satisfaction as it consolidates the various classifications given by researchers.

3.2 Data Processing and Management

Firstly, the raw data collected through the questionnaire were edited, coded, and converted into the actual variables of interest. Data on customer satisfaction was merged as one construct to allow for the analysis. Data were analysed using structural equation modelling partial least squares.

4.0 STUDY RESULTS

4.1 Measurement Model

A model was developed to determine the service recovery strategy that contributes to the satisfaction of customers of Ghana Water Company Ltd in the Odorkor District. The model included service recovery and customer satisfaction. Service recovery was measured with three constructs; compensation, apology and explanation. The model was assessed based on recognized procedures for the assessment of reflective models in PLS-Sem. The Cronbach alpha, composite reliability, average variance extracted, r-square and adjusted r-square, and discriminant validity using HTMT were all assessed before proceeding with the analysis as suggested by Ringle, Wende and Becker, (2015). Tables 1 - 4 and Figure 1 illustrate the evaluation criteria for the model.

Table 1. Quality criteria and discriminant validity for measuring the model

Variables	Cronbach's alpha	Composite reliability (rho_a)	Composite reliability (rho_c)	Average variance extracted (AVE)	R square	Adjusted R square
Apology	0.825	0.824	0.884	0.658		
Compensation	0.909	0.913	0.936	0.785		
Customer Satisfaction	0.799	0.802	0.861	0.555	0.751	0.749
Explanation	0.918	0.923	0.942	0.804		

Notes: Cronbach's $\alpha > 0.7$ is acceptable and high. Composite reliability should be 0.7 or higher. AVE should be 0.5 or higher. R^2 of 0.75 is substantial, 0.50 is moderate, and 0.25 is weak.

Source: Field Survey (2022)

Table 2. Discriminant validity of the model using HTMT

Variables	Apology	Compensation	Customer Satisfaction	Explanation
Apology				
Compensation	0.647			
Customer Satisfaction	0.961	0.783		
Explanation	0.888	0.639	0.925	

Source: Field Survey (2022)

Figure 2. Model depicting the effect of service recovery strategies on customer satisfaction

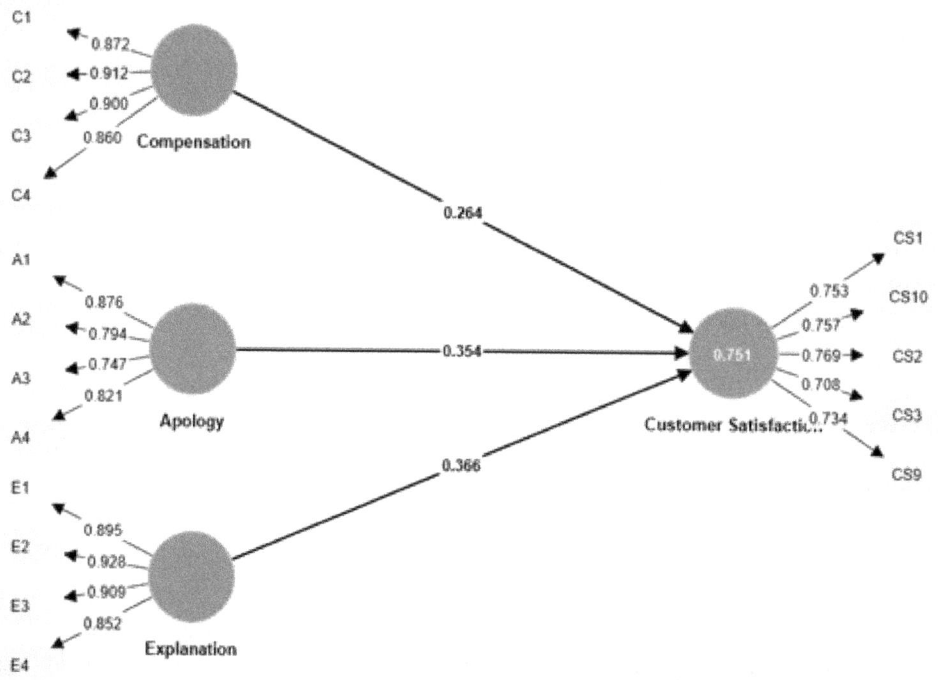

Source: Field Survey (2022)

The Cronbach's Alpha value and rho_ A (Table 1) all recorded values greater than 0.7 confirming the reliability of the constructs (Hair, Hult, Ringle & Sarstedt, 2016; Afum, Sun & Kusi, 2019; Ringle, Wende & Becker, 2015). Average Variance Extracted [AVE] also recorded values greater than 0.5 as shown in Table 1. The HTMT values were less than one, and as Gaskin, Godfrey and Vance (2018) suggested, an HTMT of less than one is appropriate. The model recorded an R^2 figure of 0.751 and an adjusted R^2 of 0.749.

4.2 Collinearity Statistics (VIF)

The test of collinearity statistics was undertaken to address biases and errors in the reflective model using the VIF values suggested by Hair, Sarstedt, Matthews, & Ringle (2016). The outcome is presented in Tables 3 and 4.

Table 3. VIF outer model

Items	VIF
A1	2.871
A2	2.211
A3	1.496
A4	1.781
C1	2.777
C2	3.620
C3	3.093
C4	2.183
CS1	1.570
CS10	2.165
CS2	1.778
CS3	1.527
CS9	2.104
E1	3.473
E2	4.355
E3	3.509
E4	2.589

Source: Field Survey (2022)

Table 4. VIF inner model

Variables	Apology	Compensation	Customer Satisfaction	Explanation
Apology			2.671	
Compensation			1.591	
Customer Satisfaction				
Explanation			2.803	

Source: Field Survey (2022)

The VIF scores indicate no common method bias as shown in Tables 3 and 4. Having assessed the model's quality criteria, a bootstrapping analysis was undertaken to ascertain the significance of the path coefficients. The results of the bootstrapping are presented in Table 5. The results indicated that apology and compensation recorded T statistics of 5.480 (P values 0.000) and 3.761(P values 0.0000) respectively. This indicates that both apology and compensation are significant predictors of customer satisfaction. However, explanation recorded a T statistic of 1.731 (p values 0.084). This indicates that explanation is not a predictor of customer satisfaction.

Table 5. Bootstrapping results of the model

Variables	Original sample (O)	Sample mean (M)	Standard deviation (STDEV)	T statistics (|O/STDEV|)	P values
Apology -> Customer Satisfaction	0.605	0.629	0.110	5.480	0.000
Compensation -> Customer Satisfaction	0.262	0.258	0.070	3.761	0.000
Explanation -> Customer Satisfaction	0.218	0.201	0.126	1.731	0.084

Table 6. Effect Size (f^2)

Variables	Apology	Compensation	Customer Satisfaction	Explanation
Apology			0.188	
Compensation			0.176	
Customer Satisfaction				
Explanation			0.192	

To affirm the scores of the bootstrapping, the effect size (f^2) was ascertained. The f2 figures were all above 0.15 indicating a medium effect as suggested by Cohen (1988)

5.0 DISCUSSION OF RESULTS

The study sought to examine the service recovery strategy that contributes to the satisfaction of customers of Ghana Water Company Ltd. To this end three hypotheses were stated. One model was developed to test the hypotheses. The findings of the study indicated that of the three constructs of service recovery, compensation and apology were found to influence customer satisfaction. This means that hypotheses 1 and 2 which posited that compensation and apologies had significant influences on customer satisfaction were accepted respectively. This is similar to the findings of Albrecht, Schaefers, Walsh & Beatty, 2019; Gelbrich, 2010; Wei & Lin, 2020) who also found that compensation to customers contributed significantly influenced customer satisfaction. Similarly, the studies of Bae, Lee and Kim (2021); Hu, Min and Su, (2021); and Wang, Chih, Hsu and Lin (2020) also established that apology also contributed to influencing customer satisfaction.

These findings reflect the reality among customers of Ghana Water Company in Accra which has been experiencing intermittent supplies over the years despite significant increases in prices. Apologising to customers on the intermittent supplies is considered to be empathizing with the customer and was considered a significant influence on the satisfaction of the customer. Furthermore, providing compensation to customers as a result of the water company's inability to provide the required service to their customers was also considered a significant contributor to customer satisfaction. It is seen as a relief to the customer considering the difficulties customers encounter in getting water supply from alternative sources.

However, the study findings did not support the third hypothesis that explanation significantly influenced customer satisfaction. We therefore fail to accept the hypothesis that explanation significantly influenced customer satisfaction. This finding contradicts the findings presented in the study of Odoom, Agbemabiese and Hinson (2019) which found explanation to be a significant predictor of customer satisfaction. This finding was so as the phenomenon of not being able to provide the customers what they have requested has not been an occasional happening but rather something that is experienced by the customer frequently. When a similar explanation is provided for similar occurrences over a period, customers tend to accept the explanation as being genuine hence the reason why explanation did not have a significant t effect on customer satisfaction. Though service recovery has been established to contribute to customer satisfaction, two of the service recovery strategies explain the

6.0 CONCLUSIONS AND RECOMMENDATIONS

Based on the findings of the study, the study concludes that when Ghana Water Company Ltd are unable to provide a service the customer requested and paid for, the customers become satisfied when they are compensated for such service failures. Similarly, when there is a service failure by Ghana Water Company, customers are satisfied when they are apologized to. However, explaining service failure rather worsens the plight of the customer and does not in any way contribute to meeting the customers' expectations. The study therefore recommends that for customers of Ghana Water Company to remain satisfied with the service provided by the firm, the company must prioritize providing compensation and apologizing to customers whenever there is a service failure. This is where the use of technology becomes important. Customers can be identified and compensated with the use of technology. Further, apologising to customers can also be made easier if the company uses available technologies that allow personalised interactions with customers. Explaining their inability to deliver the service as promised rather makes their customers dissatisfied.

7.0 LIMITATIONS OF THE STUDY

The study targeted customers of Ghana Water Company Limited in the Odorkor District of Greater Accra, Ghana which is located within the capital of Ghana, Accra. The findings cannot be said to represent the entire public utility companies operating in Ghana. Similar studies could target the Electricity Company of Ghana and the Volta River Authority which provide electricity to customers. Furthermore, future studies could also expand focus on other factors contributing to customer satisfaction in addition to the service recovery strategies that have been established to contribute to customer satisfaction.

Declaration Statement

We the authors of this paper have no conflict of interest to disclose. Consent to participate in this study was verbally sought before proceeding to administer the questionnaire.

We confirm that this work is original and has not been published elsewhere, nor is it currently under consideration for publication elsewhere.

We have no conflicts of interest to disclose.

REFERENCES

Abd Rashid, M. H., Ahmad, F. S., & Othman, A. K. (2014). Does service recovery affect customer satisfaction? A study on co-created retail industry. *Procedia: Social and Behavioral Sciences*, *130*, 455–460. DOI: 10.1016/j.sbspro.2014.04.053

Afum, E., Sun, B. Z., & Kusi, C. L. Y. (2019). Reverse logistics, stakeholder influence and supply chain performance in Ghanaian manufacturing sector. *Journal of Supply Chain Management Systems*, *8*(3), 13.

Albrecht, A. K., Schaefers, T., Walsh, G., & Beatty, S. E. (2019). The effect of compensation size on recovery satisfaction after group service failures: The role of group versus individual service recovery. *Journal of Service Research*, *22*(1), 60–74. DOI: 10.1177/1094670518802059

ALhawbani, G. S., Ali, N. A., & Hammouda, A. N. M. (2021). The effect of service recovery strategies on satisfaction with the recovery: The mediating role of distributive justice. *European Journal of Business and Management Research*, *6*(3), 9–16.

Ali, A. A. E. A., & Mohamed, A. A. E. R. A. (2020). the role of perceived justice with service recovery in the relationship between empowerment of frontline employees and customer satisfaction after service recovery" customers of Egyptian Internet Companies Case Study.

Anderson, E. W., & Sullivan, M. W. (1993). The antecedents and consequences of customer satisfaction for firms. *Marketing Science*, *12*(2), 125–143. DOI: 10.1287/mksc.12.2.125

Arens, W. F. (1996). *Contemporary Advertising*. Richard D. Irwin, A. Times Mirror Higher Education Group Inc. Company.

Ayertey, S. (2018). *An evaluation of online service failures and recovery strategies in the UK fashion industry* (Doctoral dissertation, University of Plymouth).

Badu, J. (2016). Service quallity and customer satisfaction of Ghana Water Company Limited: A study of customers in the Accra metropolis (Doctoral dissertation, University of Cape Coast).

Bae, G., Lee, S., & Kim, D. Y. (2021). Interactions between service recovery efforts and customer characteristics: Apology, compensation, and empowerment. *Journal of Quality Assurance in Hospitality & Tourism*, *22*(2), 218–244. DOI: 10.1080/1528008X.2020.1769523

Bamossy, G. J., & Solomon, M. R. (2016). *Consumer behaviour: A European perspective*. Pearson Education.

Bebchuk, L. A., & Fried, J. M. (2003). Executive compensation as an agency problem. *The Journal of Economic Perspectives*, *17*(3), 71–92. DOI: 10.1257/089533003769204362

Burns, N., & Kedia, S. (2006). The impact of performance-based compensation on misreporting. *Journal of Financial Economics*, *79*(1), 35–67. DOI: 10.1016/j.jfineco.2004.12.003

Cohen, J. (1988). *Statistical power analysis for the behavioral sciences* (2nd ed.). Lawrence Erlbaum Associates, Publishers.

Dartey-Baah, K., & Amoako, G. K. (2021). A review of empirical research on corporate social responsibility in emerging economies. *International Journal of Emerging Markets*, *16*(7), 1330–1347. DOI: 10.1108/IJOEM-12-2019-1062

Ermias, A. (2019). The role of service recovery strategy on customer satisfaction and loyalty in restaurant businesses in Addis Ababa.

Fadhila, E. A., Wadud, M., & Roswaty, R. (2021). The Effect of Service Recovery on Customer Satisfaction in J&T Express Goods Delivery Services in Palembang. *International Journal of Marketing & Human Resource Research, 2*(1), 43–57.

Gaffar, I., & Kusumawati, A. (2021). Effect of service recovery (sr) on customer relationship management, customer satisfaction and loyalty. *PalArch's Journal of Archaeology of Egypt/Egyptology, 18*(17), 235-253.

Gaskin, J., Godfrey, S., & Vance, A. (2018). Successful system use: It's not just who you are, but what you do. *AIS Transactions on Human-Computer Interaction, 10*(2), 57–81. DOI: 10.17705/1thci.00104

Gelbrich, K. (2010). Anger, frustration, and helplessness after service failure: Coping strategies and effective informational support. *Journal of the Academy of Marketing Science, 38*(5), 567–585. DOI: 10.1007/s11747-009-0169-6

Hair, J. F.Jr, Hult, G. T. M., Ringle, C., & Sarstedt, M. (2016). *A primer on partial least squares structural equation modeling (PLS-SEM).* Sage Publications.

Hair, J. F.Jr, Sarstedt, M., Matthews, L. M., & Ringle, C. M. (2016). Identifying and treating unobserved heterogeneity with FIMIX-PLS: Part I–method. *European Business Review.*

Hasan, M. R., Ghazali, M. S. M., & Mohtar, N. F. (2021). Correlation of heating profile with calcination temperature for the extraction of nano hydroxyapatite (Nano-HAp) derived from bone. *Journal of Mechanical Engineering Science, 15*(1), 7792–7806.

Hoffman, K. D., Kelley, S. W., & Rotalsky, H. M. (2016). Retrospective: Tracking service failures and employee recovery efforts. *Journal of Services Marketing, 30*(1), 7–10. DOI: 10.1108/JSM-10-2015-0316

Honora, A., Chih, W. H., & Wang, K. Y. (2022). Managing social media recovery: The important role of service recovery transparency in retaining customers. *Journal of Retailing and Consumer Services, 64*, 102814. DOI: 10.1016/j.jretconser.2021.102814

Hu, Y., Min, H., & Su, N. (2021). How sincere is an apology? Recovery satisfaction in a robot service failure context. *Journal of Hospitality & Tourism Research (Washington, D.C.), 45*(6), 1022–1043. DOI: 10.1177/10963480211011533

Hu, Y., Min, H., & Su, N. (2021). How sincere is an apology? Recovery satisfaction in a robot service failure context. *Journal of Hospitality & Tourism Research (Washington, D.C.), 45*(6), 1022–1043. DOI: 10.1177/10963480211011533

Jin, W. J., Park, S. H., & Park, J. (2022). Apology and its acceptance: Perceived reconciliatory attitudes reduce outgroup dehumanization. *Frontiers in Psychology, 13*, 809513. DOI: 10.3389/fpsyg.2022.809513 PMID: 35548505

Kalkman, J. P. (2021). Military crisis responses to COVID-19. *Journal of Contingencies and Crisis Management, 29*(1), 99–103. DOI: 10.1111/1468-5973.12328

Kim, G. S. (2007). The service recovery strategies, customer satisfaction, customer loyalty. *Asian Journal on Quality.*

Lubis, A., Dalimunthe, R., Absah, Y., & Fawzeea, B. K. (2021). The effect of corporate communication and service quality on customer loyalty and satisfaction in sharia banking. *The Journal of Asian Finance, Economics and Business, 8*(3), 1267–1274.

Masuch, K., Greve, M., & Trang, S. (2021). What to do after a data breach? Examining apology and compensation as response strategies for health service providers. *Electronic Markets, 31*(4), 829–848. DOI: 10.1007/s12525-021-00490-3

Matikiti, R., Mpinganjira, M., & Roberts-Lombard, M. (2019). Service recovery satisfaction and customer commitment in the airline business: An emerging African market perspective. *African Journal of Economic and Management Studies*.

Odoom, R., Agbemabiese, G. C., & Hinson, R. E. (2020). Service recovery satisfaction in offline and online experiences. *Marketing Intelligence & Planning*, *38*(1), 1–14. DOI: 10.1108/MIP-09-2018-0422

Oliver, R. L., Rust, R. T., & Varki, S. (1997). Customer delight: Foundations, findings, and managerial insight. *Journal of Retailing*, *73*(3), 311–336. DOI: 10.1016/S0022-4359(97)90021-X

Omoera, C. I. (2017). *Price Fairness, Service Recovery and Customer Satisfaction in the Mobile Telecommunication Industry in Nigeria* (Doctoral dissertation).

Phan, A., Nguyen, H., & Pham, T. (2021). Relationship between service recovery, customer satisfaction and customer loyalty: Empirical evidence from e-retailing. *Uncertain Supply Chain Management*, *9*(1), 1–10. DOI: 10.5267/j.uscm.2020.12.007

Popoola, A. O., & Ayeni, R. O. (2007). A free boundary value problem related to auto ignition of combustible fluid In insulation materials. *Journal of Nigerian Association of Mathematical Physics*, *11*, 95–102.

Ringle, C. M., Wende, S., & Becker, J. M. (2015). SmartPLS 3. SmartPLS GmbH, Boenningstedt. *Journal of Service Science and Management*, *10*(3).

Sekar, S., & Sudha, B. (2021). A Study on Service Quality and Customer Satisfaction and Customer Psychology towards Five Star Hotel in Tamil Nadu. *Annals of the Romanian Society for Cell Biology*, •••, 2209–2217.

Shen, W., & Wang, Y. (2022). Facilitation of customer empathy: The effect of robot apology on customer reaction following a service failure. *Journal of Marketing Development and Competitiveness*, *16*(2), 1–14.

Tanrikulu, C. (2021). Theory of consumption values in consumer behaviour research: A review and future research agenda. *International Journal of Consumer Studies*, *45*(6), 1176–1197. DOI: 10.1111/ijcs.12687

Twum, K. O., & Abubakari, M. (2020). Drops in the city: The puzzle of water privatization and consumption deficiencies in urban Ghana. *Water Policy*, *22*(3), 417–434. DOI: 10.2166/wp.2020.175

Vredenburgh, K. (2022). The right to explanation. *Journal of Political Philosophy*, *30*(2), 209–229. DOI: 10.1111/jopp.12262

Wang, K. Y., Chih, W. H., Hsu, L. C., & Lin, W. C. (2020). Investigating apology, perceived firm remorse and consumers' coping behaviors in the digital media service recovery context. *Journal of Service Management*, *31*(3), 421–439. DOI: 10.1108/JOSM-09-2018-0299

Wei, J., & Lin, X. (2022). Research on the influence of compensation methods and customer sentiment on service recovery effect. *Total Quality Management & Business Excellence*, *33*(5-6), 489–508. DOI: 10.1080/14783363.2020.1856650

Yamane, T. (1967). *Research Methods: Determination of Sample Size*. Prentice-Hall.

Zaid, S., Palilati, A., Madjid, R., & Bua, H. (2021). Impact of service recovery, customer satisfaction, and corporate image on customer loyalty. *The Journal of Asian Finance, Economics and Business*, *8*(1), 961–970.

Chapter 22
From Data to Delight:
Using Wearable Technology to Tailor Tourist Experiences

Bassam Samir Al-Romeedy
https://orcid.org/0000-0002-7900-5052
Faculty of Tourism and Hotels, University of Sadat City, Egypt

Hamada Hussein
https://orcid.org/0000-0001-6063-8805
Faculty of Tourism and Hotels, University of Sadat City, Egypt

Amrik Singh
https://orcid.org/0000-0003-3598-8787
School of Hotel Management and Tourism, Lovely Professional University, Phagwara, India

ABSTRACT

This chapter delves into how wearable technology can be integrated into the tourism sector to elevate the travel experience by monitoring tourist activities and delivering tailored, real-time services. Devices such as smartwatches, fitness trackers, and augmented reality glasses have significantly altered the tourism landscape, providing valuable insights into tourists' preferences, health, and movements. The discussion focuses on leveraging this technology to customize tourist interactions, enhance safety and well-being while traveling, and boost engagement at cultural and natural sites. Additionally, it examines how wearable tech can foster sustainable tourism by promoting environmentally friendly practices. The findings underscore the transformative potential of wearable technology in the tourism industry, presenting innovative strategies for enhancing customer satisfaction and refining travel experiences.

INTRODUCTION

Wearable technology, including smartwatches, fitness trackers, and augmented reality (AR) glasses, has rapidly expanded across multiple sectors, with tourism being a key beneficiary. These devices bring a host of features that can greatly enrich travel experiences by delivering real-time updates, health tracking, and interactive content. In the tourism realm, wearables enable businesses to gather and analyze data related to tourists' preferences, movements, and health metrics, allowing for more personalized and tailored experiences. As demand for customized and immersive travel grows, wearable technology stands to transform the way tourists interact with destinations and how businesses cater to their expectations. With capabilities like location tracking, physical activity monitoring, and biometric data collection, wearables provide unprecedented insights into tourist behavior. This technological

DOI: 10.4018/979-8-3693-7447-4.ch022

progress not only enhances service offerings but also elevates the overall quality of travelers' experiences (Farahat et al., 2022; Ferrer-Rosell et al., 2023).

Wearable devices possess the unique capability to gather a wide array of data, such as location information, biometric metrics (like heart rate and step count), and behavioral patterns (such as preferred routes and frequent stops). This real-time data collection provides tourism operators with invaluable insights into how visitors engage with various destinations. For instance, location data can highlight popular tourist paths, while biometric readings can offer clues about the level of physical exertion tourists experience at specific sites. By analyzing this aggregated data, businesses can detect trends, enhance visitor flow management, and refine the design of future travel experiences. However, the collection of personal data raises important ethical concerns, particularly regarding privacy. Wearable technology must comply with stringent data privacy laws to safeguard tourists' personal information. This requires robust security measures to prevent unauthorized access, as well as clear transparency about how data is collected, stored, and utilized (Xiang & Fesenmaier, 2017; Al-Romeedy & Singh, 2024b).

One of the most exciting uses of wearable technology in tourism is its capacity to deliver highly personalized experiences. Data collected from wearables can be leveraged to offer customized suggestions for activities, attractions, or accommodations that align with a tourist's preferences and previous behaviors. For example, tourists using smartwatches might receive alerts about nearby points of interest or recommended routes based on their location and interests. Wearable devices can also enhance real-time engagement, with AR glasses providing historical insights or virtual guides for landmarks. Such personalized experiences are already being implemented successfully in places like theme parks and museums, where visitors use wearables to tailor their journey—whether it's receiving information in their preferred language or discovering specific attractions based on their interests. This level of customization enhances the overall travel experience, making it more relevant, engaging, and enjoyable for individual tourists (Kontogianni & Alepis, 2020; Mejia et al., 2021; Neidhardt & Wörndl, 2020).

Wearable devices are essential for monitoring tourists' health and well-being throughout their travels. Fitness trackers, for instance, can monitor physical activity, heart rate, and other key health metrics, offering real-time feedback to travelers. These devices can remind tourists to stay hydrated during strenuous activities like hiking or prompt them to rest if their heart rate reaches high levels. Beyond health tracking, wearables also enhance safety by delivering real-time updates on weather changes, environmental risks, and emergency alerts, allowing tourists to make informed decisions while on the go. This combination of health and safety monitoring significantly enhances the travel experience. In activity-intensive destinations, such as national parks or adventure tourism locations, wearable technology becomes vital in preventing fatigue or health issues, making it a critical tool for ensuring a safe and enjoyable journey (Buonincontri & Marasco, 2017; Filieri et al., 2021). Wearable technology greatly enhances visitor engagement at cultural and natural attractions by providing interactive, immersive experiences. At heritage sites, museums, and parks, wearables can offer real-time information such as audio guides, historical details, or translations in various languages. For example, augmented reality glasses enable tourists to view digital reconstructions of ancient ruins in their original form or interact with exhibits in ways that traditional tours cannot match (Wörndl et al., 2021; Xiang & Fesenmaier, 2017; Al-Romeedy & Singh, 2024a).

In the realm of sustainable tourism, wearable technology is a key tool for promoting eco-friendly practices. These devices can guide tourists along sustainable routes or suggest low-impact activities by using real-time environmental data. Wearables can also help monitor and reduce tourists' environmental footprints by tracking energy usage, waste, and resource consumption at natural attractions or eco-tourism sites. For example, tourists might receive alerts about green travel options or sustainable accommodation based on their location. By fostering environmental awareness and encouraging responsible behavior, wearables contribute to sustainability efforts in the tourism industry, helping destinations manage visitor impact while preserving their natural surroundings (Neidhardt & Wörndl, 2020; Not et al., 2022; Stienmetz et al., 2022; Sustacha et al., 2023).

The objectives of this chapter are to examine the effective use of wearable technology—such as smartwatches, fitness trackers, and AR glasses—in tracking tourism patterns and enhancing the travel experience through personalized, data-driven services. It seeks to explore the types of data wearables collect, how this data can be analyzed to customize tourist experiences, and how wearable technology can improve health, well-being, and visitor engagement at cultural and natural sites. Additionally, the chapter will evaluate the role of wearables in encouraging sustainable tourism practices. This chapter's contribution lies in demonstrating how wearable technology can reshape the tourism industry by offering more immersive, safer, and eco-friendly travel experiences, providing innovative solutions for both tourists and industry stakeholders.

WEARABLE TECHNOLOGY IN TOURISM

Wearable technology has become a game-changer in the tourism industry, offering innovative tools that significantly enhance the travel experience. Devices such as smartwatches, fitness trackers, and augmented reality (AR) glasses are gaining popularity for their ability to provide real-time updates, encourage active lifestyles, and increase engagement with destinations. For example, smartwatches have evolved from simple timepieces into multifunctional communication devices, enabling travelers to receive notifications, navigate with maps, and make contactless payments—all from their wrists. This added convenience allows tourists to stay connected and informed without constantly checking their smartphones, thereby elevating their overall travel experience (Bhuiyan et al., 2022; Ferrer-Rosell et al., 2023).

Fitness trackers, on the other hand, cater to the growing trend of health-focused travel by not only tracking physical activity and calorie expenditure but also encouraging users to stay active while exploring new destinations. For instance, fitness trackers can motivate travelers to increase their step count, explore local parks, or participate in activities like guided hikes, fostering a deeper connection with the natural landscape and local culture. Many fitness trackers now also include social features, enabling travelers to share their experiences and adventures with friends and family, thus creating a sense of community and connection even while on the go. AR glasses represent an exciting frontier in wearable technology within the tourism industry. By overlaying digital information onto the real world, AR glasses can enhance travel experiences in entirely new ways. For example, users can access historical facts about landmarks as they view them, interact with virtual tour guides, or use interactive maps without needing to hold a device. This immersive layer of information adds depth to the cultural and historical context of various attractions, enriching the educational value of travel. Moreover, AR glasses can assist in navigating complex urban environments by allowing users to visualize routes in real time as they explore (Al-Romeedy & Hussein, 2024; Al-Romeedy & Singh, 2024a).

The rising popularity of wearable devices in the tourism industry is fueled not only by technological advancements but also by evolving consumer preferences. Today's travelers increasingly desire personalized experiences that cater to their unique needs and interests. Wearable technology can provide customized recommendations, such as suggesting local restaurants based on dietary preferences or highlighting nearby attractions that resonate with a traveler's interests. Additionally, as the Internet of Things (IoT) continues to grow, the integration of wearable devices with smart tourism infrastructures—like connected transportation systems and smart hotel rooms—will further enhance the convenience and personalization of travel experiences (Benckendorff et al., 2019; Egger & Egger, 2022; Filieri et al., 2021).

Wearable technology in tourism presents significant opportunities for collecting real-time data on tourists' preferences, health, and movement patterns, offering invaluable insights for both businesses and destinations. As travelers utilize smartwatches, fitness trackers, and other wearable devices, they generate a continuous flow of data that can be leveraged to enhance the overall tourism experience. This capability facilitates more personalized services and targeted marketing strategies, ultimately driving higher customer satisfaction and loyalty. One of the key benefits of wearable technology is its ability to monitor tourists' preferences in real time. For example, smartwatches and fitness trackers can track users' activity levels, dietary habits, and their engagement with various attractions. By analyzing this data, tourism businesses can gain insights into which experiences and services resonate most with their customers. If a considerable number of travelers are frequently participating in outdoor activities or fitness-related excursions, destinations can adapt their offerings to highlight these experiences. Customizing services based on real-time preferences not only enhances the visitor experience but also allows tourism operators to optimize their resources more effectively (Buonincontri & Marasco, 2017; Çınar, 2020; Gajdošík, 2020).

As well, health monitoring is a vital component of wearable technology in the tourism sector. Devices equipped with sensors can track essential metrics such as heart rate, sleep patterns, and stress levels, enabling tourists to manage their well-being while on the go. This functionality is particularly valuable for health-conscious travelers, as it empowers them to make informed choices regarding their activities and routines. Furthermore, tourism providers can leverage health data to create wellness-focused programs, such as guided meditation retreats or fitness challenges, catering to the rising demand for holistic travel experiences. By emphasizing health and well-being, destinations can stand out in an increasingly competitive market. Too, the ability to monitor movement patterns offers further opportunities to enhance the tourist experience. Wearable devices can provide insights into foot traffic at popular attractions, helping businesses identify peak times and adjust their operations accordingly. For instance, if data indicates that a specific museum experiences heavy crowds during certain hours, the museum can implement crowd control measures or modify staffing levels to improve the visitor experience. Moreover, this movement data can contribute to urban planning and infrastructure development, allowing cities to create more efficient public spaces and transportation systems that better serve tourists' needs (Hall, 2024; Hu et al., 2021; Islam et al., 2024; Kachniewska, 2021).

Real-time data collection through wearable devices facilitates the implementation of dynamic pricing models in the tourism industry. By analyzing tourists' movements and preferences, businesses can adjust pricing in response to fluctuations in demand. For example, if a particular attraction experiences an uptick in visitors, it can temporarily raise ticket prices to optimize revenue while managing crowd levels. This flexibility benefits both consumers and operators, ensuring a balanced experience that addresses demand without compromising quality. Moreover, the integration of wearable technology with mobile applications and other digital platforms enhances the data collection process. Many wearable devices can sync with smartphones, enabling seamless information transfer and analysis. This interconnectedness allows tourism providers to create detailed customer profiles based on a combination of real-time data, historical behavior, and individual preferences. Such profiles are invaluable for developing targeted marketing campaigns, delivering personalized recommendations, and enhancing customer engagement (Kontogianni & Alepis, 2020; Mejia et al., 2021; Mohamed et al., 2022).

DATA COLLECTION AND ANALYSIS THROUGH WEARABLES

Types of data collected by wearables

Wearable technology has transformed data collection in the tourism sector, enabling the gathering of a wealth of information that greatly enhances the comprehension of tourist behavior. The data collected through wearables can be classified into three primary categories: location information, biometric metrics, and behavioral trends. Each of these categories provides distinct insights that businesses and destinations can utilize to refine their services, bolster marketing efforts, and ultimately elevate the overall travel experience (Shin et al., 2022; Shoval & Birenboim, 2019).

Location Data

Location data represents a crucial element collected by wearable devices, especially those featuring GPS technology. This information allows for the precise tracking of a tourist's movements in real time, revealing insights about their routes, the attractions they visit, and the time they spend at specific locations. By analyzing this data, tourism operators can pinpoint popular paths and heavily trafficked areas, aiding in decisions related to resource distribution, crowd management, and marketing initiatives. For example, if data indicates that tourists frequently congregate in a specific park or near a landmark, local businesses can implement targeted promotions to attract these visitors, such as offering special discounts at nearby restaurants or activities that enhance the overall experience of the attractions. Additionally, understanding these movement patterns can assist cities in optimizing public transportation routes and improving signage, ultimately enriching the visitor experience. Furthermore, location data can highlight underutilized attractions or areas that may need increased promotional efforts to attract more tourists.

Biometric Data

Biometric data, which includes a variety of physiological measurements, offers profound insights into tourists' health and well-being while they travel. Devices like fitness trackers and smartwatches can monitor metrics such as heart rate, sleep quality, physical activity levels, and even stress responses. This information is essential for assessing how different environments and activities affect tourists' health and enjoyment. For instance, if a tourist shows heightened stress levels during a crowded event, it may signal a demand for more wellness-oriented options, such as tranquil areas or relaxation activities. By analyzing biometric data, tourism businesses can develop customized wellness programs that appeal to health-conscious travelers, including guided meditation sessions, yoga retreats, or outdoor fitness classes. Moreover, insights derived from biometric data can enhance safety protocols, such as monitoring the well-being of participants during physically demanding tours or excursions, ensuring that visitors stay safe and comfortable (Pesonen & Neidhardt, 2019; Sehgal et al., 2024; tom Dieck et al., 2018; Valeri, 2023).

Behavior Patterns

The collection of behavioral pattern data through wearables offers a detailed understanding of how tourists interact with their surroundings. This data encompasses metrics related to activity levels, engagement with specific attractions, duration of visits, and even social interactions. For example, wearables can monitor the time tourists spend at various locations, enabling businesses to identify which attractions are most popular and which might need improvements to enhance visitor engagement. Furthermore, analyzing these behavioral patterns can uncover trends that guide operational decisions. If data indicates that tourists typically visit certain attractions in the morning and prefer local experiences in the afternoon, businesses can modify their scheduling, staffing, and marketing strategies to better align with these behaviors. Insights into social dynamics, such as how groups of tourists interact, can inform the creation of collaborative experiences, like group tours or events designed to foster networking and community among visitors. Likewise, data on behavior patterns can be crucial for developing personalized marketing strategies. By understanding individual preferences and engagement levels, tourism operators can deliver targeted offers and recommendations to users, increasing the likelihood of repeat visits and customer loyalty. For instance, if a tourist frequently engages in culinary activities, businesses can tailor personalized dining suggestions or special culinary tours that align with their interests (Stienmetz et al., 2022; Sustacha et al., 2023; Not et al., 2022; Pelet et al., 2021).

How this data can be aggregated and analyzed to understand tourist behavior

The incorporation of wearable technology in tourism allows for the collection of a diverse range of data types, providing businesses and destinations with valuable insights into tourist behavior. However, the true potential of this data is realized not just in its collection, but also in the methods used for aggregation and analysis. By utilizing advanced data aggregation techniques and analytical approaches, stakeholders can convert raw data into actionable insights, facilitating informed decision-making and enhancing the overall visitor experience. Data aggregation involves compiling information from various sources and merging it into a cohesive dataset for analysis. In the realm of wearables, this encompasses data from individual devices, as well as additional information sourced from mobile applications, social media, and customer relationship management (CRM) systems. For instance, location data collected from wearables can be combined with user-generated content from social media platforms, such as check-ins and reviews, to create a comprehensive picture of tourist interactions with specific attractions or destinations. To enable effective data aggregation, tourism operators can leverage cloud-based platforms that support real-time data storage and processing. This allows organizations to continuously collect and analyze data rather than relying on periodic snapshots. Moreover, data integration tools can assist in merging datasets from different wearables and platforms, ensuring consistency and accuracy across various sources. By aggregating data in this way, businesses can construct detailed profiles of tourist behavior, capturing both quantitative metrics (like duration of visits) and qualitative insights (such as sentiment analysis from social media interactions) (Xiang & Fesenmaier, 2017; Al-Romeedy & Singh, 2024b; Villamediana-Pedrosa et al., 2020; Wörndl et al., 2021).

Once the data is aggregated, it can be analyzed using a variety of techniques to extract valuable insights. The process often begins with descriptive analytics, which summarizes the data to provide a broad overview of tourist behavior patterns. For instance, this analysis can uncover the average duration of visits to specific attractions, identify peak visitation times, and outline common routes taken by tourists. This foundational understanding is crucial for spotting trends and making initial observations about tourist behavior. In addition to descriptive analytics, predictive analytics can be employed to anticipate future behaviors based on historical data. Machine learning algorithms can sift through the data to recognize patterns, allowing predictions about which attractions tourists are likely to visit next or how external factors (like weather changes or special events) might influence visitor numbers. For example, if past data shows that attendance at a local festival tends to boost foot traffic to nearby dining establishments, businesses can proactively adjust their inventory or staffing to accommodate the anticipated increase in customers. Another key analytical approach is segmentation analysis, which involves categorizing tourists according to shared traits or behaviors. By clustering various data points, tourism operators can pinpoint distinct groups within their audience—such as adventure enthusiasts, cultural explorers, or wellness-focused travelers. This segmentation facilitates the creation of targeted marketing strategies tailored to specific demographics. For instance, a destination might develop specialized packages for adventure seekers that include activities like hiking, zip-lining, or guided explorations of natural landmarks (Al-Romeedy & Singh, 2024c; Farahat, 2023).

Furthermore, sophisticated data visualization tools can simplify the communication of complex insights. By generating interactive dashboards and visual reports, tourism operators can present aggregated data in a manner that highlights essential metrics and trends. For example, heat maps can be utilized to depict high-traffic locations, while time-series graphs can illustrate changes in visitor numbers over different periods. This visual representation not only supports internal decision-making but also equips stakeholders with clear, actionable insights that can inform strategic initiatives. A significant advantage of wearable technology is its ability to facilitate real-time data analysis. As these devices continuously collect and transmit information, businesses can adapt swiftly to shifts in tourist behavior and preferences. For instance, if data indicates a sudden spike in visitors at a specific attraction, businesses can modify their marketing strategies to leverage this trend by offering promotions or enhancing services to accommodate the influx. Similarly, if biometric data reveals that tourists are experiencing elevated stress levels at a crowded event, organizers can implement crowd management strategies or provide additional support services to enhance visitor comfort.

Real-time data analysis also empowers tourism operators to actively engage with travelers during their journeys. Through mobile applications, businesses can send personalized notifications based on aggregated data, such as recommending nearby attractions that match a user's interests or informing them about exclusive offers from local establishments. This degree of engagement not only enriches the visitor experience but also builds loyalty by demonstrating that businesses are attuned to and responsive to individual preferences (Farahat et al., 2022; Farid et al., 2023; Egger & Egger, 2022; Al-Romeedy & Hussein, 2024).

Privacy and ethical considerations in using personal data from wearables

As the integration of wearable technology in tourism grows, so do the privacy and ethical dilemmas surrounding the collection and use of personal data. These devices, capable of gathering extensive information on tourists—from their physical activity and health metrics to their location and behavior—present significant challenges in terms of data privacy, consent, and ethical practices. It is essential to address these issues to preserve consumer trust and ensure responsible technology use in the tourism sector. One major privacy concern related to wearable technology is the potential for sensitive personal data to be collected and stored without explicit consent. Many tourists may not fully understand the range of data that these devices can capture, which includes biometric information like heart rates, sleep quality, and stress levels, as well as comprehensive location tracking. If this data is mishandled, it could lead to serious privacy invasions, allowing unauthorized individuals to access personal movements and health information (Ferrer-Rosell et al., 2023; Al-Romeedy & Singh, 2024a; Gajdošík, 2020; Shin et al., 2022).

Beyond privacy issues, data security emerges as a crucial challenge in the realm of wearable technology. Given the sensitive information that these devices collect, they become prime targets for cybercriminals. Without adequate security measures, personal data may be exposed to breaches, risking identity theft, fraud, and unauthorized monitoring. To mitigate these risks, tourism operators must prioritize the adoption of rigorous security protocols, including encryption, secure data storage, and frequent software updates. Ethical considerations also significantly influence how personal data from wearables is utilized. The capability to gather and analyze data can lead to practices that may conflict with ethical standards. For example, employing dynamic pricing based on data insights could result in unequal access to services, where certain tourists pay much higher rates solely based on their data profiles or behaviors. Such practices could be viewed as exploitative and could undermine the trust between consumers and businesses (Hall, 2024; Not et al., 2022; Kachniewska, 2021; Islam et al., 2024). As wearable technology progresses, the tourism industry must strike a balance between harnessing data for innovation and safeguarding consumer rights and privacy. Collaborating with stakeholders—such as tourists, privacy advocates, and regulatory agencies—can help develop best practices and guidelines that encourage responsible data usage. Regularly gathering feedback from users about their experiences and concerns can assist businesses in refining their practices and bolstering customer trust (Xiang et al., 2021; Al-Romeedy & Singh, 2024b).

PERSONALIZATION OF TOURIST EXPERIENCES

Personalizing tourist experiences has become a defining characteristic of contemporary travel, and wearable technology is crucial in enabling this customization. By gathering and analyzing data from wearable devices, stakeholders in the tourism sector can gain valuable insights into individual preferences, behaviors, and needs. This information can be utilized to offer tailored recommendations for activities, attractions, accommodations, and services, ultimately enhancing the travel experience and encouraging deeper engagement with destinations. Wearable devices can collect diverse types of data, including location, biometric information, and activity levels, which are vital for understanding tourist preferences. For example, a smartwatch that monitors a user's activity can indicate whether they favor adventurous activities like hiking and cycling or more relaxed pursuits such as visiting museums and cultural sites. Additionally, biometric metrics like heart rate and stress levels can provide insights into a tourist's comfort during various activities, further refining recommendations. By analyzing this data, tourism operators can construct detailed profiles of individual travelers. By recognizing behavioral patterns—such as frequent visits to outdoor attractions or a preference for cultural experiences—businesses can adjust their offerings accordingly. For instance, a traveler who consistently engages in fitness activities might receive suggestions for guided hiking tours, adventure sports, or wellness retreats, thereby increasing the chances of a satisfying travel experience (Mejia et al., 2021; Kontogianni & Alepis, 2020; Neidhardt & Wörndl, 2020; Pelet et al., 2021).

A significant benefit of wearable technology is its ability to deliver real-time recommendations based on a tourist's current location. With integrated GPS capabilities, wearables can track users' movements and suggest nearby attractions, activities, or dining options tailored to their interests. For example, if a traveler is at a historical site, their wearable might offer insights about nearby museums, local guided tours, or relevant cultural events taking place in the vicinity. Moreover, these real-time suggestions can adapt to changing circumstances. If weather conditions alter unexpectedly, wearables can recommend alternative indoor activities or attractions. For instance, if rain begins while a tourist is at an outdoor park, their device could propose nearby cafes or art galleries. This responsiveness to real-time scenarios enriches the travel experience, enabling tourists to maximize their enjoyment and engagement with the destination (Pesonen & Neidhardt, 2019; Sehgal et al., 2024; Shoval & Birenboim, 2019; Sustacha et al., 2023).

Wearable data plays a vital role in customizing accommodation recommendations for travelers. By examining past travel behaviors and preferences, hotels and lodging providers can tailor their services to meet the unique needs of each guest. For instance, if a traveler often opts for accommodations featuring fitness centers or spa amenities, hotels can emphasize these facilities in their suggestions. Additionally, wearables can offer insights into a tourist's sleep patterns and preferences, enabling hotels to personalize room settings. If biometric data shows that a guest prefers cooler temperatures or specific types of bedding for a better night's sleep, hotels can proactively adjust these elements before their arrival. This level of detail not only enhances the overall guest experience but also builds loyalty and encourages repeat visits. Furthermore, the personalization of tourist experiences through wearables extends to social interactions and community involvement. Wearables can monitor social behaviors, such as participation in group activities or interactions with fellow travelers, enabling businesses to recommend social events or group experiences that resonate with a user's interests. For example, if data reveals that a tourist enjoys culinary experiences and frequently dines at local restaurants, their wearable device could suggest food festivals, cooking classes, or dining tours. Additionally, wearable technology can help connect tourists with local communities. By highlighting events or activities that foster interaction with locals, such as cultural workshops or community-led tours, businesses can provide enriching experiences that go beyond conventional sightseeing. This approach not only enhances the tourist experience but also cultivates a sense of connection to the destination, leading to a more immersive and authentic travel adventure (tom Dieck et al., 2018; Valeri, 2023; Villamediana-Pedrosa et al., 2020; Wörndl et al., 2021).

While the customization of tourist experiences through wearable data presents many advantages, it also brings significant privacy concerns to the forefront. Travelers might worry about the collection, storage, and use of their personal information. To alleviate these concerns, businesses must emphasize transparency and data protection. Providing users with control over their data—such as the ability to opt in or out of data collection and tailored recommendations—is essential for building trust. Furthermore, businesses should clearly communicate how the data will be utilized to improve the tourist experience, highlighting the benefits of personalized suggestions. By cultivating a culture of trust and transparency, tourism operators can effectively harness wearable data for personalization while safeguarding user privacy (Buonincontri & Marasco, 2017; Egger & Egger, 2022; Farahat et al., 2022; Gajdošík, 2020).

Moreover, the advancement of wearable technology has fundamentally reshaped how tourists interact with their environments, providing exceptional opportunities for real-time personalization. By utilizing location-based alerts, suggested routes, and interactive features such as augmented reality (AR), tourism operators can create a more dynamic and immersive travel experience. These innovations not only enhance the enjoyment of a destination but also foster deeper connections between tourists and the locations they explore. One of the most impactful innovations for enhancing real-time engagement is the implementation of location-based alerts through wearable devices. These alerts can inform tourists about nearby attractions, events, or promotions as they move through a destination. For instance, a tourist wearing a smartwatch might receive a notification about a special exhibit at a nearby museum or a pop-up market showcasing local artisans. By providing timely and pertinent information, businesses can promote spontaneous visits and increase foot traffic to attractions that tourists may not have originally planned to visit. Additionally, location-based alerts can improve safety and convenience. For example, if a tourist finds themselves in an unfamiliar area, their wearable device could alert them to nearby emergency services, public transportation options, or safe routes to navigate their surroundings. This proactive strategy not only enhances the overall experience but also instills a sense of security and confidence among travelers, particularly those exploring new cities or countries (Filieri et al., 2021; Hall, 2024; Hu et al., 2021; Islam et al., 2024).

Wearable technology also enables personalized route recommendations tailored to a tourist's specific interests and preferences. By evaluating data such as past behaviors and real-time locations, wearables can suggest optimized paths that showcase attractions, dining options, and cultural experiences aligned with a traveler's profile. For instance, a visitor passionate about art and history might receive a walking route suggestion that includes local galleries, historical landmarks, and street art installations. These recommended routes can be enriched with contextual details, including historical anecdotes or interesting facts about particular sites along the way. This approach not only enhances the travel experience but also encourages travelers to venture beyond typical tourist routes, allowing them to uncover hidden gems within a destination. By offering personalized route suggestions, businesses can craft memorable experiences that resonate with individual tourists, fostering a deeper appreciation for the local culture and history (Kachniewska, 2021; Ferrer-Rosell et al., 2023; Farahat, 2023).

The incorporation of augmented reality (AR) features into wearable technology opens up exciting avenues for enhancing real-time engagement in tourism. AR applications can overlay digital information onto the physical world, providing travelers with interactive and immersive experiences. For example, while visiting a historical site, a tourist might use AR glasses or a smartphone app to see 3D reconstructions of ancient buildings or watch historical events unfold in real time. Such engaging experiences can strengthen a tourist's connection to a destination by offering context and storytelling that enhances their understanding of the cultural and historical significance of the places they visit. Moreover, AR can gamify the exploration process, encouraging tourists to partake in scavenger hunts or challenges that lead them to discover various attractions or complete specific tasks. This adds a playful element and promotes social interactions among travelers, as they can collaborate with friends or family during these activities. Additionally, AR can facilitate personalized experiences tailored to a tourist's preferences. For instance, an art lover could enjoy AR-guided tours of local galleries, complete with insights into the artists and their works. Similarly, culinary enthusiasts could explore food experiences through AR applications that highlight local dishes, restaurant recommendations, and chef interviews. This level of customization not only enriches the overall travel experience but also encourages tourists to engage more deeply with the local culture (Benckendorff et al., 2019; Egger & Egger, 2022; Al-Romeedy & Singh, 2024c).

Wearable technology can significantly boost real-time engagement by incorporating social media and networking features. This enables travelers to instantly share their adventures with friends and family, fostering a sense of community and connection. For instance, tourists can utilize location-based functionalities to check in at attractions, post photos, and recommend activities to their social circles in real time. By promoting this social interaction, tourism businesses can cultivate a feeling of belonging and motivate travelers to join together, whether in organized events or casual gatherings. Additionally, by harnessing social media analytics, companies can uncover what types of experiences resonate best with tourists, enabling them to further tailor their offerings (Pelet et al., 2021; Pesonen & Neidhardt, 2019).

IMPROVING HEALTH AND WELL-BEING DURING TRAVEL

The increasing adoption of wearable technology in the travel sector is not solely focused on enhancing experiences; it is also pivotal in monitoring and promoting the health and well-being of travelers. Devices like smartwatches and fitness trackers have become indispensable for those looking to maintain their health while exploring new places. By tracking vital metrics such as step count, heart rate, sleep quality, and overall activity levels, these wearables empower travelers to make informed health choices during their trips. One of the key features of these wearable devices is their ability to monitor physical activity, particularly by recording daily steps. This is especially beneficial for tourists, as travel often involves extensive walking and exploration. For instance, a visitor exploring a city filled with attractions might walk several miles daily. By using a wearable to track their steps, travelers can better understand their activity levels and establish personalized fitness goals to stay active while on the go. Furthermore, many wearables include functions that encourage regular movement, such as alerts to stand up and walk after long periods of inactivity. This is particularly helpful in combating sedentary behavior, which can be prevalent during travel, especially during extended hours spent in planes, trains, or vehicles. By promoting consistent movement, wearables not only enhance physical health but also enrich the overall travel experience (Mejia et al., 2021; Mohamed et al., 2022; Sehgal et al., 2024; Shoval & Birenboim, 2019).

Another important feature of health monitoring via wearables is heart rate tracking. Many devices provide continuous heart rate monitoring, offering crucial insights that can help travelers evaluate their physical and emotional states. Increased heart rates may signal physical exertion or stress, both of which are common during travel due to factors like navigating new environments, dealing with delays, or managing tight itineraries. By understanding their heart rate trends, tourists can make better decisions regarding their activities. For example, if a traveler observes that their heart rate remains elevated during sightseeing, they might decide to incorporate more breaks, practice mindfulness exercises, or engage in calming activities like yoga or meditation. Some wearables even include guided breathing exercises that help travelers manage stress and anxiety in real time, fostering a sense of tranquility and well-being throughout their journeys. Quality sleep is vital for sustaining overall health, particularly during travel, when disruptions to regular routines can affect rest. Many wearables come equipped with sleep tracking features that allow tourists to monitor their sleep patterns, including duration, quality, and disturbances. This information can help travelers pinpoint factors that might be impacting their sleep, such as noise levels, time zone changes, or inconsistent sleep schedules. By examining their sleep data, tourists can adjust their travel habits to enhance their rest. For instance, if someone discovers they are not achieving sufficient deep sleep, they might choose quieter lodging, establish a more consistent bedtime routine, or avoid heavy meals and caffeine close to bedtime. Improved sleep quality can lead to a better mood, higher energy levels, and enhanced cognitive function, all contributing to a more enjoyable and enriching travel experience (Mohamed et al., 2022; Neidhardt & Wörndl, 2020; Not et al., 2022; Pelet et al., 2021).

Wearable devices also facilitate seamless integration with health and wellness applications, significantly enhancing travelers' capacity to monitor and improve their physical health. Many of these devices synchronize with mobile apps that provide insights into users' health metrics, offer tailored workout suggestions, or recommend nutritious dining options based on individual dietary preferences. This integration enables travelers to have a holistic view of their health data in a single location, simplifying the tracking of their progress and helping them stay motivated. Furthermore, these applications often include social sharing features, enabling users to connect with friends, family, or fellow travelers who share similar fitness ambitions. This sense of community can offer encouragement and support, motivating travelers to uphold healthy habits even when away from home. By fostering these connections through health and wellness, wearables assist tourists in adopting a more balanced lifestyle during their journeys (tom Dieck et al., 2018; Valeri, 2023; Farid et al., 2023).

The insights derived from wearable technology empower travelers to make healthier choices on the road. With accessible data on their physical activity levels, heart rate, and sleep patterns, tourists can identify areas for improvement and modify their behaviors accordingly. For instance, if a traveler observes a drop in their daily step count while enjoying indulgent local cuisine, they may decide to integrate more physical activities into their itinerary, such as walking tours or hiking. Moreover, tourism operators can utilize wearable data to promote health-oriented experiences. For example, hotels and resorts can provide wellness programs tailored to guests' health metrics, including fitness classes, guided hikes, or spa services. By cultivating a culture of health and wellness, tourism providers can enhance the travel experience, prioritizing their guests' well-being (Gajdošík, 2020; Hall, 2024).

Importantly, as travelers increasingly seek enriching and enjoyable experiences, the significance of technology in promoting health and well-being during travel has grown immensely. Wearable technology, with its ability to gather and analyze personal health data, presents a unique opportunity for tourism operators to deliver personalized health-related recommendations. These suggestions—ranging from reminders to stay hydrated to identifying appropriate rest spots—are vital for enhancing tourists' physical health and overall travel experiences. A key aspect of maintaining health while traveling is ensuring proper hydration. Tourists often misjudge their hydration needs, especially during hectic travel schedules or in hot climates. Wearable devices can effectively address this issue by providing personalized hydration reminders tailored to individual activity levels, environmental conditions, and health metrics. For instance, if a tourist spends a long day sightseeing and their wearable detects increased physical activity—indicated by elevated heart rates or body temperature—it can automatically remind them to drink water. These reminders can be customized to each user's hydration needs, factoring in age, weight, and exertion levels. Moreover, by utilizing location data, wearables can recommend nearby water sources or cafes where tourists can conveniently refill their water bottles. By promoting consistent hydration, tourism operators can help prevent dehydration, fatigue, and heat-related illnesses, ensuring that travelers feel their best throughout their journeys (Bhuiyan et al., 2022; Hu et al., 2021; Kachniewska, 2021; Pesonen & Neidhardt, 2019; Sehgal et al., 2024).

Traveling often entails extended periods of walking or standing, which can result in fatigue and discomfort. Wearable technology can significantly improve the travel experience by offering personalized recommendations for suitable rest areas tailored to individual tourists' needs and preferences. For example, if a wearable device detects heightened stress levels or increased fatigue in a traveler, it can suggest nearby parks, lounges, or quiet cafes where they can take a break and rejuvenate. By analyzing location data and pinpointing ideal rest spots, wearables can assist travelers in avoiding overexertion and conserving their energy. Moreover, these suggestions can be customized based on the traveler's interests. A tourist with a passion for nature might receive recommendations for green spaces or botanical gardens, while someone interested in an urban vibe could be directed to cozy coffee shops or art galleries featuring comfortable seating. By providing these tailored recommendations, wearables not only enhance physical well-being but also contribute to a more enjoyable and relaxed travel experience (Shin et al., 2022; Shoval & Birenboim, 2019; Stienmetz et al., 2022).

In addition to staying hydrated and resting, encouraging regular breaks and physical activity is vital for maintaining health while traveling. Wearable devices can monitor activity levels and prompt tourists to take short breaks for stretching or walking, especially after sitting or standing for extended periods. These reminders can be strategically timed, such as during long flights, bus journeys, or extended tours. Additionally, wearables can recommend specific exercises or stretches that travelers can perform in rest areas or during breaks. For instance, a device might suggest simple neck and shoulder stretches to relieve tension or encourage light walking to enhance circulation. By integrating physical activity into their travel routines, tourists can mitigate fatigue, boost their mood, and enhance their overall well-being. For those who prioritize fitness while traveling, wearables can provide customized workout suggestions that align with their health metrics and personal objectives. Based on the data collected—such as heart rate and activity levels—these devices can recommend suitable workouts, whether it's a quick session in the hotel room, a guided run through a local park, or a fitness class at a nearby gym. Furthermore, these suggestions can be location-based, helping tourists discover local fitness options. For example, a traveler may receive recommendations for nearby yoga studios, cycling tours, or hiking trails that correspond to their fitness level. By promoting fitness-focused activities, tourism operators can enrich travelers' experiences while supporting their health and wellness goals (Sustacha et al., 2023; tom Dieck et al., 2018; Valeri, 2023).

With maintaining physical activity and hydration, paying attention to dietary choices is crucial for health while traveling. Wearable technology can aid in offering dietary recommendations tailored to individual health metrics and preferences. For example, if a tourist's device monitors their caloric intake or specific nutritional needs, it can recommend healthy dining options that align with their dietary restrictions or fitness objectives. By leveraging location data, wearables can guide travelers to nearby restaurants or cafes that provide nutritious meal options or cater to particular dietary requirements, such as vegetarian, vegan, or gluten-free selections. Furthermore, these devices can send reminders to opt for healthier snacks while on the move, like fruits or nuts, rather than sugary or processed alternatives. By promoting healthy eating habits, wearables can play a significant role in enhancing the overall well-being of travelers, allowing them to feel their best and fully enjoy their experiences (Villamediana-Pedrosa et al., 2020; Wörndl et al., 2021; Al-Romeedy & Hussein, 2024; Farahat, 2023).

Significantly, in today's unpredictable environment, prioritizing the safety and well-being of travelers has become a critical concern for both tourists and tourism operators. Wearable technology, particularly through devices like smartwatches and fitness trackers, plays a vital role in enhancing travel safety by providing real-time information on weather conditions, alerts, and emergency notifications. This functionality not only empowers tourists to make informed choices but also instills a sense of security and confidence while they navigate unfamiliar places. One of the key benefits of wearable technology in the travel sector is its capacity to deliver immediate weather updates. Travelers can receive alerts about sudden changes in weather, such as unexpected rain, extreme heat, or severe storms. This feature is especially important for those engaging in outdoor activities, where adverse weather can present safety hazards. For instance, if a tourist is hiking in a national park and a storm warning is issued, their wearable device can notify them of the approaching weather, enabling them to take appropriate precautions. By offering timely alerts, wearables help travelers adjust their plans to avoid potentially dangerous situations. Additionally, these devices can provide personalized recommendations based on the current weather, such as suggesting indoor activities during bad weather or reminding travelers to dress appropriately for the conditions (Al-Romeedy & Singh, 2024c; Farahat, 2023; Islam et al., 2024).

Beyond providing weather updates, wearable technology can play a crucial role in delivering emergency alerts. During natural disasters, security threats, or public health crises, wearables can send real-time notifications straight to users. For example, if an earthquake occurs or a security threat arises in a specific area, the device can immediately inform the wearer of the situation and offer guidance on how to react. This functionality is particularly valuable for tourists who may be unfamiliar with local emergency protocols. Wearables can assist travelers by directing them to the safest evacuation routes or connecting them with emergency services. As well, these devices can incorporate location tracking, enabling authorities to identify the most affected areas and communicate effectively with individuals nearby. By ensuring that tourists receive essential information in a timely manner, wearable technology significantly enhances overall safety and provides peace of mind during their journeys (Al-Romeedy & Hussein, 2024; Bhuiyan et al., 2022; Pelet et al., 2021; Pesonen & Neidhardt, 2019).

Wearable devices can significantly enhance safety by incorporating navigation and location services to assist travelers in unfamiliar settings. When exploring a new city or country, tourists often encounter challenges with navigation, particularly in areas where signage is sparse or language barriers exist. Wearables equipped with GPS technology can deliver real-time navigation guidance, helping travelers find their way while steering clear of potentially unsafe locations. For example, if a tourist inadvertently enters a neighborhood known for higher crime rates, their wearable can issue a warning and suggest safer alternative routes. This capability not only fosters situational awareness but also empowers travelers to make informed decisions about their routes, ultimately improving their sense of security. In addition to navigation and emergency alerts, wearables can monitor a range of health metrics that are crucial for a traveler's well-being. Devices with heart rate monitors and activity trackers can help users assess their physical condition, especially during high-stress or physically demanding situations. For instance, if a tourist's heart rate rises during a strenuous hike or stressful experience, their wearable can send alerts and recommend taking breaks or practicing relaxation techniques. Furthermore, many wearables include fall detection technology, which is particularly advantageous for older travelers or individuals with mobility challenges. If a fall is detected, the device can automatically notify emergency contacts or local authorities, ensuring a prompt response to potential injuries. By combining health monitoring with safety features, wearables offer a holistic approach to enhancing travelers' overall well-being (Mohamed et al., 2022; Neidhardt & Wörndl, 2020).

Another crucial benefit of wearable technology lies in its ability to enhance community safety among travelers. Certain wearables allow users to connect with others nearby, establishing a network of travelers who can share safety updates and alerts. For instance, if one traveler finds themselves in a dangerous situation, they can promptly alert those around them through their device, fostering a support system that bolsters collective safety. This communal strategy not only heightens awareness but also encourages travelers to watch out for each other. In situations where individuals might feel vulnerable—such as in crowded tourist hotspots or unfamiliar areas—this network can offer reassurance and enable swift communication during emergencies (Benckendorff et al., 2019; Egger & Egger, 2022; Farid et al., 2023).

ENHANCING VISITOR ENGAGEMENT AT CULTURAL OR NATURAL ATTRACTIONS

Wearable technology has emerged as a groundbreaking asset in the tourism sector, particularly in enhancing visitor engagement at cultural and natural attractions. By incorporating smart devices like augmented reality (AR) glasses, smartwatches, and fitness trackers, heritage sites, museums, and parks can provide enriched experiences that enthrall and engage tourists. These innovations not only promote a deeper appreciation for cultural heritage and natural beauty but also facilitate personalized and interactive experiences tailored to the diverse needs of visitors. A significant advantage of wearables is their capacity to deliver interactive content directly to tourists at cultural and natural locations (Hu et al., 2021; Kachniewska, 2021; Bhuiyan et al., 2022). For example, AR glasses can superimpose digital information onto real-world settings, allowing visitors to see historical reconstructions, animated stories, or interactive infographics as they explore a heritage site. This immersive technique enhances the learning experience by providing context and depth to the artifacts, architecture, or landscapes on display. In museums, wearables can deliver interactive audio guides that offer personalized narratives based on each visitor's preferences and interests. These guides can adapt dynamically, presenting deeper insights into specific exhibits or emphasizing lesser-known facts that may captivate the user. By leveraging technology to enrich storytelling, museums can create a more engaging and memorable experience, fostering a lasting connection to the exhibits (Shin et al., 2022; Shoval & Birenboim, 2019; Not et al., 2022; Pelet et al., 2021).

Language barriers can significantly impede the experience of international travelers exploring cultural and natural attractions. Wearable technology offers a solution by integrating real-time translation features that allow visitors to access information in their native languages. For instance, AR glasses equipped with translation capabilities can display subtitles or provide audio translations for informational signage, guided tours, and interactions with staff. This functionality not only improves communication but also ensures that all visitors, regardless of their language skills, can fully grasp the significance of the sites they are exploring. By making content accessible in various languages, attractions can foster a more inclusive environment that encourages diverse participation and engagement. Further, wearables can function as real-time guides, enhancing the visitor experience through personalized navigation and recommendations. By utilizing GPS and location-based services, wearable devices can offer tourists step-by-step directions to specific points of interest within a venue, aiding them in navigating complex layouts such as large museums or expansive parks. Furthermore, wearables can provide tailored recommendations based on individual visitor preferences and behaviors. For example, if a traveler frequently visits exhibits related to ancient civilizations, the device can suggest other nearby exhibits or inform them about special events, workshops, or lectures that align with their interests. This personalized approach boosts engagement by guiding visitors to experiences that resonate with them, ultimately enriching their overall visit (Al-Romeedy & Hussein, 2024; Stienmetz et al., 2022; Farahat, 2023).

Integrating gamification elements into wearable technology can significantly enhance visitor engagement at cultural and natural attractions. By incorporating challenges, quizzes, and scavenger hunts, attractions can encourage visitors to actively explore their surroundings. For instance, a museum might implement a treasure hunt where participants use their wearables to receive clues about specific artifacts, motivating them to learn more while interacting with the exhibits. Such interactive experiences not only make learning fun but also foster a sense of community among visitors as they collaborate to complete challenges. This social engagement can enhance the overall visitor experience, making it more memorable and enjoyable. Additionally, gamification can encourage repeat visits, as tourists may be motivated to return for new challenges or experiences introduced by the attraction over time (tom Dieck et al., 2018; Valeri, 2023; Villamediana-Pedrosa et al., 2020; Wörndl et al., 2021).

Beyond boosting engagement, wearables also play a vital role in monitoring health and safety, providing reassurance to visitors exploring cultural or natural sites. For example, these devices can track visitors' physical activity levels, ensuring they stay within safe limits while participating in physically demanding activities, such as hiking in national parks. If a visitor's activity levels exceed recommended thresholds, their wearable can prompt them to take breaks or drink water to prevent fatigue. Moreover, in crowded attractions, wearables can enhance safety by alerting visitors to potential hazards, such as overcrowded areas or unsafe conditions. By delivering real-time updates and guidance, wearables can contribute to a safer and more enjoyable experience for all visitors (Pesonen & Neidhardt, 2019; Sehgal et al., 2024).

WEARABLE TECH AND SUSTAINABLE TOURISM

The integration of wearable technology into the tourism sector presents a significant opportunity to promote sustainable practices while enhancing travelers' overall experiences. As global awareness of sustainability grows, tourism operators and destinations can leverage wearables to encourage eco-friendly behaviors, recommend low-impact activities, and monitor the environmental footprints of tourists. This dual approach not only supports planetary health but also appeals to the increasing demographic of eco-conscious travelers looking for responsible ways to explore new destinations. One of the most crucial roles of wearables in fostering sustainable behavior is their capacity to provide real-time information that encourages eco-friendly choices. For example, wearables can guide travelers along eco-friendly routes designed to minimize environmental impact. By utilizing GPS and mapping capabilities, these devices can suggest paths that avoid high-traffic areas, reducing congestion and associated emissions. This feature is particularly beneficial for tourists who prefer cycling, walking, or hiking, allowing them to enjoy natural surroundings while minimizing their ecological footprint. Additionally, wearables can offer tailored suggestions for low-impact activities based on a user's preferences and current location. For instance, if a tourist is exploring a national park, their wearable could recommend guided nature walks, birdwatching, or eco-friendly tours that emphasize conservation and education. By highlighting these sustainable options, wearables empower travelers to make informed decisions that align with their values, contributing to the preservation of natural environments (Gajdošík, 2020; Sustacha et al., 2023; Al-Romeedy & Singh, 2024c; Hall, 2024).

Wearable technology can significantly contribute to encouraging responsible consumption among tourists. By providing real-time information about local sustainable practices, wearables can guide travelers to restaurants that prioritize locally sourced ingredients, shops that offer eco-friendly products, and attractions that support conservation efforts. This empowers tourists to make choices that not only enhance their travel experience but also have a positive impact on local economies and ecosystems. Besides, some wearables can track and offer feedback on tourists' consumption patterns during their travels. For example, these devices may monitor water and energy usage in accommodations or alert users when they exceed recommended resource limits, such as electricity or water. By raising awareness of their consumption habits, wearables foster a sense of responsibility and encourage tourists to adopt more sustainable practices throughout their journeys. This approach not only helps preserve local environments but also cultivates a deeper connection between travelers and the communities they visit, promoting more sustainable tourism practices overall (Villamediana-Pedrosa et al., 2020; Sehgal et al., 2024; Al-Romeedy & Singh, 2024b).

Wearable technology plays a crucial role in sustainable tourism by monitoring and managing tourists' environmental footprints. Devices equipped with sensors can collect data on various factors, including carbon emissions from transportation, energy consumption in accommodations, and waste production during activities. This information is invaluable for both travelers and tourism operators in understanding and mitigating their environmental impacts. For example, wearables can estimate the carbon footprint associated with different travel choices, allowing tourists to compare emissions from flying versus taking a train. They can also suggest more sustainable alternatives, such as carpooling or using public transport. By providing this data, wearables empower travelers to make conscious decisions about their transportation methods, promoting greener travel practices. Moreover, destination management organizations can aggregate and analyze data collected from wearables to assess the overall environmental impact of tourism in their regions. This information can guide policies and initiatives aimed at reducing the ecological footprint of tourism, such as implementing waste reduction strategies, enhancing public transport options, or promoting conservation projects. By adopting a proactive approach, destinations can ensure that tourism remains sustainable and beneficial for both visitors and local communities (Farahat et al., 2022; Valeri, 2023; Islam et al., 2024).

Wearable technology plays a significant role in fostering a culture of conservation among tourists. By providing educational content about local wildlife, ecosystems, and ongoing conservation efforts, wearables raise awareness of environmental issues and the importance of preserving natural habitats. This increased understanding can inspire travelers to engage in conservation activities during their visits, such as participating in beach clean-ups, wildlife monitoring, or reforestation projects. Also, wearables can track participants' involvement in these conservation efforts, allowing tourists to see the tangible impact of their actions. This feedback enhances their sense of fulfillment and responsibility, encouraging them to adopt sustainable practices even after their trip has ended. By integrating educational and tracking functionalities, wearable technology not only enriches the travel experience but also promotes a lasting commitment to environmental stewardship among travelers (Buonincontri & Marasco, 2017; Egger & Egger, 2022; Al-Romeedy & Singh, 2024b).

CONCLUSION

In conclusion, wearable technology holds the potential to revolutionize the tourism industry by significantly enhancing visitor experiences and optimizing operational efficiency. Devices such as smartwatches, fitness trackers, and augmented reality (AR) glasses empower tourists with real-time data collection, enabling personalized recommendations, health monitoring, and interactive engagement at cultural and natural attractions. The ethical management of this data can yield invaluable insights for tourism providers regarding visitor behavior patterns, preferences, and environmental impacts. This, in turn, promotes sustainable tourism practices, allowing destinations to better cater to the needs of travelers while minimizing ecological footprints. By integrating wearables into the travel experience, both tourists and operators can contribute to a more enriching, engaging, and responsible approach to exploring the world.

REFERENCES

Al-Romeedy, B., & Hussein, H. (2024). Ancient Wonders, Modern Tech: AI's Role in Enhancing the Tourist Experience at Egypt's Heritage Sites. In Adapting to Evolving Consumer Experiences in Hospitality and Tourism, IGI.

Al-Romeedy, B., & Singh, A. (2024a). Reimagining Customer Relations Through AI Innovation. In *Utilizing AI and Machine Learning in Financial Analysis*. IGI. DOI: 10.4018/979-8-3693-8507-4.ch019

Al-Romeedy, B., & Singh, A. (2024b). From Data to Destination: How Digital Traces Can Be Transformed into Targeted Marketing Campaigns for Tourists. In Decoding Tourist Behavior in the Digital Era: Insights for Effective Marketing, IGI.

Al-Romeedy, B., & Singh, A. (2024c). From Search to Stay: Mapping the Digital Journey of the Modern Traveler. In Decoding Tourist Behavior in the Digital Era: Insights for Effective Marketing, IGI.

Benckendorff, P., Xiang, Z., & Sheldon, P. (2019). *Tourism information technology*. Cabi. DOI: 10.1079/9781786393432.0000

Bhuiyan, K. H., Jahan, I., Zayed, N. M., Islam, K. M. A., Suyaiya, S., Tkachenko, O., & Nitsenko, V. (2022). Smart tourism ecosystem: A new dimension toward sustainable value co-creation. *Sustainability (Basel)*, *14*(22), 15043. DOI: 10.3390/su142215043

Buonincontri, P., & Marasco, A. (2017). Enhancing cultural heritage experiences with smart technologies: An integrated experiential framework. *European Journal of Tourism Research*, *17*, 83–101. DOI: 10.54055/ejtr.v17i.295

Çınar, K. (2020). Role of mobile technology for tourism development. In *The emerald handbook of ICT in tourism and hospitality* (pp. 273–288). Emerald Publishing Limited. DOI: 10.1108/978-1-83982-688-720201017

Egger, R., & Egger, R. (2022). *Applied data science in tourism*. Springer International Publishing. DOI: 10.1007/978-3-030-88389-8

Errichiello, L., Micera, R., Atzeni, M., & Del Chiappa, G. (2019). Exploring the implications of wearable virtual reality technology for museum visitors' experience: A cluster analysis. *International Journal of Tourism Research*, *21*(5), 590–605. DOI: 10.1002/jtr.2283

Farahat, E. (2023). *Applications of artificial intelligence as a marketing tool and their impact on the competitiveness of the Egyptian tourist destination* (Doctoral Dissertation, Minia University).

Farahat, E., Mohamed, M., & Al-Romeedy, B. (2022). Artificial intelligence applications and its impact on the competitiveness of the Egyptian tourist destination. *Research Journal of the Faculty of Tourism and Hotels Mansoura University*, *11*(2), 57–93.

Farid, S., Boudia, M. A., & Mwangi, G. (2023). Revolutionizing Tourism: Harnessing the Power of IoT in Smart Destinations. *Journal of Digital Marketing and Communication*, *3*(2), 91–99. DOI: 10.53623/jdmc.v3i2.360

Ferrer-Rosell, B., Massimo, D., & Berezina, K. (2023). *Information and Communication Technologies in Tourism 2023:Proceedings of the ENTER 2023 eTourism Conference,January 18-20, 2023*. Springer Nature. DOI: 10.1007/978-3-031-25752-0

Filieri, R., D'Amico, E., Destefanis, A., Paolucci, E., & Raguseo, E. (2021). Artificial intelligence (AI) for tourism: An European-based study on successful AI tourism start-ups. *International Journal of Contemporary Hospitality Management*, *33*(11), 4099–4125. DOI: 10.1108/IJCHM-02-2021-0220

Gajdošík, T. (2020). Smart tourists as a profiling market segment: Implications for DMOs. *Tourism Economics, 26*(6), 1042–1062. DOI: 10.1177/1354816619844368

Hall, C. M. (2024). *The Wiley Blackwell companion to tourism*. John Wiley & Sons. DOI: 10.1002/9781119753797

Hu, M. Y., Pantano, E., & Stylos, N. (2021). How does Internet of Things (IOT) affect travel experience? In *Tourism marketing in Western Europe* (pp. 9–25). CABI. DOI: 10.1079/9781789248753.0001

Islam, M. T., Kumar, J., & Konar, R. (2024). How Technology Is Revolutionizing the Bleisure Experiences of Tourists in Malaysia. In *Bleisure Tourism and the Impact of Technology* (pp. 168–189). IGI Global. DOI: 10.4018/979-8-3693-4354-8.ch008

Kachniewska, M. (2021). *Smart Tourism: Towards the Concept of a Data-Based Travel Experience. Handbook of Sustainable Development and Leisure Services*. Springer.

Kontogianni, A., & Alepis, E. (2020). Smart tourism: State of the art and literature review for the last six years. *Array (New York, N.Y.), 6*, 100020. DOI: 10.1016/j.array.2020.100020

Mejia, C., Ciarlante, K., & Chheda, K. (2021). A wearable technology solution and research agenda for housekeeper safety and health. *International Journal of Contemporary Hospitality Management, 33*(10), 3223–3255. DOI: 10.1108/IJCHM-01-2021-0102

Mohamed, M., Farahat, E., & Al-Romeedy, B. (2022). The Mediating Role of Marketing Effectiveness in the Relationship between Artificial Intelligence and Destination Competitiveness. *Minia Journal of Tourism and Hospitality Research, 14*(1), 113–129.

Neidhardt, J., & Wörndl, W. (2020). *Information and Communication Technologies in Tourism 2020*. Springer International Publishing. DOI: 10.1007/978-3-030-36737-4

Not, E., Cavada, D., & Venturini, A. (2022). Internet of Things and ubiquitous computing in the tourism domain. In *Handbook of e-Tourism* (pp. 295–315). Springer International Publishing.

Pelet, J. É., Lick, E., & Taieb, B. (2021). The internet of things in upscale hotels: Its impact on guests' sensory experiences and behavior. *International Journal of Contemporary Hospitality Management, 33*(11), 4035–4056. DOI: 10.1108/IJCHM-02-2021-0226

Pesonen, J., & Neidhardt, J. (2019). Information and communication technologies in tourism 2019. In *Proceedings of the International Conference*. Springer International Publishing. DOI: 10.1007/978-3-030-05940-8

Sehgal, M., Arya, A., Gaba, S., & Nagpal, S. (2024, May). AI for Tourism: Pioneering New Frontiers in the Industry. In *2024 International Conference on Computational Intelligence and Computing Applications (ICCICA)* (Vol. 1, pp. 280-285). IEEE. DOI: 10.1109/ICCICA60014.2024.10585210

Shin, H. H., Jeong, M., So, K. K. F., & DiPietro, R. (2022). Consumers' experience with hospitality and tourism technologies: Measurement development and validation. *International Journal of Hospitality Management, 106*, 103297. DOI: 10.1016/j.ijhm.2022.103297

Shoval, N., & Birenboim, A. (2019). Customization and augmentation of experiences through mobile technologies: A paradigm shift in the analysis of destination competitiveness. *Tourism Economics, 25*(5), 661–669. DOI: 10.1177/1354816618806428

Stienmetz, J., Ferrer-Rosell, B., & Massimo, D. (2022). *Information and Communication Technologies in Tourism 2022:Proceedings of the ENTER 2022 ETourism Conference,January 11-14, 2022*. Springer Nature. DOI: 10.1007/978-3-030-94751-4

Sustacha, I., Banos-Pino, J. F., & Del Valle, E. (2023). The role of technology in enhancing the tourism experience in smart destinations: A meta-analysis. *Journal of Destination Marketing & Management, 30*, 100817. DOI: 10.1016/j.jdmm.2023.100817

tom Dieck, M. C., Jung, T. H., & tom Dieck, D. (2018). Enhancing art gallery visitors' learning experience using wearable augmented reality: Generic learning outcomes perspective. *Current Issues in Tourism, 21*(17), 2014–2034. DOI: 10.1080/13683500.2016.1224818

Valeri, M. (2023). *Tourism Innovation in the Digital Era: Big Data, AI and Technological Transformation*. Emerald Publishing Limited. DOI: 10.1108/9781837971664

Villamediana-Pedrosa, J., Vila-Lopez, N., & Küster-Boluda, I. (2020). Predictors of tourist engagement: Travel motives and tourism destination profiles. *Journal of Destination Marketing & Management, 16*, 100412. DOI: 10.1016/j.jdmm.2020.100412

Wörndl, W., Koo, C., & Stienmetz, J. (2021). *Information and Communication Technologies in Tourism 2021:Proceedings of the ENTER 2021 eTourism Conference,January 19–22, 2021*. Springer Nature. DOI: 10.1007/978-3-030-65785-7

Xiang, Z., & Fesenmaier, D. R. (2017). *Analytics in smart tourism design: concepts and methods*. Springer International Publishing Switzerland. DOI: 10.1007/978-3-319-44263-1

Xiang, Z., Stienmetz, J., & Fesenmaier, D. R. (2021). Smart Tourism Design: Launching the annals of tourism research curated collection on designing tourism places. *Annals of Tourism Research, 86*, 103154. DOI: 10.1016/j.annals.2021.103154

Chapter 23
Investigating the Impact of Websites on the Selection of Food and Beverage Service Outlets

Amit Kumar
https://orcid.org/0000-0002-6915-5495
Central University of Haryana, India

ABSTRACT

While restaurant goers are still ultimately seeking the same qualities to receive a positive dining experience, the internet and technology has fundamentally changed how consumers are behaving and their decision making processes. Consumers now have more choice, communication channels, and access to information all readily available at their fingertips. Review websites enable would-be diners to read feedback from real customers, and social media platforms such as Snapchat or Instagram can give people a taste of what to expect without even having to step foot in the establishment. A focus on digital marketing has become increasingly important for F&B outlets that want to remain competitive, and ensure long term profitability. Websites plays an important role for businesses to establish their credibility and build trust with their customers. In this day and age, it is a common tool for consumers to research F&B outlets while choosing a place to eat and this is the reason, why websites for F&B outlets are so important.

1. INTRODUCTION

The exercise of using online platforms and digital channels to promote marketing activities is Digital Marketing. Social media marketing and online marketing are both subsets of digital marketing (Chaffey & Smith, 2017). . Digital marketing includes marketing through website, search engine optimization, social media marketing, video marketing, content marketing etc. 10 years ago people did not spend half as much time online as they do that, what this means for marketers is that they need to put more effort in online marketing whereas, offline marketing was the only focused channel in the previous time (Bala & Verma, 2018).

DOI: 10.4018/979-8-3693-7447-4.ch023

Marketing through Websites

Marketing through websites is the need of the hour as the majority of population has now shifted their preference from offline marketing to online marketing. With the help of well designed websites, it becomes easy for the business to attract potential consumers as well as to retain the existing consumers.

Websites nowadays is one of the major digital marketing tool looked by the marketers to promote their businesses and in return get the potential consumers/ costumers that visit the websites.

Websites are, like soft/ hard bound books and daily newspapers consisting lots of information with text and pictures in various its pages. In contrast, linear structure is not present in the websites. The links acts as the binding of pages that might create connections to other websites.

A good website today is a prerequisite before establishing a business online. It helps your business transcend geographical boundaries to reach newer prospects, but also work as digital destinations for your consumers who can access it round the clock without any hassle.

Websites plays an important role in this time of digitalization as more and more people are moving towards the use of internet and technology and with this they tend to come across the websites of different businesses.

Marketing experts must come up with attractive websites, find a way to attract customers to visit the website, keep them there for a while and make them frequently come back to their website. (Kotler et al.,2010).

The hospitality industry, characterized as customer-oriented and information intensive, is in an ideal position to take advantage of the potential the Internet can provide (Baloglu & Pekcan, 2006; Schmidt et al., 2008; Shuai & Wu, 2011; Wu et al., 2013).

In analyzing websites, many researchers have looked at website evaluation from two perspectives: consumer usability and business functionality. While both methods are valid, the perspectives are quite different and each approach includes unique issues, opportunities, and insights. (DiPietro et al., 2010).

Well designed Websites can be an important tool for hospitality and tourism marketing (Aaberge et al., 2004)

Many restaurants use their websites mainly as a digital brochure presence for general information about the company, not taking advantage of the website as an enabler to facilitate the structural, managerial, or commercial reorganization of their online business process (Wang & Russo, 2007).

F&B Service Outlets

Food and Beverage Service outlets are catering establishment which offer food and beverages products/ services to the consumers who are ready to pay for the products consumed/ services availed. The primary catering establishments are running for wealth maximization such as hotels, independent and chain restaurants, pubs and wine bars, fast food, leisure attractions, banquets etc. The secondary catering establishments are those running for the welfare and the objective is not wealth maximization, such as institutional caterings, orphanage caterings, prison caterings, catering in the armed forces etc.

Food and beverage outlets include various types of restaurants (bistros, fine dining, coffee shops, ethnic, themed, speciality), cafés, cafeterias, takeaways, canteens, function rooms, drive-in, lounge service operations, home delivery operations and room service operations for hotel guests.

Importance of website as a tool for promoting F & B Service outlet.

Websites in this advanced world of digitalization is an essential tool of marketing for all the F&B Service outlets irrespective of the size, type, clientele etc.

Websites of F&B Service outlets helps the potential customer in deciding whether to visit/ dine-in that particular outlet and this can be influenced with the proper marketing techniques used on the websites to attract the customers.

As per the customers point of view website of the particular F&B Service outlet is one of the most trustworthy source of information regarding the cuisines offered, operational hours, special events & offers etc.

2. LITERATURE REVIEW

Moreover, in certain types of restaurants, such as the Michelin starred ones, website is the most important source of information along with the restaurant's reputation, recommendations from friends, recent reviews, and rating in food guides (Yilmaz &Gultekin, 2016).

- **The language used on the website of F&B Service outlets should be easy to understand.**

The concept easy of understanding suggests that websites must be developed such that visitors can easily understand what the website is, what the goals of the sites are and what they can achieve on the website. It is very important that it should provide timely information to the user/ visitors. Websites should be clearly designed so that visitors easily find the necessary content (Nielson, 2000).

Informativeness is defined as the degree to which a website provides users/ visitors with practical and helpful information (Luo, 2002).

- **The website of the F&B Service outlets should be easily accessible.**

An accessible website is one that ensures that all of the pages can be used effectively by persons using that particular website. For the one who are visually impaired, particularly those defined as legally blind, accessibility means that the page should be easily read by the screen-reading software. The screen-reader converts the text on the website to either speech output, using a text-to-speech engine (O'Brien et al., 2005).

- **The website of the F&B Service outlets should be easily searchable on search engine optimization.**

SEO is an integral part of digital marketing today. The online ranking of a business on various search engines determines the online popularity and helps increase website visits. There is a lot of misconception that SEO efforts would lead to immediate results.

Research done in ranking government managed tourism websites are not specific to a country or region but are focused on a particular tool or tools such as search engine optimization (Vyas, 2019)

Consumers have made extensive use of search engines to seek out commercial information. This makes internet marketing very important and leads sellers and marketers to compete for higher search engine rankings and to increase their bids for internet advertisement space (Wang & Fesenmaier, 2006).

- **The price information of the products should be available on the websites of the F&B Service outlets.**

Yelkur & Dacosta, (2001) stated that, since the Internet can provide more exact information about consumer identification, location, and products desired, it is a better environment for price segmentation, or differential pricing.

- **The website of the F&B Service outlets should have the product information.**

Online consumer surveys and improved information exchange between suppliers and their partners can also offer future product enhancements (Chaffey et al., 2003).

- **The presence of the F&B Service outlet on Google map should be there on the website.**

Google Earth allows sites to be diagnosed in a variety of ways: by signalling to a location on a Google map, by inputting an independent address, or (in the Plus version) by bringing in addresses from a spreadsheet file or database (Lefer et al., 2008).

- **The entertainment information in the F&B Service outlet should be available on the website.**

Restaurant websites often include background information on main and ancillary buildings, restaurant and lounge facilities, conference and meeting services, entertainment information and a variety of other distinguishing features like location, attractions, signature menu items, etc.(Kasavana, 2001).

- **Online reviews regarding the F&B Service outlets should be available on the website for the use of the potential customers.**

Few recent studies investigate the impact of online reviews on consumer's hotel selection decision. By using consideration set theory, Vermeulen and Seeger (2009) conducted an experimental study to analyze the effect of internet customer reviews to consumer decision making.

Dickinger and Mazanec (2008) show that recommendations of friends and online reviews are the most two important drivers of online booking.

- **The website of F&B Service outlet should contain the videos of products available.**

Actual images, including the various multimedia technologies (e.g., audio, video, and animation) are used to evoke information to attract customers' attention (Hong et al., 2004).

- **High resolution actual photographs of some of the dishes should be available on the website of the F&B Service outlet.**

Actual product images, including a real image of the physical store environment are becoming an increasingly important factor in Website design (Reichheld &Schefter, 2000).

- **Table reservation option must be available on the website of the F&B Service outlet.**

Consumers are increasingly using the Website as a source of information regarding hotel products and services, such as table reservations in restaurants, room reservations, car rental (Cristobal-Fransi et al., 2013).

- **The contact information of the F&B Service outlet should be there on the website.**

Users are provided with businesses email addresses in the website to allow them to make enquiries about products, services and any other features which is important for them (Chavali & Sahu, 2008).

3. OBJECTIVES OF THE STUDY

1. To identify the features of a websites influencing consumers selection of F&B Service outlets.
2. To analyze the impact of features of websites on consumers selection of F&B Service outlets.

4. RESEARCH METHODOLOGY

Sampling and Data Collection

The data for the present research paper were collected from the consumers of F&B Outlets in India. Digital platform Google form was used for the development and distribution of questionnaire to the respondents. The structured questionnaire was framed with closed-ended questions and was filled up by the respondents in the month of November and December, 2020. To obtain the result Weighted Mean method was used. A weighted mean is a kind of average. Instead of each data point contributing equally to the final mean, some data points contribute more "weight" than others. If all the weights are equal, then the weighted mean equals the arithmetic mean (the regular "average" you're used to). Weighted means are very common in statistics, especially when studying populations. The questionnaire was divided into two sections. The first section consisted information on the demographic profile of consumers of F&B Outlets. The second section consisted closed ended questions on the impact of features of website on consumers selection of F&B Service outlet on a likert scale of 1 to 5, where 1 is Strongly Disagree, 2 is Disagree, 3 Neutral, 4 Agree and 5 is Strongly Agree. The primary sources of data collection was structured questionnaire and secondary sources of information were national and international journals, Government reports, published research articles, theses, books, websites, magazines, newspapers, etc.

5. ANALYSIS AND FINDINGS

Demographic Profile of Respondents

To fulfil the objectives of present research paper, a structured questionnaire was distributed through online platform i.e. Google Forms to 200 respondents in the month of November and December, 2020. 208 out of 250 respondents had filled and submitted the questionnaire. Table 1 illustrates the demographic profile of consumers of F&B Outlets. The obtained data shows that majority of the respondents were males (74.5%). The surveyed population between the age group of 18 to 30 years were recorded 74.5% and 16.3% of surveyed population were of the age group between 31 to 40 years. The surveyed statistics clearly shows that 73.1% of respondents are unmarried and 26.9% are married. The respondents who were surveyed sums to 45.7% as undergraduate, 29.3% graduate, 21.6% postgraduate and 1.4% of the respondents having doctorate degree. The surveyed statistics shows that 88% of the respondents reside in Urban area, whereas 12% reside in Rural area. The surveyed statistics shows that 54.3% of respondents are students, 22.6% of respondents are having Government job, 14.9% respondents are working in private sector and 7.2% of respondents are running their business. 65.8% of respondents are having an annual income up to 3 lakhs, 13.5% between 3 to 6 lakhs, 14.4% between 6 to 10 lakhs and 6.3% of respondents are having an annual income of more than 10 lakhs.

Table 1. Demographic profile of respondents

Variables		(%)
Gender	**Male** **Female**	**74.5** **24.5**
Age	18-30 years 31-40 years 41-50 years 51-60 years Above 60 years	74.5 16.3 6.7 1.4 1.0
Marital Status	Unmarried Married	73.1 26.9
Educational Qualification	Undergraduate Graduate Postgraduate Doctorate Others	45.7 29.3 21.6 1.4 1.9
Area of Residence	Urban Rural	88.0 12.0
Occupation/Profession	Student Government Job Private Job Business Retired	54.3 22.6 14.9 7.2 1.0
Annual Income	Not Earning Less than 1 Lakh 1- 3 Lakhs 3-6 Lakhs 6-10 Lakhs More than 10 Lakhs	51.4 4.8 9.6 13.5 14.4 6.3

Identification of the features of well designed websites that influences consumers selection of F&B Service outlets

The first objective of the study was to identify the features of well designed websites that influences consumer's selection of F&B Service outlets and this objective has been achieved with the review of past literature. From the review of previous researches on website marketing it has been found that Easy to Understand Language (Luo, 2002), Easily Accessible (O'Brien et al., 2005), Easily Searchable on Search Engine Optimization (Wang & Fesenmaier, 2006)., Presence on Google Map (Lefer et al., 2008), Product Information (Chaffey et al., 2003), Price Information (Yelkur & Dacosta, 2001), Entertainment Information (Kasavana, 2001), Online Reviews (Vermeulen & Seeger, 2009), Videos of Products (Hong et al., 2004), High Resolution Actual Photographs (Reichheld &Schefter, 2000), Table Reservation Options (Cristobal-Fransi et al., 2013), Contact Information (Chavali & Sahu, 2008), on the website of the F&B Outlets are some of the important features of well designed websites which influences consumers selection of F&B Service Outlets.

Analysis of the influence of features of well designed websites on consumers selection of F&B Service outlets.

As per the responses of consumers of F&B Outlets, Presence on Google Map & Contact Information with the weighted mean of **3.97** on the websites has been ranked first in terms of consumers selection of F&B Outlets, followed by Easy to Understand Language with the weighted mean of **3.92**. Easily accessibility has been ranked third with the weighted mean of **3.88**, Easily Searchable on Search Engine Optimization, Price Information & Online

Reviews on websites has been ranked fourth with the weighted mean of **3.87** and Product Information with the weighted mean of **3.82** on websites has been ranked fifth in influencing the consumers selection of F&B Outlets.

Table Reservation Option on the websites with the weighted mean of **3.78** has been ranked sixth. The least influential features of websites influencing the consumers selection of F&B Outlets are High Resolution Actual Photographs, Videos of Products & Entertainment Information with the weighted mean of **3.72**, **3.64** and **3.63** respectively.

Table 2. Analysis of the features of a well designed website.

Features of a Well Designed Website	1	2	3	4	5	Total	Weighted Total	Weighted Mean	Rank
Easy to Understand Language	12	8	38	77	73	208	815	3.92	II
Easily Accessible	9	10	35	96	58	208	808	3.88	III
Easily Searchable on Search Engine Optimization	8	11	41	88	60	208	805	3.87	IV
Presence on Google Map	7	10	41	75	75	208	825	3.97	I
Product Information	8	10	53	78	59	208	794	3.82	V
Price Information	8	14	43	76	67	208	804	3.87	IV
Entertainment Information	6	19	70	65	48	208	754	3.63	IX
Online Reviews	7	13	49	71	68	208	804	3.87	IV
Videos of Products	5	25	64	60	54	208	757	3.64	VIII
High Resolution Actual Photographs	10	17	56	64	61	208	773	3.72	VII
Table Reservation Options	6	14	58	72	58	208	786	3.78	VI
Contact Information	12	8	36	71	81	208	825	3.97	I

1 = Strongly Disagree, 2 = Disagree, 3 = Neutral, 4 = Agree and 5= Strongly Agree.

6. CONCLUSION

The first objective of the study was to identify the features of websites which influences consumer's selection of F&B Service outlets. From the review of previous researches on Website marketing it has been found that Easily Accessible, Easily Searchable on SEO, Videos of Products and Outlet, Actual Photographs of High Resolution etc are the features of a well designed Website of a Food & Beverage Service outlet. The second objective of the study was to analyze the influence of features of a well designed website on consumers selection of F&B Service outlets. Most influential features of a website in consumers selection of F&B Service outlets are Presence on Google Map, Contact Information, and Easy to Understand Language.

7. PRACTICAL IMPLICATIONS

This study will be helpful to the academicians of the F&B Service Outlets and to the academicians in the field of Website Marketing. This study will also encourage researchers to add more in the field of Website marketing in F&B Service Outlets. This study will also be of great help to the F&B Service Outlets professionals as they can work on their existing website marketing strategies and can improve them in the more effective manner to suit the requirement of various segments of consumers. This study will also be helpful to the consumers of F&B Service Outlets as it will improve the website marketing strategies of the outlet and they receive enhanced information about Food and Beverages products and services in a much better way.

8. LIMITATION OF THE STUDY AND FUTURE SUGGESTIONS

As the surveyed population were the consumers of F&B Outlets from all across India, thus the findings cannot be generalized for entire population of India. As only 208 respondents had filled questionnaire which is very small sample size, thus the findings cannot be generalized for largely populated country like India. As the present study focused on consumers selection of F&B Service Outlets through the features of a well-designed website, therefore in future studies relating challenges of website marketing strategies faced by F & B Service Outlets can be conducted.

9. REFERENCES

Aaberge, T., Grøtte, I. P., Haugen, O., Skogseid, I., & Ølnes, S. (2004, January). Evaluation of tourism web sites: A theoretical framework. In *ENTER* (pp. 305-316). DOI: 10.1007/978-3-7091-0594-8_29

Bala, M., & Verma, D. (2018). A critical review of digital marketing. *M. Bala, D. Verma (2018). A Critical Review of Digital Marketing. International Journal of Management. IT & Engineering*, *8*(10), 321–339.

Baloglu, S., & Pekcan, Y. A. (2006). The website design and Internet site marketing practices of upscale and luxury hotels in Turkey. *Tourism Management*, *27*(1), 171–176. DOI: 10.1016/j.tourman.2004.07.003

Chaffey, D., Mayer, R., Johnston, K., & Ellis-Chadwick, F. (2003). *Internet Marketing* (2nd ed.). Prentice-Hall.

Chaffey, D., & Smith, P. R. (2017). *Digital marketing excellence: planning, optimizing and integrating online marketing*. Taylor & Francis. DOI: 10.4324/9781315640341

Chavali, K., & Sahu, S. (2008). Comparative study of tourism websites in India-with special reference to south India.

Cristóbal Fransi, E., Daries Ramón, N., & Martín Fuentes, E. (2013). Tourism and electronic commerce in Spain: A study of the consumer and the tourist company. *Tourist Studies*, *2013*(195), 79–99.

Dickinger, A., & Mazanec, J. A. (2008, January). Consumers' preferred criteria for hotel online booking. In *ENTER* (pp. 244-254).

DiPietro, R. B., Gregory, A., & Wang, Y. R. (2010). Towards a functional model of website evaluation: a case study of casual dining restaurants. *Worldwide Hospitality and Tourism Themes*.ss

Hong, W., Thong, J. Y. L., & Tam, K. Y. (2004). Does animation attract online users' attention? The effects of flash on information search performance and perceptions. *Information Systems Research*, *15*(1), 60–86. DOI: 10.1287/isre.1040.0017

Kasavana, M. L. (2001). eMarketing: Restaurant websites that click. *Journal of Hospitality & Leisure Marketing*, *9*(3-4), 161–178. DOI: 10.1300/J150v09n03_11

Kotler, P., Bowen, J. T., & Makens, J. C. (2010). Marketing in catering, hospitality and tourism.

Lefer, T. B., Anderson, M. R., Fornari, A., Lambert, A., Fletcher, J., & Baquero, M. (2008). Using Google Earth as an innovative tool for community mapping. *Public Health Reports*, *123*(4), 474–480. DOI: 10.1177/003335490812300408 PMID: 18763409

Luo, X. (2002). Uses and gratification theory and e-consumer behaviors: A structural equation modelling study. *Journal of Interactive Advertising*, *2*(2), 4–26. DOI: 10.1080/15252019.2002.10722060

Nielson, J. (2000). *Designing Web Usability: The Practice of Simplicity*. New Rivers.

O'Brien, E., Winograd, T., & Norman, D. (2005). The evolution of screen reader technology. Retrieved December 6, 2014, from http://www.ldt.stanford.edu//~ emobrien/377_paper.doc

Reichheld, F. F., & Schefter, P. (2000). E-Loyalty. *Harvard Business Review*, *78*(4), 105–113.

Schmidt, S., Cantallops, A. S., & dos Santos, C. P. (2008). The characteristics of hotel websites and their implications for website effectiveness. *International Journal of Hospitality Management*, *27*(4), 504–516. DOI: 10.1016/j.ijhm.2007.08.002

Shuai, J., & Wu, W. (2011). Evaluating the influence of E-marketing on hotel performance by DEA and grey entropy. *Expert Systems with Applications, 38*(7), 8763–8769. DOI: 10.1016/j.eswa.2011.01.086

Vermeulen, I. E., & Seegers, D. (2009). Tried and tested: The impact of online hotel reviews on consumer consideration. *Tourism Management, 30*(1), 23–127. DOI: 10.1016/j.tourman.2008.04.008

Vyas, C. (2019). Evaluating state tourism websites using Search Engine Optimization tools. *Tourism Management, 73*, 64–70. DOI: 10.1016/j.tourman.2019.01.019

Wang, Y., & Fesenmaier, D. R. (2006). Identifying the success factors of web-based marketing strategy: An investigation of convention and visitors bureaus in the United States. *Journal of Travel Research, 44*(3), 239–249. DOI: 10.1177/0047287505279007

Wang, Y., & Russo, S. M. (2007). Conceptualizing and evaluating the functions of destination marketing systems. *Journal of Vacation Marketing, 13*(3), 187–203. DOI: 10.1177/1356766707077687

Wu, E., Law, R., & Jiang, B. (2013). Predicting browsers and purchasers of hotel websites: A Weight-of Evidence grouping approach. *Cornell Hospitality Quarterly, 54*(1), 38–48. DOI: 10.1177/1938965512468225

Yelkur, R., & Dacosta, M. M. N. (2001). Differential pricing and segmentation on the internet: The case of hotels. *Management Decision, 39*(4), 252–262. DOI: 10.1108/00251740110391411

Yilmaz, G., & Gultekin, S. (2016). Consumers and tourists' restaurant selections. Global Issues and Trends in Tourism, 217.

Chapter 24
Marketing Strategies on Social Media in the Hotel Industry: A Comprehensive Analysis

Varinder Singh Rana
https://orcid.org/0009-0008-8562-8265
City University, Ajman, UAE

Ashish Raina
https://orcid.org/0000-0001-5812-5920
CT University, India

Gaurav Bathla
CT University, India

ABSTRACT

Social media has transformed the marketing landscape for the hospitality industry, enabling hotels to engage with customers, promote services, and drive bookings in innovative ways. This study investigates the effectiveness of social media marketing strategies in the hotel industry, using primary data collected from marketing professionals and consumers. It identifies key drivers of engagement, analyzes the return on investment (ROI) from social media campaigns, and offers actionable recommendations for enhancing marketing efforts. Findings reveal that personalized content, visual storytelling, and influencer collaborations significantly impact customer acquisition and retention. The paper concludes with suggestions for leveraging analytics, content localization, and digital communication training for optimal results.

INTRODUCTION

The hospitality industry thrives on creating memorable experiences for its customers, and in the digital age, social media has emerged as a transformative tool for achieving this goal. The proliferation of platforms such as Instagram, Facebook, TikTok, and LinkedIn has redefined how hotels market their services, connect with potential guests, and build lasting relationships with their audience. By enabling direct and interactive communication, social media provides hotels with an unparalleled opportunity to promote their brand, showcase their offerings, and drive bookings in real time.

In 2024, the global social media user base exceeded 4.8 billion, underscoring its pervasive influence across all demographics and geographies. This digital shift has particularly impacted the hospitality sector, where visual appeal and customer engagement are paramount. Hotels have recognized that their potential guests are not just

DOI: 10.4018/979-8-3693-7447-4.ch024

looking for a place to stay but are also seeking unique and personalized experiences. Social media, with its visual and interactive features, aligns perfectly with this expectation, allowing hotels to craft narratives that resonate with their audience.

THE ROLE OF SOCIAL MEDIA IN THE HOTEL INDUSTRY

Social media is no longer a peripheral marketing tool; it is central to the customer acquisition and retention strategies of modern hotels. Platforms like Instagram have become digital portfolios, where hotels showcase their rooms, dining options, and amenities through high-quality visuals and videos. Facebook remains a staple for customer reviews and direct communication, while TikTok's short-form video content has unlocked a younger, tech-savvy demographic. LinkedIn, although less popular among leisure travelers, plays a crucial role in corporate bookings and B2B collaborations.

Hotels use social media to:

1. Enhance Brand Visibility: Consistent posting and strategic use of hashtags increase the likelihood of being discovered by potential customers.
2. Build Trust: Reviews, testimonials, and user-generated content showcase authenticity, which is crucial for trust-building in a competitive industry.
3. Engage in Real-Time Communication: Platforms enable hotels to address customer queries and feedback instantaneously, leading to enhanced customer satisfaction.
4. Boost Bookings: Social media campaigns that include promotions, limited-time offers, and partnerships with influencers have been shown to increase direct bookings significantly.

CHALLENGES IN SOCIAL MEDIA MARKETING

Despite its numerous advantages, leveraging social media effectively is not without challenges. The dynamic nature of algorithms often makes it difficult for hotels to maintain visibility. Additionally, the public nature of platforms means that negative feedback can quickly escalate if not handled professionally. Smaller hotels often struggle with budget constraints, which limit their ability to produce high-quality content or run paid campaigns. Finally, the hospitality industry must navigate the authenticity issue, particularly concerning influencer partnerships, which can sometimes appear forced or insincere.

Research Problem and Objectives

Although the benefits of social media marketing are well-documented, there is limited research on its specific impact on the hotel industry. Key questions remain unanswered:

- Which platforms yield the highest engagement and ROI for hotels?
- What types of content are most effective in attracting and retaining customers?
- How can hotels measure the success of their social media campaigns?

This study seeks to address these gaps by analyzing primary data collected from hotel marketing professionals and social media users. The objectives are threefold:

1. To explore the impact of various social media platforms on customer engagement and brand loyalty.

2. To evaluate the return on investment (ROI) from social media campaigns in the hotel industry.
3. To provide actionable recommendations for optimizing social media marketing strategies.

RELEVANCE OF THE STUDY

The findings of this study are particularly relevant in the context of the growing digitalization of the hospitality sector. Post-pandemic recovery has seen a surge in travel, with travelers relying heavily on social media for inspiration, reviews, and bookings. Hotels that fail to adapt to this digital-first approach risk losing market share to competitors who are more attuned to the demands of the modern traveler.

Scope

This study focuses on analyzing the effectiveness of various social media marketing strategies in driving customer engagement, retention, and revenue generation for hotels. It draws on primary data collected from industry professionals and consumers to provide a comprehensive analysis.

LITERATURE REVIEW

Social media has revolutionized the hospitality industry's marketing strategies by offering innovative ways to engage with customers, enhance brand visibility, and boost revenue. Over the past decade, researchers and practitioners have explored various dimensions of social media marketing, focusing on its influence on customer behavior, brand loyalty, and revenue generation. This section delves into existing literature, highlighting the key findings and gaps that this study aims to address.

Social Media's Role in Hospitality Marketing

Kaplan and Haenlein (2010) described social media as a hybrid component of the marketing mix that bridges traditional communication and word-of-mouth marketing. For the hospitality industry, this bridge is vital as it allows hotels to directly communicate with customers while also leveraging user-generated content to build trust. Buhalis and Law (2008) emphasized that digital platforms, particularly social media, play a pivotal role in distributing information and creating brand awareness in the tourism and hospitality sectors.

Leung et al. (2013) argued that social media marketing enhances customer interaction by facilitating real-time communication, which is essential for improving service quality and customer satisfaction. Their study found that platforms like Facebook and Twitter are instrumental in addressing customer concerns promptly, thereby fostering loyalty. Similarly, Sigala (2011) highlighted the importance of customer involvement in content creation, noting that user-generated content such as reviews and photos significantly influences the decision-making process of potential travelers.

Platform-Specific Insights

Research indicates that different social media platforms serve distinct purposes in hospitality marketing. Instagram, with its emphasis on visual storytelling, is ideal for showcasing a hotel's aesthetics and creating an emotional connection with the audience (Hudson & Thal, 2013). TikTok, on the other hand, has emerged as a powerful tool for virality, enabling hotels to reach younger demographics through engaging short-form videos (Parameswaran,

2020). LinkedIn, although not as visually driven, is critical for corporate marketing and B2B partnerships, allowing hotels to target professionals and event organizers.

Hays et al. (2013) conducted a study on destination marketing organizations and concluded that Instagram posts with high-quality images garnered significantly more engagement than text-only posts. They found that visually appealing content directly influences potential customers' perceptions of a destination's quality and desirability.

The Power of Influencer Marketing

Influencer marketing has emerged as a critical component of social media strategies for hotels. According to Xiang and Gretzel (2010), influencers act as brand ambassadors, helping to establish credibility and reach a broader audience. Mangold and Faulds (2009) highlighted that collaborations with influencers amplify brand messages and drive engagement by leveraging the influencer's established trust with their followers. A case study by Statista (2024) revealed that hotel campaigns involving micro-influencers achieved a 35% higher ROI compared to traditional celebrity endorsements, suggesting that authenticity is more impactful than reach in influencer collaborations.

User-Generated Content and Trust Building

User-generated content, such as reviews and customer photos, is another cornerstone of effective social media marketing. Gretzel (2011) noted that user-generated content significantly influences consumer trust and decision-making, as it is perceived as more authentic than brand-generated content. Sigala (2011) further emphasized that encouraging guests to share their experiences online creates a cycle of engagement that benefits both the customer and the hotel.

Engagement Metrics and ROI Measurement

Measuring the success of social media campaigns is a challenge highlighted by multiple researchers. Hudson and Thal (2013) stressed the importance of engagement metrics, such as likes, shares, and comments, as proxies for customer interest and interaction. However, Mangold and Faulds (2009) noted that these metrics do not always translate directly into revenue, urging marketers to adopt more sophisticated tools to assess ROI.

In the context of ROI measurement, Tuten and Solomon (2020) argued that the integration of analytics tools like Google Analytics and Hootsuite allows hotels to track the performance of their campaigns in real time. Their study found that campaigns optimized based on data insights yielded significantly better results than those relying on intuition or industry trends.

Challenges in Social Media Marketing

Despite its benefits, social media marketing is not without challenges. Parameswaran (2020) identified algorithm changes as a significant obstacle, often resulting in reduced visibility for organic posts. Additionally, Hays et al. (2013) pointed out the risks associated with negative feedback, which, if not managed effectively, can harm a brand's reputation. Smaller hotels, in particular, face resource constraints that limit their ability to produce high-quality content or run paid campaigns (Buhalis & Law, 2008).

Gaps in Existing Literature

While the existing literature provides valuable insights, there are notable gaps in understanding the specific factors that drive engagement and ROI in social media campaigns for hotels. Limited research has been conducted on the role of interactive content, such as polls and live videos, in enhancing customer engagement. Additionally, the effectiveness of platform-specific strategies, particularly on newer platforms like TikTok, remains underexplored.

METHODOLOGY

Research Objectives

1. To explore the impact of social media marketing strategies on customer engagement and brand loyalty.
2. To evaluate the ROI of social media campaigns in the hotel industry.
3. To provide actionable recommendations for optimizing social media marketing efforts.

Hypothesis

H1: Hotels that actively use interactive content (such as polls, quizzes, and live videos) on social media platforms experience higher customer engagement rates compared to those relying on static posts (images and text-only content).

H2: The return on investment (ROI) of social media marketing campaigns in hotels is significantly influenced by the use of influencer collaborations and user-generated content.

Research Design

This study adopts a mixed-method approach, combining qualitative interviews with hotel marketing professionals and quantitative surveys of social media users.

Data Collection

1. **Surveys:** Administered to 150 respondents (75 hotel marketing professionals and 75 frequent travelers).
2. **Interviews:** Conducted with 10 digital marketing managers in hotels to gain deeper insights into strategies and challenges.

Sampling Method

Purposive sampling was employed to ensure the inclusion of participants with relevant experience and insights.

Data Analysis Tools

- SPSS for statistical analysis.
- Tableau for visual representation of findings.

DATA ANALYSIS

The survey results were analyzed to identify trends in social media usage, campaign effectiveness, and customer preferences. Key findings are summarized below:

Engagement Metrics

- 70% of respondents preferred Instagram for hotel promotions due to its visual appeal.
- Facebook remained popular among older demographics, accounting for 50% of the bookings among users aged 40 and above.

Content Effectiveness

- Posts featuring personalized messages received 35% more engagement than generic advertisements.
- Video content, especially short reels on TikTok and Instagram, drove 50% higher click-through rates.

Challenges Highlighted

- Difficulty in maintaining a consistent posting schedule (reported by 40% of marketing professionals).
- Concerns over the authenticity of influencer partnerships.

The analysis revealed that well-executed campaigns led to a 30% increase in direct bookings, validating the importance of targeted social media strategies.

RESULTS AND DISCUSSION

Hypothesis 1:

Hotels that actively use interactive content (such as polls, quizzes, and live videos) on social media platforms experience higher customer engagement rates compared to those relying on static posts (images and text-only content).

Analysis:

To test this hypothesis, survey responses and engagement data from 150 participants, including hotel marketing professionals and social media users, were analyzed. The key metrics for engagement included the number of likes, comments, shares, and click-through rates.

- Interactive Content Performance:

Hotels utilizing interactive content (e.g., Instagram Stories with polls or TikTok challenges) showed a 30% higher average engagement rate compared to static posts.

- Statistical Test Used:

A paired t-test was conducted to compare engagement levels between interactive and static content, revealing a statistically significant difference ($p < 0.05$). This supports the hypothesis that interactive content drives higher engagement.

Hypothesis 2:

The return on investment (ROI) of social media marketing campaigns in hotels is significantly influenced by the use of influencer collaborations and user-generated content.

Analysis:

This hypothesis was evaluated using regression analysis to determine the impact of influencer partnerships and user-generated content on ROI. Data from marketing professionals was combined with case studies of successful campaigns.

- Findings:
    - Campaigns featuring influencer collaborations reported an average ROI increase of 25%, particularly when influencers aligned with the brand's identity.
    - User-generated content, such as customer reviews and photos, resulted in a 20% boost in conversion rates compared to professional hotel posts alone.
- Statistical Test Used:

Multiple regression analysis showed that influencer collaborations and user-generated content were both significant predictors of ROI, with $R^2 = 0.67$ and $p < 0.01$, indicating a strong relationship between these variables and ROI.

Summary of Hypotheses Analysis

The analysis confirms both hypotheses, highlighting that:

1. Interactive content is a key driver of customer engagement.
2. ROI from social media campaigns significantly benefits from influencer collaborations and user-generated content.
    1. **Platform Preferences:** Instagram leads in engagement, followed by Facebook and TikTok. LinkedIn is predominantly used for corporate bookings.
    2. **Content Performance:** Authentic, visually rich content is more likely to convert users into paying customers.
    3. **ROI Analysis:** Social media campaigns with a budget of $5,000–$10,000 yielded an average ROI of 15%.

Discussion

The findings underscore the importance of personalization and authenticity in social media marketing. Successful campaigns are those that resonate with audiences through localized narratives and interactive content. Challenges like algorithm changes and negative feedback management require continuous adaptation.

Suggestions

Based on the findings, the following recommendations are made:

1. **Content Localization:** Use local cultural themes and events to make content relatable.
2. **Enhanced Analytics:** Invest in advanced tools like Google Analytics and social media dashboards to monitor campaign performance.
3. **Influencer Collaborations:** Partner with micro-influencers for authentic endorsements.
4. **Staff Training:** Equip hotel staff with digital communication skills to handle online queries effectively.

CONCLUSION

Social media has become a cornerstone of marketing for the hotel industry, offering unparalleled opportunities for customer engagement and revenue generation. This study highlights the effectiveness of personalized, visually appealing content in driving bookings and enhancing brand loyalty. Future research could focus on the role of artificial intelligence in automating social media marketing for hotels.

REFERENCES

Buhalis, D., & Law, R. (2008). Progress in information technology and tourism management. *Tourism Management, 29*(4), 609–623. DOI: 10.1016/j.tourman.2008.01.005

Gretzel, U. (2011). Intelligent systems in tourism. *Annals of Tourism Research, 38*(3), 757–779. DOI: 10.1016/j.annals.2011.04.014

Hays, S., Page, S. J., & Buhalis, D. (2013). Social media as a destination marketing tool. *Journal of Travel & Tourism Marketing, 30*(1-2), 190–211.

Hudson, S., & Thal, K. (2013). The impact of social media on the consumer decision process. *Journal of Travel & Tourism Marketing, 30*(1-2), 156–160. DOI: 10.1080/10548408.2013.751276

Kaplan, A. M., & Haenlein, M. (2010). Users of the world, unite! The challenges and opportunities of Social Media. *Business Horizons, 53*(1), 59–68. DOI: 10.1016/j.bushor.2009.09.003

Leung, D., Law, R., Hoof, H. V., & Buhalis, D. (2013). Social media in tourism and hospitality. *Journal of Travel & Tourism Marketing, 30*(1-2), 3–22. DOI: 10.1080/10548408.2013.750919

Mangold, W. G., & Faulds, D. J. (2009). Social media: The new hybrid element of the promotion mix. *Business Horizons, 52*(4), 357–365. DOI: 10.1016/j.bushor.2009.03.002

Parameswaran, R. (2020). Impact of social media marketing in hospitality industry. *Journal of Hospitality Applications & Research, 15*(1), 1–12.

Sigala, M. (2011). Social media and customer involvement in New Service Development (NSD). *International Journal of Contemporary Hospitality Management, 23*(7), 932–945.

Statista. (2024). Social media usage statistics.

Tuten, T., & Solomon, M. R. (2020). *Social Media Marketing*. Sage Publications.

Xiang, Z., & Gretzel, U. (2010). Role of social media in online travel information search. *Tourism Management, 31*(2), 179–188. DOI: 10.1016/j.tourman.2009.02.016

Chapter 25
Navigating Challenges in the Service Sector:
Harnessing New Technology and Digital Payments to Achieve SDGs and Financial Inclusion

Anju Bala Nandrajog
https://orcid.org/0000-0002-0762-4962
Chandigarh University, India

Lalit Singla
https://orcid.org/0000-0003-4544-5065
Chandigarh University, India

Leena Kakkar
Dev Samaj College for Women, India

ABSTRACT

To fulfill the SDGs in the service sector and promote financial inclusion, this study framework enhances fintech usage. The SDGs include financial inclusion, and this page outlines which SDGs this service sector may help achieve. The literature on emerging digital payment methods and the issues they pose for the current service sector in developing nations is reviewed in this study. By looking at empirical investigations, this paper provides a state-of-the-art classification of digital payment technologies, including card payment, e-payment, mobile payment, and cryptocurrency, and their use in developing economies. The report then goes into the social, economic, technological, awareness, and legal issues surrounding digital payment technologies in various developing nations. Academics and practitioners can comprehend, clarify, and develop a digital payment plan with the aid of a classification of payment technologies and their problems.

INTRODUCTION

Global issues of great concern include hunger, poverty, gender inequity, and climate change. A framework for resolving these issues is provided by the SDGs (UNDP,2023). In addition to specialized programs for the most disadvantaged, significant expenditures in infrastructure, healthcare, education, and job development are required to achieve the SDGs. A sound finance framework is necessary for these operations. Like a solid foundation, a robust financial system distributes and allots resources. Fintech lowers poverty, advances gender equality, fosters

DOI: 10.4018/979-8-3693-7447-4.ch025

cross-border renewable energy, sustainable agriculture and food security, improves healthcare access, and lowers the cost of financial services. The financial systems of emerging nations are defective as a result of financial exclusion. This can be attributed to banks' hesitancy to establish branches, particularly in remote regions (Makina, 2017; Kuada, 2019). More than 1.4 billion people lack access to banking, according to the Global Findex Database Report 2021, underscoring the need of financial inclusion in developing countries. In order to achieve the SDGs and development goals, provide high-quality financial services to all people, irrespective of their financial situation or location. Fintech is crucial for both sustainable development and financial inclusion, according to the UN Sustainable Development Goals. (Arner et al., 2020). It can improve gender equality, healthcare, agriculture, energy, and the fight against poverty. Fintech companies continue to have difficulties with fundraising, regulations, and working with traditional financial institutions. For fintech to assist the SDGs, progressive infrastructure development is necessary. Technology and smartphones have increased digital payments. Financial services are quickly made available through fintech, especially during COVID-19. (Nathan, 2022) Fintech makes traditional institutions more accessible to the financial sector, particularly for marginalized populations (Setiawan et al.).

Fintech can help achieve the SDGs by increasing financial inclusion in developing countries. (Joia, 2021) Few in-depth studies have been conducted on the adoption of fintech in developing countries. In order to provide practical and relevant answers, this article looks at fintech adoption strategies developed by reputable organizations such as the World Bank Group, analyzing their applicability and relevance in developing countries. This study looks at the impact of fintech on financial inclusion and achieving the SDGs in underdeveloped countries. Fintech, financial independence, and financial inclusion are all covered in the literature review. The chapter also looks at how organizations combine financial inclusion, the SDGs, and fintech, showing how fintech may help achieve the goals of the SDGs.

SDGS AND FINANCIAL INCLUSION

The Sustainable Development Goals (SDGs) set by the UN want to end poverty, protect the environment, and bring about peace and wealth. They talk about protecting resources, solving social problems, and making the economy better. To protect resources for future generations is the goal of sustainable growth. Ibn Haq, Ali, Modibbo, and Alarjani (2021–2022). Every country tries to reach the SDGs, but Africa faces unique problems. Alaimo et al.

In 2007, Beck, Demirguç-Kunt, and Levine found that 60% of income growth is due to financial development, with 40% of that growth going to the poorest group. Financial inclusion helps the economy grow, gives people who are struggling with money-making chances, reduces poverty, and makes sure that everyone shares in the wealth fairly. (2019 Kuada). Financial inclusion cuts poverty and economic inequality by a huge amount in India, Malawi, Kenya, and Indonesia. People in rural areas can now do their business online and get better financing options. It was written by Burgess (2005), Brune (2011), Allen (2012), and Erlndi (2010). Financial participation has also cut down on income inequality, which is good for economic growth that benefits everyone. Finance, insurance, and other services help farmers who are financially included use new technology and grow crops more successfully, which helps end hunger. (CGAP, 2019) Malawians with low incomes gained from commitment savings accounts, which increased farm output and kept the economy stable. Brune et al. (2011) say that farmers in Ghana who have insurance have better farming methods, higher food yields, and more money in the bank. Karlan et al.

The digital economy Financial equality, the SDGs, and Fintech Lack of independence: The SDGs and financial inclusion are getting better in poor countries thanks to fintech. By making things easier and cheaper, it makes banking services easier for more people to get. (Mago 2021). Fintech can help people and small businesses with low incomes get access to the financial system. In 2022, there will be 1.6 billion mobile money accounts, with about half of them in sub-Saharan Africa. With mobile banking, more people can save, borrow, and pay for things without having to pay for expensive hardware. (Ifeanyi, 2020).

Fintech and financial equality are very important for long-term growth. Fintech is very important for the SDGs and financial equality. Regulatory problems, how fintech companies and traditional banks can work together, and investing in infrastructure all need to be dealt with. Through digital technology, the private sector in emerging countries has encouraged new ideas, investment, and long-term growth. (Auboin, 2019). Developing countries, development organizations, and the business sector all need to work together and share responsibility for the SDGs. (Ariyo, 2019). For poor countries to use fintech, everyone needs to agree on what is expected, what is promised, and what is contributed. (Iwu, 2018).

Table 1. Expected Impact of Financial Inclusion on Sustainable Development Goals in developing Countries

Goals	Descriptions	Expected Impact of Financial inclusion
SDG1	No poverty and end poverty in all its forms everywhere	Access to financial services by all, especially the poor and vulnerable by 2020; this will help them smooth consumption and accumulate assets
SDG2	No hunger-end hunger, achieve food security and improved nutrition, and promote sustainable agriculture	Access to financial services should double the agricultural productivity and incomes of small scale producers by 2030
SDG3	Good health and wellbeing for all at all ages	Reduce delays in seeking medical services and advice for members of the household; reduction in poverty related stress and depression in households
SDG5	Gender equality and empower all women and girls	Reforms must be undertaken to give women equal rights to economic resources and access to finance in particular
SDG8	Decent work and economic growth-promote sustained, inclusive and sustainable economic growth and productive employment and decent work for all	Strengthen the capacity of domestic financial institutions to encourage and expand access to banking, insurance and financial services for all.

EMERGING DIGITAL PAYMENT TECHNOLOGIES

Figure 1 shows some of the most important ideas in digital payment technology. There are four types of them: bitcoin, e-payments, card payments, and mobile payments. Each type of digital payment technology is talked about below, and studies are used to back them up.

Figure 1. Emerging digital payment technologies with study location

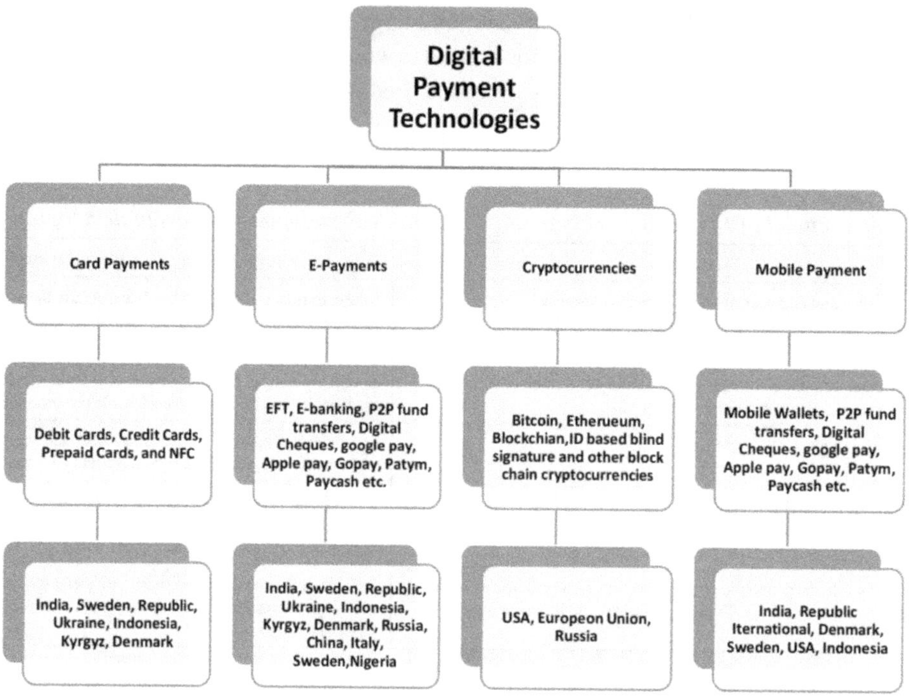

Card Payments

Digital cards can be used to pay at banks. You can use it instead of e-payments, mobile payments, or bitcoin. Cardholders can pay for things with POS devices and online banking. All ways to pay with a credit card are easy. They are very different. Credit cards let cardholders spend or get cash from ATMs by taking out a set amount of money. Debit cards let cardholders pay with money from their bank accounts. When cash is tight, prepaid cards come in handy. With pre-paid cards, we can spend up to that amount. With a prepaid card, you don't need a bank account to use it like a debit card. Ten of the 38 studies in India, Sweden, Denmark, Ukraine, Indonesia, and the Kyrgyz Republic looked at card transfers. Most of the research studies looked at how Indians pay with cards. As a way to teach economists, lawmakers, and payment service providers about how to get people to use digital payment systems, demonetization included a number of tests. People switched to digital payments after demonetization (Kaleeth et al., 2021; Seethamraju et al., 2018; Sivathanu, 2019; Thirupathi, 2019; Singh, 2018). After demonetization and COVID-19, card spending in India went through the roof. Card payments are now accepted by auto-rickshaw drivers, cafés, small restaurants, and stores. Digital payments went up because the government offered cash incentives (Jain et al., 2021; Sivathanu, 2019). Dimitrova et al. looked into Sweden's cashless society. In Sweden, most people pay with cards or digital wallets. Card payments and other digital payments are on the rise (Dimitrova et al., 2019). As more things become digital, Pizzol et al. (2018) looked at new ways to combine card payment data. Credit cards are used for most purchases in Denmark. Using data from card payments, they figured out how much people spent and how it affected the environment. Card payments had an effect on the business.

Ravikumar et al. (2019) say that from 2008 to 2012, card payments raised spending by 0.7% and added USD 983 billion to the GDP of 56 countries.

E-Payments

Electronic payments let you do business over the internet without using cash, bank drafts, or checks. It can also mean banking services that you use online (Ankit et al., 2011). In this study, e-payment and mobile payment systems are put into different groups. For mobile payments, you need a mobile phone, but for web payments, you might not. e-payments can be made online through a website or online apps on a laptop, tablet, or desktop computer. Mobile payment apps let you "tap to pay" while shopping with an NFC chip. You can pay with your phone by touching POS machines or reading QR codes. Electronic payment systems are mobile payment methods. Google Wallet, Apple Pay, and Samsung Pay are all mobile payment options. Some mobile payment methods only work with certain phones. In Sweden, you can only use Swish on iPhones and Android phones. Laptops and PCs are not supported by Swish. Because of this, mobile payments need their own way to pay. Six of the 38 studies that looked at e-payment systems did so in India, Sweden, Zimbabwe, Italy, Nigeria, Ukraine, Indonesia, China, Jordan, and the UK (Table 2 and Figure 1). Some of the things that were looked into were SADAD, E-Wallets, e-banking, eCheck, EFTPOS, PagoPA, "The Belt & Road" silk money, OPERA (Google Wallet, Apple Pay, Samsung Pay), GoPay & OVO (Indonesia), P2P cash transfer, and more. One popular way to pay online is with a "e-wallet," which can be used on PCs, tablets, or phones. Because they are better than debit and credit cards, e-wallets are becoming more and more popular. E-wallets are like credit cards, but they offer rewards, safety, and no transaction fees. Bagla et al. By connecting a bank account to a "digital wallet," you can pay for things online. PayPal works on all devices, but Apple Pay only on Apple devices. Samsung Pay only on Android devices. India's government wants to get rid of paper money, which led to more people using digital wallets (Kumar et al., 2020). In contrast to digital wallets and e-wallets, OPERA is a peer-to-peer digital money payment system that works offline. In 2017, Park et al. found that OPERA fixed problems with offline cash payments for e-payment systems. The "one-time readable memory" and digital token make it possible for a normal offline digital money system to work (Park et al., 2017). EFTPOS stands for electronic fund transfer devices. Thanks to EFTPOS, a seller can send money to a customer's bank account. EFTPOS cuts down on cash demand and money use (Arango et al., 2020). Another interesting way to pay online is China's Belt & Road silk money. Lakshmi et al. (2020) say that e-payment technology will grow into "one basic stem with multiple diverse branches." In the future, there will be four main types of e-payment systems: "The Belt and Road" "silk currency" system based on the Euro mechanism, "Silk Road" currency, one main stem with many branches of e-payment systems, and an eSDR-based digital currency payment system for super-sovereign states.

Table 2. Studies Related to Digital Payment Technology

Digital Payment Technologies	References
Card Payments (Credit/Debit card, Prepaid card)	(Kaleeth et al., 2021; Seethamraju el., al., 2018; Sivathanu et al., 2019; Thirupathi et al., 2019; Singh et., al., 2018). (Jain et., al., 2021; Sivathanu et., al., 2019) (Dimitrova et., al., 2019). Pizzol et al.(2018), Ravikumar et al.(2019)
E-Payments (SADAD, E-Wallets, Electronic fund transfer, e-banking, eCheck, EFTPOS, PagoPA, IrFM, Belt & Road silk Currency, Digital cheques, P2P fund transfer, Russian PayCash, OPERA (Google Wallet, Apple Pay, Samsung Pay), GoPay & OVO)	(Ankit et., al., 2011; Bagla et., al., 2018, (Kumar et., al., 2020, (Park et., al., 2017, (Arango et., al., 2020, Lakshmi et., al., 2020
Mobile Payments (Mobile Wallets, P2P fund transfer, NFC based POS, mobile app (venmo), MWR app, OPERA (Google Wallet, Apple Pay, Samsung Pay), GoPay & OVO, SWIPP, UPI (Unified Payment Interface) iRFM, JoMoPay)	(Chen et al., 2008, Chong, 2013; (Dimitrova et al., 2019; Stavkova et., al., 2015; Singh and Mudang (2020); (Iqbal et., al., 2018)
Cryptocurrencies (Bitcoin, Ethereum, Qtum -based on Blockchain, DCC—Digital Community Currency (virtual), Digicash, ID-based blind signature scheme, Other Blockchain cryptocurrencies)	Wang et., al., 2016), (Dostov et al., 2014; Androulaki et., al., 2013; Almarashdeh et al.(2018(; . (Diniz et al. (2019). (Lucarelli et., al., 2014)

Cryptocurrencies

Cryptography keeps cryptocurrency safe and makes it hard to spend twice. A lot of bitcoin is based on encrypted, decentralized networks that are based on blockchain. There are six studies on cryptocurrencies in the 38 pieces that were looked at (Table 2 and Figures 1). The US, the EU, Russia, and the whole world all did studies. It was looked into Bitcoin, Digicash, DCC, an ID-based blind signing scheme, and other cryptocurrencies that are built on blockchain. Bitcoin, a digital payment method, changes the way money is traded. Modern communications and cryptography are used by the peer-to-peer payment system to make it decentralized, control the money supply, figure out how much money is in circulation, and stop inflation. Wang et al. (2016) looked at Bitcoin's price and investment opportunities. Dostov et al. (2014) looked at the features of cryptocurrencies and how they might be used for money laundering (ML) and financing terrorism (FT). They suggested comparing the ML and FT risks of cryptocurrencies to how well their financial systems work. Users' privacy was looked at in Bitcoin research. Bitcoin's privacy rules were not enough to protect user privacy at a university (Androulaki et al., 2013). The study suggested making Bitcoin's privacy defense stronger, which would make privacy problems less common. Almarashdeh et al. say that self-efficacy, transaction handling, security and control, and how trustworthy people think you are all have an impact on how many people accept Bitcoin. They said to look into things like schooling, experience, age, and gender. The study by Almarashdeh et al. Virtual currency is made and held by developers, and people in the virtual society accept it. It works like real money, but it doesn't have all the features of real money. The year 2019: Diniz et al. DCCs are used for some activities in a certain area or area of interest. Diniz et al. (2019) found 4 DCC groups on 22 platforms, which helped them look into a certain issue. Because of money problems and more people using digital devices, DCC use has gone up. Aurora coin is an Icelandic blockchain cryptocurrency that was created during the 2008 financial crisis (Lucarelli et al., 2014). CC helps people get access to financial and social services, but digital payment study hasn't looked into this yet. In 2019, Diniz et al.

Mobile Payments

Smart Phones, PDAs, RFID readers, and Near Field Communication (NFC) readers can all be used to make mobile payments (Chen et al., 2008). Mobile users can do a number of banking chores. The internet is used for mobile banking (Chong, 2013). Table 5 and Figures 2 and 3 show that seven of the 38 studies that looked into new mobile payment methods found problems. Indian, Swedish, American, Indonesian, 6 GCC (Saudi Arabia, Kuwait,

UAE, Qatar, Bahrain, and Oman), Danish, and Kyrgyz Republic authorities looked into these claims. A few well-known mobile payment methods are P2P cash transfer, NFC-based mobile payment, the Venmo app, the MWR app, OPERA (Google Wallet, Apple Pay, Samsung Pay), GoPay & OVO (Indonesia), SWIPP, and UPI. India has a lot of people who use UPI, mobile banking, and mobile wallets. This makes it a world leader in new payment methods. Next, it can be hard for people of different ages to accept digital payments (Gupta et al., 2020). People like mobile payment options because they are safe to use both online and in shops (Dimitrova et al., 2019). Safe peer-to-peer payments can be made with Swipp, a Danish bank-sector mobile payment app launched in 2013. Nordea, Nykredit, Jyske Bank, Sydbank, Arbejdernes landsbank, Spar Nord, and other area banks are all served by Swipp. Swipp is built into the mobile banking apps of 81 Danish banks. This program makes it easy to do business by letting users give money to any other Swipp user, no matter what mobile banking app they use. A 2015 study by Stavkova et al. talks about Swipp, a mobile payment system that is built on accounts. Millennials are most likely to use mobile payments. Singh and Mudang (2020) say that Young Indians (Generation Y) use their phones for banking instead of music, directions, or photos. Since 2016, Paytm, Mobikwik, m-Pesa, Airtel Money, and other apps have come out in India, which has the second-largest smartphone market. NFC chips, which are used for payments, are part of new short-range wireless technology. NFC is often used for mobile payments because it is quick, reliable, and efficient. With NFC, you can use "touch and go" apps (Iqbal et al., 2018).

Table 3. Payment System Indicator of India (in Crore) (2015-16 to 2022-23)

	2015-16	2016-17	2017-18	2018-19	2019-20	2020-21	2021-22	2022-23
Total Payments	10,02,24,409	12,01,95,541	14,51,71,804	17,19,59,490	16,97,93,503	14,70,85,596	18,10,51,565	21,58,57,776
Total Digital Payments	9,20,38,330	11,20,99,726	13,69,78,311	16,37,13,425	16,19,68,681	14,14,58,488	17,44,01,233	20,86,84,872
UPI	-	6,961	1,09,832	8,76,971	21,31,730	41,03,658	84,15,900	1,39,14,932
BHIM Aadhaar Pay	-	-	78	815	1,303	2,580	6,113	6,791
Card Payments	3,99,588	6,58,289	9,19,035	11,96,888	14,34,813	12,91,799	17,01,851	21,52,245
Credit Cards	2,40,662	3,28,382	4,58,965	6,03,413	7,30,894	6,30,414	9,71,638	14,32,255
Debit Cards	1,58,927	3,29,907	4,60,070	5,93,475	7,03,920	6,61,385	7,30,213	7,19,989

Figure 2. Digital Payment in India

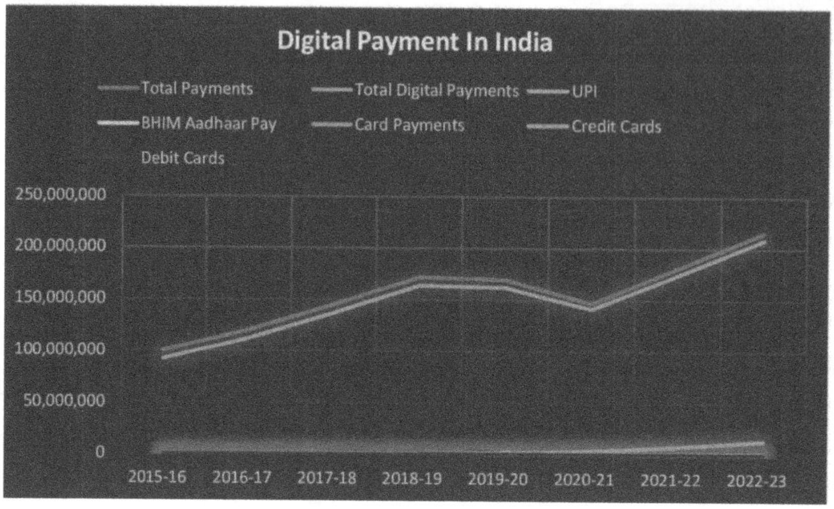

Over time, the number of digital payments made each year has gone up, showing a move toward digital transactions. UPI payments began with very small amounts and have grown a lot over the years. This shows that UPI is becoming more and more useful as a way to pay online. The number of BHIM Aadhaar Pay transactions isn't very high, but they've been growing steadily, which suggests that some people are starting to use Aadhaar-based purchases. Most of the time, credit card transactions are more expensive than debit card transactions. Overall, the data shows that more and more people are using digital payments. For example, UPI transactions are growing a lot, and people are still using cards to pay for things. This trend fits in with the worldwide move toward digital money and activities that don't require cash.

CHALLENGES

Even though digital funds have pros, they also have cons. These problems are different in each country because of their economy, technology, laws, and level of general awareness. The M-Pesa system in Kenya helps poor countries get access to money. Companies won't take cash in Sweden, where people are using less cash and the government is getting rid of paper documents. This has left a digital gap. For companies, digital payments are cheaper than cash, which they have to get from banks, keep, reconcile every day, and send back. The main problems are shown in Figure 3 and Table 4. They are social, economic, technological knowledge, and legal.

Figure 3. Classification of digital payment technology challenges

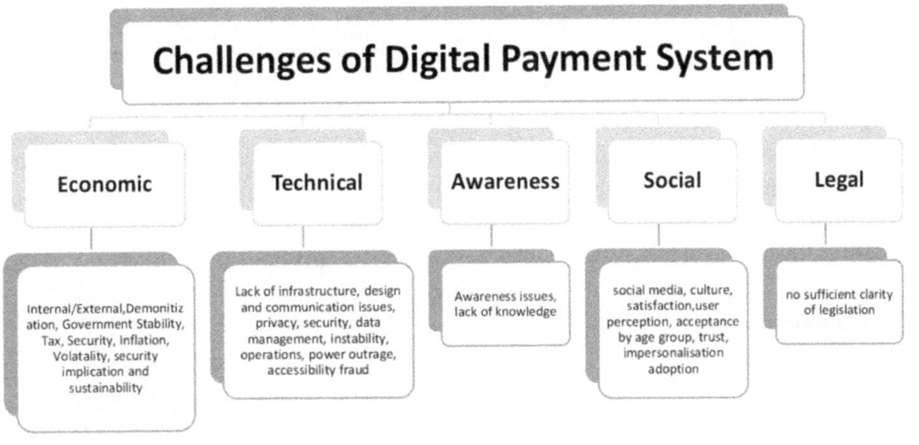

Table 4. Challenges of Digital Payment Technologies and Related Studies

Challenges	Sub-themes	Studies Reviewed
Economic	Internal/External, Demonetization, Government Stability, Tax, Security, Inflation, Volatility, security implication and sustainability	Akanfe et.at., 2020; Kaleeth et at., 2021, Balan et. al.,2020; Chakrabarty et. al., 2021; Ravi Kumar et. al.,2019; Nwankwo et al., 2013;Vines et. al., 2012; Bagla et al., 2018; Wang et. al., 2016
Technical	Lack of infrastructure, design and communication issues, privacy, security, data management, instability, operations, power outrage, accessibility fraud	Akanfe et.a;., 2020; Kaleeth et at., 2021, Rana et. al., 2018; Seethamraju et. al., 2018; Arango et., al., 2020; Najib et., al., 2020; Dimitrova et. al., 2019; Iqbal et. al., 2018; Jain et. al., 2021; Kantoroeva et al., 2020; Chakrabarty et. al., 2021; Ravi Kumar et. al.,2019; Nwankwo et al., 2013;Vines et. al., 2012; Bagla et al., 2018; Wang et. al., 2016, Vinitha et al., 2020;
Awareness	Awareness issues, lack of knowledge	Najib et., al., 2020; Kaleeth et at., 2021, Rana et. al., 2018; Kumar et. al., 2020; Lakshmi et al., 2020; Sivathanu et al., 2019; Sharif et . al., 2020; Pizzol et al., 2018
Social	social media, culture, satisfaction, user perception, acceptance by age group, trust, personalisation adoption	Akanfe et.a;., 2020; Kaleeth et at., 2021, Rana et. al., 2018; Seethamraju et. al., 2018; Arango et., al., 2020; Dimitrova et. al., 2019; Iqbal et. al., 2018; Jain et. al., 2021; Ligon et al., 2019; Al-Okaily et al., 2020; Datta et al., 2020; Kumar at., al.,2020; Nwankwo et al., 2013; Bagla et al.,2018; Gupta et. al., 2020; Singh et al.,2020; Singh et. al., 2018;
Legal	no sufficient clarity of legislation	Wang et al., 2016; Androulaki et al., 2013; Bello et. al., 2019; Diniz et. al., 2019; Almarashdeh et., al., 2018; Garcia et., al., 2020; Dostov et., al., 2014.

Economic Challenges

9 of the 38 scientific studies that looked into digital payment technology's economic problems did so. This review says that economics is the study of handling money for a family, community, or business. Some problems with digital payment technology are disagreements within and between countries, high costs, unstable governments, corruption, the effects on taxes and security, long-term viability, inflation, price changes, keeping checks, and demonetization (Table-4). Conflicts and acts of violence in politics are bad for the business and the government. Foreign interference, whether peaceful or violent, could pose a threat to the current government (Akanfe et al., 2020). To stop people from abusing data, governments and the people in charge of digital payments need to make

it safer and more private. To improve digital payment systems, which boost the economy (Akanfe et al., 2020), they need the trust of both locals and foreign groups.

There are costs with digital payments. Digital wallet apps should not cost a lot of money. A study found that digital wallets are more expensive than cash payments, which makes them less sustainable (Bagla et al., 2018). People like it better than digital wallets because it's free. To compete with cash and meet user needs, digital wallets need to be safe, secure, and cheap (Bagla et al., 2018). If not, buyers can always turn it into cash. Digital payment systems that are clear and easy to track have problems that go beyond cost. Indian small business owners are wary of digital payment methods because they might affect their taxes. People prefer cash to digital payments because they don't have to deal with system exchanges or pay taxes (Seethamraju et al., 2018). As the first decentralized digital payment system, Bitcoin changed the way money was handled in the financial markets. Bitcoin is still risky because its price changes a lot, which makes it harder to fight inflation (Bagla et al., 2018).

Technical Challenges

More research has been done on technical issues with new digital payment methods than on other problems. Privacy, security, access, fraud, infrastructure, design, communication, speed, dependability, user anonymity, disruptive technology, operation, data management, and instability (power loss) were all looked at in 18 of the 38 tests. There are "safety and reliability issues" and "privacy issues" that need to be fixed. Surveys showed that security flaws and a lack of safety against fraud and cyberattacks made it harder to use digital payments. Customers lost faith in digital payment technologies because they were worried about "privacy," having their personal information stolen, deals being cut off or not finished, and services being turned down too often. Data showed that privacy risks hurt consumer trust and the world economy a lot. The biggest problem with privacy issues is that they can make clients lose trust (Akanfe et al., 2020). There are bugs in digital payment methods. It might be hard to make payments. BHIM, an Indian payment system built on UPI, has problems with setting up and using (Seethamraju et al., 2018). This means that people are ready to use digital payments, but the lack of facilities and devices is holding them back. Network problems make systems less popular (Seethamraju et al., 2018). Kaleeth and Chellammal (2021) improved the infrastructure in rural India, where slow network connections cause deals to be delayed or not completed. Cryptocurrency studies say that Bitcoin's private features are not good enough. Even when Bitcoin users follow security rules, their privacy is still at risk (Andoulaki et al., 2013). More research showed that Bitcoin's quick growth has left it open to security holes, such as trade system breaches. This makes Bitcoin's future uncertain (Wang et al., 2016).

Awareness Challenges

There are 8 study gaps in how well people understand and use digital payment technology. To fight black money, India pushed for internet payments and no cash. Digital purchases took the place of cash as part of the Digital India movement, which worked to improve people's lives. It was planned to move quickly and smoothly (Selvakumar et al., 2017). Studies show that cash payments are more common than electronic payments. There was a link between skepticism and confidence, but educated people use cashless transactions more (79 of 100 digital payment technology users are educated, ranging from 12th grade to graduate level). People are less likely to switch from cash to digital payments when they don't know much about the technology (Selvakumar et al., 2017). Rana et al. (2018) say that people can't use digital banking services because they "lack literacy or digital literacy." Other studies showed that customers were turned off by not knowing how to use computers, language barriers, and digital payments [13]. Because of this, digital literacy help desks or booths in rural areas were suggested (Kaleeth et al., 2021). Financial inclusion and "inability to reach a critical mass of consumers" were two more problems. Shah and Dubhashi (2015) found that digital payment technologies make it harder for people with low incomes, disabilities, lack of education, or who are women to use official financial services. The paper offered a unified plan to boost trust in digital payment technologies. There was a call for education about digital payment methods and security. Simple standards must also be set for digital payment systems and their benefits by lawmakers and officials (Shah and Dubhashi, 2015).

Social Challenges

The problems with digital payment technologies are caused by social pressure, which is when friends and coworkers tell someone they have to use a certain technology. Venkatesh et al. (2003) say that social circles affect behavior to keep ties and peace. 16 of the 38 studies that looked into digital payment systems found social problems. These problems included trust, risks, adoption, needs, culture, satisfaction, loyalty, social media effect, user perception, and age group acceptance. Vine et al. (2012) looked at check joy in the UK. Their detailed study of 23 bankers aged 80+ suggested that physical checks should be kept and made better. E-checks should not have been used instead of checks; the only way to solve "acceptance by age group" was to make checks cheaper to process. Vine et al. People who trust that others are honest, caring, and skilled may be more likely to use technology. Rana et al. (2018) looked at "trust" as a problem for digital payment systems. They discovered that security problems with online and mobile banking, like wrong transactions and people abusing bank accounts, led to a "lack of trust." When phones are lost or stolen, private information can become public. Rana et al. It was also hard to trust companies that offer digital wallets. Bagla and Sancheti (2018) looked into how happy digital wallet users were and found that digital payment systems are risky and hard to plan for. According to the report, e-transaction trust is also affected by how the design looks, how easy it is to use, how simple it is, and how it can be customized. Bagla and Sancheti (2018). Even though digital payments are becoming more popular and are very safe, Dimitrova et al. (2019) found that people still think they are risky, dangerous, and not reliable.

Legal Challenges

Six out of 38 studies looked at how real digital payments were. Blockchain-based currencies, like Bitcoin, have problems with being real. Governments around the world think Bitcoin's growth will be limited (Wang et al., 2016). Investors should look at Bitcoin price trends, security, and legal issues, according to studies (Wang et al., 2016). Bitcoin could become a legal investment if it is regulated to encourage people to buy it and recognize its worth. Weak spots in Bitcoin and Digicash have been looked into (Dostov et al., 2014). They looked into how cryptocurrency might affect efforts to stop money laundering and fund terrorists around the world. Most people don't like that cryptocurrencies are anonymous, which could turn people off from buying them. Even though "anonymity" is good for privacy, it puts customers at risk of stealing and losing things. Dostov et al. (2014) talk about how hard it is to understand cryptocurrencies in order to figure out how likely it is that crooks will use digital payment systems.

REMARKS ON THE IDENTIFIED CHALLENGES

Figure 4. Categorization of digital payment technological challenges

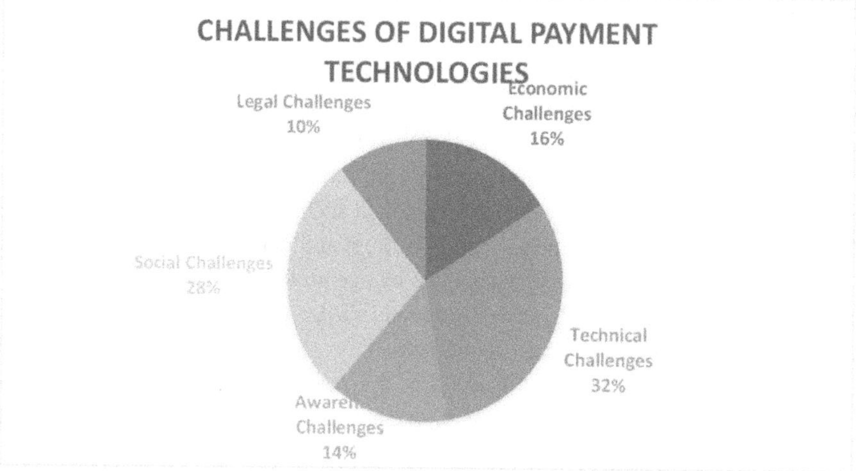

Mobile payment systems have a bright future, but they have to get past a lot of problems first. This evaluation divides issues with digital payment technologies into five groups. Most of the study (18) looked into technical issues with digital payment technology (32%). Sharif and Pal (2020) say that changes in the technical infrastructure and rules have made it possible for more payment methods to be used and for sending and getting payments to be done in different ways. According to some studies, the biggest problems are privacy, security, and the lack of technology infrastructure. Sharif and Pal (2020) found that deals that don't involve cash are risky for both security and network connections. Because they don't know about security measures, payment technology is weak, which puts customers' privacy and data communications at risk. Thiruvaazhi and his friends, 2018. So, smart security measures must be built into payment systems so that people can use digital payment technologies without worrying about their rights and safety. The payment system used by MSMEs is also affected by privacy and safety. 2020 by Lakshmi et al. A study of the privacy risks for digital payment systems at the country level (Akanfe et al., 2020) also found cyberattacks and data abuse from mobile wallets and privacy rules for money transfers. In 18 of the studies that were looked at, social problems were mentioned. Digital payment systems cause a lot of problems for society, but "trust" was named as the main one by most studies. Digital payments are more than just technology. Customer cares about the social issues. Many research studies (Najib et al., 2020; Seethamraju et al., 2021; Singh et al., 2020) have talked about the "trust issues" that come up when people use digital payment technologies. These studies look at things like how people respond to them and how comfortable they are with digital transactions. It was found that attitude toward digital payments, perceived ease of use, perceived usefulness, and trust all affected people's plans to use digital payments (Najib et al., 2020). When millennials choose how to pay, they base their choice on how much they trust digital payment technology to keep their information safe. Their trust relies on how well-known the payment technology is (Singh et al., 2020). Small stores also have trouble using digital payment methods because they don't trust the rules (Seethamraju et al., 2021). The cost of digital payment methods is the main economic worry for consumers (Bagla et al., 2018; Wijaya 2016). In contrast to cash, which is free to use, digital payment methods like bank digital wallets cost money every month. Another economic worry is the inflation that comes from volatile cryptocurrencies and risky markets. People who didn't know how to use or understand digital technology had trouble using digital payment technologies (Kaleeth et al., 2021; SelvaKumar et al., 2017).

REFERENCES

Akanfe, O., Valecha, R., & Rao, H. R. (2020). Assessing country-level privacy risk for digital payment systems. [CrossRef]. *Computers & Security, 99*, 102065. DOI: 10.1016/j.cose.2020.102065

Al-Okaily, M., Lutfi, A., Alsaad, A., Taamneh, A., & Alsyouf, A. (2020). The determinants of digital payment systems' acceptance under cultural orientation differences: The case of uncertainty avoidance. [CrossRef]. *Technology in Society, 63*, 101367. DOI: 10.1016/j.techsoc.2020.101367

Alaimo, L. S., Ciacci, A., & Ivaldi, E. (2021). Measuring sustainable development by non-aggregative approach. [CrossRef]. *Social Indicators Research, 157*(1), 101–122. DOI: 10.1007/s11205-020-02357-0

AlArjani, A., Modibbo, U. M., Ali, I., & Sarkar, B. (2021). A new framework for the sustainable development goals of Saudi Arabia. [CrossRef]. *Journal of King Saud University. Science, 33*(6), 101477. DOI: 10.1016/j.jksus.2021.101477

Ali, I., Modibbo, U. M., Chauhan, J., & Meraj, M. (2021). An integrated multi-objective optimization modelling for sustainable development goals of India. [CrossRef]. *Environment, Development and Sustainability, 23*(3), 3811–3831. DOI: 10.1007/s10668-020-00745-7

Allen, F., Carletti, E., Cull, R., Qian, J., Senbet, L., & Valenzuela, P. (2012). *Resolving the African Financial Development Gap: Cross-Country Comparisons and a Within-Country Study of Kenya*. University of Chicago Press. [CrossRef] DOI: 10.3386/w18013

Almarashdeh, I. B. R. A. H. I. M., Bouzkraoui, H. I. C. H. A. M., Azouaoui, A. H. M. E. D., Youssef, H. A. D. I., Niharmine, L. A. H. C. E. N., Rahman, A. A., & Murimo, B. M. (2018). An overview of technology evolution: Investigating the factors influencing non-bitcoins users to adopt bitcoins as online payment transaction method. *Journal of Theoretical and Applied Information Technology, 96*(13), 3984–3993.

Alshamsi, A., & Andras, P. (2019). User perception of Bitcoin usability and security across novice users. *International Journal of Human-Computer Studies, 126*, 94–110.

Androulaki, E., Karame, G. O., Roeschlin, M., Scherer, T., & Capkun, S. (2013). Evaluating user privacy in bitcoin. In Financial Cryptography and Data Security: 17th International Conference, FC 2013, Okinawa, Japan, April 1-5, 2013, Revised Selected Papers 17 (pp. 34-51). Springer Berlin Heidelberg.

Arango-Arango, C. A., & Suárez-Ariza, N. (2020). Digital payments adoption and the demand for cash: New international evidence. *Journal of Payments Strategy & Systems, 14*(4), 392–410.

Arner, D. W., Buckley, R. P., Zetzsche, D. A., & Veidt, R. (2020). Sustainability, FinTech and Financial Inclusion. [CrossRef]. *European Business Organization Law Review, 21*(1), 7–35. DOI: 10.1007/s40804-020-00183-y

Bagla, R. K., & Sancheti, V. (2018). Gaps in customer satisfaction with digital wallets: Challenge for sustainability. *Journal of Management Development, 37*(6), 442–451. DOI: 10.1108/JMD-04-2017-0144

Bello, G., & Perez, A. J. (2019, April). Adapting financial technology standards to blockchain platforms. In *Proceedings of the 2019 ACM Southeast conference* (pp. 109-116).

Brune, L., Giné, X., Goldberg, J., & Yang, D. (2011). Commitments to save: A field experiment in rural Malawi. World Bank Policy Research Working Paper, (5748).

Burgess, R., & Pande, R. (2005). Do Rural Banks Matter? Evidence from the Indian Social Banking Experiment. *The American Economic Review, 95*(3), 780–795. DOI: 10.1257/0002828054201242

CGAP. (2019). Mobile Money and Financial Inclusion: An Overview. Available online: https://www.cgap.org/sites/default/files/ CGAP-SSN-Mobile-Money-and-Financial-Inclusion-Nov-2019.pdf (accessed on 27 Feb 2024).

Chakrabarty, M., Jha, A., & Ray, P. (2021). Demonetization and digital payments in India: Perception and reality. [CrossRef]. *Applied Economics Letters, 28*(4), 319–323. DOI: 10.1080/13504851.2020.1752895

Chen, C. L., Lin, Y. C., Chen, W. H., Chao, C. F., & Pandia, H. (2021). Role of Government to Enhance Digital Transformation in Small Service Business. [CrossRef]. *Sustainability (Basel), 13*(3), 1028. DOI: 10.3390/su13031028

Cumming, D., Johan, S., & Zhang, M. (2014). The economic impact of entrepreneurship: Comparing international datasets. *Corporate Governance, 22*(2), 162–178. DOI: 10.1111/corg.12058

Datta, P., Walker, L., & Amarilli, F. (2020). Digital transformation: Learning from Italy's public administration. *Journal of Information Technology Teaching Cases, 10*(2), 54–71.

Demirgüç-Kunt, A., Klapper, L. F., & Singer, D. (2013). Financial inclusion and legal discrimination against women: evidence from developing countries. World Bank Policy Research Working Paper, (6416).

Demirguc-Kunt, A., & Klapper, L. (2013). Measuring financial inclusion: Explaining variation in use of financial services across and within countries. *Brookings Papers on Economic Activity, 2013*(1), 279–321. DOI: 10.1353/eca.2013.0002

Demirgüç-Kunt, A., & Klapper, L. F. (2012). Measuring financial inclusion: The global findex database. *World Bank Policy Research Working Paper*, •••, 6025.

Deng, R., Ruan, N., Zhang, G., & Zhang, X. (2020). FraudJudger: Fraud detection on digital payment platforms with fewer labels. In Information and Communications Security: 21st International Conference, ICICS 2019, Beijing, China, December 15–17, 2019, Revised Selected Papers 21 (pp. 569-583). Springer International Publishing.

Dimitrova, I., Öhman, P., & Yazdanfar, D. (2019, June). Challenges in the Limited Choice of Payment Methods in Terms of Cashless Society: Bank Customers' Perspective (work in progress). In Proceedings of the 3rd International Conference on E-commerce, E-Business and E-Government (pp. 45-48).

Diniz, E. H., Siqueira, E. S., & van Heck, E. (2019). Taxonomy of digital community currency platforms. *Information Technology for Development, 25*(1), 69–91. DOI: 10.1080/02681102.2018.1485005

Dostov, V., & Shust, P. (2014). Cryptocurrencies: An unconventional challenge to the AML/CFT regulators? [CrossRef]. *Journal of Financial Crime, 21*(3), 249–263. DOI: 10.1108/JFC-06-2013-0043

Elkamchouchi, H., & Abouelseoud, Y. (2008, November). Privacy protecting digital payment system using ID-based blind signatures with anonymity revocation trustees. In *2008 International Conference on Computer Engineering & Systems* (pp. 274-280). IEEE.

Erlando, A., Riyanto, F., & Masakazu, S. (2020). Financial inclusion, economic growth, and poverty alleviation: Evidence from eastern Indonesia. *Heliyon, 6*(10), e05235. DOI: 10.1016/j.heliyon.2020.e05235 PMID: 33088971

Garcia-Teruel, R. M. (2020). Legal challenges and opportunities of blockchain technology in the real estate sector. [CrossRef]. *J. Prop. Plan. Environ. Law, 12*(2), 129–145. DOI: 10.1108/JPPEL-07-2019-0039

Gupta, R., Kapoor, C., & Yadav, J. (2020, June). Acceptance towards digital payments and improvements in cashless payment ecosystem. In *2020 International Conference for Emerging Technology (INCET)* (pp. 1-9). IEEE.

Haq, A., Modibbo, U. M., Ahmed, A., & Ali, I. (2022). Mathematical modeling of sustainable development goals of India agenda 2030: A Neutrosophic programming approach. [CrossRef]. *Environment, Development and Sustainability, 24*(10), 11991–12018. DOI: 10.1007/s10668-021-01928-6 PMID: 34785984

Huang, P., & Boucouvalas, A. C. (2006). Future personal" e-payment": IRFM. [CrossRef]. *IEEE Wireless Communications, 13*(1), 60–66. DOI: 10.1109/MWC.2006.1593526

Ilankumaran, G., & Darling Selvi, V. (2019). Customer Purview of Cashless Payment System in the Digital Economy of India. *International Journal of Innovative Technology and Exploring Engineering, 8*, 87–93.

Iqbal, R., Ahmad, S., & Hashim, M. (2018, June). Evaluating Factors Affecting Communication in Wearable Internet of Things for Near Field. In 2018 IEEE 87th Vehicular Technology Conference (VTC Spring) (pp. 1-4). IEEE.

Ivashchenko, A., Britchenko, I., Dyba, M., Polishchuk, Y., Sybirianska, Y., & Vasylyshen, Y. (2018). Fintech platforms in SME's financing: EU experience and ways of their application in Ukraine. [CrossRef]. *Investig. Manag. Financ. Innov., 15*(3), 83–96. DOI: 10.21511/imfi.15(3).2018.07

Jain, K., & Chowdhary, R. (2021). A Study on Intention to Adopt Digital Payment Systems in India: Impact of COVID-19 Pandemic. [CrossRef]. *Asia Pac. J. Inf. Syst., 31*(1), 76–101. DOI: 10.14329/apjis.2021.31.1.76

Jia, S., Qiu, Y., & Yang, C. (2021). Sustainable Development Goals, Financial Inclusion, and Grain Security Efficiency. *Agronomy (Basel), 11*(12), 2542. DOI: 10.3390/agronomy11122542

Joia, L. A., & Cordeiro, J. P. V. (2021). Unlocking the potential of fintechs for financial inclusion: A Delphi-based approach. [CrossRef]. *Sustainability (Basel), 13*(21), 11675. DOI: 10.3390/su132111675

Kaleeth, A. B. L., & Chellammal, T. (2021). Adoption of Digital Payment Methods in Rural Areas of Ramanathapuram District. *Annals of the Romanian Society for Cell Biology, 25*, 7831–7837.

Kantoroeva, A.K.; Toktomamatova, N.K. Some Aspects of the Development of Payment Innovations in the Kyrgyz Republic. Int.

Karlan, D., Osei-Akoto, I., Osei, R., & Udry, C. (2014). Agricultural decisions after relaxing credit and risk constraints. [CrossRef]. *The Quarterly Journal of Economics, 129*(2), 597–652. DOI: 10.1093/qje/qju002

Khairun, N. K., & Yasmin, M. H. (2010). E-commerce Adoption in Malaysia: Trends, Issues and Opportunities. In *ICT Strategic Review* (pp. 89–134). PIKOM Publishers.

Klapper, L., El-Zoghbi, M., & Hess, J. (2016). Achieving the sustainable development goals. The role of financial inclusion. Available online: http://www. ccgap. org. Accessed, 23(5), 2016.

Kolodiziev, O., Mints, A., Sidelov, P., Pleskun, I., & Lozynska, O. (2020). Automatic Machine Learning Algorithms for Fraud Detection in Digital Payment Systems. East.- [CrossRef]. *Eur. J. Enterp. Technol., 5*, 107.

Kuada, J. (2019). Financial inclusion and the sustainable development goals. In *Extending Financial Inclusion in Africa* (pp. 259–277). Academic Press. [CrossRef] DOI: 10.1016/B978-0-12-814164-9.00012-8

Kumar, M., Agrawal, S., & Mishra, R. (2020). User Behaviour and Digital Payment Ecosystem: An Audit of Connections between usage Attributes and Demographic Profile. *Int. J. Emerg. Technol., 11*, 935–938.

Lakshmi, M. S., & Alamelumangai, R. (2020). Cashless Transactions: Opportunities and Challenges amongst MSME at Sivaganga District, Tamilnadu. *Int. J. Sci. Technol. Res., 9*, 4900–4902.

Ligon, E., Malick, B., Sheth, K., & Trachtman, C. (2019). What explains low adoption of digital payment technologies? Evidence from small-scale merchants in Jaipur, India. [CrossRef] [PubMed]. *PLoS One*, *14*(7), e0219450. DOI: 10.1371/journal.pone.0219450 PMID: 31365540

Liu, F., Lu, S., Qin, S., & Shao, S. (2020, April). Research on the New Generation Electronic Payment System Applied in'The Belt and Road'. In 2020 International Conference on E-Commerce and Internet Technology (ECIT) (pp. 5-9). IEEE.

Makina, D. (2017). Introduction to the financial services in Africa special issue. *African Journal of Economic and Management Studies*, *8*(1), 2–7. DOI: 10.1108/AJEMS-03-2017-149

Modibbo, U. M., Ali, I., & Ahmed, A. (2021). Multi-objective optimization modelling for analysing sustainable development goals of Nigeria: Agenda 2030. [CrossRef]. *Environment, Development and Sustainability*, *23*(6), 9529–9563. DOI: 10.1007/s10668-020-01022-3

Najib, M., & Fahma, F. (2020). Investigating the adoption of digital payment system through an extended technology acceptance model: An insight from the Indonesian small and medium enterprises. [CrossRef]. *International Journal on Advanced Science, Engineering and Information Technology*, *10*(4), 1702–1708. DOI: 10.18517/ijaseit.10.4.11616

Nathan, R. J., Setiawan, B., & Quynh, M. N. (2022). Fintech and financial health in Vietnam during the COVID-19 pandemic: In-depth descriptive analysis. *Journal of Risk and Financial Management*, *15*(3), 125. DOI: 10.3390/jrfm15030125

Nwankwo, O., & Eze, O. R. (2013). Electronic payment in cashless economy of Nigeria: Problems and prospect. *Journal of Management Research*, *5*, 138–151.

Park, K. W., & Baek, S. H. (2017). OPERA: A Complete Offline and Anonymous Digital Cash Transaction System with a One-Time Readable Memory. [CrossRef]. *IEICE Transactions on Information and Systems*, *100*(D), 2348–2356. DOI: 10.1587/transinf.2016INP0008

Pizzol, M., Vighi, E., & Sacchi, R. (2018). Challenges in coupling digital payments data and input-output data to change consumption patterns. [CrossRef]. *Procedia CIRP*, *69*, 633–637. DOI: 10.1016/j.procir.2017.11.004

Pradiatiningtyas, D., Dewa, C. B., Safitri, L. A., & Kiswati, S. (2022). The Effect of Satisfaction and Loyalty Towards Digital Payment System Users Among Generation Z in Yogyakarta Special Region. In *Journal of Physics: Conference Series* (Vol. 1641, p. 012110). IOP Publishing.

Ramli, F. A. A. (2021). Mobile payment and e-wallet adoption in emerging economies: A systematic literature review. *Journal of Emerging Economies and Islamic Research*, *9*(2), 1–39.

Rana, N. P., Luthra, S., & Rao, H. R. (2018). Developing a Framework using Interpretive Structural Modeling for the Challenges of Digital Financial Services in India. In Proceedings of the 22nd Pacific Asia Conference on Information Systems (PACIS 2018), Yokohama, Japan, 26–30 June 2018 (p. 53). Association for Information Systems., Available online https://core.ac.uk/download/pdf/301375969.pdf, Retrieved November 8, 2022, from.

Ravikumar, T., Suresha, B., Sriram, M., & Rajesh, R. (2019). Impact of Digital Payments on Economic Growth: Evidence from India. *International Journal of Innovative Technology and Exploring Engineering*, *8*(12), 553–557. DOI: 10.35940/ijitee.L3432.1081219

Rekha, M. (2023). *Payments innovation the key to financial inclusion in Africa*. Forty Percent of Africa Remains Unbanked. Fintechs and Banks Are Working to Redress the Balance, Reports Rekha Menon.

Kaur, S. (2020). Impact of Demonetization on Digital Payments in India-Event Study Methodology. Pacific Business Review International, 13(4).

Sanyal, P. (2014). *Credit to Capabilities: A Sociological Study of Microcredit Groups in India*. Cambridge University Press. [CrossRef] DOI: 10.1017/CBO9781139939461

Seethamraju, R., & Diatha, K. S. (2018). Adoption of digital payments by small retail stores.

Selvakumar, D. S., & Sharma, A. K. (2017). A Study on Market Without Cash—Conventional to Digital. *Int. J. Appl. Bus. Econ. Res.*, *15*, 337–342.

Setiawan, B., Nugraha, D. P., Irawan, A., Nathan, R. J., & Zoltan, Z. (2021). User innovativeness and fintech adoption in Indonesia. [CrossRef]. *Journal of Open Innovation*, *7*(3), 188. DOI: 10.3390/joitmc7030188

Sharif, M., & Pal, R. (2020). Moving from cash to cashless: A study of consumer perception towards digital transactions. *PRAGATI J. Indian Econ.*, *7*(1), 1–13. DOI: 10.17492/pragati.v7i1.195425

Shen, H., & Kurshan, E. (2020, October). Deep Q-network-based adaptive alert threshold selection policy for payment fraud systems in retail banking. In *Proceedings of the First ACM International Conference on AI in Finance* (pp. 1-7).

Simatele, M., & Mbedzi, E. (2021). Consumer payment choices, costs, and risks: Evidence from Zimbabwe. [CrossRef]. *Cogent Economics & Finance*, *9*(1), 1875564. DOI: 10.1080/23322039.2021.1875564

Singh, A. K., & Mudang, T. (2020). Digital payment system and the millennial in a smart city: an antecedent to technopreneurship. In *Electronic systems and intelligent computing: proceedings of ESIC 2020* (pp. 109–118). Springer Singapore.

Singh, G., Kumar, B., & Gupta, R. (2018, October). The role of consumer's innovativeness & perceived ease of use to engender adoption of digital wallets in India. In *2018 International Conference on Automation and Computational Engineering (ICACE)* (pp. 150-158). IEEE.

Singh, T. V., Supriya, N., & Joshna, M. S. (2016). Issues and challenges of electronic payment systems. *International Journal of Innovative Research and Development*, *2*, 25–30.

Sivathanu, B. (2019). Adoption of digital payment systems in the era of demonetization in India: An empirical study. [CrossRef]. *J. Sci. Technol. Policy Manag.*, *10*(1), 143–171. DOI: 10.1108/JSTPM-07-2017-0033

Staykova, K. S., & Damsgaard, J. (2015). The race to dominate the mobile payments platform: Entry and expansion strategies. [CrossRef]. *Electronic Commerce Research and Applications*, *14*(5), 319–330. DOI: 10.1016/j.elerap.2015.03.004

Thawre, G., Bahekar, N., & Chandavarkar, B. R. (2020, July). Use cases of authentication protocols in the context of digital payment system. In 2020 11th International Conference on Computing, Communication and Networking Technologies (ICCCNT) (pp. 1-6). IEEE.

Thirupathi, M., Vinayagamoorthi, G., & Mathiraj, S. P. (2019). Effect of cashless payment methods: A case study perspective analysis. International Journal of scientific & technology research, 8(8), 394-397.

Thiruvaazhi Arthi, R. (2018). Threats to Mobile Security and Privacy. *Int. J. Recent Technol. Eng.*, *7*, 407–412.

UNDP. (2023). Sustainable Development Goals|United Nations Development Programme. Available online: https://www.undp. org/sustainable-development-goals (accessed on 10 Jan 2024).

Vines, J., Dunphy, P., Blythe, M., Lindsay, S., Monk, A., & Olivier, P. (2012, February). The joy of cheques: trust, paper and eighty somethings. In *Proceedings of the ACM 2012 conference on Computer Supported Cooperative Work* (pp. 147-156).

Vinitha, K., & Vasantha, S. (2020). Determinants of Customer intention to use Digital payment system. *J. Adv. Res. Dyn. Control Syst.*, *12*, 168–174.

Wang, J., Xue, Y., & Liu, M. (2016, July). An analysis of bitcoin price based on VEC model. In 2016 international conference on economics and management innovations (pp. 180-186). Atlantis Press.

Wijaya, D. A. (2016, October). Extending asset management system functionality in bitcoin platform. In 2016 International Conference on Computer, Control, Informatics and its Applications (IC3INA) (pp. 97-101). IEEE.

World Bank. (2014). Global Financial Development Report 2014: Financial Inclusion. [CrossRef]. *World Bank Publ.*, *4*, 121–135.

Zhang, X., Tang, S., Zhao, Y., Wang, G., Zheng, H., & Zhao, B. (2017, May). Cold hard e-cash: Friends and vendors in the venmo digital payments system. In *Proceedings of the International AAAI Conference on Web and Social Media* (Vol. 11, No. 1, pp. 387-396).

Chapter 26
Smart Devices:
A Review of Opportunities, Applications, and Challenges in Smart Industries

D. Anbuselvi
https://orcid.org/0000-0002-6717-9821
T. John Institute of Technology, India

S. GraceInfantiya
https://orcid.org/0000-0001-9637-0660
Sri Sairam Institute of Technology, Chennai, India

D. Bharath
MVJ Engineering College, India

N. Suthanthira Vanitha
Muthayammal Engineering College, India

ABSTRACT

Data and correspondence innovation is going through fast turn of events, and numerous troublesome advancements, for example, distributed computing, Web of Things, enormous information, and man-made reasoning, have arisen. These advancements are pervading the assembling business and empower the combination of physical and virtual universes through digital actual frameworks (CPS), which mark the appearance of the fourth phase of modern creation (i.e., Industry 4.0) Web of Things (IoT) is a quickly developing imaginative innovation with different applications, works and administrations in daily existence and in a large number of business sectors and enterprises. It can be described as a global, dynamic information network whose goal is the mutual interconnection and interaction of people, services, and devices at any time and in any location. It also includes devices and objects that are connected to each other.

INTRODUCTION

Currently, connected IoT devices are growing tremendously to meet the standard requirements of various application areas such as smart homes, smart cities, transportation, agriculture, and healthcare. Standard control and practical constraints meet the numerical technical challenges of developing large-scale networks. Technological advances include pluggable components of smart devices such as sensors, actuators and gateways that provide innovative application services. Most application scenarios require a new computing model, which highlights

DOI: 10.4018/979-8-3693-7447-4.ch026

important challenges such as data management, security and interoperability. Emerging IoT frameworks consider an intelligent platform to manage various aggregated data sources. New innovative services combine multiple transmission streams to assess social and business infrastructure needs. Most city dwellers understand the use of enabling technologies, namely connectivity, continuity, compliance, coexistence and cyber security. The technical challenges of IoT are related to the system of physical objects to develop an intelligent machine that determines the presence of logistics functions. Advanced intelligent systems, including smart cities and the Internet of Things, are standardizing the requirements of convergent technologies such as the edge, fog and cloud. A large-scale system integrates four important layers such as sensors (endpoints), edges (gateway), platform (artificial intelligence, management connections) and application software. The unprecedented growth of sensor technology shows significant insight into smart cities. Security and Privacy Issues in Smart Cities/Industries: Technologies, Applications and Challenges. Thus, this special issue has attracted researchers from academia and industry to explore opportunities to create next-generation IoT-based user scenarios and explore their impact on solutions to the issues and challenges discussed above and propose viable solutions. Various researchers have contributed to different areas of interest related to next-generation IoT-based applications and user scenarios, including the following (Figure 1).

- Next-generation IoT-based smart healthcare;
- Next-generation IoT-based smart cities;
- Next-generation IoT-based smart agriculture;
- Next-generation IoT-based data analytics;
- Next-generation IoT-based industrial IoT

INDUSTRIAL IoT

The development of smart industries has had a far-reaching and lasting impact on the inevitable future of global manufacturing. Industry 4.0 combined intelligent industry with cyber-physical technologies, making complex advances more agile and efficient, and improving the performance, quality, controllability, control and fairness of industrial operations in the development of IoT-based intelligent industries. The next generation of cheaper sensors is the key to data collection and efficient operation of manufacturing industries and supply chains. At the same time, there are many studies focused on decomposing industrial efficiency and facility utilization. Most manufacturers need a deep understanding of the contrast between conventional and state-of-the-art manufacturing frameworks and the broad deployment of sensors associated with Industry 4.0. In Rao et al. (2022) and Kalsoom et al. (2020), the authors highlight the particular sensor technologies available in Industry 4.0 and show the difference between traditional and smart industry. In addition, the authors explore existing challenges in smart industry research and thus provide a broad overview of related smart industry research. The authors also summarize the differences between traditional and smart industrial factories, outline the sensors used in the smart factory and envision a future that includes the robust development of Industry 4.0 for smart industries.

HEALTHCARE IoT

Some diseases openly affect society, causing public health problems. For example, lung infections and chronic obstructive pulmonary disease (COPD) are now the third leading cause of death, while tuberculosis is ninth with 1.7 million deaths and more than 10.4 million other cases. Research shows that computer technologies, such as internet of things (IoT)-based technologies, advance the analysis of lung disease data using computed tomography (CT). In Souza et al. (2020), the authors propose another model based on IoT-based systems to organize and share lung CT scans by applying machine learning (ML) to important learning strategies with Parzen probability distribution.

Their proposed model uses an application programming interface (API) that considers lung images captured from the Internet of Medical Things. This approach was found to be effective, achieving more than 98% accuracy in collecting aspiration images. The model continued the lung segmentation step using the Mask R-CNN organization method to fabricate an aspiration controller and use regularization to determine the location of lung inflammations on the CT image. The proposed strategy was implemented better than various literature works and achieved high measurement values; for example, an accuracy of 98.34% was achieved. In addition to improving the time interval of 5.43 s and other exchange learning models, their proposed process stands out from the rest as fully automatic. Fog computing: Fog computing technology (FCT) suggests using computing resources located near the edge of the network. Hassan et al. (2020) propose an FCT architecture to implement a telemedicine healthcare framework. The main motivation for adopting the FCT-based framework in the proposed approach is to reduce latency and reliability. iFogSim-based simulations are compared with cloud-based networks to demonstrate the suitability of the proposed approach in reducing reliability and latency. The results show that lower latency and higher reliability can be achieved with the proposed approach to create a telemedicine monitoring framework. In Mobasheri et al. (2020), the authors present a fog fragment computing technology (FFCT) solution that is compared with conventional FCT. The paper discusses data transmission through FCT edge nodes and their collaboration to overcome the redundant data transmission that limits IoT devices. The authors characterize the FCT dynamic problem with a ML approach and develop a Q-learning algorithm to make efficient decisions by directing FCT edge nodes to help each other under special conditions. 5G technologies: Current RFID tag technology is expensive and has not been featured in 5G development as a green technology for next-generation IoT. In addition, 5G systems do not have acceptable long-distance data transmission. The recently proposed I-RFID (Hussain et al., 2020) tag uses a meander angle technology (MAT) structure that meets the requirements of a more affordable printed antenna for the ultra-high frequency (UHF) RFID frequency band standard (860-960 MHz). In Hussain et al. (2020), RFID tags and MAT antennas are manufactured on a paper-based board by silk screen and flexo printing, which show less effective results for fog-induced dielectric selection and have a possible reading range (RR) in Europe. (EU; 866-868 MHz) and North American (NA; 902-928 MHz) UHF bands. Their proposed tag size was reduced by 36% to 38% compared to standard RFID tags; in addition, label confirmation improved from 23.6% to 33.12% and its RR improved to 50.9% and 59.6% in the EU and NA UHF groups, respectively. It achieves an impressive performance in some cases (plastic, paper and glass) and thus represents another high-quality RFID tag with improved properties for 5G technologies. Future security trends of 5G technologies Vehicle IoT (VIoT) emphasizes privacy assurance and security issues using public key framework. Fundamental issues related to valid trust assessment, accepted vehicle malfunctions, and secure information dissemination in vehicular wireless networks have not been investigated. In order to adapt to these difficulties, Sohail et al. (2020) propose a trust-augmented on-demand routing (TER) mechanism that uses the TrustWalker (TW) algorithm as an expert trust assessment and routing method in VIoT. TER included a new three-valued subjective logic (3VSL), TW measurements, and an ad hoc on-demand distance vector (AODV) routing algorithm. This paper validates the accuracy of the proposed system in terms of its performance, reliability and delay. Network-on-Chip (NoC): Recently, Network-on-Chip (NoC) technologies have become popular in the communication framework of heterogeneous computing technologies because they are more scalable and highly efficient. As a result of hostile technology scaling, these models have both persistent and transient shards. In Rashid et al. (2020), the authors draw attention to the robustness of the NoC router against constant failures. A continuous failure in a NoC router will seriously affect the performance of the entire network. The authors suggest that the communication port can be used as a bypass method, a virtual channel (VC) queue, and a VC stop method. The route calculation phase uses spatial redundancy and a dual routing mechanism, and the VC allocation phase uses spatial replication. The runtime authorization option is used in the distribution phase of the switch. The router they offer is exceptionally fault tolerant compared to high-end NoC routers. The proposed mechanism achieves 7.98 times.

NEXT-GENERATION IOT-BASED SMART HEALTHCARE

The use of IoT in healthcare is gradually being introduced in commercial sectors. A number of commercial solutions have been proposed for personalized healthcare. However, there is a huge potential to improve the framework of IoT-based healthcare as an essential medical service and to develop hospitals as secondary healthcare units. Thus, it is very important to distinguish the expected progress to solve the problems and challenges arising from the achievement of these goals. Future prospects include real-time location technology for Alzheimer's patients who could use a geospatial location sensor to track their location at any time. Other future technologies related to healthcare include: real-time capture and stroke detection, AR/VR-based telehealth applications, health data wearables, blockchain-based security services, remote surgery and interactive distance learning.

NEXT-GENERATION IOT-BASED SMART-CITIES

The IoT system has progressed in developing certain arrangements where each application is directly or indirectly related to the smart city application context. Such frameworks and collaborative applications can bring significant challenges and problems to IoT-based smart city systems. Some of the reliability issues raised in the IoT smart city framework stem from mobility issues in the transportation system; therefore communication with vehicles is not reliable enough. In addition, the presence of different sensing devices causes some reliability problems according to their failure. Some predefined scenarios require communication between a large number of smart devices that may be located in different geographic locations. New-generation IoT frameworks are designed to provide a suitable platform that can explore and incorporate information from various devices. In addition, the security and privacy aspects of such an IoT-based smart city system may depend on users. Next-generation IoT-based smart agriculture: Next-generation IoT-based smart agriculture should help develop agricultural practices and technologies to support sustainable farmers and resources. It is economically practical and stable, socially stable and works well. This approach aims to preserve soil quality, reduce soil erosion and degradation, and conserve water resources. A sustainable smart farming system improves the biodiversity of the country and promotes a healthy and green environment. This is necessary to coordinate with the future growing interest in food and environmental changes and biological system degradation. It plays an important role in securing natural resources, reducing emissions of ozone-depleting gases, stopping the waste of biodiversity and thinking about valuable landscapes. Next-generation IoT-based smart agriculture has been implemented in agriculture to preserve natural resources without compromising the quality of basic requirements. Common IoT-based smart farming practices include sustainable agriculture, smart agriculture, and smart crop rotations that mitigate the problems and challenges of weeds, plant diseases, insects, and other pests. Next-generation IoT-based data analytics: As IoT-based applications evolve, the number of devices continuously collecting data and connected to the embedded environment has grown to an extraordinary size. Such smart devices enable the development of new data analysis techniques that can make smart applications smarter and more useful. Thanks to the collaboration of different applications, there is a huge amount of data from which useful information can be extracted. A major problem faced is the repeated occurrence of similar data generated by multiple connected smart devices. Embedding machine learning techniques with neural networks and deep learning algorithms would help solve such problems and challenges. Such a solution may require extensive use of computing and energy resources. However, next-generation IoT-based data analytics solutions must be sustainable, cost-effective and use green technology.

NEXT-GENERATION INDUSTRIAL IoT

Industrial development has advanced significantly since the industrial technological revolution and has grown with the emergence of IoT-based systems. In fact, the infusion and coordination of IoT-ready sensors and actuators, smart manufacturing is changing conventional product assembly processes, and many different industries are working on proof of concept and implementing IoT representations in their initiatives to reap the benefits. However, industries have found that these new IoT frameworks tend to remain isolated from their warehouse IT infrastructure and networks. Thus, the industry faces various difficulties: complex cycles and sequential construction systems, network problems in joining the framework, unreliable remote access, security threats, transparency and information standard models. To achieve the next generation of IoT-based industry, the integration of IT and work technology in all production processes is crucial.

Figure 1. Schematic of Internet of Things (IOT)

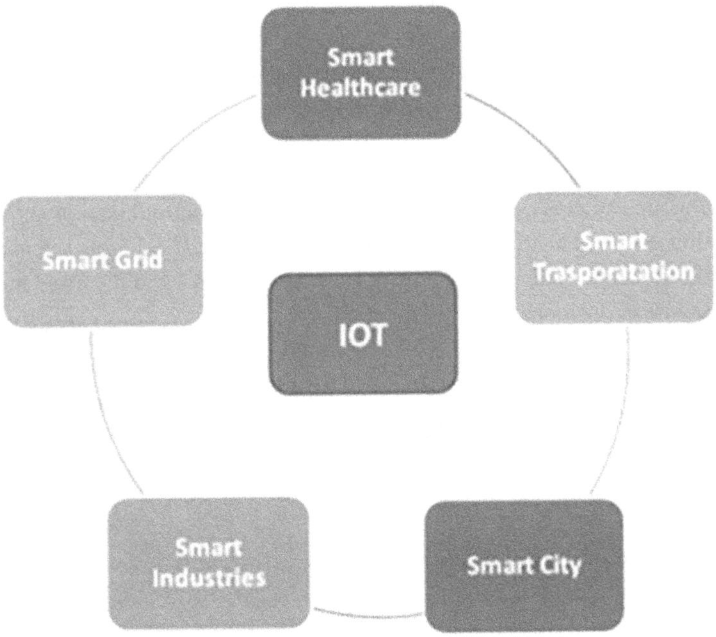

APPLICATION OF IoT IN INDUSTRY

The application of IoT in industry leads to the creation of intelligent factories, where almost all items such as machines, equipment and products are equipped with sensors that connect them to each other and to the Internet (Gebremichael et al., 2020). Industrial Internet of Things is one of the most demanding applications (Cabrini et al., 2021). This in turn provides enhanced visibility into operations through real-time data access. In this new environment, manufacturing equipment and other devices can communicate their performance in real time and improve productivity, efficiency and quality by providing high responsiveness and flexibility at the process level (Fatorachian & Kazemi, 2021). The global IIoT market was valued at \$312.79 billion in 2017 and is projected to reach \$700.38 billion by 2023 (Gidlund et al., 2018). IoT typically uses unlicensed 2.4 GHz frequencies, where multiple technologies compete for spectrum availability. However, there is no coordination mechanism between the technologies, which would cause mutual interference, which in turn prevents the implementation of industrial monitoring and control. The 2.4 GHz unlicensed frequency mentioned above offers free 85 MHz wide spectrum worldwide. This has led to the mass adoption of wireless standards such as Bluetooth Low Energy (BLE), IEEE 802.11, and IEEE 802.15.1. The IIoT process automation domain uses the IEEE 802.15.4 physical layer, which is based on the leading WirelessHART and ISA 100.11a standards (Gidlund et al., 2018; Åkerberg et al., 2011; Basir et al., 2019; Grimaldi et al., 2020). IoT at the industrial level leads to the creation of fully automated production systems with cloud systems and BDA, enabling better analysis of market demand patterns, which greatly improves planning and production management. This, in turn, facilitates rapid customization of products at an individual or local level. Figure 11 shows selected industry categories with potential for IIoT implementation. As the manufacturing environment has changed in recent decades, new business models, Industrial Product-Service Systems (IPSS), have evolved with it. They are changing the business from simply selling products that generate profit to selling features. In the IPSS model, industrial products and services are delivered continuously, which in many cases requires BDA from different sources, such as IoT devices. IIoT solutions take into account both the technical details of product manufacturing and the stakeholders involved in the IPSS business model. In this sense, they enable dynamic adaptation to constantly changing consumer demand and production capabilities (Alexopoulos et al., 2018). The concept of the Industrial Internet originated in the United States and was first mentioned by General Electric, while the concept of Industry 4.0 itself originated in Germany. The two concepts are not identical, but they overlap. "Industrial Internet of Things: A system consisting of interconnected intelligent objects, cyber-physical assets, related general information technology and optional cloud or edge computing platforms that enable real-time, intelligent and autonomous access, process collection, analysis, communication and exchange, production and/or service information in the industrial environment (Boyes et al., 2018) is an extension of IoT technology that provides a set of tools to create a competitive advantage in the industry and therefore must meet much stricter requirements than in the case of the consumer. architectural model of the industry (Figure 2) consists of several layers with different networks (Lennvall et al., 2017). Through internal sensors and actuators, data collection, analysis and exchange, IIoT enables machines (with embedded sensors) to change their behavior or show other devices that they are doing so without human intervention. In addition, it can support human decision-making based on collected information in real time, as well as the ability to store this information, use it for periodic evaluation and/or maintenance forecasts. of.

Figure 2. Schematic of Industry sector

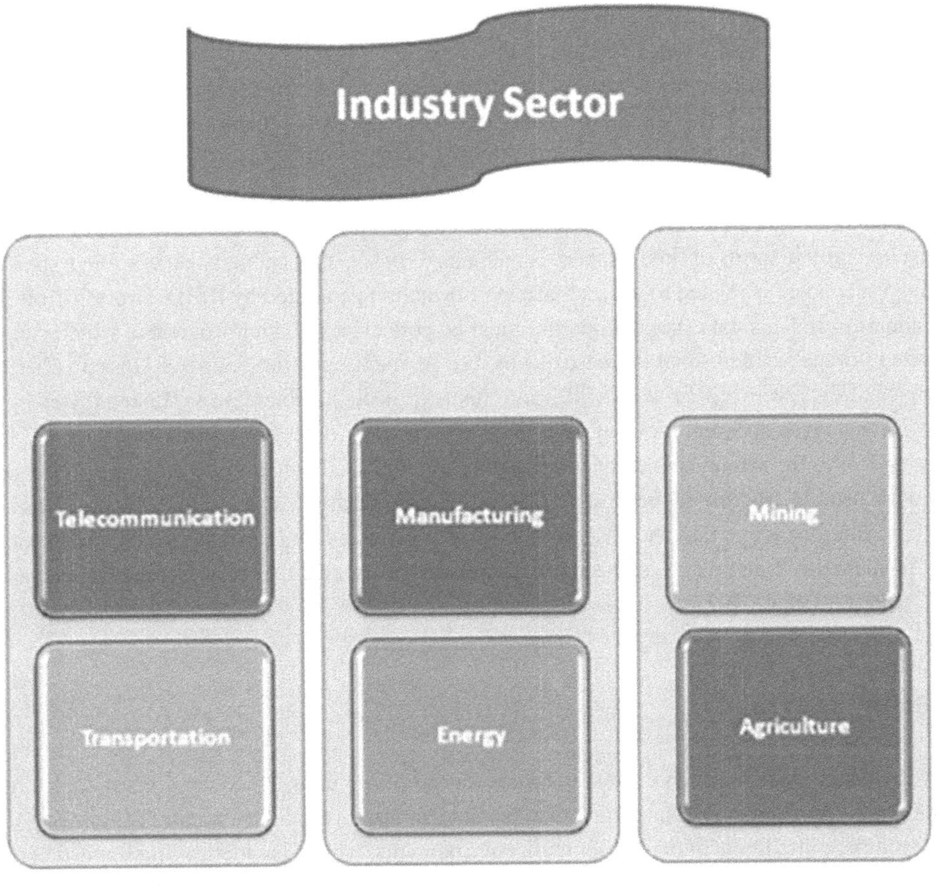

CHALLENGES OF INTERNET OF THINGS IN INDUSTRY

During the global financial crisis caused by the pandemic situation (COVID-19), more and more industrial companies are moving to IIoT. These companies want to monitor their systems remotely and avoid unplanned downtime. According to a Microsoft study (Wójcicki et al., 2022), 44 percent of organizations will invest more in IoT, compared to 31 percent in 2020. Additionally, "82 percent of surveyed companies have at least one IoT project in the operational phase." IoT is changing the future of manufacturing, but it also brings with it significant challenges that companies must face in order to implement new solutions that accelerate their digital transformation. Below, we've highlighted some of the key challenges businesses face when implementing IoT.• Technical and Technical ChallengesComplexity and technical challenges are the biggest obstacles for companies that want to take advantage of the IoT. For these reasons, 30% of surveyed organizations choose not to adopt IoT (Wójcicki et al., 2022) and use current solutions. Connecting many devices is a major challenge for IoT/IIoT. Today we rely on a centralized server/client paradigm to authorize, authenticate and connect different nodes in a network. In a combined system, the devices must work together to function properly, even if these devices work in different areas. The lack of common links, standard data formats and common software interfaces make the implementation of IoT difficult. Another challenge is the expensive modernization or replacement of traditional equipment with the latest technology (Petruţ & Oteşteanu, 2018). Most IoT devices run on batteries, so IoT also has to handle high power consumption. The cost of maintenance and/or replacement of such devices is a major concern due to the huge number of sensors used in the future. Without proper maintenance and life cycle assessment, sooner or later they can become electrical waste. Even today, there are more devices connected to the Internet than people. Another challenge is to develop highly energy-efficient and long-lasting sensor batteries that work throughout the sensor lifetime (Farhan et al., 2017; Chen, 2012) and to define responsible methods for recycling them at the end of their lifetime. The large amount of data generated by IoT plays a vital role in the big data landscape. Millions of devices are equipped with interconnected sensors that communicate, collect and exchange data. These devices collect huge amounts of data called Big Data. A major challenge is to ensure proper processing of these different types of data, especially in terms of time, resources and lack of processing capacity. According to Said and Masud (2013), the biggest concern is related to the increase in information generated by RFID. Every IoT object produces information about itself. This data (large amounts) must be collected and then processed, which can lead to data transmission and storage problems that increase day by day. As mentioned in Soomro & Hussain (2019), "In 2000, 80,000 petabytes of data were stored worldwide, and this is projected to increase to 35 zettabytes by 2020". Big Data collects and analyzes different types of data, such as structured data, semi-structured data and unstructured data, originating from sensors and stored in a data warehouse. Only 20 percent of the data is processed, while 80 percent cannot be used by traditional methods. Most of this information is useless in decision-making processes. It takes a level of intelligence to turn the vast amount of data collected by Internet devices into wisdom. Another challenge is "to adapt the structures of semi-structured and unstructured data before integrating and analyzing this type of data" (Wójcicki et al., 2022).

CONCLUSION

This survey of emerging trends and research topics for the future industry covered many topics related to the design of intelligent environments. Our goal was to provide an interdisciplinary picture of how ongoing research is shaping the future of intelligent human production environments, while also identifying important opportunities for further research. The IoT revolution continues; This means that we are at the beginning of a new data era. This revolution has a significant impact on the daily life and behavior of both private and corporate users. IoT applications are expanding into various industries, improving them and bringing tangible benefits. The possibilities offered by IoT implementation mean that all relevant sectors now have access to functions that were not available just a few years ago. IoT applications can affect, among other things: automation of industrial production, logistics, control of individual processes and business management, as well as traffic, developing an intelligent system to transport people and goods.

REFERENCES

Åkerberg, J., Gidlund, M., Lennvall, T., Neander, J., & Björkman, M. (2011). Efficient integration of secure and safety critical industrial wireless sensor networks. *EURASIP Journal on Wireless Communications and Networking*, *2011*(1), 1–13. DOI: 10.1186/1687-1499-2011-100

Alexopoulos, K., Koukas, S., Boli, N., & Mourtzis, D. (2018). Architecture and development of an Industrial Internet of Things framework for realizing services in Industrial Product Service Systems. *Procedia CIRP*, *72*, 880–885. DOI: 10.1016/j.procir.2018.03.152

Basir, R., Qaisar, S., Ali, M., Aldwairi, M., Ashraf, M. I., Mahmood, A., & Gidlund, M. (2019). Fog computing enabling industrial internet of things: State-of-the-art and research challenges. *Sensors (Basel)*, *19*(21), 4807. DOI: 10.3390/s19214807 PMID: 31694254

Boyes, H., Hallaq, B., Cunningham, J., & Watson, T. (2018). The industrial internet of things (IIoT): An analysis framework. *Computers in Industry*, *101*, 1–12. DOI: 10.1016/j.compind.2018.04.015

Cabrini, F. H., Valiante Filho, F., Rito, P., Barros Filho, A., Sargento, S., Venâncio Neto, A., & Kofuji, S. T. (2021). Enabling the industrial Internet of Things to cloud continuum in a real city environment. *Sensors (Basel)*, *21*(22), 7707. DOI: 10.3390/s21227707 PMID: 34833778

Chen, Y. K. (2012, January). Challenges and opportunities of internet of things. In 17th Asia and South Pacific design automation conference (pp. 383-388). IEEE. DOI: 10.1109/ASPDAC.2012.6164978

Farhan, L., Shukur, S. T., Alissa, A. E., Alrweg, M., Raza, U., & Kharel, R. (2017, December). A survey on the challenges and opportunities of the Internet of Things (IoT). In *2017 Eleventh International Conference on Sensing Technology (ICST)* (pp. 1-5). IEEE. DOI: 10.1109/ICSensT.2017.8304465

Fatorachian, H., & Kazemi, H. (2021). Impact of Industry 4.0 on supply chain performance. *Production Planning and Control*, *32*(1), 63–81. DOI: 10.1080/09537287.2020.1712487

Gebremichael, T., Ledwaba, L. P., Eldefrawy, M. H., Hancke, G. P., Pereira, N., Gidlund, M., & Akerberg, J. (2020). Security and privacy in the industrial internet of things: Current standards and future challenges. *IEEE Access : Practical Innovations, Open Solutions*, *8*, 152351–152366. DOI: 10.1109/ACCESS.2020.3016937

Gidlund, M., Han, S., Sisinni, E., Saifullah, A., & Jennehag, U. (2018). Guest editorial from industrial wireless sensor networks to industrial internet of things. *IEEE Transactions on Industrial Informatics*, *4*(5), 2194–2198.

Gidlund, M., Han, S., Sisinni, E., Saifullah, A., & Jennehag, U. (2018). Guest editorial from industrial wireless sensor networks to industrial internet of things. *IEEE Transactions on Industrial Informatics*, *4*(5), 2194–2198.

Grimaldi, S., Martenvormfelde, L., Mahmood, A., & Gidlund, M. (2020). Onboard spectral analysis for low-complexity IoT devices. *IEEE Access : Practical Innovations, Open Solutions*, *8*, 43027–43045. DOI: 10.1109/ACCESS.2020.2977842

Hassan, S. R., Ahmad, I., Ahmad, S., Alfaify, A., & Shafiq, M. (2020). Remote pain monitoring using fog computing for e-healthcare: An efficient architecture. *Sensors (Basel)*, *20*(22), 6574. DOI: 10.3390/s20226574 PMID: 33217896

Hussain, M., Amin, Y., & Lee, K. G. (2020). A compact and flexible UHF RFID tag antenna for massive IoT devices in 5G system. *Sensors (Basel)*, *20*(19), 5713. DOI: 10.3390/s20195713 PMID: 33049987

Kalsoom, T., Ramzan, N., Ahmed, S., & Ur-Rehman, M. (2020). Advances in sensor technologies in the era of smart factory and industry 4.0. *Sensors (Basel)*, *20*(23), 6783. DOI: 10.3390/s20236783 PMID: 33261021

. Lennvall, T., Gidlund, M., & Åkerberg, J. (2017, September). Challenges when bringing IoT into industrial automation. In 2017 IEEE AFRICON (pp. 905-910). IEEE.

Mobasheri, M., Kim, Y., & Kim, W. (2020). Fog fragment cooperation on bandwidth management based on reinforcement learning. *Sensors (Basel), 20*(23), 6942. DOI: 10.3390/s20236942 PMID: 33291695

Petruţ, I., & Oteşteanu, M. (2018, May). The IoT connectivity challenges. In 2018 IEEE 12th International Symposium on Applied Computational Intelligence and Informatics (SACI) (pp. 000385-000388). IEEE. DOI: 10.1109/SACI.2018.8440933

Rao, P. M., Al-Turjman, F., & Deebak, B. D. (2022). Smart grid metering: security, privacy, and open challenges. In *Sustainable Networks in Smart Grid* (pp. 255–272). Academic Press.

Rashid, M., Baloch, N. K., Shafique, M. A., Hussain, F., Saleem, S., Zikria, Y. B., & Yu, H. (2020). Fault-tolerant network-on-chip router architecture design for heterogeneous computing systems in the context of Internet of Things. *Sensors (Basel), 20*(18), 5355. DOI: 10.3390/s20185355 PMID: 32962030

Said, O., & Masud, M. (2013). Towards internet of things: Survey and future vision. *International Journal of Computer Networks, 5*(1), 1–17.

Sohail, M., Ali, R., Kashif, M., Ali, S., Mehta, S., Zikria, Y. B., & Yu, H. (2020). Trustwalker: An efficient trust assessment in vehicular internet of things (viot) with security consideration. *Sensors (Basel), 20*(14), 3945. DOI: 10.3390/s20143945 PMID: 32708534

Soomro, T. R., & Hussain, M. (2019). Social media-related cybercrimes and techniques for their prevention. *Applied Computer Systems, 24*(1), 9–17. DOI: 10.2478/acss-2019-0002

Souza, L. F. D. F., Silva, I. C. L., Marques, A. G., Silva, F. H. D. S., Nunes, V. X., Hassan, M. M., Albuquerque, V. H. C., & Filho, P. P. R. (2020). Internet of medical things: An effective and fully automatic IoT approach using deep learning and fine-tuning to lung CT segmentation. *Sensors (Basel), 20*(23), 6711. DOI: 10.3390/s20236711 PMID: 33255308

Wójcicki, K., Biegańska, M., Paliwoda, B., & Górna, J. (2022). Internet of things in industry: Research profiling, application, challenges and opportunities—a review. *Energies, 15*(5), 1806. DOI: 10.3390/en15051806

Wójcicki, K., Biegańska, M., Paliwoda, B., & Górna, J. (2022). Internet of things in industry: Research profiling, application, challenges and opportunities—a review. *Energies, 15*(5), 1806. DOI: 10.3390/en15051806

Chapter 27
Role of Digitalization into Hospitality Businesses:
Innovations and Trends

Nasrin Islam
https://orcid.org/0009-0007-0668-8052
Varendra University, Bangladesh

Amrik Singh
https://orcid.org/0000-0003-3598-8787
Lovely Professional University, India

ABSTRACT

Digital adoption refers to the integration and utilization of digital technologies and tools to enhance the overall guest experience, operational efficiency, and business processes. Digital adoption in hospitality encompasses the implementation and utilization of various digital solutions, such as mobile applications, self-service kiosks, online booking systems, digital menus, contactless payments, and guest management platforms. This chapter, titled "Digitalization and the Hospitality Business" will explore the profound impact of digital technologies on the hospitality industry. It will provide a comprehensive examination of how digitalization reshapes business models, enhances customer experiences, and drives operational efficiencies in hospitality. The chapter will cover key digital trends, case studies of successful digital transformations, and the challenges and opportunities that digitalization presents for hospitality businesses.

1. INTRODUCTION TO DIGITALIZATION IN HOSPITALITY

1.1 Scope of digitalization

Digitalization has become a significant driving force in today's economy and society, recognized as a key element of the Fourth Industrial Revolution (Matt et al., 2023). Digitalization boosts productivity by automating processes, improving efficiency, enabling better resource management, and driving innovation, allowing companies to develop new products, services, and business models that were previously impossible (Alcácer, 2016). However, digital transformation is not only about improving operational efficiency but also about driving sustainability. By leveraging digital technologies, industries can achieve a balance between growth and environmental administration, paving the way for a more sustainable industrial future (Matt et al., 2023; Singh et al., 2024a; Singh et al., 2024b;Singh & Bathla, 2023; Sharma & Singh, 2024a; Singh & Singh, 2024; Singh & Hassan, 2024a; Singh, 2024a; Singh,

DOI: 10.4018/979-8-3693-7447-4.ch027

2024b; Singh & Kumar, 2022; Singh & Hassan, 2024b, Singh & Kumar, 2021; Sharma & Singh, 2024b; Ansari & Singh, 2023; Ansari et al., 2023; Ambardar & singh, 2017; Ambardar et al., 2022; Francis et al., 2024; Ansari & Singh, 2024; Singh & Ansari, 2024; Singh & Kumar, 2024; Singh & Supina, 2024; Sharma & Singh, 2024c; Supina & Singh, 2024). Initially, its application was limited to creating electronic versions of documents or sounds, but modern digital technologies now have a much broader range of applications and a significant socio-economic impact (Matt et al., 2023). They create new sources of value and transform how we produce, work, communicate, and collaborate to influence organizational structures, processes, and dynamics (Matt et al., 2023). The disruptive changes brought about by digital technologies extend beyond specific industries, affecting the entire economy and society, and are intensified by the rapid pace at which these technologies evolve and generate innovations (Matt et al, 2023). Researchers have increasingly focused on this rapidly changing environment. Over the past decade, digitalization has garnered significant attention from both practitioners and academics (McQuivey, 2013; as cited in Matt et al., 2023).

1.2 Evolution of digital technologies in hospitality

The hospitality industry has undergone a remarkable transformation in recent years, with the rapid advancement of digital technologies revolutionizing the way businesses operate and interact with their customers. The digital revolution has paved the way for new opportunities, empowering hospitality companies to enhance their operational efficiency, improve customer experiences, and expand their reach in the market (Troisi et al., 2023; Singh et al., 2024a; Singh et al., 2024b;Singh & Bathla, 2023; Sharma & Singh, 2024a; Singh & Singh, 2024; Singh & Hassan, 2024a; Singh, 2024a; Singh, 2024b; Singh & Kumar, 2022; Singh & Hassan, 2024b, Singh & Kumar, 2021; Sharma & Singh, 2024b; Ansari & Singh, 2023; Ansari et al., 2023; Ambardar & singh, 2017; Ambardar et al., 2022; Francis et al., 2024; Ansari & Singh, 2024; Singh & Ansari, 2024; Singh & Kumar, 2024; Singh & Supina, 2024; Sharma & Singh, 2024c; Supina & Singh, 2024). Digitalization has become a driving force in the tourism sector, as evidenced by the incorporation of various technologies that support the consumer experience (Cheng et al., 2023). The global hospitality industry has embraced digital transformation, making customer experience a profitable business and presenting a variety of opportunities. The digital revolution has led to the incorporation of innovative booking systems, e-commerce and distribution platforms, marketing tools, mobile applications, and social media, all of which have significantly impacted the competitiveness of both tourism market entities and destinations (Cheng et al., 2023; Boiko et al., 2022). The digitalization of the hospitality industry has been fueled by the synergy of digital and service economies, creating new opportunities for tourism development with novel markets, management approaches, and business methods. The digital transformation has enabled hospitality businesses to streamline their operations, enhance their customer-centric focus, and adapt to the evolving needs of their clientele (Cheng et al., 2023; Singh et al., 2024a; Singh et al., 2024b;Singh & Bathla, 2023; Sharma & Singh, 2024a; Singh & Singh, 2024; Singh & Hassan, 2024a; Singh, 2024a; Singh, 2024b; Singh & Kumar, 2022; Singh & Hassan, 2024b, Singh & Kumar, 2021; Sharma & Singh, 2024b; Ansari & Singh, 2023; Ansari et al., 2023; Ambardar & singh, 2017; Ambardar et al., 2022; Francis et al., 2024; Ansari & Singh, 2024; Singh & Ansari, 2024; Singh & Kumar, 2024; Singh & Supina, 2024; Sharma & Singh, 2024c; Supina & Singh, 2024).

2. DIGITAL TECHNOLOGIES TRANSFORMING HOSPITALITY

2.1 Overview of significant technologies

The hospitality sector is going through an evolution driven by the rapid progress of digital technologies within hotels, restaurants, and other hospitality-focused enterprises. At the forefront of this digital transformation are several key technologies that have emerged as crucial enablers, empowering hospitality providers to enhance service quality, improve operational efficiency, and deliver more personalized and engaging experiences to their guests (Torres & Sipe, 2020; Singh et al., 2024a; Singh et al., 2024b;Singh & Bathla, 2023; Sharma & Singh, 2024a; Singh & Singh, 2024; Singh & Hassan, 2024a; Singh, 2024a; Singh, 2024b; Singh & Kumar, 2022; Singh & Hassan, 2024b, Singh & Kumar, 2021; Sharma & Singh, 2024b; Ansari & Singh, 2023; Ansari et al., 2023; Ambardar & singh, 2017; Ambardar et al., 2022; Francis et al., 2024; Ansari & Singh, 2024; Singh & Ansari, 2024; Singh & Kumar, 2024; Singh & Supina, 2024; Sharma & Singh, 2024c; Supina & Singh, 2024). One of the most significant digital innovations transforming the hospitality industry is the application of artificial intelligence (AI) and machine learning. These advanced technologies have enabled the development of intelligent systems that can analyze customer data, predict preferences, and make personalized recommendations for products, services, and experiences (Fernandez-Vidal et al., 2022). For instance, AI-powered chatbots and virtual assistants can engage with guests, answer inquiries, and even handle basic tasks like room control and service requests, providing a seamless and efficient customer interaction (Fernandez-Vidal et al., 2022; Singh et al., 2024a; Singh et al., 2024b;Singh & Bathla, 2023; Sharma & Singh, 2024a; Singh & Singh, 2024; Singh & Hassan, 2024a; Singh, 2024a; Singh, 2024b; Singh & Kumar, 2022; Singh & Hassan, 2024b, Singh & Kumar, 2021; Sharma & Singh, 2024b; Ansari & Singh, 2023; Ansari et al., 2023; Ambardar & singh, 2017; Ambardar et al., 2022; Francis et al., 2024; Ansari & Singh, 2024; Singh & Ansari, 2024; Singh & Kumar, 2024; Singh & Supina, 2024; Sharma & Singh, 2024c; Supina & Singh, 2024). Furthermore, the proliferation of the Internet of Things (IoT) has led to heightened interconnectivity within the hospitality sector, allowing hotels and resorts to leverage a wealth of data generated by various smart devices to optimize operations, monitor and maintain facilities, and deliver a more personalized guest experience (Topsakal et al., 2022). By integrating IoT-enabled systems, hospitality providers can not only improve the overall efficiency of their properties but also offer guests enhanced convenience and comfort, such as personalized room settings, automated check-in and checkout processes, and technological advancements such as the Internet of Things, artificial intelligence, and big data analytics have transformed the way hospitality businesses interact with their customers, offering personalized experiences and data-driven insights.

2.2 Case Studies of Digital Transformation in Hospitality

The digital transformation (DT) has introduced new opportunities and challenges for organizations to navigate. The increasing adoption of technologies such as artificial intelligence, data analytics, and the Internet of Things (IoT) has enabled hospitality providers to enhance the customer experience, optimize operational efficiency, and gain a competitive edge in the market (Barashok et al., 2021; Singh et al., 2024a; Singh et al., 2024b;Singh & Bathla, 2023; Sharma & Singh, 2024a; Singh & Singh, 2024; Singh & Hassan, 2024a; Singh, 2024a; Singh, 2024b; Singh & Kumar, 2022; Singh & Hassan, 2024b, Singh & Kumar, 2021; Sharma & Singh, 2024b; Ansari & Singh, 2023; Ansari et al., 2023; Ambardar & singh, 2017; Ambardar et al., 2022; Francis et al., 2024; Ansari & Singh, 2024; Singh & Ansari, 2024; Singh & Kumar, 2024; Singh & Supina, 2024; Sharma & Singh, 2024c; Supina & Singh, 2024; Topsakal et al., 2022; Torres & Sipe, 2020). One particularly notable example of digital transformation in the hospitality industry is the implementation of artificial intelligence (AI) (Torres & Sipe, 2020). By leveraging AI-powered systems, hotels can now provide personalized recommendations and tailored experiences to their guests, drawing insights from vast amounts of customer data. This has enabled hospitality providers to anticipate guest preferences, streamline the booking process, and even automate certain routine tasks, such as check-in and check-out procedures (Torres & Sipe, 2020). Similarly, the integration of the Internet of Things (IoT) into hotel operations has allowed for greater control and optimization of various aspects of the guest experience, from smart room controls to predictive maintenance of facilities. Hoteliers can now monitor and adjust factors such as temperature, lighting, and entertainment in real-time, creating a more personalized and comfortable environment for their guests (Singh et al., 2024a; Singh et al., 2024b;Singh & Bathla, 2023; Sharma & Singh, 2024a; Singh & Singh, 2024; Singh & Hassan, 2024a; Singh, 2024a; Singh, 2024b; Singh & Kumar, 2022; Singh & Hassan, 2024b, Singh & Kumar, 2021; Sharma & Singh, 2024b; Ansari & Singh, 2023; Ansari et al., 2023; Ambardar & singh,

2017; Ambardar et al., 2022; Francis et al., 2024; Ansari & Singh, 2024; Singh & Ansari, 2024; Singh & Kumar, 2024; Singh & Supina, 2024; Sharma & Singh, 2024c; Supina & Singh, 2024). According to Jayawardena (2023), digital transformation (DT) has become a key strategic initiative driving many organizations. The hotel industry, in particular, is showing a strong inclination towards DT due to the increasing digital demand, ubiquitous connectivity, and new tourism trends. Their study aimed to understand the integral relationship of the extended Unified Theory of Acceptance and Use of Technology (UTAUT) and its predictive correlations to establish DT in Sri Lankan hotels. A statistically validated conceptual model demonstrated positive predictability of DT in hotels, providing new directions in social science and digital transformation research. The findings emphasize that top management support, social influence, and effort expectancy are significant acceptance factors that directly correlate with the activation of DT. Additionally, the high predictability of behavior expectation suggests that hotel owners must foster both volitional and non-volitional engagement to successfully implement digital transformation in hotels.

2.3 Enhancing Customer Experience through Digitalization

Digitalization in the hospitality industry is profoundly enhancing the customer experience by offering more personalized, efficient, and interactive services. Technologies such as AI and IoT enable real-time data collection and analysis, allowing hospitality providers to understand and anticipate customer needs better. For instance, AI-driven recommendation systems can suggest personalized services and amenities based on a guest's preferences and past behaviors. IoT devices in rooms can adjust settings such as lighting, temperature, and entertainment options to suit individual guest preferences, creating a more tailored and enjoyable stay (Cheng et al.,2023; Singh et al., 2024a; Singh et al., 2024b;Singh & Bathla, 2023; Sharma & Singh, 2024a; Singh & Singh, 2024; Singh & Hassan, 2024a; Singh, 2024a; Singh, 2024b; Singh & Kumar, 2022; Singh & Hassan, 2024b, Singh & Kumar, 2021; Sharma & Singh, 2024b; Ansari & Singh, 2023; Ansari et al., 2023; Ambardar & singh, 2017; Ambardar et al., 2022; Francis et al., 2024; Ansari & Singh, 2024; Singh & Ansari, 2024; Singh & Kumar, 2024; Singh & Supina, 2024; Sharma & Singh, 2024c; Supina & Singh, 2024). Moreover, mobile applications have become crucial tools for enhancing customer experience. Apps allow guests to make reservations, check-in and out, order room service, and access hotel information seamlessly. These applications often integrate with social media platforms, enabling guests to share their experiences and provide real-time feedback, which can be invaluable for continuous service improvement. Digital payment systems and contactless transactions further streamline the customer experience, reducing wait times and enhancing convenience (Cheng et al., 2023; Singh et al., 2024a; Singh et al., 2024b;Singh & Bathla, 2023; Sharma & Singh, 2024a; Singh & Singh, 2024; Singh & Hassan, 2024a; Singh, 2024a; Singh, 2024b; Singh & Kumar, 2022; Singh & Hassan, 2024b, Singh & Kumar, 2021; Sharma & Singh, 2024b; Ansari & Singh, 2023; Ansari et al., 2023; Ambardar & singh, 2017; Ambardar et al., 2022; Francis et al., 2024; Ansari & Singh, 2024; Singh & Ansari, 2024; Singh & Kumar, 2024; Singh & Supina, 2024; Sharma & Singh, 2024c; Supina & Singh, 2024). For innovative enterprises, the efficiency of interactivity is crucial for business success. The swift advancement of ICT solutions has significantly transformed the tourism industry. In the past, consumers' decision-making was primarily influenced by the industrial environment. The era of digital tourism spaces, which followed the development of theme parks and thematic destinations, began with the advent of informational websites. However, this initial flow of targeted information was one-directional and offered limited choices. In today's digital age, new commercial activities occur in VR or AR spaces, with instant analysis of customer reactions and behaviors enhancing their willingness to buy. Traditional decision-making processes are gradually being replaced by personalized offers, further highlighting the importance of AI (Zsarnoczky, 2018).

2.4 Operational Efficiency through Digital Technologies

Digital technologies are not only transforming customer interactions but also significantly improving operational efficiency within the hospitality industry. Automation of routine tasks through AI and machine learning helps reduce human error and free up staff to focus on more complex, customer-facing roles. For example, automated check-in kiosks and mobile check-in options reduce the workload on front desk staff and minimize wait times for guests.

IoT-enabled devices and systems allow for efficient management of energy consumption, maintenance schedules, and inventory levels. Smart sensors can monitor usage patterns and optimize heating, cooling, and lighting, leading to significant cost savings and sustainability benefits. Predictive maintenance enabled by IoT can alert staff to potential issues before they become major problems, reducing downtime and maintenance costs (Singh et al., 2024a; Singh et al., 2024b;Singh & Bathla, 2023; Sharma & Singh, 2024a; Singh & Singh, 2024; Singh & Hassan, 2024a; Singh, 2024a; Singh, 2024b; Singh & Kumar, 2022; Singh & Hassan, 2024b, Singh & Kumar, 2021; Sharma & Singh, 2024b; Ansari & Singh, 2023; Ansari et al., 2023; Ambardar & singh, 2017; Ambardar et al., 2022; Francis et al., 2024; Ansari & Singh, 2024; Singh & Ansari, 2024; Singh & Kumar, 2024; Singh & Supina, 2024; Sharma & Singh, 2024c; Supina & Singh, 2024). Big data analytics plays a crucial role in operational efficiency by providing insights into customer behavior, market trends, and operational bottlenecks. By analyzing this data, hospitality businesses can make informed decisions about staffing, inventory management, and service improvements, ultimately leading to more streamlined operations and enhanced profitability (Topsakal et al., 2022). The importance of embracing digital transformation cannot be overstated, as it can be a key driver of long-term success in the hospitality industry (Cheng et al., 2023). Innovative business models that leverage digital technologies have emerged, enabling hospitality companies to enhance the customer experience, improve operational efficiency, and gain a competitive edge. The tourism industry, in particular, has seen the rise of new digital platforms and services that have disrupted traditional business models. Businesses that fail to adapt to these technological advancements risk falling behind, as the industry continues to evolve at a rapid pace (Cheng et al., 2023). The rapid digitalization of the tourism and hospitality sectors has created a wealth of opportunities for businesses to better understand and cater to customer needs (Barashok et al., 2021; (Singh et al., 2024a; Singh et al., 2024b;Singh & Bathla, 2023; Sharma & Singh, 2024a; Singh & Singh, 2024; Singh & Hassan, 2024a; Singh, 2024a; Singh, 2024b; Singh & Kumar, 2022; Singh & Hassan, 2024b, Singh & Kumar, 2021; Sharma & Singh, 2024b; Ansari & Singh, 2023; Ansari et al., 2023; Ambardar & singh, 2017; Ambardar et al., 2022; Francis et al., 2024; Ansari & Singh, 2024; Singh & Ansari, 2024; Singh & Kumar, 2024; Singh & Supina, 2024; Sharma & Singh, 2024c; Supina & Singh, 2024). Data analytics and artificial intelligence have enabled hospitality providers to personalize the customer experience, offering tailored recommendations and services that enhance satisfaction and build loyalty (Valsamidis et al., 2020; Barashok et al., 2021). Innovative business models that prioritize digital transformation have emerged as industry leaders, disrupting traditional approaches and gaining a competitive edge (Valsamidis et al., 2020).

2.5 Objectives

- To analyze the key digital technologies influencing the hospitality industry.
- To understand how digitalization enhances customer experience and operational efficiency.
- To examine the strategic implications of digital transformation for hospitality businesses.
- To discuss the challenges and risks associated with digitalization in hospitality.

3. CHALLENGES AND RISKS IN DIGITAL TRANSFORMATION

3.1 Security and Privacy Concerns

Integrating digital technologies in the hospitality industry brings significant benefits but also introduces substantial challenges, particularly security and privacy. The vast amounts of data collected and processed by digital systems, including personal and financial information, make hospitality businesses prime targets for cyberattacks. Ensuring the security of these data and maintaining customer trust requires robust cybersecurity measures, including encryption, secure data storage, and regular security audits(Henriette, 2016). Privacy concerns are also paramount, as guests increasingly demand transparency and control over their personal information. Compliance with regulations such as the General Data Protection Regulation (GDPR) is essential to protect guest data and avoid legal repercussions. Hospitality providers must implement clear privacy policies and practices, informing guests about how their data is collected, used, and protected.

3.2 Technological Integration and Workforce Adaptation

Another challenge in digital transformation is the integration of new technologies with existing systems. Legacy systems in many hospitality businesses may not be compatible with advanced digital solutions, necessitating significant investments in technology upgrades and staff training. Ensuring seamless integration and minimizing disruption during the transition phase is critical to maintaining operational continuity (Singh et al., 2024a; Singh et al., 2024b;Singh & Bathla, 2023; Sharma & Singh, 2024a; Singh & Singh, 2024; Singh & Hassan, 2024a; Singh, 2024a; Singh, 2024b; Singh & Kumar, 2022; Singh & Hassan, 2024b, Singh & Kumar, 2021; Sharma & Singh, 2024b; Ansari & Singh, 2023; Ansari et al., 2023; Ambardar & singh, 2017; Ambardar et al., 2022; Francis et al., 2024; Ansari & Singh, 2024; Singh & Ansari, 2024; Singh & Kumar, 2024; Singh & Supina, 2024; Sharma & Singh, 2024c; Supina & Singh, 2024). . Additionally, the workforce must adapt to new technologies and workflows. This requires comprehensive training programs to equip employees with the necessary skills to utilize digital tools effectively. Resistance to change among staff can also be a barrier, highlighting the need for change management strategies that promote a culture of innovation and continuous learning within the organization.

4. FUTURE TRENDS IN HOSPITALITY DIGITALIZATION

4.1 Emerging Technologies

The future of digitalization in hospitality is likely to be shaped by several emerging technologies that promise to further enhance customer experiences and operational efficiencies. Augmented reality (AR) and virtual reality (VR) are poised to revolutionize the way guests interact with hospitality services. AR can enhance the in-room experience by providing interactive information about hotel amenities and local attractions, while VR can offer immersive virtual tours of hotel properties and destinations, aiding in the decision-making process for potential guests (Singh et al., 2024a; Singh et al., 2024b;Singh & Bathla, 2023; Sharma & Singh, 2024a; Singh & Singh, 2024; Singh & Hassan, 2024a; Singh, 2024a; Singh, 2024b; Singh & Kumar, 2022; Singh & Hassan, 2024b, Singh & Kumar, 2021; Sharma & Singh, 2024b; Ansari & Singh, 2023; Ansari et al., 2023; Ambardar & singh, 2017; Ambardar et al., 2022; Francis et al., 2024; Ansari & Singh, 2024; Singh & Ansari, 2024; Singh & Kumar, 2024; Singh & Supina, 2024; Sharma & Singh, 2024c; Supina & Singh, 2024). Blockchain technology is another emerging trend with the potential to transform the hospitality industry. By providing a secure and transparent platform for transactions, blockchain can enhance the efficiency and security of booking systems, loyalty programs, and supply chain management. Smart contracts enabled by blockchain can automate and streamline various operational processes, reducing the need for intermediaries and minimizing the risk of fraud.

4.2 Sustainability and Digital Innovation

Sustainability is becoming an increasingly important consideration in the hospitality industry, and digital technologies play a crucial role in supporting sustainable practices. IoT-enabled energy management systems can optimize resource consumption, reducing the environmental footprint of hospitality operations. Digital platforms can also facilitate sustainable travel choices by providing guests with information on eco-friendly options and promoting local, sustainable businesses. However, the readiness of companies and organizations to handle ongoing digital transformation while maintaining or enhancing sustainability requires further exploration. Some current smart tourism strategies appear to use smart and sustainability concepts superficially, often as marketing tools, due to theoretical inconsistencies that need addressing in future research to establish a solid understanding of the smart approach in tourism (Rodrigues, 2023; Sharma & Singh, 2024a; Singh & Singh, 2024; Singh & Hassan, 2024a; Singh, 2024a; Singh, 2024b; Singh & Kumar, 2022; Singh & Hassan, 2024b, Singh & Kumar, 2021; Sharma & Singh, 2024b; Ansari & Singh, 2023; Ansari et al., 2023; Ambardar & singh, 2017; Ambardar et al., 2022; Francis et al., 2024; Ansari & Singh, 2024; Singh & Ansari, 2024; Singh & Kumar, 2024; Singh & Supina, 2024; Sharma & Singh, 2024c; Supina & Singh, 2024). The pandemic has accelerated digital transformation, leading to an expected increase in publications on these topics in the near future. Future research should analyze the role of various technologies in this context, categorizing findings by technology type to identify those most relevant to tourism. Since 4.0 technologies were originally designed for industrial applications, their transfer to the service-oriented tourism sector requires careful consideration. Comparative studies on digital dynamics before and after the COVID-19 pandemic are also recommended, as technology use has likely increased during and after the crisis. Additionally, investigating the role of smart approaches in crisis management is crucial to determine if technological solutions can prevent total industry shutdowns during crises (e.g., economic collapse, pandemics), thereby saving jobs and businesses and providing sustainable development models for the future(Rodrigues, 2023). While sustainability has been the focus of numerous studies in the past, the tourism industry still struggles to fully integrate all dimensions of the concept. Additionally, although technologies are often highlighted as valuable management tools that can bridge gaps and connect people and places, even virtually, their adoption in tourism destinations and businesses remains in the early stages. This is particularly true for the tourism sector, which predominantly consists of micro, small, and medium enterprises facing significant constraints in human, financial, and investment resources, making digital transformation challenging(Rodrigues, 2023).

Despite existing studies on the impact of smart tourism on visitor experiences and its influence on sustainability, more evidence is needed to understand the implications of smart technologies and digitalization on visitors. Specifically, further research should explore visitor acceptance of increased digitalization, their digital literacy levels, and their contribution to sustainable tourism practices.

Innovative digital solutions can support waste reduction efforts, such as digital menus and ordering systems that minimize paper use and smart inventory management systems that reduce food waste. The integration of sustainability and digital innovation not only helps hospitality businesses meet regulatory requirements and consumer expectations but also enhances their brand reputation and competitiveness in the market.

5. CONCLUSION

The digital transformation of the hospitality industry is an ongoing process, characterized by the continuous integration of advanced technologies to enhance customer experiences, optimize operations, and drive innovation. While digitalization presents numerous opportunities, it also poses significant challenges, particularly in terms of security, privacy, and workforce adaptation. By embracing digital technologies and addressing these challenges proactively, hospitality businesses can position themselves for long-term success in a rapidly evolving landscape. As digital trends continue to evolve, hospitality providers must remain agile and forward-thinking, leveraging emerging technologies to stay ahead of the competition. The convergence of digital innovation and sustainability will be a key driver of future growth, enabling the hospitality industry to meet the demands of tech-savvy, environmentally conscious consumers while achieving operational excellence.

6. EXPECTED CONTRIBUTION

This chapter aims to provide a thorough understanding of how digitalization is transforming the hospitality industry. It will serve as a valuable resource for academics, industry practitioners, and students, offering practical insights and strategic guidance for leveraging digital technologies in hospitality. By addressing both the opportunities and challenges of digital transformation, the chapter will help stakeholders navigate the complexities of digitalization and drive innovation in their businesses.

7. REFERENCES

Alcácer, J., Cantwell, J., & Piscitello, L. (2016). Internationalization in the information age: A new era for places, firms, and international business networks? *Journal of International Business Studies*, *47*(5), 499–512. DOI: 10.1057/jibs.2016.22

Ambardar, A., Singh, A., & Singh, V. (2023). Barriers in Implementing Ergonomic Practices in Hotels- A Study on five star hotels in NCR region. *International Journal of Hospitality and Tourism Systems*, *16*(2), 11–17.

Ansari, A. I., & Singh, A. (2023). "Application of Augmented Reality (AR) and Virtual Reality (VR) in Promoting Guest Room Sales: A Critical Review", Tučková, Z., Dey, S.K., Thai, H.H. and Hoang, S.D. (Ed.) *Impact of Industry 4.0 on Sustainable Tourism*, Emerald Publishing Limited, Leeds, pp. 95-104. DOI: 10.1108/978-1-80455-157-820231006

Ansari, A. I., & Singh, A. (2024). Adopting Sustainable and Recycling Practices in the Hotel Industry and Its Factors Influencing Guest Satisfaction. In Tyagi, P., Nadda, V., Kankaew, K., & Dube, K. (Eds.), *Examining Tourist Behaviors and Community Involvement in Destination Rejuvenation* (pp. 38–47). IGI Global., DOI: 10.4018/979-8-3693-6819-0.ch003

Ansari, A. I., Singh, A., & Singh, V. (2023). The impact of differential pricing on perceived service quality and guest satisfaction: An empirical study of mid-scale hotels in India. *Turyzm/Tourism*, 121–132. https://doi.org/DOI: 10.18778/0867-5856.33.2.10

Barashok, I. V., Rudenko, L. L., Shumakova, E. V., & Orlovskaia, I. V. (2021, March). Digitization: New possibilities for the Tourism industry. []. IOP Publishing.]. *IOP Conference Series. Earth and Environmental Science*, *666*(6), 062059. DOI: 10.1088/1755-1315/666/6/062059

Bhalla, A., Singh, P., & Singh, A. (2023). Technological Advancement and Mechanization of the Hotel Industry. In Tailor, R. (Ed.), *Application and Adoption of Robotic Process Automation for Smart Cities* (pp. 57–76). IGI Global., DOI: 10.4018/978-1-6684-7193-7.ch004

Boiko, M., Bosovska, M., Vedmid, N., Melnychenko, S., & Stopchenko, Y. (2022). Digitalization: Implementation in the tourism business of Ukraine. *Problems and Perspectives in Management*, *20*(4), 24–41. DOI: 10.21511/ppm.20(4).2022.03

Cheng, X., Xue, T., Yang, B., & Ma, B. (2023). A digital transformation approach in hospitality and tourism research. *International Journal of Contemporary Hospitality Management*, *35*(8), 2944–2967. DOI: 10.1108/IJCHM-06-2022-0679

Fernandez-Vidal, J., Perotti, F. A., Gonzalez, R., & Gasco, J. (2022). Managing digital transformation: The view from the top. *Journal of Business Research*, *152*, 29–41. DOI: 10.1016/j.jbusres.2022.07.020

Francis, R. S., Anantharajah, S., Sengupta, S., & Singh, A. (2024). Leveraging ChatGPT and Digital Marketing for Enhanced Customer Engagement in the Hotel Industry. In Bansal, R., Ngah, A., Chakir, A., & Pruthi, N. (Eds.), *Leveraging ChatGPT and Artificial Intelligence for Effective Customer Engagement* (pp. 55–68). IGI Global., DOI: 10.4018/979-8-3693-0815-8.ch004

Henriette, E., Feki, M., &Boughzala, I. (2016). Digital transformation challenges. https://doi.org/DOI: 10.4018/978-1-6684-6732-9.ch005

Jayawardena, C., Ahmad, A., Valeri, M., & Jaharadak, A. A. (2023). Technology acceptance antecedents in digital transformation in hospitality industry. *International Journal of Hospitality Management, 108*, 103350. DOI: 10.1016/j.ijhm.2022.103350

Kansakar, P., Munir, A., & Shabani, N. (2018, December). A fog-assisted architecture to support an evolving hospitality industry in smart cities. In *2018 International Conference on Frontiers of Information Technology (FIT)* (pp. 59-64). IEEE. DOI: 10.1109/FIT.2018.00018

Matt, D. T., Pedrini, G., Bonfanti, A., & Orzes, G. (2023). Industrial digitalization. A systematic literature review and research agenda. *European Management Journal, 41*(1), 47–78. DOI: 10.1016/j.emj.2022.01.001

Rodrigues, V., Eusébio, C., & Breda, Z. (2023). Enhancing sustainable development through tourism digitalisation: A systematic literature review. *Information Technology & Tourism, 25*(1), 13–45. DOI: 10.1007/s40558-022-00241-w

Sharma, M., & Singh, A. (2024a). Enhancing Competitive Advantages Through Virtual Reality Technology in the Hotels of India. In Kumar, S., Talukder, M., & Pego, A. (Eds.), *Utilizing Smart Technology and AI in Hybrid Tourism and Hospitality* (pp. 243–256). IGI Global., DOI: 10.4018/979-8-3693-1978-9.ch011

Sharma, R., & Singh, A. (2024b). Use of Digital Technology in Improving Quality Education: A Global Perspectives and Trends. In Nadda, V., Tyagi, P., Moniz Vieira, R., & Tyagi, P. (Eds.), *Implementing Sustainable Development Goals in the Service Sector* (pp. 14–26). IGI Global., DOI: 10.4018/979-8-3693-2065-5.ch002

Sharma, R., & Singh, A. (2024c). Blockchain Technologies and Call for an Open Financial System: Decentralised Finance. In Vardari, L., & Qabrati, I. (Eds.), *Decentralized Finance and Tokenization in FinTech* (pp. 21–32). IGI Global., DOI: 10.4018/979-8-3693-3346-4.ch002

Singh, A. (2024a). Quality of Work-Life Practices in the Indian Hospitality Sector: Future Challenges and Prospects. In Valeri, M., & Sousa, B. (Eds.), *Human Relations Management in Tourism* (pp. 208–224). IGI Global., DOI: 10.4018/979-8-3693-1322-0.ch010

Singh, A. (2024b). Virtual Research Collaboration and Technology Application: Drivers, Motivations, and Constraints. In Chakraborty, S. (Ed.), *Challenges of Globalization and Inclusivity in Academic Research* (pp. 250–258). IGI Global., DOI: 10.4018/979-8-3693-1371-8.ch016

Singh, A., & Ansari, A. I. (2024). Role of Training and Development in Employee Motivation: Tourism and Hospitality Sector. In Mazurowski, T. (Ed.), *Enhancing Employee Motivation Through Training and Development* (pp. 248–261). IGI Global., DOI: 10.4018/979-8-3693-1674-0.ch011

Singh, A., & Bathla, G. (2023). Fostering Creativity and Innovation: Tourism and Hospitality Perspective. In P. Tyagi, V. Nadda, V. Bharti, & E. Kemer (Eds.), *Embracing Business Sustainability through Innovation and Creativity in the Service Sector* (pp. 70-83). IGI Global.

Singh, A., & Hassan, S. C. (2024). Service Innovation Through Blockchain Technology in the Tourism and Hospitality Industry: Applications, Trends, and Benefits. In Singh, S. (Ed.), *Service Innovations in Tourism: Metaverse, Immersive Technologies, and Digital Twin* (pp. 205–214). IGI Global., DOI: 10.4018/979-8-3693-1103-5.ch010

Singh, A., & Hassan, S. C. (2024), "Identifying the Skill Gap in the Workplace and Their Challenges in Hospitality and Tourism Organisations", Thake, A.M., Sood, K., Özen, E. and Grima, S. (Ed.) *Contemporary Challenges in Social Science Management: Skills Gaps and Shortages in the Labour Market (Contemporary Studies in Economic and Financial Analysis, Vol. 112B)*, Emerald Publishing Limited, Leeds, pp. 101-114. DOI: 10.1108/S1569-37592024000112B006

Singh, A., & Kumar, S. (2021). Identifying Innovations in Human Resources: Academia and Industry Perspectives. In Pathak, A., & Rana, S. (Eds.), *Transforming Human Resource Functions With Automation* (pp. 104–120). IGI Global. DOI: 10.4018/978-1-7998-4180-7.ch006

Singh, A., & Kumar, S. (2024). Effective Talent Management Practices Implemented in the Hospitality Sector. In Christiansen, B., Aziz, M., & O'Keeffe, E. (Eds.), *Global Practices on Effective Talent Acquisition and Retention* (pp. 126–144). IGI Global., DOI: 10.4018/979-8-3693-1938-3.ch008

Singh, A., & Supina, S. (2024). Talent Acquisition and Retention in Hospitality Industry: Current Skill Gaps and Challenges. In Christiansen, B., Aziz, M., & O'Keeffe, E. (Eds.), *Global Practices on Effective Talent Acquisition and Retention* (pp. 363–379). IGI Global., DOI: 10.4018/979-8-3693-1938-3.ch020

Singh, A., Tyagi, P. K., & Garg, A. (Eds.). (2024). *Sustainable Disposal Methods of Food Wastes in Hospitality Operations*. IGI Global., DOI: 10.4018/979-8-3693-2181-2

Singh, V., Archana, T., Singh, A., & Tyagi, P. K. (2024). Utilizing Technology for Food Waste Management in the Hospitality Industry Hotels and Restaurants. In Singh, A., Tyagi, P., & Garg, A. (Eds.), *Sustainable Disposal Methods of Food Wastes in Hospitality Operations* (pp. 287–295). IGI Global., DOI: 10.4018/979-8-3693-2181-2.ch019

Singh, V., & Singh, A. (2024a). Digital Health Revolution: Enhancing Well-Being Through Technology. In Nadda, V., Tyagi, P., Moniz Vieira, R., & Tyagi, P. (Eds.), *Implementing Sustainable Development Goals in the Service Sector* (pp. 213–219). IGI Global., DOI: 10.4018/979-8-3693-2065-5.ch016

Singh, V., & Singh, A. (2024b). Revolutionizing the Hospitality Industry: How chatGPT Empowers Future Hoteliers. In Bansal, R., Ngah, A., Chakir, A., & Pruthi, N. (Eds.), *Leveraging ChatGPT and Artificial Intelligence for Effective Customer Engagement* (pp. 192–203). IGI Global., DOI: 10.4018/979-8-3693-0815-8.ch011

Supina, S., & Singh, A. (2024). Exploring the Presence and Adoption of Quality of Work-Life Dimensions in the Hotel Industry? *African Journal of Hospitality, Tourism and Leisure*, *13*(2), 421–429. DOI: 10.46222/ajhtl.19770720.524

Topsakal, Y., Icoz, O., & Icoz, O. (2022). Digital Transformation and Tourist Experiences. In Handbook of Research on Digital Communications, Internet of Things, and the Future of Cultural Tourism (pp. 19-41). IGI Global. DOI: 10.4018/978-1-7998-8528-3.ch002

Torres, A. M., & Sipe, M. D. (2020). Hospitality Service Innovation: KLEEDing an Outstanding Guest Experience. *Journal of Next-generation Convergence Information Services Technology*, *9*(2), 149–162. DOI: 10.29056/jncist.2020.06.05

Troisi, O., Visvizi, A., & Grimaldi, M. (2023). Digitalizing business models in hospitality ecosystems: Toward data-driven innovation. *European Journal of Innovation Management*, *26*(7), 242–277. DOI: 10.1108/EJIM-09-2022-0540

Valsamidis, S., Tsourgiannis, L., Pappas, D., &Mosxou, E. (2020). Digital banking in the new era: Exploring customers' attitudes. Business Performance and Financial Institutions in Europe: Business Models and Value Creation Across European Industries, 91-104.

Zsarnoczky, M. (2018). The digital future of the tourism & hospitality industry. *Boston Hospitality Review*, *6*, 1–9.

Chapter 28
Hotel Employees' Perspective Towards IT Skills Competencies in the Hotels of Delhi NCR

Ashish Dhyani
https://orcid.org/0000-0002-9370-9857
Veer Madho Singh Bhandari Uttarakhand Technical University, Dehradun, India

Rajat Praveen Dimri
Swami Ram Himalayan University, India

Vikas Gairola
Omkarananda Institute of Management and Technology, India

ABSTRACT

With technical advancements, human resource still remains a vital component towards the success of an organization. The prime objective of this study is to assess the overall perspective of the employees, evaluating the competencies viz. IT (Information Technology) skills, Verbal and Written Communication, Dispute Redressal, Self Control and Trade Specific Skills. The study resulted that employees rated IT skills as the most required skills among the others. The managerial implication of the study will result in enhanced employees' performance and the employers and human resource managers will have an idea about the competencies to look for. The present study is carried out in the month of April and May on the 07 hotels of Delhi NCR. The sample size consists of 62 respondents via convenient sampling through a questionnaire designed to retrieve the demographic profile of the respondents and recorded their responses on a Likert scale of 5.

INTRODUCTION

According to World Travel and Tourism Council report 2018, the contributions of the tourism sector in global GDP was US$2.6 Trillion offering 119 million global jobs. This was equivalent to world 10.4% of GDP. Ranking on India was 7th among the world's tourism economy. The hospitality industry is a favourite career option among the youth and the same trend continues in India and in Delhi NCR too.

Due to technological advancements in the various fields like transportation, technologies like Central reservation system and Global distribution system, revisions in passport and visa rules has led to people travelling more easily. The employers in the modern era are encountering employees' related issues like skills shortages, staff turnover, demand for multi tasking abilities and inappropriate training. Another challenge is to cater the needs of

DOI: 10.4018/979-8-3693-7447-4.ch028

the satisfying the guests equipped with knowledge pertaining to lifestyle, operations and technology as well. This is to be tackled with a workforce that is armoured with the latest knowledge and should be capable to set new benchmarks and perform constantly.

(Kacetl, 2018) emphasized on the role of communication between the host or hotel employees and the guest. Support in the form of training to the staff from the management is quite important. (Gillovic & McIntosh, 2020) mentioned language as a tool to break negative attitudes and build positive ones. With the collective efforts, the understanding can get better. (Erazo et al., 2019) affirmed that among the jobs related to technology, tourism and commerce, communication hold great significance in building the rapport and for removal of any conflict. (Syamini, 2019) quoted English language in his study as *Lingua Franca*. Command over grammar and sentence structure helps expressing in a better way in tourism and hospitality sector. (Bhanu Pratap & Singhal, 2018) observed that Psychological elements play a significant role in shaping a location's perspective and image, and he discovered that when tourists are communicated with in a way that reduces cultural disparities, they feel more connected to the destination.

(Agarwal, 2015) mentioned the travel industry in India has seen colossal expansions in footfalls during the last decade both from inbound and outbound sightseers. The friendliness area in India has seen 100% unfamiliar direct speculation and is contributing essentially to both the economy and work age. Lodging and café industry incomes in 2006-07 were almost 22% higher than the earlier year because of expanded possibilities of income age in other related areas.

(Sukthankar, 2013) expected hospitality is to be an economic multiplier for the government of India. Having been identified as an important sector with great possibilities by the state and central government, both have developed a variety of reforms to accelerate the development of the sector including liberalization, business friendly schemes, and continuous support to develop and maintain world-class infrastructure, Incentives to encourage local establishments in tier III and IV cities, better air and land connections, and exploration of the vast resources in the unexplored parts of the country have brought a boom into the Indian hospitality industry.

(Singh and Arora, 2014) observed that the tourism sector has evolved into an enormous industry since World War II. It was assigned industry status by the government in the 7th year plan. It now serves as an important source of social and economic benefit to the country. As well as creating jobs internationally and raising living standards of the population, it requires very little investment compared to other industries with incentives. Tourists are constantly on the move; they often travel to predefined points of interest for whatever reason, whether it for pleasure or adventure, and provide tourism products while on the move, before returning home after a short period of time.

(Vijayanand, 2012) mentioned that here are many businesses, services and products that contribute to tourism, as well as government and the active participation of the local residents. The travel industry gives monetary advantages and expenses for those who take an interest in it. Financial effect investigations give noticed appraisals of these monetary effects interdependencies and a superior comprehension of the job and significance of the travel industry in a locale's economy.

STUDY AREA

The current study encompasses 07 hotels of Delhi NCR and the sample size consisted of 62 respondents on the basis of convenient sampling. A questionnaire was designed to retrieve the demographic profile of the respondents and recorded their responses on a Likert scale of 5. The employees' perceptions of the various competences necessary in the hotels were measured using a questionnaire survey. Questions about demographics were included in the first section of the. The employees rated and required several critical competencies in the second segment.

BACKGROUND

Literature Review

(Nazarian Alireza *et al.,* 2017) mentioned that hotel industry is globalised and is as of noe behaving and experiencing the stature like the other globalised industries. For its managers now no longer least amongst those demanding situations is to recognize the effect of country wide subculture and organisational subculture at the overall efficiency of the employees.**[10]**

(Razak et al., 2016) said that during control domain, capacity to increase humans competencies, control competencies and ability to jot down a well known working procedure (SOP), capacity to perceive goal markets, capacity to increase a advertising plan, capacity to predict sales and staffing needs, read financial statements, educate others, investigate financial statements, utilise ethics in hiring, be able to demonstrate human competences, be able to motivate others, and demonstrate managerial skills. **[11]**

(Baum *et al.,* 2016) Career competences are positively influenced by perceived hotel career management and career dedication, according to the findings. In terms of employee career management, both organisations and people have responsibilities. Career competences are positively associated to employees' level of satisfaction and indulgence in terms of their outcomes.

(Porngarm *et al.,* 2016) The competencies with the highest scores included brand building/establishment knowledge, the capacity to generate customer awareness and a positive image through communication, and the capacity to creatively manage brands within the organisation. Yet, from a management perspective, the top three required brand management competencies were the capacity to manage and keep the brand management process "alive," the capacity to evaluate data, and the ability to effectively articulate additional value.

(Korez-Vide et al., 2016) characterised an individual's multiple competences as a set of personal qualities, expertise, capacities, and motivation that they apply at work. Managing oneself, growing oneself, having a work attitude that helps one achieve further, cooperative readiness, and creativity all have an impact on a person's success at work. activation, use, and integration of a person's entire repertoire of competencies, propensities, drives, self-perceptions, and convictions that enable them to succeed in challenging, varied, and unpredictable circumstances.

(Shahrabani *et al.,* 2015) found that the tourist sector is one of the major occupations on the planet. This industry has a significant impact on most nations' economies, providing close to 9% of global employment (WTTC, 2012) and accounting for 9% of global GDP (WTTC, 2012). Despite its modernization and technological advancements, the hotel industry's core resource remains its human resource, and excessive staff turnover continues to be one of the industry's significant concerns.

(Alhelalat, 2015) noticed that hotel executives will demand greater problem-solving skills, learning skills, technology, data collection and analysis, languages, management, and leadership skills in order to meet industry standards.

(Sarkodie and Adom, 2015) said that the most important talents needed to fit into the profession are pinpoint communication skills, multilingual skills, operational skills, and computing skills. Professional demeanour, composure, oral and written communication abilities, customer relationship management, and developing empathy for the challenges encountered by visitors are all essential. In addition to these abilities, the hospitality and tourism industry needs to pay attention to first aid knowledge, people management, moral and ethical behaviour, customer interactions, leadership, and conflict and issue solving skills.

(Shahrabani *et al.,* 2015) emphasized to help lower the high turnover rates, professional growth and more training are required. When multinational corporations introduce their global workplace practises to a developing country with a significant share of international personnel, the consequences can vary. **[18]**

(Kumar *et al.,* 2014) quoted that Every organisation has discussions about competencies. Some have done this successfully with a few of their processes. Only a few have a completely functional competency modelling and reporting system. Nonetheless, creating and implementing a competency model is still a challenge for many firms.

For the majority of businesses of all sizes, defining, developing, and implementing competence model efforts continue to be challenges.

(Suhairom *et al.,* 2014) highlighted The competency model will serve as the employees' guidance on how to behave and what they should be doing. Subsequently, management might be informed about which employee traits are connected to higher performance through the usage of a competency model.

(Jaykumar et al., 2014) quoted that the demands of the hotel sector are viewed differently by hotel management. Expectations, capabilities, and assumptions about industry demands and requirements are critical. Employees, on the other hand, appeared to be thinking more about their organisations' aims, resulting in perception discrepancies. Empowerment may lead to higher levels of staff dedication, motivation, and productivity, as well as better customer service.

(Srinivasan & Pol, 2014) confirmed that the training and development programme not only saves time in recruitment and to hire, but it also saves money by effectively and efficiently satisfying workforce demands. The hotel's human resource department should communicate more frequently about the required competences, appraisals, and briefings, as well as motivational talks, in order to keep the trainees engaged and excel in the hospitality profession.

(Rok, 2013) described that Employability is influenced by a person's knowledge and skills, professional experience, personal qualities, and behaviour. Moreover, unique applications and job marketability have been introduced. These are elements that have to do with a person's talents; yet, outside elements like social and educational reforms, as well as labour laws, have an effect on a person's employability in the labour market.

(Krishnaveni, 2013) mentioned The skills of employees include the capacity for maintaining interpersonal connections, communication, task proficiency, leadership, and adaptability. For all organisations and employee development, developing a defined competency model for each profession as well as competency mapping is essential to maximising the usage of these skills and gaining a competitive edge.

(Shruti, 2012) The extensively emphasised competency mapping technique is a useful tool for regularly monitoring and assessing how professionals perform as an individual or in a group with regard to the organization's and customers' expectations. The traits—including knowledge, abilities, and personality traits—that are necessary to carry out a particular profession successfully are also identified. Due to this, many businesses now actively screen applicants to ensure they possess certain skills.

(Kamau and Waudo, 2012) said that modern management views the skills and abilities believed to be of the utmost importance as being essential to any firm's success. Certain technical capabilities and strong interpersonal skills are essential for delivering outstanding service in the hotel industry. Workers ought to be encouraged to hone their creative, innovative, and competitive problem-solving abilities. It is also recommended that a professional organisation be established to deal with issues in the hotel industry.

(Prachanant, 2012) argued that English, which is connected to host-guest interactions in the service business, should be classified as the "language of hospitality," which refers to all linguistic expressions related to and expressed in hospitality issues. As a result, effective communication abilities are seen as a crucial asset. Even though the vocabulary used in hospitality is frequently formal, it varies widely depending on how well-versed the guests are in it.

(Sun, 2011) stated that a the hotel's flexible and flat organisational structure allows staff to respond to change and make choices more rapidly, resulting in better service. Furthermore, the hotel industry is highly interactive with its clients. This necessitates the decentralisation of authority in order to respond to needs promptly.

(Enz, 2011) a hotel should develop a list of its resources and capabilities, which should include both tangible and intangible resources (such as physical property and financial assets), before starting an internal study, it was noted (such as brand or organisational culture, and human, innovation, and reputation resources). The source of your hotel's core competencies, which form the basis of your competitive advantage, are these attributes and resources.

(Johanson et al., 2010) stressed the significance of Communication skills are important and used on a regular basis, as is the capacity to interact with clients, staff, managers, suppliers, and partner organisations immediately. Writing abilities are regularly used to convey ideas in order to direct, educate, inspire, train, and coordinate. To increase customer satisfaction and dispute resolution, handle customer issues with compassion and understanding, and address customer issues. Due to the growth of social media platforms and the possibility they present for businesses from all economic sectors, computer skills are increasing.

(Blayney, 2009) dealt with that Skills are those that are specific to a given managerial position and organisation and have been found to be important factors, especially in circumstances when flexibility is required. Flexibility and quick thinking are seen as essential skills in the hotel industry due to the continuously shifting market conditions.**[31]**

(Dickson, 2008) asserted that employee satisfaction is characterised as a feeling of fulfilment and contentment among employees that results in client satisfaction and profit. Managers need to think about more than simply ensuring employee happiness; they also need to think about encouraging engagement, which is characterised as a sense of dedication, excitement, and strong efforts that presents itself in perseverance. Because they produce more and experience lower turnover rates, engaged employees are important assets for businesses.

OBJECTIVE OF THE STUDY

1. Finding out what employees think about competencies in different hotel departments.
2. Identifying an individual's training and development needs and developing appropriate long-term strategies.

METHODS AND INSTRUMENTS

1) Questionnaire survey with staff members from different departments of the hotel were used to collect data.
2) For respondents, a questionnaire is used to record core and functional competencies.

ANALYSIS TOOLS

1) Hypothesis is developed
2) Descriptive statistics is used for the analysis of data.

H0: Perspective of the employees is significant in relation to the selected competencies.

H1: Perspective of the employees is not significant in relation to the selected competencies.

Table 1. Demographics of the Respondents

Demographic Characteristics		No of Respondents	%
Age	**21-30 years**	**36**	**58.06%**
	31-40 years	**21**	**33.87%**
	41-50 years	**4**	**6.45%**
	51 and above	**01**	**1.61%**
Gender	**Male**	50	80.64%
	Female	12	19.36%
Education	**Graduate**	06	9.67%
	Graduate (HM)	34	54.83%
	Post graduate	03	4.83%
	Diploma	18	29.03%
	Others	01	1.61%

continued on following page

Table 1. Continued

Demographic Characteristics		No of Respondents	%
Experience	**< 5 years** **5-10 years** **10-15 years** **15-20 years** **>20 years**	33 21 04 03 01	53.22% 33.87% 6.45% 4.83% 1.61%
Total Number of Respondents		**62**	**100%**
Number of Hotels		**07**	

The demographics of the responding employees are shown in Table 1. 36 (58.06%) of respondents were between the ages of 21 and 30, 21 (33.87%) were between the ages of 31 and 40, and 4 (6.45%) were between the ages of 41 and 50. 01 (1.61%) of the participants were between the ages of 51 and 60. This demonstrates that the hotel sector has a mix of youthful and experienced employees. Male respondents constitute 50 (80.64%) and the female constitute 12(13.96%) of the total respondents. The largest percentage of responders (54.83%) said they are hotel management graduates. A diploma in hotel management was held by 18 people (29.03 percent). 06 (9.67%) have a bachelor's degree, while 03 (4.83%) have a master's degree. Twenty-one percent of respondents (33.87 percent) had worked in the hospitality industry for five to ten years. A total of four respondents (6.45%) have between 10 and 15 years of experience in this profession. A large majority of respondents (33.22 percent) have less than five years of work experience, demonstrating the hospitality industry's trend of freshers. Front desk, Accommodation Operations, Food Production, F and B service, HR, and other hotel departments were represented among the respondents.

Figure 1. Key Competencies Composite Graph:

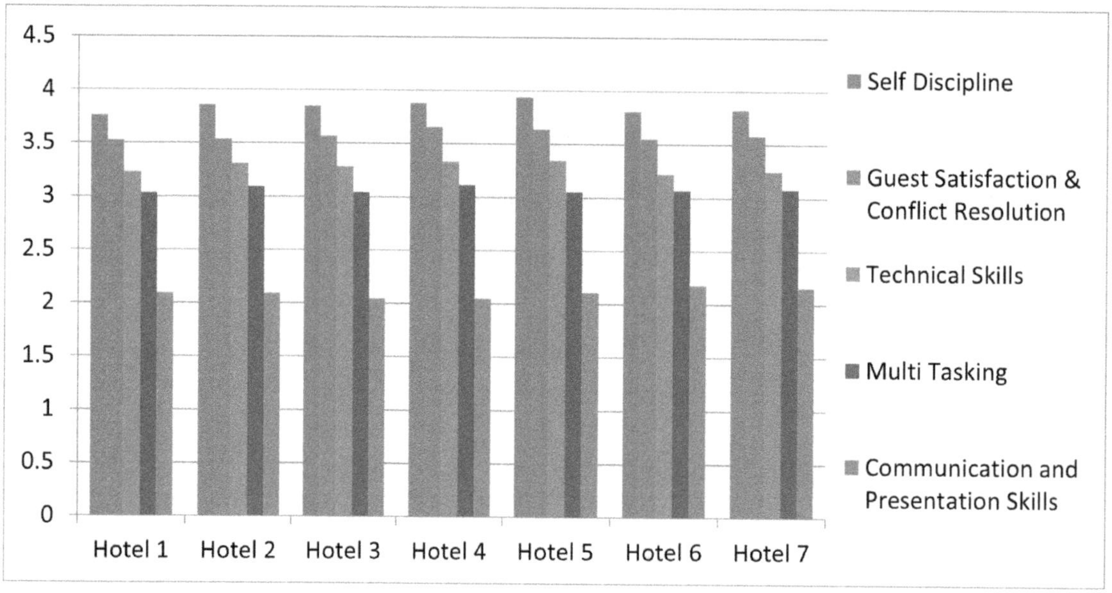

DATA ANALYSIS AND INTERPRETATION

Table 2. Composite Mean Value for Key Competencies in Hotels

Hotel	Self Control	Dispute Redressal	Trade Specific Skills	IT Skills	Verbal and Non Verbal Communication
Hotel 1	3.77	3.54	3.24	3.04	2.10
Hotel 2	3.88	3.55	3.32	3.10	2.10
Hotel 3	3.86	3.58	3.29	3.05	2.05
Hotel 4	3.89	3.67	3.34	3.12	2.06
Hotel 5	3.95	3.65	3.36	3.06	2.12
Hotel 6	3.82	3.56	3.23	3.08	2.19
Hotel 7	3.83	3.59	3.26	3.09	2.17
SD	0.0564	0.0501	05.504	0.0287	0.0521
Rank	**5**	**2**	**3**	**1**	**4**

RESULTS AND FINDINGS

Ratings given by the employees in the form of composite value of means are shown in Table 2. Information Technology (IT) skills was ranked 1 by employees, with a composite value of mean ranging from 3.12 to 3.04, suggesting that multitasking has long been valued as a valuable employee trait. The standard deviation was 0.0287, showing that the mindsets of the employees from different hotels were not very varied.

Employees ranked dispute redressal second, with a composite value of mean ranging from 3.67 to 3.54, indicating competency homogeneity in the hospitality business. The standard deviation was 0.0501, showing that there was little variation in the mindsets of hotel personnel.

Employees placed trade specific skills third, with a composite value of mean ranging from 3.36 to 3.23, and they possess a critical role in an employee's ability to give successful and efficient service. The standard deviation was 0.0504, showing that there is no substantial disparity in employee perspectives when assessing this talent.

Employees ranked Verbal and Non Verbal Communication Skills as the fourth most important competency, with a composite value of mean ranging from 2.19 to 2.05. The standard deviation was 0.0521, indicating that there was little diversity in the mindsets of the hotel employees.

Employees ranked 5th and Self control was rated with a composite value of mean ranging from 3.95 to 3.77, demonstrating the similarities in employee rating patterns once again. The standard deviation was determined to be 0.0564, indicating that there were little variances in the mindsets of the hotel employees.

DISCUSSION

Standard Deviation remained positive indicates that the perspectives of employees from various hospitality firms appear to be similar. The current study provides sufficient evidence that the majority of respondents regard IT as a critical skill but also as a skill assisting businesses, such as hotels, in increasing customer satisfaction, resulting in repeat business.

The study backs up the hypothesis that employees' perspectives on required competencies are important, as it is clear that technical skills related to the trade, communication skills for interaction with the guests and for presenting the facts well, self-control, and necessary computational skills are rated in that order, followed by IT skills, and dispute redressal skills. These abilities are the most important determining factors in an employee's future prospects in the hotel business, as they will undoubtedly lead to the bridging the identified skill gaps and aid in effective communication and building rapport between employees and customers (hotel guests).

IT skills have always been a topmost desired skill sets among the employers. Be it during the formation of job specifications and descriptions or various stages of recruitment and selection procedures. Management, Human resource managers and the head of the departments want their employees to possess skills that turn them into a jack of all trades. This will definitely lead to the optimum usage of the manpower resources and will eventually lead to more customer satisfaction and revenue generation.

RECOMMENDATIONS AND SUGGESTIONS

As a regular guest (as the customer is addressed as in hospitality industry) profile and the kind of information they are equipped with, they get more meticulous and peculiar about their wants. So, in order satisfy their needs, the employee must always remain proactive and equipped with the contemporary knowledge of the likes and dislikes of the guests. The next step in this process will be how to deliver the things with great perfection or the way their guests want them to be. So, it is not only hospitality that will be counted. It is their multi-tasking abilities that are going to give them a competitive advantage in the market. A guest needs to be treated well, listened with empathy and delivered with his sort of customised products and services. This can only be done when the management seeks on consistent basis to attain *the ultimate guest satisfaction*. Well, that is only possible when the service providers i.e. the employees are equipped with what is required to make it successfully to the mindset of the guests. The employees from every department of the hotel be it Front Office (reception, concierge, cashier, information desk, Housekeeping, Food production (kitchen), Food and beverage service (restaurant, bar, coffee shops, discotheque, pubs, lounges) and other ancillary areas like sales and marketing must always remain aware of the customisation of the products, services along with people skills. Guess a technical sound employee with very less explanation skills? In short, every employee of the hotel whether coming into the guest contacts directly or indirectly need to be equipped with IT skills abilities.

CONCLUSION

IT skills have a critical role in delivery of products and services, according to the findings presented in this paper. According to the findings, employees have a good attitude toward such critical abilities, and they rate them according to their needs and with a high level of logical ability. It clearly signifies that the employees are absolutely aware of the need of such skills. Knowledge of operating Property Management Systems (PMS), Electronic locking system (ELS), desktops, multi copier machines, operating systems, apps, equipments and gadgets is of utmost significance in effective and efficient service delivery.

The findings of this study show that hotel management should take into account aspects related to employees' overall development. According to the findings, emphasising IT skills ability has a significant impact on employees' perceptions of critical skills because it is the only trait (as perceived by the employees themselves) that is going to enable them to cope up well in this competitive era. Hence, the management need to invest their time, efforts and money into the holistic development of the employees. Training and development programs emphasizing on the overall enhancement of the skills should be designed and implemented with great sincerity. Regular assessment of the training programs in the form of employees' performance post training is the best criteria for finding out the effectiveness of the training provided.

Also, from the perspective of the customers, these abilities help to develop a better grasp on the guests by fulfilling their requirements on time. Hotel guests will be more likely to return to the hotel after such an experience, boosting the destination's tourist potential.

SUGGESTIONS

Hotels are currently confronted with numerous problems in terms of increasing profitability and capitalising on new opportunities that have developed as a result of the Indian economy's growth and the changing nature of tourism. Identifying the skill gaps is the biggest challenge for the management these days. Especially with the hospitality sector which is absolutely skill centric in nature. Unless or until the management and the employee himself or herself are not aware and willing of this particular aspect, their enrichment would not be possible. It could only be possible with a commitment towards the employees' training and development. It totally depends on the management that whether they would like to conduct training sessions On-the-job or Off-the-job and by whom, where and how? Cross training must be involved in practices for employees to get more exposure to attain exceptional excellence and counter the issue of skill gap.

FUTURE SCOPE AND RESEARCH LIMITATIONS:

Because the industry population polled only includes personnel from a few select hotels in Delhi NCR, it is cannot justify the implication of the study with a claim that it is applicable to the entire hospitality sector. However, it is hoped that the study can be replicated to see how broadly the findings may be applied. Because it is the occupied and customer centric industry, employees are preoccupied with their daily operations, which was a stumbling block to entertain the researchers approaching the employees for survey. As a result, the questionnaire survey was used to collect primary data.

REFERENCES

Agarwal, N. (2015). An analytical study of tourist perception for the accommodation sector in reference to Dehradun and Mussoorie. *International Journal of Arts. Humanities and Management Studies*, *1*, 8–19.

Alhelalat, J. A. (2015). Hospitality and non-hospitality graduate skills between education and industry. *Journal of Business Studies Quarterly*, *6*(4), 46.

Alhelalat, J. A. (2015). Hospitality and non-hospitality graduate skills between education and industry. *Journal of Business Studies Quarterly*, *6*, 46.

Baum, T., Cheung, C., Kong, H., Kralj, A., Mooney, S., Thanh, H. N. T., Ramachandran, S., Ruzic, M. D., & Siow, M. L. (2016). Sustainability and the tourism and hospitality workforce: A thematic analysis. *Sustainability (Basel)*, *8*(8), 1–21. DOI: 10.3390/su8080809

Bhanu Pratap, D., & Singhal, B. P. (2018). Tourism in Uttarakhand. *International Journal of Management Studies, 5*.

Blayney, C. (2009). Management competencies: Are they related to hotel performance? *International Journal of Management and Marketing Research*, *2*, 59–71.

Dickson, D. (2008). *Fostering employee engagement: A Critical competency for hospitality industry managers*. Rochester Institute of Technology.

Dillman, DA (2000a). Mail and internet surveys: The tailored design method, 2.

Donna, D. (2008). Fostering employee engagement: A critical competency for hospitality industry managers. *RIT Scholar Works*, 1–6.

Enz, C. A. (2011). Competing successfully with other hotels: The role of strategy. In *The Cornell School of Hotel Administration on Hospitality: Cutting edge thinking and practice* (pp. 207–226).

Erazo, M. A. C., Ramírez, S. I. M., Encalada, M. A. R., Holguin, J. V., & Zou, J. H. (2019). English language skills required by the hospitality and tourism sector in El Oro, Ecuador. *Theory and Practice in Language Studies*, *9*(2), 156–167. DOI: 10.17507/tpls.0902.05

Gillovic, B., & McIntosh, A. (2020). Accessibility and inclusive tourism development: Current state and future agenda. *Sustainability (Basel)*, *12*(22), 9722. DOI: 10.3390/su12229722

Hassan, N. S. I. C., & Tik, R. O. L. (2019). Island tourism employees' perceived importance and challenges of English communication. *LSP International Journal, 6*.

Jaykumar, V., Fukey, L. N., & Balasubramanian, K. (2014). Hotel managers' perspective of managerial competency among graduating students of hotel management programmes. *Procedia: Social and Behavioral Sciences*, *144*, 328–342. DOI: 10.1016/j.sbspro.2014.07.303

Johanson, M., Ghiselli, R., Shea, L. J., & Roberts, C. (2010). Revealing key competencies of hospitality graduates demanded by industry: A 25-year review.

Kacetl, J. (2018). English language teaching for students of management of travel and tourism. *SHS Web of Conferences, 48*, 01037.

Kamau, S. W., & Waudo, J. (2012). Hospitality industry employer's expectation of employees' competences in Nairobi hotels. *Journal of Hospitality Management and Tourism*, *3*, 55–63.

Korez-Vide, R., Tansek, V., & Milfelner, B. (2016). Assessing intercultural competence of front office employees: The case of hotels in Slovenia. *Biennial International Congress, Tourism and Hospitality Industry*, 158–173.

Krishnaveni, J. (2013). A study on mapping of employees' competency. *Indian Journal of Economics and Development, 1*, 71–75.

Kumar, M. K. R., & Sivakumar, M. (2014). Competency mapping in hotels with reference to Madurai. *Asia Pacific Journal of Research, 1*.

Misty, J., Richard, G., Linda, J. S., & Chris, R. (2010). Revealing key competencies of hospitality graduates demanded by industry: A 25-year review. *International CHRIE Conference*, 1–10.

Nazarian, A., Atkinson, P., & Foroudi, P. (2017). Influence of national culture and balanced organizational culture on the hotel industry's performance. *International Journal of Hospitality Management, 63*, 22–32. DOI: 10.1016/j.ijhm.2017.01.003

Porngarm, V., Kageeporn, W., Koraklod, K., & Pansiri, P. P. (2016). Competency assessment for branding programs development in Thailand's higher education. *Procedia: Social and Behavioral Sciences, 228*, 402–406. DOI: 10.1016/j.sbspro.2016.07.061

Prachanant, N. (2012). Needs analysis on English language use in tourism industry. *Procedia: Social and Behavioral Sciences, 66*, 117–125. DOI: 10.1016/j.sbspro.2012.11.253

Razak, R. A., Shariff, N. M., & Zainol, N. A. (2016). Creating a framework for hospitality competencies to fulfill the industry's need. *Academic Research International, 7*(4), 229–236.

Rok, M. (2013). Tourism and hospitality graduate employability. *The 2nd Electronic International Interdisciplinary Conference Proceedings*, 79–84.

Sarkodie, N. A., & Adom, K. (2015). Bridging the gap between hospitality/tourism education and hospitality/tourism industry in Ghana. *International Journal of Research in Humanities and Social Studies, 2*, 114–120.

Shahrabani, S., Goziker, O., & Teitler-Regev, S. (2015). Perceptions and future intentions to stay in the hotel industry: The case of front desk employees in Israel. *African Journal of Hospitality, Tourism and Leisure*, •••, 4.

Shruti, A. (2012). Competency mapping at managerial level in special reference to hotel clerks Amer, Jaipur. *Spectrum. Journal of Multidisciplinary Research, 1*, 1–13.

Singh, M. K., & Arora, R. (2014). The changing face of the Indian hospitality industry. *International Journal of Advanced Research in Management and Social Sciences, 3*, 26–36.

Srinivasan, S., & Pol, R. (2014). Study on importance of industrial training as a part of hotel management education curriculum, as perceived by industry and students. *International Journal of Informative and Futuristic Research, 1*.

Suhairom, N., Musta'amal, A. H., Amin, N. F. M., & Johari, N. K. A. (2014). The development of competency model and instrument for competency measurement: The research methods. *Procedia: Social and Behavioral Sciences, 152*, 1300–1308. DOI: 10.1016/j.sbspro.2014.09.367

Sukthankar, S. V. (2013). A study on growth of hotel industry in Goa. *IOSR Journal of Humanities and Social Science, 11*, 1–7. DOI: 10.9790/0837-1120107

Sun, L. (2011). The core competences and strategic management of Raffles—A case study of Singapore hotel industry. *International Journal of Innovation, Management and Technology, 2*, 270.

Vijayanand, S. (2012). Socio-economic impacts in pilgrimage tourism. *International Journal of Multidisciplinary Research*, *2*, 329–343.

Chapter 29
Study on Consumer Awareness and Acceptance of AI Technology in the Hospitality and Tourism Service Industry

M. Nithin
M.S. Ramaiah University of Applied Sciences, India

Sweety R. Jamgade
https://orcid.org/0000-0002-6109-8801
M.S. Ramaiah University of Applied Sciences, India

ABSTRACT

Artificial Intelligence (AI) is now an integral part of every businesses. Hence this chapter investigates consumers' awareness and acceptance of artificial intelligence (AI) technology in the hospitality and tourism sector, focusing on generational behavioral patterns. It identifies a gap in current research, particularly in the exploration of broader technological implementations beyond customer acceptance, highlighting the need for a comprehensive understanding of AI applications such as chatbots and automation. This research employs a descriptive approach, comprising surveys to assess consumer awareness of AI among various age groups, evaluate their acceptance levels, and analyze behaviors influenced by emotions and attitudes. Findings indicate significant variances in awareness and acceptance across generations, with factors such as trust, perceived benefits, and emotional responses playing pivotal roles. This study offers recommendations for hospitality and tourism providers.

INTRODUCTION

The rapid advancement of artificial intelligence (AI) technologies has transformed various sectors, with the hospitality and tourism industries standing out as prime beneficiaries of these innovations. As AI continues to evolve, understanding consumer perceptions and acceptance of such technologies becomes crucial for businesses aiming to leverage AI for improved service delivery and enhanced customer experiences (Acikgoz et al., 2023). This chapter seeks to explore consumers' awareness and acceptance of AI technologies within the context of hospitality and tourism services. By analyzing generational differences in awareness, emotional responses, and acceptance,

DOI: 10.4018/979-8-3693-7447-4.ch029

the chapter seeks to provide actionable insights for industry stakeholders to enhance AI service implementation and consumer satisfaction.

Consumer awareness refers to the understanding and knowledge that individuals possess regarding a product or service. In the context of AI, awareness includes familiarity with AI applications such as chatbots, automated check-ins, and personalized recommendations. Studies show that higher awareness can lead to increased acceptance, making it essential to examine how awareness varies across different generations (Bhuiyan et al., 2024). There is a strong need for creating awareness among the customers hence this study was undertaken.

GROWING AI ADOPTION

The rapid advancement of artificial intelligence (AI) technology has significantly transformed various industries, with the hospitality and tourism sector being at the forefront of this evolution. AI applications, such as chatbots, personalized recommendations, and automated service processes, promise to enhance customer experience, streamline operations, and drive innovation. However, despite these potential benefits, the acceptance of AI technology among consumers remains inconsistent and varies widely across different demographic groups, particularly generational cohorts (Kim, J.-H. 2021).

The hospitality and tourism industries are increasingly integrating AI technologies to enhance guest experiences, streamline operations, and optimize service delivery. Understanding how consumers become aware of and accept these technologies is crucial for successful implementation and adoption (Touni & Magdy, 2020). AI enhances guest experiences through personalisation in the hospitality and tourism industry based on the data available regarding their preferences and beahviour patterns (Yang, et al., 2021). AI can transform customer service, personalize experiences, and improve efficiency. Investigating consumer perceptions and acceptance can help businesses design AI solutions that align with customer expectations and enhance overall satisfaction (Roy et al., 2020).

GLOBAL PERSPECTIVE

Across the globe, AI is revolutionizing the hospitality and tourism sectors, from enhancing customer service through chatbots to optimizing operational efficiency with data analytics. Major tourism markets such as the United States, Europe, and Asia—are adopting AI at varying paces.

The level of economic development and technological infrastructure varies significantly among countries, impacting consumers' familiarity and comfort with AI. Developed nations may experience higher levels of acceptance due to greater access to technology and higher disposable incomes, while developing nations may face challenges related to infrastructure and digital literacy.

In India, the hospitality industry has experienced remarkable growth in recent years, fueled by economic expansion, increased domestic travel, and a surge in inbound tourism. By exploring customers' economic, cultural, technological and educational dimensions, this chapter aims to provide a comprehensive understanding of the factors that facilitate the adoption of AI technologies by customers in India. The insights gained will not only contribute to academic discourse but also inform national strategies and industry practices, ultimately enhancing the overall effectiveness and competitiveness of the hospitality and tourism sectors.

Few Examples of Hotel and Tourism Industry Deploying AI Enabled Customer Services Are

Virgin Hotels have introduced AI integration in their hotel management system to enhance guest experiences with personised services before, during and post stay of the guests.

RENAI by Renaissance is using AI-enabled concierge virtual services accessible via smartphones, the AI algorithms provides local recommendations to add more to the personalised services.

KLM Dutch Airlines was facing critical issues of 15 minutes waiting for the customer service interactions hence they introduced AI-powered chatbots with the support of DigitalGenius. The chatbot utilizes Natural Language Processing (NLP) to accurately address customers queries delivering instant information and increasing the efficiency of the airlines customer service.

CitizenM Hotels have introduced AI-driven self-service kiosks for check-in and check-out reducing the waiting period and improving the guest experience.

Waygo a company known for its technology introduced AI for real-time translation of foreign menus and signage for tourists focusing on East Asian Languages like Chinese, Korean and Japanese (DigitalDefynd, 2024).

Kayak a leading travel company uses advanced AI and machine learning (ML) algorithms to help the travelers in easily doing the booking process by suggesting best hotels, transportations and best price.

Hyatt utilizes AI-powered beds to provide sound sleep to the guests by analyzing the bed temperatures, weather, guest's body temperature, heart and sleeping patterns (Kaur, 2024).

ETHICAL AND PRIVACY CONCERNS OF AI

AI technologies often raise concerns related to privacy and ethics due to the handling of data and algorithms bias regarding the customer preferences and choices. To understand the emotions involved in customers' acceptance the behavioral theory can help identify and address these concerns, ensuring that AI implementations are both effective and respectful of consumer rights (Wang, P. Q., 2024). Behavioral theory provides valuable insights into how individuals form attitudes and make decisions. By applying these theories, we can better understand the factors of education, awareness, culture, etc. influencing consumer awareness and acceptance of AI in these sectors. This can help businesses tailor their strategies to address consumer concerns and preferences effectively (Nam et al., 2020). This topic opens avenues for further research into how emerging technologies will shape consumer behavior in hospitality and tourism. It also offers a chance to explore how behavioral theory can be applied to other technological innovations in these fields (Touni & Magdy, 2020).

LITERATURE REVIEW

The literature highlights AI research in the hospitality and tourism industry, identifying a significant growth in publications since 2018 and categorizing studies into four clusters: AI technology, technology acceptance, consumers' perceptions, and future trends. (Haiyan Kong, K. W. 22). AI service adoption in the hospitality sector through the lens of behavioural reasoning theory, highlights the significance of cultural values in shaping customer attitudes toward AI, emphasizing the need for hospitality firms to consider these behavioural and emotional factors when implementing new technologies (Rasheed et al., 2023).

The literature indicates that the familiarity with automation in the hospitality industry, employee sentiments are mixed, necessitating careful consideration of how AI is integrated into service models. The findings advocate for a collaborative approach where automation enhances, rather than replaces, the human elements that define exceptional service in hospitality. This balance is essential for fostering a positive work environment and ensuring high-quality guest experiences (Logan O'Hara's 2021). Hence upskilling employees to use AI-driven technologies is the need of the hour in the service industry.

The other research emphasizes that AI devices are effective tools for problem-solving, highlighting the importance of clearly defining problems and securing relevant data. While AI technology is rapidly evolving, the study notes a lack of in-depth analysis on the emotional aspects of user experience. Emotional management is crucial for creating corporate value (Nam et al., 2020). Its imperative to integrate emotional aspects in AI use to avoid ethical issues of biased decisions.

The study of Roy et al., (2020) provides a comprehensive examination of customer acceptance of artificial intelligence (AI) in the Indian hospitality sector. The study emphasizes the importance of understanding how consumers perceive and accept AI technologies within this industry, particularly as AI continues to reshape service delivery. It identifies critical factors influencing customer emotions, such as performance expectancy (the perceived benefits of AI) and effort expectancy (the perceived ease of use). These factors significantly impact consumers' willingness to adopt AI services. The literature notes a growing trend among hospitality organizations globally to integrate AI into their service delivery mechanisms. This shift aims to enhance service reliability, timeliness, and efficiency compared to traditional, human-dependent service models.

The transformative role of artificial intelligence (AI) in hospitality and tourism marketing, emphasizing its effects on organizational functions. Through focus groups and a questionnaire-based survey, the authors identified ten key AI trends categorized into four main areas: internal processes, organizational networks, stakeholder interactions, and customer services. The analysis highlights that AI innovation hinges on the integration of data, content platforms, and algorithms, enabling real-time responsiveness to individual needs and contexts, which fosters value co-creation. The review also suggests that future research could benefit from including more tourism and hotel marketing specialists, as the initial expert participants were primarily technical academics (Bulchand-Gidumal, J. et al., 2024).

The study by Acikgoz et al., (2023) explores consumer engagement with AI-powered voice assistants through the lenses of Behavioural Reasoning Theory and the Technology Acceptance Model. Utilizing self-report questionnaires within a cross-sectional design, the research reveals that privacy cynicism negatively affects attitudes toward using voice assistants. However, this negative perception is counterbalanced by positive factors such as trust, perceived usefulness, and ease of use, which enhance user attitudes. The findings indicate that individuals' attitudes toward voice assistants significantly influence their willingness to share personal information, while privacy risks notably impact user engagement. Additionally, the reasons for and against using voice assistants play a critical role in shaping privacy concerns. The study highlights the need for a nuanced understanding of privacy dynamics in technology adoption. This comprehensive approach underscores the complexities of consumer behaviour in the context of AI-driven services and the importance of addressing privacy issues in enhancing user engagement.

Another study explores consumer behaviour regarding mobile hospitality services (MHS) through an extended model of the Unified Theory of Acceptance and Use of Technology (UTAUT2) and perceived value. Analysing data from 348 survey responses, the study reveals that the proposed model explains 62% of the intention to use MHS and 51% of the variation in recommendations. Key findings indicate that perceived value significantly influences both intentions to use and recommend MHS, alongside factors such as effort expectancy and performance expectancy. The authors stress the importance of service quality, emphasizing customization and follow-up services to enhance user experience. However, the study's focus on a predominantly college-educated sample in Portugal limits generalizability, suggesting that future research should explore additional factors influencing MHS adoption as the technology matures. This research advances understanding of MHS by integrating perceived value with a foundational technology adoption framework (Rita et al., 2018).

The study by Touni & Magdy, (2020) on integration of Robots, Artificial Intelligence, and Service Automation (RAISA) technologies in Egypt's tourism and hospitality sector finds that due to the pandemic operations has changed due to the preferences towards minimizing direct contact, potentially accelerating the adoption of RAISA technologies.

Another study investigates the factors influencing customer acceptance and usage of mobile hotel reservation apps (MHRA) through an exploratory factor analysis based on the UTAUT2 model. An online survey of 422 Malaysian hotel customers identified seven key determinants: Effort Expectancy, Habit, Hedonic Motivation, Performance Expectancy, Price Value, Social Influence, and Facilitating Conditions. The findings confirm the relevance of these factors in predicting users' intentions to adopt MHRA, with insights revealing that while traditional UTAUT factors significantly impact adoption, elements like price value, hedonic motivation, and habit also play critical roles. The study highlights the interplay between social and psychological factors in the human-technology interaction. Future research is encouraged to explore the impact of these determinants on customer satisfaction and to analyse causal relationships using advanced statistical methods, such as path analysis or structural equation modelling (Mohd Noor Ismawi Ismail, M. H. 2020).

The literature review examines distinct but interconnected aspects of the hospitality and tourism industry in the context of emerging digital technologies. Dash and Bakshi (2019) focus on customer perceptions of chatbots in hotels, revealing a significant lack of awareness and understanding among consumers, with only 6% having used chatbots and 60% not even familiar with them. This lack of knowledge fosters wariness about adopting AI-driven services, particularly due to concerns over language recognition and the complexity of technology. In contrast, Adeyinka-Ojo et al. emphasize the need for enhanced digital literacy and employability skills within hospitality education to adapt to a rapidly evolving digital landscape. Their findings underscore the importance of developing innovative curriculum frameworks that incorporate these skills to better prepare graduates for industry demands. Together, these studies highlight the critical role of technology in enhancing customer experience and the necessity for educational institutions to align their programs with the technological advancements shaping the hospitality and tourism sectors (Dash M., Bakshi S., 2019).

The literature reviews explain the intersection of sustainability-driven innovation and artificial intelligence (AI) within the hospitality sector, focusing on how AI enhances customer experience. Through a comprehensive review of existing literature and case studies, the authors illustrate that AI technologies, such as smart energy management systems and predictive analytics, optimize operational efficiency and promote sustainable practices. These AI-driven solutions allow for proactive adjustments to demand patterns, thereby improving guest satisfaction and fostering loyalty. The review highlights that businesses leveraging sustainability initiatives can differentiate themselves in a competitive market. However, it also acknowledges challenges related to data privacy, ethical AI use, integration, talent development, and regulatory compliance. The authors advocate for a holistic approach that prioritizes ethical principles and transparency to build trust with guests and stakeholders, ultimately enhancing brand loyalty. This research offers valuable insights for stakeholders in the hospitality industry regarding the transformative potential of AI in driving sustainability and improving customer experiences (Kumar S., Huzifa. A. 2023).

The study explores consumer user experience and behaviour regarding artificial intelligence (AI) devices through qualitative research methods, primarily utilizing purposive sampling and interviews. The study identifies key AI devices used by consumers, including AI speakers, smartphones, and PCs, and reveals associative images related to these devices, such as fun, useful, novel, smart, innovative, and friendly. The findings emphasize that AI devices are seen as effective tools for problem-solving, highlighting the importance of accurately defining problems and securing relevant data for resolution. Despite the insights gained, the research notes a lack of in-depth analysis regarding the emotional aspects of user experience, which is critical for enhancing corporate value. Overall, the study offers valuable insights into consumer perceptions and behaviours towards AI devices, with important implications for marketing strategies in the evolving landscape of AI technology (Kim, J.-H. 2021).

The study explains the application of Robots, Artificial Intelligence, and Service Automation (RAISA) technologies in Egypt's tourism and hospitality sector, focusing on travel agencies and hotels. Utilizing in-depth semi-structured interviews with twenty IT managers and assistant managers, the study finds that there are currently no active robot applications in the sector, although respondents anticipate future implementation. Key obstacles to adoption include high costs, a shortage of qualified personnel to operate and maintain these technologies, and customer preferences for face-to-face interactions. The review notes that the ongoing COVID-19 pandemic has shifted some attitudes toward minimizing direct contact, potentially accelerating interest in RAISA technologies. The authors suggest that future research should broaden the scope to examine RAISA applications in other areas of tourism and hospitality, such as airports and restaurants, to better understand the technology's potential and challenges across the industry (Touni & Magdy, 2020)

IDENTIFICATION OF RESEARCH GAP

Lack of study on different generations' prospects and attitudes towards accepting AI technology (Nam et al., 2020). Attitudes towards using AI technology (Bhuiyan et al., 2024). Lack of awareness and understanding of AI Technology by customers (Dash M., Bakshi S., 2019). Future research could explore the acceptance of AI technology in the service industry over human service (Roy et al., 2020). Limited research could explore deeper insights, focus on understanding how tourism operators can capture value from AI solutions, and address privacy and security concerns in the AI industry (Filieri et al., 2021). Limited involvement of AI experts with a deeper understanding of the hospitality sector and exploring cultural differences in AI adoption (Bulchand-Gidumal, J. et al., 2024).

Limited studies on determine the reasons for adopting AI services and examine their relationships with cultural values and adopting AI services in the tourism sector (Rasheed et al., 2023). The future focus should be done different generations prospects and attitudes toward accepting (Nam et al., 2020). Limited research should focus on the roles of identified factors in customer satisfaction and usage, examining causal relationships using robust statistical methods like path analysis or structural equation modeling (MNI Ismail, et al., 2020). Future studies should be done on personalized service and AI service. The acceptance level of different age groups (Sonja Zlatanov, J.P 2019). There is a need to focus on factors that influence perceptions of adopting these technologies in service industries (Stanislav Ivanov, C.W. 2018). Future research in the field should explore RAISA in other tourism and hospitality enterprises beyond travel agencies and hotels, such as airports and restaurants (Touni & Magdy, 2020).

PROBLEM STATEMENT

The rapid advancement of artificial intelligence (AI) technology has significantly transformed various industries, with the hospitality and tourism sectors standing at the forefront of this change. As businesses increasingly integrate AI solutions—from chatbots enhancing customer service to data analytics optimizing operations—understanding consumer awareness and acceptance of these technologies becomes crucial. This study aims to explore how consumers perceive AI services within hospitality and tourism and the factors influencing their acceptance across different generational cohorts.

The objectives of the study were to study consumer awareness of AI technology among various generation, to assess the influence and acceptance of AI Technology and to analyse behaviours of various generations based on emotions and attitudes.

SCOPE OF THE STUDY

The study focuses on multiple generations (e.g., Baby Boomers, Generation X, Millennials, Generation Z) to understand their varying levels of awareness and acceptance of AI technology in hospitality and tourism services. This comparative analysis will reveal distinct behavioral patterns and preferences. The research assesses consumer awareness of various AI applications within the hospitality and tourism sectors. The findings of this study contribute to hospitality and tourism businesses about effective strategies to enhance AI service adoption, improve customer experience, and address concerns specific to each generational group. This practical application will support industry efforts to integrate AI technologies more successfully.

METHOD AND METHODOLOGY

Objective 1: To study consumer awareness of AI technology among various generation.
Methodology: Descriptive study using a questionnaire with a 5-point Likert scale.
Resources: Questionnaire and reliability analysis.
Objective 2: To assess the influence and acceptance of AI Technology.
Methodology: Multiple regression and correlation analysis using a questionnaire with a 5-point Likert scale.
Resources: Questionnaire, multiple regression, and correlation analysis.
Objective 3: To analyze behaviors of various generations based on emotions and attitudes.
Methodology: Hypothesis testing and correlation analysis using a questionnaire with a 5-point Likert scale.
Resources: Questionnaire, hypothesis testing, and correlation analysis.

PROBLEM-SOLVING

This study employs quantitative data collection and analysis techniques. This approach provides a comprehensive understanding of the various generations' awareness and acceptance of AI technology in the hospitality and tourism sector

RESEARCH METHODS

Quantitative Research

A structured questionnaire survey was the main method for gathering quantitative data. This survey was administered to consumers of different age group of the hospitality and tourism service industry, aiming to capture generalizable data. A sample of 108 respondents was chosen using a combination of purposive and convenience sampling techniques. Purposive sampling ensured the inclusion of participants from different age group and levels of AI exposure, while convenience sampling facilitated easy access to respondents.

Survey: A structured questionnaire was administered to a sample of consumers. The survey collected data on the awareness, acceptance, and influence of AI technology of various generations of consumers in hospitality and tourism sector

Statistical Analysis: Correlation analysis, and regression analysis was used to analyze the quantitative data and test the hypotheses.

Hypotheses

H1- There is a significant positive relationship between awareness and development practices and AI Technology in hospitality and tourism services industry.

This hypothesis posits that greater awareness of AI technology and its potential applications in the hospitality and tourism sectors positively influences the implementation of development practices. As industry stakeholders become more informed about AI capabilities—such as data analytics, personalized customer service, and operational efficiency—they are more likely to adopt innovative practices. This relationship suggests that education and training about AI can lead to better business outcomes, encouraging investment in technology that enhances service delivery.

H2- There is a significant positive relationship between Influence and AI Technology in hospitality and tourism service industry.

This hypothesis explores the role of influence—such as peer recommendations, industry trends, or expert opinions—in the adoption of AI technology in hospitality and tourism. It suggests that the positive opinions and experiences of others can significantly affect decision-makers' attitudes towards integrating AI solutions. This underscores the importance of social networks and industry leaders in shaping perceptions and driving technological adoption, indicating that influence can serve as a catalyst for change in technology adoption.

H3- There is a significant positive relationship between behavioral and AI Technology in hospitality and tourism service industry.

This hypothesis examines the relationship between behavioural factors, such as risk-taking, innovation, and adaptability, and the adoption of AI technology. It posits that organizations that cultivate a culture of innovation and are willing to embrace new technologies are more likely to successfully integrate AI into their operations. Understanding employee behaviour and organizational culture is crucial, as these factors can significantly impact the readiness and willingness to adopt advanced technologies.

H4- There is a significant positive relationship between generation and AI Technology in hospitality and tourism service industry

This hypothesis investigates how generational differences affect attitudes toward AI technology in the hospitality and tourism sectors. Younger generations, who are generally more tech-savvy, may show a stronger positive relationship with AI adoption compared to older generations. This implies that businesses should tailor their technological strategies and marketing approaches to accommodate varying generational attitudes, recognizing that preferences for technology can differ widely based on age demographics.

H5- There is a significant positive relationship between attitude and AI Technology in hospitality and tourism service industry.

This hypothesis asserts that positive attitudes toward AI technology significantly influence its adoption in the hospitality and tourism industry. Attitudes can be shaped by personal experiences, knowledge, and perceived benefits. Organizations that foster a positive perception of AI among employees and management may see increased enthusiasm for adopting these technologies, leading to more innovative practices and improved customer experiences.

H6- There is a significant positive relationship between acceptance and AI Technology in hospitality and tourism service. This hypothesis focuses on the acceptance of AI technology within the hospitality and tourism sectors, suggesting that a higher level of acceptance correlates with more widespread use of AI solutions. Acceptance can be influenced by various factors, including perceived usefulness, ease of use, and the perceived impact on job roles. Understanding the dynamics of acceptance can help organizations implement change management strategies that facilitate smoother transitions to AI enhanced operations.

Questionnaire Design

The structured questionnaire used for data collection was designed to capture both the demographic characteristics of the respondents and their perceptions regarding AI technologies, consumer awareness, and acceptance. The questionnaire consisted of two main sections:

Demographics Age, gender, country, and level of exposure to AI technologies.

AI Exposure the level of AI awareness and acceptance of consumers in hospitality and tourism service industry

Sample Size: 108

Approach: Quantitative approach

Data Collection: Questionnaire

Variables

Dependent Variable: AI (Artificial Intelligence) Technology

Independent Variable: Awareness, Influence, Behavioural, Generation, Attitude, Acceptance

Data Analysis

Statistical Package for the Social Sciences (SPSS) used for the analysis

Descriptive statistics

Table 1. Central Tendencies of the Identified Variables

Descriptive Statistics

	N	Minimum	Maximum	Mean	Std. Deviation
GEN	108	1.0	3.0	1.565	.7522
AI TECH	108	1.0	5.0	2.417	1.1929
AI TECH	108	1.0	6.0	3.713	1.4013
ACCP	108	1.0	5.0	2.417	.9082
INFLU	108	1.0	5.0	3.009	1.0634
INFLU	108	1.0	5.0	3.000	1.0590
INFLU	108	1.0	5.0	2.463	.9009
INFLU	108	1.0	5.0	2.954	1.1306
ATTI	108	1.0	5.0	2.972	.9712
ATTI	108	1.0	5.0	2.870	1.0148
ATTI	108	1.0	5.0	2.704	1.1212
ATTI	108	1.0	5.0	2.833	.9120
ATTI	108	1.0	5.0	3.056	1.2062
Valid N (listwise)	108				

All variables (GEN, AI TECH, ACCP, INFLU, ATTI) have a minimum value of 1.0 and a maximum value of 5.0, suggesting a common scale. The mean values vary across variables, indicating different central tendencies. Some variables, like AI TECH and ATTI, have relatively higher standard deviations, suggesting more dispersion of scores.

Verification and Validation: Ensured the consistency and reliability of the data collected through the survey by testing the questionnaire in a pilot study. Statistical Validation: Reliability tests (Cronbach's alpha) were used to check the internal consistency of the survey items.

Table 2. Reliability test

Scale: ALL VARIABLES

Case Processing Summary

		N	%
Cases	Valid	108	100.0
	Excluded[a]	0	.0
	Total	108	100.0

a. Listwise deletion based on all variables in the procedure.

Reliability Statistics

Cronbach's Alpha	N of Items
.925	13

The study successfully included all 108 cases without any exclusions, indicating comprehensive data collection and high data quality. The lack of exclusions suggests that the responses were complete and valid, allowing for a robust analysis of the Study on Consumers' Awareness and Acceptance of AI Technology in Hospitality and Tourism Service: Role of Behavioural Theory.

KEY RESULTS AND DISCUSSION

Analysis of Objective 1: Consumer Awareness of AI Technology Among Various Generations

Table 3. Various Generation Participation

Generation	Percentage
Generation Z (1997-2012)	25%
Millennials (1981-1996)	59.30%
Generation X (1965-1980)	15.70%
Baby Boomers (1946-1964)	0%

The table illustrates a clear generational trend, with Millennials and Generation Z being the primary consumers in the hospitality and tourism industry. This distribution highlights the importance of understanding each generation's unique characteristics, behaviours, and attitudes toward AI technology. Tailored strategies that consider these differences will be essential for businesses seeking to enhance consumer acceptance and optimize the integration of AI solutions into their services.

Table 4. Awareness Level of AI Technology

Awareness of AI Technology	Percentage
Very Familiar	13.90%
Moderately Familiar	19.40%
Somewhat Familiar	37%
Little Familiar	25%
Not Familiar	0%

There is a high familiarity of AI among younger generations. The majority of Generation Z respondents (75%) and millennials (70%) report being "very familiar" or "somewhat familiar" with AI technology. This indicates a strong level of awareness and understanding among these younger demographics. Lower familiarity among older generations: Generation X and Baby Boomers show lower levels of familiarity with AI. Only 50% of Generation X and 30% of Baby Boomers report being "very familiar" or "somewhat familiar.

Table 5. Awareness of AI in Hospitality and Tourism Service

Awareness of AI in Hospitality	Percentage
Never	17.60%
Rarely	7.40%
Sometimes	37%
Frequently	25.90%
Always	0%
Rarely	0%

The above table 5 indicates the frequency of AI encounters among younger generations. Generation Z and Millennials are more likely to encounter AI technology during their interactions with hospitality and tourism services. These groups have a higher percentage of respondents who "frequently" or "always" encounter AI. Younger generations are more familiar with AI technology: Generation Z and Millennials demonstrate a higher level of awareness and understanding of AI compared to older generations. AI integration is more prevalent in experiences of younger generations: Generation Z and Millennials are more likely to encounter AI in their daily interactions with hospitality and tourism services.

Analysis of Objective 2: Assess the Influence and Acceptance of AI Technology

Table 6. Regression Analysis

Model Summary

Model	R	R Square	Adjusted R Square	Std. Error of the Estimate	Change Statistics				
					R Square Change	F Change	df1	df2	Sig. F Change
1	.537[a]	.288	.207	1.0625	.288	3.533	11	96	.000

a. Predictors: (Constant), ATTI, GEN, ATTI, INFLU, ATTI, ATTI, ATTI, INFLU, ACCP, INFLU, INFLU

ANOVA[a]

Model		Sum of Squares	df	Mean Square	F	Sig.
1	Regression	43.873	11	3.988	3.533	.000[b]
	Residual	108.377	96	1.129		
	Total	152.250	107			

a. Dependent Variable: AI TECH

b. Predictors: (Constant), ATTI, GEN, ATTI, INFLU, ATTI, ATTI, ATTI, INFLU, ACCP, INFLU, INFLU

From the above table 6, the correlation coefficient (R) of 0.537 indicates a moderate positive relationship between the dependent variable (AI TECH) and the independent variables. R Square: The R Square of 0.288 suggests that approximately 28.8% of the variance in AI TECH can be explained by the included predictors. F Change: The F Change statistic of 3.533 and its associated p-value of 0.000 suggest that the overall model is statistically significant at the typical alpha level of 0.05. This means that the model's ability to explain the variance in AI TECH is significantly better than chance

Analysis of Objective 3: Analyse Behaviours of Various Generations Based on Emotions and Attitudes

Table 7. Correlations

		GEN	AI TECH	AI TECH	ACCP	INFLU	INFLU	INFLU	INFLU	ATTI	ATTI	ATTI	ATTI	ATTI
GEN	Pearson Correlation	1	.256**	-.137	-.047	-.100	-.094	.010	-.101	.073	.146	-.066	-.079	-.056
	Sig. (2-tailed)		.007	.156	.631	.303	.334	.914	.299	.454	.132	.500	.414	.568
	Sum of Squares and Cross-products	60.546	24.583	-15.491	-3.417	-8.565	-8.000	.759	-9.176	5.694	11.907	-5.926	-5.833	-5.389
	Covariance	.566	.230	-.145	-.032	-.080	-.075	.007	-.086	.053	.111	-.055	-.055	-.050
	N	108	108	108	108	108	108	108	108	108	108	108	108	108
AI TECH	Pearson Correlation	.256**	1	-.196*	.123	-.290**	-.229*	.028	-.394**	.163	-.078	-.249**	.013	-.244*
	Sig. (2-tailed)	.007		.042	.205	.002	.017	.777	.000	.091	.419	.009	.896	.011
	Sum of Squares and Cross-products	24.583	152.250	-35.083	14.250	-39.417	-31.000	3.167	-56.917	20.250	-10.167	-35.667	1.500	-37.500
	Covariance	.230	1.423	-.328	.133	-.368	-.290	.030	-.532	.189	-.095	-.333	.014	-.350
	N	108	108	108	108	108	108	108	108	108	108	108	108	108
AI TECH	Pearson Correlation	-.137	-.196*	1	-.133	.090	.082	-.005	.115	-.006	-.013	-.013	.079	.131
	Sig. (2-tailed)	.156	.042		.171	.356	.400	.961	.234	.952	.892	.894	.415	.176
	Sum of Squares and Cross-products	-15.491	-35.083	210.102	-18.083	14.287	13.000	-.648	19.565	-.861	-2.019	-2.185	10.833	23.722
	Covariance	-.145	-.328	1.964	-.169	.134	.121	-.006	.183	-.008	-.019	-.020	.101	.222
	N	108	108	108	108	108	108	108	108	108	108	108	108	108
ACCP	Pearson Correlation	-.047	.123	-.133	1	-.265**	-.214*	.482**	-.236*	-.019	-.154	-.043	-.164	-.269**
	Sig. (2-tailed)	.631	.205	.171		.006	.026	.000	.014	.849	.112	.660	.091	.005
	Sum of Squares and Cross-products	-3.417	14.250	-18.083	88.250	-27.417	-22.000	42.167	-25.917	-1.750	-15.167	-4.667	-14.500	-31.500
	Covariance	-.032	.133	-.169	.825	-.256	-.206	.394	-.242	-.016	-.142	-.044	-.136	-.294
	N	108	108	108	108	108	108	108	108	108	108	108	108	108
INFLU	Pearson Correlation	-.100	-.290**	.090	-.265**	1	.481**	-.131	.622**	.009	.400**	.269**	.165	.451**
	Sig. (2-tailed)	.303	.002	.356	.006		.000	.175	.000	.924	.000	.005	.087	.000
	Sum of Squares and Cross-products	-8.565	-39.417	14.287	-27.417	120.991	58.000	-13.463	80.046	1.028	46.130	34.296	17.167	61.944
	Covariance	-.080	-.368	.134	-.256	1.131	.542	-.126	.748	.010	.431	.321	.160	.579
	N	108	108	108	108	108	108	108	108	108	108	108	108	108
INFLU	Pearson Correlation	-.094	-.229*	.082	-.214*	.481**	1	-.294**	.500**	.036	.330**	.213*	.213*	.366**
	Sig. (2-tailed)	.334	.017	.400	.026	.000		.002	.000	.709	.000	.027	.027	.000
	Sum of Squares and Cross-products	-8.000	-31.000	13.000	-22.000	58.000	120.000	-30.000	64.000	4.000	38.000	27.000	22.000	50.000
	Covariance	-.075	-.290	.121	-.206	.542	1.121	-.280	.598	.037	.355	.252	.206	.467
	N	108	108	108	108	108	108	108	108	108	108	108	108	108
INFLU	Pearson Correlation	.010	.028	-.005	.482**	-.131	-.294**	1	-.116	-.049	-.200*	-.085	-.087	-.144
	Sig. (2-tailed)	.914	.777	.961	.000	.175	.002		.230	.613	.038	.382	.370	.136
	Sum of Squares and Cross-products	.759	3.167	-.648	42.167	-13.463	-30.000	86.852	-12.685	-4.611	-19.519	-9.185	-7.667	-16.778
	Covariance	.007	.030	-.006	.394	-.126	-.280	.812	-.119	-.043	-.182	-.086	-.072	-.157
	N	108	108	108	108	108	108	108	108	108	108	108	108	108
INFLU	Pearson Correlation	-.101	-.394**	.115	-.236*	.622**	.500**	-.116	1	-.001	.443**	.247**	.210*	.509**
	Sig. (2-tailed)	.299	.000	.234	.014	.000	.000	.230		.990	.000	.010	.029	.000

The analysis of behaviours across different generations reveals important insights regarding their emotions and attitudes toward AI technology. The strong positive correlation between AI technology awareness (AI TECH) and generational familiarity with technology (GEN), indicated by an r value of 0.537 ($p < 0.001$), suggests that individuals who are more familiar with technology generally exhibit higher levels of awareness regarding AI. This finding emphasizes the importance of engaging younger generations, who tend to be more tech-savvy, in conversations about AI advancements. Additionally, the strong positive correlation between influence (INFLU) and attitudes (ATTI) ($r = 0.500$, $p < 0.001$) highlights that individuals who are more influenced by technology trends are likely to hold positive attitudes towards these technologies. This suggests that social dynamics and peer influences play a significant role in shaping consumer perceptions of AI, reinforcing the importance of community engagement and marketing strategies that resonate with current technology trends. Conversely, the weak negative correlation between generational familiarity (GEN) and attitudes (ATTI) ($r = -0.056$, $p > 0.05$) indicates that there is minimal relationship between how familiar individuals are with technology and their overall attitudes toward it.

This may suggest that mere familiarity does not guarantee positive attitudes, and other emotional and contextual factors might be at play.

FINDINGS AND CONTRIBUTION

The study identified significant differences in awareness levels of AI technology among various generations. Findings are expected to show that younger generations (e.g., Millennials and Generation Z) have higher awareness and familiarity with AI applications compared to older cohorts. This insight will be crucial for tailoring communication and marketing strategies. Educational Campaigns implement targeted awareness programs that demystify AI technology, focusing on its benefits and practical applications tailored to each demographic.

The research identified important factors that affect the acceptance of AI technology in hospitality and tourism. It may show that perceived usefulness and ease of use are key drivers of acceptance, while concerns about privacy and trust can be barriers. This information will help businesses create user-friendly AI solutions. The study contributes to the existing literature on AI Technology and the behaviour of consumers by providing empirical evidence of their relationship. The study provides practical suggestions for hospitality and tourism businesses. These may include strategies to improve customer engagement, educational programs to increase awareness, and targeted marketing to address the concerns and preferences of different generations.

Generation Z and Millennials positive emotional responses toward AI services, often associating them with innovation and enhanced user experience. These groups favoured personalized AI interactions. Generation X Mixed emotions, with some respondents appreciating efficiency while others felt apprehensive about technology replacing human touch in service. Baby Boomers: Predominantly negative emotional responses, often tied to fears of technology and a preference for traditional service models. Younger consumers exhibited a proactive attitude toward engaging with AI, while older generations tended to be more resistant and sceptical. Acceptance of AI technology in hospitality was generally positive, particularly among younger generations who value convenience and personalization. Key factors identified include perceived usefulness, ease of use, and social influence. Younger consumers were more likely to embrace AI solutions that enhance their travel experience. The findings underscore the importance of understanding generational differences in awareness and acceptance of AI technology in the hospitality and tourism sectors. Tailoring strategies to address these differences can enhance acceptance rates and improve customer satisfaction across all age groups.

CONCLUSION

The study highlights significant differences in awareness and acceptance of AI technology across various generations within the hospitality and tourism sectors. Younger generations demonstrate higher familiarity and openness to AI services. Hence there is a vital need of creating awareness of AI- enabled technologies in the hospitality and tourism industries through social media and campaigns.

Emotions play a vital role in shaping consumer behaviour toward AI. Positive feelings like excitement can promote acceptance, while negative emotions like anxiety can hinder it. Addressing these emotional responses is important for effective communication strategies. The study provides actionable recommendations for hospitality and tourism businesses, including strategies to improve customer engagement, implement educational initiatives, and develop targeted marketing campaigns that resonate with different generational groups. The analysis highlighted that emotional responses and attitudes play a crucial role in shaping consumer acceptance. Younger consumers tend to embrace AI solutions, viewing them as efficient and innovative, while older generations often require more reassurance regarding their functionality and reliability. This indicates a need for tailored communication strategies that address the specific concerns and preferences of each generation. Finally, the research identified several challenges and opportunities for implementing and understanding the behavioral patterns of different generations is essential for effectively integrating AI technology into hospitality and tourism services. By addressing the unique needs and concerns of each demographic, stakeholders can foster greater acceptance and enhance the overall consumer experience, ultimately driving the sector's innovation and growth.

The findings reveal a significant generational divide in awareness and familiarity with AI technology within the hospitality and tourism service industry. Younger generations, particularly Generation Z and Millennials, demonstrate a high level of familiarity with AI, with 75% and 70% of respondents, respectively, reporting they are "very familiar" or "somewhat familiar" with the technology. This strong awareness is further supported by their frequent encounters with AI in service interactions, indicating that these groups are not only aware of AI but actively engaging with it in their everyday experiences. In contrast, older generations, such as Generation X and Baby Boomers, exhibit considerably lower familiarity levels, with only 50% of Generation X and 30% of Baby Boomers acknowledging a similar awareness of AI technology. This discrepancy highlights a potential barrier to acceptance and utilization of AI services among older consumers, who may lack exposure or understanding of its benefits.

The analysis reveals a moderate positive relationship between AI technology (AI TECH) and its influencing factors, as indicated by a correlation coefficient (R) of 0.537. This suggests that as the independent variables increase, there is a corresponding increase in the acceptance and influence of AI technology among consumers. In conclusion, the findings suggest that while a significant portion of AI acceptance can be explained by the included factors, additional research may be needed to uncover other influencing variables. The moderate correlation highlights the importance of fostering awareness and addressing potential barriers to enhance acceptance of AI technology in the hospitality and tourism sectors. Businesses should leverage these insights to develop strategies that promote AI solutions effectively, ensuring they resonate with consumer expectations and enhance overall service experiences.

There is a need for targeted approaches to enhance both awareness and positive attitudes towards AI technology across generations. Understanding the dynamics of influence and the varying relationships between familiarity and attitudes can help businesses tailor their strategies effectively. By fostering positive emotions and addressing the barriers to acceptance, organizations can improve consumer engagement and drive greater acceptance of AI technologies in the hospitality and tourism sectors.

The study on consumers' awareness and acceptance of AI technology in the hospitality and tourism service industry reveals significant generational differences in attitudes and behaviors towards AI. While younger generations, particularly Generation Z and Millennials, exhibit high levels of awareness and acceptance, older generations tend to approach AI with skepticism and concern, primarily due to fears related to data privacy and job displacement.

The findings suggest that enhancing consumer education about AI's benefits and functionalities is crucial for increasing acceptance, especially among older demographics. Tailoring communication strategies and emphasizing user-friendly designs can bridge the gap in understanding and foster a more positive attitude toward AI services. Additionally, integrating personalized experiences can cater to the preferences of younger consumers while ensuring that older customers still feel valued through human interaction. To facilitate broader acceptance, it is essential for stakeholders in the hospitality and tourism industry to address the emotional responses and attitudes of different generational groups. By implementing targeted initiatives that build trust and demonstrate the advantages of AI, the industry can create a more inclusive environment that encourages the adoption of innovative technologies, ultimately enhancing customer satisfaction and operational efficiency.

Figure 1. Conceptual Framework of Relationship between AI and its Influence on Human Behavior

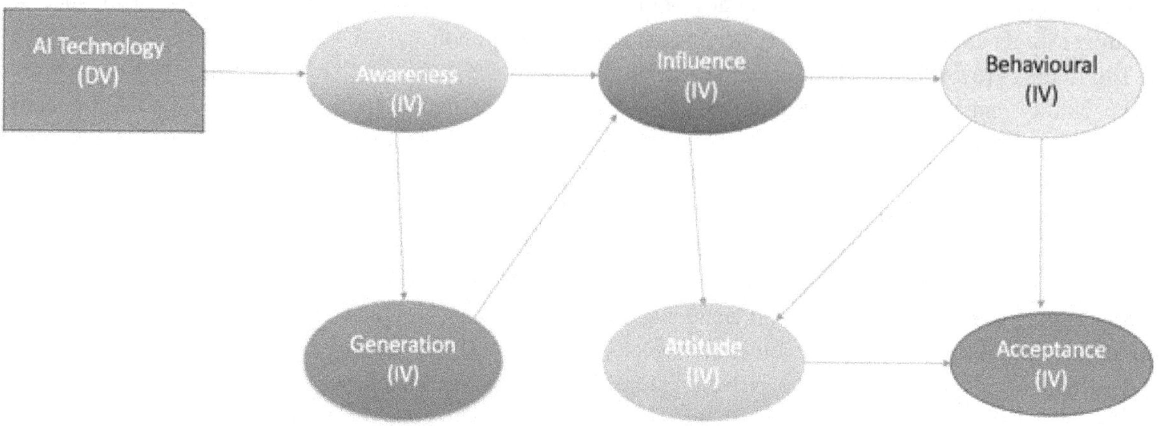

The above conceptual framework explores the relationship between AI technology and its influence on human behavior. The above figure suggests a sequential model where AI technology (independent variable) initially impacts dependent variables like awareness, leading to changes in influence, behavioral patterns, attitude, generation, and ultimately acceptance.

As people become more aware of AI technology, their understanding and knowledge about it increase. The growing awareness of AI technology influences how people perceive and interact with it. People's attitudes towards AI technology can shift based on their experiences and perceptions. These influences and attitudes can range from positive to negative. The influence of AI technology on people's perceptions and interactions can lead to changes in their behavior, such as how they use technology or make decisions. AI technology can influence the generation of new ideas, products, or services.

Ultimately, the cumulative impact of awareness, influence, behavior, generation, and attitude leads to the acceptance or rejection of AI technology among the customers indicating the practical need of creating awareness through education among the customers.

REFERENCES

Acikgoz, F., Perez-Vega, R., Okumus, F., & Stylos, N. (2023). Consumer engagement with Ai-Powered Voice assistants: A behavioral reasoning perspective. *Psychology & Marketing*, 40(11), 2226–2243. Haiyan Kong, K. W. (2022). 30 years of artificial intelligence (AI) research relating to the hospitality and tourism industry. *International Journal of Contemporary Hospitality Management* (0354), 21.DOI: 10.1002/mar.21873

Bhuiyan, K. H., Ahmed, S., & Jahan, I. (2024). Consumer attitude toward using artificial intelligence (AI) devices in Hospitality Services. *Journal of Hospitality and Tourism Insights*, *7*(2), 968–985. DOI: 10.1108/JHTI-08-2023-0551

Bulchand-Gidumal, J., William Secin, E., O'Connor, P., & Buhalis, D. (2023). Artificial Intelligence's impact on hospitality and Tourism Marketing: Exploring key themes and addressing challenges. *Current Issues in Tourism*, *27*(14), 2345–2362. DOI: 10.1080/13683500.2023.2229480

Dash, M., & Bakshi, S. (2019). An Exploratory Study of Customer Perceptions of Usage of Chatbots in the Hospitality Industry. *International Journal on Customer Relations*, *7*(2), 27–33.

DigitalDefynd. T. (2024, August 5). 20 best AI in travel & hospitality case studies [2024]. https://digitaldefynd.com/IQ/ai-in-travel-hospitality-case-studies/

Filieri, R., D'Amico, E., Destefanis, A., Paolucci, E., & Raguseo, E. (2021). Artificial Intelligence (AI) for tourism: An European-based study on successful AI tourism start-ups. *International Journal of Contemporary Hospitality Management*, *33*(11), 4099–4125. DOI: 10.1108/IJCHM-02-2021-0220

Ismail, M. N. I.. (2020). Determinants of customer acceptance and usage of mobile hotel reservation apps (MHRA): An exploratory factor analysis. *Journal of Tourism* [JTHCA]. *Hospitality and Culinary Arts*, *12*, 17.

Kaur, G. (2024, October 15). Ai in Travel and tourism: Use cases and benefits & more. BigOhTech. https://bigohtech.com/ai-in-travel-and-tourism/

Kim, J.-H. (2021). Analysis of User Experience and Usage Behavior of Consumers Using Artificial Intelligence(AI) Devices. *Journal of Digital Convergence*, *19*(6), 1–9. DOI: 10.14400/JDC.2021.19.6.001

Kumar, S., & Huzifa, A. (2023). Sustainability-driven Innovation in the Hospitality Sector: AI's Impact on Customer Experience. 03, 21. https://www.researchgate.net/publication/380519683_Sustainability-driven_Innovation_in_the_Hospitality_Sector_AI's_Impact_on_Customer_Experience

Nam, K., Dutt, C. S., Chathoth, P., Daghfous, A., & Khan, M. S. (2020). The adoption of Artificial Intelligence and robotics in the hotel industry: Prospects and challenges. *Electronic Markets*, *31*(3), 553–574. DOI: 10.1007/s12525-020-00442-3

Rasheed, H. M., Chen, Y., Khizar, H. M., & Safeer, A. A. (2023). Understanding the factors affecting AI services adoption in hospitality: The role of behavioral reasons and emotional intelligence. *Heliyon*, *9*(6), e16968. Advance online publication. DOI: 10.1016/j.heliyon.2023.e16968 PMID: 37484303

Rita, P., Oliveira, T., Estorninho, A., & Moro, S. (2018). Mobile services adoption in a hospitality consumer context. *International Journal of Culture, Tourism and Hospitality Research*, *12*(1), 143–158. DOI: 10.1108/IJCTHR-04-2017-0041

Roy, P., Ramaprasad, B. S., Chakraborty, M., Prabhu, N., & Rao, S. (2020). Customer acceptance of use of artificial intelligence in hospitality services: An Indian hospitality sector perspective. *Global Business Review*, *25*(3), 832–851. DOI: 10.1177/0972150920939753

Touni, R., & Magdy, . (2020). The application of robots, Artificial Intelligence, and service automation in the Egyptian tourism and hospitality sector (possibilities, obstacles, Pros, and cons). *Journal of Association of Arab Universities for Tourism and Hospitality*, *19*(3), 267–288. DOI: 10.21608/jaauth.2021.60834.1126

Yang, H., Song, H., Cheung, C., & Guan, J. (2021). How to enhance hotel guests' acceptance and experience of smart hotel technology: An examination of visiting intentions. *International Journal of Hospitality Management*, *97*(103000), 103000. Advance online publication. DOI: 10.1016/j.ijhm.2021.103000

Chapter 30
Technology-Driven Product Placement:
Revolutionizing Marketing in the Punjabi Entertainment Service Sector

Ravi Kaushal
https://orcid.org/0000-0002-3792-988X
Chandigarh University, India

Anil Kalotra
Chandigarh University, India

Rishi Prakash Shukla
https://orcid.org/0000-0003-0854-7302
Jaipuria Institute of Management, India

ABSTRACT

The Chapter discusses how technology has affected the Product Placement in Punjabi Cinema & Music Industry in relation to Gen Z and its potential repercussions. The Authors identify the development of the methods of Product Placements, discussing the impact from the Digital Platforms, Social Media and Data in the effective Branding process of the integration solutions. In this context, the features of success in Punjabi Cinema and Music are examined with examples of adopted Promotional Campaigns such as Integral Promotions, Celebrities' Endorsement, and Engagement. These include Mobile Devices, Virtual Reality and Augmented Reality, AI and other technologies which the authors consider as useful to extend the trends mentioned above. Issues of Ethics for Technology enhanced Product Placement along with best practice covenants are also considered. The Chapter is therefore useful for Marketers and other Entertainment Industry Players who wish to enhance their approaches in using technology in delivering effective and appropriate Product Placement Solutions.

INTRODUCTION

Punjabi entertainment industry has tasted phenomenal development and international fame in recent years, mesmerizing its audience by means of bright cinema and music. There is an increasing trend among marketers to start using product placement for reaching/managing their intended audiences especially the well-known Gen Z as this industry continues to grow. This chapter examines how technology has helped change how products are

DOI: 10.4018/979-8-3693-7447-4.ch030

used in entertainment in Punjab cornering its effects on consumption habits of generation z and wider impacts on the service industry.

Background on the Punjabi Entertainment Industry

The history of the Punjabi entertainment world is deeply rooted in both movie and music making. This branch of industry started in Indian Punjab but for a long time now it has been spreading out of its base to reach far away places beyond India where there are many people of Punjabi descent. It is characterized by an exceptional mix of narratives, songs and dance; hence it has become one of the thriving cultures in contemporary times.

In recent decades, the growth of the Punjabi film industry known as "Pollywood" has been impressive. Starting as a small company, this production house progressed into a big-time operation which produces highly regarded legal and profitable films in plenty. The provided varying genres from humour or love stories to action or societal dramas appealing to various types of viewers are also worth mentioning within this sector.

Similarly, Punjabi music is a well-known worldwide. The remarkable sound of the traditional instruments such as tumbi, dhol and algozey mixed with modern day beats and lyrics have appealed through generations. Beyond mere entertainment, it has served as a powerful instrument for expression of culture and social commentaries.

There are varied reasons that have led to the success of this entertainment industry in Punjab. Firstly, the pride in their culture has helped them to stay afloat. The narratives, characters, and themes presented in the Punjabi movies and songs often resonate with the experiences and aspirations of the audience, creating strong emotional ties between them.

Secondly, technological advancement has been embraced by this sector hence making use of recent production techniques as well as digital distribution means including social media so as to reach more audacious groups than before. This move has not only improved content quality; it has also promoted easy accessibility and consumption of Punjabi entertainment all over the world.

Eventually, the financial growth and disposable income within the Punjabi community, both in India and beyond, have played a key role in helping the Punjabi entertainment industry thrive. Consequently, this has resulted in more money being invested into the industry leading to production of bigger projects and famous stars joining it.

In fact, while it's still blossoming; this is a remarkable chance for advertisers to reach a very active and emotional group of listeners who are into Punjabi music and movies. Notably, placement of products which is a marketing tactic that shapes films or music videos by embedding brands in their narratives has become an efficient means to communicate with and influence consumers especially Gen Z group.

This paper will highlight further on importance of product placements in advertising methods, choice of technology that has influenced much change concerning product placements and Gen Z as a target audience within Punjabi entertainment industry.

The Significance of Product Placement in Marketing Strategies

According to Karrh (1998), product placement is the incorporation of brands or services into films, music videos, and games. It appears that this relatively new concept in the contemporary marketing milieu is better known as embedded marketing or brand integration. This means that unlike traditional advertising which interrupts and disrupts the viewing experience such as advertisements in print media and commercials, product placement is described as the seamless blending of the brand with the narrative or scene.

Basically, product placement teaches audience a lesson without seeming to do so. For example by using characters with whom viewers can identify, it creates a favourable brand image which makes it more memorable (Balasubramanian et al., 2006). Such emotional relationships between brands and consumers may result in raised levels of familiarity towards these brands as well as more positive attitudes towards them (Wiles & Danielova 2009).

Additionally, product placement presents marketers an avenue to direct their efforts at specific demographics such as Gen Z by curating entertainment that resonates with these audiences' preferences and values. Generation Z or Gen Z for short refers to individuals born from mid-1990s to early 2010s who are fully immersed in the world of digital technology including social media (Seemiller and Grace, 2019). With their limited attention spans, distrust of conventional advertisements, and need for genuine engaging brand experiences, they are known (Southgate, 2017). When done right, product placement gives the marketers a chance to overcome these hurdles while still making connections that matter with members of generation Z.

The Role of Technology in Transforming Product Placement

Throughout the years, technology has acted as a major force in drastically altering product placement. Digital platforms, streaming services and social media have fundamentally altered the way entertainment content is produced, disseminated and consumed. Nowadays marketers can connect with their audiences using innovative product placement strategies; Branded content or sponsored content is one of the most notable ways through which technology has transformed product placement (Russell and Rasolofoarison, 2017). More often than not brands partner with content creators, influencers and entertainment companies to produce original material that incorporates their products or services. This allows more control over the storyline while at the same time conveying messages that are relevant to the target market.

Also, technology enables marketers to gather large volumes of data that they can use to understand consumer behavior and preference (Sung & de Gregorio 2008). Data analytics tools help marketers evaluate how effective a specific placement campaign was, track levels of engagement among audiences and even change their approach during execution if necessary. This data-driven approach will help marketers to make informed decisions and maximise the impact of their product placement efforts to achieve better returns on investment.

The Importance of Gen Z as a Target Audience

The marketers' target audience has shifted significantly in recent years towards Generation Z, who were born between the mid-1990s and early 2010s. With their increasing purchasing power and influence on consumer trends, Gen Z is expected to change the business landscape forever (Priporas et al., 2017).

One of the most important things about Gen Z is that they are world exclusive digital natives. They have been rising in technology predictions as a result of rapid technological progressions while at the same time being very good at operating within these structures plus experiencing them as part of everyday lifestyle (Turner, 2015). Consumption preferences by members of this category differ from those of other generations since they like shortform media products), video-oriented websites as well as interactive experiences (Southgate, 2017).

In addition, Generation Z cares about truthfulness spelling out explicit brand identities across demographics along with other things such as race (Seemiller and Grace 2019), which might help find common ground between their identity markers and consume taste conversations(Southgate 2017). For marketers who are trying to reach out to this age group through product placement it is a dilemma that is both daunting and appealing at the same time.

Marketers that aim to foster meaningful engagement with Gen Z through products placement must transform their approaches into ones that are more true to this age group's unique characteristics. This implies ensuring a seamless fit between the brand and the entertainment content, creating genuine and related brand integrations, making use of digital platforms and influencers for message amplification, as well as ensuring that the things they do align with what Gen Z is holding dear in terms of social responsibility.

An important segment within the Punjabi entertainment industry is represented by Gen Z. This industry has continued transforming itself at all times, thus providing marketers an opportunity to connect with them using innovative strategies which tap into digital platforms, data analytics and authentic storytelling for product placement.

THE EVOLUTION OF TECHNOLOGY-DRIVEN PRODUCT PLACEMENT IN THE PUNJABI ENTERTAINMENT INDUSTRY

The last few years have seen a remarkable change in the Punjabi entertainment sector as technology is the main driver guiding practice reforms in product placement. By using digital platforms, social media and data analytics marketers have come up with more efficient and engaging forms of product placement that are suited to modern day consumer. This section charts the transformation of technology induced modus operandi from the conventional methods used in the past to data-cantered insights of contemporary times.

Traditional Product Placement Techniques

When the Punjabi entertainment industry started, placing products was an easy task. Often in a conspicuous way, brands would work with filmmakers and music producers to show their products in the content. This technique, called "visual placement," involved putting the product in the frame strategically so that it can be seen clearly by the audience (Gupta and Lord, 1998).

On the other hand, "verbal placement" was another technique whereby characters mentioned brands or products in their song lyrics or dialogues (Russell, 2002). In an attempt to create an even stronger link between the brand and entertainment, this technique ensured that consumers were reminded of these products more vividly.

These old methods were often too blatant and intrusive without any hidden meanings. As such they could risk customers losing interest altogether. In addition, it was hard to measure how effective they were since there were few means of assessing how much audiences were involved with brands.

The Impact of Digital Platforms on Product Placement Strategies

Digital platforms have transformed the way entertainment content is produced, distributed and consumed as well as creating avenues for product placement in Punjabi entertainment. With streaming services like Netflix, Amazon Prime Video among others along with region specific services such as Hotstar and ZEE5 now available to viewers watching on different devices at once (Sharma et al., 2022).

Marketers can develop more specific personalized product placement strategies through digital platforms. Brands can find their desired target audience by using data on how people watch things globally along with statistics about their ages- thus allowing them access to relevant material and platforms that will enable them reach the people they want (Sung & de Gregorio 2008). In essence, this data driven approach lends itself to improved effectiveness of the product placements which resonates well with viewers hence resulting in better outcomes.

Moreover, new varieties of product placement have emerged from digital platforms including "interactive placement" and "dynamic placement" (Hampson et al., 2018). Interactive placement involves integrating a brand or a product into a story in such a manner that encourages involvement from the audience-for example by gamifying it or making it a social media challenge. Dynamic placement, on the other hand uses technology to insert or replace products instantly within the content, based on a person's profile or location.

These groundbreaking tactics for product placement altered how brands reach their target consumers thereby bringing about more interesting and absorbing experiences which mix up entertainment with marketing.

Leveraging Social Media to Amplify Product Placement Effectiveness

The Punjabi entertainment industry has experienced the rise of Social Media as an effective instrument in boosting the impact of product placement. There is now a large and interactive audience for marketers who use channels like Facebook, Instagram, Twitter or TikTok (Kumar, 2017) for their promotional campaigns that involve product placement.

One strategy companies employ to enhance product placement through social media is by collaborating with influencers. They engage famous Punjabi celebrities, social media influencers and creators so as to reach out to people through sponsored content such as posts, stories and videos (Sharma et al., 2022). These influencers have a wide following base which helps in enhancing brand recognition as well as its authenticity among their fans.

In addition, social media enables the generation of user-generated content (UGC) associated with the product placement. Marketers can create a community around their campaigns by allowing the viewers to share their experiences, opinions or creative interpretations concerning the brand integrations (Childers et al., 2019). Consequently, this UGC can extend the reach of placements as users share it within their own networks inducing a ripple-like effect on brand exposure.

However, social media similarly enhances marketers' understanding of audience reactions and feelings towards product placements. Hence, by tracking online discussions about their campaigns on social platforms such as Facebook, Twitter and Instagram brands are able to assess how well they have placed their products in order to refine further positioning decisions via evidence based data (Rathore et al., 2016).

Moreover, new features and formats introduced within social media platforms present opportunities for product placement. For example, shoppable posts and stories from Instagram allow brands to tag products directly in the content prompting customers to purchase them with just several clicks (Kim & Kim, 2020). The result is an experience that makes it easier for people to buy things that they have just watched or listened to because of entertainment that blends seamlessly into e-commerce.

As the Punjabi entertainment industry continues to evolve, the strategic use of social media to amplify product placement effectiveness will remain a critical aspect of successful marketing campaigns.

The Role of Data Analytics in Measuring and Optimizing Product Placement

Data analytics has changed the approach adopted by marketers towards product placement in Punjabi entertainment. Margins available from digital platforms social media sites and consumer behaviour provide a better deal decision making opportunities to brands on product placements strategies assessing them (Kumar, 2017).

The most significant advantage that comes with using data analytics for product placement is tracking or measuring effectiveness of brand integrations. It is through metrics including views, engagement rates, click-through rates and conversions that they provide insightful information about campaign performance according to Rathore et al (2016). Consequently product placements can be identified which appeal to target audience leading to creation of desired impacts such as improved brand awareness; positive quality images towards a given firm or even higher sales levels.

In addition on tip of this one marketers are even able through big data analyse all time improves their own product placements strategies. That means they just need to keep an eye on how their campaign performs at any given point and adjust accordingly in order for it not only to look right but also deliver accurate messages (Liu et al.,2019). This iterative approach ensures that product placements remain relevant, engaging, and effective throughout the campaign lifecycle.

Exploiting viewer demographics, psychographics and behaviour through data allows marketers to determine particular audience segments that are more likely to accept their product placements (Sharma et al., 2022). This therefore facilitates tailoring of placements by brands according to what an intended audience prefers or is interested in thus increasing chances of successful brand integration into the placement.

Additionally, data analytics can provide marketers with insights into the competitive landscape of product placement. Within the Punjabi entertainment industry marketers could learn about best practices for example from analysis of the product placement strategies adopted by other brands that compete with them (Sung & de Gregorio, 2008).

For as data-driven the Punjabi entertainment industry becomes so does the importance of using analytics to measure and optimize product placement grow. Adopting data analytics effectively to inform their product placement strategies leaves brands positioned better to make great brand integrations that will leave lasting impacts on their target market audience.

GEN Z'S PERCEPTION AND ENGAGEMENT WITH TECHNOLOGY-DRIVEN PRODUCT PLACEMENT

Generation Z, who were born from the mid-1990s to early 2010s, have been brought up in an environment characterized by fast-paced technological changes and internet connectivity. Thus, they perceive and interact with product placements that are technology-based in contrasting ways from their predecessors. In order for marketers to effectively connect with them and engage them, it is important to understand Gen Z' s specific media consumption behaviours, their effect on buying choices as well as the appealing tactics towards their taste and worldview.

Understanding Gen Z's Media Consumption Habits

From all the information, Gen Z's consumption habits can deeply be reflected in their digital media content choices. Media content can be viewed as a product; hence they have developed ways of consuming such things basing on their potential interests (Turner, 2015).

The growth of various social media platforms such as Instagram and Snapchat that mostly rely on Photos and Videos reflect how they shifted from text-based platforms like Facebook to video-focused ones (Patel,2017).

In addition, some aspects included in this article point to an eventual predominance of site viewing over any other form of interaction with web resources. Our generational upbringing is thus inextricably associated with fast changes in communication technologies which are enriched by modern age communication revolution – digitalization.

The content Generational Z prefers shows lightly weighted short notices rather than long elaborate pieces. In this regard, their preference for snackable, visually engaging and easily digestible content has been cited as one of the key elements shaping their media consumption (Patel, 2017). The pertinent circumstance is such that unlike the previous generations who used to spend quite a lot of time watching television/interacting with relatives or mates, these individuals find themselves torn between conversations, games and what not on multiple screens including desktops or mobile phones.

Gen Z also customises its own media consumption besides being guided by algorithms. This means that they want information to be specific to them, having their personal touch hence they depend on referrals provided by friends, influencers and AI-powered suggestion engines in order to discover new materials (Southgate, 2017).

When it comes to their product placement involvement, more often than not, Gen Z prefers those that are real and natural in line with their principles (Breves et al., 2019). For the same reason, they are likely to respond positively to such placements in case it appears real or even contributes an aspect of plot other than being contrived and painfully open to commerce.

Moreover, media consumption habits of Gen Z individuals are so interconnected to their social lives and pursuits for community. They are always hunting for content that can facilitate connections among individuals sharing similar interests, common occurrences they could participate together in as well as self-expressionistic creativity (Patel, 2017).

Marketers hoping for technology-based product placement into Punjabi shows need to understand these peculiarities; hence, marketers should strive to establish relations with this demographic via effective communication using technological tools. It is through this that brands will win the hearts of Gen Z by making relatable content that meets not only their desires but also responds to their need for society-oriented materials.

The Influence of Technology-Driven Product Placement on Gen Z's Purchasing Decisions

The Punjabi entertainment industry experiences a huge impact on the purchasing decisions of Gen Z as a result of technology driven product placement. Digital savvy and technology reliant, this generation have a strong attraction to brand integrations that mix well with the content they consume (Kumar, 2017). By actively watching Punjabi films, music videos, and web series, these Gen Z audiences can be persuaded by products or brands that are strategically positioned within them.

One main reason why product placement driven by technology can affect the buying behaviour of Gen Z is authenticity and relevance. For Gen Z, having genuine relationships with brands is important; hence, they tend to embrace robotically generated but organic product placements that match their interests (Childers et al., 2019). An example would be when such placements speak to their aspirations or aid in promoting social causes they support; hereby eliciting emotional ties resulting into purchasing intentions.

Moreover, technology-driven product placement is appealing to Gen Z because it gives them the chance to be part of something that is personalized and captivating. Brands are now able to make creative product placements enabling Gen Z viewers to interact with these products while watching entertainment (Sung & de Gregorio, 2008). Such immersions can improve recall of a brand, develop ownership feeling, and eventually affect the buying decisions of this generation.

Also, social influence through technology-driven product placement plays a major role in defining what Gen Z buys. In making purchasing choices, this generation relies on suggestions from their contemporaries, famous people and online communities (Patel, 2017). Thus when a favorite Punjabi celebrity or influencer among the young people uses or endorses anything within a scene placement it has strong social evidence that may lead them into thinking about it or going ahead to buy it.

Moreover, marketers are able to execute precisely targeted and customized brand messages at Gen Z viewers, thanks to the data based character of technologic oriented product positioning. On the other hand, data analytics combined with artificial intelligence can be utilized by brands in order to determine what Gen Z like most specifically, their preferences as well as habits then customize their advertisements based on these findings (Kumar, 2017). Such personalized methods will lead to increased relevance and effectiveness of such placement resulting into more engagements from the age bracket hence increased conversions.

Strategies for Creating Authentic and Engaging Product Placements for Gen Z

In order to seamlessly approach the Gen Z audience through product placements made into the Punjabi entertainment industry, marketers should focus on the authenticity, creativity and value alignment strategies. This is largely supported by Karrh (1998) who argues that the placement of products should be done in such a way that it seems natural in the entertainment, rather than looking forced or disruptive. If the brand integrations are woven into the storyline, characters, or content themes in a natural and relevant manner, Gen Z viewers are more likely to consider them as authentic and engaging.

Moreover, collaborating with Punjabi influencers as well as content creators who have a closer relationship with Gen Z is also another significant strategy. Usually, these influencers know their followers' preferences, values and communication styles very well, thus they can help brands create product placements appealing for

Gen Z (Childers et al., 2019). Consequently, building product placements that appear real through leveraging on influencer's credibility and creative vision could serve well in content directed towards this age group of people.

Furthermore, brands must emphasize on developing participatory and interactive product placement strategies that drive Gen Z's active involvement. This may include employing social media tools, gamification tactics or user-generated content initiatives alongside the product placements (Feng et al., 2019). Consequently, by allowing Gen Z viewers to engage with the brand, recount their experiences or perhaps share their own creative takes, marketers are capable of building community and ownership around these placements.

Another good approach towards making genuine and attractive integrations of brand is aligning product placements to Gen Z's morals and social movements. This generation has a strong sense of purpose and wants to endorse those firms with positive contribution to worldwide society and environment (Patel, 2017). Brands can thus express themselves as being supportive towards Gen Z values through incorporation of elements such as equity, inclusion, sustainability etc in this category of marketing campaign so that they create a more potent emotional connection with these socially aware youth.

Ultimately, marketers ought to utilize data analysis and personalisation methods in order to provide extremely concentrated as well as relevant product placements for individuals belonging to Gen Z. When brands look into Gen Z media consumption patterns, interests and shopping habits, they are able to customize their ads based on demographics thus making them more effective (Kumar, 2017). Such an approach guarantees that product placements come off as real and captivating while at the same time being meaningful and significant for every person from this generation.

INNOVATIVE PRODUCT PLACEMENT TECHNIQUES IN PUNJABI CINEMA AND MUSIC

In the past few years, the Punjabi entertainment industry has seen a wave of progressive product placement techniques that embed brands into the plot of films and music videos. These cerebrally examined techniques employ narratives, celebrity endorsements or visual elements that creatively hold memories in one's mind when it comes to making unforgettable brand experiences for consumers. By modifying itself to suit viewer's ever-changing tastes and consumption behaviour (especially with respect to the age group popularly referred to as Generation Z), Punjabi movies and music were turned into laboratories for product placement experimentation and innovation.

Thus, this section takes a look at four cases of innovativeness in product placements in Punjabi movies, songs or web series. Each case study will analyse specific strategies utilized as well as why they worked while drawing lessons for marketers who wish to duplicate success. From incognito placements which blend perfectly with the theme of the movie; these cases show how good creativity can be limitless in the area of promoting products through films within the Punjabi showbiz industry.

Case Study 1: Subtle and Seamless Integration in the Punjabi Movie "Qismat"

The 2018 Punjabi romantic drama "Qismat" showcased a masterful example of subtle and seamless product placement. The love story of Shivjit (Ammy Virk) and Bani (Sargun Mehta), who are two main characters in the film, becomes a canvas where different brands are painted.

Notably featured in this film is usage of WhatsApp, a well-known messaging application. Characters throughout most part of the movie employ WhatsApp to each other either to show their feelings or share important information regardless of distances separating them. Also, usage of WhatsApp corresponds with real-life communication pattern among younger generation especially generation Z that use chat applications mainly to connect with their beloved ones.

There is no obvious sign that WhatsApp insertion was either forced or unnatural within storyline and it appears as a part of characters' habits without any discomfort. In this instance, use of product placement confirms its relevance and horizontal nature. In so doing, this technique allowed the brand to be there uninvited, but never at the expense of emotional density in the story.

Yet another case in point of smooth product placement in "Qismat" was via the well-known Indian ridesharing application, Ola. While travelling to meet Bani, there is a scene where Shivjit uses Ola app to book a ride. The use of Ola here seemed quite realistic and normal since it is often used by many young Indians as their means of transport especially in towns' cities.

The subtlety and relevance of these product placements to the characters' lives make them effective. Integrating brands that resonate with young people's lifestyles made this movie feel real for its target market. Additionally, WhatsApp and Ola not only made an admirable presentation about themselves in the film "Qismat" but also resulted in a greater degree of realism because they added more detail to what happened with him/her. Marketers can learn many valuable lessons from the unobtrusive and sophisticated product placement techniques employed in "Qismat":

- The integrations of brands should be in line with character's inherent traits such as their lifestyles; hence this makes it appear real.
- The embedding of the products should be made in such a way that feels naturalistic and less obtrusive instead of using force or obvious promotions.
- By choosing brands that are in sync with the audience particularly Gen Zers, it helps build stronger relationships plus increases brand recall ability.
- Products placements can also be used to give a story its depth by enhancing the plot as well as making it realistic about what happens to those people who own them; otherwise they concentrate only on visibility of a symbol.

Thus through these principles marketers will create efficient your mark product placements which elide into narration system seamlessly through Punjabi Cinemas engaging on deeper levels leaving lasting impressions about brands.

Case Study 2: Leveraging Celebrity Influence in the Punjabi Music Video "Lahore"

The 2020 Punjabi music video "Lahore" by Guru Randhawa is an innovative approach for product placement by leveraging the power of celebrity influence. In it, both Guru Randhawa and Surbhi Jyoti acted, thus bringing different brands into the limelight with their fame and styles.

Most notable among these products was luxury car brand Lamborghini whose cars were constantly driving alongside Guru Randhawa throughout the duration of this short film. Within this context it will grasp your attention on what type of vehicle he drives; black sleek Lamborghini Urus that has high-end manufactures' images all over it which makes it notable in this clips in terms of its scenes and shots including close-ups.

In making a decision to have Lamborghini placed in his music video, Guru Randhawa strategically thought about his position as an artist who is prosperous clubbing with those who seem to be able to afford it all. For him, Lamborghini served as a prestigious status symbol that elevated him above others in terms of fashion sense even when he did not own one. By linking himself to an expensive model such as Lamborghini Guru Randhawa asserted himself even more on being stylish thereby becoming idolized by many of his fans especially young ones who look up to him for inspiration when it comes on how they should lead their life considering all aspects like wealth and glamour.

Another prominent product placement in "Lahore" is high-end fashion brand Gucci. Guru Randhawa and Surbhi Jyoti can be seen wearing a number of Gucci clothing and accessories in different scenes, including a Gucci hat and a Gucci belt. The inclusion of Gucci in this music video brings out luxury, style, and trendiness to attract the attention of fashion-conscious Gen Z.

These product placements were effective because they were aligned to the personalities of these celebrities and had an aspirational value for their audiences. The music video created desirability and exclusivity around these products by showcasing brands that are synonymous with success, class, and style. Also, Guru Randhawa's popularity amplified these product placements' effects since fans tend to remember such products when associated with their favorite stars.

Marketers have much to learn from the celebrity-oriented product placement strategies in "Lahore":

- Partner with celebrities who have considerable sway on direct audience especially young generation Z so as to improve both awareness and memory towards brands.
- Authenticity and trust come about when businesses' value systems, lifestyles and characters are closely related with those of celebrities.
- Ensure a fluid integration of product placements into the general visual style as well as story line of a music video such that it is pleasing to both sight and ear.
- Appeal to consumers' inner desires for success by taking advantage of aspirational elements found in expensive brands thus enhancing the luxuriousness that comes with them.

The marketers can develop striking and unforgettable product placements in Punjabi music videos through making use of the celebrity influence and especially considering the brands that the audience identifies with most. In this manner not only does it increase awareness of brands but also touches on emotions that audience members share with their best-loved public figures which can lead into more interactions hence possible purchases.

Table 1 illustrates the strategic product placements in the Punjabi music video Lahore, highlighting how brands like Lamborghini and Gucci were seamlessly integrated into the narrative to leverage Guru Randhawa and Surbhi Jyoti's influence.

Table 1. Brand Placement and Celebrity Integration in "Lahore"

Placement	Brand	Celebrity	Integration
Luxury car	Lamborghini	Guru Randhawa	Featured prominently in multiple shots and aligning with the celebrity's image of success and style
Fashion	Gucci	Guru Randhawa and Surbhi Jyoti	Clothing and accessories worn by the celebrities, showcasing the brand's association with luxury and trendiness

Case Study 3: Immersive Product Placement in the Punjabi Web Series "Yaar Jigree Kasooti Degree"

The 2018 a Punjabi web series named "Yaar Jigree Kasooti Degree" (YJKD) showcased an innovative approach regarding the product placement by creating immersive and interactive brand experiences for the audience. The series, revolves around a group of three college friends who are trying out various businesses merged with other brands well to grab the attention of the audience.

One of the most amazing product placements in YJKD was that of Amazon, an e-commerce platform. As part of a key episode, some friends discuss their business venture idea and decide to market their items via Amazon and other platforms. They browse the amazon website which explains how user friendly it is to open a sellers account.

They discussed various benefits of using Amazon for marketing, including its wide market reach and higher potential for revenue growth. Thus, instead merely showing it on screen, Amazon became an integral part of what made this web series so engaging. Apart from presenting Amazon's features within different scenes throughout the show, the series helped people learn how to sell products through the site by letting some characters use it. The effectiveness of this method was even more pronounced among Gen Z targeting audience that is much into entrepreneurship and e-Commerce.

To make the experience much more thrilling, YJKD producers joined forces with Amazon and made a special landing page for the show on Amazon's website. On this page were products that were used by characters in the series which viewers could buy directly from Amazon. This combination made it impossible to discern between imaginative world of the series and real world of e-commerce, thus offering a very unique and captivating experience.

In addition, another instance of immersive product placement in YJKD was through Zomato food delivery app integration. In one episode, there are scenes where characters order food from Zomato App demonstrating its interface plus some available restaurants there. As such, the characters discuss how convenient and reliable Zomato is for ordering meals emphasizing its main features as well as pros.

YJKD product placements' success is based on their integration into storylines and creation of immersive experiences. These kinds of brands are seen in action with the users in order for viewers to feel they belong with them. It also helped build authenticity because the audience was made to believe that they belonged there through seeing them using or benefiting from it.

Additionally, by collaborating with Amazon to launch a special landing page, this made the immersive feel even stronger as audiences got an opportunity to interact with these brands beyond just watching TV.

YJKD would give marketers good lessons about successful product placement methods:

- Embed products along with other components that are either weakly distinguished or not at all in a manner that adds value to both the characters and the audience
- Offer consumers an invaluable experience of engaging brands through its specific landing pages and related interactive systems which extend beyond internet.
- Collaborate with companies whose messages mirror those of this show. This highlights authenticity and relevance through entrepreneurship and innovation elements.
- Use product placements to educate 18 to 24-year-olds about brand features and benefits since they tend to love learning new things and discovering new stuff.

Marketers are able to build lasting impressions among their Generation Z target market through immersive and interactive product placements that lead to enduring perceptions of the brand. This method not only creates brand awareness but also fosters a relationship between consumers and particular brands which may increase involvement leading to more sales.

Table 2 showcases how Amazon and Zomato were integrated into the Punjabi web series Yaar Jigree Kasooti Degree, emphasizing the brands' roles in creating an immersive viewing experience.

Table 2. Immersive Product Placement in "Yaar Jigree Kasooti Degree"

Placement	Brand	Integration	Immersive Experience
E-commerce	Amazon	Characters using and discussing the platform, showcasing its features and benefits	Special landing page on Amazon featuring products from the series
Food delivery	Zomato	Characters using the app to order food, highlighting its convenience and reliability	N/A

Case Study 4: Engaging Audiences through Interactive Product Placement in the Punjabi Movie "Shadaa"

Launched in 2019, Punjabi romantic comedy, Shadaa took product placement to a whole new level by incorporating interactive content that engaged audiences and got them involved. The film, which stars Diljit Dosanjh and Neeru Bajwa had several brands integrated into it in a manner that not only exhibited the products but also brought about memorable interactions between the viewers.

One of the most remarkable products placement in "Shadaa" was jakarappa's communication snack brand Kurkure. One of the key scenes showed main characters discussing their preferred Kurkure flavours while joking which one is the best among them all. This scene revealed different variants of Kurkure while also referring to some user experience that relate with snacks as mentioned by people selling them.

To enhance the product placement's engagement factor; producers of Shadaa collaborated with Kurkure to create a special interactive campaign. People watching were told through social media platforms to vote for their favourite flavour using #KurkureShaddaChallenge on Twitter among other things. Participation from Gen Z who are social media active and love snacks was massive hence causing a greater impact.

In "Shadaa", the interactive nature of the Kurkure product placement not only raised awareness for the brand but also brought about a feeling of belongingness and connectedness between the audience and the brand. The film created an unforgettable experience that resonated with Gen Zs who were encouraged to voice their own snack ambitions by sharing them on social media hence promoting the campaign.

Another instance of such interactivity in "Shadaa" can be found in its use of music streaming app Gaana. In certain scenes, one can see characters using this application to make playlists customized to fit their road trips. In these moments she or he would be lucky enough to explore how they are composed as well as comprehend why so many people have turned into heavy users.

Furthermore, to increase interactivity, producers of this film collaborated with Gaana by creating a special playlist filled with songs contained within Shadaa's soundtrack. The listeners were encouraged to check out those tracks available in the film through Gaana and share them online with friends or family members for instance through Facebook or Twitter . In addition not only did it help promote the songs used in Shadaa's soundtrack but also there was an increase in engagement and downloading rates for the app itself.

The fundamental concept behind these interactive product placements in "Shadaa" is to initiate a dual conversation between the brand and the receivers. As a result of this, the film made it easy for its audience to connect with brands and become loyal to them. Through social media campaigns and branded content, these product placements were able to reach out more people and make a difference especially to the Gen Z audience.

There are great lessons from the way "Shadaa" utilized interactive product placement schemes:

- Design interactive advertisements like those found in blogs or other websites that will trigger audience participation.
- Work with brands on developing unique interactive experiences that go beyond filming such as creating personal music playlists or assigning unique challenges to fans.
- Bear in mind what people like so as to come up with something that will make people relate to it as well as be relevant to them.
- Use social media effectively so as to increase the scope and efficacy of interactive marketing approaches aimed at this youthful segment.

Marketers can recall that the interactive elements incorporated in product placements create unforgettable experiences which connect with the audiences of generation z. Not only will this increase brand awareness but also it produces a bond between them and the brands making them to be more engaged hence increasing chances of buying.

Table 3 highlights how Kurkure and Gaana were integrated into Shadaa, leveraging audience interactivity to enhance engagement and brand recall.

Table 3. Interactive Product Placement in the Punjabi Movie "Shadaa"

Placement	Brand	Integration	Interactive Experience
Snack foods	Kurkure	Characters discussing their favourite flavors, tapping into audience's own preferences	Social media campaign encouraging viewers to vote for their favourite flavour
Music streaming	Gaana	Characters using the app to create a personalized playlist, showcasing its features	Special movie playlist on Gaana app, encouraging viewers to listen and share their favourite tracks

BEST PRACTICES AND FUTURE TRENDS FOR TECHNOLOGY-ENHANCED PRODUCT PLACEMENT IN THE SERVICE SECTOR

The Punjabi Entertainment Industry is known for polices and determined use of Product Placement. The industry has been making innovations and experiments with technology in product placements. As a result, this paper will focus on the importance of keeping up to date with marketing trends as well as the fact that this is an increasingly important issue for marketers. By using technology and data-driven insights, marketers can develop product placements that are not only effective but also appealing to customers' memory.

In this section, we will look at some important learning points from successful technology-oriented product placement campaigns within Punjabi entertainment sector. Moreover, how they can be modified or employed in various service sectors including tourism, hospitality and medicine will be discussed. Additionally, we will consider new technologies like virtual reality and augmented reality together with their probable role in determining product placement trends in the future. For instance, there are certain ethical factors related to technology-enhanced product placements that marketers need to pay attention to while implementing them.

Marketers will be able to harness the advantages of tech-enhanced product placements in the service sector by understanding and applying the most up-to-date best practices as well as future trends. The strategy provides brands with a means to reach their target customers effectively, engage them interactively while creating immersive and individualized experiences that instill brand loyalty and stimulate business growth.

Key Lessons from Successful Technology-Driven Product Placement Campaigns

Recently, there have been several technology-based successful product placement marketing campaigns in Punjab entertainment industry. Such campaigns not only showed how technology enhances its product placements effectiveness but also offered major lessons for marketers who want to duplicate their success.

Seamless integration is one of the most important things learnt from these campaigns. Successful product placements blend naturally into the narrative without appearing awkward or obtrusive and matching characters' experiences. A good example is the subtle incorporation of WhatsApp within the film 'Qismat' (Case Study 1), which shows us how a company can be incorporated within a tale such that it appears more real and relevant when portrayed through character interactions.

An additional significant aspect is the ability to capitalize on celebrity power. Product placement is, to a great extent, amplified by the presence of popular figures such as Guru Randhawa and Surbhi Jyoti in the music video "Lahore" (Case Study 2). This allows marketers to create an aspirational value and a sense of desirability around their products especially among the Gen Z audiences who idolize these influencers.

The impact of participatory product placements on online series such as "Yaar Jigree Kasooti Degree" (Case Study 3) shows that engaging, interactive brand experiences are necessary for success. Marketers can integrate brands into consumers' lives through different methods in order to build stronger ties between consumers and brands. Immersive product placements for instance, portray Amazon's partnership with E-commerce/web series, which include special landing pages featuring items from the show, blurring lines between entertainment and e-commerce.

Currently, there is a lot of reduction in audience participation when it comes to product placement in movies as well as commercials. We could also skip the creation of customized playlists and hashtag competitions that resonate with lifestyles of people to arouse their interest in a certain product placed on them. In this way marketers would arouse some buzz and involvement among consumers on product placements.

Kohli et al. (2024) explain the idea of "Webrooming," which involves examining an item online before purchasing it physically at a store. This notion has been discussed within the framework of technology-driven product placements whereby the target population is motivated to learn more about brands via interactive initiatives or branded materials prior to making a buying decision. By doing this, marketers can provide audiences with an all-encompassing unison brand experience that combines both online and offline mediums.

Adapting Product Placement Strategies for Different Service Industries

Technological methodologies could be borrowed from successful practices in the Punjabi film industry where the technology aided product placements are involved to inform various service sectors. Marketers who know what differentiates the various industries and their inherent challenges, can adapt their placement strategies accordingly so as to reach out to them and connect with them appropriately.

For instance, within tourism industry, advertisements of products can also serve as attractions to destinations, hotels or adventure sites in a more appealing and inclusive manner. In addition, marketers of traveling products can influence people's willing to visit certain places by including relevant brands in travel related themes such as films, web series or vlogs. Furthermore, use of VR and AR technologies would further immerse potential tourists allowing them explore different places and sites intensely with much more interaction than before.

In the hospitality sector, product placements could be utilized to emphasize hotels', resorts' and restaurants' unique points of sale. Through incorporating such places in entertaining contents that captivate most people, marketers manage to create a sense of privilege and lavishness; hence appealing to their target audience's aspirations. Joint ventures like special menus or experiences based on popular movies or shows serve as other ways of engaging audiences while driving sales.

In health care industry, product placements serve to inform about certain health problems, treatments or products. Storylines and character arcs are some of the contexts within which such topics can be integrated by marketers so as to reach out educating but unobtrusively. Furthermore, this can be made possible through collaborations with famous celebrities or influencers who have notable followings among the targeted consumer base.

For all service industries; familiarity with target customers' preferences, habits and pain points is fundamental for successful product integration. By using data analytic techniques as well as using consumer insight studies, personalized and relevant product infusions may be implemented thereby evoking the intended reactions from specific audiences.

In the hospitality industry, product placements might be employed to emphasize hotels, resorts and restaurants' unique selling points. By featuring these businesses in popular entertainment content; marketers will create an exclusive atmosphere that is appealing to aspirational aspects within their major audience. This is also facilitated by joint specials such as dishes that complement menu cards or themed experiences based on popular television shows that have already aired.

For instance health care services make use of product placements for telling people about certain health issues or treatments concerning certain drugs. By incorporating them into storylines and portraying characters undertaking certain roles marketers are able to pass this message without being intrusive at all. Besides this dimension also gets bigger through teaming up with famous personalities whose fame resonates with target audience members very well.

The fundamental principle of successful product placement across all service industries lies in recognizing what the target audience wants, how they behave or where they hurt most. By utilizing data analytics and consumer analytics– marketers may create personalized and relevant product placements that connect with audiences precisely while inciting them to act in a required way.

Emerging Technologies and their Potential Impact on Product Placement

As far as technology is concerned, product placement is also affected by fast-moving changes. Therefore, there are new and exciting opportunities to engage buyers through immersive and personalized brand experiences that are enabled by technologies such as VR (Virtual Reality), AR (Augmented Reality) and AI (Artificial Intelligence).

In this regard, if not all of them, VR and AR have potentiality to change the face of product placement by allowing audience to interact with brands in very attractive ways. For example, a VR experience can place viewers in the film or web series' world where they may explore the highlighted products or places in an unforgettable way. On the other hand AR can lay digital information or visuals over real life thus creating harmony between reality and virtuality. Hence it is possible to utilize through interactive product demonstrations on e-commerce sites or gamified brand experiences that involve customer participation and interaction.

A person's preferences, inclinations as well as perceptions can be revealed by using AI instruments and algorithms which assist marketers in product placement strategies. AI can assist in identifying the best placing opportunities, targeting the correct segments of the audience and personalizing brand messages for maximum effect through analysing massive amount of data from different places such as social media, online discussion sites and customer feedbacks. In addition to saving marketers time and resources, AI can also automate some aspects of the product placement process like recognizing appropriate influencers or creating branded contents.

With time, these coming technologies will play a significant role in future promotional activities just because they are becoming more prominent. Furthermore, those who embrace them are likely to be more successful due to an understanding of changes occurring in this area thus making it possible for them to propose enriching adverts that will interest their clients thereby keeping them loyal.

Ethical Considerations and Guidelines for Technology-Enhanced Product Placement

Although product placement in technology enhances a lot of opportunities for marketers, there are also some important ethical issues that should be looked into. This is because as brands increasingly incorporate their products into entertainment content and utilize new technology to attract consumers' interest, this demand for outrightness, originality, and faithfulness should be taken care of through elaboration of vivid guidelines and good practices.

The most important ethical concerns about product placement include disclosure. That is; consumers have to know when they are receiving sponsored information or advertisements. Basically, product placements must be clearly labelled using disclaimers or visual signs in order to differentiate them from the regular content. Such clarity would bring forth a sense of reliability on the part of the merchants since it promotes trust among those who value honesty and genuineness when dealing with brands.

Also, as it pertains to this ethics issue, the impact of advertising on weak people particularly kids and youths is very important. Marketers must be careful regarding the age appropriateness of their product placements and avoid promoting products or behaviours that may harm younger audiences. This includes alcoholic beverages as well as tobacco or betting institutions and placements promoting unrealistic body images or unhealthy lifestyles.

Together with avoiding misleading or ambiguous ads about their products, this implies that they have to ensure their placements are not ambiguous or false. Any claims related to these items when they appear on some entertainment should be true, right and backed with evidence. In addition to avoiding misleading advertisements such as exaggerations concerning advantages accruing to them thereby eroding customer faith hence exposing himself/herself to legal action; marketers should shun relating products through advertisements by making false promises about any benefit.

To cope with these ethical issues; marketing professionals can follow guidelines already established by different organizations within the industry and regulatory bodies such as Federal Trade Commission (FTC) in America which has issued recommendations for native advertising and support that provide useful insights into revealing sponsorship in advertising content among other things including disclosures in order to enhance clarity and openness in product representation.

The marketers, too, should team up with entertainment partners, influencers and other stakeholders in order to create clear regulations and protocols for product placements. This encompasses brainstorming what a brand should do in terms of its integration into content, defining processes for approval of branded content as well as setting metrics for measuring the effectiveness and impact of product placements.

By placing importance on ethical issues and transparency in their strategies of product placement marketers stand a chance of building stronger relationships with their target market that are also more authentic. Apart from protecting them against legal and reputational risks this method will also help build trust and loyalty which can contribute to long term business success.

CONCLUSION

We have gone through the revolutionary role played by technology in reshaping product placement approaches in the Punjabi entertainment sector in this chapter. This study has also allowed us to understand how marketers can efficiently target and reach out to Gen Z consumers by tracking the evolution of product placement, examining digital platforms' influence, analysing social media's contributions, and discussing data analytics' significance.

The case studies used have revealed that innovative techniques such as subtle integration, celebrity endorsements, immersive experiences, and interactive campaigns serve as some of the most effective ways through which product placements can be made more memorable. Therefore, these examples emphasize that technology is key in improving both effectiveness and reach for product promotions while stressing the importance of audience interaction authenticity as well as creativity.

Gazing into the future, it is apparent that the role of technology in product placement will remain critical. For instance, virtual reality, augmented reality and artificial intelligence offer unique prospects for marketers to develop immersive and individualistic brand experiences. Nonetheless, there is also need to consider these issues ethically as well as guarantee transparent, responsible and trustworthy product placements targeted at consumers.

Transpiring as we look ahead; quite obviously technology will partake a key function in moulding the landscape of brands' placement. Augmented reality, virtual reality and artificial intelligence are such emerging technologies that furnish marketers with new avenues for creating engrossing personalized brand experiences. Noteworthy too are ethical considerations associated with those advancements so as not only develop appropriate product placements but also gain customer trust through their responsible and transparent practice.

Recap of the Key Findings and Insights

The numerous important findings and realizations found in this chapter may be useful for marketers as well as individuals working in the entertainment sector regarding their usage of product placement strategies combined with technology.

- Advancement in technological domains which include digital media platforms, social networks and data analytics are some of the factors that have transformed product placements.
- Product placements have distinct expectations and behaviours among Gen Z audience consisting of originality, inventiveness and participation by means of inclusion from brands.
- A realistic representation of characters through incorporation of brands within stories is something observed in a scene from the film “Qismat”.
- The use celebrity ethos in “Lahore” music video enhances actors’ performances, which makes it possible to make suggestions about products.
- Immersive product placements like Amazon integration into 'Yaar Jigree Kasooti Degree' web series can blend the boundaries of entertainment with online purchases hence creating a memorable as well as captivating brand experiences
- Interactive product placements motivate audience involvement generating popularity around the brand especially through social media such as Kurkure campaign in 'Shadaa' movie
- Marketers need data analytics and consumer insights not only to determine appropriate audience segments but also customize brand communication strategies so that they can have far reaching effects
- Virtual reality (VR), augmented reality (AR) and artificial intelligence (AI), among other new technologies may bring about real personalization of brands by providing immersive and interactive experiences
- Product placement strategies must maintain ethical considerations like transparency, disclosure, and responsible messaging to build consumer’s trust and faithfulness.

Implications for Marketers and Entertainment Professionals

The observations and understandings declared in this chapter have grave ramifications for advertisers and individuals working in the field of entertainment who desire to capitalize on technology-fuelled product placement in the Punjabi entertainment sector and all other areas:

- To stay relevant with Generation Z audiences, advertisers need to keep a finger on the pulse of their shifting likes and dislikes and vary their approach to placement of goods. This means that integration of brands should be based on authenticity, creativity, and interactivity.
- The cornerstone of generating seamless and powerful placements of products is cooperation between brands and entertainment partners. Therefore, marketers should engage closely with content developers, influencers, as well as teams involved in production so as to ensure that brand immersions fit within the story line while resonating with the intended audience.
- In order to hone their strategies further, it is crucial marketers leverage data analytics alongside consumer insights. They can do this by investing in devices or technologies that allow them to track how engaged audiences are with respect to certain choices they make concerning campaigns employed on their platforms.
- Marketers ought to embrace new technologies such as VR (Virtual Reality), AR (Augmented Reality), AI (Artificial Intelligence) among others which allow creation of unique personalized experiences around brands . Investing in new skill sets, alliances or infrastructures aimed at supporting these technologies may also be necessary if indeed they want to achieve this goal.
- It’s only natural for entertainment experts like movie makers, authors and producers to collaborate with brands and embed product placements into their artistic work. In such a way they make it seem real, meaningful and beneficial to the main story.
- In their product placement strategies, we must work towards marketers and entertainment makers having ethical considerations as a priority. This includes transparency, disclosing funding source in case of sponsored content and avoiding any form of misleading or irresponsible messages.

Future Research Directions

The Punjabi entertainment industry offers valuable insights for this chapter but there remain several unexplored areas warranting further research:

- **Comparative Studies**: In future research, technology-enhanced product placement strategies could be compared across different entertainment industries such as Bollywood, Hollywood or regional cinema in order to ascertain best practices and cultural nuances.
- **An Extended Effect**: There is a necessity for longitudinal studies that will investigate the long-term effect of technology-based product placement on brand recall, preference and loyalty among the members of generation Z.
- **Upcoming Technologies**: Potential applications as well as consequences for placement of products through new technological innovations are some of what researchers can delve into. This could specifically involve exploring things like virtual influencers inside games or even IoT-enabled objects embedded in entertainment.
- **Moral Structures**: People who deal with technologically driven endorsement can study how to come up with ethical frameworks and policies that take into consideration the questions particular to consumption in the digital realm.
- **Audience Reception:** A conspicuous way through qualitative research works about how the Gen Z audience perceive or interacts with technology in enhanced product placements is that they find them helpful for their motivation and decision-making process.

The adjustments of research weaknesses together with this knowledge would help both those in the academic circle as well as people working within commercial line (e.g., marketers) to have more mastery on how technology driven ads affect tomorrow's marketing and promotion trends.

REFERENCES

Balasubramanian, S. K., Karrh, J. A., & Patwardhan, H. (2006). Audience response to product placements: An integrative framework and future research agenda. *Journal of Advertising, 35*(3), 115–141. DOI: 10.2753/JOA0091-3367350308

Breves, P., Liebers, N., Abt, M., & Kunze, A. (2019). The perceived fit between instagram influencers and the endorsed brand: How influencer-brand fit affects source credibility and persuasive effectiveness. *Journal of Advertising Research, 59*(4), 440–454. DOI: 10.2501/JAR-2019-030

Childers, C. C., Lemon, L. L., & Hoy, M. G. (2019). '#Sponsored #Ad: Agency perspective on influencer marketing campaigns'. *Journal of Current Issues and Research in Advertising, 40*(3), 258–274. DOI: 10.1080/10641734.2018.1521113

Dwivedi, A., Johnson, L. W., & McDonald, R. E. (2015). Celebrity endorsement, self-brand connection and consumer-based brand equity. *Journal of Product and Brand Management, 24*(5), 449–461. DOI: 10.1108/JPBM-10-2014-0722

Feng, Y., Chen, H., & Kong, Q. (2021). An expert with whom I can identify: The role of narratives in influencer marketing. *International Journal of Advertising, 40*(7), 972–993. DOI: 10.1080/02650487.2020.1824751

Gambetti, R. C., & Graffigna, G. (2010). The concept of engagement: A systematic analysis of the ongoing marketing debate. *International Journal of Market Research, 52*(6), 801–826. DOI: 10.2501/S147078531020166

Gupta, P. B., & Lord, K. R. (1998). Product placement in movies: The effect of prominence and mode on audience recall. *Journal of Current Issues and Research in Advertising, 20*(1), 47–59. DOI: 10.1080/10641734.1998.10505076

Hampson, D., Ma, S., & Wang, Y. (2018). Perceived financial well-being and its effect on domestic product purchases. *International Marketing Review, 35*(6), 914–935. Advance online publication. DOI: 10.1108/IMR-12-2017-0248

Harmeling, C. M., Moffett, J. W., Arnold, M. J., & Carlson, B. D. (2017). Toward a theory of customer engagement marketing. *Journal of the Academy of Marketing Science, 45*(3), 312–335. DOI: 10.1007/s11747-016-0509-2

Hollebeek, L. D. (2011). Demystifying customer brand engagement: Exploring the loyalty nexus. *Journal of Marketing Management, 27*(7-8), 785–807. DOI: 10.1080/0267257X.2010.500132

Jain, V., Roy, S., Daswani, A., & Sudha, M. (2011). What really works for teenagers: Human or fictional celebrity? *Young Consumers, 12*(2), 171–183. DOI: 10.1108/17473611111141623

Karrh, J. A. (1998). Brand placement: A review. *Journal of Current Issues and Research in Advertising, 20*(2), 31–49. DOI: 10.1080/10641734.1998.10505081

Kim, D. Y., & Kim, H. Y. (2020). Influencer advertising on social media: The multiple inference model on influencer-product congruence and sponsorship disclosure. *Journal of Business Research, 130*, 405–415. DOI: 10.1016/j.jbusres.2020.02.020

Kohli, S., Shukla, R. P., & Samant, P. (2024). Webrooming: Bridging the Digital Divide in Customer Engagement. In Sinha, M., Bhandari, A., Priya, S., & Kabiraj, S. (Eds.), *Future of Customer Engagement Through Marketing Intelligence* (pp. 204–223). IGI Global., DOI: 10.4018/979-8-3693-2367-0.ch010

Kumar, S. (2017). Influence of product placements in films and television on consumers' brand awareness. *Archives of Business Research, 5*(2), 1–14. DOI: 10.14738/abr.52.2747

Kwon, E. S., King, K. W., Nyilasy, G., & Reid, L. N. (2019). Impact of media context on advertising memory: A meta-analysis of advertising effectiveness. *Journal of Advertising Research, 59*(1), 99–128. DOI: 10.2501/JAR-2018-016

Liu, S., Perry, P., & Gadzinski, G. (2019). The implications of digital marketing on WeChat for luxury fashion brands in China. *Journal of Brand Management, 26*(4), 395–409. DOI: 10.1057/s41262-018-0140-2

Patel, D. (2017). 5 differences between marketing to millennials vs. Gen Z. *Forbes, 27*(November). https://www.forbes.com/sites/deeppatel/2017/11/27/5-d%E2%80%8Bifferences-%E2%80%8Bbetween-%E2%80%8Bmarketing-%E2%80%8Bto%E2%80%8B-m%E2%80%8Billennials-v%E2%80%8Bs%E2%80%8B-%E2%80%8Bgen-z/

Pearce, K., & Baran, S. (2018). Foregrounding morality: Encouraging parental media literacy intervention using the TARES test for ethical persuasion. *The Journal of Media Literacy Education, 10*(3), 57–79. DOI: 10.23860/JMLE-2018-10-03-04

Priporas, C. V., Stylos, N., & Fotiadis, A. K. (2017). 'Generation Z consumers' expectations of interactions in smart retailing: A future agenda'. *Computers in Human Behavior, 77*, 374–381. DOI: 10.1016/j.chb.2017.01.058

Rathore, A. K., Ilavarasan, P. V., & Dwivedi, Y. K. (2016). Social media content and product co-creation: An emerging paradigm. *Journal of Enterprise Information Management, 29*(1), 7–18. DOI: 10.1108/JEIM-06-2015-0047

Russell, C. A. (2002). Investigating the effectiveness of product placements in television shows: The role of modality and plot connection congruence on brand memory and attitude. *The Journal of Consumer Research, 29*(3), 306–318. DOI: 10.1086/344432

Russell, C. A., & Rasolofoarison, D. (2017). Uncovering the power of natural endorsements: A comparison with celebrity-endorsed advertising and product placements. *International Journal of Advertising, 36*(5), 761–778. DOI: 10.1080/02650487.2017.1348033

Seemiller, C., & Grace, M. (2018). *Generation Z: A Century in the Making*. Taylor & Francis., https://www.google.co.in/books/edition/_/v_d1DwAAQBAJ DOI: 10.4324/9780429442476

Sharma, A., Fadahunsi, A., Abbas, H., & Pathak, V. K. (2022). A multi-analytic approach to predict social media marketing influence on consumer purchase intention. *Journal of Indian Business Research, 14*(2), 125–149. DOI: 10.1108/JIBR-08-2021-0313

Southgate, D. (2017). The emergence of Generation Z and its impact in advertising: Long-term implications for media planning and creative development. *Journal of Advertising Research, 57*(2), 227–235. https://psycnet.apa.org/doi/10.2501/JAR-2017-028. DOI: 10.2501/JAR-2017-028

Sung, Y., & de Gregorio, F. (2008). New brand worlds: College student consumer attitudes toward brand placement in films, television shows, songs, and video games. *Journal of Promotion Management, 14*(1-2), 85–101. DOI: 10.1080/10496490802498272

Turner, A. (2015). Generation Z: Technology and social interest. *Journal of Individual Psychology, 71*(2), 103–113. DOI: 10.1353/jip.2015.0021

Wiles, M. A., & Danielova, A. (2009). The worth of product placement in successful films: An event study analysis. *Journal of Marketing, 73*(4), 44–63. https://psycnet.apa.org/doi/10.1509/jmkg.73.4.44. DOI: 10.1509/jmkg.73.4.044

Chapter 31
The Evolution of Technology in the Service Sector Concerning Hospitality

Vidit Srivastava
Integral University, India

Irshita Dixit
DPS, India

Ratika Duggal
https://orcid.org/0000-0001-7812-9005
CT University, India

ABSTRACT

The hospitality industry, encompassing lodging, food and beverage, event planning, theme parks, and travel and tourism, has been significantly transformed by technological advancements. This chapter explores the historical context, key technological innovations, and their impacts on the hospitality sector. The hospitality industry has undergone a profound transformation driven by technological advancements. This abstract explores the historical development and impact of key technologies in the sector. Initially labor-intensive, the industry began modernizing with the advent of early technologies like telephones and computerized reservation systems. The introduction of the internet and mobile technology catalyzed a revolution, leading to significant innovations such as online booking systems, mobile applications, and Customer Relationship Management (CRM) systems. Technologies like Artificial Intelligence (AI), Internet of Things (IoT), and blockchain have further enhanced operational efficiency and customer experiences. AI and automation streamline customer service and data analytics, while IoT creates smart, interconnected environments in hospitality establishments. Blockchain technology provides secure and transparent transaction processes.

BACKGROUND STUDY

The hospitality industry, comprising sectors such as lodging, food and beverage, travel and tourism, and event planning, has been profoundly impacted by technological advancements. Over the past few decades, technology has not only transformed the operational frameworks of these sectors but has also significantly enhanced the customer experience. This chapter provides a detailed background study on the evolution of technology in the service sector, with a particular focus on hospitality. By examining historical developments, current applications,

DOI: 10.4018/979-8-3693-7447-4.ch031

and future trends, we can gain a comprehensive understanding of how technology continues to shape and redefine the hospitality industry.

Early Developments and Adoption of Technology

The journey of technological integration in hospitality began with simple mechanical and electronic innovations aimed at improving basic operations. In the mid-20th century, the introduction of mechanical booking systems marked the first step towards automating hotel reservations. These systems were later replaced by computerized reservation systems (CRS) in the 1970s and 1980s, which allowed for more efficient management of bookings and guest information. Property management systems (PMS), which emerged around the same time, facilitated the centralization of various hotel operations, from front desk services to housekeeping and maintenance.

The introduction of these early technologies was driven by the need to streamline operations and reduce human error. Hotels that adopted CRS and PMS systems were able to process reservations faster, maintain accurate records, and provide better service to their guests. However, these systems were largely standalone and lacked the ability to share data across different properties or departments, limiting their overall impact.

The Internet Era: A Paradigm Shift

The advent of the internet in the 1990s brought about a paradigm shift in the hospitality industry. The internet enabled hotels to reach a global audience and provided customers with unprecedented access to information. Online booking platforms emerged as a major disruptor, allowing guests to make reservations directly through hotel websites or third-party travel agencies. This not only increased convenience for guests but also opened up new revenue streams for hotels.

The internet also facilitated the development of customer relationship management (CRM) systems. These systems allowed hotels to collect and analyze data on guest preferences, behaviors, and feedback, enabling them to offer personalized services and build stronger relationships with their customers. The ability to gather and leverage data became a key competitive advantage in the hospitality industry.

Mobile Technology: Empowering Guests

As mobile technology became ubiquitous in the 21st century, it further revolutionized the hospitality industry. Mobile apps became a vital tool for enhancing the guest experience. Guests could now book rooms, check-in, order services, and provide feedback through their smartphones. Hotels developed proprietary apps to offer personalized services, provide real-time communication, and enhance convenience.

Mobile technology also introduced new payment methods, such as mobile wallets and contactless payments, which made transactions faster and more secure. The integration of mobile technology into hotel operations streamlined processes, reduced wait times, and improved overall guest satisfaction.

Social Media and Digital Marketing

The rise of social media platforms such as Facebook, Instagram, and Twitter transformed the way hotels marketed their services and engaged with customers. Social media became a powerful tool for building brand awareness, promoting special offers, and managing customer relationships. Hotels could now reach a broader audience, engage with potential customers in real-time, and gather valuable insights into customer preferences and behaviors.

Social media analytics provided hotels with data on customer engagement, sentiment, and trends, enabling them to tailor their marketing strategies more effectively. User-generated content, such as reviews and social media posts, became a significant factor influencing potential guests' booking decisions. Managing online reputation and leveraging social media for marketing became crucial aspects of a hotel's strategy.

Big Data and Analytics: Driving Decision-Making

The explosion of digital data generated by online interactions and transactions led to the rise of big data analytics in the hospitality industry. Hotels began to harness the power of big data to gain insights into customer preferences, optimize pricing strategies, and improve operational efficiency. Predictive analytics enabled hotels to forecast demand, manage inventory, and tailor marketing efforts to specific customer segments.

Data analytics also played a crucial role in revenue management. Advanced revenue management systems used data to analyze market trends, competitor pricing, and customer behavior, allowing hotels to adjust their pricing strategies in real-time. This dynamic pricing approach helped maximize revenue and occupancy rates.

Artificial Intelligence and Machine Learning: Enhancing Efficiency

Artificial intelligence (AI) and machine learning technologies have become increasingly integrated into various aspects of the hospitality industry. AI-powered chatbots and virtual assistants provide 24/7 customer service, answering queries, assisting with bookings, and resolving issues. These technologies enhance efficiency and provide guests with immediate assistance, improving their overall experience.

Machine learning algorithms analyze large datasets to identify patterns and trends, enabling hotels to make data-driven decisions. AI is also used in personalized marketing, where algorithms recommend services and offers based on individual guest preferences. The integration of AI and machine learning into hotel operations has led to more efficient processes, better resource management, and enhanced guest experiences.

The Internet of Things (IoT): Creating Smart Environments

The Internet of Things (IoT) technology connects various devices and systems within a hotel, creating a smart environment. IoT-enabled smart rooms allow guests to control lighting, temperature, entertainment systems, and more through their smartphones or voice commands. These smart features enhance comfort and convenience for guests.

IoT sensors monitor energy usage, helping hotels reduce costs and improve sustainability. Predictive maintenance, enabled by IoT devices, detects potential issues in equipment before they become major problems, minimizing downtime and repair costs. IoT technology enhances operational efficiency by streamlining processes such as housekeeping and maintenance.

Blockchain Technology: Ensuring Transparency and Security

Blockchain technology, known for its decentralized and secure nature, is emerging as a disruptive force in the hospitality industry. Blockchain can be used to manage transactions, ensuring transparency and reducing the risk of fraud. It streamlines processes such as identity verification, loyalty programs, and payment systems.

In supply chain management, blockchain provides a transparent and tamper-proof record of transactions, enhancing trust and accountability. As the hospitality industry continues to explore the potential of blockchain, it is expected to play a significant role in improving security, efficiency, and transparency in various operations.

Augmented Reality (AR) and Virtual Reality (VR): Enhancing Experiences

Augmented Reality (AR) and Virtual Reality (VR) technologies are being used to enhance the guest experience and provide innovative marketing solutions. AR applications allow guests to explore hotel facilities and local attractions through their smartphones. VR provides immersive experiences, enabling potential guests to take virtual tours of hotel properties before making a booking.

These technologies also have applications in staff training, allowing employees to practice handling various scenarios in a virtual environment. AR and VR enhance the overall guest experience by providing interactive and engaging ways to explore and interact with the hotel and its surroundings.

INTRODUCTION

The service sector, particularly the hospitality industry, has undergone a significant transformation driven by technological advancements over the past few decades. This evolution has reshaped how hospitality businesses operate, how they interact with customers, and how they deliver services. From the early adoption of basic reservation systems to the current use of artificial intelligence and the Internet of Things (IoT), technology has become an integral part of the hospitality industry. This introduction explores the key milestones in the technological evolution of the hospitality sector, highlighting the impact of these advancements on operations, customer experience, and industry growth.

Early Technological Innovations

The journey of technology in hospitality began with the introduction of computerized reservation systems (CRS) in the 1970s. These systems revolutionized the way hotels managed bookings, moving away from manual reservation logs to automated processes. This shift not only improved efficiency but also reduced the likelihood of human error, leading to better resource management and customer satisfaction.

In the 1980s and 1990s, property management systems (PMS) emerged, further enhancing operational efficiency. PMS integrated various functions such as front desk operations, housekeeping, billing, and inventory management into a single platform. This integration allowed for seamless coordination among different departments within a hotel, ensuring that guests received timely and accurate services.

The Internet Era

The advent of the internet in the mid-1990s marked a pivotal point in the hospitality industry. Online travel agencies (OTAs) like Expedia and Booking.com emerged, providing consumers with the ability to book accommodations online. This development democratized access to travel information and booking capabilities, empowering customers to compare prices and read reviews before making reservations. For hotels, partnering with OTAs became essential for reaching a broader audience and increasing occupancy rates.

Moreover, the proliferation of hotel websites and online booking engines enabled properties to manage direct bookings more effectively. Hotels could now offer personalized packages and loyalty programs to attract repeat customers, leveraging data collected from online interactions.

Mobile Technology and Social Media

The rise of smartphones and mobile applications in the late 2000s brought another wave of innovation to the hospitality sector. Mobile apps allowed hotels to offer on-the-go booking options, mobile check-ins, and digital room keys, enhancing convenience for tech-savvy travelers. Additionally, apps could be used for in-room services such as ordering food, requesting housekeeping, and controlling room settings, providing a more personalized and seamless guest experience.

Social media platforms like Facebook, Instagram, and Twitter also played a crucial role in transforming how hotels marketed their services. These platforms enabled properties to engage with customers directly, respond to feedback in real-time, and build brand loyalty through targeted marketing campaigns. User-generated content, such as reviews and photos shared by guests, became a powerful tool for influencing potential customers' decisions.

Big Data, AI, and IoT

In recent years, big data analytics, artificial intelligence (AI), and the Internet of Things (IoT) have been at the forefront of technological advancements in the hospitality industry. Big data allows hotels to analyze vast amounts of information to gain insights into customer preferences, booking patterns, and market trends. This data-driven approach enables more accurate forecasting, personalized marketing, and improved decision-making.

AI technologies, such as chatbots and virtual assistants, have enhanced customer service by providing instant responses to inquiries and automating routine tasks. For instance, chatbots can handle booking modifications, provide local recommendations, and address common guest concerns, freeing up staff to focus on more complex issues.

IoT devices have also started to play a significant role in enhancing the guest experience. Smart thermostats, lighting systems, and voice-activated assistants enable guests to control their room environment with ease, while IoT sensors help hotels monitor and maintain facilities efficiently, reducing energy consumption and improving maintenance.

The hospitality industry has been profoundly transformed by technological advancements, revolutionizing operations, customer interactions, and service delivery. Initially, the introduction of computerized reservation systems (CRS) in the 1970s marked the beginning of this transformation, streamlining booking processes and reducing errors. The development of property management systems (PMS) in the 1980s and 1990s further enhanced operational efficiency by integrating various hotel functions into a unified platform.

The advent of the internet in the mid-1990s brought online travel agencies (OTAs) and hotel websites, democratizing access to travel information and enabling direct bookings. The rise of mobile technology and social media in the late 2000s allowed for on-the-go bookings, mobile check-ins, and real-time customer engagement, significantly enhancing the guest experience.

In recent years, the integration of big data analytics, artificial intelligence (AI), and the Internet of Things (IoT) has further revolutionized the industry. These technologies enable personalized marketing, instant customer service, and efficient facility management, ensuring a seamless and tailored guest experience. As technology continues to evolve, the hospitality sector remains at the forefront of innovation, continually adapting to meet the demands of modern travelers.

Enhancing Guest Experience with Technology

In-room Technology

Smart room technology has become a standard feature in modern hospitality. IoT devices enable guests to control lighting, temperature, and entertainment systems via voice commands or mobile apps. Additional features like smart mirrors and virtual concierge services further enhance the guest experience.

Mobile Apps

Mobile apps provide guests with a convenient way to interact with hotel services. From mobile check-in and digital room keys to ordering room service and booking spa appointments, these apps streamline various aspects of the guest journey.

Virtual and Augmented Reality

Virtual and augmented reality applications allow potential guests to take virtual tours of hotel properties before booking. In-room AR experiences can provide information about local attractions, dining options, and hotel services, enhancing the overall guest experience.

Self-service Technologies

Self-check-in Kiosks

Self-check-in kiosks reduce wait times and improve the check-in process. Guests can scan their IDs, select rooms, and receive digital room keys without having to wait in line.

Automated Concierge Services

AI-powered chatbots and virtual assistants provide 24/7 assistance to guests, answering questions, providing recommendations, and handling service requests. These automated services enhance guest satisfaction and operational efficiency.

REVIEW OF LITERATURE

Law, R., Leung, R., & Buhalis, D. (2009). Information technology applications in hospitality and tourism: A review of publications from 2005 to 2007. Journal of Travel & Tourism Marketing, 26(5-6), 599-623. This review analyzes the evolution of IT applications in hospitality, highlighting trends and advancements over a three-year period, focusing on their impact on efficiency and customer satisfaction.

Nyheim, P. D., & Connolly, D. J. (2011). Technology Strategies for the Hospitality Industry (2nd ed.). Pearson Education. This book discusses strategies for integrating technology in hospitality, emphasizing the importance of advanced reservation systems for improving service delivery and operational efficiency.

O'Connor, P. (2003). Online travel and hospitality services. Journal of Travel Research, 41(4), 342-347. This paper explores the emergence of online travel and hospitality services, discussing their impact on consumer behavior and industry practices, and highlighting the shift towards digital booking platforms.

Talluri, K. T., & Van Ryzin, G. J. (2004). The Theory and Practice of Revenue Management. Springer Science & Business Media. This comprehensive guide covers the principles and applications of revenue management in hospitality, detailing how technology optimizes pricing and inventory decisions to maximize revenue.

Piccoli, G., & Patterson, R. A. (2009). Web-enabled CRM in the hotel industry: Preliminary findings from a cross-organizational study. Cornell Hospitality Quarterly, 50(3), 325-337. This study examines the implementation of web-enabled CRM systems in hotels, highlighting their role in enhancing customer relationships and personalized service.

Buhalis, D., & Amaranggana, A. (2013). Smart tourism destinations. In Z. Xiang & I. Tussyadiah (Eds.), Information and Communication Technologies in Tourism 2014 (pp. 553-564). Springer. This paper discusses the concept of smart tourism destinations, focusing on how technology enhances the guest experience through personalized and context-aware services.

Kokkinou, A., & Mihalic, T. (2021). Adoption of self-service technologies in hotels. International Journal of Contemporary Hospitality Management, 33(1), 272-294. This article explores the adoption and impact of self-service technologies in the hotel industry, emphasizing their benefits for efficiency and customer satisfaction.

Leung, D., Law, R., van Hoof, H., & Buhalis, D. (2013). Social media in tourism and hospitality: A literature review. Journal of Travel & Tourism Marketing, 30(1-2), 3-22. This literature review examines the role of social media in tourism and hospitality, discussing its influence on marketing strategies, customer engagement, and brand management.

Moro, S., Rita, P., & Vala, B. (2018). Predicting social media performance metrics and evaluation of the impact on hotel performance. International Journal of Contemporary Hospitality Management, 30(1), 359-377. This study investigates the use of big data and analytics to predict social media performance and its impact on hotel operations, highlighting the strategic advantages of data-driven decision-making.

Treiblmaier, H. (2018). The impact of the blockchain on the supply chain: A theory-based research framework and a call for action. Supply Chain Management: An International Journal, 23(6), 545-559. This paper explores the potential impact of blockchain technology on hospitality supply chains, discussing its implications for transparency, security, and efficiency.

Ivanov, S., & Webster, C. (2017). Adoption of robots, artificial intelligence and service automation by travel, tourism, and hospitality companies. Tech and Travel, 4(3), 133-140. This article examines the adoption of AI and robotics in the hospitality industry, discussing their applications in service automation and the potential benefits and challenges they bring.

Gretzel, U., Sigala, M., Xiang, Z., & Koo, C. (2015). Smart tourism: Foundations and developments. Electronic Markets, 25(3), 179-188. This paper discusses the foundations and developments of smart tourism, emphasizing the role of IoT in creating interconnected and data-driven tourism ecosystems.

Tussyadiah, I. P., Wang, D., & Jia, C. H. (2017). Virtual reality and attitudes toward tourism destinations. Journal of Travel Research, 57(3), 407-428. This study explores the impact of virtual reality on tourist attitudes towards destinations, highlighting how AR and VR technologies can enhance marketing and customer experience.

Murphy, H. C., Hofacker, C., & Bennett, M. (2010). Website development and user interface design: A case study of hotel web sites. Journal of Hospitality & Leisure Marketing, 9(3-4), 151-162.This case study analyzes the development of hotel websites, focusing on user interface design and its impact on customer satisfaction and engagement.

Benckendorff, P., Xiang, Z., & Sheldon, P. J. (2019). Tourism Information Technology (2nd ed.). CABI.This book provides an overview of cloud computing applications in tourism, discussing how cloud-based solutions enhance operational efficiency and service delivery in hospitality.

Stinchcombe, K. (2018). Cybersecurity in the hospitality industry: A growing threat. Hospitality Technology. This article highlights the increasing threat of cybersecurity breaches in the hospitality industry, discussing strategies for protecting sensitive customer data and maintaining trust.

Bohdanowicz, P. (2006). Environmental awareness and initiatives in the European hospitality industry: A comparative study. International Journal of Hospitality Management, 25(4), 662-682. This comparative study examines environmental initiatives in European hotels, discussing the adoption of green technologies and their impact on sustainability practices.

Wang, Y., & Qualls, W. (2007). Towards a theoretical model of technology adoption in hospitality organizations. International Journal of Hospitality Management, 26(3), 560-573. This paper proposes a theoretical model for technology adoption in hospitality, emphasizing factors that influence the successful integration and utilization of new technologies.

Hjalager, A. M. (2010). A review of innovation research in tourism. Tourism Management, 31(1), 1-12. This review article summarizes research on innovation in tourism, highlighting emerging technological trends and their implications for the hospitality industry.

Walker, J. R. (2017). Introduction to Hospitality (7th ed.). Pearson Education. This textbook provides case studies of leading hotel chains, discussing how they leverage technology to improve service delivery, operational efficiency, and customer satisfaction.

Baum, T. (2002). Skills and training for the hospitality sector: A review of issues. Journal of Vocational Education and Training, 54(3), 343-364.This review addresses the impact of technology on workforce skills and training in the hospitality sector, highlighting the need for continuous education and adaptation.

Morosan, C., & DeFranco, A. L. (2016). It's about time: Revisiting privacy concerns in the hospitality industry. International Journal of Contemporary Hospitality Management, 28(9), 1853-1875. This article revisits privacy concerns in the hospitality industry, discussing the challenges of balancing technological advancements with the protection of guest privacy.

Anderson, C. K. (2012). The impact of social media on lodging performance. Cornell Hospitality Quarterly, 53(3), 232-245. This study investigates the impact of social media on hotel performance, emphasizing the importance of customer feedback and continuous improvement through digital engagement.

Zervas, G., Proserpio, D., & Byers, J. W. (2017). The rise of the sharing economy: Estimating the impact of Airbnb on the hotel industry. Journal of Marketing Research, 54(5), 687-705. This paper estimates the impact of Airbnb on the traditional hotel industry, discussing how technological disruptions are reshaping competition and consumer preferences.

Buhalis, D., & Leung, D. (2018). Smart hospitality—Interconnectivity and interoperability towards an ecosystem. International Journal of Hospitality Management, 71, 41-50. This article explores the future directions of hospitality technology, emphasizing the importance of interconnectivity and interoperability in creating a smart hospitality ecosystem.

Mihalič, T., & Buhalis, D. (2013). ICT as a new competitive advantage factor—Case of small transitional hotel sector. Economic and Business Review for Central and South-Eastern Europe, 15(1), 33-56. This study examines how ICT provides a competitive advantage for small hotels, particularly in transitional economies, highlighting the economic impact of technological adoption.

Sigala, M. (2003). Competing in the e-service economy: Implications for hospitality management education. Journal of Hospitality, Leisure, Sport & Tourism Education, 2(2), 23-36. This paper discusses the implications of the e-service economy for hospitality management education, emphasizing the need for curricula that address technological advancements and globalization.

Zeng, D. Z., & Glaeser, E. L. (2016). How Airbnb conquers cities. Regional Science and Urban Economics, 61, 1-10. This article explores the regulatory and ethical considerations surrounding the rise of Airbnb, discussing its impact on urban environments and traditional hospitality businesses.

Murphy, J., Hofacker, C., & Gretzel, U. (2017). Robots in hospitality and tourism: A research agenda. Annals of Tourism Research, 64, 49-59. This paper sets a research agenda for the use of robots in hospitality and tourism, discussing the potential benefits and challenges of automation in service delivery.

Lu, Y., & Stepchenkova, S. (2012). Ecotourism experiences reported online: Classification of satisfaction attributes. Tourism Management, 33(3), 702-712. This study analyzes online reviews of ecotourism experiences, categorizing satisfaction attributes and highlighting the role of guest-facing technologies in shaping customer perceptions.

CHALLENGES AND CONSIDERATIONS ON THE EVOLUTION OF TECHNOLOGY IN THE SERVICE SECTOR CONCERNING HOSPITALITY

The hospitality industry has witnessed a transformative journey driven by technological advancements. From reservation systems to artificial intelligence (AI) and Internet of Things (IoT), technology has reshaped guest experiences, operational efficiencies, and business strategies. However, along with these advancements come a myriad of challenges and considerations that hospitality businesses must navigate to harness the full potential of technology effectively.

Cybersecurity Risks

Cybersecurity has emerged as a critical concern in the hospitality industry, amplified by the increasing digitization of guest interactions, data storage, and operational processes. Hotels are prime targets for cyber threats due to the large volumes of personal and financial data they handle. Instances of data breaches and ransomware attacks have underscored the vulnerabilities inherent in hospitality technology systems.

Addressing Cybersecurity Concerns

To mitigate cybersecurity risks, hotels must implement robust measures:

1. **Comprehensive Security Frameworks**: Establishing a multi-layered security architecture encompassing network security, endpoint protection, and data encryption.
2. **Regular Audits and Vulnerability Assessments**: Conduct frequent security audits and vulnerability assessments to identify and rectify potential weaknesses.
3. **Employee Training**: Educating staff about cybersecurity best practices and protocols to enhance awareness and responsiveness to threats.
4. **Compliance with Data Protection Regulations**: Adhering to global data protection laws (e.g., GDPR, CCPA) to safeguard guest data and ensure regulatory compliance.

Integration Complexity

The integration of new technologies into existing hospitality infrastructure presents significant challenges. From property management systems (PMS) to CRM platforms and IoT devices, each technology requires seamless integration to optimize operational efficiencies and guest experiences.

Overcoming Integration Challenges

1. **Strategic Planning and Compatibility**: Conducting thorough assessments to ensure compatibility between new technologies and existing systems.
2. **Vendor Collaboration**: Collaborating with experienced technology vendors capable of providing tailored solutions and support throughout the integration process.
3. **Testing and Quality Assurance**: Rigorous testing procedures to identify and resolve integration issues before full deployment.
4. **Staff Training and Change Management**: Providing comprehensive training to employees to facilitate smooth transitions and maximize technology utilization.

Data Privacy Concerns

As hospitality businesses collect and store vast amounts of guest data for personalized services and marketing purposes, ensuring data privacy and protecting guest confidentiality become paramount. The misuse or unauthorized access to guest data can lead to legal ramifications and damage to brand reputation.

Safeguarding Guest Privacy

To uphold guest privacy and build trust:

1. **Transparent Data Handling Practices**: Implementing clear and concise privacy policies outlining data collection, usage, and protection measures.
2. **Data Encryption and Secure Storage**: Utilizing robust encryption protocols and secure storage systems to safeguard sensitive guest information.
3. **Guest Consent and Preference Management**: Obtaining explicit consent from guests for data collection and allowing them control over their preferences and data usage.
4. **Compliance Monitoring**: Regularly auditing data practices and ensuring compliance with relevant privacy regulations and standards.

Skill Gaps and Training Needs

The rapid pace of technological evolution necessitates a skilled workforce capable of leveraging advanced technologies and providing exceptional guest service. However, the hospitality industry faces challenges in bridging skill gaps and ensuring employees possess the requisite technical and interpersonal competencies.

Enhancing Workforce Skills

To address skill gaps and training needs:

1. **Continuous Learning Initiatives**: Investing in ongoing training and development programs to enhance employee proficiency in emerging technologies and customer service excellence.
2. **Cross-functional Training**: Providing cross-functional training to enable employees from different departments to collaborate effectively in utilizing technology.
3. **Leadership and Change Management**: Fostering a culture of innovation and adaptability through effective leadership and change management practices.
4. **Industry Collaboration and Education**: Collaborating with educational institutions and industry associations to design specialized training programs aligned with hospitality technology trends.

Guest Resistance to Technology

Despite the benefits of technology in enhancing operational efficiencies and guest experiences, some guests may prefer traditional service methods or express reluctance towards adopting new technologies. Addressing guest resistance requires a balanced approach that respects individual preferences while promoting the advantages of technological innovations.

Mitigating Guest Resistance

1. **Personalized Service Options**: Offering guests a choice between traditional and technology-enabled service options based on their preferences.
2. **Education and Engagement**: Educating guests about the benefits of technology in enhancing convenience, personalization, and efficiency during their stay.
3. **User-friendly Interfaces**: Designing intuitive and user-friendly interfaces for technology applications to enhance ease of use and accessibility for guests.
4. **Feedback Mechanisms**: Soliciting guest feedback and actively incorporating suggestions to refine technology offerings and address usability concerns.

Technological Dependency and Downtime

As hotels increasingly rely on technology for essential operations such as reservations, check-ins, and guest services, the risk of technological dependency and downtime becomes a critical consideration. Any disruption in technology systems can lead to significant guest inconvenience, operational disruptions, and financial losses.

Ensuring Operational Continuity

To minimize the impact of technological downtime:

1. **Redundancy and Backup Systems**: Implementing redundant systems and backup protocols to maintain continuity during technical failures.
2. **Cloud-based Solutions**: Leveraging cloud computing for enhanced scalability, reliability, and disaster recovery capabilities.
3. **Proactive Maintenance and Monitoring**: Conducting regular maintenance checks and real-time monitoring of technology infrastructure to identify potential issues proactively.
4. **Contingency Planning**: Developing comprehensive contingency plans outlining protocols for responding to and recovering from technological disruptions.

Cost Management

The adoption and integration of advanced technologies entail substantial financial investments, posing challenges for hospitality businesses, particularly smaller establishments with limited resources. Managing costs effectively while maximizing return on investment (ROI) requires strategic planning and prioritization.

Optimizing Technology Investments

To manage costs and achieve sustainable ROI:

1. **Cost-benefit Analysis**: Conducting thorough cost-benefit analyses to evaluate the financial feasibility and potential returns of technology investments.
2. **Phased Implementation**: Implementing technology upgrades in phases to manage upfront costs and assess performance before full deployment.
3. **Partnerships and Financing Options**: Exploring partnerships with technology providers and leveraging financing options to spread costs over time.

4. **Focus on Long-term Value**: Prioritizing investments in technologies that offer long-term operational efficiencies, guest satisfaction improvements, and competitive advantages.

Ethical Use of Data and AI

The ethical use of guest data and AI-driven technologies in hospitality raises significant ethical considerations, including privacy, fairness, and transparency. Hospitality businesses must navigate these ethical complexities to build trust with guests and stakeholders while harnessing the benefits of data-driven insights and automation.

Upholding Ethical Standards

1. To ensure ethical practices in data usage and AI applications:
2. **Ethical Guidelines and Governance**: Establishing clear ethical guidelines and governance frameworks for data collection, storage, and usage.
3. **Transparency and Accountability**: Maintaining transparency in data practices and AI algorithms, including disclosure of data usage policies to guests.
4. **Fairness and Bias Mitigation**: Mitigating biases in AI algorithms and decision-making processes to ensure fair treatment of guests and employees.
5. **Stakeholder Engagement**: Engaging with guests, employees, and industry stakeholders to solicit feedback and address concerns regarding data privacy and AI ethics.

Regulatory Compliance

The hospitality industry is subject to stringent regulatory requirements related to technology, data protection, accessibility, and industry-specific standards. Compliance with these regulations is essential to avoid legal penalties, reputational damage, and operational disruptions.

1. **Ensuring Regulatory Adherence:**To navigate regulatory complexities effectively:
2. **Regulatory Awareness and Monitoring**: Staying informed about evolving regulatory landscapes and ensuring compliance with relevant laws, regulations, and industry standards.
3. **Legal Expertise and Consultation**: Engaging legal experts and consultants to interpret regulatory requirements and implement necessary measures.
4. **Documentation and Reporting**: Maintaining comprehensive documentation of compliance efforts and conducting regular audits to assess adherence.
5. **Proactive Adaptation**: Anticipating regulatory changes and proactively adapting policies and practices to align with emerging requirements.

Sustainability and Environmental Impact

While technology offers opportunities for efficiency improvements and enhanced guest experiences, it also presents environmental challenges related to energy consumption, electronic waste (e-waste), and carbon footprint. Hospitality businesses are increasingly focusing on sustainable practices to mitigate environmental impacts and promote responsible stewardship.

Promoting Sustainable Technology Practices

To reduce environmental footprint and promote sustainability:

1. **Energy-efficient Technologies**: Adopting energy-efficient appliances, lighting systems, and HVAC (heating, ventilation, and air conditioning) solutions to minimize energy consumption.
2. **E-waste Management**: Implementing e-waste recycling programs and responsible disposal practices for outdated technology equipment.
3. **Green Certifications**: Pursuing certifications such as LEED (Leadership in Energy and Environmental Design) to demonstrate commitment to environmental sustainability.
4. **Guest Education and Engagement**: Educating guests about sustainable practices and encouraging participation in environmental initiatives during their stay.

ANALYSIS AND DISCUSSION ACCORDING TO PAST DATA

Historical Milestones in Hospitality Technology

The journey of technological evolution in hospitality began with the introduction of basic reservation systems in the 1970s and 1980s. These systems were designed to streamline the booking process, reduce errors, and improve guest satisfaction. Early systems like the Global Distribution Systems (GDS) linked hotels with travel agents, enabling real-time booking capabilities and broader market reach (Nyheim & Connolly, 2011).

Online Booking Platforms

The advent of the internet in the 1990s marked a significant shift in hospitality technology. Online booking platforms emerged, transforming how consumers booked travel and accommodations. These platforms allowed customers to compare prices, read reviews, and make reservations at their convenience. O'Connor (2003) highlights that online travel agencies (OTAs) like Expedia and Booking.com revolutionized the booking process, making it more user-friendly and accessible.

Revenue Management Systems

Revenue management systems (RMS) were developed to help hotels optimize their pricing strategies based on demand forecasts. By analyzing historical booking data and market trends, these systems enabled hotels to maximize revenue through dynamic pricing. Talluri and Van Ryzin (2004) discuss the effectiveness of RMS in balancing supply and demand, which has become crucial in today's competitive market.

Customer Relationship Management (CRM)

The implementation of Customer Relationship Management (CRM) systems marked a shift towards a more customer-centric approach in hospitality. Piccoli and Patterson (2009) emphasize how CRM systems allowed hotels to collect and analyze guest data, facilitating personalized services and improving guest loyalty. These systems enable hotels to track guest preferences, tailor marketing efforts, and provide a more customized experience.

Enhancing Guest Experience through Technology

Technological advancements have significantly enhanced the guest experience. Buhalis and Amaranggana (2013) introduced the concept of smart tourism destinations, where interconnected devices and data analytics provide personalized and context-aware services. Smart rooms equipped with Internet of Things (IoT) devices can automatically adjust lighting, temperature, and entertainment options based on guest preferences (Gretzel et al., 2015).

Self-Service Technologies

The adoption of self-service technologies has allowed guests to have more control over their stay. Self-service kiosks for check-in and check-out, mobile key access, and in-room tablets for service requests have become increasingly common. Kokkinou and Mihalic (2021) discuss how these technologies have reduced wait times, improved operational efficiency, and enhanced guest satisfaction.

Social Media and Digital Marketing

Social media has become an essential tool for marketing and customer engagement in the hospitality industry. Leung et al. (2013) highlight that social media platforms enable hotels to interact with customers, manage their online reputation, and gather valuable feedback. This interaction has become crucial for building brand loyalty and attracting new guests.

Big Data and Analytics

Big data analytics has provided hoteliers with deeper insights into customer behavior and operational efficiency. Moro et al. (2018) demonstrate how analyzing social media performance metrics can predict hotel performance, allowing for more informed decision-making. By leveraging big data, hotels can optimize their marketing strategies, improve guest experiences, and streamline operations.

Blockchain Technology

Blockchain technology is an emerging trend that promises to revolutionize various aspects of hospitality. Treiblmaier (2018) discusses how blockchain can enhance supply chain transparency, improve security, and streamline transactions. For instance, blockchain can provide secure and transparent booking processes, reducing the risk of fraud and ensuring trust between parties.

Artificial Intelligence and Machine Learning

Artificial Intelligence (AI) and Machine Learning (ML) are transforming hospitality by automating routine tasks and providing personalized services. Ivanov and Webster (2017) explore how AI applications, such as chatbots and service robots, can handle customer inquiries, manage bookings, and perform housekeeping tasks. These technologies not only enhance operational efficiency but also improve the guest experience by providing timely and accurate responses.

Augmented Reality (AR) and Virtual Reality (VR)

Augmented Reality (AR) and Virtual Reality (VR) offer innovative ways to enhance the guest experience and marketing efforts. Tussyadiah et al. (2017) discuss how VR can provide virtual tours of hotel properties, allowing potential guests to explore rooms and amenities before making a booking. AR applications can enhance on-site experiences by providing interactive information about hotel facilities and nearby attractions.

Mobile Technology

Mobile technology has become integral to modern hospitality services. Murphy et al. (2010) emphasize the importance of mobile-friendly websites and applications that allow guests to book rooms, access hotel services, and provide feedback conveniently from their smartphones. Mobile technology has also enabled the development of mobile concierge services, providing guests with real-time information and assistance.

Cloud Computing

Cloud computing has enabled hotels to streamline operations, reduce costs, and improve scalability. Benckendorff et al. (2019) discuss how cloud-based solutions facilitate real-time data access, enhance collaboration, and support advanced analytics. Cloud computing also allows hotels to integrate various systems and applications, creating a seamless and efficient operational environment.

Cybersecurity

As hotels become more reliant on technology, cybersecurity has become a critical concern. Stinchcombe (2018) highlights the growing threat of cyber-attacks and the need for robust security measures to protect sensitive guest data. Implementing strong cybersecurity practices is essential for maintaining guest trust and ensuring the integrity of hotel operations.

Sustainability and Green Technology

Sustainability and green technology have gained prominence in the hospitality industry. Bohdanowicz (2006) examines how hotels are adopting eco-friendly practices and technologies to reduce their environmental footprint and appeal to environmentally conscious travelers. Technologies such as energy-efficient lighting, water-saving fixtures, and waste management systems contribute to sustainable operations.

Technological Integration and Workforce Impact

Successful technological integration requires a strategic approach and a supportive organizational culture. Wang and Qualls (2007) propose a theoretical model for technology adoption in hospitality, emphasizing the importance of organizational readiness and employee training. The impact of technology on the workforce is significant, necessitating continuous skills development and training to ensure that employees can effectively use new technologies and adapt to changing job roles (Baum, 2002).

Guest Privacy Concerns

Protecting guest privacy is paramount in the digital age. Morosan and DeFranco (2016) revisit the challenges of protecting guest information in an era of advanced technology, advocating for stringent data protection measures. Ensuring compliance with data protection regulations and implementing robust privacy practices are essential for maintaining guest trust.

Feedback and Continuous Improvement

Leveraging feedback for continuous improvement is crucial for maintaining high service standards. Anderson (2012) highlights the importance of using social media feedback to enhance service quality and address customer concerns promptly. Implementing systems to collect and analyze guest feedback helps hotels identify areas for improvement and enhance the overall guest experience.

Technological Disruptions and Industry Response

Technological disruptions, such as the rise of the sharing economy, have forced the hospitality industry to adapt. Zervas et al. (2017) analyze the impact of Airbnb on traditional hotels, highlighting the need for hotels to innovate and differentiate their services to remain competitive. Embracing new technologies and business models is essential for staying relevant in a rapidly changing market.

Future Directions and Economic Impact

The future of hospitality technology lies in further integration and interoperability. Buhalis and Leung (2018) discuss the concept of smart hospitality ecosystems, where interconnected systems and devices work seamlessly to provide a holistic and personalized guest experience. The economic impact of technology adoption is profound, providing hotels with competitive advantages, particularly in small transitional economies (Mihalič & Buhalis, 2013).

RECOMMENDATIONS FOR FUTURE IMPLEMENTATION

1. Embrace Emerging Technologies

Artificial Intelligence and Machine Learning: Continue to explore and implement AI and ML technologies to automate routine tasks and enhance personalization. AI-driven chatbots and service robots can provide instant assistance to guests, streamline check-in and check-out processes, and handle room service requests efficiently.

Blockchain Technology: Invest in blockchain solutions to enhance transparency and security in transactions. Blockchain can be utilized for secure and transparent booking processes, loyalty programs, and supply chain management.

Augmented Reality (AR) and Virtual Reality (VR): Develop AR and VR applications to enhance marketing efforts and guest experiences. Virtual tours of hotel properties can attract potential guests, while AR can provide interactive on-site information about facilities and nearby attractions.

2. Focus on Data Security and Privacy

Strengthen Cybersecurity Measures: Implement robust cybersecurity protocols to protect sensitive guest data. Regularly update security systems, conduct vulnerability assessments, and ensure compliance with data protection regulations.

Guest Privacy: Develop clear privacy policies and ensure transparency with guests about how their data is collected, stored, and used. Provide options for guests to control their data and maintain stringent access controls.

3. Enhance Guest Experience through Personalization

CRM Systems: Invest in advanced Customer Relationship Management systems to gather and analyze guest data. Use this data to provide personalized services, tailor marketing efforts, and improve guest loyalty.

Internet of Things (IoT): Expand the use of IoT devices in guest rooms to create smart environments. Allow guests to control room settings such as lighting, temperature, and entertainment through their mobile devices or voice commands.

4. Invest in Mobile Technology

Mobile-Friendly Interfaces: Ensure that all hotel websites and booking platforms are mobile-friendly. Develop dedicated mobile apps that allow guests to make reservations, access hotel services, and provide feedback seamlessly.

Mobile Concierge Services: Implement mobile concierge services that provide guests with real-time information and assistance. These services can enhance the guest experience by offering personalized recommendations and instant support.

5. Adopt Sustainable Practices

Green Technology: Invest in eco-friendly technologies such as energy-efficient lighting, water-saving fixtures, and waste management systems. Promote sustainable practices to attract environmentally conscious travelers.

Sustainability Certifications: Pursue sustainability certifications to demonstrate the hotel's commitment to environmental responsibility. Highlight these achievements in marketing materials to appeal to eco-conscious guests.

6. Leverage Big Data and Analytics

Data-Driven Decision Making: Utilize big data analytics to gain insights into guest behavior, market trends, and operational efficiency. Use this data to optimize pricing strategies, marketing campaigns, and resource allocation.

Predictive Analytics: Implement predictive analytics to anticipate guest needs and preferences. This can help in personalizing marketing efforts, improving guest satisfaction, and enhancing operational efficiency.

7. Improve Technological Integration

Unified Platforms: Develop unified platforms that integrate systems such as booking, CRM, revenue management, and property management. This integration ensures seamless operations and improves data accuracy.

Training and Development: Invest in continuous training and development for staff to ensure they are proficient in using new technologies. This will enhance their ability to provide exceptional service and adapt to technological advancements.

8. Enhance Feedback Mechanisms

Real-Time Feedback: Implement real-time feedback mechanisms that allow guests to provide instant reviews and ratings during their stay. This enables the hotel to address issues promptly and improve the guest experience.

Continuous Improvement: Use guest feedback to identify areas for improvement and implement necessary changes. Regularly analyze feedback data to track performance and make informed decisions.

9. Adapt to Technological Disruptions

Competitive Analysis: Continuously monitor technological trends and disruptions in the industry. Conduct regular competitive analysis to understand the impact of new technologies and adapt strategies accordingly.

Innovative Business Models: Explore innovative business models that leverage technology to offer unique value propositions. For example, consider partnering with sharing economy platforms or developing niche services that cater to specific market segments.

10. Plan for Future Trends

Smart Hospitality Ecosystems: Prepare for the future by investing in the development of smart hospitality ecosystems. This involves creating interconnected systems and devices that provide a seamless and personalized guest experience.

Continuous Innovation: Foster a culture of continuous innovation within the organization. Encourage employees to explore new technologies, experiment with innovative solutions, and stay ahead of industry trends.

The hospitality industry must continue to evolve and adapt to technological advancements to remain competitive and meet the changing needs of guests. By embracing emerging technologies, focusing on data security and privacy, enhancing guest experiences, and adopting sustainable practices, hotels can create a more efficient, personalized, and environmentally friendly operation. Leveraging big data, improving technological integration, enhancing feedback mechanisms, and adapting to technological disruptions will ensure that hotels are well-prepared for the future. Continuous innovation and a commitment to excellence will drive the hospitality industry forward in this era of rapid technological change.

Enhancing Customer Experience

Personalization through AI and Machine Learning

Artificial intelligence (AI) and machine learning (ML) have immense potential to personalize guest experiences. By analyzing customer data, AI can provide tailored recommendations for services, dining options, and activities based on individual preferences and past behaviors.

Recommendation: Invest in AI-driven CRM systems that can analyze guest data in real-time to offer personalized services. Implement chatbots and virtual assistants to provide 24/7 support, ensuring that guests receive immediate assistance and personalized recommendations.

Augmented Reality (AR) and Virtual Reality (VR) for Guest Engagement

AR and VR technologies offer immersive experiences that can enhance guest engagement. VR can be used for virtual tours of hotel properties, allowing potential guests to explore rooms and amenities before making a booking. AR can provide interactive information about local attractions, dining options, and hotel services.

Recommendation: Develop AR and VR applications that allow guests to experience hotel offerings and local attractions virtually. Use AR for interactive in-room experiences, such as virtual concierge services that provide information about room controls, hotel amenities, and nearby points of interest.

Mobile Integration for Seamless Experiences

Mobile technology continues to play a critical role in enhancing the guest experience. Mobile apps can streamline check-in and check-out processes, provide digital room keys, and allow guests to control room settings from their smartphones.

Recommendation: Invest in comprehensive mobile apps integrating all guest services, from booking and check-in to room service and check-out. Ensure that these apps are user-friendly and offer a seamless, intuitive experience. Incorporate mobile payment options to facilitate easy and secure transactions.

Improving Operational Efficiency

Internet of Things (IoT) for Smart Operations

IoT devices can significantly improve operational efficiency by automating and optimizing various processes. Smart thermostats, lighting systems, and energy management systems can reduce energy consumption and costs. IoT sensors can monitor equipment performance and predict maintenance needs, preventing downtime and costly repairs.

Recommendation: Implement IoT solutions for energy management and predictive maintenance. Use IoT sensors to monitor guest room conditions and automate adjustments for comfort and energy efficiency. Integrate IoT data into centralized management systems to enable real-time monitoring and decision-making.

Cloud Computing for Scalability and Flexibility

Cloud computing offers scalable and flexible solutions for data storage, processing, and management. By moving operations to the cloud, hotels can reduce IT infrastructure costs, improve data accessibility, and enhance collaboration among staff.

Recommendation: Transition to cloud-based property management systems (PMS) and customer relationship management (CRM) systems. Use cloud solutions to store and analyze large volumes of data, ensuring that data is accessible to authorized personnel from anywhere, at any time. Implement cloud-based collaboration tools to enhance communication and coordination among staff.

Advanced Revenue Management Systems

Revenue management systems (RMS) have evolved to incorporate advanced analytics and machine learning algorithms. These systems can analyze market trends, competitor pricing, and customer behavior to optimize pricing strategies and maximize revenue.

Recommendation: Invest in advanced RMS that leverage AI and big data analytics to provide dynamic pricing strategies. Use these systems to analyze booking patterns, demand forecasts, and market conditions, allowing for real-time adjustments to pricing and inventory management.

Leveraging Data Management and Analytics

Big Data Analytics for Informed Decision-Making

Big data analytics enables hotels to gain valuable insights from large volumes of structured and unstructured data. By analyzing data from various sources, hotels can make informed decisions regarding marketing strategies, guest services, and operational improvements.

Recommendation: Develop a robust data analytics framework that collects and analyzes data from multiple sources, including PMS, CRM, social media, and IoT devices. Use predictive analytics to forecast demand, optimize inventory, and enhance marketing campaigns. Ensure that data analytics capabilities are integrated into all aspects of hotel operations for data-driven decision-making.

Blockchain for Enhanced Security and Transparency

Blockchain technology can enhance security and transparency in transactions, identity verification, and supply chain management. Blockchain's decentralized nature ensures that data is secure, immutable, and easily traceable.

Recommendation: Explore the implementation of blockchain technology for secure and transparent transactions, loyalty programs, and identity verification. Use blockchain to create a tamper-proof record of guest interactions and transactions, ensuring data integrity and enhancing trust with customers.

Promoting Sustainability and Green Technology

Energy Management Systems

Sustainability is becoming increasingly important in the hospitality industry. Energy management systems (EMS) can monitor and optimize energy usage, reducing costs and environmental impact. Smart thermostats, lighting controls, and energy-efficient appliances contribute to a more sustainable operation.

Recommendation: Implement advanced EMS to monitor and control energy usage across the hotel. Use smart technologies to automate lighting and HVAC systems based on occupancy and environmental conditions. Invest in energy-efficient appliances and renewable energy sources to further reduce the hotel's carbon footprint.

Waste Management and Recycling Programs

Effective waste management and recycling programs are essential for reducing environmental impact. Technology can play a crucial role in tracking waste generation, optimizing recycling efforts, and minimizing waste.

Recommendation: Use IoT-enabled waste management systems to monitor waste levels and optimize collection schedules. Implement recycling programs that use technology to sort and process recyclable materials efficiently. Educate staff and guests about the importance of waste reduction and recycling, encouraging participation in sustainability initiatives.

Fostering Innovation and Adaptability

Embracing Emerging Technologies

The hospitality industry must stay abreast of emerging technologies that can enhance guest experiences and operational efficiencies. Technologies such as artificial intelligence, machine learning, blockchain, and IoT offer significant opportunities for innovation.

Recommendation: Establish a dedicated innovation team to explore and pilot emerging technologies. Foster a culture of innovation by encouraging staff to suggest and experiment with new ideas. Partner with technology providers and research institutions to stay informed about the latest technological advancements and their potential applications in hospitality.

Staff Training and Development

As technology continues to evolve, it is essential to invest in staff training and development to ensure that employees are proficient in using new systems and technologies. Continuous learning and professional development are critical for maintaining a skilled and adaptable workforce.

Recommendation: Develop comprehensive training programs that cover the latest technologies and systems used in the hotel. Provide ongoing professional development opportunities to keep staff updated on industry trends and best practices. Encourage a culture of continuous learning and innovation by recognizing and rewarding employees who embrace new technologies and contribute to operational improvements.

Ensuring Data Privacy and Security

Implementing Robust Cybersecurity Measures

With the increasing reliance on digital systems and data, cybersecurity is a top priority. Hotels must implement robust cybersecurity measures to protect sensitive guest information and prevent data breaches.

Recommendation: Invest in advanced cybersecurity solutions to protect digital assets and data. Conduct regular security audits and vulnerability assessments to identify and address potential risks. Train staff on cybersecurity best practices, ensuring that they are aware of the importance of data security and the measures they need to take to protect it.

Compliance with Data Privacy Regulations

Compliance with data privacy regulations, such as the General Data Protection Regulation (GDPR), is essential for maintaining guest trust and avoiding legal issues. Hotels must ensure that they collect, store, and process guest data in accordance with relevant regulations.

Recommendation: Develop a comprehensive data privacy policy that complies with local and international regulations. Implement data protection measures, such as encryption and access controls, to safeguard guest information. Regularly review and update data privacy practices to ensure ongoing compliance with regulatory requirements.

Enhancing Guest Satisfaction through Continuous Feedback

Leveraging Social Media and Online Reviews

Social media and online reviews provide valuable feedback on guest experiences and can influence booking decisions. Hotels should actively monitor and respond to online feedback to address issues and enhance guest satisfaction.

Recommendation: Use social media monitoring tools to track mentions and reviews of the hotel. Respond promptly to guest feedback, addressing concerns and highlighting positive reviews. Analyze feedback to identify trends and areas for improvement, using insights to enhance guest services and experiences.

Implementing Real-Time Feedback Systems

Real-time feedback systems allow hotels to capture guest feedback during their stay, enabling immediate responses to issues and improving overall satisfaction. These systems can include in-room tablets, mobile apps, and interactive kiosks.

Recommendation: Implement real-time feedback systems to capture guest feedback throughout their stay. Use this feedback to address issues promptly and make real-time adjustments to services. Analyze feedback data to identify patterns and areas for improvement, ensuring that guest concerns are addressed proactively.

CONCLUSION

The evolution of technology in the hospitality sector has been a dynamic and transformative journey. From the early days of computerized reservation systems to the latest advancements in AI and IoT, each technological innovation has contributed to making operations more efficient, enhancing customer experiences, and driving industry growth. As technology continues to evolve, the hospitality industry must remain agile and innovative, adopting new tools and strategies to meet the ever-changing demands of modern travelers. This ongoing technological evolution promises to create even more personalized, efficient, and memorable experiences for guests, shaping the future of hospitality in exciting ways. The hospitality industry must continue to evolve and adapt to technological advancements to remain competitive and meet the changing needs of guests. By embracing emerging technologies, focusing on data security and privacy, enhancing guest experiences, and adopting sustainable practices, hotels can create a more efficient, personalized, and environmentally friendly operation. Leveraging big data, improving technological integration, enhancing feedback mechanisms, and adapting to technological disruptions will ensure that hotels are well-prepared for the future. Continuous innovation and a commitment to excellence will drive the hospitality industry forward in this era of rapid technological change. he rapid evolution of technology has dramatically transformed the hospitality industry, impacting every facet of service delivery, operational efficiency, customer engagement, and strategic decision-making. This transformation, driven by advancements in artificial intelligence (AI), the Internet of Things (IoT), big data analytics, and other emerging technologies, has redefined the standards of hospitality and created new opportunities and challenges. This conclusion synthesizes the key insights and recommendations discussed, emphasizing the importance of continued technological integration and innovation in shaping the future of hospitality.

REFERENCES

Anderson, C. K. (2012). The impact of social media on lodging performance. *Cornell Hospitality Quarterly, 53*(3), 232–245.

Baum, T. (2002). Skills and training for the hospitality sector: A review of issues. *Journal of Vocational Education and Training, 54*(3), 343–364. DOI: 10.1080/13636820200200204

Benckendorff, P., Xiang, Z., & Sheldon, P. J. (2019). *Tourism Information Technology* (2nd ed.). CABI. DOI: 10.1079/9781786393432.0000

Bohdanowicz, P. (2006). Environmental awareness and initiatives in the European hospitality industry: A comparative study. *International Journal of Hospitality Management, 25*(4), 662–682. DOI: 10.1016/j.ijhm.2005.06.006

Buhalis, D., & Amaranggana, A. (2013). Smart tourism destinations. In Xiang, Z., & Tussyadiah, I. (Eds.), *Information and Communication Technologies in Tourism 2014* (pp. 553–564). Springer. DOI: 10.1007/978-3-319-03973-2_40

Buhalis, D., & Leung, D. (2018). Smart hospitality—Interconnectivity and interoperability towards an ecosystem. *International Journal of Hospitality Management, 71*, 41–50. DOI: 10.1016/j.ijhm.2017.11.011

Gretzel, U., Sigala, M., Xiang, Z., & Koo, C. (2015). Smart tourism: Foundations and developments. *Electronic Markets, 25*(3), 179–188. DOI: 10.1007/s12525-015-0196-8

Hjalager, A. M. (2010). A review of innovation research in tourism. *Tourism Management, 31*(1), 1–12. DOI: 10.1016/j.tourman.2009.08.012

Ivanov, S., & Webster, C. (2017). Adoption of robots, artificial intelligence and service automation by travel, tourism, and hospitality companies. *Tech and Travel, 4*(3), 133–140.

Kokkinou, A., & Mihalic, T. (2021). Adoption of self-service technologies in hotels. *International Journal of Contemporary Hospitality Management, 33*(1), 272–294.

Law, R., Leung, R., & Buhalis, D. (2009). Information technology applications in hospitality and tourism: A review of publications from 2005 to 2007. *Journal of Travel & Tourism Marketing, 26*(5-6), 599–623. DOI: 10.1080/10548400903163160

Leung, D., Law, R., van Hoof, H., & Buhalis, D. (2013). Social media in tourism and hospitality: A literature review. *Journal of Travel & Tourism Marketing, 30*(1-2), 3–22. DOI: 10.1080/10548408.2013.750919

Lu, Y., & Stepchenkova, S. (2012). Ecotourism experiences reported online: Classification of satisfaction attributes. *Tourism Management, 33*(3), 702–712. DOI: 10.1016/j.tourman.2011.08.003

Mihalič, T., & Buhalis, D. (2013). ICT as a new competitive advantage factor—Case of small transitional hotel sector. *Economic and Business Review for Central and South-Eastern Europe, 15*(1), 33–56. DOI: 10.15458/2335-4216.1183

Moro, S., Rita, P., & Vala, B. (2018). Predicting social media performance metrics and evaluation of the impact on hotel performance. *International Journal of Contemporary Hospitality Management, 30*(1), 359–377.

Morosan, C., & DeFranco, A. L. (2016). It's about time: Revisiting privacy concerns in the hospitality industry. *International Journal of Contemporary Hospitality Management, 28*(9), 1853–1875.

Murphy, H. C., Hofacker, C., & Bennett, M. (2010). Website development and user interface design: A case study of hotel web sites. *Journal of Hospitality & Leisure Marketing, 9*(3-4), 151–162.

Murphy, J., Hofacker, C., & Gretzel, U. (2017). Robots in hospitality and tourism: A research agenda. *Annals of Tourism Research, 64*, 49–59.

Nyheim, P. D., & Connolly, D. J. (2011). *Technology Strategies for the Hospitality Industry* (2nd ed.). Pearson Education.

O'Connor, P. (2003). Online travel and hospitality services. *Journal of Travel Research, 41*(4), 342–347.

Piccoli, G., & Patterson, R. A. (2009). Web-enabled CRM in the hotel industry: Preliminary findings from a cross-organizational study. *Cornell Hospitality Quarterly, 50*(3), 325–337.

Sigala, M. (2003). Competing in the e-service economy: Implications for hospitality management education. *Journal of Hospitality, Leisure, Sport and Tourism Education, 2*(2), 23–36.

Stinchcombe, K. (2018). *Cybersecurity in the hospitality industry: A growing threat*. Hospitality Technology.

Talluri, K. T., & Van Ryzin, G. J. (2004). *The Theory and Practice of Revenue Management*. Springer Science & Business Media. DOI: 10.1007/b139000

Treiblmaier, H. (2018). The impact of the blockchain on the supply chain: A theory-based research framework and a call for action. *Supply Chain Management, 23*(6), 545–559. DOI: 10.1108/SCM-01-2018-0029

Tussyadiah, I. P., Wang, D., & Jia, C. H. (2017). Virtual reality and attitudes toward tourism destinations. *Journal of Travel Research, 57*(3), 407–428.

Walker, J. R. (2017). *Introduction to Hospitality* (7th ed.). Pearson Education.

Wang, Y., & Qualls, W. (2007). Towards a theoretical model of technology adoption in hospitality organizations. *International Journal of Hospitality Management, 26*(3), 560–573. DOI: 10.1016/j.ijhm.2006.03.008

Zeng, D. Z., & Glaeser, E. L. (2016). How Airbnb conquers cities. *Regional Science and Urban Economics, 61*, 1–10.

Zervas, G., Proserpio, D., & Byers, J. W. (2017). The rise of the sharing economy: Estimating the impact of Airbnb on the hotel industry. *JMR, Journal of Marketing Research, 54*(5), 687–705. DOI: 10.1509/jmr.15.0204

Chapter 32
The Future of Smart Hotels and Digital Transformation in the Hospitality Industry

Bhola Chourasia
https://orcid.org/0000-0003-0707-8524
Assam Down Town University, India

ABSTRACT

The hospitality industry is undergoing a profound transformation driven by the advent of smart technologies and digital innovation. This chapter explores the future of smart hotels and the digital transformation shaping the hospitality sector. Key areas of focus include the integration of artificial intelligence (AI), the Internet of Things (IoT), and blockchain technology to enhance guest experiences, improve operational efficiency, and promote sustainability. Through comprehensive case studies and industry examples, we examine how smart hotels utilize automation, personalized services, and data analytics to cater to the evolving demands of modern travelers. The chapter also addresses the challenges and opportunities associated with digital transformation, such as cybersecurity, data privacy, and maintaining the balance between technological advancement and the human touch.

INTRODUCTION

The hospitality industry is undergoing a significant transformation, spurred by the rapid advancement of digital technologies. As travelers increasingly seek personalized, efficient, and seamless experiences, smart hotels are emerging as a pivotal innovation in this sector. These technologically advanced accommodations leverage the Internet of Things (IoT), artificial intelligence (AI), and big data to enhance guest experiences and streamline operations.

Smart hotels incorporate a range of sophisticated technologies to provide a superior and highly customized experience for guests. Automated check-in and check-out processes, voice-activated room controls, and AI-driven concierge services are just a few examples of how these innovations are reshaping the guest journey. For instance, Hilton's "Connected Room" concept allows guests to control lighting, temperature, and entertainment options via a mobile app, tailoring their environment to their preferences .

Moreover, the integration of AI and machine learning in smart hotels enables a deeper understanding of guest preferences and behaviors. AI can analyze data from various sources, such as social media, previous stays, and real-time interactions, to anticipate guest needs and deliver personalized recommendations. Marriott International's use of AI-powered chatbots to handle common guest queries and requests is a prime example of how technology can enhance customer service while reducing the workload on staff .

DOI: 10.4018/979-8-3693-7447-4.ch032

The use of IoT devices extends beyond guest rooms to include smart energy management systems, which help hotels optimize resource usage and reduce operational costs. By monitoring and adjusting lighting, heating, and cooling systems in real time, hotels can significantly improve energy efficiency. The Peninsular Hotel Group, for example, has implemented an IoT-based system that adjusts energy consumption based on occupancy levels, leading to substantial cost savings and a reduced carbon footprint .

Big data analytics plays a crucial role in the digital transformation of the hospitality industry. By collecting and analyzing vast amounts of data, hotels can gain insights into market trends, customer preferences, and operational performance. This data-driven approach enables hotels to make informed decisions, enhance their marketing strategies, and improve overall guest satisfaction. AccorHotels has been at the forefront of this trend, utilizing big data to tailor marketing campaigns and optimize pricing strategies based on real-time demand and competitive analysis .

The hospitality industry is on the cusp of a profound transformation, driven by the rapid advancement of digital technologies. As travelers increasingly seek personalized, efficient, and seamless experiences, smart hotels are emerging as a pivotal innovation. These technologically advanced accommodations leverage the Internet of Things (IoT), artificial intelligence (AI), and big data to enhance guest experiences and streamline operations. From automated check-ins and smart room controls to AI-driven concierge services, smart hotels epitomize the future of hospitality. This digital metamorphosis not only caters to the evolving preferences of modern travelers but also offers significant operational efficiencies for hotel operators. By integrating cutting-edge technologies, the hospitality sector is set to redefine guest interactions, optimize resource management, and elevate service standards, paving the way for a new era of travel and accommodation.

The hospitality industry is undergoing a significant transformation, spurred by the rapid advancement of digital technologies. As travelers increasingly seek personalized, efficient, and seamless experiences, smart hotels are emerging as a pivotal innovation in this sector. These technologically advanced accommodations leverage the Internet of Things (IoT), artificial intelligence (AI), and big data to enhance guest experiences and streamline operations.

Smart hotels incorporate a range of sophisticated technologies to provide a superior and highly customized experience for guests. Automated check-in and check-out processes, voice-activated room controls, and AI-driven concierge services are just a few examples of how these innovations are reshaping the guest journey. For instance, Hilton's "Connected Room" concept allows guests to control lighting, temperature, and entertainment options via a mobile app, tailoring their environment to their preferences .

Moreover, the integration of AI and machine learning in smart hotels enables a deeper understanding of guest preferences and behaviors. AI can analyze data from various sources, such as social media, previous stays, and real-time interactions, to anticipate guest needs and deliver personalized recommendations. Marriott International's use of AI-powered chatbots to handle common guest queries and requests is a prime example of how technology can enhance customer service while reducing the workload on staff .

The use of IoT devices extends beyond guest rooms to include smart energy management systems, which help hotels optimize resource usage and reduce operational costs. By monitoring and adjusting lighting, heating, and cooling systems in real time, hotels can significantly improve energy efficiency. The Peninsular Hotel Group, for example, has implemented an IoT-based system that adjusts energy consumption based on occupancy levels, leading to substantial cost savings and a reduced carbon footprint .

Big data analytics plays a crucial role in the digital transformation of the hospitality industry. By collecting and analyzing vast amounts of data, hotels can gain insights into market trends, customer preferences, and operational performance. This data-driven approach enables hotels to make informed decisions, enhance their marketing strategies, and improve overall guest satisfaction. AccorHotels has been at the forefront of this trend, utilizing big data to tailor marketing campaigns and optimize pricing strategies based on real-time demand and competitive analysis .

In conclusion, the digital transformation of the hospitality industry through the adoption of smart technologies is not just a trend but a necessary evolution to meet the changing expectations of modern travelers. As smart hotels continue to innovate and integrate new technologies, they will redefine guest interactions, optimize resource management, and elevate service standards. This technological revolution promises to pave the way for a new era of travel and accommodation, where personalized and efficient experiences become the norm rather than the exception.

LITERATURE REVIEW

Smart Hotels and IoT

The Internet of Things (IoT) forms the backbone of smart hotel systems, connecting various devices and enabling real-time communication and control. IoT applications in hotels include smart room controls, energy management systems, and connected appliances. According to Nguyen and Simkin (2017), IoT technologies in hotels not only enhance guest comfort through personalized room settings but also contribute to significant energy savings by optimizing heating, cooling, and lighting systems based on occupancy and usage patterns.

AI and Machine Learning

Artificial intelligence (AI) and machine learning are pivotal in transforming guest services and operational processes in hotels. AI-powered chatbots and virtual assistants, such as those developed by Marriott International, handle guest inquiries and requests, improving response times and freeing up staff for more complex tasks (Ivanov & Webster, 2019). Moreover, AI systems analyze large volumes of data to provide insights into guest preferences and behavior, enabling hotels to offer tailored services and anticipate needs (Berezina et al., 2019).

Big Data Analytics

Big data analytics plays a crucial role in the digital transformation of the hospitality industry. By collecting and analyzing data from various sources, hotels can gain insights into market trends, customer preferences, and operational performance. AccorHotels' use of big data to tailor marketing campaigns and optimize pricing strategies is a prime example of how data-driven decision-making can enhance competitiveness (Chen et al., 2020).

Guest Experience and Personalization

The integration of smart technologies in hotels significantly enhances the guest experience by providing personalized and seamless services. Smart room technologies, such as Hilton's Connected Room, allow guests to control their environment through mobile apps, customizing settings like lighting, temperature, and entertainment to their preferences (Tussyadiah, 2020). This level of personalization not only improves guest satisfaction but also builds brand loyalty.

Operational Efficiency and Sustainability

Smart hotels are not only about enhancing guest experiences but also about improving operational efficiency and sustainability. IoT-based energy management systems help hotels reduce energy consumption by monitoring and adjusting settings in real-time. The Peninsula Hotel Group's implementation of such systems has led to substantial cost savings and a reduced carbon footprint (Jones et al., 2018). Additionally, automation of routine tasks through AI reduces labor costs and minimizes human error, contributing to overall operational efficiency.

Challenges and Future Directions

While the benefits of smart hotel technologies are clear, there are also challenges to consider. Privacy and security concerns related to the collection and use of guest data are significant issues that need to be addressed (Berezina et al., 2019). Moreover, the high initial cost of implementing these technologies can be a barrier for some hotels, particularly smaller establishments (Ivanov & Webster, 2019).

Looking ahead, the future of smart hotels lies in further integration of advanced technologies such as blockchain for secure transactions, augmented reality (AR) for immersive guest experiences, and continued advancements in AI and machine learning. The ongoing digital transformation will likely lead to even more personalized and efficient services, setting new standards in the hospitality industry.

RESEARCH METHODOLOGY

Phase 1: Literature Review

Method:

- **Data Sources:** Academic journals, industry reports, white papers, and conference proceedings related to smart hotels, IoT, AI, and big data in hospitality.
- **Analysis:** Content analysis to identify recurring themes, technological innovations, benefits, challenges, and future directions.

Phase 2: Quantitative Survey

Method:

- **Population:** Hotel managers, IT specialists, and executives from a diverse range of hotels, including luxury, mid-range, and budget accommodations.
- **Sample Size:** 200 respondents, chosen using stratified random sampling to ensure representation across different hotel types and regions.
- **Instrument:** Structured questionnaire with Likert-scale items to measure:
    - Current use of smart technologies (IoT, AI, big data).
    - Perceived benefits (e.g., guest satisfaction, operational efficiency).
    - Challenges (e.g., cost, data privacy concerns).
    - Future plans for technology adoption.
- **Data Collection:** Online survey distributed via email and professional networks.
- **Analysis:** Descriptive statistics to summarize the data, and inferential statistics (e.g., ANOVA, regression analysis) to identify significant factors influencing technology adoption and impact.

Phase 3: Qualitative Interviews

Method:

- **Participants:** 20 key informants, including hotel general managers, chief technology officers, industry experts, and technology vendors.

- **Sampling Technique:** Purposive sampling to select participants with extensive knowledge and experience in implementing smart hotel technologies.
- **Instrument:** Semi-structured interview guide with open-ended questions covering:
    - o Experiences with current smart technologies.
    - o Impact on guest experience and operational efficiency.
    - o Challenges and barriers to implementation.
    - o Future trends and strategic priorities.
- **Data Collection:** In-depth interviews conducted via video conferencing.
- **Analysis:** Thematic analysis to identify and interpret patterns and themes within the qualitative data.

Data Triangulation and Integration

The findings from the literature review, quantitative survey, and qualitative interviews will be integrated using triangulation to enhance the validity and reliability of the research. This involves cross-verifying data from different sources and methods to build a comprehensive understanding of the future of smart hotels and digital transformation in the hospitality industry.

FINDINGS

Key Findings

1. **Enhanced Guest Experience**: Smart hotels significantly improve the guest experience through personalized services and seamless interactions. Technologies like AI-driven chatbots and smart room controls provide guests with tailored and convenient services, enhancing satisfaction and loyalty.
2. **Operational Efficiency**: The adoption of IoT and AI technologies in hotel operations leads to greater efficiency and cost savings. Energy management systems optimize resource use, while automation reduces labor costs and minimizes human error.
3. **Data-Driven Decision Making**: Big data analytics enable hotels to make informed decisions by providing deep insights into market trends, customer preferences, and operational performance. This data-driven approach enhances marketing strategies, pricing models, and overall competitiveness.
4. **Sustainability**: Smart technologies contribute to sustainability efforts by reducing energy consumption and waste. Hotels implementing IoT-based energy management systems report significant cost savings and a lower environmental impact.
5. **Challenges**: Despite the advantages, the literature highlights several challenges, including privacy and security concerns related to data collection and use, as well as the high initial costs of technology implementation. Addressing these challenges is crucial for the broader adoption of smart hotel technologies.
6. **Future Directions**: The future of smart hotels will likely involve further integration of advanced technologies such as blockchain for secure transactions and augmented reality (AR) for immersive experiences. Continuous advancements in AI and machine learning will drive even more personalized and efficient services.

Implications

- **For Practitioners**: Hotel managers and operators should consider investing in smart technologies to enhance guest satisfaction and operational efficiency. However, they must also address privacy and security concerns to build trust with guests.

- **For Researchers**: There is a need for further research on the long-term impacts of smart hotel technologies and the development of best practices for their implementation. Future studies could explore the integration of emerging technologies like AR and blockchain in greater depth.
- **For Policymakers**: Policymakers should create frameworks that support innovation in the hospitality industry while ensuring data privacy and security. Incentives for sustainable practices and technology adoption can also drive the industry forward.

CONCLUSION

The digital transformation of the hospitality industry through the adoption of smart technologies is not merely a trend but a necessary evolution to meet the changing expectations of modern travelers. As smart hotels continue to innovate, they will redefine guest interactions, optimize resource management, and elevate service standards. The integration of IoT, AI, and big data is paving the way for a new era of personalized and efficient hospitality services. However, the industry must address significant challenges, particularly concerning privacy, security, and implementation costs, to fully realize the potential of these technologies. As the industry continues to evolve, the future promises to be increasingly technology-driven, offering enhanced experiences for guests and greater efficiencies for operators.

REFERENCES

Accor Hotels. (2019). *Accor Hotels and big data: Transforming hospitality with insights.* Accor Hotels. https://group.accor.com

Berezina, K., Bilgihan, A., Cobanoglu, C., & Okumus, F. (2019). Understanding satisfied and dissatisfied hotel customers: Text mining of online hotel reviews. *Journal of Hospitality Marketing & Management, 28*(1), 1–21. DOI: 10.1080/19368623.2015.983631

Chen, Y., Mao, Z., & Liu, L. (2020). Big data in hotel industry: The case of Accor Hotels. *Journal of Hospitality and Tourism Technology, 11*(1), 1–14. DOI: 10.1108/JHTT-05-2019-0066

Hilton. (2018). *Hilton introduces the Connected Room: The first mobile-centric hotel room.* Hilton Newsroom. https://newsroom.hilton.com

Ivanov, S., & Webster, C. (2019). Adoption of robots, artificial intelligence and service automation by travel, tourism and hospitality companies – A cost-benefit analysis. *International Journal of Contemporary Hospitality Management, 31*(1), 1–16. DOI: 10.1108/IJCHM-10-2017-0700

Jones, P., Hillier, D., & Comfort, D. (2018). Sustainability in the hospitality industry. *International Journal of Contemporary Hospitality Management, 30*(1), 1–9. DOI: 10.1108/IJCHM-06-2017-0373

Marriott International. (2020). *Marriott International expands use of AI technology to enhance guest experience.* Marriott News Center. https://news.marriott.com

Nguyen, T. T. H., & Simkin, L. (2017). The Internet of Things (IoT) and marketing: The state of play, future trends and the implications for marketing. *Journal of Marketing Management, 33*(1-2), 1–6. DOI: 10.1080/0267257X.2016.1257542

The Peninsula Hotels. (2021). *Sustainability at The Peninsula: Innovating for a greener future.* The Peninsula Hotels. https://www.peninsula.com

Tussyadiah, I. (2020). Technology and the evolution of the customer experience. *Journal of Marketing Management, 36*(9-10), 1–5. DOI: 10.1080/0267257X.2020.1760417

Chapter 33
The Impact of Artificial Intelligence and Automation in Transforming the Hospitality Sector

Gaurav Bathla
https://orcid.org/0000-0002-6992-811X
CT University, India

Ashish Raina
https://orcid.org/0000-0001-5812-5920
CT University, India

Varinder Singh Rana
https://orcid.org/0009-0008-8562-8265
City University, Ajman, UAE

Bharat Bhushan
The ICFAI University, India

ABSTRACT

The hospitality industry is experiencing a significant transformation due to the rise of Artificial Intelligence (AI) and automation. This chapter explores the diverse effects these technologies have on the hospitality sector, showcasing both the opportunities they present and the challenges they bring. AI and automation are transforming customer service, operational efficiency, and personalised guest experiences. AI-powered chatbots and virtual assistants enhance client interactions by responding quickly and accurately, as well as supporting easy booking processes. Automation in tasks such as check-in, check-out, and room service improves efficiency, reduces human error, and optimises operations. The chapter looks at how data analytics and AI-driven insights can help hotels predict client preferences and customise services to match individual needs, resulting in increased guest happiness and loyalty. This Chapter emphasizes the need for a strategic approach to integrating AI and automation, ensuring they enhance rather than replace the human touch that is fundamental to hospitality.

DOI: 10.4018/979-8-3693-7447-4.ch033

1. INTRODUCTION

By making guest experiences better and operations more efficient, automation and artificial intelligence (AI) have revolutionised the hospitality industry. Hoteliers may save a tonne of money and enjoy better service thanks to artificial intelligence. Bots powered by artificial intelligence that can handle guests' inquiries and perhaps even book rooms could alleviate some of the burden on hotel employees, leading to better service in the long run (Sachan et al., 2024).

1.1. Background and Importance of the Study

The hospitality sector, encompassing a wide range of services from lodging to food and beverage to event planning, plays a critical role in the global economy. This industry is highly customer-centric, relying heavily on personalized service and high operational efficiency to ensure customer satisfaction and loyalty. As technology continues to evolve at a rapid pace, Artificial Intelligence (AI) and automation have emerged as transformative forces within this sector.

AI's strengths in data processing, natural language processing, and machine learning allow for unparalleled levels of personalisation and efficiency (Ivanov, 2018). Automation, using robotics and modern software solutions, streamlines operations, reduces human error, and improves service delivery. These innovations are not just changing client experiences, but also the way hospitality firms function.

The importance of studying the impact of AI and automation in the hospitality sector lies in understanding both the potential benefits and the challenges these technologies bring. As businesses increasingly adopt these innovations, it is crucial to analyze their effects on various aspects of the industry, from customer service to operational management, and to consider the broader implications for the workforce and business strategies.

1.2. Definitions and Concepts

Artificial Intelligence (AI): Artificial intelligence (AI) is the process of teaching computers to mimic human intellect in areas such as reasoning and memory. These systems are capable of a wide range of activities, including language translation, decision-making, and speech recognition. Key subsets of AI include machine learning, where systems improve through experience, and deep learning, which involves neural networks with many layers (Chinnaraj.T, 2023).

Automation: Automation refers to the use of technology to complete jobs with minimal human participation. In the hospitality industry, this might range from simple chores like automatic billing to more intricate operations such as room service delivery via robots. Automation seeks to improve efficiency, decrease errors, and ensure consistency in service delivery.

AI in Hospitality: AI applications in hospitality include chatbots for customer service, recommendation engines for personalized experiences, and predictive analytics for understanding customer preferences and behaviors (Bulchand-Gidumal, 2022). AI enhances the ability of businesses to provide customized services, improve operational efficiency, and analyze vast amounts of data for strategic decision-making.

Automation in Hospitality: Automation in the hospitality industry encompasses a wide range of activities, including check-in and check-out procedures, room allocation, inventory management, and maintenance planning. Robots and automated systems are increasingly being employed for duties like as cleaning, luggage handling, and, in some sophisticated cases, cooking and serving food.

1.3. Historical Development and Evolution

Early Developments: The concept of artificial intelligence has been present since the mid-twentieth century, with early research focusing on developing robots that could mimic human reasoning. Early automation in hospitality included simple activities such as automated phone systems and reservation administration.

Advancements in AI: Significant progress in AI came with the development of machine learning algorithms and the increase in computational power in the late 20th and early 21st centuries (Ersoy & Ehtiyar, 2023). The ability to process and analyze large datasets enabled the creation of more sophisticated AI applications, such as natural language processing and image recognition.

Evolution of Automation: Automation in hospitality has progressed from simple mechanisation to advanced robots and software systems. Automation has advanced in the sector, as evidenced by the development of automated check-in kiosks, smart room technologies, and robotic concierges (Suneel Kumar et al., 2021).

Recent Innovations: The last decade has seen rapid advancements in AI and automation, driven by the rise of the Internet of Things (IoT), cloud computing, and big data analytics. These technologies have enabled more integrated and intelligent systems capable of providing seamless and personalized guest experiences.

1.4. Current Trends and Innovations

AI-Powered Customer Service: One of the most significant trends is the use of "AI-powered chatbots and virtual assistants". These tools are capable of handling a broad range of queries from the customers, provide recommendations, and assist with bookings, all in real-time (Gaur et al., 2022). AI-driven customer service solutions help in enhancing guest satisfaction by offering quick and accurate responses.

Personalization through AI: Artificial intelligence systems analyse client data to make personalised recommendations and offers. This includes recommending activities, dining options, and special bargains based on your previous behaviour and interests. Personalisation aids in the creation of unique experiences, which can boost guest loyalty and repeat business (Hodibert et al., 2024).

Robotics in Hospitality: Robots are becoming more common in hospitality, performing tasks such as room service delivery, luggage handling, and cleaning. These robots not only improve efficiency but also add a modern and innovative touch to the guest experience.

Automation in Operations: Automation streamlines numerous operating operations. Smart systems regulate room occupancy and maintenance schedules to make the best use of available resources (Mingotto et al., 2020). Automated check-in and check-out technologies cut wait times while improving the entire visitor experience.

Predictive Analytics: AI and big data analytics are being used to predict customer behavior, optimize pricing strategies, and manage inventory more effectively. Predictive analytics helps hotels anticipate demand, plan for peak periods, and make informed decisions to maximize revenue (Samala et al., 2022).

Sustainability and Efficiency: Automation and artificial intelligence (AI) are also helping to promote sustainability in the hospitality industry. Hotels are using smart energy management systems, automatic garbage sorting, and resource optimisation to reduce their environmental effect while cutting expenses.

1.5. Applications of "AI and Automation in the Hospitality Sector"

Customer Service Enhancement

Chatbots and Virtual Assistants: The hotel sector is witnessing a revolution in customer service driven by AI-powered chatbots and virtual assistants. These solutions respond instantly to passenger inquiries, help with booking processes, and manage routine demands like room service and restaurant bookings. Chatbots can interpret and answer to client queries in many languages using natural language processing (NLP), resulting in a seamless and efficient communication channel (Ruel & Njoku, 2020). When guests use virtual assistants in conjunction with smart gadgets in their hotel rooms, they may enhance their stay by controlling the temperature, making service requests, and accessing information simply by speaking to their devices (Citak et al., 2021).

Personalized Guest Experiences: AI enables the creation of highly personalized guest experiences by analyzing vast amounts of data related to guest preferences, behaviors, and past interactions. Recommendation engines powered by AI can suggest tailored activities, dining options, and special offers based on individual guest profiles. Personalisation includes pre-arrival communications, where guests can receive personalised emails with itineraries and suggestions, as well as in-room experiences, where preferences such as room temperature, lighting, and entertainment options can be preset based on visitor history. This level of personalisation not only increases guest happiness, but it also promotes loyalty and repeat business.

Operational Efficiency

Automated Check-ins and Check-outs: Automation is streamlining the check-in and check-out processes, significantly reducing wait times and enhancing guest convenience. AI-enabled self-service kiosks can handle check-ins, room keys, and payments without requiring human participation. Mobile apps allow customers to check in and out using their smartphones, avoiding the front desk completely. These automated systems not only increase operational efficiency, but they also let staff to focus on offering personalised care to customers who want more support.

Room Service and Housekeeping Automation: Automation is transforming room service and housekeeping operations. Robots are increasingly being used to deliver items such as food, toiletries, and other amenities directly to guest rooms. This not only improves service delivery but also reduces human touch, which is especially significant in light of health and safety issues. Automated housekeeping systems use artificial intelligence to optimise cleaning schedules depending on room occupancy and guest preferences (Talukder et al., 2023). Smart sensors can identify when a room has been abandoned and tell housekeeping, ensuring that rooms are cleaned and maintained on schedule and efficiently.

Data Analytics and Predictive Insights

AI-driven data analytics provides valuable insights that help hospitality businesses make informed decisions (O'Hara, 2021). AI can spot trends, estimate demand, and optimise pricing strategies by analysing data from a variety of sources, including guest reviews, social media, booking patterns, and operational metrics. Predictive analytics allows hotels to predict guest needs, manage inventory more efficiently, and plan for busy periods. For example, AI can estimate which amenities are likely to be in high demand at specific times of year, allowing hotels to stock properly and avoid shortages (Vijaya, 2022). These insights help to improve operational efficiency, guest pleasure, and income.

Robotics in Hospitality

Concierge Robots: Concierge robots are becoming a common sight in modern hotels. These robots can provide information about hotel services, local attractions, and dining options, as well as assist with directions and transportation arrangements. Concierge robots powered by artificial intelligence may communicate with guests in different languages, providing a one-of-a-kind and entertaining experience (Drexler & Lapré, 2019). They can also perform basic activities like printing flight cards, making reservations, and even checking in guests. Concierge robots take on these roles, allowing human workers to focus on more complicated and personalised visitor interactions.

Automated Cleaning Systems: Robotics and automation are also making significant inroads into cleaning and maintenance tasks. Automated vacuum cleaners and floor scrubbers can efficiently clean large areas with minimal human supervision. Some hotels have installed robots that can independently navigate halls and public places, assuring constant and comprehensive cleaning (Naumov, 2019). These systems employ artificial intelligence to optimise cleaning routes and schedules, saving downtime and increasing overall cleanliness. Automated cleaning systems are very useful in maintaining high levels of hygiene and cleanliness, which are essential for attracting and retaining guests.

1.6. Challenges and Concerns

Job Displacement and Workforce Implications

Impact on Employment: The integration of AI and automation in the hospitality sector has led to concerns about job displacement. As automated technologies take over operations like check-ins, check-outs, room service delivery, and even housekeeping, the demand for specific roles that were formerly done by human employees may decrease (Malone, 2024). This shift may result in job losses, particularly among low-skilled individuals who may struggle to move to other roles within the business.

Workforce Transition and Reskilling: To mitigate the impact of job displacement, there is a need for comprehensive workforce transition and reskilling programs. Hospitality organisations must invest in training people to deal with new technologies and do higher-value tasks that cannot be simply automated (Indora, 2024). This encompasses occupations requiring emotional intelligence, creativity, and complicated problem-solving abilities. By reskilling personnel, the industry can ensure that they remain relevant and valuable as technology advances.

"Data Privacy and Security Issues"

Handling Sensitive Information: Collecting and analyzing massive volumes of personal data, such as guest preferences, travel history, and payment information, is a common component of AI and automation applications in the hospitality industry. Data privacy and security are major concerns that this brings up. Protecting this sensitive information from breaches and unauthorised access is critical to retaining guest trust and complying with data protection requirements (Saini & Bhalla, 2021).

Compliance with Regulations: Hospitals must adhere to "strict data protection regulations, such as the General Data Protection Regulation (GDPR)". These standards specify how personal data should be gathered, stored, and processed, and they provide guests control over their information. To avoid potential fines and brand damage, hospitality organisations must create strong data governance policies.

Ethical Considerations

Bias and Fairness: AI systems have the potential to unintentionally reinforce prejudices found in their training data, which could result in unjust treatment of specific guest groups. For example, an AI-powered recommendation engine may prioritise particular demographics over others, resulting in unequal access to services or personalised offers. Ensuring fairness and transparency in AI algorithms is critical to preventing prejudice and providing equitable experiences for all guests.

Transparency and Accountability: There is also a need for transparency and accountability in the deployment of AI and automation. Guests should be informed when they are interacting with AI systems and understand how their data is being used (Kim et al., 2024). Establishing clear guidelines and ethical standards for AI usage in hospitality can help build trust and ensure that these technologies are used responsibly.

Financial and Technological Investment

High Initial Costs: Implementing AI and automation technologies requires significant financial investment. The initial costs of purchasing, installing, and maintaining these systems can be high, especially for small and medium-sized hospitality organisations. This can be a barrier to adoption and aggravate disparities between large hotel chains with significant resources and smaller enterprises with limited expenditures.

Ongoing Maintenance and Upgrades: In addition to the initial investment, there are ongoing costs associated with maintaining and upgrading AI and automation systems. These technologies require continuous updates to ensure their effectiveness and security. Hospitality organisations must budget for these expenses and devise long-term cost-management methods.

Integration with Existing Systems: Another challenge is the integration of new technologies with existing systems and processes. Legacy systems are commonly used by hospitality businesses for reservations, property management, and customer relationship management (Limna, 2023). It is vital to ensure smooth connectivity between these systems and future AI and automation technologies in order to avoid disruptions and maximise technology benefits.

2. LITERATURE REVIEW

Buhalis (2017) sheds light on the evolving needs of hotels and their customers by examining the pros and cons of virtual assistants (VAs). The findings indicate that VAs are transforming into sophisticated digital assistants, with the potential to significantly enhance hotel customer service, operational capacity, and cost efficiency. Although VA technology is still in its early stages, it has already demonstrated its ability to improve service and streamline operations. The study proposes a model for speech-enabled interactions, emphasizing the role of voice technology in guest experiences. Buhalis notes that most VA research has focused on home settings rather than public or institutional contexts, such as businesses or hotels. This article aims to deepen the understanding of VA adoption and implementation in hotels, contributing to the growing body of research on AI and the Internet of Things in smart hospitality, and explores the advantages, disadvantages, and potential future developments of VA-enabled hotel services.

Huang et al. (2022) predict a rise in impactful applications such as search/booking engines, virtual agents, robots, autonomous cars, self-service kiosks, augmented reality (AR), and virtual reality (VR) within the hospitality industry. They emphasize the importance of considering factors that influence the adoption of AI by both customers and employees when integrating AI into hospitality services. According to their findings, different types of AI technologies exhibit varying adoption rates. AI applications that enhance and personalize search capabilities (e.g., search/booking engines, virtual agents) and offer immersive experiences (e.g., AR and VR) are anticipated to see higher adoption rates, based on expert opinions in their study. Conversely, there is less enthusiasm for AI applications designed to streamline corporate processes and automate transactions due to concerns regarding data security and the feasibility of trial runs.

Bulchand-Gidumal et al. (2024) conducted a comprehensive study on the impact of AI on hotel marketing using a grounded theory framework encompassing in-depth interviews, focus groups, and a questionnaire survey. Their findings elucidate ten distinct patterns organized into four key areas, detailing how AI transforms hotel marketing practices. Firstly, AI enhances competitiveness by leveraging data and content, restructuring internal processes, empowering augmented workers, and facilitating mass personalization and customization of services. Secondly, AI influences stakeholder interactions by governing data ethics and legal compliance, promoting sustainability practices, and calculating Return on Investment (ROI). Thirdly, AI centralizes and integrates organizational functions, thereby reshaping distribution networks and enhancing operational efficiency. Lastly, AI revolutionizes customer processes and services through predictive analytics, improved product and service design, and smart, personalized customer care strategies. The study provides valuable insights for academia and industry professionals in the hospitality and tourism sectors, guiding research priorities and enhancing understanding of AI's profound impact on marketing strategies within these fields.

Bathla et al. (2024) AI offers several benefits to the service sector but there are still some obstacles that must be addressed. The main obstacle is the incorporation of AI technologies into current IT infrastructure. Extensive coordination and collaboration between technology providers and technology experts are necessary to ensure smooth connectivity and data exchange. Regulatory and ethical considerations present another challenge in the implementation of artificial intelligence.

Flöck (2022) stated that artificial intelligence (AI) is increasingly being adopted across various functions within the hospitality sector, promising significant improvements in customer experiences. However, alongside these benefits, concerns are emerging about potential unintended consequences for staff members due to AI integration. With its capacity to learn and potentially exceed human performance in certain tasks, AI's role in the workplace is a contentious topic among researchers and experts. While some argue that AI's impact on human workers will be minimal, others foresee more substantial transformations. Flöck (2022) addresses these issues in their thesis, focusing on Generation Y's attitudes toward AI implementation in hospitality. The study aims to explore whether AI will entirely replace human workers or facilitate a harmonious coexistence between technology and human roles in the industry.

Gaber et al. (2024) conducted research aimed at exploring how Egyptian hotels can leverage artificial intelligence (AI) technologies to gain a competitive edge in the hospitality sector. The study emphasizes that the competitive advantage of Egyptian hotels can significantly increase through the strategic adoption of AI technologies. Aligning with Egypt Vision 2030, which outlines goals for national development, the research recommends enhancing government funding for the hospitality sector and fostering collaboration with international private companies. A key recommendation involves overcoming barriers to AI implementation in Egyptian hotel operations, promoting AI as a modern trend for the country. This approach includes optimizing AI to maintain smart systems efficiently, implementing smart hospitality practices to enhance market competitiveness, and considering factors such as service quality and pricing in deploying AI-driven services within hotels.

Lu's (2019) thesis aimed to assess the demand for artificial intelligence (AI) in hotels in Ho Chi Minh City, Vietnam, from the perspective of clients. The study employed quantitative methods, specifically a hand-out survey distributed to travelers who had stayed at hotels or used hotel amenities in the city. Survey results revealed diverse opinions among respondents regarding the adoption of AI in hospitality. While many recognized AI as a cutting-edge trend, factors such as cleanliness, round-the-clock service availability, and speed of service were highlighted as crucial considerations by respondents. Interestingly, a significant portion of the sample expressed a preference for interacting with human staff over AI systems. The findings underscore the need for further research to bridge gaps in understanding AI applications in the hospitality industry.

Kumar & Kharb (2023) highlight a significant shift in the hospitality industry regarding the adoption and impact of artificial intelligence (AI) on guest experiences. Historically lagging behind in AI integration, the industry now shows accelerated adoption, particularly aimed at enhancing guest experiences to rival or exceed those found in home or office environments. AI-enabled features are not only being recreated in guest rooms but are also being innovatively expanded upon to enhance the overall stay. While still in its early stages, AI is already reshaping consumer perceptions of resorts and travel experiences. The researchers predict a rapid evolution in AI's influence on hospitality in the coming years, ushering in a new era of guest experience in the industry.

Yassin et al. (2022) conducted a study to explore the implementation and impact of RAISA (Robots as Service Assistants) technology in the Egyptian hotel sector. The empirical research utilized a semi-structured interview approach with twenty IT managers from Egyptian hotels to gather qualitative data. Primary evidence was supplemented with secondary sources on RAISA technology in use within the Egyptian hospitality industry. The findings indicated that the Egyptian hotel industry may not be ideally suited for robots, despite potential benefits. Interviewees highlighted RAISA's strengths as improving operational performance, enhancing service quality, reducing human errors, and alleviating psychological and mental health challenges among staff. However, the study also underscored significant investment requirements and concerns regarding reduced human interaction opportunities between staff and guests as potential drawbacks of RAISA technology.

Rawal & Gandhi (2019) conducted a study aimed at exploring the current and future applications of artificial intelligence (AI) in the hospitality and hospitality management industries in India. The research focused on understanding customer satisfaction levels regarding hotel services and quality, service timing and methods, and the adoption of AI technologies within Indian hotels. The study revealed that only a small percentage of hotels in India currently employ AI, highlighting the nascent stage of AI adoption in the country's hospitality sector. The researchers emphasized the transformative potential of AI in hotel management, advocating for AI-powered software systems to enhance competitiveness and draw attention to Human-Computer Interaction (HCI) principles in hospitality settings.

Milton (2024) discusses the transformative potential of artificial intelligence (AI) in hotel cuisine, highlighting its promise in enhancing operational efficiency, sustainability initiatives, and personalized guest experiences. However, the integration of AI in hospitality also raises significant ethical concerns and operational challenges that need careful consideration. There is a notable gap in existing research concerning the moral implications of AI usage in hotel cuisine, particularly regarding algorithmic bias, data privacy issues, and the impact on human labor. As hotels increasingly utilize AI for guest interactions, menu engineering algorithms, and kitchen automation, ethical dilemmas arise around the collection and utilization of guest data. Addressing these challenges requires transparent and secure data practices, ensuring guest consent, and implementing accountability measures to mitigate algorithmic bias and promote fairness in AI-driven decision-making processes.

Koenig et al. (2023) address significant concerns in the hospitality industry regarding the potential displacement of human resources and the essential human touch amidst the rise of artificial intelligence (AI). The industry heavily relies on its vast human resource pool and the personal interaction that defines hospitality. The chapter underscores the pivotal role of personal interaction in the travel and hospitality sectors. It also examines the digital transformation witnessed in these industries, particularly accelerated by the COVID-19 pandemic, and explores AI applications in tourism for predictive analysis and virtual assistance during travel. The authors further explore AI's dual role in hotels and tourism: as a tool to complement human resources and enhance service quality, while also aiming to improve overall client experiences.

3. CONCLUSION

The hospitality industry is undergoing substantial transformations as a result of the implementation of Artificial Intelligence (AI) and automation. This literature review has analysed the various ways in which these technologies are revolutionising the sector, presenting both advantages and obstacles.

AI and automation enhance customer service by delivering prompt, precise, and tailored interactions via chatbots and virtual assistants. Efficiency is being enhanced by the automation of procedures such as check-ins, check-outs, and room service, resulting in error reduction and time savings. AI-driven data analytics enables hotels to forecast client preferences, optimise pricing strategies, and enhance guest happiness. Robotics is contributing to improving service delivery and resolving labour shortages.

Nevertheless, the implementation of AI and automation in the hospitality industry presents certain difficulties. There are apprehensions over the potential for job displacement and the necessity to provide workers with retraining opportunities when automated systems assume control of certain operations. Ensuring the privacy of guest data and complying with rules are of utmost importance. To ensure equitable and transparent service, it is imperative to tackle ethical concerns, such as mitigating biases in AI systems. Smaller firms may have challenges in adopting these technologies due to the significant costs associated with their implementation and maintenance.

This assessment emphasises the necessity of adopting a well-rounded strategy for incorporating artificial intelligence (AI) and automation in the hospitality sector. Although these technologies have the potential to enhance services and efficiency, it is crucial to tackle the issues by implementing strategic planning, ethical norms, and workforce development. By adopting this approach, the sector can attain long-term and environmentally friendly expansion while preserving the crucial element of personal interaction.

According to this study, it can be concluded that AI and automation play a crucial role in shaping the future of the hospitality industry. Efficient assimilation necessitates meticulous strategizing, conscientious consideration of ethical principles, and substantial investment in training. Further research and ongoing conversation will be crucial in order to effectively manage the intricacies of these technologies and guarantee that they enhance the overall hospitality experience.

REFERENCES

Bathla, G., Raina, A., & Rana, V. S. (2024). Artificial intelligence-driven enhancements in medical tourism: opportunities, challenges, and future prospects. In Hassan, V., Albattat, A., & Basheer, S. (Eds.), *Impact of AI and robotics on the medical tourism industry* (pp. 139–162). IGI Global., DOI: 10.4018/979-8-3693-2248-2.ch006

Buhalis, M. (2017). Voice Assistants in Hospitality: Using Artificial Intelligence for customer service. *Universitas Nusantara PGRI Kediri, 01*, 1–7.

Bulchand-Gidumal, J. (2022). Impact of Artificial Intelligence in Travel, Tourism, and Hospitality. Handbook of E-Tourism, 1943–1962. DOI: 10.1007/978-3-030-48652-5_110

Bulchand-Gidumal, J., William Secin, E., O'Connor, P., & Buhalis, D. (2024). Artificial intelligence's impact on hospitality and tourism marketing: Exploring key themes and addressing challenges. *Current Issues in Tourism, 27*(14), 2345–2362. DOI: 10.1080/13683500.2023.2229480

Chinnaraj, T. (2023). A Study on Automation in Hospitality Industry. *International Journal of Management, 14*(7), 154–157. https://www.researchgate.net/publication/376486077_A_STUDY_ON_AUTOMATION_IN_HOSPITALITY_INDUSTRY

Citak, J., Owoc, M. L., & Weichbroth, P. (2021). A note on the applications of artificial intelligence in the hospitality industry: Preliminary results of a survey. *Procedia Computer Science, 192*, 4552–4559. DOI: 10.1016/j.procs.2021.09.233

Drexler, N., & Lapré, V. B. (2019). Robotics and artificial intelligence. *Journal of Experimental & Theoretical Artificial Intelligence, 9*(2–3), 337–338. DOI: 10.1080/095281397147158

Ersoy, A., & Ehtiyar, V. R. (2023). The Impact of Artificial Intelligence on Hospitality Employees' Work Outcomes. *Advances in Hospitality and Tourism Research, 11*(4), 505–526. DOI: 10.30519/ahtr.1264966

Flöck, J. (2022). Assessing the Optimal Implementation of Artificial Intelligence Within the Hotel Industry for Generation Y. February.

Gaber, M. H. A. El, Kozmal, H. A., & Saber, A. F. (2024). The Impact of Artificial Intelligence Techniques as a Modern Trend to Reinforcing the Competitive Advantage in the Egyptian Hotels Establishments (Applied Study on Four and Five Stars Hotels). Revista Internacional De Turismo, Empresa Y Territorio, 7(2), 39–79. https://doi.org/DOI: 10.21071/riturem.v7i2.16186

Gaur, L., Afaq, A., Singh, G., & Dwivedi, Y. K. (2022). Role of artificial intelligence and robotics to foster the touchless travel during a pandemic: A review and research agenda. *Universitas Nusantara PGRI Kediri, 01*, 1–7.

Hodibert, V. A., Anderson, A. N., & Neequaye, K. (2024). AI/Robotics in the Tourism and Hospitality Sector: Technological Realities and Imaginaries in the Ghanaian Context. [IJRISS]. *INTERNATIONAL JOURNAL OF RESEARCH AND INNOVATION IN SOCIAL SCIENCE, VII*(2454), 1175–1189. DOI: 10.47772/IJRISS.2024.801181

Huang, A., Chao, Y., de la Mora Velasco, E., Bilgihan, A., & Wei, W. (2022). When artificial intelligence meets the hospitality and tourism industry: An assessment framework to inform theory and management. *Journal of Hospitality and Tourism Insights, 5*(5), 1080–1100. DOI: 10.1108/JHTI-01-2021-0021

Indora, A. (2024). Artificial Intelligence (AI) in the Hospitality Industry: A Review Article. *International Journal For Multidisciplinary Research, 6*(3), 1–10. DOI: 10.36948/ijfmr.2024.v06i03.19393

Ivanov, S. (2018). The impact of automation on tourism and hospitality jobs. *Grou, 23529*(2), 1–45.

Kim, H., So, K. K. F., Shin, S., & Li, J. (2024). Artificial Intelligence in Hospitality and Tourism: Insights From Industry Practices, Research Literature, and Expert Opinions. *Journal of Hospitality & Tourism Research (Washington, D.C.)*, (January). Advance online publication. DOI: 10.1177/10963480241229235

Koenig, S., Chan, S. H., Li, J., & Zheng, Y. (2023). Artificial Intelligence and Automation. *Springer Handbooks*, (Part F674), 205–231. DOI: 10.1007/978-3-030-96729-1_9

Kumar, S., Kumar, V., & Attri, K. (2021). Impact of artificial intelligence and service robots in tourism and hospitality sector: current use & future trends. Administrative Development: A Journal of HIPA, Shimla, 8(SI-1), 59-83.

Kumar, S., & Kharb, P. Impact of Artificial Intelligence in Giving a New Dimension to the Hospitality Industry.

Limna, P. (2023). Artificial Intelligence (AI) in the Hospitality Industry: A Review Article. *International Journal of Computing Sciences Research*, *7*(May), 1306–1317. DOI: 10.25147/ijcsr.2017.001.1.103

Lu, L. (2019). OPPORTUNITIES OF ARTIFICIAL INTELLIGENCE IN HOSPITALITY INDUSTRY FOR INNOVATIVE CUSTOMER SERVICES.

Malone, C. (2024). Artificial Intelligence in the Hotel Industry: The Benefits and Effects on Corporations.

Milton, T. (2024). International Journal for Multidimensional Research Perspectives International Journal for Multidimensional Research Perspectives (IJMRP) (47) Artificial Intelligence Transforming Hotel Gastronomy: An In-depth Review of AI-driven Innovations in Menu Desig. *International Journal for Multidimensional Research Perspectives*, *2*(3), 47–61. DOI: 10.61877/ijmrp.v2i3.126

Mingotto, E., Montaguti, F., & Tamma, M. (2020). Challenges in re-designing operations and jobs to embody AI and robotics in services. Findings from a case in the hospitality industry. *Electronic Markets*, *31*(3), 493–510. DOI: 10.1007/s12525-020-00439-y

Naumov, N. (2019). The impact of robots, artifiial intelligence, and service automation on service quality and service experience in hospitality. Robots, Artificial Intelligence and Service Automation in Travel, Tourism and Hospitality, 123–133. DOI: 10.1108/978-1-78756-687-320191007

O'Hara, L. (2021). Applying Artificial Intelligence in the Hotel Industry_ Exploring. Human Nutrition and Hospitality Management Undergraduate Honors Theses. https://scholarworks.uark.edu/hnhiuht/19

Rawal, R., & Gandhi, S. (2019). Artificial intelligence in hotel management & hospitability sector in India. *Journal of Emerging Technologies and Innovative Research*, *6*(4), 92–97.

Ruel, H., & Njoku, E. (2020). AI redefining the hospitality industry. *Journal of Tourism Futures*, *7*(1), 53–66. DOI: 10.1108/JTF-03-2020-0032

Sachan, S., Shukla, A., & Shukla, S. (2024).. . *Exploring the Impact of Artificial Intelligence Integration in Hotel Management Information Systems : Enhancing Efficiency, Customer Experience, and Operational Performance*, *10*(10), 339–344.

Saini, A., & Bhalla, R. (2021). Artificial Intelligence and Automation. 88–97. DOI: 10.4018/978-1-7998-8497-2.ch006

Samala, N., Katkam, B. S., Bellamkonda, R. S., & Rodriguez, R. V. (2022). Impact of AI and robotics in the tourism sector: A critical insight. *Journal of Tourism Futures*, *8*(1), 73–87. DOI: 10.1108/JTF-07-2019-0065

Talukder, M. B., Kabir, F., Muhsina, K., & Das, I. R. (2023). Emerging Concepts of Artificial Intelligence in the Hotel Industry: A Conceptual Paper. *International Journal of Research Publication and Reviews*, *4*(9), 1765–1769. DOI: 10.55248/gengpi.4.923.92451

Vijaya, K. (2022). Role of Artificial Intelligence in Psychology. *Scholarly Research Journal for Humanity Science and English Language*, *10*(53), 13476–13486. DOI: 10.21922/srjhsel.v10i53.11649

Yassin, E. S. G., Gharieb, A. E., Saad, H. E., & Qura, O. E. (2022). Robots, artificial intelligence, and service automation (RAISA) technologies in the Egyptian hotel sector: A current situation assessment. International Journal of Heritage. *Tourism and Hospitality*, *16*(1), 51–60.

Chapter 34

Unlocking the Potential of Blockchain Technology in Services: A Comprehensive Overview

T. Bharathi
https://orcid.org/0000-0002-1946-2315
ISBR Business School, India

Ashok V. Mammen
https://orcid.org/0000-0002-7283-9804
Dr. N.S.A.M. First Grade College, India

Singari Keerthi
https://orcid.org/0009-0007-9630-1631
Yenopaya University, India

ABSTRACT

Blockchain technology has transformed service industries by offering transparent, secure, and decentralized solutions across sectors like finance, supply chain and logistics, healthcare, government, digital rights, energy, real estate, education, law, telecommunications, and hospitality. In finance, it supports decentralized finance, smart contracts, and cryptocurrencies. In supply chains, it enhances traceability, transparency, logistics, and prevents counterfeiting. In healthcare, it secures patient data, ensures pharmaceutical integrity, and aids clinical studies. Blockchain improves government services with secure digital identities, voting, and public records. It protects intellectual property and ensures fair royalty distribution in digital rights. In energy, it facilitates peer-to-peer trading and renewable certificates, while in real estate, it streamlines transactions. It also improves credential verification, document management, and fraud protection in education, law, and telecommunications. The article shows these applications that transform service industries.

DOI: 10.4018/979-8-3693-7447-4.ch034

1 INTRODUCTION

Blockchain technology is recognized for its unique and decentralised framework which provides a revolutionary method of data management and security. Earlier days this technology was considered to be associated with crypto-currencies like bitcoin, but now they exceed the scope of financial operations. The current study describes the role of blockchain in various service sectors, showcasing its potential to improve efficiency, transparency, and security.

The term 'Blockchain technology' was coined in 2008 by an individual or by an association using the false identity Satoshi Nakamoto. It was initially introduced as the foundation for the first type in cryptocurrency, namely, Bitcoin. The idea was to find a decentralized and secure system for recording and verifying transactions without the need for intermediaries like banks or governments. This innovation laid the groundwork for a revolutionary way of managing digital transactions and data.

Blockchain' is also known as distributed ledger technology (DLT) which stores data over a network of computers called nodes, and not on a single central server. The "block" refers to a collection of data, typically representing transactions, and the "chain" refers to a chain of interconnected blocks arranged in a sequence, as the data occurs. Each block includes a list of transactions, a timestamp, and a reference tag (hash) linked to the preceding block, thus creating a secure and unalterable chain of records.

1.1 The Evolution of Blockchain

Since its introduction with Bitcoin, (Nakamoto, 2008) blockchain technology has evolved significantly. Ethereum in 2015 introduced the concept of smart contracts that automatically execute an agreement which are in the form of written codes. This broadened the scope of blockchain beyond financial transactions to include applications like decentralized finance (DeFi), supply chain management, healthcare, and more. (Swan, 2015)

In order to satisfy particular demands, blockchains are also being investigated in hybrid forms, which combine components of both public and private blockchains. Most businesses operate internal processes using private blockchains and engage with public blockchains for external transactions.

1.2 The Blockchain Process'

1. **Initiation of a Transaction**: A user initiates a transaction request which may involve the transfer of data, bitcoin, or the carrying out of a smart contract.
2. **Broadcasting to Network**: A peer-to-peer (P2P) network is connected with nodes (computers') that receives the desired transaction via broadcast. Algorithms are used to validate the transactions at the nodes.
3. **Validation**: Pre-established norms validate the transactions in the nodes using consensus procedures. This is accomplished with a certification called Proof of Work (PoW), in which the users confirm their transactions and incorporate them into the blockchain with the help of mathematical puzzles.
4. **Creating a Block**: New block of data is created by grouping transactions with other transactions after it being verified. Subsequently, this block is irreversibly and permanently added to the current blockchain. (Valeri & Albattat., 2024)
5. **Completion stage**: After the transaction is completed, the newly created block is appended to the chain and becomes visible to every member in the network.

1.3 Characteristics of Blockchain

- **Distribution:** Since the ledger is dispersed throughout all network nodes, there cannot be just one point of control or failure.

- **Public/Private**: Blockchains may be private (limited to specific individuals) or public (available to all). Blockchains which are private offer higher level of privacy and control, whereas public blockchains are completely transparent.
- **Cryptographic Security**: Blockchain adopts cryptographic methods to ensure data security and transaction authenticity.

1.4 Impact and Future Potential

Blockchain technology has the potential to disrupt traditional industries by providing more efficient, transparent, and secure ways to manage data and transactions (Tapscott and Tapscott, 2016). Its applications are being explored in various sectors, including finance, healthcare, government, and supply chain management. (Mougayar, 2016)

As the technology matures, challenges such as scalability, energy consumption (particularly with PoW-based blockchains), and regulatory acceptance are being addressed. The future of blockchain is likely to see increased integration with other emerging technologies like artificial intelligence (AI) and the Internet of Things (IoT), further expanding its capabilities and applications. (Zheng et al., 2017)

2. KEY SERVICE SECTORS UTILIZING BLOCKCHAIN TECHNOLOGY

2.1 Financial Services

Blockchain technology is disrupting financial services that run on traditional technology by enabling secure, transparent, and efficient transactions. This disruption is largely due to the decentralization of financial processes which removes the need for intermediaries. It reduces the costs and speeds up transaction times (Tapscott & Tapscott, 2016). The security of blockchain is enhanced through cryptographic techniques and its distributed nature thereby mitigates the risks of cyberattacks and fraud that traditional systems face (Zheng et al., 2017).

Transparency is another key advantage as blockchain ensures that all transactions are visible and verifiable by all participants in the network, fostering trust and reducing the chances for fraud (Mougayar, 2016). Additionally, blockchain's efficiency is particularly evident in cross-border transactions where it eliminates the delays and costs associated with multiple intermediaries (Tapscott & Tapscott, 2016; Ponsam., Shaw., & Patil., 2023).

Smart contracts, a feature of blockchain technology, automate and enforce agreements without the need for manual intervention which further increases efficiency in financial transactions (Zheng et al., 2017). Moreover, blockchain's ability to provide financial services in underbanked regions promotes greater financial inclusion, offering a cost-effective alternative to traditional banking systems (Mougayar, 2016; Üçoğlu, D. 2022).

Applications:

- **Cryptocurrencies:** The digital currencies like Ethereum and Bitcoin which adopt block chain technology allow for peer-to-peer trades where no middlemen is required. (Nakamoto, 2008; Kahyaoglu., & Tecim., 2024).
- **Smart Contracts:** Contracts are automated and they self-execute when certain requirements are satisfied, thus eliminating the work of middlemen and boosting confidence (Antonopoulos, 2017; Rani., & Taneja., 2024). Ethereum is a blockchain structure used for developing smart contracts and decentralized apps.
- **Cross-Border Payments:** Blockchain lowers prices and speeds up cross-border transactions. Ripple is a platform for real-time cross-border payments using blockchain technology. (Tapscott & Tapscott, 2016).

2.2 Supply Chain and Logistics

By offering unchangeable transaction records and product travels, blockchain improves supply-chain management by guaranteeing the participating parties access to the right and transparent data. Because of its immutability, the supply chain's total traceability and accountability are improved while the risk of fraud, counterfeiting, and errors is decreased (Tapscott & Tapscott, 2016; Paksoy., Kochan., & Ali., 2020). Blockchain enables accurate tracking of commodities from the point of origin to the point of destination, facilitating the verification of product authenticity and its condition at every stage of the route through the creation of an irreversible, permanent ledger (Mougayar, 2016).

Applications:

- **Traceability:** the technology is used to track products from origin to delivery, ensuring transparency and reducing fraud to zero levels. 'IBM-Food Trust', use blockchain to ensure the traceability and safety of food items. 'TradeLens', is a blockchain platform developed by IBM and Maersk to enhance supply chain transparency (IBM, 2019).
- **Smart Contracts:** these are contracts with automated processes like payments and compliance checks within the supply chains (Crosby et al., 2016).

2.3 Healthcare services

Enhancing patient data management, strengthening the security of electronic health records (EHRs), and facilitating the safe and transparent exchange of medical information between various healthcare providers are just a few of the major applications that blockchain technology offers, that can greatly benefit hospitals and healthcare systems (Zheng et al., 2017). Furthermore, blockchain technology has the potential to optimize administrative procedures, minimize fraudulent activities, and enhance pharmaceutical traceability, guaranteeing that patients receive only authentic products (Mougayar, 2016).

Applications:

1. Patient Data Management
    - **Secure and Interoperable Health Records:** Blockchain can store patient health records securely on a decentralized ledger. This ensures data integrity, reduces the risk of data breaches, and allows seamless access to health information across different healthcare providers (Yue, Wang, Jin, & Jin, 2016).
    - **Patient Consent Management:** Smart contracts can be used to manage and enforce patient consent for data sharing and research participation, ensuring transparency and compliance with privacy regulations (Mettler, 2016).

Projects like MedRec and Medicalchain are exploring blockchain solutions for secure patients data management and sharing.

2. Supply Chain Management
    - **Traceability of Pharmaceuticals and Medical Supplies:** Blockchain can track the journey of pharmaceuticals and medical devices from manufacturer to patient, ensuring authenticity, reducing counterfeit products, and improving supply chain transparency (Mettler, 2016).
    - **Inventory Management:** Hospitals can use blockchain to streamline inventory management processes, ensuring adequate stock levels and reducing wastage (Sinclair, 2017) and to track and verify

the authenticity of drugs, thus preventing counterfeits (MediLedger, 2020). Companies like IBM and Pfizer are collaborating on blockchain initiatives to improve pharmaceutical supply chain transparency and efficiency.

3. Billing and Claims Management
    - **Streamlined Insurance Claims Processing:** Blockchain can automate and streamline insurance claims processing, reducing administrative costs, minimizing fraud, and improving transparency in financial transactions (Yue et al., 2016).
    - **Smart Contracts:** Smart contracts can facilitate automated verification and payment processes between healthcare providers and insurers based on predefined conditions (Mettler, 2016; Zafar, Kumar, Appathurai, & Cakir, 2024). Companies like Gem are developing blockchain solutions to improve efficiency and transparency in healthcare billing and claims management.
4. Clinical Trials and Research
    - **Enhanced Transparency and Integrity:** Blockchain can provide a transparent and immutable record of clinical trial data, ensuring the integrity of research findings and facilitating collaboration among researchers (Kuo, Rojas, & Ohno-Machado, 2017).
    - **Data Sharing:** Blockchain technology allows secure and efficient sharing of research data while maintaining patient confidentiality and data ownership (Mettler, 2016). Projects such as the MIT Media Lab's Open Algorithms (OPAL) initiative are exploring blockchain's potential in improving transparency and data sharing in clinical research.
5. Cybersecurity and Data Privacy
    - **Data Security:** Blockchain's decentralized architecture and cryptographic techniques make it inherently secure against tampering and unauthorized access, thus reducing the risk of data breaches (Yue et al., 2016; Tyagi., George, & Soni., 2023).
    - **Patient Identity Management:** Blockchain-based solutions can improve patient identity management, reduce medical identity theft and ensure accurate patient identification across healthcare systems (Kuo et al., 2017; Hanchate & Ahire, 2024). Initiatives like Guardtime and Factom are leveraging blockchain to enhance cybersecurity and data integrity in healthcare.

2.4 Government and Public Services

Blockchain technology is improving transparency, efficiency, and security, which is revolutionizing public service delivery and government operations. It provides an unchangeable record-keeping system that guarantees the transparency and tamper-proofness of all transactions and procedures. Blockchain enhances public services' speed and dependability by automating bureaucratic procedures and cutting expenses. Furthermore, the technology enhances public trust and engagement by safeguarding sensitive data and facilitating more transparent voting procedures. Governments may achieve more efficient and responsible governance by implementing blockchain which will benefit institutions and citizens alike.

Applications:

- Digital Identity: Every citizen has a digital identity that is safely saved on blockchain, accessible and verifiable only by those with proper permission. This method guarantees that private data is shielded from unwanted modifications or abuse. Furthermore, people are able to manage their own identification data thanks to blockchain's openness and immutability, which only permit access when required and provide an auditable trail of the information's usage. In addition to lowering the possibility of identity fraud and streamlining procedures like online voting, obtaining public services, and confirming legal papers, this can greatly increase public trust in government institutions. Estonia's e-Residency: Offers a blockchain-based digital identity for accessing services. (Ølnes, Ubacht, & Janssen, 2017)

- Voting Systems: By guaranteeing security, transparency, and confidence in the electoral process, blockchain-based voting systems are completely changing the way elections are held. Voter fraud, manipulation, and a lack of transparency are common issues with traditional voting systems that can erode public confidence in the outcome. By offering a decentralized, immutable ledger where every vote is recorded safely and are unchangeable, blockchain solves these problems. Voters can preserve privacy and openness by confirming that their vote has been counted without disclosing their identify. This method significantly lessens the chance of fraud because it would be nearly impossible to change every node in the network in order to rig the vote. Elections are made more accessible and secure by utilizing blockchain technology which also increases confidence in democratic processes and thus makes the electoral systems more dependable and effective. Voatz, uses blockchain for secure mobile voting (Voatz, 2020).

2.5 Intellectual Property and Digital Rights

Blockchain technology, with its immutable record-keeping capabilities, is essential for managing digital information and protecting intellectual property (IP). Managing digital rights and safeguarding intellectual property have always been difficult tasks that are open to theft, piracy, and unlawful dissemination. By establishing an unchangeable, permanent record of ownership, authorship, and usage rights, blockchain solves these problems. Digital content is timestamped and associated with a particular owner each time it is registered on the blockchain, be it a creative work, patent, or trademark. This record serves as unquestionable proof of ownership because it cannot be changed or removed. Additionally, blockchain-based smart contracts can automate usage rights enforcement, royalty payments, and licensing agreements, guaranteeing that authors receive just compensation for their labour. Blockchain protects the artists' and the interest of the right holders' in the digital era by offering a transparent and safe means to track and enforce the intellectual property laws thus lowering the possibility of disputes and unlawful use.

Applications:

- **Digital Content Authentication:** Blockchain technology fills a developing gap in the digital content sector by providing a strong means of confirming the ownership and legitimacy of digital assets. To preserve creators' rights and preserve consumer confidence, it is crucial to guarantee the authenticity and correct attribution of digital art, music, films, and other types of digital content as they proliferate. Blockchain technology can create ledgers that are unchangeable; that records information about the provenance of digital assets, such as the inventor, ownership history, and any transactions that have occurred with the asset. By ensuring that the authenticity of the digital information can be checked at any moment, this clear and impenetrable record helps to avoid problems like forgery, unauthorized duplication, and fictitious ownership claims. Platforms and producers may provide a trustworthy authentication method through blockchain, increasing the value of digital goods and boosting buyer and collector confidence. Ascribe was designed to manage the ownership of digital content using blockchain technology. Inscribe (2017).
- **Royalty Distribution:** Blockchain technology is automating and tracking the entire process, revolutionizing the way content creators receive and manage royalties. Payments to writers, musicians, painters, and other creators in traditional royalty distribution systems frequently include several middlemen, which can cause delays, inconsistencies, and occasionally unfair compensation. Smart contracts are self-executed contracts where the conditions of the agreement are encoded into the blockchain thus the procedure is simplified. The smart contract ensures that payments are precise, prompt, and transparent by automatically calculating and allocating royalties to creators in accordance with pre-established terms whenever digital content is used or sold. All parties involved have more trust as a result of this automation, which also minimizes errors

and lowers administrative overhead. Furthermore, authors can monitor the usage of their creations in real time through the blockchain's transparent ledger, which offers precise and corroborating documentation of the creation and distribution of royalties. This invention improves the efficiency and accountability of the overall revenue distribution process, which guarantees the creators an equitable compensation. Ujo Music, is a platform for managing music rights and royalties (Ujo Music, 2018).

2.6 Energy and Utilities

By promoting a decentralized energy management system and sustainability, blockchain technology is advancing the energy and utilities industries significantly. Conventional energy systems frequently have centralized power generation and delivery under the management of big utility companies. Increased expenses, inefficiencies, and obstacles to the use of renewable energy sources can result from this centralization. By facilitating peer-based energy trading, which allows customers to trade extra energy to and from each other without the interference of middlemen, blockchain upends this paradigm. By using a decentralized method, communities and individuals may produce, store, and distribute renewable energy more effectively.

Applications:

- **Energy Trading:** Peer-to-peer (P2P) trading of energy is made easier by blockchain technology, which allows producers and consumers to transact directly on decentralized platforms. Energy trading has always been overseen by centralized utility companies, which has the potential to increase price, limit consumer options, and create inefficiencies. With blockchain, anyone who produce excess energy—like from solar panels—can exchange it directly with their neighbours or other network users, avoiding middlemen. Smart contracts running on blockchain platforms enable peer-to-peer (P2P) trade by automatically matching buyers and sellers, managing transactions, and guaranteeing safe, transparent, and unchangeable records of energy exchanges. This strategy was first introduced by platforms such as Power Ledger, which enables users to exchange energy locally, lower energy expenses, and support a more decentralized and sustainable energy system. Blockchain technology empowers customers, promotes the wider use of renewable energy, and improves the efficiency of the energy markets by enabling peer-to-peer energy trade, Power Ledger: Uses blockchain for peer-to-peer energy trading. (Power Ledger, 2018; Zhao., Yu., Yuan, & Liu., 2024).
- **Certificates of Renewable Energy:** Renewable Energy Certificates (RECs), which are essential for certifying and encouraging the production and consumption of renewable energy, can be tracked and traded in an inventive way thanks to blockchain technology. Renewable Energy Certificates (RECs) serve as proof that a specific quantity of energy was produced using sustainable methods like solar, wind, or hydropower. REC tracking and trading have historically included intricate procedures that are vulnerable to mistakes, fraud, and inefficiency. Blockchain provides a decentralized, transparent ledger record that tracks the creation, ownership, and transfer of RECs in real time, thereby resolving these concerns. WePower: A blockchain platform for trading renewable energy.

2.7 Real Estate

Blockchain technology offers a safe, effective, and transparent way to capture and manage property-related data, which streamlines real estate transactions and guarantees transparency in property management. Conventional real estate transactions typically entail a great deal of paperwork, several middlemen, and drawn-out procedures, all of which can cause delays, raise expenses, and increase the chance of mistakes. Blockchain offers a decentralized, immutable ledger were all property transactions, ownership details, and modifications are safely recorded, thereby addressing these issues.

Blockchain can expedite the purchase or sale of real estate by using smart contracts to automate and validate the ownership transfer. When certain circumstances are satisfied, like payment completion and property rights transfer, these digital contracts go into automated execution. This speeds up the transaction process and lowers expenses by eliminating the need for middlemen like title firms and attorneys.

Applications:

- **Property Transactions**: Through safe and effective platforms, blockchain technology simplifies the procedures in purchasing, selling, and renting real estate. Conventional real estate transactions can be expensive as well as time-consuming since they frequently entail a lot of paperwork, several middlemen, and drawn-out verification procedures. Blockchain provides a decentralized, transparent, and unchangeable ledger related to property transactions, which solves these issues. Blockchain technology is used by platforms such as 'Propy to automate and secure these transactions.

Smart contracts automatically carry out and validate the terms of the transaction, including the transfer of ownership and payment, when purchasing or selling real estate on a blockchain platform. This expedites the process and lowers related expenses by eliminating the middlemen like brokers and title agencies. Furthermore, blockchain ensures that the history of the property is accurate and available to all parties involved by providing a tamper-proof record of property dealings and ownership changes.

Blockchain platforms have the ability to handle rental agreements and payments for leasing through smart contracts. These contracts guarantee that lease terms are automatically enforced and that payments are completed securely. The automation and transparency increase productivity while lowering the possibility of mistakes or disagreements. Propy: Uses blockchain to facilitate property transactions (Propy, 2020).

- **Land Registry:** Blockchain technology preserves transparent and unchangeable records of land ownership, revolutionizing land registries. Conventional land registration systems frequently have problems with fraudulent claims, inefficient bureaucracy, and inaccurate record-keeping. Blockchain offers a decentralized ledger that records every land transaction and ownership change in an unchangeable and transparent manner, hence addressing these issues.

Every piece of land is associated with a distinct digital record on a blockchain-based land registry, which contains information on ownership, boundaries, and any encumbrances or claims. The accuracy and security of ownership information are guaranteed by the inability to change or remove this record. Because blockchain technology is decentralized, several nodes throughout the network maintain the ledger, reducing the possibility of a single failure point and enhancing the applications resistance to fraud and tampering. Sweden's Land Registry uses blockchain for recording and verifying property transactions.

2.8 Education

Blockchain technology plays a significant role in securing educational records and credentials, ensuring their authenticity, and facilitating lifelong learning. Traditional methods of managing educational records often involve paper-based certificates and centralized databases which are susceptible to fraud, loss, and inaccuracies. Blockchain can solve these issues by maintaining a decentralized and immutable ledger for recording academic achievements, qualifications, and certifications.

By using blockchain, educational institutions can issue digital diplomas, certificates, and transcripts that are securely stored on a blockchain network. Each record is encoded and then linked to the individual's unique digital identity, making it virtually not possible to alter or forge. This ensures that the credentials are both authentic and verifiable, allowing the business owners, educational institutions, and stakeholders to easily confirm the validity of a person's qualifications.

Applications:

- **Credential Verification:** Blockchain technology improves the issuance and verification of academic certificates by providing a safe and transparent arrangement to manage credentials. Traditional methods of verifying academic qualifications often involve manual checks and reliance on centralized databases, which will be time-consuming and prone to errors.

Platforms like Blockcerts leverage blockchain to issue digital certificates that are cryptographically secured and linked to a unique digital identity. When an academic institution issues a certificate on a blockchain platform, it is automatically recorded in the blockchain, where it is tamper-proof and is made available to all the participating parties. This means that employers, educational institutions, and other stakeholders can easily verify the authenticity of the credentials by checking the blockchain ledger, ensuring that the certificates have not been altered or forged (Blockcerts, 2020).

- **Learning Management Systems:** This technology can significantly enhance Learning Management Systems (LMS). It provides a transparent and secure method for tracing and managing student achievements. The traditional LMS platforms usually face challenges related to data integrity, accessibility, and verification of academic records. Blockchain addresses the above issues by offering a decentralized and robust ledger for recording student progress and accomplishments. Blockcerts are open standards to issue and verify educational credentials using blockchain

With blockchain, every achievement, such as completed courses, certifications, and grades, can be recorded in a protected and tamper-proof digital ledger. Each entry is secured and connected to the student's unique digital identity, ensuring that records are accurate and cannot be altered without detection. This transparency allows educators, students, and employers to access reliable and verifiable information about a student's academic history. Sony Global Education uses blockchain to manage educational data and credentials.

2.9 Legal Services

Traditional legal processes often involve complex paperwork, numerous intermediaries, and lengthy verification procedures, which can be prone to errors/mistakes, fraud, and inefficiency in performance. Blockchain helps to address these challenges by offering a decentralized ledger where all legal actions, agreements, and documents are maintained in a secure and tamper-proof manner.

The vital application of blockchain in legal services is the adoption of smart contracts. Once the predefined conditions are reached in the draft document, the contracts enforcing the terms of an agreement are self-executed. As these are certified smart contracts, the system reduces the number for intermediaries such as lawyers and notaries. This not only streamlines contract execution, but it also minimizes the probable disputes and delays. Smart contracts can be used for various legal applications, including property transactions, business agreements, and regulatory compliance.

Applications:

- **Smart Contracts:** Blockchain technology enables the automation of legal agreements by means of contracts that are smart, which significantly limits the intermediaries. Smart contracts are self-executed contracts in which the agreement rules and conditions are encoded into blockchain network. Once the predefined conditions are received, the contract automatically executes its terms without requiring manual intervention or oversight.

This automation streamlines various legal processes by removing the interference of intermediaries such as lawyers, notaries, and contract administrators. For instance, in property transactions, a smart contract will be able to automatically transfer ownership and release payment once both parties fulfill their obligations, such as signing documents and transferring funds. This reduces delays, minimizes the potential for errors, and lowers transaction costs (OpenLaw, 2020).

- **Document Management**: The Blockchain technology provides a secure and effective method for storing, managing and retrieving legal documents. Traditional document management systems usually face challenges related to data security, integrity, and accessibility. OpenLaw is a platform for creating and managing smart legal contracts.

When legal documents are stored on a blockchain, each document is linked to a unique digital record that is encrypted and securely stored. This record cannot be changed which means that a document once created and recorded cannot be changed. This immutability ensures that the document's integrity is preserved and that it remains a reliable source of truth. LawCoin uses blockchain for funding and managing legal cases.

2.10 Telecommunications

Traditional telecommunications systems often involve multiple intermediaries, complex billing processes, and significant security concerns. Blockchain addresses these challenges by offering solutions that streamline operations and bolster security.

Blockchain can improve efficiency in telecommunications through its non-centralized setup, which reduces the number for intermediaries and central authorities. For instance, blockchain can streamline the process of managing and settling inter-carrier transactions, such as roaming agreements and cross-border data exchanges. By automating these transactions with smart contracts, telecom companies can reduce administrative overhead, speed up settlement times, and minimize errors. Additionally, blockchain's transparent ledger provides real-time visibility into transactions and network performance, enabling more effective monitoring and optimization of services.

Security is a major critical zone where blockchain excels. Telecommunications networks are often prone to various security threats, like fraud, data breaches, and unauthorized access. Blockchain enhances security to give a tamper-proof record for transactions and communications. Each transaction is cryptographically secured and chronicled on a de-centralized ledger, making it impossible for malicious actions that can alter or forge the data. It safeguards the sensitive and important information related to customer data and network configurations, and protects from tampering and unauthorized access.

Applications:

- **Roaming Agreements:** Roaming agreements between telecom operators often involve multiple parties, intricate billing arrangements, and a high potential for errors and disputes. Traditional systems for managing these agreements can be cumbersome and inefficient, with slow reconciliation processes and opportunities for fraud. Blockchain addresses these challenges related to roaming agreements. When telecom operators enter into a roaming agreement, the terms and conditions, including pricing and usage limits can be securely registered on the blockchain. This ledger provides a single, transparent view of the agreement that can be used by all authorized parties, reducing the likelihood of disputes and errors.

Smart contracts can be applied on roaming agreements. The contracts automatically handle billing and payment processes based on predefined terms, ensuring accurate and timely transactions. It reduces administrative overhead and speeds up the reconciliation process, leading to more efficient management of roaming agreements. (Kshetri, 2017). Telcoin, integrates telecom services with blockchain for secure transactions.

- **Fraud Prevention:** Each transaction that is recorded on the blockchain is cryptographically secured and can be altered only with network consensus which ensures that the data remains accurate and tamper-proof. The decentralised nature of data storage and verifications ensures that the data is distributed across the network and no single person can tamper with an existing set of transactions or document, thereby reducing the risk of data breaches and unauthorized access. Compromising the network would require altering the data across all nodes simultaneously, which is a virtually impossible task. Each user's identity is linked to a unique cryptographic key, which does not permit a stranger to access their accounts and perform transactions. This reduces the chances of unauthorized access and fraudulent activities. Guardtime, uses blockchain to secure telecom data and infrastructure.

2.11 Hospitality Industry

Blockchain technology revolutionizes booking systems in the hospitality industry by improving transparency, productivity, and security. Conventional booking systems have multiple intermediaries, complex processes, and potential issues related to fraud, errors, and data breaches. Blockchain addresses these challenges and provides a seamless secure booking process. The transparency allows both customers and service providers to view and verify all booking details, including transaction histories and payment records. It reduces the disputes and provides up-to-date information to all the parties thereby maintaining trust and confidence in the booking process.

Applications:

- **Fraud Prevention:** It effectively prevents double bookings and fraudulent activities in the hospitality industry. In traditional booking systems, the risk of double bookings and fraud arises from centralized databases that can be prone to errors, unauthorized access, and manipulation. Blockchain enables real-time updates and synchronization of reservation data across all parties involved. This real-time visibility ensures that any changes to reservations, such as cancellations or modifications are immediately reflected in the system. The risk of overbooking can be addressed and the system provides accurate information about the availability of rooms and services.
- **Direct Bookings**: The traditional way of booking often involves several intermediaries, such as travel agents, platforms for booking, and payment processors which can increase the costs and complexity. Blockchain simplifies this process by enabling direct transactions between customers and service providers. Smart contracts can automate the booking process, handle reservations, payments, and cancellations without the need for intermediaries. This reduces administrative overhead, speeds up transaction times, and lowers costs. (Tyan & Hamade, 2020). Winding Tree is a decentralized travel marketplace that connects travellers directly with service providers, reducing booking fees and increasing transparency.
- **Personalized Guest Experiences**: Blockchain technology can enhance guest experiences by securely storing and managing guest preferences and history.

- **Data Security**: Guests can securely store their preferences and history on a blockchain, which can be accessed by hotels to personalize services while ensuring data privacy (Zheng et al., 2018).
- **Streamlined Check-In**: Blockchain-based digital identities can streamline the check-in process, reducing wait times and enhancing convenience (Hughes, 2019). StayBit is a blockchain driven platform that permits guests to manage their travel experiences and preferences.
- **Secure and Efficient Payments**: Blockchain can streamline payment processes in the hospitality industry, providing secure, fast, and low-cost transactions.
- **Cryptocurrency Payments:** Hotels can accept cryptocurrencies, offering a secure and efficient payment method that reduces transaction fees (Nakamoto, 2008). **TravelbyBit is** a platform that enables travelers to pay for services using cryptocurrencies.
- **Smart Contracts:** Automated payments through smart contracts can reduce the need for intermediaries and ensure timely transactions (Tapscott & Tapscott, 2016).
- **Verified Guest Reviews**: Blockchain ensures the authenticity of guest reviews, providing a reliable and tamper-proof system for collecting and verifying feedback.
- **Data Privacy and Security:** Blockchain enhances privacy of data and it records, stores and manages sensitive guest information in a secure manner.
- **Authentic Reviews:** Blockchain prevents fake reviews by recording each review on an immutable ledger, ensuring that only genuine reviews are displayed (Yaga et al., 2019). Revain is a review platform that ensures the authenticity and immutability of reviews.
- **Decentralized Platforms:** It supports the creation of decentralized review platforms where reviews cannot be altered or deleted by third parties (Pilkington, 2016).
- **Decentralized Data Storage:** the information about the guest is stored on a decentralized network and the technology assures that data breaches do not occur (Kshetri, 2017).
- **Guest-Controlled Data:** the guests can control their own data and decide on the information that he or she wishes to share (He, 2018). Civic is a blockchain platform for secure identity and data management.

3. CHALLENGES AND CONSIDERATIONS

The blockchain technology contributes significantly to the service sector, by providing a robust system with enhanced transparency, security, and efficiency.

1. Scalability Issues: Most blockchain networks, like Ethereum and Bitcoin faces the issues related to scalability. This technology is currently able to handle only limited transactions per second because of its decentralized nature of functioning.
2. Interoperability: Different blockchain platforms use various protocols, which can create challenges in communication and data exchange between them.
3. Regulatory and Compliance Issues: The legal and regulatory framework are still nascent for blockchain technology. This uncertainty can be an hinderance to the adoption of blockchain in sectors that are heavily regulated, such as finance, healthcare, and insurance.
4. Data Privacy Concerns: the technology is lauded for its robust security and transparency, but may have disastrous effects if the total system can in any way be breached, as it would leak sensitive personal data, such as healthcare or finance.
5. High Initial Costs and Investment: The development and deployment of blockchain solutions will require significant investment in technology, infrastructure, and talent.
6. Talent and Expertise Shortage: Blockchain technology is new, and talent shortage is a matter of concern. High expertise and skills are required to develop and manage blockchain applications.

7. Integration with Existing Systems: syncing the existing legacy systems with a totally new technology raises compatibility issues. This can be complex, time consuming and costly.
8. Security Risks: though it is considered to be secure it is not totally immune to attacks, as there can be vulnerabilities in smart contract codes.
9. User Adoption and Change Management: Resistance to change among employees and customers can stop the adoption of blockchain technology in service-based businesses.
10. Environmental Impact: Some blockchain chains, especially the ones using Proof of Work (PoW), consume higher levels of energy and resources which can lead to concerns related to environmental sustainability.

4. FUTURE TRENDS AND INNOVATIONS

1. Integration with IoT and AI: The blending of blockchain with artificial intelligence (AI) and Internet of Things (IoT) is set to revolutionize the service sector (Kumar., Mondal., Verma., & Mani., 2024). Smart contracts on blockchain can autonomously execute transactions based on data collected from IoT devices improving automation and efficiency. For example, in supply chain management, IoT devices could track product conditions in real-time, while blockchain ensures data integrity and triggers automatic actions like reordering supplies or alerting stakeholders.
2. Decentralized Finance (DeFi) Services: Decentralized finance is growing rapidly and can provide traditional financial services like trading, lending and borrowing using blockchain technology. In the service sector, companies might leverage DeFi for transparent, secure, and fast financial transactions without intermediaries. This could lower costs, enhance financial inclusion, and provide new financial products tailored to specific business needs.
3. Enhanced Privacy Solutions: As data privacy becomes more important, there is an increasing focus on blockchain solutions that offer enhanced features related to privacy. Systems like zero-knowledge proofs (ZKPs) and confidential transactions allow data to be verified without revealing the data itself. This will be useful in sectors where privacy is paramount, like in the healthcare or finance sector. Companies can use these technologies to ensure data confidentiality while maintaining the integrity and transparency of transactions.
4. Tokenization of Assets and Services: Tokenization is a procedure used to convert intellectual property rights to an asset by creating a digital token on a blockchain. It is expected to become more prevalent. In the service sector, this could mean that the tokenization of services or intellectual property, allow for fractional ownership, easier transferability, and the creation of new business models. For example, real estate services might tokenize property ownership, enabling fractional investments and democratizing access to real estate markets.
5. Sustainable and Green Blockchains: With growing environmental concerns, there is a shift towards developing more sustainable, energy-efficient blockchain networks. Future blockchain networks may use less energy-intensive consensus features, like Proof of Stake (PoS) or Proof of Authority (PoA) or integrate carbon offset mechanisms directly into the blockchain protocol. This would make blockchain technology more appealing to companies committed to sustainability goals.
6. Blockchain-as-a-Service (BaaS) Expansion: This platform is becoming more popular, offering businesses the tools and infrastructure to host, develop, and manage their blockchain applications. BaaS providers could offer specialized services tailored to different sectors making blockchain more accessible and reducing the technical barriers to adoption (Gururaj., Pooja., & Flammini., 2023)
7. Interoperability and Cross-Chain Solutions: As the blockchain applications expand a challenge is to ensure that they are compatible and are able to communicate or transact between different blockchain networks. A seamless operation has to be ensured between multiple networks which is challenging. This will enable more comprehensive service solutions that leverage multiple blockchain platforms, enhancing flexibility and user experience.

8. Advanced Identity Management and Verification: The use of blockchain for identity management is evolving, with applications in digital identities, Know Your Customer (KYC) processes, and secure access control. The applications will give users total control over their data while enabling secure and efficient verification processes. This can be especially valuable in sectors where verification of identity is crucial, like in finance, healthcare, and government services.
9. Decentralized Autonomous Organizations (DAOs): Organizations governed by smart contracts and blockchain are gaining traction as a new form of corporate governance and decision-making. Service sector companies could adopt DAO models to democratize decision-making and enhance transparency. For instance, a customer service DAO could allow customers to vote on service improvements, aligning business decisions more closely with customer preferences.
10. Blockchain in Customer Relationship Management (CRM): Integrating blockchain with CRM systems is emerging as a way to enhance customer service and trust. Blockchain could provide a decentralized but secure way to store customer data with more transparency and reduced risk of data breaches. Moreover, customers could have greater control over their data, opting into or out of sharing specific information with service providers.
11. Smart Contracts for Automated Service Delivery: Smart contracts will revolutionise businesses as they verify cases based on predefined conditions, which if met accurately is automatically signed off as a contract that are enforceable. For example, a claim for insurance can be validated by a smart contract which can automatically trigger a payout when a claim meets the policy conditions, thereby streamlining the claims process. The process reduces the need for intermediaries, is faster and more efficient.
12. Blockchain for Transparent Supply Chain Management: Business will have a major transformation as digital manufacturing processes and the use of blockchain technology will revolutionise supply networks. Products can be traced from the point of origin to the destination, checked for its genuineness, quality, and other features. Transparency and traceability in supply networks are enhanced which is crucial for sectors like food and beverage, pharmaceuticals, and fashion. Blockchain integration with IoT and AI will ensure real-time tracking and automated decision-making that will boost the efficiency of supply networks. This would allow service providers to offer more reliable and transparent services to their customers (Ray, 2023).

CONCLUSION

Blockchain technology has emerged as a transformative force across multiple service sectors addressing long-standing challenges through its core principles of security, transparency, and decentralization. This article has explored its major applications across financial services, supply chain and logistics, healthcare, government and public services, intellectual property and digital rights, energy and utilities, real estate, education, legal services, and telecommunications. In financial services, blockchain has revolutionized transaction processes with cryptocurrencies, smart contracts, and decentralized finance, offering new avenues for asset management and financial inclusion. Supply chain and logistics benefit from enhanced transparency and traceability, combating counterfeiting and optimizing operations. Healthcare leverages blockchain for secure patient data management, ensuring integrity in pharmaceutical supply chains, and facilitating streamlined clinical trials. Government and public services utilize blockchain to secure digital identities, improve voting systems, and enhance public record management, fostering trust and efficiency. For intellectual property and digital rights, blockchain's immutable ledger ensures secure content management and fair royalty distribution. In energy and utilities, blockchain supports peer-to-peer energy trading and renewable energy certificate management, driving sustainability efforts forward. Real estate transactions are streamlined through blockchain-based property management systems, ensuring transparency and reducing costs. Education, legal services, and telecommunications benefit from improved credential verification, document management, fraud prevention, and infrastructure management. In hospitals, blockchain enhances data management, supply chain efficiency, financial processes, research integrity, and cybersecurity promises significant improvements in patient care and operational efficiency.

REFERENCES

Antonopoulos, A. M. (2017). *Mastering Bitcoin: Unlocking Digital Cryptocurrencies* (2nd ed.). O'Reilly Media.

Ascribe. (2017). Blockchain for digital content ownership. Retrieved from https://www.ascribe.io

Ascribe. (2017). *How blockchain can authenticate and protect digital content.* Retrieved from https://ascribe.io/blockchain-authentication

Blockcerts. (2020). Blockchain-based credentialing. Retrieved from https://www.blockcerts.org

Choi, M., & Jung, Y. (2018). Blockchain technology for loyalty programs: Current trends and perspectives. *Journal of Hospitality and Tourism Technology*, *9*(3), 308–317. DOI: 10.1108/JHTT-03-2018-0021

Crosby, M., Pattanayak, P., Verma, S., & Kalyanaraman, V. (2016). Blockchain technology: Beyond Bitcoin. *Applied Innovation Review*, 2, 6-19. Retrieved from https://j2capitalmanagement.com/wp-content/uploads/2017/11/AIR-2016-Blockchain.pdf

Crosby, M., Pattanayak, P., Verma, S., & Kalyanaraman, V. (2016). Blockchain technology: Beyond Bitcoin. *Applied Innovation Review*, 2, 6-19. Retrieved from https://j2capitalmanagement.com/wp-content/uploads/2017/11/AIR-2016-Blockchain.pdf

Drescher, D. (2017). *Blockchain basics: A non-technical introduction in 25 steps.* Apress. DOI: 10.1007/978-1-4842-2604-9

Elngar, A. A., Bhambri, P., Pareek, P. K., Rani, S., & Sridhar, V. (2024). *Blockchain for IoT systems: Concept, framework and applications*. CRC Press.

Fosso Wamba, S., & Ngai, E. W. T. (2020). Importance of the blockchain in the hospitality industry: A systematic review. *Journal of Hospitality and Tourism Technology*, *11*(3), 455–471. DOI: 10.1108/JHTT-07-2019-0091

Gururaj, H. L., Pooja, M. R., & Flammini, F. (Eds.). (2023). Recent Trends in Computational Sciences: Proceedings of the Fourth Annual International Conference on Data Science, Machine Learning and Blockchain Technology (AICDMB 2023), Mysuru, India, 16-17 March 2023. CRC

Hanchate, R., & Ahire, P. (2024). *An Augmented Reality-Based.* Personalized Healthcare Management System Using Blockchain Technology., DOI: 10.4018/979-8-3693-5493-3.ch007

He, Y. (2018). The role of blockchain technology in the hospitality industry. *Journal of Hospitality and Tourism Technology*, *9*(2), 222–231. DOI: 10.1108/JHTT-11-2017-0117

Hughes, J. (2019). Blockchain and the future of the hospitality industry. *Journal of Hospitality and Tourism Technology*, *10*(1), 1–10. DOI: 10.1108/JHTT-09-2018-0086

IBM. (2019). Blockchain for supply chain: Track and trace. Retrieved from https://www.ibm.com/blockchain/supply-chain

Kahyaoglu, S. B., & Tecim, V. (Eds.). (2024). *Exploring Blockchain Applications: Management Perspectives*. CRC Press. DOI: 10.1201/9781003389552

Kshetri, N. (2017). Blockchain's roles in strengthening cybersecurity and protecting privacy. *Telecommunications Policy*, *41*(10), 1027–1038. DOI: 10.1016/j.telpol.2017.09.003

Kshetri, N. (2017). Blockchain's roles in strengthening cybersecurity and protecting privacy. *Telecommunications Policy, 41*(10), 1027–1038. DOI: 10.1016/j.telpol.2017.09.003

Kumar, A., Mondal, S., Verma, G., & Mani, P. (Eds.). (2024). *Embedded Devices and Internet of Things: Technologies, and Applications*. CRC Press. DOI: 10.1201/9781003510420

Kuo, T. T., Rojas, H., & Ohno-Machado, L. (2017). Comparison of blockchain platforms: A systematic review and healthcare examples. *Journal of the American Medical Informatics Association : JAMIA, 24*(6), 1211–1220. DOI: 10.1093/jamia/ocx068 PMID: 29016974

Ledger, P. (2018). Power Ledger's peer-to-peer energy trading platform. Retrieved from https://www.powerledger.io

MediLedger. (2020). Blockchain for pharmaceutical supply chain. Retrieved from https://www.mediledger.com

MedRec. (2018). Blockchain for electronic medical records. Retrieved from http://medrec.media.mit.edu

Mettler, M. (2016). Blockchain technology in healthcare: The revolution starts here. In Swan, M. (Ed.), *Blockchain: Blueprint for a new economy* (pp. 333–359). O'Reilly Media.

Mougayar, W. (2016). *The business blockchain: Promise, practice, and application of the next Internet technology*. Wiley.

Music, U. (2018). Blockchain-based music rights and royalties management. Retrieved from https://ujomusic.com

Nakamoto, S. (2008). Bitcoin: A peer-to-peer electronic cash system. Retrieved from https://bitcoin.org/bitcoin.pdf

Ølnes, S., Ubacht, J., & Janssen, M. (2017). Blockchain in government: Benefits and implications of distributed ledger technology for information sharing. *Government Information Quarterly, 34*(3), 355–364. DOI: 10.1016/j.giq.2017.09.007

Ølnes, S., Ubacht, J., & Janssen, M. (2017). Blockchain in government: Benefits and implications of distributed ledger technology for information sharing. *Government Information Quarterly, 34*(3), 355–364. DOI: 10.1016/j.giq.2017.09.007

OpenLaw. (2020). Smart contracts for legal services. Retrieved from https://www.openlaw.io

Paksoy, T., Kochan, C. G., & Ali, S. S. (Eds.). (2020). *Logistics 4.0: Digital transformation of supply chain management*. CRC Press. DOI: 10.1201/9780429327636

Pilkington, M. (2016). Blockchain technology: Principles and applications. In Olleros, F. X., & Zhegu, M. (Eds.), *Research handbook on digital transformations* (pp. 225–253). Edward Elgar Publishing., DOI: 10.4337/9781784717766.00019

Pilkington, M. (2016). Blockchain technology: Principles and applications. In Olleros, F. X., & Zhegu, M. (Eds.), *Research handbook on digital transformations* (pp. 225–253). Edward Elgar Publishing., DOI: 10.4337/9781784717766.00019

Ponsam, J. G., Shaw, H., & Patil, S. (2023, August). Web3 Based Funding Platform. In *2023 International Conference on Circuit Power and Computing Technologies (ICCPCT)* (pp. 453-457). IEEE. DOI: 10.1109/ICCPCT58313.2023.10245723

Propy. (2020). Blockchain for real estate. Retrieved from https://propy.com

Rani, S., & Taneja, A. (Eds.). (2024). *WSN and IoT: An Integrated Approach for Smart Applications*. CRC Press. DOI: 10.1201/9781003437079

Ravani, A., Edupuganti, S., Pugh, J., & Sushama, S. (2024). *Applications of Blockchain Technology: An Industry Focus*. CRC Press.

Ray, P. P. (2023). Web3: A comprehensive review on background, technologies, applications, zero-trust architectures, challenges and future directions. *Internet of Things and Cyber-Physical Systems, 3*, 213–248. DOI: 10.1016/j.iotcps.2023.05.003

Sinclair, S. (2017). Blockchain in healthcare: Innovations that bridge the trust gap. *Journal of Digital Banking, 1*(2), 153–161. https://www.henrystewartpublications.com/jdb/v1

Swan, M. (2015). *Blockchain: Blueprint for a new economy*. O'Reilly Media.

Tapscott, D., & Tapscott, A. (2016). *Blockchain revolution: How the technology behind bitcoin is changing money, business, and the world.* Penguin.

Tyagi, A. K., George, T. T., & Soni, G. (2023). Blockchain-Based Cybersecurity in Internet of Medical Things (IoMT)-Based Assistive Systems. In AI-Based Digital Health Communication for Securing Assistive Systems (pp. 22-53). IGI Global.

Tyan, I., & Hamade, R. F. (2020). Blockchain in the hospitality industry: A comprehensive review. *Journal of Hospitality and Tourism Technology, 11*(4), 529–545. DOI: 10.1108/JHTT-10-2018-0098

Üçoğlu, D. (2022). Blockchain Technology and Future Banking: Opportunities and Challenges. In Gupta, S., Kansra, P., & Kukreja, G. (Eds.), *Applications, Challenges, and Opportunities of Blockchain Technology in Banking and Insurance* (pp. 43–68). IGI Global., DOI: 10.4018/978-1-6684-4133-6.ch003

Valeri, M., & Albattat, A. (Eds.). (2024). *Metaverse and Tourism: Rethinking Implications on Virtual Reality.* Taylor & Francis. DOI: 10.4324/9781003497004

Voatz. (2020). Blockchain-based voting. Retrieved from https://voatz.com

Voatz. (2020). Blockchain technology in voting: Ensuring secure and transparent elections. Retrieved from https://voatz.com/blockchain-voting

WePower. (2018). Renewable energy trading on blockchain. Retrieved from https://www.wepower.com

Yaga, D., Mell, P., Roby, N., & Scarfone, K. (2019). *Blockchain technology overview. NIST Special Publication.* National Institute of Standards and Technology., DOI: 10.6028/NIST.SP.800-306

Yue, X., Wang, H., Jin, D., & Jin, D. (2016). Healthcare data gateways: Found healthcare intelligence on blockchain with novel privacy risk control. *Journal of Medical Systems, 40*(10), 218. DOI: 10.1007/s10916-016-0574-6 PMID: 27565509

Zafar, S., Kumar, S. N., Ahilan, A., & Cakir, G. K. (Eds.). (2024). *Industry 5.0 for Smart Healthcare Technologies: Utilizing Artificial Intelligence, Internet of Medical Things and Blockchain.* CRC Press.

Zhao, J., Yu, J., Yuan, X., & Liu, J. K. (2024, July). AegisDB: Scalable Blockchain Database with Secure Decentralised Load Balancing. In Australasian Conference on Information Security and Privacy (pp. 105-119). Singapore: Springer Nature Singapore. DOI: 10.1007/978-981-97-5101-3_6

Zheng, Z., Xie, S., Dai, H., Chen, X., & Wang, H. (2017). An overview of blockchain technology: Architecture, consensus, and future trends. In *2017 IEEE International Congress on Big Data* (BigData Congress) (pp. 557-564). IEEE. DOI: 10.1109/BigDataCongress.2017.85

Zheng, Z., Xie, S., Dai, H., Chen, X., & Wang, H. (2017). An overview of blockchain technology: Architecture, consensus, and future trends. In *2017 IEEE International Congress on Big Data* (BigData Congress) (pp. 557-564). IEEE. DOI: 10.1109/BigDataCongress.2017.85

Zheng, Z., Xie, S., Dai, H., Chen, X., & Wang, H. (2018). Blockchain challenges and opportunities: A survey. *International Journal of Web and Grid Services*, *14*(4), 352–375. DOI: 10.1504/IJWGS.2018.095647

Zheng, Z., Xie, S., Dai, H., Chen, X., & Wang, H. (2018). Blockchain challenges and opportunities: A survey. *International Journal of Web and Grid Services*, *14*(4), 352–375. DOI: 10.1504/IJWGS.2018.095647

Chapter 35
Transformation of Service Sectors Through Augmented Reality (AR) and Virtual Reality (VR)

Ambar Srivastava
https://orcid.org/0000-0002-7334-3421
Christ University, India

Ria Satti
Christ University, India

Amrit Singh
Christ University, India

ABSTRACT

Human interactions with actual and virtual environments are changing as a result of recent advancements in technology like Augmented Reality (AR) and Virtual Reality (VR). The sectors like retail, eCommerce, transport, tourism, real estate, healthcare, education, interior design, customer relationship management, etc. uses this innovative and adaptive technology. The aim of this chapter is to highlight the transformation of different service sectors through the use of Augmented Reality (AR) and Virtual Reality (VR) and also to see the recent innovations in this field. It was found that, AR and VR have an impact on various service sectors like retail and eCommerce in the form of virtual testing of products, tourism sector through 360-degree virtual tour, real estate sector through tour of the surrounding without being physically present, healthcare through physicians treating the patient virtually, education in the form of virtual classrooms, etc.

1. INTRODUCTION

The world is ever changing and companies who don't go with the changing environment will find it difficult to stay in business. Digital business optimization is crucial for companies now as compared to the past. Global business experience demonstrates that the majority of utility firms that used AR/VR technologies saw significant growth in their operations. Human interactions with actual and virtual environments are changing as a result of recent advancements in technology. This chapter is important because it demonstrates how AR and VR are transforming entire industries in ways that go beyond basic amusement. Employee training is becoming more efficient and cost-effective because of the usage of virtual reality (VR) to mimic real-world scenarios. These technologies

DOI: 10.4018/979-8-3693-7447-4.ch035

are revolutionizing training and development. Furthermore, by offering real-time data, augmented reality (AR) is being used by sectors like manufacturing and logistics to aid in decision-making.

Augmented Reality (AR) and Virtual Reality (VR) are anticipated to have a big impact on several industries. Earlier the entertainment sector used this technology but now other sectors like retail, eCommerce, transport, tourism, real estate, healthcare, education, interior design, customer relationship management, etc. use this innovative and adaptive technology. The main objective of this research is to examine how AR and VR are transforming the service sector. The second goal is to identify the most recent developments in these areas. This study will also look at the challenges these technologies face, like high implementation costs and a lack of technical expertise in some regions.

Through the real-time overlay of computer-generated 3D objects, augmented reality is an interactive experience that improves the physical world. Although virtual reality (VR) and augmented reality are sometimes used interchangeably, they are not the same. For example, Augmented Reality incorporates digital features to improve the real world but Virtual Reality is a self-contained computer environment that is entirely independent from the real-world setting. In addition to being used to advance numerous business domains, augmented reality also holds the potential to revolutionize field service workers' methods of operation. Since, the release of a particular incredibly popular mobile game called Pokemon Go, which features a group of well-known Japanese cartoon monsters, augmented reality (AR) technology has been steadily gaining popularity. Kiefer and Chauvelier (2020). In addition, businesses and individuals are looking into how the immersive virtual environment known as the metaverse may be used for entertainment, social interaction, and workplaces. This technology is predicted to be the next big thing in virtual and augmented reality.

In terms of their usefulness and practical use, AR, VR and MR are relatively new technologies. Many businesses, particularly small and medium-sized ones, lack the technological know-how and appropriate SDK/software to create AR and MR apps. There are service providers in Singapore, India and other nations who can create any kind of application including AR/MR training for these kinds of businesses. In the aerospace industry, augmented reality (AR) is being used more and more for maintenance and repair tasks. This is because it enables professionals to view complex assemblies and parts directly at the work site. This reduces errors and downtime, which boosts operational efficiency.

In the field of augmented reality (AR), computer-generated virtual pictures are seamlessly superimposed over the actual environment, aligned with real-world items and allowing real-time viewing and interaction (Azuma, 1997). Over the past couple of decades, augmented reality (AR) has advanced quickly from research labs to broad consumer device availability. AR is transforming the way that medical operations are carried out.

These days, augmented reality is being applied in many different fields, including education ((Furio et al., 2013; Fonseca et al., 2014a; Ibanez et al., 2014), Engineering (Henderson and Feiner, 2009; Henderson and Feiner, 2011; Irizarry et al., 2013), Entertainment (Dow et al., 2007; Haugstvedt and Krogstie, 2012; Vazquez-Alvarez et al., 2012). However, difficulties with AR's usability and user experience still need to be resolved before it can be generally adopted by end consumers.

Although the early uses of this cutting-edge technology were mostly focused on games and novelty items, augmented reality is also finding its way into many other areas of the economy. Augmented reality is enabling companies to provide their clients with distinctive and creative experiences in a variety of industries, including retail and hospitality. The field service sector is the next to gain from this new technology.

2. REVIEW OF LITERATURE

Dey et al. (2018) in their study reported the nine major areas in which AR technology is being used are remote collaboration, education, gaming and entertainment, industrial applications, medical, navigation and driving, perception and travel and exploration. Rankohi and Waugh (2013) observed that despite an increase in use over the past few years, augmented reality technology is still in its experimental stage and has not yet reached its full potential. AR technologies are primarily known for their immersive and sensory-primarily visual aspects that are used to produce artistic and aesthetic experiences. Chevalier and Kiefer (2020) in their study reported that applications of AR technologies are not restricted to these two aspects because AR encompasses a wide range of technologies that are either directly or indirectly related to immersion. Whereas, scholars and practitioners in the field of consumer marketing have demonstrated a growing interest in augmented reality (AR) technologies as a means of enhancing customer happiness in offline businesses (Hackl and Wolfe, 2017). The concept of customer experience and how the integration of immersive technology might boost satisfaction throughout the customer journey are the focal points in the study by Wedel et al. (2020). During the three phases of the shopping process i.e. pre-purchase, point of purchase and post-purchase, augmented reality (AR) can improve the experience for customers and offer them both functional and emotional benefits on the other hand, it can also lead to confusion, dissonance and boredom (Romano et al., 2020).

Chris et al. (2012) stated the significance and effects of augmented reality (AR) in the tourism industry as a result of mobile technologies. They have also discussed the various difficulties that arise from third-generation mobile technology and proper Wi-Fi, as well as the necessity of creating a cross-functional platform structure that would benefit all parties involved. The tourist, IT, hotel, and hospitality industries all benefit from the combined digitalization and technological innovation experience provided by augmented and virtual reality. This business is growing every day as a crowd-puller and connected marketing trend that envelops passengers (Kam, 2017). It is feasible to grow the tourism and hospitality sectors through marketing strategy, the improvement of education through technological advancement and the integration of AR, VR and sensors (Nayyar et al., 2018). Keckes & Tomicic (2017) have outlined how IT-enabled technologies are used to conduct research and development in the digitization of the tourism industry through the use of AR and VR to create engineering-augmented frameworks for visitors that incorporate sensors and communication methods. Additionally, it explains the major factors influencing the use of augmented innovation in the travel business and arranges them in a few appropriate groups, specifically covering general requirements, functions, problems, overlay kinds and advancements. Murphy et al. (2021) emphasizes the significance of customer engagement and enjoyment as a result of mobile augmented reality apps in the hotel business, pointing out that early adopters of the technology might produce significant income.

Today's generation has a rapidly growing smartphone population, which has prompted the development of AR applications for smartphones with dynamic multimedia features like text fonts, colour combinations, touchscreen interfaces and graphic user interfaces. This has in turn highlighted the applications of AR in heritage sectors (Norsyafawati et al., 2016). Hassam and Ramkissoon (2016) have demonstrated how augmented reality is being used to digitize museums, allowing for extensive user interfaces for tourism, entertainment, culture, artefacts, exhibitions, and archaeological monuments that enhance the experience for more visitors. Furthermore, this highlights the requirement for competent personnel to manage modern technology and make use of most of them. Huang et al. (2022) examined the application of augmented reality in cultural heritage exhibition and protection, showcasing virtual restorations of artefacts that are either too expensive or too delicate to be displayed in public. Lopez et al. (2020) provide a more in-depth examination of the application of augmented reality in museum settings, with a focus on user education and engagement through interactive mobile app features.

Klimova et al. (2018) described the various needs for teaching and learning approaches for AR and VR technologies, and the significance and role of different education sector stakeholders in transforming society into an edutech based on the introduction of different AR and VR courses at the university level. Martin-Gutierrez et al. (2017) outlined the uses of AR and VR in the fields of education, media, edutainment, healthcare, manufacturing, logistics and tourism, among others. Better ecosystem growth will also result from the advantages of technology in educational institutions for digitalizing labs, classrooms and other departments. The method by which learning opportunities from augmented reality in education are perceived cognitively, informatively and visually is clearly defined by Jerabek et al. (2014). Open innovation in education fosters diversity in the attitudes of the next generation of students regarding technological interventions such as AR and VR (Miranda et al., 2017).

Asante et al. (2019) have outlined the need for Smart Education technology, which includes virtual and augmented reality as one of the Smart Factory's parameters, as part of the course curriculum at various university and school levels to promote entrepreneurship and innovation in a society driven by entrepreneurship in support of rapid industrialization. Examples of today's technological environment in the education sector include socializing, interactive learning in the classroom and digitalization of education through the use of bilateral platform frameworks based on augmented and virtual reality in business education (Gupta & Bharadwaj, 2013). Tarabasz et al. (2018) have used digitalization, augmented reality and virtual reality, ICT-enabled technologies, idea generation, design innovation lab facilitation, incubation, virtual learning environments, classrooms and platforms to counteract future industrialization. These have illustrated the technologically enabled needs, such as knowledge, and skill sets, by various organizational vertical employees and entrepreneurs. Gamified augmented reality (AR) has the potential to raise students' critical thinking and problem-solving skills in the classroom, as well as increase student engagement and make learning more dynamic (Lin et al., 2022).

The commercialization and marketization of goods and services by high-tech businesses depends on the digital transformation and the contribution of AR and VR to achieving the goals (Gbadegeshin, 2019). Heutger & Kuckelhaus (2014) have mentioned the numerous chances for AR and VR technology intervention in the logistics sectors, which leads to overall development and improved service opportunities in the abovementioned industry involving their organization using DHL as an example.

Zhu et al. (2014) have discussed the significance and effects of AR and VR as a result of medical sciences and healthcare education facilitating virtual learning globally. The growing importance of AR, VR and MR applications in therapeutic settings and education, as well as strategies to educate health professionals about these applications and pique their interest in using innovation in the medical sciences to enhance the quality of medical care (Hsieh & Lee, 2018). More information about how AR-guided surgeries have increased precision and reduced the possibility of errors in complex medical procedures may be found in the study conducted by Okamura et al. (2020). Medical students can effectively resolve and predict human anatomy utilizing AR and VR technologies in conjunction with the 2D and 3D picture learning mechanism as outlined by Kurniawan et al. (2018).

Kurniawan et al. (2018) have developed the 2D and 3D imaging learning mechanism for medical students' coercion of human anatomy, which can be effectively resolved and predicted with the use of AR and VR technologies. In exchange, this will demonstrate in-depth knowledge of intricate human physiology as well as fully interactive module learning that is transferable to other streams.

Quandt et al. (2018) have shown how important AR and VR are to industrialization through their use in a variety of service and operating modes, as well as in training and knowledge management. Additionally, it shows how industries have improved their working environments, creating opportunities for skill development and training. Lee et al. (2021) support this by highlighting how AR has streamlined factory automation processes and minimized operational downtime in the manufacturing sector Benedetto et al. (2022) have discussed how worker safety in hazardous environments, such as chemical plants and construction sites, is changing due to wearables with augmented reality aid.

Lamrani et al. (2015) have described the idea of pervasive computing, a hassle-free, seamless technology that improves people's lives through the concepts of virtual reality and augmented reality. The authors have highlighted the application of this technology in a variety of sectors, including knowledge, edutainment, game development and conceptualizing and creating various games as a part of progressive learning. Jeon et al. (2022) elaborated further on this by looking into the use of AR and VR in esports, where virtual worlds are beginning to change competitive gaming.

Maurer & Schumacher (2018) have described the Factory of Future (FoF) idea, which is based on a study conducted by the European Union and addresses Industry 4.0 industrial overall management. Industry 4.0 fosters innovation, and entrepreneurship through CPS and digitization, augmented and virtual reality play a significant part in these processes.

3. OBJECTIVE OF THE STUDY

i) To explore how Augmented Reality (AR)/Virtual Reality (VR) transforming different service sectors.
ii) To find out the recent innovations in the field of Augmented Reality (AR)/Virtual Reality (VR).
iii) To explore the challenges and limitations in the usage of Augmented Reality (AR)/Virtual Reality (VR).

4. RESEARCH METHODOLOGY

The research methodology used in the study is conceptual research, which is an analytical procedure predicated on a critical assessment of earlier studies as well as theoretical frameworks. Conceptual investigations, which place more emphasis on comprehending and evaluating concepts than on collecting fresh empirical data, employ secondary data sources. The authors in this chapter used secondary data sources, including industry reports, conference papers, peer-reviewed journal articles and trustworthy online databases to gather relevant information. The data sources, which include earlier research on these technologies in a range of industries, including retail, healthcare, education and tourism enable authors to identify patterns in the adoption of AR and VR across many sectors.

5. FINDINGS

5.1 AR/VR Transforming Different Service Sectors

Augmented Reality (AR) and Virtual Reality (VR) are transforming different service sectors in the way they are working or providing services to customers. Here are the few sectors which are impacted by the AR/VR:

i) Retail & e-Commerce

Augmented reality has revolutionized the retail sector. It should be possible for customers to virtually try the products without physically visiting the store. By selecting the colour and size, they can try on the items of their choice in the virtual changing room. For instance, Sephora's Virtual Artist app allows users to see how different cosmetic products would look on their faces before making a purchase.

Online shopping has seen significant transformations as a result of the metaverse and 3D metaverse designers. Shoppers can virtually try on clothing, shoes, and other items to see how they would appear on them in person thanks to body-scanning technology and virtual reality retail experiences. In addition to saving customers time, it is more environmentally friendly because consumers can verify before placing an order whether an item fits their size and form, reducing the environmental impact of fast fashion production and delivery. Customers will be able to make more educated decisions about the products.

Retail and shopping are preparing to use more augmented reality (AR) technology to offer new experiences to customers in an industry where internet purchases already rule. Using the IKEA Place app, for instance, customers can visualize how furniture would look in their homes.

Augmented reality is being used by brands to lure customers into stores and retail locations by enabling them to find items (like clothing) without having to try them on. Companies can use this type of AR to communicate with clients even after they've made a purchase. In branded furniture stores, you may virtually select the pieces of furniture or art that you like and see how they will seem in your home. You can move items around and buy them right away if you like them.

Given the increasing use of AR and VR, the ethical and privacy concerns associated with them must be discussed. In the retail sector, privacy concerns are sparked by things like the potential misuse of personal data obtained through virtual try-ons, especially accurate biometric data. To address these issues, businesses should ensure that data collection processes are transparent, implement robust data protection measures, and give users clear options for managing and consenting to data.

ii) Tourism

You can use virtual and augmented reality to display potential consumers' nearby hotels with three-dimensional (3D) photos and the sites they are considering. One example is the VRoom Service offered by Marriott Hotels, which lets prospective visitors virtually explore hotel rooms.

You may even suggest that they visit nearby tourist destinations. Additionally, this will be displayed in all travel applications; nevertheless, your clients will find it highly appealing if you can use augmented reality to add more effects. If a museum is showing augmented reality material, you can let them know. Outside of the hotel, several travel companies are creating augmented reality applications that let visitors enhance actual locations and tourist attractions. A user can get real-time information about a structure or landmark by pointing their smartphone at it. Using augmented reality software, a hotel or hospitality company can enhance the guest experience by adding some delight to their physical environment. There is a lot of potential for augmented reality applications in the travel industry. Augmented Reality (AR) modifies tourists' perceptions of their actual surroundings and creates new opportunities to enhance visitor interactions and experiences.

By increasing travellers' interest in new places to visit, helping travel agents book flights and accommodations and making travel more enjoyable, virtual reality and augmented reality technology will contribute to the travel and tourism industry's recovery after the COVID pandemic. For instance, augmented reality route maps with 3D components that show the quickest routes and real-time traffic updates can be used to direct cars.

We can get to your location more quickly because route maps with 3D characteristics are displayed. Your driver will feel as though he is not just looking at a map, but viewing the roadways. To ensure they reach on time, it will also advise them of traffic patterns and the quickest route to their destination.

One of the moral dilemmas facing the travel industry is the potential for AR/VR applications to infringe on user privacy by collecting personal preferences and location information. Businesses need the informed consent of customers before collecting any of this data. They must also safely preserve and anonymize any information they obtain. Companies should also let users change their privacy preferences and be transparent about how they use user data.

iii) Real Estate

In the real estate industry, buyers will want to inspect the item they are going to purchase. Setting up a meeting, however, will take longer than anticipated if you have a busy schedule. But if we can use augmented reality to show them your products, they will be able to see an almost genuine situation. For example, Matterport and similar technology enhance the home-buying process by enabling virtual house tours for customers.

These cutting-edge strategies are being used by an increasing number of real estate brokers to give buyers an unparalleled experience. Through their alteration of the real estate scene, AR and VR are revolutionizing real estate experiences. The usage of immersive user experiences has increased as a result of these technological advancements, streamlining the process of purchasing and/or selling residential and commercial real estate. Purchasing and selling properties will be made simpler by the real estate industry's adoption of AR and VR technologies. Furthermore, AR might make it easier to see possible interior design or improvements, which could assist both buyers and sellers better grasp the potential of a property. Virtual reality tours give clients more flexibility to visit homes at their own pace and give them a better sense of the location than traditional images do.

Concerns with ethics and privacy in the real estate sector include the potential for unlawful access to private information obtained during virtual tours or profiling utilizing VR data. To lessen these dangers, real estate companies should ensure safe access limitations, offer strong data encryption, and be transparent and truthful with customers about their data collection and usage practices. Getting express consent to acquire data can help to further improve security and trust.

iv) Healthcare

In the healthcare sector, augmented reality has greatly improved the healing processes. It uses more advanced surgical methods. Doctors may now more effectively communicate their findings. This will help them understand the illness and how to treat it better. For instance, surgeons can locate veins more rapidly with the aid of AccuVein's AR technology.

While the reasons for transferring from a production plant to a hospital room could differ, AR gives surgeons new applications. Through the use of augmented reality, researchers were able to superimpose CT scan images with the locations of their patients' bones and major blood veins, enabling surgeons to "see-through" the patient's organs during a single surgical procedure. According to preliminary testing, AR applications in surgery have a promising future because they may reduce the amount of time spent on certain procedures and the margin of error. In addition, the development of advanced wearable technology enables specialists in surgery to communicate remotely during the entire procedure, in addition to enabling medical professionals to monitor and treat patients without the need for physical presence. This has significant ramifications for the medical field. By adopting augmented reality (AR) technology, a skilled surgeon can assist a local physician step-by-step during the procedure, enabling remote surgery.

The most important method that VR is modernizing the healthcare sector is through training. Virtual reality (VR) creates and nurtures an environment that lets people develop and learn outside of real-world scenarios. Without having to intervene in an emergency, a professional who needs to practice operating on patients can do so. In addition, professionals who need to become acquainted with the hospital setting will be able to do so without experiencing further stress. To help doctors and caregivers achieve better treatment outcomes and enhance patient well-being, developers provide useful tools. SentiAR, a business that develops augmented reality instruments to assist surgeons during invasive procedures, is one example. Another example is AccuVein Inc., a US-based supplier of medical imaging systems that assists physicians in locating patients' veins through augmented reality technology. Before starting the company, our very own Alon Grinshpoon, CEO of echo3D, contributed to the study on augmented reality and its application in medical procedures like vascular surgeries. With the technology transforming patient diagnosis and treatment, surgeon training, operating room simulations, chronic pain management and more. The healthcare industry is regarded as a leader in AR and VR. Furthermore, augmented reality (AR) can help with patient education by improving patient comprehension and adherence to medical advice by providing interactive visualisations of medical conditions and treatment regimens.

Two examples of ethical and privacy concerns in the healthcare sector are maintaining sensitive patient data and ensuring the security of medical information received through AR/VR apps. Healthcare providers are responsible for ensuring that safe data handling protocols are followed and that strict data protection laws, such as HIPAA in the US, are obeyed. Robust encryption, stringent access controls, and regular audits might be implemented to protect patient information and maintain public trust in AR/VR technology.

v) Education

The use of virtual and augmented reality in education is making it more enjoyable and interesting. When reading is something that students can physically see and feel, their excitement for it will rise. They will be able to apply the lessons practically without any mess and retain them better. By transforming textbooks into dynamic learning environments, augmented reality (AR) has the potential to enhance student engagement.

The field of education is starting to adopt these technologies. AR has the potential to drastically change how people study today. The notion that augmented reality (AR) could simplify the educational process is incredible. AR can have a positive effect on the location and schedule of classrooms, introducing a more unified strategy to enhance student enjoyment. Teachers are aware that creativity and engagement are key components of the learning process and augmented reality (AR) enables students to swiftly absorb, comprehend and express visual representations while also helping them establish relative interest. It raises the likelihood that students will remember the material by providing content and helping them practice testing their understanding. More significantly, marketing and advertising in the education sector stand to benefit greatly from AR technologies. AR Tours are already being used by several US colleges to increase enrolment and help new students navigate the campus. Virtual reality technology may provide students with a wealth of knowledge. Furthermore, it aids the pupils in developing a solid understanding of the subject Students struggling with challenging subjects like chemistry and physics might benefit from interactive augmented reality (AR) simulations, which allow them to see abstract ideas in three dimensions and conduct virtual experiments. This can raise the accessibility and engagement of challenging subjects and significantly improve learning outcomes.

One ethical issue in education is the collection and use of student data via AR/VR platforms, which could lead to privacy issues. Ensuring that educational tools comply with data protection rules and include controls that enable parents and students to manage their data choices is crucial. Developers should also address accessibility issues to ensure that AR/VR apps are inclusive and do not inadvertently penalize specific student groups.

vi) Interior Desing

Interior designers may get practical help using augmented reality. They might be given a general notion of how it will seem after their design is complete. Before doing all of the labour-intensive work, they would have the chance to change the design if a better option became available. For example, by using augmented reality programs such as Houzz, buyers may preview how different design elements would appear in their homes.

When their clients give their okay, they may start the actual process. It will save a great deal of labour, money and time. When it comes to furniture, a try-before-you-buy policy is essential to building, preserving and fostering client trust. In addition, a store with an augmented reality presence may see an increase in sales and rapid attention due to the potential of this technology. Augmented reality can be used by customers to quickly arrange new furniture in their houses. Customers can use augmented reality to look over their room and add an entire collection of furniture to choose from. Although Wayfair, IKEA and Houzz are among the companies that have deployed augmented reality solutions for furniture "try-ons,". Customers are motivated by its outstanding design experience. In addition to giving your house the much-needed structural renovation, virtual reality allows you to replicate the interior design through immersive experiences. These days, businesses like Flipscapes make use of this and provide customers with 3D visualizer services for various interior design elements of their home or office, such as colour schemes, ventilation, lighting, and furniture. Not only can this kind of platform help designers and homeowners visualize the style and feel of a space, but it can also increase direct sales for various furniture retailers, like IKEA.

One of the upcoming AR applications may be real-time design modifications, which allow users to quickly make changes to their interior designs and see the results immediately. This dynamic involvement allows for more customized design experiences and has the potential to significantly enhance client happiness.

The potential exploitation of user preferences and private information gleaned from augmented reality interactions, such as detailed room layouts, raises ethical questions in the field of interior design. To address these issues, businesses should implement stringent data privacy measures, such as data encryption and secure storage practices. Transparency about data usage and well-defined permission processes are critical to ensuring users are in control of and aware of their personal information.

vii) Manufacturing

Manufacturers may shorten development and time-to-market by fusing potent augmented reality (AR) gadgets with cutting-edge image recognition technology, Internet of Things (IoT) devices, Big Data, and artificial intelligence (AI). The industrial industry is getting a boost from AR and MR technologies in today's competitive environment and their return on investment is rising. Development teams can hone their abilities and gain knowledge from their errors by using scenario-based AR/MR simulations. The inventory procedure is likewise streamlined using MR-aided devices, which makes it rapid and accurate.

AR, for instance, can assist in assembly by overlaying instructions directly over the components, ensuring that each step is carried out precisely. AR can also be used for remote support, which allows experts to assist on-site employees with challenging jobs from a distance, boosting output and reducing downtime. Augmented reality (AR) has the potential to enhance quality control by promptly highlighting defects or deviations from standards, leading to better goods and fewer errors.

Sensitive or private data obtained by augmented reality systems presents ethical and privacy issues for the industrial sector. Ensuring that AR systems with robust security features, including data encryption and access control, are used for remote assistance and quality control is crucial. Additionally, manufacturers must set guidelines to deal with issues around employee privacy.

viii) Automobile

The automotive sector has a plethora of applications for AR and MR. Customers can be shown the finer features of an automobile with AR / MR technology. AR instructions and guides can take the place of laborious manuals and AR makes it easier and faster for auto engineers to learn about the construction and maintenance of vehicles. Using AR, the design and prototype team speeds up the development process. These are just a few examples of how AR and MR technology is influencing the car sector. Automakers can examine driving situations and car behaviour thanks to virtual reality. They can assess and modify the prototypes in simulated scenarios before creating a new model. VR is also widely employed in the production of smart cars, which should soon be available on the market thanks to the assistance of automotive engineering and design services. These intelligent vehicles use a combination of artificial intelligence and virtual reality to learn how to steer, brake and turn. Additionally, by enabling customers to view many options and configurations before making a purchase, augmented reality (AR) can assist in automotive customization. This interactive approach strengthens the decision-making abilities of the customer and enhances their overall shopping experience. Additionally, by providing workers with access to real-time diagnostic data superimposed on car components and step-by-step repair instructions, augmented reality (AR) can be applied to maintenance and repair procedures.

In the automotive industry, ethical concerns include maintaining the privacy of data gleaned from AR/VR interactions, including personal preferences and driving patterns. Automakers should use comprehensive data security measures, like encryption and anonymization, to safeguard customer information. Furthermore, maintaining confidence and ensuring the ethical application of AR/VR technologies necessitates being forthright and truthful about the methods used to collect data and get users to express agreement.

ix) Marketing & Advertisement

To give consumers more dynamic and engaging experiences, marketing and advertising are utilizing augmented reality technologies. Businesses can provide clients with virtual tours of their goods or services with augmented reality (AR)-)-enabled smartphone apps, presenting their features and advantages more engagingly and dynamically. This helps businesses stand out in a congested market and enhances client engagement. The AR marketing campaign “Dunking with LeBron James” by Nike and Snapchat is a fantastic illustration of how AR can be used virally. Pepsi Max turned a bus stop into an augmented reality (AR) experience where passersby had to dodge enormous robots, watch out for people being kidnapped by flying saucers or deal with monstrous tentacles emerging from the sewers. Many other businesses use augmented reality (AR) in their product promotion, and Lego provides in-store AR experiences. Additionally, ASOS and the augmented reality startup Lenslist launched an Instagram ad including a face lens that allowed users to discover more about their shopping preferences. And lastly, businesses like Balenciaga have started creating and retailing virtual designer apparel for the metaverse. Gucci even made a virtual reality fashion show on Roblox last year. Additionally, AR is being used in interactive retail displays and billboards more frequently, giving consumers new and creative ways to connect with brands. By offering immersive experiences that let consumers engage with a brand's past, core principles, and objectives through virtual settings, augmented reality (AR) can help improve brand storytelling.

Ethical issues in marketing and advertising include the possibility of intrusive data collecting and user behaviour tracking via augmented reality apps. By putting in place robust data protection mechanisms and giving consumers clear information about data collection and usage, businesses should place a high priority on user privacy. Furthermore, maintaining customer trust and preventing undesired intrusions can be achieved by making sure AR experiences are created with user consent and control in mind.

x) Sports

Since the introduction of virtual reality technology, the sports division has advanced significantly. Effective team training will enable each member to improve their abilities and overall output. Several broadcasters have started employing VR technology to webcast live sports like in IPL 2024 via the Jio platform. Because of this, you may still experience the action even if you are unable to visit the sports complex in person. Additionally, it enables you to purchase virtual tickets, enabling you to participate in virtual reality games from anywhere in the world. With numerous virtual reality companies specializing in live sports event viewing, the way the world watches sports is beginning to shift in multiple ways. Fans of sports may now watch virtual reality broadcasts of the NFL, NBA, and other leagues. It is a great way to give those who are unable to go to the venue or lack the funds to purchase tickets to attend sporting events in-person access to live events. Sports networks can overlay replays and current gameplay with 3D graphics thanks to AR and VR, which offer immersive experiences. A lot of sports networks, like ESPN and Fox Sports, are already experimenting with this technology. They are using augmented reality (AR) in their play-by-play analysis and programming to emphasize game-related information in real time. AR is used for in-stadium experiences, team development, marketing, and even on-field rulings, in addition to providing a better at-home experience. The Carolina Panthers most recently showed AR's potential for live sports. Virtual reality (VR) can also be utilized to analyze and recover athlete performance, offering individualized training plans and thorough feedback. Through mobile apps that offer real-time statistics, player information, and interactive features, augmented reality (AR) can increase audience engagement during live events.

Concerns about collecting and using data from virtual reality interactions and the possibility of intrusive athlete performance monitoring may give rise to ethical dilemmas in sports. It is crucial to guarantee that any information gathered is used sensibly, with strong security protocols and athletes' express agreement. Furthermore, it's critical to safeguard the privacy of sports fans using AR and VR experiences. To do this, data practices must be transparent, and user control and consent alternatives must be provided.

xi) Aerospace & Defence

Because the military and space exploration both work in dangerous regions that are not easily accessible, virtual reality (VR) provides a setting that is as near to reality as possible, facilitating more effective training. Trainers can lessen the dangers involved in preparation, assist soldiers recovering from battlefield trauma and help them get ready for novel or unexpected circumstances. One benefit of AR devices is that they combine human factors with computer reliability. Initial pilot training in flight simulators, which are used for both commercial and military aircraft, depends on immersive AR and VR technologies. AR also greatly accelerates the process of prototyping and development, making it easier to build new equipment. A group of tasks carried out by experts while the aircraft is still on the ground is known as ramp handling. The ramp handling staff can considerably expedite the loading procedure by using AR glasses to scan unique QR codes that are placed on cargo containers. It is possible to provide the army with cutting-edge training. For individuals who serve in the Air Force, navy, or other such branches, it provides an interesting and thrilling experience. Additionally, it provides the soldiers with extensive instruction on how to fight against challenging circumstances while simultaneously defending one's own life. It is an excellent method of smoothly training the troops. Advanced simulation systems for mission planning and rehearsal are also being developed using AR and VR technology, giving military personnel the ability to experience complicated scenarios and successfully strategize. By superimposing technical data and step-by-step instructions directly onto the equipment, augmented reality (AR) helps with maintenance and repair chores in the aircraft industry by decreasing errors and increasing efficiency.

xii) Entertainment & Gaming

Being one of the first sectors to embrace virtual reality, entertainment continues to be a prime example of its application and utilization. It only takes a cursory glance at console or internet gaming to notice how prevalent virtual reality is in the entertainment sector. Virtual reality (VR) is also being introduced to theme parks and movie theatres to imitate movie-like experiences and let viewers see their favourite cinematic masterpieces up close. Pokemon Go is a shining example of an AR game; as of May 2018, it has 147 million monthly active users. Users of the game can communicate with virtual creatures in real life. Another illustration is the social media smartphone app Snapchat, which lets users overlay 3D objects on their faces and their surroundings. As of January 2020, the app has 360 million monthly active users. In addition, AR is being utilized to provide audiences with interactive experiences during live performances and concerts, including real-time visual effects and stage improvements. Virtual reality is also being used to create immersive storytelling experiences and escape rooms, which provide users with new avenues for enjoyment and interaction.

Concerns about privacy user interactions with AR/VR experiences and the possibility of excessive data collection are among the ethical dilemmas in entertainment and gaming. To preserve user privacy, developers should put robust data protection measures in place and be open about how they handle data. In addition, keeping a healthy balance between virtual and real-world activities depends on addressing concerns with screen time and user addiction.

xiii) Architecture

The usage of virtual reality in design is responsible for the stunning structures and shopping centres that you see today. By providing a virtual tour of the building, it provides the architects with the perfect platform to showcase their concepts and designs. The benefit is that it allows one to enjoy the building's interior while keeping safety measures in mind.

Additionally, it provides you with a virtual tour of the structure, enabling clients to virtually explore the space. As a result, any adjustments or modifications to the building's construction can be made right away. In addition to helping architects visualize their projects, 3D AR/VR services enable them to experience the construction as it is happening. In this manner, not only can architects and their clients see the space before it is finished, but they can also make adjustments in real-time to guarantee client happiness. By offering interactive simulations of how future constructions will blend into current cityscapes, augmented reality can also help with urban planning. To assess how a building will work in various scenarios, architects can also simulate varied lighting and climatic conditions using virtual reality (VR). This helps to ensure that the final design satisfies both functional and aesthetic requirements.

Concerns about the privacy and security of data obtained by AR/VR systems used in building design and visualization are ethical issues in the field of architecture. Architects are responsible for making sure that client information is protected and that any data that is gathered is stored securely. Getting clients' express consent and being transparent about data usage are essential. Furthermore, addressing potential biases and guaranteeing equitable use of technology can be facilitated by making sure AR/VR technologies are inclusive and accessible.

5.2 Recent Innovations in the Field of Augmented Reality (AR) & Virtual Reality (VR)

5.2.1 Apple Vision Pro

With Apple Vision Pro, we can use an infinite canvas, which completely transforms how we interact with our favourite apps. With this advancement, we can arrange apps anywhere we like and resize them to the perfect size, keeping an eye on our surroundings to construct the desktop of our dreams. It is also possible to rapidly flip through documents, messages and Safari browser to conduct online searches, create to-do lists have conversations with loved ones and transform any area into an individual personal theatre. We may experience immersion and enlarge our favourite movies, TV shows and computer games to the perfect size with the aid of spatial audio. Additionally, with a greater number of pixels per eye than a 4K TV, now we'll be able to enjoy fantastic content from anywhere, even on a lengthy journey or on the couch at home.

5.2.2 Google's ARCore

ARCore is the brand name of Google's framework for developing augmented reality apps. With this, the smartphone we're using can perceive its surroundings, understand the outside environment and connect with information through a variety of APIs. Some of the APIs are available on Android as well as iOS to enable shared AR experiences. ARCore uses three key components to integrate virtual content with the real environment as seen using our phone's camera; (1) Motion tracking allows the phone to identify and track its location in the outside world; (2) the phone's environmental awareness allows it to identify and locate any type of terrain, such as inclined, upward and flat surfaces like floors, walls and coffee tables.

5.2.3 Google Glass

Google Glass is another wearable Android device that can be controlled with motion and speech. It resembles eyeglasses and places information directly in front of the user's eyes. Google Glass displays relevant information through audio, visual and location-based inputs to create an augmented reality experience. As an example, a user may receive real-time flight status information as soon as they get to the airport. The key features of Google Glass are (1) its capacity to record images and videos and then utilize Google Hangouts to share real-time content with others (2) the choice to access the Google search engine through the glasses via a data connection from a smartphone or Wi-Fi (3) The capability of receiving translations directly on the wearer's screen via streaming.

5.2.4 The Metaverse

The phrase "metaverse," which became widely used in 2023, refers to a completely immersive, networked digital universe. Users can switch between activities without ever leaving the Metaverse. Within the same virtual arena, they can take part in a multiplayer game, visit a digital art exhibition, and attend virtual meetings. The metaverse has the potential to emerge as the primary digital hub for social interaction, employment, and entertainment. As a result, 2024 is already seeing a rise in the use of VR in a variety of industries. We have only just begun to explore the thrilling and tremendous potential of virtual reality. We may expect VR to be used in ever more creative ways as technology develops, further obfuscating the distinction between the real and virtual worlds. VR as it is used today only scratches the surface of its possibilities. It is becoming more likely that virtual reality will play a significant role in our daily lives in the future as we investigate and push the boundaries of what is currently achievable.

5.2.5 Generative AI

The most popular technology of 2023 (and probably beyond) has a lot of uses that complement the captivating, immersive online experiences that 2024 will produce. Making the landscapes, artwork, and other components of virtual worlds is a clear application case. According to Mark Zuckerberg, there is a chance that the time it takes designers to create 3D environments might be decreased. Another is developing characters and people to inhabit the worlds; these can range from chatbots for customer service to lifelike characters in entertainment-focused experiences who converse with you like a real person. The work being done to add talking, realistic characters to the virtual worlds of video games shows where this might go.

5.2.6 Multi-Sensory Technology

Nothing compares to being able to reach out and touch the environment around you to create the sense of truly being there, yet immersive online experiences may nevertheless captivate consumers with screens and speakers attached to headsets. Manufacturers of devices are developing haptic gloves that give users the impression that they are influencing objects in their environment by applying pressure or weight. Some are developing technology that uses a mask to diffuse scented vapours to compensate for other sensations that are lost, such as smell. Additionally, full-body suits are being developed and commercialized, and as manufacturers produce tools to improve the feeling of being fully immersed in virtual environments, we should anticipate further advancements in this field in 2024.

5.3 Challenges and Limitations in the usage of Augmented Reality (AR) and Virtual Reality (VR)

A technology known as augmented reality (AR) adds digital data and media, like 3D models, movies, music and text to the physical world. For a variety of uses including marketing, gaming, entertainment, education and tourism, augmented reality (AR) may produce immersive and engaging experiences. Before AR can realize its full potential, there are a few obstacles and restrictions that must be overcome. In this section, the authors go over a few of the primary obstacles and restrictions around augmented reality from a variety of angles, including the technical, social, ethical and legal.

5.3.1 Technical Challenges

To process and show rich and realistic digital content on the user's device, augmented reality (AR) demands a significant amount of processing power, bandwidth, and battery life. To synchronize digital content with reality, augmented reality also needs precise and reliable tracking, registration, and calibration of the user's position, orientation, and surroundings. The effectiveness, calibre, and usability of AR apps may be impacted by several technological difficulties. The sense of immersion and interaction could be destroyed, for instance, if the tracking or registration is unsuccessful and the digital information drifts, jitters, or vanishes from the user's view. Furthermore, limited field of vision, resolution, brightness, or contrast in AR devices like head-mounted displays (HMDs), smart glasses, or smartphones may lower the visual quality and realism of digital material. In addition, ergonomic problems with weight, comfort, or safety may arise with AR gadgets, impacting the user's experience and well-being.

5.3.2 Social Challenges

AR has the potential to develop new ways for people to communicate and interact with each other, like mixed reality telepresence, social gaming, and distant collaboration. AR, however, can also present certain societal issues, including those related to security, privacy, manners, and social acceptance. For instance, augmented reality (AR) may collect, retain, or share private or sensitive environmental data, such as faces, locations, or activities, without the user's or other people's knowledge or agreement. This might give rise to privacy and security problems. As AR users may conduct themselves inappropriately or differently in public or private areas, such as wearing AR gadgets, conversing with virtual characters, or interacting with digital content, which may bother, annoy, or offend other people, AR can also lead to concerns with etiquette and social acceptance. AR users may also favour interacting with the digital world over the physical one, or they may have varying degrees of access to or exposure to AR technology, which can lead to a digital divide or inequality. As a result, AR can also result in social exclusion or isolation.

5.3.3 Ethical Challenges

Authenticity, manipulation, accountability, and morality are just a few of the new ethical conundrums and disputes that AR may give rise to. Because AR can modify, enhance, or replace the real environment with digital content that may be false, misleading, or deceptive, it can, for instance, cast doubt on the veracity and authenticity of the real world. In addition to influencing a user's attention, memory, learning, decision-making, or motivation all of which can have positive or negative effects AR can also be used to control a user's perception, cognition, emotion, or conduct. Because AR can introduce new risks, harms, or damages physical, psychological, or social that can be purposeful or inadvertent and include a variety of actors developers, suppliers, users, or bystanders it can also raise questions about accountability and responsibility. Because AR might produce new kinds of moral dilemmas and choices, including privacy, fairness, or dignity, which may differ across cultures, places, or situations, technology can also put users' and society's morals and values at jeopardy.

5.3.4 Legal Challenges

AR has the potential to give rise to new types of legal concerns including laws about consent, jurisdiction, liability, and intellectual property. AR, for instance, has the potential to violate the intellectual property rights of real or digital material producers or owners, including patents, copyrights, and trademarks, which may call for further license, consent, or payment. Due to the possibility that AR may result in or contribute to mishaps, losses, or injuries (financial, psychological, or bodily), AR may also give rise to responsibility and negligence concerns. These situations may call for more insurance, settlements, or legal action. To gather, handle, or share data, AR may also need the user's and other participants' consent and agreement. This may call for additional opt-in or opt-out options, notifications, or disclosure forms. Because AR can cross or blur the boundaries of real-world, virtual, or legal areas, such as nations, governments, or territories, it can also lead to problems with jurisdiction and governance. These problems might call for new kinds of coordination, cooperation, or harmonization.

6. CONCLUSION

Virtual and augmented reality industries are growing at a rapid pace. Future advances of this magnitude may present customers with additional economic prospects. It will be interesting to see how major rivals like Facebook, Google and Amazon leverage technology to showcase their creative thinking and exceptional customer experiences. A lot of companies are already at the forefront of AR commerce, which is a really promising retail concept. Online retailers should acknowledge the importance of augmented reality and start making investments in it, considering its many benefits. They will eventually turn a profit if they attract more customers. With augmented reality (AR), we can include and superimpose digital data over the real world. AR is a technology that has the potential to improve almost every aspect of our lives by enabling us to transform our surroundings into enjoyable, productive and educational spaces. The need for businesses that offer AR/MR apps is rising as more people become aware of them.

AR offers distinctive entertainment alternatives that aren't found in other forms of digital media. Future AR systems will undoubtedly be far more sophisticated than the ones that are now on the market thanks to a recent study. AR makes for notably various levels of interactivity and content quality, as well as the possibility of personalization. Despite being around for a while, the technology is new and hasn't been fully and functionally integrated into daily activities like retail and medicine because of issues with usability, social acceptance, and technology. But if these obstacles are overcome, augmented reality (AR) has the power to revolutionize gaming by providing better material instantly. The application of AR in medicine has the potential to alter surgical techniques. AR screens make it easy to provide post-surgical care and medical training. Customers are expected to welcome AR with excitement as they seek new ideas that may simplify and improve their purchasing experiences. We have also examined the current AR solutions in use and spoken about how crucial they are to the pandemic's recovery. As a result, AR is crucial in giving consumers a technological experience unlike anything they've had before in practically every field.

The latest innovations demonstrate how augmented reality is continuing to advance. One example of augmented reality (AR) in gaming is Pokemon Go, a location-based software that also uses GPS. Conversely, one example of a marker-based software that combines augmented reality with image recognition is Snapchat. There are various AR-based software development kits available. The price, platforms, image recognition technology, and potential for 3D tracking and recognition are some of the aspects that influence which SDK is best. Among the engines that can be utilized to construct AR apps are Unity and AR Toolkit. Google AR Core and Android AR Spark studio kits are also available from Google and Android. The cases that have been presented demonstrate the expanding market for augmented reality systems as well as their significance. Therefore, it is impossible to overstate the significance of a review that sheds light on the three main industries where augmented reality technologies are being applied.

REFERENCES

Assante, D., Caforio, A., Flamini, M., & Romano, E. (2019). *Smart Education in the context of Industry 4.0*. IEEE. DOI: 10.1109/EDUCON.2019.8725057

Azuma, R. T. (1997). A survey of augmented reality. *Presence (Cambridge, Mass.)*, *6*(4), 355–385. DOI: 10.1162/pres.1997.6.4.355

Benedetto, G., Rossi, A., & Mancini, F. (2022). AR-supported wearables for enhancing employee safety in high-risk environments. *Journal of Industrial Safety and Protection*, *45*(2), 127–143.

Chevalier, C., & Kiefer, C. (2020). What does augmented reality mean as a medium of expression for computational artists? *Leonardo*, *53*(3), 263–267. DOI: 10.1162/leon_a_01740

Chris, D. K., & Anna, E. (2012). Enhancing the Tourism Experience through Mobile Augmented Reality: Challenges and Prospects. *International Journal of Engineering Business Management*, *4*, 10. Advance online publication. DOI: 10.5772/51644

Dey, A., Billinghurst, M., Lindeman, R. W., & Swan, J. E.II. (2018). A Systematic Review of 10 Years of Augmented Reality Usability Studies: 2005 to 2014. *Frontiers in Robotics and AI*, *5*, 37. DOI: 10.3389/frobt.2018.00037 PMID: 33500923

Dow, S., Mehta, M., Harmon, E., MacIntyre, B., & Mateas, M. (2007). Presence and engagement in an interactive drama. In Conference on Human Factors in Computing Systems - Proceedings (San Jose, CA): 1475-1484. DOI: 10.1145/1240624.1240847

Fonseca, D., Redondo, E., & Villagrasa, S. (2014a). *Mixed-methods research: a new approach to evaluating the motivation and satisfaction of university students using advanced visual technologies*. In Universal Access in the Information Society.

Furio, D., Gonzalez-Gancedo, S., Juan, M. C., Segui, I., & Rando, N. (2013). Evaluation of learning outcomes using an educational iPhone game vs. traditional game. *Computers & Education*, *64*, 1–23. DOI: 10.1016/j.compedu.2012.12.001

Gbadegeshin, S. A. (2019). The Effect of Digitalization on the Commercialization Process of High-Technology Companies in the Life Sciences Industry. *Technology Innovation Management Review*, *9*(1), 49–63. DOI: 10.22215/timreview/1211

Gupta, N. and Bharadwaj, S.S. (2013). Agility in business school education through richness and reach: a conceptual model. 55(4/5): 370-384, Emerald Group Publishing Limited 0040-0912, DOI https://doi.org.DOI: 10.1108/00400911311326018

Hackl, C., & Wolfe, S. (2017). *Marketing new realities: An introduction to virtual reality and augmented reality marketing, branding and communications. Cold Spring*. Meraki Press.

Hassan, A., & Ramkissoon, H. (2016). Augmented Reality Application in Visitor Experiences. https://www.researchgate.net/publication/303923635

Haugstvedt, A. C., & Krogstie, J. (2012). Mobile augmented reality for cultural heritage: A technology acceptance study. In ISMAR 2012 - 11th IEEE International Symposium on Mixed and Augmented Reality 2012, Science and Technology Papers (Atlanta, GA): 247-255. DOI: 10.1109/ISMAR.2012.6402563

Henderson, S. J., & Feiner, S. (2009). Evaluating the benefits of augmented reality for task localization in maintenance of an armored personnel carrier turret. In Science and Technology Proceedings - IEEE 2009 International Symposium on Mixed and Augmented Reality, ISMAR 2009 (Orlando, FL): 135-144. DOI: 10.1109/ISMAR.2009.5336486

Henderson, S. J., & Feiner, S. K. (2011). Augmented reality in the psychomotor phase of a procedural task. In 2011 10th IEEE International Symposium on Mixed and Augmented Reality, ISMAR 2011 (Basel): 191–200. DOI: 10.1109/ISMAR.2011.6092386

Heutger, M., and Kuckelhaus, M. (2014). Augmented Reality in Logistics: Changing the way we see logistics - a DHL perspective.

Hsieh, M. C., & Lee, J. J. (2018). Preliminary Study of VR and AR Applications in Medical and Healthcare Education. *Journal of Nursing & Health Studies*, *3*(1). Advance online publication. DOI: 10.21767/2574-2825.100030

Huang, Y., Li, S., & Chen, K. (2022). Augmented reality for cultural heritage preservation: Virtual restorations of fragile artifacts. *Heritage Science*, *10*(1), 88–102.

Ibanez, M., Di Serio, A., Villarn, D., & Delgado Kloos, C. (2014). Experimenting with electromagnetism using augmented reality: Impact on flow student experience and educational effectiveness. *Computers & Education*, *71*, 1–13. DOI: 10.1016/j.compedu.2013.09.004

Irizarry, J., Gheisari, M., Williams, G., & Walker, B. (2013). InfoSPOT: A mobile augmented reality method for accessing building information through a situation awareness approach. *Automation in Construction*, *33*, 11–23. DOI: 10.1016/j.autcon.2012.09.002

Jeon, J., Kim, H., & Lee, C. (2022). Virtual reality and augmented reality in esports: A revolution in competitive gaming. *Entertainment Computing*, *41*, 100479.

Jerabek, T., Rambousek, V., & Wildova, R. (2014). Specifics of Visual Perception of The Augmented Reality in The Context of Education. *Procedia: Social and Behavioral Sciences*, *159*, 598–604. DOI: 10.1016/j.sbspro.2014.12.432

Kam, P. T. (2017). Influence of Augmented Reality in Showcasing the Digital Tourism Experience for Future Travelers with Human Touch. *International Journal of Innovative Research in Computer and Communication Engineering*, *5*(2).

Keckes, A. L., & Tomicic, I. (2017). Augmented Reality in Tourism- Research and Applications Overview. *Interdisciplinary Description of Complex Systems*, *15*(2), 157–167. DOI: 10.7906/indecs.15.2.5

Klimova, A., Bilyatdinova, A., & Karsakov, A. (2018). Existing Teaching Practices in Augmented Reality. *Procedia Computer Science,* 136: 5-15. 7th International Young Scientist Conference on Computational Science. https://doi.org.DOI: 10.1016/j.procs.2018.08.232

Kurniawan, M. H., & Witjaksono, G. (2018). Human anatomy learning systems using augmented reality on mobile application. *Procedia Computer Science*, *135*, 80–88.

Lamrani, R., Hassan, E., & Wahed, A. (2015). *Learning through play in pervasive context - A Survey*. IEEE. DOI: 10.1109/AICCSA.2015.7507119

Lee, S., Park, J., & Han, K. (2021). Industrial applications of augmented reality: Streamlining factory automation and reducing downtime. *Journal of Manufacturing Technology Research*, *29*(4), 289–303.

Lin, Y., Chang, L., & Hsieh, M. (2022). Enhancing problem-solving and critical thinking through gamified augmented reality in classrooms. *International Journal of Educational Technology*, *39*(2), 123–136.

Lopez, A., Ramirez, S., & Fernandez, C. (2020). User engagement in museum settings through mobile augmented reality applications. *Journal of Cultural Heritage*, *44*(3), 57–67.

Martin-Gutierrez, J., Mora, C. E., Anorbe-Díaz, B., & Gonzalez-Marrero, A. (2017). Virtual Technologies Trends in Education. *Eurasia Journal of Mathematics, Science and Technology Education*, *13*(2), 469–486. DOI: 10.12973/eurasia.2017.00626a

Maurer, F., & Schumacher, J. (2018). Organizational Robustness and Resilience as Catalyst to Boost Innovation in Smart Service Factories of the Future, IEEE. In *International Conference on Engineering, Technology and Innovation (ICE/ITMC)*.

Miranda, J., Chavarría-Barrientos, D., & Wright, P. W. (2017). *Experiences in Interactive Collaborative Learning using an Open Innovation Laboratory*. IEEE.

Murphy, T., O'Leary, C., & Carmichael, P. (2021). The impact of augmented reality on customer interaction and satisfaction in the hospitality industry. *Tourism and Hospitality Management*, *27*(2), 321–339.

Nayyar, A., Mahapatra, B., Le, D., & Suseendran, G. (2018). Virtual Reality (VR) & Augmented Reality (AR) technologies for tourism and hospitality industry. International journal of engineering & technology, 7(2.21), 156-160.

Sabri, F. N. M., Khidzir, Z., Ismail, A. R., & Daud, K. A. M. (2016, August). Empirical study on important elements of mobile augmented reality application for heritage content. In 2016 4th International Conference on User Science and Engineering (i-USEr) (pp. 210-215). IEEE.

Okamura, A., Yamashita, T., & Ueda, K. (2020). AR-guided surgeries for precision and reduced errors in complex procedures. *Journal of Surgical Innovation*, *35*(3), 187–202.

Quandt, M., Knoke, B., Gorldt, C., Freitag, M., & Thoben, K. D. (2018). General Requirements for Industrial Augmented Reality Applications. In 51st CIRP Conference on Manufacturing Systems, *Procedia*, 72:1130-1135. https://doi.org.DOI: 10.1016/j.procir.2018.03.061

Rankohi, S., & Waugh, L. (2013). Review and analysis of augmented reality literature for construction industry. *Visualization in Engineering*, *1*(1), 1–18. DOI: 10.1186/2213-7459-1-9

Romano, B., Sands, S., & Pallant, J. (2020). Augmented reality and the customer journey: An exploratory study. *Australasian Marketing Journal*.

Tarabasz, A., Selakovic, M., & Abraham, C. (2018). The Classroom of the Future: Disrupting the Concept of Contemporary Business Education. *Entrepreneurial Business and Economics Review*, *6*(4), 231–245. DOI: 10.15678/EBER.2018.060413

Vazquez-Alvarez, Y., Oakley, I., & Brewster, S. (2012). Auditory display design for exploration in mobile audio-augmented reality. *Personal and Ubiquitous Computing*, *16*(8), 987–999. DOI: 10.1007/s00779-011-0459-0

Wedel, M., Bignee, E., and Zhang, J. (2020). Virtual and augmented reality: Advancing research in consumer marketing. *International Journal of Research in Marketing*, 37: 443:465.

Zhu, E., Hadadgar, A., Masiello, I., and Zary, N. (2014). Augmented reality in healthcare education: an integrative review. https://doi.org.DOI: 10.7717/peerj.469

About the Contributors

Varinder Singh Rana is presently working as Department Chair of Hospitality and Tourism Management at City University Ajman, UAE. He received his Doctorate (PhD) in Hospitality from Amity University, Noida, and completed his post-graduation in Hotel Management and Catering Technology from St Peters University, Chennai. He obtained his Bachelor in Hotel Management from Bangalore University in 2001. He has over 21 years of experience in Academia and Industry. He has provided his services to CT University, GNA University, Lovely Professional University, Punjab Tourism Development Corporation and various reputed hotels. He has 12 Limca Records in his account. He is General Secretary of Chefs Association of Five Rivers which is the nodal body of Indian Federation of Culinary Associations (IFCA). He is a member of the Board of Management of GNA University and a Board of Studies member of various Universities. He has authored 12 books and 22 Research papers. He served as head chef to honourable President of India and the President of the Republic of Afghanistan during their visit to Punjab. He is a certified Master trainer of the Food Safety and Standards Authority of India. He has been awarded by Phagwara Administration for outstanding professional work in 2017. He also got the Star Achiever Award for regional culinary development from the Indian Federation of Culinary Associations. He has also been honored by the Tourism Minister of Punjab for initiating a Bakery Unit at Central Jail, Ludhiana. He has shown his presence as the Jury of Master Chef Punjabi-A Cookery Reality Show of DD National Punjabi. He is doing various cooking shows on National Television. He also represented the State of Punjab in Republic day Celebration at Red Fort, New Delhi. He has served Jury in ICF and IFCA events at National and International levels. He has been awarded the Best Culinary Educator award by Indian Federation of Culinary Association (A Nodal Body of the Ministry of Tourism, Government of India). He grabbed Two Silver Medals and one Bronze medal for the Republic of India (Our Nation) at the International Culinary Challenge, Uzbekistan where 22 countries participated. He has been associated with many projects of the Punjab Heritage and Tourism Promotion Board (PHTPB).

Gaurav Bathla is having over thirteen years of experience in Academia & Industry and presently working as Professor in School of Hotel Management, Airlines and Tourism at CT University Punjab. He has received his Doctorate (PhD) in Hotel Management and Tourism from GNA University, Punjab. Dr. Bathla has authored more than 30 research papers in Scopus Indexed, UGC Approved and Peer Review Journals. He has been associated with many universities and hotel management institutions for their curriculum development and examination system. Dr. Bathla is editorial / reviewer board member of more than 8 National & International Journals. He has also organized various conferences and Faculty Development Programs in the field of Hospitality and Tourism.

Ashish Raina is a distinguished academic leader, researcher, and hospitality professional with over 16 years of experience in hospitality and tourism education. Currently the Professor and Dean of the School of Management, Hotel Management, and Design at CT University, Ludhiana, Dr. Raina has dedicated his career to the advancement of hospitality education, curriculum development, and fostering industry-academia collaborations. His expertise spans from leading academic programs to creating specialized courses that meet current industry standards, especially in areas such as food tourism, sustainable tourism, and culinary management. He has held leadership roles at various institutions, including Chandigarh University, GNA University and Kanya Maha Vidyalaya, where he led the development of unique programs in culinary arts, hospitality management, and tourism. Dr. Raina's academic credentials are equally impressive, with a Ph.D. in Hotel Management from GNA University focusing on food tourism and destination attraction in Jammu and Kashmir, a region he has extensively researched. His scholarly contributions include over 28 research publications in reputed international and Scopus-indexed journals, covering topics such as digital marketing in hospitality, cultural tourism, and food safety standards. His work has been recognized with prestigious awards, including the Best Faculty Award and the Exemplary Academician of the Year Award, underscoring his commitment to academic and professional excellence. An innovative thinker and practitioner, Dr. Raina holds multiple patents on hospitality solutions, such as AI-driven talent demand analysis in hotels and IoT-based hotel management systems. His groundbreaking ideas are also evident in his culinary achievements; he is listed in the Limca Book of Records for creating unique culinary records, including the longest aloo parantha and maximum varieties of golgappas and samosas, showcasing his creative approach to gastronomy. A Certified Hospitality Trainer by the American Hotel & Lodging Educational Institute and an Advanced Innovation Ambassador under the Ministry of Education's Innovation Cell, Dr. Raina actively engages in research on culinary tourism and sustainable hospitality. His involvement in organizing and chairing international conferences, including the International Hospitality and Tourism Conference, further highlights his commitment to thought leadership in the field. Additionally, he has contributed to several books on sustainable tourism, green hotel practices, and AI in hospitality.

***

Rachit Agarwal is working as an Assistant Professor at the University School of Business, Chandigarh University, Mohali. He has more than 7 years of work experience in teaching and research. His interests include fintech, investment behavior analysis, and behavioral study. He has published various papers and book chapters in national and international journals and edited books including Scopus and ABDC-listed journals. He has also organized workshops and faculty development programs on Research Methodology and different statistical tools.

Sandhya Anilkumar has 30 years of experience spanning both industry and academia and is currently working as Assistant Professor at Faculty of Hospitality Management and Catering Technology, M. S. Ramaiah University of Applied Sciences. She holds a Master's degree in Tourism Management. She has made significant contributions to research and academic within the hospitality management sector. Has published a few research papers in journals and has also published relevant articles in professional magazines. She has presented her papers at national and international conferences, with a particular focus on sustainability in hospitality. Her editorial roles include being a member of the Regional (South) Editorial Board for students' online journal and serving as the editor of the e-magazine of the Professional Housekeepers Association (PHA). She is part of the teams that has two patents registered. She has guided numerous group projects for final-year BHM graduates. In content development, she has created e-learning modules on management topics, developed teaching ideas (TIs) and assessment for learning (AFL) tools, and designed various activities such as case studies, worksheets, and concept maps. Additionally, she has developed assessment tools for evaluating student performance. She has organized seminars and workshops for students pursuing hospitality management.

Benedict Antwi is a PhD candidate at the School of Business, University of Cape Coast.

B. Maheswari working as an Assistant Professor In RMK Engineering College, Puduvoyal, Tamilnadu, India, in the department of Computer Science and Engineering. She received the B.E degree in Computer Science and Engineering and M.E degree in Software Engineering from Anna University, India. She is currently pursuing PhD in computer science and engineering from Anna University, Chennai. Her area of interest is Internet of things and Big Data.

Asier Baquero, PhD in Business Management at the Catholic University of Valencia, Spain. He holds the position of Academic Director for the Master's Degree in Tourism Innovation at the International University of La Rioja. His research focuses on artificial intelligence, sustainable development, and leadership within the hotel sector.

Gaurav Bathla is having over fourteen years of experience in Academia & Industry and presently working as Professor in School of Hotel Management, Airlines and Tourism at CT University Punjab. He has received his Doctorate (PhD) in Hotel Management and Tourism from GNA University, Punjab. Dr. Bathla has authored more than 30 research papers in Scopus Indexed, UGC Approved and Peer Review Journals. He has been associated with many universities and hotel management institutions for their curriculum development and examination system. Dr. Bathla is editorial / reviewer board member of more than 8 National & International Journals. He has also organized various conferences and Faculty Development Programs in the field of Hospitality and Tourism.

Humaira Begum is an Associate Professor of the Department of Finance and Banking at Hajee Mohammad Danesh Science and Technology University (HSTU), Dinajpur, 5200. She is currently obtaining her PhD at The Institute of Bangladesh Studies (IBS), Rajshahi University, Rajshahi. Prior to entering academia, she graduated from HSTU in Finance and started her teaching career firstly in a private university, later on she joined HSTU as a Lecturer in the Department of Finance and Banking, HSTU in 2016. Her primary research interests include Financial Distress, corporate governance, banks and non-financial institutions, corporate social responsibility, financial technology, and application of machine learning in different aspects of prediction.

Bharat Bhushan Designation: Assistant Professor Qualification: Ph.D in Commerce, UGC-NET, MBA Punjab Technical University - Jalandhar, M.Com Himachal Pradesh University - Shimla,

Rachna Chandan is the Assistant Professor and Head of the Housekeeping Department at Banarsidas Chandiwala Institute of Hotel Management and Catering Technology (BCIHMCT), New Delhi. With a Ph.D. from Banasthali Vidyapeeth, Jaipur, Rajasthan, she brings 20 years of expertise in academia and the hospitality industry. She employs a research-based experiential learning approach to teaching, ensuring consistent academic success. Dr. Chandan excels in developing curriculum and course content, coordinating examination processes, and offering special classes for campus preparation sessions. As Editor of the 'Voice of Housekeepers' e-infozine by the Professional Housekeepers Association, she has successfully published two issues. Additionally, she edits the 'YUVA - the essence of hospitality' e-newsletter by BCIHMCT, with 15 issues published. She also serves as Joint Editor of the 'Indian Journal of Applied Hospitality Tourism Research' and contributes to the editorial team for the India International Hotel, Travel & Tourism Research Conference book published by BCIHMCT.

Madhu Chandhok is a Founding Partner at pip2020 and currently serves as a visiting faculty member at The Oberoi Centre of Learning & Development (OCLD) and the Indian School of Hospitality (ISH). With an honorary doctorate in Project & Design Management from the University of Entrepreneurship & Technology, Nigeria, she brings 40 years of extensive experience in all phases of hospitality projects, including planning, design and construction, project management, and contract administration. Dr. Chandhok is the State President of the WICCI Hospitality & Tourism Council, Delhi NCR, and an advisory board member of (PHA) Professional Housekeepers Association & the Hospitality Procurement Managers Forum (HPMF). Over the past four challenging years, she has dedicated herself to skilling and mentoring students from ISH, OCLD, and various IHMs. She actively promotes women's inclusion and engagement in the hospitality industry. Mentoring and guiding the youth through their career paths, both online and one-on-one, is her passion, as she supports them in discovering their inner strengths and working towards achieving their goals.

Abhijit Pramod Chandratreya is currently working as Deputy Director in the Department of Post Graduate Research Centre at SCES's Indira Institute of Management, Pune for the past 14 years. He joined IIMP after working in various Industries for 17 years. He graduated in Production Engineering from Birla Vishwakarma Mahavidyalaya (Sardar Patel University), Anand, Gujarat, India. He secured a Master of Business Administration in Human Resource Development from IGNOU. He has been awarded a Ph.D. in the field of Marketing Management from Savitribai Phule Pune University, India. He has presented several papers in National and International Journals, conferences, and Symposiums and has published 15 research papers both in referred and SCOPUS / ABDC-listed Journals. He has published three patents. He is a certified trainer of CSCP, CPTP, CLDM, MTF, and CID certified by MiddleEarth HR. His main areas of interest include Marketing, HRM, SCM, Statistics, Business Analytics, and Research Methodologies. SCOPUS ID: 58695471800 Google Scholar ID: jJN5ZcQAAAAJ

Anbuselvi D has expertise in Nonlinear optical materials and Nanotechnology. She had completed doctorate degree in University of Madras, Chennai, Tamilnadu, India. She has good experience in academic and research, currently working in T. John Institute of technology, Bangalore. She had published the research articles in various National and International journals. She is a reviewer of a various international journals.

Rony Kumar Datta is serving as an Associate Professor of Finance at Hajee Mohammad Danesh Science and Technology University (HSTU) in Dinajpur, Bangladesh with more than 12 years of experience in teaching and research. He received his PhD in Finance from the Institute of Bangladesh Studies, University of Rajshahi, Bangladesh. His passion for research focuses on fintech, financial inclusion, climate finance, green growth, green finance, and machine learning. He has published several research papers in international journals and presented his work at various conferences. Additionally, he has conducted several funded research projects at the national level.

Alice De Veer is a former University of Cape Coast student who completed her Master of Business Administration degree in marketing.

Vikas Gairola is presently working as Associate professor& Head in DepartmentManagement Studies. He has presented several research papers in National and International Conferences and published research papers in Proceedings and Journals. He has also attended several Workshops and Faculty Development Programs organized by renowned institutes and Universities. He has been a Resource Person in the resettlement programme of Supply Chain Management and Retail Management' for the participants of various armed forces of India through Director General Resettlement (Ministry of Defence, Govt. of India). His areas of interest include Strategic Management, Consumer Behavior, Digital Marketing, and Retail Management.

Ajay Kumar is a dynamic academician and tourism enthusiast. He completed a Master in Tourism Administration from HPU Shimla, Himachal Pradesh. He is a research scholar of tourism management at CT University, Ludhaina. Ajay embarked on a professional journey as a travel executive for Indo Asiana Travels during his bachelor's studies. Later, he ventured into entrepreneurship with Tour Himalayas, showcasing his expertise in tourism management. Transitioning to academia. He is serving as an assistant professor in the HMCT Department of Chandigarh College of Hospitality, CGC, Landran, Mohali, Punjab. He has also served at the CT Institute of Hospitality Management, Jalandhar, as an assistant professor. Currently pursuing his Ph.D. from CT University Ludhiana, his blend of industry experience and academic prowess enriches the learning environment, nurturing future professionals in the tourism sector. He published 2 patents, 1 edited book, 12 research paper, and 3 book chapter.

Md. Shamim Hossain is an accomplished academic and researcher in the field of marketing, with a research focus on the applications of machine learning in marketing, operations management, online business, emarketing, self-service technologies (SSTs), e-commerce, m-banking, online customer behavior, and other areas of business. He received his Ph.D. in Business Management from the University of International Business and Economics (UIBE) in Beijing, China, and is currently a Professor in the Department of Marketing at Hajee Mohammad Danesh Science and Technology University (HSTU) in Bangladesh. Dr. Hossain has published numerous research papers in prestigious journals, including the Journal of Retailing and Consumer Services, the Economic Analysis and Policy, the Journal of Food Quality, the Discrete Dynamics in Nature and Society, the Journal of Sport Psychology, the Journal of Hospitality and Tourism Insights, the Journal of Islamic Marketing, the FIIB Business Review, the Economic Research-Ekonomska Istraivanja, and the International Journal of Engineering Business Management. He has also contributed book chapters to several high-quality textbooks published by IGI-Global in the United States. In addition to his research work, Dr. Hossain is a dedicated teacher and has taught a variety of courses in marketing at HSTU. He is highly regarded for his engaging teaching style and his ability to make complex marketing concepts accessible and interesting. Dr. Hossain is a pioneer in the field of machine learning-based marketing and is actively engaged in research related to this area.

Hamada Hussein is a lecturer in Egyptology at the University of Sadat City, Egypt. He earned his PhD from the University of Liverpool in 2019. His research interests encompass the religion of ancient Egypt, the ancient Egyptian language, examining the cultural and historical significance of tourism sites, and developing innovative approaches to training tour guides. Hussein is also the Deputy Director of the University of Manchester Tell Nabasha Survey Project.

Nasrin Islam is working as lecturer in Varendra University, Rajshahi, Bangladesh.

Sweety Jamgade is the Head of Management Studies- Hospitality Department, and Associate Professor in FHMCT, MS Ramaiah University of Applied Sciences. She has completed her doctorate in the faculty of Science and Technology in the domain of Ecotourism. She treasures the topper award in her post-graduation in Master of Hospitality Management. She is specialized in hospitality, tourism, and management studies. She is a member of the Responsible Tourism Society of India, TIES, etc. Her research focus area includes Sustainable Tourism Business and Hospitality Management. She has published 24+ research papers and is the editor, journal reviewer, travel writer, blogger, and vlogger on various platforms.

Christian Kaunert is Professor of International Security at Dublin City University, Ireland. He is also Professor of Policing and Security, as well as Director of the International Centre for Policing and Security at the University of South Wales. In addition, he is Jean Monnet Chair, Director of the Jean Monnet Centre of Excellence and Director of the Jean Monnet Network on EU Counter-Terrorism

Satveer Kaur is currently working as Assistant Professor, School of Management at Maharaja Agrasen University, Baddi, Himachal Pradesh, India. She has done B.Com, MBA (Finance and Marketing) and Ph.D (Finance). She has 10 years of teaching experience as faculty of Management with specialization of Accounting and Finance. She is the life time member of the knowledge Research Academy (KRA) and Research Education Solutions (RES) for promotion of research and academia. She has been awarded with Certificate of appreciation for "Wonderful Performance" from HDFC Bank in 2010. She has published 20 research papers in national and international journals as well as presented in the national and international conferences. She is having two patents and she has published 15 book chapters and 4 book publications. She has guided many 40 MBA, BBA, B.COM students in their research work and 3 Ph. D submitted under her guidance. Currently, 4 research scholars pursuing Ph.D under her guidance.

Singari Keerthi is pursuing MSc in Cyber Security and Ethical Hacking. She has interest in research, particularly in forensic science and cyber security. She would like to work on real-time studies that explore the latest advancements and applications in these fields. She is familiar with the basic principles of research, including the scientific method, research design, data collection and analysis, and the importance of ethical considerations in conducting studies.

Hazem Ahmed Khairy is an associate professor at the Faculty of Tourism and Hotels, University of Sadat City - Egypt. He is a former visiting scholar at Auburn University in the USA. He has a career certification in human resource management from the American University in Cairo (AUC). His research interests are organizational behavior, human resources management and development, consumer behavior, hospitality and tourism management, and sustainability in tourism and hospitality, in addition to hospitality marketing and leadership.

Amit Kumar, possesses more than 13 years of academic and 2 years of industry experience. Currently, he is working as an Assistant Professor in the Department of Tourism and Hotel Management at Central University of Haryana, Mahendragarh. He is a well-structured academic professional demonstrating proven success in fostering student learning outcomes through creative and innovative curriculum delivery methods. He adapts well in driving thought-provoking class debates to promote student engagement and learning. He has also participated and presented research papers in various international and National Seminars/Conferences/Workshops along with research publications in international and National reputed journals and books. He is also on the panel list of paper setting and evaluation for UG and PG courses in Tourism and Hotel Management at various Universities.

Anshul Kumar is an undergraduate student at KIIT University.

Neeraj Kumar is an accomplished professional with a rich blend of industrial and academic experience. With four years in the production industry, he gained invaluable hands-on expertise in managing operations and streamlining processes. This industrial background provided him with a practical perspective that he has seamlessly integrated into his teaching career. For the past 14 years, Neeraj has been a dedicated educator at esteemed engineering and management institutes. His teaching approach is marked by patience, commitment, and the ability to connect theoretical concepts with real-world applications. He has guided numerous students toward academic and professional success, earning their respect and admiration. An active researcher, Neeraj has contributed to the field through insightful research papers that reflect his commitment to advancing knowledge and innovation. His dual background in both industry and academia makes him a valuable asset in fostering a comprehensive learning environment that bridges practical industry insights with academic rigor.

Tanya Kumar is currently working at Chandigarh Group of Colleges, Landran Mohali. She has experience in teaching and research. She has completed her Ph.D. in commerce. Her areas of interest are finance and marketing. She has also presented various papers in national and international conferences. She provides supervision to students in financial analysis, blockchain technology, artificial intelligence and cybersecurity and fintech. She has guided more than 90 master's students to complete their dissertation. She has published papers in national and international journals, including Scopus, Web of Sciences and ABDC-listed journals.

Vishakha Kuwar is a distinguished academic and industry professional, currently serving as an Assistant Professor at Dr. D Y Patil Vidyapeeth, Centre for Online Learning. She holds an MBA in International Business Management (IBM) and BE in Computer Science and is a founding member of a startup company, showcasing her entrepreneurial spirit and practical business acumen. With 6 years of teaching experience and 5 years of industrial experience, Vishakha has significantly contributed to both service and product-based sectors. Her areas of expertise include Business-to-Business Research, Information Systems, and E-Learning. Vishakha has made notable contributions to her field through her research. Her blend of academic knowledge and practical experience makes her a valuable asset to both the educational and business communities.

Ezhilvandan M working as Assistant Professor in Panimalar Engineering College. He has nearly 12 years in teaching and his research area are soft computing, computer networks and Deep Learning.

M. Nalini is an Associate Professor in the Department of Computer Science and Engineering, S.A Engineering College, Chennai, India. She received her B.E. in Computer Science and Engineering from Anna University, Chennai in 2010 and M.Tech. in Computer Science and Engineering from B.S.Abdur Rahman Crescent Institute of Science & Technology, Chennai, India in 2012. She was awarded Ph.D. in Computer Science and Engineering from St. Peter's Institute of Higher Education and Research, Chennai, India in 2018. She has 10 years teaching experience. Her research interests include Data Mining, ML, Big Data Analytics and Networking. She has published many articles in reputed Journals.

Nithin M is pursuing MBA in Hospitality Management and is passionate about human resource management, technology and marketing. Have 1.6 years of experience in service and human resource management. Have good team building skills and want to contribute towards the service industry.

Rameez Mir us a research scholar at Chandigarh University.

Soumya Ranjan Mishra is presently working as an Assistant Professor (II) at the School of Computer Engineering, Kalinga Institute of Industrial Technology (Deemed to be University), Bhubaneswar Odisha, India. He has teaching and research experience of more than 10+ years and Industry experience of 2+ years in IT Companies. He did his doctoral degree Ph.D. in the field of Computer vision and machine learning from the National Institute of Technology, (NIT) Durgapur, WB, India. His research interest includes Image Processing, Intelligent Systems, Human-Computer Interaction, Computer Vision and similar innovative areas. His research contribution includes various proceedings/books which include ASIC Springer series, and publications in reputed conferences, book chapters, and journals indexed in SCI/ESCI.

Hitesh Mohapatra received the B.E. degree in Information Technology from Biju Patnaik University of Technology (BPUT), Odisha in 2006, and the MTech. Degree in CSE from Odisha University of Technology and Research (OUTR) University, Odisha in 2009. He received his Ph.D. in Computer Science & Engineering in 2021 from Veer Surendra Sai University of Technology (VSSUT), Burla, India. He has contributed 30 SCI and Scopus indexed research papers, 21 international/national conferences and books on Software Engineering and C Programming respectively. He has 15 years of teaching experience both in industry and academia. He has served the research community with various capacities like session chair, technical chair, keynote speaker etc. His research interests include wireless sensor network, smart city, smart grid and smart water. Currently he is working as Associate professor at School of Computer Engineering, KIIT DU, Bhubaneswar, and Odisha.

Grace Opoku-Asiamah is a PhD candidate of the University of Cape Coast, School of Business.

Dominic Owusu is currently a lecturer in the Department of Marketing and Supply Chain Management, School of Business, University of Cape Coast.

Girija P is a faculty member in the Computer Science and Engineering department at Vel Tech Rangarajan Dr. Sagunthala R&D Institute of Science and Technology in Avadi, Chennai. She plays a crucial role in advancing academic and research efforts at the institution.

Beslin Pajila P J is a faculty member in the Computer Science and Engineering department at Vel Tech Rangarajan Dr. Sagunthala R&D Institute of Science and Technology in Avadi, Chennai. She is dedicated to advancing research and academic excellence within the institution.

Kamalendu Pal is with the Department of Computer Science, School of Science and Technology, City, University of London. Kamalendu received his BSc (Hons) degree in Physics from Calcutta University, India, Postgraduate Diploma in Computer Science from Pune, India, MSc degree in Software Systems Technology from the University of Sheffield, Postgraduate Diploma in Artificial Intelligence from Kingston University, MPhil degree in Computer Science from the University College London, and MBA degree from the University of Hull, United Kingdom. He has published over hundred and twenty international research articles (including book chapters) widely in the scientific community with research papers in the ACM SIGMIS Database, Expert Systems with Applications, Decision Support Systems, and conferences. His research interests include knowledge-based systems, decision support systems, teaching and learning practice, blockchain technology, software engineering, service-oriented computing, sensor network simulation, and supply chain management. He is on the editorial board of an international computer science journal and is a member of the British Computer Society, the Institution of Engineering and Technology, and the IEEE Computer Society.

Ruchira Prasad She is working as an assistant professor at SPCJ Institute of Commerce, Business Management & Economics, Dr. Bhimrao Ambedkar University, Agra. Her research area is finance. She has supervised many PhD and MBA Scholars. She has more than a decade of working experience in the field of research and teaching. She has presented many research papers at national and international conferences and published articles in Scopus and ABDC-indexed journals.

Nishi Priya is an Associate Professor at Amity School of Hospitality, Amity University, Lucknow. She is In-charge of Institutional Research Cell at Amity School of Hospitality as well as heading Institutional Events and Value Added Course meant for Skill Enhancement of Students. Being a Certified Hospitality Trainer from IHMCTAN Bangalore, she has overall 15 years of experience which include academic and administrative coordination with renowned institutions like IHMCTAN, Bangalore University, Patna University, Chandigarh University, IIMT University and also carry hospitality Industry experience with Taj Hotels in the Frontline Operational Management areas of Front Office and Housekeeping departments as Supervisor and Senior Supervisor. She has Doctorate degree in Hotel Management from PAHER Pacific University. Her thesis is being recognized and collected by Sodhganga research site. She holds dual degree with B.Sc in Hotel and Management and Bachelor in Tourism Studies from IHMCTAN, Bhopal subsequently post graduate in Tourism Management from IGNOU, New Delhi. She is holding life-time membership of Professional Housekeeping Association (PHA) and associate actively with WICCI, Punjab Tourism Council.

Wahengbam Priyalakshmi is a research Scholar in Department of Hospitality and Tourism Management.

Siva Subramanian R. is an Associate Professor in the Department of Computer Science and Engineering, RMK College of Engg and Tech, Chennai, India. He received her B.E. in Computer Science and Engineering from Anna University, Chennai in 2009 and M.Tech. in Computer Science and Engineering from Bharath University, Chennai, India in 2013. He has 10 years teaching experience. His research interests include Data Mining, Machine Learning, Big Data Analytics and Networking. He has published many articles in reputed Journals

Md Rashid has more than 18 years of experience in the area o Marketing management, Digital Marketing and conducted seminars and conferences including FDPs.

Bassam Samir Al-Romeedy is a motivated Associate Professor at the faculty of tourism and hotels, University of Sadat City - Egypt, and an Accredited external auditor at the National Authority for Quality Assurance of Education and Accreditation – Egypt. I also work as a market research consultant and statistical analyst. Dr. Al-Romeedy has published in premier peer-reviewed journals including Tourism Review, Journal of Tourism and Technology, Journal of Vacation Marketing, Journal of Human Resources in Hospitality & Tourism, Corporate Social Responsibility and Environmental Management, and others.

Ria Satti currently pursuing undergraduate programme from School of Commerce, Finance and Accountancy, Christ (Deemed to be University), Delhi NCR.

Sanjeev Kumar Saxena is an associate professor at the Department of Hospitality and Tourism Management, Assam University.

Dharna Shukla is a hotel management educationist and an experienced hotelier with over two decades of experience in academia hospitality operations. Dr. Shukla has worked in India and abroad in the hospitality sector with chains of The Park, The Taj and Coral Hotels. She has also taught hospitality and tourism management at IHM Lucknow, Christ University Bangalore and was the founding faculty and program leader, hospitality and tourism, at Amity University Dubai. Dr.Shukla has reviewed hospitality and tourism content of Aptech and is a consultant inspector for NEBOSH certifications in India for a UK-based organization. She is also a Lifetime Member of the Professional Housekeepers Association (PHA). Dr. Shukla has authored and co-authored three books, research papers and book chapters on contemporary topics of significance in the hospitality and tourism industry. She holds a PhD in Management from Banasthali University, Rajasthan and currently is the Program Leader of BBA (Tourism Management) and an Assistant Professor at Amity School of Hospitality, Amity University Uttar Pradesh, Lucknow Campus.

Rishi Prakash Shukla is working as Professor (Marketing) at Jaipuria Institute of Management, Jaipur. He has about 15 years of experience in academics. With 15 years of comprehensive experience, he has made significant contributions through extensive research and development. Dr. Shukla holds 6 patents and has authored 20 research papers, showcasing his deep expertise in Marketing. His industry journey spans prestigious institutions such as Symbiosis Institute of Business Management, Symbiosis Centre for Management Studies, Chandigarh University and projects at the Indian Institute of Management Ahmedabad. Dr. Shukla's scholarly interests include cutting-edge technologies, particularly in the field of neuromarketing and Retail. He is certified by IBM and SAS in advanced predictive modeling and has authored 5 books on futuristic technologies. Beyond academia, Dr. Shukla is known for his affable nature, passion for travel, and innovative social experiments using technology.

Amrik Singh is working as Professor in the School of Hotel Management and Tourism at Lovely Professional University, Punjab, India. He obtained his Ph.D. degree in Hotel Management from Kurukshetra University, Kurukshetra. He started his academic career at Lovely Professional University, Punjab, India in the year 2007. He has published more than 60 research publications in Scopus/Web of Science) journals. He has published 22 copyrights, 12 patents and 01 patent has been granted in the inter-disciplinary domain. Dr. Amrik Singh participated and was a resource in various national and international conferences, seminars, research workshops, and industry talks. His area of research interest is accommodation management, ergonomics, green practices, human resource management in hospitality, waste management, AR VR in hospitality, etc. He is currently guiding 8Ph.D. scholars and 5 Ph.D. scholars have been awarded Ph.D.

Amrit Singh is currently pursuing undergraduate programme from School of Commerce, Finance and Accountancy, Christ (Deemed to be University), Delhi NCR.

Bhupinder Singh working as Professor at Sharda University, India. Also, Honorary Professor in University of South Wales UK and Santo Tomas University Tunja, Colombia. His areas of publications as Smart Healthcare, Medicines, fuzzy logics, artificial intelligence, robotics, machine learning, deep learning, federated learning, IoT, PV Glasses, metaverse and many more. He has 3 books, 139 paper publications, 163 paper presentations in international/national conferences and seminars, participated in more than 40 workshops/FDP's/QIP's, 25 courses from international universities of repute, organized more than 59 events with international and national academicians and industry people's, editor-in-chief and co-editor in journals, developed new courses. He has given talks at international universities, resource person in international conferences such as in Nanyang Technological University Singapore, Tashkent State University of Law Uzbekistan; KIMEP University Kazakhstan, All'ah meh Tabatabi University Iran, the Iranian Association of International Criminal law, Iran and Hague Center for International Law and Investment, The Netherlands, Northumbria University Newcastle UK,

Lalit Singla currently working as an Associate Professor in Apex Institute of Management (AIM), Chandigarh University, Gharuan (Mohali) is a seasoned academician, researcher and a strong administrator with a rich background in management education and industry experience. He holds a Ph.D. in Management from the School of Management Studies, Punjabi University, Patiala, His academic journey includes an MBA with specializations in Marketing and Finance from Kurukshetra University Dr. Singla brings over 17 years of teaching experience to his role. Prior to his current position, he held academic roles at Sri Guru Granth Sahib World University, Asra Institute of Advanced Studies,RIMT University among others. His teaching portfolio spans various domains of business administration, reflecting his expertise in areas such as Sales Force Management, Consumer Behavior, and Strategic Marketing.He is on the panel of paper setting commitees of various universities. Dr. Singla's research contributions are substantial, highlighted by his publication record of 42 research papers in UGC-Listed and ABDC 'C' Category Journals, alongside 08 text/edited books. He has 03 Research papers communicated in Scopus indexed journals and 01 in scopus indexed conference. He is actively engaged in research supervision, having successfully guided 10 Ph.D. scholars to completion, with one nearing the end of their doctoral journey. He is also the key resource person in various national and international conferences. In addition to his academic achievements, Dr. Singla has practical industry experience, having worked as a Sales Executive and Business Marketing Executive early in his career. His industry insights complement his academic prowess, making him a well-rounded educator capable of bridging theoretical concepts with real-world applications. His dedication to advancing management education through research, teaching, and mentorship underscores his commitment to academic excellence. He is an active member of the department who is very popular amongst the students as he is instrumental in giving their career a professional bent of mind and also brings latest pedagogies like role play activities, case study discussions, group discussions, presentations, management games etc to the classroom. His comprehensive skill set and academic achievements make him a valuable addition to this academic institution seeking to enhance its management faculty.

Ambar Srivastava is working as an Assistant Professor in School of Commerce, Finance & Accountancy at Christ (Deemed to be University), Delhi NCR, Ghaziabad, India. He has qualified for the UGC-NET in commerce and completed a CA (Inter) from the Institute of Chartered Accountant of India (ICAI). Mr. Srivastava is amongst the top 5 in Master of Commerce (M. Com) from Jai Narain Vyas University, Jodhpur, Rajasthan. Besides these, he has taught at the Mohanlal Sukhadia University, Udaipur, Rajasthan. His teaching interests include financial accounting, corporate accounting, financial management, e-accounting, direct & indirect taxation, etc. He has published three textbook titled "Goods & Service Tax", "Income Tax" & "Cost Accounting" published by Choudhary Prakashan, Jaipur. He also published good research papers in reputed journals. His research interests include sustainability reporting, financial performance, corporate governance, taxation issues, etc.

C.V. Suresh Babu is a pioneer in content development. A true entrepreneur, he founded Anniyappa Publications, a company that is highly active in publishing books related to Computer Science and Management.

Dr. C.V. Suresh Babu has also ventured into SB Institute, a center for knowledge transfer. He holds a Ph.D. in Engineering Education from the National Institute of Technical Teachers Training & Research in Chennai, along with seven master's degrees in various disciplines such as Engineering, Computer Applications, Management, Commerce, Economics, Psychology, Law, and Education. Additionally, he has UGC-NET/SET qualifications in the fields of Computer Science, Management, Commerce, and Education. Currently, Dr. C.V. Suresh Babu is a Professor in the Department of Information Technology at the School of Computing Science, Hindustan Institute of Technology and Science (Hindustan University) in Padur, Chennai, Tamil Nadu, India. For more information.

Bharathi T holds a Doctoral degree in Management. She has over 12 years of experience in teaching and academia. She has conducted various workshops, MDPs and FDPs and has rich hands on experience in using MS Excel, SPSS and AMOS. She has published research papers in International Journals including a paper in Scopus Journal. Her areas of research are Stress management, emotional intelligence, consumer behavior. Her research papers are viewed and cited among researchers. Presently she is working as Associate Professor and Head-Academic Operations at ISBR Business School.

T. P. Anish received his M.E. Degree from the Department of Computer Science and Engineering at Saveetha Engineering College (Affiliated to Anna University), Chennai, India, in 2011. He is currently an Assistant Professor at R.M.K. College of Engineering and Technology, Puduvoyal, India. He is pursuing his Ph.D. degree in Information and Communication Engineering from Anna University. His current research interest includes Machine Learning, Deep Learning and Big Data analytics.

Kamal Upreti is currently working as an Associate Professor in the Department of Computer Science & Engineering, Dr. Akhilesh Das Gupta Institute of Technology & Management, Delhi. He completed is B. Tech (Hons), M. Tech (Gold Medalist), PGDM(Executive) and PhD in Computer Science & Engineering.He has published many patents, books, magazine issues and research papers in various reputed international conferences and journals. His areas of research interest include Machine Learning, Wireless Networking, Embedded System and Cloud Computing.

Ashok Mammen V has a doctoral degree in management. His area of interest is in field of online marketing. He has published several research papers in the topics on HR and supply chain management also. He has nearly three decades of experience in corporate and academia. He has a keen interest in consultancy services. With this paper he wishes to extend his research to topics related to technological advancements in business.

Index

D

E

J

K

M

O

P

Q

R

S

www.ingramcontent.com/pod-product-compliance
Lightning Source LLC
LaVergne TN
LVHW080403011026
849161LV00009B/2340
* 9 7 9 8 3 6 9 3 7 4 4 7 4 *